MEDIA STUDIES

A READER
SECOND EDITION

Edited by
Paul Marris and Sue Thornham

EDINBURGH UNIVERSITY PRESS

Selection and editorial material © 1996,
1999 Paul Marris and Sue Thornham.
The texts are reprinted by permission
of other publishers.

Edinburgh University Press Ltd
22 George Square, Edinburgh

Typeset in Sabon and Gill Sans
by Bibliocraft Ltd, Dundee, and
printed and bound in Finland by WSOY

A CIP record for this book is available
from the British Library

ISBN 0 7486 1206 8 (paperback)

CONTENTS

INTRODUCTION
About This Reader

This book brings together sixty-five extracts from academic books and articles about the media, to provide a useful single volume for readers who want an overview of the main ways in which the media are currently studied and discussed in British higher education, either because they are university students themselves or because they are interested media professionals or audience members. Most of the readings focus on broadcasting and the press, and this limitation is quite deliberate. Film studies has a well-established critical tradition which can be traced elsewhere. Popular music, comics and popular fiction might have been given more attention, but a number of collections have been published which have as their focus the analysis of popular media culture, and the student may turn to those.[1] Broadcasting and the press have been central to the study of the mass media within a range of theoretical traditions, and this anthology echoes that centrality.

Although this volume constructs the field of media studies from a 'British' perspective, the extracts are by no means drawn solely from work by British scholars. The development of the field in Britain has been shaped partly in response to research traditions elsewhere, notably Germany and the United States. The opening section begins by outlining the different, and often theoretically and methodologically opposed, origins of the field as it is now constituted in Britain. From the arguments between the American mass communication tradition and the Europe-centred Frankfurt School in the 1940s, to the very different analyses of communication technologies by Marshall McLuhan and Raymond Williams in the 1960s, these differences have centred not only on the relative importance of the theoretical and the empirical in media research, but also – underpinning these overt arguments – on the political assumptions within the different traditions about the role and functions of the mass media in society. Baldly summarised, the approaches of both the American mass communication tradition and McLuhan's work in the 1960s derive from a position broadly supportive of the directions in which Western society was moving, whereas those of the Frankfurt School and the English culturalist tradition are profoundly critical. It is because 'the sorts of assumptions made about the broader structure of society within different bodies of theory have determined the sorts of questions that have been posed in relation to the media and the way in which those questions have been pursued' that this first section is entitled 'The Media and Social Power' (although arguably all the pieces in this collection can be seen as concerned at some level with issues of social power).[2]

The work of Stuart Hall at the Birmingham Centre for Contemporary Cultural Studies in the 1970s (see Chapter 5) constituted a crucial break for the development of media studies in Britain. He drew on paradigms from both American and European strands of thought and added to them an attention to the media text which has its origins partly in a specifically English tradition of literary criticism and partly in 1970s British film theory. But Hall's work was not merely a synthesis of previously opposed traditions. Rather, through his use of Gramsci's concept of hegemony,[3] he provided a framework by which the operation of mass media in society could be understood as a series of 'articulated' moments (where 'articulated' has the double sense of 'expressed' and 'joined together'). None of these moments 'can fully guarantee the next moment with which it is articulated',[4] and each becomes the site of 'negotiation', or cultural struggle, over meaning. Within such a framework, earlier traditions of research were both drawn upon and critiqued, positioned within a field of study which becomes reconstituted around a model which is at once a theoretical and political analysis. Hall's work helped inaugurate, and emblematises, what became by the 1980s and into the 1990s the mainstream of media studies scholarship in Britain, grounded in 'cultural studies' approaches.

It is Hall's model – with its three 'moments' of 'encoding' (production), 'meaningful discourse' (text) and 'decoding' (reception), each of which may be considered as 'relatively autonomous', but which are also understood as part of a wider process within an economically unequal and socially unjust world – that provides the central organising principle of this book. After the opening section, with its representation of the different theoretical traditions which contribute to contemporary media studies, Part One is organised into three further sections, dealing in turn with 'Production', 'Text' and 'Reception'. Within these, where appropriate, a further division into sub-sections maps the range and variety, the arguments and debates, within work in these areas.

The four case studies which make up Part Two – Soap Opera, News, Advertising and a new one on New Media – are also ordered in broad accordance with this central organising principle, so that within each one, work on the three sequenced aspects of production, text and reception has been included. Variations in the focus of attention, however, can be found between the case study topics. Work on 'News', for example, has been largely concerned with issues of public knowledge and information, and has concentrated substantially on the study of news production and organisation; in contrast, the study of 'Soap Opera' has had as its focus the analysis of popular pleasures, and has centred far more on the text-reader relationship. This difference is reflected in the balance of pieces within each case study.

For this second edition, some earlier material has been omitted, and some new material added.[5] Changes have been made partly in response to students' and colleagues' experience of using the book in teaching and learning. But many of the additions have also been made to keep abreast of developments, both within the media industries themselves, and within the field of scholarship that reflects upon them and their social role. None of these themes was wholly absent when the first edition was compiled, but several have grown more significant within the media studies literature in the four years since, and this is reflected in the selection of several of the newly included items.

These changes are perhaps best identified by the term 'postmodernisation'. 'Postmodernity' is the term adopted by many to characterise the present era through which we are living, and distinguish it from the immediate postwar world and before. Amongst the features usually associated with postmodernity are developments in the organisation of the world economy, often called 'globalisation',[6] and the increasingly salient emergence and adoption of micro-electronic and digital technologies for telecommunications, computing and consumer electronics. 'Postmodernism' refers to corresponding developments in contemporary philosophy and the arts and sciences, with the emphasis some-times on the philosophical and sometimes on the stylistic.[7] Partly because of the increasing international traffic in information goods and services, discussions of the process of 'globalisation' often focus on the cultural dimension.[8]

As the 1990s unfolded, these developments and the debates over them had a growing impact on media studies, both in the topics considered and the terms and concepts employed, and much of the material newly introduced here reflects this. In the discussion of 'encoding' or production, debates over globalisation are manifest in Chapters 54 (Gurevitch on globalisation of newsgathering) and 14 (Sinclair, Jacka and Cunningham on new patterns in global television), where a revision of the earlier concept of 'media imperialism' is registered. For consideration of media texts, there is more material exploring the nature of the postmodernist text, with its insistent intertextuality, and tendency to blur the boundaries between genres and across the rhetorics of 'fiction' and 'reality': for example, Nichols on 'reality TV' (Chapter 31) and Stratton and Ang on *Sylvania Waters* (Chapter 49). New material on reception or 'decoding' builds from Fiske's assertion that 'we have now collapsed the distinction between "text" and "audience"' (Chapter 42) to explore the forms of incorporation of media into everyday life (Jenkins, Chapter 43, and Hermes, Chapter 44).

Already at the time of the publication of the first edition of this volume in the mid-1990s, Hall's model was under pressure. We commented that 'its elaboration into a paradigm in which the "relative autonomy" of its different moments could facilitate the separate study of the text as a complex discursive structure, and of the processes of reception as ones in which the resistant, or oppositional, meanings and pleasures could be produced, can be seen as leading to the disappearance from sight of the framework as a whole'. In that period, the particular issue identified was that 'an increasing focus on theories of pleasure in studies both of the text and of the processes of reception poses problems for a model which was founded on an analysis of the operations of *power*. The result . . . is that a model which began from a perspective critical of the structure and operations of contemporary Western society has ended in an often uncritical celebration of that society's mass media output.'

The pressure of dismemberment of the encoding/decoding model and the centrifugal dispersal of its elements continued through the 1990s. The direction that 'cultural studies' overall took during the decade has continued to be the subject of criticism and debate.[9] One response for the development of a politically engaged media studies has been the renewed prominence of the 'political economy' approach to the media and communications:[10] an example in this volume is Peter Golding's piece on the World Wide Web (Chapter 63). But it has been argued of this approach (though not with particular reference to this piece) that 'there is a definite sense of . . . "the moment of the cultural" being forever deferred'.[11] Whilst political economy can track media power in its economic, legal and organisational forms, runs the argument, it cannot or does not follow it into the forests of meanings, consciousness and subjectivities.

Recent attention to the political economy of the media represents a new level of activity within an already established critical tradition.[12] Other scholarship in the 1990s has extended or opened up a variety of approaches in striving to understand what the contemporary developments of globalisation and post-modernisation might mean for a politically engaged media studies. Joyrich (Chapter 32) proposes a feminist reading of the postmodern, seeing there the power structures of modernity by another name. Some scholars frame the issue as one of more labile power relationships: 'the *shifting balance of relationships of dependency* between different participants in the network of global communications' is how Gurevitch expresses it in Chapter 54 (italics in the original). And the 1990s saw a pronounced engagement with issues of race and ethnicity, and an emphasis on the particular and localised appropriation and even transformation of media texts (examples being McClintock in Chapter 60, and Miller in Chapter 40).

Appropriately, the struggle to grasp in thought developments in the media in the period of 'globalisation' have brought forth a more globalised media studies. The study of the media in Britain has not only drawn on philosophical and social-scientific traditions from elsewhere, but – insofar as the impact of the British 'cultural studies' tradition became widely felt in the 1990s – in turn made a contribution to the development of thinking and research about the media across a broader span. The result has been the development of a more internationalised exchange of ideas and discussion in media scholarship. As one might expect, this is particularly true for the Anglophone world – the British Isles, North America, Australasia, other Anglophone postcolonial territories – but it is not confined to that; the dialogue within Northern Europe has intensified too, for example. This development has meant that this second edition includes a greater number of pieces from elsewhere, in particular the United States, Australia and the Netherlands.

In the new century, the media will remain central features of culture and society, though none of them (the media, culture or society) will remain the same, each contributing to their mutual change and transformation. By offering an overall mapping of the ways in which the media have been considered and contested from within a particular national tradition, we hope this Reader will assist the coming generation to stand on the shoulders of their twentieth century predecessors in reaching for an understanding and a re-forming of the media.

NOTES

1. For example, Simon During (ed.) *The Cultural Studies Reader* (London: Routledge, 1993), and John Storey (ed.) *Cultural Theory and Popular Culture: A Reader* (Hemel Hempstead: Harvester Wheatsheaf, 1994).
2. Tony Bennett, 'Theories of the Media, Theories of Society', in Michael Gurevitch, Tony Bennett, James Curran and Janet Woollacott (eds) *Culture, Society and the Media* (London: Methuen, 1982) p. 31.
3. The process by which economically dominant groups in society are able, through their exertion of *cultural* leadership and authority, to win the consent of subordinate groups to the *status quo*. See Antonio Gramsci *Selections from the Prison Notebooks*, ed. and trans. by Quintin Hoare and Geoffrey Nowell-Smith (London: Lawrence & Wishart, 1971) pp. 181–2.
4. Stuart Hall, 'Encoding/Decoding', Ch. 5 of this volume, p. 51.
5. Items added comprise: Hans Magnus Enzensberger, 'Constituents of a Theory of the Media'; John Sinclair, Elizabeth Jacka, Stuart Cunningham, 'New Patterns in Global Television'; Paddy Scannell, 'Public Service Broadcasting: The History of a Concept'; Bernard Berelson, 'Content Analysis in Communication Research'; Richard Dyer, 'The Role of Stereotypes'; Niki Strange, 'Perform, Educate, Entertain: Ingredients of the Cookery Programme Genre'; Norman Fairclough, 'Critical Analysis of Media Discourse'; Corinne Squire, 'Empowering Women? The *Oprah Winfrey Show*'; Jim Collins, 'Television and Postmodernism'; Bill Nichols, 'Reality TV and Social Perversion'; Lynne Joyrich, 'Critical and Textual Hypermasculinity'; Janice Radway, 'Reading the Romance'; Daniel Miller, 'The Young and the Restless in Trinidad: A Case of the Local and Global in Mass Consumption'; Henry Jenkins, '"Strangers No More, We Sing": Filking and the Social Construction of the Science Fiction Fan Community'; Joke Hermes, 'Media, Meaning and Everyday Life'; Jon Stratton and Ien Ang, '*Sylvania Waters* and the Spectacular Exploding Family'; John Hartley, 'Home Help for Populist Politics: Relational Aspects of TV News'; Lana F. Rakow and Kimberlie Kranich, 'Woman as Sign in Television News'; Michael Gurevitch, 'The Globalization of Electronic Journalism'; Sean Nixon, 'Advertising, Magazine Culture, and the "New Man"'; Anne McClintock, 'Soft-Soaping Empire: Commodity Racism and Imperial Advertising'; Brian Winston, 'How Are Media Born?'; Peter Golding,

'Worldwide Wedge: Division and Contradiction in the Global Information Infrastructure'; Eric Hirsch, 'New Technologies and Domestic Consumption'; Sadie Plant, 'On the Matrix: Cyberfeminist Simulations'. Items in the 1996 edition omitted in this edition comprise: Colin Sparks, 'The Media and the State'; Asa Briggs, 'The BBC and the 1956 Suez Crisis'; John Caughie, 'Progressive Television and Documentary Drama'; Patricia Holland, 'The Page Three Girl Speaks to Women, Too'; E. Ann Kaplan, 'Whose Imaginary? The Televisual Apparatus, the Female Body and Textual Strategies in Select Rock Videos on MTV'; Dorothy Hobson, 'Housewives and the Mass Media'; Christine Geraghty, 'The Continuous Serial: A Definition'; Ien Ang, 'Dallas and Feminism'; Philip Schlesinger, 'The Production of Radio and TV News'; Glasgow University Media Group, 'The Falklands Conflict: The Home Front'; Patricia Holland, 'When a Woman Reads the News'; Kathy Myers, 'Understanding Advertisers'; Judith Williamson, 'Decoding Advertisements'; Alan Tomlinson, 'Consumer Culture and the Aura of the Commodity'.

6. For a crisp introduction, see Waters, M. (1995) *Globalization*, London: Routledge.

7. See, variously, Lyotard, J. F. *The Postmodern Condition. A Report on Knowledge* (Manchester: Manchester University Press, trans. 1984; orig. pub. in Fr., 1979); Foster, H. (ed.) *Postmodern Culture* (London: Pluto Press, 1983); Jameson, F. 'Postmodernism, or the cultural logic of state capitalism', *New Left Review* 146, 1984; Harvey, D. *The Condition of Postmodernity* (Oxford: Basil Blackwell, 1989); Connor, S. *Postmodernist Culture* (Oxford: Blackwell, 1989); Nicholson L. J. (ed.) *Feminism/postmodernism* (London: Routledge, 1990); Best, S. and Kellner, D. *Postmodern Culture: Critical interrogations* (London: Macmillan, 1991); Docherty, T. (ed.) *Postmodernism: A Reader* (Hemel Hempstead: Harvester, 1993).

8. For example: Featherstone, M. (ed.) *Global Culture: Nationalism, Globalization and Modernity* (London: Sage, 1990); Robertson, R. *Globalization: Social Theory and Global Culture* (London: Sage, 1992).

9. See, for example, Jim McGuigan's arguments in *Cultural Populism* (London: Routledge, 1992), especially pp. 61–75, and more recently the critical reappraisals offered in Marjorie Ferguson and Peter Golding (eds) *Cultural Studies in Question* (London: Sage, 1997).

10. For a major review of this tradition, and a polemic for its renewal, see Vincent Mosco *The Political Economy of Communication* (London: Sage, 1996).

11. John Tomlinson *Cultural Imperialism* (Baltimore: John Hopkins University Press, 1991), p. 40.

12. Mosco (1996), op. cit., dates it to 1950s–60s in North America, with work of Dallas Smythe, Herbert Schiller and Thomas Guback, and the 1960s–70s in Europe, with the work of Dieter Prokop in Germany, Kaarle Nordenstreng in Finland, Armand Mattelart of Belgium, and in Britain, Nicholas Garnham, Peter Golding and Graham Murdock (though arguably Stuart Legg and Francis Klingender, *Money Behind the Screen* (Lawrence and Wishart, 1937) presaged the tradition in Britain).

PART ONE
STUDYING THE MEDIA

SECTION I
THE MEDIA AND SOCIAL POWER

THE MEDIA AND SOCIAL POWER
INTRODUCTION

When attempts at sustained and systematic consideration of the media began to be undertaken in the British academic world in the 1960s, there were essentially two relevant streams of thought available: one within social science (sociology, social psychology, political communications), the other within the humanities (notably English literary study). Social science could look to a substantial body of English-language research built up within the United States around the concept of 'mass communication'. In the USA the arrival of radio broadcasting to set alongside the popular press and mass cinema-going had first generated serious discussion about the mass media in society in the 1920s. Initially this had been of a broad general character,[1] but by the late 1930s more detailed individual empirical studies were being carried out by sociologists and social psychologists.[2] So Lazarsfeld and Merton's piece published in 1948, 'Mass Communication, Popular Taste and Organized Social Action' (Chapter 1), stands on the achievement of ten years or so of social scientific research into 'mass communication', and seeks to summarise the broad features of what they felt was then known. Robert K. Merton stands at the heart of American social science of the mid-twentieth century, and was to become acknowledged as amongst the most professionally eminent of American sociologists. His work was within the *functionalist* tradition of sociology, like that of his teacher at Harvard, Talcott Parsons. This approach is evident in the way the first part of the essay proposes a taxonomy of 'social functions of the mass media'. One of these is seen as a 'dysfunction' – the 'narcotizing dysfunction', which renders 'large masses of the population politically apathetic and inert'. Merton's collaborator in this article, Paul Lazarsfeld, had worked in Vienna as a social psychologist specialising in the study of marketing, before he emigrated to the United States in 1933 to avoid the Nazis. In the 1940s he and Merton became colleagues at Columbia University, where Lazarsfeld founded the Bureau of Applied Social Research to carry out quantitative social survey research work. Lazarsfeld is a central figure in the development of 'communication studies' in America, defining issues and methods in ways that were to prove profoundly influential for a quarter of a century. His interests in marketing, political communication and audience measurement meant that attitude change, influence and persuasive power were major preoccupations in his work – and the 'effects' of communication were long seen as consisting in attitude change and behaviour modification of a measurable kind. This theme is taken up in the final part of the joint essay, with its discussion of the best conditions for effective propaganda, which are said to be 'monopolization',[3] 'canalization' and 'supplementation'.[4] The middle passage in the piece, in which the pair 'consider the impact of the mass media upon popular taste', registers the post-war development in the United States of a substantial public debate over the consequences of the rise of the media for culture in general. Were cultural and aesthetic standards being debased, or was a historically unprecedented mass popular culture being developed by the foremost capitalist democracy? Lazarsfeld and Merton do not come down on either side, but at this early stage conclude '[t]he answer can come only from disciplined research'. The debate was to be a significant one amongst American intellectuals during the Cold War until at least the late 1950s.[5]

A sharply distinct position on the social role of the media was developed within America during the 1940s, though it did not become widely known in the United States or Britain before the 1960s. This was the position of the Frankfurt School. The Institute of Social Research had been founded in Frankfurt am Main (Germany) in 1923 as an independent scholarly research institute specialising in sociology, social psychology, philosophy and political economy, with a pronounced affiliation to Marxism. Many of its leading researchers left Germany in the mid-1930s to avoid Fascism, and the Institute was transplanted to New York, under the leadership of Max Horkheimer. The commitment to developing a Marxist understanding of society adequate to the industrial capitalist economies of the mid-twentieth century led the Frankfurt School writers to a consideration of the media. As German-speaking *émigré* intellectuals in America working within social science, Lazarsfeld and the major Frankfurt School figures were known to one another. In 1941 the Institute for Social Research collaborated with Columbia University's Office of Radio Research on a special issue of the Institute's journal, *Studies in Philosophy and Social Science*, devoted to issues in mass communication, which contained contributions by Horkheimer, Adorno and Lazarsfeld. In Lazarsfeld's piece he drew his celebrated distinction between 'administrative' and 'critical' communications research, the former being to serve the knowledge requirements of the paymasters in the mass communications industry, the latter to meet the broader needs of social progress which might not meet the approval of established interests.[6] But the views of Lazarsfeld and the Frankfurt School did not converge. Lazarsfeld wrote to Adorno 'I have great objections against ... your disregard of evidence and systematic empirical research'.[7] The Frankfurt School remained essentially peripheral and unknown within the mainstream of American social science.

In 1947 Horkheimer and Adorno published a major work, *Dialectic of Enlightenment*, whose chapter entitled 'The Culture Industry: Enlightenment as Mass Deception' set forth a general view of the media in contemporary society.[8] The term which was proposed was 'culture industry', not 'mass communication'. The dialectic expounded in the book is the play of positive and negative outcomes of the application of human reason in the modern era. The eighteenth-century Enlightenment had promised that the power of human reason could banish the forces of superstition and backwardness, end ignorance through the development of scientific knowledge, bring prosperity from a growing technical mastery of nature, and introduce justice and order to human affairs. But, argued Adorno and Horkheimer, the application of human reason within capitalism often stimulated opposing tendencies. The intellectual conquest of small areas of knowledge amounted merely to the development of technical expertises, the expression of 'instrumental' reason divorced from the wider goals of human emancipation. These contributed to the exploitation of people and nature, and made systems of social domination more efficient and effective. A traditional mitigating element had been works of art, the experience of which offered intimations of the human spirit free of domination by instrumental reason. But now, ran the argument, even this zone of human life was becoming subject to the forces of rationalisation and instrumentalisation through the industrialisation of culture. The 'culture industry' (Hollywood, the mass media, the record industry) is increasingly organised like any other commercial sector of manufacture and consumption, and culture has become commoditised. In contrast to the authenticity of folk and popular art and the human insights of genuine high art, the culture industry supplies 'substitute gratification', and promotes the cult of personality and other authoritarian attitudes. Leisure is rationalised like industrial production, and consciousness is integrated smoothly into the cycle of capitalist reproduction and accumulation. Chapter 2, Adorno's 'Culture Industry Reconsidered', usefully summarises many of the themes from *Dialectic of Enlightenment* that bear on the consideration of the media.[9] The emphasis on the media as part of a capitalist industrialisation of culture which serves to reconcile people to a dominating social order in a totalising way has made the Frankfurt School's arguments a profound exposition of what are often encountered as unsystematised colloquial opinions.

The 1960s witnessed the dramatic ascent to public celebrity of the Canadian scholar Marshall McLuhan. His book *Understanding Media*, from which the extracts that make up Chapter 3 are taken, was published in 1964. He considered that discussion of the media was too narrowly focused on their *contents* – the effect of an advertisement, the meaning of a film, the line of a newspaper editorial. These were thought to be the 'messages' the media conveyed. But for McLuhan media are technologies each of which extends a particular human sense or faculty, and the real '"message" of any medium or technology is the change of scale or pace or pattern that it introduces into human affairs'. The true significance of any medium is to be found in the overall impact of the generalised employment of that technological system. Hence, his celebrated claim that 'the *medium* is the message'. He considered that the printing press, a mechanical medium, promoted linearity, individualism and sequential rationality, which he linked to the visual. He preferred the new era of electronic media: radio, the telephone, television, and the coming 'automation' or computerisation. He associated these with instantaneity, the abolition of spatial separation, the unified field and simultaneity, and he linked them to the auditory. The global communications network that he foresaw was to be the ultimate 'extension of man', the externalisation of the central nervous system. In a period when the spread of transistor radios, television, and pop records seemed to many to be linked to the emergence of new patterns of youth behaviour, and when early communications satellites and information-processing systems seemed to herald further profound changes, many looked to McLuhan as offering an account of the significance of these developments – and a celebratory one at that. But although he spent his whole career within the academic world, McLuhan's ideas did not take deep root there. His views were rightly characterised as technological determinist, reductively attributing technological causes to social events. For instance, in what is a reference to the rise of mass movements in Europe in the 1920s and 1930s, he asserts that 'the introduction of radio in Europe' 'restore[d] a tribal pattern of intensive involvement'. Many of his preoccupations, however, now seem remarkably prescient of the themes of postmodernism: the coming of postindustrialism, the dissolution of the high culture/popular culture opposition, the eschewal of linear rationality, the information technology revolution, the contraction of time-space. The work of Jean Baudrillard owes much to McLuhan.

The second current of thought available in Britain in the 1960s to be brought to bear on the media was a native one, Leavisism within English literature. F. R. Leavis was the leading figure in a group of intellectuals connected to the Faculty of English at the University of Cambridge, whose central vehicle from 1932 was a quarterly periodical, *Scrutiny*. They were opposed to both the Edwardian belle-lettrisme that had formerly dominated the study of modern English at Cambridge, and the pseudo-aristocratic dilettantism they perceived in the Bloomsbury clique and other metropolitan literary coteries. In contrast they developed a view of the role of literary intellectuals that called for them to undertake serious tasks: above all, to uphold the continuity of culture and train discriminatory sensibilities in the face of modern mass civilisation. The felt need for such a role to be played had its precursors in Coleridge and Arnold in their views on the tasks of the 'clerisy' and the educators respectively. Because of language's important role in expressing the deepest values of a society and preserving the lines of continuity of a culture, the literary critic – and by extension, the literature teacher – comprises the key social grouping most appropriate to fulfil these functions. And a professionalisation of literary criticism is necessary: in contrast to amateurism, dilettantism and impressionism, the development of specialist professional skills in the close 'scrutiny' of literary texts and detailed analysis of how they are organised is called for – 'practical criticism'. On the other hand, the overarching concern with the state of English culture calls for consideration of how these texts are connected with the broader society and history of which they form a part. In his diagnosis of the state of English culture, made around the time of the founding of *Scrutiny*, Leavis saw the media and popular culture as integral to the 'breach in continuity' that now threatened society as a result of the strains between contemporary civilisation and the cultural tradition. In *Mass Civilization and Minority Culture* (1930) and *Culture and Environment* (1933; co-written with Denys Thompson), Leavis castigated the media of the day. Cinema trades in the 'cheapest emotional appeals', rendering it merely 'a means of passive diversion'. The levelling-down and 'standardizing influence of broadcasting hardly admits of doubt'. Advertising's copywriters abuse the language, and advertising's commercial pressures shape the press. The subtitle of *Culture and Environment* is *The Training of Critical Awareness*, and the book is an educational primer to foster the discriminatory awareness amongst pupils and students that 'films, newspapers, publicity in all its forms, commercially catered fiction – all offer satisfaction at the lowest level'.

Three elements in the Leavisite position – close attention to the (literary) text ('practical criticism'), an interest in its connections with the wider social processes, and the notion that the nature of the media's output is indicative of the general state of civilisation – were available for a reconfiguration that would treat the media with seriousness and without automatic hostility. And this reconfiguration occurred in the early 1960s amongst some literary intellectuals partly formed by Leavisism, though with a more explicit affiliation to the left, notably Raymond Williams and Stuart Hall. Raymond Williams' *Communications* (1962) was a topical book that suggested ways both for analysing press and broadcasting output and for reforming arts and media policy to remove some of the commercial pressures. The extract published here as Chapter 4 indicates how Williams is addressing issues rooted in the Leavisite problematic, but not acquiescing in its terms. In the first part he uses the term 'communications' to reconfigure effectively the ideas of 'culture' and 'civilization' and refuse the maintenance of a distinction that assigns the media solely to the latter. In the second part he discusses 'minority culture' and 'mass communications' in a way that throws doubt on the claims of minority culture – 'I see no real evidence that it is a permanent and reliable means of maintaining a living excellence' – and partially optimistic about the possibilities of mass communication – 'we often forget how many facts, how many new opinions, how many new kinds of work and new ways of seeing the world nevertheless get through'. The policy reforms proposed were designed to strengthen the institutional bases in British society for the positive development of communications. In 1964, Stuart Hall and Paddy Whannel published *The Popular Arts*. This book was an educational primer in the tradition of *Culture and Environment*, but with the crucial difference that the authors argued 'the struggle between what is good and worthwhile and what is shoddy and debased is not a struggle *against* the modern forms of communication, but a conflict *within* these media'.[10] The objective was to develop the skills of critical discrimination in young people amongst works drawn from cinema, broadcasting, popular music and other modern media, which allowed for some detailed discussion and analysis of particular examples.

Stuart Hall, however, was to go on to make a much more far-reaching break with Leavisism, as can be seen from his 'Encoding/Decoding' (Chapter 5). The version reprinted here was first published in 1980, but it is the finalised form of a piece that had started life much earlier, as an address to a 1973 conference on 'understanding television', which then appeared as an occasional paper from the Centre for Contemporary Cultural Studies at the University of Birmingham, Hall's academic home in that period. So it is fundamentally a piece from the early seventies, and can be seen as marking the inauguration of the 'cultural studies' stream in media studies, which has since become the most significant current in the academic study of the media in Britain. The paper represents the simultaneous confluence of, and rupture with, the two available relevant bodies of thinking about the media before that time, the 'mass communication' tradition rooted in American social science, and the 'culture and civilisation' tradition of Leavisism in English literary studies, even in the 'left Leavisite' version that Hall himself had inhabited previously. The residual traces of a Leavis-style concern with the particularity of the text are apparent in his denunciation of the impoverished social scientific conception of the media 'message' or 'content'. But these are no longer rich popular artworks about which a discriminatory sensibility must be cultivated. Instead the new-found influence of structural linguistics and semiology can be detected. 'Messages' should be seen as 'sign vehicles of a specific kind organized, like any form of communication or language, through the operation of codes within the syntagmatic chain of a discourse'; they are 'discursive forms' (see Chapters 14 and 15). Since the 1940s, American mass communication research had worked with a broad underlying model of the elements of (mass) communication that can be summarised as: source – message – receiver. In this piece, Hall took the model and fundamentally recast its terms to propose these 'elements' as a set of articulated moments in the circulation of social meaning. He had in mind an analogy with the value cycle set forth in Marx's account of *Capital*, in which value flows through the economy, changing its form from labour power to finished goods to realised capital and so on. The usefulness of this analogy is to illuminate that 'each [moment] has its specific modality and conditions of existence' and 'while each of the moments, in articulation, is necessary to the circuit as a whole, no one moment can fully guarantee the next moment with which it is articulated'. This point was in order to refuse the strong determinism of the Frankfurt School view of the media, in which the modern culture industry efficiently integrated the consciousness of viewers, listeners and readers to fit the reproduction needs of the capitalist social order (see Chapter 2). In its place Hall was proposing the possibility that viewers might not simply accept wholesale the media's messages just because they were exposed to them. They might make a reading according to a 'negotiated' code, or even a wholly 'oppositional' one. Hall has pointed out since that in the paper these 'are decoding positions; they are not sociological groups'.[11] That's because in a celebrated research project, his colleague David Morley did go on to test the idea of readings made according to 'hegemonic', 'negotiated' and 'oppositional' codes against actual readings made by particular groups of people (see Chapter 37).

Hall has since acknowledged a shortcoming in the paper's presentation of his position:

> I want[ed] to get rid of the notion of any originating moment ... [W]e are in history already; therefore we are in discourse already. So what the media pick up on is already a discursive universe. The encoding moment doesn't come from nowhere. *I made a mistake by drawing that bloody diagram with only the top half.* You see, if you're doing a circuit, you must draw a circuit; so I must show how decoding enters practice and discourses which a reporter is picking up on.[12]

There is, however, a reason why the 'mistake' might have been made. That's because although encoding is not intended to be seen as an 'originating moment', it's not intended either to be seen as having an equivalence or symmetry with the moment of decoding. There is a 'preferred meaning' encoded in media discourses.

> I don't want a model of a circuit which has no power in it. I don't want a model which is determinist, but I don't want a model without determination. And therefore I don't think audiences are in the same positions of power with those who signify the world to them. And preferred reading is simply a way of saying if you have control of the apparatus of signifying the world, if you're in control of the media, you own it, you write the texts – to some extent it has a determining shape.[13]

'Encoding/Decoding' is the text that marks the opening-up in Britain of study of the media to a Marxism informed by the concepts developed in structuralism and semiology. Over the same period, however, another political current was to begin addressing questions related to the media: the twentieth century's second wave of Western feminism. Like Marxism, feminism is in the first instance a politics, its aim not simply to understand but also to change, in Jane Miller's words, 'the unquestioning male possession of the structures of economic and cultural power'.[14] Such change, however, presumes understanding, and like cultural studies, feminism made use of emergent theoretical approaches – from structuralism and semiology, psychoanalysis and Althusserian Marxism, for example – in order to understand not only how and why particular images and representations of women circulate in Western culture, but also how such representations are tied to the patriarchal structure of society and to our individual sense of a gendered identity within that society. But this focus on *gender* as a structuring principle of our social and symbolic worlds could not simply be added on to the class-based model of the emerging field of cultural studies. In challenging dominant 'knowledges' of, or 'truths' about women and the feminine, feminist theory also questioned the bases of such knowledge, asking how and where knowledge is produced and by whom, what counts as knowledge and whose interests it serves. Stuart Hall has described the 'painful exercise' through which the Birmingham Centre for Contemporary Cultural Studies attempted in the late 1970s to come to terms with feminism's challenge to 'the male-oriented models and assumptions and the heavily masculine subject-matter and topics' which had until then characterised its work.[15] But this effort has not always been matched by similar adjustments within other media research traditions, and feminist theory and criticism continue to occupy an uneasy position within media studies. It is this complex relationship which Annette Kuhn's piece (Chapter 6) outlines, in a chapter which originally formed the Introduction to her 1985 book, *The Power of the Image: Essays on Representation and Sexuality*. Beginning from the insistence that 'politics and knowledge are interdependent', and in the case of feminism mutually regenerative, she describes the way in which feminism has 'both used and transformed' existing knowledge and theoretical frameworks, 'drawing strategically on ... strands of non-feminist or prefeminist thinking', but also exposing their weaknesses, and ultimately 'generating qualitatively new knowledge, ... constructing a new field'. Within this field, the questions addressed have concerned the relationship between representation, sexuality, spectatorship, knowledge and power. In asking how representations of women both 'speak to' and help to construct our gendered identities, feminist research has also explored the social and cultural contexts within which such representations circulate, and the pleasures, both complicit and resistant, which they generate. Such analysis may itself, argues Kuhn, be regarded as 'strategic practice', 'an act of resistance in itself', but it also represents that struggle over meaning which is a prerequisite for political change.

The emergence of the 'second wave' of Western feminism was connected historically with a related sociopolitical development: the New Left and student movement that burst forth in Western Europe and North America in the late 1960s. Although this was not a politically uniform movement, there were several common features: a vigorous political activism, a revolutionary rhetoric, opposition to the wars being waged against anti-colonial movements of national liberation in the 'Third World', an espousal of non-hierarchical collectivist organisation, and the search for a socialism that was neither the social democracy installed in the parliaments of the West nor the Communism in power in the Soviet Union and Eastern Europe (the two 'Old Lefts'). This search for a socialist third way beyond the frozen polarities of the Cold War was particularly acutely felt within the Federal Republic of Germany, whose state comprised the Western part of a territory politically fissured into two republics by the 'iron curtain' that had descended across Europe in the late 1940s. The New Left took the media to be central to the reproduction of social and political order in the late twentieth century, and in West Germany one of the primary political targets of the student movement was the business empire of the right-wing press magnate Axel Springer, whose titles included the mass-circulation daily *Bild Zeitung* and the weekly magazine *Der Spiegel*. In 1971, from within this German New Left milieu, the writer Hans Magnus Enzensberger published his article 'Constituents of a Theory of the Media' (Chapter 7) which set forth a significant set of ideas regarding the media.

He recognised the communications industries as being at the heart of contemporary societies industrially, economically, politically and culturally, and he shared the New Left's combination of distrust of the Communist regimes along with hostility to the capitalist social order, and consequently distrust and hostility toward the media industries within societies governed by either form of political-economic organisation. But what seemed new in his thinking was that he did not distrust the media *per se*. He drew attention to the fact that the media were 'an empty category of Marxist theory', and set out to overcome the fact that 'so far there is no Marxist theory of the media'. As a Marxist, he held to the general tenet that when the 'social relations of production' (prevailing forms of political, social and industrial organisation) come to retard the 'forces of production' (vitiating the potential of available technological and other means for producing things useful to humanity), then a social and political revolution needs to occur, to reorganise the social relations appropriately and beneficially. He did not think this transformation would take place automatically; it would require the conscious and vigorous political activism of a growing New Left to secure a successful outcome.

Taken together, these points put the media centrally at issue. If the media and communication industries increasingly formed the heartland of business and the economy (the 'productive forces'), whilst being central to the forms that political and industrial control and mainstream culture took in contemporary societies (the 'relations of production'), then they condensed what was at stake in any political struggle against the existing social order. In turn, because the media deal in ideas and meanings ('consciousness'), they offered vehicles and sites for an activist political culture to utilise. Yet the Left's attitude to the media seemed to Enzensberger to merely castigate them for a 'manipulation' before which it wavered 'between fear and surrender'. This approach seemed to him 'archaic': 'Presumably the people who produce [the socialist newspapers and journals that are so exclusive in terms of language, content and form] listen to the Rolling Stones, watch occupations and strikes on television, and go to the cinema to see a Western or a Godard; only in their capacity as producers do they make an exception, and, in their analyses, the whole media sector is reduced to the slogan of "manipulation".'

Although Enzensberger was profoundly critical of McLuhan (he describes him as promoting a 'mystique of the media'), their thinking had several shared fundamentals: a recognition of the centrality of the media for contemporary social life; an address to a generation that had grown up with television, portable record-players and the transistor radio, and was therefore not culturally fastidious toward the media; and an awareness of the accelerating lines of development of electronic technologies. On the media's technological character, Enzensberger argued that 'the new media are egalitarian in structure. Anyone can take part in them by a simple switching process. ... It is wrong to regard media equipment as mere systems of consumption. It is always, in principle, also means of production ... The contradiction between producers and consumers is not inherent in the electronic media; on the contrary, it has to be artificially reinforced by economic and administrative means.' But he stressed that whilst the spread of smaller, cheaper, more flexible cameras, tape-recorders, photocopiers, etc. provided a technological precondition, the growth of privatised, individualised, amateur media activity was not what he was promoting; what he was urging was the development of organised forms of non-commercial media communication, collectivist in method and spirit. Thus innovative 'relations of production' would release the progressive social potential of these new 'forces of production'. Although the wholesale social transformation to which Enzensberger looked was not fully realised, the social spread and collectivist use of lightweight, inexpensive electronic media and communication technologies have played a part in many of the significant democratic developments in the years since he wrote his article, including the ending of the Cold War, colonialism and apartheid, and the practice continues today. Current examples in Britain might include the video activist group Undercurrents, associated with the environmentalist and animal rights movements, or the various counter-information projects that can be accessed on the Internet.

In his article, Enzensberger was renewing a German line of argument about media technologies that derived from the thinking of Bertolt Brecht and Walter Benjamin in the Weimar period, which he acknowledges in his text. As activist artists and intellectuals, they could be said to exhibit an 'optimism of the will' about engaging with modern developments and emphasising the positive, democratic potential of the media technologies of photography, film and radio. Benjamin was peripherally associated with the Frankfurt School, but was very much in the minority in his optimism: as we have seen Adorno and Horkheimer, who more fully represent the mainstream of Frankfurt School thinking, exhibited a 'pessimism of the intellect' regarding the media. Another significant postwar German thinker, the philosopher and social scientist Jürgen Habermas, stands more centrally in the intellectual tradition of the Frankfurt School than Enzensberger. Like Adorno and Horkheimer before him, he is concerned with the legacy of the eighteenth-century European Enlightenment and all that it promised for human progress and emancipation. He identifies as a key feature of that period the formation of a 'public sphere', the (immaterial) place – not within the state or the market or private households – where public opinion can be formed. This zone is characterised by the commitment to the values of open rational debate, the public good, and the formal equality of participants. Irrationality and arbitrary or hieratic authority are in principle alien to it; argument based upon evidence is the appropriate discursive mode. One of the major institutional sites of the public sphere in the late eighteenth century was the newspaper press (along with museums and galleries, learned and debating societies, etc.), while '[t]oday, newspapers and periodicals, radio and television are the media of the public sphere'. But in the meantime, argues Habermas, the public sphere has been 'refeudalized', returned to the state of a mere display of public authority, characteristic of 'publicness' in the pre-Enlightenment 'feudal' era. Broadcasting and the press are adulterated by consumer advertising and the public relations industry: the public sphere is thus corrupted and decaying. Habermas wishes to see the fulfilment of the Enlightenment idea of the public sphere, though nowadays the participation of a 'public of private persons acting as individuals would be replaced by a public of organized private persons' in democratically based political parties, campaign groups and other civil associations. There is sometimes said to be an element of retrospective idealisation in Habermas' portrait of the public sphere. His critics point out that the eighteenth-century public sphere was for gentlemen only; artisans, waged workers and most women were excluded.[16] But this criticism overlooks Habermas' intention to register that the development of the idea itself represented a historical progress, like the ideas of 'liberty, equality, solidarity', even though the emergence of these philosophical tenets marked the inauguration of an enormous unfinished struggle to realise them. To many nowadays the concept of the public sphere is another manifestation of the false universalism of the European Enlightenment. However, Habermas' ideas have proved a rallying point for those concerned with democracy and the media, the extension of freedom of information and the curbing of commercial interests in the press and broadcasting. For instance, in the late 1980s a defence of British public-service broadcasting was mounted around the concept of the public sphere.[17]

In Chapter 9, the French philosopher Jean Baudrillard discusses a similar area of concern – the contemporary media and political and social representation – and he too acknowledges that Enlightenment ideals have not been realised, either in society at large or in the role played by the media. His is a position often called 'postmodernist' (though he is rather coy about accepting the term). In contrast to the modern era commencing with the Enlightenment –

when scientific reason sought to construct an accurate account of nature, society and history, and thus produce a truthful representation of the world – the postmodern period of today is characterised by the end of representation. For contemporary culture is a culture of 'simulation', 'the generation by models of a real without origin or reality: a hyperreal'.[18] No longer is it a case of an external real reflected or represented by scholarship or the arts; culture is dominated by the media, which exercise a fascination for the masses through the ceaseless play of hyperreal spectacle. 'Reality' becomes inseparably bound up with the media and is increasingly constituted by them. 'The situation no longer permits us to isolate reality ... as a fundamental variable. ... [B]ecause we will never in future be able to separate reality from its statistical, simulative projection in the media, [the result is] a state of suspense and of definitive uncertainty about reality.' The media, far from furnishing a public sphere in which to make social and political representations (in both senses), increasingly fill the space of that politics and society, indeed constitute the hyperreal spectacle that *is* society and politics today. This is 'the implosion of the social in the media'. Baudrillard does not mourn this development or depict it as manipulation by the media causing 'alienation' of the masses from true democratic politics. Instead he suggests it leads to a 'secret strategy' of resistance by the masses to refuse to adopt the part assigned to them by Enlightenment philosophers or power politicians, and derisively allow the rulers to assume the burdens of political responsibility while themselves remaining unknowable behind the spectacle.

These final two chapters in this section can be seen as representing the two main antagonistic poles in the major debates over the general social character of the media that took place in the last two decades of the twentieth century. The nine chapters making up the section are written from a variety of standpoints: classic American social science; Frankfurt critical theory; technological determinism; British 'culturalism' and 'cultural studies'; feminism; the activist New Left; Habermasian 'public sphere' theory; and postmodernism. Taken together, they form a representative and rich selection of the most significant traditions of thought since the 1940s on the overall role of the media in society.

NOTES

1. See, for example, Walter Lippmann, *Public Opinion* (New York: Harcourt Brace, 1922); John Dewey, *The Public and its Problems* (Chicago: Swallow Press, 1927); Harold D. Lasswell, *Propaganda Techniques in the World War* (New York: Knopf, 1927); Edward Bernays, *Propaganda* (New York: Horace Liveright, 1928).
2. See, for example, Hadley Cantril, Hazel Gaudet, Herta Herzog, *The Invasion from Mars: A Study in the Psychology of Panic* (Princeton, NJ: Princeton University Press, 1940); Paul F. Lazarsfeld and Frank N. Stanton (eds), *Radio Research: 1942–3* (New York: Duell, Sloan & Pearce, 1944); Carl I. Hovland, Arthur A. Lumsdaine, Fred D. Sheffield, *Experiments in Mass Communication* (Princeton, NJ: Princeton University Press, 1949).

3. The mention of the radio artiste Kate Smith in this section draws on the study Robert Merton and colleagues had made of the reasons for the success of the performer's marathon radio campaign to sell US war bonds: Robert K. Merton, Marjorie Fiske, Alberta Curtis, *Mass Persuasion: The Social Psychology of a War Bond Drive* (New York: Harper, 1946).

4. The idea of 'supplementation' – 'the enhanced effectiveness of th[e] joining of mass media and direct personal contact' – anticipates to some degree one of Lazarsfeld's most famous concepts, the 'two-step flow' of communication influence. This was developed through reflection on the findings of a study of mass media influence on voting in the 1940 US Presidential Election campaign (Paul F. Lazarsfeld, Bernard Berelson, Hazel Gaudet, *The People's Choice* (New York: Columbia University Press, 1944), and set forth in Elihu Katz and Paul F. Lazarsfeld, *Personal Influence: The Part Played by People in the Flow of Mass Communications* (Glencoe, Ill.: The Free Press, 1955).

5. For a sense of the range of the American post-war 'mass culture' debate, a useful anthology from the period is: Bernard Rosenberg and David Manning White (eds), *Mass Culture: The Popular Arts in America* (New York: Macmillan, 1957).

6. Paul F. Lazarsfeld, 'Remarks on Administrative and Critical Communications Research', *Studies in Philosophy and Social Science* 9:1 (1941) pp. 2–16.

7. Paul F. Lazarsfeld, unpublished letter to Theodor Adorno, n.d. [1938]. Cited in Hanno Hardt, *Critical Communication Studies: Communication, History and Theory in America* (London: Routledge, 1992).

8. 'The Culture Industry: Enlightenment as Mass Deception' is available in abridged form in James Curran, Michael Gurevitch, Janet Woollacott (eds), *Mass Communication and Society* (London: Edward Arnold, 1977).

9. In his introduction to a published translation of this essay, Andreas Huyssen detects a 'shift of emphasis' in Adorno's position towards a slightly less totalised conception of the culture industry's perpetration of mass deception, but it is for its synoptic reprise of Adorno and Horkheimer's major themes that the piece is reprinted here (Andreas Huyssen, 'Introduction to Adorno', *New German Critique* 6 (Fall 1975) pp. 3–11).

10. Stuart Hall and Paddy Whannel, *The Popular Arts* (London: Hutchinson, 1964) p. 15.

11. 'Reflections upon the Encoding/Decoding Model: An Interview with Stuart Hall', in Jon Cruz and Justin Lewis (eds), *Viewing, Reading, Listening: Audiences and Cultural Reception* (Boulder, Col.: Westview Press, 1994) p. 256.

12. Ibid., p. 260, editors' italics.

13. Ibid., p. 261.

14. Jane Miller, *Seductions: Studies in Reading and Culture* (London: Virago, 1990) p. 10.

15. Stuart Hall, 'Cultural Studies and the Centre: Some Problematics and Problems', in Stuart Hall, Dorothy Hobson, Andrew Lowe, Paul Willis (eds), *Culture, Media, Language* (London: Hutchinson, 1980) pp. 35–6.

16. Nancy Fraser, 'What's Critical about Critical Theory? The Case of Habermas and Gender', in Seyla Benhabib and Drucilla Cornell (eds), *Feminism as Critique: On the Politics of Gender* (Minneapolis: University of Minnesota Press, 1987); Oskar Negt and Alexander Kluge, 'The Proletarian Public Sphere', in Armand Mattelart and Seth Sieglaub (eds), *Communication and Class Struggle*, vol. 1 (New York: International General, 1979).

17. See especially Nicholas Garnham, 'The Media and the Public Sphere', in Peter Golding, Graham Murdock, Philip Schlesinger (eds), *Communicating Politics: Mass Communications and the Political Process* (Leicester: Leicester University Press, 1986); and Paddy Scannell, 'Public Service Broadcasting and Modern Public Life', *Media, Culture and Society* 11:2 (1989).

18. Jean Baudrillard, *Simulations* (New York: Semiotext(e), 1983) p. 2.

I

MASS COMMUNICATION, POPULAR TASTE AND ORGANIZED SOCIAL ACTION

Paul F. Lazarsfeld and Robert K. Merton

A review of the current state of actual knowledge concerning the social role of the mass media of communication and their effects upon the contemporary American community is an ungrateful task, for certified knowledge of this kind is impressively slight. Little more can be done than to explore the nature of the problems by methods which, in the course of many decades, will ultimately provide the knowledge we seek. Although this is anything but an encouraging preamble, it provides a necessary context for assessing the research and tentative conclusions of those of us professionally concerned with the study of mass media. A reconnaissance will suggest what we know, what we need to know, and will locate the strategic points requiring further inquiry.

[...]

THE SOCIAL ROLE OF THE MACHINERY OF MASS MEDIA

What role can be assigned to the mass media by virtue of the fact that they exist? What are the implications of a Hollywood, a Radio City, and a Time-Life-Fortune enterprise for our society? These questions can of course be discussed only in grossly speculative terms, since no experimentation or rigorous comparative study is possible. Comparisons with other societies lacking these mass media would be too crude to yield decisive results, and comparisons with

From: Paul F. Lazarsfeld and Robert K. Merton, 'Mass Communication, Popular Taste and Organized Social Action', in Lyman Bryson (ed.), *The Communication of Ideas* (New York: Harper & Bros., 1948). Also available in Wilbur Schramm (ed.), *Mass Communications* (Urbana: University of Illinois Press, 1960).

an earlier day in American society would still involve gross assertions rather than precise demonstrations. In such an instance, brevity is clearly indicated. And opinions should be leavened with caution. It is our tentative judgement that the social role played by the very existence of the mass media has been commonly overestimated. What are the grounds for this judgement?

It is clear that the mass media reach enormous audiences. Approximately forty-five million Americans attend the movies every week; our daily newspaper circulation is about fifty-four million, and some forty-six million American homes are equipped with television, and in these homes the average American watches television for about three hours a day. These are formidable figures. But they are merely supply and consumption figures, not figures registering the effect of mass media. They bear only upon what people do, not upon the social and psychological impact of the media. To know the number of hours people keep the radio turned on gives no indication of the effect upon them of what they hear. Knowledge of consumption data in the field of mass media remains far from a demonstration of their net effect upon behavior and attitude and outlook.

As was indicated a moment ago, we cannot resort to experiment by comparing contemporary American society with and without mass media. But, however tentatively, we can compare their social effect with, say, that of the automobile. It is not unlikely that the invention of the automobile and its development into a mass-owned commodity has had a significantly greater effect upon society than the invention of the radio and its development into a medium of mass communication. Consider the social complexes into which the automobile has entered. Its sheer existence has exerted pressure for vastly improved roads and with these, mobility has increased enormously. The shape of metropolitan agglomerations has been significantly affected by the automobile. And, it may be submitted, the inventions which enlarge the radius of movement and action exert a greater influence upon social outlook and daily routines than inventions which provide avenues for ideas – ideas which can be avoided by withdrawal, deflected by resistance and transformed by assimilation.

Granted, for a moment, that the mass media play a comparatively minor role in shaping our society, why are they the object of so much popular concern and criticism? Why do so many become exercised by the 'problems' of the radio and film and press and so few by the problems of, say, the automobile and the airplane? In addition to the sources of this concern which we have noted previously, there is an unwitting psychological basis for concern which derives from a socio historical context.

Many make the mass media targets for hostile criticism because they feel themselves duped by the turn of events.

The social changes ascribable to 'reform movements' may be slow and slight, but they do cumulate. The surface facts are familiar enough. The sixty-hour week has given way to the forty-hour week. Child labor has been progressively curtailed. With all its deficiencies, free universal education has become progressively institutionalized. These and other gains register a series of reform victories. And now, people have more leisure time. They have, ostensibly, greater access to the cultural heritage. And what use do they make of this unmortgaged time so painfully acquired for them? They listen to the radio and go to the movies. These mass media seem somehow to have cheated reformers of the fruits of their victories. The struggle for freedom for leisure and popular education and social security was carried on in the hope that, once freed of cramping shackles, people would avail themselves of major cultural products of our society, Shakespeare or Beethoven or perhaps Kant. Instead, they turn to Faith Baldwin or Johnny Mercer or Edgar Guest.

[...]

However little this sense of betrayal may account for prevailing attitudes toward the mass media, it may again be noted that the sheer presence of these media may not affect our society so profoundly as it is widely supposed.

SOME SOCIAL FUNCTIONS OF THE MASS MEDIA

In continuing our examination of the social role which can be ascribed to the mass media by virtue of their 'sheer existence,' we temporarily abstract from the social structure in which the media find their place. We do not, for example, consider the diverse effects of the mass media under varying systems of ownership and control, an important structural factor which will be discussed subsequently.

The mass media undoubtedly serve many social functions which might well become the object of sustained research. Of these functions, we have occasion to notice only three.

The status conferral function

The mass media *confer* status on public issues, persons, organizations, and social movements.

Common experience as well as research testifies that the social standing of persons or social policies is raised when these command favorable attention in the mass media. In many quarters, for example, the support of a political candidate or a public policy by *The Times* is taken as significant, and this support is regarded as a distinct asset for the candidate or the policy. Why?

For some, the editorial views of *The Times* represent the considered judgement of a group of experts, thus calling for the respect of laymen. But this is only one element in the status conferral function of the mass media, for enhanced status accrues to those who merely receive attention in the media, quite apart from any editorial support.

The mass media bestow prestige and enhance the authority of individuals and groups by *legitimizing their status*. Recognition by the press or radio or magazines or newsreels testifies that one has arrived, that one is important enough to have been singled out from the large anonymous masses, that one's behavior and opinions are significant enough to require public notice. The operation of this status conferral function may be witnessed most vividly in the advertising pattern of testimonials to a product by 'prominent people.' Within wide circles of the population (though not within certain selected social strata), such testimonials not only enhance the prestige of the product but also reflect prestige on the person who provides the testimonials. They give public notice that the large and powerful world of commerce regards him as possessing sufficiently high status for his opinion to count with many people. In a word, his testimonial is a testimonial to his own status.

[...]

This status conferral function thus enters into organized social action by legitimizing selected policies, persons, and groups which receive the support of mass media. We shall have occasion to note the detailed operation of this function in connection with the conditions making for the maximal utilization of mass media for designated social ends. At the moment, having considered the 'status conferral' function, we shall consider a second: the enforced application of social norms through the mass media.

The enforcement of social norms

Such catch phrases as 'the power of the press' (and other mass media) or 'the bright glare of publicity' presumably refer to this function. The mass media may initiate organized social action by 'exposing' conditions which are at variance with public moralities. But it need not be prematurely assumed that this pattern consists *simply* in making these deviations widely known. We have something to learn in this connection from Malinowski's observations among his beloved Trobriand Islanders. There, he reports, no organized social action is taken with respect to behavior deviant from a social norm unless there is *public* announcement of the deviation. This is not merely a matter of acquainting the individuals in the group with the facts of the case. Many may have known privately of these deviations – e.g., incest among the Trobrianders, as with political or business corruption, prostitution, gambling among ourselves – but they will not have pressed for public action. But once the behavioral deviations are made simultaneously public for all, this sets in train tensions between the 'privately tolerable' and the 'publicly acknowledgeable.'

The mechanism of public exposure would seem to operate somewhat as follows. Many social norms prove inconvenient for individuals in the society. They militate against the gratification of wants and impulses. Since many find the norms burdensome, there is some measure of leniency in applying them, both to oneself and to others. Hence, the emergence of deviant behavior and private toleration in these deviations. But this can continue only so long as one is not in a situation where one must take a public stand for or against the norms. Publicity, the enforced acknowledgment by members of the group that these deviations have occurred, requires each individual to take such a stand. He must either range himself with the non-conformists, thus proclaiming his repudiation of the group norms, and thus asserting that he, too, is outside the moral framework or, regardless of his private predilections, he must fall into line by supporting the norm. *Publicity closes the gap between 'private attitudes' and 'public morality.'* Publicity exerts pressure for a single rather than a dual morality by preventing continued evasion of the issue. It calls forth public reaffirmation and (however sporadic) application of the social norm.

In a mass society, this function of public exposure is institutionalized in the mass media of communication. Press, radio, and journals expose fairly well-known deviations to public view, and as a rule, this exposure forces some degree of public action against what has been privately tolerated. The mass media may, for example, introduce severe strains upon 'polite ethnic discrimination' by calling public attention to these practices which are at odds with the norms of non-discrimination. At times, the media may organize exposure activities into a 'crusade.'

[...]

[M]ass media clearly serve to reaffirm social norms by exposing deviations from these norms to public view. Study of the particular range of norms thus reaffirmed would provide a clear index of the extent to which these media deal with peripheral or central problems of the structure of our society.

The narcotizing dysfunction

A third social consequence of the mass media has gone largely unnoticed. At least, it has received little explicit comment and, apparently, has not been systematically put to use for furthering planned objectives. This may be called the narcotizing dysfunction of the mass media. It is termed *dysfunctional* rather than functional on the assumption that it is not in the interest of modern complex society to have large masses of the population politically apathetic and inert. How does this unplanned mechanism operate?

Scattered studies have shown that an increasing proportion of the time of Americans is devoted to the products of the mass media. With distinct variations in different regions and among different social strata, the outpourings of the media presumably enable the twentieth century American to 'keep abreast of the world.' Yet, it is suggested, this vast supply of communications may elicit only a superficial concern with the problems of society, and this superficiality often cloaks mass apathy.

Exposure to this flood of information may serve to narcotize rather than to energize the average reader or listener. As an increasing meed of time is devoted to reading and listening, a decreasing share is available for organized action. The individual reads accounts of issues and problems and may even discuss alternative lines of action. But this rather intellectualized, rather remote connection with organized social action is not activated. The interested and informed citizen can congratulate himself on his lofty state of interest and information and neglect to see that he has abstained from decision and action. In short, he takes his secondary contact with the world of political reality, his reading and listening and thinking, as a vicarious performance. He comes to mistake *knowing* about problems of the day for *doing* something about them. His social conscience remains spotlessly clean. He *is* concerned. He *is* informed. And he has all sorts of ideas as to what should be done. But, after he has gotten through his dinner and after he has listened to his favored radio programs and after he has read his second newspaper of the day, it is really time for bed.

In this peculiar respect, mass communications may be included among the most respectable and efficient of social narcotics. They may be so fully effective as to keep the addict from recognizing his own malady.

That the mass media have lifted the level of information of large populations is evident. Yet, quite apart from intent, increasing dosages of mass communications may be inadvertently transforming the energies of men from active participation into passive knowledge.

The occurrence of this narcotizing dysfunction can scarcely be doubted, but the extent to which it operates has yet to be determined. Research on this problem remains one of the many tasks still confronting the student of mass communications.

THE STRUCTURE OF OWNERSHIP AND OPERATION

To this point we have considered the mass media quite apart from their incorporation within a particular social and economic structure. But clearly, the social effects of the media will vary as the system of ownership and control varies. Thus to consider the social effects of American mass media is to deal only with the effects of these media as privately owned enterprises under profit-oriented management. It is general knowledge that this circumstance is not inherent in the technological nature of the mass media. In [Britain], for example, to say nothing of Russia, the radio is to all intents and purposes owned, controlled, and operated by government.

The structure of control is altogether different in this country. Its salient characteristic stems from the fact that except for movies and books, it is not the magazine reader nor the radio listener nor, in large part, the reader of newspapers who supports the enterprise, but the advertiser. Big business finances the production and distribution of mass media. And, all intent aside, he who pays the piper generally calls the tune.

SOCIAL CONFORMISM

Since the mass media are supported by great business concerns geared into the current social and economic system, the media contribute to the maintenance of that system. This contribution is not found merely in the effective advertisement of the sponsor's product. It arises, rather, from the typical presence in magazine stories, radio programs, and newspaper columns of some element of confirmation, some element of approval of the present structure of society. And this continuing reaffirmation underscores the duty to accept.

To the extent that the media of mass communication have had an influence upon their audiences, it has stemmed not only from what is said, but more significantly from what is not said. For these media not only continue to affirm the status quo but, in the same measure, they fail to raise essential questions about the structure of society. Hence by leading toward conformism and by providing little basis for a critical appraisal of society, the commercially sponsored mass media indirectly but effectively restrain the cogent development of a genuinely critical outlook.

This is not to ignore the occasionally critical journal article or radio program. But these exceptions are so few that they are lost in the overwhelming flood of conformist materials ...

Since our commercially sponsored mass media promote a largely unthinking allegiance to our social structure, they cannot be relied upon to work for changes, even minor changes, in that structure. It is possible to list some developments to the contrary, but upon close inspection they prove illusory. A community group, such as the PTA, may request the producer of a radio serial to inject the theme of tolerant race attitudes into the program. Should the producer feel that this theme is safe, that it will not antagonize any substantial part of his audience, he may agree, but at the first indication that it is a dangerous theme which may alienate potential consumers, he will refuse, or will soon abandon the experiment. Social objectives are consistently surrendered by commercialized media when they clash with economic gains. Minor tokens of 'progressive' views are of slight importance since they are included only by the grace of the sponsors and only on the condition that they be sufficiently acceptable as not to alienate any appreciable part of the audience. Economic pressure makes for conformism by omission of sensitive issues.

IMPACT UPON POPULAR TASTE

Since the largest part of our radio, movies, magazines, and a considerable part of our books and newspapers are devoted to 'entertainment,' this clearly requires us to consider the impact of the mass media upon popular taste.

Were we to ask the average American with some pretension to literary or esthetic cultivation if mass communications have had any effect upon popular taste, he would doubtlessly answer with a resounding affirmative. And more, citing abundant instances, he would insist that esthetic and intellectual tastes have been depraved by the flow of trivial formula products from printing presses, radio stations, and movie studios. The columns of criticism abound with these complaints.

In one sense, this requires no further discussion. There can be no doubt that the women who are daily entranced for three or four hours by some twelve consecutive 'soap operas,' all cut to the same dismal pattern, exhibit an appalling lack of esthetic judgement. Nor is this impression altered by the contents of pulp and slick magazines, or by the depressing abundance of formula motion pictures replete with hero, heroine, and villain moving through a contrived atmosphere of sex, sin, and success.

Yet unless we locate these patterns in historical and sociological terms, we may find ourselves confusedly engaged in condemning without understanding, in criticism which is sound but largely irrelevant. What is the historical status of this notoriously low level of popular taste? Is it the poor remains of standards which were once significantly higher, a relatively new birth in the world of values, largely unrelated to the higher standards from which it has allegedly fallen, or a poor substitute blocking the way to the development of superior standards and the expression of high esthetic purpose?

If esthetic tastes are to be considered in their social setting, we must recognize that the effective audience for the arts has become historically transformed. Some centuries back, this audience was largely confined to a selected aristocratic elite. Relatively few were literate. And very few possessed the means to buy books, attend theaters, and travel to the urban centers of the arts. Not more than a slight fraction, possibly not more than one or two per cent, of the population composed the effective audience for the arts. These happy few cultivated their esthetic tastes, and their selective demand left its mark in the form of relatively high artistic standards.

With the widesweeping spread of popular education and with the emergence of the new technologies of mass communication, there developed an enormously enlarged market for the arts. Some forms of music, drama, and literature now reach virtually everyone in our society. This is why, of course, we speak of *mass* media and of *mass* art. And the great audiences for the mass media, though in the main literate, are not highly cultivated. About half the population, in fact, have halted their formal education upon leaving grammar school.

[...]

Our formulation of the problem should now be plain. It is misleading to speak simply of the decline of esthetic tastes. Mass audiences probably include a larger number of persons with cultivated esthetic standards, but these are swallowed up by the large masses who constitute the new and untutored audience for the arts. Whereas yesterday the elite constituted virtually the whole of the audience, they are today a minute fraction of the whole. In consequence, the average level of esthetic standards and tastes of audiences has been depressed, although the tastes of some sectors of the population have undoubtedly been raised and the total number of people exposed to communication contents has been vastly increased.

But this analysis does not directly answer the question of the effects of the mass media upon public taste, a question which is as complex as it is unexplored. The answer can come only from disciplined research. One would want to know, for example, whether mass media have robbed the intellectual and artistic elite of the art forms which might otherwise have been accessible to them. And this involves inquiry into the pressure exerted by the mass audience upon creative individuals to cater to mass tastes. Literary hacks have existed in every age. But it would be important to learn if the electrification of the arts supplies power for a significantly greater proportion of dim literary lights. And, above all, it would be essential to determine if mass media and mass tastes are necessarily linked in a vicious circle of deteriorating standards or if appropriate action on the part of the directors of mass media could initiate a virtuous circle of cumulatively improving tastes among their audiences. More concretely, are the operators of commercialized mass media caught up in a situation in which they cannot, whatever their private preferences, radically raise the esthetic standards of their products?

In passing, it should be noted that much remains to be learned concerning standards appropriate for mass art. It is possible that standards for art forms produced by a small band of creative talents for a small and selective audience are not applicable to art forms produced by a gigantic industry for the population at large. The beginnings of investigation on this problem are sufficiently suggestive to warrant further study.

Sporadic and consequently inconclusive experiments in the raising of standards have met with profound resistance from mass audiences. On occasion, radio stations and networks have attempted to supplant a soap opera with a program of classical music, or formula comedy skits with discussions of public issues. In general, the people supposed to benefit by this reformation of program have simply refused to be benefited. They cease listening. The audience dwindles. Researches have shown, for example, that radio programs of classical music tend to preserve rather than to create interest in classical music and that newly emerging interests are typically superficial. Most listeners to these programs have previously acquired an interest in classical music; the few whose interest is initiated by the programs are caught up by melodic compositions and come to think of classical music exclusively in terms of Tschaikowsky or Rimsky-Korsakow or Dvorak.

[...]

We turn now to the third and last aspect of the social role of the mass media: the possibilities of utilizing them for moving toward designated types of social objectives.

PROPAGANDA FOR SOCIAL OBJECTIVES

This final question is perhaps of more direct interest to you than the other questions we have discussed. It represents something of a challenge to us since it provides the means of resolving the apparent paradox to which we referred previously: the seeming paradox arising from the assertion that the significance of the sheer existence of the mass media has been exaggerated and the multiple indications that the media do exert influences upon their audiences.

What are the conditions for the effective use of mass media for what might be called 'propaganda for social objectives' – the promotion, let us say, of non-discriminatory race relations, or of educational reforms, or of positive attitudes toward organized labor? Research indicates that, at least, one or more of three conditions must be satisfied if this propaganda is to prove effective. These conditions may be briefly designated as (1) monopolization, (2) canalization rather than change of basic values, and (3) supplementary face-to-face contact. Each of these conditions merits some discussion.

Monopolization

This situation obtains when there is little or no opposition in the mass media to the diffusion of values, policies, or public images. That is to say, monopolization of the mass media occurs in the absence of counterpropaganda.

In this restricted sense, monopolization of the mass media is found in diverse circumstances. It is, of course, indigenous to the political structure of authoritarian society, where access to the media of communication is wholly closed to those who oppose the official ideology. The evidence suggests that this monopoly played some part in enabling the Nazis to maintain their control of the German people.

But this same situation is approximated in other social systems. During the war, for example, our government utilized the radio, with some success, to promote and to maintain identification with the war effort. The effectiveness of these morale building efforts was in large measure due to the virtually complete absence of counterpropaganda.

Similar situations arise in the world of commercialized propaganda. The mass media create popular idols. The public images of the radio performer, Kate Smith, for example, picture her as a woman with unparalleled understanding of other American women, deeply sympathetic with ordinary men and women, a spiritual guide and mentor, a patriot whose views on public affairs should be taken seriously. Linked with the cardinal American virtues, the public images of Kate Smith are at no point subject to a counterpropaganda. Not that she has no competitors in the market of radio advertising. But there are none who set themselves systematically to question what she has said. In consequence, an unmarried radio entertainer with an annual income in six figures may be visualized by millions of American women as a hard-working mother who knows the recipe for managing life on fifteen hundred a year.

This image of a popular idol would have far less currency were it subjected to counterpropaganda. Such neutralization occurs, for example, as a result of preelection campaigns by Republicans and Democrats. By and large, as a recent study has shown, the propaganda issued by each of these parties neutralizes the effect of the other's propaganda. Were both parties to forgo their campaigning through the mass media entirely, it is altogether likely that the net effect would be to reproduce the present distribution of votes.

[...]

To the extent that opposing political propaganda in the mass media are balanced, the net effect is negligible. The virtual monopolization of the media for given social objectives, however, will produce discernible effects upon audiences.

CANALIZATION

Prevailing beliefs in the enormous power of mass communications appear to stem from successful cases of monopolistic propaganda or from advertising. But the leap from the efficacy of advertising to the assumed efficacy of propaganda aimed at deep-rooted attitudes and ego involved behavior is as unwarranted as it is dangerous. Advertising is typically directed toward the canalizing of preexisting behavior patterns or attitudes. It seldom seeks to instil new attitudes or to create significantly new behavior patterns. 'Advertising pays' because it generally deals with a simple psychological situation. For Americans who have been socialized in the use of a toothbrush, it makes relatively little difference which brand of toothbrush they use. Once the gross pattern of behavior or the generic attitude has been established, it can be canalized in one direction or another. Resistance is slight. But mass propaganda typically meets a more complex situation. It may seek objectives which are at odds with deeplying attitudes. It may seek to reshape rather than to canalize current systems of values. And the successes of advertising may only highlight the failures of propaganda. Much of the current propaganda which is aimed at abolishing deep-seated and racial prejudices, for example, seems to have had little effectiveness.

Media of mass communication, then, have been effectively used to canalize basic attitudes but there is little evidence of their having served to change these attitudes.

SUPPLEMENTATION

Mass propaganda which is neither monopolistic nor canalizing in character may, nonetheless, prove effective if it meets a third condition: supplementation through face-to-face contacts.

[...]

Students of mass movements have come to repudiate the view that mass propaganda in and of itself creates or maintains the movement. Naziism did not attain its brief moment of hegemony by capturing the mass media of communication. The media played an ancillary role, supplementing the use of organized violence, organized distribution of rewards for conformity, and organized centers of local indoctrination. The Soviet Union has also made large and impressive use of mass media for indoctrinating enormous populations with appropriate ideologies. But the organizers of indoctrination saw to it that the mass media did not operate alone. 'Red corners,' 'reading huts,' and 'listening stations' comprised meeting places in which groups of citizens were exposed to the mass media in common. The 55,000 reading rooms and clubs which had come into being by 1933 enabled the local ideological elite to talk over with rank-and-file readers the content of what they read. The relative scarcity of radios in private homes again made for group listening and group discussions of what had been heard.

In these instances, the machinery of mass persuasion included face-to-face contact in local organizations as an adjunct to the mass media. The privatized individual response to the materials presented through the channels of mass communication was considered inadequate for transforming exposure to propaganda into effectiveness of propaganda. In a society such as our own, where the pattern of bureaucratization has not yet become so pervasive or, at least, not so clearly crystallized, it has likewise been found that mass media prove most effective in conjunction with local centers of organized face-to-face contact.

Several factors contribute to the enhanced effectiveness of this joining of mass media and direct personal contact. Most clearly, the local discussions serve to reinforce the content of mass propaganda. Such mutual confirmation produces a 'clinching effect.' Secondly, the central media lessen the task of the local organizer, and the personnel requirements for such subalterns need not be as rigorous in a popular movement. The subalterns need not set forth the propaganda content for themselves, but need only pilot potential converts to the radio where the doctrine is being expounded. Thirdly, the appearance of a representative of the movement on a nation-wide network, or his mention in the national press, serves to symbolize the legitimacy and significance of the movement. It is no powerless, inconsequential enterprise. The mass media, as we have seen, confer status. And the status of the national movement reflects back on the status of the local cells, thus consolidating the tentative decisions of its members. In this interlocking arrangement, the local organizer ensures an audience for the national speaker and the national speaker validates the status of the local organizer.

This brief summary of the situations in which the mass media achieve their maximum propaganda effect may resolve the seeming contradiction which arose at the outset of our discussion. The mass media prove most effective when they operate in a situation of virtual 'psychological monopoly,' or when the objective is one of canalizing rather than modifying basic attitudes or when they operate in conjunction with face-to-face contacts.

But these three conditions are rarely satisfied conjointly in propaganda for social objectives. To the degree that monopolization of attention is rare, opposing propagandas have free play in a democracy. And, by and large, basic social issues involve more than a mere canalizing of preexistent basic attitudes; they call, rather, for substantial changes in attitude and behavior. Finally, for the most obvious of reasons, the close collaboration of mass media and locally organized centers for face-to-face contact has seldom been achieved in groups striving for planned social change. Such programs are expensive. And it is precisely these groups which seldom have the large resources needed for these expensive programs. The forward looking groups at the edges of the power structure do not ordinarily have the large financial means of the contented groups at the center.

As a result of this threefold situation, the present role of media is largely confined to peripheral social concerns and the media do not exhibit the degree of social power commonly attributed to them.

By the same token, and in view of the present organization of business ownership and control of the mass media, they have served to cement the structure of our society. Organized business does approach a virtual 'psychological monopoly' of the mass media. Radio commercials and newspaper advertisements are, of course, premised on a system which has been termed free enterprise. Moreover, the world of commerce is primarily concerned with canalizing rather than radically changing basic attitudes; it seeks only to create preferences for one rather than another brand of product. Face-to-face contacts with those who have been socialized in our culture serve primarily to reinforce the prevailing culture patterns.

Thus, the very conditions which make for the maximum effectiveness of the mass media of communication operate toward the maintenance of the going social and cultural structure rather than toward its change.

2

CULTURE INDUSTRY RECONSIDERED

Theodor W. Adorno

The term culture industry was perhaps used for the first time in the book *Dialectic of Enlightenment*, which Horkheimer and I published in Amsterdam in 1947. In our drafts we spoke of 'mass culture'. We replaced that expression with 'culture industry' in order to exclude from the outset the interpretation agreeable to its advocates: that it is a matter of something like a culture that arises spontaneously from the masses themselves, the contemporary form of popular art. From the latter the culture industry must be distinguished in the extreme. The culture industry fuses the old and familiar into a new quality. In all its branches, products which are tailored for consumption by masses, and which to a great extent determine the nature of that consumption, are manufactured more or less according to plan. The individual branches are similar in structure or at least fit into each other, ordering themselves into a system almost without a gap. This is made possible by contemporary technical capabilities as well as by economic and administrative concentration. The culture industry intentionally integrates its consumers from above. To the detriment of both it forces together the spheres of high and low art, separated for thousands of years. The seriousness of high art is destroyed in speculation about its efficacy; the seriousness of the lower perishes with the civilizational constraints imposed on the rebellious resistance inherent within it as long as

Originally a broadcast talk given on the Hessian Broadcasting System, Federal Republic of Germany in spring 1963, this piece was published in this translation by Anson G. Rabinbach, *New German Critique* no. 6 (Fall 1975) pp. 12–19; repr. as ch. 3 of Theodor W. Adorno *The Culture Industry: Selected Essays on Mass Culture*, ed. with an introduction by J. M. Bernstein (London: Routledge, 1991) pp. 85–92.

social control was not yet total. Thus, although the culture industry undeniably speculates on the conscious and unconscious state of the millions towards which it is directed, the masses are not primary, but secondary, they are an object of calculation; an appendage of the machinery. The customer is not king, as the culture industry would have us believe, not its subject but its object. The very word mass-media, specially honed for the culture industry, already shifts the accents onto harmless terrain. Neither is it a question of primary concern for the masses, nor of the techniques of communication as such, but of the spirit which sufflates them, their master's voice. The culture industry misuses its concern for the masses in order to duplicate, reinforce and strengthen their mentality, which it presumes is given and unchangeable. How this mentality might be changed is excluded throughout. The masses are not the measure but the ideology of the culture industry, even though the culture industry itself could scarcely exist without adapting to the masses.

The cultural commodities of the industry are governed, as Brecht and Suhrkamp expressed it thirty years ago, by the principle of their realization as value, and not by their own specific content and harmonious formation. The entire practice of the culture industry transfers the profit motive naked onto cultural forms. Ever since these cultural forms first began to earn a living for their creators as commodities in the market-place they had already possessed something of this quality. But then they sought after profit only indirectly, over and above their autonomous essence. New on the part of the culture industry is the direct and undisguised primacy of a precisely and thoroughly calculated efficacy in its most typical products. The autonomy of works of art, which of course rarely ever predominated in an entirely pure form, and was always permeated by a constellation of effects, is tendentially eliminated by the culture industry, with or without the conscious will of those in control. The latter include both those who carry out directives as well as those who hold the power. In economic terms they are or were in search of new opportunities for the realization of capital in the most economically developed countries. The old opportunities became increasingly more precarious as a result of the same concentration process which alone makes the culture industry possible as an omnipresent phenomenon. Culture, in the true sense, did not simply accommodate itself to human beings; but it always simultaneously raised a protest against the petrified relations under which they lived, thereby honouring them. In so far as culture becomes wholly assimilated to and integrated in those petrified relations, human beings are once more debased. Cultural entities typical of the culture industry are no longer *also* commodities, they are commodities through and through. This quantitative shift is so great that it calls forth entirely new phenomena. Ultimately, the culture industry no longer even needs to directly pursue everywhere the profit interests from which it originated. These interests have become objectified in its ideology and have even made themselves independent of the compulsion to sell the cultural commodities which must be swallowed anyway. The culture industry turns into public relations, the manufacturing of 'goodwill' *per se*, without regard for particular firms or saleable objects. Brought to bear is a general uncritical consensus, advertisements produced for the world, so that each product of the culture industry becomes its own advertisement.

Nevertheless, those characteristics which originally stamped the transformation of literature into a commodity are maintained in this process. More than anything in the world, the culture industry has its ontology, a scaffolding of rigidly conservative basic categories which can be gleaned, for example, from the commercial English novels of the late seventeenth and early eighteenth centuries. What parades as progress in the culture industry, as the incessantly new which it offers up, remains the disguise for an eternal sameness; everywhere the changes mask a skeleton which has changed just as little as the profit motive itself since the time it first gained its predominance over culture.

Thus, the expression 'industry' is not to be taken too literally. It refers to the standardization of the thing itself – such as that of the Western, familiar to every movie-goer – and to the rationalization of distribution techniques, but not strictly to the production process. Although in film, the central sector of the culture industry, the production process resembles technical modes of operation in the extensive division of labour, the employment of machines and the separation of the labourers from the means of production – expressed in the perennial conflict between artists active in the culture industry and those who control it – individual forms of production are nevertheless maintained. Each product affects an individual air; individuality itself serves to reinforce ideology, in so far as the illusion is conjured up that the completely reified and mediated is a sanctuary from immediacy and life. Now, as ever, the culture industry exists in the 'service' of third persons, maintaining its affinity to the declining circulation process of capital, to the commerce from which it came into being. Its ideology above all makes use of the star system, borrowed from individualistic art and its commercial exploitation. The more dehumanized its methods of operation and content, the more diligently and successfully the culture industry propagates supposedly great personalities and operates with heart-throbs. It is industrial more in a sociological sense, in the incorporation of industrial forms of organization even when nothing is manufactured – as in the rationalization of office work – rather than in the sense of anything really and actually produced by technological rationality. Accordingly, the misinvestments of the culture industry are considerable, throwing those branches rendered obsolete by new techniques into crises, which seldom lead to changes for the better.

The concept of technique in the culture industry is only in name identical with technique in works of art. In the latter, technique is concerned with the internal organization of the object itself, with its inner logic. In contrast, the technique of the culture industry is, from the beginning, one of distribution and mechanical reproduction, and therefore always remains external to its object. The culture industry finds ideological support precisely in so far as it carefully shields itself from the full potential of the techniques contained in its products. It lives parasitically from the extra-artistic technique of the material production of goods, without regard for the obligation to the internal artistic whole implied by its functionality (*Sachlichkeit*), but also without concern for the laws of form demanded by aesthetic autonomy. The result for the physiognomy of the culture industry is essentially a mixture of streamlining, photographic hardness and precision on the one hand, and individualistic residues, sentimentality and an already rationally disposed and adapted romanticism on the other. Adopting Benjamin's designation of the traditional work of art by the concept of aura, the presence of that which is not present, the culture industry is defined by the fact that it does not strictly counterpose another principle to that of aura, but rather by the fact that it conserves the decaying aura as a foggy mist. By this means the culture industry betrays its own ideological abuses.

It has recently become customary among cultural officials as well as sociologists to warn against underestimating the culture industry while pointing to its great importance for the development of the consciousness of its consumers. It is to be taken seriously, without cultured snobbism. In actuality the culture industry is important as a moment of the spirit which dominates today. Whoever ignores its influence out of scepticism for what it stuffs into people would be naive. Yet there is a deceptive glitter about the admonition to take it seriously. Because of its social role, disturbing questions about its quality, about truth or untruth, and about the aesthetic niveau of the culture industry's emissions are repressed, or at least excluded from the so-called sociology of communications. The critic is accused of taking refuge in arrogant esoterica. It would be advisable first to indicate the double meaning of importance that slowly worms its way in unnoticed. Even if it touches the lives of innumerable people, the function of something is no guarantee of its particular quality. The blending of aesthetics with its residual communicative aspects leads art, as a social phenomenon, not to its rightful position in opposition to alleged artistic snobbism, but rather in a variety of ways to the defence of its baneful social consequences. The importance of the culture industry in the spiritual constitution of the masses is no dispensation for reflection on its objective legitimation, its essential being, least of all by a science which thinks itself pragmatic. On the contrary: such reflection becomes necessary precisely for this reason. To take the culture industry as seriously as its unquestioned role demands, means to take it seriously critically, and not to cower in the face of its monopolistic character.

Among those intellectuals anxious to reconcile themselves with the phenomenon and eager to find a common formula to express both their reservations against it and their respect for its power, a tone of ironic toleration prevails unless they have already created a new mythos of the twentieth century from the imposed regression. After all, those intellectuals maintain, everyone knows what pocket novels, films off the rack, family television shows rolled out into serials and hit parades, advice to the lovelorn and horoscope columns are all

about. All of this, however, is harmless and, according to them, even democratic since it responds to a demand, albeit a stimulated one. It also bestows all
kinds of blessings, they point out, for example, through the dissemination of
information, advice and stress reducing patterns of behaviour. Of course, as
every sociological study measuring something as elementary as how politically
informed the public is has proven, the information is meagre or indifferent.
Moreover, the advice to be gained from manifestations of the culture industry
is vacuous, banal or worse, and the behaviour patterns are shamelessly
conformist.

The two-faced irony in the relationship of servile intellectuals to the culture
industry is not restricted to them alone. It may also be supposed that the consciousness of the consumers themselves is split between the prescribed fun
which is supplied to them by the culture industry and a not particularly well-
hidden doubt about its blessings. The phrase, the world wants to be deceived,
has become truer than had ever been intended. People are not only, as the saying
goes, falling for the swindle; if it guarantees them even the most fleeting
gratification they desire a deception which is nonetheless transparent to them.
They force their eyes shut and voice approval, in a kind of self-loathing, for
what is meted out to them, knowing fully the purpose for which it is manufactured. Without admitting it they sense that their lives would be completely
intolerable as soon as they no longer clung to satisfactions which are none at all.

The most ambitious defence of the culture industry today celebrates its spirit,
which might be safely called ideology, as an ordering factor. In a supposedly
chaotic world it provides human beings with something like standards for
orientation, and that alone seems worthy of approval. However, what its
defenders imagine is preserved by the culture industry is in fact all the more
thoroughly destroyed by it. The colour film demolishes the genial old tavern to a
greater extent than bombs ever could: the film exterminates its imago. No
homeland can survive being processed by the films which celebrate it, and
which thereby turn the unique character on which it thrives into an interchangeable sameness.

That which legitimately could be called culture attempted, as an expression
of suffering and contradiction, to maintain a grasp on the idea of the good life.
Culture cannot represent either that which merely exists or the conventional
and no longer binding categories of order which the culture industry drapes
over the idea of the good life as if existing reality were the good life, and as if
those categories were its true measure. If the response of the culture industry's
representatives is that it does not deliver art at all, this is itself the ideology with
which they evade responsibility for that from which the business lives. No
misdeed is ever righted by explaining it as such.

The appeal to order alone, without concrete specificity, is futile; the appeal
to the dissemination of norms, without these ever proving themselves in reality
or before consciousness, is equally futile. The idea of an objectively binding
order, huckstered to people because it is so lacking for them, has no claims if it

does not prove itself internally and in confrontation with human beings. But this is precisely what no product of the culture industry would engage in. The concepts of order which it hammers into human beings are always those of the status quo. They remain unquestioned, unanalysed and undialectically pre-supposed, even if they no longer have any substance for those who accept them. In contrast to the Kantian, the categorical imperative of the culture industry no longer has anything in common with freedom. It proclaims: you shall conform, without instruction as to what; conform to that which exists anyway, and to that which everyone thinks anyway as a reflex of this power and omnipresence. The power of the culture industry's ideology is such that conformity has replaced consciousness. The order that springs from it is never confronted with what it claims to be or with the real interests of human beings. Order, however, is not good in itself. It would be so only as a good order. The fact that the culture industry is oblivious to this and extols order *in abstracto*, bears witness to the impotence and untruth of the messages it conveys. While it claims to lead the perplexed, it deludes them with false conflicts which they are to exchange for their own. It solves conflicts for them only in appearance, in a way that they can hardly be solved in their real lives. In the products of the culture industry human beings get into trouble only so that they can be rescued unharmed, usually by representatives of a benevolent collective; and then in empty harmony, they are reconciled with the general, whose demands they had experienced at the outset as irreconcileable with their interests. For this purpose the culture industry has developed formulas which even reach into such non-conceptual areas as light musical entertainment. Here too one gets into a 'jam', into rhythmic problems, which can be instantly disentangled by the triumph of the basic beat.

Even its defenders, however, would hardly contradict Plato openly who maintained that what is objectively and intrinsically untrue cannot also be sub-jectively good and true for human beings. The concoctions of the culture industry are neither guides for a blissful life, nor a new art of moral responsi-bility, but rather exhortations to toe the line, behind which stand the most powerful interests. The consensus which it propagates strengthens blind, opaque authority. If the culture industry is measured not by its own substance and logic, but by its efficacy, by its position in reality and its explicit pretensions; if the focus of serious concern is with the efficacy to which it always appeals, the potential of its effect becomes twice as weighty. This potential, however, lies in the promotion and exploitation of the ego-weakness to which the power-less members of contemporary society, with its concentration of power, are condemned. Their consciousness is further developed retrogressively. It is no coincidence that cynical American film producers are heard to say that their pictures must take into consideration the level of eleven-year-olds. In doing so they would very much like to make adults into eleven-year-olds.

It is true that thorough research has not, for the time being, produced an airtight case proving the regressive effects of particular products of the culture industry. No doubt an imaginatively designed experiment could achieve this more successfully than the powerful financial interests concerned would find comfortable. In any case, it can be assumed without hesitation that steady drops hollow the stone, especially since the system of the culture industry that surrounds the masses tolerates hardly any deviation and incessantly drills the same formulas on behaviour. Only their deep unconscious mistrust, the last residue of the difference between art and empirical reality in the spiritual make-up of the masses explains why they have not, to a person long since perceived and accepted the world as it is constructed for them by the culture industry. Even if its messages were as harmless as they are made out to be – on countless occasions they are obviously not harmless, like the movies which chime in with currently popular hate campaigns against intellectuals by portraying them with the usual stereotypes – the attitudes which the culture industry calls forth are anything but harmless. If an astrologer urges his readers to drive carefully on a particular day, that certainly hurts no one; they will, however, be harmed indeed by the stupefication which lies in the claim that advice which is valid every day and which is therefore idiotic, needs the approval of the stars.

Human dependence and servitude, the vanishing point of the culture industry, could scarcely be more faithfully described than by the American interviewee who was of the opinion that the dilemmas of the contemporary epoch would end if people would simply follow the lead of prominent personalities. In so far as the culture industry arouses a feeling of well-being that the world is precisely in that order suggested by the culture industry, the substitute gratification which it prepares for human beings cheats them out of the same happiness which it deceitfully projects. The total effect of the culture industry is one of anti-enlightenment, in which, as Horkheimer and I have noted, enlightenment, that is the progressive technical domination of nature, becomes mass deception and is turned into a means for fettering consciousness. It impedes the development of autonomous, independent individuals who judge and decide consciously for themselves. These, however, would be the precondition for a democratic society which needs adults who have come of age in order to sustain itself and develop. If the masses have been unjustly reviled from above as masses, the culture industry is not among the least responsible for making them into masses and then despising them, while obstructing the emancipation for which human beings are as ripe as the productive forces of the epoch permit.

3

THE MEDIUM IS THE MESSAGE

Marshall McLuhan

In a culture like ours, long accustomed to splitting and dividing all things as a means of control, it is sometimes a bit of a shock to be reminded that, in operational practical fact, the medium is the message. This is merely to say that the personal and social consequences of any medium – that is, of any extension of ourselves – result from the new scale that is introduced into our affairs by each extension of ourselves, or by any new technology. Thus, with automation,[1] for example, the new patterns of human association tend to eliminate jobs, it is true. That is the negative result. Positively, automation creates roles for people, which is to say depth of involvement in their work and human association that our preceding mechanical technology had destroyed. Many people would be disposed to say that it was not the machine, but what one did with the machine, that was its meaning or message. In terms of the ways in which the machine altered our relations to one another and to ourselves, it mattered not in the least whether it turned out cornflakes or Cadillacs. The restructuring of human work and association was shaped by the technique of fragmentation that is the essence of machine technology. The essence of automation technology is the opposite. It is integral and decentralist in depth, just as the machine was fragmentary, centralist, and superficial in its patterning of human relationships.

The instance of the electric light may prove illuminating in this connection. The electric light is pure information. It is a medium without a message, as it

From Marshall McLuhan, *Understanding Media: the Extensions of Man* (London: Routledge & Kegan Paul, 1964) pp. 11, 15–21, 31–3, 68–9.

were, unless it is used to spell out some verbal ad or name. This fact, characteristic of all media, means that the 'content' of any medium is always another medium. The content of writing is speech, just as the written word is the content of print, and print is the content of the telegraph. If it is asked, 'What is the content of speech?' it is necessary to say, 'It is an actual process of thought, which is in itself nonverbal.' An abstract painting represents direct manifestation of creative thought processes as they might appear in computer designs. What we are considering here, however, are the psychic and social consequences of the designs or patterns as they amplify or accelerate existing processes. For the 'message' of any medium or technology is the change of scale or pace or pattern that it introduces into human affairs. The railway did not introduce movement or transportation or wheel or road into human society, but it accelerated and enlarged the scale of previous human functions, creating totally new kinds of cities and new kinds of work and leisure. This happened whether the railway functioned in a tropical or a northern environment, and is quite independent of the freight or content of the railway medium. The airplane, on the other hand, by accelerating the rate of transportation, tends to dissolve the railway form of city, politics, and association, quite independently of what the airplane is used for.

Let us return to the electric light. Whether the light is being used for brain surgery or night baseball is a matter of indifference. It could be argued that these activities are in some way the 'content' of the electric light, since they could not exist without the electric light. This fact merely underlines the point that 'the medium is the message' because it is the medium that shapes and controls the scale and form of human association and action. The content or uses of such media are as diverse as they are ineffectual in shaping the form of human association. Indeed, it is only too typical that the 'content' of any medium blinds us to the character of the medium. It is only today that industries have become aware of the various kinds of business in which they are engaged. When IBM discovered that it was not in the business of making office equipment or business machines, but that it was in the business of processing information, then it began to navigate with clear vision. The General Electric Company makes a considerable portion of its profits from electric light bulbs and lighting systems. It has not yet discovered that, quite as much as A.T. & T, it is in the business of moving information.

The electric light escapes attention as a communication medium just because it has no 'content.' And this makes it an invaluable instance of how people fail to study media at all. For it is not till the electric light is used to spell out some brand name that it is noticed as a medium. Then it is not the light but the 'content' (or what is really another medium) that is noticed. The message of the electric light is like the message of electric power in industry, totally radical, pervasive, and decentralized. For electric light and power are separate from their uses, yet they eliminate time and space factors in human association exactly as do radio, telegraph, telephone, and TV, creating involvement in depth.

[. . .]

In accepting an honorary degree from the University of Notre Dame a few years ago, General David Sarnoff[2] made this statement: 'We are too prone to make technological instruments the scapegoats for the sins of those who wield them. The products of modern science are not in themselves good or bad; it is the way they are used that determines their value.' That is the voice of the current somnambulism. Suppose we were to say, 'Apple pie is in itself neither good nor bad; it is the way it is used that determines its value.' Or, 'The smallpox virus is in itself neither good nor bad; it is the way it is used that determines its value.' Again. 'Firearms are in themselves neither good nor bad; it is the way they are used that determines their value.' That is, if the slugs reach the right people firearms are good. If the TV tube fires the right ammunition at the right people it is good. I am not being perverse. There is simply nothing in the Sarnoff statement that will bear scrutiny, for it ignores the nature of the medium, of any and all media, in the true Narcissus style of one hypnotized by the amputation and extension of his own being in a new technical form. General Sarnoff went on to explain his attitude to the technology of print, saying that it was true that print caused much trash to circulate, but it had also disseminated the Bible and the thoughts of seers and philosophers. It has never occurred to General Sarnoff that any technology could do anything but *add* itself on to what we already are.

[. . .]

[M]echanization is achieved by fragmentation of any process and by putting the fragmented parts in a series. Yet, as David Hume showed in the eighteenth century, there is no principle of causality in a mere sequence. That one thing follows another accounts for nothing. Nothing follows from following, except change. So the greatest of all reversals occurred with electricity, that ended sequence by making things instant. With instant speed the causes of things began to emerge to awareness again, as they had not done with things in sequence and in concatenation accordingly. Instead of asking which came first, the chicken or the egg, it suddenly seemed that a chicken was an egg's idea for getting more eggs.

Just before an airplane breaks the sound barrier, sound waves become visible on the wings of the plane. The sudden visibility of sound just as sound ends is an apt instance of that great pattern of being that reveals new and opposite forms just as the earlier forms reach their peak performance. Mechanization was never so vividly fragmented or sequential as in the birth of the movies, the moment that translated us beyond mechanism into the world of growth and organic interrelation. The movie, by sheer speeding up the mechanical, carried us from the world of sequence and connections into the world of creative configuration and structure. The message of the movie medium is that of transition from lineal connections to configurations. It is the transition that produced the now quite correct observation: 'If it works, it's obsolete.' When electric speed further takes over from mechanical movie sequences, then the lines of force in structures and in media become loud and clear. We return to the inclusive form of the icon.

To a highly literate and mechanized culture the movie appeared as a world of triumphant illusions and dreams that money could buy. It was at this moment of the movie that cubism occurred, and it has been described by E. H. Gombrich (*Art and Illusion*) as 'the most radical attempt to stamp out ambiguity and to enforce one reading of the picture – that of a man-made construction, a colored canvas.' For cubism substitutes all facets of an object simultaneously for the 'point of view' or facet of perspective illusion. Instead of the specialized illusion of the third dimension on canvas, cubism sets up an interplay of planes and contradiction or dramatic conflict of patterns, lights, textures that 'drives home the message' by involvement. This is held by many to be an exercise in painting, not in illusion.

In other words, cubism, by giving the inside and outside, the top, bottom, back, and front and the rest, in two dimensions, drops the illusion of perspective in favor of instant sensory awareness of the whole. Cubism, by seizing on instant total awareness, suddenly announced that *the medium is the message*. Is it not evident that the moment that sequence yields to the simultaneous, one is in the world of the structure and of configuration? Is that not what has happened in physics as in painting, poetry, and in communication? Specialized segments of attention have shifted to total field, and we can now say, 'The medium is the message' quite naturally. Before the electric speed and total field, it was not obvious that the medium is the message. The message, it seemed, was the 'content,' as people used to ask what a painting was *about*. Yet they never thought to ask what a melody was about, nor what a house or a dress was about. In such matters, people retained some sense of the whole pattern, of form and function as a unity. But in the electric age this integral idea of structure and configuration has become [...] prevalent [...].

[...]

HOT AND COLD

[...]

There is a basic principle that distinguishes a hot medium like radio from a cool one like the telephone, or a hot medium like the movie from a cool one like TV. A hot medium is one that extends one single sense in 'high definition.' High definition is the state of being well filled with data. A photograph is, visually, 'high definition.' A cartoon is 'low definition,' simply because very little visual information is provided. Telephone is a cool medium, or one of low definition, because the ear is given a meager amount of information. And speech is a cool medium of low definition, because so little is given and so much has to be filled in by the listener. On the other hand, hot media do not leave so much to be filled in or completed by the audience. Hot media are, therefore, low in participation, and cool media are high in participation or completion by the audience. Naturally, therefore, a hot medium like radio has very different effects on the user from a cool medium like the telephone.

A cool medium like hieroglyphic or ideogrammic written characters has very different effects from the hot and explosive medium of the phonetic alphabet. The alphabet, when pushed to a high degree of abstract visual intensity, became typography. The printed word with its specialist intensity burst the bonds of medieval corporate guilds and monasteries, creating extreme individualist patterns of enterprise and monopoly. But the typical reversal occurred when extremes of monopoly brought back the corporation, with its impersonal empire over many lives. The hotting-up of the medium of writing to repeatable print intensity led to nationalism and the religious wars of the sixteenth century. The heavy and unwieldy media, such as stone, are time binders. Used for writing, they are very cool indeed, and serve to unify the ages; whereas paper is a hot medium that serves to unify spaces horizontally, both in political and entertainment empires.

Any hot medium allows of less participation than a cool one, as a lecture makes for less participation than a seminar, and a book for less than dialogue. With print many earlier forms were excluded from life and art, and many were given strange new intensity.

[...]

A tribal and feudal hierarchy of traditional kind collapses quickly when it meets any hot medium of the mechanical, uniform, and repetitive kind. The medium of money or wheel or writing, or any other form of specialist speed-up of exchange and information, will serve to fragment a tribal structure. Similarly, a very much greater speed-up, such as occurs with electricity, may serve to restore a tribal pattern of intense involvement such as took place with the introduction of radio in Europe, and is now tending to happen as a result of TV in America. Specialist technologies detribalize. The non-specialist electric technology retribalizes.

[...]

By putting our physical bodies inside our extended nervous systems, by means of electric media, we set up a dynamic by which all previous technologies that are mere extensions of hands and feet and teeth and bodily heat-controls – all such extensions of our bodies, including cities – will be translated into information systems. Electromagnetic technology requires utter human docility and quiescence of meditation such as benefits an organism that now wears its brain outside its skull and its nerves outside its hide. Man must serve his electric technology with the same servomechanistic fidelity with which he served his coracle, his canoe, his typography, and all other extensions of his physical organs. But there is this difference, that previous technologies were partial and fragmentary, and the electric is total and inclusive. An external consensus or conscience is now as necessary as private consciousness. With the new media, however, it is also possible to store and to translate everything; and, as for speed, that is no problem. No further acceleration is possible this side of the light barrier.

Just as when information levels rise in physics and chemistry, it is possible to use anything for fuel or fabric or building material, so with electric technology all solid goods can be summoned to appear as solid commodities by means of information circuits set up in the organic patterns that we call 'automation' and information retrieval. Under electric technology the entire business of man becomes learning and knowing.

[...]

After three thousand years of explosion, by means of fragmentary and mechanical technologies, the Western world is imploding. During the mechanical ages we had extended our bodies in space. Today, after more than a century of electric technology, we have extended our central nervous system itself in a global embrace, abolishing both space and time as far as our planet is concerned. Rapidly, we approach the final phase of the extensions of man – the technological simulation of consciousness, when the creative process of knowing will be collectively and corporately extended to the whole of human society, much as we have already extended our senses and our nerves by the various media.

Editors' Notes

1. Automation: the 1960s term for the introduction of new information technologies; computerisation.
2. David Sarnoff (1891–1971). As a young employee of the Marconi radio company, Sarnoff is often credited with having 'invented' broadcasting as an application of the new wireless technology. He founded the first American broadcasting network, NBC, in 1926, and was head of the Radio Corporation of America from 1930 to 1966.

4

'MASS COMMUNICATION' AND 'MINORITY CULTURE'

Raymond Williams

[...]

In our own generation, there has been a dramatic tightening of interest in this world of communications. The development of powerful new means of communication has coincided, historically, with the extension of democracy and with the attempts, by many kinds of ruling group, to control and manage democracy. The development has also coincided with important changes in the nature of work and in education, which have given many people new kinds of social opportunity. There has been a great expansion in the scale of ordinary society, both through the new communications systems and through the growth of many kinds of large scale organization. Acting together, these developments have created social problems which seem to be of a quite new kind.

The growth of interest in communications is an important response to this new situation. It came, really, as a break-through in experience, cutting across our usual categories. Already some of our basic ideas of society are being changed by this new emphasis. From one familiar approach, through traditional politics, we have seen the central facts of society as power and government. From another familiar approach, through traditional economics, we have seen the central concerns of society as property, production, and trade. These approaches remain important, but they are now joined by a new emphasis: that society is a form of communication, through which experience is described, shared, modified, and preserved. We are used to descriptions of

From R. Williams, *Communications* (Harmondsworth: Penguin Special, 1962) pp. 9–12, 68–75.

our whole common life in political and economic terms. The emphasis on communications asserts, as a matter of experience, that men and societies are not confined to relationships of power, property, and production. Their relationships in describing, learning, persuading, and exchanging experiences are seen as equally fundamental. This emphasis is exceptionally important in the long crisis of twentieth-century society. Many people, starting from older versions of society, have seen the growth of modern communications not as an expansion of men's powers to learn and to exchange ideas and experiences, but as a new method of government or a new opportunity for trade. All the new means of communication have been abused, for political control (as in propaganda) or for commercial profit (as in advertising). We can protest against such uses, but unless we have a clear alternative version of human society we are not likely to make our protests effective.

My own view is that we have been wrong in taking communication as secondary. Many people seem to assume as a matter of course that there is, first, reality, and then, second, communication about it. We degrade art and learning by supposing that they are always second-hand activities: that there is life, and then afterwards there are these accounts of it. Our commonest political error is the assumption that power – the capacity to govern other men – is the reality of the whole social process, and so the only context of politics. Our commonest economic error is the assumption that production and trade are our only practical activities, and that they require no other human justification or scrutiny. We need to say what many of us know in experience: that the life of man, and the business of society, cannot be confined to these ends; that the struggle to learn, to describe, to understand, to educate, is a central and necessary part of our humanity. This struggle is not begun, at second hand, after reality has occurred. It is, in itself, a major way in which reality is continually formed and changed. What we call society is not only a network of political and economic arrangements, but also a process of learning and communication.

Communication begins in the struggle to learn and to describe. To start this process in our minds, and to pass on its results to others, we depend on certain communication models, certain rules or conventions through which we can make contact. We can change these models, when they become inadequate, or we can modify and extend them. Our efforts to do so, and to use the existing models successfully, take up a large part of our living energy. The history of a language is a record of efforts of this kind, and is as central a part of the history of a people as its changing political and economic institutions. Moreover, many of our communication models become, in themselves, social institutions. Certain attitudes to others, certain forms of address, certain tones and styles, become embodied in institutions which are then very powerful in social effect. The crisis in modern communications has been caused by the speed of invention and by the difficulty of finding the right institutions in which these technical means are to be used. In modern Britain, we have a whole range of uses of printing, of photography, of television, which do not necessarily follow from the technical means themselves. Many have been shaped by changing political and economic forces. Many, also, have been shaped by what are really particular communication models: the idea that speaking or writing to many people at once is speaking or writing to 'the masses'; the idea that there are clear types of people and interest – 'Third Programme', 'Home Service' and 'Light'[1]; 'quality' and 'popular' – that we can separate and label. These arguable assumptions are often embodied in solid practical institutions, which then teach the models from which they start. We cannot examine the process of general communication in modern society without examining the shapes of these institutions. Further, if we understand the importance of communication, in all our social activities, we find that in examining the process and the institutions we are also looking at our society – at some of our characteristic relationships – in new ways.

[…]

HIGH AND LOW

Men differ in their capacities for excellence. Yet democracy insists that everyone has an equal right to judge. Aren't we seeing, in our own time, the results of this contradiction? Isn't there great danger of the tradition of high culture being overwhelmed by mass culture, which expresses the tastes and standards of the ordinary man? Isn't it really our first duty to defend minority culture, which in its actual works is the highest achievement of humanity?

The difficulty here is that 'minority culture' can mean two things. It can mean the work of the great artists and thinkers, and of the many lesser but still important figures who sustain them. It can mean also the work of these men as received and used by a particular social minority, which will indeed, often add to it certain works and habits of its own.

The great tradition is in many ways a common inheritance, and it has been the purpose of modern education to make it as widely available as possible. Certainly this extension is never as easy as some people expect. Certainly it often happens that in the attempt to make difficult work more widely available, part of the value of the work is lost. Perhaps the whole attempt is wrongly conceived, and we should concentrate instead on maintaining the high tradition in its own terms.

The question is, however, can this in any case be done? The work of the great artists and thinkers has never been confined to their own company; it has always been made available to some others. And doesn't it often happen that those to whom it has been made available identify the tradition with themselves, grafting it into their own way of life?

[…]

Again and again, particular minorities confuse the superiority of the tradition which has been made available to them with their own superiority, an association which the passing of time or of frontiers can make suddenly ludicrous. We must always be careful to distinguish the great works of the past from the social minority which at a particular place and time identifies itself with them.

The great tradition very often continues itself in quite unexpected ways. Much new work, in the past, has been called 'low', in terms of the 'high' standards of the day. This happened to much of our Elizabethan drama, and to the novel in the eighteenth century. Looking back, we can understand this, because the society was changing in fundamental ways. The minorities which assumed that they alone had the inheritance and guardianship of the great tradition in fact turned out to be wrong. This mistake can happen at any time. In our own century, there are such new forms as the film, the musical, and jazz. Each of these has been seen as 'low', a threat to 'our' standards. Yet during the period in which films have been made, there have been as many major contributions, in film, to the world's dramatic tradition, as there have been major plays. Of course most films are nowhere near this level. But from the past we have only the best work, and we can properly compare with this only our own best work. Some forms may well be better than others, in that they contain much greater possibilities for the artist, but this cannot be settled until there has been time for development. The great period of the novel came more than a century after the form had become popular and had been dismissed as 'low'. It realized possibilities which nobody could then have foreseen. The prestige of an old form is never decisive. There is no reason, today, why a science-fiction story should be thought less serious than a historical novel, or a new musical than a naturalist play. 'Low' equals 'unfamiliar' is one of the perennial cultural traps, and it is fallen into most easily by those who assume that in their own persons, in their own learned tastes and habits, they are the high tradition.

This might be agreed, but does it go to the real issue? These mistakes are made, but new minorities set them right. Still, however, they are minorities. Most people are not interested in the great tradition, old or new. Most people are not interested in art, but merely in entertainment. Actual popular taste is for such things as variety, the circus, sport, and processions. Why force art on such people, especially since you will be in danger of reducing art to that level, mixing it up with the popular and commercial worlds? Wouldn't your effort be better spent on maintaining real art for those who value it?

This distinction between art and entertainment may be much more difficult to maintain than it looks. At its extremes, of course, it is obvious. But over the whole range, is there any easy and absolute distinction? Great art can give us deep and lasting experiences, but the experience we get from many things that we rightly call art is quite often light and temporary. The excitement of the circus, the procession, the variety sketch, can be quite easily forgotten, but at the time it is often intense. Sport, in our century, has become a popular spectacle: its excitements again are intense and often temporary. There may be a difference between such things and the minor decorative arts, the passing comedies, the fashionable artistic performers, but can it really be seen as a difference between 'high' and 'low'? And even where the difference seems absolute, what follows from this? What has to be shown, to sustain the argument that 'high culture' is in danger of being overwhelmed by 'mass culture', is that there is not only difference but conflict. Most of us can test this in our own experience. For, in fact, we do not live in these neatly separated worlds. Many of us go one day to a circus, one day to a theatre; one day to the football, one day to a concert. The experiences are different, and vary widely in quality both between and within themselves. Do we in fact feel that our capacity for any one of these things is affected by our use of the others?

But perhaps this is not the main point. Isn't the real threat of 'mass culture' – of things like television rather than things like football or the circus – that it reduces us to an endlessly mixed, undiscriminating, fundamentally bored reaction? The spirit of everything, art and entertainment, can become so standardized that we have no absorbed interest in anything, but simply an indifferent acceptance, bringing together what Coleridge called 'indulgence of sloth and hatred of vacancy'. You're not exactly enjoying it, or paying any particular attention, but it's passing the time. And in so deadly an atmosphere the great tradition simply cannot live.

Most of us, I think, have experienced this atmosphere. At times, even, we take it as a kind of drug: in periods of tiredness or convalescence, or during tension and anxiety when we have to wait and when almost anything can help us to wait. Certainly as a normal habit of mind this would be enervating and dangerous; there is a good deal of reality that we cannot afford to be cut off from, however much we may want some temporary relief.

The challenge of work that is really in the great tradition is that in many different ways it can get through with an intensity, a closeness, a concentration that in fact moves us to respond. It can be the reporter breaking through our prejudice to the facts; the dramatist reaching so deeply into our experience that we find it difficult, in the first shock, even to breathe; the painter suddenly showing us the shape of a street so clearly that we ask how we could ever have walked down it indifferently. It is sometimes a disturbing challenge to what we have always believed and done, and sometimes a way to new experience, new ways of seeing and feeling. Or again, in unexpected ways, it can confirm and strengthen us, giving new energy to what we already know is important, or what we knew but couldn't express.

Is this living world threatened by the routines of 'mass culture'? The threat is real, but it does not come only from 'mass culture'; it comes also from many kinds of routine art and routine thinking. There are many sources for the formula or routine which insulates us from reality. There is the weakness in ourselves, or at best the insufficient strength. There is also the intention of others, that we should be kept out of touch. Many interests are served by this kind of insulation: old forms of society, old and discredited beliefs, a wish to keep people quiet and uncritical. Such interests, based on power, habit, or privilege, are often served by, often actively seek, formulas and routines that insulate men from reality.

If we look at what we call 'mass culture' and 'minority culture', I am not sure that we invariably find one on the side of reality and one against it. Certainly the great works always challenge us with their own reality, and can stimulate us to active attention. But when these works are embedded in a particular minority culture, which adds to them not only its own local habits but also the facts and feelings which spring from its minority position, the effect can be very different. At best, a minority culture, in keeping the works available, offers the best that has been done and said in the world. At worst, it translates the best into its own accents, and confuses it with many other inferior things. I see no real evidence that it is a permanent and reliable means of maintaining a living excellence.

But even if it isn't permanent and reliable, isn't it bound to be better than the ordinary world of mass communications? There the construction of formulas seems almost built in. It is perhaps the only easy way of getting through quickly to a very large number of people, and the system seems to depend on this. Certainly we can only understand large-scale communications if we acknowledge the importance of formulas which can be fairly quickly and widely learned and used. Yet, in fact, formulas are necessary for all communication. What is at worst a formula for processing an experience is at best a convention for transmitting it in a widely available form. We have seen so much falsification, glamorization, and real vulgarization that we often forget how many facts, how many new opinions, how many new kinds of work and new ways of seeing the world nevertheless get through. By comparison with times when there was no highly organized communications system these are dramatic gains. We have then to adjust the balance much more carefully than a simple contrast of 'minority' and 'mass', 'high' and 'low' would suggest.

There is one further argument, that can very easily be overlooked. The great tradition is itself always in danger of being vulgarized when it is confined to a minority culture. Just because it is a mixed inheritance, from many societies and many times as well as from many kinds of men, it cannot easily be contained within one limited social form. Further, if it is so contained, there can be deep and unnecessary hostility to it from those outside the social minority. If the great tradition is not made generally available, there is often this frightening combination of hostility and a vacuum. What then usually happens is that this is penetrated and exploited from outside. In the worst cultural products of our time, we find little that is genuinely popular, developed from the life of actual communities. We find instead a synthetic culture, or anti-culture, which is alien to almost everybody, persistently hostile to art and intellectual activity, which it spends much of its time in misrepresenting, and given over to exploiting indifference, lack of feeling, frustration, and hatred. It finds such common human interests as sex, and turns them into crude caricatures or glossy facsimiles. It plays repeatedly around hatred and aggression, which it never discharges but continually feeds. This is not the culture of 'the ordinary man'; it is the culture of the disinherited. It seems to me that those who have contrived the disinheritance, by artificially isolating the great tradition, bear as heavy a responsibility for these destructive elements as their actual providers.

In Britain, we have to notice that much of this bad work is American in origin. At certain levels, we are culturally an American colony. But of course it is not the best American culture that we are getting, and the import and imitation of the worst has been done, again and again, by some of our own people, significantly often driven by hatred or envy of the English minority which has associated the great tradition with itself. To go pseudo-American is a way out of the English complex of class and culture, but of course it solves nothing; it merely ritualizes the emptiness and despair. Most bad culture is the result of this kind of social collapse. The genuinely popular tradition is despised, the great tradition is kept exclusive, and into the gap pour the speculators who know how to exploit disinheritance because they themselves are rooted in nothing.

The general situation is very difficult to understand. In part, now, the great tradition is being responsibly extended, and is finding an excellent response, both in the real increase of audiences, and in the answering vitality of new contributions to it from new kinds of experience. The purely destructive exploitation of the vacuum is also very powerful, in part because the control of our cultural organization has passed very largely into the hands of men who know no other definitions. At the same time, against all the apparent odds, elements of the really popular tradition persist, especially in variety, sport, some kinds of spectacle, and the impulse to make our own entertainment, especially in music. It seems impossible to understand this many-sided and constantly changing situation through the old formulas of 'minority' and 'mass', which are the symptoms of the collapse rather than keys to understanding it. We have to look at a new situation in new ways.

Editors' Note

1. The 'Third Programme', 'Home Service' and 'Light' were the names of the BBC's domestic wireless networks from 1945/6 to 1967, providing distinct services that in contemporary terms broadly correspond to Radio 3, Radio 4 and Radio 2 respectively.

5

ENCODING/DECODING

Stuart Hall

Traditionally, mass-communications research has conceptualized the process of communication in terms of a circulation circuit or loop. This model has been criticized for its linearity – sender/message/receiver – for its concentration on the level of message exchange and for the absence of a structured conception of the different moments as a complex structure of relations. But it is also possible (and useful) to think of this process in terms of a structure produced and sustained through the articulation of linked but distinctive moments – production, circulation, distribution/consumption, reproduction. This would be to think of the process as a 'complex structure in dominance', sustained through the articulation of connected practices, each of which, however, retains its distinctiveness and has its own specific modality, its own forms and conditions of existence. This second approach, homologous to that which forms the skeleton of commodity production offered in Marx's *Grundrisse* and in *Capital*, has the added advantage of bringing out more sharply how a continuous circuit – production–distribution–production – can be sustained through a 'passage of forms'.[1] It also highlights the specificity of the forms in which the product of the process 'appears' in each moment, and thus what distinguishes discursive 'production' from other types of production in our society and in modern media systems.

From S. Hall, 'Encoding/Decoding', Ch. 10 in Stuart Hall, Dorothy Hobson, Andrew Lowe and Paul Willis (eds), *Culture, Media, Language* (London: Hutchinson, 1980), pp. 128–38; an edited extract from S. Hall, 'Encoding and Decoding in the Television Discourse', CCCS stencilled paper no. 7 (Birmingham: Centre for Contemporary Cultural Studies, 1973).

The 'object' of these practices is meanings and messages in the form of sign-vehicles of a specific kind organized, like any form of communication or language, through the operation of codes within the syntagmatic chain of a discourse. The apparatuses, relations and practices of production thus issue, at a certain moment (the moment of 'production/circulation') in the form of symbolic vehicles constituted within the rules of 'language'. It is in this discursive form that the circulation of the 'product' takes place. The process thus requires, at the production end, its material instruments – its 'means' – as well as its own sets of social (production) relations – the organization and combination of practices within media apparatuses. But it is in the *discursive* form that the circulation of the product takes place, as well as its distribution to different audiences. Once accomplished, the discourse must then be translated – transformed, again – into social practices if the circuit is to be both completed and effective. If no 'meaning' is taken, there can be no 'consumption'. If the meaning is not articulated in practice, it has no effect. The value of this approach is that while each of the moments, in articulation, is necessary to the circuit as a whole, no one moment can fully guarantee the next moment with which it is articulated. Since each has its specific modality and conditions of existence, each can constitute its own break or interruption of the 'passage of forms' on whose continuity the flow of effective production (that is, 'reproduction') depends.

Thus while in no way wanting to limit research to 'following only those leads which emerge from content analysis'[2] we must recognize that the discursive form of the message has a privileged position in the communicative exchange (from the viewpoint of circulation), and that the moments of 'encoding' and 'decoding', though only 'relatively autonomous' in relation to the communicative process as a whole, are *determinate* moments. A 'raw' historical event cannot, *in that form*, be transmitted by, say, a television newscast. Events can only be signified within the aural–visual forms of the televisual discourse. In the moment when a historical event passes under the sign of discourse, it is subject to all the complex formal 'rules' by which language signifies. To put it paradoxically, the event must become a 'story' before it can become a *communicative event*. In that moment the formal sub-rules of discourse are 'in dominance', without, of course, subordinating out of existence the historical event so signified, the social relations in which the rules are set to work or the social and political consequences of the event having been signified in this way. The 'message form' is the necessary 'form of appearance' of the event in its passage from source to receiver. Thus the transposition into and out of the 'message form' (or the mode of symbolic exchange) is not a random 'moment', which we can take up or ignore at our convenience. The 'message form' is a determinate moment; though, at another level, it comprises the surface movements of the communications system only and requires, at another stage, to be integrated into the social relations of the communication process as a whole, of which it forms only a part.

From this general perspective, we may crudely characterize the television communicative process as follows. The institutional structures of broadcasting, with their practices and networks of production, their organized relations and technical infrastructures, are required to produce a programme. Using the analogy of *Capital*, this is the 'labour process' in the discursive mode. Production, here, constructs the message. In one sense, then, the circuit begins here. Of course, the production process is not without its 'discursive' aspect: it, too, is framed throughout by meanings and ideas: knowledge-in-use concerning the routines of production, historically defined technical skills, professional ideologies, institutional knowledge, definitions and assumptions, assumptions about the audience and so on frame the constitution of the programme through this production structure. Further, though the production structures of television originate the television discourse, they do not constitute a closed system. They draw topics, treatments, agendas, events, personnel, images of the audience, 'definitions of the situation' from other sources and other discursive formations within the wider socio-cultural and political structure of which they are a differentiated part. Philip Elliott has expressed this point succinctly, within a more traditional framework, in his discussion of the way in which the audience is both the 'source' and the 'receiver' of the television message. Thus – to borrow Marx's terms – circulation and reception are, indeed, 'moments' of the production process in television and are reincorporated, via a number of skewed and structured 'feedbacks', into the production process itself. The consumption or reception of the television message is thus also itself a 'moment' of the production process in its larger sense, though the latter is 'predominant' because it is the 'point of departure for the realization' of the message. Production and reception of the television message are not, therefore, identical, but they are related: they are differentiated moments within the totality formed by the social relations of the communicative process as a whole.

At a certain point, however, the broadcasting structures must yield encoded messages in the form of a meaningful discourse. The institution-societal relations of production must pass under the discursive rules of language for its product to be 'realized'. This initiates a further differentiated moment, in which the formal rules of discourse and language are in dominance. Before this message can have an 'effect' (however defined), satisfy a 'need' or be put to a 'use', it must first be appropriated as a meaningful discourse and be meaningfully decoded. It is this set of decoded meanings which 'have an effect', influence, entertain, instruct or persuade, with very complex perceptual, cognitive, emotional, ideological or behavioural consequences. In a 'determinate' moment the structure employs a code and yields a 'message': at another determinate moment the 'message', via its decodings, issues into the structure of social practices. We are now fully aware that this re-entry into the practices of audience reception and 'use' cannot be understood in simple behavioural terms. The typical processes identified in positivistic research on isolated elements – effects, uses, 'gratifications' – are themselves framed by structures of

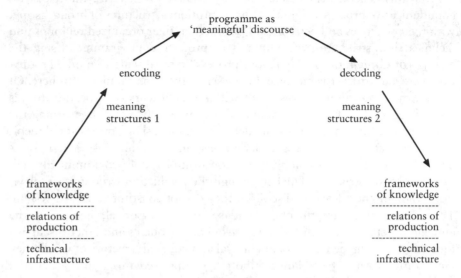

understanding, as well as being produced by social and economic relations, which shape their 'realization' at the reception end of the chain and which permit the meanings signified in the discourse to be transposed into practice or consciousness (to acquire social use value or political effectivity).

Clearly, what we have labelled in the diagram 'meaning structures 1' and 'meaning structures 2' may not be the same. They do not constitute an 'immediate identity'. The codes of encoding and decoding may not be perfectly symmetrical. The degrees of symmetry – that is, the degrees of 'understanding' and 'misunderstanding' in the communicative exchange – depend on the degrees of symmetry/asymmetry (relations of equivalence) established between the positions of the 'personifications', encoder–producer and decoder–receiver. But this in turn depends on the degrees of identity/non-identity between the codes which perfectly or imperfectly transmit, interrupt or systematically distort what has been transmitted. The lack of fit between the codes has a great deal to do with the structural differences of relation and position between broadcasters and audiences, but it also has something to do with the asymmetry between the codes of 'source' and 'receiver' at the moment of transformation into and out of the discursive form. What are called 'distortions' or 'misunderstandings' arise precisely from the *lack of equivalence* between the two sides in the communicative exchange. Once again, this defines the 'relative autonomy', but 'determinateness', of the entry and exit of the message in its discursive moments.

The application of this rudimentary paradigm has already begun to transform our understanding of the older term, television 'content'. We are just beginning to see how it might also transform our understanding of audience reception, 'reading' and response as well. Beginnings and endings have been announced in communications research before, so we must be cautious. But there seems some ground for thinking that a new and exciting phase in so-called audience research, of a quite new kind, may be opening up. At either end of the communicative chain the use of the semiotic paradigm promises to dispel the lingering behaviourism which has dogged mass-media research for so long, especially in its approach to content. Though we know the television programme is not a behavioural input, like a tap on the knee cap, it seems to have been almost impossible for traditional researchers to conceptualize the communicative process without lapsing into one or other variant of low-flying behaviourism. We know, as Gerbner has remarked, that representations of violence on the TV screen 'are not violence but messages about violence':[3] but we have continued to research the question of violence, for example, as if we were unable to comprehend this epistemological distinction.

The television sign is a complex one. It is itself constituted by the combination of two types of discourse, visual and aural. Moreover, it is an iconic sign, in Peirce's terminology, because 'it posseses some of the properties of the thing represented'.[4] This is a point which has led to a great deal of confusion and has provided the site of intense controversy in the study of visual language. Since the visual discourse translates a three-dimensional world into two-dimensional planes, it cannot, of course, *be* the referent or concept it signifies. The dog in the film can bark but it cannot bite! Reality exists outside language, but it is constantly mediated by and through language: and what we can know and say has to be produced in and through discourse. Discursive 'knowledge' is the product not of the transparent representation of the 'real' in language but of the articulation of language on real relations and conditions. Thus there is no intelligible discourse without the operation of a code. Iconic signs are therefore coded signs too – even if the codes here work differently from those of other signs. There is no degree zero in language. Naturalism and 'realism' – the apparent fidelity of the representation to the thing or concept represented – is the result, the effect, of a certain specific articulation of language on the 'real'. It is the result of a discursive practice.

Certain codes may, of course, be so widely distributed in a specific language community or culture, and be learned at so early an age, that they appear not to be constructed – the effect of an articulation between sign and referent – but to be 'naturally' given. Simple visual signs appear to have achieved a 'near-universality' in this sense: though evidence remains that even apparently 'natural' visual codes are culture-specific. However, this does not mean that no codes have intervened; rather, that the codes have been profoundly *naturalized*. The operation of naturalized codes reveals not the transparency and 'naturalness' of language but the depth, the habituation and the near-universality of the codes in use. They produce apparently 'natural' recognitions. This has the (ideological) effect of concealing the practices of coding which are present. But we must not be fooled by appearances. Actually, what naturalized codes demonstrate is the degree of habituation produced when there is a fundamental alignment and reciprocity – an achieved equivalence – between the encoding and decoding sides of an exchange of meanings. The functioning of the codes on the decoding side will frequently assume the status of naturalized perceptions. This leads us to think that the visual sign for 'cow' actually is (rather than *represents*) the animal, cow. But if we think of the visual representation of a cow in a manual on animal husbandry – and, even more, of the linguistic sign 'cow' – we can see that both, in different degrees, are *arbitrary* with respect to the concept of the animal they represent. The articulation of an arbitrary sign – whether visual or verbal – with the concept of a referent is the product not of nature but of convention, and the conventionalism of discourses requires the intervention, the support, of codes. Thus Eco has argued that iconic signs 'look like objects in the real world because they reproduce the conditions (that is, the codes) of perception in the viewer'.[5] These 'conditions of perception' are, however, the result of a highly coded, even if virtually unconscious, set of operations – decodings. This is as true of the photographic or televisual image as it is of any other sign. Iconic signs are, however, particularly vulnerable to being 'read' as natural because visual codes of perception are very widely distributed and because this type of sign is less arbitrary than a linguistic sign: the linguistic sign, 'cow' possesses *none* of the properties of the thing represented, whereas the visual sign appears to possess *some* of those properties.

[...]

The level of connotation of the visual sign, of its contextual reference and positioning in different discursive fields of meaning and association, is the point where *already coded* signs intersect with the deep semantic codes of a culture and take on additional, more active ideological dimensions. We might take an example from advertising discourse. Here, too, there is no 'purely denotative', and certainly no 'natural', representation. Every visual sign in advertising connotes a quality, situation, value or inference, which is present as an implication or implied meaning, depending on the connotational positioning. In Barthes's example, the sweater always signifies a 'warm garment' (denotation) and thus the activity/value of 'keeping warm'. But it is also possible, at its more connotative levels, to signify 'the coming of winter' or 'a cold day'. And, in the specialized sub-codes of fashion, sweater may also connote a fashionable style of *haute couture* or, alternatively, an informal style of dress. But set against the right visual background and positioned by the romantic sub-code, it may connote 'long autumn walk in the woods'.[6] Codes of this order clearly contract relations for the sign with the wider universe of ideologies in a society. These codes are the means by which power and ideology are made to signify in particular discourses. They refer signs to the 'maps of meaning' into which any culture is classified; and those 'maps of social reality' have the whole range of social meanings, practices, and usages, power and interest 'written in' to them. The connotative levels of signifiers, Barthes remarked, 'have a close communication with culture, knowledge, history, and it is through them, so to speak, that the environmental world invades the linguistic and semantic system. They are, if you like, the fragments of ideology'.[7]

The so-called denotative *level* of the televisual sign is fixed by certain, very complex (but limited or 'closed') codes. But its connotative *level*, though also bounded, is more open, subject to more active *transformations*, which exploit its polysemic values. Any such already constituted sign is potentially transformable into more than one connotative configuration. Polysemy must not, however, be confused with pluralism. Connotative codes are *not* equal among themselves. Any society/culture tends, with varying degrees of closure, to impose its classifications of the social and cultural and political world. These constitute a *dominant cultural order*, though it is neither univocal nor un-contested. This question of the 'structure of discourses in dominance' is a crucial point. The different areas of social life appear to be mapped out into discursive domains, hierarchically organized into *dominant or preferred meanings*. New, problematic or troubling events, which breach our expectancies and run counter to our 'common-sense constructs', to our 'taken-for-granted' knowledge of social structures, must be assigned to their discursive domains before they can be said to 'make sense'. The most common way of 'mapping' them is to assign the new to some domain or other of the existing 'maps of problematic social reality'. We say *dominant*, not 'determined', because it is always possible to order, classify, assign and decode an event within more than one 'mapping'. But we say 'dominant' because there exists a pattern of 'preferred readings'; and these both have the institutional/political/ideological order imprinted in them and have themselves become institutionalized.[8] The domains of 'preferred meanings' have the whole social order embedded in them as a set of meanings, practices and beliefs: the everyday knowledge of social structures, of 'how things work for all practical purposes in this culture', the rank order of power and interest and the structure of legitimations, limits and sanctions. Thus to clarify a 'misunderstanding' at the connotative level, we must refer, *through* the codes, to the orders of social life, of economic and political power and of ideology. Further, since these mappings are 'structured in dominance' but not closed, the communicative process consists not in the unproblematic assignment of every visual item to its given position within a set of prearranged codes, but of *performative rules* – rules of competence and use, of logics-in-use – which seek actively to *enforce* or *pre-fer* one semantic domain over another and rule items into and out of their appropriate meaning-sets. Formal semiology has too often neglected this practice of *interpretative work*, though this constitutes, in fact, the real relations of broadcast practices in television.

In speaking of *dominant meanings*, then, we are not talking about a one-sided process which governs how all events will be signified. It consists of the 'work' required to enforce, win plausibility for and command as legitimate a *decoding* of the event within the limit of dominant definitions in which it has been connotatively signified. Terni has remarked:

> By the word *reading* we mean not only the capacity to identify and decode a certain number of signs, but also the subjective capacity to put them into a creative relation between themselves and with other signs: a capacity which is, by itself, the condition for a complete awareness of one's total environment.[9]

Our quarrel here is with the notion of 'subjective capacity', as if the referent of a televisional discourse were an objective fact but the interpretative level were an individualized and private matter. Quite the opposite seems to be the case. The televisual practice takes 'objective' (that is, systemic) responsibility precisely for the relations which disparate signs contract with one another in any discursive instance, and thus continually rearranges, delimits and prescribes into what 'awareness of one's total environment' these items are arranged.

This brings us to the question of misunderstandings. Television producers who find their message 'failing to get across' are frequently concerned to straighten out the kinks in the communication chain, thus facilitating the 'effectiveness' of their communication. Much research which claims the objectivity of 'policy-oriented analysis' reproduces this administrative goal by attempting to discover how much of a message the audience recalls and to improve the extent of understanding. No doubt misunderstandings of a literal kind do exist. The viewer does not know the terms employed, cannot follow the complex logic of argument or exposition, is unfamiliar with the language, finds the concepts too alien or difficult or is foxed by the expository narrative. But more often broadcasters are concerned that the audience has failed to take the meaning as they – the broadcasters – intended. What they really mean to say is that viewers are not operating within the 'dominant' or 'preferred' code. Their ideal is 'perfectly transparent communication'. Instead, what they have to confront is 'systematically distorted communication'.[10]

In recent years discrepancies of this kind have usually been explained by reference to 'selective perception'. This is the door via which a residual pluralism evades the compulsions of a highly structured, asymmetrical and non-equivalent process. Of course, there will always be private, individual, variant readings. But 'selective perception' is almost never as selective, random or privatized as the concept suggests. The patterns exhibit, across individual variants, significant clusterings. Any new approach to audience studies will therefore have to begin with a critique of 'selective perception' theory.

It was argued earlier that since there is no necessary correspondence between encoding and decoding, the former can attempt to 'pre-fer' but cannot prescribe or guarantee the latter, which has its own conditions of existence. Unless they are wildly aberrant, encoding will have the effect of constructing some of the limits and parameters within which decodings will operate. If there were no limits, audiences could simply read whatever they liked into any message. No doubt some total misunderstandings of this kind do exist. But the vast range must contain *some* degree of reciprocity between encoding and decoding moments, otherwise we could not speak of an effective communicative exchange at all. Nevertheless, this 'correspondence' is not given but constructed. It is not 'natural' but the product of an articulation between two distinct moments. And the former cannot determine or guarantee, in a simple sense, which decoding codes will be employed. Otherwise communication would be a perfectly equivalent circuit, and every message would be an instance of 'perfectly transparent communication'. We must think, then, of the variant articulations in which encoding/decoding can be combined. To elaborate on this, we offer a hypothetical analysis of some possible decoding positions, in order to reinforce the point of 'no necessary correspondence'.[11]

We identify *three* hypothetical positions from which decodings of a televisual discourse may be constructed. These need to be empirically tested and refined. But the argument that decodings do not follow inevitably from encodings, that they are not identical, reinforces the argument of 'no necessary correspondence'. It also helps to deconstruct the commonsense meaning of 'misunderstanding' in terms of a theory of 'systematically distorted communication'.

The first hypothetical position is that of the *dominant-hegemonic position*. When the viewer takes the connoted meaning from, say, a television newscast or current affairs programme full and straight, and decodes the message in terms of the reference code in which it has been encoded, we might say that the viewer *is operating inside the dominant code*. This is the ideal-typical case of 'perfectly transparent communication' – or as close as we are likely to come to it 'for all practical purposes'. Within this we can distinguish the positions produced by the *professional code*. This is the position (produced by what we perhaps ought to identify as the operation of a 'metacode') which the professional broadcasters assume when encoding a message which has *already* been signified in a hegemonic manner. The professional code is 'relatively independent' of the dominant code, in that it applies criteria and transformational operations of its own, especially those of a technico-practical nature. The professional code, however, operates *within* the 'hegemony' of the dominant code. Indeed, it serves to reproduce the dominant definitions precisely by bracketing their hegemonic quality and operating instead with displaced professional codings which foreground such apparently neutral-technical questions as visual quality, news and presentational values, televisual quality, 'professionalism' and so on. The hegemonic interpretations of, say, the politics of Northern Ireland, or the Chilean *coup* or the Industrial Relations Bill are principally generated by political and military elites: the particular choice of presentational occasions and formats, the selection of personnel, the choice of images, the staging of debates are selected and combined through the operation of the professional code. How the broadcasting professionals are able *both* to operate with 'relatively autonomous' codes of their own *and* to act in such a way as to reproduce (not without contradiction) the hegemonic signification of events is a complex matter which cannot be further spelled out here. It must suffice to say that the professionals are linked with the defining elites not only by the institutional position of broadcasting itself as an 'ideological apparatus',[12] but also by the structure of *access* (that is, the systematic 'over-accessing' of selective elite personnel and their 'definition of the situation' in television). It may even be said that the professional codes serve to reproduce hegemonic definitions specifically by *not overtly* biasing their operations in a dominant direction: ideological reproduction therefore takes place here inadvertently, unconsciously, 'behind men's backs'.[13] Of course, conflicts, contradictions and even misunderstandings regularly arise between the dominant and the professional significations and their signifying agencies.

The second position we would identify is that of the *negotiated code* or position. Majority audiences probably understand quite adequately what has been dominantly defined and professionally signified. The dominant definitions, however, are hegemonic precisely because they represent definitions of situations and events which are 'in dominance', (*global*). Dominant definitions connect events, implicitly or explicitly, to grand totalizations, to the great syntagmatic views-of-the-world: they take 'large views' of issues: they relate events to the 'national interest' or to the level of geo-politics, even if they make these connections in truncated, inverted or mystified ways. The definition of a hegemonic viewpoint is (a) that it defines within its terms the mental horizon, the universe, of possible meanings, of a whole sector of relations in a society or culture; and (b) that it carries with it the stamp of legitimacy – it appears coterminous with what is 'natural', 'inevitable', 'taken for granted' about the social order. Decoding within the *negotiated version* contains a mixture of adaptive and oppositional elements: it acknowledges the legitimacy of the hegemonic definitions to make the grand significations (abstract), while, at a more restricted, situational (situated) level, it makes its own ground rules – it operates with exceptions to the rule. It accords the privileged position to the dominant definitions of events while reserving the right to make a more negotiated application to 'local conditions', to its own more *corporate* positions. This negotiated version of the dominant ideology is thus shot through with contradictions, though these are only on certain occasions brought to full visibility. Negotiated codes operate through what we might call particular or situated logics: and these logics are sustained by their differential and unequal relation to the discourses and logics of power. The simplest example of a negotiated code is that which governs the response of a worker to the notion of an Industrial Relations Bill limiting the right to strike or to arguments for a wages freeze. At the level of the 'national interest' economic debate the decoder may adopt the hegemonic definition, agreeing that 'we must all pay ourselves less in order to combat inflation'. This, however, may have little or no relation to his/her willingness to go on strike for better pay and conditions or to oppose the Industrial Relations Bill at the level of shopfloor or union organization. We suspect that the great majority of so-called 'misunderstandings' arise from the contradictions and disjunctures between hegemonic–dominant encodings and negotiated–corporate decodings. It is just these mismatches in the levels which most provoke defining elites and professionals to identify a 'failure in communications'.

Finally, it is possible for a viewer perfectly to understand both the literal and the connotative inflection given by a discourse but to decode the message in a *globally* contrary way. He/she detotalizes the message in the preferred code in order to retotalize the message within some alternative framework of reference. This is the case of the viewer who listens to a debate on the need to limit wages but 'reads' every mention of the 'national interest' as 'class interest'. He/she is operating with what we must call an *oppositional code*. One of the most significant political moments (they also coincide with crisis points within the broadcasting organizations themselves, for obvious reasons) is the point when events which are normally signified and decoded in a negotiated way begin to be given an oppositional reading. Here the 'politics of signification' – the struggle in discourse – is joined.

NOTES

1. For an explication and commentary on the methodological implications of Marx's argument, see S. Hall, 'A reading of Marx's 1857 *Introduction to the Grundrisse*', in WPCS 6 (1974).
2. J. D. Halloran, 'Understanding television', Paper for the Council of Europe Colloquy on 'Understanding Television' (University of Leicester 1973).
3. G. Gerbner *et al.*, *Violence in TV Drama: A Study of Trends and Symbolic Functions* (The Annenberg School, University of Pennsylvania 1970).
4. Charles Peirce, *Speculative Grammar*, in *Collected Papers* (Cambridge, Mass.: Harvard University Press 1931–58)
5. Umberto Eco, 'Articulations of the cinematic code', in *Cinemantics*, no. 1.
6. Roland Barthes, 'Rhetoric of the image', in WPCS 1 (1971).
7. Roland Barthes, *Elements of Semiology* (Cape 1967).
8. For an extended critique of 'preferred reading', see Alan O'Shea, 'Preferred reading' (unpublished paper, CCCS, University of Birmingham).
9. P. Terni, 'Memorandum', Council of Europe Colloquy on 'Understanding Television' (University of Leicester 1973).
10. The phrase is Habermas's, in 'Systematically distorted communications', in P. Dretzel (ed.), *Recent Sociology 2* (Collier-Macmillan 1970). It is used here, however, in a different way.
11. For a sociological formulation which is close, in some ways, to the positions outlined here but which does not parallel the argument about the theory of discourse, see Frank Parkin, *Class Inequality and Political Order* (Macgibbon and Kee 1971).
12. See Louis Althusser, 'Ideology and ideological state apparatuses', in *Lenin and Philosophy and Other Essays* (New Left Books 1971).
13. For an expansion of this argument, see Stuart Hall, 'The external/internal dialectic in broadcasting', *4th Symposium on Broadcasting* (University of Manchester 1972), and 'Broadcasting and the state: the independence/impartiality couplet', AMCR Symposium, University of Leicester 1976 (CCCS unpublished paper).

6

THE POWER OF THE IMAGE

Annette Kuhn

The twentieth century's second wave of Western feminism has distinguished itself from other social and political movements in several important respects. Its espousal of non-hierarchical approaches to organisation and action have lent themselves particularly well to issue-oriented politics – campaigns around abortion legislation and direct action on peace and disarmament, for example. The movement's insistence on bringing to centre stage areas of life hitherto considered secondary, even irrelevant, to 'serious' politics – the division of labour in the household, relations between men and women at home and in the workplace, emotions, sexuality, even the Unconscious – also sets it apart, giving ground to a conviction that the women's movement is opening up and beginning to explore a whole new country. In this process, new maps have had to be drawn, concepts constructed, systems of thought developed, in the effort to order the apparent chaos of a neglected other side of patriarchal culture. To take just one example of the effects of all this: trade union campaigns to combat sexual harassment at work would have been inconceivable before the middle or late 1970s, if only because the phenomenon simply did not have a name before that time. One can scarcely organise around a non-existent concept.

In other words, politics and knowledge are interdependent. In the ordinary way, the link between them will often go unnoticed or be taken for granted: where feminism is concerned, however, this is impossible, precisely because knowledge has had to be self-consciously produced alongside political activity.

From A. Kuhn, *The Power of the Image* (London: Routledge & Kegan Paul, 1985) pp. 1–8.

Each has regenerated the other. This is not to imply that the relationship is always a harmonious and uncontradictory one: mutual dependency always involves difficulty and struggle. Feminists may disagree, for example, on the extent to which producing knowledge is in itself a political activity. Are theory and practice in the final instance separate categories? Or is it acceptable to posit (to use a currently rather unfashionable term) a 'theoretical practice' of feminism?

Knowledge of the kind likely to be useful to the women's movement – knowledge, that is, which increases our understanding of women's lives and the institutions and structures of power which impinge on those lives in varying degrees and in different ways, structures which construct woman as 'other' in a patriarchal society – much of this knowledge is being produced under the banner of women's studies. The fact that women's studies has come to assume an existence in the Academy, apparently independent of the women's movement, may present some problems for the relationship between a body of knowledge and the movement which was its initial *raison d'être*. However, precisely because it so evidently eschews the 'neutrality' demanded by the Academy, the status of women's studies as a subject, researched and taught in universities, polytechnics and colleges, is marginal and precarious and its future uncertain: women's studies, therefore, needs the women's movement as much as *vice versa*. Women's studies also needs an institutional space to develop, and it needs, as well, the opportunity to draw on other areas of intellectual endeavour where these promise to be useful and relevant to its project. The saying that knowledge does not come from nowhere has more than one meaning.

[. . .]

From its beginnings, feminism has regarded ideas, language and images as crucial in shaping women's (and men's) lives. In the USA in 1968, feminists staged a demonstration against the Miss America contest, protesting the event on grounds that it promoted an impossible image of ideal womanhood, and was complicit in the widespread idea that all women – not only participants in beauty contests – are reducible to a set of bodily attributes. From this beginning there followed critiques of stereotypical representations of women in advertisements and in films, and studies of the ways in which language – both vocabulary and linguistic usage – defines and confines women. From the point of view of its politics, then, the women's movement has always been interested in images, meanings, representations – and especially in challenging representations which, while questionable or offensive from a feminist standpoint, are from other points of view – if they are noticed at all – perfectly acceptable.

This interest is in part responsible for the chapters in the present book [*The Power of the Image*]. I say responsible, because without the women's movement a desire to question representation in this way could not be articulated, nor would the public or even the private space to do so exist. I say in part, however, because since the early days feminist interest in images and representations has taken a variety of forms and directions. These have been determined largely by different ways in which representation has been thought about and analysed – that is, by the theories and methods brought to bear on the question. The question, I would argue, is a feminist one: the theories and methods not exclusively so. These come, at least to begin with, from elsewhere, and are appropriated and adapted to the feminist project. Knowledge does not come from nowhere, then: just as in this instance new knowledge is generated through the desire of feminist politics, so existing knowledge is both used and transformed in the service of this desire. The use and transformation of existing knowledge also partly motivates this book, then. It does not pretend to offer a comprehensive account of feminist thought on representation, however, but rather limits itself to an in-depth exploration of certain theoretical and methodological paths, hopefully opening up one or two new byways in the process. Which paths, though, and why?

The emergence of a new feminist movement in the late 1960s coincided with a renewed interest in marxist thought on 'the superstructure' – ideas, culture, ideology – and the place and effectivity of the superstructure within the social formation.[1] The different terms used here to describe the contents of the superstructure reflect a range of tendencies within marxist theory. Certain developments around the concept of ideology, for instance, were embodied in the work of the French philosopher Louis Althusser, work which – alongside that of other intellectuals, Roland Barthes and Claude Lévi-Strauss, for instance – was associated with structuralism. Barthes had written an introduction to semiotics – the study of signification, or meaning production, in society – and his book *Mythologies* comprised a series of short semiotically informed essays on specific images and representations, and on signification in general: which elements in images produce meaning, how the process operates, and so on.[2]

In the early 1970s, art historian John Berger made a series of programmes for BBC Television called *Ways of Seeing*. In these, Berger also considered how images make meaning, though in this instance without explicit recourse to semiotic concepts. Into this effectively semiotic project Berger injected a more orthodoxly marxist concern with the status of images as commodities – artifacts which are bought and sold, which have exchange value. One particularly influential programme dealt with the female nude, both in the European high art tradition and in mass-produced pinup photographs. Analysis dealt not only with the formal qualities of these images *per se*, but also with the relationship between images and their consumers – who as well as being spectators are often buyers/owners of images too.

Althusserian thought had a certain relevance to feminism because it contained a notion that human beings are constructed by ideology, that our ways of thinking about the world, of representing it to ourselves, becomes so 'naturalised' that we take our conception of that world for granted. If ideology effaces itself, the process by which this takes place could, for instance, explain (though Althusser did not in fact attempt to do so) the taken-for-granted nature of social constructs of femininity. Barthes's work on images suggested, moreover, that meanings are produced through the codes at work in representations, and that while meanings might appear to be natural, obvious, immanent, they are in fact produced: they are constructed through identifiable processes of signification at work in all representations. Finally, *Ways of Seeing* showed that meaning production takes place within social and historical contexts, and that in a capitalist society representations are no more exempt than any other products from considerations of the marketplace.

It is not difficult to see a potential for crossfertilisation between these ideas and feminist concerns with representation: indeed, the work I have described forms a backcloth to the chapters in this book [*The Power of the Image*]. It is really no more than a backcloth, though. Since the early 1970s, the study of images, particularly of cinematic images, as signifying systems has taken up and developed these 'prefeminist' concerns, bringing to the fore the issue of the spectator as subject addressed, positioned, even formed, by representations. To semiotic and structuralist approaches to representation has been added psychoanalysis, whose object is precisely the processes by which human subjectivity is formed.[3] In work on the image, the cinematic image particularly, an emphasis on subjectivity has foregrounded the question of spectatorship in new ways. This, too, informs the writing in this book.

But again, that is by no means the whole story: for feminist thought has long since entered the field of representation in its own right. These chapters may be read as inhabiting a tradition of feminist work on representation which draws strategically on the strands of non-feminist or prefeminist thinking I have described, if only because their objects (images, meanings, ideologies) and their objectives (analysis, deconstruction) have something in common with feminist concerns. At the same time, though, the very process of appropriation has exposed crucial weaknesses in these systems of thought – notably gender-blindness, formalism, and certain methodological shortcomings.[4] Not only, though, has the appropriation of pre-existing theory necessarily – fruitfully – produced criticisms of it: the particular concerns of feminism, when mapped onto that theory, have been instrumental in generating qualitatively new knowledge, in constructing a new field.

Inevitably, the[se] questions [. . .] traverse both feminist concerns and knowledge-in-process. What relation, for instance, does spectatorship have to representations of women? What sort of activity is looking? What does looking have to do with sexuality? With masculinity and femininity? With power? With knowledge? How do images, of women in particular, 'speak to' the spectator? Is the spectator addressed as male/female, masculine/feminine? Is femininity constructed in specific ways through representation? Why are images of women's bodies so prevalent in our society? Such questions may sometimes be answered by looking at and analysing actual images. But although such analysis must be regarded as necessary to an understanding of the relationship between representation and sexuality, it is not always sufficient. For, in practice, images are always seen in context: they always have a specific use value in the particular time and place of their consumption. This together with their formal characteristics, conditions and limits the meanings available from them at any one moment. But if representations always have use value, then more often than not they also have exchange value: they circulate as commodities in a social/economic system. This further conditions, or overdetermines, the meanings available from representations.

Meanings do not reside in images, then: they are circulated between representation, spectator and social formation. All of the chapters in this book [*The Power of the Image*] are concerned in one way or another with images – with films as well as still photographs of various kinds. Each chapter places a slightly different emphasis on each of the terms defining the representation– spectator– social formation triangle: though, given the central place accorded the instance of looking, the spectator undoubtedly sits at the apex. Nevertheless, each chapter marks a move further away from the model of the image/text as an isolated object of analysis, and closer to a conception of the image as inhabiting various contexts: cultural contexts of spectatorship, institutional and social/ historical contexts of production and consumption. At the same time, conceptualising texts as embedded within a series of contextual layers, and trying to do this without losing sight of texts as productive of meaning in their own right, does produce certain theoretical and methodological difficulties.

[...]

All of the texts/images discussed [...] may, in a broad sense, be regarded as 'culturally dominant'. Most of them – Hollywood films and softcore pornography, for example – are produced commercially for mass audiences. Where this is not the case they strive to slot into hegemonic 'high art' institutions. Hegemony is never without contradiction, however, which is one reason why analysing culturally dominant representations can be very productive. Contextual overdetermination notwithstanding, meaning can never be finally guaranteed. In practice, the operations of texts and various levels of context are rarely in harmony, and there is always some space for 'aberrant' reception of dominant representations.

[...]

More generally, the very existence of a book like this one is testimony to the fact that readings 'against the grain' are not only available, but often compelling. The activity of deconstruction sets loose an array of 'unintended' meanings, by their nature subversive of the apparently transparent meanings which texts offer us.

But why spend time and effort analysing images of a kind often considered questionable, even objectionable, by feminists? Why not try instead to create alternatives to culturally dominant representations? As I have argued, politics and knowledge are interdependent: the women's movement is not, I believe, faced here with a choice between two mutually exclusive alternatives, though individual feminists – if only because one person's life is too short to encompass everything – often experience their own politics in such a way. Theory and practice inform one another. At one level, analysing and deconstructing dominant representations may be regarded as a strategic practice. It produces understanding, and understanding is necessary to action.

It may also be considered an act of resistance in itself. Politics is often thought of as one of life's more serious undertakings, allowing little room for pleasure. At the same time, feminists may feel secretly guilty about their enjoyment of images they are convinced ought to be rejected as politically unsound. In analysing such images, though, it is possible, indeed necessary, to acknowledge their pleasurable qualities, precisely because pleasure is an area of analysis in its own right. 'Naive' pleasure, then, becomes admissible. And the acts of analysis, of deconstruction and of reading 'against the grain' offer an additional pleasure – the pleasure of resistance, of saying 'no': not to 'unsophisticated' enjoyment, by ourselves and others, of culturally dominant images, but to the structures of power which ask us to consume them uncritically and in highly circumscribed ways.

NOTES

1. See, for example, Robin Blackburn (ed.), *Ideology in Social Science*, London, Fontana, 1972; Raymond Williams, 'Base and superstructure in marxist cultural theory', *New Left Review*, no. 32, 1973, pp. 3–16; Louis Althusser, 'Ideology and ideological state apparatuses', *Lenin and Philosophy and Other Essays*, London, New Left Books, 1971, pp. 121–73.
2. *Elements of Semiology*, London, Jonathan Cape, 1967; *Mythologies*, London, Paladin, 1973.
3. These developments are traced in Rosalind Coward and John Ellis, *Language and Materialism*, London, Routledge & Kegan Paul, 1978.
4. See, for example, Mary Ann Doane et al., 'Feminist film criticism: an introduction', *Re-Vision: Essays in Feminist Film Criticism*, Los Angeles, American Film Institute, 1984, pp. 1–17; Annette Kuhn, 'Women's genres', *Screen*, vol. 25, no. 1, 1984, pp. 18–28.

7

CONSTITUENTS OF A THEORY OF THE MEDIA

Hans Magnus Enzensberger

If you should think this is Utopian, then I would ask you to consider why it is Utopian.

Brecht: *Theory of Radio*

With the development of the electronic media, the industry that shapes consciousness has become the pacemaker for the social and economic development of societies in the late industrial age. It infiltrates into all other sectors of production, takes over more and more directional and control functions, and determines the standard of the prevailing technology.

[In lieu of normative definitions, here is an incomplete list of new developments which have emerged in the last twenty years: news satellites, color television, cable relay television, cassettes, videotape, videotape recorders, video-phones, stereophony, laser techniques, electrostatic reproduction processes, electronic high-speed printing, composing and learning machines, microfiches with electronic access, printing by radio, time-sharing computers, data banks. All these new forms of media are constantly forming new connections both with each other and with older media like printing, radio, film, television, telephone, teletype, radar, and so on. They are clearly coming together to form a universal system.]

The general contradiction between productive forces and productive relationships emerges most sharply, however, when they are most advanced. By

From H. M. Enzensberger, *The Consciousness Industry: on Literature, Politics and the Media*, ed. Michael Roloff (New York: Seabury Press, 1974). The trans. by Stuart Hood appeared in *New Left Review*. It was published originally as 'Baukasten zu einer Theorie der Medien' in *Kursbuch* 18 (1971). The paragraphs in square brackets were printed in smaller type in the original version.

contrast, protracted structural crises, as in coal mining, can be solved merely by getting rid of a backlog, that is to say, essentially they can be solved within the terms of their own system, and a revolutionary strategy that relied on them would be shortsighted.

Monopoly capitalism develops the consciousness-shaping industry more quickly and more extensively than other sectors of production; it must at the same time fetter it. A socialist media theory has to work at this contradiction, demonstrate that it cannot be solved within the given productive relationships – rapidly increasing discrepancies, potential destructive forces. 'Certain demands of a prognostic nature must be made' of any such theory (Benjamin).

[A 'critical' inventory of the status quo is not enough. There is danger of underestimating the growing conflicts in the media field, of neutralizing them, of interpreting them merely in terms of trade unionism or liberalism, on the lines of traditional labor struggles or as the clash of special interests (program heads/executive producers, publishers/authors, monopolies/medium sized businesses, public corporations/private companies, etc.). An appreciation of this kind does not go far enough and remains bogged down in tactical arguments.]

So far there is no Marxist theory of the media. There is therefore no strategy one can apply in this area. Uncertainty, alternations between fear and surrender, mark the attitude of the socialist Left to the new productive forces of the media industry. The ambivalence of this attitude merely minors the ambivalence of the media themselves without mastering it. It could only be overcome by releasing the emancipatory potential which is inherent in the new productive forces – a potential which capitalism must sabotage just as surely as Soviet revisionism, because it would endanger the rule of both systems.

THE MOBILIZING POWER OF THE MEDIA

2. The open secret of the electronic media, the decisive political factor, which has been waiting, suppressed or crippled, for its moment to come, is their mobilizing power.

[When I say *mobilize* I mean *mobilize*. In a country which has had direct experience of fascism (and Stalinism) it is perhaps still necessary to explain, or to explain again, what that means – namely, to make men more mobile than they are. As free as dancers, as aware as football players, as surprising as guerillas. Anyone who thinks of the masses only as the object of politics cannot mobilize them. He wants to push them around. A parcel is not mobile; it can only be pushed to and fro. Marches, columns, parades, immobilize people. Propaganda, which does not release self-reliance but limits it, fits into the same pattern. It leads to depoliticization.]

For the first time in history, the media are making possible mass participation in a social and socialized productive process, the practical means of which are in the hands of the masses themselves. Such a use of them would bring the communications media, which up to now have not deserved the name, into their own. In its present form, equipment like television or film does not serve communication but prevents it. It allows no reciprocal action between transmitter and receiver; technically speaking, it reduces feedback to the lowest point compatible with the system.

This state of affairs, however, cannot be justified technically. On the contrary. Electronic techniques recognize no contradiction in principle between transmitter and receiver. Every transistor radio is, by the nature of its construction, at the same time a potential transmitter; it can interact with other receivers by circuit reversal. The development from a mere distribution medium to a communications medium is technically not a problem. It is consciously prevented for understandable political reasons. The technical distinction between receivers and transmitters reflects the social division of labor into producers and consumers, which in the consciousness industry becomes of particular political importance. It is based, in the last analysis, on the basic contradiction between the ruling class and the ruled class – that is to say, between monopoly capital or monopolistic bureaucracy on the one hand and the dependent masses on the other.

[This structural analogy can be worked out in detail. To the programs offered by the broadcasting cartels there correspond the politics offered by a power cartel consisting of parties constituted along authoritarian lines. In both cases marginal differences in their platforms reflect a competitive relationship which on essential questions is nonexistent. Minimal independent activity on the part of the voter viewer is desired. As is the case with parliamentary elections under the two-party system, the feedback is reduced to indices. 'Training in decision making' is reduced to the response to a single, three-point switching process: Program 1; Program 2; Switch off (abstention).]

'Radio must be changed from a means of distribution to a means of communication. Radio would be the most wonderful means of communication imaginable in public life, a huge linked system – that is to say, it would be such if it were capable not only of transmitting but of receiving, of allowing the listener not only to hear but to speak, and did not isolate him but brought him into contact. Unrealizable in this social system, realizable in another, these proposals, which are, after all, only the natural consequences of technical development, help towards the propagation and shaping of that *other* system.'[1]

THE ORWELLIAN FANTASY

3. George Orwell's bogey of a monolithic consciousness industry derives from a view of the media which is undialectical and obsolete. The possibility of total control of such a system at a central point belongs not to the future but to the past. With the aid of systems theory, a discipline which is part of bourgeois science – using, that is to say, categories which are immanent in the system – it can be demonstrated that a linked series of communications or, to use the technical term, switchable network, to the degree that it exceeds a certain critical size, can no longer be centrally controlled but only dealt with statistically. This basic 'leakiness' of stochastic systems admittedly allows the

calculation of probabilities based on sampling and extrapolations; but blanket supervision would demand a monitor that was bigger than the system itself. The monitoring of all telephone conversations, for instance, postulates an apparatus which would need to be *n* times more extensive and more complicated than that of the present telephone system. A censor's office, which carried out its work extensively, would of necessity become the largest branch of industry in its society.

But supervision on the basis of approximation can only offer inadequate instruments for the self-regulation of the whole system in accordance with the concepts of those who govern it. It postulates a high degree of internal stability. If this precarious balance is upset, then crisis measures based on statistical methods of control are useless. Interference can penetrate the leaky nexus of the media, spreading and multiplying there with the utmost speed, by resonance. The regime so threatened will in such cases, insofar as it is still capable of action, use force and adopt police or military methods.

A state of emergency is therefore the only alternative to leakage in the consciousness industry; but it cannot be maintained in the long run. Societies in the late industrial age rely on the free exchange of information; the 'objective pressures' to which their controllers constantly appeal are thus turned against them. Every attempt to suppress the random factors, each diminution of the average flow and each distortion of the information structure must, in the long run, lead to an embolism.

The electronic media have not only built up the information network intensively, they have also spread it extensively. The radio wars of the fifties demonstrated that in the realm of communications, national sovereignty is condemned to wither away. The further development of satellites will deal it the *coup de grâce*. Quarantine regulations for information, such as were promulgated by fascism and Stalinism, are only possible today at the cost of deliberate industrial regression.

[Example. The Soviet bureaucracy, that is to say the most widespread and complicated bureaucracy in the world, has to deny itself almost entirely an elementary piece of organizational equipment, the duplicating machine, because this instrument potentially makes everyone a printer. The political risk involved, the possibility of a leakage in the information network, is accepted only at the highest levels, at exposed switchpoints in political, military, and scientific areas. It is clear that Soviet society has to pay an immense price for the suppression of its own productive resources – clumsy procedures, misinformation, *faux frais*. The phenomenon incidentally has its analogue in the capitalist West, it in a diluted form. The technically most advanced electrostatic copying machine, which operates with ordinary paper – which cannot, that is to say, be supervised and is independent of suppliers – is the property of a monopoly (Xerox), on principle it is not sold but rented. The rates themselves ensure that it does not get into the wrong hands. The equipment crops up as if by magic where economic and political power are concentrated. Political control of the equipment goes hand in hand with maximization of profits for the manufacturer. Admittedly this control, as opposed to Soviet methods, is by no means 'watertight' for the reasons indicated.]

The problem of censorship thus enters a new historical stage. The struggle for the freedom of the press and freedom of ideas has, up till now, been mainly an argument within the bourgeoisie itself; for the masses, freedom to express opinions was a fiction since they were, from the beginning, barred from the means of production – above all from the press – and thus were unable to join in freedom of expression from the start. Today censorship is threatened by the productive forces of the consciousness industry which is already, to some extent, gaining the upper hand over the prevailing relations of production. Long before the latter are overthrown, the contradiction between what is possible and what actually exists will become acute.

CULTURAL ARCHAISM IN THE LEFT CRITIQUE

4. The New Left of the sixties has reduced the development of the media to a single concept – that of manipulation. This concept was originally extremely useful for heuristic purposes and has made possible a great many individual analytical investigations, but it now threatens to degenerate into a mere slogan which conceals more than it is able to illuminate, and therefore itself requires analysis.

The current theory of manipulation on the Left is essentially defensive; its effects can lead the movement into defeatism. Subjectively speaking, behind the tendency to go on the defensive lies a sense of impotence. Objectively, it corresponds to the absolutely correct view that the decisive means of production are in enemy hands. But to react to this state of affairs with moral indignation is naive. There is in general an undertone of lamentation when people speak of manipulation which points to idealistic expectations – as if the class enemy had ever stuck to the promises of fair play it occasionally utters. The liberal superstition that in political and social questions there is such a thing as pure, unmanipulated truth seems to enjoy remarkable currency among the socialist Left. It is the unspoken basic premise of the manipulation thesis.

This thesis provides no incentive to push ahead. A socialist perspective which does not go beyond attacking existing property relationships is limited. The expropriation of Springer is a desirable goal but it would be good to know to whom the media should be handed over. The Party? To judge by all experience of that solution, it is not a possible alternative. It is perhaps no accident that the Left has not yet produced an analysis of the pattern of manipulation in countries with socialist regimes.

The manipulation thesis also serves to exculpate oneself. To cast the enemy in the role of the devil is to conceal the weakness and lack of perspective in one's own agitation. If the latter leads to self-isolation instead of mobilizing the masses, then its failure is attributed holus-bolus to the overwhelming power of the media.

The theory of repressive tolerance has also permeated discussion of the media by the Left. This concept, which was formulated by its author with the utmost care, has also, when whittled away in an undialectical manner, become a vehicle for resignation. Admittedly, when an office-equipment firm can attempt to recruit sales staff with the picture of Che Guevara and the text *We would have hired him*, the temptation to withdraw is great. But fear of handling shit is a luxury a sewerman cannot necessarily afford.

The electronic media do away with cleanliness; they are by their nature 'dirty.' That is part of their productive power. In terms of structure, they are antisectarian – a further reason why the Left, insofar as it is not prepared to re-examine its traditions, has little idea what to do with them. The desire for a cleanly defined 'line' and for the suppression of 'deviations' is anachronistic and now serves only one's own need for security. It weakens one's own position by irrational purges, exclusions, and fragmentation, instead of strengthening it by rational discussion.

These resistances and fears are strengthened by a series of cultural factors which, for the most part, operate unconsciously, and which are to be explained by the social history of the participants in today's Left movement – namely their bourgeois class background. It often seems as if it were precisely because of their progressive potential that the media are felt to be an immense threatening power; because for the first time they present a basic challenge to bourgeois culture and thereby to the privileges of the bourgeois intelligentsia – a challenge far more radical than any self-doubt this social group can display. In the New Left's opposition to the media, old bourgeois fears such as the fear of 'the masses' seem to be reappearing along with equally old bourgeois longings for pre-industrial times dressed up in progressive clothing.

[At the very beginning of the student revolt, during the Free Speech Movement at Berkeley, the computer was a favorite target for aggression. Interest in the Third World is not always free from motives based on antagonism towards civilization which has its source in conservative culture critique. During the May events in Paris the reversion to archaic forms of production was particularly characteristic. Instead of carrying out agitation among the workers with a modern offset press, the students printed their posters on the hand presses of the École des Beaux Arts. The political slogans were hand-painted; stencils would certainly have made it possible to produce them *en masse*, but it would have offended the creative imagination of the authors. The ability to make proper strategic use of the most advanced media was lacking. It was not the radio headquarters that were seized by the rebels, but the Odéon Theatre, steeped in tradition.]

The obverse of this fear of contact with the media is the fascination they exert on left-wing movements in the great cities. On the one hand, the comrades take refuge in outdated forms of communication and esoteric arts and crafts instead of occupying themselves with the contradiction between the present constitution of the media and their revolutionary potential; on the other hand, they cannot escape from the consciousness industry's program or from its esthetic. This leads, subjectively, to a split between a puritanical view of political action and the area of private 'leisure'; objectively, it leads to a split between politically active groups and subcultural groups.

In Western Europe the socialist movement mainly addresses itself to a public of converts through newspapers and journals which are exclusive in terms of language, content, and form. These newssheets presuppose a structure of party members and sympathizers and a situation, where the media are concerned, that roughly corresponds to the historical situation in 1900; they are obviously fixated on the *Iskra* model. Presumably the people who produce them listen to the Rolling Stones, watch occupations and strikes on television, and go to the cinema to see a Western or a Godard; only in their capacity as producers do they make an exception, and, in their analyses, the whole media sector is reduced to the slogan of 'manipulation.' Every foray into this territory is regarded from the start with suspicion as a step towards integration. This suspicion is not unjustified; it can however also mask one's own ambivalence and insecurity. Fear of being swallowed up by the system is a sign of weakness; it presupposes that capitalism could overcome any contradiction – a conviction which can easily be refuted historically and is theoretically untenable.

If the socialist movement writes off the new productive forces of the consciousness industry and relegates work on the media to a subculture, then we have a vicious circle. For the Underground may be increasingly aware of the technical and esthetic possibilities of the disc, of videotape, of the electronic camera, and so on, and is systematically exploring the terrain, but it has no political viewpoint of its own and therefore mostly falls a helpless victim to commercialism. The politically active groups then point to such cases with smug *Schadenfreude*. A process of unlearning is the result and both sides are the losers. Capitalism alone benefits from the Left's antagonism to the media, as it does from the depoliticization of the counterculture.

Democratic Manipulation

5. Manipulation – etymologically, 'handling' – means technical treatment of a given material with a particular goal in mind. When the technical intervention is of immediate social relevance, then manipulation is a political act. In the case of the media industry, that is by definition the case.

Thus every use of the media presupposes manipulation. The most elementary processes in media production, from the choice of the medium itself to shooting, cutting, synchronization, dubbing, right up to distribution, are all operations carried out on the raw material. There is no such thing as unmanipulated writing, filming, or broadcasting. The question is therefore not whether the media are manipulated, but who manipulates them. A revolutionary plan should not require the manipulators to disappear; on the contrary, it must make everyone a manipulator.

All technical manipulations are potentially dangerous; the manipulation of the media cannot be countered, however, by old or new forms of censorship, but only by direct social control, that is to say, by the mass of the people, who will have become productive. To this end, the elimination of capitalistic property relationships is a necessary but by no means sufficient condition. There have been no historical examples up until now of the mass self-regulating learning process which is made possible by the electronic media. The Communists' fear of releasing this potential, of the mobilizing capabilities of the media, of the interaction of free producers, is one of the main reasons why even in the socialist countries, the old bourgeois culture, greatly disguised and distorted but structurally intact, continues to hold sway.

[As a historical explanation, it may be pointed out that the consciousness industry in Russia at the time of the October Revolution was extraordinarily backward; their productive capacity has grown enormously since then, but the productive relationships have been artificially preserved, often by force. Then, as now, a primitively edited press, books, and theater were the key media in the Soviet Union. The development of radio, film, and television is politically arrested. Foreign stations like the BBC, the Voice of America, and the *Deutschland Welle*, therefore, not only find listeners, but are received with almost boundless faith. Archaic media like the handwritten pamphlet and poems orally transmitted play an important role.]

6. The new media are egalitarian in structure. Anyone can take part in them by a simple switching process. The programs themselves are not material things and can be reproduced at will. In this sense the electronic media are entirely different from the older media like the book or the easel painting, the exclusive class character of which is obvious. Television programs for privileged groups are certainly technically conceivable – closed-circuit television – but run counter to the structure. Potentially, the new media do away with all educational privileges and thereby with the cultural monopoly of the bourgeois intelligentsia. This is one of the reasons for the intelligentsia's resentment against the new industry. As for the 'spirit' which they are endeavoring to defend against 'depersonalization' and 'mass culture,' the sooner they abandon it the better.

PROPERTIES OF THE NEW MEDIA

7. The new media are orientated towards action, not contemplation; towards the present, not tradition. Their attitude to time is completely opposed to that of bourgeois culture, which aspires to possession, that is to extension in time, best of all, to eternity. The media produce no objects that can be hoarded and auctioned. They do away completely with 'intellectual property' and liquidate the 'heritage,' that is to say, the class-specific handing-on of nonmaterial capital.

That does not mean to say that they have no history or that they contribute to the loss of historical consciousness. On the contrary, they make it possible for the first time to record historical material so that it can be reproduced at will. By making this material available for present-day purposes, they make it obvious to anyone using it that the writing of history is always manipulation. But the memory they hold in readiness is not the preserve of a scholarly caste. It is social. The banked information is accessible to anyone, and this accessibility is as instantaneous as its recording. It suffices to compare the model of a private library with that of a socialized data bank to recognize the structural difference between the two systems.

8. It is wrong to regard media equipment as mere means of consumption. It is always, in principle, also means of production and, indeed, since it is in the hands of the masses, socialized means of production. The contradiction between producers and consumers is not inherent in the electronic media; on the contrary, it has to be artificially reinforced by economic and administrative measures.

[An early example of this is provided by the difference between telegraph and telephone. Whereas the former, to this day, has remained in the hands of a bureaucratic institution which can scan and file every text transmitted, the telephone is directly accessible to all users. With the aid of conference circuits, it can even make possible collective intervention in a discussion by physically remote groups.

On the other hand, those auditory and visual means of communication which rely on 'wireless' are still subject to state control (legislation on wireless installations). In the face of technical developments, which long ago made local and international radio-telephony possible, and which constantly opened up new wavebands for television – in the UHF band alone, the dissemination of numerous programs in one locality is possible without interference, not to mention the possibilities offered by wired and satellite television – the prevailing laws for control of the air are anachronistic. They recall the time when the operation of a printing press was dependent on an imperial license. The socialist movements will take up the struggle for their own wavelengths and must, within the foreseeable future, build their own transmitters and relay stations.]

9. One immediate consequence of the structural nature of the new media is that none of the regimes at present in power can release their potential. Only a free socialist society will be able to make them fully productive. A further characteristic of the most advanced media – probably the decisive one – confirms this thesis: their collective structure.

For the prospect that in future, with the aid of the media, anyone can become a producer, would remain apolitical and limited were this productive effort to find an outlet in individual tinkering. Work on the media is possible for an individual only insofar as it remains socially and therefore esthetically irrelevant. The collection of transparencies from the last holiday trip provides a model of this.

That is naturally what the prevailing market mechanisms have aimed at. It has long been clear from apparatus like miniature and 8-mm movie cameras, as well as the tape recorder, which are in actual fact already in the hands of the masses, that the individual, so long as he remains isolated, can become with their help at best an amateur but not a producer. Even so potent a means of production as the short-wave transmitter has been tamed in this way and reduced to a harmless and inconsequential hobby in the hands of scattered radio hams. The programs which the isolated amateur mounts are always only bad, outdated copies of what he in any case receives.

[Private production for the media is no more than licensed cottage industry. Even when it is made public it remains pure compromise. To this end, the men who own the media have developed special programs which are usually called 'Democratic Forum' or something of the kind. There, tucked away in the corner, 'the reader (listener, viewer) has his say,' which can naturally be cut short at any time. As in the case of public-opinion polling, he is only asked questions so that he may have a chance to confirm his own dependence. It is a control circuit where what is fed in has already made complete allowance for the feedback.

The concept of a license can also be used in another sense – in an economic one: the system attempts to make each participant into a concessionaire of the monopoly that develops his films or plays back his cassettes. The aim is to nip in the bud in this way that independence which video equipment, for instance, makes possible. Naturally, such tendencies go against the grain of the structure, and the new productive forces not only permit but indeed demand their reversal.]

The poor, feeble, and frequently humiliating results of this licensed activity are often referred to with contempt by the professional media producers. On top of the damage suffered by the masses comes triumphant mockery because they clearly do not know how to use the media properly. The sort of thing that goes on in certain popular television shows is taken as proof that they are completely incapable of articulating on their own.

Not only does this run counter to the results of the latest psychological and pedagogical research, but it can easily be seen to be a reactionary protective formulation; the 'gifted' people are quite simply defending their territories. Here we have a cultural analogue to the familiar political judgements concerning a working class which is presumed to be 'stultified' and incapable of any kind of self-determination. Curiously, one may hear the view that the masses could never govern themselves out of the mouths of people who consider themselves socialists. In the best of cases, these are economists who cannot conceive of socialism as anything other than nationalization.

A SOCIALIST STRATEGY

10. Any socialist strategy for the media must, on the contrary, strive to end the isolation of the individual participants from the social learning and production process. This is impossible unless those concerned organize themselves. This is the political core of the question of the media. It is over this point that socialist

concepts part company with the neo-liberal and technocratic ones. Anyone who expects to be emancipated by technological hardware, or by a system of hardware however structured, is the victim of an obscure belief in progress. Anyone who imagines that freedom for the media will be established if only everyone is busy transmitting and receiving is the dupe of a liberalism which, decked out in contemporary colors, merely peddles the faded concepts of a preordained harmony of social interests.

In the face of such illusions, what must be firmly held on to is that the proper use of the media demands organization and makes it possible. Every production that deals with the interests of the producers postulates a collective method of production. It is itself already a form of self-organization of social needs. Tape recorders, ordinary cameras, and movie cameras are already extensively owned by wage-earners. The question is why these means of production do not turn up at factories, in schools, in the offices of the bureaucracy, in short, everywhere where there is social conflict. By producing aggressive forms of publicity which were their own, the masses could secure evidence of their daily experiences and draw effective lessons from them.

Naturally, bourgeois society defends itself against such prospects with a battery of legal measures. It bases itself on the law of trespass, on commercial and official secrecy. While its secret services penetrate everywhere and plug in to the most intimate conversations, it pleads a touching concern for confidentiality, and makes a sensitive display of worrying about the question of privacy when all that is private is the interest of the exploiters. Only a collective, organized effort can tear down these paper walls.

Communication networks which are constructed for such purposes can, over and above their primary function, provide politically interesting organizational models. In the socialist movements the dialectic of discipline and spontaneity, centralism and decentralization, authoritarian leadership and anti-authoritarian disintegration has long ago reached deadlock. Networklike communications models built on the principle or reversibility of circuits might give indications of how to overcome this situation: a mass newspaper, written and distributed by its readers, a video network of politically active groups.

More radically than any good intention, more lastingly than existential flight from one's own class, the media, once they have come into their own, destroy the private production methods of bourgeois intellectuals. Only in productive work and learning processes can their individualism be broken down in such a way that it is transformed from morally based (that is to say, as individual as ever) self-sacrifice to a new kind of political self-understanding and behavior.

11. An all too widely disseminated thesis maintains that present-day capitalism lives by the exploitation of unreal needs. That is at best a half-truth. The results obtained by popular American sociologists like Vance Packard are not unuseful but limited. What they have to say about the stimulation of needs through advertising and artificial obsolescence can in any case not be adequately explained by the hypnotic pull exerted on the wage-earners by mass

consumption. The hypothesis of 'consumer terror' corresponds to the prejudices of a middle class, which considers itself politically enlightened, against the allegedly integrated proletariat, which has become petty bourgeois and corrupt. The attractive power of mass consumption is based not on the dictates of false needs, but on the falsification and exploitation of quite real and legitimate ones without which the parasitic process of advertising would be redundant. A socialist movement ought not to denounce these needs, but take them seriously, investigate them, and make them politically productive.

That is also valid for the consciousness industry. The electronic media do not owe their irresistible power to any sleight-of-hand but to the elemental power of deep social needs which come through even in the present depraved form of these media.

Precisely because no one bothers about them, the interests of the masses have remained a relatively unknown field, at least insofar as they are historically new. They certainly extend far beyond those goals which the traditional working class movement represented. Just as in the field of production, the industry which produces goods and the consciousness industry merge more and more, so too, subjectively, where needs are concerned, material and nonmaterial factors are closely interwoven. In the process old psycho-social themes are firmly embedded – social prestige, identification patterns – but powerful new themes emerge which are utopian in nature. From a materialistic point of view, neither the one nor the other must be suppressed.

Henri Lefèbvre has proposed the concept of the *spectacle*, the exhibition, the show, to fit the present form of mass consumption. Goods and shop windows, traffic and advertisements, stores and the world of communications, news and packaging, architecture and media production come together to form a totality, a permanent theater, which dominates not only the public city centers but also private interiors. The expression 'beautiful living' makes the most commonplace objects of general use into props for this universal festival, in which the fetishistic nature of the commodities triumphs completely over their use value. The swindle these festivals perpetrate is, and remains, a swindle within the present social structure. But it is the harbinger of something else. Consumption as spectacle contains the promise that want will disappear. The deceptive, brutal, and obscene features of this festival derive from the fact that there can be no question of a real fulfillment of its promise. But so long as scarcity holds sway, use-value remains a decisive category which can only be abolished by trickery. Yet trickery on such a scale is only conceivable if it is based on mass need. This need – it is a utopian one – is there. It is the desire for a new ecology, for a breaking down of environmental barriers, for an esthetic which is not limited to the sphere of 'the artistic.' These desires are not – or are not primarily – internalized rules of the game as played by the capitalist system. They have physiological roots and can no longer be suppressed. Consumption as spectacle is – in parody form – the anticipation of a utopian situation.

The promises of the media demonstrate the same ambivalence. They are an answer to the mass need for nonmaterial variety and mobility – which at present finds its material realization in private car ownership and tourism – and they exploit it. Other collective wishes, which capital often recognizes more quickly and evaluates more correctly than its opponents, but naturally only so as to trap them and rob them of their explosive force, are just as powerful, just as unequivocally emancipatory: the need to take part in the social process on a local, national, and international scale; the need for new forms of interaction, for release from ignorance and tutelage; the need for self-determination. 'Be everywhere!' is one of the most successful slogans of the media industry. The readers' parliament of *Bild-Zeitung* [The Springer press mass publication] was direct democracy used against the interests of the *demos*. 'Open space,' and 'hee time' are concepts which corral and neutralize the urgent wishes of the masses.

[There is corresponding acceptance by the media of utopian stories: e.g., the story of the young Italo-American who hijacked a passenger plane to get home from California to Rome was taken up without protest even by the reactionary mass press and undoubtedly correctly understood by its readers. The identification is based on what has become a general need. Nobody can understand why such journeys should be reserved for politicians, functionaries, and businessmen. The role of the pop star could be analyzed from a similar angle; in it the authoritarian and emancipatory factors are mingled in an extraordinary way. It is perhaps not unimportant that beat music offers groups, not individuals, as identification models. In the productions of the Rolling Stones (and in the manner of their production) the utopian content is apparent. Events like the Woodstock Festival, the concerts in Hyde Park, on the Isle of Wight, and at Altamont, California, develop a mobilizing power which the political Left can only envy.]

It is absolutely clear that, within the present social forms, the consciousness industry can satisfy none of the needs on which it lives and which it must fan, except in the illusory form of games. The point, however, is not to demolish its promises but to take them literally and to show that they can be met only through a cultural revolution. Socialists and socialist regimes which multiply the frustration of the masses by declaring their needs to be false, become the accomplices of the system they have undertaken to fight.

12. Summary

Repressive use of media	Emancipatory use of media
Centrally controlled program	Decentralized program
One transmitter, many receivers	Each receiver a potential transmitter
Immobilization of isolated individuals	Mobilization of the masses

Passive consumer behavior	Interaction of those involved, feedback
Depoliticization	A political learning process
Production by specialists	Collective production
Control by property owners or bureaucracy	Social control by self-organization

THE SUBVERSIVE POWER OF THE NEW MEDIA

13. As far as the objectively subversive potentialities of the electronic media are concerned, both sides in the international class struggle – except for the fatalistic adherents of the thesis of manipulation in the metropoles – are of one mind. Frantz Fanon was the first to draw attention to the fact that the transistor receiver was one of the most important weapons in the Third World's fight for freedom. Albert Hertzog, ex-Minister of the South African Republic and the mouthpiece of the right wing of the ruling party, is of the opinion that 'television will lead to the ruin of the white man in South Africa.'[2] American imperialism has recognized the situation. It attempts to meet the 'revolution of rising expectations' in Latin America – that is what its ideologues call it – by scattering its own transmitters all over the continent and into the remotest regions of the Amazon basin, and by distributing single-frequency transistors to the native population. The attacks of the Nixon Administration on the capitalist media in the USA reveal its understanding that their reporting, however one-sided and distorted, has become a decisive factor in mobilizing people against the war in Vietnam. Whereas only twenty-five years ago the French massacres in Madagascar, with almost one hundred thousand dead, became known only to the readers of *Le Monde* under the heading of 'Other News' and therefore remained unnoticed and without sequel in the capital city, today the media drag colonial wars into the centers of imperialism.

The direct mobilizing potentialities of the media become still more clear when they are consciously used for subversive ends. Their presence is a factor that immensely increases the demonstrative nature of any political act. The student movements in the USA, in Japan, and in Western Europe soon recognized this and, to begin with, achieved considerable momentary success with the aid of the media. These effects have worn off. Naive trust in the magical power of reproduction cannot replace organizational work; only active and coherent groups can force the media to comply with the logic of their actions. That can be demonstrated from the example of the Tupamaros in Uruguay, whose revolutionary practice has implicit in it publicity for their actions. Thus the actors become authors. The abduction of the American ambassador in Rio de Janeiro was planned with a view to its impact on the media. It was a television production. The Arab guerillas proceed in the same way. The first to experiment with these techniques internationally were the Cubans. Fidel appreciated the revolutionary potential of the media correctly from the first (Moncada, 1953). Today illegal political action demands at one and the same time maximum security and maximum publicity.

14. Revolutionary situations always bring with them discontinuous, spontaneous changes brought about by the masses in the existing aggregate of the media. How far the changes thus brought about take root and how permanent they are demonstrates the extent to which a cultural revolution is successful. The situation in the media is the most accurate and sensitive barometer for the rise of bureaucratic or Bonapartist anticyclones. So long as the cultural revolution has the initiative, the social imagination of the masses overcomes even technical backwardness and transforms the function of the old media so that their structures are exploded.

['With our work the Revolution has achieved a colossal labor of propaganda and enlightenment. We ripped up the traditional book into single pages, magnified these a hundred times, printed them in color and stuck them up as posters in the streets ... Our lack of printing equipment and the necessity for speed meant that, though the best work was hand-printed, the most rewarding was standardized, lapidary and adapted to the simplest mechanical form of reproduction. Thus State Decrees were printed as rolled-up illustrated leaflets, and Army Orders as illustrated pamphlets.'[3]]

In the twenties, the Russian film reached a standard that was far in advance of the available productive forces. Pudovkin's *Kinoglas* and Dziga Vertov's *Kinopravda* were no 'newsreels' but political television magazine programs *avant l'écran*. The campaign against illiteracy in Cuba broke through the linear, exclusive, and isolating structure of the medium of the book. In the China of the Cultural Revolution, wall newspapers functioned like an electronic mass medium – at least in the big towns. The resistance of the Czechoslovak population to the Soviet invasion gave rise to spontaneous productivity on the part of the masses, which ignored the institutional barriers of the media. Such situations are exceptional. It is precisely their utopian nature, which reaches out beyond the existing productive forces (it follows that the productive relationships are not to be permanently overthrown), that makes them precarious, leads to reversals and defeats. They demonstrate all the more clearly what enormous political and cultural energies are hidden in the enchained masses and with what imagination they are able, at the moment of liberation, to realize all the opportunities offered by the new media.

THE MEDIA: AN EMPTY CATEGORY OF MARXIST THEORY

15. That the Marxist Left should argue theoretically and act practically from the standpoint of the most advanced productive forces in their society, that they should develop in depth all the liberating factors immanent in these forces and use them strategically, is no academic expectation but a political necessity. However, with a single great exception, that of Walter Benjamin (and in his footsteps, Brecht), Marxists have not understood the consciousness industry and have been aware only of its bourgeois-capitalist dark side and not of its

socialist possibilities. An author like George Lukács is a perfect example of this theoretical and practical backwardness. Nor are the works of Horkheimer and Adorno free of a nostalgia which clings to early bourgeois media.

[Their view of the cultural industry cannot be discussed here. Much more typical of Marxism between the two wars is the position of Lukács, which can be seen very clearly from an early essay on 'Old Culture and New Culture'[4] 'Anything that culture produces' can, according to Lukács, 'have real cultural value only *if it is in itself* valuable, if the creation of each individual product is from the standpoint of its maker a single, finite process. It must, moreover, be a process conditioned by the *human* potentialities and capabilities of the creator. The most typical example of such a process is the work of art, where the entire genesis of the work is exclusively the result of the artist's labor and each detail of the work that emerges is determined by the individual qualities of the artist. In highly developed mechanical industry, on the other hand, any connection between the product and the creator is abolished. *The human being serves the machine, he adapts to it.* Production becomes completely independent of the human potentialities and capabilities of the worker.' These 'forces which destroy culture' impair the work's 'truth to the material,' its 'level,' and deal the final blow to the 'work as an end in itself.' There is no more question of 'the organic unity of the products of culture, its harmonious, joy-giving being.' Capitalist culture must lack 'the simple and natural harmony and beauty of the old culture – culture in the true, literal sense of the word.' Fortunately things need not remain so. The 'culture of proletarian society,' although 'in the context of such scientific research as is possible at this time' nothing more can be said about it, will certainly remedy these ills. Lukács asks himself 'which are the cultural values which, in accordance with the nature of this context, *can be taken over from the old society* by the new *and further developed.*' Answer: Not the inhuman machines but 'the idea of mankind as an end in itself, the basic idea of the new culture,' for it is 'the inheritance of the classical idealism of the nineteenth century.' Quite right. 'This is where the philistine concept of *art* turns up with all its deadly obtuseness – an idea to which all technical considerations are foreign and which feels that with the provocative appearance of the new technology its end has come.'[5]

These nostalgic backward glances at the landscape of the last century, these reactionary ideals, are already the forerunners of socialist realism, which mercilessly galvanized and then buried those very 'cultural values' which Lukács rode out to rescue. Unfortunately, in the process, the Soviet cultural revolution was thrown to the wolves; but this esthete can in any case hardly have thought any more highly of it than did J. V. Stalin.]

The inadequate understanding which Marxists have shown of the media and the questionable use they have made of them has produced a vacuum in Western industrialized countries into which a stream of non-Marxist hypotheses and practices has consequently flowed. From the Cabaret Voltaire to Andy Warhol's Factory, from the silent film comedians to the Beatles, from the first comic-strip artists to the present managers of the Underground, the apolitical have made much more radical progress in dealing with the media than any grouping of the Left. (Exception – Münzenberg.) Innocents have put themselves in the forefront of the new productive forces on the basis of mere intuitions with which communism – to its detriment – has not wished to concern itself. Today this apolitical avant-garde has found its ventriloquist and prophet in Marshall McLuhan, an author who admittedly lacks any analytical categories for the understanding of social processes, but whose confused books serve as a quarry of undigested observations for the media industry. Certainly his little finger has experienced more of the productive power of the new media than all the ideological commissions of the CPSU and their endless resolutions and directives put together.

Incapable of any theoretical construction, McLuhan does not present his material as a concept but as the common denominator of a reactionary doctrine of salvation. He admittedly did not invent but was the first to formulate explicitly a mystique of the media which dissolves all political problems in smoke – the same smoke that gets in the eyes of his followers. It promises the salvation of man through the technology of television and indeed of television as it is practiced today. Now McLuhan's attempt to stand Marx on his head is not exactly new. He shares with his numerous predecessors the determination to suppress all problems of the economic base, their idealistic tendencies, and their belittling of the class struggle in the naive terms of a vague humanism. A new Rousseau – like all copies, only a pale version of the old – he preaches the gospel of the new primitive man who, naturally on a higher level, must return to prehistoric tribal existence in the 'global village.'

It is scarcely worthwhile to deal with such concepts. This charlatan's most famous saying – 'the medium is the message' – perhaps deserves more attention. In spite of its provocative idiocy, it betrays more than its author knows. It reveals in the most accurate way the tautological nature of the mystique of the media. The one remarkable thing about the television set, according to him, is that it moves – a thesis which in view of the nature of American programs has, admittedly, something attractive about it.

[The complementary mistake consists in the widespread illusion that media are neutral instruments by which any 'messages' one pleases can be transmitted without regard for their structure or for the structure of the medium. In the East European countries the television newsreaders read fifteen-minute-long conference communiqués and Central Committee resolutions which are not even suitable for printing in a newspaper, clearly under the delusion that they might fascinate a public of millions.]

The sentence 'The medium is the message' transmits yet another message, however, and a much more important one. It tells us that the bourgeoisie does indeed have all possible means at its disposal to communicate something to us, but that it has nothing more to say. It is ideologically sterile. Its intention to hold on to the control of the means of production at any price, while being incapable of making the socially necessary use of them, is here expressed with complete frankness in the superstructure. It wants the media *as such* and *to no purpose.*

This wish has been shared for decades and given symbolical expression by an artistic avant-garde whose program logically admits only the alternative of negative signals and amorphous noise. Example: the already outdated 'literature of silence,' Warhol's films in which everything can happen at once or nothing at all, and John Cage's forty-five-minute-long *Lecture on Nothing* (1959).

THE ACHIEVEMENT OF BENJAMIN

16. The revolution in the conditions of production in the superstructure has made the traditional esthetic theory unusable, completely unhinging its fundamental categories and destroying its 'standards.' The theory of knowledge on which it was based is outmoded. In the electronic media, a radically altered relationship between subject and object emerges with which the old critical concepts cannot deal. The idea of the self sufficient work of art collapsed long ago. The long-drawn discussion over the death of art proceeds in a circle so long as it does not examine critically the esthetic concept on which it is based, so long as it employs criteria which no longer correspond to the state of the productive forces. When constructing an esthetic adapted to the changed situation, one must take as a starting point the work of the only Marxist theoretician who recognized the liberating potential of the new media. Thirty-five years ago, that is to say, at a time when the consciousness industry was relatively undeveloped, Walter Benjamin subjected this phenomenon to a penetrating dialectical-materialist analysis. His approach has not been matched by any theory since then, much less further developed.

> One might generalize by saying: the technique of reproduction detaches the reproduced object from the domain of tradition. By making many reproductions it substitutes a plurality of copies for a unique existence and in permitting the reproduction to meet the beholder or listener in his own particular situation, it reactivates the object reproduced. These two processes lead to a tremendous shattering of tradition which is the obverse of the contemporary crisis and renewal of mankind. Both processes are intimately connected with the contemporary mass movements. Their most powerful agent is the film. Its social significance, particularly in its most positive form, is inconceivable without its destructive, cathartic aspect, that is, the liquidation of the traditional value of the cultural heritage.
>
> For the first time in world history, mechanical reproduction emancipates the work of art from its parasitical dependence on ritual. To an ever greater degree the work of art reproduced becomes the work of art designed for reproducibility ... But the instant the criterion of authenticity

ceases to be applicable to artistic production, the total function of art is reversed. Instead of being based on ritual, it begins to be based on another practice – politics ... Today, by the absolute emphasis on its exhibition value, the work of art becomes a creation with entirely new functions, among which the one we are conscious of, the artistic function, later may be recognized as incidental.[6]

The trends which Benjamin recognized in his day in the film and the true import of which he grasped theoretically, have become patent today with the rapid development of the consciousness industry. What used to be called art, has now, in the strict Hegelian sense, been dialectically surpassed by and in the media. The quarrel about the end of art is otiose so long as this end is not understood dialectically. Artistic productivity reveals itself to be the extreme marginal case of a much more widespread productivity, and it is socially important only insofar as it surrenders all pretensions to autonomy and recognizes itself to be a marginal case. Wherever the professional producers make a virtue out of the necessity of their specialist skills and even derive a privileged status from them, their experience and knowledge have become useless. This means that as far as an esthetic theory is concerned, a radical change in perspectives is needed. Instead of looking at the productions of the new media from the point of view of the older modes of production we must, on the contrary, analyze the products of the traditional 'artistic' media from the standpoint of modern conditions of production.

> Earlier much futile thought had been devoted to the question of whether photography is an art. The primary question – whether the very invention of photography had not transformed the entire nature of art – was not raised. Soon the film theoreticians asked the same ill-considered question with regard to the film. But the difficulties which photography caused traditional esthetics were mere child's play as compared to those raised by the film.[7]

The panic aroused by such a shift in perspectives is understandable. The process not only changes the old burdensome craft secrets in the superstructure into white elephants, it also conceals a genuinely destructive element. It is, in a word, risky. But the only chance for the esthetic tradition lies in its dialectical supersession. In the same way, classical physics has survived as a marginal special case within the framework of a much more comprehensive theory.

This state of affairs can be identified in individual cases in all the traditional artistic disciplines. Their present-day developments remain incomprehensible so long as one attempts to deduce them from their own prehistory. On the other hand, their usefulness or otherwise can be judged as soon as one regards them as special cases in a general esthetic of the media. Some indications of the possible critical approaches which stem from this will be made below, taking literature as an example.

THE SUPERSESSION OF WRITTEN CULTURE

17. Written literature has, historically speaking, played a dominant role for only a few centuries. Even today, the predominance of the book has an episodic air. An incomparably longer time preceded it in which literature was oral. Now it is being succeeded by the age of the electronic media, which tend once more to make people speak. At its period of fullest development, the book to some extent usurped the place of the more primitive but generally more accessible methods of production of the past; on the other hand, it was a stand-in for future methods which make it possible for everyone to become a producer.

The revolutionary role of the printed book has been described often enough and it would be absurd to deny it. From the point of view of its structure as a medium, written literature, like the bourgeoisie who produced it and whom it served, was progressive. (See the *Communist Manifesto*.) On the analogy of the economic development of capitalism, which was indispensable for the development of the industrial revolution, the nonmaterial productive forces could not have developed without their own capital accumulation. (We also owe the accumulation of *Das Kapital* and its teachings to the medium of the book.)

Nevertheless, almost everybody speaks better than he writes. (This also applies to authors.) Writing is a highly formalized technique which, in purely physiological terms, demands a peculiarly rigid bodily posture. To this there corresponds the high degree of social specialization that it demands. Professional writers have always tended to think in caste terms. The class character of their work is unquestionable, even in the age of universal compulsory education. The whole process is extraordinarily beset with taboos. Spelling mistakes, which are completely immaterial in terms of communication, are punished by the social disqualification of the writer. The rules that govern this technique have a normative power attributed to them for which there is no rational basis. Intimidation through the written word has remained a widespread and class-specific phenomenon even in advanced industrial societies.

These alienating factors cannot be eradicated from written literature. They are reinforced by the methods by which society transmits its writing techniques. While people learn to speak very early, and mostly in psychologically favorable conditions, learning to write forms an important part of authoritarian socialization by the school ('good writing' as a kind of breaking-in). This sets its stamp forever on written communication – on its tone, its syntax, and its whole style. (This also applies to the text on this page.)

The formalization of written language permits and encourages the repression of opposition. In speech, unresolved contradictions betray themselves by pauses, hesitations, slips of the tongue, repetitions, anacoluthons, quite apart from phrasing, mimicry, gesticulation, pace, and volume. The esthetic of written literature scorns such involuntary factors as 'mistakes.' It demands, explicitly or implicitly, the smoothing out of contradictions, rationalization, regularization of the spoken form irrespective of content. Even as a child, the writer is urged to hide his unsolved problems behind a protective screen of correctness.

Structurally, the printed book is a medium that operates as a monologue, isolating producer and reader. Feedback and interaction are extremely limited, demand elaborate procedures, and only in the rarest cases lead to corrections. Once an edition has been printed it cannot be corrected; at best it can be pulped. The control circuit in the case of literary criticism is extremely cumbersome and elitist. It excludes the public on principle.

None of the characteristics that distinguish written and printed literature apply to the electronic media. Microphone and camera abolish the class character of the mode of production (not of the production itself). The normative rules become unimportant. Oral interviews, arguments, demonstrations, neither demand nor allow orthography or 'good writing.' The television screen exposes the esthetic smoothing out of contradictions as camouflage. Admittedly, swarms of liars appear on it, but anyone can see from a long way off that they are peddling something. As at present constituted, radio, film, and television are burdened to excess with authoritarian characteristics, the characteristics of the monologue, which they have inherited from older methods of production – and that is no accident. These outworn elements in today's media esthetics are demanded by the social relations. They do not follow from the structure of the media. On the contrary, they go against it, for the structure demands interaction.

It is extremely improbable, however, that writing as a special technique will disappear in the foreseeable future. That goes for the book as well, the practical advantages of which for many purposes remain obvious. It is admittedly less handy and takes up more room than other storage systems, but up to now it offers simpler methods of access than, for example, the microfilm or the tape bank. It ought to be integrated into the system as a marginal case and thereby forfeit its aura of cult and ritual.

[This can be deduced from technological developments. Electronics are noticeably taking over writing: teleprinters, reading machines, high-speed transmissions, automatic photographic and electronic composition, automatic writing devices, typesetters, electrostatic processes, ampex libraries, cassette encyclopedias, photocopiers and magnetic copiers, speedprinters.

The outstanding Russian media expert El Lissitsky, incidentally, demanded an 'electro library' as far back as 1923 a request which, given the technical conditions of the time, must have seemed ridiculous or at least incomprehensible. This is how far this man's imagination reached into the future:
'I draw the following analogy:

Inventions in the field of verbal traffic	Inventions in the field of general traffic
Articulated language	Upright gait
Writing	The wheel
Gutenberg's printing press	Carts drawn by animal power

| ? | The automobile |
| ? | The airplane |

'I have produced this analogy to prove that so long as the book remains a palpable object, i.e. so long as it is not replaced by auto-vocalizing and kino-vocalizing representations, we must look to the field of the manufacture of books for basic innovations in the near future.

'There are signs at hand suggesting that this basic innovation is likely to come from the neighborhood of the collotype.'[8]

Today, writing has in many cases already become a secondary technique, a means of transcribing orally recorded speech: tape-recorded proceedings, attempts at speech pattern recognition, and the conversion of speech into writing.]

18. The ineffectiveness of literary criticism when faced with so-called documentary literature is an indication of how far the critics' thinking has lagged behind the stage of the productive forces. It stems from the fact that the media have eliminated one of the most fundamental categories of esthetics up to now – fiction. The fiction/nonfiction argument has been laid to rest just as was the nineteenth century's favorite dialectic of 'art' and 'life.' In his day, Benjamin demonstrated that the 'apparatus' (the concept of the medium was not yet available to him) abolishes authenticity. In the productions of the consciousness industry, the difference between the 'genuine' original and the reproduction disappears – 'that aspect of reality which is not dependent on the apparatus has now become its most artificial aspect.' The process of reproduction reacts on the object reproduced and alters it fundamentally. The effects of this have not yet been adequately explained epistemologically. The categorical uncertainties to which it gives rise also affect the concept of the documentary. Strictly speaking, it has shrunk to its legal dimensions. A document is something the 'forging' – i.e. the reproduction – of which is punishable by imprisonment. This definition naturally has no theoretical meaning. The reason is that a reproduction, to the extent that its technical quality is good enough, cannot be distinguished in any way from the original, irrespective of whether it is a painting, a passport, or a bank note. The legal concept of the documentary record is only pragmatically useful; it serves only to protect economic interests.

The productions of the electronic media, by their nature, evade such distinctions as those between documentary and feature films. They are in every case explicitly determined by the given situation. The producer can never pretend, like the traditional novelist, 'to stand above things.' He is therefore partisan from the start. This fact finds formal expression in his techniques. Cutting, editing, dubbing – these are techniques for conscious manipulation without which the use of the new media is inconceivable. It is precisely in these work processes that their productive power reveals itself – and here it is completely immaterial whether one is dealing with the production of a reportage or a play. The material, whether 'documentary' on 'fiction,' is in each case only a prototype, a half-finished article, and the more closely one examines its origins, the more blurred the difference becomes.

The Desacralization of Art

19. The media also do away with the old category of works of art which can only be considered as separate objects, not as independent of their material infrastructure. The media do not produce such objects. They create programs. Their production is in the nature of a process. That does not mean only (or not primarily) that there is no foreseeable end to the program – a fact which, in view of what we are at present presented with, admittedly makes a certain hostility to the media understandable. It means, above all, that the media program is open to its own consequences without structural limitations. (This is not an empirical description but a demand. A demand which admittedly is not made of the medium from without; it is a consequence of its nature, from which the much-vaunted open form can be derived – and not as a modification of it – from an old esthetic.) The programs of the consciousness industry must subsume into themselves their own results, the reactions and the corrections which they call forth, otherwise they are already out-of-date. They are therefore to be thought of not as means of consumption but as means of their own production.

20. It is characteristic of artistic avant-gardes that they have, so to speak, a presentiment of the potentiality of media which still lie in the future.

> It has always been one of the most important tasks of art to give rise to a demand, the time for the complete satisfaction of which has not yet come. The history of every art form has critical periods when that form strives towards effects which can only be easily achieved if the technical norm is changed, that is to say, in a new art form. The artistic extravagances and crudities which arise in this way, for instance in the so-called decadent period, really stem from art's richest historical source of power. Dadaism in the end teemed with such barbarisms. We can only now recognize the nature of its striving. Dadaism was attempting to achieve those effects which the public today seeks in film with the means of painting (or of literature).[9]

This is where the prognostic value of otherwise inessential productions, such as happenings, flux, and mixed-media shows, is to be found. There are writers who in their work show an awareness of the fact that media with the characteristics of the monologue today have only a residual use-value. Many of them admittedly draw fairly shortsighted conclusions from this glimpse of the truth. For example, they offer the user the opportunity to arrange the material provided by arbitrary permutations. Every reader as it were should write his own book. When carried to extremes, such attempts to produce interaction, even when it goes against the structure of the medium employed, are nothing more than invitations to freewheel. Mere noise permits of no articulated interactions. Short cuts, of the kind that Concept Art peddles, are based on the banal and false conclusion that the development of the productive forces renders all work superfluous. With the same justification, one could leave a computer to its own devices on the assumption that a random generator will organize material production by itself. Fortunately, cybernetics experts are not given to such childish games.

21. For the old-fashioned 'artist' – let us call him the author – it follows from these reflections that he must see it as his goal to make himself redundant as a specialist in much the same way as a teacher of literacy only fulfills his task when he is no longer necessary. Like every learning process, this process too is reciprocal. The specialist will learn as much or more from the nonspecialists as the other way round. Only then can he contrive to make himself dispensable.

Meanwhile, his social usefulness can best be measured by the degree to which he is capable of using the liberating factors in the media and bringing them to fruition. The tactical contradictions in which he must become involved in the process can neither be denied nor covered up in any way. But strategically his role is clear. The author has to work as the agent of the masses. He can lose himself in them only when they themselves become authors, the authors of history.

22. 'Pessimism of the intelligence, optimism of the will' (Antonio Gramsci).

NOTES

1. Bertolt Brecht, *Theory of Radio* (1932). *Gesammelte Werke*, Band VIII. pp. 129 seq. 131.
2. *Der Spiegel*, 20/10/1969.
3. El Lissitsky, 'The Future of the Book,' *New Left Review*, No. 41. p. 42.
4. *Kommunismus, Zeitschrift der Kommunistischen Internationale für die Länder Südosteuropas*, 1920, pp. 1538–49.
5. Walter Benjamin, *Kleine Geschichte der Photographie* in *Das Kunstwerk im Zeitalter seiner technischen Reproduzierbarkeit* (Frankfurt: 1963), p. 69.
6. Walter Benjamin, 'The Work of Art in the Age of Mechanical Reproduction,' *Illuminations* (New York: 1969), pp. 223–7.
7. Ibid., p. 229.
8. Op. cit., p. 40.
9. Benjamin, op. cit., p. 42.

THE PUBLIC SPHERE

Jürgen Habermas

Concept

By 'public sphere' we mean first of all a domain of our social life in which such a thing as public opinion can be formed. Access to the public sphere is open in principle to all citizens. A portion of the public sphere is constituted in every conversation in which private persons come together to form a public. They are then acting neither as business or professional people conducting their private affairs, nor as legal consociates subject to the legal regulations of a state bureaucracy and obligated to obedience. Citizens act as a public when they deal with matters of general interest without being subject to coercion; thus with the guarantee that they may assemble and unite freely, and express and publicize their opinions freely. When the public is large, this kind of communication requires certain means of dissemination and influence; today, news- papers and periodicals, radio and television are the media of the public sphere. We speak of a political public sphere (as distinguished from a literary one, for instance) when the public discussions concern objects connected with the practice of the state. The coercive power of the state is the counterpart, as it were, of the political public sphere, but it is not a part of it. State power is, to be sure, considered 'public' power, but it owes the attribute of publicness to its task of caring for the public, that is, providing for the common good of all legal consociates. Only when the exercise of public authority has actually been

From S. Seidman (ed.), *Jürgen Habermas on Society and Politics: A Reader*, trans. S. W. Nicholson (Boston: Beacon Press, 1989); originally published as 'Öffentlichkeit', in J. Habermas, *Kultur und Kritik* (Frankfurt am Main: Suhrkamp Verlag, 1973).

subordinated to the requirement of democratic publicness does the political public sphere acquire an institutionalized influence on the government, by the way of the legislative body. The term 'public opinion' refers to the functions of criticism and control of organized state authority that the public exercises informally, as well as formally during periodic elections. Regulations concerning the publicness (or publicity [*Publizität*] in its original meaning) of state-related activities, as, for instance, the public accessibility required of legal proceedings, are also connected with this function of public opinion. To the public sphere as a sphere mediating between state and society, a sphere in which the public as the vehicle of public opinion is formed, there corresponds the principle of publicness – the publicness that once had to win out against the secret politics of monarchs and that since then has permitted democratic control of state activity.

It is no accident that these concepts of the public sphere and public opinion were not formed until the eighteenth century. They derive their specific meaning from a concrete historical situation. It was then that one learned to distinguish between opinion and public opinion, or *opinion publique*. Whereas mere opinions (things taken for granted as part of a culture, normative convictions, collective prejudices and judgements) seem to persist unchanged in their quasi-natural structure as a kind of sediment of history, public opinion, in terms of its very idea, can be formed only if a public that engages in rational discussion exists. Public discussions that are institutionally protected and that take, with critical intent, the exercise of political authority as their theme have not existed since time immemorial – they developed only in a specific phase of bourgeois society, and only by virtue of a specific constellation of interests could they be incorporated into the order of the bourgeois constitutional state.

HISTORY

It is not possible to demonstrate the existence of a public sphere in its own right, separate from the private sphere, in the European society of the High Middle Ages. At the same time, however, it is not a coincidence that the attributes of authority at that time were called 'public'. For a public representation of authority existed at that time. At all levels of the pyramid established by feudal law, the status of the feudal lord is neutral with respect to the categories 'public' and 'private'; but the person possessing that status represents it publicly; he displays himself, represents himself as the embodiment of a 'higher' power, in whatever degree. This concept of representation has survived into recent constitutional history. Even today the power of political authority on its highest level, however much it has become detached from its former basis, requires representation through the head of state. But such elements derive from a pre-bourgeois social structure. Representation in the sense of the bourgeois public sphere, as in 'representing' the nation or specific clients, has nothing to do with *representative publicness*, which inheres in the concrete existence of a lord. As long as the prince and the estates of his realm 'are' the land, rather than merely 'representing' it, they are capable of this kind of representation; they represent their authority 'before' the people rather than for the people.

The feudal powers (the church, the prince, and the nobility) to which this representative publicness adheres disintegrated in the course of a long process of polarization; by the end of the eighteenth century they had decomposed into private elements on the one side and public on the other. The position of the church changed in connection with the Reformation; the tie to divine authority that the church represented, that is, religion, became a private matter. Historically, what is called the freedom of religion safeguarded the first domain of private autonomy; the church itself continued its existence as one corporate body under public law among others. The corresponding polarization of princely power acquired visible form in the separation of the public budget from the private household property of the feudal lord. In the bureaucracy and the military (and in part also in the administration of justice), institutions of public power became autonomous vis-à-vis the privatized sphere of the princely court. In terms of the estates, finally, elements from the ruling groups developed into organs of public power, into parliament (and in part also into judicial organs); elements from the occupational status groups, insofar as they had become established in urban corporations and in certain differentiations within the estates of the land, developed into the sphere of bourgeois society, which would confront the state as a genuine domain of private autonomy.

Representative publicness gave way to the new sphere of 'public power' that came into being with the national and territorial states. Ongoing state activity (permanent administration, a standing army) had its counterpart in the permanence of relationships that had developed in the meantime with the stock market and the press, through traffic in goods and news. Public power became consolidated as something tangible confronting those who were subject to it and who at first found themselves only negatively defined by it. These are the 'private persons' who are excluded from public power because they hold no office. 'Public' no longer refers to the representative court of a person vested with authority; instead, it now refers to the competence-regulated activity of an apparatus furnished with a monopoly on the legitimate use of force. As those to whom this public power is addressed, private persons subsumed under the state form the public.

As a private domain, society, which has come to confront the state, as it were, is on the one hand clearly differentiated from public power; on the other hand, society becomes a matter of public interest insofar as with the rise of a market economy the reproduction of life extends beyond the confines of private domestic power. The *bourgeois public sphere* can be understood as the sphere of private persons assembled to form a public. They soon began to make use of the public sphere of informational newspapers, which was officially regulated, against the public power itself, using those papers, along with the morally and critically oriented weeklies, to engage in debate about the general rules governing relations in their own essentially privatized but publicly relevant sphere of commodity exchange and labor.

THE LIBERAL MODEL OF THE PUBLIC SPHERE

The medium in which this debate takes place – public discussion – is unique and without historical prototype. Previously the estates had negotiated contracts with their princes in which claims to power were defined on a case-by-case basis. As we know, this development followed a different course in England, where princely power was relativized through parliament, than on the Continent, where the estates were mediatized by the monarch. The 'third estate' then broke with this mode of equalizing power, for it could no longer establish itself as a ruling estate. Given a commercial economy, a division of authority accomplished through differentiation of the rights of those possessing feudal authority (liberties belonging to the estates) was no longer possible – the power under private law of disposition of capitalist property is non-political. The bourgeois are private persons; as such, they do not 'rule.' Thus their claims to power in opposition to public power are directed not against a concentration of authority that should be 'divided' but rather against the principle of established authority. The principle of control, namely publicness, that the bourgeois public opposes to the principle of established authority aims at a transformation of authority as such, not merely the exchange of one basis of legitimation for another.

In the first modern constitutions the sections listing basic rights provide an image of the liberal model of the public sphere: they guarantee society as a sphere of private autonomy; opposite it stands a public power limited to a few functions; between the two spheres, as it were, stands the domain of private persons who have come together to form a public and who, as citizens of the state, mediate the state with the needs of bourgeois society, in order, as the idea goes, to thus convert political authority to 'rational' authority in the medium of this public sphere. Under the presuppositions of a society based on the free exchange of commodities, it seemed that the general interest, which served as the criterion by which this kind of rationality was to be evaluated, would be assured if the dealings of private persons in the marketplace were emancipated from social forces and their dealings in the public sphere were emancipated from political coercion.

The political daily press came to have an important role during this same period. In the second half of the eighteenth century, serious competition to the older form of news writing as the compiling of items of information arose in the form of literary journalism. Karl Bücher describes the main outlines of this development: 'From mere institutions for the publication of news, newspapers became the vehicles and guides of public opinion as well, weapons of party politics. The consequence of this for the internal organization of the newspaper enterprise was the insertion of a new function between the gathering of news and its publication: the editorial function. For the newspaper publisher, however, the significance of this development was that from a seller of new information he became a dealer in public opinion.' Publishers provided the commercial basis for the newspaper without, however, commercializing it as such. The press remained an institution of the public itself, operating to provide and intensify public discussion, no longer a mere organ for the conveyance of information, but not yet a medium of consumer culture.

This type of press can be observed especially in revolutionary periods, when papers associated with the tiniest political coalitions and groups spring up, as in Paris in 1789. In the Paris of 1848 every halfway prominent politician still formed his own club, and every other one founded his own *journal*: over 450 clubs and more than 200 papers came into being there between February and May alone. Until the permanent legalization of a public sphere that functioned politically, the appearance of a political newspaper was equivalent to engagement in the struggle for a zone of freedom for public opinion, for publicness as a principle. Not until the establishment of the bourgeois constitutional state was a press engaged in the public use of reason relieved of the pressure of ideological viewpoints. Since then it has been able to abandon its polemical stance and take advantage of the earning potential of commercial activity. The ground was cleared for this development from a press of viewpoints to a commercial press at about the same time in England, France, and the United States, during the 1830s. In the course of this transformation from the journalism of writers who were private persons to the consumer services of the mass media, the sphere of publicness was changed by an influx of private interests that achieved privileged representation within it.

THE PUBLIC SPHERE IN MASS WELFARE-STATE DEMOCRACIES

The liberal model of the public sphere remains instructive in regard to the normative claim embodied in institutionalized requirements of publicness; but it is not applicable to actual relationships within a mass democracy that is industrially advanced and constituted as a social-welfare state. In part, the liberal model had always contained ideological aspects; in part, the social presuppositions to which those aspects were linked have undergone fundamental changes. Even the forms in which the public sphere was manifested, forms which made its idea seem to a certain extent obvious, began to change with the Chartist movement in England and the February Revolution in France. With the spread of the press and propaganda, the public expanded beyond the confines of the bourgeoisie. Along with its social exclusivity the public lost the cohesion given it by institutions of convivial social intercourse and by a relatively high standard of education. Accordingly, conflicts which in the past were pushed off into the private sphere now enter the public sphere. Group needs, which cannot expect satisfaction from a self-regulating market, tend toward state regulation. The public sphere, which must now mediate these demands, becomes a field for competition among interests in the cruder form of forcible confrontation. Laws that have obviously originated under the 'pressure of the streets' can scarcely continue to be understood in terms of a consensus achieved by private persons in public discussion; they correspond, in more or less undisguised form, to compromises between conflicting private interests. Today it is social organizations that act in relation to the state in the political public sphere, whether through the mediation of political parties or directly, in interplay with public administration. With the interlocking of the public and private domains, not only do political agencies take over certain functions in the sphere of commodity exchange and social labor; societal powers also take over political functions. This leads to a kind of 'refeudalization' of the public sphere. Large-scale organizations strive for political compromises with the state and with one another, behind closed doors if possible; but at the same time they have to secure at least plebiscitarian approval from the mass of the population through the deployment of a staged form of publicity.

The political public sphere in the welfare state is characterized by a singular weakening of its critical functions. Whereas at one time publicness was intended to subject persons or things to the public use of reason and to make political decisions susceptible to revision before the tribunal of public opinion, today it has often enough already been enlisted in the aid of the secret policies of interest groups; in the form of 'publicity' it now acquires public prestige for persons or things and renders them capable of acclamation in a climate of nonpublic opinion. The term 'public relations' itself indicates how a public sphere that formerly emerged from the structure of society must now be produced circumstantially on a case-by-case basis. The central relationship of the public, political parties, and parliament is also affected by this change in function.

This existing trend toward the weakening of the public sphere, as a principle, is opposed, however, by a welfare state transformation of the functioning of basic rights: the requirement of publicness is extended by state organs to all organizations acting in relation to the state. To the extent to which this becomes a reality, a no longer intact public of private persons acting as individuals would be replaced by a public of organized private persons. Under current circumstances, only the latter could participate effectively in a process of public communication using the channels of intra-party and intra-organizational public spheres, on the basis of a publicness enforced for the dealings of organizations with the state. It is in this process of public communication that the formation of political compromises would have to achieve legitimation. The idea of the public sphere itself, which signified a rationalization of authority in the medium of public discussions among private persons, and which has been preserved in mass welfare-state democracy, threatens to disintegrate with the structural transformation of the public sphere. Today it could be realized only on a different basis, as a rationalization of the exercise of social and political power under the mutual control of rival organizations committed to publicness in their internal structure as well as in their dealings with the state and with one another.

9

THE MASSES: THE IMPLOSION OF THE SOCIAL IN THE MEDIA

Jean Baudrillard

Up to now there have been two great versions of the analysis of the media (as indeed that of the masses), one optimistic and one pessimistic. The optimistic one has assumed two major tonalities, very different from one another. There is the technological optimism of Marshall McLuhan: for him the electronic media inaugurate a generalized planetary communication and should conduct us, by the mental effect alone of new technologies, beyond the atomizing rationality of the Gutenberg galaxy to the global village, to the new electronic tribalism – an achieved transparency of information and communication. The other version, more traditional, is that of dialectical optimism inspired by progressivist and Marxist thought: the media constitute a new, gigantic productive force and obey the dialectic of productive forces. Momentarily alienated and submitted to the law of capitalism, their intensive development can only eventually explode this monopoly. 'For the first time in history,' writes Hans Enzensberger, 'the media make possible a mass participation in a productive process at once social and socialized, a participation whose practical means are in the hands of the masses themselves.'[1] These two positions more or less, the one technological, the other ideological, inspire the whole analysis and the present practice of the media.[2]

It is more particularly to the optimism of Enzensberger that I formerly opposed a resolutely pessimist vision in 'Requiem for the Media.' In that I

A lecture delivered at the University of Melbourne; trans. Marie MacLean, *New Literary History*, 16:3 (Spring 1985) pp. 577–89; reprinted as Ch. 9 in Jean Baudrillard, *Selected Writings*, ed. Mark Poster (Cambridge: Polity Press, 1988) pp. 207–19.

described the mass media as a 'speech without response.' What characterizes the mass media is that they are opposed to mediation, intransitive, that they fabricate noncommunication – if one accepts the definition of communication as an exchange, as the reciprocal space of speech and response, and thus of *responsibility*. In other words, if one defines it as anything other than the simple emission/reception of information. Now the whole present architecture of the media is founded on this last definition: they are what finally forbids response, what renders impossible any process of exchange (except in the shape of a simulation of a response which is itself integrated into the process of emission, and this changes nothing in the unilaterality of communication). That is their true abstraction. And it is in this abstraction that is founded the system of social control and power. To understand properly the term *response*, one must appreciate it in a meaning at once strong, symbolic, and primitive: power belongs to him who gives and to whom no return can be made. To give, and to do it in such a way that no return can be made, is to break exchange to one's own profit and to institute a monopoly: the social process is out of balance. To make a return, on the contrary, is to break this power relationship and to restore on the basis of an antagonistic reciprocity the circuit of symbolic exchange. The same applies in the sphere of the media: there speech occurs in such a way that there is no possibility of a return. The restitution of this possibility of response entails upsetting the whole present structure; even better (as started to occur in 1968 and the '70s), it entails an 'antimedia' struggle.

In reality, even if I did not share the technological optimism of McLuhan, I always recognized and considered as a gain the true revolution which he brought about in media analysis (this has been mostly ignored in France). On the other hand, though I also did not share the dialectical hopes of Enzensberger, I was not truly pessimistic, since I believed in a possible subversion of the code of the media and in the possibility of an alternate speech and a radical reciprocity of symbolic exchange.

Today all that has changed. I would no longer interpret in the same way the forced silence of the masses in the mass media. I would no longer see in it a sign of passivity and of alienation, but to the contrary an original strategy, an original response in the form of a challenge; and on the basis of this reversal I suggest to you a vision of things which is no longer optimistic or pessimistic, but ironic and antagonistic.

I will take the example of opinion polls, which are themselves a mass medium. It is said that opinion polls constitute a manipulation of democracy. This is certainly no more the case than that publicity is a manipulation of need and of consumption. It too produces demand (or so it claims) and invokes needs just as opinion polls produce answers and induce future behavior. All this would be serious if there were an objective truth of needs, an objective truth of public opinion. It is obvious that here we need to exercise extreme care. The influence of publicity, of opinion polls, of all the media, and of information in general would be dramatic if we were certain that there exists in opposition to it an authentic human nature, an authentic essence of the social, with its needs, its own will, its own values, its finalities. For this would set up the problem of its radical alienation. And indeed it is in this form that traditional critiques are expressed.

Now the matter is at once less serious and more serious than this. The uncertainty which surrounds the social and political effect of opinion polls (do they or do they not manipulate opinion?), like that which surrounds the real economic efficacy of publicity, will never be completely relieved – and it is just as well! This results from the fact that there is a compound, a mixture of two heterogeneous systems whose data cannot be transferred from one to the other. An operational system which is statistical, information-based, and simulational is projected onto a traditional values system, onto a system of representation, will, and opinion. This collage, this collusion between the two, gives rise to an indefinite and useless polemic. We should agree neither with those who praise the beneficial use of the media, nor with those who scream about manipulation, for the simple reason that there is no relationship between a system of meaning and a system of simulation. Publicity and opinion polls would be incapable, even if they wished and claimed to do so, of alienating the will or the opinion of anybody at all, for the reason that they do not act in the time–space of will and of representation where judgement is formed. For the same reason, though reversed, it is quite impossible for them to throw any light at all on public opinion or individual will, since they do not act in a public space, on the stage of a public space. They are strangers to it, and indeed they wish to dismantle it. Publicity and opinion polls and the media in general can only be imagined; they only exist on the basis of a disappearance, the disappearance from the public space, from the scene of politics, of public opinion in a form at once theatrical and representative as it was enacted in earlier epochs. Thus we can be reassured: they cannot destroy it. But we should not have any illusions: they cannot restore it either.

It is this lack of relationship between the two systems which today plunges us into a state of stupor. That is what I said: stupor. To be more objective one would have to say: a radical uncertainty as to our own desire, our own choice, our own opinion, our own will. This is the clearest result of the whole media environment, of the information which makes demands on us from all sides and which is as good as blackmail.

We will never know if an advertisement or opinion poll has had a real influence on individual or collective wills, but we will never know either what would have happened if there had been no opinion poll or advertisement.

The situation no longer permits us to isolate reality or human nature as a fundamental variable. The result is therefore not to provide any additional information or to shed any light on reality, but on the contrary, because we will never in future be able to separate reality from its statistical, simulative projection in the media, a state of suspense and of definitive uncertainty about reality. And I repeat: it is a question here of a completely new species of uncertainty, which results not from the *lack* of information but from information itself and even from an *excess* of information. It is information itself which produces uncertainty, and so this uncertainty, unlike the traditional uncertainty which could always be resolved, is irreparable.

This is our destiny: subject to opinion polls, information, publicity, statistics; constantly confronted with the anticipated statistical verification of our behavior, and absorbed by this permanent refraction of our least movements, we are no longer confronted with our own will. We are no longer even alienated, because for that it is necessary for the subject to be divided in itself, confronted with the other, to be contradictory. Now, where there is no other, the scene of the other, like that of politics and of society, has disappeared. Each individual is forced despite himself or herself into the undivided coherency of statistics. There is in this a positive absorption into the transparency of computers, which is something worse than alienation.

There is an obscenity in the functioning and the omnipresence of opinion polls as in that of publicity. Not because they might betray the secret of an opinion, the intimacy of a will, or because they might violate some unwritten law of the private being, but because they exhibit this redundancy of the social, this sort of continual voyeurism of the group in relation to itself: it must at all times know what it wants, know what it thinks, be told about its least needs, its least quivers, *see* itself continually on the videoscreen of statistics, constantly watch its own temperature chart, in a sort of hypochondriacal madness. The social becomes obsessed with itself; through this auto-information, this permanent autointoxication, it becomes its own vice, its own perversion. This is the real obscenity. Through this feedback, this incessant anticipated accounting, the social loses its own scene. It no longer enacts itself; it has no more time to enact itself; it no longer occupies a particular space, public or political; it becomes confused with its own control screen. Overinformed, it develops ingrowing obesity. For everything which loses its *scene* (like the obese body) becomes for that very reason *ob-scene*.

The silence of the masses is also in a sense obscene. For the masses are also made of this useless hyperinformation which claims to enlighten them, when all it does is clutter up the space of the representable and annul itself in a silent equivalence. And we cannot do much against this obscene circularity of the masses and of information. The two phenomena fit one another: the masses have no opinion and information does not inform them. Both of them, lacking a scene where the meaning of the social can be enacted, continue to feed one another monstrously – as the speed with which information revolves increases continually the weight of the masses as such, and not their self-awareness.

So if one takes opinion polls, and the uncertainty which they induce about the principle of social reality, and the type of obscenity, of statistical pornography to which they attract us – if we take all that seriously, if we confront all that with the claimed finalities of information and of the social itself, then it all seems very dramatic. But there is another way of taking things. It does not shed much more credit on opinion polls, but it restores a sort of status to them, in terms of derision and of play. In effect we can consider the indecisiveness of their results, the uncertainty of their effects, and their unconscious humor, which is rather similar to that of meteorology (for example, the possibility of verifying at the same time contradictory facts or tendencies); or again the casual way in which everybody uses them, disagreeing with them privately and especially if they verify exactly one's own behavior (no one accepts a perfect statistical evaluation of his chances). That is the real problem of the credibility accorded to them.

Statistics, as an objective computation of probabilities, obviously eliminate any elective chance and any personal destiny. That is why, deep down, none of us believes in them, any more than the gambler believes in chance, but only in Luck (with a capital, the equivalent of Grace, not with lower case, which is the equivalent of probability). An amusing example of this obstinate denial of statistical chance is given by this news item: 'If this will reassure you, we have calculated that, of every 50 people who catch the metro twice a day for 60 years, only one is in danger of being attacked. Now there is no reason why it should be *you*!' The beauty of statistics is never in their objectivity but in their involuntary humor.

So if one takes opinion polls in this way, one can conceive that they could work for the masses themselves as a game, as a spectacle, as a means of deriding both the social and the political. The fact that opinion polls do their best to destroy the political as will and representation, the political as meaning, precisely through the effect of simulation and uncertainty – this fact can only give pleasure to the ironic unconscious of the masses (and to our individual political unconscious, if I may use this expression), whose deepest drive remains the symbolic murder of the political class, the symbolic murder of political *reality*, and this murder is produced by opinion polls in their own way. That is why I wrote in *Silent Majorities* that the masses, which have always provided an alibi for political representation, take their revenge by allowing themselves the theatrical representation of the political scene.[3] The people have become *public*. They even allow themselves the luxury of enjoying day by day, as in a home cinema, the fluctuations of their own opinion in the daily reading of the opinion polls.

It is only to this extent that they believe in them, that we all believe in them, as we believe in a game of malicious foretelling, a double or quits on the green baize of the political scene. It is, paradoxically, as a game that the opinion polls recover a sort of legitimacy. A game of the undecidable; a game of chance; a game of the undecidability of the political scene, of the equifinality of all tendencies; a game of truth effects in the circularity of questions and answers. Perhaps we can see here the apparition of one of these collective forms of game which Caillois called *aléa*[4] – an irruption into the polls themselves of a ludic, aleatory process, an ironic mirror for the use of the masses (and we all belong to the masses) of a political scene which is caught in its own trap (for the politicians are the only ones to believe in the polls, along with the pollsters obviously, as the only ones to believe in publicity are the publicity agents).

In this regard, one may restore to them a sort of positive meaning: they would be part of a contemporary cultural mutation, part of the era of simulation.

In view of this type of consequence, we are forced to congratulate ourselves on the very failure of polls, and on the distortions which make them undecidable and chancy. Far from regretting this, we must consider that there is a sort of fate or evil genius (the evil genius of the social itself?) which throws this too beautiful machine out of gear and prevents it from achieving the objectives which it claims. We must also ask if these distortions, far from being the consequence of a bad angle of refraction of information onto an inert and opaque matter, are not rather the consequence of an offensive resistance of the social itself to its investigation, the shape taken by an occult duel between the pollsters and the object polled, between information and the people who receive it?

This is fundamental: people are always supposed to be willing partners in the game of truth, in the game of information. It is agreed that the object can always be persuaded of its truth; it is inconceivable that the object of the investigation, the object of the poll, should not adopt, generally speaking, the strategy of the subject of the analysis, of the pollster. There may certainly be some difficulties (for instance, the object does not understand the question; it's not its business; it's undecided; it replies in terms of the interviewer and not of the question, and so on), but it is admitted that the poll analyst is capable of rectifying what is basically only a lack of adaptation to the analytic apparatus. The hypothesis is never suggested that all this, far from being a marginal, archaic residue, is the effect of an offensive (not defensive) counterstrategy by the object; that, all in all, there exists somewhere an original, positive, possibly victorious strategy of the object opposed to the strategy of the subject (in this case, the pollster or any other producer of messages).

This is what one could call the evil genius of the object, the evil genius of the masses, the evil genius of the social itself, constantly producing failure in the truth of the social and in its analysis, and for that reason unacceptable, and even unimaginable, to the tenants of this analysis.

To reflect the other's desire, to reflect its demand like a mirror, even to anticipate it: it is hard to imagine what powers of deception, of absorption, of deviation – in a word, of subtle revenge – there is in this type of response. This is the way the masses escape as reality, in this very mirror, in those simulative devices which are designed to capture them. Or again, the way in which events themselves disappear behind the television screen, or the more general screen of information (for it is true that events have no probable existence except on this deflective screen, which is no longer a mirror). While the mirror and screen of alienation was a mode of production (the imaginary subject), this new screen is simply its mode of disappearance. But disappearance is a very complex mode: the object, the individual, is not only condemned to disappearance, but *disappearance is also its strategy*; it is its way of response to this device for capture, for networking, and for forced identification. To this *cathodic* surface of recording, the individual or the mass reply by a *parodic* behavior of disappearance. What are they; what do they do; what do they become behind this screen? They turn themselves into an impenetrable and meaningless surface, which is a method of disappearing. They eclipse themselves; they melt into the superficial screen in such a way that their reality and that of their movement, just like that of particles of matter, may be radically questioned without making any fundamental change to the probabilistic analysis of their behavior. In fact, behind this 'objective' fortification of networks and models which believe they can capture them, and where the whole population of analysts and expert observers believe that they capture them, there passes a wave of derision, of reversal, and of parody which is the active exploitation, the parodic enactment by the object itself of its mode of disappearance.

There is and there always will be major difficulties in analyzing the media and the whole sphere of information through the traditional categories of the philosophy of the subject: will, representation, choice, liberty, deliberation, knowledge, and desire. For it is quite obvious that they are absolutely contradicted by the media; that the subject is absolutely alienated in its sovereignty. There is a distortion of principle between the sphere of information, and the moral law which still dominates us and whose decree is: you shall know yourself, you shall know what is your will and your desire. In this respect the media and even technics and science teach us nothing at all; they have rather restricted the limits of will and representation; they have muddled the cards and deprived any subject of the disposal of his or her own body, desire, choice, and liberty.

But this idea of alienation has probably never been anything but a philosopher's ideal perspective for the use of hypothetical masses. It has probably never expressed anything but the alienation of the philosopher himself; in other words, the one who *thinks himself or herself other*. On this subject Hegel is very clear in his judgement of the *Aufklärer*, of the *philosophe* of the Enlightenment, the one who denounces the 'empire of error' and despises it.

Reason wants to enlighten the superstitious mass by revealing trickery. It seeks to make it understand that it is *itself*, the mass, which enables the despot to live and not the despot which makes it live, as it believes when it obeys him. For the demystifier, credulous consciousness is mistaken *about itself*.

> The Enlightenment speaks as if juggling priests had, by sleight of hand, spirited away the being of consciousness for which they substituted something absolutely *foreign* and *other*; and, at the same time, the Enlightenment says that this foreign thing is a being of consciousness, which believes in consciousness, which trusts it, which seeks to please it.[5]

There is obviously a contradiction, says Hegel: one cannot confide oneself to an other than oneself and be mistaken about oneself, since when one confides in another, one demonstrates the certainty that one is safe with the other; in consequence, consciousness, which is said to be mystified, knows very well where it is safe and where it is not. Thus there is no need to correct a mistake which only exists in the *Aufklärer* himself. It is not *consciousness*, concludes Hegel, which takes itself for another, but it is the *Aufklärer* who takes himself for another, another than this common man whom he endeavors to make aware of his own stupidity. 'When the question is asked if it is allowable to deceive a people, one must reply that the question is worthless, because it is impossible to deceive a people about itself.'[6]

So it is enough to reverse the idea of a mass alienated by the media to evaluate how much the whole universe of the media, and perhaps the whole technical universe, is the result of a secret strategy of this mass which is claimed to be alienated, of *a secret form of the refusal of will*, of an in-voluntary challenge to everything which was demanded of the subject by philosophy – that is to say, to all rationality of choice and to all exercise of will, of knowledge, and of liberty.

In one way it would be no longer a question of revolution but of massive *devolution*, of a massive delegation of the power of desire, of choice, of responsibility, a delegation to apparatuses either political or intellectual, either technical or operational, to whom has devolved the duty of taking care of all of these things. A massive de-volition, a massive desisting from will, but not through alienation or voluntary servitude (whose mystery, which is the modern enigma of politics, is unchanged since La Boétie because the problem is put in terms of the consent of the subject to his own slavery, which fact no philosophy will ever be able to explain). We might argue that there exists another philosophy of lack of will, a sort of radical antimetaphysics whose secret is that the masses are deeply aware that they do not have to make a decision about themselves and the world; that they do not have to wish; that they do not have to know; that they do not have to desire.

The deepest desire is perhaps to give the responsibility for one's desire to someone else. A strategy of ironic investment in the other, in the others; a strategy toward others not of appropriation but, on the contrary, of expulsion, of philosophers and people in power, an expulsion of the obligation of being responsible, of enduring philosophical, moral, and political categories. Clerks are there for that, so are professionals, the representative holders of concept and desire. Publicity, information, technics, the whole intellectual and political class are there to tell us what we want, to tell the masses what they want – and basically we thoroughly enjoy this massive transfer of responsibility because perhaps, very simply, it is not easy to want what we want; because perhaps, very simply, it is not very interesting to know what we want to decide, to desire. Who has imposed all this on us, even the need to desire, unless it be the philosophers?

Choice is a strange imperative. Any philosophy which assigns man to the exercise of his will can only plunge him in despair. For if nothing is more flattering to consciousness than to know what it wants, on the contrary nothing is more seductive to the other consciousness (the unconscious?) – the obscure and vital one which makes happiness depend on the despair of will – than not to know what it wants, to be relieved of choice and diverted from its own objective will. It is much better to rely on some insignificant or powerful instance than to be dependent on one's own will or the necessity of choice. Beau Brummel had a servant for that purpose. Before a splendid landscape dotted with beautiful lakes, he turns toward his valet to ask him: 'Which lake do I prefer?'

Even publicity would find an advantage in discarding the weak hypothesis of personal will and desire. Not only do people certainly not want to be *told* what they wish, but they certainly do not want to *know* it, and it is not even sure that they want to *wish* at all. Faced with such inducements, it is their evil genius who tells them not to want anything and to rely finally on the apparatus of publicity or of information to 'persuade' them, to construct a choice for them (or to rely on the political class to order things) – just as Brummel did with his servant.

Whom does this trap close on? The mass knows that it knows nothing, and it does not want to know. The mass knows that it can do nothing, and it does not want to achieve anything. It is violently reproached with this mark of stupidity and passivity. But not at all: the mass is very snobbish; it acts as Brummel did and delegates in a sovereign manner the faculty of choice to someone else by a sort of game of irresponsibility, of ironic challenge, of sovereign lack of will, of secret ruse. All the mediators (people of the media, politicians, intellectuals, all the heirs of the *philosophes* of the Enlightenment in contempt for the masses) are really only adapted to this purpose: to manage by delegation, by procuration, this tedious matter of power and of will, to unburden the masses of this transcendence for their greater pleasure and to turn it into a show for their benefit. *Vicarious*: this would be, to repeat Thorstein Veblen's concept, the status of these so-called privileged classes, whose will would be, in a way, diverted against themselves, toward the secret ends of the very masses whom they despise.

We live all that, subjectively, in the most paradoxical mode, since in us, in everyone, this mass coexists with the intelligent and voluntary being who condemns it and despises it. Nobody knows what is truly opposed to consciousness, unless it may be the repressive unconscious which psychoanalysis has imposed on us. But our true unconscious is perhaps in this ironic power of nonparticipation of nondesire, of nonknowledge, of silence, of absorption of all powers, of *expulsion* of all powers of all wills, of all knowledge, of all meaning onto representatives surrounded by a halo of derision. Our unconscious would not then consist of drives, of *pulsions*, whose destiny is sad repression; it would not be repressed at all; it would be made of this joyful *expulsion* of all the encumbering superstructures of being and of will.

We have always had a sad vision of the masses (alienated), a sad vision of the unconscious (repressed). On all our philosophy weighs this sad correlation. Even if only for a change, it would be interesting to conceive the mass, the object-mass, as the repository of a finally delusive, illusive, and allusive strategy, the correlative of an ironic, joyful, and seductive unconscious.

About the media you can sustain two opposing hypotheses: they are the strategy of power, which finds in them the means of mystifying the masses and of imposing its own truth. Or else they are the strategic territory of the ruse of the masses, who exercise in them their concrete power of the refusal of truth, of the denial of reality. Now the media are nothing else than a marvellous instrument for destabilizing the real and the true, all historical or political truth (there is thus no possible political strategy of the media: it is a contradiction in terms). And the addiction that we have for the media, the impossibility of doing without them, is a deep result of this phenomenon: it is not a result of a desire for culture, communication, and information, but of this perversion of truth and falsehood, of this destruction of meaning in the operation of the medium. The desire for a show, the desire for simulation, which is at the same time a desire for dissimulation. This is a vital reaction. It is a spontaneous, total resistance to the ultimatum of historical and political reason.

It is essential today to evaluate this double challenge: the challenge to meaning by the masses and their silence (which is not at all a passive resistance), and the challenge to meaning which comes from the media and their fascination. All the marginal alternative endeavors to resuscitate meaning are secondary to this.

Obviously there is a paradox in the inextricable entanglement of the masses and the media: is it the media that neutralize meaning and that produce the 'formless' (or informed) mass; or is it the mass which victoriously resists the media by diverting or by absorbing without reply all the messages which they produce? Are the mass media on the side of power in the manipulation of the masses, or are they on the side of the masses in the liquidation of meaning, in the violence done to meaning? Is it the media that fascinate the masses, or is it the masses who divert the media into showmanship? The media toss around sense and nonsense; they manipulate in every sense at once. No one can control this process: the media are the vehicle for the simulation which belongs to the system and for the simulation which destroys the system, according to a circular logic, exactly like a Möbius strip – and it is just as well. There is no alternative to this, no logical resolution. Only a logical *exacerbation* and a catastrophic resolution. That is to say, this process has no return.

In conclusion, however, I must make one reservation. Our relationship to this system is an insoluble 'double bind' – exactly that of children in their relationship to the demands of the adult world. They are at the same time told to constitute themselves as autonomous subjects, responsible, free, and conscious, and to constitute themselves as submissive objects, inert, obedient, and conformist. The child resists on all levels, and to these contradictory demands he or she replies by a double strategy. When we ask the child to be object, he or she opposes all the practices of disobedience, of revolt, of emancipation; in short, the strategy of a subject. When we ask the child to be subject, he or she opposes just as obstinately and successfully resistance as object; that is to say, exactly the opposite: infantilism, hyperconformity, total dependance, passivity, idiocy.

Neither of the two strategies has more objective value than the other. Subject resistance is today given a unilateral value and considered to be positive – in the same way as in the political sphere only the practices of liberation, of emancipation, of expression, of self-constitution as a political subject are considered worthwhile and subversive. This is to take no account of the equal and probably superior impact of all the practices of the object, the renunciation of the position of subject and of meaning – exactly the practices of the mass – which we bury with the disdainful terms *alienation* and *passivity*. The liberating practices correspond to *one* of the aspects of the system, to the constant ultimatum we are given to constitute ourselves as pure objects; but they do not correspond at all to the other demand to constitute ourselves as subjects, to liberate, to express ourselves at any price, to vote, to produce, to decide, to speak, to participate, to play the game: blackmail and ultimatum just as serious as the other, probably more serious today. To a system whose argument is oppression and repression, the strategic resistance is to demand the liberating rights of the subject. But this seems rather to reflect an earlier phase of the system; and even if we are still confronted with it, it is no longer a strategic territory: the present argument of the system is to maximize speech, to maximize the production of meaning, of participation. And so the strategic resistance is that of the refusal of meaning and the refusal of speech; or of the hyperconformist simulation of the very mechanisms of the system, which is another form of refusal by overacceptance. It is the actual strategy of the masses. This strategy does not exclude the other, but it is the winning one today, because it is the most adapted to the present phase of the system.

NOTES

1. Hans Magnus Enzensberger, 'Constituents of a Theory of the Media,' *New Left Review* 64 (1970) 13–36.
2. Armand Mattelart, *De l'usage des média en temps de crise* (Paris, 1979).
3. Jean Baudrillard, *A l'ombre des majorités silencieuses* (Paris, 1978).
4. Roger Caillois, *Man, Play and Games*, trans. Meyer Barash (London, 1962), ch. 8.
5. Georg Wilhelm Friedrich Hegel, *Phänomenologie des Geistes*, ed. Johannes Hoffmeister (Hamburg, 1952) pp. 391–2.
6. Hegel, ibid., p. 392.

FURTHER READING

AMERICAN MASS
COMMUNICATION THEORY

Berelson, B. and Janowitz, M., *Reader in Public Opinion and Communication* (Glencoe, Illinois: Free Press, 1953).

Bryson, L. (ed.), *The Communication of Ideas* (New York: Harper, 1948).

De Fleur, M., *Theories of Mass Communication* (New York: David McKay Co. Inc., 1966); 5th edn, with Ball-Rokeach, S. (New York: Longman, 1989).

Dexter, L. and White, D. M. (eds), *People, Society and Mass Communications* (New York: Free Press, 1964).

Gitlin, T., 'Media Sociology: The Dominant Paradigm', *Theory and Society* 6:2 (1978) pp. 205–53.

Hardt, H., *Critical Communication Studies: Communication, History and Theory in America* (London and New York: Routledge, 1992).

Lazarsfeld, P., Berelson, B. and Gaudet, H., *The People's Choice: How the Voter Makes up his Mind in a Presidential Campaign* (New York: Duell, Sloan & Pearce, 1944).

Merton, R., *Social Theory and Social Structure*, Part III (Glencoe, Illinois: Free Press, 1957).

Morrison, D., 'The Beginnings of Modern Mass Communication Research', *European Journal of Sociology* 19:2 (1978) pp. 347–59.

Rosenberg, D. and White, D. M., *Mass Culture: The Popular Arts in America* (New York: Free Press, 1957).

Schramm, W. (ed.), *Communications in Modern Society* (Urbana: University of Illinois Press, 1948).

Schramm, W. (ed.), *Mass Communications* (Urbana: University of Illinois Press, 1960; 2nd edn, 1975).

Wright, C. R., *Mass Communications: A Sociological Perspective* (New York: Random House Inc., 1959).

FRANKFURT SCHOOL

Adorno, T., *The Culture Industry: Selected Essays on Mass Culture*, ed. with an introduction by J. M. Bernstein (London: Routledge, 1991).

Adorno, T. and Horkheimer, M., 'The Culture Industry: Enlightenment as Mass Deception', in Curran, J., Gurevitch, M. and Woollacott, J. (eds), *Mass Communication and Society* (London: Open University/Edward Arnold, 1977).

Arato, A. and Gebhardt, E. (eds), *The Essential Frankfurt School Reader* (Oxford: Basil Blackwell, 1978).

Jay, M., *The Dialectical Imagination: A History of the Frankfurt School and the Institute of Social Research 1923–1950* (London: Heinemann, 1973).

Rose, G., *The Melancholy Science: An Introduction to the Thought of T. W. Adorno* (London: Macmillan, 1978).

Slater, P., *Origin and Significance of the Frankfurt School: A Marxist Perspective* (London: Routledge & Kegan Paul, 1977).

Tar, Z., *The Frankfurt School: The Critical Theories of Max Horkheimer and Theodor W. Adorno* (New York: Wiley, 1977).

MARSHALL MCLUHAN AND
TECHNOLOGICAL DETERMINISM

Ferguson, M., 'Marshall McLuhan Revisited: 1960s Zeitgeist Victim or Pioneer Postmodernist?' *Media, Culture and Society* 13:1 (1991) pp. 71–90.

Kroker, A., *Technology and the Canadian Mind: Innis, McLuhan, Grant* (New York: St Martin's Press, 1984).

McLuhan, M., *Understanding Media: The Extensions of Man* (London: Routledge & Kegan Paul, 1964).

McLuhan, M. and Fiore, Q., *The Medium is the Massage: An Inventory of Effects* (New York: Bantam Books, 1967).

Marchand, P., *Marshall McLuhan: The Medium and the Messenger* (New York: Tichnenor & Fields, 1989).

Miller, J., *McLuhan* (London: Fontana/William Collins, 1971).

Stearn, G. (ed.), *McLuhan: Hot and Cool* (London: Penguin Books, 1967).

Williams, R., *Television: Technology and Cultural Form* (London: Fontana/William Collins, 1974).

Winston, B., *Misunderstanding Media* (London: Routledge, 1986).

LEAVISISM TO CULTURALISM

Hall, S. and Whannel, P., *The Popular Arts* (London: Hutchinson, 1964).

Hunter, W., *Scrutiny of Cinema* (London: Wishart, 1932); reprinted (New York: Arno Press, 1972).

Leavis, F. R., *Mass Civilisation and Minority Culture* (Cambridge: Minority Press, 1930).

Leavis, F. R. and Thompson, D., *Culture and Environment: The Training of Critical Awareness* (London: Chatto & Windus, 1933); reprinted (Westport, Connecticut: Greenwood Press, 1977).

O'Connor, A., *Raymond Williams: Writing, Culture, Politics* (Oxford: Basil Blackwell, 1989).

Storey, J., *An Introductory Guide to Cultural Theory and Popular Culture*, chaps 2 and 3 (Hemel Hempstead: Harvester Wheatsheaf, 1993).

Thompson, D. (ed.), *Discrimination and Popular Culture* (Hardmondsworth: Penguin Books, 1964); 2nd edn, 1973.

Williams, R., *The Long Revolution* (London: Chatto & Windus, 1961).

Williams, R., *Communications* (Harmondsworth: Penguin Special, 1962).

CULTURAL STUDIES

Fiske, J., 'British Cultural Studies and Television', in Allen, R. C. (ed.), *Channels of Discourse: Television and Contemporary Criticism* (London: Methuen, 1987); also *Channels of Discourse, Reassembled* (London: Routledge, 1992).

Hall, S., 'Introduction' to Smith, A. C. H. et al., *Paper Voices: The Popular Press and Social Change 1935–1965* (London: Chatto & Windus, 1975).

Hall, S., 'Culture, the Media and the "Ideological Effect"', in Curran, J., Gurevitch, M. and Woollacott, J. (eds), *Mass Communication and Society* (London: Open University/Edward Arnold, 1977).

Hall, S., 'The Rediscovery of "Ideology": Return of the Repressed in Media Studies', in Gurevitch, M., Bennett, T., Curran, J. and Woollacott, J. (eds), *Culture, Society and the Media* (London: Methuen, 1982).

Hall, S., Hobson, D., Lowe, A. and Willis, P. (eds), *Culture, Media, Language*, pt three, chaps 8–13, 'Media Studies' (London: Hutchinson, 1980).

Turner, G., *British Cultural Studies: An Introduction* (London: Unwin Hyman, 1990).

FEMINISM

Butcher, H., Coward, R. et al., 'Images of Women in the Media', CCC stencilled paper no. 31 (University of Birmingham, 1974).

Coward, R., *Female Desire* (London: Paladin, 1984).

Doane, M. A., Mellencamp, P., Williams, L. (eds), *Re Visions. Essays in Feminist Film Criticism* (Los Angeles: American Film Institute, 1984).

Friedan, B., *The Feminine Mystique* (New York: Norton & Co. Inc., 1963).

Kaplan, E. A., 'Feminist Criticism and Television', in Allen, R. C. (ed.), *Channels of Discourse* (London: Methuen, 1987); also *Channels of Discourse, Reassembled* (London: Routledge, 1992).

Kuhn, A., *Women's Pictures* (London: Routledge & Kegan Paul, 1982).

Kuhn, A., 'Women's Genres', *Screen* 25:1 (1984) pp. 18–28.

Mulvey, L., 'Visual Pleasure and Narrative Cinema', *Screen* 16:3 (1975) pp. 6–18.

Tuchman, G. et al. (eds), *Hearth and Home: Images of Women in the Media* (New York: Oxford University Press, 1978).

Women's Studies Group, *Women Take Issue* (London: CCCS/Hutchinson, 1978).

Zoonen, L. van, 'Feminist Perspectives on the Media', in Curran, J. and Gurevitch, M. (eds), *Mass Media and Society* (London: Edward Arnold, 1991).

Zoonen, L. van, *Feminist Media Studies* (London: Sage, 1994).

See also 'Further Reading' for 'Feminist Readings' below.

THE GERMAN NEW LEFT

Benjamin, W., 'The Work of Art in the Age of Mechanical Reproduction', *Illuminations*, ed. H. Arendt (London: Jonathon Cape, 1969); available in Curran, J., Gurevitch, M. and Woollacott, J. (eds) *Mass Communication and Society* (London: Open University/Edward Arnold, 1977).

De Lauretis, T., Huyssen, A. and Woodward, K. (eds) *The Technological Imagination* (Madison, Wisconsin: Coda Press, 1980).

Enzensberger, H. M., *The Conciousness Industry: On Literature, Politics and the Media*, ed. M. Roloff (New York: Seabury Press, 1974).

Huyssen, A., *After the Great Divide: Modernism, Mass Culture, Postmodernism* (London: Macmillan, 1986).

THE PUBLIC SPHERE

Calhoun, C., *Habermas and the Public Sphere* (Cambridge, Mass.: MIT Press, 1992).

Curran, J., 'Rethinking the Media as a Public Sphere', in Dahlgren, P. and Sparks, C. (eds), *Communication and Citizenship* (London: Routledge, 1991).

Garnham, N., 'The Media and the Public Sphere', in Golding, P., Murdock, G. and Schlesinger, P. (eds), *Communicating Politics: Mass Communications and the Political Process* (Leicester: Leicester University Press, 1986); also available in Garnham, N., *Capitalism and Communications: Global Culture and the Economics of Information*, ed. F. Inglis (London: Sage, 1990).

Habermas, J., *The Structural Transformation of the Public Sphere*, transl. T. Burger (Cambridge: Polity Press, 1989); originally publ. as *Strukturwandel der Offentlichkeit* (Frankfurt am Main: Suhrkamp-Verlag, 1962).

Keane, J., '"Liberty of the Press" in the 1990s', *New Formations* no. 8 (1989).

McCarthy, T., *The Critical Theory of Jürgen Habermas* (Cambridge: Polity Press, 1978).

Scannell, P., 'Public Service Broadcasting and Modern Public Life', *Media, Culture and Society* 11: 2 (1989) pp. 134–66.

Thompson, J. B. and Held, D. (eds), *Habermas: Critical Debates* (London: Macmillan, 1982).

POSTMODERNISM

Baudrillard, J., *Simulations*, transl. P. Foss, P. Patton and P. Beithman (New York: Semiotext(e), 1983).

Baudrillard, J., 'The Ecstasy of Communication', in Foster, H. (ed.), *Postmodern Culture* (London: Pluto Press, 1985).

Baudrillard, J., *Selected Writings*, ed. and introduced by M. Poster (Cambridge: Polity Press, 1988).

Best. S. and Kellner, D., *Postmodern Theory: Critical Interrogations* (London: Macmillan, 1991).

Collins, J., 'Postmodernism and Television', in Allen, R. C. (ed.), *Channels of Discourse, Reassembled* (London: Routledge, 1992).

Connor, S., *Postmodernist Culture: An Introduction to Theories of the Contemporary* (Oxford: Basil Blackwell, 1989).

Fiske, J., 'Postmodernism and Television', in Curran, J. and Gurevitch, M. (eds), *Mass Media and Society* (London: Edward Arnold, 1991).

Harvey, D., *The Condition of Postmodernity* (Oxford: Basil Blackwell, 1989).

Jameson, F., 'Postmodernism, or the Cultural Logic of Late Capitalism', *New Left Review* 146 (1984) pp. 53–92.

SECTION 2
PRODUCTION

PRODUCTION
INTRODUCTION

The prevailing tradition in thinking about cultural production, since at least the Romantic period, has been to focus on the individual artist, writer or composer. The mainstream of literary studies, for instance, is notoriously indifferent to the realities of the publishing industry in the various periods when its authors wrote or were read. But in media studies attention has persistently been paid to the economic, sociological, industrial and political factors contributing to and shaping media production. In part this is because – although individual talented journalists, performers and technicians can sometimes command high salaries and acquire celebrity – the work of assembling a newspaper or a broadcast programme more apparently requires teams of people. In addition, the very scale of the investment and turnover involved makes it harder to overlook the economic dimension, and the very nature of much of journalism's material makes obvious a connection with political affairs. But it is also because much of the research has been carried out by scholars in the Marxist tradition, concerned to link the political economy of capitalism with an understanding of the nature and role of the symbolic realm in the maintenance and reproduction of the social order. The first three chapters in this section can be said to fall broadly within that tradition.

The Frankfurt School coined the term 'the culture industry' to refer to the mass media, and Nicholas Garnham is prominent among the scholars who have found this a suggestive formulation. He has sought to pursue the implications of the industrialisation of culture for the nature of cultural production. In Chapter 11 he analyses the economic trends at work within the cultural industries that drive from the commodification of labour power and cultural goods and services within a capitalist economy. Although some individual points of fact have changed since the mid-1980s when the paper from which this piece is extracted was originally written,[1] the account remains a penetrating explanatory overview, allowing us to understand certain fundamental features of the media industry. Garnham's final observation here on the course of development of the cultural market ('a complex hegemonic dialectic of liberation and control') indicates that he does not fully accept the wider Frankfurt School pessimism about media culture in the twentieth century, but takes a more Gramscian view.

Garnham is explicitly concerned with the 'political economy' of the media.[2] In contrast to neo-classical economics, the 'political' in 'political economy' draws attention to the constituting role of the political in the organisation and conduct of economic life. This is particularly plain for the early phases of the history of broadcasting in Britain, where in the 1920s a conscious political decision was made that the production and distribution of programmes would be undertaken within another logic than that of the competitive drive for commercial profits. A public corporation was established by Royal Charter, to which Parliament granted a monopoly of broadcasting and the right to levy a household charge on the possessors of receiving equipment, in exchange for which the corporation was required to provide a programme service which educates, entertains and informs the public, within a party-politically neutral position. Thus, with the founding of the British Broadcasting Corporation, was established a tradition of 'public service broadcasting'. Paddy Scannell's piece (Chapter 10) traces the background, emergence and evolution of this concept over the course of British broadcasting up to 1990. For the purposes of considering 'production' in the media circuit, this history highlights several key aspects: the role of institutions as supraindividual, corporate subjects of 'media discourse'; legislation and other forms of political regulation as active factors in determining the nature of media output, or at least in setting boundaries which are then administratively and artistically interpreted; the part played by institutional address in constituting audiences. With regard to the particular history of British broadcasting, the history reveals how the concept of public service broadcasting evolved and was modified to contribute to the legal structuring of other forms of broadcasting institution (for example: the private sector, advertising-supported ITV companies, which nevertheless have programming obligations; the unique institutional form with which Channel Four was furnished in the 1980s).[3] For the media in general, public policy and regulation has a significant determining role in a variety of ways: competition policy, for example, or privacy law or censorship practices.

In the years following the original publication of this piece, as its ending anxiously foresaw, the reregulation of British broadcasting by the 1990 Broadcasting Act reduced the 'public service' requirements placed on broadcasters, and gave rise to a far greater commercialism and market liberalism than had previously been the case. The 1990s saw the transmitter systems privatised;

ITV franchises effectively auctioned and permitted to be bought and sold; Channel Four becoming directly advertising dependent; a new commercial television channel (Channel Five) created which had next to no specific programming obligations; the establishment of the first three national commercial radio stations in Britain; the formation of the subscription- and pay-per-view supported BSkyB programming service; the authorisation of direct programme sponsorship.[4] These developments in Britain were in a broadly similar direction to those elsewhere: the strengthening of commercial interests in the media, including the growth in private sector ownership and its capacity to operate unconstrainedly. The roots of these developments in the 1980s are discussed in a 1990 piece by Graham Murdock (Chapter 12). Murdock is a leading critical political economist of the media who is concerned with the significance of ownership for communications. His essay begins from the contradiction between the ownership of the major means of communication by private interests and the need for unfettered circulation of a diversity of information and opinion in a democracy in the public interest. Murdock proceeds to trace the increasing penetration of private business interests within the media sector during the 1980s, and points to a corresponding diminution and weakening of 'the countervailing power of public cultural institutions'. He writes in the conviction that – provided the fact that it 'largely excluded the working class, women and ethnic minorities'[5] can be remedied – 'the idea of the public sphere is worth retaining' (see Chapter 8). Further developments within the media business sector and its relations with public institutions have occurred since those charted in the essay.

At the end of the twentieth century, ten megacorporations – which are among the largest firms in the world – dominate the global media market: Time-Warner, Disney, Bertelsmann, Viacom, Tele-Communications Inc. (TCI), News Corporation, Sony, Seagram, General Electric and Philips (owner of Polygram).[6] These are private sector companies which often own portions of each other, share directors and engage in numerous joint ventures around the globe. This state of affairs confirms the continuing relevance of the themes explored in Chapter 12.

Seven of these companies are headquartered in the United States, and in international terms, this relevance is sometimes thought to be straightforward: that Western, particularly American, media products saturate media outlets throughout the world, which in turn fill up people's minds with Western (mostly pro-American) ideas. American movies, records and TV programmes certainly are sold around the globe, but John Sinclair, Elizabeth Jacka and Stuart Cunningham, the three Australian authors of Chapter 14, judge – at least with regard to television – that this idea of 'media imperialism' does not accurately convey the international situation at the turn of the century. The unchallenged dominance of American programming in the export market may have been a feature of the 1960s and 1970s, but by the 1990s Mexico, Brazil, India, Australia, Hong Kong, Egypt, Taiwan and India had all come to have flourishing export trades in programmes. Furthermore, in practically all territories of the world, a minority of the programming viewed on television is American in origin. They also go on to express their doubts that the watching of these programmes necessarily means that the viewers are imbued with Western ideologies. The piece provides a useful overview of the sources of production for television services around the world and the new patterns of exchange in the global media marketplace.

Another line of approach to exploring the range of production determinants shaping media output is to look within the media institutions, at their labour processes, management practices, divisions of labour, work routines and occupational patterns. This is to examine in detail the implications of the fact that media products are made by teams; the subject of the media 'message' is a collective one. Much of the research in British sociology with this focus was carried out in the 1970s.[7] The sociologist Jeremy Tunstall has carried out studies of a number of groups of media workers, including advertisers, parliamentary lobby correspondents, and journalists. Chapter 13 is drawn from a recent investigation of his into the occupational group television producers. This group is pivotal for the television industry, being the lynchpin between the creative and technical staff on the one hand, and the industry's controlling and managerial layers on the other. Tunstall's study draws out how the changing regulation and business practices of the television industry in the 1990s are sustaining this pivotal role of producers, while worsening their conditions of remuneration and security within the occupation.

'Production' embraces all the factors that contribute to the shaping and making of media output: economic and business, legal and regulatory, technological, managerial and organisational, employment patterns and divisions of labour, artistic skills and professional routines and understandings, including operational concepts of markets and audiences. These can be seen as the determinants of the text, all that is 'prior' to the text. This section provides a sample of the kinds of understanding of media production that the social sciences can bring to bear.

NOTES

1. For instance: the Association of Cinematograph, Television and Allied Technicians no longer exists as a separate organisation, having merged with another media workers' union to form the Broadcasting, Entertainment and Cinematograph Union (thereby contributing to the trend to unification of industrial bargaining organisation to march the conditions of an increasingly unified labour market within the cultural industries); the growth of the Maxwell Communications Corporation ceased abruptly following the sudden death of its founder Robert Maxwell in 1991; in 1989 Time-Life merged with Warner Bros. to form Time-Warner, which in 1996 acquired Turner Broadcasting (producers of the CNN channels) and makes up the largest corporate media group in the world.
2. His major statement of 1979 was entitled 'Contribution to a Political Economy of Mass Communication' (*Media, Culture and Society 1*, pp. 123–46; also available in his *Capitalism and Communication: Global Culture and the Economics of Information* (London: Sage, 1990)).

3. A useful survey of the history of broadcasting in Britain is Andrew Crisell, *An Introductory History of British Broadcasting* (London: Routledge, 1997).

4. See Tom O'Malley, *Closedown? The BBC and Government Broadcasting Policy 1979–1992* (London: Pluto Press, 1994); and Peter Goodwin, *Television under the Tories: Broadcasting Policy 1979–1997* (London: British Film Institute, 1998). It is noteworthy, that in contrast to its usage from the mid-50s to the 1980s, the term 'public service broadcasting' has increasingly become used to mean 'public *sector* broadcasting', i.e. to refer to the BBC alone.

5. Peter Golding and Graham Murdock, 'Culture, Communication and Political Economy', in James Curran and Michael Gurevitch (eds), *Mass Media and Society* (London: Edward Arnold, 1991) p. 22.

6. Robert W. McChesney, 'Media convergence and globalisation', ch. 2 of Daya Kishan Thussu (ed.), *Electronic Empires: Global Media and Local Resistance* (London: Arnold, 1998) p. 31.

7. For example: Philip Schlesinger, *Putting 'Reality' Together: BBC News* (London: Methuen, 1978).

10

PUBLIC SERVICE BROADCASTING: THE HISTORY OF A CONCEPT

Paddy Scannell

It is well known that broadcasting in Britain is based on the principle of public service, though what exactly that means, on close inspection, can prove elusive. The last parliamentary committee to report on broadcasting – the 1986 Peacock Committee – noted that it had experienced some difficulty in obtaining a definition of the principle from the broadcasters themselves. A quarter of a century earlier, the members of the Pilkington Committee on broadcasting were told by the chairman of the BBC's Board of Governors that it was no use trying to define good broadcasting – one recognized it. Maybe. Yet for the sake of reasonable discussion of the relevance or otherwise of public service broadcasting today it is worth trying to pin down the characteristics that define the British system. A useful starting point is to distinguish between public service as a responsibility delegated to broadcasting authorities by the state, and the manner in which the broadcasting authorities have interpreted that responsibility and tried to discharge it.

Government intervention to regulate broadcasting has been, in many cases, the outcome of wavelength scarcity and problems of financing. The portion of the electromagnetic spectrum suitable for broadcasting is limited and governments have had to assume responsibility for negotiating international agreements about wavelength allocations to particular countries as well as deciding how to parcel out the wavelengths available in their own country amongst the competing claims of broadcasting and those of the armed forces, merchant

From Andrew Goodwin and Gary Whannel (eds), *Understanding Television* (London: Routledge, 1989).

shipping, emergency services, telecommunications, and so on. The problem of financing arises because it is not immediately obvious how people are to be made to pay for a broadcast service. Most forms of culture and entertainment are funded by the box-office mechanism – people pay to enter a special place to enjoy a play, concert, film, or whatever. But radio and television are enjoyed in people's homes and appear as natural resources available, at the turn of a switch, like gas, water, or electricity. The two means of financing broadcasting in universal use, until recently, have been either a form of annual taxation on the owners of receiving sets (the licence fee), or advertising.

The British solution, back in the early 1920s, was the creation of a single company, the British Broadcasting Company, licensed to broadcast by the Post Office and financed by an annual licence fee charged on all households with a wireless. How the concept of public service came to be grafted onto what were originally a set of *ad hoc*, practical arrangements and the shifting terms of debate about what it has meant, can best be traced through the various committees on broadcasting set up by successive governments from the beginning through to the present. These committees, usually known by the name of their chairmen, have been given the task of reporting to Parliament on the conduct of the broadcasters, the general nature of the service provided, and its possible future development. They have been the means whereby Parliament has kept an eye on the activities of those to whom it has delegated responsibility for providing broadcast services in this country.

The very first broadcasting committee, set up by the Post Office in 1923 under the chairmanship of Major-General Sir Frederick Sykes, was asked to consider broadcasting in all its aspects and the future uses to which it might be put. In the minuted proceedings of this committee and its report we find the earliest attempts to formulate what the general purposes of broadcasting should be. A crucial move was the definition of broadcasting as 'a public utility' whose future should be discussed as such.

> The wavebands available in any country must be regarded as a valuable form of public property; and the right to use them for any purpose should be given after full and careful consideration. Those which are assigned to any particular interest should be subject to the safeguards necessary to protect the public interest in the future. (Sykes, 1923: 11)

Bearing in mind the cheapness and convenience of radio, and its social and political possibilities ('as great as any technical attainment of our generation'), the committee judged that 'the control of such a potential power over public opinion and the life of the nation ought to remain with the state' (Sykes, 1923: 15). The operation of so important a national service ought not to be allowed to become an unrestricted commercial monopoly.

The report rejected direct government control of broadcasting. Instead, it argued, indirect control should be operated through the licence which by law must be obtained from the Post Office for the establishment of any broadcasting station. The terms of the licence would specify the general responsibilities of the broadcasters and hold them answerable for the conduct of the service to that state department.

Thus the definition of broadcasting as a public utility, and the mandate to develop it as a national service in the public interest, came from the state. The interpretation of that definition, the effort to realize its meaning in the development of a broadcasting service guided by considerations of a national service and the public interest, came from the broadcasters and above all from John Reith, the managing director of the British Broadcasting Company from 1923 to 1926, and the first Director-General of the British Broadcasting Corporation from 1927 to 1938. The Sykes Committee had made only short-term recommendations about the development of a broadcasting service and the BBC had been granted a licence to broadcast for only two more years. The Crawford Committee was set up in 1925 to establish guidelines for the future of broadcasting on a more long-term basis. Reith was invited by the committee to present it with a statement of his views about the scope and conduct of broadcasting and he did so in a memorandum which he wrote as an impartial statement, presented in the interests of broadcasting not the British Broadcasting Company, and intended to show the desirability of the conduct of broadcasting as a public service.

In Reith's brief and trenchant manifesto for a public service broadcasting system there was an overriding concern for the maintenance of high standards and a unified policy towards the whole of the service supplied. The service must not be used for entertainment purposes alone. Broadcasting had a responsibility to bring into the greatest possible number of homes in the fullest degree all that was best in every department of human knowledge, endeavour, and achievement. The preservation of a high moral tone – the avoidance of the vulgar and the hurtful – was of paramount importance. Broadcasting should give a lead to public taste rather than pander to it: 'He who prides himself on giving what he thinks the public wants is often creating a fictitious demand for lower standards which he himself will then satisfy' (Reith, 1925: 3). Broadcasting had an educative role and the broadcasters had developed contacts with the great educational movements and institutions of the day in order to develop the use of the medium of radio to foster the spread of knowledge.

Here we find a cogent advocacy of public service as a cultural, moral, and educative force for the improvement of knowledge, taste, and manners, and this has become one of the main ways in which the concept is understood. But radio, as Reith was well aware, had a social and political function too. As a national service, broadcasting might bring together all classes of the population. It could prove to be a powerful means of promoting social unity particularly through the live relay of those national ceremonies and functions – Reith cited the speech by George V when opening the British Empire Exhibition: the first time the king had been heard on radio – which had the effect, as he put it, of 'making the nation as one man' (Reith, 1925: 4). By providing a common access for all to a wide range of public events and ceremonies – a royal wedding, the FA Cup Final, the last night of the Proms, for example – broadcasting would act as a kind of social cement binding people together in the shared idioms of a public, corporate, national life.

But, more than this, broadcasting had an immense potential for helping in the creation of an informed and enlightened democracy. It enabled men and women to take an interest in many things from which they had previously been excluded. On any great public issue of the day ratio could provide both the facts of the matter and the arguments for and against. Reith had a vision of the emergence of 'a new and mighty weight of public opinion' with people now enabled by radio to make up their own minds where previously they had to accept 'the dictated and partial versions of others' (Reith, 1925: 4). The restrictive attitude of the Post Office which, at the time, had forbidden the BBC to deal with any matters of public controversy, was severely restricting the development of this side of broadcasting, and Reith bitterly denounced the shackles imposed on radio's treatment of news and politics. Only when freed from such chains would broadcasting be able to realize one of its chief functions. The concept of public service, in Reith's mind, had, as a core element, an ideal of broadcasting's role in the formation of an informed and reasoned public opinion as an essential part of the political process in a mass democratic society.

Finally, Reith argued strongly for continued 'unity of control' in broadcasting – that is, for the maintenance of the BBC's monopoly of broadcasting in the United Kingdom. The monopoly granted to the BBC in 1922 was merely for the administrative convenience of the Post Office – it found it easier to deal with one licensed broadcasting service than several. At first there had been a considerable outcry (particularly from the popular press) against this 'trade monopoly' as a restrictive practice which inhibited the development of a range of competing programme services for listeners to choose from. But Reith defended what he later called the 'brute force of monopoly' as the essential means of guaranteeing the BBC's ability to develop as a public service in the national interest. The monopoly was, Reith argued, the best means of sorting out a technically efficient and economical system of broadcasting for the whole population – and universal availability was the cornerstone of the creation of a truly national service in the public interest. Second, unity of control was essential ethically in order that 'one general policy may be maintained throughout the country and definite standards promulgated' (Reith, 1925: 10).

Reith favoured changing the status of the BBC from a company in the private sector, set up originally in the interests of the British radio industry, to a corporation in the public sector under the authority of the state, because he believed it would give broadcasting a greater degree of freedom and independence in the pursuit of the ideals of public service. On the one hand it was necessary to be freed from commercial pressures. If radio continued to be part of a profit-oriented industry then the programme service would be influenced by commercial considerations and the need to appeal to popular demand. Entertainment, a legitimate aim of broadcasting, would become a paramount consideration to the detriment of other kinds of programming with a more educative or culturally improving aim. On the other hand, broadcasting needed to be free of interference and pressure from the state in order to develop its political role as a public service.

Reith's advocacy of a public service role for broadcasting in 1925 had the support of Post Office officials. Public opinion too had come round in favour of continuing broadcasting as a monopoly in the custody of the BBC, and there was no opposition to its transformation into a corporation at the end of the following year. Thereafter, for nearly thirty years, secure in its monopoly, the BBC was uniquely empowered to develop a service along the lines envisaged by its first Director-General.

There were two crucial decisions made by Reith and a handful of senior BBC staff about how to organize and deliver the programme service. The mandate of national service was interpreted most basically as meaning that anyone living anywhere in the United Kingdom was entitled to good quality reception of the BBC's programmes. They should be universally available to all. To achieve this a small number of twin transmitters were set up in strategically chosen locations to deliver two programmes to listeners: a regional programme produced from a handful of provincial centres, and a national programme produced from London. Wherever they lived listeners had the choice either of the national or their own regional programme. Second, the policy of mixed programming offered listeners on either channel a wide and varied range of programmes over the course of each day and week. Typically it included news, drama, sport, religion, music (light to classical), variety, and light entertainment. Not only did this mix cater for different needs (education, information, entertainment), but for different sectional interests within the listening public (children, women, farmers, businessmen, and so on).

These decisions had farreaching consequences. In the first place they brought into being a radically new kind of public – one commensurate with the whole of society. On behalf of this public the broadcasters asserted a right of access to a wide range of political, cultural, sporting, religious, ceremonial, and entertainment resources which, perforce, had hitherto been accessible only to small, self-selecting, and more or less privileged publics. Particular publics were replaced by the *general* public constituted in and by the general nature of the mixed programme service and its general, unrestricted availability. The fundamentally democratic thrust of broadcasting – of which Reith was well aware – lay in the new kind of access to virtually the whole spectrum of public life that radio made available to everyone. It equalized public life through the common access it established for all members of society – and it is worth noting that initially in nearly every case the broadcasters had a hard fight to assert that right on behalf of their audiences. In one particular case – the access of TV cameras to the House of Commons – the principle has only just been won.

In the long run these structural arrangements for the distribution of the service and the range of programmes on offer were far more important than the actual style and content of particular programmes at the time. The BBC soon succeeded in winning a reputation for itself as a purveyor of moral and cultural 'uplift' in the well established tradition of improvement for the masses. It was far less successful in establishing its news and political programmes. The monopoly, a source of strength in some areas of programming such as music, was a source of weakness in relation to parties, governments, and state departments. Throughout the era of its monopoly the BBC's independence of government was frail and it was widely regarded (especially overseas) as government's semi-official mouthpiece.

In the decade after the Second World War the monopoly came under increasing pressure, and the first postwar committee of inquiry into broadcasting – the 1950 Beveridge Committee – made the question of the monopoly its central concern. The BBC produced a classic defence of its position in its written submission to the committee. To introduce competition for audiences into broadcasting by establishing other programme services would inevitably lead to a lowering of programme standards. By that the BBC meant 'the purpose, taste, cultural aims, range and general sense of responsibility of the broadcasting service as a whole'.

> Under any system of competitive broadcasting all these things would be at the mercy of Gresham's Law. For, at the present stage of the nation's educational progress, it operates as remorselessly in broadcasting as ever it did in currency. The good, in the long run, will inevitably be driven out by the bad. It is inevitable that any national educational pyramid shall have a base immeasurably broader than its upper levels. The truth of this can be seen by comparing those national newspapers which have circulations of over four millions with those whose circulations are counted in hundred-thousands. And because competition in broadcasting must in the long run descend to a fight for the greatest number of listeners, it would be the lower forms of mass appetite which would more and more be catered for in programmes. (Beveridge, 1950: para. 163)

In the event, the Beveridge Committee endorsed the BBC's monopoly, but its days were numbered. Within a couple of years a general election returned a Conservative government that rejected the recommendations of Beveridge and opted to establish commercial television, funded by advertising, in competition with the BBC's television service.

The British system is sometimes presented as a mixture of public service and commercial broadcasting as represented respectively by the BBC and ITV, but this is misleading. The terms under which commercial broadcasting was established by government made it part of the public service system from the beginning. A public corporation, the Independent Television Authority, was created by Act of Parliament with general responsibilities to establish a commercial television service that would inform, educate, and entertain. This service, known as Independent Television (ITV), was subject to state regulation and control by an authority charged with maintaining high standards of programme quality. It was an extension of public service broadcasting, not an alternative.

Even so, when the next committee on broadcasting, chaired by Sir Harry Pilkington, set about examining the impact of commercial television in 1960 and comparing its programme service with that of the BBC it found much to complain of in the doings of ITV. If the main concern of Beveridge had been with the monopoly, Pilkington was concerned with programme standards and the ominous threat of 'triviality'. Pilkington defined the concept of public service broadcasting as always to provide 'a service comprehensive in character; the duty of the public corporations has been, and remains, to bring to public awareness the whole range of worthwhile, significant activity and experience' (Pilkington, 1960: 9). Against this criterion the committee noted the widespread public anxiety about television which had, in the last few years, taken over from radio as the dominant broadcasting medium. The commonest objection was that television programmes were too often designed to get the largest possible audience, and that to achieve this they appealed to a low level of public taste (Gresham's Law again). There was a lack of variety and originality, an adherence to what was safe, and an unwillingness to try challenging, demanding, and, still more, uncomfortable subject matter.

The committee had no hesitation in identifying commercial television as the culprit. The BBC was praised for its responsible attitude to the power of the medium of television. In the review of the BBC's performance there was a short paragraph on triviality – 'The BBC are aware of the liability of TV to fall into triviality, but have not always been successful in preventing this happening' (Pilkington, 1960: 42) – but a whole page and a half were devoted to the problem of triviality in commercial television. The ITA was scolded for equating quality with box-office success, and was scathingly condemned for its inability to 'understand the nature of quality or of triviality, nor the need to maintain one and counter the other' (Pilkington, 1960: 65). In short, commercial television was regarded as failing to live up to its responsibilities as a public service. It was not fit, in its present form, to extend its activities, and the plum that the committee had on offer – a third television channel – was unhesitatingly awarded to the BBC.

By the mid-1970s the terms in which the role of broadcasting in society was discussed had changed again, and the representations made to the committee on the future of broadcasting chaired by Lord Annan raised issues that would have seemed astonishing fifteen years earlier. The Annan Report, published in 1977, noted a marked shift in the social, political, and cultural climate in Britain since the deliberations of its predecessor.

For years British broadcasting had been able successfully to create, without alienating Government or the public, interesting and exciting popular network programmes from the world of reality as well as the world of fantasy – programmes on the arts and sciences, international reportage, political controversy, social enquiry, local investigation. These now began to stir up resentment and hostility, and protests against their political and social overtones.

Hitherto it had been assumed – apart from the occasional flurry over a programme – that Britain had 'solved' the problem of the political relations of broadcasting to Government, Parliament and the public. Now people of all political persuasions began to object that many programmes were biased or obnoxious. But some, with equal fervour, maintained that broadcasters were not challenging enough and were cowed by Government and vested interests to produce programmes which bolstered up the *status quo* and concealed how a better society could evolve. (Annan, 1977: 15)

Pilkington had praised the BBC and blamed ITV. Annan found both wanting – and the BBC rather more than ITV. The old monopoly had given way to a cosy 'duopoly' between the BBC and ITV who had both come to terms with competition by providing a broadly similar programme service with a roughly equal share of the audience. A significant spectrum of opinion, both among politicians and among the general public, was now calling a plague on both broadcasting houses. Broadcasting had become 'an overmighty subject' answerable neither to its political masters nor the general public. It was no longer representative of the increasingly diverse tastes, interests, and needs of an increasingly diverse society. Perhaps the only way to deal with the problem was to break up the existing broadcasting institutions.

The committee's response to the barrage of conflicting opinion it encountered was to opt for 'pluralism' – 'Pluralism has been the *leitmotiv* of all of us in this Report' it noted (Annan, 1977: 108). It wanted to create a wider range of programmes that spoke not to the mass audience addressed by the existing duopoly but to those minorities and social groups whose needs and interests were not adequately served under the existing arrangements. It therefore recommended that the available fourth television channel should go to neither of the existing authorities but should be given to an independent Open Broadcasting Authority charged with the responsibility to develop a service that catered for all those interests presently underrepresented or excluded in the output of the BBC and ITV. The new authority would not produce any of its own programmes but, like a publishing house, would commission its programmes from a wide range of sources, including independent programme makers. The essential basis of what, in 1980, became Channel 4 was contained in Annan's concept of the Open Broadcasting Authority.

If hitherto public service broadcasting had been widely accepted in a largely unquestioning way, from Annan onwards old certainties crumbled. The defence of the original monopoly had been linked to a claim to a unified policy for programming that rested on a presumed social, cultural, and political consensus whose values were widely shared. But when that consensus collapsed what case could there be for a monopoly or a duopoly, or even the modest pluralism advocated by Annan? In the last decade there have been striking technological developments in broadcasting and telecommunications which, coupled with a sharp change in the political climate, have undermined all the old arguments in favour of public service broadcasting.

Today the key topic in debates about broadcasting is deregulation. Should the state cease to control and regulate broadcasting, and let market forces shape its future development? State regulation, the argument goes, was necessary from the beginning through to the end of the 1970s because in that period the scarcity of suitable wavelengths for broadcasting necessitated the intervention of the state to regulate their allocation and use. In this country there are at present [1990] only four national television channels, regulated by two authorities, broadcasting to the whole population, but change is only just around the corner. As the Peacock Report puts it:

> We are now in an unusually rapid technological advance in broadcasting. People can buy video recorders and watch films whenever they choose. Cable networks are beginning to develop in various parts of the country. There is already some broadcasting by satellite and, although it is impossible to predict its future precisely, it seems certain that its effects will be very large ... There is no reason why a large – indeed an indefinitely large – number of channels should not be brought into use. In the case of cable television fibre optic communication techniques allow for two way communication and make pay TV a live possibility. (Peacock, 1986: 2)

What will soon be available, at a price it is argued, is multi-channel access to a wide range of different video services and television programmes supported either by advertising, or by a fixed monthly charge or on a pay as you view basis. Whatever the precise mix of ways in which these services are financed and paid for it will not be by the licence fee method which has always been the means of financing the BBC. In this context why should people go on paying for the BBC as they do at present? It will become, after all, only one service out of many. It was this question that the Peacock Committee was asked by the government to consider in 1985 and its report was published the following year.

Other committees had considered broadcasting in social, cultural, and political terms. Peacock, set up to consider alternatives to the licence fee as a means of financing the BBC, applied a stringent economic approach and in so doing completely shifted the grounds of discussion. For Peacock, broadcasting was a commodity – a marketable good like any other – provided for consumers, and

the establishment of consumer sovereignty in broadcasting through a sophisticated market system was the aim of the report. It defined a satisfactory
broadcasting market as offering 'full freedom of entry for programme makers,
a transmission system capable of carrying an indefinitely large number of
programmes, facilities for pay-per-programme or pay-per-channel and differentiated charges for units of time' (Peacock, 1986: 134). Consumer sovereignty
meant the greatest freedom of choice for individuals via the widest provision of
alternative broadcast goods. Neither the state nor delegated broadcasting
authorities should continue to determine the nature and scope of the available
broadcasting services. In future consumers should be the best judges of their
own welfare.

Peacock envisaged a three-stage transition to a free market in broadcasting.
In the crucial second stage (some time in the 1990s) it recommended that the
BBC should be financed by subscription. Eventually, in the next century, a full
market for broadcasting, with a very wide range of services via geo-stationary
satellites and fibre-optic cable systems as well as traditional terrestrial broadcast services, would be based wholly on direct payment either for particular
channels or programmes.

The committee recognized that these proposals might well lead to the
erosion of public service broadcasting, and it was concerned to identify how
the essential elements of public service broadcasting – which it defined as the
production of a wide range of high quality programmes – might be retained. It
wanted to protect those programmes of merit which, it acknowledged, would
not survive in a market where audience ratings were the sole concern. To this
end it suggested – though only in general terms – the establishment of a Public
Service Broadcasting Council to secure the funding of public service programmes on any channel from stage two onwards. In spite of this gesture
the whole tenor of the Peacock Report reversed the thinking of all previous
parliamentary committees on broadcasting. Hitherto commercial considerations had taken second place to a public service commitment. Peacock, however, placed public service a long way second to commercial considerations and
consumer choice. Public service broadcasting would no longer be the definitive
feature of the British system.

Raymond Williams has identified the idea of *service* as one of the great
achievements of the Victorian middle class, and one that deeply influenced
later generations (Williams, 1961: 313–17). It was certainly a crucial component of the ideal of public service as grafted onto broadcasting in its formative
period from the 1920s to the 1950s. The Victorian reforming ideal of service
was animated by a sense of moral purpose and of social duty on behalf of the
community, aimed particularly at those most in need of reform – the lower
classes. It was institutionalized in the bureaucratic practices of the newly
emerging professional classes – especially in the reformed civil service of the
late nineteenth century whose members saw themselves as public servants. At

its best this passion for improving the lot of those below was part of a genuinely humane concern to alleviate the harsh consequences of a newly industrialized society. But it did nothing to change the balance of power in society, and maintained the dominance of the middle classes over the lower ranks.

One strand in this general concern for the conditions of the poor focused on their educational and cultural needs. A key figure in this development was Matthew Arnold (an inspector of schools for most of his working life) who believed that everyone was entitled to the enjoyment of those cultural treasures which, in his day, were available only to the educated classes. Arnold defined culture as 'the best that has been thought and written in the world' (quoted in Williams, 1961: 124), a definition echoed by Reith in his advocacy of public service broadcasting. The radical element in Arnold's thinking was this claim that the state should use its authority to establish a fully national education system with a curriculum that included the study of the arts and humanities. Culture, for Arnold, was a means of alleviating the strain and hostility between classes in a deeply divided society, and the task of 'civilizing' the masses had a prudent political basis. It was a means of incorporating the working classes within the existing social and political order, and thus preventing the threat of revolt from below. Arnold's best known essay, *Culture and Anarchy*, expressed that fear in its very title.

The idea that the state should intervene in the terrain of culture and education, so daring in Arnold's time, had won a much wider acceptance some fifty years later at the time that broadcasting was established. Indeed, government intervention to control and regulate broadcasting and to define its general purposes is an early and classic instance of state intervention to regulate the field of culture. Victorian ideals of service laced with Arnoldian notions of culture suffused all aspects of the BBC's programme service in the thirty years of its monopoly. Such attitudes, in broadcasting as elsewhere, did not outlast the 1950s – or at least not with the degree of unself-critical certainty that they had hitherto possessed. 'The ideals of middle class culture', as the Annan Report put it, 'so felicitously expressed by Matthew Arnold a century ago ... found it ever more difficult to accommodate the new expressions of life in the sixties' (Annan, 1977: 14). Even so, it noted that at some levels the 'old Arnoldian belief in spreading "sweetness and light" still inspired the BBC' (Annan, 1977: 80).

Underlying Arnoldian ideals of sweetness and light was a concern for social unity mingled with national pride. In the epoch of the BBC's monopoly both concerns were central to its role as a public service in *the national interest*. The linking of culture with nationalism – the idea of a national culture – was given new expression in broadcasting through those kinds of programme that had the effect of, in Reith's words, 'making the nation as one man'. From the 1920s through to today the BBC has continued this work of promoting national unity through such programmes. Sir Michael Swann, chairman of the BBC's Board of Governors, told the Annan Committee that 'an enormous amount of the

BBC's work was in fact social cement of one sort or another.' Royal occasions, religious services, sports coverage, and police series, 'all reinforced the sense of belonging to our country, being involved in its celebrations, and accepting what it stands for' (Annan, 1977: 263). The report described the BBC as 'arguably the most important single cultural institution in the nation', and recommended preserving it as 'the natural interpreter of [great national occasions] to the nation as a whole' (Annan, 1977: 79, 114).

Such occasions – exemplified by, say, the wedding of Prince Charles and Lady Diana Spencer – may indeed be moments of national unity in which all sections of society participate. But what of moments of crisis? The question then arises as to whose interests, in the last resort, broadcasting is there to serve – those of the state or the people? Governments claim the right to define the national interest and expect the broadcasters, particularly in a crisis, to uphold their definition of it. To defend the public interest may mean challenging the government of the day – a risky thing for institutions which derive their authority to broadcast from the government.

This politicized concept of the public interest has a very different history to that of public service, for the former relates to the news function of modern media and was elaborated in struggles for press freedom from the late eighteenth to the mid-nineteenth century. Against the power of the state, radical publics – bourgeois and proletarian – emerged to claim universal political and civil rights; the right to vote, to free speech and free assembly. A new kind of 'public sphere' was formed, independent of church and state, claiming the right to criticize both and committed to the establishment of public life, grounded in rational discussion, in which all members of society might participate (for a discussion of this concept in relation to broadcasting see Garnham, 1986). The struggle to establish an independent press, both as a source of information about the activities of the state and as a forum for the formation and expression of public opinion, was part of this process, and an important aspect of the long battle for a fully democratic representative system of government.

The establishment of broadcasting coincided with the moment that the vote was finally conceded to all adult men and women, and the development of mass democracy is closely connected with broadcasting's role in that process. Reith was well aware of the importance of radio as a new organ of public opinion and as an instrument of democratic enlightenment, and was keen to move it in those directions. If the BBC was slow to develop a robust independence from the state it was not, as some have argued, the fault of its first Director-General. Nevertheless it is true to say that the political independence of broadcasting goes back no further than the mid-1950s. The introduction of strictly limited competition for audiences between the BBC and ITV gave the BBC something else to worry about other than its political masters. Competition in the sphere of news and current affairs had the effect of detaching the BBC from the apron strings of the state. Deference to political authority was replaced by a more populist, democratic stance as the broadcasters asserted the public's right to know by making politicians answerable and accountable to the electorate for their conduct of the nation's affairs. In news interviews, studio discussions and debates, current affairs magazine programmes, documentaries, and documentary dramas a whole clutch of political and social issues came onto the agenda through the medium of television – became part of the public domain, matters of common knowledge and concern. In this way broadcasting came to fulfil – never without difficulty, always under pressure – its role as an independent 'public sphere' and a forum for open public discussion of matters of general concern.

The extent of 'openness' is, however, something that varies according to the social, economic, and political climate. The thresholds of tolerance are not fixed. It is arguable, for instance, that television was more 'open' in the mid-1960s than the late 1970s. It is notable, however, that a Conservative government enhanced the 'public sphere' role of broadcasting at the beginning of the 1980s by authorizing Channel 4 to give special attention to the interests of minority groups and to commission a significant amount of its programmes from independent programme makers. The establishment of Channel 4 must be seen as the expression of a continuing political commitment to regulating broadcasting as a public good and in the public interest.

The pursuit of these aims has to date been underpinned by a disregard for commercial considerations as either the only or the primary objective of the broadcast services. This has manifested itself in two ways that are crucial to the realization of public service objectives: a policy of mixed programming on national channels available to all. Where commercial motives are primary broadcasters will go only for the most profitable markets – which lie in densely populated urban areas that can deliver large audiences without difficulty. The markets for cabled services are likely to prove even more selective: the affluent districts of major towns and cities will be wired up, while the poorer areas will be neglected. More sparsely populated, remoter areas will be ignored entirely. The long-term commitment of the BBC and IBA to make their services available to all has meant an investment out of all proportion to the returns in order to reach those regions that strictly economic considerations would simply neglect. The BBC set up sixty-five new transmitting stations in order to extend its service from 99 per cent of the population to the 99.1 per cent it reaches at present.

The alternative to mixed programming is generic programming – a channel that provides a service in which all or most of the programmes are of the same kind. Typically this has – on radio – meant particular kinds of music channel: classical, top forty, country and western, reggae or whatever. More recently, in the United States, generic TV channels have been established in cable services – Home Box Office (mainly movies), MTV (music videos), CNN (Cable News Network), as well as pay-per-view channels that offer mainly sporting fixtures. Generic programming fragments the general viewing public as still constituted, for instance, in the mixed programme service offered on the four national UK television channels. In so doing it destroys the principle of equality of access for all to entertainment and informational and cultural resources in a common public domain. The hard-won 'public sphere' created over the last thirty years on national television may shatter into splinters under the impact of deregulated multi-channel video services.

The Peacock Report has redefined broadcasting as a private commodity rather than a public good. Individual consumers, in the media universe of the next century as envisaged by Peacock, will choose what they want and pay for what they get. But consumers are not all equal in their purchasing power. The privatization of informational and cultural resources may well create a two-tiered society of those who are rich and poor in such resources. Such a development would undercut the fundamentally democratic principles upon which public service broadcasting rests.

In the political climate of today, public service broadcasting may seem a concept that has outlived its relevance. I do not think so. The history of its development in Britain has undoubtedly been coloured by the patrician values of a middle-class intelligentsia, and a defence of public service broadcasting in terms of quality and standards tied to prescriptive and elitist conceptions of education and culture is no longer feasible. But that has proved to be a contingent historical feature in the development of the BBC. Far more crucial has been the political will, until very recently, to maintain, against the grain of economic considerations, a commitment to properly public, social values and concerns in the system as a whole, that is, in the services provided by both the BBC and IBA. In my view equal access for all to a wide and varied range of common informational, entertainment, and cultural programmes carried on channels that can be received throughout the country must be thought of as an important citizenship right in mass democratic societies. It is a crucial means, perhaps the only means at present, whereby a common culture, common knowledge, and a shared public life are maintained as a social good equally available to the whole population. That was the basis of public service broadcasting as envisaged by John Reith, the much misunderstood first Director-General of the BBC. It is the basis of the present system. It should continue to be so in the future.

REFERENCES

Annan Committee, *Report of the Committee on the Future of Broadcasting* (Annan Report), Cmnd. 6753, London: HMSO, 1977.

Beveridge Committee, *Report of the Broadcasting Committee* (Beveridge Report), Cmnd. 8116, London: HMSO, 1951.

Crawford Committee, *Report of the Broadcasting Committee* (Crawford Report), Cmnd. 2599, London: HMSO, 1925.

Garnham, N., 'The media and the public sphere', in P. Golding, G. Murdock, and P. Schlesinger (eds), *Communicating Politics*, Leicester: Leicester University Press, 1986.

Peacock Committee, *Report of the Committee on Financing the BBC* (Peacock Report), Cmnd. 9284, London: HMSO, 1986.

Pilkington Committee, *Report of the Broadcasting Committee* (Pilkington Report), Cmnd. 1753, London: HMSO, 1960.

Reith, J., *Memorandum of Information on the Scope and Conduct of the Broadcasting Service*, Caversham, Reading: BBC Written Archive, 1925.

Sykes Committee, *Broadcasting Committee Report* (Sykes Report), Cmnd. 1951, London: HMSO, 1923.

Williams, R., *Culture and Society*, Harmondsworth: Penguin, 1961.

11

ON THE CULTURAL INDUSTRIES

Nicholas Garnham

[...]

An analysis of culture structured around the concept of the cultural industries [...] sees culture, defined as the production and circulation of symbolic meaning, as a material process of production and exchange, part of, and in significant ways determined by, the wider economic processes of society with which it shares many common features.

Thus, as a descriptive term, 'cultural industries' refers to those institutions in our society which employ the characteristic modes of production and organization of industrial corporations to produce and disseminate symbols in the form of cultural goods and services, generally, although not exclusively, as commodities. These include newspapers, periodical and book publishing, record companies, music publishers, commercial sports organizations, etc. In all these cultural processes, we characteristically find at some point the use of capital-intensive, technological means of mass production and distribution, highly developed divisions of labour and hierarchical modes of managerial organization, with the goal, if not of profit maximization, at least of efficiency. I refer to this as a descriptive use of the term 'cultural industries' because it describes characteristics common to the cultural process in all industrial societies, whether capitalist or socialist. Within the descriptive usage we need to note a further distinction made by Adorno, who originally coined the term, between

From N. Garnham, 'Public Policy and the Cultural Industries', Ch. 10 in Nicholas Garnham, *Capitalism and Communication: Global Culture and the Economics of Information* (London: Sage, 1990) pp. 154–68.

those cultural industries which employ industrial technology and modes of organization to produce and distribute cultural goods or services which are themselves produced by largely traditional or preindustrial means (for example, books and records) and those where the cultural form itself is industrial (such as newspapers, films and TV programmes). We need to remember this distinction because the two forms tend to give rise to different relations of production and types of economic organization.

But the term 'cultural industries' can also be used analytically to focus upon the effects on the cultural process within the capitalist mode of production of cultural goods and services produced and distributed as commodities by labour, which is itself a commodity.

A key point here is that the cultural sector operates as an integrated economic whole because industries and companies within it compete:

1. for a limited pool of disposable consumer income;
2. for a limited pool of advertising revenue;
3. for a limited amount of consumption time;
4. for skilled labour.

[1]

Consumer expenditure on cultural goods and services has been rising slowly as a proportion of total expenditure, as consumption of basic essentials, such as food and clothing, reaches saturation point. However, this movement has been within limits, and studies have shown this expenditure to be inelastic not only in general but also in the sense that for individuals and families expenditure does not rise in line with income. This is probably linked to the question of limited consumption time.

[2]

[There is a] close relationship between total advertising expenditure and both consumer expenditure and GNP. From 1952 to 1982 it [...] varied between 1.94 and 1.15 per cent of consumer expenditure, and between 1.43 and 0.89 per cent of GNP. Moreover, in real terms, total advertising expenditure has remained remarkably stable. [...] Against a background of a high level of advertising in the UK in relation to GNP compared with other European economies, the limits of the advertising revenue pool are plain.

[3]

For most people, cultural consumption is confined to a so-called free time, the extension of which is limited by the material necessities of work and sleep. If we assume a working week including travel of 45 hours and sleep time of 48 hours per week, that leaves 75 hours per week in which all other activities have to be fitted. On average, 20 hours per week are taken up by TV viewing.

Cultural consumption is particularly time-consuming in the sense that the most common and popular form of culture, namely narrative and its musical equivalent, are based upon manipulation of time itself, and thus they offer deep resistances to attempts to raise the productivity of consumption time. This scarcity of consumption time explains:

1. the acute competition for audiences in the cultural sector;
2. the tendency to concentrate cultural consumption in the home, thus cutting out travel time;
3. as [...] Swedish studies have shown, a sharp rise in the unit cost of each minute of consumption time, in particular as investment on domestic hardware increases while the time for using such hardware does not. Thus in Sweden between 1970 and 1979 time spent listening to music rose by 20 per cent while the cost rose by 86 per cent, with each hour of listening costing 55 per cent more.

|4|

The various cultural industries compete in the same market for labour. Individual film-makers, writers, musicians or electricians may move in their work from film, to television, to live theatre. The electronic engineer may work in manufacturing or broadcasting. The journalist may work in newspapers, periodicals, radio or television.

This unified labour market is reflected in trade-union organizations. The Association of Cinematograph, Television and Allied Technicians (ACTT) organizes across film, television and radio, the National Union of Journalists (NUJ) across newspapers, books, magazines, radio and television. The Musicians' Union members work in film, radio, television and records as well as live performances, and so on.

As a result of these levels of integration within the cultural sector, a shift in one new television channel, such as Channel 4, restructures the broadcasting, film and advertising market in specific ways. Even more, of course, will this be the case with cable and satellite services. The introduction of a new colour supplement has repercussions upon the finances of other publications, but may well also have cross-effects on broadcasting revenue.

[...]

[5]

The particular economic nature of the cultural industries can be explained in terms of the general tendencies of commodity production within the capitalist mode of production as modified by the special characteristics of the cultural commodity. Thus we find competition driving the search for profits via increased productivity, but it takes specific forms.

There is a contradiction at the heart of the cultural commodity. On the one hand, there is a very marked drive towards expanding the market share or the form this takes in the cultural sector, audiences. This is explained by the fact that in general, because one of the use-values of culture is novelty or difference, there is a constant need to create new products which are all in a sense proto-types. That is to say, the cultural commodity resists that homogenization pro-cess which is one of the material results of the abstract equivalence of exchange to which the commodity form aspires. This drive for novelty within cultural production means that in general the costs of reproduction are marginal in relation to the costs of production (the cost of each record pressing is infinitesimal compared to the cost of recording, for instance). Thus the margin-al returns from each extra sale tend to grow, leading in turn to a powerful thrust towards audience maximization as the preferred profit maximization strategy.

On the other hand, the cultural commodity is not destroyed in the process of consumption. My reading of a book or watching of a film does not make it any less available to you. Moreover, the products of the past live on and can be relatively easily and cheaply reproduced anew. Thus it has been difficult to establish the scarcity on which price is based. And thus cultural goods (and some services, such as broadcasting, for technical reasons) tend towards the condition of a public good. Indeed, one can observe a marked tendency, where they are not *de jure* so treated, for consumers to so treat them *de facto* through high levels of piracy, as is now the case with records, video cassettes and books. (It should be noted that this in its turn relates to another contradiction in the cultural sphere, on which I shall comment shortly, between the producers of cultural hardware and software. It is the development of a market in cheap reproduction technology that makes piracy so difficult to control.) In contra-diction, then, to the drive to maximize audiences, a number of strategies have had to be developed for artificially limiting access in order to create scarcity.

The drive to audience maximization leads to the observed tendency towards a high level of concentration, internationalization and cross-media ownership in the cultural industries. The strategies to limit access have taken a variety of forms:

1. Monopoly or oligopolistic controls over distribution channels, sometimes, as in broadcasting, linked to the state. One often finds here a close relation-ship between commercial interests and those of state control.
2. An attempt to concentrate the accumulation process on the provision of cultural hardware – e.g. radio and television receivers, hi-fi, VCRs, etc. – with the programmes, as in the early days of British broadcasting, as necessary loss-leaders. The rationale for the introduction of cable in the UK is an example of this.
3. The creation of the audience as a commodity for sale to advertisers, where the cultural software merely acts as a free lunch. This has proved itself the most successful solution; both the increased proportion of advertising to sales revenue in the press and periodicals market, culminating in the growth

of free newspapers and magazines, and the steady expansion of wholly advertising-financed broadcasting services, are indications of this.

4. The creation of commodities, of which news is the classic example, which require constant reconsumption.

[6]

The third key characteristic of the cultural commodity lies in the nature of its use-values. These have proved difficult if not impossible to pin down in any precise terms, and demand for them appears to be similarly volatile. As I have already remarked, culture is above all the sphere for the expression of difference. Indeed, some analysts would claim that cultural goods are pure positional goods, their use-value being as markers of social and individual difference. While this aspect of culture merits much deeper and more extended analysis, it is only necessary here to draw one key conclusion, namely that demand for any single cultural product is impossible to predict. Thus the cultural industries, if they are to establish a stable market, are forced to create a relationship with an audience or public to whom they offer not a single cultural good, but a cultural repertoire across which the risks can be spread. For instance, in the record industry only one in nine singles and one in sixteen LPs makes a profit, and 3 per cent of the output can account for up to 50 per cent of turnover. Similarly, in films the top ten films out of 119 in the UK market in 1979 took 32 per cent of the box-office receipts and the top forty took 80 per cent.

Thus the drive to audience maximization, the need to create artificial scarcity by controlling access and the need for a repertoire bring us to the central point in this analysis. *It is cultural distribution, not cultural production, that is the key locus of power and profit.* It is access to distribution which is the key to cultural plurality. The cultural process is as much, if not more, about creating audiences or publics as it is about producing cultural artefacts and performances. [...]

We need to recognize the importance, within the cultural industries and within the cultural process in general, of the function which I shall call, for want of a better word, editorial: the function not just of creating a cultural repertoire matched to a given audience or audiences but at the same time of matching the cost of production of that repertoire to the spending powers of that audience. These functions may be filled by somebody or some institution referred to variously as a publisher, a television channel controller, a film distributor, etc. It is a vital function totally ignored by many cultural analysts, a function as creative as writing a novel or directing a film. It is a function, moreover, which will exist centrally within the cultural process of any geographically dispersed society with complex division of labour.

Taking these various factors into account, we are now in a position to understand why our dominant cultural processes and their modes of organization are the way they are. The newspaper and the television and radio schedule are montages of elements to appeal to as wide a range of readers, viewers and listeners as possible. The high levels of concentration in the international film, record and publishing industries are responses to the problem of repertoire. The dominance of broadcast television stems from its huge efficiency as a distribution medium, with its associated economies of scale.

For this reason, the notion that the new technologies of cable and VCR are fragmenting the market rather than shifting the locus of oligopolistic power needs to be treated with caution, since there are strict limits to how far such fragmentation can go economically.

[7]

As I have noted, power in the cultural sector clusters around distribution, the channel of access to audiences. It is here that we typically find the highest levels of capital intensity, ownership concentration and multinationalization, the operation of classic industrial labour processes and relations of production with related forms of trade-union organization. These characteristics are exhibited to their highest degree in the manufacture of the hardware of cultural distribution, especially domestic hardware. This is a sub-sector increasingly dominated by a few Japanese corporations such as Matsushita, Sony, Sanyo, Toshiba and Hitachi, together with Eastman Kodak, Philips and RCA.

[...]

Then there are the major controllers of channels of software distribution, often closely linked to specific modes of reproduction, such as record pressing or newspaper printing. In non-print media there is again a high level of concentration and internationalization, and US firms dominate, owing to the large size of the domestic US market. Here we find some of the same firms as in hardware, e.g. RCA, Thorn-EMI and Philips joined by firms such as Warner, CBS, Time-Life, Gulf-Western and MCA. The multinationalization of print media has been limited by barriers of language. None the less, apart from the high levels of concentration in the national UK market, with three groups controlling 74 per cent of daily newspaper circulation, two of these groups – News International and Reed International (now owned by Maxwell) – have extensive foreign interests.

The increasing tendency in this field, as an extension of the principle of repertoire, is the formation of multi-media conglomerates. Examples are Pearson-Longman and Robert Maxwell in the UK, who own interests across a number of media, thus enabling them both to exploit the same product, be it a film, a book or a piece of music, across several media, and also to expand the principles of risk-spreading not only across a range of consumer choice in one medium but also across consumers' entire range of cultural choice. The development of such centres of cultural powers also, of course, raises barriers to entry.

Around these centres of power cluster groups of satellites. These satellites can be either small companies, for instance independent production companies in relation to Channel 4, or individual cultural workers such as freelance journalists, writers, actors and film directors. In these satellite sectors we find high levels of insecurity, low levels of profitability, low levels of unionization and, where they exist, weak trade-union organizations. Often labour is not waged at all, but labour power is rented out for a royalty.

The existence of this dependent satellite sector fulfils a very important function for the cultural industries because it enables them to shift much of the cost and risk of cultural research and development off their own shoulders and on to this exploited sector, some of which is then [. . .] supported from the public purse. It also enables them to maintain a consistently high turnover of creative cultural labour without running the risk of labour unrest, or bearing the cost of redundancy or pension payments. Their cup brimmeth over when, as is often the case, the workers themselves willingly don this yoke in the name of freedom.

[8]

[. . .]

What should be our attitude to the relation between the market and the cultural process? There is that general tradition which regards culture and the market as inherently inimical. This view is powerfully reinforced within the socialist tradition by opposition to the capitalist mode of production. I think it is crucial, however, to separate the concept of the market from the concept of the capitalist mode of production, that is to say from a given structure of ownership and from the special features derived from labour as a market commodity. In terms of this relationship between consumers, distributors and producers of cultural goods and services, the market has much to recommend it, provided that consumers enter that market with equal endowments and that concentration of ownership power is reduced, controlled or removed. However, we must be clear that removal of the power vested in private or unaccountable public ownership will not remove the need for the function I have described as editorial, whether such a function is exercised individually or collectively. It also has to be stressed that even within the capitalist mode of production the market has, at crucial historical junctures, acted as a liberating cultural force. One thinks of the creation of both the novel and the newspaper by the rising bourgeoisie in the eighteenth century and of working-men's clubs and the working-class seaside holiday in the late nineteenth century.

Indeed, the cultural market, as it has developed in the past 150 years in the UK as a substitute for patronage in all its forms, cannot be read either as a destruction of high culture by vulgar commercialism or as a suppression of authentic working-class culture, but should be read as a complex hegemonic dialectic of liberation and control.

[. . .]

12

CONCENTRATION AND OWNERSHIP IN THE ERA OF PRIVATIZATION

Graham Murdock

At the outset of the modern media age, in the first half of the nineteenth century, most commentators generally saw no contradiction between the private ownership of the press (the major medium of the time) and its public, political roles as a channel for strategic information and a forum for political debate. Freedom of the press was synonymous with the absence of government censorship and licensing and the freedom to operate unhindered in the market-place. Newspapers were viewed as a voice on a par with individual voices, and the advocation of press freedom was seen as a logical extension of the general defence of free speech. This was plausible so long as most proprietors owned only one title and the costs of entering the market were relatively low. As the century wore on, however, and newspaper production became more sophis-ticated both technologically and operationally, rising costs increasingly re-stricted entry to major markets and drove smaller titles out of business, while the larger, wealthier concerns expanded their operations. By the beginning of this century the age of chain ownership and the press barons had arrived, prompting liberal democratic commentators to acknowledge a growing con-tradiction between the idealized role of the press as a key resource for citizen-ship and its economic base in private ownership. As the American writer, Delos Wilcox, author of one of the earlier systematic analyses of press content, observed in 1900:

From G. Murdock, 'Redrawing the Map of the Communications Industries: Concentration and Onwership in the Era of Privatization', Ch. 1 in Marjorie Ferguson (ed.), *Public Communication: The New Imperatives* (Beverly Hills: Sage, 1990) pp. 1–15.

The newspaper is pre-eminently a public and not a private institution, the principal organ of society for distributing what we might call working information ... The vital question is, from the social standpoint, the question of control. Who shall be responsible for the newspaper? It is rationally absurd that an intelligent, self-governing community should be the helpless victim of the caprice of newspapers managed solely for individual profit. (Wilcox, 1900: 86–9)

Wilcox's concern is more pertinent than ever as we move into an era where the combination of technological change and privatization policies are creating massive communications conglomerates with an unrivalled capacity to shape the symbolic environment which we all inhabit.

OLD PROBLEMS, NEW CONTEXTS

The last two years or so have seen a series of major acquisitions and mergers in the communications industries in Europe, North America and around the world. They include: Sony's acquisition of CBS's record division; General Electric's take-over of the US television network, NBC; the German multi-media group, Bertelsmann's, purchase of the Doubleday book company and RCA records; the Maxwell Communications Corporation's take-over of the New York publisher, Macmillan; and Rupert Murdoch's acquisition of a string of important communications concerns. These include the Twentieth Century Fox film interests; the major British publisher, Collins; Australia's biggest media company, the Herald and Weekly Times, and the Triangle Group of publications, which includes America's best-selling weekly magazine, *TV Guide*. By extending the activities of the leading media groups in such a visible way, these moves have breathed new life into long-standing concerns about concentration and ownership in the communications industries. To assess the significance of these developments, however, we must go beyond the immediate activity of bids, deals and buy-out, and analyse the longer-term movements which underpin them. As a first step we need to identify the key changes in the operating environment of the leading corporations that are facilitating the current wave of expansion and shaping its direction.

Two processes have been particularly important in restructuring the corporate playing field: technological innovation and 'privatization'. The 'digital revolution' which allows voice, sound, text, data and images to be stored and transmitted using the same basic technologies opens up a range of possibilities for new kinds of activity and for novel forms of convergence and interplay between media sectors. At the same time, we must be careful not to overstress the importance of technological innovation or to assign it an autonomous and determining role in the process of corporate development. New technologies create new opportunities, but before corporations can take full advantage of them there has to be a change in the political context which extends their freedom of action. And here the major force has undoubtedly been the growing momentum of privatization initiatives over the last decade. Before we examine the implications of this movement for corporate structures and strategies in more detail, however, we need to answer the prior question of why these changes matter.

MEDIA OWNERSHIP AND SOCIAL THEORY

Part of the answer is that investigation of the emerging patterns of media enterprise and ownership, and the tracing of their consequences for the range and direction of cultural production, is not just a specialized topic in communications enquiry. It also helps to illuminate the general relations between structure, culture and agency in the modern world. This classic problem lies at the heart not just of media research but also of the human sciences more generally, and presents both the greatest challenge to anyone specializing in the social investigation of communications and the best opportunity to reconnect our particular concerns to general developments in the social sciences to the mutual benefit of both. The relations between structure and action have moved steadily up the agenda for debate within social theory, to the extent that they now constitute its central problem (for example, Bourdieu, 1977: Giddens, 1984). More recently, theorists have begun to examine the parallel issue of culture and agency (for example, Archer, 1988), but as yet there has been no systematic attempt to link these general concerns to a detailed investigation of the media system. This is a double loss, to social theory and to communications research.

The question of mass media ownership provides a particularly pertinent point of entry into the structure–culture–agency triangle for two reasons. First, the power accruing to ownership entails both action and structural components (see Layder, 1985). The potential control it bestows over production does not arise solely from specific exercises of power within the corporations directly owned or influenced. It is also a function of pre-existing and enduring asymmetries in the structure of particular markets or sectors, which deliver cumulative advantages to the leading corporations, and enables them to set the terms on which competitors or suppliers relate to them (see Mintz and Schwartz, 1985). Consequently, a close study of the interplay between the structural and action components of control within media industries helps considerably in illuminating the core issues at stake in current debates about the nature of power.

The second theoretical pay-off of analysing media ownership arises from the pivotal role that the communications industries play in organizing the symbolic world of modern capitalist societies and hence in linking economic structures to cultural formations. More particularly, they connect a productive system rooted in private ownership to a political system that presupposes a citizenry whose full social participation depends in part on access to the maximum possible range of information and analysis and to open debate on contentious issues. Since this dual formation of liberal democratic capitalism first emerged, sceptics have been asking how far a communications system dominated by private ownership can guarantee the diversity of information and argument required for effective citizenship.

This question is more pertinent than ever today when the modal form of media enterprise is no longer a company specializing in one particular activity, but a conglomerate with interests in a wide range of communications industries, often linked to other key economic sectors through shareholdings, joint ventures and interlocking directorships. Before we examine the ways in which this structure facilitates certain kinds of control over cultural production, however, we need to distinguish between different types of conglomerate.

VARIETIES OF CONGLOMERATE

On the basis of their core activities we can distinguish three basic kinds of conglomerates operating in the communications field: industrial conglomerates; service conglomerates; and communications conglomerates.

Industrial conglomerates are companies which own media facilities but whose major operations are centred on industrial sectors. The Italian press provides a particularly good example of this pattern. The country's leading industrial group, Fiat, controls two major dailies: *La Stampa*, which it owns outright, and *Corriere della Sera* which it controls through its strategic stake in the paper's publisher, Rizzoli. The second largest group, the Ferruzzi-Montedison food and chemicals giant, controls *Il Messaggero* and *Italia Oggi* in Milan, while the third main group, which is run through Carlo de Benedetti's master holding company, Cofide, has a controlling interest in the country's second largest publishing house, Editore Mondadori, which own 50 per cent of the best-selling daily, *La Repubblica*. Altogether it is estimated that over 70 per cent of the Italian press is controlled or significantly influenced by these three groups, with other major industrial companies accounting for significant parts of the balance. The widely read paper, *Il Giorno*, for example, is owned by the state energy company, ENI. Not surprisingly, this situation has led to allegations that press coverage is coloured by the owners' corporate interests. Critics include the broadcasting magnate, Silvio Berlusconi, who recently complained that 'Our newspapers are not written by journalists but by industrial competitors with special interests' (Friedman, 1988a: 32).

Berlusconi's own master company, Fininvest, is a good example of the second main type of conglomerate, which is centred on service sectors such as real estate, financial services, and retailing. In addition to owning a national newspaper, a major cinema chain and Italy's three main commercial television networks, Berlusconi's interests include the country's leading property company; a substantial insurance and financial services division; a major chain of department stores, La Standa; and an advertising operation which accounts for around 30 per cent of the nation's billings.

In contrast to this highly diversified structure, the major interests of communications conglomerates are centred mainly or wholly in the media and information industries. Well-known examples include Rupert Murdoch's News International; the Maxwell Communications Corporation; and Bertelsmann. Until recently it was not unusual for communications conglomerates to own companies in unrelated industries. But lately there have been signs that the leading players are shedding these marginal subsidiaries in order to concentrate on expanding their core interests. In 1988, for example, Robert Maxwell disposed of his engineering interests, Associated Newspapers sold their North Sea oil division, and Reed International shed the paper and packaging division which had been their original base.

At the same time, the major communications companies have been making strenuous efforts to expand their core interests. These moves take several forms. First, there is a growing integration between hardware and software, prompted by a desire to ensure a supply of programming to service the new distribution technologies. Sony, for example, recently acquired the CBS record division, giving it a major stake in the international music industry to add to its already dominant position in the world market for compact disc players through its partnership with Philips. Second, there is a growing interpenetration between old and new media markets as major players in established sectors move into emerging areas which offer additional opportunities to exploit their resources. Newspaper and journal publishers, for example, have moved into the provision of on-line data services and broadcasting networks have branched out into cable programming. The rationale behind these moves is the desire for greater 'synergy' between the companies' various divisions so that activity in one sector can facilitate activity in another.

The rise of conglomerates as the modal form of media enterprise considerably increases the major players' potential reach over the communications and information system and makes the old questions of ownership and control more pertinent than ever.

PERSONAL AND IMPERSONAL POSSESSION

Changes in the organization of corporate enterprise have also been accompanied by shifts in ownership, though these are by no means uni-directional. Although there is a discernible trend towards the forms of impersonal possession outlined by John Scott (1986) in which the controlling interests in major corporations are held by other companies and financial institutions, older patterns of personal ownership, where effective control remains in the hands of the founding family or group, have also proved remarkably resilient within the communications industries. According to one recent estimate, for example, sixteen of the top twenty-four media groups in the United States 'are either closely held or still controlled by members of the originating family' (Herman and Chomsky, 1988: 8). They include both old-established companies such as the *New York Times* (the Sulzbergers) and Dow Jones and Co. (the Bancroft and Cox families) and newer arrivals such as Turner Broadcasting. At the same time, as the recent battles for control of the Springer press empire in West Germany and the Fairfax publishing interests in Australia clearly show, maintaining family or founder control can be a precarious and often expensive business.

The form of ownership is important since in combination with the structure and size of the company, it has an important bearing on the forms of control that proprietors want and are able to exercise. Although concern about the ways in which owner power may operate to curtail the diversity of publicly available information and debate can be traced back to the beginning of the modern media system in the second half of the nineteenth century, they are arguably more important than ever now, for three main reasons.

First, the fact that many of the leading communications companies command interests that span a range of key media sectors and operate across the major world markets gives them an unprecedented degree of potential control over contemporary cultural life. Second, as we shall see presently, the process of privatization has eroded the countervailing power of public cultural institutions. This is a significant loss, since at their best they embodied a genuine commitment to diversity and open argument, and at their minimum they filled a number of important gaps in commercially organized provision. Third, the privately owned media are becoming both more concentrated and more homogenized at a time when a range of new social concerns and movements, around ecological issues, women's rights and racial, regional and religious identities, are emerging in a number of countries. As a consequence, 'there is a growing gap between the number of voices in society and the number heard in the media' (Bagdikian, 1985: 98). What then are the powers of ownership? In what ways are proprietors able to shape the range and direction of cultural production?

THE POWERS OF OWNERSHIP

Owners possess two basic kinds of potential control over the symbolic environment. First and most obviously, they are able to regulate the output of the divisions they own directly, either by intervening in day-to-day operations, or by establishing general goals and understandings and appointing managerial and editorial staff to implement them within the constraints set by the overall allocation of resources (see Murdock, 1982). Second, they may also be able to influence the strategies of companies they do not own in their roles as competitors or suppliers.

In the area of direct intervention, attention has mostly been focused on proprietors' efforts to use the media outlets under their control as megaphones for their social and political ambitions. As the more perceptive commentators recognized when the trend first became apparent at the turn of the century, the movement towards conglomeration offered additional opportunities for the abuse of power. It was no longer simply a question of an individual owner giving himself and his views free publicity. As Edward Ross noted in 1910, the growing integration of newspapers into the core sectors of capital threatened to create new 'no-go' areas for critical reporting on corporate affairs and to undermine the press's role as a Fourth Estate, keeping watch over all those institutions – whether governmental or corporate – with significant power over people's lives. As he pointed out:

> newspapers are subject to the tendency of diverse businesses to become tied together by the cross-investments of their owners. But naturally, when the shares of a newspaper lie in a safe-deposit box cheek by jowl with gas, telephone, and pipe-line stock, a tenderness for these collateral interests is likely to affect the news columns. (Ross, 1910: 305)

Contemporary cases of such 'instrumental' abuses of power are not hard to find. In the summer of 1988, for example, Toshiba, one of Japan's leading contractors for nuclear power plants, withdrew a record protesting against the country's nuclear programme commissioned by its Toshiba–EMI music subsidiary. As is often the case in these situations, a political judgement was presented as a disinterested commercial decision, with a company spokesman claiming that 'this music is just too good to put before the market right now' (*Marketing Week*, 1988: 18). Direct interventions are also used to denigrate the activities of competitors. In March 1988, for example, the Fiat-controlled daily, *Corriere della Sera*, carried an abusive front-page story and editorial ridiculing the attempts of one of the company's main business rivals, Carlo de Benedetti, to take control of the leading Belgian holding company, Société Générale de Belgique. Although Fiat intervention was denied, it was clear that, however engineered, the story was designed to boost the company's position, and no one in Italy was surprised when the magazine *L'Expresso* produced a mock version of the paper's front page with the title altered to *Corriere della Fiat* (Friedman, 1988b: 115–16).

In both these cases we are dealing with industrial conglomerates defending their corporate interests. With service and communications conglomerates the dynamics of influence are somewhat different. Here the major impetus comes from commercial initiatives designed to maximize the 'synergy' between the company's various operations. When Silvio Berlusconi bought the Standa department store chain in July 1988, he immediately announced a programme of cross-promotion whereby his television stations would carry daily slots featuring the bargains on offer in the stores, thereby reducing the space available for other kinds of programming. When the publishing group Reed International acquired Octopus Books in 1987, it made no secret of the fact that it was looking to develop titles based on its substantial stable of magazines. Other publishing companies are actively exploring ways of making television programming for satellite distribution using the same editorial resources employed to produce newspapers and magazines (Handley, 1988). These are purely commercial decisions, but by promoting multiplicity over diversity they have a pertinent effect on the range of information and imagery in the public domain. In a cultural system built around 'synergy', more does not mean different; it means the same basic commodity appearing in different markets and in a variety of packages. But owner power does not end with these kinds of interventions.

As we noted earlier, as well as determining the actions of the companies they control directly, the strategies pursued by the major media owners also have a considerable knock-on effect on smaller competitors operating in the same markets and on potential take-over targets. The deeper their corporate pockets, the greater their potential influence. In the autumn of 1988, for example, in an effort to strengthen its defences against the hostile attentions of Rupert Murdoch who had built up a 20 per cent stake in the company, the Pearson group (whose interests include Penguin Books and the *Financial Times*) entered into an alliance with the Dutch publisher, Elsevier, who had been the target of another major media mogul, Robert Maxwell. Whether this tie-up is in the best long-term interests of Pearson or whether another partner would have been more advantageous is open to debate, but there is no doubt that this link will materially affect the company's future options.

The leading corporations' extensive power to shape the future of the communications and information system both directly and indirectly is not in itself new, of course. What is new is the rapid enlargement of these powers produced by a decade of privatization initiatives.

DIMENSIONS OF PRIVATIZATION

Since the term 'privatization' has acquired a variety of meanings in recent debates, I should make it clear that I am using it here in its most general sense to describe all forms of public intervention that increase the size of the market sector within the communication and information industries and give entrepreneurs operating within it increased freedom of manoeuvre. Two general features of this process are particularly worth noting. First, although such initiatives are usually associated with conservative administrations – most notably, the three Thatcher governments in Britain and Reagan's terms of office in the United States – they are by no means confined to them. The socialist government of Spain, for example, recently used its majority in the lower house to push through legislation authorizing three new commercial television franchises in the face of strong opposition from both conservative and left parties. More significantly, both the Soviet Union and the People's Republic of China have recently allowed commercial programme providers from overseas into their broadcasting systems. The second, and equally important, feature of privatization is its relative irreversibility. Although the popularity of specific initiatives may decline in the future and the original almost messianic impetus wane somewhat, there is little doubt that the previous balance between public and private enterprise has been tipped permanently in favour of the market in a growing number of societies. It is difficult, for example, to imagine any socialist or social democratic government capable of being elected in Western Europe in the near future, successfully renationalizing the key communications companies that have been sold off to private investors.

Privatization as I am defining it here is a multi-dimensional movement with four distinct components: de-nationalization; liberalization; the commercialization of the public sector; and the regearing of the regulatory environment. Each has important implications for the overall structure of the communications industries, for patterns of ownership, and for corporate strategies, which we need to trace, but it is important to separate them since they are not always pursued together.

DENATIONALIZATION: FROM PUBLIC TO PRIVATE OWNERSHIP

Because denationalization involves selling shares in public companies to private investors, its most significant impact is on patterns of ownership. However, this varies depending on how the shares are placed. Where they are put out to competitive tender and awarded to a particular consortium, as in France under the conservative administration of Chirac, the advantage clearly lies with companies which are already well financed and positioned and who can use the opportunity to extend their interests into areas from which they were previously locked out. For example, the group that took over TF1, which had been France's major public broadcasting network, included the Maxwell media conglomerate, the Bouygues construction group and the major banking group, Société Générale (which also had important stakes in two other denationalized communications concerns: the Havas advertising agency, and the telecommunications and engineering group, Companie Générale d'Electricité).

In contrast, the British strategy of public flotation was expressly designed to create a 'popular capitalism' in which shareholding would be widely dispersed. To this end, shares in the most important communications utility to be sold to date, British Telecom, were underpriced in order to attract first-time investors. Not surprisingly, their value rose sharply as soon as they were traded on the Stock Exchange, and many small shareholders opted to sell and pocket the profit. In the two years between December 1984 and the end of November 1986, the total number of BT shareholders fell by almost 30 per cent from 2.1 million to 1.48 million, reducing the public's overall share to less than 12 per cent and leaving the bulk of BT's equity in the hands of financial institutions, many based overseas.

Overall, then, denationalization has operated to reinforce and extend the power of the leading communications, service and industrial conglomerates rather than to disperse it, or to create new sources of countervailing power. By the same token, liberalization has enabled them to extend their reach into new markets.

LIBERALIZATION

Liberalization policies are designed to introduce competition into markets that were previously served solely by public enterprise. Here the impact depends on the terms on which this competition is allowed to proceed. Broadcasting provides a good example. Britain was the first major European country to introduce a commercial television service in competition with the public broadcasting system, when the ITV network was launched in 1954. However, the private sector was carefully regulated to ensure a reasonable spread of ownership and to limit foreign programming to 14 per cent of the total output. Without these safeguards, moves to liberalize broadcasting serve to open up national markets to the major international corporations. The major shareholders in the new French commercial channels, for example, include the Italian television magnate, Silvio Berlusconi, who has a 25 per cent stake in La Cinq, and Companie Luxembourgeoise de Télédiffusion (which operates the Luxembourg based television service RTL-Plus), which owns 25 per cent of the sixth channel, M6. In addition, the rapid expansion of commercial television paved the way for a sharp rise in the amount of foreign programming imported into the system since the proliferation of new distribution systems outstripped the supply of nationally originated material by a very considerable margin. This effect is noticeable even where broadcasting remains a public monopoly, as in Norway, where the decision to allow local cable systems to take advertising-supported pan European satellite channels has already acted as a stalking horse for full liberalization by deepening the crisis of public broadcasting.

COMMERCIALIZING THE PUBLIC SECTOR

One response to this crisis is to commercialize the public sector itself. Faced with rising costs and government ceilings imposed on the income they derive from the public purse, this has become an imperative for many public institutions, but it is one which a number are now embracing with enthusiasm. It takes several forms. The first is to allow broadcasters to supplement their income by taking spot advertising, as the state broadcasting network RAI does in Italy. So far this option has been resisted in Britain, but as recent developments at the BBC show, audiences and indeed resources can be opened up to private enterprise in other ways.

In the spring of 1988, the BBC offered two new services to the corporate sector. The first provided for 100 new data channels for use by retailers and other service companies wishing to advertise to their customers. The second allowed a private company, British Medical Television, to use time after regular broadcasts had finished for the night to relay a programme with advertising from the major pharmaceutical companies to VCRs in doctors' homes and surgeries for later viewing. In return, the Corporation will receive a £1 million fee in the first year. As well as gaining access to transmission resources for the first time, private corporations are also gaining a foothold in programme production as a result of the Government's decision that the BBC should move rapidly towards a situation in which at least 25 per cent of its programming is obtained from independent producers. Although the independent sector has only been established for a few years in Britain, prompted by the launch of Channel Four, which buys in almost all its programming, there is already a movement towards concentration which senior figures in the industry expect to continue. As Charles Denton, the Chief Executive of Zenith Productions, one of the country's most successful television independents, told an interviewer: 'I think there will be a move to agglomeration, and to cope with the economic realities there will be some very complex cross-holding. When this industry matures, you will find maybe half a dozen, even fewer, large independents. And we intend to be one of them' (Fiddick, 1988: 21). Recent examples of this trend include Robert Maxwell's takeover of the creative consortium Witzend; the purchase of Goldcrest Films and Elstree Studios by the leisure group Brent Walker; and the acquisition of Zenith itself by Carlton Communications, one of Britain's leading facilities houses. These movements, coupled with the partial relaxation of the rules governing corporate underwriting and sponsorship for programming (particularly on cable), open the way for greater corporate influence over what appears on the domestic screen. This erosion of the traditional 'Chinese walls', separating programming from product or corporate promotion, which we now see in a number of countries, is part of a much wider re-gearing of the regulatory environment in which the communications industries operate.

RE-REGULATION: FROM PUBLIC TO CORPORATE INTERESTS

This process is often called de-regulation. This is a misnomer. What is at stake is not so much the number of rules but the shift in their overall rationale, away from a defence of the public interest (however that was conceived) and towards the promotion of corporate interests. Communications corporations benefit from this shift at two levels. They not only gain from changes to the general laws governing corporate activity in areas such as trade-union rights but, more importantly, they have also gained considerably from the relaxation of the additional rules designed to prevent undue concentration in the market-place of ideas and to ensure diversity of expression.

One of the most important changes has been the general loosening of the restrictions on concentration of ownership. In Britain, for example, Rupert Murdoch's bid for the mid-market daily *Today* was judged not to be against the public interest on the grounds that, although he owned the country's most popular tabloid paper, the *Sun*, and one of the leading quality titles, *The Times*, he did not have an interest in the middle range and that his acquisition would not therefore increase concentration – a judgement that conveniently leaves aside the question of concentration in the national daily market as a whole.

In the broadcasting field, changes to the rules limiting the number of stations a single owner can possess have led to a significant increase in concentration in both the United States and Australia. In America, in April 1985, the old 7–7–7 limit which had operated since 1953 was replaced by a new 12–12–12 rule which allowed one company to own up to twelve AM and FM radio stations plus twelve television stations, providing that their total audience did not exceed 25 per cent of the country's television households. This made network ownership a more attractive proposition (despite the steady erosion of their overall audience share by cable and independent stations), and all three became the subject of bids. ABC was merged with Capital Cities; NBC was acquired by General Electric; and CBS narrowly fought off a bid from Ted Turner. A similar relaxation occurred in Australia in November 1986 when Bob Hawke's Labour Government replaced the old two-station rule with a new arrangement which allows owners to have as many stations as they like as long as they do not reach more than 60 per cent of the national audience. Here again, the result has been a marked movement towards greater concentration of ownership as companies in the two major markets – Sydney and Melbourne – have branched out to build national networks. Between December 1986 and September 1988, twelve out of the fifteen stations in capital cities changed hands, leaving the commercial television system as a virtual duopoly divided between the media wing of Alan Bond's industrial conglomerate and Christopher Skase's Quintex Group (Brown, 1988).

Changes to the regulatory regime are not uni-directional, however. At the same time as they relaxed the rule on the number of television stations that could be owned, the Australian government imposed new restrictions forbidding cross-ownership of radio stations, television stations or newspapers in the same markets. This accelerated the shake-up in newspaper ownership already under way, though here again the major beneficiaries were the leading groups. At the beginning of 1987, Rupert Murdoch successfully bid for the country's largest press concern, the Herald and Weekly Times, bringing his total share of the Australian newspaper market to 59 per cent. In the United States, in contrast, the rules on cross-ownership have recently been relaxed, though not without a struggle. Senator Edward Kennedy, for example, appended a clause to the Federal government's spending authorization for 1988, tightening the restrictions on owning television stations and newspapers in the same city. This was directed expressly at Murdoch whose *Boston Herald* had been consistently hostile to Kennedy. Murdoch contested it, and in the spring of 1988 it was overturned by the Circuit Court of Appeals in Washington on the grounds that since it was clearly aimed at one person it violated constitutional guarantees of equal treatment. This ruling was in line with the general trend of recent regulatory thinking typified by the Federal Communication Commission's decision to lift the ban on local telephone companies owning cable systems.

The FCC has also been in the forefront of the drive to loosen the public service requirements governing commercial broadcasting so as to give station owners maximum freedom to make profits. One of the bitterest rows in this area has been over children's television, which during the Reagan years had become one more or less continuous advertisement for toys and other products both in and around the programmes. After a concerted campaign, a citizens' lobby was successful in getting a Bill passed in both the House of Representatives and the Senate, limiting advertising time during children's programmes to twelve minutes in the hour and requiring franchisees to show a commitment to education. However, in one of his last acts as President, Ronald Reagan killed the measure by the simple expedient of omitting to sign it, declaring that its provisions 'simply cannot be reconciled with the freedom of expression secured by our constitution' (*The Economist*, 1988: 50). This statement exemplifies the general view which sees corporate promotion as continuous with individual speech, a position neatly encapsulated in the description of advertising as 'commercial speech'. The cumulative result of these shifts, and the other dimensions of the privatization process I have outlined here, has been to strengthen and extend the power of the leading corporations and to pose more sharply than ever the dilemma that faces a liberal democratic society in which most key communications facilities are held in private hands.

Detailing the way in which our existing maps of the cultural industries are being redrawn by the twin processes of technological changes and privatization policies and tracing their consequences for the range and nature of cultural production is a key task for future research. By the same token, anyone interested in formulating alternative policies for communications urgently needs to grapple with ways of regulating the new multi-media concerns, both nationally and internationally, and with the problem of developing novel forms of public initiative and institution which avoid the overcentralized, unresponsive structures of the past and are capable of responding creatively to the new poly-cultural formations now emerging. This is perhaps the major issue facing those of us interested in the future of communications as an essential resource for developing and deepening democracy.

REFERENCES

Archer, M. S. (1988) *Culture and Agency: the Place of Culture in Social Theory*, Cambridge: Cambridge University Press.

Bagdikian, B. (1985) 'The US Media: Supermarket or Assembly Line?', *Journal of Communication* 35:3, pp. 97–109.

Bourdieu, P. (1977) *Outline of a Theory of Practice*, Cambridge: Cambridge University Press.

Brown, A. (1988) 'Restructure of Australian Commercial Television', paper presented to Oz Media National Conference, Brisbane, 24 Sept.

Economist, The (1988) 'Pocket Vetoes: Licence to Kill', 19 Nov., p. 50.

Fiddick, P. (1988) 'Risk-risk at the Top-top', *Guardian*, 15 Feb., p. 21.

Friedman, A. (1988a) 'Putting Himself in the Picture', *Financial Times*, 1 Aug., p. 32.

Friedman, A. (1988b) *Agnelli and the Network of Italian Power*, London: Harrap.

Giddens, A. (1984) *The Constitution of Society: Outline of a Theory of Structuration* Cambridge: Polity Press.

Handley, N. (1988) 'Multiple Choices in the Single Market', *Marketing Week*, 25 Nov., pp. 73–7.

Herman, E. and Chomsky, N. (1988) *Manufacturing Consent: the Political Economy of the Mass Media*, New York: Pantheon Books.

Layder, D. (1985) *Structure, Interaction and Social Theory*, London: Routledge & Kegan Paul.

Marketing Week (1988) 'Toshiba Forced to Turn Down Music', 15 July, p. 18.

Mintz, B. and Schwartz, M. (1985) *The Power Structure of American Business*, Chicago: University of Chicago Press.

Murdock, G. (1982) 'Large corporations and the control of the communications industries', pp. 118–50 in Michael Gurevitch, Tony Bennett, James Curran and Janet Woollacott (eds), *Culture, Society and the Media*, London: Methuen.

Ross, E. (1910) 'The Suppression of Important News', *Atlantic Monthly* 105, pp. 303–11.

Scott, J. (1986) *Capitalist Property and Financial Power: A Comparative Study of Britain, the United States and Japan*, Brighton: Wheatsheaf.

Wilcox, D. (1900) 'The American Newspaper: A Study of Political and Social Science', *Annals of the American Academy of Political and Social Science* 16, July, pp. 56–92.

13

PRODUCERS IN BRITISH TELEVISION

Jeremy Tunstall

[...]

An important characteristic of British television is its tradition of covering a wide range of different programme types, and of carrying this range within the high-audience hours of the evening. Part of the traditional 'public-service broadcasting' project is that both popular and less-popular programming should be scheduled in the most popular hours on the main channels. It is also characteristic of British television that several of the genres are factual – including not only news, current affairs and sport, but also documentary and mixed-goal or 'edinfotainment' programming.

[...]

Each specific genre has its particular requirements and working cycles, which tend to cut its producers off from producers and others working in different fields with different timetables. Most British producers spend between 4 and 6 months each year locked into the intensive effort involved in meeting deadlines for a series of programmes; during this intensive phase they may well work 7 days a week for many weeks in succession. The other half of the year includes vacation time and perhaps 5 months of less intensive work. During these other months the producer may be supervising writing, casting supporting roles, engaging in research, looking at locations, seeing possible interviewees, talking

From Jeremy Tunstall, *Television Producers* (London: Routledge, 1993) pp. 2–13, 202–7, 212–16.

to actors' agents, and so on. Producers spend much of the time out of their offices – in the studio, at the location, viewing the raw rushes and, later, the rough edited film or tape.

Even at the quieter times of the year most producers do not arrive home until after the London rush-hour. They often take home with them scripts and programme outlines to read, as well as cassettes of programmes submitted by available writers, directors or performers. Much of their domestic TV viewing is of programming in their own genre. Thus producers tend to be locked into a genre-specific world even when at home.

Each of the genres is located within a department or departments; and even independent production companies specialize, so that here also producers are locked into the private world of a single genre. Each genre has its own specific goal or goals; it has a characteristic style of production – location film, or live studio, or the 'outside broadcasts' of sport. Each genre has its own internal system of status and prestige, its own values and its own world-view.

Departments and genres also function as career-ladders. There is continuing movement between organizations: many producers have started in the BBC, moved to ITV, then back to the BBC, only finally to go freelance or to set up as independent producers; but such job-moves all take place within one small world which shares one broad career-ladder. It is common for a producer's career to have involved several job-moves, each move following one particular senior colleague. Producers also in turn tend to be surrounded by production team-members with whom they have worked on several previous programmes and projects.

Thus the producer's own work-career advances within the private world of a particular genre whose peculiar work-mix of timetables, goals, production schedules and world-view largely shuts its members off from the members of other private genre-worlds.

WHERE THE PRODUCER CAME FROM

The producer role (like television itself) has multiple origins. The British TV producer historically is derived from the civil servant, the radio producer and the film producer, as well as from show business and the stage.

The BBC in the 1920s emerged from the Post Office, which was a department of government. The producer role in the BBC and in advertising-financed television derives from an inter-war civil service which still had colonial responsibilities; there are echoes of the district officer, gallantly attempting to administer one small corner of a vast empire. There is also a military element in this history: the BBC was set up in the 1920s by men who had served in and survived the first world war. British television in the 1940s and 1950s was built by men who had served in the second war or had done two years of post-1945 military service. Many young producers of the 1950s had been 'national-service' officers, and the television producer was seen as a leader of men (not women).

Political neutrality was a key element. The producer, like the civil servant and the army officer, avoided partisanship. In contrast to France or Germany, the British producer role was not, and still has not been, politicized. In Britain the BBC gradually evolved the tradition of being non-partisan while quietly patriotic. This non-partisanship has also been supported by the BBC's early reliance on neutral news agencies as a model for radio news. The non-partisan tradition acquired in 1955 a non-commercial element; when advertising was introduced with ITV, the relevant legislation and regulatory authority required producers to be sheltered from any direct advertising connections.

The BBC, modelled on the Post Office with its monopoly of post and telephone, was a vertically integrated monopoly. This conception of vertical integration was only modified by the ITV and its cartel of fifteen regional companies. The British TV-producer role developed within a pattern of two large systems – BBC and ITV – both of which made the bulk of their own programming and also transmitted it to a national audience.

This pattern, which reached maturity in the 1970s, involved two large cultural bureaucracies with an occupational hierarchy. Like the civil service, television had three main occupational categories. At the top were the managers, amongst whom former and current programme producers were the largest subgroup; producers mingled with general administrators, accountants and senior engineers, constituting a managerial elite. In the middle was a large category of TV skills and crafts; there were the men (and a few women) who operated TV studios and the outside broadcasts, the outdoor filming, the post-production and editing functions and other craft skills. Third and last were the clerical and lower service functions, in which women predominated. These latter two groupings were again reminiscent of the civil-service executive and clerical levels.

Another crucial civil-service-style feature in the 1970s was job security. It was required by the trade unions, and accepted by both BBC and ITV, that 70 per cent or more of the employees were in permanent and pensionable employment. In the 1970s a substantial minority of producers and directors were freelances; but many of these had been in staff positions previously and had chosen to go freelance. At the skilled levels and above in both the BBC and ITV there were very low rates of employee turnover, and 86 per cent of BBC employees in 1989 had been in the BBC for all their broadcasting work-careers. The numbers of producers and other personnel employed in British television expanded steadily – buoyed up by expanding revenue – in almost every single year from 1946 to 1988.

Producers were integrated into general management. Within this broad category, several levels of programme decision-making can be identified in 1990s terms:

Channel Heads
Departmental Head (BBC); Director of Programmes (ITV)

Executive Producer (BBC); Department Head (ITV)
Series Producer; Editor
Producer; Assistant Producer.

In this study we are focusing primarily upon the series producer or editor; this is the highest level of person who is in regular daily editorial or 'hands-on' control of the content of a series of programmes. At the executive-producer levels and above, the responsibility is typically for more than one series and has a lower 'hands-on' component.

Many producers are hesitant about accepting promotion out of the series-producer level; they often express their dilemma by referring to parallel cases of people promoted above the core-activity level – the teacher who is too senior to teach, the sailor who is too senior to go to sea. The tradition in British television is that the producer is part of management. The producer is made aware of what the senior people are thinking; the producer receives a flow of advice and guidance – much of it spoken, some of it written. Words such as 'guidance', 'guidelines' and 'consultation' are heavily used.

The emphasis placed on 'flexibility' and the avoidance of rigid rules in turn reflects the vague collection of goals towards which British broadcasting traditionally strives; each one of the public-service trio 'education, entertainment and information' is fairly vague, and how these can, or should, be mixed together in a particular series of programmes is very uncertain indeed.

There is inevitably a substantial degree of tension in such a system. From time to time conflicts between creative autonomy and organizational hierarchy surface into press publicity and political controversy; this may involve a channel controller vetoing the work of a series producer. However, much more frequently these tensions are managed quietly within the system; often the disciplinary intervention takes the form of a 'Don't do that again' retrospective memo, rather than an actual veto.

Many, or most, difficult decisions for the producer focus, in fact, on logistics and money. If television is an art-form, it is a cumbersome and expensive one. If the producer is an auteur or author, he is an author who needs the active involvement of thirty or forty other people, expensive equipment, studio space and – not least – a network to transmit the end-product. Few people who have not been involved in television recognize how much work, energy and time in programme preparation go into polishing and refining small details; dotting the 'i's and crossing the 't's is an elaborate undertaking in this thousands-of-pounds-per-minute medium.

The producer role encompasses elements not only of the civil servant but of a latter-day Renaissance Man, capable of playing all the parts. The producer ideally should be good with both words and pictures, the two main building blocks of television. He or she needs some basic grasp of TV technology, of tape against film, of sound, lighting and sets; requires (usually extensive) specialist knowledge of the particular programme genre, such as drama or news; needs to be able to juggle ideas against finance; needs plenty of sheer energy; needs some performance skills – the ability to enthuse and activate others during a long working day; and needs diplomatic skills to smooth ruffled egos and to persuade outsiders to do things at different times and for less money than they would prefer.

This civil servant, macho-military, Renaissance Man, creative manager was in practice usually a man – a white, responsible, British male who could be trusted to do a decent job in difficult circumstances. Some of this tradition has now changed in ways favourable to women – if not to ethnic minorities – but the point remains that the producer role was traditionally conceived as male.

FROM INTEGRATED-FACTORY PRODUCTION

Until 1982 British television consisted of just two vertically integrated organizations (BBC and ITV) which each made the bulk of the programmes in its own factories (or studios), assembled the schedule and transmitted it over a national network. This 'integrated-factory' approach derives from BBC radio, where the radio studios could be tucked quietly away in the basement. In the case of television the studios were larger, but were still placed at the lower levels of buildings; above ground were the programme-makers' offices and on the top floor were the senior managers. British television was vertically integrated both as an industry and within its own buildings.

There are two other possible production systems which in the 1990s are both increasingly important. In 1982 Channel Four introduced the 'publisher' concept to Britain; it 'published' (assembled and transmitted) programming commissioned and acquired from other producers. By the early 1990s, on government direction, this publisher model was also increasingly followed in both ITV and BBC television.

There is also a third model, that of the 'packager', which prevails in cable and satellite systems. Cable did not get far in 1980s Britain, but from 1990 satellite offerings did attract customer-households in increasing numbers. These satellite and cable channels are typically themed to one specific genre such as news, sport or movies. The cable or satellite provider typically packages the channels with programming acquired in bulk from large suppliers of news, sport, movies, and so on.

By 1990 the Channel Four publisher model was well established and, along with it, a distinction between, on the one hand, 'commissioning editors' inside Channel Four, and, on the other hand, outside producers who actually made the programming. The packager model was also starting to become entrenched; the packager, of course, only directly employs very small numbers of producers.

Up to about 1990, however, the integrated-factory system of production remained the normal and dominant pattern. In the 1970s the British TV producer had been largely insulated from fierce head-to-head competition and from harsh financial pressures. For a period of eighteen years (1964–82) there were just three channels, with the audience in effect amicably shared 50/50 between one ITV channel and two BBC channels. The audience was offered large rations of educational and informational programming as well as entertainment. There was plenty of money – with all the booming advertising revenue supporting just one channel, and a steadily growing licence fee (as consumers switched to colour sets) going to the BBC; British television in the 1970s was much more generously funded than was western Europe's television overall.

Television producers lived a sheltered life within a system based on consensus and cartel. There was a consensus between the political parties and between broadcasters schooled in the BBC and ITV versions of public service. The trade unions also played a central role, favouring good-quality British programming, a broad mix of programming genres, and strict quotas of cheap programme imports. The unions got secure employment for their members, with extremely generous levels of manning and overmanning.

The ITV network was a cartel of non-competing regional companies which had a monopoly on TV advertising; the regulatory body, the Independent Broadcasting Authority, required it to carry quotas of non-entertainment, mainly factual, programming. Each of the ITV companies bargained fiercely to keep its share of programming airtime, which meant that even ITV's entertainment programming was supplier-driven and less than 100 per cent market-orientated.

[...]

While a few established (popular or prestige) successes might run for 25 or 35 weeks per year, most British TV series conformed to a mini-series pattern of as few as 6, and no more than 13, programmes per year. Popular situation comedies, for example, could take 15 years to accumulate 100 episodes. This mini-series emphasis fitted both ITV cartel-bargaining and BBC deference towards TV writers; it fitted also with the producers' perception that quantity often led to reduced quality.

This mini-series system of short runs – but lengthy preparation and extended filming/recording – reflected producers' interests. The performers (such as actors) were not very highly rewarded in British television; nor were the army of (mainly women) clerical and support staff. The people who did well were the producers and their teams and the highly unionized technicians; they were fairly well paid, securely employed, not over-worked on very long series runs, and provided with interestingly varied work.

[...]

British producers, as late as 1990, still lived in a world in which cash and specific sums of money were not the effective currency. A producer in practice worked primarily within a budget, not of money, but of resources. These resources would involve people – such as researchers, reporters, actors, the design people and the studio crew; second, there would be the studio spaces and the use of outdoor film or outside broadcast units; and third, there was the time for which these people and resources were allocated – often very generous by international standards. In addition, the producer would have some cash (for travel, staying in hotels and so on) but knew that the cash element was only a fraction of the total cost. The producer had little idea of the real cost and often suspected, or knew, that the ITV company itself or the BBC also did not know the real cost: so why should the producer bother? Even the concept of 'over-spending' the budget was a vague one, because – in these vertically integrated organizations with their permanent facilities and staff – there was no agreed cost that could be attached to, say, one extra day for forty people and a studio.

With many short runs of 6 or 7 programmes, the producer might have only a hazy idea of the intended audience, the real cost, or the real goal (from the company's viewpoint). Given this degree of vagueness, the producer was also likely to be unclear how 'success' could be defined.

In keeping with this traditional lack of concern for financial detail, produ-cers – despite being managers – were given little or no management prepara-tion. Indeed, the recruitment process, which focused broadly on artistic skills and education in the humanities, selected and promoted some people who were not good at arithmetic. Finance was seen by some producers as a tiresome chore which could safely be entrusted to a unit manager or some other member of the production team.

AROUND 1990: BRITAIN'S TV REVOLUTION

[...]

The publisher element in British broadcasting gradually expanded in the decade after 1982. Initially, Channel Four only had a few per cent of the British TV audience; by the late 1980s both it and the independent-production sector were getting larger. The Thatcher Government then set a 25 per cent inde-pendent-production target for ITV and later (in the 1990 Act) for the BBC. During the early 1990s it became increasingly clear that both the BBC and ITV would contract out more than 25 per cent of the production to outside prod-ucers. The four new ITV companies which in 1991 won new franchises from the previous incumbents all began broadcasting in 1993 using the publisher model. By 1993 the four conventional British channels were operating two production systems alongside each other. The two advertising-financed chan-nels – Channel Four and ITV – now operated predominantly the publisher model. The BBC still operated mainly as an integrated factory but was also moving towards the publisher model.

What made the changes around 1990 indeed revolutionary – compared with normal British slow evolution – was that around 1990 not only the second publisher system but also the third system – the packager – was arriving on the British scene. This was a move not just to one additional channel but to multiple additional channels.

[...]

[From about 1988 'casualization' became a major trend.]

'Casualization' had several aspects. First, there was a massive reduction in regular employment. In 1987–8 the ITV companies were employing 17,000 people to run a single national channel (with some regional programming); by 1993 ITV employed 6,000 fewer. The BBC – especially from 1990 – began cutting staff, although it favoured many small bites of a hundred or two hundred redundancies rather than the ITV big-bang approach.

Second, there was a marked shift towards employing people on short contracts, usually for a few months. Consequently in the early 1990s some people (mainly aged over 40) were permanently employed on the old life-long basis; some senior people were on contracts of a few years; many producers were on contracts of one year or six months; more junior production personnel were often employed for the few months of the series run. In the technical studio areas there was a similar range.

Third, another major facet was the closing of studio buildings. In their vertical factories both the BBC and ITV companies had too much production capacity, too many buildings and too many studios. With the move towards contracting production out to independents it gradually became evident that this over-capacity was on a massive scale. In late 1991 the BBC announced a 40 per cent cut in its capacity for studios and facilities.

Fourth, there was a quite overt attack on the trade unions. This had been a repeated theme in Thatcher Government rhetoric and policy documents in the 1980s. The broadcasting trade unions – in the 1970s of legendary strength – now saw their power rapidly reduced. There was a spate of trade-union mergers, resulting in one main union, BECTU (its full name – Broadcasting, Entertainment, Cinematograph and Theatre Union – indicates its genealogy).

These numerous changes and forms of casualization had multiple impacts on British TV producers. Many producers interviewed for this study had entered television in the 1960s or 1970s when it offered extremely secure employment:

> If you were any good, they expected and wanted you to stay there for life.

By the early 1990s producers felt themselves to be in a fairly insecure job, which now involved working here for a year or two before moving on to some other organization.

The 1990 changes also involved various forms of slimming-down and speeding-up. The slimming-down affected not only the number of people on a camera-crew but the number of people responsible for researching, filming and editing a programme. Speeding-up took different forms in different genres; but in drama, for instance, a producer who in the mid-1980s might have had 15 days to film an hour's drama would by the early 1990s have been reduced to 10 or 11 days.

[...]

LESS SECURE, MORE AUTONOMOUS

During the recent years of turbulence, British TV producers have undergone a paradoxical combination of changes: they have become less secure but more autonomous.

Few British TV producers would deny that producers overall have become less secure in recent years. This study has focused on producers whose names were in the *Radio Times* attached to productions just being transmitted. Many other producers were becoming ex-producers; indeed, a number of the producers we interviewed in 1990 were already ex-producers by 1992.

How, then, can they have become more autonomous at the same time? The paradox derives from a significant shift in the nature of the producer's job. Those producers who are (still) working are being asked to do more things than was the case before 1986. First, producers have been forced to take budgeting more seriously. Second, producers (especially in fields such as documentary and drama) are increasingly expected to take part in raising finance. Third, with the increasing contracting-out of programming by the BBC and ITV, many working producers are not only producing programmes but commissioning them out to other producers.

Fourth, producers are required to make more decisions about resources and encouraged to use outside freelance camera-crews, studios or graphics specialists, instead of the BBC's or the ITV company's own in-house facilities. The BBC in 1992 launched its new effort of this kind called 'Producer Choice'; the BBC made clear that choices would rest with series producers and not with heads of output departments.

All this adds up to more work, more responsibility, more control and more autonomy – for those producers who are still producing.

A PROFESSION?

Television producers do not constitute a profession.

Television producers collectively have some similarities to the many occupations which have been professionalizing in recent decades; but TV producers have not tried very hard to do the classic things normally done by occupations which have a strong urge to professionalize.

Television producers have not tried to control entry; on the contrary, entry has become more open. Television producers have not set up a 'qualifying association' which vets qualifications, establishes standards and the like. Television producers lack 'clients' of the kind that doctors, lawyers, architects or teachers claim to serve. Although TV producers are serving the general public, their 'hands-on' work refers not to clients or patients but to cameras, scripts, editing, performers – the business of TV production, not TV consumption.

There is another simple reason why British TV producers are not likely to go much further in a professional direction. In British television the producers –

more than any other occupational category – are, or become, the general managers. Apprentice producers can start as 'researcher' and eventually become chief executive. This occupation of producer is not only a lengthy career-ladder, but also fits closely with the organizational hierarchy from bottom to top.

The TV-producer role covers a very wide horizontal range in terms of genres and types of output. In recent years the producer role has become further fragmented by the introduction of two new industrial systems, each of which introduced new definitions of producer to the British scene. The publisher model introduced the 'commissioning editor' and the 'independent producer'; the satellite or cable channels give weight to the acquisition and packaging of large flows of pre-existing production.

Some associations and organizations of a 'professional' kind do exist. There is the Royal Television Society which holds conferences and awards prizes. There are bodies which lobby on behalf of independent producers. Trade unions, although now weaker, still exist.

There is, however, no single body which seeks to preserve, defend and advance the interests of TV producers in Britain. The producers are too involved in their organizations – many devote their 'professional' loyalty to the BBC which they see as preserving the kind of television they believe in; indeed, many ITV and independent producers also express deep loyalty to the BBC and what it stands for.

Producers' deep involvement in their private genre-worlds is also in part both cause and effect of this lack of professional feeling or organization.

AN ELITE OCCUPATION?

Television production is not an elite occupation.

This study indicates that TV production is a well-established occupational category but the term 'elite' certainly does not fit many producers' social backgrounds. The [254] producers interviewed in this study are not a representative sample of all TV producers. Of those interviewed about one-quarter were educated at either Oxford or Cambridge; about another quarter were at one of another small group of institutions (including two London University colleges – the London School of Economics and University College – as well as Bristol, York, East Anglia and Manchester Universities). The majority of these producers did not attend fee-paying schools; more went to grammar schools or comprehensives. In terms of their social and educational origins these producers' backgrounds are broadly middle-class and meritocratic. Despite having lived in London most of their adult lives, many of these producers speak with some trace of a British regional accent. In this respect, and in others, the producers are probably very similar to their presenters whose faces appear on the screen.

These are jobs, however, which many young people would like to do. A number of producers complained about the huge numbers of applicants that a single newspaper advertisement for a 'TV researcher' would attract. This occupation, of course, has no specific entry-qualification.

[...]

PRODUCER AS EMPLOYER

In British television, the producer (of various kinds) has taken over some functions previously performed by management and also by trade unions; increasingly, the producer is becoming the effective employer.

'We have removed an entire tier of management' said one senior executive of an ITV company. Some of the functions previously performed by both specialist and general management are now heaped on to the producer.

The same is true of the trade unions, which until about 1986 in practice managed much of what went on in the craft areas. For example, the unions operated penally high overtime rates of pay which greatly affected the entire practice of location filming. The construction of sets, the operation of studios, the outside broadcasting of sporting events – all of these areas of work were partly managed by unions and partly managed by management. When trade-union power radically declined after 1986, these management tasks were not given back to management, which itself was slimming down radically.

The producer of a series run often has one, two or three million pounds to spend; and there are several possible strategic paths which could be followed. Do you do all the location filming first? Do you work alternate weekends? Do you start in the studio when the days are shorter in March? In the past all such decisions were heavily influenced by union rules. Now it is the producer who sits down, maybe for quite a long time, worrying away at the cheapest and most efficient use of the available time, resources and people. The producer makes a management plan, carries it out and is held responsible for it.

Increasingly, the producer is not just a general manager; the producer is also coming to be the effective employer. This latter has happened most obviously in independent production; but it is happening also within the BBC and ITV. With the short series runs so common in British television, employment is very often for a few months; it is the producer who effectively employs the production team, and increasingly also the technical crew, for those weeks or months. The producer who from 'inside' the BBC or an ITV company takes on a production team – via the personnel department – is increasingly likely to be either a freelance producer employed for that short series run, or a producer on a contract of perhaps one year.

British television is no less – probably more – producer-driven today than before 1986. The production systems have changed and the publisher system has become central; but the production culture has remained the same, in focusing on the producer as the person who holds the reins. The overall system has increasingly fragmented into smaller programme-making units. Everyone seems to agree that to the question of who should be in charge, in most cases the answer has to be the producer. If the producers are not driving the system, no other suitable occupational category – under British conditions – is available to do the job.

[...]

TOWARDS 2022

In the 1990s the competitive pressures and industrial changes will continue to make for major changes in the working conditions of producers. As the average series size (in hours and episodes) increases – and there are fewer very-short series – the balance between the numbers of 'executive producers' and 'series producers' will shift. The executive producer, instead of being in charge of several short series and their series producers, will increasingly be in charge of just one big series.

The executive producer will be supported by a larger team of fairly senior producers and script editors. It will become more rare for one director or producer-director to direct all the programmes in a series. The typical series will employ not only more producers, but also more writers and more directors. The status of the individual director is likely to decline since he or she will only be directing, say, 4 programmes in a series of 26 programmes. Directors will have less say in the script–filming–editing sequence overall, some directors may cease to be involved in the post-production editing of their 'own' work.

WOMEN PRODUCERS

The proportion of producers who are women will greatly increase, especially in the BBC; in more and more genres within the BBC women will be in the majority. This advance of women producers will have a massive impact across British broadcasting and beyond.

Around 1989–90 the BBC began to take seriously equal opportunities for women (it was slower in the case of ethnic minorities). Even though there was a pause or small falling back in the early 1990s, this policy has a big head of steam. The proportions of women producers at all levels will increase; and there will be a 'the more, the more' effect. Women tend to promote other women; some men do not want to work for women.

By 1992 the majority of the BBC's science TV programmes were produced by women. This trend will continue most strongly in documentary and edinfotainment areas. Drama will be in a middle position. Bringing up the rear will be sport, entertainment and comedy, although women will advance here also.

Not all producers, male or female, want to become executive producers. Probably a higher proportion of women producers prefer to stay in their present working-niche. Nevertheless, the proportions of women producers will increase for several reasons.

First, within the private worlds of the separate genres the promotion of even one or two women producers can have a big impact. When a success like *One Foot in the Grave* was produced by a woman, who could any longer say that women could not produce comedy?

Second, the BBC is especially attractive to women because of its vigorous equal-opportunities policy. There are large numbers of women in the BBC in the junior-producer ranks. They appear more willing than men to accept the BBC's lower rates of pay; although some women do become independent producers, they may be less inclined than men to go independent. As the independent sector continues to be so insecure and stressful, it looks increasingly a better bet for a woman – especially with children – to remain in the somewhat less insecure BBC.

Third, there may be a tendency for men to occupy BBC executive-producer jobs, employing a team of mainly women producers; but the BBC is committed to equality at all levels.

ITV can be expected to follow the BBC – as it often has – but at something of a distance. A number of men, as well as women, producers denounced the whole of ITV as 'male-chauvinist'. This was somewhat sweeping; but the ITC, although proclaiming its equal-opportunities loyalty, wasted a unique moment in the 1991 franchise round. However, the ITC will doubtless focus its attention on this issue in due course. There may also be anxiety within ITV that the BBC has an advantage in its greater proportion of women producers. The argument will be made that ITV depends on advertising aimed primarily at women consumers. This argument will eventually prove compelling, especially combined with the point that you may be able to pay women slightly less.

Increasingly in the later 1990s it will become apparent that the BBC is going to be the first major organization in Britain in which around half the senior management are women. This in turn will have consequences, not all of which can easily be predicted. One probable consequence is that still-stronger flows of well-qualified young women will be attracted to the BBC; it will be interesting to see how young men react.

This advance of women may not hugely change the programming output. BBC1 and ITV are already strongly ratings-driven and will get more so. However, the advance of women will finally remove those earlier conceptions of the TV producer as an ex-military man in charge of men.

[...]

PRODUCER-DRIVEN TELEVISION

British television during the 1990s will continue to be producer-driven.

The extent to which British television has fragmented, and will fragment, can be exaggerated. However, in so far as further fragmentation does occur in the 1990s, it will be producers who are in charge of the fragments. In this, as in much else, the new independent producers of the 1980s were showing the way which others would follow.

Increasingly sharp distinctions will be made between different categories of producers. One important distinction will be between buyers and sellers – the commissioning editor in the network who buys and the seller, who will be an independent production company or a freelance.

Executive Producers will be distinguished more sharply from the working, or line, producer. Increasingly, EP could as appropriately stand for 'Entrepreneur Producer'. The range of skills and knowledge ideally required of the senior producer will not be found in any single human being. Some producers will focus more on the creative side and still think of themselves as producer-directors or producer-writers; such creative producers may need especially strong support in finance and management. Other producers will be strongest on the financial and deal-making side of things; the packager, or deal-maker, or more finance-orientated producer may require stronger support on the creative side. Producers who combine both artistic and managerial creativity will be highly regarded and more highly paid than today's producers. British television will throughout the 1990s continue to be producer-driven.

[...]

So long as a mix of in-house production and the publisher system continues to predominate, then the broad producer-driven style of television [...] will prevail; but if, or when, the themed channels become the predominant, and no longer the minority, pattern, then the driving forces will be the operators of batches of themed channels and the operators of delivery systems. British producer-driven television will then be a thing of the past.

14

NEW PATTERNS IN GLOBAL TELEVISION

John Sinclair, Elizabeth Jacka, Stuart Cunningham

A sea-change in television systems around the world began in the late 1970s. An integral element in the various complex phenomena usually captured under the rubric of 'globalization', this transformation has forced the West to confront the television cultures of the more 'peripheral' regions of the world. Shifting geopolitical patterns within the world system, most notably the partial dismantling of national boundaries in Europe, the demise of communism, and the rise of the Asian economies, are having a profound effect on cultural ecologies and the consequent receptiveness of many regions of the world to new cultural influences, including new sources and kinds of television. Alongside this, and related to it, the last ten years have seen major changes in the television cultures of many countries as technological innovation, industrial realignments, and modifications in regulatory philosophy have begun to produce a new audiovisual landscape.

THE TRANSFORMATION OF THE AUDIOVISUAL LANDSCAPE

All these changes in turn have been part of a broader movement in the Western world, spearheaded by the USA and the UK, towards a 'post-Fordist' mode of organization of the economy, composed of four major elements – globalization, trade liberalization, increased national and international competition, and a decrease in the centrality of the state as a provider of goods and services. These tendencies in the advanced Western economies were all reflected in the arena of

From John Sinclair, Elizabeth Jacka, Stuart Cunningham (eds), *Peripheral Vision: New Patterns in Global Television* (Oxford: Oxford University Press, 1996) Ch. 1.

communications and the cultural industries, but with the added factor of a revolution in technology which promised, at least according to its enthusiasts, to provide many more channels than had ever been possible on the traditional bandwidth, and bring about a new era of diversity and choice in broadcasting services.

At the forefront of the technological changes in broadcasting technology was the satellite, which abolished distance and allowed for the first time the linking of remote territories into new viewing communities. There is no doubt that the satellite has acted as a kind of 'Trojan horse' of media liberalization. Although evidence from Europe and elsewhere indicates that satellite services originating outside national borders do not usually attract levels of audience that would really threaten traditional national viewing patterns, the ability of satellite delivery to transgress borders has been enough to encourage generally otherwise reluctant governments to allow greater internal commercialization and competition.

Until the late 1970s only three regions of the world (North America, Latin America, and Australia) had mixed systems of broadcasting, that is, some combination of public and private sectors. The ITV sector in the UK, though technically a privately owned commercial system, was so heavily regulated and protected from competition up until 1992 that to all intents and purposes it operated as a second public service network after the BBC. Everywhere else state-owned broadcasting dominated, either in the traditional public service version characteristic of Europe, or the state-controlled model common in Asia and the Middle East. As the 'Fordist' mode of capitalist economic and political organization began to crumble, this pattern began to change. First in Italy in the late 1970s, then in the mid- to late 1980s in other European countries, including Germany, France, The Netherlands, and the UK, privately owned commercial competitors to the public service monopoly were introduced. This process often proceeded in a back-door and rather chaotic fashion and the regulatory repercussions are still being felt. The process in Europe was enormously complicated by the contemporaneous move towards a united Europe with its parallel set of regulatory requirements (Silj, 1992).

The result of these upheavals was a very large increase in the number of channels available, and a consequent spreading of audience and revenue across a much greater range of services. This led to a shortage of product at the same time as the capacity of each service to pay for programmes was strained. In the early stages of the new services there was heavy dependence on USA imports, but it also led to a demand for programmes from new sources, including some formerly peripheral regions, such as Australia and Canada. Similarly, Latin American *telenovelas* began to enjoy popularity in southern Europe. At the same time, new satellite and cable delivery systems permitted the opening up of viable international channels for minority audiences, such as services available in Europe which carry entertainment and news programming from India and the Middle East.

By the beginning of the 1990s similar changes had begun to occur in Asia. The rapid development and opening up of Asian economies has not excluded the media industries. Advances in telecommunications are an inherent component of economic development, and the commercial entertainment possibilities of convergent telecommunication and television technologies have proved attractive to Asian entrepreneurs. However, [...] this development has produced an intense contradiction, harder and harder to reconcile, between liberalization at the economic level and a continued desire for political control and censorship at the cultural level. The same pattern of privately owned, entertainment-driven media that appeared in Europe in the 1980s can be seen in most of the emergent economies of Asia in the 1990s. Thus, the hunger for programmes seen in Europe also operates in the Asian market, and while the traditionally strong production industries of Hong Kong and India will continue to be major sources of product, programming from other sources, especially in the English language, will also be important. Furthermore, the emergence of new media services in countries like Malaysia, Indonesia, Singapore, and Korea has stimulated indigenous production industries in those countries, so that in the future they in turn might develop an export capacity, even if it were to remain a regional rather than a global one.

The most significant innovation has undoubtedly been the advent of STAR TV, the pan-Asian satellite service which operates from Hong Kong. Asian television cultures traditionally have been heavily controlled politically and protected from a high level of Western programming, but STAR TV has introduced them to new sources of programming, especially from the West, and exposed them to diverse sources of news reporting. Although the advent of STAR TV seems to demonstrate that attempts to control the national television space are fruitless, some Asian governments still seek to maintain bans on satellite receiver dishes, notably China, Malaysia, and Singapore.

In the Americas, where the privately owned commercial model has been the norm since television's inception in the 1950s, the 1980s have also brought significant changes, again stimulated by the potential of the new technologies and a more deregulatory mood. In the USA cable technology has facilitated the proliferation of new specialist channels which cater for all sorts of minorities, including ethnic minorities. This has created new viewing sub-communities on both a national and a transnational basis. While some programming for these services is produced inside the USA, a great amount of it is imported from those countries from which the immigrant and exile communities are drawn, including many countries of Asia and Latin America. [...] [T]he strongest television economy of Latin America, Mexico, has not been slow to exploit the possibilities offered by the very sizeable Spanish-speaking population of the largest and richest television market in the world, and has benefited from both its programme exports to the USA and its ownership of the major Spanish-language network within it.

Even in the Middle East, which is undoubtedly the most closed and controlled television region in the world, the satellite has brought transnational
services which cross borders within the Arab world. [...] [T]his is a cause of
some friction between countries which share a common language but have
distinct political and cultural orientations. Furthermore, comparable to some
international Asian services, the existence of sizeable Arab populations outside
the Middle East, mainly in Europe, North America, and Asia, opens up new
overseas markets for Arab-language programming.

What emerges from this sketch of changes in world television is indeed an
extremely complex picture, better described by Michael Tracey's image of a
'patch-work quilt' (1988: 24), than by Kaarle Nordenstreng and Tapio Varis's
'one-way street' metaphor of the 1970s (1974). In this new vision, global,
regional, national, and even local circuits of programme exchange overlap and
interact in a multi-faceted way, no doubt with a great variety of cultural effects,
which are impossible to conceptualize within the more concentric perspective
appropriate to previous decades. Instead of the image of 'the West' at the centre
dominating the peripheral 'Third World' with an outward flow of cultural
products, this book [Sinclair et al., 1996] sees the world as divided into a
number of regions which each have their own internal dynamics as well as their
global ties. Although primarily based on geographic realities, these regions are
also defined by common cultural, linguistic, and historical connections which
transcend physical space. Such a dynamic, regionalist view of the world helps us
to analyse in a more nuanced way the intricate and multi-directional flows of
television across the globe.

NEW PATTERNS OF TELEVISION FLOW

Public discourse about television and the media-studies literature are both
replete with anxiety about the supposed cultural effects of the global spread
of programmes like *Dallas* (Silj, 1988: 22–58) or, more recently, *Beverly
Hills 90210*. The unquestioned basis for this anxiety is expressed in the
orthodox critical paradigm for analysing the connection between international
power relations and the media, the thesis of 'cultural imperialism', or more
particularly, 'media imperialism'. According to this view, world patterns of
communication flow, both in density and in direction, mirror the system of
domination in the economic and political order. Thus, world centres like New
York, Los Angeles, London, and Tokyo are major nodes for international
telecommunications traffic, as well as for other kinds of flows, such as television
programmes. The media imperialism perspective more particularly sees that the
major world sources for programme exports are located in the USA and
secondarily in Europe, mainly the UK, and that these centres act as nodes
through which all flows of cultural products must pass, including those from
one peripheral part of the world to another.

The *locus classicus* of the cultural imperialism thesis is found in the work of
Herbert Schiller. As recently as 1991, in an article tellingly entitled 'Not Yet the

Post-Imperialist Era', he has restated his position in the following way: 'The role of television in the global arena of cultural domination has not diminished in the 1990s. Reinforced by new delivery systems – communication satellites and cable networks – the image flow is heavier than ever. Its source of origin also has not changed that much in the last quarter of the century' (p. 15). The classic study for UNESCO by Nordenstreng and Varis in 1974 cited earlier documented the dominance of the USA in world television programme exports at that time. Television programme flows became an integral issue for the New World Information Order movement and its debate within UNESCO. As this continued into the 1980s, the cultural imperialism view of international domination stood challenged only by those who were seen as apologists for the USA and its demand for a 'free flow' international regime for trade in cultural products. Neither critics nor apologists questioned the oft-quoted factoid that entertainment is second only to aerospace as an export industry for the USA (Carveth, 1992: 707).

Indeed, as long as the flows of television programme exports seemed to continue along the 'one-way street' from the West (and the USA in particular) to the rest of the world, the critical discourse of cultural imperialism was a plausible theoretical response, at least in its more subtle variations, notably that of 'cultural dependence' (Salinas and Paldán, 1974), and 'media imperialism' (Boyd-Barrett, 1977). In an essential respect, the cultural imperialism perspective was the then-current neo-Marxist analysis of capitalist culture projected on to an international scale: the 'dominant ideology' thesis writ large. As such, it had the all-embracing appeal of a comprehensive theory, and also provided the high moral ground from which the international activities of USA networks and the ideological content of their television programmes could be analysed, and then denounced.

However, by the mid-1980s it became evident that the cultural imperialism discourse had serious inadequacies, both as theory and in terms of the reality which the theory purported to explain. Actual transformation of the world television system made it less and less sustainable on the empirical level, and shifting theoretical paradigms, including postmodernism, postcolonialism, and theories of the 'active' audience, made its conceptual foundations less secure (Sinclair, 1990; Tomlinson, 1991; McAnany and Wilkinson, 1992; Naficy, 1993). To take the empirical aspect first, Jeremy Tunstall had long since pointed out that the 'television imperialism thesis' of such writers as Schiller (1969) and Wells (1972) was based on the quite incorrect assumption that the high levels of USA programme imports into Latin America in the 1960s were a permanent condition rather than a transitional stage in the development of television in these regions (1977: 38–40). The other empirical development which ought to have given pause to theorists of cultural imperialism was the research reported by Varis as an update of the original 'one-way street' project, in which he noted 'a trend toward greater regional exchanges', in spite of continued USA and European dominance in television programme flows

(1984). This finding was reinforced by other studies around the same time which, although absurdly exaggerated in their estimation of how far the flows had formed new patterns, were able nevertheless to document just how one such regional market was taking shape, in the case of Latin America (Rogers and Antola, 1985).

Thus, even in Latin America, virtually the cradle of the theorization of cultural imperialism, USA imports were prominent only in the early stages. As the industry matured in Latin America, and as it developed 'critical mass', USA imports were to some extent replaced by local products, a pattern that can be found repeated many times over around the world, and which is currently shaping Europe's new privately owned services. Of course, not all countries in Latin America have the capacity to develop sizeable indigenous television production industries. Rather, the pattern in Latin America, as in Asia and the Middle East, is that each 'geolinguistic region', as we shall call them, is itself dominated by one or two centres of audiovisual production – Mexico and Brazil for Latin America, Hong Kong and Taiwan for the Chinese-speaking populations of Asia, Egypt for the Arab world, and India for the Indian populations of Africa and Asia. The Western optic through which the cultural imperialism thesis was developed literally did not see these non-Western systems of regional exchange, nor understand what they represented. Yet by the late 1980s, Tracey could observe that the 'very general picture of TV flows ... is not a one-way street; rather there are a number of main thoroughfares, with a series of not unimportant smaller roads' (1988: 23).

We have noted how, as theory, the cultural imperialism critique tended to identify the USA as the single centre of a process of mediacentric capitalist cultural influence which emanated out to the rest of the world in the form of television programmes. It also assumed that these programmes had an inevitable and self-sufficient ideological effect upon their helpless audiences in the periphery. Although this rationale established a theoretical connection between US television programmes and 'consumerism', it did not address the question of just how such a mechanism of effect might work, nor how it could be observed in action upon actual audiences. In the discourse of cultural imperialism, the mystique of television entertainment's multivalent appeal for its audiences, and how specific audiences responded to it, were never on the agenda.

Other shortcomings arose from the theory's emphasis on external forces from the USA, and the corresponding disregard for the internal sociological factors within the countries seen to be subject to them. In its eagerness to hold US companies, and behind them, the US government, responsible for regressive sociocultural changes in the 'Third World', the cultural imperialism critique neglected the internal historical and social dynamics within the countries susceptible to their influence. This left out of consideration the strategic social structural position of the individuals and interest groups who benefited from facilitating US market entry or even from taking their own initiatives. Some of these have subsequently built up their own international media empires, as have Mexico and Brazil. Other players have more recently joined the game, such as investors from Saudi Arabia, while investment in the new channels in India by expatriates [...] shows that media entrepreneurism also can be widespread on a small scale. The cultural imperialism theory failed to see that, more fundamental than its supposed ideological influence, the legacy of the USA in world television development was in the implantation of its systemic model for television as a medium – the exploitation or entertainment content so as to attract audiences which could then be sold to advertisers. American content may have primed this process, but as the experience of many parts of the peripheral world shows, it is not required to sustain it.

We should also note that with its dichotomized view of 'the West' versus the 'Third World', the cultural imperialism theory was unable to give an adequate account of semi-peripheral settler societies such as Australia and Canada, where the experience or colonialism, and postcolonialism, has been quite distinct from that of nations in other former colonized zones, a distinctiveness manifest in the television systems which they developed.

The basic assumption of Western domination via television is worth further comment. Paradoxically, even though the cultural imperialism thesis has been articulated in the name of defending the 'Third World' against domination by audiovisual products from the USA, it is more inclined to reinforce Western cultural influence by taking it as given, when it should be challenging it. A more postcolonial perspective in theory has forced us to realize that USA domination always was limited, either by cultural or political 'screens', or both. A related weakness or 'blind spot' of the cultural imperialism thesis has been its over-emphasis on the significance of imported *vis-à-vis* local television. Television has always been more of a local than a global medium, and remains so, although the increasingly multichannel and globalized nature of the industry may alter the balance at the margin in the longer term. According to figures from 1989, the volume of purely domestic material in national markets is twenty-nine times higher than that which is traded (O'Regan, 1992). Television is still a gloriously hybrid medium, with a plethora of programming of an inescapably and essentially local, untranslatable nature.

Although US programmes might lead the world in their transportability across cultural boundaries, and even manage to dominate schedules on some channels in particular countries, they are rarely the most popular programmes where viewers have a reasonable menu of locally produced material to choose from. And even where there is imported content, it is no longer acceptable to read off from that fact alone any presumed effects of a cultural or political kind. Hamid Naficy captures this vividly in his brilliant study of television amongst Iranian exiles in Los Angeles. Describing how his exclusively English-speaking Iranian daughter, Shayda, and his exclusively German-speaking Iranian niece, Setarah, communicated through the Disney film, *The Little Mermaid*, he goes on to comment:

> The globalization of American pop culture does not automatically translate into globalization of American control. This globalized culture provides a shared discursive space where transnationals such as Setarah and Shayda can localize it, make their own uses of it, domesticate and indigenize it. They may think with American cultural products but they do not think American. (Naficy, 1993: 2)

If the discourse of cultural imperialism has proven inadequate to understand the more complex international patterns of television production, distribution, and consumption as they became evident in the 1980s, and the responses which audiences make to the television available to them, what new theories have become available which might serve these purposes? As Richard Collins has observed, there has been no adequate replacement for the fallen 'dominant ideology paradigm' in which cultural imperialism theory had grounded its view of the world (1990: 4–5). One important reason for this is that in the process by which postmodernism has succeeded neo-Marxism as the master paradigm in social and cultural theory, the new orthodoxy has taught us to be sceptical of such 'grand narratives' or totalizing theories as that of cultural imperialism.

Yet, it must also be said that within postmodernism itself there is no clear theoretical model with which to understand the international trade in television programmes. On the contrary, postmodernism has tended to valorize the fractured cultural meanings of all images and goods, and to conflate the actual processes by which they are produced, distributed, and consumed. In this context, it is ironic to recall the exhortation of Jorge Schement and his colleagues more than a decade ago that we disengage from the 'grand theory' of both the 'free flow' and the 'American hegemony' paradigms in favour of Robert Merton's 'theory of the middle range' (1984), yet this now appears to be just the level of abstraction to which we should now climb down the ladder.

HOME ON THE MIDDLE RANGE: GEOLINGUISTIC REGIONS

Germane amongst theories at this more modest rung of explanation is the classical economists' notion of 'comparative advantage', which now has been renovated as 'competitive advantage' (Porter, 1986), and applied to explain the traditional dominance enjoyed by the USA in the international trade in audiovisual products. Colin Hoskins and Stuart McFadyen argue that of the several comparative advantages enjoyed by audiovisual producers in the USA, the most crucial is their 'unique access to the largest market' (1991: 211–12). The US domestic market, while heterogeneous in terms of its cultural mix, is more or less homogeneous in terms of language, and so represents the largest English-language market in the world. The economies of scale and scope offered by the huge size of the domestic market can be exploited as a platform for audiovisual exports to the rest of the English-speaking world. In this respect, Collins's observations on English as 'the language of advantage' are fundamental:

> Works in English enjoy enormous advantages, for not only are anglo-
> phones the largest and richest world language community – excluding
> non-market economies . . . but English is the dominant second language
> of the world. The size and wealth of the anglophone market provides
> producers of English language information with a considerable compara-
> tive advantage *vis-à-vis* producers in other languages. But it is important
> to recognize that this is a *potential* advantage which may or not be
> realizable. (1990: 211)

He goes on to point out that the converse also holds, that is, that the USA and
other anglophone markets exhibit resistance against imported programmes in
languages other than English. Of course, such a 'cultural discount' (Hoskins
and Mirus, 1988) is also applied against English-language programmes in non-
anglophone markets, but nowhere near as much. Language is thus a natural
protective barrier as well as a basic source of advantage in the process by which
the USA has built up its pre-eminence within what we can call the 'geolinguistic
region' of English. This includes not only the anglophone countries, but also
those where English is widely used as a second language, or perhaps just by a
particular social stratum. It is worth emphasizing Collins's point that language
of production is a potential rather than necessary advantage, but [. . .] it is
clearly one which has been exploited with increasing success by both Canada
and Australia respectively, in spite of the relative disadvantages of their small
market size and their semi-peripheral, postcolonial, and derivative status within
the world that speaks English.

An even more striking feature of the new international media landscape
beyond the traditional anglophone centre, however, is the consolidation of the
trend to regional markets. As noted above, these also are geolinguistic rather
than just large, geographically contiguous regions, as international satellite
networks enable the television production centres of the major domestic
markets in the world's largest language regions to beam programmes across
the world to the 'imagined communities' of their diasporic concentrations and
former colonial masters in the metropolises of Europe and the USA. It is worth
noting, too, how far these new regional centres have been built upon already
existing centres of film production identified with characteristic popular tradeable 'hybrid' genres of their own, such as the Hong Kong action movie or Hindi
musical. [. . .] [T]his has been true to a considerable extent in the case of India in
particular. Latin America, which the 'geolinguistic region' explanation fits
particularly well, also has had its film production centres, but its tradeable
hybrid became the *telenovela*, a commercial television serial genre, reflecting
the long-standing commercialization of Latin American broadcasting.

Although some of these regions appear to have been victims of cultural
imperialism in the past, at least in terms of their heavy importation of US films
or television programmes, the pattern which had emerged by the mid-1970s
was that the 'countries which are strong regional exporters of media tend

themselves to be unusually heavy importers of American media' (Tunstall, 1977: 62). This suggests a process of indigenization in which the US generic models, in establishing themselves as 'international best practice', also invite domestic imitation. However, the substitute products become adapted to the local culture in the process, whether for market reasons, for the sake of diversity, or to diminish foreign influence, and new 'hybrid' genres are created.

The resulting situation is not the passive homogenization of world television which cultural imperialism theorists feared, but rather its heterogenization. Within the anglophone world, Australia and Canada, and even the UK, produce programmes which have assimilated the genre conventions of US television, but with their own look and feel. Outside of it, US genres (such as the MGM musical and the soap opera) have been adapted beyond recognition in a dynamic process of cultural syncretism. For it is cultural similarities in general, not just language in particular, that binds geolinguistic regions into television markets. Pan-Sino cultural elements allow programmes produced in Cantonese to cross easily into Mandarin, just as Spanish and Portuguese readily translate into each other in 'Latin' markets. Religion, music, humour, costume, nonverbal codes, and narrative modes are all elements in what Joe Straubhaar calls 'cultural proximity'. He hypothesizes that audiences will first seek the pleasure of recognition of their own culture in their programme choices, and that programmes will be produced to satisfy this demand, relative to the wealth of the market. Similar to Tunstall's prediction of the growth of a level of hybrid programme choice between the global and the local, Straubhaar argues that, in general:

> audiences will tend to prefer that programming which is closest or most proximate to their own culture: national programming if it can be sup-ported by the local economy, regional programming in genres that small countries cannot afford. The US continues to have an advantage in genres that even large Third World countries cannot afford to produce, such as feature films, cartoons, and action-adventure series. (1992: 14–15)

This is consistent with Hoskins and McFadyen's prognosis that US production will continue to increase, finding its strength especially in the prosperous 'North American/West European/Australasian market', but that it will also 'constitute a smaller share of an expanding market' in world terms as regional and national production also expands (1991: 221). This expansion will occur to the extent that competitors also develop comparative advantages such as the USA has enjoyed historically. As well as dominance of the largest market within a geolinguistic region, these include economies of scale, high levels of commercialization, and 'first mover advantage', especially where that is based on technical and stylistic innovation. Thus, with the important proviso that the flow of peripheral production is not so much displacing US production as finding its own intermediate level, the way is open to enquire into how these levels might be impacting upon the cultural identification and restratification of television audiences on a global scale. First, however, we should consider some other middle range theories which strive to account for the rise of peripheral nations' television export markets.

CROSS-CULTURAL TEXTUAL AND AUDIENCE ANALYSIS

Just as the cultural imperialism thesis has governed the analysis of industrial, technological, and linguistic factors which underpin peripheral nations' export activity, so has it informed how we should grasp the cross-cultural implications of such activity. John Tomlinson, in his careful examination of the discourse of cultural imperialism, contends that 'there is a definite sense of . . . "the moment of the cultural" being forever deferred' (1991: 40) in favour of the more solid evidence that seems to be delivered by a political economy approach. By this he means that factual accounts of media production and distribution too often have stood in place of an attempt to analyse exactly how domination, resistance, and negotiation work in the transfer and 'consumption' of cultural meaning by actual audiences. In his wide-ranging overviews of the idea of dominance in international television culture, Michael Tracey (1985, 1988) caustically draws attention to the 'curious . . . way the level of analysis employed for understanding the implications of the mass media at the international, as opposed to the national and individual level, has remained frozen at the stage of intellectual development achieved by communications research in the first three or four decades of this century' (1985: 44). In other words, cultural imperialism theory has been dogged by the outdated notion of an automatic media effect that, paradoxically, it shares with traditional US social science. Tracey submits that these crude models of cultural transmission and of the assumed cultural impact of economic and political influence are patently inadequate for the task of tracking cultural transfer.

Part of the reason for this inadequacy is that traditional grand theories have not given sufficient attention to the middle range factors that ought to be taken into account in explaining the relationship between the world television trade, the changing character of transmission technologies, and questions of cultural proximity and cultural screens. Current explanations for the popularity and success of imported television drama in particular range from arguments about textual form and content, to fortuitous placement in programme schedules. There is also the approach, most closely associated with John Fiske (1987), which focuses on the use to which particular programmes might be put by audiences – the pleasures they might gain and the cognitive, intersubjective and social experiences that might be generated around particular programmes.

In all these approaches the programmes that have attracted the most attention have been those which have had the greatest success in terms of ratings, high industrial or critical regard, or number of territories into which they have been sold. Commercial success is not a necessary precondition for choosing programmes for audience use studies, although in practice the two have gone together. It is generally more feasible and perhaps of more significance to study cross-cultural audience use of programmes with high and lasting international visibility. For these reasons, in the English-speaking literature it has been American programmes, almost without exception, which have been the object of critical or ethnographic audience studies.

We must ask what precisely it means, and how might it be possible, to carry out research on how audiences respond to television programmes from other cultures, and not just the dominant ones. Methodological protocols central to this line of investigation need modification to account for peripheral programme reception. When studies are restricted to reporting and analysis of the self-understanding of selected audience respondents, wider factors affecting the impact of programmes are often bracketed out, or treated superficially as just 'background'. Instead, the middle range research advocated here looks at the broader context of viewer reception set by the social environment; the professional practices of trading in, marketing, and scheduling television programmes, and the strategic role played by the 'gatekeepers' of the television industries, including owners, managers, and programme buyers.

In recent years a tradition of micro-situational audience analysis, influenced in some measure by 'ethnographic' anthropological methodologies, has been used to demonstrate the great variety of ways in which programmes are interpreted by different audiences in different 'places'. The best-known of these is undoubtedly the Tamar Liebes and Elihu Katz (1990) study of the reception of *Dallas*, the series which became 'the perfect hate symbol' of cultural imperialism critics in the 1980s (Mattelart *et al.*, 1984: 90). While this line of investigation is welcome as far as it goes, we want to argue that, just in itself, a micro approach is also inadequate to track the fortunes of the television exports of peripheral nations.

However, it is worth giving some attention to this landmark study to show why we believe this to be the case. It is an investigation of cross-cultural audience decodings of *Dallas* on three continents, in which the authors argue that the key reasons for the international popularity of US prime-time television, and especially serial/soap formats like *Dallas*, lie in:

> (1) the universality, or primordiality, of some of its themes and formulae, which makes programmes psychologically accessible; (2) the polyvalent or open potential of many of the stories, and thus their value as projective mechanisms and as material for negotiation and play in the families of man [*sic*]; and (3) the sheer availability of American programmes in a marketplace where national producers – however zealous – cannot fill more than a fraction of the hours they feel they must provide. (1990: 5)

However, it is clear that universality and primordiality are features of the genre as a whole rather than peculiar to US soap opera; even a cursory examination of, for example, Mexican and Brazilian *telenovelas* or Egyptian soap opera makes this clear. This criticism also holds for the second reason given. Thus, universality cannot account for the international success of US serials. The third reason that Liebes and Katz adduce is the one they least explore, yet it is far more significant than they allow. Indeed, there is something strangely decontextualized about the detailed recording and elegant analyses of their selected respondents in Israel, Japan, and the USA. 'Vigorous marketing', they say, 'is certainly a reason for the international success of *Dallas*' (1990: 4), but they pay almost no attention to this level of explanation.

This treatment should be compared with the analyses of the programme's introduction into foreign markets presented by Jean Bianchi (1984), and the *East of Dallas* research team led by Alessandro Silj (1988), which indicate that factors like scheduling, programme philosophy, and the cultural environment prior to the programme's reception militated against its success in countries such as Peru, or, for unexpected and surprising reasons, enhanced its success in countries such as Algeria. In the latter, a one-party nation with one television station (state-owned), *Dallas* was a popular success. 'One wonders', says Silj, 'why the television of an anti-imperialist, anti-capitalist state, the guardian of a social and family morality deeply marked by the Islamic religion, a pioneer of collective values ... should wish to put on a programme so imbued with antagonistic, "American" values' (1988: 36).

In the Peruvian case, where *Dallas* was not successful – it ran for less than a year – Silj's mode of explanation is industrial and cultural. *Dallas* became the losing card in a ratings battle between the two leading commercial channels when it was pitted against a local comedy programme. This seems to bear out Straubhaar's hypothesis, that successful local programming will tend to relegate US material to second or lower place. However, Silj is careful to remind us that the situation in Peru was a contingent one – had the local programme been of lesser quality the outcome may well have been reversed. Bianchi's and Silj's conclusions are that viewer reception is a dynamic process governed by the cultural identities of audiences and the 'sedimentation of other social practices' (Silj, 1988: 40); which we can take to mean, amongst other factors, the industrial and institutional conditions obtaining prior to any audience seeing any foreign programme.

'GATEKEEPERS' AND CULTURAL INDUSTRY FACTORS IN TELEVISION FLOWS

Many cross-cultural studies emphasize the diverse, localized character of international audience responses, and are imbued with a sense of the viability and integrity of the cultures of peripheral or 'small' nations. So it is somewhat ironic, because of the dominance of American programmes at highly visible though only provisionally premium places in schedules, that such studies should focus on US programmes almost exclusively. As Ellen Seiter argues strongly with regard to the theoretical field from which this position draws, 'in our concern for audiences' pleasures ... we run the risk of continually validating Hollywood's domination of the worldwide television market' (Seiter *et al.*, 1989: 5).

Far more than for the USA, the success or otherwise of peripheral nations' exports is contingent on factors other than those captured by established modes of audience study. This explains why so little audience reception research has been able to be conducted on their products in international markets, and why we need instead middle range analysis to do so. In the middle range between political economy approaches and reception analysis, a number of factors are mediating. How are programmes acquired overseas? Who engages in their appraisal and acquisition and what perceptions have they formed of peripheral programming? This 'primary audience' is the major source of informed 'gate-keeping' which regulates (in the widest sense) the flow of peripheral programming in international markets. And what are the characteristics of the major territories which influence the success or failure of such programmes internationally? All these mediating factors embody legitimate, indeed central, aspects of cultural exchange, as virtually all the significant research on non-dominant nations' television production and reception indicates (Lee, 1980; Silj, 1988; de la Garde *et al.*, 1993).

The actual structure of major international television trade markets is central to middle range analysis. There is an ever-wider variety of modes of contracting for international programme production and exchange: offshore, co-production, official co-production, co-venture (including presales), and straight purchase of territorial rights for completed programmes in the major trade markets such as MIP-TV and MIPCOM. These run on annual cycles suited to the programming and scheduling patterns of the major northern hemisphere territories, but a notable shift in the patterns of global television traffic was indicated in 1994 when the first MIP-Asia was held, a trade market specifically for the Asian region. At such events, programming is often bought (or not bought) on the basis of company reputation or distributor clout, in job lots and sight unseen. Very broad, rough-and-ready genre expectations are in play; judgements may seem highly 'subjective' and arbitrary.

Universalist explanations such as those of Liebes and Katz may prove useful in accounting for the international successes of historically universal forms like US series drama, but there is solid evidence that cultural specificities, along with other middle range industrial factors, are unavoidable and, at times, enabling factors for international success in peripheral countries' export activity. Studies which compare viewers' engagement with US as against other sources of television programming confirm that there tends to be a more distanced realm of 'pure entertainment' within which US programmes are processed – as markers of modish modernity, as a 'spectacular' world – compared to more culturally specific responses made to domestic and other sources (Biltereyst, 1991).

The capacity for peripheral countries to export their programmes across diverse markets is to some extent based on their substitutability or non-substitutability for US material, although this also depends in part on the type of channel they are purchased for. [...] Australian productions have provided useful models from which the protocols of commercial popularity may be learnt in rapidly commercializing European broadcasting environments, but the fact that Australian programmes are perceived as imitations of US formats constitutes a problem for both commentators and regulators in Europe (de Bens *et al.*, 1992).

To be sure, the structure of content and the form of internationally popular serial drama in particular are widely shared and may even be 'borrowed' from US practice, as the *telenovela* was decades ago. But the 'surface' differences, nevertheless, almost always are consequential, and contribute to the acceptance or rejection or non-US material, depending on whether the 'primary audience' of gatekeepers and the viewing audience respond positively or negatively to those differences. As Anne Cooper-Chen (1993) has shown, even that most transparently internationalized of television formats, the game show, contains significant differences in the widely variant cultures in which it is popular. After looking at popular game shows in fifty countries, she regards them as having at least three structural variants – the East Asian, Western, and Latin models – and innumerable surface particularities. Hamid Mowlana and Mehdi Rad (1992) show that the Japanese programme *Oshin* found acceptance in Iran because its values of perseverance and long-suffering were compatible with cultural codes prevalent in what might appear a distinctly different society. The evidence for the popularity of *Neighbours* in Britain demonstrates that, while Australian soaps arguably were brought into the market as substitutes for US material, their popularity built around textual factors based on projections and introjections of Australian 'life-style'. Australia has served in many ways as a kind of 'other' to Britain – the younger, more upstart and hedonistic vision of how the British might like to see themselves.

The 'export of meaning' is not just a matter of viewer reception. Many nations, both core and peripheral, place special importance on the international profile they can establish with their audiovisual exports. These are fostered both as a form of cultural diplomacy, and for intrinsic economic reasons, although national cultural objectives and audiovisual industry development are not always compatible, as Australia and Canada have long been aware, and some Asian countries are now learning. In the case of the Middle East, one commentator has observed that the popularity of Egyptian television exports in the Arab states has a number of cultural and even political 'multiplier effects'. This popularity was preceded by the success of Egyptian films, and carries with it a potential acceptance and recognition of Egyptian accents and performers that can operate as 'a soft-sell commercial for Egyptian values' which then carries over into indirect political leverage (M. Viorst, quoted in Tracey 1988: 12). While it might be difficult to isolate and measure them, it is not unreasonable to infer cultural, trade, and political multiplier effects from what can be seen of peripheral nations' products on the world's television screens.

'GLOBALIZATION': MORE THAN MEETS THE EYE

While it is fundamental that we recognize the new patterns of television programme exchange and service distribution to be global in their scale, this does
not mean that we must therefore conceive of them in any facile framework of
'globalization'. As Marjorie Ferguson has so vigorously pointed out, the concept
of globalization is shrouded in myth, and it is not at all clear that its protagonists
all mean the same thing by it (1992). At best, it is no more than a catch-all
category to refer to various trends towards more complex patterns of international circulation, not only of media products, but also of technologies, finance, people, and ideas (Appadurai, 1990). At worst, it is the ideological gloss
which the beneficiaries of these trends put upon them – the global village, at your
service. Ien Ang has argued that talk about globalization may have been 'part of a
short-lived rhetoric which coincided with a precise historical moment' during
the late 1980s and early 1990s. This was a period when news of major political
transformations, notably the end of the Cold War, and events such as Tiananmen Square and the Gulf War, were carried to the world by media with instantaneous global reach, such as CNN. These produced 'an apocalyptic sense of
globalised reality', but she suggests that our present and immediate future is
better characterized as a '*post*-globalised world rife with regional realignments
and fracturings, nationalist and ethnic separatisms, and, in parallel, a proliferation of overlapping and criss-crossing media vectors which undermine a unified
and singular notion of the "global"' (1994: 325). Thus, globalization has already
become a cliché that it is time to move beyond, and analysis of the new patterns
discernible in global television show a useful way in which this can be done.

Discussions of globalization often counterpose the global with the local, and
the local is in turn equated with the national. However, as we have already
suggested, in the analysis of television production and distribution on a world
scale it is important to distinguish not just the local from the national, but the
regional from the global. Of these distinct but related levels, it is the local and
the regional which have been most neglected in the literature to date. [...] Yet
several television industries of significant non-metropolitan countries have
built a presence outside their own borders. This includes the phenomenon of
'contra-flow' (Boyd-Barrett and Kishan Thussu 1992), where countries once
thought of as major 'clients' of media imperialism, such as Mexico, Canada,
and Australia, have successfully exported their programmes and personnel into
the metropolis – the empire strikes back.

For the regional level, and the national within the context of the regional,
'region' must now be understood to be geolinguistic and cultural as well as
geographic. A regional perspective on the development of television markets
brings to light national similarities, such as the widespread adoption of
commercial television in Latin America, or to take a familiar example from
the old metropolis, the wave of privatization and new services which has
transformed television in Europe since the mid-1980s. A regional, rather than

a global, perspective elucidates the connections between trade and culture, particularly in the potential impact which the formation of regional free-trade zones might have upon programme exchange, and in the clash of free-trade rhetoric with national cultural objectives. Again, the prominent example of a regional position is the EU's refusal to allow their audiovisual industries to be opened up to free trade under the GATT trade-in-services agreement, and instead seek to implement a European content quota. An instance which emphasizes the tension of the national and regional is NAFTA (North American Free Trade Agreement), in which Canada's insistence that its audiovisual industries be excluded contrasted with Mexico's position in which the protection of these industries was never an issue.

So long as television remained a terrestrial technology, there was less distance between the local and the national levels on one hand, and the national and the global on the other. However, satellite distribution has opened up regional and transcontinental geolinguistic markets, as we have argued, while terrestrial broadcasting and videocassettes have provided an additional but less immediate means for the distribution of television products to diasporic communities, notably those of Chinese, Arab, and Indian origin. Attention to this regionalization of markets gives greater insight into what is happening in the world than does the hollow rhetoric of globalization. Two instances of trends elucidated by a regional perspective are the rise of the regional entrepreneurs, and the restratification or audiences into 'imagined communities' beyond national boundaries.

Although Rupert Murdoch severed his national ties with Australia by taking up US citizenship in 1986, it remains the case that his rise to become perhaps the world's most spectacular media entrepreneur was based upon his initial accumulation of media assets in Australia, where he still controls almost 70 per cent of the daily press. From this base, literally on the periphery of the English-speaking world, he launched his ventures into the largest countries of that geolinguistic region, first Britain and then the USA. Even more peripheral in origin were the two generations of Azcárragas, whose dominance of the world's largest Spanish-speaking market in an erstwhile 'Third World' country has been turned into a platform for extensive operations in the USA as well as South America, and a toehold in Spain. In this respect, 'El tigre' (the tiger) Azcárraga is not 'Mexican' any more than Murdoch is Australian. If the term 'globalization' is to mean anything, it must take account of such deracination of corporations and entrepreneurs from 'their' nation-states, and furthermore, the more recent moves of these entrepreneurs in particular even beyond their geolinguistic regions. With Murdoch's purchase of STAR TV and Azcárraga's return to partnership in the PanAmSat international satellite corporation, we see both of them ratcheting up the scale of their operations so as to establish a strong presence in Asia, expected to be the fastest-growing regional media market of the next century. Also of note is the strategic alliance which they have made to exchange programming from each other's regions.

Benedict Anderson's concept of 'imagined communities' has been one of the most influential tropes in theories of national consciousness for more than a decade (1983), but as satellite television distribution transcends the borders of the nation-state, there is some value in applying it to the new audience entities which that process creates. Similarly, in the decades since Nordenstreng and Varis first drew attention to the transnational media's action upon 'the non-homogeneity of the national state' (1973), there have arisen international services which stratify audiences across national boundaries not just by class and education, but by 'taste culture' and age – the ostensible international youth culture audience for MTV, for example. Of more interest to us are the imagined communities of speakers of the same language and participants in similar cultures which form the geolinguistic regions exploited by the media entrepreneurs, especially the diasporic communities of émigrées on distant continents.

Even amongst the globalization theorists, it is becoming a commonplace to observe that the globalizing forces towards 'homogenization', such as satellite television, exist in tension with contradictory tendencies towards 'heterogenization', conceived pessimistically as fragmentation, or with post-modernist optimism, as pluralism. Thus, 'identity and cultural affiliation are no longer matters open to the neat simplifications of traditional nationalism. They are matters of ambiguity and complexity, of overlapping loyalties and symbols with multiple meanings' (Castles et al., 1990: 152). To the extent that we can assume that television is in fact a source of identity, and that audiences for the same programme derive similar identities from it, it becomes possible to think of identities which are multiple, although also often contradictory, corresponding to the different levels from which the televisual environment is composed in a given market. An Egyptian immigrant in Britain, for example, might think of herself as a Glaswegian when she watches her local Scottish channel, a British resident when she switches over to the BBC, an Islamic Arab expatriate in Europe when she tunes in to the satellite service from the Middle East, and a world citizen when she channel surfs on to CNN. In both the positivist mainstream and critical traditions of communication theory in the past, disregard for actual content, disdainful stereotypes of 'lowest common denominator' programming, and dichotomous thinking about tradition and modernity, all have prevented this more pluralistic conception of audience identity to surface. What it has required has been, firstly, the more recent theorization of multiple social identities being overlaid in the individual subject, and then the perception argued for here, that these identities are related to the local, national, regional, and global levels at which cultural products such as television programmes circulate.

REFERENCES

Anderson, Benedict (1983) *Imagined Communities: Reflections on the Origin and Spread of Nationalism* (Verso, London).

Ang, Ien (1994) 'Globalisation and Culture', *Continuum*, 8/2: 323–5.

Appadurai, Arjun (1990) 'Disjunction and Difference in the Global Cultural Economy', *Public Culture*, 2/2: 1–24.

Bianchi, Jean (1984) *Comment comprendre le succes international des séries de fiction a la television? – Le cas 'Dallas'*, Laboratoire CNRS/IRPEACS, Lyon.

Biltereyst, Daniel (1991) 'Resisting American Hegemony: A Comparative Analysis of the Reception of Domestic and US Fiction', *European Journal of Communication*, 7: 469–97.

Boyd-Barrett, Oliver (1977) 'Media Imperialism: Towards an International Framework for the Analysis of Media Systems', in J. Curran, M. Gurevitch, and J. Woollacott (eds.), *Mass Communication and Society* (Edward Arnold, London), 116–35.

—— and Kishan Thussu, Daya (1992) *Contra-flow in Global News: International and Regional News Exchange Mechanisms* (John Libbey, London).

Carveth, Rod (1992) 'The Reconstruction of the Global Media Marketplace', *Communication Research*, 19/6: 705–23.

Castles, Stephen, Kalantzis, Mary, Cope, Bill, and Morrissey, Michael (1990) *Mistaken Identity: Multiculturalism and the Demise of Nationalism in Australia* (2nd edn., Pluto Press, Sydney).

Collins, Richard (1990) *Television: Policy and Culture* (Unwin Hyman, London).

Cooper-Chen, Anne (1993) 'Goodbye to the Global Village: Entertainment TV Patterns in 50 Countries', paper presented to the conference of the Association for Education in Journalism and Mass Communication, Kansas City, August.

de Bens, Els, Kelly, Mary, and Bakke, Marit (1992) 'Television Content: Dallasification of Culture?', in K. Siune and W. Treutzschler (eds.), *Dynamics of Media Politics: Broadcast and Electronic Media in Western Europe* (Sage, London).

de la Garde, Roger, Gilsdorf, William, and Wechselmann, Ilja (eds.) (1993) *Small Nations, Big Neighbour: Denmark and Quebec/Canada Compare Notes on American Popular Culture* (John Libbey, London).

Ferguson, Marjorie (1992) 'The Mythology about Globalization', *European Journal of Communication*, 7: 69–93.

Fiske, John (1987) *Television Culture* (London, Routledge).

Hoskins, Colin, and McFadyen, Stuart (1991) 'The U.S. Competitive Advantage in the Global Television Market: Is it Sustainable in the New Broadcasting Environment?' *Canadian Journal of Communication*, 16/2: 207–24.

—— and Mirus, Roger (1988) 'Reasons for the US Dominance of International Trade in Television Programmes', *Media, Culture and Society*, 10/4: 499–515.

KPMG Management Consulting (1992) *A History of Offshore Production in the UK: A Report for the Australian Film Commission*, April.

Lange, André, and Renaud, Jean-Luc (1989) *The Future of the European Audiovisual Industry*, Media Monograph No. 10, European Institute for the Media, Dusseldorf.

Lee, Chin-Chuan (1980) *Media Imperialism Reconsidered: The Homogenizing of Television Culture* (Sage, London).

Liebes, Tamar, and Katz, Elihu (1990) *The Export of Meaning: Cross-Cultural Readings of 'Dallas'* (Oxford University Press, New York).

Mattelart, Armand, Delcourt, Xavier, and Mattelart, Michèle (1984) *International Image Markets* (Comedia, London).

McAnany, Émile, and Wilkinson, Kenton (1992) 'From Cultural Imperialists to Takeover Victims? Questions on Hollywood's Buyouts from the Critical Tradition', *Communication Research*, 19/6: 724–48.

Mowlana, Hamid, and Rad, Mehdi Mohensian (1992) 'International Flow of Japanese Television Programs: The "Oshin" Phenomenon', *KEIO Communication Review*, 14: 51–68.

Naficy, Hamid (1993) *The Making of Exile Cultures: Iranian Television in Los Angeles* (University of Minnesota Press, Minneapolis).

Nordenstreng, Kaarle, and Varis, Tapio (1973) 'The Nonhomogeneity of the National State and the International Flow of Communication', in G. Gerbner, L. Gross, and W. Melody (eds.), *Communications Technology and Social Policy* (Wiley, New York), 393–412.

—— and —— (1974) *Television Traffic – A One-Way Street?* (UNESCO, Paris).

O'Regan, Tom (1992) 'New and Declining Audiences: Contemporary Transformations in Hollywood's International Market', in Elizabeth Jacka (ed.), *Continental Shift* (Local Consumption Publications, Sydney), 74–98.

Porter, Michael (1986) *Competition in Global Industries* (Harvard Business School Press, Boston).

Rogers, Everett, and Antola, Livia (1985) '*Telenovelas*: A Latin American Success Story', *Journal of Communication*, 35/4: 24–35.

Salinas, Raquel, and Paldán, Leena (1974) 'Culture in the Process of Dependent Development: Theoretical Perspectives', in K. Nordenstreng and H. Schiller (eds.), *National Sovereignty and International Communication* (Ablex, Norwood, NJ), 82–98.

Schement, Jorge, González, Ibarra, Lum, Pairicia, and Valencia, Rosita (1984) 'The International Flow of Television Programmes', *Communication Research*, 11/2: 163–82.

Schiller, Herbert (1969) *Mass Communications and American Empire* (Augustus M. Kelley, New York).

—— (1991) 'Not Yet the Post Imperialist Era', *Critical Studies in Mass Communication*, 8: 13–28.

Seiter, Ellen, Borchers, H., Kreutzner, G., and Warth, E. (eds.), (1989) *Remote Control* (Routledge, London), 'Introduction', 1–15.

Silj, Alessandro (1988) *East of Dallas: The European Challenge to American Television* (British Film Institute, London).

—— (1992) *The New Television in Europe* (John Libbey, London).

Sinclair, John (1990) 'Neither West nor Third World: The Mexican Television Industry Within the NWICO Debate', *Media Culture and Society*, 12/3: 343–60.

Straubhaar, Joseph (1992) 'Assymetrical Interdependence and Cultural Proximity: A Critical Review of the International Flow of TV Programs', paper presented to the conference of the Asociación Latinoamericana de Investigadores de la Comunicación, São Paulo, August.

TBI (Television Business International) (1994) 'The 1994 TBI 100', *Television Business International* (March), 22.

Tomlinson, John (1991) *Cultural Imperialism* (John Hopkins University Press, Baltimore).

Tracey, Michael (1985) 'The Poisoned Chalice? International Television and the Idea of Dominance', *Daedalus*, 114/4: 17–56.

——, (1988) 'Popular Culture and the Economics of Global Television', *Intermedia*, 16/2: 9–25.

Tunstall, Jeremy (1977) *The Media Are American* (Constable, London).

Varis, Tapio (1984) 'The International Flow of Television Programmes', *Journal of Communication*, 34/1: 143–52.

Wells, Alan (1972) *Picture-Tube Imperialism? The Impact of US Television on Latin-America* (Orbis, Maryknoll, NY).

FURTHER READING

Boyce, G., Curran, J. and Wingate, P. (eds), *Newspaper History from the Seventeenth Century to the Present Day* (London: Constable, 1978).

Briggs, A., *The History of Broadcasting in the United Kingdom*, vols 1–5 (London: Oxford University Press, 1961–95).

Burns, T., *The BBC: Public Institution and Private World* (London: Macmillan, 1977).

Collins, R., *Television: Policy and Culture* (London: Unwin Hyman, 1990).

Collins, R., Curran, J., Garnham, N., Scannell, P., Schlesinger, P. and Sparks, C. (eds), *Media, Culture and Society: A Critical Reader* (London: Sage, 1989).

Collins, R., Garnham, N. and Locksley, G., *The Economics of Television: The UK Case* (London: Sage, 1988).

Curran, J. and Seaton, J., *Power without Responsibility: The Press and Broadcasting in Britain* (London: Routledge, 1992).

Drummond, P. and Paterson, R. (eds), *Television in Transition* (London: BFI, 1985).

Elliott, P., *The Making of a Television Series: A Case Study in the Sociology of Culture* (London: Constable, 1972).

Garnham, N., *Capitalism and Communication: Global Culture and the Economics of Information* (London: Sage, 1990).

Golding, P. and Murdock, G., 'Culture, Communications and Political Economy', in Curran, J. and Gurevitch, M. (eds), *Mass Media and Society* (London: Edward Arnold, 1991).

Halmos, P. (ed.), *The Sociology of Mass Media Communicators*, Sociological Review Monographs 13 (Keele: University of Keele, 1969).

Harvey, S., 'Deregulation, Innovation and Channel Four', *Screen* 30:1/2 (1989) pp. 60–78.

Koss, S., *The Rise and Fall of the Political Press in Britain*, 2 vols (London: Hamish Hamilton, 1981 and 1984).

Lee, A. J., *The Origins of the Popular Press* (London: Croom Helm, 1976).

Lewis, P. M. and Booth, J., *The Invisible Medium: Public, Commercial and Community Radio* (London: Macmillan, 1989).

MacCabe, C. and Stewart, O. (eds), *The BBC and Public Service Broadcasting* (Manchester: Manchester University Press, 1986).

Murdock, G., 'Large Corporations and the Control of the Communications Industries', in Gurevitch, M., Bennett, T., Curran, J. and Woollacott, J. (eds), *Culture, Society and the Media* (London: Methuen, 1982).

O'Malley, T., *Closedown? The BBC and Government Broadcasting Policy 1979–92* (London: Pluto Press, 1994).

Potter, J., *Independent Television in Britain*, vols 3 and 4 (London: Macmillan, 1987 and 1990).

Scannell, P. and Cardiff, D., *A Social History of British Broadcasting*, vol. 1, *1922–1939: Serving the Nation* (Oxford: Basil Blackwell, 1991).

Schlesinger, P., *Media, State and Nation* (London: Sage, 1991).

Sendall, B., *Independent Television in Britain*, vols 1 and 2 (London: Macmillan, 1982 and 1985).

Seymour-Ure, C., *The British Press and Broadcasting since 1945* (Oxford: Blackwell, 1991).

Tracey, M., *The Production of Political Television* (London: Routledge & Kegan Paul, 1978).

Tunstall, J., *Journalists at Work* (London: Constable, 1971).

Tunstall, J., *The Media in Britain* (London: Constable, 1983).

Tunstall, J., *Television Producers* (London: Routledge, 1993).

Tunstall, J. and Palmer, M., *Media Moguls* (London: Routledge, 1991).

SECTION 3
TEXT

1. TEXTUAL STRUCTURES

TEXTUAL STRUCTURES
INTRODUCTION

The 'mass communication' tradition of investigating the media was part of the American social-scientific project of the 1940s and 1950s, whose predominant character was scientistic, functionalist and quantitative. Its main approach to the question of the media 'message' was 'content analysis', which reflected these characteristics. Research in content analysis was given a substantial boost in World War II, when the United States government funded efforts to investigate and analyse propaganda materials and campaigns from the Allied and Axis nations. Chapter 15 is an extract from Bernard Berelson's *Content Analysis in Communication Research* (1952), which was an expanded, published book version of what had originally been an introductory handbook for wartime researchers. He aims to give an overview of content analysis methodology, and the extract reveals the 'scientific' model which underpinned it. '[T]he categories of analysis should be defined so precisely that different analysts can apply them to the same body of content and secure the same results' he states, echoing the idea from the natural sciences that experimental findings must be replicable to be verified: '[t]his requirement ... is necessary to give some scientific standing to content analysis.' Furthermore, in content analysis findings must be expressible quantitatively: 'The *requirement of quantification*, the single characteristic on which all the definitions agree, is perhaps the most distinctive feature of content analysis' he emphasises. Any categories of analysis of the message must therefore be capable of quantitative expression, and the extract includes an interesting discussion of generating categories with which to analyse the portrayal of different ethnic groups in American magazine fiction of the mid-1940s. Content analysis had some impact in Britain, and is still amongst the repertoire of methods sometimes deployed when considering the treatment of particular topics or themes by the media.[1]

Berelson's definition of content analysis implicitly acknowledges some limitations of the approach: 'content analysis is ordinarily limited to the manifest content of the communication and is not normally done directly in terms of the latent intentions which the content may express nor the latent responses which it may elicit',[2] he writes, and goes on to point out that '[i]n general ... content analysis must deal with relatively denotative communication materials and not with relatively connotative materials.' The method had an impoverished conception of its object, the 'message', a point which was argued contemporarily by Siegfried Kracauer, a scholar of German origin working in America.[3] In Britain this thin legacy was to be counteracted from the direction of the humanities, where in English Literature there was a rich Leavisite tradition of close consideration of literary texts in all their complexity. Some of those influenced by this tradition – notably Richard Hoggart, Raymond Williams, and Stuart Hall and Paddy Whannel – turned to the consideration of the texts of the media and popular culture. Thus, in an important conceptual shift, the 'message' was to become seen as a 'text'. The elaboration of detailed attention to media texts – to the forms, structures and meanings of newspapers or broadcast programmes – came to assume an important place in the study of the media from the 1960s.

Film studies in this period drew on the ideas of semiology to examine the workings of meaning-making in films,[4] and the study of other media began to follow suit in the 1970s. (Semiology is the study of signs and their processes of generating meaning.) The development of semiology – originating in a suggestion by the Swiss linguist Ferdinand de Saussure[5] – had accelerated in the 1960s through the work of the French critic Barthes. 'A sign has three essential characteristics: it must have a physical form, it must refer to something other than itself, and it must be used and recognised by people as a sign.'[6] Media texts are composed of signs (images, words, sounds) from which meaning or significance is derived. In 'Radio Signs' (Chapter 16), Andrew Crisell classifies and discusses the kinds of signs that are to be found in radio broadcasts. At one level, radio sets simply emit sound waves that make a variety of noises, yet listeners derive information, emotions and understandings from these; so at another level, radio broadcasts consist of complicated sequences of signs.

Collections of signs are organised in certain rule-governed ways that are called 'codes'. In Chapter 17 John Fiske selects as an example two scenes from the 1980s American television series *Hart to Hart* in order to anatomise the codes at work in a programme. For each element of the programme, the programme-makers have made a choice from among possible options, and each of these elements carries a meaning in accordance with socially established (though rarely spelt out) codes – some of which are specific to television, many of which are not. Fiske brings out the connection between the term 'code' and the concept of 'ideology'. Ideologies are interlinked groups of ideas that circulate socially, and the possibility of understanding the elements of a text – of 'decoding' them – requires the mental mobilisation, consciously or unconsciously, of particular ideologies. Codes are not given by Nature, nor are they invariantly meaningful throughout time or across cultures. Semiology's historic – and persisting – value lies in the way it compels a close regard for how meanings are made by a text, which thereby 'denaturalises' these meanings and highlights their socially produced character.

The next two chapters are also concerned with formal properties of media texts, in both cases those which derive from the particular social institutionalisation of a specific media technology. Chapter 18 is an extract from Raymond Williams' book *Television: Technology and Cultural Form*, whose title signals a concern with this relationship. The ideas of Marshall McLuhan about media technologies, though widely popularised, did not gain many adherents in the academic development of media studies in Britain, and Williams' book is in many ways an explicit refutation of McLuhan's claims for the strong determining role of technologies, taking television as a specific instance. But Williams does not argue that the technological nature of television has no effectivity; here he suggests that the technical character of broadcasting as the continuous emission of a signal for domestic reception, combined with its institutionalisation within a fundamentally commercial system that aims to retain audiences' attention maximally, makes for an output whose 'characteristic organisation ... is one of sequence or flow'. The continuous availability of television, the heterogeneity of programme types, the intermixing of commercials and programme chunks, the constant station announcements, promotions and trailers, the ceaseless flux, the remorseless onward drive through time: taken together, these features mean that 'both internally, in its immediate organisation, and as a generally available experience, this characteristic as flow seems central'.

In his study of the contrasting characters of cinema and broadcast television, John Ellis builds on Williams' insight. Both writers suggest that the best definition of the broadcast text should not necessarily be taken to be the individual programme; instead the 'text' might usefully be seen as both greater and lesser than that. Perhaps, Williams implies, the text for analysis should be an evening's viewing (though that transmutes nowadays imperceptibly into night-time broadcasting, rather than exhibiting sharp boundaries). Ellis points in two other directions as well. First, to the micro-unit: there is the reliance by broadcast television on the unit of the 'segment' to organise and present (or 'narrate') its material. In the domestic setting of its reception, broadcast television cannot be sure of commanding unbroken attention, so it proceeds segment by segment, often with loose connections between them and a stress on sound as the principal track. Secondly, there are the connections that are made across time – a day, a week – within series and serials and long-running magazine shows, which adopt a pattern of repetition and novelty. Chapter 19 contributes to an illuminating exploration of certain general formal features of the broadcast television text.

A textual feature that is often said to be found in both the press and broadcasting, in actuality and fictional forms, is the 'stereotype'. This refers to the representation of people by endowing them with particular recognisable characteristics which are implicitly or explicitly attributed in general to the social group of which they are a member, or a particular fraction of it. The social group may be defined by occupation, age, gender, nationality, ethnicity, sexual orientation, class, religious affiliation, and so on. In semiotic terms, the collection of signs that make up the stereotype mobilise a social mythology about the group. These characteristics are frequently negative, and 'stereotyping' is usually seen as prejudiced. Colloquially, to observe that a representation is a 'stereotype' is to make a pejorative comment about the representation. Although the term was first put into circulation in the 1920s by the American writer and journalist Walter Lippmann,[7] the concept has received renewed attention since the 1970s in large measure arising from the development of the new social movements (for example of women, black people, gays, people with disabilities), which have often actively contested their representations in the public sphere. In Chapter 20 Richard Dyer agrees that many stereotypes are prejudiced and oppressive, whilst asserting that *this is not necessarily intrinsic to stereotyping*. It would be – and on occasion is – possible to 'stereotype' in the sense of making a deft and evocative summary representation of a particular type of person, that can communicate their social location and personality traits through a few well-chosen attributes, without this needing to be deprecatory. What overwhelmingly makes stereotypes prejudiced is the source of representations: media representations especially tend to emanate from the side of power in society, disparaging less powerful social groups and defining them as 'out' or 'other' in some way. Dyer summarises his argument: 'it is not stereotypes, as an aspect of human thought and representation, that are wrong, but who controls and defines them, what interests they serve.'

In a development from the study of painting and literature, film studies adopted a method of classifying texts according to 'genre'. Within Film Studies the topic of genre has accumulated a significant literature, but when we turn to the broader media field it is fair to say as Andrew Tolson has commented '[p]erhaps more than any other area of contemporary media studies, the theory of genre remains in a state of uncertainty and confusion.'[8] 'Genre' is literally French for kind or type. Clearly media output can be classified not just by medium (newspaper, radio, comics), but also into further subsets, according to the various kinds or types of content or material. Thus amongst magazines there are women's magazines, car magazines, computer magazines. But also within these there are a variety of kinds of material: reports, features, personal columns, readers' letters, reviews, and so on. Where the term genre operates is not a settled question in media studies. Keith Selby and Ron Cowdery adopt the wider term 'categorisation' to refer to the recognisable broad features of a media text that are shared with other texts.[9] Perhaps what is required next is a provisional, heuristic, empirical exploration of the question through examination of particular groups of media texts. In Chapter 21 Niki Strange does this for a set of television programmes which she calls the 'cookery genre', thereby selecting an example that is not a sanctioned genre, but is more akin to the matter of everyday broadcast output. She considers content, style, mode of verbal address, ideology, and how these elements are distributed across different kinds of cookery programmes. The chapter furnishes a fruitful example for a return to the issue of genre in media studies.

NOTES

1. For examples, see David Deacon and Peter Golding, *Television and Representation: the media, political communication and the Poll Tax* (London: John Libbey, 1993) or Anders Hansen, 'Greenpeace and press coverage of environmental issues' in Anders Hansen (ed.) *The Mass Media and Environmental Issues* (Leicester: Leicester University Press, 1993).
2. 'Manifest' and 'latent' were key terms in the vocabulary of functionalism: see Robert K. Merton, 'Manifest and Latent Functions' in *Social Theory and Social Structure* (New York: Free Press, 1957).
3. Siegfried Kracauer, 'The challenge of qualitative content analysis', *Public Opinion Quarterly* 16, winter 1952, pp. 631–42.
4. Peter Wollen, 'Cinema and Semiology: Some Points of Contact', *Form*, no. 7 (1968); id., *Signs and Meaning in the Cinema* (London: Secker & Warburg, 1969).
5. 'A science that studies the life of signs within society is conceivable ... I shall call it semiology.' Ferdinand de Saussure, *Course in General Linguistics* (London: Fontana, 1974); orig. pub. 1916.
6. Tim O'Sullivan, John Hartley, Danny Saunders, John Fiske, *Key Concepts in Communications*, 1st edn (London: Methuen, 1983).
7. Walter Lippmann, *Public Opinion* (New York: Harcourt Brace, 1922).
8. Andrew Tolson, *Mediations: Text and Discourse in Media Studies* (London: Arnold, 1996), p. 91.
9. Keith Selby and Ron Cowdery, *How to Study Television* (London: Macmillan, 1995), pp. 34–7.

15

CONTENT ANALYSIS IN COMMUNICATION RESEARCH

Bernard Berelson

In the communication process a central position is occupied by the content. By communication content is meant that body of meanings through symbols (verbal, musical, pictorial, plastic, gestural) which makes up the communication itself. In the classic sentence identifying the process of communication – *'who* says *what* to *whom, how,* with *what effect'* – communication content is the *what.* This book [Berelson, 1952] deals with the analysis of what is said in communications of various kinds.

Since the content represents the means through which one person or group communicates with another, it is important for communication research that it be described with accuracy and interpreted with insight. Communication content is so rich with human experience, and its causes and effects so varied, that no single system of substantive categories can be devised to describe it. However, a scientific *method* has been developed – and is being developed further – for describing various facets of communication content in summary fashion. That method is called content analysis. It has been used to answer such diverse questions as these:

How have the slogans of May Day propaganda in the U.S.S.R. changed during the Soviet regime?

What are the dominant images in Shakespeare's plays?

How is the writer's personality structure reflected in what he writes?

How do the values in American plays differ from those in German

From Bernard Berelson, *Content Analysis in Communication Research* (New York: Free Press, 1952) pp. 13–20, 147, 165–8.

plays of the same time? How do the values in Boy Scout literature in the United States differ from those in *Hitlerjugend* literature?

What are the major trends in the use of research literature by chemists and physicists since 1900?

How are minority ethnic groups treated in short stories in popular magazines?

How can communications suspected of subversion be tested for their 'propaganda' component?

How do newspapers and radio compare in their treatment of a sensational murder case?

What makes writing readable?

In what ways do motion pictures reflect popular feelings and desires?

What are the similarities and differences in the political symbols which come to the attention of people in the major power states?

What happens to a 'good book' when it is made into a movie?

What intelligence data can be secured from analysis of enemy propaganda?

This is a report on the technique of content analysis, which has been used with increasing frequency in recent years. This report attempts critically to survey the applications of content analysis through 1950, to relate it to marginal developments in other fields, to note the major types and categories of analysis, and to review certain technical problems. After a general introductory section, the report discusses the major uses of content analysis, the nature of 'qualitative' analysis, the units and the categories of analysis, and such technical matters as sampling, reliability, presentation, and modes of inference.

DEFINITION OF CONTENT ANALYSIS

What is meant by the term 'content analysis'? Review of several definitions which have appeared in the technical literature will serve to identify the major characteristics of content analysis.

> 'Systematic content analysis attempts to define more casual descriptions of the content, so as to show objectively the nature and relative strength of the stimuli applied to the reader or listener' (Waples & Berelson, 1941, p. 2).

> 'A social science sentence may be called one of "content analysis" if it satisfies all of the following requirements: 1) it must refer either to syntactic characteristics of symbols ... or to semantic characteristics ... 2) it must indicate frequencies of occurrence of such characteristics with a high degree of precision. One could perhaps define more narrowly: it must assign numerical values to such frequencies. 3) it must refer to these characteristics by terms which are general ... 4) it must refer to these characteristics by terms which occur ... in universal propositions of social

science. One may consider adding to this definition another requirement: 5) a high precision of the terms used to refer to the symbol characteristics studied' (Leites & Pool, 1942, pp. 1–2).

'The content analyst aims at a quantitative classification of a given body of content, in terms of a system of categories devised to yield data relevant to specific hypotheses concerning that content' (Kaplan & Goldsen, 1943, p. 1).

'"Content analysis" may be defined as referring to any technique for the *classification* of *sign-vehicles*; which relies solely upon the *judgments* – which, theoretically, may range from perceptual discriminations to sheer guesses – of an analyst or group of analysts as to which sign-vehicles fall into which categories; on the basis of *explicitly formulated rules*; provided that the analyst's judgments are regarded as the reports of a *scientific observer*. The results of a content analysis state the frequency of occurrence of signs – or groups of signs – for each category in a classification scheme' (Janis, 1943, p. 429; his emphasis).

'... The technique known as content analysis ... attempts to characterize the meanings in a given body of discourse in a systematic and quantitative fashion' (Kaplan, 1943, p. 230).

This group of definitions provides six distinguishing characteristics of content analysis:

1. it applies only to social science generalizations: Leites & Pool
2. it applies only, or primarily, to the determination of the effects of communications: Waples & Berelson
3. it applies only to the syntactic and semantic dimensions of language: Leites & Pool
4. it must be 'objective': Waples & Berelson, Leites & Pool, Janis, Kaplan
5. it must be 'systematic': Leites & Pool, Kaplan & Goldsen, Kaplan
6. it must be quantitative: Waples & Berelson, Leites & Pool, Kaplan & Goldsen, Janis, Kaplan

As we shall see, the first and second of these characteristics define the field of content analysis too narrowly. The review of the literature will show that it has been applied successfully in other fields than the social sciences and for other purposes than the description of the effects of communications upon readers and listeners. But the other four characteristics are required for a proper definition of content analysis.

The *syntactic-and-semantic requirement* is meant to rule out the analysis of communication content for the pragmatic dimension of language (the third branch of semiotic, the general science of signs, as developed by Charles Morris). That is, content analysis is ordinarily limited to the manifest content of the communication and is not normally done directly in terms of the latent intentions which the content may express nor the latent responses which it may elicit. Strictly speaking, content analysis proceeds in terms of what-is-said, and not in terms of why-the-content-is-like-that (e.g., 'motives') or how-people-react (e.g., 'appeals' or 'responses'). Three reasons have been given for this delimitation: 1. the low validity of the analysis, since there can be little or no assurance that the assigned intentions and responses actually occurred, in the absence of direct data on them; 2 the low reliability of such analysis, since different coders are unlikely to assign material to the same categories of intention and response with sufficient agreement; and 3. the possible circularity involved in establishing relationships between intent and effect on the one hand, and content on the other, when the latter is analyzed in terms referring to the former.[1]

The *requirement of objectivity* stipulates that the categories of analysis should be defined so precisely that different analysts can apply them to the same body of content and secure the same results.[2] Like the first requirement, this ordinarily limits content analysis to the manifest content. This requirement, of course, is necessary in order to give some scientific standing to content analysis.

The *requirement of system* contains two different meanings. In the first place, it states that *all* of the relevant content is to be analyzed in terms of *all* the relevant categories, for the problem at hand. This requirement is meant to eliminate partial or biased analyses in which only those elements in the content are selected which fit the analyst's thesis. Thus 'system' means that if some occurrences of the category are taken into consideration, within a specified body of content, then all occurrences must be – or the definition of the problem changed.

The second meaning of 'system' is that analyses must be designed to secure data relevant to a scientific problem or hypothesis. The results of a content analysis must have a measure of general application. Thus a tabulation simply reporting the numbers of books of different kinds acquired by a particular library in a given year would not represent a content analysis study (unless the results were used for a trend or comparative analysis, or for some other generalization).[3] By this requirement, content analysis is designed for the establishment of scientific propositions.

The *requirement of quantification*, the single characteristic on which all the definitions agree, is perhaps the most distinctive feature of content analysis. It is this characteristic of content analysis which goes farthest toward distinguishing the procedure from ordinary reading. Of primary importance in content analysis is the *extent* to which the analytic categories appear in the content, that is, the relative emphases and omissions. Now this requirement of quantification does not necessarily demand the assignment of *numerical* values to the analytic categories. Sometimes it takes the form of quantitative words like 'more' or 'always' or 'increases' or 'often.' Although results of this kind may be appropriate for certain studies, it should be recognized that such terms are just as 'quantitative' as the terms 37 or 52 per cent; they are only less exact and precise. In most applications of content analysis, numerical frequencies have been assigned to occurrence of the analytic categories.

This review of the distinguishing characteristics of content analysis, then, results in the following definition: *Content analysis is a research technique for the objective, systematic, and quantitative description of the manifest content of communication.*[4]

ASSUMPTIONS OF CONTENT ANALYSIS

This definition of content analysis implies certain assumptions which should be made explicit. Different types of content analyses and particular studies have their own specific assumptions, but we are not concerned with them here. At this point we are concerned only with those general assumptions which apply to all studies of content analysis. There are three such general assumptions.

1. Content analysis assumes that inferences about the relationship between intent and content or between content and effect can validly be made, or the actual relationships established. We say 'inferences' (i.e., 'interpretations') because most studies utilizing content analysis have been limited to inferences; there have been extremely few studies which concretely demonstrate the nature or the extent of the relationship between communication content, on the one hand, and intentions or effects, on the other. This assumption that knowledge of the content can legitimately support inferences about non-content events is basic to a central contribution of content analysis, namely, to illuminate certain non-content areas. Content analysis is often done to reveal the purposes, motives, and other characteristics of the communicators as they are (presumably) 'reflected' in the content; or to identify the (presumable) effects of the content upon the attention, attitudes, or acts of readers and listeners. The nature of such inferences is discussed in the section on technical problems.

2. Content analysis assumes that study of the manifest content is meaningful. This assumption requires that the content be accepted as a 'common meeting-ground' for the communicator, the audience, and the analyst. That is, the content analyst assumes that the 'meanings' which he ascribes to the content, by assigning it to certain categories, correspond to the 'meanings' intended by the communicator and/or understood by the audience. In other words, the assumption is that there is a common universe of discourse among the relevant parties, so that the manifest content can be taken as a valid unit of study.

This requirement that the analysis deal with manifest content raises the question of whether, in a psychological sense, there is such a thing as 'manifest content.' The argument runs like this: the only sense in which 'manifest content' exists is in the form of black-marks-on-white. As soon as meanings are attached to the symbols, the psychological predispositions of the reader become involved and to some degree they distort his comprehension of the 'manifest content.' Thus there is no guarantee that the meanings in the 'manifest content' are the same as the meanings actually understood by the different readers or intended by the writer; and thus only latent content can exist wherever meanings are involved. To some degree the argument goes, every reader takes his own peculiar meanings away from the common content. Without going into the meta-psychology of this argument, we suggest that there are various kinds and 'levels' of communication content and that analysis of the manifest content for meanings can apply to some and not to others. If one imagines a continuum along which various communications are placed depending upon the degree to which different members of the intended audience get the same understandings from them, one might place a simple news story on a train wreck at one end (since it is likely that every reader will get the same meanings from the content) and an obscure modern poem at the other (since it is likely that no two readers will get identical meanings from the content).[5] Other kinds of content will fall at various points along this continuum. The analysis of manifest content is applicable to materials at the end of the continuum where understanding is simple and direct, and not at the other. Presumably, there is a point on the continuum beyond which the 'latency' of the content (i.e., the diversity of its understanding in the relevant audience) is too great for reliable analysis. In general, then, content analysis must deal with relatively denotative communication materials and not with relatively connotative materials. Under such conditions, analysis of the manifest content of communications takes on a certain uniformity of comprehension and understanding.

3. Content analysis assumes that the quantitative description of communication content is meaningful. This assumption implies that the frequency of occurrence of various characteristics of the content is itself an important factor in the communication process, under specific conditions. Whenever one word or one phrase is as 'important' as the rest of the content taken together, quantitative analysis would not apply. It does apply only when the content units have a more or less equal weight, for purposes of the analysis. To some extent, but not entirely, this is simply a matter of selecting the important categories for analysis. In any case, content analysis should be undertaken only when relative frequencies of content categories are relevant to the problem at hand.

(There are two related considerations which are *not* involved in this assumption: 1. the assumption does not imply that different items of the same length – e.g., a front page newspaper story and a story on an inside page – are necessarily given the same 'weight' in the final quantitative formulation; and 2. the assumption does not imply that all the members of the audience, or the typical members of the audience, necessarily expose to the communication content in the proportions in which the categories appear; that is, there is no assumption that audience exposure and content emphasis are necessarily parallel.)

[...]

Content Analysis stands or falls by its categories. Particular studies have been productive to the extent that the categories were clearly formulated and well adapted to the problem and to the content. Content analysis studies done on a hit-or-miss basis, without clearly formulated problems for investigation and with vaguely drawn or poorly articulated categories, are almost certain to be of indifferent or low quality, as research productions. Although competent performance in other parts of the analytic process is also necessary, the formulation and the definition of appropriate categories take on central importance. Since the categories contain the substance of the investigation, a content analysis can be no better than its system of categories.

[...]

THE FORMULATION PROCESS ILLUSTRATED IN A SINGLE STUDY

Let us now describe the process concretely in terms of one illustrative study – the analysis of the treatment given different ethnic groups in popular magazine fiction (Berelson & Salter, 1946).

The problem derived from concern about the tensions affecting inter-group understanding in this country [USA]. This concern was focused upon the role of the mass media of communication in affecting inter-group attitudes, and more particularly it was localized upon the role of popular magazine fiction in this regard. Thus the problem became to describe the treatment given the members of different ethnic groups in short stories in mass magazines. This was as full and as precise a statement of the problem as was ever formulated.

Next came the crucial step of putting substance into the problem through the formulation of appropriate hypotheses for investigation. These hypotheses were secured partly from introspection on the part of the analysts, partly from reading short stories of the type selected for analysis, partly from reviewing previous studies of this general kind, and partly from reading material on inter-ethnic relations and on American society in general. From these sources a set of some fifteen hypotheses were constructed; here are some examples from the original list:

> The overwhelming majority of the major sympathetic (or approved) characters are from the majority group; the minorities are more likely to be unsympathetic or minor characters.
>
> The majority group receives more of society's rewards than the minority group: they are in better economic positions, they have 'higher' occupations, they are better-educated, they wield more power, they receive more deference, they have pleasanter personalities.
>
> Social interaction between the majority and minority characters seldom exists on a basis of equality (even between majority and minority children). When such social interaction does occur, the minority character usually appears in a subordinate position and never in a super-ordinate position.
>
> The problems to be solved by majority and minority groups differ: the majority mainly has individual problems to solve (usually courtship)

whereas the minority has social and economic problems (of which they are often the 'cause').

The wants of the majority are more generally approved than the wants of the minority (e.g., the majority want love, the minority want material gain or personal advancement).

This original list of hypotheses was constructed before any of the actual analysis was undertaken, and even before the analysis scheme was set up. During the entire balance of the study – through the rest of the formulation stage, the pre-testing of the analysis, the instruction of the various analysts, the incorporation of their suggestions, and the actual analysis itself – only a very few additional hypotheses were formulated and they referred to minor aspects of the problem. The maximum return is almost always apparent by this stage.

The hypotheses were systematically translated into categories by noting every separate item on which analytic results must be secured. Thus the first hypothesis noted above yielded three categories for analysis: ethnic identification of the characters (majority, minority), role in the story (major, minor), and degree of approval (sympathetic, unsympathetic). Content analysis of the sample of stories in terms of these three categories would provide a full testing of the initial hypothesis. The other hypotheses add various categories, e.g., socio-economic status of the characters, the amount and kind of their interaction, their problems, their wants. When all such categories are listed, then the hypotheses are completely covered by the potential data.

To find suitable indicators in the content becomes the next and final step in the formulation of the analysis. The first and most general category necessary in the present case was the ethnic identification of the character. Even a cursory reading of the material under analysis revealed that such identifications are seldom made explicitly (i.e., in such terms as, 'he was an Italian-American'); hence, in addition to noting as many such explicit identifications as possible, it was necessary to formulate certain indirect indicators of ethnic position. Among the indicators used for this purpose were the name of the character, his language, his appearance, his membership in voluntary organizations, and so on; in several cases more than one indicator was found for the same character. Another general category was the character's role in the story – major or minor; the indicator for this category was the relative amount of space given in the story to the character. Those characters who appeared throughout the story were termed major and those who appeared incidentally and briefly were termed minor. The socio-economic status of the character was analyzed in terms of such indicators as occupation, education, income, material possessions, living standards, and residence. In this way, the entire list of categories was re-stated in terms of concrete evidences appearing in the textual material under analysis.

During this stage in which the categories were redefined in terms of concrete indicators, the necessary immersion in the content sometimes suggested additional ideas. The present study was no exception. For example, it was noticed that some form of violence – a fight, a murder – occurred rather frequently in the stories under investigation. On the hypothesis that this might reveal differential treatment of the majority and minority groups (the former fighting 'fair' and the latter 'foul'), the category of violence was formulated and the indicators stated in terms of the methods and means used by the character (e.g., fists, knives, brass knuckles). Again, social etiquette was elaborated as another category, with the obvious hypothesis about differential treatment between the two groups; the indicators in this case were the particular kinds of manners exhibited by the characters (e.g., using the right fork, introducing people properly, talking with one's hands). Although these categories were systematically analyzed, it happened that they did not produce meaningful results, simply through their too-infrequent occurrence. However, another category which turned up at this stage of the study did yield significant data. That derived from the insight that the stories under consideration contained an explanation when members of minority groups appeared in high status positions. From this indicator was elaborated a hypothesis concerning the implicit assumption of status position for the majority group and the 'need' for an explanation for the minorities. Thus even at a late stage in the design of a content analysis study, ideas may emerge from careful scrutiny of the content and add their contribution to the final results.

NOTES

1. For an extended discussion of this problem, see Janis, 1943. See also the following section on the assumptions of content analysis.
2. For the fulfillment of this requirement in actual content analysis studies, see the section of this report on reliability.
3. For a discussion of this point, see the distinction between 'topical' analysis and 'presentation' analysis in Lasswell, 1942.
4. It should be made explicit here that content analysis can be applied to private communications like conversation or the psychoanalytic interview just as it can be applied to public or 'mass' communications like newspapers and radio programs. One proposal suggests enlarging the scope of the definition beyond communication content: '... description of human behavior, particularly linguistic' (Schutz, 1950, p. 3).
5. The poem might still be analyzed for certain non-meaning categories, e.g., use of certain terms (e.g., as in Miles, 1951, and Hamilton, 1949).

REFERENCES

Berelson, B. and Salter, P. (1946) 'Majority and Minority Americans: an Analysis of Magazine Fiction', *Public Opinion Quarterly*, 10, pp. 168–90.
Hamilton, G. R. (1949) *The Tell-Tale Article: a Critical Approach to Modern Poetry*, Heinemann.
Janis, I. L. (1943) 'Meaning and the Study of Symbolic Behaviour', *Psychiatry*, 6, pp. 425–39.
Kaplan, A. (1943) 'Content Analysis and the Theory of Signs', *Philosophy of Science*, 10, pp. 230–47
Kaplan, A. and Goldsen, J. (1943) 'The Reliability of Content Analysis Categories', in Lasswell, H. D. and Leites, N. C. (eds) (1949), *Language of Politics*, Stewart.

Lasswell, H. D. (1942) *Analyzing the Content of Mass Communication: a Brief Introduction*, Library of Congress Experimental Division for Study of War-Time Communications Document no. 11.

Leites, N. C. and Pool, I. de S. (1942) *On Content Analysis*, Library of Congress Experimental Division for Study of War-Time Communications Document no. 26.

Miles, J. (1951) *The Continuity of Poetic Language: Studies in English Poetry from the 1540s to the 1940s*, University of California Press.

Schutz, W. (1950) *Theory and Methodology of Content Analysis*, PhD dissertation, UCLA.

Waples, D. and Berelson, B. (1941) *What the Voters were Told: an Essay in Content Analysis*, Graduate Library School University of Chicago (mimeo).

16

RADIO SIGNS

Andrew Crisell

[...]

[I shall here examine] the raw material of radio, [...] the signs which its codes make use of in order to convey messages, and for this purpose I shall borrow some rudimentary distinctions from what is in fact a highly sophisticated classification of signs devised by the American philosopher, C. S. Peirce (1839–1914). Peirce, who is commonly regarded as a founding father of semiotics or semiology, the study of signs, distinguishes between the *icon* – a sign which resembles the object which it represents, such as a photograph; the *index* – a sign which is directly linked to its object, usually in a causal or sequential way: smoke, for instance, is an index of fire; and the *symbol* – a sign which bears no resemblance or connection to its object, for example the Union Jack as a symbol of Great Britain (Peirce, 1960: I, 196; II, 143, 161, 165, 168–9; Hawkes, 1977: 127–30; Fiske, 1982: 50). In radio all the signs are auditory: they consist simply of noises and silence, and therefore use *time*, not space, as their major structuring agent (Hawkes, 1977: 135). The noises of radio can be subdivided into words, sounds and music, and we will look at each of these in turn and also at the nature and functions of silence [...].

WORDS

Since words are signs which do not resemble what they represent (we may represent a canine quadruped by the word 'dog' but we may equally refer to it

From Andrew Crisell, *Understanding Radio*, 1st edn (London: Methuen, 1986) pp. 45–56.

as 'chien', 'hund' or 'cur' or even invent a private word of our own), they are symbolic in character. Their symbolism is the basis of radio's imaginative appeal, for if the word-sign does not resemble its object the listener must visualize, picture or *imagine* that object. But there is an important difference between words which are written or printed on a page and words on the radio, and that is that words on the radio are always and unavoidably *spoken*. They therefore constitute a binary code in which the words themselves are symbols of what they represent, while the voice in which they are heard is an index of the person or 'character' who is speaking – a fact which was perceived and researched fairly early in the medium's history (Pear, 1931). In other words such factors as accent and stress have semiotic functions, or at least effects (O'Donnell and Todd, 1980: 95). Almost irrespective of what is said in a French accent, for example, the listener may automatically ascribe a romantic person-ality to its speaker. In fact, voice can be so powerful an expression of personality that merely by virtue of some well-delivered links a presenter or disc jockey can impose a unifying and congenial presence on the most miscellaneous of maga-zine or record programmes. Moreover, the voice of a continuity announcer is an index not only of herself, whom she may identify by name from time to time, but of the whole station or network. As a matter of deliberate policy she will give a kind of composite unity to its various programmes, set the tone or style of the whole network (Kumar, 1977: 240–1). Indeed an announcement such as 'You're listening to Radio 4' is ambivalent, for it means not only 'The pro-grammes you're presently hearing are the output of Radio 4' but 'Since the network has no other self-conscious means of expression, *I* am Radio 4'. The ambivalence can be seen rather more clearly, and is taken even further, in the name of the USA's world service where at intervals we can hear 'You're listening to the Voice of America' in which the 'voice' is an index not only of the con tinuity announcer and the radio station, but of the entire nation.

By now it will be clear that signification is not static or rigid, but a highly fluid or elastic process which varies according to context and the preconcep-tions we bring to it – a fact which is not sufficiently acknowledged by some semioticians. A voice may be interpreted merely as the index of a human presence; or on another level as the index of a personality (a country bumpkin, seductive French woman, and so on); or on yet a third level as the index of a programme, broadcasting institution or entire nation. It might be useful to see the latter two levels as examples of *extended* signification.

SOUNDS

Unlike words, which are a human invention, sound is 'natural' – a form of signification which exists 'out there' in the real world. It seems never to exist as an isolated phenomenon, always to manifest the presence of something else. Consequently we can say that sounds, whether in the world or on the radio, are generally indexical. We could of course say that recorded sound on the radio is iconic in the elementary sense that it is an icon or image of the original sound or that a sound in a radio play is an icon of a sound in the real world, but if we do we are still faced with the question of what the sound *signifies*, what it is that is *making* the sound. Thus sounds such as the ringing of a door-bell or the grating of a key in a lock are indexical in signifying someone's presence. Shut your eyes for a moment and listen. The chances are that you will become aware of sounds which you have been hearing for some time but which you have not been aware of before. You have not been aware of them because you are reading such a fascinating book that you have ignored the messages coming from your ears. Suppose, however, that your desire for a cup of coffee is almost equal to your absorption in this book and that a friend has agreed to bring one to you about now. You will be quite capable of picking out from the welter of unimportant noises which surround you the keenly awaited sounds of rattling cup and turning door-handle. But the radio medium is such that the listener cannot select his own area of attention in this way: the broadcasters must prioritize sounds for him, foregrounding the most important ones and eliminating the irrelevant ones, or if this is not possible reducing them to the level of the less important ones. This has been illustrated in respect of radio drama by Erving Goffman (1980: 162–5). Taking a conversation at a party as his scenario Goffman points out that whereas in real life we would be able to distinguish the important from the less important strand of sound, this has to be done for us on the radio by certain conventions. Among the possibilities he instances:

1. Fading in party chatter then fading it down and holding it under the conversation, or even fading it out altogether.
2. Allowing one or two low sounds to stand for what would actually be a stream of background noise.

What Goffman is concerned to stress about these conventions is their artificiality, which is aptly conveyed in the stock phrase 'sound *effects*': 'the audience is not upset by listening in on a world in which many sounds are not sounded and a few are made to stand out momentarily; yet if these conditions suddenly appeared in the off-stage world, consternation would abound' (ibid., 163). Nevertheless it is important to realize that such conventions are indispensable even in radio which deals with real life. In a location interview, for instance, the interviewer will set the recording-level on her portable tape-machine so that the sound of her voice and that of the person she is interviewing will be foregrounded against all the other noises of the location. Let us imagine an interview which takes place against a background of traffic noise. If the interview is with a superintendent of highways about noise pollution the traffic noise, while of less importance – and therefore less loud – than the interview, will still be of relevance to it. If, however, the interview is with the Chancellor of the Exchequer about his Budget proposals the noise of traffic will be quite irrelevant, an unavoidable evil, and the listener will be fully capable of distinguishing between these positive and negative functions of background noise. This second type of location interview is, of course, a *faute de mieux*: it brings a broadcasting facility to an interviewee who cannot be brought into the studio, for an important function of the studio with its sound-proofing is that it eliminates irrelevant noise altogether. My point, then, is that radio does not seek to reproduce the chaotic, complex and continuous sounds of actual life: it may tolerate them to a degree, but seeks to convey only those sounds which are relevant to its messages and to arrange them in their order of relevance. Nevertheless the ultimate test of relevance is the verbal context: it is the subject under discussion in the interview which will tell us whether we should be paying any attention to the traffic noise.

Yet even when the relevant sounds have been distinguished from the irrelevant, the *level* of that relevance often needs to be determined. Let us imagine a programme which begins with an owl-hoot. The 'relevance' or importance of the sound is not in doubt since we can hear virtually nothing else. But what does that relevance consist in? Are we to take the sound simply as an index of the bird, as we would in a documentary about wild-life or the countryside? Or does it carry what I have termed an extended signification in evoking not merely a solitary owl but an entire setting – an eerie, nocturnal atmosphere, as it would in a radio melodrama or a programme about the occult? In the first place, how do such sounds as owl-hoots acquire an extended signification? A crowing sound, for instance, frequently signifies not only 'a cock' but 'daybreak', while the sound of strumming may suggest not only a guitar but a Spanish setting. Because radio broadcasters seldom walk while broadcasting, the sound of footsteps, frequently heard – and ignored – in real life, acquires a peculiar suggestiveness on the radio. Drama producers will use it sparingly, and to convey not only that a person is moving but also that an atmosphere of tension or solitude is developing. This extended signification seems to be established through a process of custom and habit. It is likely that such sounds were originally chosen as an effective way of reinforcing particular pieces of dialogue or description. But since they *are* effective and part of what is a rather limited range of resources open to the radio producer they were chosen again and again and came to acquire the status of a convention, an acoustic shorthand, in that they could *replace* or absorb much of the adjacent language. In hearing the hoot of the owl the listener would begin to brace himself for darkness and mystery before a word had been uttered. Nevertheless, while such conventions may be useful in replacing *much* of adjacent language they cannot *wholly* replace it, for ultimately it is only the words which follow upon our owl-hoot which will tell us whether what we are listening to is *Sounds Natural* or *Afternoon Theatre*.

But it is not simply the case that radio broadcasters must discriminate between important and unimportant sounds on their listeners' behalf and that they must also make the *level* of that importance clear: in some cases they must clarify the very *nature* of those sounds. Why? Shut your eyes and listen again to the sounds around you. You may be surprised at how few of them you can identify with any precision. The frequency range of most sounds is narrow and what we often overlook about the way in which we normally recognize them are the clues our other senses afford, notably the visual sense. When we do not actually see what is causing them they often mean nothing at all. Moreover studio simulations of sounds can often sound more 'real' on the radio than the actual sounds themselves would. Among the better known and genuine examples of these studio simulations are the clapping together of coconut shells to convey horses' hooves and the rustle of a bunch of recording tape to convey someone walking through undergrowth (McLeish, 1978: 252). These are not straightforwardly indexical, since the sounds made by coconut shells and recording tape have no *direct* connections with horses and people in undergrowth. They are 'images' of the sounds made by horses and people and are therefore best described as iconic indexes. They might also be described as 'non-literal signifiers' analogous to an actor in the theatre who represents a table by kneeling on all fours (Elam, 1980: 8); but in radio such signifiers must approximate rather more closely to that which they signify than signifiers in the visual media. Yet however carefully selected and 'realistic' the sounds may be, the listener may still be unclear as to what aspect of reality they are meant to signify. The rustle of recording tape may sound like someone walking through undergrowth, but it also sounds like the swish of a lady's gown and remarkably like the rustle of recording tape. In a radio play which of these things would it signify?

Accompanied by 'Damn! I don't often hit it off the fairway': a golfer searching for his ball in the rough.

Accompanied by 'Darling, you'll be the belle of the ball tonight': a lady in an evening gown.

Accompanied by 'This studio's a pig-sty. Throw this old tape out': a bunch of recording tape.

In other words, sounds require textual pointing – support from the dialogue or narrative. The ear will believe what it is led to believe. This pointing might be termed 'anchorage', which is how Roland Barthes describes the function of words used as captions for photographs. Visual images, he argues, are polysemous. But so are sounds. Hence words help '*Fix* the floating chain of signifieds in such a way as to counter the terror of uncertain signs' (Barthes, 1977: 39).

MUSIC

Music on the radio, as on television, seems to perform two main functions. It is an object of aesthetic pleasure in its own right, in record shows, concerts, recitals, and so on; and either by itself or in combination with words and/or sounds it performs an ancillary function in signifying something outside itself.

As an object of pleasure in its own right, music is quite simply the mainstay of radio's output. Some stations offer little or nothing else. Even on the four BBC networks, one of which – Radio 4 – devotes over three-fifths of its output to news and current affairs, music accounted for 61.3 per cent of total radio output in 1983–4 (BBC *Annual Report and Handbook 1985*, 1984: 145). The difficulty is to define such music in semiotic terms since there is some doubt as to the sense in which music can be said to signify. Broadly speaking, words and images refer to something outside themselves but the assertion cannot be quite so confidently made about music. Music with lyrics seems to present less of a difficulty since we could say that the significance or meaning of the music means one thing and the lyrics mean another and that they are quite capable of counterpointing as well as complementing each other. Quite apart from this, the question of what meaning (if any) attaches to wordless music is a formidable one. It can of course be seen as an index of the instruments and musicians that are playing it. When we hear a record on the radio but miss the disc jockey's introduction to it, we may still be able to identify which group is playing by the characteristic sound it has evolved. But to leave the matter there is rather like saying that spoken words are signs of nothing but the identity of their speaker. Dictionary definitions of music generally ascribe an emotional significance to it, and some compositions (for example Tchaikovsky's *1812 Overture*) evoke historical events: but while acknowledging this we would have to point out that music does not convey these emotions or events with anything like the precision that words do. Indeed there is room for disagreement about the emotional significance of certain compositions with unrevealing titles like 'Opus No. 3' or 'Study in E Flat' – and who could tell merely from hearing it that Chopin's *Minute Waltz* is about a dog chasing its tail? This means that written commentaries which point to particular features of a piece of music as referring to particular emotional or historical conditions tend to rely consciously or unconsciously on circumstantial evidence – the title of the piece and/or the famous legend which it 'narrates', the situation in which it was composed, the biographical and psychological details of the composer, and so on. Hence our very difficulty in discerning what music refers to means that if it does signify, then apart from its local imitations of 'natural' sounds its mode of signification will be almost entirely symbolic.

This virtual absence, or at any rate imprecision, of meaning in music makes it at once highly suited to the radio medium and somewhat unilluminating as to its nature. It is highly suited because in being largely free of signification it allows us to listen without making strenuous efforts to imagine what is being referred to, but to assimilate it, if we wish, to our own thoughts and moods – a fact which helps to explain why music has become even more popular since radio's rebirth as a secondary medium. But it is unilluminating in the sense that in its fully realized form (that is, not as a written score) it consists almost purely of sound, refers scarcely at all to anything outside itself, and is therefore one code which is not distinctively shaped by radio since radio is itself a purely acoustic medium. This was recognized fairly early in broadcasting history by a features producer who wished to dismiss the idea that there was anything especially 'radiogenic' about music:

> There is no such thing as radio music. Composers go on composing music just as if wireless had never been invented, and the music of all periods is played before microphones in exactly the same way as it has always been played. It does not have to be 'adapted'.   (Sieveking, 1934: 24)

Apart from the fact that radio allowed the listener to hear music without visual distractions (and even in this was anticipated by the gramophone), the point is that music is rather less revealing about the nature and possibilities of the medium than, say, news, drama and light entertainment: for whereas we can compare radio versions of the latter with their corresponding forms on the stage, screen or in newspapers and see the distinctive way in which the medium has adapted them, music in its essential form is always and everywhere the same. Not modified by radio, it does not particularly illuminate it.

Nevertheless the broad emotive power of music enables it to be combined with words and/or sounds as a way of signifying something outside itself, and some of these forms of signification are worth considering in detail.

1. Music as a 'framing' or 'boundary' mechanism. Musical jingles (sometimes known as 'IDs') identify or 'frame' radio stations just as signature or theme music frames an individual programme by announcing its beginning and/or end. Station IDs are similar in function to the voice of the continuity announcer, they set the style or tone of the station and could be seen as both index and symbol. It is interesting to speculate why musical IDs are more closely associated with 'popular' and verbal IDs with 'quality' networks; but it is certainly the case that the work done by continuity announcers on Radios 3 and 4 is performed largely by jingles on Radios 1 and 2!

   As a way of framing individual items theme music is also common in film and television, but it is of particular significance in radio because of the blindness of the medium. Silence, a pause, can also be used as a framing mechanism, but unlike that of film and television it is *total*, devoid of images. To give the programmes connotations, an overall style or mood, music is therefore an especially useful resource on radio – less bald, more indefinitely suggestive, than mere announcements. Let us take a formal but lively piece of eighteenth-century music played on a harpsichord – a gavotte or bourrée composed by Bach, perhaps – and consider its possibilities for the radio producer. It is highly structured and symmetrical in form and therefore commonly regarded as more cerebral or 'intellectual' than the Romantic compositions of the following century. She might therefore regard it as ideal theme music for a brains trust or quiz programme. But its characteristics have other possibilities. The 'period' quality of both the harpsichord and the music is unmistakable and might lend itself to a programme about history or antiques. Alternatively the 'tinny' tone of the instrument combined with the rhythmic nature of the piece might introduce a children's programme about toys or music boxes or with a faery or fantasy theme. You can doubtless imagine other possibilities for yourself, and I would simply make two further points. The first is that depending on the specific contents of the programmes I have suggested, it would be possible to discern all three modes of signification in such theme music – the symbolic, the indexical and the iconic. Secondly I would stress that these are *extrinsic* meanings of the music: we could not say that it is 'about' cerebration or history or toys. Another way we might describe them is as 'associative' meanings: in a serial, for instance, the theme music will bring to the listener's mind what he already knows about the story-line; even more than this, it is a 'paradigm' of that *genre* of programme (Fiske and Hartley, 1978: 169). This function of music as a framing mechanism and the two following functions are noticed by Goffman (1980: 164–5).

2. Music as a link between the scenes of a radio play or the items of a programme. Such links are analogous to curtain drops in the theatre, since they keep certain aspects of the programme apart and may additionally signal advertising breaks. But as well as keeping apart they bridge the changes of scene or subject, thus providing a kind of continuity.

3. 'Mood' music during a play, a background enhancement which is understood not to be heard by the characters, but is heard by the listeners as a clue to the characters' feelings or thoughts. These last two functions of music could be seen as symbolic, but there is another which Goffman appears to overlook:

4. Music as a kind of stylized replacement for naturalistic sound effects in a play, for example musical simulations of storms or battles. It has an imitative function and is a sort of iconic index. It is heard by the characters in the play, but not in that form.

5. Music in an indexical function, as part of the ordinary sounds of the world which radio portrays. These sounds are usually known collectively as 'actuality'. Here is a typical example from a news programme:

FADE IN SOUND OF BAGPIPES AND DRUMS

Presenter: The Band of the Argyll and Sutherland Highlanders, who were today granted the freedom of Aldershot.

The semiotic function of the music would be much the same whether it were live actuality from the freedom ceremony, or a recording of the actuality, or simply taken from a gramophone record (radio producers often 'cheat'). In the first instance the music would be indexical and in the other two instances the recordings would simply be acting as icons of the sounds the band was making at the ceremony – sounds which are an index of its presence. They would therefore be iconic indexes.

SILENCE

Though it is natural for us to speak of radio as a sound medium we should remember that the *absence* of sound can also be heard. It is therefore important to consider silence as a form of signification. It has both negative and positive functions which seem to be indexical. Its negative function is to signify that for the moment at least, nothing is happening on the medium: there is a void, what broadcasters sometimes refer to as 'dead air'. In this function silence can resemble noise (that is, sounds, words and music) in acting as a framing mechanism, for it can signify the integrity of a programme or item by making a space around it. But if the silence persists for more than a few seconds it signifies the dysfunction or non-functioning of the medium: either transmitter or receiver has broken down or been switched off.

The positive function of silence is to signify that something is happening which for one reason or another cannot be expressed in noise. Because radio silence is total (unlike film and theatrical silences, which are visually filled) it can be a potent stimulus to the listener, providing a gap in the noise for his imagination to work: 'Pass me the bottle. Cheers. Ah, that's better!' But such silences or pauses can suggest not only physical actions but abstract, dramatic qualities, generate pathos or irony by confirming or countering the words which surround them. They can also generate humour, as in a famous radio skit which featured Jack Benny, a comedian with a reputation for extreme miserliness:

> The skit consists of a confrontation between Benny and a mugger on the street. Says the mugger: 'Your money or your life'. Prolonged pause: growing laughter; then applause as the audience gradually realises what Benny *must* be thinking, and eventually responds to the information communicated by the silence and to its comic implications. (Fink, 1981: 202)

How, then, does the listener discriminate among these various negative and positive functions of silence? His guide is clearly the context – in the first instance whether any noise frames the silence and in the second, what that noise signifies.

REFERENCES

Barthes, R. (1977) *Image – Music – Text* (trans. S. Heath) Glasgow: Fontana.
BBC Annual Report and Handbook 1985 (1984) London: British Broadcasting Corporation.
Elam, K. (1980) *The Semiotics of Theatre and Drama*, London: Methuen.
Fink, H. (1981) 'The sponsor's v. the nation's choice: North American radio drama' in Lewis, P. (ed.) *Radio Drama*, London and New York: Longman.
Fiske, J. (1982) *An Introduction to Communication Studies*, London: Methuen.
Fiske, J. and Hartley, J. (1978) *Reading Television*, London: Methuen.
Goffman, E. (1980) 'The radio drama frame' in Corner, J. and Hawthorn, J. (eds) *Communication Studies*, London: Edward Arnold.
Hawkes, T. (1977) *Structuralism and Semiotics*, London: Methuen.
Kumar, K. (1977) 'Holding the middle ground: the BBC, the public and the professional broadcaster' in Curran, J., Gurevitch, M. and Woollacott, J. (eds) *Mass Communication and Society*, London: Edward Arnold.
McLeish, R. (1978) *The Technique of Radio Production*, London: Focal Press.

O'Donnell, W. and Todd, L. (1980) *Variety in Contemporary English*, London: George Allen & Unwin.

Pear, T. H. (1931) *Voice and Personality*, London: Chapman & Hall.

Peirce, C. S. (1960) *Collected Papers*, vols I and II, (eds) Hartshorne, C. and Weiss, P., Cambridge, Mass: Harvard University Press.

Sieveking, L. (1934) *The Stuff of Radio*, London: Cassell.

17

THE CODES OF TELEVISION

John Fiske

[...]

[To demonstrate] a traditional semiotic account of how television makes, or attempts to make, meanings that serve the dominant interests in society, [...I shall analyse...] a short segment of two scenes from a typical, prime-time, long-running series, *Hart to Hart*.

[...]

The Harts are a wealthy, high-living husband and wife detective team. In this particular episode they are posing as passengers on a cruise ship on which there has been a jewel robbery. In scene 1 they are getting ready for a dance during which they plan to tempt the thief to rob them, and are discussing how the robbery may have been effected. In scene 2 we meet the villain and villainess, who have already noticed Jennifer Hart's ostentatiously displayed jewels.

SCENE 1

HERO: He knew what he was doing to get into this safe.

HEROINE: Did you try the numbers that Granville gave you?

HERO: Yeh. I tried those earlier. They worked perfectly.

HEROINE: Well you said it was an inside job, maybe they had the combination all the time.

HERO: Just trying to eliminate all the possibilities. Can you check this out for me. (*He gestures to his bow tie.*)

From John Fiske, *Television Culture* (London and New York: Methuen, 1987) pp. 1–13.

HEROINE: Mm. Yes I can. (*He hugs her.*) Mm. Light fingers. Oh, Jonathon.

HERO: Just trying to keep my touch in shape.

HEROINE: What about the keys to the door?

HERO: Those keys can't be duplicated because of the code numbers. You have to have the right machines.

HEROINE: Well, that leaves the window.

HERO: The porthole.

HEROINE: Oh yes. The porthole. I know they are supposed to be charming, but they always remind me of a laundromat.

HERO: I took a peek out of there a while ago. It's about all you can do. It's thirty feet up to the deck even if you could make it down to the window, porthole. You'd have to be the thin man to squeeze through.

HEROINE: What do you think? (*She shows her jewelry.*) Enough honey to attract the bees?

HERO: Who knows? They may not be able to see the honey for the flowers.

HEROINE: Oh, that's the cutest thing you've ever said to me, sugar. Well, shall we? (*Gestures towards the door.*)

SCENE 2

VILLAIN: I suppose you noticed some of the icing on Chamberlain's cup cake. I didn't have my jeweler's glass, but that bracelet's got to be worth at least fifty thousand. Wholesale.

VILLAINESS: Patrick, if you're thinking what I know you're thinking, forget it. We've made our quota one hit on each ship. We said we weren't going to get greedy, remember.

VILLAIN: But darling, it's you I'm thinking of. And I don't like you taking all those chances. But if we could get enough maybe we wouldn't have to go back to the Riviera circuit for years.

VILLAINESS: That's what you said when we were there.

VILLAIN: Well maybe a few good investments and we can pitch the whole bloody business. But we are going to need a bit more for our retirement fund.

Figure 1 shows the main codes that television uses and their relationship. A code is a rule-governed system of signs, whose rules and conventions are shared amongst members of a culture, and which is used to generate and circulate meanings in and for that culture. (For a fuller discussion of codes in semiotics see Fiske, 1983, or O'Sullivan *et al.*, 1983.) Codes are links between producers, texts, and audiences, and are the agents of intertextuality through which texts interrelate in a network of meanings that constitutes our cultural world. These codes work in a complex hierarchical structure that Figure 1 oversimplifies for the sake of clarity. In particular, the categories of codes are arbitrary and slippery, as is their classification into levels in the hierarchy; for instance, I have put speech as a social code, and dialogue (i.e. scripted speech) as a technical one, but in practice the two are almost indistinguishable: social psychologists

---

Figure 1 The Codes of Television

Level one:
'REALITY'

An event to be televised is already encoded
by *social codes* such as those of:

appearance, dress, make-up, environment, behavior,
speech, gesture, expression, sound, etc.

Level two:
REPRESENTATION

these are encoded electronically by
technical codes such as those of:

camera, lighting, editing, music, sound

which transmit the
conventional representational codes, which shape the
representations of, for example:
narrative, conflict, character, action, dialogue, setting,
casting, etc.

Level three:
IDEOLOGY

which are organised into coherence and social
acceptability by the *ideological codes*, such as those of:
individualism, patriarchy, race, class, materialism,
capitalism, etc.

---

such as Berne (1964) have shown us how dialogue in 'real life' is frequently scripted for us by the interactional conventions of our culture. Similarly, I have called casting a conventional representational code, and appearance a social one, but the two differ only in intentionality and explicitness. People's appearance in 'real life' is already encoded: in so far as we make sense of people by their appearance we do so according to conventional codes in our culture. The casting director is merely using these codes more consciously and more conventionally, which means more stereotypically.

The point is that 'reality' is already encoded, or rather the only way we can perceive and make sense of reality is by the codes of our culture. There may be an objective, empiricist reality out there, but there is no universal, objective way of perceiving and making sense of it. What passes for reality in any culture is the product of that culture's codes, so 'reality' is always already encoded, it is never 'raw.' If this piece of encoded reality is televised, the technical codes and representational conventions of the medium are brought to bear upon it so as to make it (a) transmittable technologically and (b) an appropriate cultural text for its audiences.

Some of the social codes which constitute our reality are relatively precisely definable in terms of the medium through which they are expressed – skin color, dress, hair, facial expression, and so on.

Others, such as those that make up a landscape, for example, may be less easy to specify systematically, but they are still present and working hard. Different sorts of trees have different connotative meanings encoded into them, so do rocks and birds. So a tree reflected in a lake, for example, is fully encoded even before it is photographed and turned into the setting for a romantic narrative.

Similarly the technical codes of television can be precisely identified and analyzed. The choices available to the camera person, for example, to give meaning to what is being photographed are limited and specifiable: they consist of framing, focus, distance, movement (of the camera or the lens), camera placing, or angle and lens choice. But the conventional and ideological codes and the relationship between them are much more elusive and much harder to specify, though it is the task of criticism to do just that. For instance, the conventions that govern the representation of speech as 'realistic dialogue' in Scene 1 result in the heroine asking questions while the hero provides the answers. The representational convention by which women are shown to lack knowledge which men possess and give to them is an example of the ideological code of patriarchy. Similarly the conventional representation of crime as theft of personal property is an encoding of the ideology of capitalism. The 'naturalness' with which the two fit together in the scene is evidence of how these ideological codes work to organize the other codes into producing a congruent and coherent set of meanings that constitute the *common sense* of a society. The process of making sense involves a constant movement up and down through the levels of the diagram, for sense can only be produced when 'reality,' representations, and ideology merge into a coherent, seemingly natural unity. Semiotic or cultural criticism deconstructs this unity and exposes its 'naturalness' as a highly ideological construct.

A semiotic analysis attempts to reveal how these layers of encoded meanings are structured into television programs, even in as small a segment as the one we are working with. The small size of the segment encourages us to perform a detailed analytical reading of it, but prevents us talking about larger-scale codes, such as those of the narrative. But it does provide a good starting point for our work.

Camera Work

The camera is used through angle and deep focus to give us a perfect view of the scene, and thus a complete understanding of it. Much of the pleasure of television realism comes from this sense of omniscience that it gives us. Camera distance is used to swing our sympathies away from the villain and villainess, and towards the hero and heroine. The normal camera distance in television is mid-shot to close-up, which brings the viewer into an intimate, comfortable relationship with the characters on the screen. But the villain and villainess are also shown in extreme close-up (ECU). Throughout this whole episode of *Hart to Hart* there are only three scenes in which ECUs are used: they are used only to represent hero/ine and villain/ess, and of the twenty-one ECUs, eighteen are of the villain/ess and only three of the hero/ine. Extreme close-ups become a codified way for representing villainy.

This encoding convention is not confined to fictional television, where we might think that its work upon the alignment of our sympathies, and thus on our moral judgement, is justified. It is also used in news and current affairs programs which present themselves as bringing reality to us 'objectively.' The court action resulting from General Westmoreland's libel suit against the CBS in 1985 revealed these codes more questionably at work in television reporting. Alex Jones recounts their use in his report of the trial for the *New York Times*:

> Among the more controversial techniques is placing an interviewee in partial shadow in order to lend drama to what is being said. Also debated is the use of extreme close-ups that tend to emphasize the tension felt by a person being interviewed; viewers may associate the appearance of tension with lying or guilt.
>
> The extreme close-up can be especially damaging when an interview is carefully scripted and a cameraman is instructed to focus tightly on the person's face at the point when the toughest question is to be asked. Some documentary makers will not use such close-ups at all in interviews because they can be so misleading.
>
> The CBS documentary contained both a shadowed interview of a friendly witness and 'tight shots' of General Westmoreland. Such techniques have been used in documentaries by other networks as well.
>
> Even the wariest viewer is likely to find it difficult to detect some other common techniques. 'I can't imagine a general viewer getting so sophisticated with techniques that they could discount them,' said Reuven Frank, a former president at NBC News who has been making documentaries for about 30 years. (*NYT*, February 17, 1985: 8E)

There are two possible sources of the conventions that govern the meanings generated by this code of camera distance. One is the social code of interpersonal distance: in western cultures the space within about 24 inches (60 cm) of us is encoded as private. Anyone entering it is being either hostile, when the entry is unwelcome, or intimate, when it is invited. ECUs replicate this, and are used for moments of televisual intimacy or hostility, and which meanings they convey depends on the other social and technical codes by which they are contextualized, and by the ideological codes brought to bear upon them. Here, they are used to convey hostility. The other source lies in the technical codes which imply that seeing closely means seeing better – the viewer can see *into* the villain, see *through* his words, and thus gains power over him, the power and the pleasure of 'dominant specularity.'

These technical and social codes manifest the ideological encoding of villainy.

Most of the other technical codes can be dealt with more quickly, with only brief comments.

Lighting

The hero's cabin is lit in a soft, yellowish light, that of the villains in a harsh, whiter one. (I am reminded of Hogben's (1982) anecdote about the occasion when he was given a hostile treatment in a television interview. He did, however, manage to convince the interviewer that his point of view deserved more sympathy, whereupon the interviewer insisted they record the interview again, but this time without the greenish-white studio lighting.)

Editing

The heroes are given more time (72 secs) than the villains (49), and more shots (10 as against 7), though both have an average shot length of 7 seconds. It is remarkable how consistent this is across different modes of television (see Fiske, 1986): it has become a conventional rhythm of television common to news, drama, and sport.

Music

The music linking the two scenes started in a major key, and changed to minor as the scene changed to the villains.

Casting

This technical code requires a little more discussion. The actors and actresses who are cast to play hero/ines, villain/esses and supporting roles are real people whose appearance is already encoded by our social codes. But they are equally media people, who exist for the viewer intertextually, and whose meanings are also intertextual. They bring with them not only residues of the meanings of other roles that they have played, but also their meanings from other texts such as fan magazines, showbiz gossip columns, and television criticism. Later on in the book [*Television Culture*] we will discuss intertextuality and character portrayal in greater depth: here we need to note that these dimensions of meaning are vital in the code of casting, and that they are more important in the casting of hero/ines than of villain/esses.

Characters on television are not just representations of individual people but are encodings of ideology, 'embodiments of ideological values' (Fiske, 1987a). Gerbner's (1970) work showed that viewers were clear about the different characteristics of television heroes and villains on two dimensions only: heroes were more attractive and more successful than villains. Their attractiveness, or lack of it, is partly the result of the way they are encoded in the technical and social codes – camera work, lighting, setting, casting, etc., but the ideological codes are also important, for it is these that make sense out of the relationship between the technical code of casting and the social code of appearance, and that also relate their televisual use to their broader use in the culture at large. In his analysis of violence on television, Gerbner (1970) found that heroes and villains are equally likely to use violence and to initiate it, but that heroes were successful in their violence, whereas villains finally were not. Gerbner worked out a killers-to-killed ratio according to different categories of age, sex, class, and race. The killers category included heroes and villains, but the killed category included villains only. He found that a character who was white, male, middle class (or classless) and in the prime of life was very likely, if not certain, to be alive at the end of the program. Conversely characters who deviated from these norms were likely to be killed during the program in proportion to the extent of their deviance. We may use Gerbner's findings to theorize that heroes are socially central types who embody the dominant ideology, whereas villains and victims are members of deviant or subordinate subcultures who thus embody the dominant ideology less completely, and may, in the case of villains, embody ideologies that oppose it. The textual opposition between hero/ine and villain/ess, and the violence by which this opposition is commonly dramatized, become metaphors for power relationships in society and thus a material practice through which the dominant ideology works. (This theory is discussed more fully in Fiske and Hartley, 1978, and in Fiske, 1982.)

The villain in this segment has hints of non-Americanness; some viewers have classed his accent, manner, and speech as British, for others his appearance has seemed Hispanic. But the hero and heroine are both clearly middle-class, white Americans, at home among the WASPs (White Anglo-Saxon Protestants). The villainess is Aryan, blonde, pretty, and younger than the villain. Gerbner's work would lead us to predict that his chances of surviving the episode are slim, whereas hers are much better. The prediction is correct. She finally changes sides and helps the hero/ine, whereas he is killed; hints of this are contained in her condemnation of the villain's greed, which positions her more centrally in the ideological discourse of economics (see below).

These technical codes of television transmit, and in some cases merge into, the social codes of Level 1. Let us look at how some of them are working to generate meanings and how they embody the ideological codes of Level 3.

Setting and Costume

The hero/ine's cabin is larger than that of the villain/ess: it is humanized, made more attractive by drapes and flowers, whereas the other is all sharp angles and hard lines. The villain wears a uniform that places him as a servant or employee and the villainess's dress is less tasteful, less expensive than the heroine's. These physical differences in the social codes of setting and dress are also bearers of the ideological codes of class, of heroism and villainy, of morality, and of attractiveness. These abstract ideological codes are condensed into a set of material social ones, and the materiality of the differences of the social codes is used to guarantee the truth and naturalness of the ideological. We must note, too, how some ideological codes are more explicit than others: the codes of heroism, villainy, and attractiveness are working fairly openly and acceptably. But under them the codes of class, race, and morality are working less openly and more questionably: their ideological work is to naturalize the correlation of lower-class, non-American with the less attractive, less moral, and therefore villainous. Conversely, the middle and the white American is correlated with the more attractive, the more moral and the heroic. This displacement of morality onto class is a common feature of our popular culture: Dorfman and Mattelart (1975) have shown how Walt Disney cartoons consistently express villainy through characteristics of working-class appearance and manner; indeed they argue that the only time the working class appear in the middle-class world of Ducksville it is as villains. Fiske (1984) has found the same textual strategy in the *Dr Who* television series.

Make-up

The same merging of the ideological codes of morality, attractiveness, and heroism/villainy, and their condensation into a material social code, can be seen in something as apparently insignificant as lipstick. The villainess has a number of signs that contradict her villainy (she is blonde, white American, pretty, and more moral than the villain). These predict her eventual conversion to the side of the hero and heroine, but she cannot look too like them at this early stage of the narrative, so her lips are made up to be thinner and less sexually attractive than the fuller lips of the heroine. The ideology of lipstick may seem a stretched concept, but it is in the aggregate of apparently insignificant encodings that ideology works most effectively.

Action

There are a number of significant similarities and differences between the actions of the hero/ine and the villain/ess. In both cabins the women are prettying themselves, the men are planning. This naturalizes the man's executive role (Goffman, 1979) of instigating action and the woman's role as object of the male gaze – notice the mirror in each cabin which enables her to see herself as 'bearer of her own image' (Berger, 1972): the fact that this is common to both hero/ine and villain/ess puts it beyond the realm of conflict in the narrative and into the realm of everyday common sense within which the narrative is enacted. The other action common to both is the getting and keeping of wealth as a motive for action, and as a motor for the narrative: this also is not part of the conflict-to-be-resolved, but part of the ideological framework through which that conflict is viewed and made sense of.

A difference between the two is that of co-operation and closeness. The hero and heroine co-operate and come physically closer together, the villain and villainess, on the other hand, disagree and pull apart physically. In a society that places a high value on a man and woman being a close couple this is another bearer of the dominant ideology.

Dialogue

The dialogue also is used to affect our sympathy. That of the villain and villainess is restricted to their nefarious plans and their mutual disagreement, whereas the hero and heroine are allowed a joke (window/porthole/laundromat), an extended metaphor (honey and the bees), and the narrative time to establish a warm, co-operative relationship. Both the hero/ine and villain/ess are allowed irony.

Ideological Codes

These codes and the televisual codes which bring them to the viewer are both deeply embedded in the ideological codes of which they are themselves the bearers. If we adopt the same ideological practice in the decoding as the encoding we are drawn into the position of a white, male, middle-class American (or westerner) of conventional morality. The reading position is the social point at which the mix of televisual, social, and ideological codes comes together to make coherent, unified sense: in making sense of the program in this way we are indulging in an ideological practice ourselves, we are maintaining and legitimating the dominant ideology, and our reward for this is the easy pleasure of the recognition of the familiar and of its adequacy. We have already become a 'reading subject' constructed by the text, and, according to Althusser (1971), the construction of subjects-in-ideology is the major ideological practice in capitalist societies.

This ideological practice is working at its hardest in three narrative devices in this segment. The first is the window/porthole/laundromat joke, which, as we have seen, is used to marshal the viewer's affective sympathy on the side of the hero/ine. But it does more than that. Freud tells us that jokes are used to relieve the anxiety caused by repressed, unwelcome, or taboo meanings. This joke revolves around the 'feminine' (as defined by our dominant culture) inability to understand or use technical language, and the equally 'feminine' tendency to make sense of everything through a domestic discourse. 'Porthole' is technical discourse – masculine: 'window-laundromat' is domestic-nurturing discourse – feminine. The anxiety that the joke relieves is that caused by the fact that the heroine is a detective, is involved in the catching of criminals – activities that are part of the technical world of men in patriarchy. The joke is used to recuperate contradictory signs back into the dominant system, and to smooth over any contradictions that might disrupt the ideological homogeneity of the narrative. The attractiveness of the heroine must not be put at risk by allowing her challenge to patriarchy to be too stark – for attractiveness is always ideological, never merely physical or natural.

The metaphor that expresses the sexual attractiveness of women for men in terms of the attraction of honey and flowers for the bees works in a similar way. It naturalizes this attraction, masking its ideological dimension, and then extends this naturalness to its explanation of the attractiveness of other people's jewelry for lower-class non-American villains! The metaphor is working to naturalize cultural constructions of gender, class, and race.

The third device is that of jewelry itself. As we have seen, the getting and keeping of wealth is the major motor of the narrative, and jewelry is its material signifier. Three ideological codes intersect in the use of jewelry in this narrative: they are the codes of economics, gender, and class.

In the code of economics, the villain and villainess stress the jewelry's investment/exchange function: it is 'worth at least fifty thousand wholesale,' it forms 'a retirement fund.' For the hero and heroine and for the class they represent this function is left unstated: jewelry, if it is an investment, is one to hold, not cash in. It is used rather as a sign of class, of wealth, and of aesthetic taste.

The aesthetic sense, or good taste, is typically used as a bearer and naturalizer of class differences. The heroine deliberately overdoes the jewelry, making it vulgar and tasteless in order to attract the lower-class villain and villainess. They, in their turn, show their debased taste, their aesthetic insensitivity, by likening it to the icing on a cupcake. As Bourdieu (1968) has shown us, the function of aesthetics in our society is to make class based and culture-specific differences of taste appear universal and therefore natural. The taste of the dominant classes is universalized by aesthetic theory out of its class origin; the metaphor of 'taste' works in a similar way by displacing class differences onto the physical, and therefore natural, senses of the body.

The meaning of jewelry in the code of gender is clear. Jewels are the coins by which the female-as-patriarchal-commodity is bought, and wearing them is the sign both of her possession by a man, and of his economic and social status. Interestingly, in the code of gender, there is no class difference between hero/ine and villain/ess: the economics of patriarchy are the same for all classes, thus making it appear universal and natural that man provides for his woman.

This analysis has not only revealed the complexity of meanings encoded in what is frequently taken to be shallow and superficial, but it also implies that this complexity and subtlety has a powerful effect upon the audience. It implies that the wide variety of codes all cohere to present a unified set of meanings that work to maintain, legitimate, and naturalize the dominant ideology of patriarchal capitalism. Their ideological effectivity appears irresistible, [although I do not think it is, and argue elsewhere why it is not (Fiske, 1987b: chs. 5 and 6).] For the moment, however, it serves to demonstrate that popular television is both complex and deeply infused with ideology.

REFERENCES

Althusser, L. (1971) 'Ideology and Ideological State Apparatuses' in *Lenin and Philosophy and Other Essays*, New York and London: Monthly Review Press, 127–86.

Berger, J. (1972) *Ways of Seeing*, Harmondsworth: Penguin.

Berne, E. (1964) *Games People Play: the Psychology of Human Relationships*, Harmondsworth: Penguin.

Bourdieu, P. (1968) 'Outline of a Sociological Theory of Art Perception', *International Social Sciences Journal* 2: 225–54.

Dorfman, A. and Mattelart, A. (1975) *How to Read Donald Duck*, New York: International General.

Fiske, J. (1982) *Introduction to Communication Studies*, London: Methuen.

Fiske, J. (1983) 'The Discourses of TV Quiz Shows or School + Luck = Success + Sex', *Central States Speech Journal* 34, 139–50.

Fiske, J. (1984) 'Popularity and ideology: A Structuralist Reading of Dr Who' in W. Rowland and B. Watkins (eds) (1984) *Interpreting Television: Current Research Perspectives*, Beverley Hills: Sage, 165–98.

Fiske, J. (1986) 'Television: Polysemy and Popularity', *Critical Studies in Mass Communication* 3:4, 391–408.

Fiske, J. (1987a) 'British Cultural Studies' in R. Allen (ed.) (1987) *Channels of Discourse: Television and Contemporary Criticism*, Chapel Hill: University of North Carolina Press, 254–89.

Fiske, J. (1987b) *Television Culture*, London and New York: Methuen.

Fiske, J. and Hartley, J. (1978) *Reading Television*, London: Methuen.

Gerbner, G. (1970) 'Cultural Indicators: the Case of Violence in Television Drama', *Annals of the American Association of Political and Social Science* 338, 69–81.

Goffman, E. (1979) *Gender Advertisements*, London: Macmillan.

Hogben, A. (1982) 'Journalists as Bad Apples', *Quadrant*, January/February, 38–43.

O'Sullivan, T., Hartley, J., Saunders, D., and Fiske, J. (1983) *Key Concepts in Communication*, London: Methuen.

18

PROGRAMMING AS SEQUENCE OR FLOW

Raymond Williams

[...]

In all developed broadcasting systems the characteristic organisation, and therefore the characteristic experience, is one of sequence or flow. This phenomenon, of planned flow, is then perhaps the defining characteristic of broadcasting, simultaneously as a technology and as a cultural form.

In all communications systems before broadcasting the essential items were discrete. A book or a pamphlet was taken and read as a specific item. A meeting occurred at a particular date and place. A play was performed in a particular theatre at a set hour. The difference in broadcasting is not only that these events, or events resembling them, are available inside the home, by the operation of a switch. It is that the real programme that is offered is a *sequence* or set of alternative sequences of these and other similar events, which are then available in a single dimension and in a single operation.

Yet we have become so used to this that in a way we do not see it. Most of our habitual vocabulary of response and description has been shaped by the experience of discrete events. We have developed ways of responding to a particular book or a particular play, drawing on our experience of other books and plays. When we go out to a meeting or a concert or a game we take other experience with us and we return to other experience, but the specific event is ordinarily an occasion, setting up its own internal conditions and responses. Our most general modes of comprehension and judgement are then

From Raymond Williams, *Television: Technology and Cultural Form* (London: Fontana, 1974) pp. 86–96.

closely linked to these kinds of specific and isolated, temporary, forms of attention.

Some earlier kinds of communication contained, it is true, internal variation and at times miscellaneity. Dramatic performances included musical interludes, or the main play was preceded by a curtain-raiser. In print there are such characteristic forms as the almanac and the chapbook, which include items relating to very different kinds of interest and involving quite different kinds of response. The magazine, invented as a specific form in the early eighteenth century, was designed as a miscellany, mainly for a new and expanding and culturally inexperienced middle-class audience. The modern newspaper, from the eighteenth century but very much more markedly from the nineteenth century, became a miscellany, not only of news items that were often essentially unrelated, but of features, anecdotes, drawings, photographs and advertisements. From the late nineteenth century this came to be reflected in formal layout, culminating in the characteristic jigsaw effect of the modern newspaper page. Meanwhile, sporting events, especially football matches, as they became increasingly important public occasions, included entertainment such as music or marching in their intervals.

This general trend, towards an increasing variability and miscellaneity of public communications, is evidently part of a whole social experience. It has profound connections with the growth and development of greater physical and social mobility, in conditions both of cultural expansion and of consumer rather than community cultural organisation. Yet until the coming of broadcasting the normal expectation was still of a discrete event or of a succession of discrete events. People took a book or a pamphlet or a newspaper, went out to a play or a concert or a meeting or a match, with a single predominant expectation and attitude. The social relationships set up in these various cultural events were specific and in some degree temporary.

Broadcasting, in its earliest stages, inherited this tradition and worked mainly within it. Broadcasters discovered the kinds of thing they could do or, as some of them would still normally say, transmit. The musical concert could be broadcast or arranged for broadcasting. The public address – the lecture or the sermon, the speech at a meeting – could be broadcast as a talk. The sports match could be described and shown. The play could be performed, in this new theatre of the air. Then as the service extended, these items, still considered as discrete units, were assembled into programmes. The word 'programme' is characteristic, with its traditional bases in theatre and music-hall. With increasing organisation, as the service extended, this 'programme' became a series of timed units. Each unit could be thought of discretely, and the work of programming was a serial assembly of these units. Problems of mix and proportion became predominant in broadcasting policy. Characteristically, as most clearly in the development of British sound broadcasting, there was a steady evolution from a general service, with its internal criteria of mix and proportion and what was called 'balance', to contrasting types of service, alternative programmes. 'Home', 'Light' and 'Third', in British radio, were the eventual names for what were privately described and indeed generally understood as 'general', 'popular' and 'educated' broadcasting. Problems of mix and proportion, formerly considered within a single service, were then basically transferred to a range of alternative programmes, corresponding to assumed social and educational levels. This tendency was taken further in later forms of reorganisation, as in the present specialised British radio services One to Four. In an American radio programme listing, which is before me as I write, there is a further specialisation: the predominantly musical programmes are briefly characterised, by wavelength, as 'rock', 'country', 'classical', 'nostalgic' and so on. In one sense this can be traced as a development of programming: extensions of the service have brought further degrees of rationalisation and specialisation.

But the development can also be seen, and in my view needs to be seen, in quite other ways. There has been a significant shift from the concept of sequence as *programming* to the concept of sequence as *flow*. Yet this is difficult to see because the older concept of programming – the temporal sequence within which mix and proportion and balance operate – is still active and still to some extent real.

What is it then that has been decisively altered? A broadcasting programme, on sound or television, is still formally a series of timed units. What is published as information about the broadcasting services is still of this kind: we can look up the time of a particular 'show' or 'programme'; we can turn on for that item; we can select and respond to it discretely.

Yet for all the familiarity of this model, the normal experience of broadcasting, when we really consider it, is different. And indeed this is recognised in the ways we speak of 'watching television', 'listening to the radio', picking on the general rather than the specific experience. This has been true of all broadcasting, but some significant internal developments have greatly reinforced it. These developments can be indicated in one simple way. In earlier phases of the broadcasting service, both in sound and television, there were *intervals* between programme units: true intervals, usually marked by some conventional sound or picture to show that the general service was still active. There was the sound of bells or the sight of waves breaking, and these marked the intervals between discrete programme units. There is still a residual example of this type in the turning globe which functions as an interval signal in BBC television.

But in most television services, as they are currently operated, the concept of the interval – though still, for certain purposes, retained as a concept – has been fundamentally revalued. This change came about in two ways, which are still unevenly represented in different services. The decisive innovation was in services financed by commercial television. There was a specific and formal undertaking that 'programmes' should not be interrupted by advertising; this could take place only in 'natural breaks': between the movements of a

233

symphony, or between the acts in *Hamlet*, as the Government spokesman said in the House of Lords! In practice, of course, this was never complied with, nor was it ever intended that it should be. A 'natural break' became any moment of convenient insertion. News programmes, plays, even films that had been shown in cinemas as specific whole performances, began to be interrupted for commercials. On American television this development was different; the sponsored programmes incorporated the advertising from the outset, from the initial conception, as part of the whole package. But it is now obvious, in both British and American commercial television, that the notion of 'interruption', while it has still some residual force from an older model, has become inadequate. What is being offered is not, in older terms, a programme of discrete units with particular insertions, but a planned flow, in which the true series is not the published sequence of programme items but this sequence transformed by the inclusion of another kind of sequence, so that these sequences together compose the real flow, the real 'broadcasting'. Increasingly, in both commercial and public-service television, a further sequence was added: trailers of programmes to be shown at some later time or on some later day, or more itemised programme news. This was intensified in conditions of competition, when it became important to broadcasting planners to retain viewers – or as they put it, to 'capture' them – for a whole evening's sequence. And with the eventual unification of these two or three sequences, a new kind of communication phenomenon has to be recognised.

Of course many people who watch television still register some of these items as 'interruptions'. I remember first noticing the problem while watching films on British commercial television. For even in an institution as wholeheartedly commercial in production and distribution as the cinema, it had been possible, and indeed remains normal, to watch a film as a whole, in an undisturbed sequence. All films were originally made and distributed in this way, though the inclusion of supporting 'B' films and short features in a package, with appropriate intervals for advertising and for the planned selling of refreshments, began to develop the cinema towards the new kind of planned flow. Watching the same films on commercial television made the new situation quite evident. We are normally given some twenty or twenty-five minutes of the film, to get us interested in it; then four minutes of commercials, then about fifteen more minutes of the film; some commercials again; and so on to steadily decreasing lengths of the film, with commercials between them, or them between the commercials, since by this time it is assumed that we are interested and will watch the film to the end. Yet even this had not prepared me for the characteristic American sequence. One night in Miami, still dazed from a week on an Atlantic liner, I began watching a film and at first had some difficulty in adjusting to a much greater frequency of commercial 'breaks'. Yet this was a minor problem compared to what eventually happened. Two other films, which were due to be shown on the same channel on other nights, began to be inserted as trailers. A crime in San Francisco (the subject of the original film) began to operate in an extraordinary counterpoint not only with the deodorant and cereal commercials but with a romance in Paris and the eruption of a prehistoric monster who laid waste New York. Moreover, this was sequence in a new sense. Even in commercial British television there is a visual signal – the residual sign of an interval – before and after the commercial sequences, and 'programme' trailers only occur between 'programmes'. Here there was something quite different, since the transitions from film to commercial and from film A to films B and C were in effect unmarked. There is in any case enough similarity between certain kinds of films, and between several kinds of film and the 'situation' commercials which often consciously imitate them, to make a sequence of this kind a very difficult experience to interpret. I can still not be sure what I took from that whole flow. I believe I registered some incidents as happening in the wrong film, and some characters in the commercials as involved in the film episodes, in what came to seem – for all the occasional bizarre disparities – a single irresponsible flow of images and feelings.

Of course the films were not made to be 'interrupted' in this way. But this flow is planned: not only in itself, but at an early stage in all original television production for commercial systems. Indeed most commercial television 'programmes' are made, from the planning stage, with this real sequence in mind. In quite short plays there is a rationalised division into 'acts'. In features there is a similar rationalised division into 'parts'. But the effect goes deeper. There is a characteristic kind of opening sequence, meant to excite interest, which is in effect a kind of trailer for itself. In American television, after two or three minutes, this is succeeded by commercials. The technique has an early precedent in the dumbshows which preceded plays or scenes in early Elizabethan theatre. But there what followed dumbshow was the play or the scene. Here what follows is apparently quite unconnected material. It is then not surprising that so many of these opening moments are violent or bizarre: the interest aroused must be strong enough to initiate the expectation of (interrupted but sustainable) sequence. Thus a quality of the external sequence becomes a mode of definition of an internal method.

At whatever stage of development this process has reached – and it is still highly variable between different broadcasting systems – it can still be residually seen as 'interruption' of a 'programme'. Indeed it is often important to see it as this, both for one's own true sense of place and event, and as a matter of reasonable concern in broadcasting policy. Yet it may be even more important to see the true process as flow: the replacement of a programme series of timed sequential units by a flow series of differently related units in which the timing, though real, is undeclared, and in which the real internal organisation is something other than the declared organisation.

For the 'interruptions' are in one way only the most visible characteristic of a process which at some levels has come to define the television experience. Even when, as on the BBC, there are no interruptions of specific 'programme units', there is a quality of flow which our received vocabulary of discrete response and description cannot easily acknowledge. It is evident that what is now called 'an evening's viewing' is in some ways planned, by providers and then by viewers, *as a whole*; that it is in any event planned in discernible sequences which in this sense override particular programme units. Whenever there is competition between television channels, this becomes a matter of conscious concern: to get viewers in at the beginning of a flow. Thus in Britain there is intense competition between BBC and IBA in the early evening programmes, in the belief – which some statistics support – that viewers will stay with whatever channel they begin watching. There are of course many cases in which this does not happen: people can consciously select another channel or another programme, or switch off altogether. But the flow effect is sufficiently widespread to be a major element in programming policy. And this is the immediate reason for the increasing frequency of programming trailers: to sustain that evening flow. In conditions of more intense competition, as between the American channels, there is even more frequent trailing, and the process is specifically referred to as 'moving along', to sustain what is thought of as a kind of brand-loyalty to the channel being watched. Some part of the flow offered is then directly traceable to conditions of controlled competition, just as some of its specific original elements are traceable to the financing of television by commercial advertising.

Yet this is clearly not the whole explanation. The flow offered can also, and perhaps more fundamentally, be related to the television experience itself. Two common observations bear on this. As has already been noted, most of us say, in describing the experience, that we have been 'watching television', rather than that we have watched 'the news' or 'a play' or 'the football' 'on television'. Certainly we sometimes say both, but the fact that we say the former at all is already significant. Then again it is a widely if often ruefully admitted experience that many of us find television very difficult to switch off; that again and again, even when we have switched on for a particular 'programme', we find ourselves watching the one after it and the one after that. The way in which the flow is now organised, without definite intervals, in any case encourages this. We can be 'into' something else before we have summoned the energy to get out of the chair, and many programmes are made with this situation in mind: the grabbing of attention in the early moments; the reiterated promise of exciting things to come, if we stay.

But the impulse to go on watching seems more widespread than this kind of organisation would alone explain. It is significant that there has been steady pressure, not only from the television providers but from many viewers, for an extension of viewing hours. In Britain, until recently, television was basically an evening experience, with some brief offerings in the middle of the day, and with morning and afternoon hours, except at weekends, used for schools and similar broadcasting. There is now a rapid development of morning and afternoon 'programmes' of a general kind. In the United States it is already possible to begin watching at six o'clock in the morning, see one's first movie at eight-thirty, and so on in a continuous flow, with the screen never blank, until the late movie begins at one o'clock the following morning. It is scarcely possible that many people watch a flow of that length, over more than twenty hours of the day. But the flow is always accessible, in several alternative sequences, at the flick of a switch. Thus, both internally, in its immediate organisation, and as a generally available experience, this characteristic of flow seems central.

Yet it is a characteristic for which hardly any of our received modes of observation and description prepare us. The reviewing of television programmes is of course of uneven quality, but in most even of the best reviews there is a conventional persistence from earlier models. Reviewers pick out this play or that feature, this discussion programme or that documentary. I reviewed television once a month over four years, and I know how much more settling, more straightforward, it is to do that. For most of the items there are some received procedures, and the method, the vocabulary, for a specific kind of description and response exists or can be adapted. Yet while that kind of reviewing can be useful, it is always at some distance from what seems to me the central television experience: the fact of flow. It is not only that many particular items – given our ordinary organisation of response, memory and persistence of attitude and mood – are affected by those preceding and those following them, unless we watch in an artificially timed way which seems to be quite rare (though it exists in the special viewings put on for regular Reviewers). It is also that though useful things may be said about all the separable items (though often with conscious exclusion of the commercials which 'interrupt' at least half of them) hardly anything is ever said about the characteristic experience of the flow sequence itself. It is indeed very difficult to say anything about this. It would be like trying to describe having read two plays, three newspapers, three or four magazines, on the same day that one has been to a variety show and a lecture and a football match. And yet in another way it is not like that at all, for though the items may be various the television experience has in some important ways unified them. To break this experience back into units, and to write about the units for which there are readily available procedures, is understandable but often misleading, even when we defend it by the gesture that we are discriminating and experienced viewers and don't just sit there hour after hour goggling at the box.

For the fact is that many of us do sit there, and much of the critical significance of television must be related to this fact. I know that whenever I tried, in reviewing, to describe the experience of flow, on a particular evening or more generally, what I could say was unfinished and tentative, yet I learned from correspondence that I was engaging with an experience which many viewers were aware of and were trying to understand. There can be 'classical' kinds of response, at many different levels, to some though not all of the discrete units. But we are only just beginning to recognise, let alone solve, the problems of description and response to the facts of flow.

19

BROADCAST TV NARRATION

John Ellis

Commercial entertainment cinema is overwhelmingly a narrative fiction medium. Non-fiction films have always had a precarious place in the commercial cinema, and nowadays they are practically non-existent. Broadcast TV on the other hand carries large amounts of non-fiction: news, documentaries, announcements, weather forecasts, various kinds of segments that are purely televisual in their characteristic forms. It could be argued, therefore, that any model of televisual narration would have to give pride of place to this division of TV products between fiction and non-fiction. Whereas the classical narrative model, basically a fiction model, still underlies our assumptions about the entertainment film, it would seem that no such generalised conception of TV narration would be possible. In fact, this does not seem to be the case. Quite the reverse, the non-fiction and fiction modes of exposition of meanings seem to have converged within TV, under the impulsion of the characteristic broadcast TV forms of the segment and the series, and the pervasive sense of the TV image as live. This has produced a distinctive regime of fictional narration on TV which owes much to its non-fictional modes. After all, the first true use of the open-ended series format would seem to be the news bulletin, endlessly updating events and never synthesising them.

The mode of narration on TV does not have to be divided into two distinct models, one appropriate to fiction, the other to non-fiction. Instead, one model seems to be enough, a model that is capable of inflection by fictional or

From John Ellis, *Visible Fictions: Cinema, Television, Video* (London: Routledge and Kegan Paul, 1982) Ch.9.

non-fictional concerns. This explains the case that TV has long since had of producing programmes that are ambiguous in their status: the documentary-drama, or the drama-documentary, forms that seem to have existed in the late 1950s at least on the BBC. The divisions between fiction and non-fiction exist at another level to that of narration; they are chiefly concerned with the origin of material used in the programme.

Any model of narration on broadcast TV therefore has to be based on the particular institutional and material nature of that TV as we now know it. It depends on the conception of the broadcast output as that of segment following segment, segments which by no means always have any connection between them. It depends on the counterpart to this segmental process, the programme series with its distinctive forms of repetition and favoured forms of problematic. It depends on the conception of TV as a casual, domestic form, watched without great intensity or continuity of attention. It assumes the ideology of TV as a medium which transmits events as they happen, even though (especially in Britain) this is virtually never the case. It is worth repeating in this connection that, although the overwhelming mass of TV output is recorded, it still carries a different sense of immediacy from the cinematic image. Broadcast TV is capable of adopting a filmic mode of narration as a kind of borrowing from an already established medium. This will almost always be announced as such: by the form of the TV movie (often a 'pilot' for a series), or by the designation of a programme as a prestigious cultural event. This tends to mean that the programme will not so much have been made on film as made within a cinematic mode of narration. In this sense, TV acknowledges a certain inferiority to cinema. Cinema, for TV, means the culturally respectable, the artistic text. The designation 'film' for a TV transmission indicates that this transmission is to be viewed despite TV; it is not to be segmented, interruptions in terms of advertisements breaks or viewer attention 'at home' are to be kept to a minimum. The 'film' transmission on TV will then proceed to construct a more cinematic narration. The vast majority of such events, indeed, are cinema films which have already been exhibited in a cinematic context. Cinema is currently not capable of a similar borrowing of broadcast TV forms, however: the collective exhibition of TV material is still a novelty or an aberration.

Cinema narration has a strong internal dynamic, a movement from an initial equilibrium that is disrupted towards a new harmony that is the end of the fiction. Broadcast TV narration has a more dispersed narrational form: it is extensive rather than sequential. Its characteristic mode is not one of final closure or totalising vision; rather, it offers a continuous refiguration of events. Like the news bulletin series, the broadcast TV narrative (fiction and non-fiction) is open-ended, providing a continuous update, a perpetual return to the present. Since closure and finality is not a central feature of TV narration (though it does occur in specific major ways), it follows that the hermetic nature of the cinema narrative, with its patterns of repetition and novelty, is also absent. Repetition in the TV narrative occurs at the level of the series:

formats are repeated, situations return week after week. Each time there is novelty. The characters of the situation comedy encounter a new dilemma; the documentary reveals a new problem; the news gives us a fresh strike, a new government, another earthquake, the first panda born in captivity. This form of repetition is different from that offered by the classic cinema narrative, as it provides a kind of groundbase, a constant basis for events, rather than an economy of reuse directed towards a final totalisation.

The series is composed of segments. The recognition of the series format tends to hold segments together and to provide them with an element of continuity and narrative progression from one to the next. The segment form itself has a strong internal coherence. Certain forms of segments are free-standing: the spot advertisement and the item in the news bulletin are both examples. They occur alongside similar segments which have no connection with them except a similarity of class. Other segments, those in a documentary exposition of a particular situation, or a fictional depiction of characters, will have definite connections of a narrative kind. But again, the movement from event to event is not as concentrated and causal as it tends to be in classic cinema narration. Broadcast TV's fictional segments tend to explore states and incidents in real time, avoiding the abbreviation that is characteristic of cinema. Hence a certain sense of intimacy in TV drama, a different pace and attention from entertainment cinema.

The segment is self-contained in TV production partly because of the fragmentary nature of much broadcast TV (especially if it carries spot advertising), but also because of the attention span that TV assumes of its audience, and the fact that memory of the particular series in all its detail cannot be assumed. People switch on in the middle and get hooked; they miss an episode or two; someone phones up in the middle. The TV production cannot be hermetic in the way that the film text is, otherwise the audience for a long-running soap opera like *Coronation Street* would now consist of half a dozen ageing addicts. The segment and the series are the repository of memory, and thus of the possibility of repetition and coherence.

The segment is a relatively self-contained scene which conveys an incident, a mood or a particular meaning. Coherence is provided by a continuity of character through the segment, or, more occasionally, a continuity of place. Hence many fictional segments consist of conversations between two or three characters, an encounter which produces a particular mood (embarrassment, relief, anger, love-at-first-sight, insults, anxiety) and tends to deliver a particular meaning which is often encapsulated in a final line. The segment ends and, in conventional TV fiction, is succeeded by another which deals with a different set of (related) characters in a different place, or the same characters at a different time. There is a marked break between segments. The aspect of break, of end and beginning, tends to outweigh the aspect of continuity and consequence. The non-fiction segment tends to operate in the same way, though in the expository or investigatory documentary it is a series of fragments (interviews, stills, captions, studio presenters, reporter-to-camera in locations) which are held together as a segment by the fact that they all combine to deliver a particular message. Each segment then represents a 'move' in the argument of the overall programme. In both drama and investigatory documentary, the segment is relatively self-contained and usually does not last longer than five minutes.

Being self-contained, the segment tends to exhaust its material, providing its own climax which is the culmination of the material of the segment. It is a characteristic of soap operas that they withhold the climactic revelation or action to the end of the segment and the end of the episode. [. . .] This process of climaxing directly followed by a break to other forms of segments (title sequences, advertisements, programme announcements, etc.) generates a series of segments in the next episode which effectively chart the repercussions of the climactic event. A series of conversations and actions exhaustively explores and, in the process, recapitulates the climactic action or revelation. The discovery of a husband's affair is followed by a rush of disconnected segments, adverts and so on; a week's wait produces a series of conversations: wife to friend, children, neighbours; husband to lover, colleague; and perhaps even The Couple them selves. Each depicts a certain attitude and mood, produces subsidiary revelations and mulls over the situation. These segments are self-exhausting: enough is said, done and shown to convey a particular meaning. This completion and internal coherence means that movement from one segment to the next is a matter of succession rather than consequence.

This effect of the self-containedness of the segment is intensified, especially in fiction and observational documentary work, by the use of real time. Where cinema elides actions within a scene by cutting out 'dead time' (a character's movement across a room that has no directly narrative function, for example), TV tends to leave this 'dead time' in. This stems directly from the studio multiple camera technique, where events are staged in temporal sequence and picked up by a number of cameras one of whose images is selected at any one moment by the director. Where cinema stages events in a very fragmentary way (sometimes just a gesture, a look), TV will stage much more like a theatrical scene. The result is that events unroll in real time for the audience, in the time that they took. A segment will tend to hold to temporal unity, especially if it is a conversation. This produces a sense of intimacy within the segment, and a sharp break between segments.

[. . .]

The narrative movement between segments does not follow the cinematic pattern of a relatively rapid transition from event to event in causal sequence. The movement from event to event is more circumspect. This circumspection shows itself in two ways. The first is the multiplication of incidents whose consequences and conclusion are suspended. This is a characteristic of the TV action series like the cop saga *Starsky and Hutch*. Our heroes perpetually encounter fresh incidents, and equally often find themselves suspended in an ambiguous position at the end of a segment (cue for commercial break). The second form of circumspect movement from event to event is that characterised by the soap opera and the drama alike. Events are at a premium: when they occur they generate tidal waves of verbiage, of gossip, discussion, speculation, recrimination. Guilt, jealousy, worry and an immense curiosity about people is generated by this form. The action series tends to generate car journeys, car chases, interrogations and the segment that reveals the furtive goings-on that the action-heroes will head off.

In each form, the events that take place are anticipated. For the soap opera/ drama, the deliciousness of the anticipation is worth in many instances more than the event itself. Speculation abounds; the event is perfunctory; the mulling over of the repercussions is extended. But it is a characteristic of the action series too that it carries few surprises. Its form of suspense is more incidental. Rather than proposing a central 'whodunnit' problem, it is more characteristic to find the central mystery revealed fairly early in the programme. Suspense then becomes a serial affair: the heroes and villains become entangled in a series of different situations, each of which involves escape, chase, shoot-out, etc. Narration in the cinematic sense is relatively perfunctory. Little play is made with the fact that the solution to the 'whodunnit' has been revealed to the audience before it has to the heroes. This differential knowledge and analytic attittude to the actions of the heroes, characteristic of a cinema director like Fritz Lang (who usually reveals the narrative enigma to the audience), is relatively absent.

[...]

The unifying principle behind TV programmes is not as it is in cinema (significant patterns of repetition and innovation of meanings; narrative sequence; central problematic); it is the series which provides coherence between segments. The series provides the unity of a particular programme, pulling together segments into a sense of connection which enables a level of narrative progression to take place between them. The series is the major point of repetition in TV, matching the innovation that takes place within each segment. This pattern of repetition and innovation is very different from the cinematic model. Where the cinematic form is a closed system which aims to reuse as much material as possible and to balance kinds of repetition and innovation against each other, the TV form is more open-ended. It is a pattern of repetition that is far more centred on the narrative problematic than in cinema. Cinema's single texts tend to inaugurate a novel problematic, a new story subject, for each film. The TV series repeats a problematic. It therefore provides no resolution of the problematic at the end of each episode, nor, often, even at the end of the run of a series. Hence again the reduction of onward narrative progression. The TV series proposes a problematic that is not resolved; narrative resolution takes place at a less fundamental level, at the level of the particular incidents (clinches, confrontations, conversations) that are offered each week (in the case of situation comedies) or between one week and the next (with the cliff-hanger serial ending). Fundamentally, the series implies the form of the dilemma rather than that of resolution and closure. This perhaps is the central contribution that broadcast TV has made to the long history of narrative forms and narrativised perception of the world.

The series is based on the repetition of a problematic. It repeats a situation, a situation which can be fictional or non-fictional. Hence the news series and the current affairs series both present a certain inquiring, fact-finding vision: the situation of reporters observing and collating information, then organising it for presentation to an uninformed public. This is as much a situation as a father and son running a scrap business with a totter's horse and cart and a crowded London yard (*Steptoe and Son*). The news and current affairs series present a problematic of vision and of explanation. Specific characters encounter a specific set of circumstances every week. But across the specificity of the week's circumstances runs the generality of the same problematic: that of how to see, how to understand. The terms of the understanding are always specified by the programme format. It will be 'we go behind the scenes' (*Panorama*), 'we ask the awkward questions' (*World in Action*), 'we update and see how this affects London' (*The London Programme*), 'we glance around' (*Nationwide*). In addition to these specific forms of understanding, there are the terms in which these understandings are cast: 'moderate/extremist', 'the housewife', 'But surely you don't think that . . . ?' The role of presenter is fundamental to these opera-tions. The characters who investigate and explain for us are a loose group remarkably similar to the cast of a soap opera: some are central, long-running figures (presenters, anchor-persons); others come and go (reporters). In some areas of current affairs, the soap opera aspect becomes more or less explicit. *Nationwide* and *That's Life* are specific examples. The series format constitutes a stable basis of repetition in the programme format, its cast of characters, and its particular kind of reporting attention. Novelty in each edition is provided by the specific circumstances that these characters and their vision run up against. It is often explicit that the particular focus of attention for the characters is provided by outside forces over which they have no control, the world of current events. This world tends to be constituted as a place where problems occur. The political actions that the current events series is constituted to explain thus become a particular modality of action: they are problems, troubles, disturbances. The current events series provides a security against these disturbances. The result is that the political arena tends to be given the same status as the emotional problems encountered by soap opera characters. This is one effect of the series format, and one aspect of it.

The fictional series, too, repeats a basic problematic or situation week after week. Like the news and current affairs series, the situation comedy, the crime drama and the hospital series all return to the stability of the basic dilemma at the end of the week's episode. There is no development at all across the series. The serial marks a long slow narrative movement towards a conclusion, but often that conclusion is tentative (allowing a second series) or incidental (the dispersion of the characters). The situation that provides the steady core is a state of permanent or semi-permanent relationships between a stable but antagonistic group of characters. This is most fully developed in the situation comedy. *Steptoe and Son* may well hate each other, but they also love each other, and Harold's repeated threats to leave his father were never serious. This is exactly the dilemma that situation comedy deals with: it presents conflicting forces or emotions that can never be resolved. Hence the series situation is highly suited to present a particular static vision of the family and of work relations. What is particularly marked about the situation series is that the characters lose all memory of the previous week's incidents. They never learn.

[...]

Repetition across the series is one of problematic, of both characters and the situation (or dilemma) in which they find themselves. These situations provide a steady state to which audience and fiction return each week. Specific incidents are fed into this steady state, to provide fresh ammunition for our embattled family to fire at each other and the world, or for our reporters to look into and arrange for our inspection and concern. The incidental problems are solved, but the series format provides no real place for its own resolution. There is no final closure to the series' own recurring problematic. The run of a series ends without resolving its basic dilemma. This marks a basic difference between the cinema narrative and the TV series narrative. The film text aims for a final coherent totalising vision, which sets everything back into order. The series does not share this movement from stable state to stable state. The basic problematic of the series, with all its conflicts, is itself a stable state.

[...]

20

THE ROLE OF STEREOTYPES

Richard Dyer

The word 'stereotype' is today almost always a term of abuse. This stems from the wholly justified objections of various groups – in recent years, blacks, women and gays, in particular – to the ways in which they find themselves stereotyped in the mass media and in everyday speech. Yet when Walter Lippmann coined the term, he did not intend it to have a wholly and necessarily pejorative connotation. Taking a certain ironic distance on his subject, Lippmann none the less lays out very clearly both the absolute necessity for, and the usefulness of, stereotypes, as well as their limitations and ideological implications:

> A pattern of stereotypes is not neutral. It is not merely a way of substituting order for the great blooming, buzzing confusion of reality. It is not merely a short cut. It is all these things and something more. It is the guarantee of our self-respect; it is the projection upon the world of our own sense of our own value, our own position and our own rights. The stereotypes are, therefore, highly charged with the feelings that are attached to them. They are the fortress of our tradition, and behind its defenses we can continue to feel ourselves safe in the position we occupy. (1956: 96)

We can begin to understand something of how stereotypes work by following up the ideas raised by Lippmann – in particular his stress on stereotypes as (i) an ordering process, (ii) a 'short cut', (iii) referring to 'the world', and (iv)

From Jim Cook and Mike Lewington (eds) *Images of Alcoholism* (London: British Film Institute, 1979). Reprinted as Ch. 3 of Richard Dyer, *The Matter of Images: Essays on Representations* (London: Routledge, 1993).

expressing 'our' values and beliefs. The rest of this essay is structured around these topics, concluding with some tentative remarks on the relevance of what has gone before [in Dyer, 1993] to the representation of alcoholism. Throughout, I move between the more sociological concern of Lippmann (how stereotypes function in social thought) and the specific aesthetic concerns (how stereotypes function in fictions) that must also be introduced into any consideration of media representations. The position behind all these considerations is that it is not stereotypes, as an aspect of human thought and representation, that are wrong, but who controls and defines them, what interests they serve.

AN ORDERING PROCESS

Stereotypes as a form of 'ordering' the mass of complex and inchoate data that we receive from the world are only a particular form – to do with the representation and categorization of persons[1] – of the wider process by which any human society, and individuals within it, make sense of that society through generalities, patternings and 'typifications'. Unless one believes that there is some definitively 'true' order in the world which is transparently revealed to human beings and unproblematically expressed in their culture – a belief that the variety of orders proposed by different societies, as analysed by anthropology and history, makes difficult to sustain – this activity of ordering, including the use of stereotypes, has to be acknowledged as a necessary, indeed inescapable, part of the way societies make sense of themselves, and hence actually make and reproduce themselves. (The fact that all such orderings are, by definition, partial and limited does not mean that they are untrue – partial knowledge is not false knowledge, it is simply not absolute knowledge.)

There are, however, two problems about stereotypes within this perspective. Firstly, the need to order 'the great blooming, buzzing confusion of reality' is liable to be accompanied by a belief in the absoluteness and certainty of any particular order, a refusal to recognize its limitations and partiality, its relativity and changeability, and a corresponding incapacity to deal with the fact and experience of blooming and buzzing.

Secondly, as the work of Peter Berger and Thomas Luckmann, amongst others, on the 'social construction of reality' stresses, not only is any given society's ordering of reality an historical product but it is also necessarily implicated in the power relations in that society – as Berger and Luckmann put it, 'he who has the bigger stick has the better chance of imposing his definitions of reality' (1967: 127). I shall return below to these two problems of Lippmann's formulation – order (stereotypes) perceived as absolute and rigid, order (stereotypes) as grounded in social power.

A SHORT CUT

Lippmann's notion of stereotypes as a short cut points to the manner in which stereotypes are a very simple, striking, easily-grasped form of representation but are none the less capable of condensing a great deal of complex information and a host of connotations. As T. E. Perkins notes in her key article 'Rethinking Stereotypes', the often observed 'simplicity' of stereotypes is deceptive:

> to refer 'correctly' to someone as a 'dumb blonde', and to understand what is meant by that, implies a great deal more than hair colour and intelligence. It refers immediately to *her* sex, which refers to her status in society, her relationship to men, her inability to behave or think rationally, and so on. In short, it implies knowledge of a complex social structure. (1979: 139)

The same point emerges from Arnold S. Linsky's analysis (1970–1) of the representation of the alcoholic in popular magazines between 1900 and 1966, where changing depictions of alcoholics are shown to express complex and contradictory social theories not merely of alcoholism but of free will and determinism.

REFERENCE

Lippmann refers to stereotypes as a projection on to the 'world'. Although he is not concerned primarily to distinguish stereotypes from modes of representation whose principal concern is not the world, it is important for us to do so, especially as our focus is representations in media *fictions*, which are aesthetic as well as social constructs. In this perspective, stereotypes are a particular subcategory of a broader category of fictional characters, the type. Whereas stereotypes are essentially defined, as in Lippmann, by their social function, types, at this level of generality, are primarily defined by their aesthetic function, namely, as a mode of characterization in fiction. The type is any character constructed through the use of a few immediately recognizable and defining traits, which do not change or 'develop' through the course of the narrative and which point to general, recurrent features of the human world (whether these features are conceptualized as universal and eternal, the 'archetype', or historically and culturally specific, 'social types' and 'stereotypes' – a distinction discussed below).[2] The opposite of the type is the novelistic character, defined by a multiplicity of traits that are only gradually revealed to us through the course of the narrative, a narrative which is hinged on the growth or development of the character and is thus centred upon the latter in her or his unique individuality, rather than pointing outwards to a world.

In our society, it is the novelistic character that is privileged over the type, for the obvious reason that our society privileges – at any rate, at the level of social rhetoric – the individual over the collective or the mass. For this reason, the majority of fictions that address themselves to general social issues tend nevertheless to end up telling the story of a particular individual, hence returning social issues to purely personal and psychological ones. Once we address ourselves to the representation and definition of social categories – e.g. alcoholics –

we have to consider what is at stake in one mode of characterization rather than another. Where do we want the emphasis of the representation to lie – on the psychological (alcoholism as a personal problem), on the social (alcoholism as an aspect of society) or in some articulation of the two? The choice or advocacy of a more novelistic or a more typical representation implicitly expresses one or other of these emphases.

THE EXPRESSION OF VALUES

It is Lippmann's reference to *our* tradition, and indeed his use of 'our' and 'we' throughout the passage quoted, that takes us into the most important, and most problematic, issue in stereotyping. For we have to ask, who exactly are the 'we' and 'us' invoked by Lippmann? – is it necessarily you and me?

The effectiveness of stereotypes resides in the way they invoke a consensus. Stereotypes proclaim, 'This is what everyone – you, me and us – thinks members of such-and-such a social group are like', as if these concepts of these social groups were spontaneously arrived at by all members of society independently and in isolation. The stereotype is taken to express a general agreement about a social group, as if that agreement arose before, and independently of, the stereotype. Yet for the most part it is *from* stereotypes that we get our ideas about social groups. The consensus invoked by stereotypes is more apparent than real; rather, stereotypes express particular definitions of reality, with concomitant evaluations, which in turn relate to the disposition of power within society. Who proposes the stereotype, who has the power to enforce it, is the crux of the matter – *whose* tradition is Lippmann's 'our tradition'?

Here Orrin E. Klapp's distinction between stereotypes and social types is helpful. In his book *Heroes, Villains and Fools* (1962) Klapp defines social types as representations of those who 'belong' to society. They are the kinds of people that one expects, and is led to expect, to find in one's society, whereas stereotypes are those who do not belong, who are outside of one's society. In Klapp, this distinction is principally geographic – i.e. social types of Americans, stereotypes of non-Americans. We can, however, rework his distinction in terms of the types produced by different social groups according to their sense of who belongs and who doesn't, who is 'in' and who is not. Who does or does not belong to a given society as a whole is then a function of the relative power of groups in that society to define themselves as central and the rest as 'other', peripheral or outcast.

In fictions, social types and stereotypes can be recognized as distinct by the different ways in which they can be used. Although constructed iconographically similarly to the way stereotypes are constructed (i.e. a few verbal and visual traits are used to signal the character), social types can be used in a much more open and flexible way than can stereotypes. This is most clearly seen in relation to plot. Social types can figure in almost any kind of plot and can have a wide range of roles in that plot (e.g. as hero, as villain, as helper, as light relief, etc.), whereas stereotypes always carry within their very representation an implicit narrative. Jo Spence has argued in the context of the representation of women that, despite the superficial variety of images, they all carry within them an implicit narrative pattern:

> visual representations which may appear to deal with diverse ideas but which are all aimed at women tend to act as part of an implicit narrative. This has a 'beginning' and a 'middle' (birth, childhood, marriage, family life) but there is only minimal representations of its 'end', of growing old and dying. (1980: 29–45)

In an article dealing with the stereotyping of gays in films, I tried to show how the use of images of lesbians in a group of French films, no matter what kind of film or of what 'artistic quality', always involved an identical plot function (1977: 33–5). Similarly, we surely only have to be told that we are going to see a film about an alcoholic to know that it will be a tale either of sordid decline or of inspiring redemption. (This suggests a particularly interesting potential use of stereotypes, in which the character is constructed, at the level of dress, performance, etc., as a stereotype but is deliberately given a narrative function that is not implicit in the stereotype, thus throwing into question the assumptions signalled by the stereotypical iconography.)

The social type/stereotype distinction is essentially one of degree. It is after all very hard to draw a line between those who are just within and those definitely beyond the pale. This is partly because different social categories overlap – e.g. men 'belong', blacks do not, but what of black men? It is also because some of the categories that the social type/stereotype distinction keeps apart cannot logically be kept apart in this way. The obvious examples here are men and women, and it is this that causes T. E. Perkins to reject the distinction (1979: 140–1). As applied to men and women, the social type/stereotype distinction implies that men have no direct experience of women and that there could be a society composed entirely of men: both of these are virtually impossible. Yet it seems to me that what the distinction points to, as applied to women and men, is a tendency of patriarchal thought[3] to attempt to maintain the impossible, by insisting on the 'otherness' of women and men (or rather the 'otherness' of women, men being in patriarchy the human norm to which women are 'other') in the face of their necessary collaboration in history and society. (The distinction does also refer in part to a real separation in social arrangements, i.e. the fact of male and female 'preserves': the pub, the beauty salon, the study, the kitchen, etc.) What the distinction also maintains is the *absolute* difference between men and women, in the face of their actual relative similarity.

This is the most important function of the stereotype: to maintain sharp boundary definitions, to define clearly where the pale ends and thus who is clearly within and who clearly beyond it. Stereotypes do not only, in concert with social types, map out the boundaries of acceptable and legitimate behaviour, they also insist on boundaries exactly at those points where in reality there are none. Nowhere is this more clear than with stereotypes dealing with social categories that are invisible and/or fluid. Such categories are *invisible*, because you cannot tell just from looking at a person that she or he belongs to the category in question. Unless the person chooses to dress or act in a clearly and culturally defined manner (e.g. the working-class man's cloth cap, the male homosexual's limp wrist) or unless one has a trained eye (as those dealing with alcoholics have?), it is impossible to place the person before one, whereas many social groups – women and men, different races, young and old – are visibly different, and this difference can be eradicated only by disguise. Social categories can be *fluid*, in the sense that it is not possible in reality to draw a line between them and adjacent categories. We make a fuss about – and produce stereotypes about – the difference between women and men, yet biologically this is negligible compared to their similarity. Again, we are led to treat heterosexuality and homosexuality as sharply opposed categories of persons when in reality both heterosexual and homosexual responses and behaviour are to some extent experienced by everybody in their life. Alcohol use is clearly in this category – it is notoriously difficult to draw the line between harm-free and harmful drinking. But stereotypes can.

The role of stereotypes is to make visible the invisible, so that there is no danger of it creeping up on us unawares; and to make fast, firm and separate what is in reality fluid and much closer to the norm than the dominant value system cares to admit.

In the widest sense, these functions of rendering visible and firm can be connected to Lippmann's insistence on stereotypes as ordering concepts, and to the tendency towards rigidity that may be implied by this. All societies need to have relatively stable boundaries and categories, but this stability can be achieved within a context that recognizes the relativity and uncertainty of concepts. Such a stability is, however, achieved only in a situation of real, as opposed to imposed, consensus. The degree of rigidity and shrillness of a stereotype indicates the degree to which it is an enforced representation that points to a reality whose invisibility and/or fluidity threatens the received definitions of society promoted by those with the biggest sticks. (E.g. if women are not so very different from men, why are they subordinated?; if alcoholism is not so easily distinguished from social drinking, can we be so comfortable in our acceptance of the latter and condemnation of the former?)

[...]

NOTES

1. I confine myself here to the discussion of stereotypes as a form of representing persons, although the word itself (especially in adjectival form) is also used to refer to ideas, behaviour, settings, etc.

2. It is important to stress the role of conceptualization in the distinction between, on the one hand, archetypes, and, on the other, social and stereotypes, since what may be attributed to a type as a universal and eternal trait, hence making it archetypal, may only be a historically and culturally specific trait misunderstood as a universal and eternal trait – it is, after all, the tendency of dominant value systems in societies to pass their values off as universally and eternally valid.

3. By patriarchy I mean the thought system that legitimates the power of men and the subordination of women in society; I do not mean that it is necessarily and simply how all men think of women, although it is an overwhelming determinant on that.

REFERENCES

Berger, Peter and Luckmann, Thomas (1967) *The Social Construction of Reality*, London: Allen Lane/Penguin Press.

Dyer, Richard (1977) 'Stereotyping', in Richard Dyer (ed.) *Gays and Film*, London: British Film Institute.

Klapp, Orrin E. (1962) *Heroes, Villains and Fools*, Englewood Cliffs: Prentice-Hall.

Linsky, Arnold S. (1970–1) 'Theories of Behaviour and the Image of the Alcoholic in Popular Magazines 1900–1960', *Public Opinion Quarterly* 34: 573–81.

Lippmann, Walter (1956) *Public Opinion*, New York: Macmillan. (First published 1922.)

Perkins, T. E. (1979) 'Rethinking Stereotypes', in Michèle Barrett, Philip Corrigan, Annette Kuhn and Janet Wolff (eds) *Ideology and Cultural Production*, London: Croom Helm, 135–59.

Spence, Jo (1980) 'What Do People Do All Day? Class and Gender in Images of Women', *Screen Education* 29.

21

PERFORM, EDUCATE, ENTERTAIN: INGREDIENTS OF THE COOKERY PROGRAMME GENRE

Niki Strange

Food, at the most fundamental level, is a biological necessity for life. At a more sophisticated level, cultural work such as Roland Barthes's semiological analysis of food advertising (Barthes, 1973) and Pierre Bourdieu's studies of 'taste' (Bourdieu, 1984) has acknowledged the profound significance of food.

One area within which the general cultural concern with food and cookery is manifest is the media. Indeed, cookery programmes have long formed a staple of the televisual diet fed to viewers. By contrast, the genre, as an object of study, has remained absent from the academic menu. This neglect suggests the assumption that cookery programmes (and other lifestyle/leisure genres such as gardening and home decoration) are transparent: that they are merely about food and the instruction of cookery methods and, as such, do not merit closer examination. Influenced by the existing rich cultural work about food, I turned a long-overdue critical eye to four cookery series (*Delia Smith's Christmas, Far Flung Floyd, Rhodes Around Britain* and *Madhur Jaffrey's Flavours of India*) and have developed the following terms which broadly characterise the main ingredients of the cookery programme genre and offer a framework for its study:

- 'Cookery-Educative' (Cook-Ed.): The most easily identifiable element, this term refers to instruction through cookery demonstration. It consists of an instructor; a verbal, written or visually articulated instructive discourse; and a textually inscribed tutee to whom the discourse is addressed.

From Christine Geraghty and David Lusted (eds), *The Television Studies Book* (London: Arnold 1998) Ch. 19.

- 'Personality' (Per.): Refers specifically to the instructor/presenter who is placed within the format and beyond it. I have used the term personality rather than instructor because of the useful connotations of entertainment.
- 'Tour-Educative' (Tour-Ed.): Travelogue aspects are often evident in cookery programmes. The Tour-Ed. category may serve as a channel for wider educational projects of a series.
- 'Raw-Educative' (Raw-Ed.): This category refers to the way in which the food's journey from raw state to finished dish is accommodated within a series. It may also act as a cipher for wider educational projects.

Though identifiable in their own right, these elements often interact, inflecting, affirming and sometimes short-circuiting each other. A particular construction of Per., Tour-Ed., and/or Raw-Ed., for example, may significantly alter the mode of Cook Ed. While cookery programmes have common characteristics, their configuration may thus dramatically differ. It is at these points that the programmes offer fascinating insights that serve to problematize any charge of 'transparency'.

All programmes contain some element from all of these categories, though some will be more evident than others. I intend, therefore, to explore the genre by analysing these categories more fully, using examples from particular programmes to demonstrate both the paradigm itself and the way in which it is deployed in particular instances.

COOKERY-EDUCATIVE: *DELIA SMITH'S CHRISTMAS* AND *FAR FLUNG FLOYD*

The average number of cookery demonstrations in each of the six-part series studied is four per programme. In *Delia Smith's Christmas* (or *Delia*), the length of each demonstration tends to be five minutes, whereas in *Far Flung Floyd* (or *Floyd*) it is three minutes. This broad survey indicates, firstly, the contrast between the time that may be given over to Cook-Ed.: over two-thirds of a typical *Delia* is taken up by demonstration; for *Floyd* it is under one half. Secondly, and as *Floyd* illustrates, substantial parts of a cookery programme may consist of non-demonstrative, and even non-cookery related items – something that will be explored in the following sections.

A characteristic *Delia* demonstration features in programme one in the series. The item – about Christmas cakes – opens with a sequence introducing three cakes in turn. The audio-visual repertoire is made up of medium close-up, close-up and extreme close-up shots of each of the cakes, laid out as parts of a tableau with dishes of selected ingredients and table arrangements, accompanied by Delia Smith's voice-over comments about ingredients, look, texture and taste. Three-key lighting works with the beautifully constructed tableaux to articulate that time has been spent to create an appealing context for the demonstration, working with the Cook-Ed. in two ways. By underlining that time, labour and presentation skills are fundamental to cookery, and by showing the 'finished dishes' before the demonstration, the programme reassures us that it is possible for the viewer/cook to recreate such pleasing dishes if they carefully follow the ensuing demonstration.

This sequence dissolves into a mid-shot of Delia Smith standing in her kitchen. Addressing the camera she says, 'Now if you've never made a Christmas cake before, a classic Christmas cake, and you're a little bit worried about it, what I'd like to do first of all is just go through the basic principles with you.' Following her speech are a series of inset images showing the step-by-step preparatory stages in making a classic Christmas cake. Smith's hands occasionally enter the frame: otherwise her only active participation is via voice-over, telling of precise measurements, timings and methods.

Here, the mode of Cook-Ed. address – the comforting and encouraging register of Smith's dialogue and delivery, and the chronological simplicity of the step-by-step demonstration – serves to textually inscribe a viewer/cook whose knowledge of cookery is elemental. If the aim of Cook-Ed. is to teach the viewer how to cook, then this demonstration exemplifies Cook-Ed. proper, though the real proof is in one's recreation of the 'pudding'. Even so, the Cook-Ed. is disrupted by the programme's use of elliptical editing to negotiate time constraints and lulls in action – literally watching a cake rise doesn't tend to make for entertaining television.

'Lesson two' follows immediately, with a return to Smith's kitchen. Smith addresses the camera, saying, 'Well, those were some of the basic principles of classic cake-making. Now we're going to move onto something completely different and that's a new Christmas cake called Creole cake. It comes from Trinidad . . .' The viewer/cook has been promoted from beginner to intermediary level, without shifting from armchair to kitchen. Assessing her viewers to be advanced enough to follow, and potentially at least to recreate the 'new' recipe, Smith introduces an 'exotic' twist on the standard fare. In actuality, the ingredients are typical cake ingredients; the differences occur in her use of certain alcohol, and in the particular amalgamation of those ingredients. That this recipe uses readily available raw materials typifies those featured by Smith and, in the somewhat rare instances that Smith uses ingredients that are not commonly accessible to the viewer/cook, the stampede that has ensued on the days following the broadcast has ensured that the product will be stocked on supermarket shelves from thereon.

The easy-to-follow visual and verbal instructions and relatively simple recipes that characterise the mode of Cook-Ed. in *Delia* sharply contrast to those of *Floyd*. Whilst Smith's recipes are largely selected from a menu composed of a normative British conception of a Christmas feast, Keith Floyd's dishes are drawn from a range of foreign cuisine, relating to the specific location that he is visiting on his journey. His recipes thus involve ingredients that may be less familiar and accessible to the viewer/cook: 'If you want to do this at home, cook your cobra for at least five minutes.' In the unlikelihood that the intrepid viewer/cook managed to obtain a cobra, the next obstacle in their path would be to follow Floyd's demonstration.

In order to capture the 'authenticity' of the dish, and of the place that it represents (and here, characteristically, we see an example of the Tour-Ed. element that will be discussed later), Floyd's demonstrations often use temporary 'kitchens' set up on boats, on bustling street-corners and outside village huts. Whereas Smith's demonstrations are predominantly shot in MCU, CU and ECU, with wide-shots merely utilised to establish her location and to take us into and out of a demonstrative sequence, Floyd's consist of many more wide-shots to allow for the camera to capture his surroundings. The action is thus spread across the frame; cookery is not the focal point. Indeed the demonstrations tend to be punctuated with scenic cutaways to, for example, onlooker's faces (registering their often bemused reaction to Floyd). The combination of wide-shots and scenic cutaways serves to distract the viewer/cook, and also Floyd himself, from the cooking and influences the character of the Cook-Ed.

Illustrative of this is a sequence featuring Floyd in the jungle, cooking a curry for a regiment of Vietnamese soldiers who are playing football in the background. At one point, there is a crash caused by something off-screen, and Floyd says 'That's fine. That was just a ball hitting me. You didn't see that, did you? I was injured by an enemy b- by a ball, [he giggles embarrassedly] depending on which side you were on. B-Team got me there, you see. I'm hoping the reds will win [laughs and covers mouth with hand]. Sorry . . . [another crash]. There goes the whisky.'

Despite these, albeit entertaining, distractions Floyd completes the curry and offers plates of it to the surrounding soldiers to taste. Their local knowledge enables them to assess his cookery skills and how well he has learnt about local cuisine. Such a process of judgement tends to conclude Floyd's demonstrations: in programme six, for example, he is observed by four chefs who bear testimony to his knowledge. Thus even though Floyd's demonstrations are instructive in that he talks the viewer/cook through the ingredients he is adding, and the processes by which he is creating a dish, his position as authoritative tutor is ultimately short-circuited by his construction as tutee.

My analysis of the two series demonstrates that, whilst cookery programmes may share common elements: presenter/cooks and demonstrations, they may involve dramatically different modes of Cook-Ed. In *Delia*, priority is placed upon the communication of cookery methods to the viewer/cook, with the relatively simple menu and verbal and visual clarity of demonstration designed to ensure this. In *Floyd*, the viewer/cook is not the object of the Cook-Ed., but rather the observer of Floyd's culinary adventures. As Pearson Phillips writes from an interview with Floyd: 'There are apparently people who watch Floyd with a pencil and paper at the ready, hoping to note down a recipe. "That's not what it's about", he (Floyd) says. There is one thing that he is not trying to do and that is to give cookery lessons' (Phillips, 1991: 23).

As Floyd himself asserts, his series is not about giving cookery lessons. This raises the issue that if we concentrate only on cookery we may actually miss other crucial aspects of a programme. This is even true of the most normative –

by virtue of its prioritisation of the Cook-Ed. – of the series I have looked at, *Delia Smith's Christmas*.

PERSONALITY: *DELIA SMITH'S CHRISTMAS* AND *FAR FLUNG FLOYD*

In both *Delia Smith's Christmas* and *Far Flung Floyd* the presenter lends their name to the title, implying that they are judged to be of sufficient popularity to entice viewers familiar with them as personalities. The presenters of cookery programmes may thus operate generically, as conventional sites for viewer expectations. An exploration of the genre, commonsensically and historically defined by its subject matter, should acknowledge and account for the role of the personality presenter within and beyond the immediate text.

One of the ways in which a presenter's personality is inscribed in a programme is location. The vast majority of *Delia* is set within Delia Smith's house. In the opening sequence of the series, Smith stands on her doorstep and, addressing the camera, says that by sharing her own Christmas with the viewers she hopes to help with their Christmas preparations. She even regrets that she cannot take the panic and pressure away. As she speaks, the camera zooms in from a wide-shot of Smith and her cottage to a mid-shot of Smith, doubly framed by the doorway. After a cut-away of trees gently bobbing in Smith's garden, there is a cut to Smith walking into her kitchen, the camera panning to follow her movement as she says: 'In this series I'm very pleased to be able to invite you all into my own home ...'

From the outset the register is of domestic intimacy; the viewer is welcomed into Smith's personal space. Her verbal articulation of this is compounded visually by the closing-in movement of the zoom, added to the framing within a frame expressive of enclosed space. Here, Delia Smith as televisual construct is conflated with Delia Smith as 'real' person via a shared *mise-en-scène*. The specificities of this *mise-en-scène* – domestic, private, enclosed and secure – serve as an extension of Smith's personality, reinforcing her solid, rooted and reliable presence. These characteristics in turn resonate within her mode of Cook-Ed. As Matthew Fort describes (Fort, 1995: 22): 'Short of charisma maybe, but much more importantly, you feel that Delia will never let you down. She is completely reliable, and given the anxiety – nay, terror – most of us feel when boiling an egg, having Delia at our side is very comforting.'

Unlike the static setting of *Delia*, *Far Flung Floyd* is structured around Keith Floyd's journey through the Far East. The opening sequence features Floyd at the airport, addressing the camera-operator, trying to persuade him to come on the trip: 'We'll have wonderful fun, you know. There are wonderful curries and rice dishes. We can go fishing, we can go into the jungle, we can even eat coconut milk!' Floyd's discussion of the 'wonderful fun' that he will have sets up the Personality/Cook-Ed./Tour-Ed. configuration as being framed by his role as *male* adventurer, as traditionally masculine in its dynamic journey through the public sphere as Smith's private sphere stasis is traditionally feminine.

The contrast between Smith's 'interiority' and Floyd's 'exteriority' – manifest in the different locations of the series – is also present in their verbal and gestural repertoires. Whereas Smith's delivery is measured and methodical, Floyd's is flamboyant and chaotic. Moreover, whilst both presenters directly address the camera, Floyd actively directs it. In programme six, for example, he directs the camera-operator on some thirteen occasions, with comments such as 'Follow me please, Paul ... good close-up on that please ... Paul, back to there ... okay, that's long enough'. His transgression, as registered by both his exposure of the mechanics of television and his disruption of the Cook-Ed. discourse, is subsumed to become a trait of his televised personality. In this way he stamps his authority within the format, with the demonstrations functioning as sketches (as he himself terms them, with all the connotations of comedic entertainment) in which he performs.

A significant element within his performance is his relationship with alcohol. Floyd's hedonism is in diametric opposition to Delia Smith's sobriety. In one introduction to a cookery sketch he says, after arriving at his hotel, 'Normally I'd head straight for the bar, but it was nearly morning and I was ravenous, so I made a beeline for the kitchen to cook a classic Vietnamese dish for early breakfast.' In programme six, he appears to subvert his own discourse of excess by declaring that the viewer will see a 'new him', who will be 'so fit and bright-eyed and bushy-tailed because this month not a drop of alcohol is going to pass my lips'. As the viewer would expect, he is shown guzzling red wine later on in the same programme.

These examples illustrate Floyd's role as active consumer – he performs a cookery sketch because *he's* hungry. In a wider sense his role, as adventurer, within the journey is to consume the people he meets and places he visits. It is via his impressions that the viewer learns something: as much of his uniquely personal experience of the place as the place itself. Thus, as with the Cook-Ed., a personality register may shape the mode of the Tour-Ed. within a series.

TOUR-EDUCATIVE: *RHODES AROUND BRITAIN* AND *MADHUR JAFFREY'S FLAVOURS OF INDIA*

In *Floyd*, the Cook-Ed., Personality and Tour-Ed. came together via Keith Floyd's *education* in and recreation of local cuisine drawn from his peripatetic location. By contrast, the presenters of *Rhodes Around Britain* (*Rhodes*) and *Madhur Jaffrey's Flavours of India* (*Madhur*) are constructed, via an alternative configuration, as knowledgeable tourists in their own countries. Unlike *Delia* and *Floyd*, *Rhodes* (BBC Education Department) and *Madhur* (BBC Multicultural Programmes Unit) were produced by departments within the corporation working to educational, racial and cultural remits. As I shall demonstrate, the particular configurations of the Cook-Ed., Per., Tour-Ed. and Raw-Ed. within the two series may be explained within the context of their wider educational projects.

One important way in which both presenters' knowledge is expressed is within the Cook-Ed. Gary Rhodes takes up recipes characteristic of a popular and traditional British menu. In programme five, Rhodes returns to Thanet College, where he took a basic training course in 1976, and asks the students, 'So what's cooking today, gents?' On hearing that traditional British faggots and 'good old' rhubarb are on the menu, he comments, 'I knew I'd leave an impression; back to tradition.' Yet, at the same time, Rhodes's typically intricate methods of presentation belie the simplicity of the dishes themselves. As he states in programme five, when introducing a cookery demonstration of a leek pie: 'I'm going to take a simple dish and make it special' articulating his investment in the presentation as a site of fantasy, before going on to pipe mashed potatoes onto a bed of peppered leeks. This juxtapositional celebration of the classic (recipe) and the modern (trendy notions of culinary aesthetics) resonates within Rhodes's Personality construct and the series' Tour-Ed. discourse.

Rhodes's journey features a tour of the iconography of British heritage, from a Punch and Judy show to a number of fish and chip shops and public houses. Epitomising the British 'have-a-go' spirit of amateurism, he joins in with a group of Morris dancers, drinks Guinness and argues with the locals in a bar in Belfast, and celebrates Burns night with a party of Glaswegians (Wales is conspicuous by its absence). At one end of the axis is his gaining experience of a region through being indigenized by local communities, and at the other is knowledge, which involves Rhodes imparting cookery methods in live demonstration to groups of spectators. Via Rhodes's tour, the series constructs a British community that is regionally differentiated and paradoxically unified by a shared heritage. This celebration of 'the past' and of its traditions and cuisine may be set against the modern modes of transport that Rhodes uses to 'travel back in time' to these communities: he returns to Thanet College in a blue Lotus, flies to Glasgow in a helicopter and travels by speed-boat to the oyster beds off Whitstable. He is constructed as a working-class boy (or the equivalent of a classic British recipe) made good, as expressed by his presentation/packaging. Moreover, just as his tour serves as the adhesive which binds the disparate elements of the British 'community' construct, so it paradoxically renders him as a perpetual outsider, a transient drifter.

It is possible to identify a number of bi-polar oppositions within this text:

The authenticity of classic British cuisine	Presentation of the cuisine as site of fantasy
Experience	Knowledge
Tradition	Change
Classicism	Modernity
The Raw	The Cooked
Nature	Culture

which will be explored further in the following section

These oppositions are reminiscent of structuralist definitions of the Western as: 'a series of antinomic elements defined in opposition as the axis around which the drama and its [the Western genre] conflicts are structured' (Neale, 1980: 58). Indeed, Stephen Neale's discussion of the male hero of the Western provides a useful perspective from which to view *Rhodes*'s Tour-Ed. and Gary Rhodes's position within it. The Western, Neale suggests,

> is marked by a spatial economy whose polar instances are natural land-scape on the one hand and the township/homestead on the other. Here the body of the hero is located dynamically at their intersection, oscillating between them ... the Western offers maximum scope for variations and permutations on the relation of the male figure ... as well as variations and permutations on the speed and mode of its movements.

Like the Western hero, Rhodes stands between Nature and Civilisation, Tradition and Change. He offers both a sense of adventure and the reassurance of culinary knowledge and skill; it is thus appropriate that his recipes consistently offer adventurous 'variations and permutations' on traditional national themes. As a cook, though, Rhodes perhaps has to work harder than the conventional male hero to assert his masculinity; not only is there an emphasis on the physical hunting for food – which will be discussed in the next section – but Rhodes, like a lad on a package holiday, flirts outrageously with the women he meets on his travels.

In the first programme of the *Madhur* series, Jaffrey states that 'Every part of India has a dish, a vegetable or fruit that in some way characterises the place or cuisine.' This articulates the central premise of the series: that the spirit of a region may be uncovered by looking at its use of a particular food, its methods of production and preparation, and for whom it is prepared. Whilst this mode of Tour-Ed. would appear to target an unfamiliar viewer, this is complicated by the particular formation of the Cook-Ed.

Jaffrey's recipes tend to be complex, involving many stages of preparation. In programme one she demonstrates a recipe for lamb encrusted with spices, which involves some fourteen preparatory stages and takes over one and a half hours to prepare and cook. This sequence, like many of her other demonstrations, is edited elliptically, using dissolves to mark time-shifts, and a number of preparatory stages such as the boning of the lamb are passed over. The omission of stages which require a somewhat advanced culinary knowledge renders her recipes less easily reproducible by the inexperienced viewer/cook. Moreover, Jaffrey rarely makes any concession to the viewer/cook who may be unfamiliar with the ingredients that she uses. On the one hand, then, the demonstrations address a viewer/cook who is relatively familiar with Indian cuisine. On the other, the series' premise – to demystify culture through an exploration of its cuisine – suggests that it is the unfamiliar viewer who is the object of the series' address. Though apparent in the mode of Cook-Ed., the primary site of the negotiation of the dual address is the Tour-Ed.

As with the Tour-Ed. in *Floyd* and *Rhodes*, the formal characteristics in *Madhur* consist of long-shots, to allow maximum exposure of landscapes; rapidly cut montage sequences, in a style reminiscent of a tourist's snap-shots; narration relaying historical, geographical and cultural information, as well as personal impression; and the use of local people's kitchens as locations for the cookery demonstrations to invoke an 'authenticity' in the representation of culture and cuisine.

In *Madhur*, this picturesque register involves a spectacularization of the exotic other which serves to complicate the project of demystification articulated by Jaffrey's commentaries. Ironically, one of the only visual references to Western influence upon India is found in programme four, where *tourists* are shown arriving on a beach in Goa. This sequence is particularly interesting in that Jaffrey's accompanying voice-over states:

> Welcome to Goa ... over the seas the Arabs have come and ruled, the Portuguese came and stayed for four hundred and fifty years. And the latest invasion is that of tourists ... the hippies were the forerunners of the tourist invasion. Now its coastline hotels increasingly draw middle-class Europeans.

Her analogy between the 'tourist invasion' and past colonisation of the region suggests that both are ideologically unsound. Yet the stunning beauty of the region, as rendered by the Tour-Ed.'s particular visual repertoire, will undoubtedly tempt some viewers from arm-chair to sun-chair. In addition, Jaffrey is herself constructed as a tourist elsewhere in the text. In programme three, there is a sequence of eight shots of the Golden Temple in the Punjab, lit up by fireworks against the night sky. Jaffrey's voice-over informs the viewer that 'Many tourists come just to stand and marvel at the beautiful spectacle'. As she finishes speaking, there is a cut from a long-shot of the Temple to a medium-shot of Jaffrey standing and marvelling at the temple in the background. On the one hand, then, Jaffrey is constructed as a tourist, in a way similar to Keith Floyd. On the other, she has pre-existing local knowledge, which she imparts to the viewer, in a way similar to that of Gary Rhodes.

However, the processes by which she demonstrates her knowledgeability differ from that of Rhodes. Whereas he pitches in, catching fish with local fish-farmers that he later cooks, for example, Jaffrey maintains her distance, so much so that she is often only involved in the action via her voice-over. The contrast may be understood in terms of gender. Jaffrey, by virtue of her femininity, is freed from the necessity of having to legitimize her interest in cookery by being presented as a hunter-gatherer. Furthermore, unlike Rhodes, who learns something of the community by the experience of joining them, Jaffrey 'already knows', and is thus constructed as part of the community by virtue of her pre-existing knowledge of its customs and cuisine.

To a British audience, particularly within the context of white-dominated television presentation, Jaffrey is marked by her ethnicity. In the series she is shown to be returning to her homeland, as exemplified in programme four, where she visits an old friend. This is despite the fact that she is an actress who comes from a wealthy family who has lived in the West for much of her life. Whilst all televisual cooks (and, one may argue, presenters in general) are mediators, it is particularly evident that both Jaffrey's personality construction and her role within the text are sites for the mediation of discourses of ethnicity. This mediation is articulated by her dress, which oscillates between saris and baseball caps; her use of two languages, situating her as (cultural) translator; and by her knowledge and experience of both cultures. Her status is thus akin to a cultural ambassador, occupying an informed yet distanced vantage point across two landscapes. Thus whilst Rhodes and Jaffrey function similarly as agents of the Tour-Ed., they operate in strikingly different ways. Rhodes swings between the antinomic groupings, his *movement* serving as the site of the interplay of Cook-Ed., Personality and Tour-Ed. Jaffrey is herself the primary site upon which such elements are mapped.

RAW-EDUCATIVE: *RHODES AROUND BRITAIN* AND *MADHUR JAFFREY'S FLAVOURS OF INDIA*

The Raw-Ed. pertains to the contextualization of ingredients in their original state/habitat, the methods by which produce may be harvested/hunted and, relating to this, the labour involved in such processes. As with the Tour-Ed., the Raw-Ed. may serve as the cipher for educational projects of a series that go beyond the Cook-Ed.

Each programme in the *Rhodes* series contains at least one item focusing on Rhodes travelling to the 'source' of a (potential) raw ingredient, motivated by a range of reasons. In the case of programme one, he visits an Ostrich farm, and during an interview with a farmer discovers that the meat is high in fibre and low in cholesterol and thus 'good' for anyone with a heart condition. Here, the motivation is largely Cook-Ed. in that it informs the viewer, who is assumed to be unfamiliar with the newly available meat product. In contrast to this is an item featured in programme five, which shows Rhodes joining in with some workers harvesting oysters, and getting waterlogged boots as a result. This contributes to Rhodes's Personality construct and the Tour-Ed. as previously discussed. In both cases, though, the emphasis on origins also serves to introduce the Raw-Ed. discourse into the text.

The foregrounding of the origin of a raw ingredient, as well as the labour involved in the production of a commodity, invokes an 'authenticity' that contributes to the educational project of the series. Rhodes preaches that one must embrace the raw in order to transform it. However, to convince the viewer Rhodes has to counter the pervading cultural distaste for lumps of raw meat uneffacedly connected to their animal origin by providing constant reassurance. For example, during the demonstration of the recipe for salmon, he says: 'Well, look at this, it really is wonderful. Clean both sides. The texture, the muscle, look at the lovely lines . . . it really is beautiful . . . it's going to be succulent and juicy.'

The sensuality of his verbal and gestural registers (he often kisses his fingers and caresses the produce) serves to eroticize the recipes. This is interesting when seen in the light of Lisa M. Heldke's (Curtin and Heldke, 1992: 222) assertion that:

> Growing and preparing food are activities which often require and generate emotional energy – and which see emotion and eroticism as vital to the activity. In contrast to the received view of theory and practice, which tends to divorce reason from emotion and eroticism, a transformed conception of food-making practice views them as thoughtful practices in which these forms of interaction are interrelated and mutually constitutive.

Recalling the Personality construction of Delia Smith, I would argue that the predominantly normative cookery instruction and efficient mode of presentation are related to the received view of theory and practice – cooking is contextualized as a practical and social skill. By contrast, *Rhodes*'s eroticization of food, in part to sanction the discourse of the Raw-Ed., allows a reading of a transformed conception of food-making practice which repositions even British food as sensual and pleasurable. As such, Rhodes's mode of presentation of the Cook-Ed. and Raw-Ed. is framed by a wider 'Food-Educative' project.

This Raw-Ed. project can be found in *Madhur* also. As in *Rhodes*, the cookery demonstrations often follow a linked item focusing on a particular raw ingredient, method of harvest or social custom. For example, in programme four, a sequence of ten shots of fishermen and trawlers is accompanied by Jaffrey's voice-over commentary, which states:

> Behind the tourism and hotels is the real economy. It employs thousands and still uses traditional nets. They've just been fishing on this trawler and caught a whole load of fish. And amongst the things they have are prawns … I'm going to make a delicious fish dish.

Another example is found in programme three, where Jaffrey traces the 'narrative' of a coconut from a tree, through various ways in which the by-products are used – as she informs us, we probably have a doormat made from a coconut by-product – to a cookery demonstration using coconut milk. However, Jaffrey's mode of Raw-Ed. discourse differs from that of Rhodes in a number of ways, going beyond simply embracing the raw in order to transform it.

Her contextualization of the ingredients that she prepares, via commentaries on processes of production, labour and export, often hints at a critique. In programme one there is a sequence featuring women sorting black peppercorns, accompanied by Jaffrey's voice-over, which states 'The work is very labour intensive', highlighting the labour element of the production-consumption equation. This is further emphasised during a later sequence, which depicts women harvesting tea, bent double by the weight of the bundles they are carrying. Jaffrey comments 'and of course all these spices are as fundamental to an Indian meal as tea is in Britain'. Her statement works with the visual images to expose the intensive manual labour involved in the production of a commodity so avidly consumed in a country that seemingly eschews consideration of the product's origins. In programmes two and three one finds examples, in Jaffrey's commentary, of a shift in this focus on manual labour to issues of exportation of products to the West. In a sequence featuring nomads, Jaffrey informs the viewer of their continual battle for survival against the elements, before going on to discuss how they are famous for their embroidery, which fetches hundreds of pounds in the West. In programme three her voice-over, which accompanies images of fishermen returning to shore states: 'Whatever they bring back, be it squid or shrimp, it is auctioned off as soon as the boat touches land. The big fish, like these huge rays, or the best of the prawns, crabs and lobsters are sold off for export. Local villagers can only afford the little fish.'

As these examples suggest, Jaffrey's mode of Raw-Ed. contains oblique references to a potential, or actual, exploitation in every stage of the production-consumption process that points to the existence of a progressive educational dynamic. However, drawing on my previous discussion of the picturesque register of the Tour-Ed., one sees that the critical charge of the Raw-Ed. may often be short-circuited by other elements within the text.

CONCLUSION

I started by questioning the notion of the transparency of cookery programmes. Certainly, food and the instruction of cookery methods feature in each of the case-study series. However, the Cook-Ed. is not immutable and isolated; its formation varies according to the nature of its inflection by the other identifiable elements such as the Per., Tour-Ed. and Raw-Ed. To deny the impact of these aspects is to overlook a fundamental part of the internal mechanics of the genre, and of its making of meaning.

My concern has been with these internal mechanics. However, the elements that I have identified extend beyond the immediate texts. In order to reproduce a recipe one often needs to refer to the (lucrative) series spin-off book to locate precise measurements and methods: illustrative of the ongoing Cook-Ed. discourse. Presenter/cooks move outside of their programmes into a range of other texts, from cookery books, advertising and product endorsements, to web-sites and to chat-shows, their personality constructions continually being affirmed or transformed by these contexts. Bennett and Woollacott (1987: 44) discuss the similarly expansive 'Bond phenomenon', saying: 'the figure of Bond has been constructed and been operative in the relations between a considerable and accompanying set of texts, different in its total size and composition as well as in its internal configuration at different moments'. They go on to list some of the various textual sites of 'Bond', from novels and films to photo-features of the 'Bond Girls', before stating:

Added to these have been the sedimentations of Bond in the world of objects. Through its uses in advertising and commodity design, the figure of Bond has become tangled up in the world of things . . . functioning like textual meteorites.

One may similarly view the various manifestations of the cookery programmes as 'textual meteorites': sites for the extension, disruption or transformation of the discourses within the original text. A study of the processes of extension and circulation upon the elements identified here would, I believe, offer up considerable currency. Perhaps my research will serve as an *apéritif*, to whet the critical appetite sufficiently for such a project to be undertaken.

REFERENCES

Barthes, R. (1973) *Mythologies*, London: Paladin.
Bennett, T. and Woollacott, J. (1987) *Bond and Beyond: The Political Career of a Popular Hero*, London: Macmillan.
Bourdieu, P. (1984) *Distinction*, London: Routledge and Kegan Paul.
Curtin, D. W. and Heldke, L. M. (eds) (1992) *Cooking, Eating, Thinking: Transformative Philosophies of Food*, Indianapolis: Indianapolis University.
Fort, M. (1995) 'The TV dinners: chefs on the box – a recipe for culinary success?', *Guardian*, 3 March.
Neale, S. (1980) *Genre*, London: British Film Institute.
Phillips, P. (1991) 'Floyd on the tucker trail', *Radio Times*, 6–12 April.

FURTHER READING

Barthes, R., *Elements of Semiology*, transl. A. Lavers and C. Smith (London: Jonathan Cape, 1967); Orig. 1964.

Barthes, R., *Image–Music–Text*, transl. S. Heath (Glasgow: Fontana/William Collins, 1977).

Burgelin, O., 'Structural Analysis and Mass Communication', in McQuail, D. (ed.), *Sociology of Mass Communications* (Harmondsworth: Penguin Books, 1972).

Eco, U., 'Towards a Semiotic Inquiry into the Television Message', WPCS no. 3 (1972); and Corner, J. and Hawthorn, J. (eds), *Communication Studies: An Introductory Reader* (London: Edward Arnold, 1980).

Ellis, J., *Visible Fictions: Cinema, Television, Video* (London: Routledge & Kegan Paul, 1982).

Fiske, J., *Introduction to Communication Studies* (London: Methuen, 1982).

Fiske, J. and Hartley, J., *Reading Television* (London: Methuen, 1978).

Hartley, J., *Understanding News* (London: Metheun, 1982).

Hawkes, T., *Structuralism and Semiotics* (London: Methuen, 1977).

Heath, S. and Skirrow, G., 'Television: A World in Action', *Screen* 18:2 (1977) pp. 7–59.

Screen Education no. 20 (1976). Special issue on '*The Sweeney*': TV Crime Series'.

Woollacott, J., 'Messages and Meanings', in Gurevitch, M., Bennett, T., Curran, J. and Woollacott, J. (eds), *Culture, Society and the Media* (London: Methuen, 1982).

SECTION 3
TEXT

2. IDEOLOGY AND DISCOURSE

IDEOLOGY AND DISCOURSE
INTRODUCTION

Much of the thinking about the media has concerned itself with the connection between the media as institutions with social power and the ideas that they circulate. In the tradition that has developed in Britain, the term 'ideology' has come to play a substantial role in articulating this relationship. The concept of ideology, taken generally from Marxism, was given an influential inflection by the French philosopher Louis Althusser, and although his use of the term has not survived unmodified, it still underlies most of the ways in which it is employed.[1] 'Ideologies' rather than 'ideas' is used to bring out several significant aspects. It loses the association of individually generated notions that can adhere to 'ideas', in order to stress the social, transindividual nature of the thinking that circulates. It carries the consideration that *clusters* of *interlinked* ideas are being referred to: 'ideologies do not consist of isolated and separate concepts, but in the articulation of different elements into a distinctive set or chain of meanings', as Stuart Hall expresses it. And most importantly, it is intended to convey the fact that in an unequal society ideas and clusters of ideas are inevitably implicated in the differential allocation and operation of social power and the struggles over this, even though it may not be their manifest focus.

Stuart Hall's abridged essay (Chapter 22) begins with some useful general points about ideologies and the media, and then discusses racist ideology in the British media in particular. He discerns two major streams of racist ideology, which he calls the 'overt' and the 'inferential'. These roughly correspond to the right-wing and the liberal. He points to the fact that British imperial culture has provided a capacious repertoire of racist elements available for remobilisation, reworking and recombining by the media. Not surprisingly, the essay bears the traces of the historical moment of its composition (1979–81), and it provokes consideration of how racist ideology has evolved over the intervening period, of the nature of the ideologies operative in a changed political conjuncture.

The previous section introduced the term 'genre'. Some scholars have posed the question as to whether particular genres – because they shape certain kinds of material into certain recognisable, because conventionalised, textual forms – are inherently ideological in some way. In her piece on the situation comedy genre (Chapter 23), Janet Woollacott discusses the distinctive nature of the sitcom narrative, that lacks 'progression' and tends towards a different kind of resolution or (temporary) closure. Given this tendency to return to the 'situation', combined with the use of stereotyping, leads to the question of whether the humour is necessarily ideologically reactionary. Does it serve to reconcile people to their conditions of social existence? Or is it a cultural vehicle for resisting grim conformism and symbolically defying social power? Woollacott's response is that examination of the text alone cannot reveal the answer to this, and suggests that it will partly depend on the nature of the connections between the ideology of the particular sitcom and the conjuncturally important ideologies circulating elsewhere in society, including in other media and other genres. This question, and its answer, can be seen to be underpinned by the Gramscian version of Marxism that Stuart Hall has done so much to introduce within British cultural studies. Indeed, Woollacott explicitly references a collaborative work (*Policing the Crisis*, 1978) in which Hall had participated, and from which 'The Social Production of News' in Part Two is taken (Chapter 51). The other part of her answer – that it will depend on the 'reading formations' which viewers inhabit – has affinities with the work of David Morley (see Chapter 37) as well as drawing explicitly on the work of Tony Bennett.[2]

Over the last twenty years, another term has come into circulation in discussing the media: discourse. Overlaid upon the routine meaning of the word – 'formal and orderly expression of ideas in speech and writing' – are a number of more complex associated meanings, drawing particularly on the writings of the French scholar Michel Foucault.[3] He saw discourses as 'practices that systematically form the objects of which they speak', and which often emanate from institutional sources, such as the discourse of the Church, say, or the discourse of the Microsoft corporation. For him, social speech and writing is intimately linked to social power; often it is literally the *expression* of power, though not always, since socially subordinate groups speak – generate a discourse – too. Discourses are often in conflict with other discourses in their explicit or implicit claims to define the 'truth' of things.

Foucault's exploration of the connection between the emission of statements and social power has proved insightful for many students of the media. In many ways, he adopted and inflected the term 'discourse' in conscious opposition to the concept of 'ideology' which had also come to be used in thinking through the connection between utterances and power. Of the wider debate that has arisen in the wake of his work, it has been commented: 'For some, discourse is the larger term within which there exist a range of different ideologies, whilst for others ideologies are made manifest through a variety of different discourses.'[4] Norman Fairclough is a linguist who calls his approach Critical Discourse Analysis.[5] Influenced by the kinds of ideas which Foucault and others have explored about language and power, he has developed a more linguistically informed analysis of discourses.

In Chapter 25 he summarises his general approach to media discourse analysis, and offers a sample analysis of an article that appeared in *The Sun* newspaper in 1985. This is informative and revealing, and throws up a number of insights, particularly in its employment of the idea of 'transform[ation] across a chain of linked communicative events'. But as an example it displays an uncertainty about the nature of media 'language'. He states 'Like many linguists, I shall use "discourse" to refer to spoken or written language use, though I also want to extend it to include other types of semiotic activity (i.e. activity which produces meanings), such as visual images (photography, film, video, diagrams) and non-verbal communication (e.g. gestures).' In practice, the piece is more secure in approaching the verbal language dimension of his chosen item, than in issues of, say, typographical design.[6]

Andrew Tolson in Chapter 24 is also interested in the verbal language dimension of media texts, and here takes his examples from the *Wogan* chat show that ran on early evening television during the 1980s. Though by no means innocent of the contribution that linguistics can make to the analysis of media output, Tolson is working in a more mainstream 'cultural studies' vein,[7] and employs his textual study to illuminate a historical shift in the nature of the chat show genre – and arguably in the wider culture – towards the mediated personality as ironic performance staged for a media-savvy audience. Although Tolson himself eschews the conclusion, this shift could be seen as consonant with many of the broader claims in the late twentieth century regarding the diffusion of a postmodern sensibility.[8]

NOTES

1. Louis Althusser, 'Ideology and Ideological State Apparatuses', *Lenin and Philosophy and Other Essays*, trans. Ben Brewster (London: New Left Books, 1971).
2. Tony Bennett, 'Text, Readers, Reading Formations', *Literature and History* 9:2 (1983) pp. 21–27.
3. Michel Foucault, *The Order of Discourse: An Archaeology of the Human Sciences* (London: Tavistock, 1970); Michel Foucault, *Power/knowledge: Selected Interviews 1972–77*, ed. C. Gordon (Brighton: Harvester, 1980); Michel Foucault, 'The order of discourse' in Robert Young (ed) *Untying the Text: a Poststructuralist Reader* (London: RKP, 1981), David Couzens Hoy (ed) *Foucault: a Critical Reader* (Oxford: Blackwell, 1986).
4. Sara Mills, *Discourse* (London: Routledge, 1997), p. 46.
5. Norman Fairclough, *Language and Power* (London: Longman, 1989); Norman Fairclough and Ruth Wodak, 'Critical Discourse Analysis', ch. 10 of Teun A. van Dijk (ed) *Discourse as Social Interaction*, vol 2 of *Discourse Studies: a Multidisciplinary Introduction* (London: Sage, 1997).
6. Some of Fairclough's peers working in the field of linguistics are addressing such

issues. See for example Gunther Kress and Theo van Leeuwen, *Reading Images: the Grammar of Visual Design* (London: Routledge, 1996).

7. An early example of this is Stuart Hall, Ian Connell, Lidia Curri, 'The "Unity" of Current Affairs Television', *Working Papers in Cultural Studies* 9 (1976) which examines a 1974 edition of *Panorama*.

8. In the full version of the article from which Chapter 24 is extracted, Tolson writes 'I am not going to argue here that . . . we have moved into some kind of "postmodern" world where people no longer speak honestly or sincerely, or where experience is no longer taken to be a source of truth.'

22

RACIST IDEOLOGIES AND THE MEDIA

Stuart Hall

[...]

'Racism and the media' touches directly the problem of *ideology*, since the media's main sphere of operations is the production and transformation of ideologies. An intervention in the media's construction of race is an intervention in the *ideological* terrain of struggle. [...] I am using the term [ideology] to refer to those images, concepts and premises which provide the frameworks through which we represent, interpret, understand and 'make sense' of some aspect of social existence. Language and ideology are not the same – since the same linguistic term ('democracy' for example, or 'freedom') can be deployed within different ideological discourses. But language, broadly conceived, is by definition the principal medium in which we find different ideological discourses elaborated.

Three important things need to be said about ideology in order to make what follows intelligible. First, ideologies do not consist of isolated and separate concepts, but in the articulation of different elements into a distinctive set or chain of meanings. In liberal ideology, 'freedom' is connected (articulated) with individualism and the free market; in socialist ideology, 'freedom' is a collective condition, dependent on, not counterposed to, 'equality of condition', as it is in liberal ideology. The same concept is differently positioned within the logic of different ideological discourses. One of the ways in which ideological struggle

From S. Hall, 'The Whites of Their Eyes: Racist Ideologies and the Media', in George Bridges and Rosalind Brunt (eds), *Silver Linings* (London: Lawrence & Wishart, 1981); also available in Manuel Alvarado and John O. Thompson (eds), *The Media Reader* (London: British Film Institute, 1990).

takes place and ideologies are transformed is by articulating the elements differently, thereby producing a different meaning: breaking the chain in which they are currently fixed (e.g. 'democratic' = the 'Free' West) and establishing a new articulation (e.g. 'democratic' = deepening the democratic content of political life). This 'breaking of the chain' is not, of course, confined to the head: it takes place through social practice and political struggle.

Second, ideological statements are made by individuals: but ideologies are not the product of individual consciousness or intention. Rather we formulate our intentions *within ideology*. They pre-date individuals, and form part of the determinate social formations and conditions in which individuals are born. We have to 'speak through' the ideologies which are active in our society and which provide us with the means of 'making sense' of social relations and our place in them. The transformation of ideologies is thus a collective process and practice, not an individual one. Largely, the processes work *unconsciously*, rather than by conscious intention. Ideologies produce different forms of social consciousness, rather than being produced by them. They work most effectively when we are not aware that how we formulate and construct a statement about the world is underpinned by ideological premisses; when our formations seem to be simply descriptive statements about how things are (i.e. must be), or of what we can 'take-for-granted'. 'Little boys like playing rough games; little girls, however, are full of sugar and spice' is predicated on a whole set of ideological premisses, though it seems to be an aphorism which is grounded, not in how masculinity and femininity have been historically and culturally constructed in society, but in Nature itself. Ideologies tend to disappear from view into the taken-for-granted 'naturalised' world of common sense. Since (like gender) race appears to be 'given' by Nature, racism is one of the most profoundly 'naturalised' of existing ideologies.

Third, ideologies 'work' by constructing for their subjects (individual and collective) positions of identification and knowledge which allow them to 'utter' ideological truths as if they were their authentic authors. This is not because they emanate from our innermost, authentic and unified experience, but because we find ourselves mirrored in the positions at the centre of the discourses from which the statements we formulate 'make sense'. Thus the same 'subjects' (e.g. economic classes or ethnic groups) can be differently constructed in different ideologies.

[...]

Ideologies therefore work by the transformation of discourses (the disarticulation and rearticulation of ideological elements) and the transformation (the fracturing and recomposition) of subjects-for-action. How we 'see' ourselves and our social relations *matters*, because it enters into and informs our actions and practices. Ideologies are therefore a site of a distinct type of social struggle. This site does not exist on its own, separate from other relations, since ideas are not free-floating in people's heads. The ideological construction of black people as a 'problem population' and the police practice of containment in the black communities mutually reinforce and support one another. Nevertheless, ideology is a practice. It has its own specific way of working. And it is generated, produced and reproduced in specific settings (sites) – especially, in the apparatuses of ideological production which 'produce' social meanings and distribute them throughout society, like the media.

[...]

Amongst other kinds of ideological labour, the media construct for us a definition of what *race* is, what meaning the imagery of race carries, and what the 'problem of race' is understood to be. They help to classify out the world in terms of the categories of race.

The media are not only a powerful source of ideas about race. They are also one place where these ideas are articulated, worked on, transformed and elaborated. We have said 'ideas' and 'ideologies' in the plural. For it would be wrong and misleading to see the media as uniformly and conspiratorially harnessed to a single, racist conception of the world. Liberal and humane ideas about 'good relations' between the races, based on open-mindedness and tolerance, operate inside the world of the media – among, for example, many television journalists and newspapers like the *Guardian* – alongside the more explicit racism of other journalists and newspapers like the *Express* or the *Mail*. In some respects, the line which separates the latter from the extreme right on policies, such as, for example, guided repatriation for blacks, is very thin indeed.

[...]

[An] important distinction is between what we might call 'overt' racism and 'inferential' racism. By *overt* racism, I mean those many occasions when open and favourable coverage is given to arguments, positions and spokespersons who are in the business of elaborating an openly racist argument or advancing a racist policy or view. Many such occasions exist; they have become more frequent in recent years – more often in the press, which has become openly partisan to extremist right-wing arguments, than in television, where the regulations of 'balance', 'impartiality and neutrality' operate.

By *inferential* racism I mean those apparently naturalised representations of events and situations relating to race, whether 'factual' or 'fictional', which have racist premises and propositions inscribed in them as a set of *unquestioned assumptions*. These enable racist statements to be formulated without ever bringing into awareness the racist predicates on which the statements are grounded.

Both types of racism are to be found, in different combinations, in the British media. Open or overt racism is, of course, politically dangerous as well as socially offensive. The open partisanship of sections of the popular press on this front is an extremely serious development. It is not only that they circulate and popularise openly racist policies and ideas, and translate them into the vivid populist vernacular (e.g. in the tabloids, with their large working-class reader-ship) it is the very fact that such things can now be openly said and advocated which *legitimates* their public expression and increases the threshold of the public acceptability of racism. Racism becomes 'acceptable' – and thus, not too long after, 'true' – just common sense: what everyone knows and is openly saying. But *inferential racism* is more widespread – and in many ways, more insidious, because it is largely *invisible* even to those who formulate the world in its terms.

An example of *this* type of racist ideology is the sort of television programme which deals with some 'problem' in race relations. It is probably made by a good and honest liberal broadcaster, who hopes to do some good in the world for 'race relations' and who maintains a scrupulous balance and neutrality when questioning people interviewed for the programme. The programme will end with a homily on how, if only the 'extremists' on *either side* would go away, 'normal blacks and whites' would be better able to get on with learning to live in harmony together. Yet every word and image of such programmes are impregnated with unconscious racism because they are all predicated on the unstated and unrecognized assumption that the *blacks* are the *source of the problem*. Yet virtually the whole of 'social problem' television about race and immigration – often made, no doubt, by well-intentioned and liberal-minded broadcasters – is precisely predicated on racist premises of this kind. This was the criticism we made in the CARM programme, *It Ain't Half Racist, Mum*[1] and it was the one which most cut the broadcasters to their professional quick. It undermined their professional credentials by suggesting that they had been partisan where they are supposed to be balanced and impartial. It was an affront to the liberal consensus and self-image which prevails within broad-casting. Both responses were, in fact, founded on the profound misunderstand-ing that racism is, by definition, mutually exclusive of the liberal consensus – whereas, in inferential racism, the two can quite easily cohabit – and on the assumption that if the television discourse could be shown to be racist, it must be because the individual broadcasters were intentionally and deliberately racist. In fact, an ideological discourse does *not* depend on the conscious intentions of those who formulate statements within it.

[...]

[There is a] rich vocabulary and syntax of race on which the media have to draw. Racism has a long and distinguished history in British culture. It is grounded in the relations of slavery, colonial conquest, economic exploitation and imperialism in which the European races have stood in relation to the 'native peoples' of the colonised and exploited periphery.

Three characteristics provided the discursive and power-coordinates of the discourses in which these relations were historically constructed. (1) Their imagery and themes were polarised around fixed relations of subordination and domination. (2) Their stereotypes were grouped around the poles of 'superior' and 'inferior' natural species. (3) Both were displaced from the 'language' of history into the language of Nature. Natural physical signs and racial characteristics became the unalterable signifiers of inferiority. Subordinate ethnic groups and classes appeared, not as the objects of particular historical relations (the slave trade, European colonisation, the active underdevelopment of the 'underdeveloped' societies), but as the given qualities of an inferior *breed*. Relations, secured by economic, social, political and military domination were transformed and 'naturalised' into an order of *rank*, ascribed by Nature. Thus, Edward Long, an acute English observer of Jamaica in the period of slavery wrote (in his *History of Jamaica*, 1774) – much in the way the Elizabethans might have spoken of 'the Great Chain Of Being' – of 'Three ranks of men [sic], (white, mulatto and black), dependent on each other, and rising in a proper climax of subordination, in which the whites hold the highest place'.

[Often it is] 'forgotten' [the] degree to which in the period of slavery and imperialism popular literature is saturated with these fixed, negative attributes of the colonised races. We find them in the diaries, observations and accounts, the notebooks, ethnographic records and commentaries, of visitors, explorers, missionaries and administrators in Africa, India, the Far East and the Americas. And also something else: the 'absent' but imperialising 'white eye'; the unmarked position from which all these 'observations' are made and from which, alone, they make sense. This is the history of slavery and conquest, written, seen, drawn and photographed by The Winners. They cannot be *read* and made sense of from any other position. The 'white eye' is always outside the frame – but seeing and positioning everything within it.

[T]elling sequences [can be found in] early film of the British Raj in India – the source of endless radio 'reminiscences' and television historical show-pieces today. The assumption of effortless superiority structures every image – even the positioning in the frame: the foregrounding of colonial life (tea-time on the plantation), the background of native bearers ... In the later stages of High Imperialism, this discourse proliferates through the new media of popular culture and information – newspapers and journals, cartoons, drawings and advertisements and the popular novel. Recent critics of the literature of imperialism have argued that, if we simply extend our definition of nineteenth-century fiction from one branch of 'serious fiction' to embrace popular literature, we will find a second, powerful strand of the English literary imagination to set beside the *domestic* novel: the male-dominated world of imperial adventure, which takes *empire*, rather than *Middlemarch*, as its microcosm. I remember a graduate student, working on the construction of race in popular literature and culture at the end of the Nineteenth Century, coming to me in despair – racism was so *ubiquitous*, and at the same time so *unconscious* – simply assumed to be the case – that it was impossible to get any critical purchase on it. In this period, the very idea of *adventure* became synonymous with the demonstration of the moral, social and physical mastery of the colonisers over the colonised.

Later, this concept of 'adventure' – one of the principal categories of modern *entertainment* – moved straight off the printed page into the literature of crime and espionage, children's books, the great Hollywood extravaganzas and comics. There, with recurring persistence, they still remain. Many of these older versions have had their edge somewhat blunted by time. They have been distanced from us, apparently, by our superior wisdom and liberalism. But they still reappear on the television screen, especially in the form of 'old movies' (some 'old movies', of course, continue to be made). But we can grasp their recurring resonance better if we identify some of the base-images of the 'grammar of race'.

There is, for example, the familiar *slave-figure*: dependable, loving in a simple childlike way – the devoted 'Mammy' with the rolling eyes, or the faithful field-hand or retainer, attached and devoted to 'his' Master. The best known extravaganza of all – *Gone With The Wind* – contains rich variants of both. The 'slave-figure' is by no means limited to films and programmes *about* slavery. Some 'Injuns' and many Asians have come on to the screen in this disguise. A deep and unconscious ambivalence pervades this stereotype. Devoted and childlike, the 'slave' is also unreliable, unpredictable and undependable – capable of 'turning nasty', or of plotting in a treacherous way, secretive, cunning, cut-throat once his or her Master's or Mistress's back is turned: and inexplicably given to running way into the bush at the slightest opportunity. The whites can never be sure that this childish simpleton – 'Sambo' – is not mocking his master's white manners behind his hand, even when giving an exaggerated caricature of white refinement.

Another base-image is that of the 'native'. The good side of this figure is portrayed in a certain primitive nobility and simple dignity. The bad side is portrayed in terms of cheating and cunning, and, further out, savagery and barbarism. Popular culture is still full today of countless savage and restless 'natives', and sound-tracks constantly repeat the threatening sound of drumming in the night, the hint of primitive rites and cults. Cannibals, whirling dervishes, Indian tribesmen, garishly got up, are constantly threatening to overrun the screen. They are likely to appear at any moment out of the darkness to decapitate the beautiful heroine, kidnap the children, burn the encampment or threatening to boil, cook and eat the innocent explorer or colonial administrator and his lady-wife. These 'natives' always move as an anonymous collective mass – in tribes or hordes. And against them is always counterposed the isolated white figure, alone 'out there', confronting his Destiny or shouldering his Burden in the 'heart of darkness', displaying coolness under fire and an unshakeable authority – exerting mastery over the rebellious natives or quelling the threatened uprising with a single glance of his steel-blue eyes.

A third variant is that of the 'clown' or 'entertainer'. This captures the 'innate' humour, as well as the physical grace, of the licensed entertainer – putting on a show for The Others. It is never quite clear whether we are laughing with or at this figure: admiring the physical and rhythmic grace, the open expressivity and emotionality of the 'entertainer', or put off by the 'clown's' stupidity.

One noticeable fact about all these images is their deep *ambivalence* – the double vision of the white eye through which they are seen. The primitive nobility of the ageing tribesman or chief, and the native's rhythmic grace, always contain both a nostalgia for an innocence lost forever to the civilised, and the threat of civilisation being over-run or undermined by the recurrence of savagery, which is always lurking just below the surface; or by an untutored sexuality, threatening to 'break out'. Both are aspects – the good and the bad sides – of *primitivism*. In these images, 'primitivism' is defined by the fixed proximity of such people to Nature.

Is all this so far away as we sometimes suppose from the representation of race which fill the screens today? These *particular* versions may have faded. But their *traces* are still to be observed, reworked in many of the modern and up-dated images. And though they may appear to carry a different meaning, they are often still constructed on a very ancient grammar. Today's restless native hordes are still alive and well and living, as guerilla armies and freedom fighters in the Angola, Zimbabwe or Namibian 'bush'. Blacks are still the most frightening, cunning and glamorous crooks (and policemen) in New York cop series. They are the fleet-footed, crazy-talking under-men who connect Starsky and Hutch to the drug-saturated ghetto. The scheming villains and their giant-sized bully boys in the world of James Bond and his progeny are still, unusually, recruited from 'out there' in Jamaica, where savagery lingers on. The sexually-available 'slave girl' is alive and kicking, smouldering away on some exotic TV set or on the covers of paperbacks, though she is now the centre of a special admiration, covered in a sequinned gown and supported by a white chorus line. Primitivism, savagery, guile and unreliability – all 'just below the surface' – can still be identified in the faces of black political leaders around the world, cunningly plotting the overthrow of 'civilisation': Mr Mugabé,[2] for example, up to the point where he happened to win both a war and an election and became, temporarily at any rate, the best (because the most politically credible) friend Britain had left in that last outpost of the Edwardian dream.

The 'Old Country' – white version – is still often the subject of nostalgic documentaries: 'Old Rhodesia', whose reliable servants, as was only to be expected, plotted treason in the outhouse and silently stole away to join ZAPU in the bush . . . Tribal Man in green khaki. Black stand-up comics still ape their ambiguous incorporation into British entertainment by being the first to tell a racist joke. No Royal Tour is complete without its troupe of swaying bodies, or its mounted tribesmen, paying homage. Blacks are such 'good movers', so *rhythmic*, so *natural*. And the dependent peoples, who couldn't manage for a day without the protection and know-how of their white masters, reappear as the starving victims of the Third World, passive and waiting for the technology or the Aid to arrive, objects of our pity or of a *Blue Peter* appeal. They are not represented as the subjects of a continuing exploitation or dependency, or the global division of wealth and labour. They are the Victims of Fate.

These modern, glossed and up-dated images seem to have put the old world of Sambo behind them. Many of them, indeed, are the focus of a secret, illicit, pleasurable-but-taboo admiration. Many have a more active and energetic quality – some black athletes, for example, and of course the entertainers. But the connotations and echoes which they carry reverberate back a very long way. They continue to shape the ways whites see blacks today – even when the white adventurer sailing up the jungle stream is not *Sanders of the River*,[3] but historical drama-reconstructions of Stanley and Livingstone; and the intention is to show, not the savagery, but the serenity of African village life – ways of an ancient people 'unchanged even down to modern times' (in other words, still preserved in economic backwardness and frozen in history for our anthropological eye by forces unknown to them and, apparently, unshowable on the screen).

'Adventure' is one way in which we *encounter* race without having to *confront* the racism of the perspectives in use. Another, even more complex one is 'entertainment'. In television, there is a strong counterposition between 'serious', informational television, which we watch because it is good for us, and 'entertainment', which we watch because it is pleasurable. And the purest form of pleasure in entertainment television is *comedy*. By definition, comedy is a licensed zone, disconnected from the serious. It's all 'good, clean fun'. In the area of fun and pleasure it is forbidden to pose a serious question, partly because it seems so puritanical and destroys the pleasure by switching registers. Yet race is one of the most significant themes in situation comedies – from the early Alf Garnett to *Mind Your Language, On The Buses, Love Thy Neighbour* and *It Ain't Half Hot, Mum*. These are defended on good 'anti-racist' grounds: the appearance of blacks, alongside whites, in situation comedies, it is argued, will help to naturalise and normalise their presence in British society. And no doubt, in some examples, it does function in this way. But, if you examine these fun occasions more closely, you will often find, as we did in our two programmes, that the comedies do not simply include blacks: they are *about race*. That is, the same old categories of racially defined characteristics and qualities, and the same relations of superior and inferior, provide the pivots on which the jokes actually turn, the tension-points which move and motivate the situations in situation comedies. The comic register in which they are set, however, protects and defends viewers from acknowledging their incipient racism. It creates disavowal.

This is even more so with the television stand-up comics, whose repertoire in recent years has come to be dominated, in about equal parts, by sexist and racist jokes. It's sometimes said, again in their defence, that this must be a sign of black acceptibility. But it *may* just be that racism has become more normal: it's hard to tell. It's also said that the best teller of anti-Jewish jokes are Jews themselves, just as blacks tell the best 'white' jokes against themselves. But this is to argue as if jokes exist in a vacuum separate from the contexts and situations of their telling. Jewish jokes told by Jews among themselves are part of the self-awareness of the community. They are unlikely to function by 'putting down' the race, because both teller and audience belong on equal terms to the same group. Telling racist jokes across the racial line, in conditions where relations of racial inferiority and superiority prevail, reinforces the *difference* and reproduces the unequal relations because, in those situations, the point of the joke depends on the existence of racism. Thus they reproduce the categories and relations of racism, even while normalizing them through laughter. The stated good intentions of the joke-makers do not resolve the problem here, because they are not in control of the circumstances – conditions of continuing racism – in which their joke discourse will be read and heard. The time *may* come when blacks and whites can tell jokes about each other in ways which do not reproduce the racial categories of the world in which they are told. The time, in Britain, is certainly *not yet arrived*.

Two other arenas [. . .] relate to the 'harder' end of television production – news and current affairs. This is where race is constructed as *problem* and the site of *conflict* and debate. There have been good examples of programmes where blacks have not exclusively appeared as the source of the 'problem' (ATV's *Breaking Point* is one example) and where they have not been exclusively saddled with being the aggressive agent in conflict (the London Weekend Television *London Programme* and the Southall Defence Committee's *Open Door* programme on the Southall events are examples). But the general tendency of the run of programmes in this area is to see blacks – especially the mere fact of their existence (their 'numbers') – as constituting a problem for English white society. They appear as law-breakers, prone to crime; as 'trouble'; as the collective agent of civil disorder.

In the numerous incidents where black communities have reacted to racist provocation (as at Southall) or to police harassment and provocation (as in Bristol)[4] the media have tended to assume that 'right' lay on the side of the law, and have fallen into the language of 'riot' and 'race warfare' which simply feeds existing stereotypes and prejudices. The precipitating conditions of conflict are usually *absent* – the scandalous provocation of a National Front march through one of the biggest black areas, Southall, and the saturation police raiding of the last refuge for black youth which triggered off Bristol – to take only two recent examples. They are either missing, or introduced so late in the process of signification, that they fail to dislodge the dominant definition of these events. So they testify, once again, to the disruptive nature of black and Asian people *as such*.

The analysis of the media coverage of Southall contained in the NCCL Unofficial Committee of Inquiry Report, for example, shows how rapidly, in both the television and press, the official definitions of the police – Sir David McNee's statement on the evening of 23 April, and the ubiquitous James Jardine, speaking for the Police Federation on the succeeding day – provided the media with the authoritative definition of the event. These, in turn, shaped and focused what the media reported and how it explained what transpired. In taking their cue from these authoritative sources, the media reproduced an account of the event which, with certain significant exceptions, translated the conflict between racism and anti-racism into (a) a contest between Asians and the police, and (b) a contest between two kinds of extremism – the so-called *'fascism'* of left and right alike.

This had the effect of downgrading the two problems at the centre of the Southall affair – the growth of and growing legitimacy of the extreme right and its blatantly provocative anti-black politics of the street; and the racism and brutality of the police. Both issues had to be *forced* on to the agenda of the media by a militant and organized protest. Most press reports of Southall were so obsessed by embroidering the lurid details of 'roaming hordes of coloured youths' chasing young whites 'with a carving knife' – a touch straight out of *Sanders of the River*, though so far uncorroborated – that they failed even to mention the death of Blair Peach. This is selective or tunnel-vision with a vengeance.

A good example of how the real causes of racial conflict can be absorbed and transformed by the framework which the media employ can be found in the *Nationwide* coverage of Southall on the day following the events. Two inter-locking frameworks of explanation governed this programme. In the first, conflict is seen in the conspiratorial terms of far-left against extreme-right – the Anti-Nazi League against the National Front. This is the classic logic of television, where the medium identifies itself with the moderate, consensual, middle-road, Average viewer, and sets off, in contrast, extremism on both sides, which it then equates with each other. In this particular exercise in 'balance', fascism and anti-fascism are represented as *the same* – both equally *bad*, because the Middle Way enshrines the Common Good under all circumstances. This balancing exercise provided an opportunity for Martin Webster of the National Front to gain access to the screen, to help set the terms of the debate, and to spread his smears across the screen under the freedom of the airwaves: 'Well,' he said, 'let's talk about Trotskyists, extreme Communists of various sorts, raving Marxists and other assorted left-wing cranks.' Good knockabout stuff. Then, after a linking passage – 'Southall, the day after' – to the second framework: rioting Asians *vs* the police. 'I watched television as well last night,' Mr Jardine argued, 'and I certainly didn't see any police throwing bricks . . . So don't start making those arguments.' The growth of organised political racism and the circumstances which have precipitated it were simply not visible to *Nationwide* as an alternative way of setting up the problem.

In the CARM programme *It Ain't Half Racist, Mum*, we tried to illustrate the inferential logic at work in another area of programming: the BBC's 'Great Debate' on Immigration. It was not necessary here to start with any precon-ceived notions, least of all speculation as to the personal views on race by the broadcasters involved – though one can't expect either the BBC hierarchy or Robin Day to believe that. You have simply to look at the programme with one set of questions in mind: Here is a problem, defined as 'the problem of immigration'. What is it? How is it defined and constructed through the programme? What logic governs its definition? And where does that logic derive from? I believe the answers are clear. The problem of immigration is that 'there are too many blacks over here', to put it crudely. It is *defined* in terms of *numbers of blacks* and what to do about them. The *logic* of the argument is 'immigrants = blacks = too many of them = send them home'. That is a racist logic. And it comes from a chain of reasoning whose representative, in respectable public debate and in person, on this occasion, was Enoch Powell. Powellism set the agenda for the media. Every time (and on many more occasions than the five or six we show in the programme) the presenter wanted to define the base-line of the programme which others should address, Mr Powell's views were indicated as representing it. And every time anyone strayed from the 'logic' to question the underlying premiss, it was back to 'as Mr Powell would say ... ' that they were drawn.

It certainly does not follow (and I know of no evidence to suggest) that Robin Day subscribes to this line or agrees with Mr Powell on anything to do with race. I know absolutely nothing about his views on race and immigration. And we made no judgement on his views, which are irrelevant to the argument. If the media function in a systematically racist manner, it is not because they are run and organised exclusively by active racists; this is a category mistake. This would be equivalent to saying that you could change the character of the capitalist state by replacing its personnel. Whereas the media, like the state, have a *structure*, a set of *practices* which are *not* reducible to the individuals who staff them. What defines how the media function is the result of a set of complex, often contradictory, social relations; not the personal inclinations of its members. What is significant is not that they produce a racist ideology, from some single-minded and unified conception of the world, but that they are so powerfully constrained – 'spoken by' – a particular set of ideological discourses. The power of this discourse is its capacity to constrain a very great variety of individuals: racist, anti-racist, liberals, radicals, conservatives, anarchists, know-nothings and silent majoritarians.

What we said, however, about the *discourse* of problem television was true, despite the hurt feelings of particular individuals: and demonstrably so. The premiss on which the Great Immigration Debate was built and the chain of reasoning it predicated was a racist one. The evidence for this is in what was said and how it was formulated – how the argument unfolded. If you establish the topic as 'the numbers of blacks are too high' or '*they* are breeding too fast', the opposition is obliged or constrained to argue that 'the numbers are not as high as they are represented to be'. This view is opposed to the first two: but it is also imprisoned by the same logic – the logic of the 'numbers game'. Liberals, anti-racists, indeed raging revolutionaries can contribute 'freely' to this debate, and indeed are often obliged to do so, so as not to let the case go by default: without breaking for a moment the chain of assumptions which holds the racist proposition in place. However, changing the terms of the argument, questioning the assumptions and starting points, breaking the logic – this is a quite different, longer, more difficult task.

[...]

Editors' Notes

1. Stuart Hall worked with colleagues in the Campaign Against Racism in the Media (CARM) to make a programme for the BBC TV Community Programmes Unit *Open Door* slot about racism on television. *It Ain't Half Racist, Mum* was transmitted on 1 March 1979. For an account of the resistance encountered in the production of the programme, see Carl Gardner, *It Ain't Half Racist Mum: Fighting Racism in the Media* (London: Comedia, 1982) pp. 85–9.
2. Robert Mugabe, leader of ZANU, one of the two main armed political movements which fought against white minority rule in Rhodesia. (The other movement was ZAPU.) In 1979 free elections were held, and Mugabe became the first president of the new Zimbabwe.
3. *Sanders of the River* (prod. Alexander Korda, 1935), a British feature film based on Edgar Wallace's stories about a white district commissioner in West Africa.
4. In April 1979 the Metropolitan Police attacked Anti-Nazi League (ANL) supporters who had gathered in the Southall district of London to protest against a public parade being held by the racist National Front. ANL supporter Blair Peach died as a result. On 2–3 April 1980, provoked by months of saturation policing, black youth in the St Paul's district of Bristol fought with the police.

23

FICTIONS AND IDEOLOGIES:
THE CASE OF SITUATION COMEDY

Janet Woollacott

Escapist fiction, that which purportedly allows its viewers or readers to 'escape' from the problems of the real world, was the category within which situation comedies found their home in terms of television criticism. Whereas some popular genres show obvious connections with the more general ideological formations in play at the time of their popularity (the spy thriller during the 1960s, for example, or the television crime series during the seventies), situation comedies could be held to have a more general grip on their audience. Over a longer period of time, at least for the last three decades, they have been a consistent part of the flow of the evening's television entertainment, a necessary and vital ingredient in the television controller's strategy for keeping the audience 'tuned in'. Moreover, the popularity of situation comedies has remained, throughout major shifts in more general ideological configurations in the period, and through the rise and decline of other popular genres such as the crime series. It is the aim of this article to outline some of the general characteristics of situation comedies, their narrative and comic strategies, use of character and performance; to consider some of the 'pleasures' of situation comedies and to suggest some of the issues raised by the role of situation comedies in considering the relations between fictions and other ideologies.

Despite the very wide range of targets for joking and humour in situation comedies, the programmes do conform to relatively strict conventions. Clearly some aspects of their formal organisation are related to institutional constraints;

From T. Bennett, C. Mercer and J. Woollacott (eds), *Popular Culture and Social Relations* (Milton Keynes: Open University Press, 1986) pp. 196–218.

the weekly half-hour slot, the limited number of characters and the cheap sets. In this respect and others they can be considered as a television genre. Ryall suggests in relation to film genres that 'genres may be defined as patterns/forms/styles/structures which transcend individual films and which supervise both their construction by the film-maker and their reading by an audience'.[1] In the mutual expectations of television producers and audiences, genre conventions are constantly varied but rarely totally exceeded or broken. Generally situation comedies are pre-eminently texts which are linked to a comfortable practice of reading. As Stephen Neale remarks of all popular genres, 'the existence of genres means that the spectator, precisely, will always know that everything will be made right in the end, that everything will cohere, that any threat or danger in the narrative process itself will always be contained.'[2]

[...]

In Eaton's attempt to outline a typology of situation comedy, he suggests that the two basic 'situations' of situation comedy are those of home and work. [...] Within these parameters, he argues that the narrative form of situation comedies is organised around an 'inside/outside' dichotomy. Moreover, the dichotomy 'affects every aspect of production down to its finest budgetary details'.[3] In plot terms, this means that events or characters from the outside can be allowed to enter the situation but only in such a way that the outsiders don't affect the situation which can be maintained for future weekly episodes. [...] In Eaton's typology, the inscription of the viewer within situation comedies is made manifest rather than being rendered invisible as in so many forms of novelistic fiction. However, this particular form of inscription is not typical of [...] many [...] situation comedies. Moreover, as Eaton acknowledges, he pays little attention to the pleasures of situation comedy, suggesting only that an analysis of such pleasures would not be incompatible with his typology. One of the problems of Eaton's analysis is the extent to which it relies on simply listing the typical characteristics of situation comedies. For example, the circumstances which Eaton perceptively categorises as 'typical', the small number of characters 'stuck with one another' at work or at home, or in some other boundaried setting, may occur in other genres. The situation of *Blake's Seven*, for example, in which the characters are confined to their spaceship, with fleeting teleported trips to other worlds, is not markedly dissimilar to that described by Eaton as a feature of situation comedies, and for rather similar institutional reasons. Even jokes or comic situations are not limited to situation comedies. Soap operas usually have their comic characters and situations. Regan's wit, in a crime series like *The Sweeney* is one much quoted reason for his popularity, while part of the format of a James Bond film is to follow an exciting 'action' sequence with a one-line joke from the hero. Indeed, the generic specificity of situation comedy is not really a question of certain exclusive elements ('situation', jokes, etc.) but of particular combinations of elements. In Neale's terms, it's a matter of 'the exclusive and particular weight given in any one genre to elements which in fact it shares with other genres'.[4]

NARRATIVE AND SITUATION COMEDY

Most forms of popular fiction involve a narrative which is initiated through the signification of a disruption, a disturbance, which the narrative proceeds to resolve. The narrative offers to the readers or the viewers a transformation of the initial equilibrium through a disruption and then a reordering of its components. Hence, it could be argued that one of the pleasures of reading a Bond novel rests on the simultaneous existence within the Bond novels of a disturbance both in a discourse of sexuality and in a discourse of imperialism and a progression towards the resolution of those disturbances through the activities of the hero. It is possible to suggest that all genres play with a disturbance, process and closure within the narrative, although in different ways. In so doing, genres construct particular temporal sequences. In the detective story, for example, the enigma with which the narrative begins structures suspense not simply by organising the narrative as a puzzle, but also by setting up a particular temporal sequence. The enigma or disturbance involves separate times; the time of the story behind the crime and the time of its reconstruction in the narrative. Closure is effected through the bringing together of the two times. Thus detective films construct a memory from instances of the story of the crime, from the story of its investigation and from the process of the text itself so that the 'memory constructed within the film duplicates the memory constructed by the film'. The temporal tension produced is the main characteristic of the suspense of a detective story.

The suspense of the thriller form is achieved slightly differently, but one common structure is that of the playing of the protagonist against a grouping of apparently disparate threats. In the Bond novels, the symbolic phallic threat takes a number of forms, that of Bond's substitute father M, that of the villains and that of the heroine. In a crime series programme such as *The Sweeney*, Jack Regan is threatened by criminals and by bureaucratic elements in the law and on occasion by problems with his family or private life. This doubling and occasionally trebling of threats to the hero not only increases the danger to him, but also sets up a temporal sequence involving both the number and complexity of the tasks which have to be performed for an effective and coherent closure to the narrative, for the story to 'end satisfactorily'. Suspense resides in the tension between the viewer's desire for the narrative to progress, although this involves a degree of risk for the hero, and the viewer's desire for the narrative to end, although this requires the full working out of the complex interconnections of the threats to the hero or heroine.[5]

Situation comedies also order the narrative and effect a particular closure, setting up a temporal sequence and positioning the subject, not in suspense but amusement and laughter. Eaton's argument suggests one aspect of the narrative of situation comedies, the lack of 'progression' involved in many situation comedies. In a sense, this lack of progression can only be identified in comparison with other genres, in which the progressive aspect of the narrative, that is the impetus towards the resolution of the initial disturbance, is more strongly weighted. In the opening episode of *Steptoe and Son*, the disturbance from the 'outside', the 'offer' does not lead to an obvious resolution in which either Harold takes the offer and leaves or rejects the offer and stays, but to Harold's inability to take the offer and his remaining without acceptance. In situation comedies, the viewer's pleasure does not lie in the suspense of puzzle-solving nor in the suspense surrounding the hero's ability to cope through action with various tasks and threats. Rather the tension of the narrative to which the viewer responds revolves around the economy or wit with which two or more discourses are brought together in the narrative. The pleasure of situation comedy is linked to the release of that tension through laughter.

Eaton's account of the 'inside/outside' dichotomy in situation comedies indicates the narrative structuring of many situation comedies around an intersection of two discourses. The resolution of the disturbance, the contradictions and resistances of the bringing together of the two discourses has to be accomplished with economy and wit, with conscious and overt fictional manipulation. The 'circularity' of many situation comedy plots is precisely an indication of that formally articulated wit. In Tony Hancock's 'The Blood Donor', you may remember the narrative follows this type of economic circularity. The episode begins with Hancock's entry into the Blood Donor Department of a hospital.

[. . .]

The two discourses are present from the beginning. On the one hand there is Hancock's discourse, in which the hero constantly and ineffectively seeks higher status, from his name ('Anthony Aloysius St John Hancock' rather than Tony Hancock), his conviction that he has aristocratic connections, to his desire to be given a badge for giving blood. [. . .] On the other hand, there is the discourse of the hospital and the older blood donors, the resisting world against which Hancock's delusions normally clash. The intersection of the two discourses is finally marked in the text of 'The Blood Donor', by Hancock's return to the hospital to be given the pint of blood he had donated earlier. He has cut himself with a kitchen knife.

[. . .]

The pleasure and coherence of this ending is partly one of Hancock's triumph over the hospital and blood donorship. Hancock overcomes the resistance of the hospital and subordinates it to his personal demands, thus reordering the discourses in another relationship to that of the beginning, from one of altruism to one of self-interest. But our amusement is also linked to the way in which Hancock's mixture of self-interest and would-be altruism comes full circle.

The narratives of most popular situation comedies within each episode tend to follow this pattern, although over a whole series the narrative sometimes develops beyond a constant return to square one. *Whatever Happened to the Likely Lads?* sees Terry's return from the army, the re-establishment of his friendship with Bob and the events leading up to Bob's wedding to Thelma and his removal to the Elm Lodge housing estate. The three series of *Agony* see the breakup of agony aunt Jane Luca's marriage to Laurence, her living alone, her affair with Vincent Fish and with Laurence, her pregnancy, return to Laurence and the birth of her child.[6] At the same time, although events happen, the discursive relationships often remain the same. In *Whatever Happened to the Likely Lads?* the clash between Bob and Terry's long-established friendship and common interests and Bob's new relationship with Thelma remains at the centre of the narrative of each episode. Similarly, in *Agony*, the contradiction between Jane's public image of helping others and her private difficulties in helping herself, her husband and friends, continues to provide the mainspring for the comic strategies of each episode.

In one sense, it is quite clear that while watching situation comedies we already know the likely outcome, just as we know the likely outcome of a detective story or a thriller. This does not, however, eradicate a sense of narrative tension. The tension and suspense of situation comedy is produced through a particular organisation of narrative time. A simple internal example of this is the use in situation comedies of the 'anticipation of the inevitable'. The joke is telegraphed in advance and the pleasurable effects are achieved through the viewer's foreknowledge of it. The comedy stems from the timing and economy with which a scene or a series of scenes are treated.

[. . .]

IDEOLOGY AND [STEREOTYPES]

One of the recurring interests in the study of comedy is the issue of its 'subversive' nature. In the British Film Institute's Dossier on situation comedy, the question of whether situation comedy is ideologically incorporative or ideologically subversive is broached time and again and with conclusions varying from seeing situation comedy as essentially conservative despite its reputation for subversion to seeing it as a fictional form which is capable of both inflections.[7]

[. . .]

In the case of situation comedies, one characteristic mode of identifying ideological 'bias' has been that concerned with the use of stereotypes. Stereotypes are forms of characterisation which are simple, memorable, widely recognised and frequently repeated. 'Dumb blondes', for example, are a recognisable type through a range of texts from Judy Holliday in *Born Yesterday*, to Marilyn Monroe in *Some Like It Hot*, to Lucy in the *I Love Lucy* show, to Wendy Craig in situation comedies such as *And Mother Makes Five*. The notion of stereotype assumes, not altogether unjustifiably, that there are important consequences stemming from the repetition of character types.

Stereotyping is not simply a 'neutral' exercise. Forms of stereotyping in the media have been identified as part of the way in which the media define and reinforce the deviant status of particular groups. Pearce sums up news coverage of homosexuality as 'How to be immoral, and ill, pathetic and dangerous, all at the same time'.[8] In a monograph on *Gays and Films*, Sheldon suggests the difficulties for homosexuals of responding to films with negative stereotypes: 'I remember being depressed for days after seeing *Sister George*, feeling "Sure, such a relationship may exist, but what a miserable one, and what's it doing on film to pervert young minds about lesbians"'.[9] Particular stereotypes are often attacked for their failure adequately to convey the 'real', either in terms of the complexity of any one individual or in terms of the range of real concrete individuals, homosexuals, blacks or women, who make up the membership of any particular stereotyped group. Criticism of the characterisation offered in stereotypes often explicitly demands more 'realism', in the sense of being truer to the real individuals outside the text, but it may also, of course, implicitly endorse some forms of signification at the expense of others. The typical characterisation of the nineteenth-century bourgeois novel, for example, is normally seen to be more adequate than that of a popular, contemporary situation comedy. Stereotypes are also attacked, however, for their failure to offer an ideal, a positive rather than a negative image.

Richard Dyer attempts to theorise the positive and negative aspects of stereotypes, by taking up Klapp's distinction between social types and stereotypes:

> stereotypes refer to things outside one's social world, whereas social types refer to things with which one is familiar; stereotypes tend to be conceived of as functionless or dysfunctional (or, if functional, serving prejudice and conflict mainly), whereas social types serve the structure of society at many points.[10]

As Dyer makes clear, most social types turn out to be white, middle class, heterosexual and male, and the distinction between social type and stereotype refers to those characters or types who are to be seen within and outside the boundaries of normal acceptability. Stereotypes in this formulation are inevitably negative. Indeed, Dyer suggests that they form part of a wider strategy of social control.

> The establishment of normalcy through social and stereotypes is one aspect of the habit of ruling groups – a habit of such enormous political consequences that we tend to think of it as far more premeditated than it actually is – to attempt to fashion the whole of society according to their own world-view, value system, sensibility and ideology. So right is the

worldview for the ruling groups that they make it appear (as it does to them) as 'natural' and 'inevitable' – and for everyone – and insofar as they succeed, they establish their hegemony.[11]

There are one or two problems with this outline of the ideological functions of social types and stereotypes. One problem is simply the extent to which a focus on stereotypes and on their repetition leads to the neglect of differences between characters in situation comedies. Wendy Craig's Ria in the BBC2 series *Butterflies*, for example, undoubtedly plays upon certain aspects of the 'dumb blonde' stereotype, but it also differs substantially from the earlier version. Moreover, any analysis which works on the assumption of relatively unambiguous identification between the viewer or reader and the stereotype, ignores the way in which identification works through textual and inter-textual formations. Identification with a character in a situation comedy follows both from the articulation of a character within a text and from the spectator's position within a particular reading formation. Neale suggests in relation to film that identification with character depends upon identification with the text itself. 'It is this primary identification that provides the basis of the spectator's relationship to the text and its characters and so requires initial attention and analysis.'[12] In one sense, this simply appears as understanding the function of the character in the text. Hence, the appearance of homosexual characters in *Whatever Happened to the Likely Lads?* appears to function simply to reinforce the 'healthy' heterosexuality of Bob and Terry, despite their intimate friendship. In 'Strangers on a Train' after Bob and Terry have re-established their friendship, they quarrel in the train buffet over Bob's marriage to Thelma. As Bob leaves, full of affronted dignity, Terry orders a Scotch and remarks to the barman that he gave the best years of his life for that man (an implicit reference to his stint in the army). The barman, however, who has been listening sympathetically, puts a comforting hand over Terry's and remarks, 'Never mind, sailor, lots of other pebbles on the beach'. The camera focuses on Terry's aghast reaction to this. The typical and dominant response of the viewer is with Bob and Terry and the camera ensures that it remains with Terry in this case rather than with the barman.

Yet to a large extent, the 'reading' relationships or 'viewing' relationships have to be conceived of in terms of an interrelationship between the reading formations of the viewers and the internal characteristics of the situation comedy. Questions about the subversive or incorporative qualities of stereotypes in situation comedy are fraught with problems, but particularly so when dependent simply on a textual analysis of a situation comedy. Medhurst and Tuck, for example, argue that situation comedies such as *Butterflies* or *Solo* lie outside the main pattern of situation comedy, moving towards melodrama because they involve themes untypical of situation comedy, that the woman rather than the male is seen as the victim of marriage and domesticity. To a certain extent this is seen as an explanation of differing views of these two series.

They are controversial series, liable to cause radical disagreements (not least between the two writers of this essay). Does *Butterflies*, for example, represent any kind of breakthrough in representations of women in comedy, or does it stand as the most insidious example of the method of inoculation? Ria is shown to be unable to cook; do we read this as a positive rejection of the housewifely role or a tired revival of the old jokes about female incompetence? Similarly, in the last episode of the first series of *Solo*, Gemma remarks of her relationship with Danny, 'If only the world hadn't changed and shown me things I really didn't want to see.' This can be taken as a positive acknowledgement of the impact of contemporary feminism, or as a glibly inoculatory gesture towards such an acknowledgement.[13]

But many 'non-controversial' situation comedies allow for different strategies of identification. In *Whatever Happened to the Likely Lads?*, the dominant critical reading undoubtedly involved identification with the 'lads'. Clive James summarises this 'male' view.

> Back from forces, Terry has spent the last couple of months trying to pull the birds. Bob, however, is on the verge of the ultimate step with the dreaded Thelma, and last week felt obliged to get rid of his boyhood encumbrances. Out of the old tea chest came the golden stuff: Dinky toys, Rupert and Picturegoer Annuals, all the frisson inducing junk that Thelma would never let weigh down the shelf units. 'I need those for reference', whined Bob with his arms full of cardboard covered books. There were Buddy Holly 78s – never called singles in those days, as Terry observed with the fantastic pedantry typical of the show. Obviously Bob will have a terrible time with Thelma.[14]

But discussions with Open University Summer School students showed a substantial proportion of them, predominantly women, who identified with Thelma as a strong maternal figure, similar to those in soap operas such as *Coronation Street*, against which the activities of Bob and Terry are simply the amusing antics of children. Clearly, this does not show that *Whatever Happened to the Likely Lads?* is a subversive text, but it does indicate that there can be very different readings of a situation comedy depending upon the operations of gendered reading formations and it itself suggests that any judgement about ideological subversion or incorporation can only be made in relation to the analysis of reading formations or viewing formations over time.

Of course, stereotypes are one attempt to bridge the gap between individual readings and more general ideological formations, but they tend to work in terms of a view in which ruling class ideas are handed down to the masses. Dyer, for example, suggests that stereotypes are one way through which ruling class groups project their own worldview. If however, the sphere of popular fiction is viewed as occupying an area of exchange and negotiation between ruling groups and subordinate classes, it could still be said to be the case that stereo-types play a particular role in establishing elements of the ideologies of dom-inant groups. Homosexuals, blacks and women could all be said to have negative images in contrast with white heterosexual males but it can also be argued that there is considerable negotiation around the use of stereotypes, indicated by the shifts and differences in one stereotype across a range of texts and by the way in which social subjects established in different reading for-mations negotiate identification with a stereotyped character. Thus, the use of stereotypes in popular fictional forms such as situation comedies may be rather less unambiguously a reflection of dominant group views than Dyer suggests.

POPULAR FICTION AND CONSENT

Mick Eaton in a recent article quotes a Tony Allen routine in which the comic is approached by the Anti-Nazi League to perform at one of their benefits. He is questioned over the phone by the organiser over whether his humour is 'anti-black' and replies that it isn't. He is then asked whether his humour is 'anti-women' – he thinks that it isn't. Allen then warns the organiser that his humour has a broader span, 'it's anti-life'. 'That's all right', says the organiser, 'that's not an area of current concern'. Eaton uses the joke to argue that discussions of comedy cannot be separated from the ideological/political positions available in a class society. One way of conceiving the relationships between ideologies and situation comedies is to focus rather less on the 'progressive' or 'non-progres-sive', 'subversive' or 'non-subversive' polarities of situation comedies and more on the way in which situation comedies perform alongside and in relation to other ideologies.

Traditionally, Marxist theories of ideology were centrally concerned with determination. Indeed, the preoccupation with questions of determination, with the determining relationship between economic base and ideological superstructures, led to the problems of reductionism referred to earlier. Changes in Marxist theories of ideology, initiated largely through the work of Althusser, involved some crucial reformulations in this area. Althusser's 'structuralist' reworking of Marxist theory stressed not the view of ideology as distortion, involving false consciousness, but the notion that ideology constituted the forms and representations through which men and women 'live' in an imaginary relation, their relationship to their real conditions of existence. Althusser's work generally, with its conceptualisation of ideology as determined only 'in the last instance' by the economic base, and in conjunction with developments in semiology, refocused attention on the autonomy and materiality of the ideo-logical and on the notion of articulation, on the relationships between parts within a structure rather than solely on determination. Theories of hegemony make use of the idea of articulation in a particular way to suggest that within a given mode of hegemony, popular consent is won and secured around an articulating principle, which ensures the establishment and reproduction of the interests of ruling groups while at the same time winning popular consent. The success of hegemonic ideological dominance can then be judged by the degree to which the articulating principle secures an ordering of different and potentially oppositional ideological discourses.

The area of popular fiction and popular culture generally works to shift and secure subject positions with the active consent of its readers and viewers. It constitutes a crucial area of negotiation of consent. When forms of popular fiction such as situation comedy rework the subject positions available to viewers they move their viewers on into different ideological frameworks. For example, regardless of whether a series like *Butterflies* truly 'subverts' or really 'incorporates', it does move its viewers on to a different set of ideological coordinates in relation to extramarital sex on the woman's part in terms of past handlings of this theme in situation comedies. In a reading framework of feminist criticism, of course, this move to a new set of ideological coordinates may not appear to be an improvement but it does occur. The popularity of a particular situation comedy or other fictional forms is an indicator of the success of that securing or shifting of subject positions.

In *Policing the Crisis*,[15] the authors outline a number of changes which have taken place in the ideological configurations of post-war Britain. *Policing the Crisis* takes as its starting point the orchestration by the media of mugging as a 'moral panic' and seeks to establish that this represents a movement from a 'consensual' to a more 'coercive' management of the class struggle, which in itself stems from the declining international competitiveness of the British economy following the post-war period, the erosion of which led to attempts to secure 'consent' by more coercive although legitimate means. The immediate post-war period saw the construction of a consensus based on the politics of affluence. Economic decline triggered the disintegration of the 'miracle of spontaneous consent' based on these politics and there was an attempt to put forward a Labourist variant of consent to replace it. The exhaustion of this form of consent, however, combined with the rise of social and political conflict, the deepening of the economic crisis and the resumption of more explicit class struggle, culminated in the 'exceptional' form of class domination through the state in the 1970s, in which the ideological articulating principle was a discourse of 'law and order'.

The media play a central part in this analysis. They are described as a 'key terrain where "consent" is won or lost', as 'a field of ideological struggle'.[16] The key to the media's involvement in the construction of consent lies in the authors' analysis of news as performing a crucial transformative but secondary role in defining social events. The primary definers are those to whom the media turn, their accredited sources in government and other institutions. Although *Policing the Crisis* emphasises the transformative nature of media news reporting, in the selection and structuring of themes and topics, the conception of the media role is one of 'structured subordination' to the primary definers. Further, the creative media role serves to reinforce a consensual viewpoint, by using public idioms and by claiming to voice public opinion. Thus, in

the 'crisis' described, the media have endorsed and enforced primary definitions of industrial militancy, troublesome youth cultures, mugging, student
protest movements, as part of a 'law and order' problem.

Policing the Crisis confines its account of the media largely to the area of
news coverage and only touches upon the area of popular culture tangentially.
Yet clearly the idea of the dominant articulating principle of ideological
hegemony, a principle which structures ideological discourses and which
involves the media in the construction of that articulation, could and should
be extended beyond the confines of news coverage. One obvious area for
development is in establishing the relationship between the dominant articulating principle and particular popular fictional genres. Given that genres themselves constitute specific articulations of ideological and formal elements, it
would seem to follow that shifts in the dominant articulating principle would be
registered in the area of popular fiction by the increased popularity of appropriate genre articulations. The police crime series, for example, became popular
at a time when there were major shifts in the dominant articulating principle,
from the terrain of ideologies of 'affluence' to that of 'law and order'. The
television crime series was a form in which both arguments for and reservations
about current 'law and order' issues could be put into play in terms of the
subject positions produced by the genre.

Similarly the thriller format developed around notions of Britain's internal
and external security in programmes such as *The Professionals* and *Sandbag-
gers*. *The Professionals* stands at one end of a range of programmes which
focus directly on themes of 'law and order' and which extend the notion of
policing quite radically. Where programmes such as *The Sweeney* suggested the
dissatisfactions of a working policeman in the Flying Squad in terms of the
barriers placed by bureaucratic police procedures on the arrest of criminals,
The Professionals begins from the premise that the ordinary police cannot
handle certain problems. One of the books derived from the programmes
describes the heroes as the 'hard men'. 'They're the hard men. The Professionals. Doing society's dirty work in the ever more bloody war against
violence and destruction ...'[17]

The process of articulation with a hegemonic principle may help explain one
of the continuing problems of the study of genre – why particular genres are
popular at any one historical moment and why they may increase or decrease in
popularity over time. Works of fiction and specific genres are popular precisely
because they articulate, work upon and attempt in different ways to resolve
contemporary ideological tensions. The case of situation comedies raises two
important issues in relation to this, however. In the first place any comparison
of situation comedies and television crime series will indicate something of the
complexities of the process whereby popular genres both organise ideological
themes differently and interpellate their subjects differently. Thus the episode
of *Till Death Us Do Part*, 'If we want a proper democracy we've got to start
shooting a few people' (transmission October 1972), constructs one version of

the 'law and order' discourse with Garnett 'pulling in' a range of problems into the same problem of law and order.

Alf	... Enoch's wrong, having a go at the coons.
Mike and Rita	(astonished) Oh!!!
Alf	Yes! He ain't seen the real danger. It's not the coons. We don't want 'em over here stinking the country out with their curries and making a row on their dustbin lids. But they're bloody harmless – not like yer bloody Russian Unions and yer Chinese *Take-Aways* ... Hot beds of bloody fifth column they are. But we're on to 'em, don't worry. You'll see the next time one of them commy shop stewards goes in the nick he'll rot there. All they organise them bloody strikes for is so they can get on the bleedin' telly. I blame the BBC for encouraging 'em. They'll put anyone on the bloody telly, they will. Rock an' roll vicars ... and sex maniacs, an' bloody Irish gunmen. Admit they put stockings over their heads first, but still. They only let the Queen go on for one show at Christmas – I don't know what they've got against that woman. She should have her own series, 'cos she's better'n Lulu. (*Rita giggles.*) Blimey, she's the best thing on at Christmas.

Garnett's mad logic takes the argument on to cover both prison conditions and the unions and the solution to it all.

Alf	And why shouldn't they get bloody slops? Prisons supposed to be a bloody deterrent annit? They ain't supposed to sit about all day scoffing and shagging! (*Else is shocked.*) I mean, blimey, they'll be putting yer Billy Butlin in charge of the prisons soon, and have bloody red-coats for warders! I mean in the old days, they used to put 'em in bloody chains and ship 'em out to the Colonies. But we can't do that now, 'cos your bloody Labour Party gave all the Colonies away. So we have to keep 'em here and feed 'em out of our taxes. And what if five of their ring leaders [of the prison officer's union] defy the law, eh? They can't bung them in prison, 'cos they're already in there.
Else	They'll have to fine their union.
Alf	Don't be so bloody daft. What are they gonna fine them? Eighty gallons of porridge? A hundredweight of hardtack? And another thing what would yer Russians have done, eh? They wouldn't have put them in prison, would they, eh? And your Chinese, eh? If five of their

	dockers had defied their laws, eh? They wouldn't have put them in prison, would they? Eh? No. They'd have bloody shot 'em.
Mike	And I suppose you'd like to see 'em shoot our dockers, eh?
Alf	We wouldn't! That's the trouble with this country. That's our weakness! If we want a proper democracy here, we've got to start shooting a few people ... like yer Russians do.[18]

Till Death Us Do Part quite clearly registers a political concern with the ideological themes which were the focal point of other popular genres, notably the television crime series. At the same time, it could be argued that *Till Death Us Do Part* handles those themes rather differently. Garnett's suggestion that 'we've got to start shooting a few people' may sound more than reminiscent of the solution that is found in most episodes of *The Professionals*, but it is also a conclusion that we are supposed to laugh at rather than applaud. Moreover while *Till Death Us Do Part* was relatively unusual amongst the popular situation comedies of its period in its direct concern with political issues, it was also organised like many other situation comedies to pull the right-wing views of the inimitable Alf Garnett into a family narrative, playing off his position outside a liberal consensus against his position within the family. Later situation comedies such as *Shelley, Citizen Smith* or *Agony* dealt with characters and problems relevant to 'law and order' issues (unemployment in *Shelley*, political radicalism in *Citizen Smith* and sexual permissiveness in *Agony*) in a manner which also tended to pull 'deviance' into a familiar sitcom world of 'universal' problems of family, sexuality and class. The crime series, however, tended to place those same problems and characters as threatening to and outside the parameters of the family, class and 'normal' sexuality. In important ways then situation comedies and the crime series in the 1970s work against one another rendering their themes and subjectivities in opposed directions and in so doing indicating something of the complexity of the relationship between a hegemonic principle and the fictional field.

In the second place, popular and controversial situation comedies such as *Till Death Us Do Part* raise certain questions about the relationship between specific fictional forms and more general ideological formations. It is clearly the case that some fictions are not simply popular but also play a particular part in relation to the ordering of other ideologies. Such fictions have a place in the public arena above and beyond their immediate textual base. The public outcry which surrounded *Till Death Us Do Part* and the way in which Alf Garnett became a figure in the popular imagination even for people who didn't watch television indicates this process at work. At specific historical moments, some fictions, rather than working alongside and in relation to other ideologies, come to provide a nexus through which ideologies may be actively reorganised, shifting the subjectivities at their core, while other fictions work precisely to stabilise existing subjectivities. It is in this area that it is possible to establish in historical rather than formal terms the subversive or incorporative qualities of situation comedies. Without work of this order, the discussion of situation comedies in terms of their potentially subversive effects is simply an exercise in criticism, an attempt to organise situation comedies to mean some things and not others, to establish the protocols of viewing: a perfectly legitimate but rather different exercise.

NOTES

1. T. Ryall, 'Teaching through Genre', *Screen Education*, 1976, p. 27.
2. S. Neale, *Genre*, British Film Institute, London, 1980, p. 28.
3. M. Eaton, 'Laughter in the Dark', *Screen Education*, 1981, p. 33.
4. Neale, *Genre*, p. 9.
5. Ibid., p. 27.
6. G. Hickman, *Agony*, Arrow Books, London, 1980.
7. *Television Sitcom*, BFI Dossier no. 17, British Film Institute, London, 1982.
8. F. Pearce, 'How to be immoral and ill, pathetic and dangerous, all at the same time: mass media and the homosexual' in S. Cohen and J. Young (eds), *The Manufacture of News*, Constable, London, 1973, p. 284.
9. Sheldon, quoted in R. Dyer (ed.), *Gays and Films*, British Film Institute, London, 1977, p. 16.
10. Klapp, quoted in Dyer (1977), p. 29.
11. Ibid., p. 30.
12. S. Neale, 'Stereotypes', *Screen Education*, 1979, p. 35.
13. A. Medhurst and L. Tuck, 'The Gender Game' in *British Film Institute Dossier, Television Sitcom*, p. 52.
14. C. James, *The Observer*, 11 March 1972.
15. S. Hall, C. Critcher, T. Jefferson, J. Clarke and B. Roberts, *Policing the Crisis: Mugging, the State and Law and Order*, Macmillan, London, 1978.
16. Ibid., p. 220.
17. K. Blake, *The Professionals 4: Hunter Hunted*, Sphere, London, 1978.
18. J. Speight, *Till Death Us Do Part*, The Woburn Press, London, 1973, pp. 136–7.

24

TELEVISED CHAT AND THE SYNTHETIC PERSONALITY

Andrew Tolson

Just as television, and broadcasting more generally, has developed its own particular dramatic genres (e.g. situation comedy), so too it has developed certain forms of broadcast talk which have identifiable generic structures. These forms of talk are, in general terms, 'informal and conversational' (Scannell, 1988), but more precisely, they should be seen as institutionalized variants of 'conversation' as such. Moreover, these forms of talk occur across the different programme formats within which 'talk' predominates. For instance, it would be interesting to undertake a study of the art of 'live commentary' as a speech genre which clearly takes different forms on radio and television, but which occurs across sports programmes, state occasions, live political events and, sometimes, disasters. Live commentary is one broadcast speech genre; and 'chat', I am suggesting, is another. Chat is a form of studio talk, which can be found in all types of interviews, panel discussions, game shows and human interest programmes (e.g. *That's Life!*) – wherever in fact there is a studio.

What then characterizes 'chat' as a broadcast speech genre? In many contexts [...] chat is apparent in a clear shift of *register* within the programme format where it occurs, such that the primary business of the format is temporarily delayed or suspended. Thus in the context of a game show, chat between participants delays the actual playing of the game (a prime example would be *Blankety Blank* [a celebrity quiz show]); whereas in the context of a current affairs interview chat introduces a suspension within the 'main' discourse,

From Andrew Tolson, 'Televised Chat and the Synthetic Personality', Ch. 9 in Paddy Scannell (ed.), *Broadcast Talk* (London: Sage, 1991) pp. 179–87.

whilst a 'subsidiary' discourse (an aside, a metadiscursive comment) is briefly formulated (cf. Montgomery, 1977). It is this functional contrast between main and subsidiary levels of discourse which frequently allows us to recognize chat when we hear it:

Robin Day	Mrs Thatcher do you intend to lead the Conservative Party into the next election in say '87?
Mrs Thatcher	I hope so.
Day	Because if you do that and let's say that the next is in the autumn of 1987 do you realise then that you would have been, held the office of Prime Minister for a longer, for the longest continuous period this century and possibly long before that?
Thatcher	Yes.
Day	Eight-and-a-half-years, and you'll be six ...
Thatcher	Not very long.
Day	Eight-and-a-half-years.
Thatcher	Yes it's not very long if you look back to other times.
Day	And you'll be sixty-two. You still think you want to go ahead at the next election?
Thatcher	Yes. I shall be a very fit sixty-two. You might be a little bit nearer that than I am, but you feel all right?
Day (chuckles)	Forgive me if I don't answer that question Prime Minister, towards the end of this interesting interview. (*Panorama*, April 1984)

Actually, I think Brown and Yule [1983] have overestimated the difficulties in arriving at a formal definition of 'chat'. There are at least three main identifying features of this speech genre, not all of which may be operating at once. First, there is often a topical shift towards the 'personal' (as opposed to the institutional), or towards the 'private' (as opposed to the public). Secondly, this shift may be accompanied by displays of wit (e.g. foregrounding lexical ambiguities) or humour (double entendres, etc.). But thirdly, and this is the vital point, in any context 'chat' always works by opening up the possibility of transgression. Chat does not simply reproduce norms and conventions, rather it flirts with them, for instance, it opens up the possibility of the interviewee putting questions to the interviewer. Certainly, in the context of a *Panorama* interview, Robin Day must appear to 'manage' this behaviour; but at the same time (as this example shows) it is not simply disavowed. For in this momentary transgression of convention, both Mrs Thatcher, and in his response Day himself, are constructed as 'television personalities'.

Defined in these terms, I would suggest that 'chat' is a central feature of televised public discourse, and I shall return to a discussion of its effects. For not only is chat a ubiquitous and constant possibility for nearly every kind of televised studio talk; it is also, because of the studio's pivotal location in the regime of broadcasting, in a certain position of dominance. However, from a discursive point of view, perhaps the most interesting of all programme formats is the contemporary 'chat' or 'talk' show (I will use the American term 'talk show' to emphasize that 'chat' is a genre which occurs in several formats). In the 1980s, the talk show attained new heights of sophistication, both in Britain and in the USA. In America, David Letterman might be compared and contrasted to the earlier format personified by Johnny Carson; whilst in Britain, the genre dominated in the 1970s by Michael Parkinson (previously, a journalist) was taken over and developed by Terry Wogan (previously, a disc jockey). The talk show is, by definition, devoted to the production of 'chat'; but by the mid-1980s the BBC's prime-time Saturday night show *Wogan* had developed 'chat' to the point where it was virtually an art form.

TELEVISION CHAT AND THE 'PERSONALITY EFFECT'

Consider for example the following exchange between Terry Wogan and Shelley Winters (*Wogan*, 10 March 1984):

Winters	You had to give away my age, huh?
Wogan	No no.
Winters	You had to say how old I was. When was it, 1939?
Wogan	1957 or something, wasn't it?
Winters	When was *Gone With The Wind* done?
Wogan	I'm not sure.
Winters	The only reason I didn't get the part was that I had a Brooklyn accent. Vivien Leigh spoke better otherwise I would have got it.
Wogan	You would have walked that.
Winters	* What was that accent, that man, who just talked for fifteen minutes?
Wogan	What, Terry Venables?
Winters	Yes.
Wogan	I'm not sure, a type of East End accent I think. I think he makes it up as he goes along.
Winters	I did a picture with Michael Caine a while ago called *Alfie* which was sort of a good picture but I never knew what he was saying. Whenever he took a breath I said my line, it was like that.
Wogan	Many of us have difficulty with Michael Caine, yes.
Winters	It seems like the same language but it isn't. I mean sometimes you get in a lot of trouble.
Wogan	What sort of trouble have you been in?
Winters	I'm not discussing it.
Wogan	Come on.

Winters	There are millions of people watching I mean you say anything on your television ...
Wogan	That's what you think.
Winters	I know er, but you know, no there's nothing. Well you say anything. Last night I watched something on BBC2 about sex.
Wogan	Yes we have that over here. What do you call that in America?
Winters	You don't talk about it you do it (*laughter*). I mean, I never saw a show *Sex Education for Adults*. That's what it was.
Wogan	Yes, I saw it myself. I learned quite a lot.
Winters	[*] It was slides and pictures and diagrams and er, I was, did it shock you?
Wogan	No, because I know where I'm going wrong now.
Winters	[*] Well, listen how long have you done this show, three years?
Wogan	Feels like it. Only a year.
Winters	No, you don't.
Wogan	Still a boy, still a boy at the game. Yes, before I did this there was a very old man who used to do it called Dartington or something.
Winters	Have you thought, now Saturday nights because of inflation and everything, I learned from the crew – I've just been doing a picture called *Always*, and I think it will be done always. It's all about, I play a Russian psychic lesbian I think, I'm not sure.
Wogan	I'm glad you looked at that sex instruction film.
Winters	I know er.
Wogan	I can see the problems you'd have with that part.
Winters	Well, anyway, it was a sort of weird love story that takes place between 1936 and now and the people they have trouble making out. Do you say making out?
Wogan	No. Making up? Making it?
Winters	No, when you do it.
Wogan	Doing it?
Winters	Yeah, do you say making out?
Wogan	No, we say doing it.
Winters	Well, in the still of the night if you can't sleep do you ever wonder, because people don't go out much on Saturday nights as they used to, it used to be a regular thing.
Wogan	They do now, look they usen't to, but they do now since we started.

Winters	* This interview. OK. Now have you ever wondered sort of if people are at home Saturday nights and they're watching you and its warm and they stretch out in the bedroom or the living room wherever the telly is (*TW*: steady, yes). Have you ever thought how many babies you're responsible for?
Wogan	No, I'm responsible for no babies whatsoever.
Winters	Well you are though.
Wogan	No I'm not (*SW*: Yes you are) No, people nod off to me.
Winters	I didn't nod off last week when Joan Rivers said all those terrible things.
Wogan	Didn't she, didn't she say some shocking ... You talk about us saying some shocking things, I mean she really does.
Winters	No we don't let her say those things on television in America.
Wogan	Yes you do.
Winters	No we don't. We laugh at night clubs and then we are ashamed we laughed. I mean I'm not exactly a Women's Libber but I mean I get so angry when I laugh at her (...)
Wogan	* You've been a bit of a shocker yourself though, haven't you?
Winters	Yes, but I put it in print I don't do it on television.

I will begin my formal analysis of this exchange by recognizing that as a species of interviewing, it contains some peculiar, and in other contexts abnormal, features. Just in straight quantitative terms Winters (interviewee) puts nine questions to Wogan, whilst he (interviewer) puts seven questions to his guest. Furthermore, at least four of Winters' questions (marked by asterisks in the transcript) can be counted as major topical initiations, requiring developed responses from Wogan, which Winters then follows up with supplementary questions and comments. Wogan himself makes three such topical initiations, the first of which is rejected by the interviewee ('I'm not discussing it'). Equally, many of the utterances in this exchange are hearable neither as questions nor as answers, but rather as initiating propositions or as contributions to sequences of argument.

Nor is this exactly the intimate and cosy 'fireside chat', casting the audience in the position of 'eavesdroppers' to a private conversation, which some previous forms of the talk show have attempted to simulate (Greatbatch, 1987: 35). Rather, the Wogan/Winters dialogue seems to be much more aware of itself as a public performance: at times it is a kind of double act, with mock pantomimic arguments ('Oh yes you do'; 'Oh no I don't') and with Wogan playing the straight man to Winters' humorous lines. In a word, the talk show interview is now dedicated to *banter*. It is as if the conventions of interviewing have now become a pretext for the development of clever and complex forms of verbal improvisation in which both parties more or less equally participate. Within this space, Winters in particular stretches her position as interviewee to the limit: not only does she ask most of the questions and introduce most of the topics; as she comments on Wogan's introduction and interrogates his career as a talk show host she seems to be highlighting the artificiality of his role.

However, my principal reason for reproducing this extract here is because it provides a particularly rich illustration of my three defining features of 'chat' as a speech genre. First then, in terms of content, there is the characteristic focus on the 'personal', which in *Wogan* was often equated with the sexual, but also was more generally articulated in terms of gossip – both about other stars/personalities (Leigh, Caine) and previous performances on the programme (Rivers). Also at this level a common cultural knowledge is invoked (e.g. the date of *Gone With The Wind*, the joke about 'Dartington' i.e. Parkinson, the BBC's best-known talk show interviewer before Wogan). This is the kind of mass-mediated cultural knowledge which is classified in many contexts today as 'trivia'.

Secondly, and building on this foundation, there is a sustained and highly self-reflexive metadiscourse about television as a cultural institution. Here participants not only invoke the cultural knowledge of the viewer, they also draw attention to the construction of their own performances. It is assumed for instance, that the viewer has a knowledge of the history of television, of its genres, and is reflexively aware of the domestic conditions of its reception. Indeed, when Winters refers to these, in her speculations about viewers and babies, she comes very close to transgressing the formal distance between television and its audience – the next step would be to address the viewer directly. It is certainly very far from a realistic simulation, where disbelief is 'suspended', because here the reflexive nature of the talk assumes a viewer who is consciously aware of the forms as well as the contents of television.

In my view, however, it is at a third level that this kind of talk becomes really clever. There is a level at which the dialogic improvisation is somewhat similar to a jazz performance, not only because it is apparently unrehearsed, but also in so far as it involves a play of thematic repetition and variation. In this dialogue the metadiscursive level ('Here we are on television'/'How are people watching this at home?') is articulated to a repetition of two topics (both introduced by the interviewee): i.e. language/cultural difference and sex/the limits of public discourse. A form of *wit* is demonstrated by interweaving these various topics, so that each is inflected in terms of the other. Thus the topic of linguistic difference is inflected into the terminology of sex ('Do you say making out?'), whilst the topic of sexual discourse is inflected into cultural differences in the publicly sayable ('We don't let her say those things on television'). Two or three topics are in the air at once and the skill of the participants consists in their ability to manipulate the dialogue to ensure that the verbal juggling act continues.

And the performance is of course given added impetus by the fact that it is apparently 'live'. Will the participants be able to sustain this spontaneous flow of wit and repartee? In fact, in this case, the programme was recorded, the 'liveness' is an illusion; but an effect of liveness and immediacy is constructed in a number of ways. In this context, with its 'live' studio audience, liveness is an effect of the studio location; but it is also reinforced by deictic features of the reflexive metadiscourse: 'What was that accent that just talked?', 'How long have you been doing this show?' When Shelley Winters talks about the viewer's domestic situation she indirectly refers to immediate conditions of viewing. My point here is that whilst the metadiscourse does, on one level, 'demystify' the institution of television, it also simultaneously contributes to a 'liveness' effect which helps to sustain it. At this level then, the metadiscourse *re-mystifies*: it reaffirms a bond between television performers, studio audience and, by extension, the domestic viewer which implicates all parties in a common and immediate situation.

All of which serves to reproduce a particular kind of 'personality effect'. It is instructive at this point to refer to the discussion of 'personality' in television studies which, in some accounts, has made reference to the effects of televised 'chat'. For instance, John Langer (1981) has defined television's 'personality system' in terms of a 'complex unity [of] heterogenous and multi-faceted codes', amounting to a 'systematic tendency' across many forms of television (Langer, 1981: 352). But after talking in general terms about the effects of 'speaking for oneself' in television interviews, and in close-up, Langer comes to focus specifically on a notion of 'disclosure':

> In the context of the talk-show's carefully orchestrated informality, with its illusion of lounge-room casualness and leisurely pace, the host and guest engage in 'chat'. During the course of this chat, with suitable questions and tactful encouragement from the host, the guest is predictably 'drawn in' to making certain 'personal' disclosures, revealing aspects of what may be generally regarded as the private self, in fact becoming incorporated into television's personality system by disclosing for the purposes of television, one's 'personality'.
>
> ... What prevails in the end is not the talk show's diluted hucksterism and commercial 'hype' but its capacity to provide a special setting for personal disclosure where guests appear to be showing us their 'real' selves, where they can discuss how they 'feel' and reflect on their private lives with impunity. If these guests are among the great and powerful or are well-known celebrities, which is most frequently the case, this is the place where the cares and burdens of high office or public life can be set aside, where we can see them as they 'really are', which in the end after all, as these programmes set out to illustrate, is just like us, 'ordinary folks'. (Langer, 1981: 360–1)

On this basis, Langer goes on to attribute an ideological effect to this discourse of personality, in so far as it displaces social and political criteria. But perhaps his frequent recourse to inverted commas ('real' selves, etc.) already begins to suggest some doubts about the sincerity of personal disclosure in the contemporary talk show. In fact, what Langer really seems to be describing here is an earlier form of 'human interest' interview programme, of which John Freeman's *Face to Face* (BBC, 1959–62) would be an exemplary instance, where indeed a populist personality discourse was frequently reflected in the open and apparently sincere disclosure of 'real feelings'. In these programmes, Freeman's interviewing technique might certainly be characterized as a strategy of 'tactful encouragement', allied to a rigorous, probing use of the camera. But today, I would suggest, this kind of transparent populism appears old-fashioned. Although its rhetorical structure (i.e. public/private persons; apparent/real selves, etc.) persists as a generic formula for the talk show, it seems to me that a fundamental shift has taken place in the way this formula is reproduced.

Increasingly, as the Winters interview illustrates, 'personality' now appears not in transparent revelation, but in the interviewee's capacity to negotiate the terms of 'disclosure'. This is precisely not the context for a 'true confession' (as Winters herself indicates) and so part of the pleasure for the audience in this speech genre consists in working out the different degrees of truth/untruth in what is then spoken. A certain level of complexity, which implicates the 'knowingness' of the viewer, is related to a form of speaking from 'experience' where *the experiences may or may not be real*. [...] [C]learly at this level 'personality' is no longer reducible to 'people as they really are'. Rather, it seems to me that the personality effect now consists in the willingness of stars and celebrities, like Winters, to take the risk of playing this kind of public verbal game. In the contemporary talk show the interview is explicitly and transparently a *performance* of 'chat' – that is its *raison d'être* – and there are moments in this performance when the very concept of 'personality' is up for discussion.

Personality as Performance

In the *Wogan* series, regularly and in various ways, the whole notion of 'personality' was called into question. But it was not that the populist personality discourse, with its emphasis on sincerity and authenticity, was entirely redundant; rather the earlier formula was now explicitly interrogated, and other rhetorics of 'authenticity' were on display. Consider, first of all, the following dialogue between two established television 'personalities':

> (*Terry Wogan interviewing Bob Monkhouse, 10 March 1984*)
>
> *Wogan*   You've done your chat show series for BBC 2. How do you like being an interviewee rather than an interviewer?
>
> *Monkhouse* I found being an interviewer very very difficult. I have watched this series of course I have, and the last one and the previous one. And I think you are, I hate to do this, I think you're very good (*laughter*). I really do ... I found

	it very difficult. I find the biggest problem for me is, that my admiration for my guests, because they were all comedians, is so considerable that I can't disguise it, I can't hide it, and therefore it's possible to appear erm obsequious and er over enthusiastic about a guest when that is a genuine emotion, and that's been criticised. I noticed er (W: Yes). Well I should develop the same contempt that you obviously have for your guests.
Wogan	No, only for some of them.
Monkhouse	(*Laughs*) Adsum.
Wogan	Do you think then that erm, being honest or showing honest emotions on television is not a good idea, if they could be misinterpreted, as they have been in your case, they're called smarm which is genuine admiration?
Monkhouse	(*Laughs*) Yes, er I don't think er, television is a place for me to show my genuine emotions. I think it's a place for, I would rather, I'm much happier, er Joan Rivers when you interviewed her the other week so, so excellently said the cabaret stage was her psychiatrist er that she regarded her job as to entertain, to get laughs. And that's the way I feel I, I came into the business in eighteen hundred and forty five in order to get laughs but that meant inventing a persona, offering something which is not necessarily me, it's an invention, it's a construction.
	I, I've known you long enough to know that there are er, inconceivably deeper parts of you than are actually visible on the TV screen. There are parts of you which have never been seen on the TV screen (*audience laughter*). I for one hope that they will never be seen.
Wogan	You nearly got into a compliment there. And you decide to duck out of it. Because a little bit of the real Bob came out there and you quickly shoved it back again.
Monkhouse	Yes, yes I don't really want to, no, exposing myself on the TV screen is not my idea of fun.

In a previous article (Tolson, 1985) I have analysed another extract from this interview in which Monkhouse tells a couple of very funny anecdotes about a television programme he used to compere, *The Golden Shot*. The aim of that article was to highlight certain similarities between the formal structure of the anecdote and the regime of broadcast television – arguing that the rhetoric of much contemporary television can be characterized as 'anecdotal'. However, that discussion also makes a further point which is more immediately relevant to this extract, where Monkhouse and Wogan are directly discussing the activity in which they are simultaneously engaged. This point is again that increasingly, talk on television is self-reflexive. It is not only talk, but also talk about talk: that is 'metatalk', and talk about television in general (Tolson, 1985: 23).

Moreover, I think it is very significant that some of the talk about television in the contemporary talk show, now extends to the notion of 'television personality' as such. There now seems to be a space for Monkhouse to engage in what is effectively a *critique* of his own television personality. In the light of Langer's account this is a very interesting discussion: for Monkhouse is now saying that his television personality is a 'construction' – and that the same point applies to our host, Wogan himself. Not that this critique is particularly disturbing, however – for somehow Monkhouse appears as an even more authentic and sincere personality ('the real Bob') in so far as he admits that his television personality is a sham.

Also, of course, Monkhouse is making an attempt to inject some (not very subtle) humour into the discussion. Again, in comparison with *Face to Face* (recall Freeman's interview with Tony Hancock) the rhetoric of personality has changed. The terms of an acceptable talk show performance now extend to an ability to play with conventions of sincerity and personal disclosure, and to develop jokes at their expense. Joan Rivers herself is particularly adept at this kind of strategy:

(Terry Wogan interviewing Joan Rivers, 3 March 1984)

Wogan	You do chat shows yourself I know in the States. You sit in for the biggest chat show they have there, *Johnny Carson*, and he hates you because you're more popular than he is.
Rivers	No no he loves me. He found me, he found me. He's my mentor.
Wogan	So you're his protegee.
Rivers	I'm his protegee.
Wogan	Mm. And when you hosted that show you had a bit of a run in with one of our own lovely ladies Joan Collins, didn't you?
Rivers	The best, she's the best. She's the best because she's bitchy back. Do you know what fun it is, Joan Collins is so ...' Cause that's what television should be, it should be fun. And she gets on, and I'll be bitchy to her. It's like a tennis match and she goes whack back. I said to her, you know 'cause we call her the British Open, I mean she's just had everybody, so but *(laughter, applause)*
Wogan	But did you say that to her face?
Rivers	Yes, so I said to her, you know 'who is the best man you ever had?' And she said to me 'your husband'. *(laughter)* Well, that's great. You just want to say that's what television should be.

Of course, not everyone tells them like Joan Rivers, and in fact when the Rivers talk show was shown subsequently on British television it was not particularly successful. But in both content and form I think this exchange with Wogan is indicative of a transformation in the talk show genre, and its attendant concept of 'good television', as compared for instance to the kind of talk show interview which Langer has described. Two essential points can be made. First, the grounds for speaking from 'experience' have changed. In so far as personal experiences still remain the focus for such interviews, and in so far as they are 'disclosed', they may be recounted sincerely (Monkhouse), but equally they may be represented as constructions, even fabrications (Rivers) for the 'game' which is 'good television'. But, secondly, the reason why the grounds for disclosure have shifted is that a key generic development has taken place in the history of the talk show interview. The Rivers interview (and there were several similar interviews in the 1984 series of *Wogan*) is in fact indicative of an institutional 'mixing' of genres, where the talk show interview meets stand-up comedy. The interview provides a vehicle and the interviewer poses as the straight-man, for an established and rehearsed comedy routine. Thus 'chat' may still be serious, or it may be comic; but more often than not it has now become a complex and entertaining mixture of the two.

REFERENCES

Brown, G. and G. Yule (1983) *Discourse Analysis* Cambridge: Cambridge University Press.

Greatbatch, D. (1987) 'A Turn Taking System for British News Interviews', Warwick Working Papers in Sociology, University of Warwick, Department of Sociology.

Langer, J. (1981) 'Television's "Personality System"' *Media, Culture and Society* 3: 351–65.

Montgomery, M. (1977) 'Discourse Structure and Cohesion in Selected Science Lectures', MA thesis, University of Birmingham.

Scannell, P. (1988) 'The Communicative Ethos of Broadcasting'. Paper presented at the International Television Studies Conference, London (BFI).

Tolson, A. (1985) 'Anecdotal Television' *Screen* 26(2): 18–27.

25

CRITICAL ANALYSIS OF MEDIA DISCOURSE

Norman Fairclough

[My framework for analysing media discourse] is a version of the theory of 'critical discourse analysis' which I have developed in previous publications (Fairclough 1989, 1992, 1993). [This piece] first briefly describes in general terms the theory of discourse I am operating with, and then focuses attention upon media discourse. The framework is described and then applied to an example.

THEORY OF DISCOURSE

Recent social theory has produced important insights into the social nature of language and how it functions in contemporary societies. Social theorists have tended to put such insights in abstract ways, without analysis of specific texts. To develop a form of discourse analysis which can contribute to social and cultural analysis, we need to combine these insights with traditions of close textual analysis which have developed in linguistics and language studies – to make them 'operational', practically usable, in analysis of specific cases.

Calling the approach 'critical' is a recognition that our social practice in general and our use of language in particular are bound up with causes and effects which we may not be at all aware of under normal conditions (Bourdieu, 1977). Specifically, connections between the use of language and the exercise of power are often not clear to people, yet appear on closer examination to be vitally important to the workings of power. For instance, ways in which a

From Norman Fairclough, *Media Discourse* (London: Arnold, 1995) pp. 53–74. Cross-references to other sections of Fairclough's book have been removed here.

conventional consultation between a doctor and a patient is organized, or a conventional interview between a reporter and a politician, take for granted a whole range of ideologically potent assumptions about rights, relationships, knowledge and identities. For example, the assumption that the doctor is the sole source of medically legitimate knowledge about illness, or that it is legitimate for the reporter – as one who 'speaks for' the public – to challenge the politician. Such practices are shaped, with their common-sense assumptions, according to prevailing relations of power between groups of people. The normal opacity of these practices to those involved in them – the invisibility of their ideological assumptions, and of the power relations which underlie the practices – helps to sustain these power relations.

'Discourse' is a concept used by both social theorists and analysts (e.g. Foucault, 1972; Fraser, 1989) and linguists (e.g. Stubbs, 1983; van Dijk, 1985). Like many linguists, I shall use 'discourse' to refer to spoken or written language use, though I also want to extend it to include other types of semiotic activity (i.e. activity which produces meanings), such as visual images (photography, film, video, diagrams) and non-verbal communication (e.g. gestures). In referring to use of language as discourse, I am signalling a wish to investigate it in a way that is informed by the [insights of] social theory, as a form of social practice.

Viewing language use as social practice implies, first, that it is a mode of action, as linguistic philosophy and the study of pragmatics have recognized (Austin, 1962; Levinson, 1983). It also implies that language is a socially and historically situated mode of action, in a dialectical relationship with other facets of the social. What I mean by a dialectical relationship is that it is socially shaped, but is also socially shaping – or socially *constitutive*. Critical discourse analysis explores the tension between these two sides of language use, the socially shaped and socially constitutive, rather than opting one-sidedly for one or the other.

Language use – any text – is always simultaneously constitutive of (1) social identities, (2) social relations and (3) systems of knowledge and belief (corresponding respectively to identities, relationships and representations). That is, any text makes its own small contribution to shaping these aspects of society and culture. In particular cases, one of the three might appear to be more important than the others, but it is a sensible working assumption that all three are always going on to some degree. Language use is, moreover, constitutive both in conventional ways which help to reproduce and maintain existing social identities, relations and systems of knowledge and belief, and in creative ways which help to transform them. Whether the conventional or the creative predominates in any given case will depend upon social circumstances and how the language is functioning within them.

The relationship between any particular instance of language use – any particular text – and available discourse types may be a complex and (in the terms of the last paragraph) creative one. It is always possible to find relatively straightforward instances of particular discourse types – a conventional and typical political interview on the radio, for instance. But many texts are not so simple. They may involve complicated mixtures of different discourse types – a political interview which is in part rather like a friendly conversation and in part like a political speech, for example. Given my concern with changing discursive practices in the media, such complex texts are of particular interest.

The critical discourse analysis approach thinks of the discursive practices of a community – its normal ways of using language – in terms of networks which I shall call 'orders of discourse'. The order of discourse of a social institution or social domain is constituted by all the discursive types which are used there. The point of the concept of 'order of discourse' is to highlight the relationships between different types in such a set (e.g. in the case of a school, the discursive types of the classroom and of the playground): whether, for instance, a rigid boundary is maintained between them, or whether they can easily be mixed together in particular texts. The same question applies to relationships between different orders of discourse (e.g. those of the school and the home): do they commonly overlap and get mixed together in language use, or are they rigidly demarcated? Social and cultural changes very often manifest themselves discursively through a redrawing of boundaries within and between orders of discourse, and I shall be showing that this is true of the media. These boundaries are also sometimes a focus of social struggle and conflict. Indeed, orders of discourse can be seen as one domain of potential cultural hegemony, with dominant groups struggling to assert and maintain particular structuring within and between them.

It is useful to distinguish two main categories of discourse type, which are constituents of orders of discourse: genres, and discourses. A discourse is the language used in representing a given social practice from a particular point of view. Discourses appertain broadly to knowledge and knowledge construction. For instance, the social practice of politics is differently signified in liberal, socialist and Marxist political discourses; or again, illness and health are differently represented in conventional ('allopathic') and homoeopathic medical discourses. A genre, by contrast, is a use of language associated with and constituting part of some particular social practice, such as interviewing people (interview genre) or advertising commodities (advertising genre). Genres can be described in terms of their organizational properties – an interview, for instance, is structured in quite different way from an advertisement. See Kress and Threadgold (1988) and van Leeuwen (1993).

The analysis of any particular type of discourse, including media discourse, involves an alternation between twin, complementary focuses, both of which are essential:

- communicative events
- the order of discourse.

On the one hand, the analyst is concerned with the particular, with specific communicative events, for instance a particular newspaper editorial or television documentary. The concern here is always with both continuity and change – in what ways is this communicative event normative, drawing upon familiar types and formats, and in what ways is it creative, using old resources in new ways? On the other hand, the analyst is concerned with the general, the overall structure of the order of discourse, and the way it is evolving in the context of social and cultural changes. The focus here is upon the configuration of genres and discourses which constitute the order of discourse, the shifting relationships between them, and between this order of discourse and other socially adjacent ones. These are not, let me stress, alternatives, but complementary perspectives on the same data which we can shift between during analysis. My presentation of a framework for critical analysis of media discourse will discuss the two perspectives in turn.

ANALYSIS OF COMMUNICATIVE EVENTS

Critical discourse analysis of a communicative event is the analysis of relationships between three dimensions or facets of that event, which I call *text*, *discourse practice*, and *sociocultural practice*. 'Texts' may be written or oral, and oral texts may be just spoken (radio) or spoken and visual (television). By 'discourse practice' I mean the processes of text production and text consumption. And by 'sociocultural practice' I mean the social and cultural goings-on which the communicative event is a part of. The analytical framework is summarized in Figure 1.

[P]ractices of media text production and consumption [are] aspects of *discourse practice*. [A]spects of *sociocultural practice* [include] mass communication as a particular type of situation, the economics of the media, the politics of the media, and the wider cultural context of communication in the mass media. These two features are addressed further below.

Texts

The analysis of texts covers traditional forms of linguistic analysis – analysis of vocabulary and semantics, the grammar of sentences and smaller units, and the sound system ('phonology') and writing system. But it also includes analysis of textual organization above the sentence, including the ways in which sentences are connected together ('cohesion'), and things like the organization of turn-taking in interviews or the overall structure of a newspaper article. I shall refer to all this as 'linguistic analysis', though this is using the term in an extended sense.

Analysis of texts is concerned with both their meanings and their forms. Although it may be useful analytically to contrast these two aspects of texts, it is in reality difficult to separate them. Meanings are necessarily realized in forms, and differences in meaning entail differences in form. Conversely, it is a sensible working assumption that where forms are different, there will be some difference in meaning.

I work with a multifunctional view of text. This sees any text, and indeed even the individual clauses and sentences of a text, as simultaneously having three main categories of function, each of which has its own systems of choices: *ideational, interpersonal*, and *textual*. This view of text harmonizes with the constitutive view of discourse outlined above, providing a way of investigating the simultaneous constitution of systems of knowledge and belief (ideational function) and social relations and social identities (interpersonal function) in texts. Or with *representations, relations* and *identities*. So, for instance, in analysing a sentence in a written text, the analyst might focus upon how three aspects are articulated:

- particular representations and recontextualizations of social practice (ideational function) – perhaps carrying particular ideologies
- particular constructions of writer and reader identities (for example, in terms of what is highlighted – whether status and role aspects of identity, or individual and personality aspects of identity)
- a particular construction of the relationship between writer and reader (as, for instance, formal or informal, close or distant).

The analysis is sensitive to absences as well as presences in texts – to representations, categories of participant, constructions of participant identity or participant relations which are not found in a text.

Analysis of text needs to be multisemiotic analysis in the case of the press and television, including analysis of photographic images, layout and the overall visual organization of pages, and analysis of film and of sound effects. A key issue is how these other semiotic modalities interact with language in producing meanings, and how such interactions define different aesthetics for different media.

Discourse practice

The discourse practice dimension of the communicative event involves various aspects of the processes of text production and text consumption. Some of these have a more institutional character, whereas others are discourse processes in a narrower sense. [W]ith respect to institutional processes, [these can include] institutional routines such as editorial procedures involved in producing media texts, and how, for instance, watching television fits into the routines of the household. I shall call [the two aspects] 'institutional processes' and 'discourse processes'. (One could also include here more psychological and cognitivist concerns with how people arrive at interpretations for particular utterances – 'interpretative processes'. [V]an Dijk works with a more cognitively oriented framework which is otherwise rather similar in conception to mine.)

The analytical framework of critical discourse analysis is summarized in Figure 1.

The visual representation of the relationships between the three dimensions of communicative events in the diagram is significant: I see discourse practice

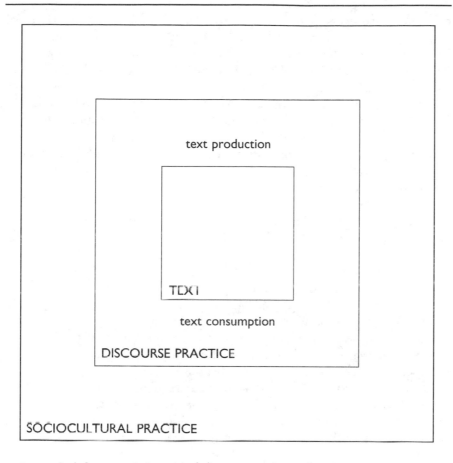

Figure 1: A framework for critical discourse analysis of a communicative event

as mediating between the textual and the social: and cultural, between text and sociocultural practice, in the sense that the link between the sociocultural and the textual is an indirect one, made by way of discourse practice: properties of sociocultural practice shape texts, but by way of shaping the nature of the discourse practice, i.e. the ways in which texts are produced and consumed, which is realized in features of texts. Notice also that, as we have just seen with the distinction between 'institutional processes' and 'discourse processes', discourse practice straddles the division between society and culture on the one hand, and discourse, language and text on the other.

In referring to 'the nature of the discourse practice', I have in mind particularly the polarity alluded to earlier between broadly conventional and broadly creative discourse processes, involving either a normative use of discourse types (genres and discourses) or a creative mixture of them. This is where the two perspectives within critical discourse analysis – on the communicative event, and on the order of discourse – intersect. The question here is how the communicative event draws upon the order of discourse (normatively or creatively), and what effect it has upon the order of discourse – whether it helps reproduce its boundaries and relationships, or helps restructure them. Creative discourse practice can be expected to be relatively complex, in terms of the number of genres and discourses mixed together and the way they are mixed together. But complex discourse practice may also become conventionalized – for instance, there are now in documentary quite conventional combinations of genres of informing, persuading, and entertaining.

In very general terms, a conventional discourse practice is realized in a text which is relatively homogeneous in its forms and meanings, whereas a creative discourse practice is realized in a text which is relatively heterogeneous in its forms and meanings. Of course, it is the particular nature of the creativity of the discourse practice and of the heterogeneity of the text that is of interest in a specific analysis – and their relationship to the sociocultural practice that frames them. Also in general terms, one would expect a complex and creative discourse practice where the sociocultural practice is fluid, unstable and shifting, and a conventional discourse practice where the sociocultural practice is relatively fixed and stable. [M]edia texts are sensitive barometers of cultural change which manifest in their heterogeneity and contradictoriness the often tentative, unfinished and messy nature of change. Textual heterogeneity can be seen as a materialization of social and cultural contradictions and as important evidence for investigating these contradictions and their evolution.

The focus on discursive creativity, hybridity, and heterogeneity in my analysis of media discourse corresponds to the nature of the times. We are living through a period of rapid and continuous change in society and culture, the media play a significant role in reflecting and stimulating more general processes of change, and the practices of the media are correspondingly in constant flux. This includes the discursive practices of the media. The general point to emphasize is that creativity in discursive practices is tied to particular social conditions – conditions of change and instability. The term 'creativity' can be misleading in its individualistic connotations: discursive creativity is an effect of social conditions, not an achievement of individuals who have particular (creative) qualities.

I want to contrast the linguistic analysis of texts (in the extended sense I explained above) with the *intertextual* analysis of texts (see Bakhtin, 1986; Fairclough, 1992; Kristeva, 1986). Intertextual analysis focuses on the borderline between text and discourse practice in the analytical framework. Intertextual analysis is looking at text from the perspective of discourse practice, looking at the traces of the discourse practice in the text. Intertextual analysis aims to unravel the various genres and discourses – often, in creative discourse practice, a highly complex mixture – which are articulated together in the text. The question one is asking is, what genres and discourses were drawn upon in producing the text, and what traces of them are there in the text? To use a familiar example, the traces in a documentary text of a mixture of genres of information, persuasion and entertainment. Intertextual complexity in the mixing of genres and discourses is realized linguistically in the heterogeneity of meaning and form.

Linguistic analysis is descriptive in nature, whereas intertextual analysis is more interpretative. Linguistic features of texts provide evidence which can be used in intertextual analysis, and intertextual analysis is a particular sort of interpretation of that evidence – an interpretation which locates the text in relation to social repertoires of discourse practices, i.e. orders of discourse. It is a cultural interpretation in that it locates the particular text within that facet of the culture that is constituted by (networks of) orders of discourse. The linguistic analysis is, in an obvious sense, closer to what is 'there' on paper or on the audio- or video-tape, whereas the intertextual analysis is at one remove in abstraction from it. Consequently, in intertextual analysis the analyst is more dependent upon social and cultural understanding. This can seem problematic to those who expect more 'objective' forms of analysis, though it is easy to overstate the objectivity of linguistic analysis. Nevertheless, linking the linguistic analysis of texts to an intertextual analysis is crucial to bridging the gap between text and language on the one hand, and society and culture on the other.

Sociocultural practice

Analysis of the sociocultural practice dimension of a communicative event may be at different levels of abstraction from the particular event: it may involve its more immediate situational context, the wider context of institutional practices the event is embedded within, or the yet wider frame of the society and the culture. All of these layers may be relevant to understanding the particular event – and indeed particular events cumulatively constitute and reconstitute social and cultural practice at all levels. Many aspects of sociocultural practice may enter into critical discourse analysis but it may be useful to broadly differentiate three: economic, political (concerned with issues of power and ideology), and cultural (concerned with questions of value and identity).

[...]

ANALYSIS OF THE ORDER OF DISCOURSE

I come now to the second of the twin perspectives within a critical discourse analysis of the media, the order of discourse – how it is structured in terms of configurations of genres and discourses, and shifts within the order of discourse and in its relationship to other socially adjacent orders of discourse.

[T]he media [are positioned] between public orders of discourse and private orders of discourse, and [they] transform their source public discourse for consumption in domestic settings. This mediating position, and the *external* relations between the order of discourse of the media and socially adjacent public and private orders of discourse such as those of books and magazines, is the key to understanding the media order of discourse and the *internal* relations between its constituent genres and discourses. The order of discourse of the media has been shaped by the tension between its contradictory public sources and private targets, which act as contrary poles of attraction for media discourse; it is constantly being reshaped through redefining its relationship to – redrawing its boundaries with – these public and private orders of discourse. Moreover, the negotiation and renegotiation of the relationship between public and private discursive practices which takes place within the order of discourse of the media has a general influence on the relationship between these practices, and between the public and the private in an overall sense, in other domains of social life. Research on media orders of discourse is thus of more than parochial interest, because it impinges upon major changes in society and culture. Similar remarks apply, for instance, to the (re)negotiation within broadcast media discourse of the relationship between the more traditional order of discourse of public service broadcasting and the commercial order of discourse of the market and consumerism.

The general point here is that the relationship between institutions and discursive practices is not a neat or simple relationship. Different institutions come to share common discursive practices, and a particular discursive practice may have a complex distribution across many institutions. For instance, advertising may be rooted in the orders of discourse of commodity production, distribution and consumption, but it has come to be an element in the orders of discourse of diverse institutions – education, medicine, the arts, and so forth. It follows that discourse analysis should always attend to relationships, interactions and complicities between social institutions/domains and their orders of discourse, and be sensitive to similarities in social organization and discursive practices between different institutions. Although the media may be a particularly clear case of such fluid relationships between institutions, this property is widely shared.

It should also be emphasized that media discourse may shape socially adjacent orders of discourse as well as being shaped by them. For instance, television formats have considerable cultural salience, and one finds them as models in a variety of public domains. An example would be the way in which the celebrity-interview format is now quite widely used in higher education for introductory books on the thinking of prominent figures, as well as in magazines (such as the left-wing political magazine *Red Pepper*).

[...]

Media discourse also influences private domain discourse practices, providing models of conversational interaction in private life which are originally simulations of the latter but which can come to reshape it. A complex dialectic seems to exist between the media and the conversational discourse of everyday life.

External relations between orders of discourse, and internal relations between discourses and genres within the media order of discourse, may be difficult to disentangle, but the distinction between these two concerns in analysis of orders of discourse is a useful one. Both external and internal relations include *choice* relations, and *chain* relations. What I have said so far appertains to choice relations. ('Choice' does not here imply free choice on the part of participants – selection among alternatives is generally socially conditioned.) Externally, the issue is how the order of discourse of the media chooses within, and appropriates, the potential available in adjacent orders of discourse. Internally, the issue is to describe the paradigms of alternative discursive practices available within the order of discourse of the media, and the conditions governing selection amongst them. Discursive practices are functionally differentiated, providing contrasting formats for the main types of output in the media. Thus there are different discursive practices for news, documentary, drama, quiz and 'soap' programmes on television, and there are different discursive practices for hard news, soft news, comment and feature articles in newspapers. (As these two examples show, the classification of functionally different discursive practices may be at various levels of generality.) But there are also alternatives for any given type of output whose selection is governed by different conditions, which I come to shortly.

[A] communicative event in the mass media can be regarded as in fact a chain of communicative events. Such chains are partly internal – the process of text production within a media institution is a chain of communicative events – and partly external – the source communicative events at one end of the chain lie outside the media, as do the communicative events (conversations, debates, reports) which media texts may themselves be sources for. A description of the media order of discourse is concerned to specify what communicative events, internal and external, are chained together in this way; and the sorts of transformations that texts undergo in moving along such chains, and how earlier texts in the chain are embedded in later ones. Choice relations and chain relations intersect in an account of the order of discourse: one needs to specify the choice relations that apply at each link in the chain.

The distinction between choice and chain relations suggests a refinement of the intertextual analysis of texts discussed in the section on discourse practice above. Part of the intertextual analysis of a text is concerned with unravelling mixtures of genres and discourses which are in a choice relationship in the order of discourse. But the intertextual analysis of a text is also concerned with embedding – with how the transformations which texts undergo in shifting along chains leave traces in embedding relations within texts.

In trying to arrive at a characterization of the media order of discourse, the analyst constantly has in mind two important questions, which may receive different answers for different parts of this complex order of discourse: (a) how unitary, or how variable, are media discursive practices? and (b) how stable, or how changeable are they?

The questions are linked: typical of a settled and conservative society are unitary and stable discursive practices, typical of an unsettled society are variable and changeable discursive practices. There are also more local institutional pressures towards unitary practice – standardized formats reduce production costs, and conform to audience expectations. In describing the order of discourse, one is trying to capture the particular balance that exists between what Bakhtin called 'centripetal' (unitary and stable) and 'centrifugal' (variable and changeable) pressures, and in which direction that balance is tending (Bakhtin, 1981). The variability question links back to my mention above of alternatives for a particular type of output, such as television documentary. Where there is variability, selection between alternatives may, for instance, involve political and ideological differences and struggles, attempts to cater for different 'niche' audiences, as well as differences of professional or artistic judgement. Variability is also an issue in text consumption: what orders of discourse do audiences draw upon to appropriate media texts? Do they, for instance, talk or write about them in the genres and discourses of private life, or in those of public (e.g. academic) domains they are familiar with? And what social factors are relevant to that choice?

Changing media discursive practices can be conceptualized in terms of shifting external or internal, chain or choice relations. An account of the media order of discourse should particularly highlight major points of tension affecting internal or external boundaries, [such as]: the public/private boundary and the privately oriented communicative ethos of broadcasting, with extending use of a conversational, public-colloquial discourse style; the boundary between public service and information on one side and the market on the other, with the construction of audiences as consumers and the colonization of even the news media by entertainment; and, related to this, the boundary between fiction and non-fiction, with non-fictional programmes such as documentary often drawing upon fictional, dramatic, formats.

I want to use the term *discourse type* for relatively stabilized configurations of genres and discourses within the order of discourse. One issue here is that genres occur in particular combinations with discourses – particular genres are predictably articulated with particular discourses. For instance, party political broadcast is a genre which predictably draws upon economic discourse, discourse of law and order and educational discourse, but not, for instance, on the discourses of science, cookery, or craft (e.g. knitting). But discourse types also standardly involve configurations of genres rather than a single genre. So, for instance, a party political broadcast may combine political oratory, interview, and simulated fireside conversation. Or again, 'chat' has emerged as an important studio-based discourse type in television, involving an articulation of elements of conversation with elements of entertainment. A major concern here is capturing the distinctive discourse types which have emerged in the order of the discourse of the media, such as chat, or what passes for discussion on television, and properties which cut across types, such as the 'communicative ethos' identified by Scannell (1992). Another concern is a historical focus on the stabilization and destabilization of the configurations which constitute discourse types.

One might see the mass media as an interrelated set of orders of discourse, in that the orders of discourse of television, radio, and the press are distinct in important ways which relate to differences of technology and medium while also having significant similarities. There are also sufficient differences between different outlets to distinguish at a more detailed level separate orders of discourse for different newspapers, radio stations, or television channels.

The media order of discourse can, I think, usefully be examined as a domain of cultural power and hegemony. The media have in the past often been described as if they were dominated by stable unitary practices imposed from above. This is certainly not an adequate characterization of the contemporary media, though it may have some truth for certain aspects of media practice, and was markedly less inadequate thirty years ago than it is now. It implies a code model of the media order of discourse: that it is made up of a number of well-defined, unitary and stable codes which dictate practice.

It does not, however, follow that because the code model is inadequate, questions of power and domination do not arise. One common picture of contemporary media stresses cultural diversity – a view of the media as highly pluralistic in practices, with no single web of power running through the whole system. This would perhaps compromise entirely the notion of a media order of discourse, or at least lead to a very different model of it as a *mosaic* of practices. Another possible approach, however, is to ask how the relative diversity and pluralism of the media might itself operate within a system of domination. Gramsci's concept of *hegemony* (Forgacs, 1988; Gramsci, 1971) is helpful here as a theory of power and domination which emphasizes power through achieving consent rather than through coercion, and the importance of cultural aspects of domination which depend upon a particular articulation of a plurality of practices. The issue with respect to a hegemony model becomes one of whether and how diverse discursive practices are articulated together within the order of discourse in ways which *overall* sustain relations of domination. See Fairclough (1992) for a discussion of code, mosaic and hegemony models.

[...]

A SAMPLE CRITICAL DISCOURSE ANALYSIS

I conclude this chapter with a sample analysis to make the critical discourse analysis framework a little more concrete. My example is a report which appeared in 1985 in the British newspaper, the *Sun*, about a government document on hard-drug abuse. It is reproduced in Figure 2.

My objective is to give readers a quick overview of how the framework applies in a particular case, so I shall be very selective in my comments (for instance, not referring to consumption at all), and certainly will not attempt a full analysis (the example is more fully analysed in Fairclough 1988).

I shall shift slightly from the order in which I presented the framework, first analysing this as a communicative event in terms of *discourse practice* and *text*, but deferring discussion of *sociocultural practice* until after I comment on what the example indicates about the media order of discourse.

The communicative event

The *discourse practice* here involves transformations of source texts – most obviously the Committee report, but also presumably a press conference or interview alluded to in the penultimate paragraph – into an article. The text is likely to have gone through a number of versions, as it was transformed across a chain of linked communicative events. For a reconstruction of such a trans-formational history in detail, see Bell (1991). The discourse practice is complex, in the sense that it articulates together features of the source discourse (the report) and features of the target discourse, the discourse of consumption, the informal, colloquial language of private life.

This is shown in an *intertextual analysis* of the text, an analysis which looks at the text from the perspective of discourse practice, aiming to unravel the genres and discourses which are articulated together in it. I shall focus on dis-courses, in particular how official discourses of drug trafficking and law enforcement are articulated with colloquial discourses of drug trafficking and law enforcement, within a genre of hard news (described below). Compare the article with a short extract from the source report:

> The Government should consider the use of the Royal Navy and the Royal Air Force for radar, airborne or ship surveillance duties. We recommend, therefore, that there should be intensified law enforcement against drug traffickers by H. M. Customs, the police, the security services and possibly the armed forces.

In part, the *Sun* article draws upon the official discourses which are illustrated in this extract. This is most obvious where the report and the Committee chairman are directly quoted, but it is also evident elsewhere.

What is striking about the text is that these contrasting official and colloquial discourses are both used within what is traditionally called 'reported speech' – or more precisely, the reporting of the source written document. Although the direct quotation is marked as coming directly from the report, the borderline between what the report actually said and the *Sun*'s transformation of it into colloquial discourse is not always clear. For instance, the main headline is in the form of a direct quotation, though it is not in quotation marks. The newspaper itself seems to be taking on the prerogative of the Committee to call for action, though its call is translated into a colloquial discourse, becomes a demand rather than a recommendation, and loses the nuances and caution of the original (*the Government should consider the use of* becomes *call up!*).

To show some of this in detail, I now move to *linguistic analysis* of the text, though in this case I shall focus upon certain relatively superficial linguistic

1 **Britain faces a war to stop pedlars, warn MPs**

CALL UP FORCES
2
IN DRUG BATTLE!

By DAVID KEMP

3 **THE armed forces should be called to fight off a massive invasion by drug pushers, MPs demanded yesterday.**

4 Cocaine pedlars are the greatest threat ever faced by Britain in peacetime–and could destroy the country's way of life, they said.

5 The MPs want Ministers to consider ordering the Navy and the RAF to track suspected drug-running ships approaching our coasts.

6 On shore there should be intensified law enforcement by Customs, police and security services.

Profits

7 The all-party Home Affairs Committee visited America and were deeply shocked by what they saw.

8 In one of the hardest-hitting reports for years, the committee–chaired by Tory lawyer MP Sir Edward Gardner–warned gravely:

❝ Western Society is faced by a warlike threat from the hard-drugs industry.

The traffickers amass princely incomes from the exploitation of human weakness, boredom and misery.

They must be made to lose everything –their homes, their money and all they posess which can be attributed to their profits from selling drugs. ❞

9 Sir Edward said yesterday: "We believe that trafficking in drugs is tantamount to murder and punishment ought to reflect this."

The Government is expected to bring in clampdown laws in the autumn.

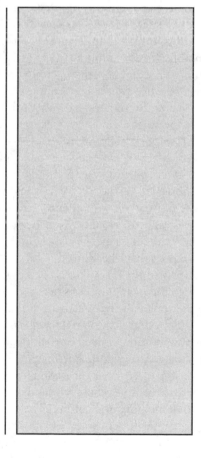

Figure 2: Extract from the *Sun*, 24 May 1985

features of vocabulary and metaphor. In accordance with the complex dis-course practice and intertextual relations, this is a relatively heterogeneous text linguistically. For instance, in the directly quoted sections the article uses the same term (*traffickers*) as the report to refer to those dealing in drugs, whereas elsewhere it uses colloquial terms not found at all in the report – *pushers* and *pedlars*. But even in the parts of the article where the report is summarized rather than quoted, official discourse is sometimes used – for instance *armed forces*, *law enforcement*, and *security services*. Compare *forces* in the headline with *armed forces* in the first (lead) paragraph; the former is an expression from colloquial discourse, whereas the latter belongs to official discourse.

Why does the article use such pairs of terms? Perhaps because it is translating official discourse into colloquial discourse and thereby giving a populist force to official voices, but at the same time preserving the legitimacy of official discourse. The position and point of view of the newspaper is contradictory, and that contradiction is registered here in the heterogeneity of the language. Hall *et al.* (1978: 61) refer to a trend in media towards 'the translation of official viewpoints into a public idiom' which not only 'makes the former more "available" to the uninitiated' but also 'invests them with popular force and resonance, naturalizing them within the horizon of understanding of the various publics'. Notice that use of colloquial vocabulary in the *Sun* article has both ideational and interpersonal functions: it draws upon a particular representa-tion of the social reality in question, but at the same time the newspaper, by using it, implicitly claims co-membership, with the audience, of the world of ordinary life and experience from which it is drawn, and a relationship of solidarity between newspaper and audience. (These implicit claims are modu-lated, however, by the use of the vocabulary of official discourse as well.) Thus this vocabulary is simultaneously functional with respect to representations, identities, and relations. It is also worth noting how a visual semiotic works together with language: it is colloquial and not official discourse that dominates the visually salient headlines.

Notice also the metaphor of dealing with drug traffickers as fighting a war. Although the metaphor does occur at one point in the report, it is elaborated in the *Sun* article in ways which are wholly absent from the report – the mobiliza-tion (again using a colloquial term, *call up*) of armed forces in the headline, and the representation of drug trafficking as an invasion in the lead paragraph. The metaphor is also significant in terms of the newspaper's implicit claim to a relationship of solidarity and common identity with the audience. It draws upon war as an evocative theme of popular memory and popular culture, claiming to share that memory and culture. The metaphor also links this text *intertextually* to popular media coverage of the drugs issue over a long period, where the representation of the issue as a war against traffickers is a standard feature of the discourse. It is an ideologically potent metaphor, construing drugs in a way which helps to marginalize other constructions from the perspective of opposi-tional groups – drugs as a symptom of massive alienation associated with the effects of capitalist reconstruction, unemployment, inadequate housing, and so forth.

The order of discourse

Turning to the second of the twin perspectives within critical discourse analysis, what does this example indicate about the order of discourse? The discourse type is a 'hard-news' story from the popular press. As a hard-news story, it is different in genre from other types of article which are in a choice relation within the order of discourse – soft-news stories, comments and features. It has the typical generic structure of a hard-news story: a 'nucleus' consisting of a headline (in fact both a major and a minor one) and a lead paragraph which gives the gist of the story; a series of 'satellite' paragraphs which elaborate the story in various directions; and a final 'wrap-up' paragraph which gives a sense of resolution to the story (Media Literacy Report, 1993). In this discourse type within the order of discourse of the *Sun* (and other similar tabloid newspapers, though not the broadsheet newspapers), this genre is standardly articulated with the combination of official and colloquial discourses I have discussed above. So the discourse type here is a relatively stabilized, and recognizable, one.

An obvious external aspect of *choice* relations is the 'public-colloquial' nature of the style – indicative of a redrawing of boundaries between (external) public and private orders of discourse within the media order of discourse to produce this hybrid style. One feature of *chain* relations which is striking in this case is the way in which the source text is transformed into, and embedded in, the article. I have already commented in this regard on the ambivalence of voice, an ambivalence at times about whether the article is giving the words of the report or the newspaper's (radically transformed) reformulation of them. I suspect this ambivalence is common in this discourse type. It is linked in this case, and more generally, to a mixing of genre – the combination of the informative hard-news genre with elements of persuasive genre. Notice in particular that the main headline is an imperative sentence which, as I have already indicated, functions as a demand. In addition to reporting, the *Sun* article is characteristically also campaigning for particular policies and actions. Another feature of chain relations is the way the article is intertextually linked into another chain which consists of previous coverage of the drugs issue in the popular media. This sort of chaining is a quite general feature of media texts.

Let me finally comment, briefly and partially, on the sociocultural practice which has framed the stabilization of this sort of discourse type. The newspaper is mediating source events in the public domain to a readership in a private (domestic) domain under intensely competitive economic conditions. The maximization of circulation is a constant preoccupation, in a wider economic context in which the accent is upon consumption and consumers and leisure, and a wider cultural context of detraditionalization and informalization which are problematizing traditional authority relations and profoundly changing traditional constructions and conceptions of self-identity. These features of sociocultural context have shaped, and are constituted in, the complex discourse practice that I have described, and the shift towards that discourse practice which has taken place over a period of time. The discourse practice mediates between this unstable sociocultural practice and heterogeneous texts.

Turning to the politics of this type of article, one important likely effect of the translation of official sources and official positions into colloquial discourse is to help legitimize these official sources and positions with the audience, which in this case means within sections of the British working class. (Notice, though, that one would need to investigate consumption, how people read such articles, to see what the effects actually are in detail.) In the terms I used earlier, this would seem to be a powerful strategy for sustaining the hegemony of dominant social forces, based upon a hybridization of practices which gives some legitimacy to both official and colloquial discourses (though the preservation of the former alongside the latter perhaps covertly signals their continuing greater legitimacy, while using the latter as a channel for official 'messages'). At the same time, the newspaper, as I have pointed out, not only takes on a persuasive role in campaigning for (its version of) the report's recommendations, but also, through the war metaphor, helps to sustain and reproduce dominant ideological representations of the drugs issue.

I have suggested that this example is representative of a relatively stable discourse type, but the restructuring within media discourse of boundaries between public and private orders of discourse, and the emergence of various forms of public-colloquial discourse, are striking features of the modern media which invite historical analysis. What we have here is a creative articulation of public and private orders of discourse which has become conventionalized. But the picture is rather more complex, in the sense that in the context of constant renegotiation of the public/private boundary, the heterogeneity of texts such as this might under certain circumstances be perceived as contradictions, and the relatively stable discourse type might come to be destabilized.

References

Austin, J. L. (1962) *How to do things with words*, Oxford University Press

Bakhtin, M. (1981) *The dialogical imagination*, trans. Emerson, C. and Holquist, M., University of Texas Press

Bakhtin, M. (1986) *Speech genres and other late essays*, ed. Emerson, C. and Holquist, M., University of Texas Press

Bell, A. (1991) *The language of news media*, Blackwell

Bourdieu, P. (1977) *Outline of a theory of practice*, trans. Nice, R., Cambridge University Press

Fairclough, N. (1988) 'Discourse representation in media discourse', *Sociolinguistics*, 17: 125–39

Fairclough, N. (1989) *Language and power*, Longman

Fairclough, N. (1992) *Discourse and social change*, Polity Press

Fairclough, N. (1993) 'Critical discourse analysis and the marketisation of public discourse: the universities', *Discourse and Society*, 4(2): 133–68

Forgacs, D. (1988) *A Gramsci reader*, Lawrence & Wishart

Foucault, M. (1992) *The archaeology of knowledge*, trans. Sheridan-Smith, A. M., Penguin Books

Fraser, N. (1989) *Unruly practice: power, discourse and gender in contemporary social theory*, Polity Press

Gramsci, A. (1971) *Selections from the prison notebooks*, trans. Hoare, Q. and Nowell-Smith, G., Lawrence & Wishart

Hall, S., *et al.* (1978) *Policing the crisis: mugging, the state, and law and order*, Methuen

Kress, G. and Threadgold, T. (1988) 'Towards a social theory of genre', *Southern Review*, 21: 215–43

Kristeva, J. (1986) 'Word, dialogue and novel', in Moi, T. (ed.), *The Kristeva reader*, Basil Blackwell

Levinson, S. (1983) *Pragmatics*, Cambridge University Press

Media Literacy Report (1993) (draft) WIR Industry Research, Sydney

Scannell, P. (1992) 'Public service broadcasting and modern public life', in Scannell, P., *et al.* (eds) *Culture and power*, Sage

Stubbs, M. (1983) *Discourse analysis*, Basil Blackwell

van Dijk, T. (ed.) (1985) *Handbook of discourse analysis*, 4 vols, Academic Press

van Dijk, T. (1988a) *News as discourse*, Erlbaum

van Dijk, T. (1988b) *News analysis*, Erlbaum

van Dijk, T. (1991) *Racism and the press*, Routledge

van Leeuwen, T. (1993) 'Genre and field in critical discourse analysis', *Discourse and Society*, 4(2): 193–223

FURTHER READING

Allen, R. C. (ed.), *Channels of Discourse* (Chapel Hill: University of North Carolina Press, 1987).

Allen, R. C. (ed.), *Channels of Discourse, Reassembled* (London: Routledge, 1992).

Alvarado, M. and Stewart, J. (eds), *Made for Television: Euston Films Limited* (London: BFI, 1985).

Alvarado, M. and Thompson, J. O. (eds), *The Media Reader* (London: BFI, 1990).

Barthes, R., *Mythologies* (London: Paladin, 1973).

Bennett, T., Boyd-Bowman, S., Mercer, C. and Woollacott, J. (eds), *Popular Television and Film* (London: BFI, 1981).

Bennett, T., Martin, G., Mercer, C. and Woollacott, J. (eds), *Culture, Ideology and Social Process* (London: Batsford Academic and Educational Ltd., 1981).

Bennett, T., Mercer, C. and Woollacott, J. (eds), *Popular Culture and Social Relations* (Milton Keynes: Open University Press, 1986).

Bennett, T. and Woollacott, J., *Bond and Beyond: The Political Career of a Popular Hero* (London: Macmillan Education, 1987).

Boys from the Blackstuff, British Film Institute Dossier 20 (1984).

Brandt, G. W. (ed.), *British Television Drama* (Cambridge: Cambridge University Press, 1981).

Brunsdon, C. and Morley, D., *Everyday Television: 'Nationwide'* (London: BFI, 1978).

Caughie, J. (ed.), *Television, Ideology and Exchange* (London: BFI, 1978).

Caughie, J., 'Rhetoric, Pleasure, and "Art Television" – *Dreams of Leaving*', *Screen* 22: (1981) pp. 9–31.

Corner, J. (ed.), *Documentary and the Mass Media* (London: Edward Arnold, 1986).

Corner, J. (ed.), *Popular Television in Britain* (London: BFI, 1991).

Curran, J., Ecclestone, J., Oakley, G. and Richardson, A. (eds), *Bending Reality: The State of the Media* (London: Pluto Press, 1986).

Curran, J., Smith, A. and Wingate, P. (eds), *Impacts and Influences: Essays on Media Power in the Twentieth Century* (London: Methuen, 1987).

Davis, H. and Walton, P. (eds), *Language, Image, Media* (Oxford: Blackwell, 1983).

Drama-Documentary, British Film Institute Dossier 19 (1984).

Elliott, P., Murdock, G. and Schlesinger, P., '"Terrorism" and the State: A Case Study of the Discourses of Television', *Media, Culture and Society* 5:2 (1983) MTM: pp. 155–77.

Feuer, J., 'Narrative Form in Television', in C. MacCabe (ed.), *High Theory/Low Culture: Analysing Popular Television and Film* (Manchester: Manchester University Press, 1986).

Feuer, J., Kerr, P. and Vahimagi, T., '*Quality Television*' (London: BFI, 1984).

Fiske, J., *Television Culture* (London: Methuen, 1987).

Fiske, J. and Hartley, J., *Reading Television* (London: Methuen, 1978).

Gilbert, W. S., 'The TV Play: Outside the Consensus' *Screen Education* 35 (1980) pp. 35–44.

Gitlin, T., *Inside Prime Time* (New York: Panthcon, 1985).

Goodwin, A. and Whannel, G. (eds), *Understanding Television* (London: Routledge, 1990).

Hall, S., Hobson, D., Lowe, A. and Willis, P. (eds), *Culture, Media, Language* (London: Hutchinson, 1980).

Hartley, J., *Tele-Ology: Studies in Televison* (London: Routledge, 1992).

Heath, S. and Skirrow, G., 'Television: A World in Action', *Screen* 18:2 (1977) pp. 7 59.

Kaplan, E. A. (ed.), *Regarding Television: Critical Approaches – An Anthology* (Frederick, Md.: University Publications of America, 1983).

McArthur, C., *Television and History* (London: BFI, 1978).

MacCabe, C. (ed.), *High Theory Low Culture: Analysing Popular Film and Television* (Manchester: Manchester University Press, 1986).

McGrath, J., 'TV Drama: The Case Against Naturalism', *Sight and Sound* 46:2 (1977) pp. 100–5.

Masterman, L. (ed.), *Television Mythologies: Stars, Shows and Signs* (London: Comedia, 1984).

Mellencamp, P. (ed.), *Logics of Television* (Bloomington and London: Indiana University Press and BFI, 1990).

Millington, B. and Nelson, R., '*Boys from the Blackstuff*: The Making of TV Drama (London: Comedia, 1986).

Modleski, T. (ed.), *Studies in Entertainment: Critical Approaches to Mass Culture* (Bloomington: Indiana University Press, 1986).

Morse, M., 'Talk, Talk, Talk – the Space of Discourse in Television', *Screen* 26:2 (1985) pp. 2–15.

Murdock, G., 'Authorship and Organization', *Screen Education* 35 (1980) pp. 19–34.

Neale, S., *Genre* (London: BFI, 1980).

Neale, S. and Krutnik, F., *Popular Film and Television Comedy* (London: Routledge, 1990).

Nichols, B., *Representing Reality: Issues and Concepts in Documentary* (Bloomington: Indiana University Press, 1991).

Silverstone, R., 'Narrative Strategies in Television Science – A Case Study', *Media, Culture and Society* 6:4 (1984) pp. 377–410.

Skovmand, M. and Schroder, K. C. (eds), *Media Cultures: Reappraising Transnational Media* (London: Routledge, 1992).

Strinati, D. and Wagg, S. (eds), *Come on Down? Popular Media Culture* (London: Routledge, 1992).

Television Sitcom, British Film Institute Dossier 17 (1982).

Tulloch, J., *Television Drama: Agency, Audience, and Myth* (London: Routledge, 1990).

Tulloch, J. and Alvarado, M., '*Doctor Who*': *The Unfolding Text* (London: Macmillan, 1983).

White, M., 'Television Genres: Intertextuality', *Journal of Film and Video* 37: (1985) pp. 41–47.

Williams, R., 'A Lecture on Realism', *Screen* (Spring 1977).

Williams, R., *Raymond Williams on Television*, ed. A. O'Connor (London: Routledge, 1989).

SECTION 3
TEXT

3. FEMINIST READINGS

FEMINIST READINGS
INTRODUCTION

Feminist readings of media texts have, as Annette Kuhn (Chapter 6) indicates, both an academic and a political focus. Whatever their differences, they share an insistence on gender as a structuring principle of both our material existence and the symbolic forms through which it is represented.[1] As a result, they have also shared an uneasy, and often marginalised, position within Media Studies. John Corner[2] has described what he sees as the 'two projects' evident within media analysis: one, the '*public knowledge* project', focusing on the media as agents of public information and power, and the other, the '*popular culture* project', focusing on entertainment texts, pleasure and subjectivity. It is not difficult to recognise this as both a gendered and a hierarchical division.[3] Thus feminist media critics, in concerning themselves with 'women's genres'[4] and the construction of femininity – in insisting on *taking seriously* popular media forms for women – have extended and radically challenged the definitions within Media Studies of what constitutes the 'political'.[5] But they have also tended to reproduce the public/private, knowledge/pleasure, masculine/feminine split which is the object of their analysis. Feminist readings of television texts have drawn on the insights gained from feminist film theory and criticism, where work on the visual construction of women as spectacle and the gendering of visual pleasure has been developed in relation both to mainstream Hollywood film and to melodrama, or 'the woman's film'. But such work has placed them outside, or at odds with, Corner's '*public knowledge* project'.

Much feminist research, then, has focused on what Charlotte Brunsdon calls 'mass cultural fictions of femininity',[6] popular forms for women such as soap opera, mass produced romantic fiction and girls' and women's magazines, and on the (often contradictory) pleasures and ideological positionings which they offer. This research has in its turn raised issues around the theorising of pleasure, the relationship of gender to genre, to narrative modes and patterns of address, and the relationship of the 'ideal' spectator addressed by the text to the real social subject who responds to that address. More recent work, however, has shown a number of shifts. First, as popular media forms have themselves given evidence of an increased engagement with feminist concerns, feminist analysis has broadened its focus to include hitherto 'masculine' genres like the detective series. Second, there has been a growing challenge to the assumption by white feminist critics that they could speak about an inclusive category of 'the feminine', and ignore the ways in which gender, 'race' and ethnicity interact in the construction of both social power and individual subjectivity. Finally, the influence of postmodern theory, in which popular media forms such as television and the pop video are seen as marked by the collapse of boundaries – including those of gender – and the producion of a viewing subjectivity characterised by fragmentation and distraction, has shifted feminist critics away from the influence of film theory, with its emphasis on a gendered division into the male 'gaze' and female 'to-be-looked-at-ness'.[7] Further evidence of this last shift can be found throughout this volume, but particularly in Sections 3.4 and 4.3 and the Case Studies.

The first extract in this section (Chapter 26) is taken from Janice Winship's *Inside Women's Magazines* (1987). Winship begins by addressing the public/private split described above. 'As TV soap opera is to news and current affairs,' she writes, 'so women's magazines are the soaps of journalism', disparaged within both critical and popular discourse. The 'Woman's World' which they claim to offer us is both an affirmation of women's interests and identity, and an indication of women's marginality: 'Men do not have or need magazines for "A Man's World"; it *is* their world, out there, beyond the shelves'. This ambiguity characterises the magazines: the 'gaze between cover model and women readers' marks the extent to which women see themselves 'in the image which a masculine culture has defined'; at the same time the model is 'centre stage and powerful', affirming the importance of 'women's territory'. The magazines, then, offer us 'survival skills' to deal with the real dilemmas of femininity, and 'daydreams' that these strategies might actually work.

Danae Clark's '*Cagney & Lacey*: Feminist Strategies of Detection' (Chapter 27), which follows, addresses the separation between public and private worlds in a different way. The 1980s series *Cagney & Lacey* is a hybrid text, mixing the police drama series, whose episodes end in narrative closure, with an 'open and fragmented' central narrative, which centres on the lives of the two major characters. It is a text, argues Clark, which both addresses women and 'challenges the boundaries of patriarchal discourse'. First, it centres on women's active control over *decision-making*, in situations where this process is facilitated through female bonding: female viewers are thus invited to consider their own demands and how they might articulate them, within a context of female support. Second, as a detective series, *Cagney & Lacey* assigns to its female characters the traditionally male role of investigation and judgement. In this investigation public and private are merged: it is the institution of the family which is frequently the object of investigation, and the personal may become political in the form of a 'social issue'. Third, the series challenges male control of the 'gaze' in a number of ways. In giving its female characters 'possession of the look', it privileges the woman's point of view without reducing its male characters to 'fetishised objects of female desire and power'. In establishing relations of looking *between* women it also permits women to 'interact as *subjects*', in relationship with each other. Its privileging of women's *voices,* too, in the characters' frequent 'rest room' conversations, undercuts the power of the gaze to determine meaning. Finally, in the disguises adopted by its detectives, *Cagney & Lacey* comments on the issue of female representation, sometimes critically and sometimes playfully. Whilst the series' overt politics might belong to liberal feminism, therefore, its textual strategies are far more radical.

The final chapter of this section (Chapter 28) takes us into the 1990s and the fragmented, 'atomistic' address of the daytime talk show. In her analysis of the *Oprah Winfrey Show*, Corinne Squire addresses its claims to empower women. Taking issue with claims that such a dispersed, often incoherent form can only support ideological consensus, she argues that in fact its mixture of 'fluff and gravity' and its emotional and empirical excess are better able to register the complex connections between subjectivity, gender and 'race' than is much feminist theory. *Oprah*, she argues, is a 'polysemous, difficult but readable text', infused with a feminism rooted in black women's histories and writing. Its declared commitment to empowering women may be manifest through a multiplicity of representations of women in which differing conceptions of feminism are apparent, but it is consistent in assuming a commonality between women which must ground any feminist project. The fragmentation and excess which make the show so difficult to read, she argues, also serve a valuable function, unsettling common assumptions about gender, 'race' and class. *Oprah* offers no explanatory closure, but in its 'super-realism' is able to speak the 'unspeakable' in ways which mark it as oppositionally feminist. The diversity and interrelationship of its representations of gender, 'race', class, sexuality and subjectivity in turn offer new ways of understanding *to* feminism.

NOTES

1. Liesbet van Zoonen, *Feminist Media Studies* (London: Sage, 1994) p. 3.
2. Corner, 'Meaning, Genre and Context: The Problematics of 'Public Knowledge' in the New Audience Studies', in J. Curran and M. Gurevitch (eds), *Mass Media and Society* (London: Edward Arnold, 1991) p. 268.
3. van Zoonen, p. 9.
4. See Annette Kuhn, 'Women's Genres', *Screen*, 25:1 (1984) pp. 18–28.

5. See Charlotte Brunsdon, Julie D'Acci, and Lynn Spigel, 'Introduction', in C. Brunsdon, J. D'Acci, and L. Spigel (eds), *Feminist Television Criticism: A Reader* (Oxford: Oxford University Press, 1997) p. 5.
6. Brunsdon, 'Pedagogies of the feminine: feminist teaching and women's genres', *Screen* 32:4 (1991) p. 365.
7. Laura Mulvey, 'Visual Pleasure and Narrative Cinema', *Screen* 16:3 (1975) pp. 6–18.

26

SURVIVAL SKILLS AND DAYDREAMS

Janice Winship

[...]

'... A Story about Men; and Women'

Women's magazines, perhaps especially *Woman* and *Woman's Own*, have become as well known nationally in Britain as any of the daily or Sunday newspapers. Yet though a million of *Woman*'s 5 to 6 million readers and around one-third of *Cosmopolitan*'s, for example, are men, magazines are very specifically associated with femininity and *women's* culture. Indeed, it is impossible to think about femininity and women without considering, among other things, motherhood and family life, beauty and fashion, love and romance, cooking and knitting – and therefore romantic novels, cookery books and women's magazines. It is difficult to envisage a masculine culture without contemplating work and careers, brawls in the boxing ring or on the 'real' battlefields of war, train spotting and messing around with cars, the pub and pulling girls – and therefore newspapers, hobby journals and 'girlie' magazines. No matter that not all women are mothers or read women's magazines, and that many men loathe boxing and have rarely glanced at a 'girlie' magazine; no matter either that feminism has chipped away at the stereotypes of femininity and masculinity, those versions of two genders are still profoundly influential in our experiences of growing up. Our lives as women and men continue to be culturally defined in markedly different ways, and both what we read and how it is presented to us reflects, and is part of, that difference.

From J. Winship, *Inside Women's Magazines* (London: Pandora Press, 1987) pp. 5–14.

The cultural image of father-reading-newspaper-at-breakfast, mother-busy-on-the-domestic-front may have been starkly present in my family thirty years ago. But it has not yet disappeared, either literally or symbolically.

The same cultural gap can be seen at any local newsstand. There on the rack marked 'Woman's World' are the women's magazines which women are glancing through and buying. A short distance away is another stand marked 'Leisure' or 'Hobbies'. There are all the 'girlie' magazines, the photography, computing and do-it-yourself magazines (crochet, cooking and sewing magazines are, of course, with the women's magazines), and *their* voyeurs and purchasers are almost exclusively men. All this we take for granted as we amble or scurry through the shop for our own purchase. Yet those labels and that separation between a 'woman's world' and 'leisure' or 'hobbies' reveal much about our gendered culture. Men do not have or need magazines for 'A Man's World'; it *is* their world, out there, beyond the shelves: the culture of the workplace, of politics and public life, the world of business, property and technology, there they are all 'boys' together. Women have no culture and world out there other than the one which is controlled and mediated by men. The 'girls' are drawn in to support the masculine quest: 'boys will be boys' whatever the game being played.

Women tend to be isolated from one another, gathering together briefly and in small huddles, stealing their pleasures in the interstices of masculine culture so graciously allowed them: family gatherings, rushed coffee mornings or the children's events, and the occasional night out with the 'girls'. The tasks they immerse themselves in, the priorities they believe in, constantly take second place to the concerns of men. In men's presence women are continually silenced, or they are ridiculed, scolded or humiliatingly ignored. Thus the 'woman's world' which women's magazines represent is created precisely because it does not exist outside their pages. In their isolation on the margins of the men's world, in their uneasiness about their feminine accomplishments, women need support – desperately. As Jane Reed, long-time editor of *Woman's Own* and then editor-in-chief of *Woman*, put it, 'a magazine is like a club. Its first function is to provide readers with a comfortable sense of community and pride in their identity' (Hughes-Hallett, 1982: 21).

Yet such is the power of masculine wisdom that women's magazines and their millions of readers are perennially belittled – by many women no less than by most men. As TV soap opera is to news and current affairs, so women's magazines are the soaps of journalism, sadly maligned and grossly misunderstood. Over the years critics have disparagingly opined that women's magazines are 'a journalism for squaws ... you find yourself in a cosy twilit world' (1965); it is a world of 'the happy ever after trail' (1976); 'cooking and sewing – the woman's world' (1977); 'kitchen think' (1982). They lament that women's magazines do not present a true and real picture of women's lives: 'Why ... does the image deny the world?' (1965). Worse, magazines are 'completely schizophrenic' (1958); 'experience and make-believe merge in a manner conductive to the reader's utter bewilderment' (1971).

But if the focus of women's magazines *is* predominantly home and hearth, if the world they present *is* a happy-ever-after one, if they *do* refuse the reality of most women's lives, if they *do* offer a schizophrenic mix – and none of these characteristics is quite accurate – then there are pertinent cultural reasons why this is so. I want [...] to delve beneath this simple and dismissive description in order both to explain the appeal of the magazine formula and to critically consider its limitations and potential for change.

HIDDEN COVER LINES: TALKING TO 'YOU'

If the profile of women's magazines is partly determined by the state of play between women and men, it is also (as indeed is the 'game' between women and men) shaped by a consumer culture geared to selling and making a profit from commodities, and whose sales are boosted (it's firmly believed) through the medium of advertising. As commodities, women's magazines sell their weekly or monthly wares not only by advertising proper but also by the 'advertisement' of their own covers.

On any magazine stand each women's magazine attempts to differentiate itself from others also vying for attention. Each does so by a variety of means: the title and its print type, size and texture of paper, design and lay-out of image and sell-lines (the term the magazine trade aptly uses for the cover captions), and the style of model image – but without paying much attention to *how* a regular reader will quickly be able to pick out her favourite from others nestling competitively by it. Cover images and sell lines, however, also reveal a wealth of knowledge about the cultural place of women's magazines. The woman's face which is their hallmark is usually white, usually young, usually smoothly attractive and immaculately groomed, and usually smiling or seductive. The various magazines inflect the image to convey their respective styles – domestic or girl-about-town, cheeky or staid, upmarket or downmarket – by subtle changes of hairstyle, neckline and facial pose. They waver from it occasionally rather than regularly with royals and male celebrities, mothers-and-babies and couples. Only magazines on the fringes of women's magazines, like *Ideal Home* (concentratedly home-oriented and with a high male readership) never use the female model. It is no profundity to say that as the sign of 'woman' this cover image affirms and sells those qualities of white skin, youth, beauty, charm and sexuality as valuable attributes of femininity. In marked contrast *Spare Rib* covers break sharply with the stereotyped plasticity of the model face, and communicate immediately how far that magazine distances itself from such an evaluation of femininity.

There is one other important and defining characteristic of this cover image: the woman's gaze. It intimately holds the attention of 'you', the reader and viewer. Such an image and gaze also has a wide currency in ads directed at women and men, has a daily venue on page 3 of the *Sun* and *Star*, and appears on the cover of 'girlie' magazines like *Mayfair* and *Fiesta*. The woman's image in these latter is obviously caught up in a provocatively sexual significance. Her partially revealed body speaks the sexuality about which the facial expression often equivocates. Her gaze holds that of the male voyeur; but it is he who has the controlling look: to look or not to bother, to choose to be sexually aroused or to turn over the page. She is the object and toy for his sexual play. It would be pushing it to suggest that the covers of women's magazines work in quite this way. For one thing many completely play down the 'come-on' look, for another the covers are primarily addressed to women. Nevertheless, what I would argue is that the gaze between cover model and women readers marks the complicity between women that we see ourselves in the image which a masculine culture has defined. It indicates symbolically, too, the extent to which we relate to each other as women through absent men: it is 'the man' who, in a manner of speaking, occupies the space between model image and woman reader.

In fact few women readers will make an immediate identification with these cover images: they are too polished and perfect, so *un*like us. Paradoxically, though, we do respond to them. Selling us an image to aspire to, they persuade us that we, like the model, can succeed. For the image is a carefully constructed one, albeit that it sometimes apes a 'natural look'. The model is only the cipher, the (often) anonymous face for others' skills and a range of commodities to fill. As *Company* puts it: 'Cover photograph of Joanne Russell by Tony McGee. Vest dress by Sheridan Barnett; necklace by Pellini. Hair by Harry Cole at Trevor Sorbie. Make-up by Philippe at Sessions' (April 1983). Easy then, 'you' too can create the look – given the ready cash. *Company* continues, 'Our cover girl look can be achieved by using Charles of the Ritz signature Collection for spring. complexion, Amboise Ritz Mat Hydro Protective Make-up; cheeks, Cinnamon Glow Revenescence Cheekglow; eyes, Country Plums Perfect Finish Powder, Eyecolour Trio, Black, Ritz Eye Pencil, Black Perfect Lash Mascara; lips, Pink Carnation Perfect Finish Lip Colour; nails, Champagne Rose Superior Nail Lacquer.' Phew! Etched though the final image is here by the combined talents of men and the myriad make-up offerings of consumer culture, it also offers 'you' hope – of sorts: she is 'successful'; why not 'you'? It is a seductive appeal.

There is, however, a counterthread to this image which perhaps provides the stonger attraction for women. Woman is placed first here; she is centre stage and powerful. The gaze is not simply a *sexual* look between woman and man, it is the steady, self-contained, calm look of unruffled temper. She is the woman who can manage her emotions and her life. She is the woman whom 'you' as reader can trust as friend; she looks as one woman to another speaking about what women share: the intimate knowledge of being a woman. Thus the focus on the face and the eyes – aspects which most obviously characterise the person, the woman – suggests that inside the magazine is a world of personal life, of emotions and relationships, clearly involving men and heterosexuality, but a world largely shunned by men. This is all women's territory.

More than that, the careful construction of the model's appearance not only points to the purchase of certain commodities but also covertly acknowledges the *creative work* involved in producing it, a work executed in everyday life not by the 'experts' but by women themselves.

The cover image shouts that this woman's world of personal life and feminine expressivity is one worth bothering about, engendering a feel for the reader that such pursuits are successful, and moreover bring happiness: the model smiles. Idealistic as all this is (some would say oppressive), it is less a denial of the 'real world' than an affirmation of how much women and feminine concerns are neglected in that 'real world'.

With the model's gaze on 'you', the magazine invites 'you' into its world. It may address you directly: 'Self-esteem: a little more will take you a long way' declares *Company*; or (You) 'Win a speed boat worth £4000' urges *Options*, the magazine 'For your way of living'. Like the language of advertising, these sell-lines for that issue's inside delights ambiguously address 'you' as an individual. There is the suggestion that the relationship being struck up is the intimate one between the magazine and 'you' – just one reader. The same is implied in the title *My Weekly*. This address to the individual [. . .] heightens the sense of, on the one hand, the magazine speaking to the 'lonely woman', and, on the other, the strength of the support the magazine provides for its readers.

What 'you' are also offered on the cover is a careful balance between practical items linked to daily life and those which draw you, dreamily, into another world. Regarded by some critics as 'conducive to the readers' utter bewilderment', this mixture of entertainment and advice has been consciously promoted by editors since the inception of women's magazines. For example, *The Lady's Magazine* of 1770 aimed to combine 'amusement with instruction'; *The Englishwoman's Domestic Magazine*, published in 1852 by Samuel Beeton (husband of that doyenne of cookery Mrs Isabella Beeton) and one of the forerunners of modern middle-class home magazines, combined 'practical utility, instruction and amusement'. More contemporarily, in 1976 Beatrix Miller, then editor of *Vogue*, remarked, 'We are 60% selling a dream and 40% offering practical advice.' And in the launch issue of *Options* in April 1982 its editor Penny Radford hopefully declared, 'We want *Options* to be a lot of information, a lot of help and a lot of fun. So enjoy it.'

Why should women's magazines offer this mix? Men's magazines seem to settle for one or the other: 'entertainment' ('girlie' magazines) or 'information' (all the hobby journals). But then men's lives tend to be more clearly compartmentalised and – often thanks to women's hidden labour – men are singular about their activities: they are at work *or* at leisure; they are watching TV *or* engaged in their hobby. Many of the activities women carry out – often several at once – cut across categories: at work they can find themselves 'being mother', entertaining visitors or giving the feminine (sensitive) ear to others' work problems; lunch breaks are devoted to the 'work' or 'pleasure' of shopping; running a home can be both 'work' and a 'hobby' – cooking and sewing are tasks which can eat up leisure time, while ironing can be done in front of the TV.

After my father had glanced through the newspaper at breakfast he would go out to work and my brother and I would rush off to school, but my mother would stay put. Working mainly in the house, she often had to take 'time off' there too. When we all came home she had to cater to our needs, switching hats according to our various moods, and moving from one thing to another as we each in turn wanted this – a clean collar (my father rushing out to a meeting) – or that – a hem of a dress pinned up (me) – even as she was baking, tidying up or doing her own sewing.

At odd moments in this many-faceted and disrupted routine she would snatch the time to escape into her *Woman's Weekly*. At other times *Woman's Weekly* would deliver 'the recipe' or the answer to a stubborn stain. Women's magazines provide for these rhythms and routines of women's lives in which private time and space are precious, work and leisure merge, activities overlap, and dreams and escape often feed on a modest vocabulary of everyday possibilities: modest partly because the horizons of women's lives are still limited and partly because women's desires are constantly forestalled. The predominantly masculine world neither welcomes women nor women's ways of doing things. Notwithstanding its (often empty) tributes to mothers and wives and page 3 pin-ups, it will do its damnedest to exclude them from certain domains, frighten them on the streets, hassle them in the pub, or stamp on their hopes and ambitions.

No wonder that women need the 'refuge' of women's magazines.

For their part most women tolerate these harassments because, whatever the costs of being a woman, there are also compensations. The balance sheet of feminine qualities far outweighs that of masculinity. Women do not want to be the kind of people men are and it is difficult to envisage *other* ways of being women (and men). Women's magazines provide a combination of (sometimes wholly inadequate) survival skills to cope with the dilemmas of femininity, and daydreams which offer glimpses that these survival strategies *do* work. They are dreams of a better and different life, but one that remains well within a spectrum of familiar possibilities.

The survival skills offered by feminist magazines like *Spare Rib* and *Everywoman* may be more political, aimed at getting women off the 'desert island' of femininity and encouraging their daydreams of a radical future. Yet the formula is similar. They offer help and, above all, hope. They present a catalogue, both sad and heartening, of women's ability to survive in a world where the odds are stacked against them.

[...]

REFERENCES

Adams, Carol and Laurikietis, Rae (1980), *The Gender Trap 3: Messages and Images*, Virago, London.

Adamson, Lesley (1977), 'Cooking and sewing – the woman's world', *Guardian*, 3 November.

Berger, John (1972), *Ways of Seeing*, Penguin, Harmondsworth.

Braithwaite, Brian and Barrel, Joan (1979), *The Business of Women's Magazines*, Associated Business Press, London.

Connell, Myra (1981), 'Reading Romance', MA thesis, University of Birmingham.

Coward, Rosalind (1983), *Female Desire*, Paladin, London.

Curran, Charles (1965), 'Journalism for squaws', *Spectator*, 19 November.

Ferguson, Marjorie (1978), 'Imagery and ideology: the cover photographs of traditional women's magazines', in Gay Tuchman, Arlene Kaplan Daniels and James Benet (eds), *Hearth and Home*, Oxford University Press, New York.

Ferguson, Marjorie (1983), 'Learning to be a woman's woman', *New Society*, 21 April.

Greer, Germaine (1972), *The Female Eunuch*, Paladin, London.

Hall, Stuart, Hobson, Dorothy, Lowe, Andy and Willis, Paul (eds) (1980), *Culture, Media, Language*, Hutchinson, London.

Hughes-Hallett, Lucy (1982) 'The cosy secret of a jolly good Reed', *The Standard*, 8 February.

King, Josephine and Stott, Mary (1977), *Is This Your Life?*, Virago, London.

Lefebvre, Henri (1971), *Everyday Life in the Modern World*, Allen Lane, London.

McRobbie, Angela (1977), '*Jackie*', stencilled paper, Centre for Contemporary Cultural Studies, University of Birmingham.

McRobbie, Angela and McCabe, Trisha (1982) *Feminism is Fun: An Adventure Story for Girls*, Routledge & Kegan Paul, London.

Reed, Jane (1982), 'The story so far', *Guardian*, 20 October.

Root, Jane (1983), *Pictures of Women: Sexuality*, Pandora, London.

Sharpe, Sue (1976), *Just Like a Girl*, Penguin, Harmondsworth.

Tolson, Andrew (1977), *The Limits of Masculinity*, Tavistock, London.

Toynbee, Polly (1977), 'At the end of the happy ever after trail', *Guardian*, 21 June.

White, Cynthia (1977), *Royal Commission on the Press, the Women's Periodical Press in Britain 1946–76*, Working Paper 4, HMSO, London.

27

CAGNEY & LACEY:
FEMINIST STRATEGIES OF DETECTION

Danae Clark

The connection between *Cagney & Lacey* and feminism can be traced back to 1974 when Barbara Corday, one of the show's creators, made her husband, producer Barney Rosenzweig, read Molly Haskell's feminist attack on the film industry, *From Reverence to Rape: The Treatment of Women in the Movies.* According to Corday, Rosenzweig became 'enlightened' when he encountered Haskell's point that women had never been portrayed as buddies in film or television, and thereafter he was committed to producing a female buddy movie.[1] Unfortunately, executives in the entertainment industry had still not attained enlightenment. Corday developed a movie script of *Cagney & Lacey* along with Barbara Avedon in 1974, but it was not until 1981 that CBS finally produced it as a TV-movie and (based on its high ratings) subsequently developed *Cagney & Lacey* into a weekly series.

While *Cagney & Lacey* may have been inspired by feminist film criticism, its continued existence has been attributed to its predominantly female viewing audience. When the show was cancelled during its first season, executive producer Rosenzweig managed to keep it on the air. But when *Cagney & Lacey* was cancelled again after its second season (1982–3), thousands of letters sent in by viewers convinced CBS that *Cagney & Lacey* had a dedicated and sizeable audience. According to Rosenzweig, 'a lot of women, especially younger women, had been identifying almost fiercely with the show'.[2] They were not the traditional starstruck fans, he added. 'They were affluent, well-educated

From M. E. Brown (ed.), *Television and Women's Culture* (London: Sage, 1990) pp. 117–33.

people ... working women [and] college students'.[3] Overwhelmingly, women responded to *Cagney & Lacey*'s 'complex, real women characters' and 'honestly portrayed women's friendships'.[4] This held true even among women who tended not to care for 'the usual cop shows'.

Cagney & Lacey has certainly challenged the stereotypes found in earlier police dramas such as *Police Woman*, in which a highly sexualised Angie Dickinson was put into dangerous, suggestive situations only to be rescued by her male partners. But the importance of *Cagney & Lacey* to feminism lies beyond its presentation of a new or 'better' image of women. As a text that specifically addresses women and women's issues, *Cagney & Lacey* potentially challenges the boundaries of patriarchal discourse at the same time as it allows viewers to actively enter into the process of its meaning construction. Thus, as I hope to demonstrate in this essay, the 'fierce identification' experienced by the show's female viewers may derive from their participation in and empowerment by the show's discursive strategies. In particular, I will argue that *Cagney & Lacey* empowers women and encourages women-identified constructions of meaning through a combination of its narrative form, its representational codes, and its structures of looking.

NARRATIVE STRATEGIES/FEMINIST STRATEGIES

Barney Rosenzweig summarises *Cagney & Lacey*'s narrative construction when he says '[t]his is not a show about two cops who happen to be women; it's about two women who happen to be cops'.[5] While *Cagney & Lacey* is categorised as a police drama, this aspect assumes only minor significance. The major aspect, or real drama of the show, revolves around the personal lives of Christine Cagney (Sharon Gless) and Mary Beth Lacey (Tyne Daly) both inside and outside the 14th Precinct. Although these two aspects are interwoven in any given episode, they differ significantly in their narrative structure. As in other police dramas, the protagonists of *Cagney & Lacey* are presented with a case to solve, the criminal is apprehended or outwitted, and a sense of order is restored at the end when the case is either solved or dismissed. But the drama of Cagney and Lacey's lives continues beyond a single episode. Unlike the linear, cause and effect progression of the police subplot, the main plot is open and fragmented. We don't know from any cause and effect structure what Chris will decide about marriage or how Mary Beth will cope with having breast cancer. More importantly, we eventually learn about their decisions and feelings through dialogue, not action. Because of this, the narrative structure of *Cagney & Lacey*'s major plotline seems more characteristic of the soap opera than the classical realist text.

According to Tania Modleski, one of the chief differences between these types of texts is that the soap opera appears to be participatory in a way that the realist text almost never is. In soap operas, 'action is less important than *rea*ction and *inter*action', and this is one reason, she says, that fans insist on the soap opera's 'realism':

Despite the numerous murders, kidnappings, blackmail attempts, emergency operations, amnesia attacks, etc., ... [one] knows that these events are not important in themselves; they merely serve as occasions for characters to get together and have prolonged, involved, intensely emotional discussions with each other.[6]

Cagney & Lacey differs from soap operas in relegating the more outrageous events to the police drama subplot, while the more 'realistic' events of the two women's lives provide the occasions for intense, ongoing discussion. Yet, like the soap opera, Cagney & Lacey contains a combined narrative structure that permits closure on a subsidiary level while remaining open on another level.

[...]

Another major difference between the soap-like structure of Cagney & Lacey and soap operas themselves, is the way that viewers are invited to participate in the problem-solving process of characters' lives. According to Modleski, soap operas provide the spectator with training in 'reading' other people, in being sensitive to their needs and desires. She equates this skill in reading with the function of the woman in the home who must be attuned to the effects of the world upon her family.

[...]

In relation to Cagney & Lacey, however, a viewer's active reading is potentially influenced by two important factors: the experience of female bonding that is strengthened and explored through Cagney and Lacey's interaction, and the emphasis that their interaction places on decision-making – a skill not generally associated with traditionally feminine competencies.

Various strategies are used in emphasising the decision-making process in Cagney & Lacey. In some cases, viewers are not presented with the outcome or immediate effects of the characters' decisions. For example, [...] when Mary Beth learns that she has breast cancer, textual emphasis is placed on her deliberation over the options available to her rather than the treatment she decides to receive. In a soap opera, her medical treatment would have become the object of spectacle as well as an occasion for other characters to engage in prolonged, involved discussion. The absence of this occasion in Cagney & Lacey, however, serves to emphasise women's active control over the decision-making process.

From time to time, other female characters are brought into the decision-making process. In the two-part episode on sexual harassment, for example, Chris decides to press charges against a superior officer who threatens to withhold a job promotion if she refuses to comply with his sexual demands. To ensure his conviction, she seeks the testimony of a woman who has been also harassed by him. But because the woman had succumbed to his threats, she is afraid that her co-operation will result in the loss of her job and the promotion she had been promised. Although Chris' statements about the need for women to speak out against sexual harassment in the workplace are met with resistance, the woman finally comes forward. But the episode concludes *before* she delivers her testimony. The outcome of her decision (winning or losing the case) thus becomes less important than the decision-making process itself. In this way textual emphasis is placed on the difficulties and risks that such decisions pose for women within patriarchy. Or, more significantly, emphasis is placed on the need to reach effective and empowering decisions on such matters.

[...]

In other situations, the follow-up action becomes an integral part of the decision-making process. When Chris finally admits to having an alcohol problem, for example, her realisation is not in itself constituted as a solution. The process also includes her decision to attend Alcoholics Anonymous and announce publicly: 'My name is Christine, and I am an alcoholic'.

When the decision process is represented in terms of reaction and interaction, rather than action, *Cagney & Lacey* invites the participation of the spectator to complete the process of meaning construction in ways that are meaningful to her. Cagney, Lacey, and the show's other characters, provide a 'concert of voices' that interchangeably listen to and provide feminist as well as non-feminist options to problems that affect women and women's autonomy (e.g., rape, sexual harassment, pregnancy, and breast cancer).[7] While not all women have had the same experience of these situations, the knowledge and experience they do have *as women* allow them to identify with discussions of what options are available, what decisions might put them in control, and what discursive strategies are appropriate for arriving at these decisions. When the characters' subsequent actions are represented, viewers may additionally identify with the desire and courage to follow through on such decisions.

Above all, viewers are encouraged to identify with the role that female bonding plays in decision-making. Although the relationship between Chris and Mary Beth has been strained and challenged over the six years of the show's existence, the two women depend upon each other for support and constantly reaffirm their friendship. The text thus acknowledges women's need to talk to each other (without male intervention) and also suggests to the female viewer that the positive support of women can help her in coping with the problems encountered under patriarchy.

[...]

When decisions involve the issue of female bonding itself, additional strategies come into play. These strategies are less compromising in the sense that divisions among women are not easily tolerated. For example, after Chris is made sergeant, she occasionally pulls rank on Mary Beth and insists on a plan of action that her partner opposes. Mary Beth's confrontation with Chris on this issue often produces heated accusations and threats (including the dissolution of their partnership). But, ultimately, Chris recognises that her attempt to establish a hierarchical relationship is an improper and intolerable option that only serves to weaken their collective power. In other instances, patience and silence are shown to be necessary correlatives to verbal confrontation. When Chris is struggling with alcoholism, Mary Beth aggressively confronts her with the truth of her situation, but thereafter quietly stands vigil at her bedside. When the two women are shown together, clasping hands at the AA meeting, the unspoken and unquestioning support between them makes the issue of female bonding as important as the issue of alcoholism.

The viewer's relation to *Cagney & Lacey* thus contrasts markedly with the viewer-text relation Modleski suggests for the soap opera. Although both texts provide women with multiple points of view, the *Cagney & Lacey* viewer is not addressed as an 'ideal mother' with no demands of her own. On the contrary, *Cagney & Lacey* calls upon women to examine what their demands might be and how they might articulate them. This relation between textual strategies and reading practices most closely resembles the framework and goals of feminist consciousness-raising groups in the sense that women are encouraged to join in the discussion of women's issues and find answers that will empower them. The aspect of female bonding, which privileges trust among women and assumes a crucial, supportive role in the process of women's decision-making, has prompted one critic to suggest that *Cagney & Lacey* offers 'a nascent feminist ideology within the context of mass art'.[8]

CODES OF DETECTION

At the risk of contradicting the points made in the previous section, I would now like to suggest that no discernible separation exists between the police drama subplot of *Cagney & Lacey* and the drama of the main characters' lives, and that the show can also be read in relation to certain textual strategies found in the detective genre.

It is commonly thought, for example, that the detective undertakes two simultaneous investigations – one involving the world of crime, and the other the sphere of sexuality. In the process of detecting the truth, the former precipitates the latter and, ultimately, the question of sexuality assumes primary importance. The typical male hero of such texts is forced to encounter his own sexual anxieties in relation to another (usually female) character. Annette Kuhn explains it thus:

> It is often the woman ... who constitutes the motivator of the narrative, the 'trouble' that sets the plot in motion, [and] the film's resolution depends on [his] resolution of the particular 'woman question'.[9]

Cagney & Lacey works against the generic boundaries of traditional detective fiction by usurping the male's privileged role as representative of the (patriarchal) Law. Yet, significantly, the text continues to centre on the 'woman question'. This focus challenges and often reverses the relations of power that structure traditional (male-defined) detective genres such as *film noir*. Within *film noir*, for example, the woman question is generally resolved by determining the guilt or innocence of women, and guilty women (by virtue of their independence or expression of sexual desire) are killed, punished, or otherwise eradicated from the text. But within *Cagney & Lacey*, women (i.e. Chris and Mary Beth) assume the voice(s) of judgement concerning female sexuality while attempting to resolve the trouble that patriarchal structures create for women. Resolution of the woman question thus becomes a resolution of the issues that affect women's autonomy and expression.

The power and credibility of Cagney and Lacey as heroines derive from the text's refusal to separate the public and private aspects of their lives. In other words, Cagney and Lacey are not defined solely by a private (sexual and familial) identity, but also in relation to a public (professional) role. According to Jane Tompkins, '[The] public-private dichotomy, which is to say the public-private *hierarchy*, is a founding condition of female oppression'.[10] This dichotomy, in other words, results in women's objectification and confinement, privatising their functions within the home while privileging the role of men as decision-makers in the public sphere. The dissolution of this distinction in *Cagney & Lacey* can thus be read as an attempt to represent women in more empowering social relations. As women engaged in a demanding profession, work forms an integral part of Cagney's and Lacey's experiences and provides a context outside the home in which decisions are discussed and acted upon.

[...]

The representation of the institution of the family may, on the other hand, serve as a vehicle for the expression of frustration and non-fulfilment of desire. According to Sylvia Harvey, 'one of the defining characteristics of *film noir* is to be found in its treatment of the family and family relations'.[11] While the presence of the family may appear to legitimate and naturalise the dominant social values embodied in the patriarchal nuclear family, it may also serve to expose the 'intolerable contradictions' and suppression of desires that this institution sustains. If, as I am suggesting, *Cagney & Lacey* can be read according to certain textual strategies found in the detective genre (which finds its most exaggerated interpretation in *film noir*), then the show's representation of 'broken, perverted, peripheral' family relations may actually be founded upon the *absence* of the family.[12]

[...]

The institution of the family also provides a context in which other issues, such as racial and economic differences, can be explored. Differences between Cagney and Lacey, for example, are defined as much by class standing as by marital status. While Cagney claims the working-class background of her father, she more obviously embraces the upper-class interests of her (deceased) mother. Chris regards Mary Beth's 'low culture' tastes with some disdain, and Mary Beth often feels impelled to defend her latch-key childhood and working-class husband against Chris' more economically-privileged existence. While these conflicts are never resolved, neither are they erased. The exploration of class differences within the context of the family rather serves to create greater awareness of the family's social and economic effects on women.

This awareness is heightened through Cagney and Lacey's contacts with other women. Welfare mothers, for example, are not represented simply as women without husbands, but as economically-disadvantaged women who are victimised by a variety of patriarchal, capitalist institutions. During one investigation, Cagney and Lacey encounter a woman who is sleeping with her slum tenement landlord. When Cagney tells her that she does not have to exchange sexual favours for a place to live, the woman replies, 'You mean *you* don't'. This exchange foregrounds the experience of a woman (or class of woman) who is ordinarily absent from televisual representation; at the same time it foregrounds differences between women. Thus, far from being a commentary on family life, such an exchange points to the larger issues of women's oppression and offers a 're-visioning' of women's social relations. Within this context, the traditional family loses its force. *Cagney & Lacey* challenges a unified concept of the family by exposing its internal strife, by exploring the economic and political conflicts that exist *between* families, and by insisting on establishing a connection among women across family lines in spite of – or, rather, because of – their differences. As Teresa de Lauretis notes, textual representations of feminism succeed to the extent that they can generate an understanding of how women are 'constructed and defined in gender across multiple representations of class, race, language and social relations'.[13]

As these examples suggest, the lack of separation between public and private in *Cagney & Lacey* works as a narrative strategy to highlight social issues while reinforcing the idea that the personal is political. The investigative structure can translate personal conflict into public concerns and anchor viewer identification to a specific political stance, especially when the police subplot and the drama of characters' lives are integrally connected in an episode. For example, at a time when Mary Beth is trying to cope with her son's decision to enlist in the military, her police work brings her into contact with a WW II veteran who proudly shows off his war decorations. The man becomes a target for Mary Beth's displaced frustrations (since she feels she cannot interfere with Harv Jr.'s decision). But the fact that this man turns out to be a murderer in civilian life substantiates her outrage towards the stupidity and false pride of war. Harvey, Mary Beth's husband, occupies an important position in relation to this issue. He not only shares his wife's views about the military, but explicitly critiques Reagan's Central American policies. In this particular case, then, the personal and the political coincide to reinforce viewer sympathy with a pacifist stance and to discourage identification with militarism.

Aside from Harvey's supportive role as husband in *Cagney & Lacey*, his character is often used to signify opinions or positions that the show's stars do not articulate. Other minor characters who take up controversial stances are also featured in episodes – especially when the social issue in question is not explicitly feminist. In addition to Harvey's liberal (sometimes bordering on socialist) working-class position, for example, Detective Marcus Petrie repeatedly takes a stand against racism, insisting on the recognition of his racial difference as a way of confronting the racist attitudes of others. [...] The positions assumed by minor characters may be seen by some as a diversion tactic or safe method of keeping a more conservative representation of Cagney and Lacey intact. On the other hand, it could be argued that these additional voices work in concert with the women's own political agendas to suggest a broad based approach to social problems.

The investigative structure of *Cagney & Lacey* can be summarised as a 'struggle between different voices for control over telling the story'.[14] Working in conjunction with its soap opera strategies to provide multiple points of view and identification, *Cagney & Lacey* uses codes of detection to uncover the 'truth' of women's social relations. While the show departs from the traditional detective genre in significant ways, and its investigative structure might work just as well if Cagney and Lacey were members of a different profession (e.g., medicine), the authority invested in these women as representatives of the Law makes its comparison with the detective genre both profitable and unavoidable. According to *Cagney & Lacey's* newly-emerging law governing crime and sexuality, women are presumed innocent, the voices of many different women are examined, and women's struggle to assert control over their own lives is legitimised.

RECLAIMING THE LOOK

One final way in which *Cagney & Lacey* challenges patriarchal discourse and encourages women-identified constructions of meaning is through its economy of vision. In fact, it is this aspect, more than any other, that most clearly distinguishes *Cagney & Lacey* from other texts. Dominant theories of spectatorship maintain that traditional (male-governed) texts are founded on a subject/object dichotomy that places a male subject in control of the 'gaze' and positions the woman as object of his look. Since the woman becomes the passive raw material for the active gaze and visual pleasure of the male, the female viewer's possibilities for identification become extremely limited; she must choose between adopting the voyeuristic (sadistic) position of the male subject or the masochistic position of the female object.[15] But this model of spectatorship does not describe the viewer's relation to *Cagney & Lacey*. As I have pointed out in the previous sections, female viewers are more likely to feel empowered by their identifications with Cagney and Lacey. Thus they experience a pleasure in viewing that cannot be explained in masochistic terms.

Cagney & Lacey provides an alternative viewer-text relation that breaks up traditional structures of looking in several different ways. First of all, the show's female characters are in possession of the look. By virtue of their authority to control the process of detection and narrative action, Cagney and Lacey define the text's point of view and vision of social relations. Thus, they not only act as subjects of narration, but rarely become the objects of a male gaze. It could be argued that it is precisely because Cagney and Lacey are not the fetishised objects of male desire that they are able to assert control [...]. However, this control is not necessarily a control *over* men. Instead of reversing the traditional relations of looking and objectifying men as the fetishised objects of female desire and power, *Cagney & Lacey* attempts to break the pattern of dominance and submission altogether. Even though the text privileges the woman's point of view, reverse discrimination is not seen as the answer to women's empowerment.

Cagney & Lacey actively works to frustrate the traditional relations of voyeurism and fetishism by avoiding scenes which would ordinarily result in an objectification of women. For example, in episodes on spouse abuse and child abuse, viewers are not privy to scenes in which women or female children are physically assaulted, thus discouraging a sadistic and voyeuristic identification with violence against women.

[...]

The relations of looking established between women in *Cagney & Lacey* also challenge traditional economies of vision. Since women are not isolated from each other as objects for male consumption, women have more freedom to initiate and act upon relations with each other. The de-eroticised images of women, in other words, permit women to interact as *subjects*. This sort of re-visioning requires women to look beyond the surface level of a woman's image and to place into question male-defined images of women. Thus, women are perceived by other women not as sexual objects, but as the victimised subjects of patriarchal desire. *Cagney & Lacey* does not foreclose the possibility of erotic identification – a point that lesbian viewers can substantiate – but the female viewer's *objectification* of female characters is discouraged. Since *Cagney & Lacey* looks behind the image to examine women's oppression and encourages identification with the various struggles that women encounter, viewers are less likely to identify these women as fetish objects. In this way, *Cagney & Lacey* offers a vision of female bonding that simultaneously threatens patriarchal definitions of sexual relations and offers female viewers a point of identification that is neither sadistic nor masochistic. This results in more empowering (rather than power-filled) social relations for and among women.

Another way that *Cagney & Lacey* avoids the objectification of women is by shifting the viewer's attention from sight to sound. In other words, greater emphasis is placed on the voice (what women say) than on the image (how women look). As Mary Ann Doane notes, '[the] voice displays what is inaccessible to the image, what exceeds the visible: the "inner life" of the character'.[16] Thus the voice can be seen as 'a potentially viable means whereby the woman can make herself heard'.[17] *Cagney & Lacey* provides 'an isolated haven' for the voice of women within patriarchy, through the creation of woman's space. Within the enclosed space of the police car or the rest room at the 14th Precinct House (spaces which are both public and private), Cagney and Lacey speak to each other without male intervention and are free to explore and affirm the dimensions of female partnership. The importance of this woman's space (and the female bonding that occurs within it) is underscored by the fact that the show includes at least one such scene in every episode.

Other textual strategies in *Cagney & Lacey* rely on the voice (e.g., the reaction and interaction evident in the process of women's decision-making). But when examined in relation to the gaze, strategies involving the voice take on added significance. The voice is sometimes placed in counterpoint to the gaze – a strategy that allows *Cagney & Lacey* to play with the conventions of voyeurism. For instance, when Cagney and Lacey are in the precinct house rest room, the camera often focuses on their reflections as they primp themselves in front of the mirror. But within this woman's space, the role of the image becomes undermined. Either the woman's concern with her image is shown to be a diversionary tactic (a way to avoid discussing the real issues at hand), or the image itself turns out to be a false or incomplete source of information (it is, after all, only a reflection). Viewers are thus discouraged from investing any identification or voyeuristic pleasure in the image. To gain access to the character's inner feelings we must actively look beyond the image and listen to rather than look at the characters.

In other instances, the voice and the image combine in ways that explicitly usurp male privilege. In the episode on spouse abuse, for example, Chris' ACLU boyfriend, David, is the trial lawyer who gets the accused husband convicted. But instead of showing the actual courtroom scene, the site of David's authority and expertise, the event is recounted verbally in the women's rest room. Mary Beth performs for Chris the details of the trial by playing David's role and speaking in his place. In this way, the woman's voice is privileged and Mary Beth, instead of David, receives recognition for all the hard work she put in on the case. Although Mary Beth makes a 'spectacle' of herself during this scene, the woman's space provides a safe environment for her performance while it, once again, allows a woman to speak and to be heard.

Finally, *Cagney & Lacey* tampers with the conventions of voyeurism through the use of masquerade. As Mary Ann Doane notes, '[t]here is always a certain excessiveness, a difficulty associated with women who appropriate the gaze, who insist on looking'.[18] In order to maintain control – over the narrative, the look, and her own body – a woman must destabilise the image and confound the masculine structure of the look. One option is to give (male) viewers more than they bargain for. Thus, instead of refusing the familiar trappings of femininity, a woman might *flaunt* her femininity, play the game of femininity, by using her own body as a disguise. This masquerade allows a woman to distance herself from the image (to refuse complicity with objectification) while she demonstrates and controls the representation of her body.

In *Cagney & Lacey*, the detectives often adopt disguises in the service of their undercover work. While these disguises generally connote a power of action that extends beyond a woman's sexualised form, the occasions of feminine masquerade provide a direct commentary on the issue of female representation. In a 1987 episode, for example, Cagney and Lacey go undercover as hookers to catch a mugger. In their role as women dressed up as women, they display an excess of femininity – mounds of makeup and hair (wigs of unnatural color), revealing dresses, feathers, jewellery – that creates a ridiculous image of the female form. The masquerade allows Cagney and Lacey to expose the sadism of male desire, i.e., 'those "ogling" eyes that turn women into pieces of meat', as Cagney remarks. Moreover, when the detectives change into their street clothes and assume a different identity, they deconstruct this fetishised image of woman and expose male-defined femininity as a mask that can be worn or simply removed. At the end of the episode (after they have successfully closed the case), Cagney and Lacey return to the privacy of the woman's rest room and conduct a ceremonial ritual in which they burn their costumes. Once free of the burden of their feminised images, Cagney remarks, 'We are better cops now, Mary Beth'. 'And smarter', replies her partner.

[...]

Other uses of masquerade are more celebratory than pedagogical. When Cagney and Lacey dress up as fruits for a game show, and when they perform a Rockettes number for a police awards banquet, their disguises invite laughter rather than critical reflection. In circumstances such as these, masquerade provides an occasion for play and the detectives do not comment directly on the conventions of female representation. Nonetheless, their disguises act as a visual statement on the fluid, potentially subversive quality of the female image and women's ability to change and control the parameters of its representation. And this is finally what *Cagney & Lacey* is all about: the empowerment and pleasure that women gain from representing themselves (to themselves). If the makers of *Cagney & Lacey* occasionally celebrate and flaunt this pleasure, many female viewers, including myself, feel that they have earned the right to do so.

Visual playfulness and other disruptions of conventional representation do not automatically mark *Cagney & Lacey* as a radical text however.[19] As Julie D'Acci has noted, the show's representations are often rooted in liberal notions of feminist politics which perceive 'social change and difference for women (as) simply a matter of equal rules, equal jobs and equal representation'.[20] Its liberal politics thus tend to promote individual accomplishment (i.e., representations of women who have 'made it') and pluralism (i.e., many different types of successful women) as a means to correct the social imbalance of a white male dominated culture.[21] Yet, *Cagney & Lacey*'s pluralism of representation should not be confused or equated with the show's discursive strategies of detection. In spite of its apparent liberalism, the text opens up the possibility of a reading practice that goes beyond a mere identification with certain stereotypes or roles and engages its female viewers in a process of locating and (re)articulating women's positioning within social practices. This becomes possible because *Cagney & Lacey* actively works to create viewing positions which empower the text's female viewers as political subjects.

NOTES

1. *American Film*, July–August 1985, pp. 11–12.
2. O'Connor, J. 1984.
3. Farber, S. 1984.
4. Reilly, S. 1985, p. 14.
5. McHenry, S. 1984, p. 23.
6. Modleski, T. 1983, p. 68.
7. White, M. 1987, p. 158.
8. Ibid.
9. Kuhn, A. 1982, p. 34.
10. Tompkins, J. 1987, p. 169. This quotation occurs slightly out of context. Tompkins is referring to the public-private dichotomy within the academy that berates women for combining emotionality (personal response) with rationality (scholarly discourse). This said, I would add that the form this paper takes, and the positive reading of the text that I argue for here, emerges out of my own 'fierce identification' with and sense of empowerment by *Cagney & Lacey*.
11. Harvey, S. 1980, p. 23.
12. Ibid., p. 25.
13. de Lauretis, T. 1985, pp. 167–68.
14. Gledhill, C. 1980, p. 16.
15. Mulvey, L. 1975, p. 17.
16. Doane, M. A. 1980, p. 41.
17. Ibid., p. 49.
18. Doane, M. A. 1982, p. 83.
19. Brower states that *Cagney & Lacey* is 'by no means a radical show', even though its aesthetic and political marginalisation has been equated with 'quality' (i.e. progressive) television programming (p. 28).
20. D'Acci, J. 1987, p. 222.
21. Ibid., p. 205.

REFERENCES

Brower, S. 'TV "Trash" and "Treasure": Marketing *Dallas* and *Cagney & Lacey*', *Wide Angle* 11.1, 1989: pp. 18–31.

D'Acci, J. 'The Case of Cagney and Lacey'. *Boxed In: Women and Television*. Baehr, H., and Dyer, G. (eds). Pandora Press, London. 1987.

de Lauretis, T. 'Aesthetic and Feminist Theory: Rethinking Women's Cinema'. *New German Critique* 34. Winter 1985, pp. 154–75.

Doane, M. A. 'The Voice in the Cinema: The Articulation of Body and Space'. *Yale French Studies* 60, 1980: pp. 33–50.

Doane, M. A. 'Film and the Masquerade: Theorising the Female Spectator'. *Screen* 23, 3–4, 1982, pp. 74–88.

Farber, Stephen. 'A New Chance for *Cagney & Lacey*'. *New York Times* 14 March 1984, Sec. C: 26.

Gledhill, C. '*Klute 1*: A Contemporary Film Noir and Feminist Criticism'. *Women in Film Noir*. Kaplan, E. A. (ed). British Film Institute, London. 1980.

Harvey, S. 'Woman's Place: The Absent Family in Film Noir'. *Women in Film Noir*. Kaplan, E. A. (ed). British Film Institute, London. 1980.

Kuhn, A. *Women's Pictures: Feminism and Cinema*. Routledge & Kegan Paul, London. 1982.

McHenry, S. 'The Rise and Fall – And Rise of TV's *Cagney & Lacey*'. *Ms*, April 1984. pp. 23–6.

Modleski, T. 'The Rhythms of Reception: Daytime Television and Women's Work'. *Regarding Television*. Kaplan, E. A. (ed). American Film Institute, Los Angeles. 1983.

Mulvey, L. 'Visual Pleasure and Narrative Cinema'. *Screen* 16. 3. Autumn 1975. pp. 6–18.

O'Connor, J. *Cagney & Lacey*, Police Series on CBS. *New York Times* 2 July 1984.

Reilly, S. 'The Double Lives of Cagney and Lacey'. *McCall's*. April 1985: pp. 14, 204.

Tompkins, J. 'Me and My Shadow'. *New Literary History* 19. 1. Autumn 1987, pp. 169–78.

White, M. 'Ideological Analysis and Television'. *Channels of Discourse*. Allen, R. C. (ed). University of North Carolina Press, Chapel Hill. 1987.

28

EMPOWERING WOMEN?
THE *OPRAH WINFREY SHOW*

Corinne Squire

The Oprah Winfrey Show, *the most-watched US daytime talk show, aims to empower women. This article examines the show's representations of gender and how images of 'race', sexuality and class cross-cut them. It considers the show's status as television psychology. It explores the show's translation of aspects of black feminism to television, and discusses the social implications of its 'super-real' representations.*

> *Winfrey*: Listen ... obviously I come from a very biased point of view here.
>
> *Female guest*: Because you're a woman.
>
> *Winfrey*: Yes. Well, and because I – what we try to do – we do program these shows to empower women (*Oprah Winfrey Show*, 1989b).

INTRODUCTION

Every weekday in the USA, 20 million people watch the *Oprah Winfrey Show*, making it the most-watched daytime talk programme. Snaring an unassailable 35 percent of the audience, it acts as a lead-in for local stations' lucrative early evening news programmes (McClellan, 1993; Boemer, 1987). The show has become a common source of information and opinions about relationships, psychopathology and gender. It is a cultural icon, signifying at the same time lurid dilemmas, emotional intensity, fame and black women's success. It is even a well-known chronological marker, as in 'I worked so hard I was done in time for *Oprah*', or, 'I did my shopping so quick I was home by *Oprah*'.

From *Feminism and Psychology*, 4/1 (1994) pp. 63–79.

Winfrey, the first African-American woman to host a national talk show[1] is also well known for her television specials on self-esteem and child abuse, for her role as Sophia in the film *The Color Purple*, as an advocate for abused children and as a philanthropist supporting programmes for poor black youth. The tabloids chronicle her fluctuating weight and self-esteem and her long-standing relationship with a businessman, Stedman Graham. She is one of the richest women in the world, with a yearly income of around $40 million, $16 million more than Madonna (Goodman, 1991). In 1989 she was voted the second most-admired woman in the USA – after Nancy Reagan. The Oprah phenomenon is interesting in itself but this essay will restrict itself to considering Oprah, 'day-time queen' (Guider, 1987), in the context of the show.

In this article, I will treat the television programme as a polysemous, difficult but readable text; examine its compliance with and departure from television conventions; investigate its framing by broader 'texts' of social power and history; and see it as suffused with the intensity and fragmentariness of subjectivity.

[. . .]

Like other daytime talk shows, *Oprah* aims to entertain, inform and encourage communication about difficult issues. It is a kind of popular psychology, lacing advice and catharsis with comedy and melodrama. But the show also tries, Winfrey says, to empower women: to be a televisual feminism. Not only the host but many guests and the majority of the studio and watching audiences are women, and most episodes address female-identified topics: relationships, communication, physical appearance. Host, guests and the studio audience also spend a lot of time in animated, messy discussions of injustices that are at the centre of much contemporary feminist campaigning, like job discrimination, male violence and sexual abuse.

While Winfrey often says the show transcends 'race', it features black guests and issues of concern to black people in the USA more than comparable shows and focuses particularly on black women's perspectives. Since the 1980s such perspectives have had a major impact on US feminism as black women activists and writers make their voices heard within the largely US women's movement (see, for instance, Butler, 1990; de Lauretis, 1986; Hill Collins, 1990; hooks, 1981, 1989; Moraga and Anzaldua, 1981; Spelman, 1990; Spivak, 1988). Differences in class and sexuality between women, which are also concerns of contemporary feminism (Lorde, 1984; Rich, 1986) have only a small place on the *Oprah* show however. Edginess characterizes *Oprah's* occasional mentions of lesbian and gay sexuality, and class is rarely explicitly discussed.

I am going to explore the show's diverse and intricate representations of gender, 'race', sexuality, class and subjectivity, and how the nature of television affects these representations. In the process I aim to develop an account of *Oprah's* relationship to feminism. I am adopting a very general definition of feminism here, assuming that it is concerned, first, to understand gender relationships as fully as possible, in their interrelationships with other social differences, with history, with subjectivity and with different representational media like television; and second, that it tries to make gender relations and relationships between women less oppressive (Coward, 1983). Does *Oprah*, much watched by women, and a secular authority on gender issues, speak to these feminist concerns? I shall argue that it does and that its most interesting contributions are first, a feminism generalized from black women's histories and writing, and second, its super-realism – an unsettling combination of emotional and empirical excess that puts common assumptions about gendered subjectivities in doubt.

[...]

REPRESENTATIONS OF GENDER ON *OPRAH*

Sometimes the *Oprah* show seems simply to endorse traditional notions of femaleness. In the woman-dominated world of daytime television, it appears, the predominantly female audience watches the mainly female casts of the early afternoon soap operas endlessly play out relationship dilemmas – and then listens to a female talk-show host, her many female guests and her largely female studio audience discuss how to improve your looks, marriage and parenting. The advertisements in the breaks, like most advertisements and indeed most programming (Bretl and Cantor, 1988; Davis, 1990), show women in traditional roles, worrying about their weight and their children. While the show encourages women to speak frankly about their lives, including their sexualities, the conventional limits apply. In one episode Winfrey assured a woman who had employed a male surrogate sex therapist to teach her to reach orgasm that she could be 'explicit'. 'Well, he started by using his finger inside me, very gently. I felt a contraction ...', the woman said, and was abruptly cut off by a commercial. During the break Winfrey said, 'I didn't mean *that* explicit' (King, 1987: 126). Conventionally, the show uses women to conjure prohibited pleasures; their transgressive, cathartic confessions become the apotheosis of television's voyeurism (Ellis, 1982).

Winfrey touches audience members a lot, cries and laughs, and they touch, laugh and cry back. These exchanges signify an empathy that is traditionally feminine, but also feminist in its insistence on the 'personal', and that is largely free of the inflections of authority and sexuality mixed in with male hosts' touching.

The show also presents feminist arguments about women's lower economic and social status, men's difficulties in close relationships, women's difficulties in combining paid work and parenting, the suppression of women's sexuality and men's physical and sexual abuse. Moreover, since television representations often have more than one meaning, even the show's apparently conservative representations of gender can support feminist readings. The show's representations of the female body for instance are not simply incitements to female self-hatred. In one notorious episode Winfrey hauled onstage 67 pounds of lard – the amount of weight she had lost; since then she has forsworn dieting. Today, the show routinely notes the oppressiveness and irrelevance of dominant images of the female body, explores how preoccupations with food and weight cloak depression and feelings of low self-worth and acknowledges the comforting, social and sensual nature of eating and one episode focused exclusively on discrimination against fat people. Winfrey's own size acts as a reminder of how women's bigness can be a form of power, perhaps especially when they are black women in a field dominated by white men. As Gracie Mae Still, the narrator of Alice Walker's '1955' put it, 'fat like I is looks distinguished. You see me coming and know somebody's *there!*' (1982: 13).

The show sometimes considers motherhood with conventional reverence, but also treats it as a matter of hard work or discusses it in a more flexible way, as when Maya Angelou calls Winfrey her 'daughter-friend' (*Oprah Winfrey Show*, 1993). It has also problematized motherhood, as in an episode on maternal child abuse.

The show's feminism is most explicit, however, in its often-declared commitment to empowering women. This term has multiple meanings, indicating variously an interest in women's political, economic and educational advancement; in women getting help for personal and relationship problems; and most generally, in women perceiving a range of individual and social choices as open to them and deciding among them. Each meaning implies a different version of feminism. The first suggests a public, the second a personal focus for feminism and the last founds feminist politics in psychological wellbeing. Nevertheless the show's representations of empowerment all assume a commonality between women that allows the representations to make the category 'women' their unproblematic center. Feminism must use this category to ground its analyses and claims, but the category always has a social and historical context that gives it a specific meaning (Riley, 1988; Spelman, 1990). *Oprah*, however, represents women as sharing emotional and social qualities – communication skills, for instance – regardless of the differences between women. The show's aim is to empower this shared womanhood.

The dominant presence of women on the show is underwritten by a complementary male presence. The show continually solicits men's opinions, runs episodes on men as lovers and parents, and raises and counters the suggestion that *Oprah* is 'anti-men'. The show's 'woman-centred' talk is always, silently, about men, for gender is a relationship: one term evokes the other.

The complementariness of *Oprah*'s representations of gender raises an important question about its relationship to feminism. Might women's disempowerment, against which the show defines itself, nevertheless be its most powerful message? A narrative of empowerment structures each episode but the show's repeated accounts of victimization often seem to overwhelm them. After the daily success story of women getting their lives in order, you know that tomorrow you will start off once more with the harrowing experiences of women whose lives have been taken from them by abuse, illness or poverty. Feminism has to describe structures of male power in order to resist them and to this degree it is complicit with them. But on the *Oprah Winfrey Show*, self-consciously complicit description often seems to collapse into a fruitless reiteration of stories of personal suffering. Domestic violence, child abuse and eating disorders support regular episodes, each claiming to bring to light a horrible and hitherto secret oppression, each by this claim implicitly reinstating the horror and prohibitions around the topic; for talking about a forbidden subject may maintain as much as disperse a taboo. *Oprah*'s current emphasis on health and exercise at the expense of diets, for example, is undercut by a conventional subtext of the female body as subject to control (Bordo, 1989; Coward, 1989), and by the frequency with which diets are mentioned, only to be dismissed.

[. . .]

If we view *Oprah*'s multiple representations of gender in a context wider than the show, their relationship to feminism often starts to seem closer. Despite the limits the show sets on what can be said, for instance, and its tendency to present talk as a cure-all, its stress on 'explicit' speech seems oppositional in the broader context of US pro-censorship campaigns, especially since explicit talk on *Oprah* is often talk about a common censorship target, female sexuality. The show's representations of men also appear more resistant if they are read against the power relationships generally obtaining between women and men. Episodes shift from description to prescription, from problems with men or men's problems, to women's solutions. Even if a similar move will be made all over again in the very next episode, the move cuts against the cultural grain. Viewed historically, too, *Oprah*'s repeated and apparently unchanging considerations of some sensational topics may indicate not just unsated voyeurism or stalled feminism but a series of historically distinct concerns. A show about rape survivors, for example, means something different after the Palm Beach case, in which William Smith, a nephew of Edward Kennedy, was acquitted of raping a lower middle class white woman, than it does after the Central Park case, in which black youths were convicted of beating and raping a white woman stockbroker who was running in the park.

'RACE' AND RACISM

Henry Louis Gates (1989) describes how, in the 1950s, his family would rush to see African Americans on television, and how concerned they were that the performers be good. More African Americans are on television now but blacks are still underrepresented and appear mainly as a set of sitcom and drama cliches or as news anchors. The concern of people of color about their television representation remains strong (Fife, 1987; Grey, 1989; Ziegler and White, 1990). Shows like *Oprah* generate big expectations and concomitant criticism. *Oprah* has been said to absolve white guilt by presenting a rags-to-riches black, unthreatening female, who hugs whites in the audience more than people of color. The show has also been accused of being negative about African-American men, having few minorities on the production team, and giving racist white organizations air-time rather than confronting more subtle and pervasive racisms. Winfrey ridicules calls for her to be more black, asking, 'How black do you have to be?' (King, 1987: 187). The demand that she 'represent' African Americans is indeed a sign of her token status on television. As Isaac Julien and Kobena Mercer have written of film, the notion that one instance 'could "speak for" an entire community of interests reinforces the perceived secondariness of that community' (1989: 4).

The *Oprah* show is, in any case, permeated with 'race' as much as it is with gender. Winfrey's own Chicago-based production company, the first owned by an African American, makes it. This, together with her ratings, gives her Cosby-like powers – to determine topics and how to treat them, for instance – that black people rarely have in television. The show itself consistently addresses racism, explicitly, by calling for equal opportunities and recruiting people of color for the production team and, implicitly, by challenging casual instances of racism. In an episode on interracial relationships, Winfrey ironizes a white male guest's history of dating only black women, saying, 'It's that melanin that got you ... that melanin count just overwhelmed him'. *Oprah* avoids overt racial politics but towards the end this episode featured audience members' political analyses of interracial relationships:

> *Female audience member:* ... the reason people are taking it so terribly is that we are part of a racist society period, and that has to change for anything to change.
> *Female guest:* That's right (*Oprah Winfrey Show*, 1989a).

Less overtly, the show often features visual representations of racial difference without verbal comment, a silence that may be the result of television's caution about 'race' but that may work, as Kum-Kum Bhavnani (1990) has described, as anti-racist empowerment. In one segment of the '1991 Follow-up Show' (*Oprah Winfrey Show*, 1992), for instance, an African-American family, identified simply as a 'family' living in a project, got a 'dream house'. Two other segments showed dramatic reunions between adopted children and birth parents. In both cases children of mixed parentage met previously unknown white or black parents, while 'race' went unmentioned. These silences allowed racial differences to appear but refused them legitimacy in the narratives. In the silences, the cultural mythology of a de-raced all-American 'family' achieved a tactical defeat of other more clearly racist mythologies of black welfare mothers and tragic mulatto children.

The show's representations of black America are also telling. It regularly features successful African-American business people, professionals and entertainers, generating a picture of black culture and achievement rare in mainstream media. After a long absence, rappers now appear on the show occasionally; there are indeed parallels between *Oprah*'s woman-empowering aims and those some women rappers express (Rose, 1990). The show regularly considers issues that are important and controversial among blacks: education, self-esteem, class tensions, conflicts between black women and men over black women's alleged disrespectful and money-grabbing, 'ain't nothing going on but the rent' approach to black men and black men's claimed irresponsibility, black discrimination against dark-skinned black people, interracial adoption and relationships, and black hair and skin care. Black-oriented advertisements and public service announcements are more frequent than on most other network shows. More generally, Winfrey's and her black guests' stories of their lives combine with the show's references to black struggles, especially those of strong black women, to provide a perpetually renewed and reformulated television history of African America, not as comprehensive as those produced during Black History Month, but there all year round.

Winfrey sometimes talks black American, usually to make a joke. Television conventionally allows such language for comedic purposes but it remains language infrequently heard outside sitcoms, dramas and documentary representations of inner cities. Winfrey even induces similar speech in others. Once, trailing one of her specials on the early evening news after her show, she talked with the black newsreader Roz Abrams, and the somewhat formal Abrams called her 'girlfriend'. For a hallucinatorily brief moment black women's acquaintanceship and talk displaced the bland chumminess and linguistics common in such exchanges.

Occasionally Winfrey addresses whites in the studio audience to explain some aspect of black life. This move homogenizes both the life and the audience, and can seem to offer a quasi-anthropological supplement to talk shows' usual peeping-tom pleasures. But it gives a public voice to marginalized phenomena and acknowledges an ignorance and distance that usually goes unspoken, while Winfrey's blunt pedagogy circumvents voyeurism.

Finally, black feminism seems, as much as woman-centered feminism, to define the show. This black feminism recognizes the different history of patriarchy among African Americans (Gaines, 1988), writes the history of black women's resistance in the anti-slavery and civil rights movements and in every family and celebrates the strength and creativity of black women (Walker, 1983). Winfrey often invokes the film *The Color Purple*, the writing of Gloria Naylor (1982) and the work of Maya Angelou (1970), whose account of growing up in the black South she says describes her own life and whom she calls her mentor (*Oprah Winfrey Show*, 1993). Men's abuse, which Patricia Hill Collins (1990: 185) says needs to be the object of black feminist analysis, implicitly receives this attention through the host's and black audience members' repeated engagements with it. Angelou and Walker are often said to ignore the history and problematic of black masculinity, and in the process collude with white racism. *Oprah* is subject to similar criticisms but tackles the issues by presenting positive images of African American fatherhood and male mentoring. Winfrey still Signifies on black men though, as Gloria-Jean

Masciarotte (1991), citing Gates (1988) citing Hurston, says; and other African American women on the show do the same. This Signifyin(g) is, as Gates says, both a verbal game and a serious cultural engagement. A black woman in the audience raised a laugh when she admonished a black male guest, a Lothario vacillating between two white women, one with dark, one with light hair, 'She over there on the light side, she over there on the dark side, you in the middle on the *grey* side' (*Oprah Winfrey Show*, 1992). The show itself also Signifies, in Gates's broad sense of textual revision, on the texts of African American women writers, rewriting them in a different medium and for a larger racially diverse audience. For many of the white and black viewers of *Oprah*, the show's enduring canon of these writers – along the more variable set of female self-help gurus and high-achieving women who guest – must constitute the dominant cultural representation of feminism.

SEXUALITIES

In common with the rest of television, the *Oprah Winfrey Show* is heterosexist Openly lesbian or gay guests appear rarely, the show carefully establishes the heterosexuality of well-known guests, and when it addresses homosexuality directly it tends either to problematize it or to mainstream it as a human issue, distanced from sex and politics (Gross, 1989). Bisexuality is a special problem. In an episode presented jointly with the hunt-the-criminal programme *America's Most Wanted*, a man's bisexuality became the emblem of his ability to elude the criminal justice system: 'The problem with John Hawkins is he's a very good-looking guy, he's a very good con, and he's bisexual, so he has the ability to basically adapt into any community or any type of social structure', said a police officer (reshown on *Oprah Winfrey Show*, 1992).

Sometimes *Oprah* gives screen time to camp men who function briefly and conventionally as jesters. More of a challenge to dominant assumptions about sexuality is the show's marking of differences within heterosexuality, for instance the line it draws between abusive and non-abusive heterosexual relationships. This acknowledgement of plural heterosexualities coexists with the show's more traditional representations of sexual relationships between women and men either as always involving the same desires and social patterns, as in episodes along the lines of 'Save Your Marriage' and 'Best Husband Contest' or as infinitely various, as in 'Men Who Married Their Divorced Wives' and 'Women Who Married Their Stepsons'. Finally, the show's overwhelmingly female spectacle and spectatorship might conceivably be read as a kind of televisual lesbianism but the link between female spectatorship, sexuality and sexual politics is very unclear (de Lauretis, 1991; Stacey, 1988).

CLASS

Despite a late-1980s' burst of class-conscious sitcoms, television is not very interested in class relationships. On *Oprah* though the all-American narrative of Winfrey's progress from poverty to wealth is often invoked, and her riches legitimized as the rightful reward of her struggle for a piece of the pie. The wealth is frequently represented as exuberant consumption by references to Winfrey's restaurant, her condo, her farm and her furs. In a study of women's reactions to *Dynasty*, Andrea Press (1990) writes that working class women have a particular affinity with such representations; the *Oprah* show's periodic ditchings of gritty emotion in favour of glitz may then be a part of its success. But the show represents Winfrey's good works and her dispensations of wealth to the poor too. Taken together, these representations turn wealth into something new, strange and full of responsibilities. The show also refers often and unromantically to poverty, in episodes on project life for instance, and points up class differences in values and lifestyles. At the start of a show on 'Stressed-out Dads', Winfrey showed two clips from *thirtysomething* of yuppie fathers caring for their children and then said, laughing and sarcastic, 'I know that happens in y'all's house every night' (*Oprah Winfrey Show*, 1990b).

The show may present Winfrey as a de-raced all-American success story but it gives a strong presence to middle class African Americans and pays attention to the responsibilities and close historical relationships middle class blacks have with and for poorer blacks, especially young people. Many issues debated between black women and men on the show involve class: the averred paucity of suitable black men available to educated black women; these women's alleged prejudices about ordinary working black men, and whether black women or men, especially those in the middle class, should have interracial relationships. No other networked shows give these topics the acrimonious airings they get on *Oprah*; the other daytime talk shows seem unable to see their contentiousness. *Oprah* is indeed at times better able to recognize the shifting and intersecting agendas of class, gender and 'race' than is much feminist theory.

OPRAH AS PSYCHOLOGY

Alongside the show's investment in social relationships runs a much more explicit preoccupation with psychological issues and explanations. The daytime talk show is a psychological genre (Carbaugh, 1988). Most *Oprah* episodes focus on overtly psychological phenomena like 'obsessions' and 'negotiation skills', psychologists are the show's commonest 'expert' guests, Winfrey's interventions and those of audience members are mostly directed at clarifying experiences and emotions, and interpersonal communication is presented as a cathartic and enabling solution to social as well as personal problems. The show gives almost all the problems it addresses, even those like unemployment, some psychological content, usually in terms of 'feelings'. Each episode's narrative moves towards psychological closure: people end up 'feeling' better because they have 'expressed themselves' or 'started to think about what they really want'. Winfrey's psychological democracy, her representation as a person just like the audience members, is also very powerful. Showing an extreme version of the usual perception of television as the mass medium closest to interpersonal communication (Ellis, 1982; Pfau, 1990), women in *Oprah*'s audience frequently preface their contributions by telling Winfrey how much they like her and the show, and how they feel they know her almost as a friend (Waldron, 1987: 182).

[...]

Antiprofessionalism is a common stance in the USA but *Oprah*'s lay psychology has other connotations too. Its emphasis on getting people to communicate is part of a utopian picture of a viewing community and a world in which everyone knows they are not alone. Often the stress on communication recalls a religious commitment to testifying (see also Masciarotte, 1991), and this convergence of talk show with worship (Fogel, 1986) takes on a specific resonance in *Oprah* from the history of black churches as places where African American women's voices could be raised and heard. The show's persistent focus on self-esteem ties into an implicit liberal democratic politics of rights, responsibilities and choice, and, through the non specific spirituality the show attaches to self-worth, to New Ageism. *Oprah*'s optimism about psychological improvement is associated with beliefs in religious redemption and in social progress, for which redemption is itself a metaphor. Andrea Stuart (1988; see also Bobo, 1988) has suggested that black women watching *The Color Purple* read its happy ending not within the film narrative, where it seems inconsistent and sentimental, but within broader religious, social and historical narratives where it offers an important antidote to hopelessness. Perhaps *Oprah*'s daily psychological resolutions of dramatic suffering support a similar reading.

An individual woman may be represented on *Oprah* as shaped by social forces like racism and male violence but also as fully and only responsible for her own actions. An odd melange can result, of growth psychology, religious devotion, political analysis and personal hubris. An emblematic example on *Oprah* itself was Angelou's presentation of herself and her work. Describing her composition of a poem for Clinton's inauguration, she said she was not nervous: all she had to do was 'get centered' and write. No false humility was required: after all, 'I come from the Creator trailing wisps of glory'. And telling of her own overcoming of abuse, poverty and racism she recalled the key realization: 'God loves *me*. Oprah, Oprah, the skies opened up. I can do *anything*' (*Oprah Winfrey Show*, 1993). Winfrey looked deeply touched, they clasped hands and the show broke for commercials. The show's loose concatenations of ideas are easy to deride but they build up a complicated picture of psychological, as well as social and historical relationships, relationships which the show does not try to resolve. Some might see the ambiguities as disabling and claim television audiences cannot cope with them. But I think it is productive for a talk show to display, as *Oprah* does, the contradictions that traverse our subjectivities, rather than to opt for social determinist explanations of problems, victimologies that allow subjectivity no clear place or to invoke an unproblematic human agency as the general solution, as talk shows usually do. *Oprah*'s infusion by black feminism seems to be what generates this complexity.

OPRAH, TELEVISION AND SUPER-REALISM

Oprah's reflexivity about being television calls attention to how the characteristics of television, and of the daytime talk show in particular, shape it. More than most television (see Ellis, 1982), the daytime talk show is a casual form, not watched continuously. To compensate, it is made eye-catching, with clear, immediate images and plenty of camera movement and cutting to offset the slowness of talk. Daytime viewers may be attending to things other than television or just passing through a room where the television is on, so the shows favor soundbites: punchy questions; short, clear encapsulations of arguments and feelings; brief passages of incoherent speech, tears or silence to signal deep emotion; bursts of laughter and applause, snatches of theme music bracketing breaks and the programme itself, and enticing cliffhanger trails before each break: 'when we get back, are strong-thinking, decisive women a threat to you men?' (*Oprah Winfrey Show*, 1989b). These characteristics produce a currency of rapid, intense, simple and repetitive aural and visual representations, from the six-note sequence that means *Oprah*, to the screwed-up, crying faces of incest survivors asked 'How did it feel?' These fragmented representations are always breaking up the coherence and continuity of the talk show's narrative of psychological improvement.

It might be said of *Oprah*, as is often argued of talk shows and television in general, that its dispersed, atomistic representations do not disturb but only support the cultural consensus (Ellis, 1982; Fogel, 1986; Miller, 1990; Minnini, 1989). From this perspective, *Oprah* is too frivolous to be feminist. Some feminists have, however, interpreted television representations that reach *Oprah*'s level of disruption as carnivalesque or melodramatic challenges to television's conventional representations of gender (Ang, 1985; Brown, 1990; Deming, 1990). I am going to argue that *Oprah*'s televisual characteristics produce rather a *super-realism* that has some modest feminist value.

Daytime talk shows like *Oprah* try to reach a realist truth by interleaving information and entertainment, and deploying narratives of psychological growth to pull this 'infotainment' together. Sometimes, they do not manage the integration and super-realism, a realism torn out of shape by excesses of emotion or empiricism, disrupts the explanatory framework. On *Oprah*, this disruption happens in one of two ways. First, super-realism may take over when a 'psychological' truth recurs so often on the show that it begins to shed its individual psychological character and starts to look more like a social, political or religious fact. The narratives of sexual abuse on *Oprah*, for example, very similar and endlessly repeated, seem to go beyond psychological understanding to become facts about gender relationships that demand explanation in other, social terms. It is the televisual superficiality and facility of the show that allows this super-real excess to register.

Oprah's second type of super-realism appears when the emotions in the show get so intense that the show forgoes any claim to provide information and simply displays an extreme effect – accessible to psychoanalytic interpretation, perhaps, but not to the kinds of psychological explanations most of us are familiar with and use. For instance, when the show featured an abused woman with 92 personalities, it could not provide a coherent account of her subjectivity. Abuse started to seem utterly idiosyncratic and affectively overwhelming. Again, this registering of excess relied on the show's super-real televisual character: on snappy formulations of monstrous feelings and quick moves to commercial breaks ('back in a moment') that left the unspeakable and the unimaginable resounding around American living rooms.

I would argue that *Oprah* owes its cultural effects largely to its super-realist emotional and empirical excesses, which rework or Signify on television and culture, something talk shows' more conventional psychological explanations are unlikely to do. Its contribution to US debates about the education of black children or the relationships between black women and black men comes not so much from its explicit consideration of these debates as from their unannounced, unasked for and unmarked recurrence within the show, so frequently and pervasively that they become super-real facts, uncontainable within the show's psychological narratives.

Henry Louis Gates (1989) wrote that he hopes 'blacks will stop looking to tv for (their) social liberation'. Feminists of color and white feminists rarely look to television for social liberation. But television can achieve what feminist writing finds difficult: *Oprah*'s interwoven explorations of 'race', class and gender and its popularization of aspects of black feminist thought are examples. And feminists may discover something about how to deal with the complex connections between subjectivity, gender and other social relationships from the suspension of the *Oprah Winfrey Show* between fluff and gravity; psychology, social analysis and emotions; realism and super-realism; and from their own difficulties in addressing this mixture.

NOTES

1. Another African-American woman, the comedian Marsha Warfield, has had a half-hour networked morning show, and Montel Williams, the 'male Oprah', has an hour long morning show on CBS. A new crop of *Oprah* challengers, several with African-American hosts, appeared in 1993 (Freeman, 1992). The earliest African-American talk-show host was Ellis Haizlip who, in the late 1960s and early 1970s, fronted *Soul*, 'a live performance/talk show inspired by the burgeoning cultural nationalist movement' (Jones, 1991).

REFERENCES

Ang, I. (1985) *Watching Dallas: Soap Opera and the Melodramatic Imagination*. London: Methuen.
Angelou, M. (1970) *I Know Why The Caged Bird Sings*. New York: Random House.
Bhavnani, K-K. (1990) 'What's Power Got To Do With It?', in I. Parker and J. Shotter (eds) *Deconstructing Social Psychology*. London: Routledge.

Bobo, J. (1988) 'The Color Purple: Black Women as Cultural Readers', in D. Pribram (ed.) Female Spectators Looking at Film and Television. London: Verso.

Boemer, M. (1987) 'Correlating Lead-in Show Ratings with Local Television News Ratings', Journal of Broadcasting and Electronic Media 31: 89–94.

Bordo, S. (1989) 'Reading the Slender Body', in M. Jacobus, E. Foxkeller and S. Shuttleworth (eds) Body/Politics. New York: Routledge.

Bretl, D. and Cantor, J. (1988) 'The Portrayal of Men and Women in US Television Commercials: A Recent Content Analysis and Trends over 15 years', Sex Roles 18: 595–609.

Brown, M. E. (1990) 'Motley Moments: Soap Operas, Carnival, Gossip and the Power of the Utterance', in M. E. Brown (ed.) Television and Women's Culture: The Politics of the Popular. London: Sage.

Butler, J. (1990) Gender Trouble. New York: Routledge.

Carbaugh, D. (1988) Talking American: Cultural Discourses on Donahue. Norwood, NJ: Ablex.

Coward, R. (1983) Patriarchal Precedents. London: Routledge and Kegan Paul.

Coward, R. (1989) The Whole Truth. London: Faber and Faber.

Davis, D. (1990) 'Portrayals of Women in Prime-time Network Television: Some Demographic Characteristics', Sex Roles 23: 325–32.

de Lauretis, T. ed. (1986) Feminist Studies/Critical Studies. Bloomington, IN: Indiana University Press.

de Lauretis, T. (1991) 'Film and the Visible', in Bad Object-Choices (ed.) How Do I Look? Queer Film and Video. Seattle: Bay Press.

Deming, C. (1990) 'For Television-centred Television Criticism: Lessons from Feminism', in M. E. Brown (ed.) Television and Women's Culture: The Politics of the Popular. London: Sage.

Ellis, J. (1982) Visible Fictions. London: Routledge and Kegan Paul.

Fife, M. (1987) 'Promoting Racial Diversity in US Broadcasting: Federal Policies Versus Social Realities', Media, Culture and Society 9: 481–505.

Fogel, A. (1986) 'Talk Shows: On Reading Television', in S. Donadio, S. Railton and S. Ormond (eds) Emerson and His Legacy. Carbondale, IL: Southern Illinois University Press.

Freeman, M. (1992) 'Can We Talk? New for 1993', Broadcasting and Cable (December): 14.

Gaines, J. (1988) 'White Privilege and Looking Relations: Race and Gender in Feminist Film Theory', Last Special Issue on 'Race', Screen 29: 12–27.

Gates, H. L. (1988) The Signifying Monkey. New York: Oxford University Press.

Gates, H. L. (1989) 'TV's Black World Turns – But Stays Unreal', New York Times (Nov.): 12.

Goodman, F. (1991) 'Madonna and Oprah: the Companies They Keep', Working Women. 16: 52–5.

Grey, H. (1989) 'Television, Black Americans, and the American Dream', Critical Studies in Mass Communication 6: 376–86.

Gross, L. (1989) 'Out of the Mainstream: Sexual Minorities and the Mass Media', in E. Seiter, H. Borchers, G. Kretscner and E. Warth (eds) Remote Control. New York: Routledge.

Guider, E. (1987) 'Katz Advises How to Handle Daytime Queen', Variety (July): 8

Harrison, B. (1989) 'The Importance of Being Oprah', New York Times Magazine (June): 11.

Hill Collins, P. (1990) Black Feminist Thought. Cambridge, MA: Unwin Hyman.

hooks, b. (1981) Ain't I A Woman? Black Women and Feminism. Boston: South End Press.

hooks, b. (1989) Talking Back: Thinking Feminist, Thinking Black. Boston: South End Press.

Jones, L. (1991) 'Hot Buttered "Soul"', Village Voice (March): 12.

Julien, I. and Mercer, K. (1988) 'Introduction: De Margin and De Center', Last 'Special Issue' on 'Race', *Screen* 29(4): 2–10.

King, N. (1987) *Everybody Loves Oprah*. New York: Morrow.

Lorde, A. (1984) *Sister Outsider: Essays and Speeches*. Trumansburg, NY: Crossing Press.

McClellan, S. (1993) 'Freshman "Deep Space Nine" Records Stellar Sweep Debut', *Broadcasting and Cable* (April): 24–6.

Masciarotte, G-J. (1991) 'C'mon Girl: Oprah Winfrey and the Discourse of Feminine Talk', *Genders* 11: 81–110.

Miller, M. C. (1990) *Boxed In: The Culture of Television*. Evanston, IL: Northwestern University Press.

Minnini, G. (1989) 'Genres de discourse et types de dialogue: Le "Talk-show"', in E. Weigand and F. Hundnurscher (eds) *Dialoganalyse* II. Tubingen: Niemeyer.

Moraga, C. and Anzaldua, G. (1981) *This Bridge Called My Back*. Watertown, MA: Persephone Press.

Naylor, G. (1982) *The Women of Brewster Place*. New York: Viking.

Oprah Winfrey Show (1989a) 'Blacks and Whites Dating', New York: Journal Graphics, 1 March.

Oprah Winfrey Show (1989b) 'Home Fights', New York: Journal Graphics, 25 April.

Oprah Winfrey Show (1990a) 'A Mother's Plea: Marry My Daughter', 23 May, author's transcript.

Oprah Winfrey Show (1990b) 'Stressed-Out Dads', 30 May, author's transcript.

Oprah Winfrey Show (1992) '1991 Follow-up Show', 8 January, Channel 4, Britain, author's transcript.

Oprah Winfrey Show (1993) 'Maya Angelou Interview', 13 July, author's transcript.

Pfau, M. (1990) 'A Channel Approach to Television Influence', *Journal of Broadcasting and Electronic Media* 34: 195–214.

Press, A. (1990) 'Class, Gender and the Female Viewer: Women's Responses to *Dynasty*', in M. E. Brown (ed.) *Television and Women's Culture: The Politics of the Popular*. London: Sage.

Rich, A. (1986) 'Compulsory Heterosexuality and Lesbian Existence', in *Blood, Bread and Poetry*. New York: Norton.

Riley, D. (1988) *Am I That Name? Feminism and the Category of 'Women' in History*. Minneapolis, MN: University of Minnesota Press.

Rose, T. (1990) 'Never Trust a Big Butt and a Smile', *camera obscura* 23: 109–32.

Spelman, E. (1990) *Inessential Woman*. London: Women's Press.

Spivak, G. (1988) *In Other Worlds*. New York: Routledge, Chapman and Hall.

Stacey, J. (1988) 'Desperately Seeking Difference', in L. Gamman and M. Marshment (eds) *The Female Gaze*. London: Women's Press.

Stuart, A. (1988) '"The Color Purple": in Defence of Happy Endings', in L. Gamman and M. Marshment (eds) *The Female Gaze*. London: Women's Press.

Waldron, R. (1987) *Oprah!* New York: St Martin's Press.

Walker, A. (1982) *You Can't Keep A Good Woman Down*, London: Women's Press.

Walker, A. (1983) *In Search of Our Mothers' Gardens*, New York: Harcourt Brace Jovanovich.

Ziegler, D. and White, A. (1990) 'Women and Minorities on Network Television News: An Examination of Correspondents and Newsmakers', *Journal of Broadcasting and Electronic Media* 34: 215–23.

FURTHER READING

Ang, I., 'Feminist Desire and Female Pleasure'. *Camera Obscura*, 16 (1988) pp. 179–91.

Baehr, H. and Dyer, G. (eds), *Boxed In: Women and Television* (London: Pandora, 1987).

Baehr, H. and Gray, A. (eds), *Turning it On: A Reader in Women and Media* (London: Arnold, 1996).

Ballaster, R., Beetham, M., Frazer, E. and Hebron, S., *Women's Worlds: Ideology, Femininity and the Woman's Magazine* (London: Macmillan, 1991).

Betterton, R. (ed.), *Looking On: Images of Femininity in the Visual Arts and Media* (London: Pandora, 1987).

Brown, M.E. (ed.), *Television and Women's Culture* (London: Sage, 1990).

Brunsdon, C., *Screen Tastes* (London: Routledge, 1996).

Brunsdon, C., D'Acci, J. and Spigel, L. (eds), *Feminist Television Criticism: A Reader* (Oxford: Oxford University Press, 1997).

Holland, Patricia, 'The Page Three Girl Speaks to Women, Too'. *Screen* 24:3 (1983) pp. 84–102.

Brunsdon, C., 'Pedagogies of the Feminine: Feminist Teaching and Women's Genres'. *Screen* 32:4 (1991) pp. 364–81.

Brunt, R. and Rowan, C. (eds), *Feminism, Culture and Politics* (London: Lawrence and Wishart, 1982).

Butcher, H. et al., 'Images of Women in the Media'. CCCS Stencilled Paper, University of Birmingham (1974).

Byars, J., 'Gazes/Voices/Power: Expanding Psychoanalysis for Feminist Film and Television Theory'. In E.D. Pribram (ed.), *Female Spectators* (London: Verso, 1988).

Coward R., *Female Desire* (London: Paladin, 1984).

Creedon, P. (ed.), *Women in Mass Communication: Challenging Gender Values* (London: Sage, 1989).

D'Acci, J., *Defining Women: Television and the Case of* Cagney and Lacey (Chapel Hill: University of North Carolina Press, 1993).

Davies, K., Dickey, J. and Stratford, T. (eds), *Out of Focus: Writing on Women and the Media* (London: The Women's Press, 1987).

Ferguson, M., *Forever Feminine: Women's Magazines and the Cult of Femininity* (London: Heinemann, 1983).

Feuer, J., 'Melodrama, Serial Form and Television Today'. *Screen* 25:1 (1984) pp. 4–16.

Gallagher, M., 'Women and Men in the Media'. *Communication Research Trends*, Special Issue 12:1 pp. 1–36.

Gamman, L. and Marshment, M. (eds), *The Female Gaze: Women as Viewers of Popular Culture* (London: The Women's Press, 1988).

Gledhill, C., 'Pleasurable Negotiations'. In E.D. Pribram (ed.), *Female Spectators* (London: Verso, 1988).

Holland, P., 'The Page Three Girl Speaks to Women, Too'. *Screen* 24:3 (1983) pp. 84–102

hooks, b., *Black Looks: Race and Representation* (London: Turnaround, 1992).

Journal of Communication Inquiry (1987) 'The Feminist Issue', Special Issue 11:1.

Kaplan, E.A. (ed.), *Regarding Television* (Los Angeles: American Film Institute, 1983).

Kaplan, E.A., 'Feminist Criticism and Television'. In R.C. Allen (ed.), *Channels of Discourse, Reassembled* (London: Routledge, 1992).

Kirkham, P. and Skeggs, B., '*Absolutely Fabulous*: Absolutely Feminist?' in C. Geraghty and D. Lusted (eds), *The Television Studies Book* (London: Arnold, 1998) pp. 287–98.

Kuhn, A., 'Women's Genres'. *Screen* 25:1 (1984) pp. 18–28.

Mattelart, M., *Women, Media, Crisis: Femininity and Disorder* (London: Comedia, 1986).

McCracken, E., *Decoding Women's Magazines* (London: Macmillan, 1993).

McRobbie, A., '*Jackie*: An Ideology of Adolescent Femininity'. In B. Waites, T. Bennett and G. Martin (eds), *Popular Culture: Past and Present* (London: Croom Helm, 1982).

McRobbie, A., *Feminism and Youth Culture: From "Jackie" to "Just Seventeen"* (London: Macmillan, 1991).

Mellencamp, P. (ed.), *Logics of Television* (Bloomington and London: Indiana University Press and BFI, 1990).

Modleski, T., *Loving with a Vengeance: Mass Produced Fantasies for Women* (London: Methuen, 1984).

Modleski, T. (ed.), *Studies in Entertainment: Critical Approaches to Mass Culture* (Bloomington: Indiana University Press, 1986).

Modleski, T., 'Femininity as Mas(s)querade: A Feminist Approach to Mass Culture'. In C. MacCabe (ed.), *High Theory/Low Culture: Analysing Popular Television and Film* (Manchester: Manchester University Press, 1986).

Modleski, T., *Feminism Without Women.* (London: Routledge, 1991).

Mulvey, L., 'Visual Pleasure and Narrative Cinema'. *Screen* 16:3 (1975) pp. 6–18.

Pribram, E.D. (ed.), *Female Spectators: Looking at Film and Television* (London: Verso, 1988).

Skirrow, G., '*Widows*'. In M. Alvarado and J. Stewart (eds), *Made for Television: Euston Films Limited* (London: BFI, 1985).

Steeves, L., 'Feminist Theories and Media Studies'. *Critical Studies in Mass Communication* 4:2 (1987) pp. 95–135.

Tuchman, G. et al. (eds), *Hearth and Home: Images of Women in the Media* (New York: Oxford University Press, 1978).

van Zoonen, L., 'Feminist Perspectives on the Media'. In J. Curran and M. Gurevitch (eds), *Mass Media and Society* (London: Edward Arnold, 1991).

van Zoonen, L., *Feminist Media Studies* (London: Sage, 1994).

Winship, J., *Inside Women's Magazines* (London: Pandora Press, 1987).

Women: A Cultural Review (issue on 'Women Both Sides of the Camera') 2:1 (1991).

Women's Studies Group (eds), *Women Take Issue.* Centre for Contemporary Cultural Studies (London: Hutchinson, 1978).

SECTION 3
TEXT

4. POSTMODERN MEDIA

POSTMODERN MEDIA
INTRODUCTION

A focus on postmodern theory has increasingly characterised the analysis of popular media forms. Television in particular, with its 'segmentation' and 'flow' (see Chapters 18 and 19), its multiplicity of narratives, its emphasis on the 'now', its inter-referentiality and intercutting of images, and its technical reproducibility, seems to invite such readings, as does its increasingly fragmented patterns of use, particularly among the young. For Jean Baudrillard, indeed, television and its technologies are seen as both symptom and cause of the universe of simulation which Western culture has become. In the endless proliferation and circulation of signs characteristic of 'television culture', the domination of 'screen and network' is seen to collapse old distinctions between public and private space, and between representation and the real. Instead, there is 'the ecstasy of communication' and the 'obscenity' of a culture in which all is image, surface and transparency.[1]

Quite what the implications of such an identification of 'postmodern' media forms might be, is less certain. The collapse of boundaries which is seen to characterise the postmodern may be read as negative, as the absorption and neutralisation of resistant strategies and oppositional forms, and the substitution of meaningless surface and style. Alternatively, it may be seen as positive, offering liberating possibilities of difference, multiplicity and de-centredness, destabilizing old hierarchies of power. It may, finally, be seen as neither: as a continuation rather than a break with earlier forms and hierarchies. Feminists, for example, have been critical of postmodern theory's claims of a collapse of hierarchies and divisions. Thus, in a critique of Baudrillard's position, Tania Modleski[2] has attacked his 'implicit denial of the contemporary relevance of sexual difference', as all differences are supposedly absorbed into the post-modern universe of simulation. It is only the powerful, she argues, who can argue in this way for the collapse of the social into a universe of signs. For women, as for other disempowered groups, the dominance of style and surface does not signal the end of oppression. Indeed, the social order, far from being absorbed into an intertextual 'hyperreal', is 'alive enough to ensure the continuance of that oppression'.

The chapter by Jim Collins which opens this section (Chapter 29) begins by exploring the varying ways in which television has been conceptualised within postmodern thought. Whilst television has appeared as central within postmodern theorising, he writes, such theorising is complicated by the fact that neither television nor postmodernism have any agreed-upon definitions. 'Postmodern', then, may be used to describe a socio-historical period (postmodernity), a form of textual organisation, or a mode of cultural analysis. In all of these, television occupies a central place. As a medium, argues Collins, television is characterised by *'hyperconsciousness* . . . a hyperawareness on the part of the text itself of its cultural status, function and history, as well as of the conditions of its circulation and reception'. Its texts are thus marked by self-reflexivity and intertextual referencing. Such ironic knowingness, however, is not necessarily either emancipatory (offering *critical* awareness) or disempowering (meaningless repetition). Instead, it marks a new kind of viewing subject, one who is neither wholly defined by television's mass cultural images nor able wholly to stand outside them. Instead, the viewer is 'a technologically sophisticated *bricoleur*', negotiating meanings and values from the eclectic site of television's textuality.

Collins' optimism is echoed by Angela McRobbie in the chapter which follows (Chapter 30). Recent debates on postmodernism, argues McRobbie, possess 'both a positive attraction and a usefulness to the analyst of popular culture'. Postmodernism, in its insistence on the collapse of boundaries between image and lived reality, challenges the narrowness of earlier forms of textual analysis. Moreover, the phenomena which it describes – the 'frenzied expansion of the mass media', the intertwining of image and reality, of media and society, the self-referentiality and endless cross-referencing of media output, the inescapability of images from popular culture – themselves hold critical potential. Postmodernism's collapsing of boundaries challenges old dualisms – between the 'self' and 'other', between 'the West' and its postcolonial 'other' – and forges new alliances. The outburst of energy released can produce new resistances and a 'vibrant critique' through its use of pastiche, its 'ransacking and recycling of culture'. As an example, McRobbie points to black urban culture, which thrives on its 'assertive re-assembling of bits and pieces' and 'fake, forged identities'. Black women writers, too, she argues, have produced an 'explosion of the written word' whose rhythms approximate 'the jazz sounds of the city'. Postmodernism's emphasis on fragmentation, she concludes, describes the experience of many groups of young people, and far from being its victims, they are 'putting it to work for them'.

A very different approach is taken by Bill Nichols in his account of 'Reality TV' (Chapter 31). Reality TV – by which Nichols means 'all those shows that present dangerous events, unusual situations, or actual police cases, often reenacting aspects of them and sometimes enlisting our assistance in apprehending criminals still at large' (shows like *Crimewatch UK* or *999* in Britain, or *America's Most Wanted* in the USA) – represents a postmodern blurring of boundaries between fact and fiction, reality and representation. As such it signals the death of the documentary form, with its claims to authenticity and sense of a historical world beyond representation. Reality TV absorbs reality into spectacle, offering talk as distraction and news as non-history, a perpetual 'now'. Here, then, is Baudrillard's universe of tele-visual simulation, and the viewer response invited, argues Nichols, is one of detached consumption, distracted viewing and episodic amazement ('Isn't that amazing!'). Unlike documentary, reality TV does not address us as citizens who might act in the real world in response to the argument it makes. Instead, it absorbs us into its screen-world, substituting sensation for argument and the random and unforeseen for order and cohesion. It is a symptom, argues Nichols, of a collapse in the authority of the powerful: their explanations (or 'master narratives') are no longer believed. But it is not a *critical* response: its focus on localised events may produce a politics of sorts, but it will be a decontextualised and reactive politics, mobilised around emotion not explanation.

The final chapter in this section (Chapter 32) offers a critique of postmodern television from a very different perspective. Like Tania Modleski, Lynne Joyrich argues that, if television has been characterised as a postmodern medium, these characteristics – of fluidity, proximity, surface and emotional excess – are also characteristics traditionally identified with the feminine. Similarly, the distracted gaze of the television viewer, consuming and consumed by the flow of images, marks this viewer as the typically feminine consumer of popular imagination. But this appropriation of markers of the feminine by television and postmodern critics alike does not mean, argues Joyrich, the dissolution of gendered binaries: in fact, 'the very rupture of traditional modes of thought provokes a panicked attempt to create new divisions rather than working to dispel our society's felt need for oppositions'. Thus, just as the postmodern critic's embrace of a 'feminine' fluidity can be used to deny the specificity of the historical and cultural positioning of women, so the 'feminine' textuality of television obscures crucial gender differences. The first of these, argues Joyrich, is the split between production and consumption, in which men control the former and women are positioned within the latter. The second is television's own response to the threat of 'feminization' by the construction within much of its output of 'a violent hypermasculinity'. Thus 'postmodern' programmes like *Miami Vice* and *Max Headroom* may show masculinity to be a matter of spectacle and display, but they are also characterised by the neutralisation or absence of women and a violent excess which is masculinity's defence against 'the contagion of feminization'.

NOTES

1. Baudrillard, 'The Ecstasy of Communication', in H. Foster (ed.), *Postmodern Culture* (London: Pluto Press, 1985), p.126.
2. Modleski, 'Femininity as Mas(s)querade', in Modleski, *Feminism Without Women: Culture and Criticism in a "Postfeminist" Age* (New York and London: Routledge, 1991), p.34.

29

TELEVISION AND POSTMODERNISM

Jim Collins

The development of some kind of working relationship between television and postmodernism within the realm of critical studies is inevitable, almost impossible, and absolutely necessary. Inevitable, because television is frequently referred to as the quintessence of postmodern culture, and postmodernism is just as frequently written off as mere 'television culture.' Close to impossible, because of the variability of both television and postmodernism as critical objects; both are currently undergoing widespread theorization in which there are few, if any, commonly agreed-upon first principles. Necessary, because that very lack, the absence of inherited critical baggage, places television studies in a unique position vis-à-vis postmodernism. Unlike the critical work devoted to other media, television studies does not have to 'retrofit' critical paradigms developed in modernist or premodernist periods and therefore should ideally be able to provide unprecedented insights into the complex interrelationships between textuality, subjectivity, and technology in contemporary cultures.

There is no short definition of *postmodernism* that can encompass the divergent, often contradictory ways the term has been employed. One reason for this divergence is that the term is used to describe: (1) a distinctive style; (2) a movement that emerged in the sixties, seventies, or eighties, depending on the medium in question; (3) a condition or milieu that typifies an entire set of socioeconomic factors; (4) a specific mode of philosophical inquiry that throws

From R. C. Allen (ed.), *Channels of Discourse Reassembled* (London: Routledge, 1992) pp. 327–51.

into question the givens of philosophical discourse; (5) a very particular type of 'politics'; and (6) an emergent form of cultural analysis shaped by all of the above.

This terminological confusion is exacerbated by the contentiousness of the various definitions. As Jonathan Arac has written, 'It remains even now typically the case that to "have a position" on postmodernism means not just to offer an analysis of its genesis and contours, but to let the world know whether you are for it or against it, and in fairly bold terms.'[1] One could argue that the chief drawback of most of this work is that the latter inevitably takes precedence over the former, producing little in the way of actual description but a great deal in the way of critical ax grinding. But although easy moralizing about postmodernism may often reveal little besides the presuppositions of the critical languages used to demonize or valorize it, the contested nature of the term – the fact that no definition of contours can ever be ideologically neutral, that description is inseparable from evaluation – reveals one of the most significant lessons of postmodern theory: all of our assumptions concerning what constitutes 'culture' and 'critical analysis' are now subject to intense debate.

If there is a common denominator in all of these contentious definitions of postmodernism, it is the determination to define it as something other than *modernism*, a term that is likewise given variable status. Modernism is generally characterized in one of two ways, depending on the individual critic's perspective on postmodernism: as a heroic period of revolutionary experimentation that sought to transform whole cultures, in which case postmodernism is seen as a neoconservative backlash; or as a period of profound elitism, in which case postmodernism signals a move away from the self-enclosed world of the avant-garde back into the realm of day-to-day life.

[...]

Although it is possible to list the tell-tale stylistic features of postmodern design – the move away from abstraction and geometrics to the overly familiar and mass-produced; the replacement of purity with eclecticism, internationalism with cultural specificity, and invention with rearticulation – the cultural significance of these changes and their ideological ramifications remains a matter of intense debate. It is also especially difficult to relate television to these debates in any kind of one-to-one correspondence. Television, unlike architecture, literature, or painting, never had a modernist phase that could serve as a point of departure for postmodern television. The emergence of postmodernism is decidedly an 'uneven' development; its appearance and eventual impact vary from one medium to another.

Because neither an etymology, nor an evolutionary schema, nor an all-encompassing theoretical paradigm can provide an adequate working definition of postmodernism that allows for diverse applications to television, I will set forth a series of recurring themes developed by theoreticians working in different media that, in aggregate, provide a sense of the conflictedness but also the potential cohesiveness of postmodern theory. These themes, considered together, allow for a reconsideration of the semiotic, technological, and ideological dimensions of television.

A Semiotics of Excess: 'The Bombardment of Signs'

One of the key preconditions of the postmodern condition is the proliferation of signs and their endless circulation, generated by the technological developments associated with the information explosion (cable television, VCRs, digital recording, computers, etcetera). These technologies have produced an ever increasing surplus of texts, all of which demand our attention in varying levels of intensity. The resulting array of competing signs shapes the very process of signification, a context in which messages must constantly be defined over and against rival forms of expression as different types of texts frame our allegedly common reality according to significantly different ideological agendas.

Television is obviously a central factor in this information explosion. Many critics on both the left and the right insist that television is likewise instrumental in the devaluation of meaning – the reduction of all meaningful activity to mere 'non-sense,' to a limitless televisual universe that has taken the place of the real. Such critics as Allan Bloom and Jean Baudrillard have made grandiose claims about the destructive power of mass culture (most especially television).[2] The former has claimed that television has brought about the ruination of true learning and morality. The latter has claimed that contemporary culture *is* television culture – endless simulations in which reality simply disappears. In Bloom's view, the culprit is not television alone, but the more general democratization of culture, which threatens the elite values that once formed the basis of real learning: the acquisition of Truth. But to Baudrillard (who is no more a postmodernist than Bloom), television is cause as well as symptom, allegedly constructing a seamless realm of simulations that hinder our acquisition of the *really real*.

The problem with these critiques is their contention that all signs are encoded and decoded according to exactly the same logic, or encoded so differently that, as a whole, they produce one and only one effect. They insist that the technological developments of the recent past have made 'meaning' an antiquated concept, because all signs are supposedly exhausted, mere electronic pulses disconnected from any referent. The chief limitation of these critics who are so anxious to demonize television is that they insist on making dire predictions about the devastating effects of this technological explosion (which alters everything, everywhere, in the same way), but they fail to recognize that the rate of absorption of those technological changes has increased commensurately. The medium may indeed be the message, but twenty minutes into the future the technological novelty is already in the process of being absorbed. In the same way that a figure of speech enjoys a certain novelty at its initial appearance but then begins to become absorbed into the category of the already familiar, the 'figures of technology' that produce an initial disorientation are quickly made manageable (*secondarized*) through different strategies of absorption as they are worked over by popular texts and popular audiences. This absorption/secondarization process involves the manipulation of the array by texts operating within it – television programs (as well as rock songs, films, bestsellers, and so forth) that demonstrate an increasingly sophisticated knowledge of the conditions of their production, circulation, and eventual reception.

[...]

IRONY, INTERTEXTUALITY, AND HYPERCONSCIOUSNESS

The all-pervasiveness of different strategies of rearticulation and appropriation is one of the most widely discussed features of postmodern cultural production. Umberto Eco has argued that this ironic articulation of the 'already said' is the distinguishing feature of postmodern communication. In his often-quoted example, he insists that we can no longer make innocent statements. A lover cannot tell his beloved, 'I love you madly,' because it would very probably produce only a laugh. But if he wants to make such a declaration of love, he could say, 'As Barbara Cartland would put it, "I love you madly."' The latter indicates a mutual awareness of the 'already said,' a mutual delight in ironically manipulating it for one's own purposes.[3] This emphasis on irony is often written off as mere 'camp' recycling, but such a view fails to account for the diversity of possible strategies of rearticulation, which range from the simple revivalism found in the buildings of Robert Stern, the interior design collections of Ralph Lauren, or the clothing of Laura Ashley to the more explicitly critical reworking of the 'already said' in films like *Thelma and Louise*, the photographs of Barbara Kruger, or the radicalized cover versions of pop standards by the Sex Pistols or The Clash, in which the past is not just accessed but 'hijacked,' given an entirely different cultural significance than the antecedent text had when it first appeared. What is postmodern in all of this is the simultaneity of these competing forms of rearticulation – the 'already said' is being constantly recirculated, but from very different perspectives ranging from nostalgic reverence to vehement attack or a mixture of these strategies. Linda Hutcheon argues very convincingly that what distinguishes postmodern rearticulations of the past is their ambivalent relationship to the antecedent text, a recognition of the power of certain texts to capture the imagination, but at the same time a recognition of their ideological or stylistic limitations (this ambivalent parody will be discussed in more detail below).[4]

There is no other medium in which the force of the 'already said' is quite so visible as in television, primarily because the already said is the 'still being said.' Television programming since the fifties has depended on the recycling of Hollywood films and the syndication of past prime-time programs. The proliferation of cable channels that re-present programs from the past four decades of television history marks the logical extension of this process, in which the various pasts and presents of television now air simultaneously. Television programming as accessing of the accumulated past of popular culture ranges from K-Tel offers for old *Honeymooners* and *I Love Lucy* episodes to the explicitly parodic demolitions of television programs to be found on *In Living Color David Letterman*, and *Saturday Night Live*. This diversity in the forms and motivations of televisual rearticulation is even more apparent in the simultaneous but conflictive 're-presentations' of early sitcoms on rival cable networks. The Christian Broadcasting Network and Nickelodeon both broadcast series from the late fifties and early sixties, but whereas the former presents these series as a model for family entertainment the way it used to be, the latter offers them as fun for the contemporary family, 'camped up' with parodic voice-overs, super-graphics, and reediting designed to deride their quaint vision of American family life, which we all know never really existed even 'back then.'

The foregrounding of intertextual references has become a marker of 'quality television' (for example, prime-time network programs like *Hill Street Blues* and *St. Elsewhere*, which reflect a more sophisticated 'cinematic style,' feature ensemble casts, etc.) as well. Jane Feuer has traced this self-conscious intertextuality as it developed in the MTM style, but more recently, as 'quality television' has developed across production companies and networks, the explicit referencing has played a vital role in situating a given program in relation to other forms of quality and nonquality programs.[5] During the 1990 fall season, for example, Michael and Hope of ABC's *thirtysomething* referred to watching *L.A. Law*, while on NBC's *L.A. Law*, attorney Anne Kelsey spoke of wanting to get home and watch *thirtysomething* because it was 'responsible television.'

This sort of referencing-as-positioning is not restricted to quality TV. On a recent episode of *Knots Landing* (a nighttime soap that airs opposite *L.A. Law* and makes no claims whatsoever to be quality television), two minor characters argue about their favorite TV programs. One states that he has to turn down a dinner invitation because 'I forgot to set my VCR. I gotta see what Corbin Bernsen is wearing tonight.' When his friend states that he 'never watches that show' because he's a 'newshound,' the *L.A. Law* fan says derisively, 'News my foot. You're crazy about Diane Sawyer.' When his colleague protests that 'she's very intelligent,' his friend responds, 'Right, you're in love with her mind.' The referencing here, within the context of an evening soap, presupposes three important factors: (1) that viewers will possess a televisual literacy developed enough to recognize programs from the actors' names and that they will know the television schedule well enough to appreciate the reference to the programs that air opposite *Knots Landing* on the two other major networks (*L.A. Law* and *Prime Time Live*); (2) that VCR time-shifting is now commonplace, especially for dedicated viewers of *L.A. Law* but also for those fans who exist within the fictional world of programs that air on competing channels; and (3) that the 'irresponsible,' nonquality program informs us why viewers *really* like quality television – for the wardrobes and the sexiness of the stars involved, which, as the characters of *Knots Landing* know, constitute the *real* pleasure of the televisual text.

These intertextual references are emblematic of the *hyperconsciousness* of postmodern popular culture: a hyperawareness on the part of the text itself of its cultural status, function, and history, as well as of the conditions of its circulation and reception. Hyperconsciousness involves a different sort of self-reflexivity than that commonly associated with modernist texts. Highly self-conscious forms of appropriation and rearticulation have been used by postmodern painters, photographers, and performance artists (David Salle, Cindy Sherman, Laurie Anderson, and others), and their work has enjoyed a great deal of critical attention. In the 'metapop' texts that we now find on television, on newsstands, on the radio, or on grocery store book racks, we encounter, not avant-gardists who give 'genuine' significance to the merely mass cultural, but a hyperconscious rearticulation of media culture by media culture.[6]

The self-reflexivity of these popular texts of the later eighties and early nineties does not revolve around the problems of self-expression experienced by the anguished creative artist so ubiquitous in modernism but instead focuses on antecedent and competing programs, on the ways television programs circulate and are given meaning by viewers, and on the nature of televisual popularity. A paradigmatic example of this is the opening scene of *The Simpson's Thanksgiving Special* (1990), in which Bart and his father, Homer, are watching television in their living room on Thanksgiving morning. *The Simpsons*, as a concept, is already a mean-spirited parody of the traditional family sitcom, and this particular scene adds an attack on the imbecilic chatter of 'color commentators.' But the scene goes beyond simple parody. As they watch the Thanksgiving Day parade, Bart keeps asking Homer to identify the balloon float characters, complaining that they could use some characters that 'were made in the last fifty years.' His father tells him that the parade is a tradition, that if 'you start building a balloon for every flash-in-the-pan cartoon character, you'll turn the parade into a farce.' At this point the television-within-the-television depicts a Bart Simpson balloon floating by while the 'real' Bart Simpson looks on. Thus Bart watches himself as a popular phenomenon on television. *The Simpsons* television program thereby acknowledges its own characters' status as popular icons whose circulation and reception are worked back into the 'text' itself.

SUBJECTIVITY, BRICOLAGE, AND ECLECTICISM

The 'Bart watches Bart' example may be emblematic of a postmodern textuality, but what are the effects of this hyperconscious irony on television viewers? Is its ultimate effect emancipatory, leading to a recognition that television's representations are social constructions rather than value-neutral reflections of the 'real' world? Or does this irony produce a disempowering apathy, in which no image is taken at all seriously? John Caughie has described this problem very effectively:

The argument, then, is that television produces the conditions of an ironic knowingness, at least as a possibility ... [which] may offer a way of thinking subjectivity free of subjection. ... Most of all, it opens identity to diversity, and escapes the notion of cultural identity as a fixed volume. ... But if it does all this, it does not do it in that utopia of guaranteed resistance which assumes the progressiveness of naturally oppositional readers who will get it right in the end. It does it, rather, with terms hung in suspension ... tactics of empowerment, games of subordination with neither term fixed in advance.[7]

The crux of the matter here is the notion of the subject that is presupposed. Caughie's insightful point about irony vis-à-vis subjectivity suggests that television viewers are individual subjects neither completely programmed by what they are watching nor completely free to choose as self-determining individuals, captains of their fates, masters of their souls.[8] One of the significant developments in postmodern theory (put forward in an increasing number of disciplines) is the recognition that a new theory of the subject must be developed, one that can avoid the deterministic conception of the individual as programmable android without resurrecting a romantic 'Self' that operates as a free agent, unfettered and uninfluenced by ideology.

[...]

The concept of the postmodern subject as multiple and contradictory, acted upon but also acting upon, has also led to reconsideration of the 'effect' that popular culture, most especially television, has on its viewers. The *hypodermic* model of media effects (in which mass media allegedly 'injects' values directly into passive viewers) has been challenged by John Fiske, Ien Ang, and others who share a cultural studies perspective.[9] Many of them use de Certeau's concept of 'poaching' to characterize audiences' skillful abduction of televisual texts, focusing on the ways in which audiences make the meanings they want or need out of television programs.[10] It is at this point that British cultural studies begins to share a number of concerns with postmodern theory per se, positing a subject who operates as a technologically sophisticated *bricoleur*, appropriating and recombining according to personal need. The term *bricolage*, developed by anthropologists to describe the ways primitive tribespeople piece together a meaningful cosmogony (or simply a way of operating) out of random elements they encounter in their day-to-day lives, has recently been applied to the behavior of individuals in contemporary media cultures. The culturalist and postmodernist positions differ, however, in regard to 'mass culture.' The former presupposes that mass culture may still be pernicious and homogeneous, but that it may be transformed into something resembling a genuine folk culture at the moment of reception because viewers tend to disregard the intended effects of television and take from it what best fits into their lives. This is a very attractive political position in that it allows for the continued demonization of capitalism and mass culture while it celebrates the resourcefulness of ordinary people. However, it fails to recognize the eclecticism of postmodern cultural *production*.

[...]

The eclecticism associated with postmodernism takes on a more complicated dimension in regard to television. Individual programs like *Pee-Wee's Play House*, *Max Headroom*, and *Twin Peaks* are as radically eclectic in their use of diverse stylistic conventions as any postmodern building. Furthermore, the eclecticism of television textuality operates on a technological/institutional level as well because it has been institutionalized by cable television and the VCR, which together produce infinite programming variations. Postmodernist eclecticism might only occasionally be a preconceived design choice in individual programs, but it is built into the technologies of media-sophisticated societies. Thus television, like the postmodern subject, must be conceived as a *site* – an intersection of multiple, conflicting cultural messages. Only by recognizing this interdependency of *bricolage* and eclecticism can we come to appreciate the profound changes in the relationship of reception and production in postmodern cultures. Not only has reception become another form of meaning production, but production has increasingly become a form of reception as it rearticulates antecedent and competing forms of representation.

COMMODIFICATION, POLITICS, VALUE

Another major concern of postmodern cultural analysis has been the impact of consumerism on social life. Fredric Jameson argues that postmodernism is best understood as the end result of capitalism's relentless commodification of all phases of everyday existence. He sees pop culture's radical eclecticism as mere 'cannibalization' of the past and as 'sheer heterogeneity' without 'decidable' effects.[11] For Jameson, all such cultural activity is driven by the logic of 'late' capitalism, which endlessly develops new markets that it must neutralize politically by constructing a vision of success and personal happiness, expressible solely through the acquisition of commodities.

The relevance of Jameson's work for television studies has already been explored by a number of critics, not surprising given the advertiser-driven nature of the medium in the United States, where commercials not only interrupt programs but have actually emerged as a form of programming. The blurring of the distinction between programs and commercials has become even greater with the development of 'infomercials,' shopping channels, product lines generated by Saturday morning cartoons (as well as by evening soaps like *Dynasty*), and so on. If television is defined by its semiotic complexity, its intertextuality, and its eclecticism, it is also just as surely defined by its all-pervasive appeals to consumerism.

The problem for television studies, as it tries to come to terms with postmodernism, is how to reconcile the semiotic and economic dimensions of television. Stressing the semiotic to the exclusion of the economic produces only a formalist game of 'let's count the intertexts,' but privileging the economic to the point that semiotic complexity is reduced to a limited set of moves allowed by a master system is just as simplistic. The attempt to turn television into a master system operating according to a single logic is a fundamentally nostalgic perspective; the culture of the 1990s, though judged to be the sheer noise of late capitalism, is nevertheless expected to operate according to nineteenth-century models of culture as homogeneous totality.

Making postmodernism coterminous with late capitalism offers a theoretical neatness by providing an all-purpose, master explanation: postmodern culture is a symptom of more fundamental economic and political trends. But this position is fraught with a number of problems. The limitations of this view of postmodernism become especially apparent in Jameson's notion of 'cognitive mapping.'[12] He argues that a new aesthetics that will make sense of multi-national capitalism has yet to emerge and that there exists as yet no way of mapping the chaotic spaces of postmodern cultures. But the 'map' he hopes will be drawn will not be acceptable to him unless it envisions this space according to the contours of traditional Marxist theory.[13] Jameson doesn't entertain the notion that mere mass culture may itself provide a mapping function or that television is not just a chaotic terrain in need of mapping but is itself a proliferation of maps. Lifetime, MTV, Black Entertainment Television, and the Family Channel all envision contemporary cultural life from specific generational, racial, and gendered perspectives. Taken together, they don't coalesce into one big picture but rather a composite of overlapping views that visualize the terrain of contemporary life in reference to its specific uses. The desire to formulate one master map, despite the multiple ways that the terrain can be envisioned and put to use by individual subjects as *bricoleurs*, exposes not just the limitations of traditional Marxist paradigms, but also the need to develop far more sophisticated forms of materialist analysis that recognize the multiple uses and effects of consumerism.[14]

[...]

Within this politics of diversity and difference, 'value' is not abandoned – only absolute 'truth values,' or what Herrnstein Smith has called the automatic 'axiomatics' of traditional critical theory that relied on transcendent, universal qualities as proof or verification for all evaluation. She insists that both value and evaluation are radically contingent. 'That which we call "value" may be seen neither as an inherent property of objects, nor an arbitrary projection of subjects but, rather, as the product of the dynamics of some economy or, indeed, of any number of economies (that is, systems of apportionment and circulation of "goods") in relation to a shifting state, of which an object or entity will have a different (shifting) value.'[15]

The ramifications of this point for television study – specifically for developing a theory of postmodern television – are far reaching, because Smith argues that we need to continue to debate the value of any given text but also insists on the contingent nature of those judgements. Evaluation always depends on criteria that are culturally determined and therefore culturally specific rather than transcendent. This is a vitally important point, because it allows for an analysis of television that recognizes the variable nature of televisual signs. Their value cannot be explained in reference to one logic but will be channel-, program-, and audience-sensitive. Even more important, by focusing on the dynamics of the economies that determine these shifting values, we can begin to understand the interconnectedness of the semiotic and the economic dimensions of postmodern television.

NOTES

1. Jonathan Arac, *Critical Genealogies* (New York: Columbia University Press, 1987), p. 284.
2. Allan Bloom, *The Closing of the American Mind* (New York: Simon and Schuster, 1987); Jean-Louis Baudrillard, 'The Implosion of Meaning in the Media and the Information of the Social in the Masses', in *Myths of Information: Technology and Post-Industrial Culture*, ed. Kathleen Woodward (Madison, Wis.: Coda Press, 1980), pp. 137–48.
3. Umberto Eco, postscript to *The Name of the Rose* (New York: Harcourt Brace Jovanovich, 1984).
4. Linda Hutcheon, 'The Politics of Postmodernism, Parody, and History', *Cultural Critique 5* (Winter 1986–87): 179–207.
5. Jane Feuer, 'The MTM Style', in *MTM: 'Quality Television'*, ed. Jane Feuer, Paul Kerr, and Tise Vahimagi (London: British Film Institute, 1984), pp. 32–60.
6. Jim Collins, 'Appropriating Like *Krazy*: From Pop Art to Meta-Pop', in *Modernity and Mass Culture*, ed. James Naremore and Patrick Brantlinger (Bloomington: Indiana University Press, 1991), pp. 203–23.
7. John Caughie, 'Playing at Being American: Game and Tactics', in *Logics of Television: Essays in Cultural Criticism*, ed. Patricia Mellencamp (Bloomington: Indiana University Press, 1990), pp. 54–55.
8. For a detailed analysis of the changes in theories of the subject, see Paul Smith, *Discerning the Subject* (Minneapolis: University of Minnesota Press, 1988).
9. John Fiske, 'Popular Discrimination', in *Modernity and Mass Culture*, ed. James Naremore and Patrick Brantlinger (Bloomington: Indiana University Press, 1991), pp. 103–16; Ien Ang, *Watching 'Dallas': Soap Opera and the Melodramatic Imagination*, trans. Della Couling (London: Methuen, 1985).
10. Michel de Certeau, *The Practice of Everyday Life* (Berkeley: University of California Press, 1984).
11. See Fredric Jameson, 'Postmodernism, or the Cultural Logic of Late Capitalism', *New Left Review* 146 (July/August 1984), and 'Postmodernism and Consumer Society', in *The Anti-Aesthetic: Essays on Postmodern Culture*, ed. Hal Foster (Port Townsend, Wash.: Bay Press, 1983), pp. 111–25.
12. Jameson, 'Cognitive Mapping', in *Marxism and the Interpretation of Culture*, ed. Cary Nelson and Lawrence Grossberg (Urbana: University of Illinois Press, 1988), pp. 347–57.
13. Raymond Williams, *Culture and Society, 1780–1950* (New York: Columbia University Press, 1983).
14. See especially Hilary Radner, *Shopping Around: Feminine Culture and the Will to Pleasure* (New York: Routledge, 1992).
15. Barbara Herrnstein Smith, 'Value without Truth Value', in *Life after Postmodernism*, ed. John Fekete (New York: St. Martin's Press, 1987), p. 1.

30

POSTMODERNISM AND POPULAR CULTURE

Angela McRobbie

THE 'SOWETO DASH'

Rather than starting with a definition of postmodernism as referring either to a condition of contemporary life, or a textual, aesthetic practice, I want to begin by suggesting that the recent debates on postmodernism possess both a positive attraction and a usefulness to the analyst of popular culture. This is because they offer a wider, and more dynamic, understanding of contemporary representation than other accounts to date. Unlike the various strands of structuralist criticism, postmodernism considers images as they relate to and across each other. Postmodernism deflects attention away from the singular scrutinizing gaze of the semiologist, and asks that this be replaced by a multiplicity of fragmented, and frequently interrupted, 'looks'.

The exemplary text or the single, richly coded, image, gives way to the textual *thickness* and the visual *density* of everyday life, as though the slow, even languid 'look' of the semiologist is, by the 1980s, out of tempo with the times. The field of postmodernism certainly expresses a frustration, not merely with this seemingly languid pace, but with its increasing inability to make tangible connections between the general conditions of life today and the practice of cultural analysis.

Structuralism has also replaced old orthodoxies with new ones. This is apparent in its re-reading of texts highly placed within an already existing literary or aesthetic hierarchy. Elsewhere it constructs a new hierarchy, with

From ICA Documents 4: *Postmodernism* (1986) pp. 54–8.

Hollywood classics at the top, followed by selected advertising images, and girls' and women's magazines rounding it off. Other forms of representation, particularly music and dance, are missing altogether. Andreas Huyssen[1] in his recent introduction to postmodernism draws attention to this 'high' structuralist preference for the works of high modernism especially the writing of James Joyce or Mallarmé:

> There is no doubt that center stage in critical theory is held by the classical modernists: Flaubert ... in Barthes; ... Mallarmé and Artaud in Derrida; Magritte ... in Foucault; ... Joyce and Artaud in Kristeva ... and so on *ad infinitum*.

He argues that this reproduces unhelpfully the old distinction between the high arts and the 'low', less serious, popular arts. He goes on to comment,

> Pop in the broadest sense was the context in which a notion of the postmodern first took shape, and ... the most significant trends within postmodernism have challenged modernism's relentless hostility to mass culture.

High theory was simply not equipped to deal with multi-layered pop. Nor did it ever show much enthusiasm about this set of forms, perhaps because pop has never signified within one discrete discourse, but instead combines images with performance, music with film, or video, and pin ups with the magazine form itself. As a *Guardian* journalist recently put it, 'Rock and pop performers today have to speak in multi-media tongues' (3.1.86).

With the exception of Barthes, 'heavy weight' criticism has been focused towards memorable texts, while lightweight cultural analysis is given over to the more forgettable images of everyday life. And the 'purity' of the about-to-be-decoded-image is reflected in the pivotal position occupied by semiology and structuralist criticism in media courses up and down the country. Despite gestures towards intertextuality and interdisciplinarity, this centrality given to *the structualisms* in effect squeezes all the other complex relations which locate the text, or the image, and allow it to produce meaning, out of the picture. These relations include those which mark out its physical place within the world of commodities, its sequencing, and its audience as well as consumers. Such issues are frequently relegated, with some disregard, to the realm of sociology or 'empiricism' as though these were the same thing. And while critics argue that this outside reality is really nothing more than a series of other texts, they are in the meantime happy to treat questions about consumers, readers, audience, and viewers, as intrinsically uninteresting, as though this entails hanging about street corners with a questionnaire and clipboard.

Postmodernism allows what were respectable sociological issues to reappear on the intellectual agenda. It implicitly challenges the narrowness of structuralist vision, by taking the deep interrogation of every breathing aspect of lived experience by media imagery as a starting point. So extensive and inescapable is this process that it becomes conceptually impossible to privilege one simple moment.

[. . .]

Postmodernism has entered into a more diverse number of vocabularies more quickly than most other intellectual categories. It has spread outwards from the realms of art history into political theory and onto the pages of youth culture magazines, record sleeves, and the fashion pages of *Vogue*. This seems to me to indicate something more than the mere vagaries of taste. More also, than the old Marcusian notion of recuperation, where a radical concept which once had purchase, rapidly becomes a commodity, and in the process is washed, laundered, and left out to dry.

[. . .]

Postmodernism certainly appeared in the UK like a breath of fresh air. It captured in a word, a multitude of experiences, particularly what Baudrillard[2] has called the 'instantaneity of communication'. This refers to the incursion of imagery and communication into those spaces that once were private – where the psyche previously had the chance to at least explore the 'other', to explore, for example, alienation. Baudrillard claims this space now to be penetrated by the predatory and globally colonialist media. But as the frontiers of the self are effaced and transformed, so too are the boundaries which mark out separate discourses and separate politics. Baudrillard interprets the new associative possibilities thrown up by 'instantaneity' gloomily. 'Everything is exposed to the harsh and inexorable light of information and communication', which in turn generates only an 'ecstasy of communication' . . . But need Baudrillard be quite so pessimistic? Why must this speeding-up process, this intensification or exchange be greeted with such foreboding?

The remainder of this paper will be given over to arguing the case for postmodernism. It will suggest that the frenzied expansion of the mass media has political consequences which are not so wholly negative. This becomes most apparent when we look at representations of the Third World. No longer can this be confined to the realist documentary, or the exotic televisual voyage. The Third World refuses now, to 'us', in the West, to be reassuringly out of sight. It is as adept at using the global media as the old colonialist powers. Equally the 'we' of the British nation no longer possesses any reliable reality. That spurious unity has been decisively shattered. New alliances and solidarities emerge from within and alongside media imagery. A disenchanted black, inner city population in Britain, can look in an 'ecstasy of communication' as black South Africans use every available resource at hand to put apartheid into crisis. Jokily, and within a kind of postmodern language Dick Hebdige wrote, in *Subculture*,[3] that TV images of Soweto in 1976 taught British youth 'the Soweto dash'. Ten years later this connection has amplified. The image is the trigger and the mechanism for this new identification.

IMPLOSION

Of course it's not quite so simple. The South African government has recently banned journalists from the black townships. And in less politically sensitive arenas, the media continues, relentlessly, to hijack events and offer in their place a series of theatrical spectacles whose points of relevance are only tangentially on what is going on, and whose formal cues came from other, frequently televisual, forms of representation. 1985 was rich in examples. Reagan's illness was relayed to the public, overwhelmingly in the language of soap opera. A *Guardian* correspondent pointed out that nobody would have been convinced if his doctors had not appeared at the press conferences dressed in white coats. A few weeks earlier Shi'ite militiamen took over a TWA airline office in Athens. In what was largely a bid for space on Western prime-time television, the captors could afford to appear smiling and jubilant as they offered their victims a Lebanese banquet, against a backdrop of random gunfire at the ceiling, before packing them off to the United States.

This easing out of the real in favour of its most appropriate representation makes it more difficult to talk about the media and society today. It creates even greater difficulties in assessing the relationship between images, or between popular cultural forms, and their consumers. The consciousness industries have changed remarkably over the last ten years, but so have the outlook and the expectations of their audiences.

Against a backdrop of severe economic decline, the mass media continues to capture new outlets, creating fresh markets to absorb its hi-tech commodities. Symbolically the image has assumed a contemporary dominance. It is no longer possible to talk about the image and reality, media and society. Each has become so deeply intertwined that it is difficult to draw the line between the two. Instead of referring to the real world, much media output devotes itself to referring to other images, other narratives. Self-referentiality is all-embracing, although it is rarely taken account of. The Italian critic and writer, Umberto Eco, recently contrasted what TV was (paleo-TV), with what it now is, (neo-TV). 'Its prime characteristic is that it talks less and less about the external world. Whereas paleo-television talked about the external world, or pretended to, neo-television talks about itself and about the contacts it establishes with its own public.[4]

Self-referentiality occurs within and across different media forms. One TV programme might be devoted to the production of another (Paul Gambaccini 'on' the Tube), just as television films based on the making of other large-scale cinema productions are becoming increasingly common. There is a similar dependency for material and content, as well as a relatively recent redefinition of what is interesting, and what readers and viewers want, in the print media's use of *televisual stories*. *The Face* magazine ran a piece on The Tube, and more recently on Michelle, the pregnant schoolgirl, in EastEnders ... The *NME* carried a major feature on Brookside, and *City Limits* sent two journalists to the Coronation Street set, for a week. It's not so much that fiction is being mistaken for fact; more that one set of textual practices (in this case British soap) has become the reference point for another (reading the newspaper or glancing at a headline).

Media interdependency is both an economic and a cultural imperative. Children's TV on a Saturday morning revolves entirely around the pop music industry, offering an exclusive showcase for new 'promo' videos. The contents of these programmes are orchestrated around all the familiar pop business, phone-in to the stars, interviews, the new single, the talent competition for young hopefuls. This shows the feeding-off effect between mass media today. Where once the middle class world of Blue Peter documented children's initiatives for charity, now Capital, in the form of culture and visual communications, penetrates further into the youth market. In the *classless* world of these programmes this means pushing back the frontiers of young people as consumers by transforming children and even toddlers into fans and thus part of the record-buying public.

The implications of this endless cross-referencing are extensive. They create an ever-increasing, but less diverse verbal and visual landscape. It is these recurring fictions, and the characters who inhabit them which feed into the field of popular knowledge, and which in turn constitute a large part of popular culture. It would be difficult not to know about Victoria Principal, it would be impossible not to know about Dallas.

Texts have always alluded to or connected with others. Simone De Beauvoir's *Memoirs of a Dutiful Daughter* gives up many pages to all the other books she read during her childhood, adolescence and early adult years.[5] Indeed this critical bibliography forms a major strand of the work. The difference now is that the process is less restricted to literature, more widespread, and most apparent in the commercial mass media where there are more spaces to be filled. And such an opening up doesn't necessarily mean an extension of rights of access, only rights of consumption. More often it means a form of cosy, mutual congratulatory, cross-referencing and repetition. (Wogan in Denver, Clive James in Dallas.) Baudrillard greets these recent changes with some cynicism. He claims that more media offers less meaning in the guise of more information: 'All secrets, spaces and scenes abolished in a single dimension of information'.[6] Eco follows this when he describes the scrambling effect of multi-channel choice on TV. 'Switching channels reflects the brevity and speed of other visual forms. Like flicking through a magazine, or driving past a billboard. This means that "our" TV evenings no longer tell us stories, it is all a trailer!'[7]

Images push their way into the fabric of our social lives. They enter into how we look, what we earn, and they are still with us when we worry about bills, housing and bringing up children. They compete for attention through shock tactics, reassurance, sex, mystery and by inviting viewers to participate in series of visual puzzles. Billboard advertisements showing an image without a code, impose themselves, infuriatingly, on the most recalcitrant passer-by.

[...]

And, if media forms are so inescapable 'if unreality is now within everyone's grasp' (Eco),[8] then there is no reason to assume that the consumption of pastiche, parody or high camp is, by definition, without subversive or critical potential. Glamour, glitter, and gloss, should not so easily be relegated to the sphere of the insistently apolitical. For the left, necessarily committed to endorsing the real and the material conditions of peoples' lives, there remains still an (understandable) stiffness about Neil Kinnock's appearance in a Tracy Ullman video. This need not be the case.

If, as Jameson suggests, life has been dramatised to the level of soap, if love is always like a *Jackie* story, then yes, the sharp distinction between real life and fictional forms must give way to a deep intermingling, unmeasurable and so far captured most precisely in fictive or cinematic forms. Scorsese's *King of Comedy* traced this 'overdetermination by the image', as did Woody Allen's *Stardust Memories*, as well as his more recent *Zelig* and *The Purple Rose of Cairo*. But Gore Vidal's novel *Duluth* outstrips all of these.[9] It is a model of postmodern writing. Gore Vidal has his tongue firmly in his cheek. *Duluth* is a witty multi-layered fiction which moves from the town of the title, to the soap series based on the place, outwards to the novel of the soap, backwards into the historical romances favoured by the town's top woman cop, and forwards into a science fiction setting where Roland Barthes makes a guest appearance. Obligingly Vidal ends the novel by handing over to a word processor.

All of this comes close to what Baudrillard infuriatingly calls implosion.[10] It's a vague but appropriate term. It implies an outburst of energy which is nonetheless controlled and inclining inwards. Baudrillard, Eco and Jameson all see this as a totalising and all-immersing process. But none of them consider the new associations and resistances which have come into prominence by way of these processes in the last fifteen years. Many of these share more in common with the shattered energy of implosion, with Jameson's fragmented schizo-phrenic consciousness, than with the great narratives of the old left:

> It was especially the art, writing, film-making and criticism of women and minority artists, with their recuperation of buried and mutilated traditions, their emphasis on exploring forms of gender- and race-based subjectivity in aesthetic productions and experiences, and their refusal to be limited to standard canonizations, which added a whole new dimen-sion to the critique of high modernism and to the emergence of alter-native forms of culture.[11]

In the British context one would want to append to this formidable production not just the proliferation of pop culture and the challenge it has mounted to the mainstream arts, but also the involvement of youth in the creation of an egalitarian avant-garde. Of course this is no longer an avant-garde proper, since the privileging of the forms have been abandoned in favour of a cross referencing between forms, and notably between pop music and 'art', between aesthetics and commerce, between commitment and the need to make a living. This leads directly to a further failing in Jameson's account. There is no recognition that those elements contained within his diagnosis of postmodernism – including pastiche, the ransacking and recycling of culture, the direct invocation to other texts and other images – can create a vibrant critique rather than an inward-looking, second-hand aesthetic. What else has black urban culture in the last few years been, but an assertive re-assembling of bits and pieces, 'whatever comes to hand', noises, debris, technology, tape, image, rapping, scratching, and other hand me downs? Black urban music has always thrived on fake, forged identities, creating a façade of grand-sounding titles which reflect both the 'otherness' of black culture, the extent to which it is outside that which is legitimate, and the way in which white society has condemned it to be nameless. Who, after all, is Grandmaster Flash or Melle Mel? Or who was Sly and the Family Stone? Who mixed the speech by Malcolm X onto a haunting disco funk backing track? Reggae also parodies this enforced namelessness. Many of its best known musicians suggest a deep irony in their stagenames: Clint Eastwood, Charlie Chaplin, and so on.

In America graffiti remains the best example of fleeting, obsolescent urban aesthetics. It gives its creators fame once they get into the galleries but otherwise only faint notoriety:

> It is a cultural identity which half mocks, half celebrates, the excesses of mainstream white culture. The graffiti painter is the Spiderman of the ghettos, projecting pure fantasy. A terminal vantage point on white consumer culture. Hip hop is a subculture which feeds for its material upon the alien culture which needs make no concession to blacks. The spray paints and comic book images of graffiti painting, to the disco beats and found sounds of rapping, are diverted from their mainstream domestic use and put out on the streets as celebration. For the white middle class kid, the comic heroes occupy a space of boredom. For the black ghetto kid they are transformed by graffiti art into fantastic visions invested with secret meanings.[12]

Alongside these largely male forms, must be placed the writing of black women, the great explosion of the written word which writes a history otherwise condemned to remain only within popular memory. Toni Cade Bambara's[13] prose is closest in rhythm to the jazz sounds of the city. It is breath-taking, agile writing, insisting on the pleasures, the wit and the idiosyncracies of a community more often characterised as monolithic and deprived. All of this is taking place within the cracks of a crumbling culture where progress is in question and society seems to be standing still.

There *is* no going back. For populations transfixed on images which are themselves a reality, there is no return to a mode of representation which politicizes in a kind of straightforward 'worthwhile' way. Dallas is destined to sit alongside images of black revolt. And it is no longer possible, living within postmodernism, to talk about unambiguously negative or positive images. But this need not be seen as the end of the social, or the end of meaning, or for that matter the beginning of the new nihilism. Social agency is employed in the activation of *all* meanings. Audiences or viewers, lookers or users are not simple-minded multitudes. As the media extends its sphere of influence, so also does it come under the critical surveillance *and* usage of its subjects.

The reason why postmodernism appeals to a wider number of young people, and to what might be called the new generation of intellectuals (often black, female, or working class) is that they themselves are experiencing the enforced fragmentation of impermanent work, and low career opportunities. Far from being overwhelmed by media saturation, there is evidence to suggest that these social groups and minorities are putting it to work for them. This alone should prompt the respect and the attention of an older generation who seem at present too eager to embrace a sense of political hopelessness.

NOTES

1. Andreas Huyssen, 'Mapping the Postmodern', *New German Critique* 1984.
2. Jean Baudrillard, 'The Ecstasy of Communication', *Postmodern Culture* ed. Hal Foster [Pluto Press 1985].
3. Dick Hebdige, *Subculture, The Meaning of Style*, Methuen 1979.
4. Umberto Eco, 'A Guide to the Neo Television of the 1980s', *Framework no. 25*.
5. Simone De Beauvoir, *Memoirs of a Dutiful Daughter*, Penguin 1984.
6. Jean Baudrillard see above.
7. Umberto Eco see above.
8. Umberto Eco see above.
9. Gore Vidal, *Duluth*, Heinemann 1983.
10. Jean Baudrillard [*For a Critique of the Political Economy of the Sign*, trans. C. Levin, St. Louis, MO: Telos Press, 1981].
11. Andreas Huyssen see above.
12. Atlanta and Alexander, 'Wild Style ... Graffiti Painting', *ZG no. 6*.
13. Toni Cade Bambara, *Gorilla, My Love*, The Women's Press 1983.

31

REALITY TV AND SOCIAL PERVERSION

Bill Nichols

Isn't it time you felt that way again?
– Saturn car ad

It protects you like a man, treats you like a woman.
– Lady Speed Stick ad

Kill the germs. Keep the kids.
– Liquid Dial ad

Reality TV is to the documentary tradition as sexual 'perversion' was to 'normal' sexuality for Freud. The biological purpose of sexuality – reproduction – is no longer served by perversions that have purposes of their own. Similarly, representations whose purpose is to absorb and neutralize all questions of magnitude no longer serve the ostensible purpose of news: to facilitate collective action based on fresh information. (Perverse purposes need not necessarily be condemned; perversity's willingness to disregard social and moral codes lends it great potential for subversions of all kinds. Each case requires separate assessment. Sexual perversities can have great value for what they reveal, and refuse, of our culture's prohibitions and constraints; the value of the perversity of reality TV may lie in the gleeful abandon with which it mocks, or rejects, civic-mindedness and the positivist social engineering behind it.)

Reality TV extends into the zones that threaten to erupt within network news itself but normally remained repressed. Reality TV anneals the felt gap opened by historical consciousness between representation and referent. Dan

From Nichols, *Blurred Boundaries: Questions of Meaning in Contemporary Culture* (Bloomington: Indiana University Press, 1994) pp. 51–60.

Rather's strangely hallucinatory tour of an Iraqi bunker reveals the symptomatic return of this repressed. Believing himself surrounded by booby traps, in constant bodily peril, Rather acts out a tableau of vicarious concern for American lives that might have been lost. News becomes dramatic spectacle, a simulacrum of eventfulness for which there is no original (this *is* the moment of discovery, and danger, such as it is, for Rather).[1]

> It's sorta like havin' a seat in the front row of life.
> — Patrol car officer, speaking of his job, *Top Cops*

> While most of the outrageous events the realities and tabs are concerned with actually happen, they fortunately happen somewhere else, to someone else. And that allows us to be discrete voyeurs, occupying front-row seats for these displays of human folly.
> — Van Gordon Sauter, 'Rating the Reality Shows,' *TV Guide*

Reality TV's perverse kinship with traditional documentary film, network newscasting, and ethnographic film lies in its ability to absorb the referent. The digestive enzymes of reality TV (its distracting quality and spectacle, its dramatic story lines and self-perpetuation) break the referent down into palatable confections that do not represent an absent referent so much as cannibalize and assimilate it into a different type of substance. The historical world becomes reduced to a set of simulations and idle talk (Heidegger's *gerede*). The webs of signification we build and in which we act pass into fields of simulation that absorb us but exclude our action. Referentiality dissolves in the nonbeing and nothingness of TV.

What characterizes reality TV most broadly is the production of a feeling tone in the viewer similar to that produced by an exceptional acrobatic feat, superb magic tricks, or the sudden appearance of a full-scale helicopter thirty feet above the stage in *Miss Saigon*: 'Isn't that amazing!'

> Now, how are they going to get the wife over here, because she can't swim.
> — Elderly husband of a woman still trapped in her car by a torrential flood in the Arizona desert, *Code 3*

A reality TV special, *Miracles and Other Wonders* (June 5, 1992), reported the story of Barney, a black truck driver, who played good samaritan by deviating from his route to answer a distress call from a driver suffering a heart attack. Voice-over comments by the host accompany a reconstruction of the events, like the traditional *benshi* presenter of Japanese silent films. Barney finds the man and radios for paramedics who are able to stabilize the man and get him to a hospital where he recovers. The oddest part of the story, though, is that when they examine the man's car, they see no trace of the CB radio he would have needed in order to contact truck driver Barney.

This apparent act of telepathy would have been amazing enough, but several years later Barney succumbs to a heart attack of his own while trekking through remote country on a fishing trip. Friends manage to get him to a nearby Indian village but despair that the nurse who only visits once a month will not be there. Miraculously, she is. Even more miraculously, she is not alone. Her father, a cardiologist, happens to accompany her. The man steps into the room where Barney rests and, lo and behold, it is the very man Barney saved all those years before! His quick action spares Barney from certain death.

Isn't that amazing!

> When we return a woman needs your help to find her long-lost twin brother.
>
> *– Unsolved Mysteries*

This ebb and flow of detached consumption, distracted viewing, and episodic amazement exists in a time and space outside history, outside the realm in which physical, bodily engagement marks our existential commitment to a project and its realization. 'Project' refers to Sartre's idea of an engaged, committed life in the world, and in the body, where every 'experience' remains charged with importance in this larger context – exactly what reality TV denies or perverts. Here we have disembodied but visceral experience, a freewheeling zone in which the same set of emotional responses recycle with gradually diminishing force until the next raise of the ante in the production of spectacle.

These responses are keyed to a conventional story format. It is something like a perversely exhibitionistic version of the melodramatic imagination: provide a 'hook' by underlining an important aspect of the case – its scale, severity, uniqueness, or consequences; offer a dab of location realism; sketch in characters quickly; dramatize sensational aspects of the case – usually aspects of intense threat to human life and bodily integrity; move swiftly to an emotional climax; and urge a specific response – grief, alarm, fear, consolation, shock. Conclude the episode with a resonant moment and perhaps a pause for affective response to the marvelous and terrifying, the challenging and remarkable, the extraordinary and corrupt.

In a phrase, 'Isn't that amazing!'[2]

A chronicle of contingent, futureless moments strung together in a protracted morality play produces an entire telescape that does not so much screen us off from reality, or refer us back to it, as beam us aboard a tele-visual simulation. Our subjectivity streams toward the videoscreen that welcomes us to its cyborg circuits of information, noise, feedback, and homeostatic redundancy. Instead of a charge up San Juan Hill (filmed by Vitagraph employees J. Stuart Blackton and Albert E. Smith in 1898), we see a charge into a suspected amphetamine lab (on *Cops* in 1992). The first charge was represented as news, as a report on the finality of the already done (with clear awareness of how public opinion might be shaped by such reports).[3] The second charge, even if news in some sense that is not examined, hangs in suspended animation: every moment, every action, takes shape around the sensation of contingency. We *are* at the moment of filming: 'Nothing has been changed, except, You are there.' Desperate criminals or terrified children may pop into the frame. Shots may be fired or profuse apologies offered. Suspects may submit immediately, in resigned silence or sullen anger, or they may resist, shouting, twisting, flailing at their captors. The stress on a sense that 'You never know what might happen next,' and the parallel admonition to 'Do your part to help bring criminals to justice,' makes this richly constructed sense of contingency a vital element in the pervasive 'now' of tele-reality. Social responsibility dissolves into tele-participation.

Our subjectivity is less that of citizens, social actors or 'people,' than of cyborg collaborators in the construction of a screen-world whose survival hinges on a support system designed to jack us into the surrounding commodity stream, around which an entire aesthetic of simulated pleasure exists. We cannot read these shows as built upon a prefigurative ground that would entail a particular moral or political stance toward the surrounding world.[4] Documentary film had a vested interest in our behavior and disposition beyond the theater. Reality TV has a vested interest in subsuming everything beyond itself into its own support system of circulating exchange values. This circulatory system incorporates the only behavior that really matters: consuming. Careful explication of episodes or shows serves little point at all, at least in the conventional terms of textual analysis and narrative structure. Their meaning comes from elsewhere, from the tele-world to which they belong and in which 'we' are constituted as messages-in-the-circuit of contingency, participation, consumption.

Reality TV, then, plays a complex game. It keeps reality at bay. It succeeds in activating a sense of the historical referent beyond its bounds but also works, constantly, to absorb this referent within a tele-scape of its own devising. Reference to the real no longer has the ring of sobriety that separates it from fiction. Such reference now *is* a fiction. Participation is fully absorptive. The gap is sealed, the referent assimilated. We enter the twilight border zone of virtual reality.

THE TELE-SACRAMENTAL

An odd characteristic of this ebb and flow of sensation and banality is its simulation of a spiritual dimension, well beyond the televangelism that exhorts us to participate by phoning in our donations as the crime shows urge us to call in our tips. Reality TV offers a continuous confessional for the sins of the world. It promises the absolution of sins when we participate in the redemption of everyday life. (Phone in, stay tuned, consume.)

Reality TV tenders charity for 'those poor people' it parades before us as victims of violence and disaster. It urges faith – in the ceaseless baptism in the tele-real for those wishing never to be bored again. It offers hope for a future constantly collapsing into an ever-expanding present.

Now, when her daughter's killer escaped the death sentence, police say she showed up with a loaded gun. More in a moment.

> – *Hard Copy*

Reality TV may not be 'intimately bound up with women's work,' as Tania Modleski argued on behalf of daytime soap operas, but it is bound up with everyday experience.[5] Reality TV shares many of the characteristics Modleski assigns to fictional soap operas such as a participatory quality (connection to versus separation from); a sense that characters or social actors are 'like me' – unlike stars who are of decidedly different status; an emphasis on knowledge of what others might do or think (troubled characters, potential dates, criminals at large) rather than strictly factual 'know how';[6] acceptance and acknowledgment that viewers are subject to 'interruption, distraction, and spasmodic toil';[7] multiple plot lines; and casts of characters who may not know each other. As Modleski argues, soaps have a special meaningfulness for their target audience; they are more than filler, audiovisual wallpaper or escape. So is reality TV.

> All suspects are innocent until proven guilty in a court of law.
>
> – Voice-over introduction, *Cops*

We asked for your help last week and you provided some good leads. If you see Peter Fisher, call 1–800-CRIME-92.

If you see James Ashley, call us right now.

If you think you know who kidnapped little Terry Molini, call our hot line tonight. . . . Please have the courage to call.

> – John Walsh, host, *America's Most Wanted*

'Shrift': the confession of one's sins, especially to a priest in the sacrament of penance (*Websters*).

'Short shrift' originally meant the abbreviated sacrament offered to criminals condemned to die and thence took on the meaning of summary treatment. The tele-confessional offers only short shrift. Now, see this. Act now. Tomorrow is too late.

If you know anything that can help solve this case, call us at 1–800–876–5353.

> – Robert Stack, *Unsolved Mysteries*

Thanks for a nation of finks.

> – William S. Burroughs

Reality TV patrols borders and affirms the law. It also offers a therapeutic ritual for encounter with what lies beyond the law. Reality TV substitutes the confessional dynamics of viewers who phone in their response for the confession that cannot be: the criminal's penance. Neither we nor the tele-confessional itself can grant forgiveness for those whose guilt is not the point. But we can obtain it for ourselves. What Foucault says of confession as a strategy for the regulation of sexuality seems to apply vividly, but not to the suspects whom we encounter as much as to our own vicariously participatory dynamic:

> [The confession] is a ritual that unfolds within a power relationship, for one does not confess without the presence (*or virtual presence*) of a partner who is not simply the interlocutor but the authority who requires the confession, prescribes and appreciates it and intervenes in order to judge, punish, forgive, console, and reconcile; ... and finally, *a ritual in which the expression alone, independently of its external consequences,* produces intrinsic modifications in the person who articulates it: it exonerates, redeems, and purifies him; it unburdens him of his wrongs, liberates him, and promises him salvation.[8] (italics mine)

But the redemptive virtue of our calling, as it were, is not stressed as much as the purgation of fear through the sensation/pleasure of vicariously participating – a simulation of the form of the confessional without its content. Our engagement is less in terms of a civic duty than in terms of the perpetuation of a moment, here and now, when confessional engagement is always possible. We have the pleasure of situating ourselves within a cybernetic feedback loop, absolved, over and over, of all necessity to step beyond it.

The spiritual quality of this appeal permeates a dimensionless surface of sensation. The phatic bond – the open channel, the phone operators 'standing by,' the pleas of 'Don't go away,' the possibility that you may have something to contribute at any moment – offer the sensation of connectedness, of tele-communion. Here is a connectedness that affirms the work patterns and social hierarchies from which we allegedly escape. Vicarious participation as (virtual) confession constructs spirals of power and pleasure:

> The power that lets itself be invaded by the pleasure it is pursuing; and opposite it, power asserting itself in the pleasure of showing off, scandalizing, or resisting. ... These attractions, these evasions, these circular incitements have traced around bodies and sexes, not boundaries not to be crossed, but *perpetual spirals of power and pleasure*.[9]

Reality TV offers communion drawn from atomized, dissociated figures who remain so; a sense of engagement, empathy, charity, and hope built on a disengaged, detached simulation of face-to-face encounter; and a sense of coherence and continuity, if not suspended animation, at a time when ideas and values *feel* worn, ineffective, abused, and bandied about. Here is another form of televisual perversion: the (virtual) conversion of spiritual ritual to social, institutional, hierarchical purposes of its own.

SPECTACLE: GROUNDED SENSATION

Tele-spectacle treats sensations the way an electrical circuit treats shorts: it runs them to ground. The very intensity of feeling, emotion, sensation, and involvement that reality TV produces is also discharged harmlessly within its dramatic envelope of banality. The historical referent, the magnitudes that exceed the text, the narratives that speak of conduct in the world of face-to-face encounter, bodily risk, and ethical engagement ground themselves harmlessly in circuits devoted to an endless flux of the very sensations they run to ground, a perfect balancing act of homeostatic regulation.

Transitions from one attraction to the next are moments of risk. Alternatives to 'Isn't it amazing' threaten to intrude. 'Stay turned,' 'Don't go away,' 'More in a minute.' These endless pleas to maintain the phatic connection between show and viewer while our hosts mysteriously 'go away' underscore the urgency of self-promotion. The pleas implore us to grant these denizens in a box the right to persist, as though it were in our power to annihilate them. And perhaps for a fleeting moment we believe they are at our mercy as we decide whether or not to grant them a continuing presence in the telescape they hope to share with us.

An orchestrated sense of distraction saves the day.

> After an extensive profile of ex-baseball pitcher Denny McLain which touched on his jail term for drug use, his rehabilitation as a radio talk-show host, and the death of his daughter at the hands of a drunk driver, the male co-host intones, speaking to the camera (us), 'No family should endure that much tragedy.'
>
> His female co-host looks toward her partner, pauses, then, looking back toward the camera, responds, 'Now, if you need to try pulling a few rabbits out of the boudoir, try the *magic* of making love.'
>
> A set of ads follow, then a story on Dr. Miriam Stoppard's new book, *The Magic of Sex*. At its conclusion the co-host says, 'Now, when her daughter's killer escaped the death sentence, police say she showed up with a loaded gun. More in a moment' (another set of ads follow).
>
> – *Hard Copy*

The melodramatic novel arose at a time when contending classes, the aristocracy and bourgeoisie, could see their own precarious class situation played out in fiction (for example, the sentimental novels and romantic dramas of the eighteenth century that surround the French revolution, such as *Clarissa* and *Nouvelle Héloïse*, *Emilia Galiotti* and *Kabale und Liebe*).[10] Reality TV offers another version of this effort to represent anxieties of social stability and mobility at a time when economic solvency, let alone prosperity, hangs in doubt. The fate of middle-class 'in-betweeners' is uncertain, split as it is between a richer and more insulated upper class and a despondent and more isolated 'underclass.' White-collar, mid-level managers in Ohio may suddenly find their work delegated to a monitoring system and computer network based in Osaka in these days of transnational globalization. Paranoia may be one form of response to a system without a center; in this case, responsibility diffuses into an amorphous, unrepresentable 'they.'[11]

Reality TV, though, stems anxiety less with paranoia than with a schizoid-like detachment from and reconstruction of the 'reality' it re-presents. Beset by dreams of rising and nightmares of falling, plagued by the terror of pillage, plunder, and rape, the 'target' audience for reality TV (white, middle-class consumers with 'disposable' income) attends to a precarious world of random violence and moment-to-moment contingency (as inexplicable to viewers as it was to Tom Brokaw).

> The decimation of the men within the population is quite nearly total. Four of five births in East St. Louis are to single mothers. Where do the men go? Some to prison. Some to the military. Many to an early death. Dozens of men are living in the streets or sleeping in small, isolated camps behind the burnt-out buildings. There are several of these camps out in the muddy stretch there to the left.
> – Safir Ahmed, *St. Louis Post-Dispatch* reporter, quoted in Jonathan Kozol, *Savage Inequalities*

> In 1991, 21,859 white students earned Ph.D. degrees. In the same year, 933 black students earned Ph.D.s, the first year the percentage of black students earning doctorates had increased in thirteen years.
> – *S.F. Chronicle*, May 4, 1992

The aesthetics of immediacy, conjured in a timeless, spaceless telescape of mediated reality, drowns out the descriptions, like Ahmed's, that urge us to further action beyond exclamation or dismay. An aesthetics of sensation underlies reality TV: Its claims of authenticity, its construction of an endless 'now,' its preference for the chronicle, the random and the unforeseen over the order and cohesion of historiography and the problem-solving discourses of a technocratic order all come at a time when master narratives are a target of disparagement.

Under what conditions does the need to represent contingency and to reject order prevail? One answer is: Contingency looms when an elite, or ruling class, can no longer convince others or itself of its rightful primacy (when hegemony fails). Unpredictability, uncertainty, contingency: they loom as symptoms of incomprehension masquerading behind an aesthetics of sensation when those for whom hegemony has failed demand alternative visions and different futures. These demands cannot be understood in the form they are spoken. 'A riot is the language of the unheard,' asserted Martin Luther King, Jr. Instead these demands register as noise, confusion, chaos. Their negation of what is and their transformative call for what ought to be cannot be contained. They lie beyond the law. Those who speak no longer convince us that they can speak for others; a dumb silence haunts the endless talk. 'We' may be 'the people,' but 'we' are also many, and among that many are diverse cultures and subcultures, affinity groupings and collectivities that lie beyond the pale of reality TV.

An insistence on *differences that make a difference* confounds a sense of hierarchy, undermines standard reference points, and questions received notions of quality or excellence. This diffusion of power and control may seem closely akin to the form of reality TV. But there is a major difference that makes a difference. Reality TV may be as sensational as it wishes, it may be as seemingly decentered, ahistorical, and futureless as it chooses, but, in its present manifestations, it is never critical of the hierarchy perpetuated by its own form or of the power rooted in its dynamic of vicarious (or virtual) participation. Reality TV can be as heterogenous, dispersive, self-conscious, and reflexive as all get out, but it never calls our own position as virtual participant and actual consumer into question. It can tolerate our talking back and mocking its own self-mocking forms but not our refusal to listen to its (empty) talk at all.[12]

We presume immunity from this perversion or dis-ease at some peril, however. There is a risk that the *form* of political struggle may take on qualities akin to those of reality TV. The simple dramatic envelopes placed around localized events that rapidly play themselves out, passing our attention on to their successor, are a dangerous model for political struggle. Such dramatic protest rituals allow for sharply focused moral outrage but often channel it into partial or token victories that leave basic structural conditions unchanged. Celebrating the conviction of two LAPD officers for beating Rodney King 'ends' the story, on the episodic level, but does nothing to address the social conditions that underpin it structurally.

The danger exists that actual struggles will take their cue from the rhythms of reality TV: specific issues and events will become a target of concern or outrage; emotions will wax and wane in keeping with the dramatic curve of televised coverage (Three Mile Island, the Gulf War, Anita Hill and Clarence Thomas, the Panama invasion, 'ethnic cleansing,' Rodney King). Coalitions, support groups, ad hoc committees and rallies will spring up. Collective identities take shape and a common agenda will emerge. But the specific event will eventually reach a point of resolution. The forces once mobilized with fervor and outrage will disperse, potentially available for the next contingency. Such a pattern constructs a reactive politics that may mirror, in disturbing ways, the very forms of absorption and distraction that should be among its primary targets.

Reality TV seeks to reimagine as broad a collectivity or target audience for its sponsors as possible. Hence the tendency to represent experience as spectacle framed only by the banalities of a crude morality play. This form of orchestrated spectacle stands in an antithetical relationship to the project of an existential phenomenology.

REALITY TV AND POLITICAL CONSCIOUSNESS

What reality TV (a phrase that shows no embarrassment at its oxymoronic ring) eliminates is any coming to historical consciousness. By historical consciousness I mean something akin to consciousness raising: an awareness of the present in relation to a past active within it and a future constantly being made in the thick of the present, together with a heightened consciousness of one's relation to others in the common project of the social construction of reality. Such a consciousness holds production and consumption, past and future, in a dialectical relationship. It is what films like *Who Killed Vincent Chin?* and *JFK* may bring into being, and what reality TV perverts. We can turn off the tube to go shopping with no alteration in the distracted state of consciousness a perpetual 'now' encourages.

The founding principle of surrealism – the juxtaposition of incommensurate realities as a jarring act that forces the beholder to see things anew, casting off old habits and assumptions, seeing the strange quality of the familiar in ways that propose alternative values and action – this collage principle becomes absorbed by a telescape from which it cannot escape. There is no 'Aha!' on reality TV. A subsuming 'logic' absorbs all incommensurate juxtapositions. It denies contradiction by refusing to propose any frame from which more local gaps, disturbances, or incompatibilities could be rearranged coherently. Reality TV is one significant piece of a postmodern aesthetic in which what was once incompatible, incommensurate, and contradictory – experiences that compelled us to search for resolution, if not revolution – coexist inside a boundless envelope of presence that banishes historical consciousness from its bounds.

NOTES

1. The appeal of reality TV approximates that of snuff movies, but tailored to the codes of taste required by prime-time broadcasting. The sober-minded trappings of respectable hosts and corporate sponsors, of documentary details and eyewitness reports, successfully deflect anger away from this perverse mode of production itself, allowing reality TV shows to prompt a discharge of anger and amazement at people who can be so extraordinary. 'How could this happen?' we ask of what we see rather than of what produces what we see.

2. This format has a ring of the familiar to it not only as a primal recipe for spectacle or for its own banality. It also cannibalizes many of the melodramatic elements of the morality plays of early films such as Edwin S. Porter's *The Life of an American Fireman* (1902) and *The Great Train Robbery* (1903); Cecil Hepworth's *Rescued by Rover* (1905); or D. W. Griffith's *A Corner in Wheat* (1909), *The Lonely Villa* (1909), *The Lonedale Operator* (1911), and *The Musketeers of Pig Alley* (1912). Characters are quickly sketched out in stereotypic fashion, playing roles that frequently recapitulate those of the nuclear family: strong and benevolent patriarchs, earnest sons and respectful suitors, devious rivals and underhanded villains, honorable but vulnerable women, corrupted women of the night, innocent children, and devoted mothers. Conflict centers around the struggle between good and evil, between virtuous Abels and immoral Cains, in domestic wars on drugs, robbery, theft, kidnapping, murder, gambling, and cruel confidence games.

   Reality TV, however, absorbs melodrama, like documentary, perversely. Its purposes may still allow us to think of these forms in terms of class (they both speak to the precariousness of a world order when perceived from a middle-class point of view), but seldom in terms of domestic drama, the affective domain of women's experience, the maternal dilemma imposed on women of choosing either self-fulfillment or sacrifice, or in terms of the use of stylistic excess to draw our attention to the very force of repression itself.

3. See Raymond Fielding, *The American Newsreel: 1911–1967* (Norman: University of Oklahoma Press, 1972), for a useful account of the blurred boundaries and social purposes of early news reporting. During the Spanish-American War, the Battle of Santiago Bay, for example, was reenacted on movie lots more than once, in one case using cutout photographs of the actual warships.

4. The reference here is to Hayden White's *Metahistory*, in which he argues that historiographic writing undergoes prefiguration as its authors opt for various modes of narrative representation. These choices then establish the moral tone of historical accounts that use reference to 'what happened' in a sort of *trompe d'oeil* move in which it now seems that the historical world itself has authorized this particular tone, this particular understanding of history. Reality TV, since it does not offer narratives on the level of historiography, also does not choose among prefigurative options. Its function and effect rely on its implosive quality: it does not so much account for the historical world as subsume it into a world of its own.

5. Tania Modleski, 'The Rhythms of Reception: Daytime Television and Women's Work', in E. Ann Kaplan, ed., *Regarding Television* (Frederick, MD: University Publications of America, 1983), 74.

6. 'How to' shows are another genre, testing another boundary. They, too, substitute vicarious participation for face-to-face encounter but also allow for viewers to 'follow along,' as they learn how to imitate what their mentors do. Cooking, home renovation, and gardening shows also activate a sense of the referent beyond and promise of easy passage to it. This *ease* of passage (no budget or bills, no issues of ownership or privacy, no questions of crime or poverty intrude) allows for everyday experience to effortlessly transform nature into culture, the raw into the cooked. The patrol-car duties performed elsewhere provide the guarantee for this ease.

7. Modleski, 'The Rhythms of Deception', 71.

8. Michel Foucault, *The History of Sexuality*, vol. 1 (New York: Vintage Books, 1980), 61–62.

9. Foucault, *The History of Sexuality*, 45.

10. For a superb sketch of the backdrop to Hollywood melodrama of the 1940s and '50s in the eighteenth and nineteenth-century novel, see Thomas Elsaesser, 'Tales of Sound and Fury', *Monogram*, no. 4 (1972): 2–15, reprinted in Bill Nichols, ed., *Movies and Methods*, vol. II (Berkeley: University of California Press, 1985).

11. See Fredric Jameson's *The Geopolitical Aesthetic: Cinema and Space in the World System* (Bloomington: Indiana University Press, 1992) for an extended discussion of representations of paranoia, particularly in Western cinema.

12. The variable, historically contingent linkage between subversion and form is made quite succinctly by Judith Butler in an interview: 'There is no easy way to know whether something is subversive. Subversiveness is not something that can be gauged or calculated. In fact, what I mean by subversion are those effects that are incalculable. I do think that for a copy to be subversive of heterosexual hegemony it has to both mime and displace its conventions. And not all miming is displacing.' Interview with Liz Kotz, 'The Body You Want', *Artforum* (November 1992): 84.

32

CRITICAL AND TEXTUAL HYPERMASCULINITY

Lynne Joyrich

I'd like to begin my discussion of TV, postmodernism, and the cultural connotations of femininity by referring to an image from David Cronenberg's film *Videodrome*. In this film, video signals are used to literally open their viewers to total control: exposure to these signals transforms the human body into a living VCR which can then be penetrated by videotapes, preventing the subject from differentiating reality from video simulation. Not only does this illustrate the worst fears of mass culture critics (fears concerning the power of the media to seduce and rape the viewer), but it clearly and violently marks the receptive TV body as feminine – the tapes are thrust into a gaping wound that pierces the hero's stomach. *Videodrome* thus brings together the image of the cyborg body – a postmodern hybrid of human, animal, and machine – and the image of the 'feminine body' – a body yielding to manipulation, too close to the image to properly evaluate it.[1]

Such conceptual ties between TV, postmodernism, and femininity (or, more accurately, the meanings our culture assigns to 'femininity' are symptomatic of shifting gender relations in our technologically mediated culture. Television, today's cyborgian 'machine-subject,'[2] can be seen as playing out these relations in all their contradictions, revealing a terrain in which gender figures prominently in a network of differences we have only begun to explore. By 'reading' several television texts against texts marking TV's critical reception, I will attempt to map out the connections forged between TV and postmodern

From P. Mellencamp (ed.), *Logics of Television: Essays in Cultural Criticism* (Bloomington: Indiana University Press / London: BFI, 1990) pp. 156–72.

culture, focusing on the veiled references to sexual difference and the figuration of gender constituted within this field.

Noting the ways in which TV has been portrayed as feminine in both film and mass culture criticism – a situation exacerbated by the fluctuating ground of postmodernism – I argue that while such tropes of analysis are seductive, they are also potentially dangerous, encouraging critics to ignore the complexities and contradictions of gender inscription as well as the other fields of difference (race, class, age, and so on) which traverse the TV text and audience alike.[3] In fact, attending to the complex dynamics of gender within both television and TV criticism might lead us to a very different conclusion from that implied by *Videodrome*'s sexual imagery. Despite the prevalence of such figures and images in accounts of TV, we cannot simply claim that television is itself either feminine or feminizing. Rather, this ontological premise recuperates the feminine and the critical insights of feminism within a new version of masculinity which inhabits television studies as well as television texts. In other words, the focus on TV as 'feminine' masks a deeper cultural concern with masculinity – a concern which may express itself through the construction of a 'hypermasculinity' that renders the presence of women within TV representation and TV criticism unnecessary.

Several theorists have noted that consumer culture and the culpable masses blamed for its existence have often been figured as feminine. Tania Modleski examines this aspect of historical accounts and emphasizes the problems involved in either simply condemning or celebrating these feminine inscriptions.[4] Andreas Huyssen has also explored attacks on sentimental culture – slurs based on fears of the engulfing ooze of the masses which provoked the 'reaction formation' of a virile and authorial modernism. Yet he concludes his analysis by claiming that such gendered rhetoric has diminished with the decline of modernism: 'mass culture and the masses as feminine threat – such notions belong to another age, Jean Baudrillard's recent ascription of femininity to the masses notwithstanding ...'.[5] Nonetheless, despite Huyssen's optimistic conclusion, such gendered imagery can still be seen in many analyses of television.

[...]

[T]he use of feminine imagery to describe our 'lowest' cultural form (in opposition to whatever is held up as more respectable and 'masculine' – print or film) has not faded away with the passing of modernism.[6] In fact, such gender implications take on new meaning in the postmodern age as the threat of fluctuating signs, unstable distinctions, and fractured identities provokes a retreat toward nostalgia for firm stakes of meaning.[7] As the '"natural" grounding principle' once seemingly offered by sexual difference erodes, new anxieties are created which are often projected onto television (a medium which stands as the ultimate in fluctuating signs even as it tries to remain a bastion of family values). Describing television in a world in which distance and contemplation are impossible, for example, Baudrillard writes, 'the opposing poles of determination vanish according to a nuclear contraction ... of the old polar schema which has always maintained a minimal distance between a cause and an effect, between the subject and an object. ...'[8] In the circular logic of simulation, classical reason threatens to vanish, and separate positions merge. In Baudrillard's words, 'positivity and negativity engender and overlap ... there is no longer any active or passive ... linear continuity and dialectical polarity no longer exist.'[9] As dialectics collapse, the oppositions which maintain sexual difference and the stability of the sexed gaze seem to shift, if not fully disappear.

This collapse of the oppositions which have always upheld the primacy of the masculine subject is further suggested in Baudrillard's description of television as he discards what film theory has taken to be the terms of sexual difference: 'TV is no longer the source of an absolute gaze ... no longer ... a system of scrutiny ... playing on the opposition between seeing and being seen. ...'[10] In rejecting the applicability of the categories subject/object, active/passive, and seeing/being seen, Baudrillard rejects the divisions that have been seen by many feminist film critics as constitutive of the male spectator.[11] In other words, for Baudrillard, postmodernism – and television in particular – seems to disallow the security and mastery of the masculine position, and as this stable site disappears, we are all left floating in a diffuse, irrational space – a space traditionally coded as feminine.

[...]

Baudrillard is not the first male theorist to claim the position of the feminine as a way to signify ironic strength (whether deemed political or not). His analysis of hyperaffirmation recalls Jacques Derrida's discussion of the feminine in *Spurs* (part of which occurs, interestingly, in a section entitled 'Simulations'). Considering Nietzsche's 'affirmative woman,' Derrida writes, 'she plays at dissimulation, at ornamentation, deceit, artifice, at an artist's philosophy. Hers is an affirmative power. ...' Woman is thus an indeterminable identity, 'a non-figure, a simulacrum.'[12] It is the very breakdown in logic that dismays readers of Baudrillard's *Simulations* that delights Derrida here, and the creation of a space between the self and the image through an exaggeration of this breakdown, the hypersimulation associated with feminine irony, is the only 'hopeful' possibility that even Baudrillard seems to offer.

Yet feminists must approach a hope figured as feminine salvation with suspicion. As Modleski points out, figuring both the masses and their subversive mode as feminine does not necessarily give feminists concerned with the historical and cultural position of women any cause for celebration. Noting the (masculine) sexual indifference that arises when the position of feminine difference is claimed by everyone, Modleski insists that the ascription of femininity to the anonymous mass glosses over crucial distinctions.[13] Attending similarly to Nancy Miller's warning, we must not lose sight of the ways in which a theoretical position that deems the question 'who speaks?' irrelevant can also maintain the institutional silencing of women. As Miller states, 'Only those who have it can play with not having it.'[14]

Not only must we be leery of male theorists playing with the demise of a social and political representation that we have never had, but we must not obscure the differences that do exist for men and women within the realm of mass culture. Returning to Huyssen's claim that images of a feminized mass culture no longer apply to the postmodern world, let me continue his point: 'If anything, a kind of reverse statement would make more sense: certain forms of mass culture, with their obsession with gendered violence, are more of a threat to women than to men. After all, it has always been men rather than women who have had real control over the productions of mass culture.[15] In other words, while television spectatorship may be figured as generically feminine, two crucial differences are overlooked: the historical split between consumption and production (in which women are the primary consumers while men largely control television production) and TV's reaction against the feminine through the construction of a violent hypermasculinity.

Turning first to the issue of a gendered consumption, many television critics and historians have explored the material conditions of female consumption, women's viewing patterns, and advertisers' address to this audience.[16] Furthermore, several theorists suggest a relationship between constructions of femininity and the consumer subject. Elsewhere, I have argued that such theoretical accounts of femininity accord in many ways with popular images of women in relation to looking and buying.[17] In the popular imagination, the woman is too close to what she sees – she is so attached that she is driven to possess whatever meets her eye (or, as the pun suggests, her 'I'). The labels commonly applied to film and television genres addressing a female audience – 'weepies' and 'tearjerkers' – convey the same assessment: there is an almost physical closeness assumed to exist between the overinvolved female spectator and the image which forces her tearful response. Such everyday appraisals of women as subjects who lack the distance required for 'proper' reasoning and viewing are mirrored by theoretical and psychoanalytic accounts of femininity which similarly stress women's lack of subject/object separation.[18]

While feminist theorists may offer these tropes of female proximity, fluidity, and 'nearness' as a subversive or hopeful alternative to the masculine model of identity, such overpresence cannot be divorced from consumer desires. As several critics have remarked, it is the emphasis on self-image that invites the consumer to attend to the images of advertised products, and the woman who must purchase in order to enhance her own status as valued commodity becomes the prototypical consumer – the same overpresence that ties her to the image allows her to be situated as both the subject and the object of consumerism at once.[19] It is thus no coincidence that (what has been seen as) the particular 'feminine' textuality of television supports the psychology of the perfect consumer. One of TV's most devalued genres, the soap opera, clearly exposes this intersection of cultural notions of femininity and consumerism:

within the form seen by many critics as emblematic of female subjectivity, there are almost twice as many commercials as occur on prime-time TV. Furthermore, television theorists have suggested a relationship between soap opera form – a continuously interrupted present which refuses closure – and the effectivity of its commercials which, rather than truly interrupting the soap opera, continue its narrative patterns while offering 'oases of narrative closure.'[20]

Yet the conditions that link consumerism and femininity (both related to an overidentification with the image and commodity object) affect all of postmodern culture – today men also attend to self-image and their value of exchange, similarly losing the distinction between subject and object that has characterized the female consumer. Not only, then, are women presumed to be the best of consumers, but all consumers are figured as feminized – a situation yielding tension in a culture desperately trying to shore up traditional distinctions even as its simulations destabilize such attempts. As the distance between subject and object diminishes in the weightless space of postmodern culture, the threat of feminization as well as an all-encompassing consumerism hangs over all subjects, and television (discussed, like femininity, through tropes of proximity, overpresence, and immediacy) is central to this process.

While TV's appeal then does not stop with women, its consumers have been belittled in such terms in the critical and popular imagination alike, provoking contemptuous assessments of genres in addition to those traditionally associated with female audiences. Music Television, for example – a form which also addresses a culturally devalued (but economically desirable) audience, youths in this case – further reveals the relations between a fractured Oedipal logic, postmodern form, and consumerism: these videos completely dissolve the distinction between program, product, and ad in texts which can only be described as commercials for themselves.[21] TV soap operas and music videos, the programs most disparaged, are thus in many ways the most telling, displaying the conventions of continuity and difference, presence and interruption, viewing and consuming invoked by the television apparatus. In other words, the forms that seem to best illustrate TV's specificity also reveal a consumerism associated with the address to an audience deemed infantile or feminine, a spectator 'not fully a man.'

Yet as the 'feminine' connotations attached to television and consumer closeness are diffused onto a general audience, contradictions of gender and spectatorship emerge, and television is placed in a precarious position as it attempts to induce consumer overpresence even as it tries to achieve cultural status by mimicking the more respectable cinema. It is interesting in this context to look at texts which exaggerate or foreground the specific representational strategies and discursive configurations of contemporary television. For example, a program such as ABC's on-again, off-again series *Max Headroom* rejects the cinematic model as it self-consciously announces television's difference, and as it calls attention to the characteristics of television (which are, as we have seen, shot through with connotations of gender), it would also seem to be among the shows most vulnerable to charges of feminization.

Max Headroom does, in many ways, raise this fear as it both extends and defends itself against the vacuum of simulation and the threat of a feminized world. In the premiere episode, for example, we are introduced to Max, a computer-generated 'video subject' who is born in an attempt to answer an enigma. The enigma at the root of this 'birth' centers on a mysterious death and cover-up – an event investigated by ace news reporter Edison Carter, the man who furnished the mind given to Max. In the scene in which this enigma is made visible, we see a large and lazy man at home in his armchair, watching television as an ad comes on the air. The ad he sees makes use of a diegetically new representational form – instead of presenting a logical and linear argument, a miniature narrative, or a coherent series of associational images, it involves a rapid flow of sound and images, chaotically thrown together so that nothing can be clearly identified or isolated. In other words, this ad is simply an intensified microcosm of TV as we, the home viewers, know it. The effect of this commercial on the diegetic viewer, however, is that of a literal inflation – the man swells up as consumer s(t)imulation builds inside of him until he actually explodes (or, for Baudrillard, implodes). What we witness, then, can almost be described as a form of hysterical pregnancy – TV provokes a generation of sensations, meaning, and animated force until this energy short-circuits and bursts to the surface, destroying the human body but providing the narrative origin of the cyborg, Max. Because Edison Carter has seen this event (although on videotape), he is captured, and his brain is scanned by a computer in order to disclose the full extent of his knowledge. In the process, Max Headroom is created. Eventually, of course, Edison recovers, solves the case, and reports the crime through another simulation – he broadcasts the contents of Max's memory which contains the videotape of the viewer explosion.

Exploring the sexual and textual issues raised in this episode, it is first of all apparent that TV is caught up in a web of simulations – any access to 'the real' is mediated through a series of video images (the original video ad, the videotape of the ad and explosion, the computer scan of Edison's memory of the tape, and finally, Edison's retaping of Max's computerized memory of the tape – a broadcast which is at that point at least four times removed) ... *Max Headroom*, in other words, presents a completely technologically mediated world, the ultimate in postmodern hyperreality that, as the program's logo tells us, is only twenty minutes into our own future. Furthermore, in its form as well as content, this show draws on postmodern textual devices – the program is known for the ways in which it refuses to subordinate its visual effects to a clear narrative progression and multiplies the look through a dense layering of simulated images and a fractured diegesis. As this program plays with TV's multiplicity of signs, time flow and shifting space, editing techniques derived from advertising, and fluctuating levels of reality/reproduction/

fabrication, it carries TV form to its limits, shifting the critique of television into a celebration of its specificity.

But like critical accounts of television, *Max Headroom*'s depiction of TV simulation is not divorced from questions of gender: this scene figures both the receptive TV body and the threat of a simulated world in terms of denigrating images of femininity. The viewer-victim, while a man, is an emasculated one – flabby and passive, he sits in front of his TV set until his body blows up in the pregnancy that ultimately results in Max. As (literally) a 'talking head,' Max himself is likewise feminized – he lacks the body of a man and constantly tries to sort out a man's sexual memories that he can't really understand. While Max masquerades as male, his constantly shifting contours provide him with a fluctuation of being that refuses even the illusion of unity and stability. Unable to differentiate himself from the matrices that bear him, he does not master the order of hyperreality but can only flow within it, losing the distinction between self and other that is (however fictionally) required to attain the status of a man. This condition, however, is not confined to Max – even the experts of this simulation, the computer operators who help Edison solve his cases, lack powerful masculinity: Max is created by a pre-adolescent (and pre-sexual) whiz kid, while Edison's computer guide is female. Here, as in Baudrillard's vision, the dangers of hyperreality, as well as its perpetrators, are feminized.

Yet while it plays with textual figures and devices that have been theoretically linked not only to postmodernism but also to feminine subjectivity, various strategies with which to contain TV's 'feminine' connotations are also employed. *Max Headroom* literally splits its hero in two, displacing postmodern consumer consciousness onto Max and leaving Edison Carter free to play the role of traditional hero. While Max is there for comic effect (much of the show's humor is based on his lack of a stable identity and his literal existence in the perpetual present of the TV mosaic – in the show's jargon, Max is 'in the system,' essentially bound to the flow of TV), it does, nonetheless, take a 'real man' to free us from the adverse effects of this simulated world. Edison Carter, a typical melodramatic hero, battles crime and exposes wrongdoing in order to keep his world in line. This program thus exists in the tension between modern and postmodern forms, projecting the 'feminine' cyborgian elements onto a dominated other (Max) while still allowing its male protagonist to control the diegetic space and the flow of the narrative.

In a similar way, television as a whole exists in an odd tension, balanced between the modern and the postmodern (its reliance on melodrama, for example, in the midst of its own self-referential texts) and between culturally constituted notions of the feminine and the masculine (both sustaining and rejecting the positions offered by critical, as well as commercial, discourses). This places television in a curious bind – a situation perhaps most evident in many prime-time programs which, in order to be 'culturally respectable' and appeal to male viewers, attempt to elevate the infantile and deny the feminine conventionally associated with television (particularly with the texts I have noted). A common strategy of television is thus to construct a violent hyper-masculinity – an excess of 'maleness' that acts as a shield. In this way, TV's defense against the feminine may be seen to correspond with television theory's attempts to dispense with the same – by their either resisting the feminine position (as many television texts do) or else incorporating and so speaking for it (as occurs in many recuperative critical texts, as discussed above), the real presence of women within these particular TV representations and critical texts is deemed unnecessary.

Within the realm of TV itself, there are a number of possible methods of defense. By aiming for the status of 'quality' television (producing texts that can function under the name of an author), creating 'proper' spectator distance by mimicking cinematic conventions, or obsessively remarking the masculinity of their thematics, some programs attempt to evade TV's feminization. Yet attempts at denial and male masquerade can produce problems which emerge on the surface of 'masculine' texts.[22] Faced with the contradictions created by the imperative to inscribe order in a medium that disallows resolution and the demand to be 'manly' in the 'feminized' world of TV, these texts yield a realm of masculine excess that demonstrates their fragile position within both TV's hyperreality and a 'hypermasculinity' that is its defense.

In her article on televised sports, Margaret Morse notes that despite cultural inhibition, 'the gaze at "maleness" would seem necessary to the construction and ... replenishment of a shared ... ideal of masculinity'[23] – an ideal that, in the light of my earlier remarks on consumer culture, particularly needs replen-ishing. Morse examines the discourse on sport as 'a place of "autonomous masculinity," freed even from dependence on woman-as-other to anchor identity.'[24] Sport, however, is not the only area in which the male body is displayed. In her analysis of *Magnum, p.i.*, for example, Sandy Flitterman traces the mobilization of the male spectacle, revealing the ways in which an eroticized masculinity is foregrounded.[25] Furthermore, such displays do not necessarily establish a masculinity free from relation to the feminine, despite their location within the (generally) all-male preserves of sports and the cop/detective show. They can instead be seen as an attempt to save masculinity even in the 'feminized' world of TV, even in the vacuum of a crisis-ridden postmodernism (which, not incidentally, also includes the crisis of Vietnam – a crisis in masculinity which has been dealt with explicitly in several cop/detective shows, including *Magnum, p.i.*, and which may also be partially responsible for the popularity of the genre in general).[26]

Even more than *Magnum, p.i.*, *Miami Vice* is a show of male excess and display which can be analyzed as a response to a feminine 'contagion.' In his insightful analysis, Jeremy Butler reveals the ways in which *Miami Vice* aspires to the cultural position of the cinema through its use of *film noir* conventions.[27] Yet *Vice* differs from *film noir* in some important ways. In place of the dup-licitous woman – the trouble that sets the cinematic plot in motion – the motiv-ating forces in *Miami Vice* are all men. Women may be visible as background detail or decor, but in a world in which male criminals are the primary enigmas and objects of voyeurism, the woman is divested of all potency, including, and most importantly, her power of masquerade, her ability to manipulate her femininity. Here, the power of masquerade belongs to men, most frequently Crockett and Tubbs who display themselves as criminals in order to lure their prey into captivity. (This display can also be seen in the ways in which the images of Crockett and Tubbs have been taken up by advertising and fashion – again, it is the male image which is now the focus, the men who masquerade.) While *film noir* investigates female identity and masquerade, *Miami Vice*'s central dilemma revolves around the identity of 'V/vice' and the possibility of differentiating between the cops and the crooks, the men and their roles.[28] Clearly at stake here is a question of masculinity in a world in which all stable distinctions have dissolved, in which the feminized object of the look and trouble of the text constitute a position shared by everyone. This is a crucial question for postmodern, post-Vietnam America as well as an issue for television – the 'feminine' cultural form of our time.

An episode entitled 'Duty and Honor' (one of the episodes confronting Vietnam) exemplifies the textual disturbances provoked by such displays of manliness. The narrative traces the paths of both an assassin – a black Vietnam veteran, called only 'the Savage,' who is responsible for a series of prostitute murders (all of the victims are marked by the words 'VC Whore' despite the fact that most of them are not Vietnamese) – and a Vietnamese police officer, a former friend of Lieutenant Castillo who comes to Miami to solve the murders that have haunted the two since their meeting in Vietnam. From our first sight of the Savage, he is marked as an object of the gaze as he appears before a mirror, eyeing himself and rehearsing a pose. He is thus constituted as spectacle – the spectacle of a perfect machine, a cyborg weapon of war, and a feminized icon demanding to be looked at.

[...]

While the politically progressive 'message' of this episode is striking in relation to the usual fare of TV cop shows, it exposes the problematic of which I am speaking in chillingly clear terms, embodying the hypermasculine defense against a feminization associated with TV, postmodernism, and post-Vietnam America in the cyborg character of the Savage. As such, it reveals TV's masquerade of masculinity – a masquerade which may be seen as a violent response to the feminine connotations attached to television and its receptive viewers. In other words, while theoretical and popular discourses alike may figure television in terms of femininity, we should not accept such views uncritically, failing then to notice other crucial differences which run through television – differences related to class and racial positioning, for example – as well as the contradictions of gender that do exist within television's multiple address. While the gender inscriptions of U.S. broadcast television are complex, intertwined, and unstable, it is important to note that even the temporary securities offered in shows of male spectacle require the neutralization or absence of women (while still disavowing any overt homosexual eroticism). The family offered is a family of man, and the gender positions cast arc significant for both the men and women watching. In a medium in which the familial is the dominant theme as well as mode of address, this is the final irony that cannot yet be explained by current theories of sexual and textual difference – the masculine threat that lurks 'within the gates' of a medium deemed feminine.

NOTES

1. The concept of the cyborg body comes from Donna Haraway, 'A Manifesto for Cyborgs: Science, Technology, and Socialist Feminism in the 1980s', *Socialist Review* 80 (Mar.-Apr. 1985): 65–107. See also Tania Modleski's discussion of *Videodrome* in 'The Terror of Pleasure: The Contemporary Horror Film and Postmodern Theory', in *Studies in Entertainment: Critical Approaches to Mass Culture*, ed. Tania Modleski (Bloomington: Indiana University Press, 1986), p. 159.
2. The term 'machine-subject' comes from Margaret Morse who analyzes the ways in which TV seems to address its viewers from a position of subjectivity in 'Talk, Talk, Talk – The Space of Discourse in Television', *Screen* 26.2 (Mar.–Apr. 1985): 6.
3. For a related analysis, see Patrice Petro, 'Mass Culture and the Feminine: The "Place" of Television in Film Studies', *Cinema Journal* 25.3 (Spring 1986): 5–21.
4. Tania Modleski, 'Femininity as Mas(s)querade: A Feminist Approach to Mass Culture', in *High Theory/Low Culture*, ed. Colin MacCabe (New York: St. Martin's Press, 1986), pp. 37–52.
5. Andreas Huyssen, 'Mass Culture as Woman: Modernism's Other', in *After the Great Divide: Modernism, Mass Culture, Postmodernism* (Bloomington: Indiana University Press, 1986), pp. 62 and 53–55.
6. Perhaps the most obvious case of this tendency to associate television with the feminine is the Lacanian reading offered by Beverle Houston in the article 'Viewing Television: The Metapsychology of Endless Consumption', *Quarterly Review of Film Studies* 9.3 (Summer 1984): 183–95. I don't discuss this analysis in the text precisely because the thesis that TV is feminine is so clear in her work. The more interesting cases, in my opinion, arc those in which gendered metaphors creep into discussions of television by critics not expressly making this claim.
7. See, for example, Huyssen's discussion of nostalgia as a response to postmodernism's 'various forms of "otherness"' (including feminism) on pp. 199 and 219–20. Janice Doane and Devon Hodges discuss the anxiety provoked by the erosion of traditional categories of gender in *Nostalgia and Sexual Difference: The Resistance to Contemporary Feminism* (New York: Methuen, 1987).
8. Jean Baudrillard, *Simulations* (New York: Semiotext[e], 1983), p. 56.
9. Ibid., pp. 30–31. See also pp. 52, 54.
10. Ibid., pp. 52, 54.
11. See, in particular, Laura Mulvey, 'Visual Pleasure and Narrative Cinema', *Screen* 16.3 (Autumn 1975): 6–18. Recently, many feminist film theorists have re-theorized spectatorship so as to account for shifting and contradictory identifications and more powerful and pleasurable positions for the female viewer. See, for example, Elizabeth Cowie, 'Fantasia,' *m/f* 9 (1984): 71–105; Teresa de Lauretis, *Alice Doesn't: Feminism, Semiotics, Cinema* (Bloomington: Indiana University Press, 1984); Tania Modleski, *The Women Who Knew Too Much: Hitchcock and Feminist Theory* (New York: Methuen, 1988); Kaja Silverman, *The Acoustic Mirror: The Female Voice in Psychoanalysis and Cinema* (Bloomington: Indiana University Press, 1988); and Linda Williams, 'Something Else Besides a Mother:

Stella Dallas and the Maternal Melodrama', *Cinema Journal* 24.1 (Fall 1984): 2–27.

In discussing the female spectator in the latter part of this paper in terms of narcissism and tropes of proximity, I am not claiming that these are the only or essential positions available for an actual female viewer. Rather, I am focusing on the *representation* of women in both popular and critical accounts of cinematic spectatorship. In other words, the historically and culturally sanctioned positions for female viewers are quite limited even though other constructions of viewing pleasure are certainly possible, particularly for viewers who have been positioned 'differently' by the discourses of feminism.

12. Jacques Derrida, *Spurs: Nietzsche's Styles*, trans. Barbara Harlow (Chicago: University of Chicago Press, 1978), pp. 67, 57, 49.
13. Modleski, pp. 50–51.
14. Nancy Miller, 'The Text's Heroine: A Feminist Critic and Her Fictions', *Diacritics* 12.2 (Summer 1982): 53. Also addressing this issue is Naomi Schor, 'Dreaming Dissymmetry: Barthes, Foucault, and Sexual Difference', in *Men in Feminism*, ed. Alice Jardine and Paul Smith (New York: Methuen, 1987), pp. 98–110; and Patricia Mellencamp who examines sit-com simulations that are inflected differently by the female voice in 'Situation Comedy, Feminism, and Freud: Discourses of Gracie and Lucy', in *Studies in Entertainment*, especially p. 87.
15. Huyssen, p. 205. The 'threat to women' revealed by mass culture's gendered violence can also be seen in my example of *Videodrome* – a film that thus demonstrates how TV has been figured as feminine as well as how this figuration masks a violent hypermasculinity.
16. See, for example, the essays in *Camera Obscura*'s special issue on 'Television and the Female Consumer', *Camera Obscura* 16 (Jan. 1988), and in the anthology *Boxed In: Women and Television*, ed. Helen Baehr and Gillian Dyer (New York: Pandora Press, 1987).
17. Lynne Joyrich, 'All That Television Allows: TV Melodrama, Postmodernism, and Consumer Culture', *Camera Obscura* 16 (Jan. 1988): 141–47.
18. See, for example, Nancy Chodorow, *The Reproduction of Mothering: Psychoanalysis and the Sociology of Gender* (Berkeley: University of California Press, 1978); Carol Gilligan, *In a Different Voice: Psychological Theory and Women's Development* (Cambridge: Harvard University Press, 1982); Irigaray, *This Sex Which Is Not One*; and Michèle Montrelay, 'Inquiry into Femininity', *m/f* 1 (1978): 83–102. For an illuminating discussion of such tropes of feminine proximity, see Mary Ann Doane, *The Desire to Desire: The Woman's Film of the 1940s* (Bloomington: Indiana University Press, 1987).
19. On advertising and self-image, see T. J. Jackson Lears, 'From Salvation to Self-realization: Advertising and the Therapeutic Roots of Consumer Culture, 1880–1930', in *The Culture of Consumption: Critical Essays in American History, 1880–1980*, ed. Richard Wightman Fox and T. J. Jackson Lears (New York: Pantheon, 1983), pp. 3–38. Relating this to the specific position of women is Rosalind Coward, *Female Desires: How They Are Sold, Bought, and Packaged* (New York: Grove Press, 1985), and Doane, *The Desire to Desire*, especially pp. 13 and 22–33.
20. See Sandy Flitterman, 'The *Real* Soap Operas: TV Commercials', in *Regarding Television: Critical Approaches – An Anthology*, ed. E. Ann Kaplan (Frederick, Md.: University Publications of America, 1983), pp. 84, 94. See also the essays on soaps by Tania Modleski, Charlotte Brunsdon, and Robert Allen in the same volume.
21. On MTV and postmodernism, see, for example, E. Ann Kaplan, *Rocking Around the Clock: Music Television, Postmodernism, and Consumer Culture* (New York: Methuen, 1987); Peter Wollen, 'Ways of Thinking about Music Video (and Postmodernism)', *Critical Quarterly* 28.1–2 (Spring-Summer 1986): 167–70; and the essays on music video in *Journal of Communication Inquiry* 10.1 (1986).

22. The analysis of such shows as 'hysterical' texts that yield contradictions emerging as textual fissures suggests a reading of these programs as 'male melodramas.' Noting that melodrama's search for clearly marked oppositions historically arises in periods of crisis, one can analyze television – the medium of hyperreality which is defined as *the* age of crisis – as the melodramatic forum of postmodernism. Because of both the specific suitability of melodrama for television and the demands of postmodernism, even genres not typically associated with the melodrama – such as the cop show – have turned toward the more personal issues associated with melodramatic form, thereby inheriting some of this genre's tensions as well as the tensions provoked by such generic hybrids. See Joyrich, 'All That Television Allows', pp. 129–53.

23. Margaret Morse, 'Sport on Television: Replay and Display', in *Regarding Television*, p. 45.

24. Ibid., p. 44.

25. Sandy Flitterman, 'Thighs and Whiskers – the Fascination of *Magnum, p. i.*', *Screen* 26.2 (Mar.–Apr. 1985): 42–58.

26. The crisis in masculinity provoked by Vietnam has also been discussed by Andrew Ross, 'Masculinity and *Miami Vice*: Selling In', *Oxford Literary Review* 8.1–2 (1986): 150. Comparing *Miami Vice* to *film noir*, Jeremy Butler reminds us of the historical connection between *noir* style and postwar disillusionment – a connection which suggests that the popularity of *Miami Vice* may be related to post-Vietnam despair. See '*Miami Vice*: The Legacy of Film Noir', *Journal of Popular Film and Television* 13.3 (Fall 1985): 129.

27. For Butler's analysis of these issues of sexual difference, see pp. 129–30, 132–33.

28. On this core dilemma, see Butler, pp. 131–32. On the double meaning of 'Vice' as it relates to masquerade and the 'right stuff' of masculinity, see Ross, p. 152.

FURTHER READING

Bordo, Susan, '"Material Girl": The Effacements of Postmodern Culture'. From Bordo, *Unbearable Weight: Feminism, Western Culture and the Body* (Berkeley: University of California Press, 1993) pp. 245–75.

Brooker, P. and Brooker, W. (ed.), *Postmodern After-images: A Reader in Film, Television and Video* (London: Arnold, 1997).

Collins, J., *Uncommon Cultures: Popular Culture and Post-modernism* (London: Routledge, 1989).

Connor, S., *Postmodernist Culture: An Introduction to Theories of the Contemporary* (Oxford: Blackwell, 1989).

Docherty, T. (ed.), *Postmodernism: A Reader* (Hemel Hempstead: Harvester Wheatsheaf, 1992).

Featherstone, M., *Consumer Culture and Postmodernism* (London: Sage, 1991).

Fiske, J., 'MTV: Post Structural Post Modern'. *Journal of Communication Enquiry* 10:1 (1986) pp. 74–9.

Fiske, J., 'Postmodernism and Television'. In J. Curran and M. Gurevitch (eds), *Mass Media and Society* (London: Edward Arnold, 1991).

Frith, S., Goodwin, A. and Grossberg, L. (eds), *Sound and Vision: The Music Video Reader* (London and New York: Routledge, 1993).

Goodwin, A., 'Music Video in the (Post)Modern World'. *Screen* 28:3 (1987) pp. 36–55.

Goodwin, A., 'Popular Music and Postmodern Theory'. *Cultral Studies* 5:2 (1991) pp. 174–90.

Goodwin, A., *Dancing in the Distraction Factory: Music Television and Popular Music* (Minneapolis: University of Minnesota Press, 1992).

Grossberg, L., 'The In-difference of Television'. *Screen* 28:2 (1987) pp. 28–45.

Grossberg, L., *We Gotta Get Out of this Place: Popular Conservatism and Postmodern Culture* (London: Routledge, 1992).

Hartley, J., *Popular Reality: Journalism, Modernity, Popular Culture* (London: Arnold, 1996).

Hebdige, D., *Hiding in the Light: On Images and Things* (London: Routledge, 1988).

Huyssen, A., *After the Great Divide: Modernism, Mass Culture, Postmodernism* (London: Macmillan, 1986).

Joyrich, L., 'All That Television Allows: TV Melodrama, Postmodernism, and Consumer Culture'. *Camera Obscura,* 16 (1988) pp. 128–53.

Kaplan, E.A., *Rocking Around the Clock: Music Television, Postmodernism and Consumer Culture* (London: Methuen, 1987).

Kaplan, E. A., 'Whose Imaginary? The Televisual Apparatus, The Female Body and Textual Strategies in Select Rock Videos on MTV'. From E. D. Pribram (ed.) *Female Spectators: Looking at Film and Television* (London: Verso, 1988).

Kaplan, E.A. (ed.), *Postmodernism and its Discontents: Theories, Practices* (London: Verso, 1988).

McRobbie, A., *Postmodernism and Popular Culture* (London: Routledge, 1994).

Mellencamp, P. (ed.), *The Logics of Television* (Bloomington and London: Indiana University Press and BFI, 1990).

Modleski, T. (ed.), *Studies in Entertainment: Critical Approaches to Mass Culture* (Bloomington: Indiana University Press, 1986).

Sim, S. (ed.), *The Icon Critical Dictionary of Postmodern Thought* (Cambridge: Icon Books, 1998).

Strinati, D., 'Postmodernism and Popular Culture'. *Sociology Review,* April, 1992, pp. 2–7.

Wollen, P., 'Ways of Thinking about Music Video (and Post-modernism)'. *Critical Quarterly* 28:1 & 2 (1986).

SECTION 4
RECEPTION

1. FROM 'EFFECTS' TO 'USES'

FROM 'EFFECTS' TO 'USES'
INTRODUCTION

When British social science began to give attention to media reception, it turned to the existing American social scientific tradition for its ideas and models. This tradition was marked by a behaviourist psychology and a functionalist sociology, and tended to focus on the search for direct, palpable, short-term effects of media messages.

One of the leading figures in the British psychological establishment, Hans Eysenck, Professor of Psychology at the University of London from 1955, had himself long researched within a behaviourist paradigm, and was thus in tune with the underlying approach of much of the American experimental research when he came to take up the topic of the media. In his book *Sex, Violence and the Media*, co-written with Nias, he draws largely on this American research to sustain a case for the judicious employment of censorship to prevent the ill-effects of the portrayal of violence (and some kinds of sexual conduct) in the media. The experiments cited are noteworthy for the degree to which they aim to screen out – laboratory-style – all other cultural and social factors besides the 'pure' exposure to audiovisual material depicting violence; for the immediate and analogic nature of the effects they expect to capture; and for the incorporation in several instances of even a measurable *physiological* definition of media effects. The reported consequences of exposure to media portrayals of violence include a tendency for viewers to become 'disinhibited' about employing violence themselves, a tendency for some direct 'imitation', and – as covered by Chapter 33 – a tendency to become 'desensitized' to 'violent materials', to fail to feel appropriate revulsion from them. Eysenck summarises 'effects' research within a particularly extreme behaviourist paradigm of the human animal, who can be consciously or inadvertently trained or conditioned, so that certain stimulus inputs will generate certain behavioural outputs. The publication in Britain in the late 1970s of this summary account of American behaviouristic research into the 'effects' of media 'violence' was taken by many as implicit endorsement for the main lines of approach of the pro-censorship campaign being mounted by the Christian fundamentalist-led National Viewers' and Listeners' Association and the Festival of Light.

But by then the mainstream of American social science had long been doubtful about the notion of strong, direct, measurable attitude changes attributable to individual mass communication messages. Mass communication was turning out to have very 'limited effects'. A widely read review of the American research, published in 1960, concluded that 'mass communication does not ordinarily serve as a necessary and sufficient cause of audience effects, but rather functions through a nexus of mediating factors'.[1] This was the predominant drift of thinking by the 1960s when the pioneering social scientists of mass communication in Britain began their work – notably Denis McQuail, Jeremy Tunstall, Jay G. Blumler and James Halloran.[2] Since the platform for this work was, not surprisingly, a reading of the American mass communication literature, the objective was to grasp this complex nexus. Chapter 34 comprises two extracts from *The Effects of Television* (1970), edited by James Halloran, head of the Centre for Mass Communication Research at the University of Leicester from 1966. The first extract registers the view that 'attitude change has been over-used as the primary criterion of influence ... Influence must not be equated with attitude change.' The second extract discusses studies of the reception of particular British television programmes (*Children of Revolution, Nature of Prejudice* and *Rainbow City*) that confirmed this view. The need for a more complex and comprehensive conception of the reception of broadcast transmissions had been demonstrated by these native studies. David Morley later remarked that 'The empirical work of the Leicester Centre at this time marked an important shift in research from forms of behavioural analysis to forms of cognitive analysis.'[3]

Denis McQuail took up another, subordinate, strand in the American literature, one which concerned itself with audience 'gratifications'.[4] This inverted the 'effects' approach, and set out 'to concentrate less on what the media do to people than on what people do *with* the media.'[5] What are people's motives in reading a newspaper or listening to a particular radio programme? What are the uses for them of such activities? What needs are gratified, what satisfactions derived? The posing of these questions, and the pursuit of their answers, often within the framework of a functionalist sociology, had become known as the 'uses and gratifications' approach.[6] In the study reported in Chapter 35, McQuail and his colleagues Jay G. Blumler and J. R. Brown investigated what functions the television quiz shows *University Challenge, TV Brain of Britain* and *Ask the Family* served for a sample of viewers in Leeds. From the viewers' responses when questioned, they developed a four-part inventory of gratifications and uses, which they suggested might have a general applicability for media use. These four types of 'media-person interaction' are: surveillance (information gathering); personal identity; personal relationships (social integration and interaction); and diversion (entertainment). The attempt to correlate instances of the expression of each of these kinds of satisfaction with social and demographic variables, however, proved rather inconclusive: the results 'were not without ambiguity and left many questions unanswered'. Also, in relation to the various kinds of programmes, it seemed that 'people can look to quite different kinds of material for essentially the same gratification and, correlatively, find alternative satisfactions in the same televised material'.

Two of the commonplace colloquial views on popular media had been to despise them as trivially 'escapist', while regarding them as powerful agents of mental influence. As American empirical research – and the British research that followed in its footsteps – had come to eclipse the latter view, the former threatened to maintain its sway. So it was a gain for British media studies that McQuail and his colleagues simultaneously refused both a one-dimensional view of the irresistible power of the media to impose itself upon passive audiences, *and* the widespread unquestioning disdain for popular media consumption as simply 'escapist'. But the 'uses and gratifications' approach came under attack from within a Marxian sociology hostile to functionalism. Philip Elliott of the University of Leicester Centre for Mass Communication Research, in a paper abridged here as Chapter 36, pointed to a fundamental problem of logic within the exponents' arguments:

> In both variants – use leads to the gratification of need or need leads to satisfaction through functional behaviour – need is the residual factor and yet it is also put forward as an explanation for the process. . . . [Much uses and gratifications] research invites the accusation that it lacks explanatory power.

McQuail himself was troubled by something similar to this. He had written:

> The guiding assumption of utility can lead the analyst to impute a social function where none may exist, with a resulting circularity of argument: a regularity in the pattern of media content is observed, linked to an assumed configuration of social and individual needs which fit this pattern, and mass communication may then be 'explained' in terms of these needs.[7]

But Elliott's criticism goes further than simply identifying a circularity in the argumentation. 'Uses and gratifications' research findings may add up to generalisations about 'aggregates of individuals, but they cannot be converted in any meaningful way into social structure and process'. To him it is a profound shortcoming, implicit in the functionalist origins of the approach, that '[n]o attempt is made to differentiate between media or people on the basis of the interests they represent or the power they possess'. He sees the approach as fundamentally conservative:

> In themselves, uses and gratifications data can only point in one direction, towards a justification of the present situation ... If the media-output audience-satisfaction nexus were explored in uses and gratifications terms, the only possible conclusion would be that the audience was getting something out of it. But that is not in dispute. The issue in dispute is whose interests are being served in the process, and that is an issue which the approach itself is powerless to elucidate.

But Elliott acknowledged that '[t]o reject the idea of a purposive audience out of hand would be to adopt a completely determinist view'. He was reaching towards a similar view to that of Stuart Hall's 'Encoding/Decoding' (Chapter 5). In the mass communication process, production and reception are distinct moments, yet the two moments are not equivalent: there is an asymmetry of power.

NOTES

1. Joseph T. Klapper, *The Effects of Mass Communication* (Glencoe, Ill.: Free Press, 1960).
2. William Belson, Hilde Himmelweit and Joseph Trenaman also carried out significant pioneering research in Britain.
3. David Morley, *The 'Nationwide' Audience* (London: British Film Institute, 1980) p. 7. See especially James D. Halloran, Philip Elliott, Graham Murdock, *Demonstrations and Communication: A Case Study* (Harmondsworth: Penguin, 1970), ch. 7.
4. Examples of 'gratification' studies from the classic period of American mass communication research include: Herta Herzog, 'Professor Quiz: A Gratification Study', in Paul F. Lazarsfeld (ed.), *Radio and the Printed Page* (New York: Duell, Sloane & Pearce, 1940); Bernard Berelson, 'What "Missing the Newspaper" Means', in Paul F. Lazarsfeld and Frank N. Stanton (eds), *Communication Research 1948–49* (New York: Harper & Bros., 1949); Katherine M. Wolfe and Marjorie Fiske, 'The Children Talk about Comics', in Paul F. Lazarsfeld and Frank N. Stanton (eds), *Communication Research 1948–49* (New York: Harper & Bros., 1949).
5. Denis McQuail, *Towards a Sociology of Mass Communications* (London: Collier Macmillan, 1969) p. 71.
6. From a phrase in Elihu Katz, 'Mass Communication Research and the Study of Culture', *Studies in Public Communication* 2 (1959) pp. 1–60.
7. McQuail, *Towards a Sociology*, p. 88. Also, in Chapter 35, McQuail and his colleagues express certain reservations over adopting functionalism *tout court*: 'However appropriate otherwise, the language of functionalism is so overworked, ambiguous and imprecise that we prefer to avoid it, and to attempt a new start. ... [W]e propose to use the expression "media–person interaction", to refer to the orientations distinguished in the typology.'

33

DENSENSITIZATION, VIOLENCE AND THE MEDIA

Hans Eysenck and D. K. B. Nias

[...]

Civilized man everywhere has erected barriers to the simple expression of sexual and violent impulses in direct action – rape and murder are universally prohibited, and punished by law. These barriers are internalized, probably through some form of conditioning (Eysenck, 1977), although it is quite possible and even likely that innate factors also play some part – even animals tend to act out their intraspecific conflicts in a more or less symbolic way. Lions seldom kill lions, nor do gorillas normally kill gorillas. Humans are almost unique in having ritualized murder by inventing 'war', but even so humans tend on the whole to have some seemingly innate aversion to taking human life. It seems probable that these innate tendencies are strengthened by a process of conditioning, but for the purpose [here ...] it is not really vital to know the precise provenance of the very obvious barriers to the direct expression of primitive impulses which characterize civilized man (and even primitive man).

Let us now consider how we could weaken these barriers, supposing that we wanted to. Clearly it could be done by using the methods of desensitization. What would be required would be the portrayal, at second hand (i.e. through the written word, or in pictures, or film, or on TV) of acts of violence or abnormal sex which, had they occurred normally in our presence, would have aroused strong negative emotions of disgust, dislike and fear. By viewing them in this second-hand, indirect form we immediately reduce the impact and

From H. J. Eysenck and D. K. B. Nias, *Sex, Violence and the Media* (London: Maurice Temple Smith, 1978) pp. 50–1, 178–84.

relegate the images to the lower ranks of our hierarchy. At the same time we view them under conditions of relaxation – in our own homes in the case of TV, or in a comfortable seat in the cinema, in the case of films. Thus the situation combines all the vital elements of desensitization – relaxation and exposure to low-ranking items in the hierarchy of fears and anxieties. We are in fact free to select for ourselves the precise images which are low enough in our own, individual hierarchy to make the viewing tolerable, and not excite too much anxiety – we usually have some information about the film or play to be seen, or the TV series to be viewed. And if we are wrong in our choice, we can always walk out of the cinema, or turn off the TV, to reduce anxiety. It would not be too much to say that if the Martians had in mind the brutalization of our civilization by incitement to violence and sexual exploitation, they could not have hit upon a better method than making use of the media in their present form to achieve their aims.

Desensitization, then, is a method of changing conduct and emotional reactions which is well documented experimentally, both in animals and in humans; it has been widely used, with considerable success, to cure neurotic fears and anxieties; it seems highly unlikely that under the conditions under which pornographic and violent materials are shown these should have no effect on the viewer whatsoever. Desensitization in this case is the technical term for what many critics of the media call 'brutalization'; the idea is the same. It would need a very powerful argument indeed to persuade anyone familiar with the extensive literature on desensitization (Bergin and Garfield, 1971) to take seriously the proposition that viewing large numbers of scenes of explicit sex and violence on film or TV would leave the viewers completely unaffected. Most writers who favour the view that such scenes have no effect do not in fact argue the point; they simply disregard the evidence and the theory, as if it did not exist. This is a simple way of dealing with the difficulty, but it does not impress the unbiased critic as a good way of disposing of an inconvenient argument. It is true that the conditions of viewing are not scientifically prearranged to produce optimum effects, as could only be done in individual therapy; it is the large number of people exposed to the 'treatment', and the large number of exposures, which create the effect.

Some readers may object that Pavlovian conditioning is a very primitive method which surely does not apply to human beings in the same manner as to dogs, rats and other mammals. The evidence is strong that this is not true; humans follow the same laws of conditioning as do animals.

[. . .]

People, by constant exposure to violence, will eventually become 'desensitized' and no longer be upset or aroused by witnessing violence.

When feeling emotional we tend to sweat, and very slight increases in moisture can be detected electrically by what is known as a 'galvanic skin response' or 'skin conductance' measure. This highly sensitive indicator of emotional arousal, which is used in 'lie detector' tests, was being used in a study in which students were shown a film of an aboriginal ceremony that vividly depicted a sequence of crude operations performed with a piece of flint on several adolescent boys (Lazarus *et al.*, 1962). Skin conductance tended to 'peak' every time there was a particularly gory scene, but these peaks were not as high towards the end of the film as they were at the beginning. This is evidence of desensitization, but, because this demonstration was not the main point of the study, no attempt was made to control for alternative interpretations such as the later scenes being less horrific and so accounting for the decline in emotional responsiveness.

Fortunately this necessary control was incorporated in the design of an experiment by Berger (1962). Galvanic skin responses were monitored in fifteen subjects who either watched a man being given a series of electric shocks in order 'to see what level he could take' or the same man merely having his galvanic skin responses recorded. The 'victim' was in fact a confederate of the experimenter, and the subjects were reassured that it would not be necessary to give them shocks. Skin responses were evident in the experimental subjects each time the victim jerked his arm at the shock, but their emotional response became less with each repetition of the procedure.

Heart rate and self-reported distress were monitored as well as skin conductance in a study of habituation to an industrial accident film (Averill *et al.*, 1972). Male students were shown twenty repetitions of either a gruesome accident or a benign scene, and then the complete film involving three accidents. This procedure was repeated on three occasions, and each time prior exposure to the accident scene was found to reduce emotional arousal when that same scene was viewed in the context of the whole film. There was, however, little evidence of generalization since emotional responses to the other two accidents were similar for the control and experimental subjects. This lack of desensitization to the new accidents helps explain why the interest of existing TV audiences is maintained if producers provide them with new forms of violence. Nevertheless, generalization is known to occur in other situations and it may not have become apparent in this study simply because it may need more than three days of brief exposure to one type of violence in order to manifest itself. Evidence from a field study does in fact suggest that generalization to TV violence occurs in real life; this study is listed together with the above in Table [33.1].

Boys were shown a sequence, including a brutal boxing scene, from a Kirk Douglas film (Cline *et al.*, 1973). Galvanic skin response and blood volume pulse amplitude were recorded before and during this film for two groups of boys. One group had been selected on the basis of having watched TV for twenty-five hours or more a week over the previous two years, and the other for four hours or less a week. Emotional arousal during the violent scene was less for the 'hardened' viewers than it was for the 'low exposure' controls, whereas before this scene the physiological measures were similar for the two

---

Table [33.1]

Lazarus et al. (1962)   A progressive drop in skin conductance was noted for 70 students while watching a seventeen-minute film of primitive mutilation.

Berger (1962)   Compared with a control group, galvanic skin responses occurred more frequently for subjects who were witnessing a man being shocked, but these responses steadily declined over thirteen trials.

Averill et al. (1972)   For three days, 45 students watched a twenty-five second accident scene twenty times at half-minute intervals before seeing a twelve-minute film in which this was one of three accidents. Compared with 23 control subjects, emotional arousal was significantly reduced only for the accident to which they had been desensitized.

Cline et al. (1973)   Boys aged 5 to 14 years were selected on the basis of high or low exposure to TV. While watching an eight-minute violent scene in a fourteen-minute film, emotional responses were lower for 17 'high exposure' than for 15 'low exposure' boys.

---

groups. Because this was a field study, the results suffer from a weakness inherent in the method, namely that alternative interpretations are always apparent. For example, if boys who are particularly sensitive to violence are less inclined to watch TV, then this alone could be sufficient to account for the results obtained. Because of this limitation we shall return to laboratory studies, which also provide important evidence of desensitization to violence generalizing to another situation.

In one of the few studies in the Surgeon General's Commission to be concerned with desensitization, children were shown either a violent *Peter Gunn* or a neutral *Green Acres TV* episode, and then compared in a test for awareness of violence (Rabinovitch *et al.*, 1972). The test involved a stereoscopic projector by which two slides can be presented simultaneously to each eye so quickly that only one is seen. Nine pairs of slides were used in which one portrayed a violent and the other a neutral scene. For example, a man hitting another over the head with a gun was paired with a picture of a man helping another hit a pole into the ground with a gun butt. The children were asked to write down descriptions of what they saw, and it was the group who had just seen *Peter Gunn* who identified fewer of the violent pictures. This constitutes evidence that the violent programme, by making them temporarily less sensitive to violence, blunted their awareness of the violent pictures. It is difficult to think of an alternative interpretation of this result unless it was catharsis making the violent group think of peaceful rather than violent scenes.

Evidence that attitudes in real life can be influenced by a violent film is provided in an ingenious experiment by Drabman and Thomas (1974). Children who had watched a violent scene from *Hopalong Cassidy* were compared with a control group, who had not seen a film, for tolerance of violent acts. This was done by asking each subject to keep an eye on a couple of children who were playing in another room, and to summon the experimenter if there was any trouble. They were able to watch the children by way of a videotape monitor; by this technique it was possible to arrange for both groups of subjects to see exactly the same sequence of events. After playing peacefully the two children started to abuse each other verbally and then to fight during the course of which the TV camera was knocked over and contact was eventually lost. The measure of attitude to aggression was the time taken before the subject sought help from the experimenter, and these results are presented in Table [33.2].

Table [33.2] Effects of films on toleration of aggression

	Violent film	No film
Boys	104 seconds	63 seconds
Girls	119 seconds	75 seconds

Time taken before notifying the experimenter of an altercation between two younger children for whom the subject had taken responsibility.

(*Based on Drabman and Thomas, 1974*)

Just over half the control subjects notified the experimenter of the argument before physical fighting began, whereas only 17 per cent of the film group did so. Whether these results were obtained because of a temporary reduction in emotional responsivity in the film group, or simply because the argument and fighting appeared trivial in comparison with the filmed violence, they constitute strong evidence that violent film can lead to increased tolerance of aggression. One criticism, however, is apparent and this concerns the possibility that the film group took less notice of their responsibility because they were still thinking of the exciting film. It would have been better if the control subjects had been shown an exciting but non-violent film instead of nothing. This was duly done in a replication by Thomas and Drabman (1975) and the result still held; children who had watched an excerpt from *Mannix* took an average of 145 seconds before summoning help, whereas those who had watched an exciting baseball film took only 88 seconds.

Thomas *et al.* (1977) attempted to produce temporary desensitization by showing children a violent TV police drama, and then assessed the effect in terms of their response to a videotape of two pre-school children fighting. Compared with a control group who were shown an exciting volleyball game, the 'desensitized' children responded with fewer galvanic skin responses when shown the videotape of 'real' aggression. This again provides evidence that the viewing of TV violence can make children inured to real-life violence, only this time there is the additional information that after watching TV they feel less emotional when witnessing scenes of real fighting. The study was repeated with students, except that news films of riots were used instead of the fighting scenes, and similar results were obtained at least for males.

The above studies, which are summarized in Table [33.3] have all provided evidence of desensitization to violence. That desensitization occurs is not really in doubt, although we have noted that generalization to other forms of violence is a very gradual process. It probably requires years of ardent viewing before people become immune to whatever type of violence is next to appear on the screens. According to the reports of cinema managers, some members of the audience fainted or were sick during the screening of *Soldier Blue* and *A Clockwork Orange*. Presumably these viewers had not been sufficiently 'de-sensitized' for films of such a violent nature. Carruthers and Taggart (1973) took electrocardiogram recordings and other physiological measures from adult men and women watching these two films. Reactions to the violent scenes were assessed relative to baseline measures taken during pre-film commercials. The interesting observation was made that although there was increased adrenaline excretion, indicating excitement or arousal, there was also a slowing of the heart, indicating horror or revulsion, during the most violent scenes. In some people the heart rate slowed even below forty beats per minute; this provides an explanation for the fainting attacks since with a

---

Table [33.3]

Rabinovitch et al. (1972)   57 children, aged 11 to 12 years, watched either a violent or a neutral TV programme, and were then shown pictures of violent and neutral scenes flashed momentarily before them. The violent group were less likely than the controls to notice the violent pictures.

Drabman and Thomas (1974)   44 children, aged 8 to 10 years, watched either an eight-minute violent film or nothing, and were then asked to keep an eye on two younger children. The violent group were less likely than the controls to call the experimenter when the children started to fight.

Thomas and Drabman (1975)   In a replication of the above study, 20 children who had just seen a fifteen-minute violent detective film on TV were slower to summon help than were 20 controls who saw an exciting non-violent film. This result was not apparent, however, for younger children aged 6 to 7 years.

Thomas et al. (1977)   28 boys and 16 girls, aged 8 to 10 years, were shown either a violent police drama or an equally emotion-arousing sports film. Subsequently, a videotape of real-life aggression (children fighting) produced less emotional re-sponse (skin resistance) in the violent group. Similar results were obtained for 29 male students, but not 30 females, in a replication. In both studies, amount of TV violence normally viewed was negatively related to responsivity while viewing aggression.

---

drastically slowed heart beat insufficient blood may be reaching the brain to retain consciousness. A very interesting extension to this research would be to observe changes in these physiological measures during a process of desensitization. If the aversive reaction habituates more rapidly than the excitement reaction, then we would have the ominous prospect of the 'hardened' viewer responding to such films only with excitement.

In an earlier review of the desensitization evidence, Howitt and Cumberbatch (1975) commented that 'it is very likely that this process of habituation does occur for mass media violence ... but the social consequences of this are unclear'. One such consequence is that desensitization, by reducing anxiety, may make people more likely to carry out acts of aggression in the future. In other words, in order to commit an act of aggression it may be necessary to overcome certain inhibitions, and this is where prior exposure, even if only to acts of a similar nature on the screen, probably helps. The experiment by Drabman and Thomas indicates another social consequence. As people become more and more used to violence, there is the danger that they will come to accept and tolerate it. If witnessed continually, violence may eventually come to be regarded as normal behaviour.

The effects of desensitization to violence have been generally overlooked by theorists in favour of the imitation and disinhibition effects. [...] But it seems to us that the consequences of a nation 'desensitized' to violence are just as serious, if not more so, than one which is merely exposed to examples of how to be violent.

REFERENCES

Averill, J. R., Malmstrom, E. J., Koriat, A. and Lazarus, R. S. (1972). Habituation to complex emotional stimuli. *Journal of Abnormal Psychology*, 80, 20–8.

Berger, S. M. (1962). Conditioning through vicarious instigation. *Psychological Review*, 69, 450–66.

Bergin, A. E. and Garfield, S. L. (Eds) (1971). *Handbook of Psychotherapy and Behaviour Change*. London: Wiley.

Carruthers, M. and Taggart, P. (1973). Vagotonicity of violence: Biochemical and cardiac responses to violent films and television programmes. *British Medical Journal*, 3, 384–9.

Cline, V. B., Croft, R. G. and Courrier, S. (1973). Desensitization of children to television violence. *Journal of Personality and Social Psychology*, 27, 360–5.

Drabman, R. S. and Thomas, M. H. (1974). Does media violence increase children's tolerance of real-life aggression? *Developmental Psychology*, 10, 418–21.

Eysenck, H. J. (1977). *Crime and Personality* (3rd Edition). London: Routledge & Kegan Paul.

Howitt, D. and Cumberbatch, G. (1975). *Mass Media Violence and Society*. New York: Halstead.

Lazarus, R. S., Speisman, J. C., Mordkoff, A. M. and Davison, L. A. (1962). A laboratory study of psychological stress produced by a motion picture film. *Psychological Monographs*, 76 (Whole No. 553).

Rabinovitch, M. S., McLean, M. S., Markham, J. W. and Talbot, A. D. (1972). Children's violence perception as a function of television violence. In *TV and Social Behaviour* (Vol. 5). Washington DC: US Government Printing Office.

Thomas, M. H. and Drabman, R. S. (1975). Toleration of real life aggression as a function of exposure to televised violence and age of subject. *Merrill-Palmer Quarterly*, 21, 227–32.

Thomas, M. H., Horton, R. W., Lippincott, E. C. and Drabman, R. S. (1977). Desensitization to portrayals of real-life aggression as a function of exposure to television violence. *Journal of Personality and Social Psychology*, 35, 450–8.

34

ON THE SOCIAL EFFECTS
OF TELEVISION

James D. Halloran

[...]

The early view of mass communication assumed that people could be persuaded by the media to adopt almost any point of view desired by the communicator. Manipulation, exploitation and vulnerability were the key words. In this crude sense this extreme view is no longer accepted, although some of the implications of this initial position are still with us. In one way or another it has provided a base from which so much of our thinking about mass communication (pessimistic as well as optimistic) has stemmed. Some people still write and talk about television as a powerful direct influence and of its tremendous potential for good or evil. In some quarters the myth of omnipotence dies hard.

Social science has undergone many changes since the days of instinct theory and the early ideas about mass society. Models of society, concepts of human nature and images of man, all change. Learning theory, work on motives and attitudes, the development of personality theory, the emphasis on selectivity in attention and perception, recognition of the importance of individual differences, the formulation of psychodynamic models of persuasion, the use of social categories in surveys and empirical work generally, the 'rediscovery' of the primary group, the acceptance of the influence of informal group ties, the development of such concepts as reference group and the work on diffusion of

From James D. Halloran, 'Studying the Effects of Television' and James D. Halloran, 'The Social Effects of Television', in James D. Halloran (ed.), *The Effects of Television* (London: Panther Books, 1970) pp. 18–20 and 39–43.

information and social interaction, have all played their part in producing more refined and elaborate approaches and more developed theories than the one referred to above.

It is sometimes said that one of the dangers today is that so much attention is given to the intervening or associated factors that we are in danger of neglecting what should always be central to our work, namely, the medium itself – television. In general the trend has been away from the idea of exploitation, away from an emphasis on the viewer as tabula rasa, as someone wide open just waiting to soak up all that is beamed at him. Now we think more in terms of interaction or exchange between medium and audience, and it is recognized that the viewer approaches every viewing situation with a complicated piece of filtering equipment. This filter is made up not only of his past and present, but includes his views of and hopes for the future. We should welcome this change in emphasis but there is always a possibility that in making the shift the baby might be thrown out with the bath water. Instead of having the false picture of the all-powerful influence of television presented to us we now run the risk of getting an equally false picture of no influence whatsoever.

Even today despite all the changes and developments the picture should not be regarded as final. Granted the state of our knowledge, we could not afford to let things stay as they are. One of the healthy signs about the current situation is that in research the established ways of doing things are being questioned and challenged. [...] There is, of course, plenty of room for change. For example, although we have seen that the viewer is no longer *thought of* as an isolated individual in front of a television set – the importance of his background, experiences and relationships are recognized – he is still frequently researched as though he were an isolated individual. In many research exercises the individual remains the main sampling unit, and *in practice* there would still appear to be a fairly widespread acceptance of the atomistic nature of the audience.[1]

Attitude has been one of the central concepts in both social psychology and mass communication research for a long time, but there is a growing body of opinion which holds that attitude change has been over-used as the primary criterion of influence. [...] [T]here is much more to television's influence than can be studied through direct changes in attitude and opinion as these have normally been defined and assessed. Television may provide models for identification, confer status on people and behaviour, spell out norms, define new situations, provide stereotypes, set frameworks of anticipation and indicate levels of acceptability, tolerance and approval. Influence must not be equated with attitude change.

It is neither necessary nor desirable to confine or even to concentrate our research on conventional approaches which seek to study viewer reactions before and after exposure to television programmes. Whilst accepting that quite often a concern with media content, to the exclusion of other factors, has led to misleading predictions about effects, we still cannot afford to ignore content. A *systematic* study of what television provides, whilst not telling us what happens to people, will tell us what is available, what there is for them to use. If we have also studied the patterns of use and the relevant relationships, predispositions and background experience of those who use television, then it is possible for predictions to be made about the consequence of that use.

[...]

A study[2] carried out at the Centre for Mass Communication Research at the University of Leicester on a programme which dealt with the lives of young people in Czechoslovakia, in addition to providing further support for the principle that different people get different things from the same programme, indicated that it could be misleading to think of the effects of television solely in terms of visual impact. The effects of this particular programme seemed to follow the commentary. Whilst accepting that any television programme is essentially a complex audio-visual message, it seemed that the clear and unambiguous statements about Czech life made in the programme had considerable impact. Several years ago the late Joe Trenaman also drew attention to the importance of the verbal element in what is sometimes regarded as a purely visual medium.[3]

This research also showed that it might be possible for a programme to produce short-term changes in attitude about certain topics covered by the programme (in this case favourable changes about specific aspects of Czech life) and yet produce no change at the more general or overall level (in this case, favourable change in attitude about Czechoslovakia as a political state).

The programme in question, *Children of Revolution*, was an Intertel programme, and Intertel aims to produce programmes which promote 'a wider knowledge of contemporary world affairs and a better mutual understanding of world problems'. We might ask if this is a realistic policy – can television hope to do this? It would be unwise to rely too much on the results from one small piece of research but this research did show that, after viewing the programme, people not only had more knowledge about life in Czechoslovakia but in general took a more favourable view of life in that country. In a sense then, the objectives of the programme were met. However, we have already seen that the favourable change in attitude did not extend to the government and the state. These were often more negatively evaluated after the programme. It is possible, as Roger Brown suggests, that people had their prior beliefs in the tensions supposedly inherent in a Communist society strengthened by the programme. The favourable shifts in attitude with regard to the parts of the programme (e.g. Czech youth) may have been bought at the price of a less favourable image of the Czech state. In this complex situation is it possible to assess whether or not the programme-makers really achieved their objectives?

What can one hope to achieve by presenting social and political issues on television? Unfortunately, good intentions are no guarantee of success, as the reactions to many a programme (drama, documentary and educational) clearly show. Research on the ATV seven-programme series *Nature of Prejudice*, presented in 1968, showed – like the findings from many other studies – that the same message can be used in different ways by different people. From this study it is possible to argue that audience members saw in the programme what was uppermost in their own minds, rather than what the programme itself stressed most. In general, viewers found a way of avoiding the anti-prejudice message. Different sorts of viewers did see different things in the programmes, and did respond in different ways. This comes out clearly both in the comparison between prejudiced and non-prejudiced respondents, and in that between adolescent and adult viewers. But this is only another way of saying that individuals brought to the viewing situation a range of differing interests, beliefs, concepts and levels of knowledge, and that these acted as filters through which the programmes were viewed. This latter description of the situation, in its turn, raises questions about the 'success' of the programme in penetrating the defences which all of us raise against alien ideas, and about the particular processes which take place between the time our eyes and ears receive a particular sort of stimulation and the time when we arrive at some vision of the original message which fits in as well as possible with our initial needs and predispositions.[4]

In a different genre, the BBC produced a six-episode serial, *Rainbow City*, in 1967. The avowed purpose of these programmes was to contribute to the reduction of inter-racial tensions and to promote a sympathetic understanding of coloured immigrants. The evidence available from a minor research project on these programmes indicates that sympathy was enlisted for particular characters, but that the attitudes of viewers to coloured people or immigrants in general were not modified. Identification or empathy with individual screen personalities belonging to an outgroup or minority group does not necessarily rub off on the group in general.

In view of the American experience over the years (e.g. with musicians, sporting personalities etc.) it might be argued that we do not require research to teach us this lesson. Nevertheless, it is worth emphasizing, with regard to prejudice as with other attitudes, that as far as this form of attitude change is concerned, television can only work within the existing climate.[5] If the general climate is hostile to the message, there is even the possibility of a boomerang effect, i.e. the hostility being increased. Although in this particular case we can say nothing about the overall quality of the series or about the form of presentation, it is possible that – with issues that produce strong reactions – these factors may not be particularly relevant. It seems reasonable to suggest that certain topics in television programmes will produce predictable reactions from given sections of the viewing audience independently of quality and mode of presentation.

In considering the presentation of social issues on television and the effects of such presentations, it is essential to make the distinction between a gain in knowledge or information, and a change in attitude. It is usually easier to convey knowledge than to change attitudes. Research carried out several years ago by the BBC Audience Research Department, on programmes dealing with such topics as crime and the death penalty,[6] showed that although in the latter case attitudes were modified (not changed), the former programme had very little effect on either knowledge or attitudes. Even where there was a considerable increase in knowledge about a particular topic or item covered in the programme, the majority of the viewing audience still remained ignorant on the same topic after viewing. It may be easier to impart knowledge than to change attitudes, but powerful restricting factors, external to the programme itself, would appear to operate in both cases.

Several points can be made about the apparent lack of effects of these programmes which dealt with social and political issues.[7] The first is that even within the limited terms of reference and possibilities of this type of research, it would be quite unreasonable to expect a single programme or even a series of programmes to bring about appreciable changes in attitudes. Change just doesn't take place so easily. The second is that it is a mistake to equate lack of change, in the sense of people not changing from a pro to a con position (or vice versa) after seeing a programme with the overall lack of influence of that programme. The programme may confirm or reinforce the existing attitudinal position or, on the other hand, as we have just seen, the attitude may be modified in intensity. Many researchers have confined their attention to the narrower interpretation of change (from a pro to a con position) and this has undoubtedly contributed to the idea, still widely held in some quarters, that the media have little influence.

There have, of course, been many occasions when the media have been credited with, or accused of having, too much influence. Perhaps television does not have the influence that some people would have us believe but it must be recognized that influence can take several forms. Influence should certainly not be equated with these relatively narrow definitions of change.

NOTES

1. Marten Brouwer. 'Prolegomena to a Theory of Mass Communication', in *Communication Concepts and Perspectives*, Ed. Lee Thayer, Spartan Books, 1967.
2. Roger L. Brown. *Some Effects of the Television Programme 'Children of Revolution'*. A Report prepared for the Television Research Committee, Centre for Mass Communication Research, University of Leicester. 1967. 160 p. & vi p.
3. Joseph Trenaman. 'The Effects of Television', in *Twentieth Century*. Nov. 1959. pp. 332–42.
4. Television Research Committee. *Second Progress Report and Recommendations*. Leicester University Press 1969. p. 34.
5. The part played by television in creating the climate remains to be considered.
6. See B. P. Emmett. 'The Design of Investigations into the Effects of Radio and Television Programmes and other Mass Communications'. *Journal of the Royal Statistical Society*. Vol. 129. 1966.
7. Some studies have demonstrated that other programmes have been *slightly* more effective.

35

THE TELEVISION AUDIENCE:
A REVISED PERSPECTIVE

Denis McQuail, Jay G. Blumler and J. R. Brown

The single concept which seems to have assumed most prominence in discussions of mass media experience has been that of 'escape'.

[...]

When all due allowance is made for distinctions and reservations, it must be admitted that the escapist hypothesis still occupies much of the central ground in discussion and study of the television audience.

Like several other notions that are deeply entrenched in the vocabulary of discourse about culture and society, the concept of escape is exceptionally potent because it inextricably intermingles what might otherwise be a merely descriptive assertion in the scientific spirit (hypothesizing that most viewers predominantly use television in order to forget stressful and disliked features of their environment) with a strongly held normative standpoint. Deployed in the latter sense, the escapist thesis has helped to precipitate and perpetuate certain derogatory assumptions about the typical relationship between television and the viewer, from which even the qualifications and reservations mentioned above are usually excluded.

Firstly there is the view that popularity is inconsistent with high quality, since the latter is assumed to connote educational attainment, critical standards, sensitivity of judgement, effort and creativity, all of which stand in

From Denis McQuail, Jay G. Blumler and J. R. Brown, 'The Television Audience: A Revised Perspective', Ch. 7 in Denis McQuail (ed.), *Sociology of Mass Communications* (Harmondsworth: Penguin, 1972).

contrast to the dominant meanings of the escape concept. Second, there is an assumption of homogeneity; the content of a mass medium like television is regarded virtually as a single commodity, in which one programme could stand in quite readily for any other. The audience is unselective because all or most programmes offer essentially the same satisfaction and are watched for broadly the same motive. A third and related point is that the experience of television is uninvolving and, by implication, unimportant according to a widely held scale of values. It is regarded as shallow, undemanding and trivial. Fourth, television is regarded as a residual category of leisure activity; it is a time-filler, a substitute for doing nothing or something more worthwhile, shaped more by variations in other demands on one's time than by any positive attractions or considered motivations. This view finds some support in the phenomenal *quantity* of time devoted to it. The general bearing of this set of views is to see the experience of watching television as largely lacking in meaning, hardly deserving of serious interest or respect, a chance outcome of a set of market circumstances. The explanatory formula is thus closed and virtually self-validating. So the evidence showing long hours of time spent watching television is not interpreted as pointing to the influence of powerful attraction or strong need, but as indicative instead of a vacancy of outlook, an emptiness of life and a uniformity of response. And when evidence shows that people do actually depend a good deal on television and are upset when it is not available, this is taken more as a sign of their stupidity than of the constructive role which the medium plays in their lives.

[...]

The danger is that an uncritical acceptance of the escapist thesis will go hand-in-hand with a simplistic view of the relations between audience and media content and an underestimation of the diversity and complexity of motives that may sustain the mass audience. It could also have undesirable consequences for the organization of television and the evolution of policies that determine its place in society – undesirable, that is, if television is not in fact so constrained as the escapist theory makes out from performing a wider range of social functions than is generally assigned to it in western societies today.

In this essay we aim, then, to advance, on the basis of empirical research evidence, a typology of viewer gratifications which can both enlarge our understanding of what escape implies and help to place it in a context of a number of other equally important orientations, motives and links between people and television. We strive to substantiate the claim that escape does not represent the only, or even the invariably most appropriate, formulation of the needs served by the mass communication process and to direct attention towards several other formulations of what this process may fundamentally involve and signify.

The evidence presented for illustration and support derives from a programme of investigation initiated in 1969 at the Centre for Television Research in the University of Leeds. It was designed to further in a systematic way the tradition of inquiry which has been concerned with audience 'uses and gratifications', and which seeks to explain, usually on the basis of the audience member's own subjective account of the media experience, just what functions a particular kind of content serves in particular circumstance.

[...]

Our work was guided by certain presuppositions, which should be briefly outlined. Most fundamentally, we adopted the view that an important part of television viewing is goal-directed. While this premise may seem question-begging, we could not proceed far with our investigation without it, and it does not imply in advance any single kind of motive. Second, we assumed that the goals of television viewing can only be discovered from viewers themselves and that people will be sufficiently self-aware to be able to report their interests and motives in particular cases or at least to recognize them when confronted with them in an intelligible and familiar verbal formulation. Third, we were prepared to find diverse and overlapping patterns of motive and satisfaction; if a viewer was moved by several different concerns to follow the same content, we want our instruments of investigation to disclose, not to ignore, this fact. Fourth, we were prepared to treat as a conceptually independent unit of analysis something which might variously be described as a satisfaction, a motive, a gratification, an interest or a function. These units could be distributed in varying ways amongst a given population of television viewers and also be associated with different programmes and programme types in varying degrees.

Because it stands on the same plane of generality as the assumptions specified above, a final orientation deserves to be mentioned here, even though it only emerged explicitly as evidence was collected and analysed. This is that media use is most suitably characterized as an interactive process, relating media content, individual needs, perceptions, roles and values and the social context in which a person is situated. Our model of this process is that of an open system in which social experience gives rise to certain needs, some of which are directed to the mass media of communication for satisfaction. It is also possible that media content may occasionally help to generate in the audience member an awareness of certain needs in relation to his social situation. The linkage is necessarily a complex one and may take diverse forms; it may involve a process of deprivation-compensation in which the media offer substitute satisfactions for something desired or valued, but relatively unavailable; or it may involve a process of value reinforcement in which salient values, beliefs or attitudes are sustained by attention to certain content forms; or materials taken from the media may contribute to certain processes of social interchange which go with the occupancy of certain roles. The essential point to be stressed is our belief that media use is interactive. That is, it does not conform to the typical lineaments of a subject-object relationship, and should not be treated merely as a one-way tension-reducing mechanism. Such a model would leave out of account the many ways in which, according to our evidence, audience members seem to bring back into their lives, their patterns of activity and their circles of familiar acquaintances some of the broadcast programmes to which they have become attached.

[...]

[An] account follows of one programme study, that which was concerned with television quiz programmes. This was the second study carried out and the first in which a group of programmes as a type, rather than a single programme, was examined. The choice was influenced by the fact that quiz programmes form a distinctive and popular category of television content with a seeming diversity of associations. In addition, there existed a link with early research in the form of an interesting study of a small sample of listeners to an American radio quiz programme, providing material for comparison and a source of some hypotheses (Herzog, 1940).

A series of tape-recorded discussions was first held with followers of television quiz programmes, and a questionnaire compiled in the light of the analysis of material thus obtained. This questionnaire was then administered to a quota sample of seventy-three Leeds residents (with controls for sex, age, housing type and social grade), all of whom had designated as among their favourite television programmes one of several quiz programmes from a wider list. The three quiz programmes were *University Challenge*, *TV Brain of Britain*, and *Ask the Family*, each of them involving genuine tests of knowledge rather than being merely parlour games with big prizes, gimmicks and a prominent element of chance.

The most relevant part of the questionnaire consisted of an inventory of forty-two statements about quiz programmes, divided into three sections, which were presented to respondents for endorsement on a four-point scale. The first section contained statements indicating expected satisfactions and accompanied by the wording: 'When I think of watching a quiz [the statement] applies very much, quite a lot, a little, not at all.' The second referred to experienced satisfactions in the following way: 'When watching quizzes [the experience] has happened very often, quite often, only now and then, never.' In the third section respondents were asked whether certain descriptive phrases applied 'very well', 'slightly', or 'not at all' to quiz programmes.

[...]

The pattern of the gratifications viewers seek from quiz programmes emerged from an analysis involving two stages. First, associations between endorsements of the scales were set out in a 42×42 matrix of intercorrelations. Second, the statements were re-arranged into sub-sets by means of a cluster analysis (McQuitty's elementary linkage analysis, 1957). This technique is designed to arrange intercorrelated items into clusters which maximize the average internal correlation of the clustered items and minimize the correlation between sub-sets. It is an approximate method, easy to apply, which provides an entirely empirical solution to the problem of ordering interrelated data. Every item is assigned to one and only one cluster, although it may be the case that a particular statement could equally well fit in more than one cluster.

The results of the quiz programme cluster analysis are presented in Table [35.1]. We find four main clusters of items emerging, with several small groups in pairs also separated out.

[...]

[T]hey form a strikingly clear and interpretable pattern, or so we can conclude about the four relatively large clusters. The six later clusters add little to the results, partly because most of their meanings have already been covered and partly because two- or three-item groups are inevitably low in reliability.

According to this analysis, then, four main kinds of gratifications are involved in the viewing of quiz programmes. One stems from a *self-rating appeal*, whereby watching a quiz enables the viewer to find out something about himself. Inspection of the individual items in Cluster 1 suggests that it embraces several related elements. There is the possibility of assessing one's ability by comparing one's own responses to the questions with the performance of other contestants. There is the possibility of testing one's judgement by guessing which group of competitors will turn out to be the winners. There is the theme of projection, whereby the viewer can imagine how he would fare if he were on the programme himself. And there is the possibility of being reminded of what one was like as a schoolchild. In the last context it is interesting to note that Herzog also detected a self-rating appeal of quiz programmes and speculated that one of its ingredients was the attraction of 'being taken back to one's own school days' (1940).

The meaning of Cluster 2 seems equally definite. A second major appeal of quiz programmes is their provision of a *basis for social interaction* with other people. Each item in the cluster (with only one exception) bears this interpretation. A quiz programme offers shared family interest; there is the possibility of observing 'what the children get out of it'; the whole family can work together on the answers; alternatively, viewers can compete with each other in trying to answer the questions; and the occasion can form a topic of conversation afterwards. Clearly quiz programmes are well adapted to serving a 'coin of exchange' function.

A third main appeal of TV quizzes arises from the *excitement* they can engender. Many of the items in Cluster 3 convey this emphasis. Quiz programmes apparently offer the excitement of competition itself, guessing who might win and seeing how one's forecast turns out, and the prospect of a close finish. Herzog seemed to have this gratification in mind when referring to the so-called 'sporting appeal' of *Professor Quiz* (1940). Perhaps what is distinctive about the composition of Cluster 3 in this study is its injection of an 'escapist' note into the associated group of items ('I like to forget my worries for a while', and 'I completely forget my worries'). It is as if the various tensions of a quiz programme facilitate its 'escapist' function and help the viewer to shed his everyday cares for a while.

Finally, Cluster 4 picks out an *educational appeal* of quiz programmes. Here, too, several ingredients are involved. It is not just that quizzes can help to stimulate thought ('I think over some of the questions afterwards'). In addition, two of the items sound a note of 'self-improvement' ('I feel I have improved myself', and 'I find I know more than I thought'), in terms which suggest that people who feel insecure in their educational status may use quizzes to reassure themselves about their own knowledgeability. And this suggests yet another way of interpreting Cluster 4 – as expressive of the function of quiz programmes in projecting and reinforcing educational values.

Subsequent analysis involved the testing of relationships between the appeals represented by these main clusters and variables representative of social experience and attitudes. In effect we wished to know what kinds of people were most attracted to quiz programmes for reasons implied in these different clusters [. . .] [and] what kinds of social circumstances are associated with, and hence possibly causative of, liking the programme in question for a given type of reason. The results are of interest both as tests of certain hypotheses and as means of validating the distinctiveness of two separate clusters. The findings are complex, but for each of four quiz clusters we can report the sub-group or groups which are maximally involved.

Cluster 1 Self-rating appeal

The analysis separates out as relatively high scorers those members of the sample (thirty-six out of seventy-three) living in council housing. This suggests that the working-class fans of a programme type which in fact had a generally stronger appeal for middle-class people were more concerned to use it to 'learn things about themselves' than were other viewers.

Cluster 2 Basis for social interaction

Here the strongest associations were with social contact variables. The first high-scoring group to emerge from the analysis consisted of those respondents who reported having a very large number of acquaintances in their neighbourhoods. Among the other sample members, those with a large extended family were then distinguished as particularly high-scoring on this cluster. The use of quiz material as a 'coin of exchange' seemed, then, to be directly related to the number of opportunities for interaction available in the individual's immediate social environment.

Cluster 3 Excitement

The highest scoring group consisted of working-class viewers who had measured low on an index of acts of sociability and who were late-born children of large families. While the significance of the role of family background here is not clear, the predominant meaning of the link to low sociability seems to favour an escapist or compensatory explanation of this motive for watching quiz programmes.

Cluster 4 Educational appeal

The strongest and most clearcut association here was with educational background, since the analysis, after first distinguishing Leeds-born respondents from the 'immigrants' to the city, then split the former into a high-scoring group whose education had finished at the minimum school-leaving age. Thus the educational appeal of quiz programmes was strongest for those individuals with the most limited school experience.

These and other results which related to quiz programmes were not without ambiguity and left many questions unanswered, but they appeared to lend support to some of our basic working assumptions. They also foreshadowed some of the categories that figure in the typology of viewer gratifications which stemmed from our attempt to organize the results of several different studies, of which the quiz investigation was but one example.

The four most successful studies yielded a total of nineteen clusters to which substantive labels could be attached, and when these were regarded as a whole a relatively small number of recurrent categories were found to emerge. It was this striking, and only partly anticipated, degree of overlapping in the gratification clusters which makes it possible, without further detailed research, to prepare the outlines of the overall framework of appeals by which television may meet the needs of its audience. A major implication of this phenomenon of overlapping dispositions is that people can look to quite different kinds of material for essentially the same gratification and, correlatively, find alternative satisfactions in the same televised material. Thus an 'escape' motive seemed to feature in the structure of orientations to broadcast materials as diverse as *The Dales* radio serial, *The Saint*, television news and quiz programmes. It should be noted that these types of content are hardly comparable in terms of the degree to which they provide a faithful representation of reality; yet they still offer a recognizably similar kind of satisfaction to audience members. Other gratification types ranged with equal facility across a similarly diverse set of programme areas.

In fact, this repetition of a small number of themes was the starting point for the development of an overall framework of gratification types.

[...]

The conceptual status of the typology calls for a brief comment. What, exactly, it may be asked, *are* the sorts of things that we are classifying? However appropriate otherwise, the language of functionalism is so overworked, ambiguous and imprecise that we prefer to avoid it, and to attempt a

Table [35.1] Results of cluster analysis of statements relating to television quiz programmes

	Coefficients of homogeneity	reliability
Cluster 1 Self-rating appeal	0.24	0.69
I can compare myself with the experts		
I like to imagine that I am on the programme doing well		
I feel pleased that the side I favour has actually won		
I imagine that I was on the programme and doing well		
I am reminded of when I was in school		
I laugh at the contestant's mistakes		
Hard to follow		
Cluster 2 Basis for social interaction	0.31	0.79
I look forward to talking about it with others		
I like competing with other people watching with me		
I like working together with the family on the answers		
I hope the children get a lot out of it		
The children get a lot out of it		
It brings the family together sharing the same interest		
It is a topic of conversation afterwards		
Not really for people like myself		
Cluster 3 Excitement appeal	0.34	0.78
I like the excitement of a close finish		
I like to forget my worries for a while		
I like trying to guess the winner		
Having got the answer right I feel really good		
I completely forget my worries		
I get involved in the competition		
Exciting		

	Coefficients of homogeneity	reliability
Cluster 4 Educational appeal	0.30	0.68

Cluster 4 Educational appeal

I find I know more than I thought

I feel I have improved myself

I feel respect for the people on the programme

I think over some of the questions afterwards

Educational

Cluster 5

It is nice to see the experts taken down a peg

It is amusing to see the mistakes some of the contestants make

Cluster 6

I like to learn something as well as be entertained

I like finding out new things

Cluster 7

I like trying to guess the answers

I hope to find that I know some of the answers

Cluster 8

I find out the gaps in what I know

I learn something new

A waste of time

Cluster 9

Entertaining

Something for all the family

Cluster 10

I like the sound of voices in the house

I like seeing really intelligent contestants showing how much they know new start. In keeping with our view of mass media use as being potentially highly involving and also two-way, we propose to use the expression, 'media-person interaction', to refer to the orientations distinguished in the typology. Our clusters of items seem to reveal certain types of relationship between the user and the communicated content that depend on the perceptions of the audience member. A good deal of imprecision remains in the concept, but this stems from the variability inherent in the situation. What we wish to avoid is any specific inference about the presence of a discrete motive or the occurrence of a precise 'effect'. The audience member temporarily occupies a particular position in relation to what he is viewing, a position affected by a large number of factors, including those deriving from his personality, social background, experience, immediate social context, and, of course, from the content itself. He brings certain expectations and responds in line with these, and he derives certain affective, cognitive and instrumental satisfactions.

The typology of media–person interactions is intended to differentiate certain common constellations of disposition and response. It does so only very approximately and at present hypothetically. Its main strength as a heuristic device or source of hypotheses derives from its empirical base and its main weakness from the possibly limited character of this base.

The categories of our typology can first be presented in a summary form and then elaborated and illustrated more fully:

1. Diversion
   (a) Escape from the constraints of routine
   (b) Escape from the burdens of problems
   (c) Emotional release
2. Personal Relationships
   (a) Companionship
   (b) Social utility
3. Personal Identity
   (a) Personal reference
   (b) Reality exploration
   (c) Value reinforcement
4. Surveillance

Diversion

The meaning of the three sub-types listed under this heading can be illustrated from the results of the programme studies mentioned above. The first sub-type of the category labelled 'diversion' is instanced by the first main clustering of responses to *The Saint*. This cluster included the following set of empirically linked items:

> 'It helps you escape from the boredom of everyday life'
> 'It takes you out of yourself'
> 'The stories often have interesting backgrounds'

'It does you good to see somebody doing things you can't do yourself'
'*The Saint* keeps me in suspense'

What a programme of this kind offers is a fantasy world which is attractive in itself, and which the viewer can temporarily occupy.

A somewhat different relationship, justifying a second sub-type, is indicated by one of the clusters concerning quiz programmes where the item 'I completely forgot my worries' is closely linked with two others that refer to the mechanism involved: 'I like the excitement of a close finish', and 'I like trying to guess the winner'. Another expression of this kind of diversion seems implicit in one of the news-viewing clusters which linked the following items:

'It helps me to get away from my problems'
'It's like having a good gossip'
'I like the sound of voices in my house'

Third, the category of media function, which we have labelled 'emotional release' (familiar from Herzog's pioneering study (1944) of radio soap operas of thirty years ago) appeared in connection with *The Dales* radio serial. Only two linked items of response can bear this meaning – 'Sometimes I think "I wish that were me"', and 'Sometimes it makes me want to cry' – and probably it applies to only a minority of the audience for certain limited kinds of media material. Even so, the appropriate content may have been under-represented in the small sample of programmes studied, and additional evidence obtained in a follow-up study of the original sample of *The Dales* listeners seemed to confirm the presence of this kind of response. Thus, when fifty-five members of the sample were reinterviewed and asked directly if *The Dales* did provide an opportunity 'to relieve their feelings', sixteen answered affirmatively. The existence of this kind of reaction to books, films and plays is so familiar that it perhaps needs no further proof. More important is our wish to treat it as a form of 'diversion' and to distinguish it from an escape into a more desirable imaginary world or out of an oppressive reality.

Personal Relationships

Two gratification types have been placed under this heading because they both refer to the viewer's relationships with other people – either real-life persons or media personalities. The 'companionship' category stands for a process whereby the audience member enters into a vicarious relationship with media personalities (fictional characters, entertainers, or presenters) as if he was on friendly terms with them, and as if they could stand in for real persons. Two perceptive observers have termed this tendency a 'para-social relationship' (Horton and Wohl, 1956). The clearest expression of the wish to use media in this way is represented in one of *The Dales* clusters, the most frequently endorsed item of which was 'It is good company when you're alone'. Some of the other related items were:

'The characters have become like close friends to me'
'It gives me something in common with other *Dales* listeners'
'I like the sound of the characters' voices in my house'

A familiar assumption about the mass media, and a phenomenon which will be within the experience of most people is attested to by the occurrence of this set of attitudes in relation to a programme which attracted a large number of solitary listeners, *The Dales*. What our evidence about this programme suggested, however, was that the companionship element was even stronger than is often supposed: the characters may become virtually real, knowable and cherished individuals, and their voices are more than just a comforting background which breaks the silence of an empty house. This point can be illustrated by some further data, relating this time to the TV serial, *Coronation Street*. In the course of interviewing the sample of viewers, an opportunity arose of asking respondents how they felt about a road crash which had occurred in the programme. Amongst the many replies demonstrating the ease with which fictional events are integrated into real life were a number relevant to the idea of substitute companionship: 'I'm sorry. I like all of them. Minnie's just like Auntie; you feel you know them. You know you feel as if they had been in a real accident and you'd like to do something for them'; or 'Shattered. I'm very upset. I hope they'll be all right'; and 'My wife was very upset. So was I. I hope they'll be all right.'

The category we have called 'social utility' is a disparate one, but would cover those uses of the media which are instrumental for social interaction with real people in familiar surroundings. Social utility here may refer to media use as a source of conversational material, as a subject of conversation in itself, as a common activity for a family or other group engaging, say, in viewing together, or as something that helps an individual to discharge a definite social role or to meet the membership requirements of one or more of his peer groups. The research literature includes a number of examples describing a 'coin of exchange' function served by the media in conversational and other social situations (Riley and Riley, 1951). One of the clearest illustrations from our own work is provided by many of the items included in the second cluster of responses to television quiz programmes:

'I look forward to talking about it with others'
'I like competing with other people watching with me'
'I like working together with the family on the answers'
'It brings the family together sharing the same interest'
'It is a topic of conversation afterwards'

And a prominent cluster in the analysis of television newsviewing located a somewhat more specific information-relaying use of television, grouping the following items:

'I like to be the first with the news so that I can pass it on to other people'
'It satisfies my sense of curiosity'
'Keeping up with the news gives you plenty to talk about'
'Somehow I feel more secure when I know what is going on'

Perhaps this category of media use provides the best support for our contention that the relationship between medium and audience is not one-sided and that the role and social situation of the viewer may help to govern his selection and response. It also serves to make plausible the view that the specific content of the media can be relatively unhelpful in predicting the grounds of audience response; consequently, categorization of content based on overt meaning may have a limited value in mass communications research. The 'meaning' of an example of viewing behaviour is not self-evident from knowledge of content alone, or of the social-demographic parameters of the audience.

Personal Identity

The set of gratification types classified under this heading brings together ways of using programme materials to reflect upon or to give added salience to something important in the viewer's own life or situation. One such disposition – a use of television for what has been termed 'personal reference' – provided perhaps that most novel outcome of the exploratory research, for few previous uses and gratification studies have reported anything like it. This reflected a use of programme content to characterize or highlight for the viewer some feature of his own situation, character or life, past or present. For example, the dominant item of the first *Dales* cluster was worded 'The programme reminds me that I could be worse off than I am', while other items with which this was associated included:

'I can compare the people in the programme with other people I know'
'It reminds me of things that have happened in my own life'
'It sometimes brings back memories of certain people I used to know'

In addition, the first quiz cluster brought together a group of items which reflected the viewer's interest in rating his abilities by responding to the questions asked on the programmes and comparing his achievement with that of the performers. This orientation is reminiscent of the perspective of symbolic interactionism, according to which a central element in the world of every person is some notion of himself, and such a notion is formed in great part by looking at oneself through the eyes of others. Apparently, not only interpersonal exchanges but also mass communications can help some people to form or reassess impressions of their own 'selves'.

A second version of this concern of people to explore their own personal identity was distinguished from the first mainly by the kind of reflection that was evoked. In contrast to the more descriptive activities of classification and labelling subsumed under 'personal reference', the process of 'reality exploration' involved a use of programme content to stimulate ideas about certain problems which the viewer was experiencing, or might at some time experience, in his more immediate social environment. The *Dales* cluster which seemed to express this tendency included such items as: 'The people in *The Dales* sometimes have problems that are like my own', and 'It sometimes helps me to understand my own life'. The emergence of a similar cluster from the *Saint* analysis – centering on the dominant item 'It provides food for thought' – was more surprising, since this series would seem to many observers to provide no more than a succession of wish-fulfilling fantasies. The result suggests that keen 'fans' of almost any kind of fictional content may regard it as a stimulus relevant to their own real-life problems.

Less surprisingly, amongst the appeals of television news, we located a small group of items which together indicated an empathic response to news viewing. This cluster separated out the following: 'It helps me realize my life is not so bad after all'; 'It helps me to understand some of the problems other people have'; 'It sometimes makes me feel sad'. While the allocation of this type of response between the categories of 'personal reference' and 'reality exploration' is uncertain, there is little doubt that news enters into the process of establishing and maintaining identity and of relating the self to the wider society.

The third gratification category under 'personal identity' in the typology, termed 'value reinforcement', is more or less self explanatory. It locates the appeal to a viewer of a programme which upholds certain values that he also believes in. This particular mode of media–person interaction is most clearly illustrated by one of the *Dales* clusters, the dominant item of which, worded, 'It's nice to know there are families like the Dales around today', was linked with two others: 'It reminds me of the importance of family ties', and 'It puts over a picture of what family life should be like'. Two other instances of a value-reinforcing relationship involving broadcast material may be noted. One of these emerged from the quiz study where a set of items expressive of a positive attitude to self-improvement and educational values generally was picked out by the analysis. The second was also found in *Dales* study and involved a valuation of the serial as a programme for women, including in this assessment an appreciation of its gentility and moral respectability in contrast to other media content deemed to emphasize sex and violence.

Surveillance

We have no empirical basis for subdividing this category which has been labelled in accordance with Lasswell's original classification of media functions (1948), although further research might make this necessary. As one would expect, our own work shows it to have an important place in news viewing dispositions. One large cluster included the following items:

'Television news provides food for thought'
'It tells me about the main events of the day'
'I like to see how big issues are finally sorted out'
'I follow the news so I won't be caught unawares by price increases and that sort of thing'
'Watching the news helps me to keep an eye on the mistakes people in authority make'
'Television news helps me to make my mind up about things'

Although the meaning of this cluster seems similar to that of the 'reality exploration' category, its main thrust is directed elsewhere – more towards having some information and opinions about events in the wider world of public affairs than towards stimuli for reflecting upon a set of more immediately experienced personal problems. In fact this very distinction was preserved in the analysis itself, since another cluster of attitudes to the news conveyed just such a more personal emphasis.

Conclusions

[...]

[I]t is unlikely that any universally valid structure of media–person interactions could ever be erected on an empirical basis, since the phenomena in question are to some extent variable according to changes in audience experience and perception and also to changes in communication content and differences of social context. But there is no reason why, with further research along the reported lines, a good deal more precision could not be attained. Moreover, we would be surprised if more extensive inquiry, using the same methods, were to necessitate a fundamental revision of the pattern we have located and described.

The main implications for the problems discussed at the outset of this essay are also fairly self-evident. If the typology is accepted as approximating to the true state of affairs, then the escapist formula, as it has often been applied to the television viewing experience, is clearly inadequate. For one thing the motives and satisfactions to which the term 'escape' has customarily been applied are far from exhaustive of audience orientations. Although we have grouped an important set of interactions under the heading of 'diversion' in our typology, it is clear that in many people these coexist with several other very important kinds of expectation and outlook.

[...]

Second, the relationship between content categories and audience needs is far less tidy and more complex than most commentators have appreciated. It is not just that most popular programmes are multi-dimensional in appeal. It is also the case that we have no single scale by which we can reliably attach a value to any given content category. Given the heterogeneity of materials transmitted over the broadcast media, not only is one man's meat another man's poison, but one man's source of escape from the real world is a point of anchorage for another man's place in it, defining or underlining certain features of his personality, of the problems he has encountered in daily living, and of the values he adheres to. There is neither a one-to-one correspondence between communication content and audience motivation, nor any such correspondence between the place on a presumed scale of cultural worth to which programme material may be assigned (according to prevailing standards of aesthetic judgement) and the depth of meanings that may be drawn from them by many of their most keen attenders.

And third, the supports of any sweepingly dismissive attitude to the popular viewing experience tend to crumble in so far as the predominantly escapist interpretation of its meaning is successfully challenged. Of course mass communications research is still unable to shed much light on the lasting contributions made by time spent viewing television, but at least much of what they look for no longer seems quite so ignoble as depicted in the light of the escapist perspective.

But why should so many of the common assumptions about the television audience [...] have proven to be at odds with the evidence? Several explanations suggest themselves. An obvious one is the paucity in the past of the kind of data that might have better informed the views of critics and commentators. In addition, many vocal commentators are culturally disposed to adopt a superior attitude towards a popular medium like television, perhaps supposing that people deprived of the richness and diversity of the communication materials made available by literature, the arts, the specialist press and personal association with educated people, must simply go without altogether. In reality, people who, for whatever reason, lack access to multiple communication sources are much less functionally specific in their use of television; for them it is much more of an all-purpose medium than for the kinds of special population groups from which many critics and students of the mass media tend to be drawn. Finally, one must point to the dominance in television content of material which, on the face of it, is oriented to escape and diversion and which is often represented as such by its presenters because they believe that this will help to attract larger audiences. If one assumes a one-to-one relationship between the overt category of content and the kind of response it elicits, and if one also assumes a determining power in the media to shape audience response beyond what evidence and theory warrants, then the escapist interpretation becomes virtually inevitable. [...] The research we have described should pose a challenge to closed ways of thinking about mass communications. The typology which has emerged from it should provide a stimulus to further studies of the place of television in the lives of members of its audience.

REFERENCES

Herzog, H. (1940), 'Professor Quiz: A gratification study', in P. F. Lazarsfeld (ed.) *Radio and the Printed Page*, Duell, Sloan & Pearce.

Herzog, H. (1944), 'What do we really know about daytime serial listeners?', in P. F. Lazarsfeld and F. N. Stanton (eds), *Radio Research, 1942–1943*, Duell, Sloan & Pearce.

Horton, D., and Wohl, R. (1956) 'Mass communication and para-social interaction', *Psychiat*, vol. 19, pp. 215–19.

Lasswell, H. D. (1948), 'The structure and function of communication in society', in L. Bryson (ed.), 1964, *The Communication of Ideas*, Institute for Religious and Social Studies, New York.

McQuitty, L. L. (1957), 'Elementary linkage analysis', *Educ. Psychol. Measurement*, vol. 17, pp. 207–29.

Riley, J., and Riley, M. W. (1951) 'A sociological approach to communications research', *Pub. Opinion Q.* vol. 15, pp. 445–60.

36

USES AND GRATIFICATIONS
RESEARCH: A CRITIQUE

Philip Elliott

[...]

[The] distinction between size and satisfaction has dogged broadcast audience research from its infancy. In addition, research using traditional socio-demographic background variables has proved singularly unrevealing when applied to the consumption of the mass media and especially television. Research using such variables as education and social class has established that while people may differ in what they say they do, they differ very little in actual patterns of consumption behavior (Abrams, 1959, 1968; McQuail, 1970; Marplan, 1965; Steiner, 1963; Wilensky, 1964). But the main focus of empirical methods in social research is on explaining differences between groups. This has led to the proposition that there is a set of intervening variables between media output and media consumption that may provide more effective predictors of media behavior differences than crude classifications of output or demographic indicators.

This proposition links the various approaches to be found under the uses and gratifications heading. The proposition is most commonly formulated in psychological terms emphasizing the needs and gratifications experienced by the individual in the mass communication process, but there are also variants that appear to be more sociological and employ the language of

From Philip Elliott, 'Uses and Gratifications Research: A Critique and Sociological Alternative', Ch. 12 in Jay G. Blumler and Elihu Katz (eds), *The Uses of Mass Communications: Current Perspectives on Gratifications Research* (Beverly Hills: Sage, 1974).

functionalism (Rosengren and Windahl, 1972, 1973). There is some uncertainty within the approach about whether these internal states are independent, dependent, or intervening variables. There is also considerable variation in terminology and in whether explicit reference is made to needs as well as gratifications. In general, it seems that whereas the early studies carried out in the United States in the 1940s were content to deal with gratifications, more recent work has made more explicit reference to needs. Even so there are exceptions (Fearing, 1947). The trend, however, seems to be toward identifying general patterns of gratification and need and using these as independent variables to explain media consumption (Katz, Blumler and Gurevitch, 1974).

The functional variant also relies on the concept of need (Rosengren and Windahl, 1972, 1973). Individuals experience basic human needs that may be met through media use or by other patterns of behavior. In this case there is less emphasis on the individual purposively using one channel in place of another to find his satisfaction. Rather the frustration of some natural way to satisfy a need will necessarily lead to the substitution of a 'functional alternative' – media consumption.

The concept of need is the source of most of the difficulties to be found in uses and gratifications research in general. In the psychological formulation individuals are allowed to identify their own needs or at least the gratifications from which needs may be inferred. The difficulty of providing independent evidence for the existence and importance of the intervening mental states and processes becomes more acute as they proliferate. The more one aspect of the process has to be used as evidence for another the more the argument becomes circular and unnecessarily complex. In both variants – use leads to the gratification of need or need leads to satisfaction through functional behavior – need is the residual factor and yet it is also put forward as an explanation for the process. As explanatory variables, 'needs' appear to exist outside time and space. In searching for 'basic human needs' the aim is to find needs that are true of human beings qua human beings. The basic concept tends to set the approach off in a direction that is too general, too static, and too asocial for it to be effectively redirected at a later stage by the reintroduction of social or psychological variables. Such variables are unlikely to turn out to be powerful predictors of need distribution and satisfaction if the needs themselves have been selected to represent the general human condition.

[...]

The uses and gratifications approach is basically *mentalistic*, relying as it does on intervening mental states and processes. But their introduction only adds to the confusion and circularity of the argument because their existence and importance can only be assessed indirectly. The approach is *individualistic* in the sense that it deals with intra-individual processes. These can then be generalized to aggregates of individuals, but they cannot be converted in any meaningful way into social structure and process. It is *empiricist*. The existence of the intervening states and processes appears to be proved by the methods used, but they may also be an artifact of these methods. Moreover, although there are exceptions in the literature, the methods are usually imposed upon the subjects rather than taken from them. Tests too often contain items that cannot be answered and that no self-respecting researcher would (or should) consider trying to answer himself.[1] As the approach is not informed by any initial social theory, findings have to be explained post hoc. Given an association between variables, the difficulty is to know what they mean.[2]

This lack of social theory contributes to another characteristic of the approach, its *static-abstraction*. The mass communication process is treated in isolation from any other social process. Social variables may be introduced at a late stage in the analysis, but these too are abstracted from the social context, posing once again the problem of meaning. The sampling and analysis techniques used ensure that respondents are wrenched from their social situation, from ongoing social process, from the groups and subcultures that provide a framework of meaning for their activities, especially in a symbolic field like media consumption.

Static-abstraction is largely responsible for another general problem with the approach – its *low explanatory power*. There seems to be an inverse relationship between the level of abstraction and generality of the studies and the interest of the results produced. Although uses and gratifications studies seem to have developed partly because demographic variables proved so ineffective in explaining different patterns of media consumption, uses and gratifications variables themselves have not so far been spectacularly revealing or effective. This may be because they are simply a more cumbersome way of tapping the original demographic variables.

Finally, the approach raises all the problems commonly associated with *functionalism*, and more besides, since it is based on a peculiarly individualistic variant of functionalism. Because of the inferences involved, the argument that use leads to the gratification of needs is at best circular and at worst imprisons research within a stable system of functional interdependencies from which there is no escape. Functionalism at the individual level is matched by a very generalized view of society. No attempt is made to differentiate between media or people on the basis of the interests they represent or the power they possess; no analysis is made in terms of the functions and dysfunctions for different power groups and their ideologies.[3] Dysfunctions, when they appear at all, tend to be negatively labelled phenomena which might prevent society (as a whole) from reaching its ideals, as for example the narcotizing dysfunction identified by Lazarsfeld and Merton (1948).

[...]

THEORY AND ASSUMPTIONS

[...]

[T]he idea of an active audience consciously selecting its media fare in order to maximize its gratifications, brings out the ideological ambiguities involved in this supposedly value-free approach. The idea of an active audience has its attractions when fitted into a broader model of the communication process. Overarching the stimulus-response model was the fear that the new media had put people and society directly at the mercy of those who controlled them. The idea of an active audience is apparently more optimistic. People are credited with more control over their own activities. [...] Active in this case means purposive. The activity of media consumption is directed toward the achievement of certain goals – the gratification of certain needs.

[...]

'Needs' are founded on the idea of deficit motivation, but, as Maslow (1964) has pointed out, this is only plausible when applied to basic or deficiency needs, cases where lack of satisfaction produces physiological consequences. Maslow contrasts these needs with the growth needs that motivate healthy people toward 'self-actualization (defined as ongoing actualization of potential capacities and talents, as fulfilment of mission ... as a fuller knowledge of, and acceptance of, the person's own intrinsic nature, as an unceasing trend toward unity ... within the person).' If we must talk of needs in relation to media consumption, then, it seems clear that they are growth needs, not deficiency needs, that they are learned, not innate, that media consumption is founded on growth rather than deficiency motivation. But learned needs are a product of social experience. In that case media consumption should be explained as part of a positive process of self-development taking place in a series of social situations.

To reject the idea of an active, purposive audience out of hand would be to adopt a completely determinist view. But the problem lies in the equation of goals and needs. To reinstate man as a conscious actor, it is only necessary to suggest that he orients his behavior toward the external world rather than internal mental states. To translate this into a verstehen perspective, the task then becomes one of identifying the social meaning of different media and their outputs for groups differentially located in society. This also sidesteps another difficulty with the goal-needs equation. Need-goals appear to operate outside time and space. On occasion they are used as if they were once for all properties of individuals forming a basis from which the media consumption behavior of groups with different needs can be assessed. At bottom there is something fundamentally illogical in the claim that basic human needs are differentially distributed through society; that this distribution can be explained by reference to social and psychological factors; and that the needs themselves will explain differences in behavior. What is more, there seems every reason to declare the needs redundant and to go back to social and psychological factors as direct explanations of behavior.

Method and Findings

[...]

If it can be shown that the methods of data collection themselves construct reality, and that the new processes identified coincide with and obscure ones that were already known, then the foundations are cut away from the impressive edifices of statistical analysis that are the tour de force of contemporary uses and gratifications researchers. [...] The argument that the methods used themselves construct reality rests on the type of questions commonly asked. The aim is to assess the importance of various need-goals to the respondent and the importance he attaches to different media and other types of behavior as means of achieving them. Both the need-goals and the media are selected on the assumption that they are important (Lundberg and Hultén, 1968; Kjellmor, 1973; Katz et al., 1973). In most cases respondents can only be differentiated according to the degree of importance they attach to goals and means.

Given the level of generality at which the questions are aimed, it is not surprising to find that people will subscribe to them. One can hardly reject truisms out of hand. The difficulty is whether they are truisms about the people – whether, for example, some people really have a greater need than others to avoid boredom – or whether they are truisms about the situations in which people find themselves – boredom varies according to situation and also according to the social meaning of the concept. But as soon as this possibility is introduced, it becomes clear that measuring boredom avoidance or indeed any other need-goal is liable to be a way of measuring variance in the social situation, or available social meanings, variance that could be more directly expressed in terms of familiar demographic variables.

For all their methodological ingenuity Rosengren and Windahl (1972, 1973) seem to have run into the same difficulty in their studies of mass media consumption as a functional alternative to actual interaction. Their claim that people less involved in actual interaction will become more involved in media consumption is backed up by data collected around four indices: degree of involvement in mass media output, interaction potential, actual interaction, and amount of mass media consumption. The names given to these indices make the argument sound plausible, but it must be questioned whether the first three indices are such discrete measures of newly identified phenomena as is suggested.

Degree of involvement, for example, is based on whether respondents answer in personal terms when asked what type of media output they like. The authors themselves recognize that the tendency to think in personal terms may be a class phenomenon. More than that, however, when dealing with television output there is more scope for giving a personal answer about entertainment programs which commonly include well-known stars, than about news or information programs. The whole notion of personal involvement has some problems when applied to newspapers, but answers in terms of local people seem much more likely to come from geographically stable, lower-class people with a local orientation to their community.

The construction of the next two indices, interaction potential and actual interaction, seems to confirm these suspicions that what we are really dealing with is a class phenomenon. Among the six indicators of interaction potential are education, car ownership, and leisure time. Actual interaction is based on the number of contacts at work and with friends outside. It seems, therefore, that the association between lack of interaction and degree of involvement can be translated into the more familiar terms that lower-class people tend to say they like entertainment programs (and tend to be locally oriented) more than middle-class.

Such a conclusion is the stock in trade of many uses and gratifications studies (Weiss, 1971).[4] It is also a reason why such research invites the accusation that it lacks explanatory power. The contrast between information and entertainment usually turns up in some guise as a classification both of media output and of audience need-goals. It is then not surprising to find that these differences in tastes, reported consumption behavior, or need-goals can in turn be related to social class and similar variables. It may be questioned, however, whether this is a step forward, since it is already known that, at least so far as television is concerned, it is reported behavior, not actual behavior, which differs along this dimension (Steiner, 1963; Marplan, 1965; Wilensky, 1964). Uses and gratifications researchers often make a virtue out of the fact that they have to rely on their respondents' ability to recognize and verbalize their needs and gratifications. It may be a good thing to trust people, but it is naive to suppose that people can give answers as if they were in a social vacuum. The various media and the consumption behaviors associated with them are already socially stratified (Murdock and McCron, 1973). Their social meaning will be clear to people and so too will the social meaning of the associated need-goals.

[...]

CRITIQUE – POLICY IMPLICATIONS

The uses and gratifications approach is commonly put forward as an advance on traditional 'head-counting' techniques of broadcast audience research (Emmett, 1968). The substance of this claim was questioned in the previous section. But the claim also includes the idea that measuring audience gratifications and needs would provide more useful data to guide broadcasting policy. Audience figures have an accepted place in program planning. We may all agree that broadcasters should know more about their audience, but it seems unlikely that they will learn much from uses and gratifications data. The approach is effectively neutered by its assumptions.

The difficulty stems from the basic tautology that use leads to gratification. Different gratifications may be identified independently of use, but there is no way of distinguishing between them according to the level of satisfaction they supply. The difficulty is well illustrated by the few references to dysfunctions that are to be found in the uses and gratifications literature. In most cases dysfunctions are types of gratifications that the researchers suppose will have harmful consequences for society. At the individual level, to label some gratifications functional, others dysfunctional, would clearly be to reintroduce the critical judgements of popular culture theorists by the back door. But the social dysfunctions identified have no firmer basis, especially so long as they are applied to society as a whole or to the general quality of life within it. Thus the only basis for policy is to decide normatively which gratifications should be encouraged, which suppressed.[5]

This problem also underlies Brian Emmett's scheme to replace the maximization of audience size with the maximization of audience satisfaction. If audience satisfaction can be concluded from use, it is just as effective to count heads. If not, then some place will have to be found in the uses and gratifications approach for dissatisfaction. But even if it were, the fundamental difficulty would remain. Different types of gratification are not additive. It may also be questioned how far they are stable entities dependent directly on media content, as Emmett's model would suppose. Taking the view that media consumption is a specifically situated, social process, on the other hand, would suggest that gratification depends on a dynamic relationship between the individual and his whole social environment. Of course the problem could always be sidestepped by throwing the onus on the long-suffering respondents and asking them to provide a general satisfaction score. While the respondent tries to work out what he is being asked, the researcher will have time to pause and wonder what the answer will be worth when he gets it. Uses and gratifications research is effectively hoist with its own petard. Research has led to 'a growing consensus that almost any type of content may serve practically any type of function' (Rosengren and Windahl, 1972), but research cannot produce any criteria for differentiating between them.

Having argued that the approach provides no basis for policy making, it may seem perverse, if not illogical, to go on to argue that if it were used, its effect would be positively harmful. But this follows given the tautological and functional assumptions behind the approach. In themselves, uses and gratifications data can only point in one direction, toward a justification of the present situation. One example is the finding cited above that any content may serve any function (yield a variety of gratifications). In other words, the audience may not be getting what was intended from media output, but at least they are getting something.

Another example may be taken from Katz, Blumler and Gurevitch's (1974) attempt to defuse the radical critique of mass communications as a dysfunctional 'latter-day opiate of the masses' by suggesting that uses and gratifications research would be peculiarly suited to exploring the supposed 'media-output audience-satisfaction nexus.' The implication is that 'dysfunction' as used here is simply a negative evaluation, as it would be in the uses and gratifications approach itself. It rests, however, on a social analysis in which it is seen to be in the interests of those controlling the media to distract others in society from a true recognition of their own interests. If the media-output audience-satisfaction nexus were explored in uses and gratifications terms, the only possible conclusion would be that the audience was getting something out of it. But that is not in dispute. The issue in dispute is whose interests are being served in the process, and that is an issue which the approach itself is powerless to elucidate.

Nordenstreng (1970) raised the same issue when he pointed out that needs develop within the existing social structure and so that any approach based on identifying such needs would inevitably provide support for the status quo. The conclusion to be drawn from this critique is not that individual opinions do not matter, as Katz, Blumler and Gurevitch interpret it, but that some prior analysis of social structure is necessary to know what such opinions are worth. The quest to identify functions for 'society as a whole' or basic underlying human needs must inevitably rule out any consideration of the differential distribution of power and opportunity in society, of the conflict of interests between different groups, and of the development and use of different ideologies to protect them.

[...]

NOTES

1. For example, 'How important is it for you to understand the true quality of our leaders?' or 'How important is it for you to feel satisfied with the way of life in Israel as compared with other countries?' (Katz et al., 1973).
2. For example, in describing the correlates of a tendency to seek 'excitement' from quiz program viewing, McQuail et al. (1972) state that 'The highest scoring group consisted of working-class viewers who were late-born children of large families. While the significance of the role of family background here is not clear. ... ' And, in presenting data from a functional study of children's media uses, Brown et al. (1973) write: 'As with the earlier table we cannot attempt to explain many of the findings. Instead we will conclude by offering a few conjectures which might help to integrate and explain the somewhat disjointed data presented.'
3. Thus 'not all effects of mass communication are germane to functional analysis, only those which are relevant and important if the system under analysis is to continue to function normally' (Wright, 1960).
4. The same argument, that uses and gratifications concepts only work because class relationships are already built into them, applies especially to Schramm, Lyle and Parker (1961).
5. Emmett (1968) recognizes this: ' ... one other matter has to be considered. That is the relative importance, or weight, to be given to the gratification of various needs. The decision about these weights is crucial, since they ultimately determine the solution. It is not too extreme to say that they must encapsulate the philosophy or value system of the organisation. ... '

REFERENCES

Abrams, M. (1968) Education, Social Class and Readership of Newspapers and Magazines. London: JICNARS.

Abrams, M. (1959) 'The mass media and social class in Great Britain.' Paper presented at the Fourth World Congress of Sociology, Stresa, Italy.

Brown, J. R., J. K. Cramond, and R. J. Wilde (1973) 'Children's use of the mass media: a functional approach.' Paper presented at the Annual Conference of the Social Psychology Section of the British Psychological Society, Bristol.

Emmett, B. P. (1968) 'A new role for research in broadcasting.' Public Opinion Quarterly 32: 654–65.

Fearing, F. (1947) 'Influence of the movies on attitudes and behaviour.' Annals of the American Academy of Political and Social Science 254: 70–80.

Katz, E., J. G. Blumler, and M. Gurevitch (1974) 'Utilization of mass communication by the individual: an overview,' in J. G. Blumler and E. Katz (eds) The Uses of Mass Communications: Current Perspectives on Gratifications Research. Beverly Hills: Sage.

Katz, E., M. Gurevitch, and H. Haas (1973) 'On the use of the mass media for important things.' American Sociological Review 38 (April): 164–81.

Kjellmor, S. (1973) 'Basic subjective broadcasting media functions.' Paper presented to the Stockholm Conference on Uses and Gratifications Studies

Lazarsfeld, P. F. and R. K. Merton (1948) 'Mass communication, popular taste and organized social action,' [abridged as Chapter 1 of this volume] in B. Rosenberg and D. M. White (eds) Mass Culture – The Popular Arts in America. New York: Free Press, 1957.

Lundberg, D. and O. Hulten (1968) Individen och Mass Media. Stockholm: Norstedts.

McQuail, D. (1970) 'The audience for television plays,' in J. Tunstall (ed.) Media Sociology. London: Constable.

McQuail, D., J. G. Blumler, and J. R. Brown (1972) 'The television audience: a revised perspective,' [abridged as Chapter 35 of this volume] in D. McQuail (ed.) Sociology of Mass Communications. Harmondsworth: Penguin.

Marplan Ltd. (1965) Report on a Study of Television and the Managerial and Professional Classes. London: ITA.

Maslow, A. B. (1964) 'Deficiency motivation and growth motivation,' in R. C. Teevan and R. C. Birney (eds) Theories of Motivation in Personality and Social Psychology. London: Van Norstrand.

Murdock, G. and R. McCron (1973) 'Scoobies, skins and contemporary pop.' New Society (March 29).

Nordenstreng, K. (1970) 'Comments on "gratifications research" in broadcasting.' Public Opinion Quarterly 34: 130–132.

Rosengren, K. E. and S. Windahl (1973) 'Mass media use: causes and effects.' Lund (mimeo).

Rosengren, K. E. and S. Windahl (1972) 'Mass media consumption as a functional alternative,' in D. McQuail (ed.) Sociology of Mass Communications. Harmondsworth: Penguin.

Schramm, W., J. Lyle, and E. B. Parker (1961) Television in the Lives of Our Children. Stanford: Stanford University Press.

Steiner, G. A. (1963) The People Look at Television. New York: Knopf.

Weiss, W. (1971) 'Mass Communications.' Annual Review of Psychology 22.

Wilensky, H. (1964) 'Mass society and mass culture: interdependence or independence.' American Sociological Review 29, 2: 173–97.

Wright, C. R. (1960) 'Functional analysis and mass communication.' Public Opinion Quarterly 24: 605–20.

FURTHER READING

Belson, W., *The Impact of Television* (London: Crosby Lockwood, 1967).

Blumler, J. G. and Katz, E., *The Uses of Mass Communications: Current Perspectives on Gratifications Research* (London: Sage, 1974).

Blumler, J. G. and McQuail, D., *Television in Politics: Its Uses and Influence* (London: Faber & Faber, 1968).

Chaney, D., *Processes of Mass Communication* (London: Macmillan, 1972).

Halloran, J. D., *The Effects of Mass Communication; with Special Reference to Television* (Leicester: Leicester University Press, 1964).

Halloran, J. D. (ed.), *The Effects of Television* (London: Panther Books, 1970).

Halloran, J. D., Elliott, P. and Murdock, G., *Demonstrations and Communication: A Case Study* (Harmondsworth: Penguin, 1970).

Himmelweit, H., 'A Theoretical Framework for the Consideration of the Effects of Television – a British Report', *Journal of Social Issues* XVIII: 2 (1962) pp. 16–27.

Himmelweit, H., Oppenheim, A. and Vince, P., *Television and the Child* (London: Oxford University Press, 1958).

Howitt, D. and Cumberbatch, G., *Mass Media, Violence and Society* (New York: John Wiley, 1975).

Klapper, J. T., *The Effects of Mass Communication* (New York: Free Press, 1960).

Lazarsfeld, P. F. and Stanton, F. N. (eds), *Radio Research 1942–3* (New York: Duell, Sloan & Pearce, 1944).

Lazarsfeld, P. F. and Stanton, F. N. (eds), *Communications Research 1948–9* (New York: Harper & Bros., 1949).

McQuail, D., *Towards a Sociology of Mass Communications* (London: Collier Macmillan, 1969).

McQuail, D. (ed.), *Sociology of Mass Communications* (Harmondsworth: Penguin, 1972).

McQuail, D., 'The Influence and Effects of Mass Media', in Curran, J., Gurevitch, M. and Woollacott, J. (eds), *Mass Communication and Society* (London: Edward Arnold, 1977).

McQuail, D., *Mass Communication Theory: An Introduction*, 2nd edn (London: Sage, 1983).

Trenaman, J., 'The Effects of Television', *Twentieth Century*, Nov. (1959) pp. 332–42.

Trenaman, J. and McQuail, D., *Television and the Political Image* (London: Methuen, 1961).

Tunstall, J. (ed.), *Media Sociology: A Reader* (London: Constable, 1970).

SECTION 4
RECEPTION

2. THE POLITICS OF READING

THE POLITICS OF READING
INTRODUCTION

Stuart Hall's introduction to the six chapters on Media Studies included in the 1980 Birmingham CCCS collection, *Culture, Media, Language* outlines the 'paradigm break' which differentiates the Birmingham Centre's approach from earlier approaches to the media as 'mass-communications'. It broke with the models of 'direct influence', he writes, 'into a framework which drew much more on what can broadly be defined as the "ideological" role of the media'.[1] As a result, it also 'broke with the passive and undifferentiated conceptions of the "audience"' which had dominated earlier research, replacing them with more active conceptions of the 'audience', of the process of 'reading' and of the relation between 'encoding' (the construction of the media message), text, and 'decoding' (the various audience readings).[2] This account has since been criticised as over-simplistic,[3] but it signals a decisively different approach to the study of the audience from those represented in preceding chapters of this volume, one which begins from *overtly* theoretical and political concerns.[4] Hall's encoding/decoding model (see Chapter 5), further developed by David Morley in an early paper, *Reconceptualizing the Audience*,[5] provided the theoretical model, which Morley's empirical research into audience readings of the BBC's early evening magazine programme, *Nationwide*, would seek to test. The television audience, writes Morley, must be seen neither as an undifferentiated mass nor as autonomous individuals. Instead, it comprises 'clusters of socially situated individual readers', whose readings 'will be framed by shared cultural formations and practices'. These formations are in turn determined by the 'position of the individual reader in the class structure'.[6]

Chapter 37 is David Morley's (1983) account of the theoretical context, the methods, and the findings of his study of *The 'Nationwide' Audience*. Morley's starting point is the 'potential disjuncture between the codes of those sending and those receiving messages' through the mass media. This 'disjuncture' is a product of power structures within society, and 'the subcultures and codes inhabited by different classes and class fractions within British society'. The meaning of a text, then, 'cannot be "read off" straight from textual character-istics'; it must be 'interpreted in terms of which set of discourses it encounters in any particular set of circumstances'. Morley's project, therefore, set out to analyse the discourse of 'Nationwide', and then to study the readings made of the programme by twenty-nine groups drawn from different social back-grounds. The framework he used was that proposed by Stuart Hall: audience decodings would fall into the 'preferred/dominant', the 'negotiated' or the 'oppositional' category. In fact, Morley's empirical research revealed a more complex picture. A 'multiplicity of discourses' was evident in the decodings made by his twenty-nine audience groups, and these could not be matched unproblematically with social class. His findings indicated the importance of socio-cultural forces and divisions beyond those of social class, and they suggested that each of us has access to 'a number of discourses, some of which are in parallel and reinforce each other, some of which are contradictory'.[7] Nevertheless, Morley insisted, these discourses remained the product of 'cul-tural differences embedded within the structure of society'. The task of the new audience research was to explore empirically the processes by which textual codes interact with those of audience groupings to produce a range of 'social meanings'.

The importance of the 'critical' model of audience research inaugurated by Morley's *Nationwide* study is the subject of the chapter by Ien Ang (Chapter 38). Writing in 1989, she perceives an erosion of the 'paradigm break' described by Hall and Morley, as 'mainstream' uses and gratifications research increas-ingly embraces Morley's 'ethnographic' approach. Against this proposed 'con-vergence of antagonistic traditions',[8] Ang offers a forceful reassertion of their fundamental incompatibility. Despite a certain commonality of research ques-tions and methods of enquiry, there are, Ang insists, fundamental differences between the two approaches 'not only in epistemological, but also in theoretical and political attitudes towards the aim and status of doing empirical research'. Uses and gratifications research, she argues, is conceptualised as a 'scientific' enterprise, whose aim is to categorise, systematise, and explain its object of study, 'the audience'. Its findings aspire to the status of 'total knowledge' and objective 'truth'. The purposes of cultural studies approaches are very different. Cultural studies scholars are concerned with issues of social and cultural power, seeing media consumption as a 'site of struggle' over meanings and pleasures. The cultural studies researcher is therefore engaged in the process of *inter-pretation*, in a 'dialectic between the empirical and the theoretical' which is always political. What are produced in this encounter between researcher and informants are 'historically and culturally specific' knowledges and interpretations, inevitably incomplete and partial. To interpret recent developments in audience research as a convergence of the two traditions is therefore to 'misconceive the issues at stake'.

Janice Radway's concluding chapter to her (1984) *Reading the Romance* (Chapter 39) has been central in the development of feminist approaches to 'the politics of reading'. Whilst her research into the reading practices of a group of forty-two women romance readers did not begin – as her introduction to the British edition of the book points out – as a contribution to the cultural studies tradition outlined above, it was, she argues, 'eventually hijacked by its own theory and subject and, en route to its intended destination, gradually found itself directed to another'.[9] Through questionnaires, group discussions, face-to-face interviews, informal discussions and observations, as well as textual analysis and a survey of the 'institutional matrix' of mass-produced romance novels, Radway explored 'the phenomenon of romance reading'. Her explorations of why her women readers read romance fiction, how and where they read, how they understand themselves as readers, and what they see as an 'ideal' or a 'failed' romance, lead her to complex and contradictory conclusions. As *texts*, romance novels are conservative, 'a simple recapitulation and recommendation of patriarchy and its social practices and ideologies'. The *act of reading*, however, may be oppositional. In taking space and time for her own pleasure, the reader refuses momentarily her 'self-abnegating social role' – though in satisfying her needs through the private consumption of a conservative text, she may also be preparing herself for a return to that role. Romance reading is thus both perpetuator of the ideological status quo *and* the locus of protest against it. Its exploration reveals both the ideological power of contemporary cultural forms and the many ways in which subordinate groups appropriate and use them to refuse or contest that power.

Radway's work on romance readers, then, explores the ways in which a mass-produced media text may be appropriated for the local and often resistant meanings and pleasures of its users. Such appropriation, however, may occur not only on the part of subordinate groups *within* a national culture. As media texts increasingly become products of a global and globalising culture, their consumption may be localised within very different domestic and national cultures. The final chapter in this section (Chapter 40) is an exploration by Daniel Miller of one such example of consumption and appropriation: the reception by Trinidadians of the American soap opera, *The Young and the Restless*. Miller's concern is with the way in which this imported programme is appropriated and transformed in the production of local identities. The imported text, he argues, may actually lend itself more easily than can 'serious' local programming to the expression and mediation of tensions between Trinidad's culture of 'bacchanal' (lack of restraint, disorder and excess) and its more sober domestic culture of respectability. In this context, then, we should see the relationship between global media and their localised audiences not as one of straightforward cultural and ideological domination – of 'Americanisation' – but rather as a complex interaction in which cultural transformations of imported media products may actually serve in the construction and affirmation of local identities.

NOTES

1. Hall, 'Introduction to Media Studies at the Centre', in S. Hall, D. Hobson, A. Lowe and P. Willis (eds), *Culture, Media, Language* (London: Hutchinson, 1980), p. 117.
2. Ibid., p. 118.
3. See James Curran's 'The New Revisionism in Mass Communication Research: A Reappraisal', in the *European Journal of Communication* Vol. 5 (1990), pp. 146 ff.
4. As Curran, Gurevitch and Woollacott point out, all empirical audience research 'is based upon theoretical models of society even if these are often unexamined and unstated'. See J. Curran, M. Gurevitch and J. Woollacott, 'The study of the media: theoretical approaches', in M. Gurevitch, T. Bennett, J. Curran and J. Woollacott (eds), *Culture, Society and the Media* (London: Methuen, 1982), p. 15.
5. Morley, *Reconceptualizing the Audience*, CCCS Stencilled Paper, no. 9.
6. Morley, *The 'Nationwide' Audience* (London: BFI, 1980), p. 15.
7. Ibid., p. 162.
8. This phrase is taken from Kim Christian Schroder, 'Convergence of Antagonistic Traditions? The Case of Audience Research', in the *European Journal of Communication* Vol. 2 (1987) pp. 7–31.
9. Radway, *Reading the Romance* (London: Verso, 1987), p. 2.

37

CULTURAL TRANSFORMATIONS:
THE POLITICS OF RESISTANCE

David Morley

Mattelart has pointed to the fact that forms of popular resistance to, and subversion of, dominant cultures have rarely been studied. The point here, he argues, is that while the 'receiver' of communications is often considered as a passive consumer of information or leisure commodities, it is nonetheless true that the audience does not necessarily read the messages sent to it within the cultural code of the transmitters. The way in which the subaltern groups and classes in a society reinterpret and make sense of these messages is therefore a crucial problem for any theory of communications as a mode of cultural domination. At the macro level of international cultural relations, he argues, the consequences of a message being interpreted in a different way from what its senders intended may be quite radical. He asks:

> In how many countries do the Aryan heroes of the television series, Mission Impossible, fighting against the rebels, undergo a process of identification which is the exact opposite of that intended by the imperialist code, and how often are they viewed as the 'bad guys' in the story? (Mattelart & Siegelaub, 1979: 27)

Mattelart warns that any notions of ideological domination must be employed with great care and recommends that the idea that imperialism invades different sectors of society in a uniform way be abandoned in favour of an analysis of the particular milieux which favour or resist penetration.

From H. Davis and P. Wilson (eds), *Language, Image, Media* (Oxford: Blackwell, 1983) pp. 104–17.

In the domestic context, the argument alerts us to the relation between the dominant ideological forms of the media, and the subcultures and codes inhabited by different classes and class fractions within British society.

[...]

This is to argue that the structures of imperialism and of class domination, when introduced into the study of communications, pose the problem of audience responses to and interpretations of the mass media as a critical area of research.

COMMUNICATIONS: A BROKEN CIRCUIT?

We are faced with a situation in which there is a potential disjunction between the codes of those sending and those receiving messages through the circuit of mass communications (cf. Hall, 1973: 18–19; Eco, 1972: 121). The problem of (non-)complementarity of codes at the production and reception ends of the chain of communications is indissolubly linked with the problem of cultural domination and resistance. In a research project on Nationwide (a popular current affairs magazine programme on BBC television), we attempted to pose this as a specific problem about the degree of complementarity between the codes of the programme and the interpretative codes of various sociocultural groups (Brunsdon & Morley, 1978; Morley, 1980). We were concerned to explore the extent to which decodings take place within the limits of the preferred (or dominant) manner in which the message has been initially encoded. However, there is a complementary aspect to this problem, namely the extent to which these interpretations, or decodings, also reflect, and are inflected by, the codes and discourses which different sections of the audience inhabit, and the ways in which these decodings are determined by the socially governed distribution of cultural codes between and across different sections of the audience – that is, the range of decoding strategies and competencies in the audience.

To raise this as a problem for research is already to argue that the meaning produced by the encounter of text and subject cannot be 'read off' straight from textual characteristics. The text cannot be considered in isolation from its historical conditions of production and consumption. And an analysis of media ideology cannot rest with an analysis of production and text alone.

[...]

Thus the meaning of the text must be interpreted in terms of which set of discourses it encounters in any particular set of circumstances, and how this encounter may restructure both the meaning of the text and the discourses which it meets. The meaning of the text will be constructed differently according to the discourses (knowledges, prejudices, resistances etc.) brought to bear by the reader, and the crucial factor in the encounter of audience/ subject and text will be the range of discourses at the disposal of the audience. The crucial point here is that individuals in different positions in the social formation defined according to structures of class, race or sex, for example, will tend to inhabit or have at their disposal different codes and subcultures. Thus social position sets parameters to the range of potential readings by structuring access to different codes.

Whether or not a programme succeeds in transmitting the preferred or dominant meaning will depend on whether it encounters readers who inhabit codes and ideologies derived from other institutional areas (e.g. churches or schools) which correspond to and work in parallel with those of the programme or whether it encounters readers who inhabit codes drawn from other areas or institutions (e.g. trade unions or 'deviant' subcultures) which conflict to a greater or lesser extent with those of the programme.

[...]

THE MESSAGE: ENCODING AND DECODING

In outline, the premises on which we base our approach are as follows:

a The production of a meaningful message in television discourse is always problematic 'work'. The same event can be encoded in more than one way.

b The message in social communication is always complex in structure and form. It always contains more than one potential 'reading'. Messages propose and prefer certain readings over others, but they cannot be entirely closed around one reading: they remain polysemic.

c The activity of 'getting meaning' from the message is also problematic practice, however transparent and natural it may seem. Messages encoded in one way can also be read in a different way.

Thus, the communicative form and structure of the encoded message can be analysed in terms of its preferred reading: the mechanisms which prefer one, dominant reading over the other readings; the means which the encoder uses to try to win the assent of the audience to his particular reading of the message. Special attention can be given here to the control exercised over meaning, and to 'points of identification' within the message which transmit the preferred reading to the audience.

It is precisely the aim of the presenter to achieve identification with the audience through mechanisms which gain the audience's complicity and 'suggest' preferred readings. If and when these identificatory mechanisms are attenuated or broken, will the message be decoded in a different framework of meaning from that in which it was encoded? Broadcasters undoubtedly make the attempt to establish a relationship of complicity with the audience (Brunsdon & Morley, 1978) but there is no justification for assuming that the attempt will always be successful.

THE STRUCTURE OF THE AUDIENCE: DECODINGS IN CULTURAL CONTEXT

We might profitably think of the media audience not so much as an undifferentiated mass of individuals but as a complex structure of socially organized individuals in a number of overlapping subgroups and subcultures, each with its own history and cultural traditions. This is not to see cultural competence as automatically determined or generated by social position but to pose the problem of the relation between, on the one hand, social categories and social structure and, on the other, codes, subcultures and ideologies. In this perspective the primary relationships for analysis are those between linguistic and cultural codes and patterns of class (cf. Bernstein, 1971; Rosen, 1972), race (cf. Labov, 1969) and sex (cf. Lakoff, 1976; Spender, 1980). We are therefore proposing a model of the audience, not as an atomized mass of individuals, but as composed of a number of subcultural formations or groupings whose members will share a cultural orientation towards decoding messages in particular ways. Individual members' readings will be framed by shared cultural formations and practices. Such shared 'orientations' will in turn be determined by factors derived from the objective position of the individual reader in the social structure. These objective factors must be seen as setting parameters to individual experience although not determining consciousness in a mechanistic way: people understand their situation and react to it by way of subcultures and meaning systems (Critcher, 1975).

Bernstein's work on sociolinguistic codes and his hypothesis of a correlation between particular social (class) categories and codes is of obvious relevance to any theory of the media audience, in terms of how different sections of that audience may relate to different kinds of messages – perhaps through the employment of different codes of interpretation. However, Bernstein's scheme is highly simplified: it contains only two classes (working and middle) and two codes (restricted and elaborated), and no attempt is made to differentiate within these classes, nor within their 'corresponding' codes.

[...]

Bernstein's oversimplistic formulation of the relation between classes and cultural codes, and his neglect of cultural differentiation within classes, is to some extent paralleled in Parkin's attempt to produce a typology of 'meaning systems' in relation to class structure. Parkin's treatment of class structures as the ground of different meaning systems (1971, Ch. 3) is a fruitful if crude point of departure which provided some basic categories for Hall's (1973) hypotheses about typical decoding positions. The key question at issue is that of the nature of the fit between, say, class, socioeconomic or educational position and interpretative codes.

Following, but adapting Parkin, we have suggested three hypothetical-typical positions which the decoder may occupy in relation to the encoded message. He or she may take the meaning fully within the interpretative framework which the message itself proposes and 'prefers': if so, decoding proceeds within, or is aligned with, the dominant or 'hegemonic' code. Second, decoders may take the meaning broadly as encoded; but by relating the message to some concrete, located or situational context which reflects their position and interests, they may modify or partially inflect the meaning. Following Parkin, we would call this a 'negotiated' position. Third, the decoder may recognize how the message has been contextually encoded, but bring to bear an alternative frame of interpretation, which sets aside the encoding framework and superimposes on the message an interpretation which works in a directly oppositional way – an oppositional, or 'counter-hegemonic' decoding.

Parkin elaborated these positions as three possible and typical positions of different classes in relation to a class-based hegemonic ideology. We have transposed them in order to describe possible alternative ways of decoding ideologically constructed messages. Of course, Parkin's conceptual framework is limited in that it provides only a statement of the three logical possibilities: that a given section of the audience may either share, partly share, or not share the dominant code in which the message has been transmitted (Morley, 1974). If the three basic decoding positions have any sociological validity it will necessarily be at the very broad level of what one might call class competencies in the reading of ideological messages. Even at this level, further distinctions may have to be made: for example between a version of the negotiated position which reflects a deferential stance towards the use of the hegemonic code, or one which reflects a subordinate stance, as defined by Parkin, where messages cast at a general or abstract level are subject to negotiation when referred to a more limited or sectional interest.

Much of the important work in this respect consists in differentiating Parkin's catch-all category of 'negotiated code' into a set of empirically grounded subvariants of this basic category, which are illustrated in the sociological work on different forms of sectional and corporate consciousness (cf. Parkin, 1971; Mann, 1973; Nichols & Armstrong, 1976). The crucial development from this perspective has been the attempt to translate Parkin's three ideal types (which are themselves a considerable advance on any model which sees the audience as an unstructured aggregate of individuals) into a more sensitive model of actual decoding positions within the media audience.

There remains, however, one critical problem in the attempt to integrate the sociological work of authors such as Parkin into a theory of communications. This is the tendency to directly convert social categories (e.g. class) into meanings (e.g. ideological positions) without attending to the specific factors which govern this conversion. It is simply inadequate to present demographic and sociological factors such as age, sex, race or class position as objective correlates or determinants of differential decoding positions without any attempt to specify *how* they intervene in the process of communication. The relative autonomy of signifying practices means that sociological factors cannot be 'read in' directly as affecting the communication process. These factors can only have effect through the (possibly contradictory) action of the discourses in which they are articulated.

AUDIENCES AND IDEOLOGIES: METHODOLOGICAL AND EMPIRICAL QUESTIONS

I will now attempt to illustrate some of these theoretical arguments by drawing on material from the Nationwide research project (see Brunsdon & Morley, 1978 and Morley, 1980 for a full account of this project). The research was designed to provide an analysis of the programme discourse and then to ascertain which sections of the programme's audience decoded in line with the preferred/dominant codes, and which sections operated negotiated/oppositional decodings.

Two videotaped Nationwide programmes were shown to 29 groups drawn from different social and cultural backgrounds, and from different levels of the educational system. Our procedure was to gain entry to a situation where the group already had some existence as a social entity – at least for the duration of a course. The videotape showings and the subsequent interviews were arranged to slot into the context of their established institutional settings as far as possible.

The groups usually consisted of between five and ten people. After the viewing session the discussion was taperecorded (usually about 40 mins duration) and this was later transcribed in full to provide the basic data for the analysis. The project used the 'focused interview' method originally developed by Merton and Kendall (1946). Thus the interviews began with non-directive prompting designed to establish the 'working vocabulary' (Mills, 1939) and frame of reference of the groups, and the order of priority in which *they* raised issues, before moving on to a more structured set of questions based on our programme analysis.

We were particularly concerned to identify the nature of the groups' 'lexico-referential systems' (Mills, 1939) and to examine how these systems related to those employed by the broadcasters. Our questions were designed to reveal whether audiences used the same words in the same ways as the broadcasters, in discussing different topics in the programme; whether the groups ranked issues and topics in the same order of priority as that given in the programme discourse; and whether there were aspects of topics not discussed by the broadcasters that were specifically mentioned by these groups. The decision to work with group rather than individual interviews followed from our desire to explore the extent to which individual 'readings' are shaped by the socio-cultural groupings within which they are situated.

We attempted to work as far as possible with the raw data of actual speech instead of trying to convert responses into immediately categorizable forms. Although this choice raised problems which we cannot claim in any sense to have solved, it did allow us to bring into focus the question of the relation between the forms of speech employed by broadcasters and those employed by respondents.

[...]

CLASSES, CODES, DECODINGS

The problematic proposed here does not attempt to derive decodings directly from social class position or 'reduce' them to it. It is always a question of how social position, as it is articulated through particular discourses, produces specific kinds of readings or decodings. These readings can then be seen to be patterned by the way in which the structure of access to different discourses is determined by social position. The question is which cultural repertoires and codes are available to which groups, and how do they utilize these symbolic resources in their attempt to make sense of messages coming from the media?

Although the project as a whole investigated decodings made by groups across a range of class positions, I shall, in order to focus the comparisons more sharply, deal here only with the differences between the decodings made by three kinds of groups, all sharing a roughly similar working-class position or background. These groups were, first, young apprentice engineers and metal-lurgists, second, groups of trade union officials and of shop stewards, and third, young black students at a college of further education.

Of these groups it was the apprentices who most closely inhabited the dominant code of the programme. Their decodings were mostly closely in line with the dominant/preferred meanings of Nationwide. This seemed to be accounted for by the extent to which the lads' use of a form of populist discourse ('damn all politicians – they're all as bad as each other ... it's all down to the individual in the end, isn't it?') was quite compatible with that of the programme. Although the dominant tone of these groups' responses to Nationwide was one of cynicism, a resistance to anyone 'putting one over' on them, most of the main items in the programme were, in fact, decoded by these groups within the dominant framework or preferred reading established by the programme. They tended to accept the perspectives offered by and through the programme's presenter. The situation here seems to be the converse of that outlined by Parkin: here we have working-class groups who cynically claim to be distanced from the programme at a general level but who accept and repro-duce its ideological formulations of specific issues. The 'commonsense' inter-pretations which the programme's presenters offer seem 'pretty obviously OK' to these groups too, and Nationwide's questions are justified as 'natural' or 'obvious' – and therefore unproblematic: 'They just said the obvious comment didn't they?'

The groups involved in the activities and discourse of trade unionism produced differently inflected versions of negotiated and oppositional decod-ings, depending on their social position and positioning in educational and political discourses. There is a profound difference between the groups who are non-union, or are simply members of trade unions, and those with an active involvement in and commitment to trade unionism – the latter producing much more negotiated or oppositional readings of Nationwide. So the structure of decoding is not a simple function of class position, but rather the result of differential involvement and positioning in discourse formations.

Further, there are the significant differences between the articulate, fully oppositional readings produced by the shop stewards as compared with the negotiated/oppositional readings produced by the trade union officials. This, we would suggest, is to be accounted for by the greater distancing of the stewards from the pressures of incorporation which full-time officials experience, which thus allows them to inhabit a more 'left-wing' interpretation of trade unionism.

The trade union officials on the whole inhabit a dominant/populist inflected version of negotiated code and espouse a right-wing Labour perspective. They are regular Nationwide watchers and approve both the programme's mode of address and ideological stance – 'I find that quite interesting ... here's something in that programme for everyone to have a look at ...'; 'It seems to be a programme acceptable to the vast majority of people.' They accept the individualistic theme of the programme and accept the programme's construction of an undifferentiated national community which is currently suffering economic hardship: to this extent they can be said to identify with the national 'we' which the programme discourse constructs. However, this is at an abstract and general level: at a more concrete, local level – that of directly economic 'trade union' issues – they take a more critical stance, and specific items within this category are then decoded in a more oppositional way (the classic structure of the negotiated code).

It is the shop stewards who spontaneously produce by far the most articulate, fully oppositional reading of the programme. They reject the programme's attempt to tell us what 'our grouse' is and its attempt to construct a national 'we' – 'They want "*we*" ... they want the average viewer to all think "we" ...' And they identify this Nationwide form of presentation as part of a general pattern: 'I mean, take Nationwide, add the *Sun* ... the *Mirror* and the *Daily Express* to it ...' This is a pattern in which: 'Union leaders are always being told "You're ruining the country!" '

Finally, the black students made hardly any connection with the discourse of Nationwide. The concerns and the cultural framework of Nationwide are simply not the concerns of their world. They do not so much produce an oppositional reading as refuse to 'read' it at all. These groups are so totally alienated from the discourse of Nationwide that their response is in the first instance 'a critique of silence'. In a sense they fail, or refuse, to engage with the discourse of the programme enough to deconstruct or redefine it. They are clear that it's not a programme for them, it's for 'older people, middle-class people'; it doesn't deal with their specific interests – 'Why didn't they never interview Bob Marley?' – and it fails to live up to their standards of 'good TV' defined in terms of enjoyment and entertainment (in which terms Today and ITV in general are preferred to Nationwide and BBC).

To this group Nationwide is 'so boring it's not interesting at all': they 'don't see how anyone could watch it'. There is a disjunction between the discourse of their own culture and that, not simply of Nationwide in particular, but of the whole field of 'serious TV' ('BBC is definitely boring') and of party politics ('God that's rubbish'). Moreover, these groups reject the descriptions of their life offered by the programme. They can find no point of identification within the programme's discourse about the problems of families in Britain today – a discourse into which, the programme presenters have claimed, 'most people in Britain' should fit. Their particular experience of family structures among the black, working-class, inner city community is simply not accounted for. The programme's picture of family life is as inappropriate to them as that offered in a 'Peter and Jane' reading scheme:

> It didn't show one-parent families ... the average family in a council estate – all these people seemed to have cars, their own home ... property ... Don't they ever think of the average family?

Now this is precisely what Nationwide would claim to think of: the point here is that the representation of 'the family' within the discourse of Nationwide has no purchase on the representation of that field within the discourse and experience of these groups – and is consequently rejected.

However these are statements at the level of gross differences of orientation between the groups, and they should not blind us to the differences, divisions and overlaps which occur within and among these groups. For example, although the apprentice groups were generally in sympathy with the programme and identified with the perspectives on events offered by its presenters, they did at times find it hard to relate to the programme's style of presentation or 'mode of address' (Neale, 1977). At this point they frequently invoked Nationwide's ITV competitor as being 'more of a laugh' or 'better entertainment' and were, to this extent, alienated from the discourse of the BBC programme.

Moreover, if we are to characterize the apprentice group as decoding in a dominant mode, we must recognize that this is only one version, or inflection, of 'dominant code': within the study there were groups from quite different social positions (bank managers, schoolboys, teacher training students) whose decodings shared some of the dominant characteristics of those made by the apprentice groups, but which diverged from theirs at other points. Thus the category of dominant code would need to be differentiated, in terms of the material in this study, to account for different versions (radical and traditional Conservative, deferential, Leavisite) of the dominant code.

Equally, we must distinguish between different forms and formulations of negotiated and oppositional readings, between the 'critique of silence' offered initially by the black students, the critical reading (from an educational point of view) articulately expressed by some of the higher-education groups (though this itself varied, with topic-critical readings being made by these groups on moral and social issues, but dominant code readings being made by the same groups on economic and trade union issues), and the various forms of 'politicized' negotiated and oppositional readings made by the trade union groups.

These are simply instances of a more general phenomenon of differentiation within and across the basic categories derived from Parkin's scheme which we would need to take account of in developing an adequate model of the media audience. We need to understand the process through which the multiplicity of discourses in play in any social formation intersect with the process of decoding media material. The effect of these discourses is precisely to lend variety to decodings. Thus, in each of the major categories of decoding (dominant, negotiated, oppositional) we can discern a number of varieties and inflections of what, for purposes of gross comparison only, is termed the same 'code'.

CONCLUSIONS

This quick sketch of a large quantity of material at least allows us to see clearly the fundamental point that social position in no way directly, or unproblematically, correlates with decoding. The apprentice groups, the trade union and shop stewards groups and the black college students can all be said to share a common class position, but their decodings of a television programme are inflected in different directions by the discourses and institutions in which they are situated. In one case the framework derives from a tradition of mainstream working-class populism, in another from trade unions and Labour party politics, in another, from black youth subcultures. In each case the discourses in play inflect and organize the groups' responses to and decodings of the media material shown.

Any superficial resemblance between this study of television audience and the 'uses and gratifications' perspective in media research is misleading. In the latter, the focus would be entirely on what individuals 'do with' messages.[1] But the different responses and interpretations reported here are not to be understood simply in terms of individual psychologies. They are founded on cultural differences embedded within the structure of society; cultural clusters which guide and limit the individual's interpretation of messages. To understand the potential meanings of a given message we need a cultural map of the audience to whom that message is addressed – a map showing the various cultural repertoires and symbolic resources available to differently placed subgroups within that audience. Such a map will help to show how the social meanings of a message are produced through the interaction of the codes embedded in the text with the codes inhabited by the different sections of the audience.

NOTES

1. Carey & Kreiling 1974 give an account of the relation between 'cultural studies' and the 'uses and gratifications' approach. The present work [Davis and Walton, 1983] owes its main categories and concepts to the cultural studies tradition.

REFERENCES

Bernstein, B. 1971: *Class, codes and control*, vol. 1. London: Routledge & Kegan Paul.
Blumler, J. & Katz, E., editors, 1974: *Uses and gratification studies: theories and methods*. London: Sage.

Brunsdon, C. & Morley, D. 1978: *Everyday television: Nationwide*. London: British Film Institute.

Carey, J. & Kreiling, A. 1974: Cultural studies and uses and gratifications. In Blumler & Katz 1974.

Corner, J. 1980: Codes and cultural analysis. In *Media, Culture and Society* 2, 73–86.

Critcher, C. 1975: Structures, cultures and biographies. *Working Papers in Cultural Studies* 7/8, 167–73.

Eco, U. 1972: Towards a semiotic enquiry into the television message. *Working Papers in Cultural Studies* 3, 103–21.

Giglioli, P. (ed.) 1972: *Language and Social Context*. Harmondsworth: Penguin.

Hall, S. 1973: Encoding and decoding in the television discourse. Stencilled occasional paper, Centre for Contemporary Cultural Studies, University of Birmingham. [See Chapter 5 of this volume.]

Labov, W. 1969: The logic of nonstandard English. In Giglioli 1972.

Lakoff, R. 1976: *Language and woman's place*. New York: Harper & Row.

Mann, M. 1973: *Consciousness and action among the western working class*. London: Macmillan.

Mattelart, A. & Siegelaub, S., editors, 1979: *Communication and class struggle*, vol. 1. New York: International General.

Merton, R. & Kendall, P. 1946: The focused interview. *American Journal of Sociology*, 11, 541–57.

Mills, C. Wright 1939: *Power, politics and people*. London/New York: OUP.

Morley, D. 1974: Reconceptualising the media audience. Stencilled occasional paper, Centre for Contemporary Cultural Studies, University of Birmingham.

Morley, D. 1980: *The 'Nationwide' audience*. London: British Film Institute.

Neale, S. 1977: Propaganda. *Screen* 18, 3, 9–40.

Nichols, T. & Armstrong, P. 1976: *Workers divided*. London: Fontana.

Parkin, F. 1971: *Class inequality and political order*. London: MacGibbon & Kee (also Paladin, 1972).

Rosen, H. 1972: *Language and class*. Bristol: Falling Wall Press.

Spender, D. 1980: *Man made language*. London: Routledge & Kegan Paul.

38

WANTED: AUDIENCES.
ON THE POLITICS OF
EMPIRICAL AUDIENCE STUDIES

Ien Ang

In his pioneering book *The 'Nationwide' Audience*, David Morley situates his research on which the book reports as follows: 'The relation of an audience to the ideological operations of television remains in principle an empirical question: the challenge is the attempt to develop appropriate methods of empirical investigation of that relation.'[1]

Although this sentence may initially be interpreted as a call for a technical discussion about empirical research methods, its wider meaning should be sought in the theoretical and political context of Morley's work. To me, the importance of *The 'Nationwide' Audience* does not so much reside in the fact that it offers an empirically validated, and thus 'scientific' account of 'the ideological operations of television,' or merely in its demonstration of some of the ways in which the television audience is 'active.' Other, more wide-ranging issues are at stake.

[...]

ACADEMIC CONVERGENCE?

The 'Nationwide' Audience has generally been received as an innovative departure within cultural studies, both theoretically and methodologically. If *Screen* theory can be diagnosed as one instance in which critical discourse on television suffered from the problem of the 'disappearing audience,'[2] Morley's project is an indication of a growing acknowledgment within cultural studies

From E. Seiter, H. Borchers, G. Kreutzner and E.-M. Warth (eds), *Remote Control: Television, Audiences and Cultural Power* (London: Routledge, 1989) pp. 96–115.

that television viewing is a practice that involves the active production of meanings by viewers.

But the book has also been welcomed by some adherents of the influential uses and gratifications approach, who see it as an important step on the part of 'critical' scholars in their direction, that is as an acceptance of, and possible contribution to, a refinement of their own basic axiomatic commitment to 'the active audience.' On the other hand, some uses and gratifications researchers, for their part, have begun to take over semiologically informed cultural studies concepts such as 'text' and 'reader,' thereby indicating an acknowledgment of the symbolic nature of negotiations between media texts and their readers which they, in their functionalist interest for the multiple relationships between audience gratifications and media 'uses,' had previously all but ignored.[3]

On top of this conceptual rapprochement, these social scientists have also expressed their delight in noticing a methodological 'concession' among 'critical' scholars: finally, so it is argued, some 'critical' scholars at least have dropped their suspicion of doing empirical research. In a benevolent, rather fatherly tone, three senior ambassadors of the uses and gratifications approach, Blumler, Gurevitch, and Katz, have thus proclaimed a gesture of 'reaching out' to the other 'camp,' calling for incorporating some of the insights developed within the 'critical' perspective into their own paradigm.[4] Evoked then is the prospect of merging the two approaches, to the point that they may ultimately fuse into a happy common project in which the perceived hostility between the two 'camps' will have been unmasked as academic 'pseudo-conflicts.' As one leading gratifications researcher, Rosengren, optimistically predicts: 'To the extent that the same problematics are empirically studied by members of various schools, the present sharp differences of opinion will gradually diminish and be replaced by a growing convergence of perspectives.'[5]

However, to interpret these recent developments in audience studies in terms of such a convergence is to simplify and even misconceive the issues at stake. For one thing, I would argue that the two perspectives only superficially share 'the same problematics,' and that what separates a 'critical' from a 'mainstream' perspective is more than merely some 'differences of opinion,' sharp or otherwise: it concerns fundamental differences not only in epistemological, but also in theoretical and political attitudes toward the aim and status of doing empirical research as such.

The academic idealization of joining forces in pursuit of a supposedly common goal as if it were a neutral, scientific project is a particularly depoliticizing strategy, because it tends to neutralize all difference and disagreement in favor of a forced consensus. If I am cautious about this euphoria around the prospect of academic convergence, it is not my intention to impose a rigid and absolute eternal dichotomy between 'critical' and 'mainstream' research. Nor would I want to assert that Morley's project is entirely 'critical' and the uses and gratifications approach completely 'mainstream.' As I have noted before, the relationship between 'critical' and 'mainstream' is not a fixed one; it does not concern two mutually exclusive, antagonistic sets of knowledge, as some observers would imply by talking in terms of 'schools' or 'paradigms.' In fact, many assumptions and ideas do not intrinsically belong to one or the other perspective. For example, the basic assumption that the television audience is 'active' (rather than passive) and that watching television is a social (rather than an individual) practice is currently accepted in both perspectives. There is nothing spectacular about that.[6] Also, I would suggest that the idea that texts can generate multiple meanings, and that the text/reader relationship takes the form of negotiations, is not in itself a sufficient condition for the declared convergence.[7]

In other words, in evaluating whether we can really speak of convergence, it is not enough to establish similar research questions, or to identify a common acknowledgment of the usefulness of certain methods of inquiry. Of course, such commonalities are interesting enough and it would be nonsense to discard them categorically. I do think it is important to get rid of any dogmatism or antagonism-for-the-sake-of-it, and to try to learn from others wherever that is possible. But at the same time we should not lose sight of the fact that any call for convergence itself is not an innocent gesture. It tends to be done from a certain point of view and therefore inevitably involves a selection process in which certain issues and themes are highlighted and others suppressed. And it is my contention that an all too hasty declaration of convergence could lead to neglecting some of the most important distinctive features of cultural studies as a critical intellectual enterprise.

A difference in conceptualizing the object of study is a first issue that needs to be discussed here. Thus, to take the common interest in 'audience activity' as an example in a cultural studies perspective, 'audience activity' cannot and should not be studied in isolation. Rather than dissecting 'audience activity' into variables and categories in order to be able to study them one by one, so that we could ultimately have a complete and generalizable formal 'map' of all dimensions of 'audience activity,' which seems to be the drive behind the uses and gratifications project,[8] the aim of cultural studies, as I see it, is to arrive at a more historicized insight into the ways in which 'audience activity' is related to social and political structures and processes. In other words, what is at stake is not the understanding of 'audience activity' as such as an isolated and isolable phenomenon and object of research, but the embeddedness of 'audience activity' in a network of ongoing cultural practices and relationships.

As a result, an audience researcher working within a cultural studies sensibility cannot restrict herself or himself to 'just' studying audiences and their activities (and, for that matter, relating those activities with other variables such as gratifications sought or obtained, dependencies, effects, and so on). She or he will also engage with the structural and cultural processes through which the audiences she or he is studying are constituted and being constituted. Thus, one essential theoretical point of the cultural studies approach to the television audience is its foregrounding of the notion that the dynamics of watching television, no matter how heterogeneous and seemingly free it is, is always related to the operations of forms of social power. It is in this light that we should see Morley's decision to do research on viewers' decodings: it was first of all motivated by an interest in what he – in the quote at the beginning of this chapter – calls 'the ideological operations of television.'

It is important then to emphasize that the term 'active audience' does not occupy the same symbolic status in the two approaches. From a cultural studies point of view, evidence that audiences are 'active' cannot simply be equated with the rather triumphant, liberal-pluralist conclusion, often expressed by gratificationists, that media consumers are 'free' or even 'powerful' – a conclusion which allegedly undercuts the idea of 'media hegemony.' The question for cultural studies is not simply one of 'where the power lies in media systems' (i.e. with the audience or with the media producers),[9] but rather how relations of power are organized within the heterogeneous practices of media consumption. In other words, rather than constructing an opposition between 'the' media and 'the' audience, as if these were separate ontological entities, and, along with it, the application of a distributional theory of power (that is, power is a property that can be attributed to either side of the opposing entities), cultural studies scholars are interested in understanding media consumption as a site of cultural struggle, in which a variety of forms of power are exercised, with different sorts of effects.[10] Thus if, as Morley's study has shown, viewers can decode a text in different ways and sometimes even give oppositional meanings to it, this should not be conceived as an example of 'audience freedom,' but as a moment in that cultural struggle, an ongoing struggle over meaning and pleasure which is central to the fabric(ation) of everyday life.

I hope to have made clear by now that in evaluating the possibility or even desirability of convergence, it is important to look at how 'audience activity' is theorized or interpreted, and how research 'findings' are placed in a wider theoretical framework. So, if one type of 'audience activity' which has received much attention in both approaches recently has been the interpretative strategies used by audiences to read media texts (conceptualized in terms of decoding structures, interpretative communities, patterns of involvement, and so on), how are we to make sense of those interpretative strategies? The task of the cultural studies researcher, I would suggest, is to develop *strategic interpretations* of them, different not only in form and content, but also in scope and intent, from those offered in more 'mainstream'-oriented accounts.[11] I will return to this central issue of interpretation.

BEYOND METHODOLOGY

A troubling aspect about the idea of (and desire for) convergence, then, is that it tends to be conceptualized as an exclusively 'scientific' enterprise. Echoing the tenets of positivism, its aim seems to be the gradual accumulation of scientifically confirmed 'findings.' It is propelled by the hope that by seeking a shared agreement on what is relevant and by developing shared methodological skills the final scientific account of 'the audience' can eventually be achieved. In this framework, audience studies are defined as just another branch of an academic discipline (i.e. mass communication), in which it is unproblematically assumed that 'the audience' is a proper object of study whose characteristics can be ever more accurately observed, described, categorized, systematized, and explained, until the whole picture is 'filled in.' In principle (if not in practice), this scientific project implicitly claims to be able to produce total knowledge, to reveal the full and objective 'truth' about 'the audience.' Audience here is imagined as and turned into an object with researchable attributes and features (be it described in terms of arrays of preferences, decodings, uses, effects, or whatever) that could be definitively established – if only researchers of different breeding would stop quarreling with each other and unite to work harmoniously together to accomplish the task.[12]

From such an academic point of view, the question of methodology becomes a central issue. After all, rigor of method has traditionally been seen as the guarantee *par excellence* for the 'scientific' status of knowledge. In positivist social science, the hypothetico-deductive testing of theory through empirical research, quantitative in form, is cherished as the cornerstone of the production of 'scientific' knowledge. Theory that is not empirically tested, or that is too complex to be molded into empirically testable hypotheses, is dismissed as 'unscientific'. These assumptions, which are central to the dominant version of the uses and gratifications approach as it was established in the 1970s, are now contested by a growing number of researchers who claim that reality cannot be grasped and explained through quantitative methods alone. Furthermore, they forcefully assert that to capture the multidimensionality and complexity of audience activity the use of qualitative methods – and thus a move towards the 'ethnographic' – is desperately called for.[13]

From an academic point of view, it is this methodological challenge that forms the condition of possibility of the perceived convergence. However, although I think that the struggle for legitimization of qualitative research is a very important one, I do believe that it is not the central point for critical cultural studies. This is because the struggle is cast primarily in methodological terms, and therefore its relevance is confined to the development of audience research as an *academic* enterprise. Given the decade-long hegemony of positivism and the quantifying attitude in audience research, this development is a significant one indeed. Unfortunately, however, many discussions about the usefulness of qualitative methods still do not question the epistemological distinction between science and common sense that lies at the heart of positivism. The aim is still the isolation of a body of knowledge that can be recognized as 'scientific' (in its broadest meaning), the orientation is toward the advancement of an academic discipline, and concomitantly, the technical improvement of its instruments of analysis.

A cultural studies perspective on audience research cannot stop short at this level of debate. For a critical cultural studies, it is not questions of methodology or academic struggle as such that prevail. On the contrary, we should relativize the academic commitment to increasing knowledge for its own sake and resist the temptation to what Stuart Hall has called the 'codification' of cultural studies into a stable realm of established theories and canonized methodologies.[14] In this respect, the territorial conflict between 'mainstream' and 'critical,' quantitative and qualitative, humanistic and social scientific, and so on, should perhaps not bother us too much at all in the first place. As James Carey once remarked, 'perhaps all the talk about theory, method, and other such things prevents us from raising or permits us to avoid raising, deeper and disquieting questions about the purposes of our scholarship.'[15] And indeed: why are we so interested in knowing about audiences in the first place? In empirical audience research, especially, it is important to reflect upon the status of the knowledge produced. After all, scrutinizing media audiences is not an innocent practice. It does not take place in a social and political vacuum. Historically, the hidden agenda of audience research, even when it presents itself as pure and objective, has all too often been its commercial or political usefulness. In other words, what we should reflect upon is the *political* interventions we make when talking about audiences – political not only in the sense of some distant societal goal, but, more importantly, in that we cannot afford ignoring the political dimensions of the *process* and practice of knowledge production itself. What does it mean to subject audiences to the researcher's gaze? How can we develop insights that do not reproduce the kind of objectified knowledge served up by, say, market research or empiricist effects research? How is it possible to do audience research which is 'on the side' of the audience?[16] These are nagging political questions which cannot be smoothed out by the comforting canons of epistemology, methodology, and 'science.'

Of course, it is not easy to pin down what such considerations would imply in concrete terms. But it could at least be said that we should try to avoid a stance in which 'the audience' is relegated to the status of exotic 'other' – merely interesting in so far as 'we,' as researchers, can turn 'them' into 'objects' of study, and about whom 'we' have the privileged position to acquire 'objective' knowledge.[17] To begin with, I think, critical audience studies should not strive and pretend to tell 'the truth' about 'the audience.' Its ambitions should be much more modest. As Lawrence Grossberg has suggested, 'the goal of [critical research] is to offer not a polished representation of the truth, but simply a little help in our efforts to better understand the world.'[18] This modesty does not have so much to do with some sort of false humility as with the basic acknowledgment that every research practice unavoidably takes place in a particular historical situation, and is therefore principally of a partial nature. As Hammersley and Atkinson have provocatively put it, 'all social research takes the form of participant observation: it involves participating in the social world, in whatever role, and reflecting on the products of that participation.'[19] The collection of data, either quantitative or qualitative in form, can never be separated from their interpretation; it is only through practices of interpretative theorizing that unruly social experiences and events related to media consumption become established as meaningful 'facts' about audiences. Understanding 'audience activity' is thus caught up in the discursive representation, not the transparent reflection, of realities having to do with audiences.

These considerations lead to another, more politicized conception of doing research. It is not the search for (objective, scientific) knowledge in which the researcher is engaged, but the construction of *interpretations*, of certain ways of understanding the world, always historically located, subjective, and relative. It is the decisive importance of this interpretative moment that I would like to highlight in exploring the possibilities of critical audience studies.[20]

In positivism, interpretation is assigned a marginal place: as a result of its emphasis on the empirical testing of theory, interpretation is assumed to follow rather automatically from the so-called 'findings.' Achieved then is an apparent innocence of interpretation, one that is seemingly grounded in 'objective social reality' itself. In fact, the term 'interpretation' itself would seem to have definite negative connotations for positivists because of its connection with 'subjectivism.' And even within those social science approaches in which the interpretative act of the researcher – not only at the moment of data analysis, but also at that of data collection – is taken more seriously, interpretation is more often than not problematized as a methodical rather than a political matter, defined in terms of careful inference making rather than in terms of discursive constructions of reality.

It should be recognized, however, that because interpretations always inevitably involve the construction of certain representations of reality (and not others), they can never be 'neutral' and merely 'descriptive.' After all, the 'empirical,' captured in either quantitative or qualitative form, does not yield self-evident meanings; it is only through the interpretative framework constructed by the researcher that understandings of the 'empirical' come about. The choice of empirical methods of investigation is only one part of a double venture: it is in the dialectic between the empirical and the theoretical, between experience and explanation, that forms of knowledge, that is interpretations, are constructed. Here then the thoroughly political nature of any research manifests itself. What is at stake is a *politics of interpretation*: 'to advance an interpretation is to insert it into a network of power relations.'[21]

This also implies a shift in the position of the researcher. She or he is no longer a bearer of truth, but occupies a 'partial' position in two senses of the word. On the one hand, she or he is no longer the neutral observer, but is someone whose job it is to produce historically and culturally specific knowledges that are the result of equally specific discursive encounters between researcher and informants, in which the subjectivity of the researcher is not separated from the 'object' s/he is studying. The interpretations that are produced in the process can never claim to be definitive: on the contrary, they are necessarily incomplete (for they always involve simplification, selection, and exclusion) and temporary. 'If neither history nor politics ever comes to an end, then theory (as well as research) is never completed and our accounts can never be closed or totalized.'[22] And on the other hand, and even more important, the position of the researcher is also more than that of the professional scholar: beyond a capable interpreter, she or he is also inherently a political and moral subject. She or he is an intellectual who is not only responsible to the Academy, but to the social world she or he lives in as well. It is at the interface of 'ethics' and 'scholarship' that the researcher's interpretations take on their distinctive political edge.[23]

Of course, all this entails a different status for empirical research. Material obtained by ethnographic fieldwork or depth-interviews with audience members cannot simply be treated as natural 'data.' Viewers' statements about their relation to television cannot be regarded as self-evident facts. Nor are they immediate, transparent reflections of those viewers' 'lived realities' that can speak for themselves. What is of critical importance, therefore, is the way in which those statements are made sense of, that is interpreted. Here lies the ultimate political responsibility of the researcher. The comfortable assumption that it is the reliability and accuracy of the methodologies being used that will ascertain the validity of the outcomes of research, thereby reducing the researcher's responsibility to a technical matter, is rejected. In short, to return to Morley's opening statement, audience ethnographies are undertaken because the relation between television and viewers is an empirical *question*. But the empirical is not the privileged domain of the *answers*, as the positivist would have it. Answers (temporary ones, to be sure) are to be constructed, in the form of interpretations.[24]

[...]

NOTES

1. David Morley, *The 'Nationwide' Audience: Structure and Decoding* (London: British Film Institute, 1980), p. 162.
2. See Fred Feyes, 'Critical Communications Research and Media Effects: The Problem of the Disappearing Audience,' *Media, Culture, and Society* 6 (1984): 219–32.
3. 'Gratifications researchers, in their paradigmatic personae, have lost sight of what the media are purveying, in part because of an overcommitment to the endless freedom of the audience to reinvent the text, in part because of a too rapid leap to mega-functions, such as surveillance or self-identity' (Jay G. Blumler, Michael Gurevitch, and Elihu Katz, 'Reaching Out: A Future for Gratifications Research,' in K. E. Rosengren, L. A. Wenner, and Ph. Palmgreen (eds) *Media Gratifications Research: Current Perspectives* (Beverly Hills, Calif.: Sage, 1985), p. 272).
4. Ibid.
5. Karl Erik Rosengren, 'Communication Research: One Paradigm, or Four?' *Journal of Communication* 33 (1983): 203; also Tamar Liebes, 'On the Convergence of Theories of Mass Communication and Literature Regarding the Role of the Reader' (paper presented to the Conference on Culture and Communication, 1986); and Kim Christian Schroder, 'Convergence of Antagonistic Traditions? The Case of Audience Research,' *European Journal of Communication* 2 (1987): 7–31. Such an insistence upon convergence is not new among 'mainstream' communication researchers. For example, Jennifer Daryl Slack and Martin Allor have recalled how in the late 1930s Lazarsfeld hired Adorno in the expectation that the latter's critical theory could be used to 'revitalize' American empiricist research by supplying it with 'new research

ideas.' The collaboration ended only one year later because it proved to be impossible to translate Adorno's critical analysis into the methods and goals of Lazarsfeld's project. Lazarsfeld has never given up the idea of a convergence, however. See Jennifer Daryl Slack and Martin Allor, 'The Political and Epistemological Constituents of Critical Communication Research,' *Journal of Communication* 33 (1983): 210.

6. Note, for instance, the striking similarities between the following two sentences, one from a uses and gratifications source, the other from a cultural studies one: 'There seems to be growing support for that branch of communications research which asserts that television viewing is an active and social process' (Katz and Liebes, 'Mutual Aid in the Decoding of *Dallas*: Preliminary Notes for a Cross-Cultural Study,' in Phillip Drummond and Richard Paterson (eds) *Television in Transition* (London: British Film Institute, 1985), p. 187); 'Television viewing, the choices which shape it and the many social uses to which we put it, now turn out to be irrevocably active and social processes' (Stuart Hall, 'Introduction,' in David Morley, *Family Television. Cultural Power and Domestic Leisure* (London: Comedia, 1986), p. 8).

7. Tamar Liebes suggests that 'the focus of the convergence is on the idea that the interaction between messages and receivers takes on the form of negotiation, and is not predetermined' ('On the Convergence,' p. 1). However, as I will try to show, what makes all the difference in the theoretical and political thrust of ethnographic audience studies is the way in which 'negotiation' is conceived. Furthermore, 'not predetermined' does not mean 'undertermined,' – and how (complex, structural, conjunctural) determinations should be conceived remains an important point of divergence between 'critical' and 'mainstream' studies. It is also noteworthy to point out that, while uses and gratifications researchers now seem to be 'rediscovering the text,' researchers working within a cultural studies perspective seem to be moving away from the text. This is very clear in Morley's second book, *Family Television*. In fact, it becomes more and more difficult to delineate what 'the television text' is.

8. See, for example, M. R. Levy and S. Windahl, 'Audience Activity and Gratifications: A Conceptual Clarification and Exploration,' in Rosengren et al., *Media Gratifications Research*, pp. 109–22.

9. Blumler et al., 'Reaching Out,' p. 260.

10. In stating this I do not want to suggest that cultural studies is a closed paradigm, or that all cultural studies scholars share one – say, Foucaultian – conception of power. Thus, the Birmingham version of cultural studies, with its distinctly Gramscian inflection, is critized by Lawrence Grossberg for its lack of a theory of pleasure. An alternative, postmodernist perspective on cultural studies is developed by Grossberg in his 'Cultural Studies Revisited and Revised,' in Mary S. Mander (ed.) *Communications in Transition* (New York: Praeger, 1983), pp. 39–70.

11. Strategic interpretations, that is interpretations that are 'political' in the sense that they are aware of the fact that interpretations are always concrete interventions into an already existing discursive field. They are therefore always partial in both senses of the word, and involved in making sense of the world in specific, power-laden ways. See Mary Louise Pratt, 'Interpretive Strategic Interpretations: On Anglo-American Reader-Response Criticism,' in Jonathan Arac (ed.) *Postmodernism and Politics* (Minneapolis: University of Minnesota Press, 1986), pp. 26–54.

12. Rosengren expresses this view in very clear cut terms, when he reduces the existence of disagreements between 'critical' and 'mainstream' researchers to 'psychological reasons' ('Communication Research: One Paradigm, or Four?,' p. 191).

13. Cf. James Lull, 'The Naturalistic Study of Media Use and Youth Culture,' in Rosengren et al., *Media Gratifications Research*, pp. 209–24; Klaus Bruhn Jensen, 'Qualitative Audience Research: Towards an Integrative Approach to Reception,' *Critical Studies in Mass Communication* 4 (1987): 21–36; Thomas R. Lindlof and

Timothy P. Meyer, 'Mediated Communications as Ways of Seeing, Acting and Constructing Culture: The Tools and Foundations of Qualitative Research,' in Lindlof, *Natural Audiences: Qualitative Research and Media Uses and Effects* (Norwood, NJ: Ablex Publishing Company, 1987), pp. 1–30.

14. Lawrence Grossberg (ed.) 'On Postmodernism and Articulation: An Interview with Stuart Hall,' *Journal of Communication Inquiry* 10, no. 2 (summer 1986): 59.

15. James Carey, 'Introduction,' in Mander, *Communications in Transition*, p. 5.

16. I borrowed this formulation from Virginia Nightingale, 'What's Happening to Audience Research?,' *Media Information Australia* 39 (February 1986): 21–2. Nightingale remarks that audience research has generally been 'on the side' of those with vested interests in influencing the organization of the mass media in society, and that it is important to develop a research perspective that is 'on the side' of the audience. However, it is far from simple to work out exactly what such a perspective would mean. The notion of the 'active audience,' for example, often put forward by uses and gratifications researchers to mark the distinctive identity of the 'paradigm,' is not in itself a guarantee for a stance 'on the side of the audience.' In fact, the whole passive/active dichotomy in accounts of audiences has now become so ideologized that it all too often serves as a mystification of the real commitments behind the research at stake.

17. Reflections on the predicaments and politics of research on and with living historical subjects have already played an important role in, for example, feminist studies and anthropology, particularly ethnography. At least two problems are highlighted in these reflections. First, there is the rather awkward but seldom discussed concrete relation between researcher and researched as human beings occupying certain positions invested with power; second, there is the problem of the discursive form in which the cultures of 'others' can be represented in non-objectifying (or better, less objectifying) ways. See, for example, Angela McRobbie, 'The Politics of Feminist Research,' *Feminist Review* 12 (October 1982): 46–57; James Clifford, 'On Ethnographic Authority,' *Representations* 1, no. 2 (1983): 118–46; James Clifford and George E. Marcus (eds) *Writing Culture. The Poetics and Politics of Ethnography* (Berkeley, Los Angeles, London: University of California Press, 1986). Researchers of media audiences have, as far as I know, generally been silent about these issues. However, for a perceptive and thought-provoking engagement with the problem, see Valerie Walkerdine, 'Video Replay: Families, Films and Fantasy,' in Victor Burgin, James Donald and Cora Kaplan (eds) *Formations of Fantasy* (London and New York: Methuen, 1986), pp. 167–99.

18. Lawrence Grossberg, 'Critical Theory and the Politics of Empirical Research,' in Michael Gurevitch and Mark R. Levy (eds) *Mass Communication Review Yearbook*, vol. 6 (Newbury Park, Calif.: Sage, 1986), p. 89.

19. Martyn Hammersley and Paul Atkinson, *Ethnography: Principles in Practice* (London and New York: Tavistock, 1983), p. 16.

20. For a general overview of the interpretative or hermeneutic turn in the social sciences, see Paul Rabinow and William M. Sullivan (eds) *Interpretive Social Science* (Berkeley, Los Angeles, London: University of California Press, 1979). A more radical conception of what they call 'interpretive analytics' is developed by Hubert Dreyfuss and Paul Rabinow in their *Michel Foucault: Beyond Structuralism and Hermeneutics* (Chicago, Ill.: University of Chicago Press, 1982).

21. Pratt, 'Interpretative Strategies/Strategic Interpretations,' p. 52.

22. Grossberg, 'Critical Theory,' p. 89.

23. Cf. Paul Rabinow, 'Representations Are Social Facts: Modernity and Post-Modernity in Anthropology,' in Clifford and Marcus, *Writing Culture*, pp. 234–61.

24. A more general, lucid criticism of empiricist mass communications research is offered by Robert C. Allen in his *Speaking of Soap Operas* (Chapel Hill and London: University of North Carolina Press, 1985), chapter 2.

39

READING THE ROMANCE

Janice Radway

If in concluding [these chapters], the reader remains unsure as to whether the romance should be considered fundamentally conservative on the one hand or incipiently oppositional on the other, that is not surprising. Until now, I have deliberately refrained from the formulation of a definitive conclusion. Indeed, the picture that emerges from this study of the romance-reading phenomenon is less distinct, though not less complete, than previous investigations of other mass-produced literary forms. Although the indistinctness is perhaps frustrating because it hinders the elaboration of a single conclusive statement about the meaning and effect of the romance, it is also an indistinctness born of ambiguity resulting from the planned superimposition or double exposure of multiple images. Those images are themselves produced by the several perspectives brought to bear upon the complicated, polysemic event known as romance reading. The indistinctness is not, then, simply the result of a faulty focus in a singular, comprehensive portrait of a fixed and unified object, the romantic text.

Had I looked solely at the act of reading as it is understood by the women themselves or, alternately at the covert significance of the romance's narrative structure, I might have been able to provide one clear-cut, sharp-focus image. In the first case, the image would suggest that the act of romance reading is oppositional because it allows the women to refuse momentarily their self-abnegating social role. In the second, the image would imply that the romance's

From Radway, 'Conclusion', *Reading the Romance* (London: Verso, 1987) pp. 209–22.

narrative structure embodies a simple recapitulation and recommendation of patriarchy and its constituent social practices and ideologies. However, by looking at the romance-reading behavior of real women through several lenses, each trained on a different component or moment of a process that achieves its meaning and effect over time, each also positioned differently in the sense that one attempts to see the women's experience from within while the other strives to view it from without, this study has consciously chosen to juxtapose multiple views of the complex social interaction between people and texts known as reading. Although I think each view accurately captures one aspect of the phenomenon of romance reading, none can account fully for the actual occurrence or significance of the event as such. In part, this is a function of the complexity inherent in any human action, but it is also the consequence of the fact that culture is both perceptible and hidden, both articulate and covert. Dot and the Smithton women know well both how and why they read romances. Yet at the same time, they also act on cultural assumptions and corollaries not consciously available to them precisely because those givens constitute the very foundation of their social selves, the very possibility of their social action. The multiple perspectives employed here have been adopted, therefore, in the hope that they might help us to comprehend what the women understand themselves to be gaining from the reading of romances while simultaneously revealing how that practice and self-understanding have tacit, unintended effects and implications.

Although it will be impossible, then, to use this conclusion to bring a single, large picture into focus simply because there is no context-free, unmarked position from which to view the activity of romance reading in its entirety, I can perhaps use it to remind the reader of each of the snapshots provided herein, to juxtapose them rapidly in condensed space and time. Such a review will help to underscore the semantic richness and ideological density of the actual process known as romance reading and thus highlight once and for all the complicated nature of the connection between the romance and the culture that has given rise to it.

If we remember that texts are read and that reading itself is an activity carried on by real people in a preconstituted social context, it becomes possible to distinguish *analytically* between the meaning of the act and the meaning of the text as read. This analytic distinction then empowers us to question whether the significance of the act of reading itself might, under some conditions, contradict, undercut, or qualify the significance of producing a particular kind of story. When this methodological distinction is further complicated by an effort to render real readers' comprehension of each of the aspects of the activity as well as the covert significance and consequences underlying both, the possibilities for perceiving conflict and contradiction are increased even more. This is exactly what has resulted from this account of the reading preferences and behavior of Dorothy Evans and the Smithton women.

Ethnographic investigation, for instance, has led to the discovery that Dot and her customers see the act of reading as combative and compensatory. It is combative in the sense that it enables them to refuse the other-directed social role prescribed for them by their position within the institution of marriage. In picking up a book, as they have so eloquently told us, they refuse temporarily their family's otherwise constant demand that they attend to the wants of others even as they act deliberately to do something for their own private pleasure. Their activity is compensatory, then, in that it permits them to focus on themselves and to carve out a solitary space within an arena where their self-interest is usually identified with the interests of others and where they are defined as a public resource to be mined at will by the family. For them, romance reading addresses needs created in them but not met by patriarchal institutions and engendering practices.

It is striking to observe that this partial account of romance reading, which stresses its status as an oppositional or contestative act because the women use it to thwart common cultural expectations and to supply gratification ordinarily ruled out by the way the culture structures their lives, is not far removed from the account of folkloric practices elaborated recently by Luigi Lombardi-Satriani and José Limon.[1] Although both are concerned only with folkloric behavior and the way indigenous folk performances contest the hegemonic imposition of bourgeois culture on such subordinate groups as 'workers, ... peasants, racial and cultural minorities, and women,'[2] their definitions of contestation do not rule out entirely the sort of behavioral activity involving mass culture that I have discovered among the Smithton readers.

[...]

When romance reading is examined, then, as an activity that takes place within a specific social context, it becomes evident that this form of behavior both supplements and counter-valuates in Limon's sense. Romance reading supplements the avenues traditionally open to women for emotional gratification by supplying them vicariously with the attention and nurturance they do not get enough of in the round of day-to-day existence. It counter-valuates because the story opposes the female values of love and personal interaction to the male values of competition and public achievement and, at least in ideal romances, demonstrates the triumph of the former over the latter. Romance reading and writing might be seen therefore as a collectively elaborated female ritual through which women explore the consequences of their common social condition as the appendages of men and attempt to imagine a more perfect state where all the needs they so intensely feel and accept as given would be adequately addressed.

I must stress here [...] that this is *not* the only view of romance reading that might be taken. Women's domestic role in patriarchal culture, which is simultaneously addressed and counter-valuated in the imagination through a woman's encounter with romantic fiction, is left virtually intact by her leisure-time withdrawal. Although in restoring a woman's depleted sense of self romance reading may constitute tacit recognition that the current arrangement of the sexes is not ideal for her emotional well-being, it does nothing to alter a woman's social situation, itself very likely characterized by those dissatisfying patterns. In fact, this activity may very well obviate the need or desire to demand satisfaction in the real world because it can be so successfully met in fantasy.

By the same token, it should also be pointed out that although romance writing and reading help to create a kind of female community, that community is nonetheless mediated by the distances that characterize mass production and the capitalist organization of storytelling. Because the oppositional act is carried out through the auspices of a book and thus involves the fundamentally private, isolating experience of reading, these women never get together to share either the experience of imaginative opposition, or, perhaps more important, the discontent that gave rise to their need for the romance in the first place. The women join forces only symbolically and in a mediated way in the privacy of their individual homes and in the culturally devalued sphere of leisure activity. They do nothing to challenge their separation from one another brought about by the patriarchal culture's insistence that they never work in the public world to maintain themselves but rather live symbiotically as the property and responsibility of men.

In summary, when the act of romance reading is viewed as it is by the readers themselves, from within a belief system that accepts as given the institutions of heterosexuality and monogamous marriage, it can be conceived as an activity of mild protest and longing for reform necessitated by those institutions' failure to satisfy the emotional needs of women. Reading therefore functions for them as an act of recognition and contestation whereby that failure is first admitted and then partially reversed. Hence, the Smithton readers' claim that romance reading is a 'declaration of independence' and a way to say to others, 'This is my time, my space. Now leave me alone.'

At the same time, however, when viewed from the vantage point of a feminism that would like to see the women's oppositional impulse lead to real social change, romance reading can also be seen as an activity that could potentially disarm that impulse. It might do so because it supplies vicariously those very needs and requirements that might otherwise be formulated as demands in the real world and lead to the potential restructuring of sexual relations. The question of whether the activity of romance reading does, in reality, deflect such change by successfully defusing or recontaining this protest must remain unanswered for the moment. Although it may appear on the surface that the leisure-time activity of reading an admittedly fantastic story could never provoke the women who recognize that they need such a 'crutch' to act to change their situation, the women themselves indicate otherwise. In fact, they claim to be transformed by their hobby. Because recent developments in the social practices of romance writing and reading and variations in the romantic plot structure suggest that some change *is* being generated as a consequence of the phenomenon, I will return to this question of the cumulative effect of romance reading shortly after reviewing the significance of the traditional narrative itself, both as it is consciously constructed by the Smithton women and as I think they experience it unconsciously.

If one begins, as I have here, with the premise that the construction of a narrative is an activity that takes place over time, it becomes clear that the significance of the whole process of assembling and understanding the romantic story itself is as ambiguous and conflicted as the simple act of reading the book that contains the tale. As with the act of reading, the women construct and understand the story in a positive manner that both underscores their capabilities as readers and interprets the heroine's actions in the most favorable of ways. Nonetheless, it can also be shown that those conscious processes have tacit and sometimes contradictory consequences. They do so because the activities of constructing the narrative world and of interpreting the heroine's role within it leave intact the very cultural categories, assumptions, and institutions that prompt the readers' desire to demonstrate repeatedly that they are capable and to be told again and again of the worth and power of a romantic heroine.

The narrative discourse of the romantic novel is structured in such a way that it yields easily to the reader's most familiar reading strategies. Thus the act of constructing the narrative line is reassuring because the romantic writer's typical discourse leads the reader to make abductions and inferences that are always immediately confirmed. As she assembles the plot, therefore, the reader learns, in addition to what happens next, that *she* knows how to make sense of texts and human action. Although this understanding of the process must be taken into account and attributed to a positive desire to assert the power and capability of the female self, it cannot be overlooked that the fictional world created as its consequence also reinforces traditional female limitations because it validates the dominance of domestic concerns and personal interaction in women's lives. The reader thus engages in an activity that shores up her own sense of her abilities, but she also creates a simulacrum of her limited social world within a more glamorous fiction. She therefore inadvertently justifies as natural the very conditions and their emotional consequences to which her reading activity is a response.

Similarly, in looking at the Smithton readers' conscious engagement with the manifest content of the ideal romance, it becomes evident that these women believe themselves to be participating in a story that is as much *about* the transformation of an inadequate suitor into the perfect lover-protector as it is about the concomitant triumph of a woman. Her triumph consists of her achievement of sexual and emotional maturity while simultaneously securing the complete attention and devotion of this man who, at least on the surface, admits her preeminent claim to his time and interest. The act of constructing the romantic tale thus provides the reader first with an opportunity to protest vicariously a man's initial inability to understand a woman and to treat her with sensitivity. Secondarily, the process enables a woman to achieve a kind of mastery over her fear of rape because the fantasy evokes her fear and subsequently convinces her that rape is either an illusion or something that she can control easily. Finally, by witnessing and approving of the ideal romantic conclusion, the reader expresses her opposition to the domination of commodity values in her society because she so heartily applauds the heroine's ability to draw the hero's attention away from the public world of money and status and to convince him of the primacy of her values and concerns.

It seems apparent, then, that an oppositional moment can be said to characterize even the production of the romantic story if that process is understood as the women themselves conceive it. I have elsewhere called this stage of aspect of the reading process a 'utopian' moment,[3] drawing on Fredric Jameson's important argument that every form of mass culture has a dimension 'which remains implicitly, and no matter how faintly, negative and critical of the social order from which, as a product and a commodity, it springs.'[4] In effect, the vision called into being at the end of the process of romance reading projects for the reader a utopian state where men are neither cruel nor indifferent, neither preoccupied with the external world nor wary of an intense emotional attachment to a woman. This fantasy also suggests that the safety and protection of traditional marriage will not compromise a woman's autonomy or self-confidence. In sum, the vision reforms those very conditions characterizing the real world that leave so many women and, most probably, the reader herself, longing for affective care, ongoing tenderness, and a strong sense of self-worth. This interpretation of the romance's meaning suggests, then, that the women who seek out ideal novels in order to construct such a vision again and again are reading not out of contentment but out of dissatisfaction, longing, and protest.

Of course, in standing back from this construction of the romance's meaning, once again to assess the implications of its symbolic negation and criticism of the social order, it becomes possible to see that despite the utopian force of the romance's projection, that projection actually leaves unchallenged the very system of social relations whose faults and imperfections gave rise to the romance and which the romance is trying to perfect. The romance manages to do so because its narrative organization prompts the reader to construct covert counter-messages that either undercut or negate the changes projected on an overt level. To begin with, although the narrative story provides the reader with an opportunity to indulge in anger at the initial, offensive behavior of the hero, we must not forget that that anger is later shown to be unwarranted because the hero's indifference or cruelty actually originated in feelings of love. Thus while the experience of reading the tale may be cathartic in the sense that it allows the reader to express in the imagination anger at men that she would otherwise censor or deny, it also suggests to her that such anger as the heroine's is, in reality, unjustified because the offensiveness of the behavior prompting it was simply a function of the heroine's inability to read a man properly. Because the reading process always confirms for the reader that she knows how to read male behavior correctly, it suggests that her anger is unnecessary because her spouse, like the hero, actually loves her deeply, though he may not express it as she might wish. In the end, the romance-reading process gives the reader a strategy for making her present situation more comfortable without substantive reordering of its structure rather than a comprehensive program for reorganizing her life in such a way that all needs might be met.

In this context, I should also call attention once again to the hole in the romance's explanatory logic with respect to the hero's transformation from the heroine's distant, insensitive, and cold superior into her tender, expressive intimate. Although this crucial transformation in the romance clearly derives from writers' and readers' desires to believe in the possibility of such an ideal partner, the manner in which it is effected implies once again that the transfiguration is accomplished largely by a shift in the heroine's perceptual gestalt. Of course, the ideal hero does become more expressive in the course of the story, but because the early descriptions of him emphasized that this tender side was always part of his true character even though it was suppressed, the narrative structure places ultimate responsibility for its nurturance and flowering on the heroine herself. In reassuring him about the purity of her motives, it is *she* who frees him to respond warmly to her. This structure covertly suggests, then, that male reticence and distance cannot be transmuted into something else entirely. All that is possible, really, is the cultivation and encouragement of tendencies already there in the personalities of particular men. If a woman wants to be treated tenderly and attentively, the story ultimately suggests, she must find a man who is already capable of such expression though perhaps fearful of indulging in it. By having it both ways to begin with, that is, by beginning with a hero who is traditionally masculine and somewhat expressive in a feminine way, the romance manages to sidestep the crucial issue of whether the traditional social construction of masculinity does not rule out the possibility of nurturant behavior in men.

Little need be said here about the way in which the romance's treatment of rape probably harms romance readers even as it provides them with a sense of power and control over their fear of it. Although their distaste for 'out-and-out' violation indicates that these women do not want to be punished or hurt as so many have assumed, their willingness to be convinced that the forced 'taking' of a woman by a man who 'really' loves her is testimony to her desirability and worth rather than to his power suggests once again that the romance is effectively dealing with some of the consequences of patriarchy without also challenging the hierarchy of control upon which it is based. By examining the whole issue of rape and its effect on the heroine, the romance may provide the reader with the opportunity to explore the consequences of related behavior in her own life. Nonetheless, by suggesting that rape is either a mistake or an expression of uncontrollable desire, it may also give her a false sense of security by showing her how to rationalize violent behavior and thus reconcile her to a set of events and relations that she would be better off changing.

Finally, it must also be noted here that even though the romance underlines the opposition between the values of love and those associated with the competitive pursuit of status and wealth, by perpetuating the exclusive division of the world into the familiar categories of the public and the private, the romance continues to justify the social placement of women that has led to the very discontent that is the source of their desire to read romances. It is true, certainly, that the romance accepts this dichotomy in order to assert subsequently that the commonly devalued personal sphere and the women who dominate it have higher status and the evangelical power to draw the keepers of the public realm away from their worldly interests. Yet despite this proclamation of female superiority, in continuing to relegate women to the arena of domestic, purely personal relations, the romance fails to pose other, more radical questions. In short, it refuses to ask whether female values might be used to 'feminize' the public realm or if control over that realm could be shared by women and by men. Because the romance finally leaves unchallenged the male right to the public spheres of work, politics, and power, because it refurbishes the institution of marriage by suggesting how it might be viewed continuously as a courtship, because it represents real female needs within the story and then depicts their satisfaction by traditional heterosexual relations, the romance avoids questioning the institutionalized basis of patriarchal control over women even as it serves as a locus of protest against some of its emotional consequences.

Given the apparent power of the romance's conservative counter-messages, then, it is tempting to suggest that romantic fiction must be an active agent in the maintenance of the ideological status quo because it ultimately reconciles women to patriarchal society and reintegrates them with its institutions. It appears that it might do so by deflecting and recontaining real protest and by supplying vicariously certain needs that, if presented as demands in the real world, might otherwise lead to the reordering of heterosexual relationships. If true, romances would do all of this within the already fenced-off realm of leisure and the imaginary and thereby protect the more important arenas of the culture from women's collective elaboration of their dissatisfaction with patriarchy's effects on their lives.

[...]

Other developments on the national romance scene suggest that the utopian current running through the experience of reading may move women in ways that conflict significantly with the more conservative push effected by the story's reaffirmation of marriage's ability to satisfy female needs completely. I am thinking here of the recent decision to organize among romance writers themselves. Founded by several Texas women in the spring of 1981, the Romance Writers of America has developed rapidly as a national organization that draws together writers and editors of romances and even some readers. Communicating through a monthly newsletter and at both regional and national conferences, these women are now sharing tips, techniques, and information about romance writing and reading. Indeed, the writers are, for the first time, disclosing facts and figures about their contracts with the express purpose of forcing better deals from publishers who the women now know are making enormous profits from the sales of their books.

[. . .]

Whether such developments will be widespread and general in the future is impossible to say since we have no way of knowing how many women will give up their safe, limited, and barely conscious contestation of patriarchy for the uncertainty of feminism's conscious assault on both its categorization of the world and its institutional structure. The developments bear watching, however, for they may indicate that the romance's long-present but covert challenge to the notion that traditional marriages satisfy all women's needs is about to take on a more combative, questioning tone. This could occur if romance writers and readers ever discover through the collective sharing of experiences that together they have strength, a voice, and important objections to make about current gender arrangements. However, because I suspect a demand for real change in power relations will occur only if women also come to understand that their need for romances is a function of their dependent status *as women* and of their acceptance of marriage as the only route to female fulfillment, I think we as feminists might help this change along by first learning to recognize that romance reading originates in very real dissatisfaction and embodies a valid, if limited, protest. Then by developing strategies for making that dissatisfaction and its causes consciously available to romance readers and by learning how to encourage that protest in such a way that it will be delivered in the arena of actual social relations rather than acted out in the imagination, we might join hands with women who are, after all, our sisters and together imagine a world whose subsequent creation would lead to the need for a new fantasy altogether.

Perhaps one final observation about the implications of this study for future investigation of mass-cultural forms is necessary before bringing the work to its conclusion. I do not think it would be claiming too much to suggest that the very fruitfulness of the methodology employed here indicates that we may not yet understand the complexity of mass culture's implication in social life as well as we might. Certainly, my study does not challenge absolutely the notion that mass-produced art forms like the romance are ideologically conservative in the sense that they restore at least temporarily the claims of presently existing institutions and practices to the loyalty of those who participate vicariously in these forms. After all, the romance does assert on one level that the perfect heterosexual lover is a possibility as is an ideal marriage in which a woman achieves independence, dependence, excitement, and nurturance all at the same time. Nonetheless, the study's investigation of reading as act suggests that real people can use the romance to address their unmet needs experienced precisely because that ideal relationship is made highly improbable by the institutional structure and engendering practices of contemporary society. Furthermore, the focus on reading as a process of construction reveals that the early stages of a reader's interpretation and response to the romantic form can be characterized by the expression of repressed emotions deriving from dissatisfaction with the status quo and a utopian longing for a better life. The methodology highlights, then, the complicated and contradictory ways in which the romance recognizes and thereby protests the weaknesses of patriarchy and the failure of traditional marriage even as it apparently acts to assert the perfection of each and to teach women how to *re*-view their own imperfect relationships in such a way that they seem unassailable.

All of this suggests that we must be careful not to reproduce the reifying tendencies of late capitalism and its supportive perceptual and analytical strategies in our methodologies and interpretive work. We must not, in short, look only at mass-produced objects themselves on the assumption that they bear all of their significances on their surface, as it were, and reveal them automatically to us. To do so would be to assume either that perceptible, tangible things alone are worth analyzing or that those commodified objects exert such pressure and influence on their consumers that they have no power as individuals to resist or alter the ways in which those objects mean or can be used.

Commodities like mass-produced literary texts are selected, purchased, constructed, and used by real people with previously existing needs, desires, intentions, and interpretive strategies. By reinstating those active individuals and their creative, constructive activities at the heart of our interpretive enterprise, we avoid blinding ourselves to the fact that the essentially human practice of making meaning goes on even in a world increasingly dominated by things and by consumption. In thus recalling the interactive character of operations like reading, we restore time, process, and action to our account of human endeavor and therefore increase the possibility of doing justice to its essential complexity and ambiguity as practice. We also increase our chances of sorting out or articulating the difference between the repressive imposition of ideology and oppositional practices that, though limited in their scope and effect, at least dispute or contest the control of ideological forms.

If we can learn, then, to look at the ways in which various groups appropriate and use the mass-produced art of our culture, I suspect we may well begin to understand that although the ideological power of contemporary cultural forms is enormous, indeed sometimes even frightening, that power is not yet all-pervasive, totally vigilant, or complete. Interstices still exist within the social fabric where opposition is carried on by people who are not satisfied by their place within it or by the restricted material and emotional rewards that accompany it. They therefore attempt to imagine a more perfect social state as a way of countering despair. I think it absolutely essential that we who are committed to social change learn not to overlook this minimal but nonetheless legitimate form of protest. We should seek it out not only to understand its origins and its utopian longing but also to learn how best to encourage it and bring it to fruition. If we do not, we have already conceded the fight and, in the case of the romance at least, admitted the impossibility of creating a world where the vicarious pleasure supplied by its reading would be unnecessary.

NOTES

1. Luigi Lombardi-Satriani, 'Folklore as Culture of Contestation', *Journal of the Folklore Institute* 11 (June–August 1974), 99–121. José Limon, 'Folklore and the Mexican in the United States: A Marxist Cultural Perspective' (unpublished paper), 1–21.
2. Ibid., 3.
3. Janice Radway, 'The Utopian Impulse in Popular Literature: Gothic Romances and "Feminist" Protest', *American Quarterly* 33 (summer 1981), 140–62.
4. Fredric Jameson, 'Reification and Utopia in Mass Culture', *Social Text* 1 (winter 1979), 144.

40

THE YOUNG AND THE RESTLESS IN TRINIDAD: A CASE OF THE LOCAL AND THE GLOBAL IN MASS CONSUMPTION[1]

Daniel Miller

[...]

The Young and the Restless may be introduced through a particularly Trinidadian perspective. Below is an edited transcript of one of the two calypsos launched in 1988 called 'The Young and the Restless'. This one was rapturously received by audiences from the moment it started with a copy of the soap's theme tune, and the laughter, provoked by what is largely a summary of plot, usually continued to the end.

Hear how it go,

> Philip and Cricket did love bad.
> For some reason Jack Abbott dohn like Brad.
> Nina, the old lady dohn like she,
> Nina stick Philip with a baby.
> Jack Abbott, he went crazy
> over Cricket' mummy,
> so though the woman got Aids
> he still went and marry she.
> You talk of commess
> check the young and restless,
> commess at its best
> check the young and restless.
> Everyday at noon precisely

From R. Silverstone and E. Hirsch (eds), *Consuming Technologies: Media and Information in Domestic Spaces* (London and New York: Routledge, 1992) pp. 163–82.

old and young in front their TV.
Well believe me this ain no joke
some people carry TV to work,
to watch (he bacchanal
to watch the confusion,
I tell you the picture
is a sensation.
It was *Dallas* and *Dynasty*
that had TV fans going crazy,
then came *Falcon Crest*
but they can't touch *Young and Restless*,
when it comes to bacchanal

(Extract from 'The Young and the Restless' by
calypsonian 'The Contender')

The Young and the Restless fits the narrow category of true soap opera as given by Cantor and Pingree (1983) of afternoon serials as opposed to the prime-time series such as *Dallas*. It has been produced since 1973, though by Columbia pictures for CBS rather than the original 'soap' group produced by Proctor and Gamble. The targeted audience is the housewife, reflected in the emphasis on dialogue rather than visual content, so that it is compatible with domestic work. According to these same authors, *The Young and the Restless* is one of a group which tends to a greater orientation towards sex and breakdown than the prime-time series. Within the field of soap opera *The Young and the Restless* is situated in the 'liberal' group, which is particularly so inclined (ibid.: 94).

The Young and the Restless was introduced to Trinidad following other lunch-hour soaps and was not therefore expected to have the same weight as serials such as *Dynasty* and *Dallas*. Advertising space was consequently cheaper at that period, which is seen as the housewives' slot, although by the end of fieldwork retailers were insisting that the producers target this time slot. Evidence that the effect of this soap opera emanates from the salience of its content and is not merely the product of well-targeted television comes from the manner in which it has completely overthrown the power of the prime-time slot and that Trinidadians have refused the logistical constraints and insisted on watching the series even when conditions should have constrained them. The case reveals something of the flexible potential of television as technology. Many of the favourite stories surrounding the aura of *The Young and the Restless* are about the extremes people go to in order to see what is generally termed the 'show' on a daily basis, although it is repeated in full at weekends. Particularly important are battery-operated miniature televisions, which are vital for those wishing to see the show at work. These are particularly conspicuous in retailing, where shop assistants have one eye to the screen, even as they serve, but many also find their way into office lunching areas. The miniature televisions are generally purchased abroad on shopping trips to places such as Caracas or Miami, or brought in by relatives resident in Canada or the USA. The disruptive impact of the show on work was heightened by the desire of those without access to a television to use the subsequent hour to pick up the details they had missed.

Much less common because of their relative scarcity, was the use of videos to reschedule watching to a more convenient time after work. Those with low income, for example, a large squatting community amongst whom I worked, were amongst the most resourceful in gaining access. The bulk of these homes have neither water nor electricity, but given the imperative to watch the 'show' many homes have televisions connected to car batteries which are recharged at a small fee per week by those who have electricity supplies.

A local marketing survey carried out early in 1988, I suspect before *The Young and the Restless* had peaked, suggested 70 per cent of those with TV watched the show regularly, slightly more than those who watched the news, both of these being well ahead of the third highest rating, which was less than 30 per cent. In my own survey of 160 households,[2] out of the 146 who had access to a television all but 20 watched *The Young and the Restless* regularly. There was no evident association with ethnicity, but only 5 out of 71 in the lower income bracket did not watch this show while 15 out of 75 in the higher income bracket did not watch it. In a separate question, where 44 households mentioned their favourite programmes, 37 gave *The Young and the Restless* as one of them.

The viewing of the soap opera is often both a social and a participatory affair. Few televisions fail to attract a neighbour or two on a regular basis. Individuals may shout deprecations or advice to the characters during the course of the programme. Afterwards there is often collective commentary and discussion. There is a considerable concern to spread news of important events quickly. I was slightly 'shocked' in my vicarious sense of propriety, when an important Muslim festival I was viewing was interrupted by three ladies who collectively announced to the assembled group some new development which we had missed by taking part in the ceremony. Typically also, people telephone each other to confirm that they knew all along that some event was going to occur.

For most of this century and particularly since the stationing of American troops there during the Second World War, Trinidad has been the recipient of sustained influences from the United States, reinforced by the number of families with relatives who have emigrated to North America, by macro-economic pressures and by the American dominance of the media. The nature of American society and the implications of its current influence upon Trinidad are certainly contentious issues, and one might have expected that the soap opera would be viewed in relation to these issues, but a review of the conversations in which the soap opera is discussed or used for illustrative purposes shows that this is not the case. Indeed, one of the most common comments about the show was its relevance to contemporary conditions in Trinidad. Typical would be:

'The same thing you see on the show will happen here, you see the wife blackmailing the husband or the other way around, I was telling my sister-in-law, Lianna in the picture, just like some bacchanal woman.'

'It really happening this flirtatious attitude, this one they living together that partner working this partner, and have a date with the next one or in bed with another.'

'People look at it because it is everyday experience for some people. I think they pattern their lives on it.'

From this sense of relevance comes also the idea that there are direct lessons to be learnt from the narrative content for moral issues in Trinidad, e.g.

'It teach you how husbands could lie and cheat and how a wife could expect certain things and never get it, the women always get the short end of the stick.'

'I believe marriage should be 50–50 not 30–70 the woman have to be strong she have to believe in her vows no matter what ... that make me remember *The Young and the Restless*, Nicky want her marriage to work but Victor is in love with somebody else, but she still holding on.'

Or (as in a current story)

'You always to go back to the first person you loved, in my own family my elder sister went with a Moslem boy, and so was married off by parents to a Hindu man, but she left her husband, gone back to the first man and had a child by him.'

As evidenced in the study of *Dallas* in Israel this moral use of the show will depend upon the perspective it is being viewed from. The Trinidad evidence supports Buckingham in arguing that the audience feels quite able to retain both a sense of critical distance which breaks the frame of realism and yet have intense involvement in the 'as if scenario' which results (Buckingham, 1988: 200; see also Vink, 1988: 232–40). This may emerge in the desire to intervene in or comment on the construction, as in the following two comments on AIDS:

'We find that Jessica so nice they shouldn't have given her Aids they should have given Jill, somebody nice shouldn't have been given Aids.'

'I like the idea of Aids, since there was an episode which explain to Cricket how you get it, that you can't get it through swimming pools, so I find that was good, it's educational especially to housewives. It also show two sides to each person like Victor who would be warm and loving but cruel and nasty. In *Dallas* you hate JR and I don't think you would be able to like him again, but it is not like that on *The Young and the Restless*. I like the way they do their make-up, the Australian soap operas seem very dull make-up, but this one outstanding shades of lipstick, eye

make-up, earring and kinds of jewellery, the way they dress and everything goes with everything else.'

There can also be criticism of over identification, as in

'With my mother in the USA she so involved you would actually think it
is some of she children she is talking about.'

BACCHANAL

From both the calypso and the above quotations it is clear that Trinidadians
have themselves developed a set of ideas which accounts for the attraction and
success of this particular soap opera. This is encapsulated in the phrase 'they
like the bacchanal'. Outside Trinidad this term would connote some kind of
orgiastic or frenzied celebration, and so it is not surprising that the term is also
frequently applied to the annual Carnival. But within Trinidad bacchanal has
far more complex connotations. If one looks at the use of the term in calypso
the first synonym is clearly 'scandal'. In 1988 David Rudder sang 'Bacchanal
Woman, sweet scandal where she walks', while Carl and Carol Jacobs sang,
'We people like scandal. We people like bacchanal.' In the 1988 Carnival
queen competition there was an entry with the title of 'Bacchanal Woman', the
costume consisting of a voluminous pink/scarlet dress with exaggerated breast
and buttocks, but above this was a spreading fan of layers like a peacock's tail
emblazoned with a series of open eyes.

The second clear connotation of the term 'bacchanal' is confusion or disorder. The two major connotations are linked by the other unfamiliar term in
the calypso, that is 'commess'. In dictionaries commess is translated as extreme
confusion, but it will normally carry the connotation of confusion which results
from scandal. Indeed, it seems that Trinidadian language has retained a set of
terms from earlier French patois for constructing a network of concepts which
are not well covered by English. My work as an anthropologist in uncovering or
listening in to gossip rendered me a Maco, or Macotious, potentially instrumental in spreading news or Movay-Lang (*mauvaise-langue*) which again leads
to commess and to bacchanal.

A final semantic linkage is the connotation of the term 'bacchanal' as truth,
as in the notion of bringing to light. It is not just that scandal reveals the
hidden, but for many Trinidadians there is a moral value in this exposure.
Scandal and confusion have highly ambiguous moral overtones, at once undermining patiently constructed systems of order and stability but also bringing us
closer to the true nature of social being. The benign element of bacchanal is
most evident in the affection for Carnival, which is the moment of the year
given to the exploration of bacchanal as an ideal. Indeed the central motif for
many in Carnival is the ritual of Jouvert, where groups dressed in mud and
ashes organized into bands such as 'Barbarians' or 'Kids in Hell', full of ironic
commentary parodying topical items such as advertisements, TV evangelists or
The Young and the Restless, throng the streets before dawn. The event is

dominated by dawn itself, the bringing into light of that which is normally hidden.

Having established this semantic network for the term 'bacchanal', we may now reintroduce it into two contexts as the instrument which relates them: that is the concept of the domestic, and the reception of *The Young and the Restless*.

In one of the most influential anthropological accounts of Caribbean society, Wilson (1973) divides Caribbean societies into two opposing cultural projects, which he terms 'respectability' and 'reputation'. Respectability is seen as the abiding influence of colonial pressures towards the kind of domesticity which is enshrined by the colonial female. This includes the drive to social stratification, religiosity, familial forms sanctioned by the church, and its major enshrinement is through women's involvement in the construction of a domestic domain. This becomes, however, in the Caribbean context an even more gendered distinction, since most men are entirely uninvolved in this arena. Rather they embody an oppositional tendency termed 'reputation', in which they are mainly engaged in male-only activities with transient peer rivalry but longer term egalitarian pressures, involving drinking, gambling and above all verbal play, resistant to the hierarchizing and constraining pressures of the domestic. Working from the perspective of Trinidad, I would wish to modify elements of Wilson's portrayal of the origins and implications of these projects, and a dualism he associates most closely with gender I see as being projected equally onto ethnicity in Trinidad and class in Jamaica. However, I would confirm a framework based on two opposed cultural projects, which in the Trinidadian case I have termed 'transient' and 'transcendent', emphasizing an orientation either to the event, or to descent or continuity respectively.[3] It is fair, then, to attempt to derive some sense of the domestic from within the transcendent end of this polarity and associate this with a commonly gendered division. Furthermore, these projects refer back to the global discourse of the domestic, incorporating images from television sit-coms or feminism respectively.

[...]

As already noted, the term 'bacchanal' is deeply ambivalent, but certain groups do manage to transform it either into an almost entirely derisory or a benign assertion. From the perspective of transcendence it was commonly asserted that the current government, which is called the National Alliance for Reconstruction, but which was in practice falling apart into warring factions, was a clear case of bacchanal. The previous government's insistence, through fairly heavy-handed control, on keeping its internal divisions from public view was seen as a much more 'serious' form of rule. In my interviews with people within the very private and protected houses of the middle class, I found that women, in particular, were extremely fearful, sometimes literally terrified, that their husbands would get to know that they had been talking to me (but equally to my female research assistant) about their domestic circumstances. Women are understood as being responsible for the domestic world.

They not only build it but equally they are seen as the weak link whose revelations or wrong behaviour would lead to its collapse. It is here that the centripetal aesthetic is clearest, in the strategies for enclosure, layering and covering up to protect themselves from revelation and exposure. When, as often happens within the realm of the transcendent, an apparently stable and close family is broken asunder into disordered fragments following a dispute over inheritance, the appellation of 'bacchanal' has nothing good about it.

Equally common, however, is the use of the term 'bacchanal' from the perspective of the transient. Here the term was most frequently used in relation to domestic scandal and exposure. The quintessential case is the woman or family that has gradually built up an aura of respectability, has entered fully into the spirit of transcendence, when suddenly some behaviour is revealed which indicates the false or hollow nature of the claims to respectability. In the context of the domestic, this may also be seen as the collapse of culture into nature, of chastity into lust, of façades of domestic calm into revelations of domestic violence and strife. One of the clearest expressions of bacchanal is what are called 'cuss-outs', in which two people stand before their houses and exchange insults, often for hours, while an audience gathers to appreciate the quality of the verbal invective.

The background to this is the centrality of gossip to social relations and the control of access to potentially revelatory information. Gossip is both highly stylized and frequently leads to confusion. For the transient of the squatting community there may be a positive identification with this culture of gossip, as they see themselves as the true objectification of bacchanal. This was the area where you would hear the most elaborate cussing-out, where gossip flowed free and far, where the walls of houses built from the boxes in which car parts are imported could scarcely hope to conceal the activities of the domestic arena. From their perspective it is the connotations of truth and nature which are particularly important. It is they who can condemn as façade the 'social' (meaning anti-social) ways of the suburb, and who insist that eventually all such attempts to respectability will fail, as all will succumb to the natural drives which lead them into scandalous situations. One of the strongest instruments of bacchanal is clearly the sexual imperative, and the term 'nature' is as equally connotative of sex itself as it is of the male's world in nature outside the domestic.

[...]

As in other accounts of soap opera it is clear that the 'realism' with which it is identified has little to do with the environmental context of domestic presentation; the scenes cannot look like Trinidad. Realism rather is based on the truth of the serial in relation to key structural problematics of Trinidadian culture. It is the realism of myth. The soap opera is a meta-commentary on the nature of truth itself. It explores through its stories the processes by which natural forces such as lust and gossip break open the global discourse of the domestic into the confusion and disorder of true life.

A major preoccupation in the soap opera is the manner in which individuals are thrown off course or driven to extreme actions by sexual desire. So a person writing a critical biography, almost against her will, starts an affair with the object of her work. A female working hard to be integrated within the respectable family of her child's father is seduced from these efforts by a good-looking male recruited for the purpose. Here, as in the Trinidadian ideology of the domestic, it is often the females who assert one morality but find themselves inexorably drawn through sexual attraction into overturning these same principles. The viewer notes, 'look how she is a commess maker, just so some women come to some people house and do the same thing'.

For some of the squatters there is not enough bacchanal:

> 'People in *The Young and the Restless* can't have fun like people in Trinidad, their sort of fun is boring. There's more bacchanal here than in *The Young and the Restless*, in each soap you can tell what's going to happen but around here you can't tell.'

Almost all the literature on soap opera emphasizes the forms of identification between the audience and the characters portrayed as central to the attraction of the genre. When I reviewed the occasions upon which informants noted personal identifications, it became evident that these almost always take a particular form that I had not encountered in the comparative literature (though see Vink, 1988: 227–8, 236, on the work of Milanesi). It is rarely the character or personality of the individual which is seen as the point of identification. In the first instance it is almost always the clothing which mediates the act of identification [...] This identification may often translate into direct copying of clothes, so that seamstresses may conceive of watching the soap operas as part of their job.

[...]

The important point about this use of clothing is not that it shows the superficial level at which the programme is absorbed, but quite the opposite. Given the principal exteriorizing, centrifugal aesthetic of bacchanal, it shows the centrality of the programme to that aspect of Trinidadian culture. In the approach to ontology espoused by transience it is precisely in the response to stylistic display that one finds out who one really is. This being is based on the event and is not accretative or institutionalized in social structures. It is reconstructed with each performance, which ideally requires a new set of clothing. During the oil boom, when families who had been brought up in poverty obtained wealth, they outdid the hegemonic classes in the transience of their fashions, not out of some 'crass' materialism, but rather as an appropriation of goods which opposed their incorporation into longer standing accretative structures (see Miller, 1990). The identification through fashion is therefore evidence for the profundity of the experience of this programme rather than its inverse.

[...]

TRANSFORMING THE DOMESTIC

A question remains as to the impact of these images upon the nature of the domestic in Trinidad. Clearly the serial represents a displaced form of gossip. Bacchanal is generally associated with innuendo and is not entirely provenanced. This is not a new phenomena, however. 'Town talk', as it used to operate, was also often based on the circulation of generalized genre suspicions before they could be pinned onto any particular person or place. Nevertheless, *The Young and the Restless* is still more displaced, which means that a considerable amount of gossip can take place in which people's actual interests are not involved, as in

> 'I prefer that, you see it is safer to talk about the celebrities' business than to talk about people's business. You won't get into trouble, nobody will cuss you if you say Chancellor was with this one husband . . . but it is just bacchanal . . . all them soaps is bacchanal.'

This comment helps account for the particular significance of *The Young and the Restless* at this point of time. Trinidad is an extraordinarily dynamic society. With the oil boom post-1973 it was catapulted into the world of mass consumption, but with the decline of the oil price, especially in 1986, it has suffered an almost equally precipitous recession. I would argue that bacchanal is more important than wealth *per se* in determining the local equivalent of class. The disdain felt by the suburban for the squatters is based on the uncontrolled commess of the latter. Wealth, however, is of considerable importance in allowing groups to struggle towards the respectability of transcendence and its instruments of interiorization and enclosure.

The oil boom gave a tremendous impetus to the growth of the middle class, to the extent that they emerged at its peak as dominant both numerically and culturally. With the recession, however, many of the more fragile pretensions of the *nouveau* element within this class are becoming exposed. There is a continual discourse about the financial plight that exists behind the closed doors of the domestic, which is only brought to light by events such as cutting off the phone because of unpaid bills. Even in the suburbs there were frequent rumours about how many properties were back in the hands of the banks or deserted by migrants to Canada. The crisis was largely financial but it is very possible that this was instrumental in the displaced crescendo of activity around the concept of exposure based on the more familiar theme of sexuality. Therefore this unprecedented orientation towards an imported soap opera may well have its roots in the near-exquisite tension that had built up between transcendence and transience and which is highlighted by the focus upon bacchanal.

Many of the writings on soap opera and serials tend to assume that these lend some reassurance, stability and so forth as part of their power. Much of this may stem from the legacy of the mass culture critique which treated soap operas as a kind of visual Valium that stupefies its audience in the interest of some dominant will. In certain cases this may well be the impact, but not in Trinidad. Here, so far from patching up a wound, or 'functioning' in the interests of social cohesion, the attraction of the programme is that it forces its point into the key fissure which manifests the basic contradiction of Trinidadian culture, at a time when this is especially sensitive. This is precisely why Trinidadian television cannot produce a programme of this kind. *The Young and the Restless* reinforces bacchanal as the lesson of recession which insists that the domestic and the façade of stability is a flimsy construction which will be blown over in the first storm created by true nature.

As such, the soap opera is merely a new transformation of a concept of bacchanal which has already a number of alternative forms of objectification, for example in Carnival. It is, nevertheless, innovatory in certain respects. The soap opera is closer to the everyday activities of those for whom bacchanal is a more constant experience, the world of gossip, scandal and confusion that generates the constant narrative structure of community life. It may thereby comment more directly on the current dynamics of the domestic while Carnival reflects more on a slower moving structural dualism within which the domestic is implicated. *The Young and the Restless*, in particular, colludes with the local sense of truth as exposure and scandal. The soap opera is not just Trinidadian but, as in a popular local expression, 'True True Trini'.

CONCLUSION: THE LOCAL AND THE GLOBAL

The terms 'global' and 'local' as used here are dialectical categories, which are proposed only to be productively dissolved in analysis. Indeed, the impossibility of a simple dualist approach to the local and the global is given by the juxtaposition of two points. On the one hand, bacchanal is the term many people gave as their one-word description of the essential character of Trinidadian society, and at the same time the principal form used to exemplify bacchanal in 1988 was not an indigenous production but an imported American soap opera. The mistake made by some studies is to assume that we are dealing with an 'American' product which others may not have the cultural knowledge to interpret 'properly', or that it simply slips into some local context (e.g. Katz and Liebes, 1986; Schroder, 1988). Although, in terms of production, we are dealing with what might be called the unintended consequence of international media marketing for profit, this chapter has argued that at the level of consumption we can observe both the recreation of the soap opera as Trinidadian and also its role in the refinement of the concept of Trinidad as the culture of bacchanal.

The term 'global' is useful because it does not exclude Trinidad, which is by definition as much a part of the world as, say, France. It accepts, then, that the work of writers such as V. S. Naipaul and C. L. R. James or music such as the steel band may be found today in shops in virtually any country in the world. At the same time we should not assume that the term 'global' connotes the massive homogenization presupposed by the debate on consumer culture. The influence of America includes everything from full gospel black churches and Miami brand names to youth music, to the creation of all of which the Caribbean contributed, and which represent the United States as an extremely heterodox society. Trinidadians are very keen on dissecting the stylistic distinctions between, say, New York and California, not to mention Puerto Rico.

Trinidadians sense their disadvantage in being small scale compared to larger national or multi-national forces. In particular, they are well aware of the highly authoritarian and ideologically charged pressures represented by the IMF, which presently dictates Trinidadian politics to what is regarded as a quite unacceptable degree. At the same time many see their fellow Trinidadians as often highly successful entrepreneurially and otherwise within the United States, which, while it is held in a kind of awe as the centre of metropolitan style, is simultaneously derided as often less sophisticated, less highly educated and a bit of a pushover by comparison with their own social milieu. The soap opera might have been used to comment upon the relationship between America and Trinidad or the nature of American 'bacchanal' but, as is often the case with melodrama, the setting is taken as a fantasy, under the cover of which viewers can consider intensely personal and local relations.

An individual case study tends to stress certain conclusions which need to be qualified in a comparative context. The example described here suggests that, in the production of one's own culture, indigenously created forms may provide for easier cultural appropriation, but imported forms may also have transformative potential as vehicles for objectification. A broader understanding of mass consumption within the global and the local, however, requires appreciation of the many constraints on possible appropriation. It also requires acknowledgement that in other cases the effects of an import may be detrimental, and what is produced is merely that sense of alienation which comes from an inability to appropriate that which is given by larger corporations as the means of cultural identity. To achieve a balance, a case study such as this one needs to be seen in conjunction with the findings of Mattelart (1983) on the deleterious effects of international media imperialism.

Trinidad was never, and will never be, the primary producer of the images and goods from which it constructs its own culture. To that extent an analysis of Trinidadian culture has at least in part to incorporate a theory of consumption. As with most nation-states today, Trinidad is largely the recipient of global discourses for which the concept of spatial origin is becoming increasingly inappropriate. This applies both to finance capital and to media ownership, which are becoming increasingly stateless (Harvey, 1989:163). If Trinidad wishes to participate in the wealth of images created through mass production, then it cannot hope to manufacture them all locally. This is merely the original lesson of the industrial revolution writ large. Trinidadians themselves are perfectly well aware of the advantages of global products made to higher specifications than they can manage, while being alert to inequalities in the terms of trade and potential insensitivity of global marketing to the needs of small markets. The fact that Carnival is derived from French colonial culture, Anansi stories from Africa, Divali from India, *Sesame Street* from the United States, Rasta from Jamaica does not dictate the process of local consumption with its considerable transformative properties. The mistake is to assume this means the end of specificity for Trinidadian culture. As noted at the beginning of this chapter, authenticity has increasingly to be judged a posteriori not a priori, according to local consequences not local origins.

NOTES

1. The fieldwork on the topic of mass consumption took place in 1988–9. The major component consisted of work in four communities in and around the town of Chaguanas in central Trinidad. Although often viewed as a centre for East Indians, the communities studied – which comprised a middle-class suburban residential area, a government housing project, an incorporated village and a settlement of squatters – reflected the ethnic make-up of the national census with approximately 40 per cent ex-East Indian, 40 per cent ex-African and 20 per cent Mixed and others. As one part of the fieldwork, a survey of forty households from each of the communities was carried out.
2. Although I conducted no interviews directly on the topic of *The Young and the Restless*, which was not an intended object of study, I frequently tape-recorded general conversations between informants, once it become evident that this did not seem to detract from their spontaneity. The quotations given in this section come from the transcriptions of these conversations. It may be noted that the bulk of these quotations are from women, partly because most of my fieldwork was conducted with women, but also because it was they who were more ready to acknowledge or refer to the soap opera in casual conversation.
3. These two terms, 'transient' and 'transcendent', are used here as analytical categories. I do not want to overextend their literal meaning, but they are intended to express polarized sets of values which are fundamental to Trinidadian culture, the former associated with individualism, the outside, and a refusal of institutionalization, the latter expressive of a concern for the longer term (e.g. roots or planning) and often conventional religion. There are some groups of people whose lifestyles and values seem clearly to embody such values, so that the text may speak of the transient from the squatting area, i.e. those in that neighbourhood who consistently embody transient ideals. Most Trinidadians, however, will affirm both sets of values, depending on circumstances or season. The terms may also refer to these values as expressed in some cultural form, as with the transcendence found in living-room decorations.

REFERENCES

Buckingham, D. (1988) *Public Secrets*: EastEnders *and its Audience*, London: British Film Institute.

Cantor, M. and Pingree, S. (1983) *The Soap Opera*, Beverly Hills: Sage.

Harvey, D. (1989) *The Condition of Postmodernity*, Oxford: Blackwell.

Katz, E. and Liebes, T. (1986) 'Mutual aid in the decoding of *Dallas*: preliminary notes from a cross-cultural study', in P. Drummond and R. Paterson (eds) *Television in Transition*, London: British Film Institute, 197–8.

Mattelart, A. (1983) *Transnationals and the Third World*, Massachusetts: Bergin & Garvey.

Miller, D. (1990) 'Fashion and ontology in Trinidad', *Culture and History* 7: 49–77.

Schroder, K. (1988) 'The pleasure of *Dynasty*: the weekly reconstruction of self-confidence', in P. Drummond and R. Paterson (eds) *Television and its Audience*, London: British Film Institute, 61–82.

Silj, A. (ed.) (1988) *East of* Dallas, London: British Film Institute.

Vink, N. (1988) *The Telenovela and Emancipation*, Amsterdam: Royal Tropical Institute.

Wilson, P. (1973) *Crab Antics*, New Haven: Yale University Press.

FURTHER READING

Ang, I., *Watching 'Dallas': Soap Opera and the Melodramatic Imagination* (London: Methuen, 1985).

Ang, I., 'The Battle Between Television and its Audiences: The Politics of Watching Television'. In P. Drummond and R. Paterson (eds), *Television in Transition* (London: BFI, 1985).

Ang, I., 'Culture and Communication: Towards an Ethnographic Critique of Media Consumption in the Transnational Media System'. *European Journal of Communication* 5:2/3 (1990) pp. 239–60.

Ang, I., *Desperately Seeking the Audience* (London: Routledge, 1991).

Baehr, H. and Dyer, G. (eds), *Boxed In: Women and Television* (London: Pandora, 1987).

Bourdieu, P., *Distinction: A Social Critique of the Judgment of Taste*, trans. R. Nice (London: Routledge, 1984).

Bourdieu, P., 'Social Space and Symbolic Power'. *Sociological Theory* 7:1 (1989) pp. 14–25.

Brown, M. E. (ed.), *Television and Women's Culture* (London: Sage, 1990).

Collett, P. and Lamb, R., *Watching Families Watching Television*. Report to the Independent Broadcasting Authority (1986).

Curran, J., 'The New Revisionism in Mass Communication Research': A Reappraisal'. *European Journal of Communication* 5: 2/3 (1990) pp. 135–64.

Curran, J. and Gurevitch, M., *Mass Media and Society* (London: Edward Arnold, 1991).

Drummond, P. and Paterson, R. (eds), *Television in Transition* (London: BFI, 1985).

Drummond, P. and Paterson, R. (eds), *Television and its Audiences: International Research Perspectives* (London: BFI, 1988).

Feyes, F., 'Critical Communications Research and Media Effects: the Problem of the Disappearing Audience'. *Media, Culture and Society* 6:3 (1984) pp. 219–32.

Fiske, J., *Television Culture* (London: Methuen, 1987).

Fiske, J., *Reading the Popular* (London: Unwin Hyman, 1989).

Fiske, J., *Understanding Popular Culture* (London: Unwin Hyman, 1989).

Frazer, E., 'Teenage Girls Reading Jackie'. *Media, Culture and Society* 9 (1987) pp. 407–25.

Gillespie, M., 'Technology and Tradition: Audio-Visual Culture among South Asian Families in West London'. *Cultural Studies* 3:2 (1989) pp. 226–239.

Gillespie, M., *Television, Ethnicity and Cultural Change* (London: Routledge, 1995).

Gray, A., 'Reading the Audience'. *Screen* 28:3 (1987) pp. 24–35.

Hall, S., Hobson, D., Lowe, A. and Willis, P. (eds), *Culture, Media, Language* (London: Hutchinson, 1980).

Hobson, Dorothy, 'Housewives and the Mass Media'. From Hall, S., Hobson, D., Lowe, A. and Willis, P. (eds), *Culture, Media, Language* (London: Hutchinson, 1980) pp. 105–114.

Hodge, R. and Tripp, D., *Children and Television* (Cambridge: Polity, 1986).

Jensen, K. B., 'Qualitative Audience Research: Towards an Integrative Approach to Reception'. *Critical Studies in Mass Communication* 4 (1987) pp. 21–36.

Katz, E. and Liebes, T., 'Mutual Aid in the Decoding of *Dallas*: Preliminary Notes from a Cross-Cultural Study', in P. Drummond and R. Paterson (eds), *Television in Transition* (London: BFI, 1985).

Lewis, J., 'The Encoding/Decoding Model: Criticisms and Redevelopments for Research on Decoding'. *Media, Culture and Society* 5: 2 (1983) pp. 179–97.

Lewis, J., 'Are You Receiving Me?'. In A. Goodwin & G. Whannel (eds), *Understanding Television* (London: Routledge, 1990).

Lewis, J., *The Ideological Octopus: An Exploration of Television & its Audience* (London: Routledge, 1991).

Liebes, T. and Katz, E., *The Export of Meaning: Cross-Cultural Readings of Dallas* (Oxford: Oxford University Press, 1990).

Livingstone, S. M., *Making Sense of Television: The Psychology of Audience Interpretation* (New York: Pergamon Press, 1990).

Lull, J. (ed.), *World Families Watch Television* (London: Sage, 1988).

Lull, J., *Inside Family Viewing: Ethnographic Research on Television's Audiences* (London: Routledge, 1990).

McRobbie, A., *Feminism and Youth Culture: From 'Jackie' to 'Just Seventeen'* (London: Macmillan, 1991).

Modleski, T., 'The Rhythms of Reception: Daytime Television and Women's Work'. In E. A. Kaplan (ed.), *Regarding Television: Critical Approaches – An Anthology* (Frederick, Md.: University Publications of America, 1983).

Moores, S., 'Texts, Readers and Contexts of Reading: Developments in the Study of Media Audiences'. *Media, Culture and Society* 12:1 (1990) pp. 9–30.

Moores, S., *Interpreting Audiences: The Ethnography of Media Consumption* (London: Sage, 1993).

Morley, D., 'Reconceptualizing the Media Audience'. CCCS Stencilled Paper 9, University of Birmingham (1974).

Morley, D., *The 'Nationwide' Audience* (London: BFI, 1980).

Morley, D., 'Texts, Readers, Subjects'. In S. Hall, D. Hobson, A. Lowe and P. Willis (eds), *Culture, Media, Language* (London: Hutchinson, 1980).

Morley, D., '"The Nationwide Audience": A Critical Postscript'. *Screen Education* 39 (1981) pp. 3–14.

Morley, D., *Family Television: Cultural Power and Domestic Leisure* (London: Comedia, 1986).

Morley, D., 'Where the Global meets the Local: Notes from the Sitting Room'. *Screen* 32:1 (1991) pp. 1–15.

Morley, D., *Television, Audiences and Cultural Studies* (London: Routledge, 1992).

Nava, M., *Changing Cultures: Feminism, Youth and Consumerism* (London: Sage, 1992).

Nightingale, V., 'Women as Audiences'. In M. E. Brown (ed.), *Television and Women's Culture* (London: Sage, 1990).

Oakley, A., 'Interviewing Women: A Contradiction in Terms'. In H. Roberts (ed.), *Doing Feminist Research* (London: Routledge, 1981).

Press, A. L., *Women Watching Television: Gender, Class and Generation in the American Television Experience* (Philadelphia: University of Pennsylvania Press, 1991).

Radway, J., *Reading the Romance* (London: Verso, 1987).

Radway, J., 'Reception Study: Ethnography and the Problems of Dispersed Audiences and Nomadic Subjects'. *Cultural Studies* 2:3 (1988) pp. 359–76.

Schlesinger, P., Dobash, R. E., Dobash, R. P. and Weaver, C. K., *Women Viewing Violence* (London: BFI, 1992).

Schroder, K. C., 'Convergence of Antagonistic Traditions? The Case of Audience Research'. *European Journal of Communication* 2 (1987) pp. 7–31.

Seiter, E., 'Making Distinctions in TV Audience Research: Case Study of a Troubling Interview'. *Cultural Studies* 4:1 (1990) pp. 61–84.

Seiter, E., Borchers, H., Kreutzner, G. & Warth, E.-M. (eds), *Remote Control: Television, Audiences and Cultural Power* (London: Routledge, 1989).

Willis, P., *Common Culture* (Milton Keynes: Open University Press, 1990).

Wilson, T., *Watching Television* (Cambridge: Polity Press, 1993).

SECTION 4
RECEPTION

3. BEYOND HEGEMONY?

BEYOND HEGEMONY?
INTRODUCTION

The chapters in Section 4.2 all in their different ways define media reception as, in Ang's words, a 'site of cultural struggle'. In some way, then, all draw their theoretical framework from the Gramscian model of 'hegemony' developed by Stuart Hall and the Birmingham Centre in the 1970s. Gramsci's model, argues Tony Bennett, provided a conceptual framework for such studies because it insisted that 'the cultural and ideological relations between ruling and subordinate classes in capitalist societies consist less in the domination of the latter by the former than in the struggle for *hegemony* – that is, for moral, cultural, intellectual and, thereby, political leadership of society' between the ruling class and its subordinate others.[1] It is this concept which underpins both Hall's encoding/decoding model and the studies of media reception as negotiation, resistance or appropriation which we saw in Section 4.2.

More recently, however, the impact of theorists of the postmodern has challenged the capacity of 'Gramscianism' to provide a framework for a 'critical' audience studies. Two thinkers, in particular, deserve mention here. Michel Foucault's view of power as dispersed and decentred, manifest throughout the system of social networks and operating as 'a fundamentally enabling force',[2] whilst it opens up consideration of power relations other than those of class, fits uneasily with a model of cultural consumption as *struggle*. The influence of Pierre Bourdieu's work on the correspondence between socioeconomic positioning and patterns of taste, on the other hand, has been to shift emphasis away from the text–reader relationship and towards *contexts* of consumption, and 'the issue of how popular taste and popular pleasures can be understood'.[3] As a result, the media audience has become less easy to conceptualise or even to distinguish. Indeed, John Hartley has suggested that the very idea of the audience is an imaginary construction, an 'invisible fiction', fashioned to serve the needs of the imagining institution, whether that is the advertising industry or the 'institution' of cultural studies research.[4] The chapters which follow offer different examples of these shifts in the field of audience research.

Ann Gray's study of women's use of video recorders in the home (Chapter 41) focuses on the domestic and family context for video viewing, arguing that the text–reader relationship is one that itself 'has to be negotiated, struggled for, won or lost, in the dynamic and often chaotic processes of family life'. Gray's work, therefore, has links with that of Dorothy Hobson (see Chapter 48), as well as the later work of David Morley.[5] The domestic sphere, argues Gray, is increasingly becoming women's only leisure space, but it is a space which is structured by gendered power relationships which determine how and when women may make choices in leisure activities. Video technology is itself gendered, with women usually having access to the VCR's most basic functions but not to the operation of the timer or remote control. The hiring of tapes for family viewing, too, is usually done by men. In her study, Gray found two contexts in which women could exercise choice over video viewing; both were in the absence of men. The first is alone, as a 'breathing space' between daytime domestic tasks. The second, which Gray sees as giving more grounds for optimism, is one in which several women meet to watch a video which they have hired jointly. These latter contexts 'give a focus to an almost separate female culture', with pleasures and gratifications which would be derided by the women's male partners. The domestic context, concludes Gray, is not a 'singular and unchanging' one; the domestic use of the VCR demonstrates the way in which its gendered power structures construct and limit women's ability to negotiate their own viewing pleasures.

John Fiske's recent work, whilst continuing to insist that 'the text [i]s a site of struggle for the power to make meanings', nevertheless demonstrates the collapse of the hegemonic model under the pressure of a Foucauldian concept of a decentred and 'productive' power. For Fiske, then (Chapter 42), the concepts of 'text' and 'audience' should be abandoned, to be replaced by 'textuality' and the 'intertextuality' of 'moments of viewing'. Fiske's model of society is of 'a vast shifting range of subcultures and groups' whose members form shifting alliances and become different viewing subjects at different times, producing a range of meanings and pleasures from the semiotic potential that television offers. Fiske proposes the existence of a 'cultural economy' which operates with 'relative autonomy' from the 'financial economy'. In the latter, audiences are commodities, but in the former, which Fiske grants 'equal, if not greater, power', they are free to act as producers – of their own pleasures and meanings. The task of the critic is, then, to 'understand popular pleasures and popular discrimination', not by examining texts, audience readings or the processes of production, but through the 'investigation of instances', 'moments of television' in which the 'variety of cultural activities that take place in front of the screen' can be glimpsed.

This focus on audiences as active and autonomous producers of their own pleasures and meanings has led to a growing interest in the culture of 'fandom'. Fans are after all, we assume, the ultimate undiscriminating consumers of mass culture: to see them instead as active producers of meaning offers a decisive challenge to accounts of the hegemonic power of media producers. Henry Jenkins' chapter on the cultural productions of science fiction fans (Chapter 43) presents such a view. Jenkins offers a model of fandom which situates fans as employing a specific and conscious mode of media reception, as active interpretive communities, as producers and distributors of a distinctive 'Art World', and as inhabitors of an 'alternative social community'. Fans, he writes, are producers of meanings, of art-works, of communities and of alternative identities. Their materials are those of dominant media but these 'borrowed materials' are fashioned through the tools and conventions of a specific subcultural community. Fandom is a 'scavenger' culture, and the fan perhaps the ultimate postmodern 'bricoleur' (see Jim Collins' description, Chapter 29).

Joke Hermes (Chapter 44) takes up the interest in mass media cultural forms for women which we have seen already in the work of Janice Winship, Janice Radway and Ann Gray (Chapters 26, 39 and 41, and see also Section 5). Her work, however, marks a shift away from explanations rooted in a politics of gender, and in particular from the explicitly feminist political agenda articulated by Janice Radway. Her point of departure is that all of us, for much of the time, engage in media use which is 'virtually meaningless'. 'Reducing everyday life to power relations' as for example David Morley does, she argues, 'means skipping over the particularities of everyday routines that also, partly, explain media use'. But neither should her casual readers of women's magazines be romanticised as postmodern 'bricoleurs'. Understanding how her subjects – everyday readers rather than fans – make sense of popular media texts has to begin, on the one hand, from an analysis of the range of 'interpretive repertoires' (culturally available explanatory structures) to which they have access. On the other, analysis must start from 'everyday life', acknowledging that for all of us this is the product of specific reading histories which will encompass both 'periods of uncomplicated making do' and moments of 'rupture and change'. Like John Fiske, then, Hermes dissolves the boundaries between text and context, arguing that on its own the media text 'never becomes fully meaningful'. In her account the media audience, too, dissolves (as does the possibility of explanatory frameworks), to be replaced with the routines and contradictions of everyday life.

NOTES

1. Bennett, 'Introduction: Popular Culture and 'the Turn to Gramsci'. In T. Bennett, C. Mercer and J. Woollacott (eds), *Popular Culture and Social Relations* (Milton Keynes: Open University Press, 1986) p. xiv.

2. Lois McNay, *Foucault: A Critical Introduction* (Cambridge: Polity Press, 1994) p. 3.
3. David Morley, 'Changing paradigms in audience studies', in E. Seiter, H. Borchers, G. Kreutzner and E.-M. Warth (eds), *Remote Control: Television, Audiences and Cultural Power* (London: Routledge, 1989) p. 28.
4. Hartley, 'Invisible Fictions', in J. Hartley, *Tele-Ology: Studies in Television* (London: Routledge, 1992) p. 105.
5. Morley, *Family Television: Cultural Power and Domestic Leisure* (London: Comedia, 1986).

41

BEHIND CLOSED DOORS:
VIDEO RECORDERS IN THE HOME

Ann Gray

The video cassette recorder is arguably the major innovation in home entertainment in Britain since television. When we address questions of how women watch television and video we inevitably raise a complex set of issues which relate to women and their everyday lives. In talking to women about home video cassette recorders (VCR) and television use, I have identified some of the determining factors surrounding these activities which take place within the domestic environment.[1] With the development of VCRs and other products such as home computers and cable services, the 1980s is seeing an ever increasing trend towards home-centred leisure and entertainment. New technology in the home has to be understood within a context of structures of power and authority relationships between household members, with gender emerging as one of the most significant differentiations. This far from neutral environment influences the ways in which women use popular texts in general and television and video in particular, and the pleasures and meanings which these have for them.

[...]

VIDEO AND FAMILY LIFE

Although there are many aspects of the video phenomenon which are worthy of study, my research initially focuses on the potential choice which the VCR offers for viewing within the domestic and family context. The major reason for

From H. Baehr and G. Dyer (eds), *Boxed In: Women and Television* (London: Pandora Press, 1987) pp. 38–54.

this is that, until recently, attention to the context of viewing seems to have been largely neglected in media and cultural studies.[2] The relationship between the viewer and television, the reader and text, is often a relationship which has to be negotiated, struggled for, won or lost, in the dynamic and often chaotic processes of family life. As video recorders offer, above all, extended choice of content and time management for viewing within the home, research into its use has to be focused within that very context. The context of 'the family' is, for my purposes, conceived of as a site of constant social negotiation within a highly routinised framework of material dependency and normative constraint,[3] and all these elements enter into the negotiations which surround viewing decisions. This family setting, with its power relationships and authority structures across gender, is an extremely important factor in thinking more generally of 'leisure' and, specifically, home-based leisure. The home has increasingly become the site for entertainment, and we can see VCRs as yet one more commodity which reduces the necessity for household members to seek entertainment outside the home, a situation reinforced by the present economic climate in Britain:

> JS: Well, we can't really afford to go out to the pictures, not any more. If we all go and have ice-creams, you're talking about eight or nine pounds. It's a lot of money.

What is especially important for women is that the domestic sphere is increasingly becoming defined as their only leisure space. Many married women are in paid work outside the home, but women are still largely responsible for the domestic labour in the home. Childcare, food provision, laundry, shopping and cleaning the living space, are ultimately women's responsibility even if their male partners help. While men in paid employment come home to a non-work environment, women who either work in the home all day or go out to paid employment still have to work at home in the evenings and at weekends:

> AS: Him? Oh, he sits on his backside all night, from coming in from work to going to bed.

Indeed, many women do not consider themselves as having any leisure at all. (Deem, 1984). And many certainly would not allow themselves the luxury of sitting down to watch television until the children are fed and put to bed and the household chores have been completed:

> JK: I'd feel guilty, I'd feel I was cheating. It's my job and if I'm sat, I'm not doing my job.

This is a context which, at the most basic and practical level, positions women in relation to the whole area of leisure, but particularly in relation to television and video viewing:

> AS: Like, if he comes in and he's rented a video, straight after tea he wants to put it on. I say 'well let me finish the washing-up first'. I mean, I just wouldn't enjoy it if I knew it was all to do.

VIDEO AS TECHNOLOGY

Women and men have differential access to technology in general and to domestic technology in particular. The relations between domestic technology and gender are relatively unexplored,[4] though there is more work on gender and technology in the workplace where, as Jan Zimmerman notes, new technology is entering existing and traditional sets of relations. Old values in this way become encoded in new technologies (Zimmerman, 1981; Cockburn, 1983, 1985). It is interesting to note that American researchers discovered that in the early 1970s the full-time housewife was spending as much time on housework as her grandmother had done fifty years earlier. Domestic technology may be labour-saving, replacing the drudgery of household work, but it is time-consuming in that each piece of equipment requires work if it is to fulfil its advertised potential. Rothschild argues that far from liberating women from housework, new technology, embedded as it is in ideological assumptions about the sexual division of labour, has further entrenched women in the home and in the role of housewife (Rothschild, 1983).

When a new piece of technology is purchased or rented, it is often already inscribed with gender expectations. The gender specificity of pieces of domestic technology is deeply implanted in the 'commonsense' of households, operating almost at an unconscious level. As such it is difficult for the researcher to unearth. One strategy I have employed which throws the gender of domestic technology into high relief is to ask the women to image pieces of equipment as coloured either pink or blue.[5] This produces almost uniformly pink irons and blue electric drills, with many interesting mixtures along the spectrum. The washing machine, for example, is most usually pink on the outside, but the motor is almost always blue. VCRs and, indeed, all home entertainment technology would seem to be a potentially lilac area, but my research has shown that we must break down the VCR into its different modes in our colour-coding. The 'record', 'rewind' and 'play' modes are usually lilac, but the timer switch is nearly always blue, with women having to depend on their male partners or their children to set the timer for them. The blueness of the timer is exceeded only by the deep indigo of the remote control switch which in all cases is held by the man:

> SW: Oh, yes, that's definitely blue in our house. He flicks from channel to channel, I never know what I'm watching – it drives me mad.

It does appear that the male of the household is generally assumed to have knowledge of this kind of technology when it enters the household, or at least he will quickly gain the knowledge. And certain knowledges can, of course, be withheld and used to maintain authority and control:

> AS: Well, at first he was the only one who knew how to record things, but then me and my young son sat down one day and worked it out. That meant we didn't have to keep asking him to record something for us.

Although women routinely operate extremely sophisticated pieces of domestic technology, often requiring, in the first instance, the study and application of a manual of instructions, they often feel alienated from operating the VCR. The reasons for this are manifold and have been brought about by positioning within the family, the education system and the institutionalised sexism with regard to the division of appropriate activities and knowledges in terms of gender. Or there may be, as I discovered, 'calculated ignorance':

> CH: If I learnt how to do the video it would become my job just like everything else.

If women do not feel confident or easy in approaching and operating the recorders, let alone in setting the timer for advance recording, they are at an immediate and real disadvantage in terms of exercising the apparent choices which the VCR offers. This, combined with constraints in the hiring of video tapes, either financial or simply normative, means that for women the idea of increased freedom and choice of viewing may well be spurious.

GENRE AND GENDER

If women are 'positioned' within the context of consumption, it seems that they are also positioned, or even structured in absence, by the video industry itself in terms of the kind of audience it seems to be addressing. To enter a video library is to be visually bombarded by 'covers' depicting scenes of horror, action adventure, war, westerns and 'soft' pornography, traditionally considered to be 'male' genres.[6] Is it therefore mainly men who are hiring video tapes, and if so, what do women feel about the kinds of tapes they are watching at home? Do women ever hire tapes themselves, or do they feel alienated from both the outlets and what they have to offer? In other words, what are the circumstances surrounding the use of video libraries and what is the sexual division of labour associated with the hiring and viewing of tapes? I have already made reference to the so-called 'male' genres which imply that certain kinds of films address themselves to and are enjoyed by a male audience and the same, of course, could be said for 'female' genres. But why do certain kinds of texts or genres appeal to women and not to men and *vice versa* and how should we conceive of the audience for these texts made up of women and men?

The 'gendered audience' has a theoretical history which, as Annette Kuhn usefully points out, has developed within two different perspectives, one emerging from media studies and the other from film theory (Kuhn, 1984). This has resulted in two quite different notions of the gendered audience. The sociological emphasis of media studies has tended to conceive of a 'social audience', that is, an audience made up of already constituted male and female persons who bring (among other things) maleness or femaleness to a text, and who decode the text within that particular frame of reference. Film theory on the other hand, has conceived of a 'psychological audience', a collection of individual spectators who do not read the text, but rather the text 'reads' them.

In other words, the film offers a masculine or feminine subject position and the spectator occupies that position. Of course, this is not automatic and there is nothing to prevent, for example, a female spectator taking up a masculine subject position. However, the construction of masculinity and femininity across the institutions within society is so powerfully aligned to the social categories 'male' and 'female' that the two usually coincide apparently seamlessly. But, as Kuhn points out, what is suggested by these two perspectives is a distinction between femaleness as a social gender and femininity as a subject position. The problem here is that neither of these two perspectives is sufficient in themselves to gain a full understanding of what happens when men and women watch films. In the former case, context is emphasised over text and in the latter text over context. The spectator–text relationship suggested by the psychoanalytic models used in film theory tend to disregard those important factors of social context involved in film and TV watching. Also, they find it difficult to allow for the subject constituted outside the text, across other discourses, such as class, race, age and general social environment. The social audience approach, conversely, sees the response to texts as a socially pre-determined one, and in this way does not allow for consideration of how the texts themselves work on the viewers/readers.

There have been some attempts to link text with context by examining the particular features of 'women's genres'. Soap operas, for example, have been looked at in terms of their distinctive narrative pattern, which is open-ended and continuous; their concern with so-called 'female' skills; their scheduling on television which fits into the rhythm of women's work at home, all of which can be seen as specifically addressing a social audience of women (Brunsdon, 1981; Modleski, 1982). However, this would still seem to stress context over text and in this area the film theory perspective has certainly been limited by its implicit assumption of an intense and concentrated relationship between spectator and text in a darkened cinema. For television this relationship is more likely to be characterised by distinction and diversion. As Kuhn points out:

> This would suggest that each medium constructs sexual difference through spectatorship in rather different ways: cinema through the look and spectacle, and TV – perhaps less evidently – through a capacity to insert its flow, its characteristic modes of address and the textual operations of different kinds of programmes into the rhythms and routines of domestic activities and sexual divisions of labour in the household at various times of day. (Kuhn, 1984, p. 25)

This distinction is important and useful, but when thinking about the use of VCRs the two media are viewed in the same context. Movies have long been a part of television's nightly 'flow' as well as part of daytime viewing. But in video recording movies off television for watching at a later date, and in hiring movies, we have a discrete 'event' which disrupts the flow of television and its insertive scheduling:

AC: Oh yes, we all sit down and watch – 'we've got a video, let's sit down' – TV's different, that's just on.

Concepts of the psychological audience and the social audience are not sufficient in themselves to explore the whole complexity of text, subject and context and the ways in which they intersect. But both are necessary, representing as they do different instances within the process of consumption of popular texts. While the psychological model posits an unacceptably homogeneous and 'universal' audience, it docs allow us to consider the importance of how texts work, not only in terms of subject positioning and interpellation, but also in terms of pleasure and desire. The social model demands that the audience is heterogeneous and requires us to explore those other differences and contexts which, to a greater or lesser extent, determine the ways in which women and men read those texts. It seems clear that the problem of the relationship between text and gendered audience cannot be resolved at the theoretical level, but rather must be kept in play and, if possible, problematised throughout the research enterprise.

VIEWING CONTEXTS

It would seem that women do have certain preconceptions about what constitutes a 'film for men' as against a 'film for women', and furthermore, a typology of viewing contexts is beginning to emerge, along with appropriate associated texts (see Table [41.1]).

I wish to focus mainly on Context (Female alone), but before I do it is worth mentioning the difference between the negotiations around Contexts (Male alone) and (Female alone). For the latter to exist, the male partner must normally be out of the house, either at work or at leisure, whereas, Context (Male alone) would be likely to exist when both male and female were in the house together. The women simply wouldn't watch:

BA: If he's watching something I'm not enjoying, I'll either knit or read.

JS: Well, I can read when the telly's on if it's something I don't like.

DS: I usually go to bed with a book, or sometimes I'll watch the portable in the kitchen, but it's damned uncomfortable in there.

CH: Well, when he's in, Father has priority over what's on. Yes, he does, but I can go in the other room if I don't want to watch it.

WOMEN ONLY

For women who are at home all day, either with very small children or children of school age, and whose husbands are out at work, there are obvious opportunities for them to view alone. However, most of the women I have talked to are constrained by guilt, often referring to daytime viewing as some kind of drug:

SW: No, I've got too many things to do during the daytime, I couldn't do it to myself, I'd be a total addict.

JK: Well, I watch *Falcon Crest* – it's a treat, when I've done my work, then I sit down and it's my treat. But I'm not one to get videos during the day because I think you can get really addicted, then everything else suffers.

The second woman quoted indicates what is a fairly common strategy – that of using daytime television programmes to establish some time for herself as a reward to which completion of household tasks will lead. This assuages the guilt to a certain extent and the pleasure afforded by this particular viewing context seems to go far beyond the pleasures of the text itself. What it represents is a breathing space when the busy mother can resist the demands of her children and domestic labour for a brief period of time. One of the most popular daytime programmes cited was *Sons & Daughters*, an Australian imported soap opera, transmitted three afternoons a week in the Yorkshire region. Most of the women preferred to watch this alone, some taking the telephone off the hook to ensure uninterrupted concentration, but they would watch it with a friend if they happened to be in each other's houses at the time. Janice Radway in her study of women and romantic fiction talks with regret of

Table [41.1] *Typology of viewing contexts*[7]

Context	Film	TV
1 Family together	*Superman*	Children's TV
	Walt Disney	Quiz shows
	Jaws	Comedy
2 Male and female partners together	*An Officer and a Gentleman*	Aufwiedersehen Pet
	Kramer v. Kramer	*Minder*
	The Rockys	Shows
	Any Clint Eastwood	*Coronation Street*
		EastEnders
3 Male alone	War	Sport
	Action adventure*	News
	Horror*	Documentaries
	Adults*	
4 Female alone	*Who Will Love My Children?*	*Coronation Street*
	Evergreen	*Crossroads*
	Romance	*Dallas*
		Dynasty
		A Woman of Substance
		Princess Daisy

* These are the category headings used by many video libraries

the isolated context within which popular romances are consumed by women (Radway, 1984). The next viewing context I wish to discuss reveals a more optimistic state of affairs for women.

This context is again female only, but is one in which several women get together to watch a video which they have hired jointly. This would normally happen during the day when their children are at school. Far from being instrumental in isolating women, it would seem that there is a tendency to communal use of hired videos, mainly on economic grounds, but also on the grounds that the women can watch what they want together without the guilt or the distraction of children:

> BS: There are three of us, and we hire two or three films a week and watch them together, usually at Joyce's house when the kids are at school. We can choose what we want then.
>
> JK: Yes, if there's something we want to see we wait 'til the kids have gone back to school so's we can sit and watch it without them coming in saying 'can I have ... can I have ... ' it makes it difficult.

The idea of viewing together during the day for this particular network of women living on the same street came when one of them found herself continually returning the video tapes which her husband had hired the night before. She discovered that there were films which she would like to watch but which her husband never hired. A good relationship was established with the woman who worked in the video library who would look out for good films:

> BS: She comes into the shop where I work and I go 'have any new videos come out?' She tells me. She knows what we like.

One favoured form for this viewing network is that of the long family saga, often running to two or three tapes:

> JK: We like something in two or three parts; something with a really good story to it so's you can get involved.
>
> BS: Mm ... the other week we had a Clint Eastwood and Burt Reynolds film because she [MD] likes Clint Eastwood but we talked all the way through that, didn't we?

When the group views sagas which extend over two or three tapes there is obvious pleasure in anticipating both the outcome of the narrative and the viewing of the following tape. A considerable amount of discussion and speculation ensues and a day for the next viewing is fixed:

> MD: We like to spread them out – every other day, it helps to break the week up. Sometimes we have them on an evening, if our husbands are away or out. We'll have a bottle of wine then, then we don't even have to get up to make a cup of tea.

These women are also devotees of the American soap operas and operate a 'failsafe' network of video recording for each other, refusing to discuss each episode until they have all seen it. These popular texts form an important part of their friendship and association in their everyday lives and give a focus to an almost separate female culture which they can share together within the constraints of their positions as wives and mothers. Furthermore, they are able to take up the feminine subject positions offered by these texts comfortably and pleasurably. In contrast, the films which their husbands hire for viewing Context (Male & female partners together) mainly offer a masculine subject position which the women seem to take up through their male partners, who in turn give their approval to such texts.

The major impetus for a viewing group like this is that films which women enjoy watching are rarely, if ever, hired by their male partners for viewing together because they consider such films to be 'trivial' and 'silly' and women are laughed at for enjoying them:

> BA: I sit there with tears running down my face and he comes in and says 'you daft thing.'

This derision also applies to soap operas, and is reproduced in male children:

> JK: Oh, my son thinks I'm stupid because I won't miss *Dallas* – perhaps I am.

It is the most powerful member within the household who defines this hierarchy of 'serious' and 'silly', 'important' and 'trivial'. This leaves women and their pleasures in films downgraded, objects and subjects of fun and derision, having to consume them almost in secret. But the kinds of films and television soap operas which women enjoy watching alone deal with things of importance to them, highlighting so-called 'female' concerns – care of children, concern for members of one's own family, consideration for one's own sexual partner, selflessness in characters – all of which are the skills of competence, the thought and caring which husbands and children expect of women and assume as a matter of natural course.[8] This is a deeply contradictory position for women, lying between the realities of their day to day lives and the pleasures and gratifications that they seek to find in texts that their partners and very often their children, look upon as so much rubbish:

> JS: I think a lot of storylines in soap operas are very weak and I think a man needs something to keep his interest more than a woman. That makes a man sound more intelligent, but that's not what I mean. It's got to be something worth watching before he'll sit down and actually watch it, but I'd watch anything. I think he thinks its unmanly to watch them.

> SW: All the soap operas are rubbish for men, fantasy for women.

AG: *Do you think men need fantasy?*

SW: They need fantasy in a different way, detectives and wars, that's their fantasy world, and science fiction, a tough, strong world. Not sloppy, who's fallen in love with who, who's shot JR – it's rubbish. Men know it's rubbish, that's the difference.

Here are two women talking about a genre they love in relation to their male partners, giving us a sense of the 'power of definition' within the partnerships, but also the ways in which the women themselves think of their own pleasures.

CONCLUSION

Theories of the gendered audience as they have been developed are useful, but when women and men watch movies and television they become that hybrid, the *social spectator* (Kuhn, ibid.) and, in understanding the subject–text–context relationship, the social and the psychological have to be kept in play to a proportionately greater or lesser degree. This allows us to consider how texts and contexts (both the specific and the wider social context) combine together in producing the gendered reading subject. Charlotte Brunsdon, writing on *Crossroads*, has attempted to resolve this dualism and suggests that, 'The relation of the audience to the text will not be determined solely by that text, but also by positionalities in relation to a whole range of other discourses – discourses of motherhood, romance and sexuality for example' (Brunsdon, 1981, p. 32).

This enables us to think of the subject in the social context occupying different positions in relation to different discourses which change across time. As particular discourses become central issues, they will affect the ways in which the social subject occupies, or resists, the subject position constructed by a text.

The viewing and reading of texts takes place, for the majority of people, within the domestic context. However, this is a context which is not singular and unchanging, but plural and open to different permutations, dependent upon the negotiations between members of the household and the particular texts involved. The VCR offers the potential for extended choice of viewing in terms of text and context. But in order to explore how this potential is being used the particular conditions of its consumption must be addressed. The viewing contexts and their associated texts which I have outlined here have emerged from my discussions with women who occupy different social positions and there are remarkable similarities in the ways in which all the women have spoken about their domestic viewing practices. However, it is simply not sufficient to have identified these similarities, and my analysis of the interview 'texts' continues in an attempt to make visible the important differences between the women's accounts of these practices. These differences must be seen in relation to their particular social positioning and the various specific discourses which they inhabit. The interview material I have gathered demands a framework of analysis which uses theories and concepts developed within different disciplines and will, I am sure, test their relative strengths and weaknesses in revealing the complexity of how women relate to television and video in their everyday lives.

NOTES

1. This research was initially funded by the Economic and Social Research Council and has taken the form of long, open-ended discussions with women whose age, social position, employment and family circumstances differ (race is a variable which has not been introduced). Part of my strategy has been to encourage open discussion and allow the women themselves to introduce topics which are of importance to them. By keeping the discussions open they can take pleasure in having the opportunity to explore and express their own ideas and feelings on these matters. For discussions on feminist research methods see Roberts (ed.), 1981; Stanley and Wise, 1983; Bell and Roberts, 1984.
2. There are notable exceptions (Hobson, 1981 and 1982; Morley, 1986; Collett, 1986).
3. I am grateful to Elizabeth Shove and Andrew Tudor for this working definition.
4. However, a recent publication by W. Faulkner and E. Arnold (eds), *Smothered by Invention Technology in Women's Lives*, Pluto Press, 1985, does address issues of domestic technology and gender.
5. These were ideas discussed at a seminar given by Cynthia Cockburn at York University, June 1985. See also Cockburn, 1985.
6. It is interesting to note that video tapes are now being distributed which are specifically aimed at a female audience; IPC and Videospace combined magazine and video to market their *Woman's Own Selection*, along with their more recent label *Image of Love*, while Polygram Video are offering a label, *Women's Choice*. However, in the North of England certainly, these have a very limited distribution.
7. These are the names which the women themselves gave to the different texts and genres.
8. Charlotte Brunsdon has made this point in relation to *Crossroads*, but we can see that it can apply to other 'women's genres' (Brunsdon, 1981).

REFERENCES

Barker, M. (ed.) (1984), *The Video Nasties*, London, Pluto Press.
Bell, C. and Roberts, H. (eds) (1984), *Social Researching*, London, Routledge & Kegan Paul.
Brunsdon, C. (1981), 'Crossroads: Notes on a soap opera', *Screen*, vol. 22, no. 4, pp. 32–7. [See Chapter 47 of this volume.]
Cockburn, C. (1983), *Brothers*, London, Pluto Press.
Cockburn, C. (1985), *Machinery of Dominance*, London, Pluto Press.
Collett, P. (1986), 'Watching the TV audience', paper presented to International Television Studies Conference 1986.
Deem, R. (1984), 'Paid work, leisure and non-employment: shifting boundaries and gender differences', paper presented to British Sociological Association Conference 1984.
Hobson, D. (1981), 'Housewives and the mass media', in Hall, S. *et al.* (eds), *Culture, Media, Language*, London, Hutchinson.
Hobson, D. (1982), *'Crossroads': The Drama of a Soap Opera*, London, Methuen. [See Chapter 48 of this volume.]
Kuhn, A. (1984), 'Women's genres', *Screen*, vol. 25, no. 1, Jan/Feb, pp. 18–28.
Modleski, T. (1982), *Loving With a Vengeance*, Hamden, Connecticut, Shoe String Press. [See Chapter 46 of this volume.]

Morley, D. (1986), *Family Television: Cultural Power and Domestic Leisure*, London, Comedia.

Radway, J. A. (1984), *Reading the Romance*, Chapel Hill, University of North Carolina Press.

Roberts, H. (ed.) (1981), *Doing Feminist Research*, London, Routledge & Kegan Paul.

Rothschild, J. (1983), *Machina ex Dea*, New York, Pergamon Press.

Stanley, L. and Wise, S. (1983), *Breaking Out*, London, Routledge & Kegan Paul.

Zimmerman, J. (1981), 'Technology and the future of women: haven't we met somewhere before?', *Women's Studies International Quarterly*, vol. 4, no. 3, p. 355.

42

MOMENTS OF TELEVISION: NEITHER THE TEXT NOR THE AUDIENCE

John Fiske

A group of people in front of the television set, spines curved weakly on the couch, drinks or snacks in hand, eyes glued to the screen is, I suppose, the commonsense model of television and its audience. What is on the screen is the text, the people watching, multiplied a millionfold, are the audience. In the not too distant past there have been theories of both the text and the audience that, unfortunately for them and us, have taken this model for the uninspected base of their assumptions, for the scene the model paints is both typical and realistic. Its problem lies in its easy categorization of the viewers into 'the audience' and the screen into 'the text'.

I wish to dissolve both categories. First, there is no such thing as 'the television audience,' defined as an empirically accessible object, for there can be no meaningful categories beyond its boundaries – what on earth is 'not the television audience'? The 'television audience' is not a social category like class, or race, or gender – everyone slips in or out of it in a way that makes nonsense of any categorical boundaries: similarly when in 'it' people constitute themselves quite differently as audience members at different times – I am a different television 'audience' when watching my football team from when watching *The A-Team* with my son or *Days of our Lives* with my wife. Categories focus our thinking on similarities: people watching television are best modeled according to a multitude of differences.

From E. Seiter, H. Borchers, G. Kreutzner and E.-M Worth (eds), *Remote Control: Television, Audiences and Cultural Power* (London: Routledge, 1989) pp. 56–78.

Similarly, the television text, or program, is no unified whole delivering the same message in the same way to all its 'audience.' The old literary idea of the organic, self-contained text has been exploded so comprehensively that there is no need for me here to contribute further to its demolition. But we still need the term, or something like it to refer to television's meaning-making potential, though we might do better to make it less concrete, less comfortable to handle, and to use the word 'textuality' whose abstraction signals its potentiality rather than its concrete existence. What the set in the living-room delivers is 'television,' visual and aural signifiers that are potential provokers of meaning and pleasure. This potential is its textuality which is mobilized differently in the variety of its moments of viewing.

Textuality is realized in the making of sense and the production of pleasure, and central to this process is the inescapable intertextuality of our culture, a point I shall return to later. For the moment I wish only to point out that we have now collapsed the distinction between 'text' and 'audience.' The textuality of television, the intertextuality of the process of making sense and pleasure from it, can only occur when people bring their different histories and subjectivities to the viewing process. There is no text, there is no audience, there are only the processes of viewing – that variety of cultural activities that take place in front of the screen which constitute the object of study that I am proposing.

THE VIEWER

[...]

Watching television is a process of making meanings and pleasures, and this process is determined by two parallel and interlocking sets of forces. I use the word 'determine' in its literal sense of setting the boundaries, not in its more common mis-sense of authoritarian social imperatives – thou shalt be, do, feel, react as society determines. Determination, then, refers to a bounded terrain within which people have the space to exercise some power over their meanings, pleasures, subjectivities. People can and do make their own culture, albeit within conditions that are not of their own choosing. How much power is available within this terrain, and how fixedly its boundaries are determined are matters of considerable debate, in which I align myself with those who propose that ideological and hegemonic theories of popular culture have overestimated the power of the determinations and underestimated that of the viewer.

The two intertwined sets of determination are the social and the textual, the one working upon the subjectivity of the viewer, the other upon the textuality of television, and I wish to argue that the correspondence between subjectivity and textuality is so close that the two leak into each other at every point of contact.

Viewers within this determined terrain are subjects constituted by late-capitalist societies. Such societies are characterized by heterogeneity – a vast shifting range of subcultures and groups which are finally structured by their relationship to the system by which power is unequally distributed in them. Any one person, or television viewer, forms a number of shifting alliances within this heterogeneity, she or he enters the social system via differently constituted and shifting social formations: the metaphor of a nomadic subjectivity is a productive one here.[1] Any one viewer, then, may at different times be a different viewing subject, as constituted by his or her social determinants, as different social alliances may be mobilized for different moments of viewing: to return to our spatial metaphor, the socially constituted viewing subject may occupy different spaces within the determined terrain according to the social alliances appropriate to this specific moment of making sense of and finding pleasure in the television experience. Hall refers to a similar process as 'articulation.'[2] Here he uses both senses of the word, first as speech, that is a symbolic system used to make sense of both self and experience, and second as flexible linkage. Hodge and Tripp's school students who made sense of *Prisoner* by aligning themselves with the prisoners, the wardens with school teachers, and the prison with the school were articulating, in both senses of the word.[3] They were using the television program to 'speak,' or make sense of their experience of institutionalized subordination and thus to make sense of themselves as subordinated subjects, and they did this by articulating (linking) their viewing of a soap opera set in a women's prison with their social experience of school.

But many of the same students also enjoyed *Sale of the Century* – *Prisoner* and *Sale of the Century* were the most popular programs amongst Australian junior high school students in 1983. Here, the program was articulated with school in a way that produced quite different meanings and pleasures.[4] Making sense of popular television, then, is the process of activating meanings from it, and this process is controlled within more or less determined boundaries by the socially situated viewer. The text will be a source of popular pleasure when these meanings become part of that larger cultural process by which the subject makes sense of his or her material existence. For social experience is like a text: it can only be made meaningful when a social subject brings his or her discursive competencies to bear upon it. The shifting alliance of formations that constitute social experience for the subject allows for a potentially unlimited range of social differences so that each person may be constituted differently, yet these differences are to be explained not by the individual differences of psychology but by the variety of intersections of social alliances and social relations.

Social experience is like intertextuality. It is a vast interlocking potential of elements that can be mobilized in an unpredictable number of ways. Any social system needs a system of meanings to underpin it, and the meanings that are made of it are determined only to an extent by the system itself. This determination allows adequate space for different people to make different meanings though they may use a shared discursive repertoire in the process. The subject is not fully subjected – the sense we make of our social relations is partly under our control – and making sense of social experience necessarily involves making sense of ourselves within that experience.

This potential of meanings that constitutes our social experience must not be seen as amoeba-like and structureless. Just as post-structuralism and discourse theory must not be allowed to evacuate a notion of material social relations, so too, my argument in favor of difference and a relatively empowered, relatively loosely subjected, subject must not blind us to the determining framework of power relations within which all of this takes place. In a similar vein, the emphasis on the power of the viewer to achieve certain meanings from the potential offered by the text can only be understood in terms of a textual power and a textual struggle that are remarkably similar to social power and social struggle. Making sense of social experience is an almost identical process to making sense of a text.

What television delivers is not programs but a semiotic experience. This experience is characterized by its openness and polysemy. Television is not quite a do-it-yourself meaning kit but neither is it a box of ready-made meanings for sale. Although it works within cultural determinations, it also offers freedoms and the power to evade, modify, or challenge these limitations and controls. All texts are polysemic, but polysemy is absolutely central to television's textuality.

TELEVISION AS CULTURAL COMMODITY

Television is a cultural commodity. It works within an economically determined capitalist economy, but when we have said that about it we have said both much and remarkably little. There is a financial economy within which wealth circulates, and a cultural economy within which meanings and pleasures circulate, and the relationship between them is not as deterministic as some theorists have proposed. In the financial economy television is programs and advertisements, not textuality. A program is a commodity produced and then sold to distributors. In distribution its role changes and it becomes not a commodity, but a producer, and what it produces is a new commodity, the audience which is then, in its turn, sold as a commodity to advertisers. The ramifications of this financial economy are fascinating, but they are not the topic of this paper. I wish to concentrate more on the cultural economy.

Here the role shift undergone by the program in the financial economy – that from commodity to producer – is now undergone by the audience, whom I left as a commodity sold to the advertiser. But in the cultural economy the audience rejects its role as commodity and becomes a producer, a producer of meanings and pleasures, and at this moment stops being 'an audience' and becomes different materializations of the process that we call 'viewing television.'

While the metaphor of a cultural economy is a productive one, we must not let it blind us to differences between it and the financial. Meanings and pleasures do not circulate in the cultural economy in the same way that wealth does in the financial. In the first place there is no exchange of money at the point of sale or consumption. Television *appears* to be free, however it may actually be paid for. Payment has no direct relationship to consumption – people can consume as much as they wish and what they wish with no thought of what they are able to afford. Watching an opera or a concert by Dire Straits costs no more than a quiz show or a rerun sitcom.

This liberation from economic constraints frees the viewer from the subordinate role in the market economy, that of 'consumer' who, by definition, gives more than he or she receives. This crucial difference between the television commodity and other more material goods in the market-place foregrounds the considerable freedom won by the viewer in the shift from consumer in the financial economy to producer in the cultural. Meanings and pleasures cannot be owned or bought and sold in a way that grants proprietorial rights over them to some but denies them to others. Bourdieu's theory of cultural capital needs re-examination: for him cultural capital works for one section of the bourgeoisie (the intelligentsia) similarly to the way that economic capital works for the business section.[5] It works to maintain power in the hands of the powerful, advantaged minority, whether that power be expressed in economic or cultural terms. We need to add to this notion that of a popular cultural capital that puts bourgeois culture under constant pressure. Hobson, for instance, has shown how the women viewers of Crossroads had made the program theirs, had constituted it as their cultural capital that they could draw upon to articulate their social relations and social identities – the meanings and pleasures of the program were theirs, not the male producers'.[6] Similarly, Hodge and Tripp have shown how Australian Aboriginal children have made American westerns into their cultural capital.[7] They constructed a cultural category, a tool to think with, that included them, American Indians, and American blacks in a way that enabled them to find in the western some articulation of their subordination to white imperialism and, presumably, to identify with instances of resistance to it. Such a reading position will, we may predict, affect the sense they make of the inevitability of the final narrative defeat of the Indians or non-whites. It was their ability to make a non-white sense from, and find non-white pleasures in, a genre of white imperialism and colonialism that made it popular with them. Without this ability to be the producers of their own culture, the makers of their own meanings and pleasures, it would be difficult to account for Aboriginals' choosing to watch westerns.

This freedom of the viewer to make socially pertinent meanings and pleasures out of television is considerable. Tulloch and Moran found that school students in working-class and middle-class areas made completely different sense out of an episode of the Australian soap A Country Practice which dealt with youth unemployment.[8] The working-class students articulated it with their social experience and found in it the sense that the economic system was at fault in not providing enough jobs for the people. The middle-class students, on the other hand, found meanings that supported the system and placed the blame upon the failures of the (working-class) individuals: for them the unemployed were the undereducated, and the episode's meanings for them were produced by the socially derived discourses of class, education, and economics that they brought to bear upon it. A group of Arab viewers in Katz and Liebes' study of different ethnic group readings of *Dallas* found it incompatible with their own culture that Sue Ellen, escaping with her baby from her husband, should return to her father; so they 'rewrote' it in their conversation about the program, making her return to her former lover, not to her father.[9] Of course, this freedom is inherent in all popular art, not just television: Michaels, for instance, has found that Aboriginal viewers of *Rambo*, who derived great pleasure from the movie, 'rewrote' considerable areas of it.[10] They found pleasure in Rambo's conflict with authority (presumably his Hispanic, non-white appearance, his verbal inarticulateness, and his opposition to the white officer class will have helped here), but could find neither sense nor pleasure in his 'patriotic' nationalistic motivation. Instead they constructed for him a tribal or family motivation by inserting him into an elaborate kinship network with those he was rescuing, which enabled them to make sense of the movie in a way that paralleled the way they made sense of their social relations both with each other and with white power. The fact that the film was a favorite with both Ronald Reagan and Australian Aboriginals must not lead us to assume any affinity between the two, nor between the meanings and pleasures that each produced from the same cultural commodity.

The (usually) scatological versions of television commercial jingles produced by school children provide an extreme example of this 'rewriting' process which is itself typical.[11] Most viewers of course do not need to rewrite television to this extent to find pleasurable meanings in it, but these examples demonstrate that the freedom is there; they are not a distinct form of perverse or aberrant viewing, but an exaggerated and therefore explicit example of the normal process of making meanings and pleasures from television.

This model differs essentially from that underlying political economy in stressing the relative autonomy of the cultural economy from the financial to which political economy traditionally grants considerable, if not total, determinate power. The political economy model is thus unable to progress beyond seeing the audience as a commodity, or in defining it other than in market terms, those of demographic headcounting. Equally it cannot conceive of the text except as the free lunch that catches the audience for the advertisers. Of course the audience is a commodity, of course the text is a free lunch: but neither definition comes within a mile of adequacy. Political economy cannot conceive of television audiences as being socially diverse and therefore capable of producing different socially pertinent meanings from the same commodity, nor of conceiving of this productive activity as pleasurable. It thus cannot conceive of the cultural commodity as a text that requires reading, and thus as capable of serving the contradictory interests of both the producers in the financial economy and of the viewers in the cultural: it cannot conceive of the text as a site of struggle for the power to make meanings; or of the notion that what finally determines the meanings and pleasures provoked by a text is the social situation of the viewer-reader, *not* the interests of the producers and their ideological investment in consumer capitalism. This leads to another crucial factor in the cultural economy which political economy is unable to take into account, and that is popular discrimination. The people choose to make some texts popular, and some not, and this process of choice is essentially a popular one: however hard the industry may try through market research, promotion, advertising, and scheduling to influence popular choice, its failure rate is enormous. It has thus been forced into producing what Garnham calls a 'repertoire' of products from which the public is invited to choose.[12] And it does not know which of its products will be chosen: if it did, it could concentrate on producing a narrower and thus more profitable repertoire. As it is, twelve out of thirteen records fail to make a profit, as do the vast majority of films on their cinema release. Television shows are regularly axed in mid-run. Political economy cannnot conceive of any audience activity that opposes the interests of the producers, whether this activity be one of semiosis or of discrimination.

My position differs from that of political economy in locating at least equal, if not greater, power in the cultural economy. The interests of the financial economy would be best served by producing and reproducing the smallest number of hit products: the cultural needs of the constantly shifting alliances of its audiences force the industry into its constant search for products that have enough originality to meet these shifts, but yet retain enough familiarity to meet both the audience expectations and developed competencies, and the routinized production practices of the producers. The major drive for innovation and change comes from the audience activity in the cultural economy, and from the relationship of this activity to larger movements in the political and social system. Television's rehabilitation of Vietnam in shows like *Magnum PI*, *Simon and Simon* or *The A-Team* has participated in the 1980s shift of American values to the Reaganite masculine right, but did not originate it. Similarly, shows like *Designing Women*, *Golden Girls*, and *Cagney and Lacey* are part of the redefinition of gender meanings, but the spur to redefine them came from the changing material conditions of women. In both cases, it was the cultural economy's dialectic relationship with the socio-political system at the level of the meanings of social experience that fed into the financial economy and caused the economic success and therefore the reproduction of these genres. Theorizing the audience as commodity blinds us to the subtleties and complexities of these social forces.

Of course the audiences' freedom and ability to make their socially pertinent meanings out of television's text, even though these meanings may be beyond both the prediction and the control of the producers, is, at one level, exactly what producers want: they neither know nor care what meanings and pleasures their audiences produce, their concern is solely with the headcount and the demographics. But only a tiny proportion of audience members are converted into purchasers or even potential purchasers. We must be chary of singular definitions of such multifarious (and ultimately untenable) categories as text and audience. Just as television's textuality can simultaneously serve the economic needs of its producers and the cultural pleasures of its audiences, however oppositional these functions may be to each other, so the audience can, at one and the same time, fill the contradictory roles of commodity and cultural producer. Russian Jews, newly arrived in Israel, read *Dallas* as capitalism criticizing itself: such a process can hardly be described as one of commodification.[13] Of course the industry will attempt, often successfully, to produce programs that invite and encourage the audiences' powers as meaning-producers, but their commercial intention can only describe a part and, I would argue, a small part, of the audiences' activities within the cultural economy.

[...]

CRITICAL INTERVENTION

Television's textuality is not bounded by the titles and credits of a program, subjectivity cannot be confined within the skin or history of an individual, and similarly viewing television cannot be confined to the periods when the set is switched on. Television is not only part of the process of viewing, or reading or talking about it, but it is also part of our cultural lives when its presence is less direct, less obvious. We need to investigate ways in which a television fan watches movies in a cinema or attends a live ballgame: we need to probe how a middle-aged fan of *Miami Vice* makes sense of his own shabby dress. Television is part of family relations and family politics, it is part of gender relations and politics, part of consumer relations and politics. Again, a comprehensive map of all the cultural processes, of which television viewing is only one, is both impossible and unnecessary. What is needed is the investigation of instances that are no more and no less typical than other instances. And the emphasis should be not on what people do, not on what their social experience is, but on how they make sense of it. Their recorded words and behaviors are not data giving us their reactions and meanings, but instances of the sense-making process that we call culture, clues of how this process works and can be actualized.

The ability of the critic to intervene in the politics of popular culture, to counter the forces of domination and support those of resistance or evasion, depends upon a far more sympathetic and detailed understanding of the cultural economy than we have so far achieved. The traditional critical emphasis from the left has focused upon the power of the industry and upon the power of ideology and hegemony. This has led us to locate the appropriate sites of intervention in the processes of production and representation. A more effective, if methodologically much more difficult, focus for intervention might be the diversity of sites of reception, but instrumental simplicity should not be the only factor in our choice of appropriate political action.

The main problem facing the critic today is to understand popular pleasures and popular discrimination, and on the basis of this understanding to decide how and if to intervene in both the production and reception of texts. It may be that open heteroglossic texts such as *Dallas* (which Altman characterises as a 'menu' from which viewers choose)[14] are actually socially and politically more progressive than more closed, monoglossic texts, even ones that prefer more apparently progressive meanings. The progressiveness of popular television may lie in heteroglossic programs that not only promote the dominant ideology but that also offer opportunities to resist, oppose, and evade it. As yet, we just do not know.

We can only find out by paying more attention to the moments of reception for only here can we determine which texts and which characteristics of those texts offer their polysemy for semiotic mobilization by the subordinate, and how these semiotic differences are produced and circulated subculturally. We also need to discover why some members of subordinated groups are more productive or more resistant viewers than others. The critic can only intervene effectively on the basis of adequate understanding, and on the basis of a deep respect for the pleasure that the subordinate make from their popular culture. It may seem unfortunate that it is commercially motivated mainstream television that is best able to offer these pleasures, but possibly the commercial imperative has brought its producers to a closer relationship with popular social experience than the more distantly theorized political-moral-aesthetic position of those with both a social conscience and a social power has been able to achieve.

The question facing progressive critics may now need reversing: rather than asking how it is that the culture industry makes people into commodities that serve its interests, we should now be asking how it is that the people can turn the products of the industry into *their* popular culture and can make them serve *their* interests.

Social differences are produced by the social system but the meanings of these differences are produced by culture: the sense of them has to be constantly produced and reproduced as part of the subject's experience of these differences. Viewer-driven meanings made from texts and subculturally driven meanings made of social experience involve the pleasures of producing meanings rather than the subjection of being produced by them, and make it possible to maintain a consciousness of those abrasive, uncomfortable social differences that hegemonic common sense works so hard to smooth over.

And television plays a crucial role in this; though it is produced by the culture industry and bears within it the lines of hegemonic force, it is met by the tactics of the everyday. De Certeau argues that social power and the power to make meanings that serve the interests of the dominant work strategically, that is, they work in the manner of an occupying army, in a massively organized structure of power.[15] But they are met by the tactics of guerrilla warfare, by tactical, fleeting raids upon their weak points which are not organized into any master plan, but which exploit the particularities and possibilities of each tactical moment. According to de Certeau, 'people make do with what they have,' and in the heavily bureaucratized and industrialized society of late capitalism, what people have is what is provided for them by the institutions and industries of capitalism. It is through these that the social strategy is put into practice, but its effectivity must not be read simply from its intent or from the strength of the forces at its disposal. It is not only the US army in Vietnam and the Soviet army in Afghanistan that have been unable to devise a strategy to beat guerrilla tactics. What we need to investigate, after de Certeau's provocative theorizing, is the everyday tactical, and therefore pleasurable, uses of these cultural resources (albeit industrially produced), the everyday deployment of the tactics of evasion, expropriation, and resistance.

The links between semiotic power/resistance/pleasure and the maintenance of resistive social differences, the role of television in this, and the part that all this can play in social change are theoretically arguable. What I would like to see is the methodologically daunting project of tracing actual instances of these links being made, of these processes being actualized, of the delineation of the multitude of cultural processes at work in the different moments of viewing television.

NOTES

1. Lawrence Grossberg, 'The In-Difference of Television,' *Screen* 28, no. 2 (spring 1987): 28–46.
2. Lawrence Grossberg (ed.) 'On Postmodernism and Articulation: An Interview with Stuart Hall,' *Journal of Communication Inquiry* 10, no. 2 (summer 1986): 45–60.
3. Robert Hodge and David Tripp, *Children and Television* (Cambridge: Polity Press, 1986). *Prisoner* (screened in the US under the title *Prisoner – Cell Block H*) is an Australian soap opera set in a women's prison. Hodge and Tripp (p. 49) found that school students identified many similarities between school students and prisoners:
   1. pupils are shut in;
   2. pupils are separated from their friends;
   3. pupils would not be there if they were not made to be;
   4. pupils only work because they are punished if they do not and it is less boring than doing nothing at all;
   5. pupils have no rights; they can do nothing about an unfair teacher;
   6. some teachers victimize their pupils;
   7. there are gangs and leaders amongst the pupils;
   8. there are silly rules which everyone tries to break.
   These similarities enable *Prisoner* to provide the students with an imaginative 'language' with which to think through their experience of powerlessness in the school. The meanings of subordination were those of the subordinate, not of the dominant, and there is evidence that students found these meanings both pleasurable and empowering.
4. *Sale of the Century* and *Prisoner* were both 'articulations' of school in that both could be linked with school and could be used differently to 'speak,' or make sense of, the school experience. See John Fiske, *Television Culture* (London and New York: Methuen, 1987).
5. Pierre Bourdieu, 'The Aristocracy of Culture,' *Media, Culture, and Society* 2, no. 3 (July 1980): 225–54.
6. Dorothy Hobson, '*Crossroads*': *The Drama of a Soap Opera* (London: Methuen, 1982). [See Chapter 48 of this volume.]
7. Hodge and Tripp, *Children and Television*.
8. John Tulloch and Albert Moran, '*A Country Practice*': '*Quality Soap*' (Sydney: Currency Press, 1986).
9. Elihu Katz and Tamar Liebes, 'Mutual Aid in the Decoding of *Dallas*: Preliminary Notes from a Cross-Cultural Case Study,' in Philip Drummond and Richard

Paterson (eds) *Television in Transition* (London: British Film Institute, 1985), pp. 187–98.

10. Eric Michaels, 'Aboriginal Content: Who's Got it – Who Needs it' (paper presented at the Australian Screen Studies Association Conference, Sydney, December 1986).

11. Fiske, *Television Culture*; e.g. Sydney children in 1982 and 1983 were singing their version of a Tooheys beer commercial: 'How do you feel when you're having a fuck, under a truck, and the truck rolls off? I feel like a Tooheys', I feel like a Tooheys', I feel like a Tooheys' or two' (Children's Folklore Archives, Australian Studies Centre, Curtin University).

12. Nicholas Garnham, 'Concepts of Culture: Public Policy and the Cultural Industries,' *Cultural Studies* 1, no. 1. (January 1987): 23–37.

13. See Tamar Liebes and Elihu Katz, in [Ellen Seiter et al. (eds), *Remote Control*: *Television, Audiences and Cultural Powers* (London: Routledge, 1989)].

14. Rick Altman, 'Television/Sound,' in Tania Modleski (ed.) *Studies in Entertainment*: *Critical Approaches to Mass Culture* (Bloomington: Indiana University Press, 1986), pp. 39–54.

15. Michel de Certeau, *The Practice of Everyday Life* (Berkeley, Calif.: University of California Press, 1984).

43

'STRANGERS NO MORE, WE SING': FILKING AND THE SOCIAL CONSTRUCTION OF THE SCIENCE FICTION FAN COMMUNITY

Henry Jenkins

Media fans are consumers who also produce, readers who also write, spectators who also participate.

On the one hand, these claims seem counter-intuitive. We tend to think of fans almost exclusively in terms of relations of consumption rather than production. For many critics of mass culture, the fan has been emblematic of the most obsessive and slavish forms of cultural consumption, consumption which has been understood primarily in terms of metaphors of addiction, religious zealotry, social aberration or psychological imbalance. Journalistic accounts of fan culture tend to give primary attention to the exchange of mass-produced commodities, often at excessive prices, and to the worshipful approach the fans take to media producers.

On the other hand, claims about producerly fans can seem banal and self-evident. As cultural studies, cognitive film theory, reader-response criticism, and other contemporary theoretical movements have come to characterize all media spectators as 'active audiences,' the notion of textual production has been extended from reference to specific types of cultural activities which result in material artifacts to encompass all forms of interpretive activity. In this move, the fan becomes the emblematic example of the reader's activity in making meaning and finding pleasure within commercial texts; the fan's activity is treated as different only in degree from those types of interpretive strategies adopted by all consumers of mass culture (see, for example, Fiske,

From L. A. Lewis (ed.), *The Adoring Audience: Fan Culture and Popular Media* (London and New York: Routledge) pp. 208–36.

1987 and 1989). Fan communities are characterized as 'audiences' and they are read exclusively in terms of their relationship to a privileged primary text, a formulation which, as Janice Radway (1988) notes, still tends to keep the media text, rather than the reader's use of it, as the central focus of analysis. Fans as audiences defined through their attachment to particular programs or genres (Madonna 'wanna-bes,' romance readers, Trekkers) are still seen as constituted by texts rather than as appropriating and reworking textual materials to constitute their own varied culture. Moreover, the fans' own cultural creations are not read as the artifacts of a larger cultural community but as the material traces of personal interpretations – or at least, of interpretations defined primarily in terms of a singular and stable social identity (housewives, children, punks, and so on). Such an account of fannish production, thus, gains general applicability at the expense of a more precise understanding of the social and cultural specificity of the fan community, allows for the construction of a theory of dominant reading practices without offering a sharper sense of the particular character of the fans' fundamental break with those practices.

To proceed, then, with any concrete discussion of fannish cultural production, we must start with a more precise definition of fandom, a definition which from the very outset recognizes that part of what distinguishes fans as a particular class of textual consumers is the social nature of their interpretive and cultural activity (Jenkins, 1990). I would propose a model of fandom which operates on at least four levels:

1. *Fans adopt a distinctive mode of reception*: Ethnographic research has begun to focus more and more on understanding the specific modes of reception which are characteristic of specific social and cultural communities – the selective attention of the child viewer (Jenkins, 1989; Palmer, 1986) or the housewife (Brunsdon, 1981; Morley, 1986), who for very different reasons divide their interest between television programming and other household activities, the more focused attention of the husband (Morley, 1986), who may watch television somewhat indiscriminately but who often makes the broadcast the focus of undivided concentration, the social interaction which surrounds viewing programs within a group context (Amsley, 1989), and so on. These different modes of reception reflect different interests the viewers bring to their relationship with the media and are shaped by the different social conditions which these viewers experience in their everyday lives.

Fannish viewing can be understood, then, as yet another mode of reception. First, fan viewing is characterized by a conscious selection of a specific program which is viewed faithfully from week to week and is often reread repeatedly either through reruns or through videotape archiving. Second, fans are motivated not simply to absorb the text but to translate it into other types of cultural and social activity. Fan reception goes beyond transient comprehension of a viewed episode towards some more permanent and material form of meaning-production. Minimally, fans feel compelled to talk about viewed programs with other fans. Often, fans join fan organizations or attend conventions which allow for more sustained discussions. Fans exchange letters. Fans chat on computer nets. Fans trade tapes so that all interested parties have a chance to see all the available episodes. And, as we will see, fans use their experience of watching television programs as the basis for other types of artistic creation – writing new stories, composing songs, making videos, painting pictures. It is this social and cultural dimension which distinguishes the fannish mode of reception from other viewing styles which depend upon selective and regular media consumption. Fan reception can not and does not exist in isolation, but is always shaped through input from other fans.

2. *Fandom constitutes a particular interpretive community*: Given the highly social orientation of fan reading practices, fan interpretations need to be understood in institutional rather than personal terms.[1] Fan club meetings, newsletters, and letterzines provide a space where textual interpretations get negotiated: new readings or evaluations of shared texts are proposed and supported by appeal to certain generally accepted forms of evidence or types of inferential moves ('Roj Blake is going progressively mad throughout the second season of "Blake's 7"'), others debate the merits of these interpretations, offering counter-examples, proposing alternative readings, or challenging them according to their conformity to the group's standards of what constitutes an appropriate use of textual materials ('No, Roj Blake makes rational but unpopular decisions necessary for the conduct of a paramilitary campaign against the Federation'). Each party appeals to the primary text episodes, interviews with program producers, or general social and cultural knowledge to explore differences in the ways they make sense of the narrative events. Moreover, fans debate the protocols of reading, the formation of canons, and the ethical dimension of their relationship to primary textual producers almost as much as they discuss the merits and significance of individual program episodes. The meanings generated through this process certainly reflect, to some degree, the personal interests and experiences of individual fans; one may also locate meanings which originate from the fans' specific position within the larger social formation, meanings which reflect, say, characteristically 'feminine' perspectives on dominant culture. Yet, these readings must also be understood in terms of the ways they reflect and conform to the particular character of fandom as a specific institution of interpretation with its own distinctive reading protocols and structures of meaning.

3. *Fandom constitutes a particular Art World*: Howard Becker (1982) has adopted the term, 'Art World,' to describe 'an established network of cooperative links' (p. 34) between institutions of artistic production, distribution, consumption, interpretation and evaluation: 'Art Worlds produce works and also give them aesthetic values' (p. 39). An expansive term, 'Art World' refers to systems of aesthetic norms and generic conventions, systems of professional training and reputation building, systems for the circulation, exhibition and/or

sale of artworks, systems for critical evaluation. In one sense, fandom simply constitutes one component of the mass-media Art World. Fan conventions play a central role in the distribution of knowledge about media productions and in the promotion of comic books, science fiction novels, and new film releases. They provide a space where writers and producers may speak directly with readers and may develop a firmer sense of audience expectations. Fan awards, such as the Hugo, which is presented each year at the World Science Fiction Convention, play a key role in building the reputations of emerging science-fiction writers and in recognizing outstanding accomplishment by established figures. Historically, fan publishing has provided an important training ground for professional writers, a nurturing space in which to develop skills, styles, themes, and perhaps most importantly, self-confidence before entering the commercial marketplace (Bradley, 1985).

Yet, fandom constitutes as well its own distinctive Art World founded less upon the consumption of pre-existing texts than on the production of fan texts which draw raw materials from the media as a basis for new forms of cultural creation. Fans write short stories, poems, and novels which use the characters and situations of the primary text as a starting point for their own fiction. Fans take found footage from television texts and edit them to construct their own videos which comment, sometimes with irony, sometimes in celebration, on the programs which gave them birth. Fan artists paint pictures, construct sculptures, or fashion elaborate costumes. Fan musicians record and market tapes of their perform-ances. Much as science fiction conventions provide a market for commercially-produced goods associated with media texts and as a showcase for professional writers, illustrators, and performers, the conventions also provide a marketplace for fan-produced artworks and a showcase for fan artists. Fan paintings are auctioned, fanzines are sold, performances staged, videos screened, and awards are given in recognition of outstanding accomplishments. Semi-professional companies are emerging to assist in the production and distribution of fan pro-ducts – songs tapes, zines, and so on – and publications are appearing whose primary function is to provide technical information and commentary on fan art (*Apa-Filk* for fan music, *Art Forum* for fan artists, *Treklink* and *On the Double* for fan writers) or to publicize and market fan writing (*Datazine*). Fan artists develop their talent in a nurturing environment and reputations, sometimes international in scope, while remaining unknown to the world outside of fandom.

4. *Fandom constitutes an alternative social community*: The fans' appropria-tion of media texts provides a ready body of common references that facilitates communication with others scattered across a broad geographic area, fans who one may never – or only seldom – meet face to face but who share a common sense of identity and interests. The collapse of traditional forms of cultural solidarity and community within an increasingly atomistic society has not des-troyed a felt need to participate within a cultural community and to adopt an identity which is larger than the type of isolated individual demanded by the

alienated workplace (Lipsitz, 1988). What fandom offers is a community not defined in traditional terms of race, religion, gender, region, politics, or profession, but rather a community of consumers defined through their common relationship with shared texts. Fans view this community in conscious opposition to the 'mundane' world inhabited by non-fans, attempting to construct social structures more accepting of individual difference, more accommodating of particular interests, and more democratic and communal in their operation. Entering into fandom means abandoning pre-existing social status and seeking acceptance and recognition less in terms of who you are than in terms of what you contribute to this new community. Fandom is particularly attractive to groups marginalized or subordinated in the dominant culture – women, blacks, gays, lower-middle-class office workers, the handicapped – precisely because its social organization provides types of unconditional acceptance and alternative sources of status lacking in the larger society. For many fans, this social dimension – their allegiance to fandom – often takes precedence over their allegiance to particular media texts with fans moving from 'Star Trek' to *Star Wars*, from 'Blake's 7' to 'The Professionals,' while remaining active within the larger social structures of the fan community. Some forms of fan cultural production exist, then, not so much as a vehicle for interpreting and commenting upon primary texts, than as a means of building and maintaining solidarity within the fan community.

So, fans are consumers who also produce, readers who also write, spectators who also participate. What do fans produce? Fans produce meanings and interpretations; fans produce artworks; fans produce communities; fans produce alternative identities. In each case, fans are drawing on materials from the dominant media and employing them in ways that serve their own interests and facilitate their own pleasures. In each case, the nature of fannish production is shaped through the social norms, aesthetic conventions, interpretive protocols, technological resources and technical competence of the larger fan community. Fan texts, then, do not give us any pure, 'authentic' or unmediated access to the personal interpretive activities of individual fans; nor do they provide a very good basis for constructing a theory of dominant reading practices, since fannish production reflects the particular demands and expectations of a subcultural community which are different in kind as well as degree from the types of semiotic production occurring within the larger culture. They can, however, teach us about tactics of cultural appropriation and the process by which artworks produced for one context may be remade to serve alternative interests.

'Star Trek' fan fiction offers a particularly vivid example of some key aspects of fan cultural production (Jenkins, 1988). Over the twenty-five years since 'Star Trek' was first aired, fan fiction has achieved a semi-institutional status. Fan magazines, sometimes hand typed, photocopied and stapled, other times offset printed and commercially bound, are distributed through the mails and sold at conventions. Fanzines publish both nonfiction essays speculating on

technical or sociological aspects of the program world, and fiction which elabo-
rates on the characters and situations proposed by the primary text, but often
pushing them into directions quite different from those conceived by the
original textual producers.

'Star Trek' fan writing is a predominantly feminine response to mass media
texts, with the majority of fanzines edited and written by women for a largely
female readership. These fan writers rework the primary text in a number of
significant ways: they shift attention from action and adventure aspects of the
show onto character relationships, applying conventions characteristic of traditionally feminine genres, such as the romance, to the interpretation and continuation of materials drawn from traditionally masculine genres; female
characters who were marginalized and subordinate in the original series
(Uhura, Chapel) become the focus of fan texts which attempt to examine the
types of problems women might experience as active contributors to Star Fleet
and, in the process, these characters must be strengthened and redefined to
accommodate more feminist interests; fan writers explore erotic aspects of the
texts which could not be directly represented on network television and,
sometimes, move from homosocial representations of male bonding and friendship towards the depiction of a homoerotic romance between Kirk and Spock.
Fan writing, then, can be characterized as a type of textual 'poaching'
(de Certeau, 1984), as a strategy for appropriating materials produced by the
dominant culture industry and reworking them into terms which better serve
subordinate or subcultural interests. In this way, fan writing employs 'Star
Trek' characters as a means of working through social experiences and concerns
of particular interest to the female writing community, concerns which were
given little or no attention by the original series.

Fanzine stories grow out of gender-specific reading strategies and speak to
feminist issues but they do not simply duplicate the types of individual interpretive activity which initially generated fannish interest in the series. Fanzine
stories are created to be circulated within the fan Art World. They conform to
particular generic traditions which originate within the fan community. They
foreground meanings which are of interest to other fans; they accept certain
common rules about what types of uses of textual materials are desirable or
appropriate. They tend to build upon characterizations and worlds already
elaborated by earlier fan writers. In short, these fanzine stories are as much the
artifacts of a particular cultural community as they are the expressions of
personal meanings and interests.

Fan music-making (or filking, as fans call it) offers us another point of entry
into the cultural logic of fandom, another way of understanding the nature and
structure of the fan community and its particular relationship to dominant
media content.[2] Filking, like fan fiction, may be a vehicle for extending or
commenting upon pre-existing media texts; it may be a way of taking textual
materials and pulling to the surface characters or concerns which have been
marginalized (Jenkins, 1991). Fans often write songs from the perspective of

fictional characters, singing in their voices, and expressing through musical performance aspects of their personalities or their particular perspectives on narrative events. Just as a fan writer may develop a story around the character of Uhura, a filker may develop a song centered around a Chapel or Yar, female characters whose voices are rarely allowed to be heard within the aired episodes. Singing as these characters may allow filkers to explore issues which remain unresolved by the primary text and to offer challenges to its preferred meanings; singing as these characters may also allow them to play with the possibility of shifting between existing social categories, of seeing the world from a variety of different perspectives. Moreover, filking may add yet another dimension to the practice of textual poaching since motifs and themes from media texts are often attached to tunes scavenged from popular or folk music, often with a keen awareness of the types of meanings which may be sparked by the careful juxtaposition of the two.

Yet, filking differs from fan writing in a number of significant ways. First, while fan writers tend to focus their output primarily if not exclusively around a single program text, filkers draw references from a much broader range of media products, exemplifying the more 'nomadic' aspects of textual 'poach ing.' While fan writing represents a predominantly female response to the media, men and women play equally prominent roles within filk, sometimes collaborating on songs, other times exploring themes or subjects of a more gender-specific interest. If fan writing encourages individual creativity, filk more persistently promotes a communal conception of cultural production, though, as we will see, this type of folk ideology is being challenged by the promotion and marketing of individual filk artists as star musicians. Finally, if fan writing can still be understood primarily in terms of textual interpretation and appropriation, filking more often attempts to speak directly about fandom as a distinctive social community, to celebrate its characteristic values and activities and to articulate a fannish perspective on political topics, such as the space program, environmentalism, and the arms race.

Filk takes many forms: lyrics are published in fan songbooks or as one element among many in fanzines; filk clubs host monthly meetings; filk conventions are held several times a year; filk is circulated on tapes, either informally (through barter) or more commercially (through several semi-professional filk tape distributors). Yet, it is important to position filk songs initially within their original and primary context as texts designed to be sung collectively and informally by fans gathered at science fiction conventions.

[...]

One constantly meets a sense of filking as a spontaneous and ongoing process of popular creation, one which builds upon community traditions but which is continually open to individual contribution and innovation. Some traditional filk songs have acquired literally hundreds of verses as new filkers have tried their hands at adding to the general repertoire. In other cases, popular filk songs are parodied or pirated, sometimes numerous times, and such parodies are generally regarded as compliments by filk composers since they mark the songs' general acceptance within the fan community. Several times during the evening, a traditional filk or folk song was followed by one or more of its parodies advanced by another singer in the circle. Filk songs are not closed or completed, but rather open and fluid, not so much personal expressions as communal property, a contribution to fan culture. The 'flying island' of fandom ensures that a song performed at one con may quickly be accepted into the general repertoire to be sung at other cons scattered throughout the country and, sometimes, refitted to the new context and occasion.

[...]

A number of different yet interrelated conceptions of fans run through the filk-song repertoire. Fans are represented as both passionate lovers and harsh critics of media culture. Fans are defined in opposition to the values and norms of everyday life, as people who live more richly, feel more intensely, play more freely, and think more deeply than the 'mundanes' who constantly surround them. Fans are seen as people who carry the dreams and fantasies of childhood into their adult life. Fans are represented as technological utopians who maintain an active commitment to humanity's future in space. The communal quality of the filk sing allows such claims to be made not *for* or *to* but *by* the fan community itself, enabling them to be read as reflexive artifacts that collectively shed light on the ideals, values, and lifestyle of the group which produced them. Such songs play a pivotal role in articulating and maintaining a common identity for fans which reflects and integrates the group's own diverse interests and which challenges the dominant negative stereotyping of fans.

[...]

Filk, then, offers us a particularly vivid illustration of the various dimensions of fan cultural production. Filk songs may, like fan writing, serve as a vehicle for interpreting and commenting upon media texts, a way of opening favorite texts to new interests and making them produce new meanings; filk is indeed a form of textual 'poaching.' Yet filk also plays a vital role in the construction and maintenance of the fan community, as a means of articulating a group identity and expressing collective ideals. Finally, filk is becoming one of the aesthetic commodities which circulate within the fan Art World, becoming the basis for the creation of institutionalized systems of artistic creation and distribution, and offering a new arena within which fan artists may build their reputations.

Filk songs are far more than simply the material trace of individual fans' reception and interpretation of media texts. To read them in such a fashion is to offer an impoverished account of fan cultural production. The significance of fan cultural production must necessarily be understood in relation to the larger social and cultural institutions of the fan community and understood in terms of its aesthetic norms and generic conventions. Such communities draw upon media materials as an important resource, one which forms the basis for interpretive debates, one which provides the raw materials for aesthetic creation, one which facilitates social interaction with people who otherwise might not have a common frame of reference.

Yet it is important to see these communities not as constituted by single media texts, but rather as constituting themselves from a multitude of borrowed materials. Fandom is a 'scavenger' culture built from poached fragments of many different media products, woven together into a coherent whole through the meanings the fans bring to those fragments and the uses they make of them, rather than by meanings generated from the primary texts. Any understanding of fan cultural productions, then, requires not simply sensitivity to the relationship of those products to their media origins but also their particular function within the larger cultural logic of fandom.

NOTES

1. My discussion of fandom as an interpretive institution draws inspiration from Bordwell (1989) and from extensive conversations with its author.
2. According to Jackson (1986), the term filk is the result of a typo on a conference program which turned 'folk music' into 'filk music.' The word was retained out of a certain perverse pleasure, but it functions nicely to show both the continuity and discontinuity between fan music and traditional filk music. Filk adopts many folk music practices and often bases its songs on tunes from the folk repertoire, but borrows its contents from mass media and popular culture. As a result, the form, like most fan culture, mediates between folk culture and mass culture, suggesting an intermediate form wherein mass culture can be turned back into something akin to folk culture.

REFERENCES

Amsley, Cassandra. (1989) How to Watch *Star Trek*. *Cultural Studies* Fall: 323–39.

Becker, Howard. (1982) *Art Worlds*. Berkeley: University of California Press.

Bradley, Marion Zimmer. (1985) Fandom: Its Value to the Professional. In *Inside Outer Space: Science Fiction Professionals Look at Their Craft*, ed. Sharon Jarvis. New York: Frederick Ungar.

Brunsdon, Charlotte. (1981) *Crossroads*. Notes on Soap Opera. *Screen* 22(4): 32–7.

de Certeau, Michel. (1984) *The Practice of Everyday Life*. Berkeley: University of California Press.

Fiske, John. (1987) *Television Culture*. London: Methuen.

——. (1989) *Understanding Popular Culture*. Boston: Unwin Hyman.

Jenkins, Henry. (1988) *Star Trek* Rerun, Reread, Rewritten: Fan Writing as Textual Poaching. *Critical Studies in Mass Communication* 5(2): 85–107.

——. (1989) Going Bonkers!: Children, Play and Pee Wee. *Camera Obscura* 18.

——. (1990) 'If I Could Speak With Your Sound': Textual Proximity, Liminal Identification and the Music of the Science Fiction Fan Community. *Camera Obscura* 23.

——. (1991) *Textual Poachers: Television Fans and Participatory Culture*. London: Routledge.

Lipsitz, George. (1988) Mardi Gras Indians: Carnival and Counter Narrative in Black New Orleans. *Cultural Critique* Fall: 99–122.

Morley, David. (1986) *Family Television*. London: Comedia.

Palmer, Patricia. (1986) *The Lively Audience: A Study of Children Around the TV Set*. Sydney: Unwin Hyman.

Radway, Janice. (1988) Reception Study: Ethnography and the Problem of Dispersed Audiences and Nomadic Subjects. *Cultural Studies* 2(3): 359–76.

44

MEDIA, MEANING AND EVERYDAY LIFE

Joke Hermes

Stuart Hall's 'We are all in our heads different audiences at once', for me marks the definitive move away from a paradigm that was organized around texts producing subjectivies. Even though Hall related the different audiences we are to the text, he also said: 'We have the capacity to deploy different levels and modes of attention, to mobilise different competences in our viewing. At different times of the day, for different family members, different patterns of viewing have different "saliences".' (1986: 10) The departing point for this paper exactly is the question of salience. Or, more to the point, given the shift in media studies towards the audience and contexts of viewing, how and when everyday media use becomes meaningful needs to be carefully thought through. One of David Morley's respondents in *Family Television*, who has a habit of putting the television on in the early morning, says: 'Sometimes I intend to look at it . . . but . . . at the end of it I've seen everything but I've heard nothing. You know what I mean?' (1986: 56) Do we know what she means?

I suggest that from time to time, all of us (some perhaps more often than others), engage in virtually meaningless media use. In this paper I will argue that the consequences of such a point of departure, of radically decentring the media text in favour of an understanding of the specific routines of the everyday that media use is part of, are a challenge epistemologically and will constitute more space politically than a number of recent audience studies have done. I will draw upon my own research on women's magazines, based on

From *Cultural Studies* 7/3 (1993) pp. 493–506.

seventy-five lengthy interviews with readers; upon David Morley's work on families watching television and a small number of texts addressing the issues involved in studying media use and/or everyday life.

[...]

My respondents described their everyday lives as singularly stable and set routines. Routine easily associated with daily drag. But built into the routines was potential pleasure, too. It ranged, indeed, from sitting down with a cup of tea and a magazine that has just been bought, or in the summer going to a trailer that has been rented year after year with a shopping bag, passed on by a sister or a neighbour, crammed full with romances. There also was potential boredom: watching television is more rewarding if one is prepared for the occasional uninteresting items. And, only occasionally acknowledged, there is danger of the routines and pleasures breaking up ... Everyday life is something of an enigma. Bausinger stresses its stability. Schutz (1973) defines everyday life by its taken-for-grantedness. Birte Bech Jørgensen, in her research on female youth employment, found that such a perspective didn't fit her interview material, nor does it fit mine.

> Modern everyday life is created as doubleness on the one hand of continuity, of trust and certainty, made possible by the norms, rules and routines of everyday life. And, on the other hand, change and a more or less frightening and joyful urge for autonomy. (Bech Jørgensen, 1990: 22)

Bech Jørgensen feels that the ways of handling the conditions of everyday life are basically repetitive, intuitive *and* inventive (1990: 22). Lodged deep within the everyday there is also transformative power, perceptible especially in the case of ruptures and dramas when the taken-for-grantedness is broken (1990: 23). Routines may fall short of their reassuring function, because of tensions in a relationship, unemployment or chance happenings. The point is to recognize that the everyday, on the one hand, is the site of the utterly superficial and repetitive that we need to respect for the sense of security it gives and, on the other hand, potentially is the site of major personal and societal change. (The women's movement is a case in point. In the early seventies women were mobilized on their feelings of dissatisfaction regarding their everyday routines.) Both sides to the everyday need to be part of media research.[1] Before I turn to the question of how to recognize routines, the boredom, the pleasures and the faultlines, the account needs to be settled regarding the issue of superficiality and everyday taken-for-grantedness.

The superficiality of accounts of media use partly is real, in the sense that it reflects taken-for-grantedness and pleasure derived from things being the way they are. Repetitiveness, knowing where to find what in a magazine or being familiar with the routines of a quiz show, or the formula of a popular genre can be reassuring, a guarantee one's viewing or reading pleasures will not be interfered with or uprooted. As one women's magazine reader put it: 'Reading those tips, you are reminded of all sorts of things that you knew already but kind of had forgotten.' In a sense then, media use may quite often be relatively meaningless.

The superficiality of interview transcripts also needs to be understood as an academic artefact, however. Media texts have been invested with so much meaning, anyone would be hard put to come up with an interesting reading. The audiences that have been researched, have, more often than not, been fans. Knowledgeable, ardent readers and television viewers have come to be confused with 'average' viewers and readers.[2] In other cases researchers switch from a reader perspective to a text-based perspective which saves them from engaging with questions regarding how media ordinarily become meaningful in everyday life.

[...]

Since we have some knowledge of how fans experience their favourite texts as meaningful and pleasurable[3] and also of how choice, use and pleasure are caught up in specific arrangements of the domestic[4] the issue is: how to deal with media use as a secondary, relatively meaningless activity; how to understand people's descriptions of such media use? How are all those texts one is not a 'fan' of, but that are used regularly, made sense of? In my own research project I have tried to foreground that a major part of media use is routine triggered behaviour that isn't meaningful in itself but as part of how (everyday) life is organized. Not *all* media use is meaningless. Meaninglessness, I believe, is part of media use in the sense that one simply cannot stop and think about every single thing one does during a normal day's work and leisure, in and outside of the home. Life is largely organized around routines that do not allow for elaborate self-reflection.

To use the word 'meaninglessness' is to dive headlong into a sea full of mines. The least one can do is defuse a number of them. No, I am not writing up yet another way of putting down not just everyday media use but also the quintessential everyday media consumer: someone supposedly lacking in cultural capital, or lacking in ambition to make her surroundings meaningful. This is not about different types of readers but about different ways of reading that all of us engage in. And no, I don't think that in this case the relative 'meaninglessness' of media use must be understood to mean that it is unresearchable. To clarify the position I take here, I will briefly turn to the work of Michel de Certeau, widely read expert on everyday life and how/whether it becomes meaningful.

De Certeau in *The Practice of Everyday Life* (1984) suggests we need to differentiate between tactics, (ways of making-do, *arts de faire*) and strategies. Strategies are used by such total institutions as armies, cities or supermarket chains to create and delimit their own place. Tactics, calculated actions determined by the absence of a proper locus, tend to insert themselves in these spaces that are created for the maintenance of power (de Certeau, 1984: 36–7).

Reading, in the framework sketched by de Certeau, like poaching, strolling, cooking or dwelling is 'to wander through an imposed system (that of the text, analogous to the constructed order of a city or a supermarket)' (1984: 169). Wanderers don't acquire status or build their memories and pleasures into recollectable structures, monuments so to speak.

> Writing accumulates, stocks up, resists time by the establishment of a place and multiplies its production through the expansionism of reproduction. Reading takes no measures against the erosion of time (one forgets oneself and also forgets), it does not keep what it acquires, or it does so poorly, and each of the places through which it passes is a repetition of the lost paradise. (1984: 174)

Theoretically, I couldn't agree more with the point put forward. Texts cannot impose upon readers how they are to be read. But, the nomadic imagery de Certeau offers is in fact a description (or so I believe) of having to serve your family meals seven days per week; or go to work every day; of going to the shops to find bargains in order to stretch a limited budget. Not only does de Certeau romanticize everyday life to an unacceptable extent; he also closes off all possibilities of change using a polar model of domination that is strengthened rather than changed by the tactics 'ordinary' people use and, thirdly, theorizing everyday life along these lines amounts to saying that the meanings and doings (one hesitates to say 'pleasures') of ordinary people can only be understood by actually doing it. As Frow points out:

> In the absence of realized texts which can be subject to determinate analysis – in the absence of a definite and graspable object – the analyst will inevitably reconstruct such an object. ... [The result of which] ... is a politically fraught substitution of the voice of a middle-class intellectual for that of the users of popular culture; and it is characteristically in the space of this substitution that the category of the popular is constructed. (1991: 60)

De Certeau's polar model of domination has high romantic quality. But it totally discounts that viewers will try to explain and legitimize their media use. It might well be the case that we have to do without academic understanding of the transient and fleeting qualities of media use, and that using 'meaninglessness' as a descriptive label is an act of power that delimits a proper space for academic knowledge. But for a researcher there is more to be found in interview transcripts, be it fragmented and in bits and pieces here and there, than either de Certeau or Frow would give one reason to believe. The issue is to understand the relative importance of the media text and media use. Relative, that is, to other practices people engage in at the same time. These other practices, in the case of such media use as reading women's magazines or viewing television, will quite often be routines that can be described; for the practices themselves exists widely spread legitimatory discourse. The two together, descriptions of routines and legitimatory discourse, add up to a strong description of how media are used, that put 'meaninglessness' in perspective and make it researchable by default as it were, as a residue. The superficiality of interview transcripts that deal with the most ordinary of media use is a warning sign but not an impregnable barrier.

It is my point of view that people are rational, social actors who within the limited space and means available to them will have good reasons for doing the things they do, even if these 'good reasons' cannot always be clearly stated or articulated. Going back to the interview transcripts, there seem to be two sources of knowledge that one may draw on to come to an understanding of everyday media use. In the accounts people gave me they explained about their daily routines (which is one source), superimposed on these routines, specific legitimatory discourse, schemata that explain and justify media use, can be recognized. These schemata I will call interpretive repertoires. To analyze how media texts are made sense of, I propose that one has to make these repertoires explicit. Secondly, one has to map the sedimented, everyday routines readers give accounts of, on to how they have come to understand themselves as readers and viewers over the years, bearing in mind that for most this is accepted knowledge, not something to question or reflect upon.

During the course of my peregrinations I taped interviews with about sixty women, fifteen men and the occasional child ...

I asked these readers to tell me about their 'reading histories', their everyday lives, their ambitions and their use of women's magazines and other mass media. The interviews were modelled on everyday lengthy conversation, as between friends. Most of the interview usually wasn't taken up with women's magazines but with my respondents describing themselves, their lives and their specific vantage points on life. While trying to explain how they read and chose particular magazines, apart from wandering off to tell me about themselves (encouraged, usually, by me – as these stories provided me with much needed background information that made other things that were said more comprehensible), readers would in a pragmatic and functionalist way use different interpretive repertoires. Interpretive repertoires are defined by Jonathan Potter and Margaret Wetherell as common interpretations or 'recurrently used systems of terms, used for characterizing and evaluating actions, events and other phenomena' (1987: 149).

[...]

Reconstructing the repertoires readers use resembles simultaneously doing a series of jigsaw puzzles. In the interviews one will find bits and pieces of different repertoires. Combined, the interviews will allow a number of repertoires, or regularities really, to emerge. The repertoires are an explanatory and justificatory discursive system. As Western culture is a class-based culture, justificatory systems come in hierarchies. (See Bourdieu, 1980.) Some ways of describing why and how one views, television or reads women's magazines are more legitimate than others.

[...]

As regards women's magazines, repertoires that underline the practical use of women's magazines and that one can learn from them (about human mature, relationships, oneself) are clearly the most legitimate. ... Reading women's magazines these repertoires say, is not wasting your time on drivel, or, taking time for yourself. One is keeping up with the trade journals to do the best possible job caring and providing for one's family. Again, a repertoire running counter to this one is mentioned as well, although it is much less clear or articulate. It mainly describes reading as a very pleasurable and relaxing activity; what is actually read may vary. Some respondents had a clear order in which they'd read what was available. One of the men I interviewed would read the free broadsheets with local news that are financed by advertising revenue after he had finished the newspaper and then read *Viva*, a magazine his wife buys occasionally, when he comes home from work and makes himself a cup of tea.

Another much used and legitimate repertoire to talk about magazines ranging from feminist magazines and glossies to traditional and gossip magazines was the therapeutical repertoire: a way to stress how one may learn about oneself by reading about the experiences of others. ... Remarkably, the only repertoire that counters outright 'legitimate' reasons for reading, is a repertoire voiced usually by men. It is rooted in camp readings of popular culture. It presents the reader as one who has set out to 'rise below the vulgar'.[5] This is a repertoire strongly tied to gay subculture which bespeaks a totally different relation *vis-à-vis* the cultural spectrum. ... To reconstruct these repertoires from the interview transcripts involved a considerable *tour de force* that would make any self-respecting researcher slightly suspicious of the value of such a reconstruction. To understand these repertoires as what reading women's magazines is about, is to grossly misread the interview transcripts. The repertoires are available cultural sources to explain and justify reading women's magazines and a range of other cultural practices. More important to understanding how women's magazines become meaningful are the everyday routines that over the years constitute specific reading histories, the historical counterpart to the contemporary repertoires.

Reading histories offer a different kind of understanding of how women's magazines become meaningful than do simple accounts of where, when and how magazines are read or than mapping available interpretative repertoires does. Reading histories evaluate routines and reading magazines or watching television in their own way, closely related to personal histories, to periods of uncomplicated making-do as well as to rupture and change, encompassing a series of understandings of the self. Going back and forth between everyday routines and understandings of the self, one is given a picture of how life for people is structured by having to go out to work, taking care of children, or pursuing education. Thus, a link can be forged between reading women's magazines, living one's life the way one does and how society is structured. Obviously, most of the stories one is told are safe stories to tell. Only occasionally and usually by chance one gets an inkling of the unfinished business people have to find ways to deal with: feeling unhappy in a marriage, having post-natal depression. Such things will be of some importance in what one will read and how. A historical perspective on daily life and routines, I expect, is the closest social research will come to understanding how everyday life is a mixture of being much the same from year to year and sudden, radical changes.

Everyday talk is not self-reflective. It is pragmatic, it is used to explain and to justify and therefore is no easy way to come to understand how women's magazines (or other media) are made sense of. Solely understanding how people come to love texts that offer spellbinding escape, a learning experience, suspense, moral outrage or good melodrama that carries one off, is equivalent to understanding the media landscape to be Nepal: nothing but peaks. Such a view easily confuses the ordinary viewer with a media critic: someone who has built up a specific knowledge of a particular kind of text. Media use is also a fleeting, transient experience that doesn't leave much trace except in how everyday practices are structured. There seems to be a gradual slope along which media use will slowly change from an intense, well-defined experience into an inextricable part of everyday life, in which the media text as such has no meaning of its own. I can see no other way to understand such media use, than by reconstructing how routines have led to specific ways of understanding the self and how this informs how a reader will feel about the magazines she reads, the television programmes she watches and by making explicit the repertoires that are used to describe and legitimate media use.

An analysis that, on the one hand, starts from everyday routines and, on the other, from repertoires, politically and epistemologically enriches our understanding of media use. Politically, by recognizing the double-edgedness of everyday life, i.e., by recognizing the repetitiveness and the legitimatory force of everyday life as well as its being a site of personal and social change, the image of ordinary viewers as being cultural dupes is undermined. The repertoires, politically, can be used to criticise dominant interpretations; despite their hierarchical organization repertoires will change over time.

Epistemologically, recognizing the importance of routines for media use, means that text and context cannot always be distinguished from one another, consequently the media text as such never becomes fully meaningful. Furthermore, the two sides to routines entails recognizing their internal dynamic which underlines that there is no essential meaning that can be actualized nor is there an essential viewing mode or practice of media use. A repertoire approach, last but not least, has the invaluable advantage of not imposing academic standards on everyday discourse; it doesn't require closure or consistency. It works with rather than against the contradictions no one in an everyday context feels are necessary to sort out.

NOTES

1. They may be less represented in Morley's interviews because he interviewed a group of families who for all of their lives had been living in the same area (1986: 53). The point is that he did not choose to read them that way.
2. Examples are Livingstone (1990) on soap opera viewers; Ang (1985) on watching *Dallas*; Walkerdine (1986) on a family's use of a Rocky video; Radway (1984) on romance reading.
3. E.g., Livingstone (1990); Schrøder (1988); Ang (1985); Radway (1984).
4. Gray (1992 and 1987); Morley (1986).
5. As Mel Brooks put it, quoted in Ross (1989: 153).

REFERENCES

Ang, Ien (1985) *Watching Dallas. Soap Opera and the Melodramatic Imagination*, London and New York: Methuen.

Ang, Ien and Joke Hermes (1991) 'Gender and/in media consumption', in James Curran and Michael Gurevitch (1991) editors, *Mass Communication and Society*, London: Edward Arnold: 307–28.

Bausinger, Herman (1984) 'Media, technology and daily life', *Media, Culture and Society* 6 (1984) 343–51.

Bech Jørgensen, Birte (1990) 'The impossibility of everyday life', in *Every Cloud has a Silver Liming. Lectures on Everyday Life, Cultural Production and Race*, Flemming Røgilds (1990) editor, Studies in Cultural Sociology, No. 28, Copenhagen: Akademisk Forlag: 20–8.

Bourdieu, Pierre (1980) 'The aristocracy of culture', *Media, Culture and Society* 2(3) 225–54.

Certeau, Michel de (1984) *The Practice of Everyday Life*, trans. Steven Randall, Berkeley, Los Angeles: University of California Press.

Frow, John (1991) 'Michel de Certeau and the practice of representation', *Cultural Studies* 5(1) 52–60.

Gray, Ann (1987) 'Behind closed doors: video recorders in the home', in Helen Baehr and Gillian Dyer (1987) editors, *Boxed In: Women and Television*, New York and London: Pandora: 38–54.

—— (1992) *Video Playtime: The Gendering of a Leisure Technology*, London: Comedia/Routledge.

Hall, Stuart (1986) 'Introduction', in Morley (1986) 7–10.

Livingstone, Sonia (1990) *Making Sense of Television*, Oxford: Pergamon.

Morley, David (1986) *Family Television, Cultural Power and Domestic Leisure*, London: Comedia.

Potter, Jonathan and Margaret Wetherell (1987) *Discourse and Social Psychology*, London: Sage.

Radway, Janice (1984) *Reading the Romance, Women, Patriarchy and Popular Literature*, Chapel Hill and London: The University of North Carolina Press.

Ross, Andrew (1989) *No Respect. Intellectuals and Popular Culture*, New York and London: Routledge.

Schrøder, Kim Christian (1988) 'The pleasure of Dynasty: the weekly reconstruction of self-confidence', in Philip Drummond and Richard Paterson (1988) editors, *Television and its Audience*. London: BFI: 61–82.

Schutz, Alfred (1973) 'On multiple realities', in *Collected Papers I*, The Hague: Martinus Nijhoff: 207–59.

Walkerdine, Valerie (1986) 'Video Replay: families, films and fantasy', in Victor Burgin, James Donald and Cora Kaplan (1986) editors, *Formations of Fantasy*, London and New York: Methuen: 167–99.

FURTHER READING

Ang, I., *Living Room Wars: Rethinking Media Audiences for a Postmodern World* (London and New York: Routledge, 1996).

Ang, I. and Hermes, J., 'Gender and/in Media Consumption'. In J. Curran and M. Gurevitch (eds), *Mass Media and Society* (London: Edward Arnold, 1991).

Bausinger, H., 'Media, Technology and Daily Life'. *Media, Culture and Society* 6:4 (1984) pp. 345–51.

Featherstone, M., *Consumer Culture and Postmodernism* (London: Sage, 1991).

Fiske, J., *Power Plays/Power Works* (London: Verso, 1993).

Gray, A., *Video Playtime; the Gendering of a Leisure Technology* (London: Comedia/ Routledge, 1992).

Grossberg, L., 'Wandering Audiences, Nomadic Critics'. In *Cultural Studies* 2:3 (1988) pp. 377–91.

Hartley, J., 'Invisible Fictions: Television Audiences, Paedocracy, Pleasure'. *Textual Practice* 1:2 (1987) pp. 253–74.

Hartley, J., *Tele-Ology: Studies in Television* (London: Routledge, 1992).

Hermes, J., 'Media, Meaning and Everyday Life'. *Cultural Studies* 7:3 (1993) pp. 493–506.

Hermes, J., *Reading Women's Magazines* (Cambridge: Polity Press, 1995).

Jenkins, H., *Textual Poachers: Television Fans and Participatory Culture* (London and New York: Routledge, 1992).

Kolar-Panov, D., 'Video and the Diasporic Imagination of Selfhood: A Case Study of the Croatians in Australia'. *Cultural Studies* 10:2 (1996) pp. 288–314.

Lewis, L. A. (ed), *The Adoring Audience: Fan Culture and Popular Media* (London and New York: Routledge, 1992).

McGuigan, J., *Cultural Populism* (London: Routledge, 1992).

McRobbie, A., *Postmodernism and Popular Culture* (London: Routledge, 1994).

Morley, D., 'Where the Global meets the Local: Notes from the Sitting Room'. *Screen* 32:1 (1991) pp. 1–15.

Morley, D., *Television, Audiences and Cultural Studies* (London: Routledge, 1992).

Morley, D. and Robins, K., 'Spaces of Identity: Communications, Technologies and the reconfiguration of Europe'. *Screen* 30:4 (1989) pp. 10–34.

Morley, D. and Silverstone, R., 'Domestic Communications: Technologies and Meanings'. *Media, Culture and Society* 12:1 (1990) pp. 31–55.

Morris, M., 'Banality in Cultural Studies', in P. Mellencamp (ed.), *Logics of Television: Essays in Cultural Criticism* (Bloomington: Indiana University Press, 1990).

Naficy, H., *The Making of Exile Cultures: Iranian Television in Los Angeles* (Minneapolis: University of Minnesota Press, 1993).

Nightingale, V., 'What's "Ethnographic" about Ethnographic Audience Research?'. *Australian Journal of Communication* 16 (1989) pp. 50–63.

Nightingale, V., *Studying Audiences: The Shock of the Real* (London: Routledge, 1996).

Rose, A. and Friedman, J., 'Television Sport as Mas(s)culine Cult of Distraction'. *Screen* 35:1 (1994) pp. 22–35.

Shields, R., *Lifestyle Shopping: The Subject of Consumption* (London: Routledge, 1992).

Silverstone, R., 'Television and Everyday Life: Towards an Anthropology of the Television Audience'. In M. Ferguson (ed.), *Public Communication: The New Imperatives* (London: Sage, 1990).

Silverstone, R., 'From Audiences to Consumers: The Household and the Consumption of Information and Communication Technologies'. *European Journal of Communication* 6:2 (1991) pp. 135–54.

Silverstone, R. and Hirsch, E. (eds), *Consuming Technologies: Media and Information in Domestic Spaces* (London: Routledge, 1992).

Stacey, J., *Star Gazing: Hollywood Cinema and Female Spectatorship* (London: Routledge, 1994).

Walkerdine, V., 'Video Replay: Families, Films and Fantasy', in V. Burgin, J. Donald and C. Kaplan (eds), *Formations of Fantasy* (London: Methuen, 1986).

Walkerdine, V., *Daddy's Girl: Young Girls and Popular Culture* (Basingstoke and London: Macmillan, 1997).

PART TWO
CASE STUDIES

SECTION 5
SOAP OPERA

SOAP OPERA
INTRODUCTION

Over the past twenty years, soap opera has moved from being an object of academic and popular contempt to a major area of media study.[1] Much of the research which has contributed to this shift has been produced by feminist scholars, and can be seen as part of a wider commitment within feminist research to the re-evaluation of popular forms aimed at and enjoyed by women.[2] If this political commitment is one hallmark of feminist work on soap opera, a second is its focus upon the relationship of the popular text to its audience and the question of where, in this relationship, lies the power to determine meaning. This concern takes up many of the issues raised in Sections 3.3 and 4.2–4.3 above, in particular that of the relationship between the 'ideal' spectator constructed, or envisaged, by the text, and the socially situated 'real' spectator who reads, enjoys, and uses it. More recently, the soap opera form – always more variable than some critics have presented it – has itself undergone further shifts. Both the 'postmodern soap opera' (*Twin Peaks* is an example) and the 'docusoap' have appeared. In the latter, we can see a further blurring of the boundaries between fiction and 'real life' – always difficult to draw in the case of soap opera – as the 'soap' becomes the mode through which are represented the private lives of 'ordinary people'.

The extract from David Buckingham's *Public Secrets: EastEnders and its Audience* (Chapter 45), which opens the section, focuses on the production determinants of the genre. In this chapter, which details the launch of the BBC's new soap opera in 1985, Buckingham describes the programme's promotion as a 'product', designed to fulfil a key role in the BBC's search for ratings and the reconstruction of its 'rather staid and middle-class "Auntie" image' – extremely important to the Corporation at a time in the mid-1980s when it was under threat from government moves towards privatisation. The extract also shows the problems which a popular soap like *EastEnders* can pose for a public service institution like the BBC, whose dominant discourse of 'quality' in television drama adapts uneasily, and not without contradiction, to a popular success like *EastEnders*.

The chapter by Tania Modleski (Chapter 46) which follows, focuses on the gendered address of soap opera. Modleski analyses soap opera's structural features (its lack of resolution and closure, its multiple and interrupted narratives and shifting points of identification, its constant use of close-ups and use of dialogue as gossip) in relation both to psychoanalytically informed theories of female subjectivity and to the rhythms of women's work in the home. Insisting that in their address to women's desires and 'collective fantasies', soap operas not only allay '*real* anxieties', and satisfy '*real* needs' but can also be said to make a contribution to the development of a feminist aesthetics, she is nevertheless critical. Soap operas may satisfy real needs and desires, but it also distorts them. Like Radway (Chapter 39), she argues that feminists must find new and more empowering ways of meeting the utopian needs and desires which are at present expressed through mass cultural forms like soap opera.

Charlotte Brunsdon's 1981 article (Chapter 47) asks what we mean when we assume a gendered audience for soap opera. Are we talking about a quality of the *text* – a 'feminine' subject position which it constructs for its spectator – or the member of the audience who is of course already gendered when she watches it? Her answer draws an important distinction between the subject positions proposed for their readers by texts and a 'social subject' who may or may not take up these positions. Brunsdon argues that in both their narrative structures and their 'moral and ideological frameworks', soap operas demand and set in play specific understandings and assumptions, discourses and cultural competencies which our society traditionally genders feminine. In turn, these 'repertoires of understandings and assumptions' about personal and familial relationships and 'traditionally feminine competencies' in managing the domestic sphere, are more likely to be possessed by female viewers. Thus, the gendered address of soap opera is both appeal to and also helps to construct the 'femininity' of its audiences.

It is the 'social subject' of Brunsdon's model which is the object of investigation in the chapter by Dorothy Hobson (Chapter 48). This extract from Hobson's (1982) study of the producers and audience of ATV's soap opera, *Crossroads* (1964–88), is taken from her ethnographic study of the viewers of the Midlands soap opera. Hobson went into the homes of viewers, watched the programme with these women and their families, and then discussed with them the meanings and pleasures which they found in it. Her conclusion, that 'there are as many different Crossroads as there are viewers', very much asserts the power of the audience in determining the meanings (and definition) of a text, and can be contrasted in this respect with Modleski's work. Indeed, her observation that 'the audience do not watch programmes as separate or indi-vidual items' can be seen as preparing the way for the later work of John Fiske and Henry Jenkins (Chapters 42 and 43), in which audiences are viewed as being free to construct their own meanings, and the power of the text (and of its producers) disappears completely.

The final chapter in this section (Chapter 49) takes us into the postmodern world of the 'docusoap'. Jon Stratton and Ien Ang's analysis of the 1992 British-made study of a 'typical' Australian family, *Sylvania Waters*, focuses on the 'intimate connection between television and the family', and hence to tele-vision's role in the construction of myths of a stable nation. The utopian ideal of family has underpinned soap opera – even if its actual families are always seen to be in crisis – and rendered it a key site for the negotiation of gendered roles and regional and national identities. Now, however, argue Stratton and Ang, the 'explosion' of the nuclear family has destabilised the soap opera form, and rendered it unable to perform this function. *Sylvania Waters*, doubly coded as both documentary and soap opera, represents both the postmodern family (hardly a nuclear family at all) and the postmodern transformation of the soap opera form. In it, the boundaries between fiction and fact have disappeared, and its protagonists become soap 'stars', coded as 'good' or 'bad' characters, the 'reality' of their lives absorbed into spectacle. *Sylvania Waters*, then, becomes a 'simulation', rather than (re)presentation, of 'an Australian family'. Its 'specta-cular' family exists as image with no utopian ideal against which it might be set, and indicates the collapse of television's (and soap opera's) ability to 'represent the nation to itself'.

NOTES

1. This is not to deny that important research on soap opera was carried out before this period. See, in particular, Herta Herzog, 'On Borrowed Experience: An Analysis of Listening to Daytime Sketches' in *Studies in Philosophy and Social Science*, 9, 1 (1941), and 'What do we Really Know about Daytime Serial Listeners?' in P. F. Lazarsfeld and F. M. Stanton (eds), *Radio Research: 1942–1943* (New York: Duell, Sloan & Pearce, 1944).
2. See, for example, the work by Janice Radway on romance (*Reading the Romance*, London: Verso, 1987), Janice Winship on women's magazines (*Inside Women's Magazines*, London: Pandora Press, 1987), and Tania Modleski on Harlequin romances and Gothic novels (*Loving with a Vengeance: Mass Produced Fantasies for Women*, London: Methuen, 1984). See also Chapters 39 and 26 in this volume.

45

EASTENDERS: CREATING THE AUDIENCE

David Buckingham

GRABBING THE RATINGS?

The BBC's decision to produce a new bi-weekly continuing serial dates back to 1981, well before the concern about declining viewing figures became a matter of urgency. The initial 'in principle' decision was made by Bill Cotton, then Controller of BBC1, and the early planning was commissioned by his successor, Alan Hart.

Michael Grade, who subsequently inherited *EastEnders*, certainly perceived its value in terms of the competition for ratings, and in particular as a means of increasing the BBC's early evening share, which had slumped to little more than half that of ITV:

> I think it was clear to the BBC that one of the reasons for the discrepancy in the share between ITV's audience and the BBC's audience was down to *Coronation Street*, *Emmerdale Farm* and *Crossroads*. The BBC did not have anything of that kind in its locker. ITV certainly didn't invent the soap opera. The BBC were doing *The Groves* and *Mrs Dale's Diary* and *The Archers* years before. So it was nothing new for the BBC to be in the soap business. But it had somehow gotten out of the soap business over the years, and it seemed the right time to get back into it, as a means also to boost the early evening schedule, which had been languishing for some time.[1]

From David Buckingham, *Public Secrets*: EastEnders *and its Audience* (London: BFI, 1987) pp. 7–33.

The choice of a continuing serial as a means of building ratings would therefore appear at first sight to be an obvious one. Yet there were clearly significant risks. A new serial would involve a far greater financial outlay than any of the likely alternatives, such as game shows. While the running costs of a regular soap opera are comparatively small, it takes many years to recoup the substantial initial investment, and an early exit from the schedules would mean financial disaster as well as public embarrassment.

Furthermore, the number of soaps already being screened led many to doubt whether the public would be willing to accept yet another: indeed, the BBC's first audience research report on the subject in early 1984 concluded that enthusiasm for a new bi-weekly serial was 'at best moderate'.[2] The BBC's own past experience with continuing television serials could hardly be said to inspire confidence either: although 1970s serials like *The Brothers* and *Angels* had done fairly well in terms of ratings, and had lasted for several years, they had not been screened continuously for the full 52 weeks. The BBC's only experience in producing continuing serials on television was as long ago as the 1960s, with *Compact* (1962–65), *United* (1965–67) and *The Newcomers* (1965–69), of which only the first had achieved any substantial success in the ratings.

[...]

The decision to opt for a continuing serial was thus not merely informed by the desire to reach a large audience. Soap operas possess a symbolic importance for television institutions, above and beyond their function in terms of ratings. By building a loyal audience, often over decades, they can become a highly significant element in the way viewers perceive the institutions themselves. *Coronation Street*, for example, can be seen as providing a specific regional identity for Granada Television, despite the fact that the majority of its productions have no such regional flavour. If, as recent research has suggested, popular perceptions of the BBC remain to some extent tied to the rather staid and middle-class 'Auntie' image, a successful soap opera could clearly do much to alter these.[3]

Jonathan Powell, who became Head of Series & Serials in November 1983, and played a key role in the development of *EastEnders*, felt that a continuing serial could also serve as an important training ground for new talent, just as *Coronation Street* has done at Granada. Using new writers and directors alongside more experienced ones would provide his own department, and the industry in general, with 'a substantial injection of talent'.

While Powell acknowledged *EastEnders'* considerable strategic value in terms of ratings, he also saw it as filling a gap in the overall spread of drama programming:

> It was clearly an area of popular drama in which the BBC wasn't offering something to the public. ... I think that the point of any department in the BBC as a matter of fact – although it's not my business to say so – is to

offer the correct balance of material across the whole spectrum of taste. And I think that a drama department of this size without a bi-weekly is a drama department without a very important linchpin in the panoply of ground that it's covering.[4]

At the same time, Jonathan Powell and Michael Grade refuted the suggestion that *EastEnders* was merely a means of keeping the mass audience happy, and thereby enabling the BBC to get on with its real business of producing 'serious' television: both were keen to emphasise its dramatic 'quality' and the 'responsibility' with which it dealt with controversial issues. *EastEnders* was regarded as tangible proof that popularity did not necessarily mean 'catering to the lowest common denominator'.

If the drive for ratings was therefore not the only motivation behind the decision to produce *EastEnders*, it certainly assumed a central significance in the period immediately before and subsequent to its launch in February 1985. The Peacock Committee, the latest in a series of government enquiries into the running of the BBC, appeared set to recommend a degree of privatisation, which many advocates of public service broadcasting saw as the thin end of a very thick wedge which would eventually destroy the Corporation. More was clearly at stake in the 'Soap Wars' so enthusiastically reported by the tabloid press than the success or failure of individual programmes. If the supremacy of *Coronation Street* was in some sense symbolic of ITV's overall dominance of the ratings, the failure of *EastEnders* would doubtless have been seized upon with relish by the BBC's enemies.

[...]

LOCATING THE SERIAL

In re-entering the highly competitive 'soap business', the BBC inevitably had to exercise a considerable degree of caution. Key decisions in planning the serial had to be made with extreme care and forethought, as they would for the most part be impossible to reverse once the programme was on the air. The price of failure, in terms of both money and reputation, was very high indeed.

The choice of a location for the serial was clearly crucial, and required a number of considerations to be held in the balance.

[...]

As an area which has historically been populated by waves of different immigrant groups, and which has recently begun to be 'gentrified', the East End would provide a setting which could plausibly contain a broad mixture of characters. Furthermore, it would allow a greater potential for turnover of new characters, thus enabling the serial to remain contemporary – a distinct advantage over the relatively static community of *Coronation Street*, which they felt had become stuck in a 'timewarp' of the early 1960s, when it had been originated.

Like Julia Smith and Tony Holland[*], Jonathan Powell felt that the East End location would provide 'roots' and 'identity', 'an attractive folklore and a sense of history', which was essential for the genre. He also argued that a 'flagship' programme like a continuing serial should provide a regional identity for the BBC, even though the Corporation as a whole has a national role. If the independent television companies had soap operas set in their own regions, then the BBC's should, he felt, be set in London.

Logistical factors were also significant here. In 1983 the BBC had purchased Elstree Studios, just outside London, from the independent company Central Television. Although the location of the new serial had not yet been decided at this stage, Elstree was clearly earmarked for it. While it would theoretically have been possible to make the programme at Elstree and set it in Manchester, Julia Smith was strongly opposed to the idea. In order to achieve the degree of authenticity she felt was essential, actors would have to be moved from Manchester down to London, and the cost of this operation would certainly have been prohibitive.

[...]

The balance of characters also had clear implications in terms of the kind of audience *EastEnders* was attempting to build. Prior to the launch of the BBC's new early evening package, its audience at this time of day tended to be predominantly middle-aged and middle-class. In order to broaden that audience, *EastEnders* would have to appeal both to younger and older viewers, and also to the working-class audience which traditionally watched ITV. The choice of a working-class setting, and the broad age range of the characters thus also made a good deal of sense in terms of ratings.

In addition, *EastEnders* sought to extend the traditional audience for British soaps, which is weighted towards women and towards the elderly. Having a number of strong younger characters, it was argued, meant that the programme would have a greater appeal for young viewers than other British soaps, as well as providing a means of regenerating the narrative in the longer term. Strong male characters would also serve to bring in male viewers who were traditionally suspicious of the genre. Julia Smith had a definite idea of her potential audience profile:

> I'm not going for the stereotypical middle-class, BBC audience. The professional classes won't get home early enough to see the programme. I expect the audience to consist of working people who watch television around tea-time before going to bingo or the pub. Soap operas traditionally appeal to women, but we have to remember that men watch them too – even if they don't admit to it. And with at least five teenagers in the cast I expect to pick up a lot of young viewers.[5]

[...]

THE LAUNCH

After almost a year of frenetic activity, *EastEnders* was launched at 7 p.m. on 19 February 1985. Julia Smith's original target date of September 1984 had been postponed twice: firstly at the instigation of the new Controller of BBC1, Michael Grade, who had preferred a January start; and secondly when *East-Enders'* companion in the BBC's new early evening package, the chat show *Wogan*, had not been ready in time. Julia Smith was certainly uneasy about the late start: *EastEnders* no longer had the long winter months in which to build up a loyal following before the summer downturn in the ratings.

If the initial projections of *EastEnders'* audience size had been relatively modest, the publicity which surrounded its launch was rather less so. In an unprecedented move, the BBC had appointed a publicity officer specifically to promote the new serial. The programme had been trailed in *Radio Times* and on screen for many weeks beforehand, leading many newspaper critics to accuse the BBC of 'hype'. An ostentatious press launch, complete with lavish press pack and 'showbiz walkpast' of the cast, only fuelled their scepticism. The high profile certainly succeeded in giving the programme public visibility – and encouraged as many as 13 million viewers to tune in to the first episode – but it also increased the risks attached to failure. If *EastEnders* was going to make mistakes, it would do so in the public eye, without the opportunity to ease itself in gently.

[...]

One major reason for *EastEnders'* eventual success in the ratings was its careful scheduling. Michael Grade had arrived at the BBC with a reputation derived from his work at London Weekend Television of being a scheduling wizard. One of the problems he had identified very early on was the lack of fixed points in the BBC schedule – and in particular in the early evening. *EastEnders* and *Wogan*, in addition to pulling ratings, would also provide a much-needed stability at the start of the evening's viewing. The sheer longevity of a soap opera was also a significant point in its favour: as Grade observed, the BBC's past attempts to dent the ratings for *Coronation Street*, for example by scheduling a popular situation comedy against it, had only proved successful in the short term.

At the same time, Grade did not subscribe to the view that 'inheritance' was all-important – the idea that if you caught an audience at the start of the evening, it would stay with you until close down. Particularly in an era of remote control keypads, this approach was largely outdated. Nevertheless, if *EastEnders* were to be followed by a sequence of popular programmes, it would certainly go a long way to increase the BBC's overall audience share:

> If you've got good programmes that are following it, the audience look at it as a package. They say, 'Right, I'll watch BBC from 7.00 to 9.00 and

then I'll switch to ITV because I want to watch their drama.' They'll watch a package of programmes, with a gem like that in the middle which attracts. So there is a package idea, but the pieces around it have to be the right pieces.

Nevertheless, the initial decision to schedule *EastEnders* at 7 p.m. represented something of a gamble since it meant competing with ITV's *Emmerdale Farm*, a rural soap opera with a steady and respectable share of the ratings. Michael Grade described this first phase of the 'Soap Wars' with considerable relish:

> I put *EastEnders* at 7.00 because *Emmerdale Farm* was not networked. As a response to it going at 7.00, ITV for once got its act together and networked *Emmerdale Farm*. That was a blow, but I knew – from my knowledge of ITV – that *Emmerdale Farm* went off the air in the summer for a number of weeks, and I only had to wait for that window, and then I would be away. What they did was that they somehow squeezed extra episodes and repeats, so there was no break in the clouds. So I thought, this is crazy, this is silly now, I'm going to have to move it. And because of the sort of press we have in this country, I didn't want them rubbishing the show – 'panic move' – they'd have written that as a failure story. I had to dress up the presentation of that move in such a way as to protect the show, so I gave all kinds of reasons for the move, trying to disguise the fact that I was having to move it because it had reached a plateau and wasn't moving off.

[. . .]

Following the shift to 7.30 in September 1985, *EastEnders'* ratings began a meteoric rise which eventually peaked at around 23 million in February and March of 1986. This rise coincided with the regular seasonal upturn in the ratings, and also with the ending of the latest series of *Dallas*, but *EastEnders'* climb to the top of the ratings charts was both faster and earlier than even its most enthusiastic advocates could have expected. The appreciation indices also continued to rise, averaging a phenomenal 85 in the early months of the new year. Studies of the demographic profile of the audience showed that the programme was successfully reaching a genuine cross-section of the population in a way that no British soap opera had previously managed to do, and that it was particularly popular with teenagers, traditionally the least captive section of the television audience. Ironically, qualitative research suggested that it was precisely those features which had initially been found alienating – and in particular its abrasive treatment of 'social issues' – which viewers were now ready to praise.

[. . .]

SERVING THE PUBLIC

EastEnders' extraordinary popularity nevertheless means that it enjoys a rather ambiguous relationship with the 'official' Reithian definition of 'public service broadcasting'. The charge of 'catering to the lowest common denominator' could be made not only by the BBC's enemies, but also by those within the Corporation who believe in broadcasting as a means of uplifting public taste. While Tony Holland agreed that the BBC had allowed Julia Smith and himself a considerable degree of autonomy, he also acknowledged that their work was 'very commercial', and in some respects had more in common with the ethos of independent television than with that of the BBC. For example, part of the 'craft of script-making', as he defined it, lay in knowing the correct time of year to 'blow the big story': getting in a good story at Christmas meant that you might stand some chance of keeping your audience until Easter, despite the seasonal drop in the ratings.

> We are, in that sense, not typical of the BBC. It has been considered for some years, although I think it's changing, that to actually promote a product – and we're the only people in the BBC that I know of who call our show a product – a lot of people in the corridors of power think it's terribly vulgar. But we like the packaging, we like the promotion, we like the hype.[6]

As Holland indicated, this Reithian view of public service broadcasting is gradually changing, although it remains influential. Michael Grade and Jonathan Powell both contested the view that popularity was incompatible with the principle of public service – a view which they described as both outdated and condescending:

> MICHAEL GRADE That's a patronising argument by people who believe that the BBC should be an elitist ghetto of cultural high ground, inaccessible to the working classes, or inaccessible to people who aren't highly educated, appreciative of the finer things of life.

At the same time, they refuted the suggestion that *EastEnders* was primarily about 'grabbing the ratings', or about popularity at any price. The idea that it was 'a lowest common denominator show' was incorrect, both on the basis of its broad demographic appeal, and on the grounds of its 'quality':

> JONATHAN POWELL If we really wanted to grab the ratings, we wouldn't make *EastEnders* like we make *EastEnders*. I think *EastEnders* has attracted a large audience because it's good, it's mature, it's grown up and it talks to people on their level. It talks to them on a mature level. It's an entertainment programme, fine: but entertainment is not a dirty word. It addresses, within a quite wide interpretation of an entertainment format, quite significant and human problems. There are good episodes and there are bad episodes, sure, but there are 104 a year, so there are

bound to be. But there are episodes of *EastEnders* which I would frankly be very happy to put up as a one-off play.

Significantly, although popularity is clearly valued, 'quality' is still defined here by standards which derive from the 'cultural high ground' of the single play.

While Grade and Powell were therefore keen to argue the case for *East-Enders* as 'quality' television, they were also aware of its strategic role within the broader range of BBC programming, and within the context of public criticism of the Corporation. There was a sense in which the popularity of *EastEnders* enabled other, less popular, programmes to exist:

> JONATHAN POWELL I'm sure it helps our image to have programmes like this. I'm sure it helps to attract people to other programmes. And it creates space, too. ... You have to create your space, allow yourself the space for specialised programming. It works when the balance is right. I don't think this department works with just *EastEnders* and *Bergerac*, but equally I don't think it just works with *Bleak House* and *Edge of Darkness*. They all complement each other.

Michael Grade argued that the BBC had always been in the business of producing popular programmes, although in the current context a major success like *EastEnders* could perform a particularly important function for the Corporation as a whole:

> It's a problem for our enemies, because they don't want us to be popular. If we weren't popular, then there is a case for breaking up the BBC and selling it off to private enterprise. We do stand in the way of a lot of people making a lot of money. My belief is that we need to be popular, but we don't need to be popular all the time, every day, every week of the year. We need to *prove* that we can be as popular as the other side with quality programmes when we want to be.

In many ways these comments reflect the broader dilemma which has faced public service broadcasting in this country since the introduction of commercial television, and which was brought to a head in the period immediately preceding the launch of *EastEnders*. On the one hand, the BBC is obliged to justify its monopoly over the licence fee by producing programmes of artistic 'quality' and 'responsibility'. Yet on the other hand, that monopoly can only be sustained if the BBC is seen to speak to the nation as a whole, rather than to a privileged minority, and it is therefore obliged to compete with ITV for a reasonable share of the mass audience. As Michael Grade argued, the BBC has always resisted the idea of catering merely to the educated middle class, yet in the context of a dwindling audience share, and a government committed to 'free market' economics, its delicate attempts to retain a balance between popular and minority tastes have inevitably been fraught with uncertainty.[7]

[...]

The very popularity of *EastEnders* thus highlights a number of tensions and contradictions in the relationships between the broadcasting institution, the programme-makers and the audience.

On the one hand, the programme has clearly served a very useful function for the BBC, in a period of increasing uncertainty. As a significant element within its early evening schedule, it has managed to maximise ratings, and to reverse the downturn in its audience share, thereby staving off a certain amount of public criticism. Yet, on the other hand, its success has also provoked further attacks on the Corporation from those on the political Right. *EastEnders* has been seen as a symptom of the BBC's abandonment of its 'public service' obligations, whereby 'quality' and 'responsibility' have simply been sacrificed in a cynical drive for ratings.

[...]

NOTES

1. All quotations from Michael Grade are taken from an interview with the author.
2. BBC Broadcasting Research Special Report, *Bi-Weekly Serial: The Appeal of Different Regional and Social Class Concepts*, February 1984.
3. Laurie Taylor and Bob Mullan, *Uninvited Guests: the Intimate Secrets of Television and Radio* (London: Chatto & Windus, 1986).
4. All quotations from Jonathan Powell are taken from an interview with the author.
5. *Broadcast*, 26 October 1984.
6. All quotations from Julia Smith and Tony Holland are taken from an interview with the author, unless otherwise indicated.
7. For a useful account of contemporary developments, see Michael Leapman, *The Last Days of the Beeb* (London: Allen & Unwin, 1986).

Editors' Note

* Julia Smith and Tony Holland, producer and script-editor, originators of the *East-Enders* proposal.

46

THE SEARCH FOR TOMORROW
IN TODAY'S SOAP OPERAS

Tania Modleski

[...]

Whereas the meaning of Harlequin Romances depends almost entirely on the sense of an ending, soap operas are important to their viewers in part because they never end. Whereas Harlequins encourage our identification with one character, soap operas invite identification with numerous personalities. And whereas Harlequins are structured around two basic enigmas, in soap operas, the enigmas proliferate: 'Will Bill find out that his wife's sister's baby is really his by artificial insemination? Will his wife submit to her sister's blackmail attempts, or will she finally let Bill know the truth? If he discovers the truth, will this lead to another nervous breakdown, causing him to go back to Springfield General where his ex-wife and his illegitimate daughter are both doctors and sworn enemies?' Tune in tomorrow, not in order to find out the answers, but to see what further complications will defer the resolutions and introduce new questions. Thus the narrative, by placing ever more complex obstacles between desire and fulfillment, makes anticipation of an end an end in itself. Soap operas invest exquisite pleasure in the central condition of a woman's life: waiting – whether for her phone to ring, for the baby to take its nap, or for the family to be reunited shortly after the day's final soap opera has left *its* family still struggling against dissolution.

According to Roland Barthes, the hermeneutic code, which propounds the enigmas, functions by making 'expectation ... the basic condition for truth:

From T. Modleski, *Loving With a Vengeance: Mass-produced Fantasies for Women* (London: Methuen, 1984) pp. 85–109.

truth, these narratives tell us, is what is *at the end* of expectation. This design implies a return to order, for expectation is a disorder.[1] But, of course, soap operas do not end. Consequently, truth for women is seen to lie not 'at the end of expectation,' but *in* expectation, not in the 'return to order,' but in (familial) disorder.

[...]

The family is, for many women, their only support, and soap operas offer the assurance of its immortality.[2] They present the viewer with a picture of a family which, though it is always in the process of breaking down, stays together no matter how intolerable its situation may get. Or, perhaps more accurately, the family remains close precisely because it is perpetually in a chaotic state. The unhappiness generated by the family can only be solved in the family. Misery becomes not, as in many nineteenth-century women's novels, the consequence and sign of the family's breakdown, but the very means of its functioning and perpetuation. As long as the children are unhappy, as long as things *don't* come to a satisfying conclusion, the mother will be needed as confidante and adviser, and her function will never end.

[...]

The subject/spectator of soap operas, it could be said, is constituted as a sort of ideal mother: a person who possesses greater wisdom than all her children, whose sympathy is large enough to encompass the conflicting claims of her family (she identifies with them all), and who has no demands or claims of her own (she identifies with no one character exclusively). The connection between melodrama and mothers is an old one. Harriet Beecher Stowe, of course, made it explicit in *Uncle Tom's Cabin*, believing that if her book could bring its female readers to see the world as one extended family, the world would be vastly improved. But in Stowe's novel, the frequent shifting of perspective identifies the reader with a variety of characters in order ultimately to ally her with the mother/author and with God who, in their higher wisdom and under-standing, can make all the hurts of the world go away, thus insuring the 'essential "rightness" of the world order.' Soap opera, however, denies the 'mother' this extremely flattering illusion of her power. On the one hand, it plays upon the spectator's expectations of the melodramatic form, continually stimulating (by means of the hermeneutic code) the desire for a just conclusion to the story, and, on the other hand, it constantly presents the desire as unreal-izable, by showing that conclusions only lead to further tension and suffering. Thus soap operas convince women that their highest goal is to see their families united and happy, while consoling them for their inability to realize this ideal and bring about familial harmony.

This is reinforced by the character of the good mother on soap operas. In contrast to the manipulating mother who tries to interfere with her children's lives, the good mother must sit helplessly by as her children's lives disintegrate;

her advice, which she gives only when asked, is temporarily soothing, but usually ineffectual. Her primary function is to be sympathetic, to tolerate the foibles and errors of others.

[...]

It is important to recognize that soap operas serve to affirm the primacy of the family not by presenting an ideal family, but by portraying a family in constant turmoil and appealing to the spectator to be understanding and tolerant of the many evils which go on within that family. The spectator/ mother, identifying with each character in turn, is made to see 'the larger picture' and extend her sympathy to both the sinner and the victim. She is thus in a position to forgive all. As a rule, only those issues which can be tolerated and ultimately pardoned are introduced on soap operas. The list includes careers for women, abortions, premarital and extramarital sex, alcoholism, divorce, mental and even physical cruelty. An issue like homosexuality, which could explode the family structure rather than temporarily disrupt it, is simply ignored. Soap operas, contrary to many people's conception of them, are not conservative but liberal, and the mother is the liberal par excellence. By constantly presenting her with the many-sidedness of any question, by never reaching a permanent conclusion, soap operas undermine her capacity to form unambiguous judgements.

[...]

These remarks must be qualified. If soap operas keep us caring about everyone; if they refuse to allow us to condemn most characters and actions until all the evidence is in (and, of course, it never is), there is one character whom we are allowed to hate unreservedly: the villainess, the negative image of the spectator's ideal self.[3] Although much of the suffering on soap opera is presented as unavoidable, the surplus suffering is often the fault of the villainess who tries to 'make things happen and control events better than the subject/spectator can.' The villainess might very possibly be a mother trying to manipulate her children's lives or ruin their marriages. Or perhaps she is a woman avenging herself on her husband's family because it has never fully accepted her.

This character cannot be dismissed as easily as many critics seem to think.[4] The extreme delight viewers apparently take in despising the villainess testifies to the enormous amount of energy involved in the spectator's repression and to her (albeit unconscious) resentment at being constituted as an egoless recep tacle for the suffering of others.[5] The villainess embodies the 'split-off fury' which, in the words of Dorothy Dinnerstein, is 'the underside of the "truly feminine" woman's monstrously overdeveloped talent for unreciprocated empathy.'[6]

[...]

Soap operas, then, while constituting the spectator as a 'good mother,' provide in the person of the villainess an outlet for feminine anger: in particular, as we have seen, the spectator has the satisfaction of seeing men suffer the same anxieties and guilt that women usually experience and seeing them receive similar kinds of punishment for their transgressions. But that anger is neutralized at every moment in that it is the special object of the spectator's hatred. The spectator, encouraged to sympathize with almost everyone, can vent her frustration on the one character who refuses to accept her own powerlessness, who is unashamedly self-seeking. Woman's anger is directed at woman's anger, and an eternal cycle is created.

And yet, if the villainess never succeeds, if, in accordance with the spectator's conflicting desires, she is doomed to eternal repetition, then she obviously never permanently fails either. When, as occasionally happens, a villainess reforms, a new one immediately supplants her. Generally, however, a popular villainess will remain true to her character for most or all of the soap opera's duration. And if the villainess constantly suffers because she is always foiled, we should remember that she suffers no more than the good characters, who don't even try to interfere with their fates. Again, this may be contrasted to the usual imperatives of melodrama, which demand an ending to justify the suffering of the good and punish the wicked. While soap operas thrive they present a continual reminder that women's anger is alive, if not exactly well.

[...]

Another way in which soap opera stimulates women's desire for connectedness is through the constant, claustrophobic use of close-up shots. Often only the audience is privileged to witness the characters' expressions, which are complex and intricately coded, signifying triumph, bitterness, despair, confusion – the entire emotional register, in fact. Soap operas contrast sharply with other popular forms aimed at masculine visual pleasure, which is often centered on the fragmentation and fetishization of the female body. In the most popular feminine visual art, it is easy to forget that characters even have bodies, so insistently are close-ups of faces employed. One critic significantly remarks, 'A face in close-up is what before the age of film only a lover or a mother ever saw.'[7] Soap operas appear to be the one visual art which activates the gaze of the mother – but in order to provoke anxiety about the welfare of others. Close-ups provide the spectator with training in 'reading' other people, in being sensitive to their (unspoken) feelings at any given moment.

Chodorow* stresses the 'connectedness' of women's work in the home, but this is only half the picture. The wife's job is further complicated by the fact that she must often deal with several people with different, perhaps conflicting moods; and further she must be prepared to drop what she is doing in order to cope with various conflicts and problems the moment they arise. Unlike most workers in the labor force, the housewife must beware of concentrating her energies exclusively on any one task – otherwise, the dinner could burn or the baby could crack its skull (as happened once on 'Ryan's Hope' when the villainess became so absorbed in a love encounter that she forgot to keep an eye on her child). The housewife functions, as many creative women have sadly realized, by distraction. Tillie Olsen writes in *Silences*, 'More than in any other human relationship, overwhelmingly more, motherhood means being instantly interruptable, responsive, responsible. . . . It is distraction, not meditation, that becomes habitual: interruption, not continuity; spasmodic, not constant toil.'[8] Daytime television plays a part in habituating women to distraction, interruption, and spasmodic toil.

These observations have crucial implications for current television theory. In his book *Television: Technology and Cultural Form* Raymond Williams suggests that the shifts in television programming from one type of show to another and from part of a show to a commercial should not be seen as 'interruptions' – of a mood, of a story – but as parts of a whole. What at first appear to be discrete programming units in fact interrelate in profound and complex ways. Williams uses the term 'flow' to describe this interaction of various programs with each other and with commercials. 'The fact of flow,' he says, defines the 'central television experience.'[9] Against Williams I would argue that the flow within soap operas as well as between soap operas and other programming units reinforces the very principle of interruptability crucial to the proper functioning of women in the home. In other words, what Williams calls 'the central television experience' is a profoundly decentering experience.

'The art of being off center,' wrote Walter Benjamin in an essay on Baudelaire, 'in which the little man could acquire training in places like the Fun Fair, flourished concomitantly with unemployment.'[10] Soap operas also provide training in the 'art of being off center' (and we should note in passing that it is probably no accident that the nighttime 'soap opera' *Dallas* and its spinoffs and imitators are flourishing in a period of economic crisis and rising unemployment). The housewife, of course, is in one sense, like the little man at the Fun Fair, unemployed, but in another sense she is perpetually employed – her work, like a soap opera, is never done. Moreover, as I have said, her duties are split among a variety of domestic and familial tasks, and her television programs keep her from desiring a focused existence by involving her in the pleasures of a fragmented life.

Interruptions may be, as Benjamin thought, one of the fundamental devices of all art, but surely soap opera relies on them to a far greater extent than any other art.[11] Revelations, confrontations, and reunions are constantly being interrupted and postponed by telephone calls, unexpected visitors, counter-revelations, catastrophes, and switches from one plot to another. These interruptions are both annoying and pleasurable: if we are torn away from one exciting story, we at least have the relief of picking up the thread of an unfinished one. Like the (ideal) mother in the home, we are kept interested in a number of events at once and are denied the luxury of a total and prolonged absorption. Commercials constitute another kind of interruption, in this case from *outside* the diegesis. Commercials present the housewife with mini-problems and their resolutions, so after witnessing all the agonizingly hopeless dilemmas on soap operas, the spectator has the satisfaction of seeing something cleaned up, if only a stained shirt or a dirty floor.

Although daytime commercials and soap operas are both set overwhelmingly within the home, the two views of the home seem antithetical, for the chief concerns of commercials are precisely the ones soap operas censor out. The saggy diapers, yellow wax build-up and carpet smells making up the world of daytime television ads are rejected by soap operas in favor of 'Another World,' as the very title of one soap opera announces, a world in which characters deal only with the 'large' problems of human existence: crime, love, death and dying. But this antithesis embodies a deep truth about the way women function in (or, more accurately, around) culture: as both moral and spiritual guides and household drudges: now one, now the other, moving back and forth between the extremes, but obviously finding them difficult to reconcile.[12]

Similarly, the violent mood swings the spectator undergoes in switching from quiz shows, the other popular daytime television fare, to soap operas also constitute a kind of interruption, just as the housewife is required to endure monotonous, repetitive work but to be able to switch instantly and on demand from her role as a kind of bedmaking, dishwashing automaton to a large sympathizing consciousness. It must be stressed that while nighttime television certainly affords shifts in mood, notably from comedy to drama, these shifts are not nearly as extreme as in daytime programming. Quiz shows present the spectator with the same game, played and replayed frenetically day after day, with each game a self-contained unit, crowned by climactic success or failure. Soap operas, by contrast, endlessly defer resolutions and climaxes and undercut the very notion of success.

The formal properties of daytime television thus accord closely with the rhythms of women's work in the home. Individual soap operas as well as the flow of various programs and commercials tend to make repetition, interruption, and distraction pleasurable. But we can go even further and note that for women viewers reception itself often takes place in a state of distraction. According to Benjamin, 'reception in a state of distraction ... finds in the film its true means of exercise'.[13] But now that we have television we can see that it goes beyond film in this respect, or at least the daytime programs do. For, the consumption of most films as well as of nighttime programs in some ways recapitulates the work situation in the factory or office: the viewer is physically passive, immobilized, and all his attention is focused on the object before him. Even the most allegedly 'mindless' program requires a fairly strong degree of concentration if its plot is to make sense. But since the housewife's 'leisure' time is not so strongly demarcated, her entertainment must often be consumed on the job. As the authors of *The Complete Soap Opera Book* tell us:

> The typical fan was assumed to be trotting about her daily chores with her mop in one hand, duster in the other, cooking, tending babies, answering telephones. Thus occupied, she might not be able to bring her full powers of concentration to bear on *Backstage Wife*.[14]

This accounts, in part, for the 'realistic' feel of soap operas. The script writers, anticipating the housewife's distracted state, are careful to repeat important elements of the story several times. Thus, if two characters are involved in a confrontation which is supposed to mark a final break in their relationship, that same confrontation must be repeated, with minor variations, a few times in order to make sure the viewer gets the point. 'Clean breaks' – surely a supreme fiction – are impossible on soap operas.

[...]

Ironically, critics of television untiringly accuse its viewers of indulging in escapism. In other words, both high art critics and politically oriented critics, though motivated by different concerns, unite in condemning daytime television for *distracting* the housewife from her real situation. My point has been that a distracted or distractable frame of mind is crucial to the housewife's efficient functioning *in* her real situation, and at this level television and its so-called distractions, along with the particular forms they take, are intimately bound up with women's work.

Given the differences in the ways men and women experience their lives, it is not surprising to find that 'narrative pleasure' can sometimes mean very different things to men and women. This is an important point. Too often feminist criticism implies that there is only one kind of pleasure to be derived from narrative and that it is an essentially masculine one. Hence, it is further implied, feminist artists must first of all challenge this pleasure and then out of nothing begin to construct a feminist aesthetics and feminist form. This is a mistaken position, in my view, for it keeps us constantly in an adversary role, always on the defensive, always, as it were, complaining about the family but never leaving home. Feminist artists don't have to start from nothing; rather, they can look for clues to women's pleasure which are already present in existing forms, even if this pleasure is currently placed at the service of patriarchy. Claire Johnston, a feminist film theorist, has argued for a strategy combining 'both the notion of film as a political tool and film as entertainment':

> For too long these have been regarded as two opposing poles with little common ground. In order to counter our objectification in the cinema, our collective fantasies must be released: women's cinema must embody the working through of desire: such an objective demands the use of the entertainment film. Ideas derived from the entertainment film, then, should inform the political film, and political ideas should inform the entertainment cinema: a two way process.[15]

Clearly, women find soap operas eminently entertaining, and an analysis of the pleasure these programs afford can provide feminists with ways not only to challenge this pleasure but to incorporate it into their own artistic practices.

The fact that soap operas never reach a full conclusion has usually been viewed in an entirely negative light. Here are the words of Dennis Porter, who, working from Roland Barthes' theories of narrative structures and ideology, completely condemns soap operas for their failure to resolve all problems:

> Unlike all traditionally end-oriented fiction and drama, soap opera offers process without progression, not a climax and a resolution, but mini-climaxes and provisional denouements that must never be presented in such a way as to eclipse the suspense experienced for associated plot lines. Thus soap opera is the drama of perepetia without anagnorisis. It deals forever in reversals but never portrays the irreversible change which traditionally marks the passage out of ignorance into true knowledge. For actors and audience alike, no action ever stands revealed in the terrible light of its consequences.[16]

These are strange words indeed, coming from one who purports to be analyzing the ideology of narrative form. They are a perfect illustration of how a high art bias, an eagerness to demonstrate the worthlessness of 'low' art, can lead us to make claims for high art which we would ordinarily be wary of professing. Terms like 'progression,' 'climax,' 'resolution,' 'irreversible change,' 'true knowledge,' and 'consequences' are certainly tied to an ideology; they are 'linked to classical metaphysics,' as Barthes observes. '[The] hermeneutic narrative in which truth predicates an incomplete subject, based on expectation and desire for its imminent closure, is . . . linked to the kerygmatic civilization of meaning and truth, appeal and fulfillment.'[17] To criticize classical narrative because, for example, it is based on a suspect notion of progress and then criticize soap opera because it *isn't* will never get us anywhere – certainly not 'out of ignorance into true knowledge.' A different approach is needed.

Luce Irigaray, describing woman's 'rediscovery' of herself, writes, 'It is a sort of universe in expansion for which no limits could be fixed and which, for all that, would not be incoherence.'[18] The similarities between this description and soap opera as a form are striking. They suggest the possibility that soap operas may not be an entirely negative influence on the viewer; they may also have the force of *a negation*, a negation of the typical (and masculine) modes of pleasure in our society. This challenge, is, moreover, very like the one being mounted in current literary and film theory. Theorists have recently been pointing out the pleasures of the kind of text which breaks the illusion of unity and totality provided the reader or spectator by the 'classic text.' Hence the emphasis since the structuralists has been on 'decentering the subject.' But, as we have seen, women are, in their lives, their work, and in certain forms of their pleasure, already decentered – 'off center.' As Mark Poster remarks in his *Critical Theory of the Family*, 'the feeling of being the center of creation is typical of the ego-structure of the bourgeois male.'[19] This fact seems to me to be of crucial importance to anyone interested in formulating a feminist aesthetic. Indeed, I would like to argue that soap operas are not altogether at odds with an already developing, though still embryonic, feminist aesthetics.

'Deep in the very nature of soaps is the implied promise that they will last forever.'[20] This being the case, a great deal of interest necessarily becomes focused upon those events which retard or impede the flow of the narrative. If, on the one hand, these constant interruptions provide consolation for the housewife's sense of missed opportunities, by illustrating for her the enormous difficulty of getting from desire to fulfillment, on the other hand, the notion of what Porter contemptuously calls 'process without progression' is one endorsed by many innovative women artists. In praising Nathalie Sarraute, for example, Mary Ellmann observes that she is not

> interested in the explicit speed of which the novel is capable, only in the nuances which must tend to delay it. In her own discussions of the novel, Nathalie Sarraute is entirely anti-progressive. In criticizing ordinary dialogue, she dislikes its haste: there not being 'time' for the person to consider a remark's ramifications, his having to speak and to listen frugally, his having to rush ahead toward his object – which is of course 'to order his own conduct.'[21]

Soap opera is similarly antiprogressive.[22] Just as Sarraute's work is opposed to the traditional novel form, soap opera is opposed to the classic (male) film narrative, which, with maximum action and minimum, always pertinent dialogue, speeds its way to the restoration of order.

In soap operas, the important thing is that there always be time for a person to consider a remark's ramifications, time for people to speak and to listen lavishly. Actions and climaxes are only of secondary importance. This may seem wilfully to misrepresent soap operas. Certainly they appear to contain a ludicrous number of climaxes and actions: people are always getting black-mailed, having major operations, dying, conducting extra-marital affairs which inevitably result in pregnancy, being kidnapped, going mad, and losing their memories. But just as in real life (one constantly hears it said) it takes a wedding or a funeral to reunite scattered families, so soap opera catastrophes provide convenient occasions for people to come together, confront one another, and explore intense emotions. One advantage of placing people in hospitals, for example, is that because they are immobilized they are forced to take the time to talk to others and listen to what others have to say to them. And friends and family members, imprisoned in waiting rooms (in some ways an apt metaphor for women's homes), can discuss their feelings about the latest tragedy, and, from there, since the waiting often seems interminable, go on to analyze the predicaments of their mutual friends, as well as the state of their own relationships. Thus, in direct contrast to the typical male narrative film, in which the climax functions to resolve difficulties, the 'mini-climaxes' of soap opera function to introduce difficulties and to complicate rather than simplify the characters' lives.

Furthermore, as with much women's narrative (such as the fiction of Ivy Compton-Burnett, who strongly influenced Sarraute), dialogue in soap operas is an enormously tricky business. Again, I must take issue with Porter, who says, 'Language here is of a kind that takes itself for granted and assumes it is always possible to mean no more and no less than what one intends.[23] More accurately, in soap operas the gap between what is intended and what is actually spoken is often very wide. Secrets better left buried may be blurted out in moments of intensity, or they are withheld just when a character most desires to tell all. This is very different from nighttime television programs and classic Hollywood films with their particularly naive belief in the beneficence of communication. The full revelation of a secret on these shows usually begins or proclaims the restoration of order. Marcus Welby can then get his patient to agree to treatment; Perry Mason can exonerate the innocent and punish the guilty. The necessity of confession, the means through which, according to Michel Foucault, we gladly submit to power, is wholeheartedly endorsed.[24] In soap operas, on the other hand, the effects of confession are often ambiguous, providing relief for some of the characters and dreadful complications for others. (Here too we can see how soap opera melodrama diverges from traditional melodrama, which Peter Brooks, following Eric Bentley, has defined by its impulse to excess, to the overcoming of inhibition and repression: 'The genre's very existence is bound to [the] possibility, and necessity, of saying everything.'[25]) Moreover, it is remarkable how seldom in soap operas a character can talk another into changing his/her ways. Ordinarily, it takes a major disaster to bring about self-awareness – whereas all Marcus Welby has to do is give his stop-feeling-sorry-for-yourself speech and the character undergoes a drastic personality change. Perhaps more than men, women in our society are aware of the pleasures of language – though less sanguine about its potential use as an instrument of power.

Not only do soap operas suggest an alternate kind of narrative pleasure experienced by women, but they also tell us a great deal about what Johnston calls women's 'collective fantasies.' To the dismay of many feminist critics, the most powerful fantasy embodied in soap operas appears to be the fantasy of a fully self-sufficient family. Carol Lopate complains:

> Daytime television . . . promises that the family can be everything, if only one is willing to stay inside it. For the woman confined to her house, daytime television fills out the empty spaces of the long day when she is home alone, channels her fantasies toward love and family dramas, and promises her that the life she is in can fulfill her needs. But it does not call to her attention her aloneness and isolation, and it does not suggest to her that it is precisely in her solitude that she has a possibility for gaining a self.[26]

This statement merits close consideration. It implies that the family in soap operas is a mirror-image of the viewer's own family. But for most viewers, this is definitely not the case. What the spectator is looking at and perhaps longing for, is a kind of *extended* family, the direct opposite of her own isolated nuclear family. Most soap operas follow the lives of several generations of a large family, all living in the same town and all intimately involved in one another's lives. The fantasy here is truly a 'collective fantasy' – a fantasy of community, but put in terms with which the viewer can be comfortable. Lopate is wrong, I believe, to end her peroration with a call for feminine solitude. For too long women have had too much solitude and, quite rightly, they resent it. In her thought-provoking essay on the family, Barbara Easton points out that since the family is for many women their only support, those women who are abandoned to solitude by feminists eager to undermine this support are apt to turn to the right. People like Anita Bryant and Marabel Morgan, says Easton, 'feed on fears of social isolation that have a basis in reality.'[27] So do soap operas.

For it is important to recognize that soap opera allays *real* anxieties, satisfies *real* needs and desires, even while it may distort them. The fantasy of community is not only a real desire (as opposed to the 'false' ones mass culture is always accused of trumping up), it is a salutary one. As feminists, we have a responsibility to devise ways of meeting these needs that are more creative, honest, and interesting than the ones mass culture has supplied. Otherwise, the search for tomorrow threatens to go on, endlessly.

NOTES

1. Barthes, *S/Z*, p. 76.
2. Not only can women count on a never ending story line, they can also, to a great extent, rely upon the fact that their favorite characters will never desert them. To take a rather extreme example: when, on one soap opera, the writers killed off a popular female character and viewers were unhappy, the actress was brought back to portray the character's twin sister. See Madeleine Edmondson and David Rounds, *From Mary Noble to Mary Hartman: The Complete Soap Opera Book*, p. 208.
3. There are still villains on soap operas, but their numbers have declined considerably since radio days – to the point where they are no longer indispensable to the formula. 'The Young and the Restless', for example, does without them.
4. According to Kathryn Weibel (*Minor Mirror*), we quite simply 'deplore' the victimizers and totally identify with the victim (p. 62).
5. 'A soap opera without a bitch is a soap opera that doesn't get watched. The more hateful the bitch the better. Erica of "All My Children" is a classic. If you want to hear some hairy rap, just listen to a bunch of women discussing Erica.
   "Girl, that Erica needs her tail whipped."
   "I wish she'd try to steal my man and plant some marijuana in my purse. I'd be mopping up the street with her new hairdo."' Bebe Moore Campbell, 'Hooked on Soaps,' p. 103.
6. Dorothy Dinnerstein, *The Mermaid and The Minotaur*, p. 236.
7. Dennis Porter, 'Soap Time: Thoughts on a Commodity Art Form,' p. 786.
8. Tillie Olsen, *Silences*, pp. 18–19.
9. Williams, p. 95.
10. Benjamin, 'On Some Motifs in Baudelaire,' in *Illuminations*, p. 176.
11. Benjamin, 'What is Epic Theater?' in *Illuminations*, p. 151.

12. See Sherry B. Ortner's brilliant discussion of women's position in culture, 'Is Female to Male as Nature Is to Culture?'
13. Benjamin, 'The Work of Art in the Age of Mechanical Reproduction,' in *Illuminations*, p. 240.
14. Edmondson and Rounds, pp. 46–47.
15. Claire Johnston, 'Women's Cinema as Counter-Cinema,' p. 217.
16. Porter, pp. 783–84.
17. Barthes, *S/Z*, p. 45.
18. Luce Irigaray, 'Ce sexe qui n'en est pas un,' p. 104.
19. Mark Poster, *Critical Theory of the Family*, p. 9.
20. Edmondson and Rounds, p. 112.
21. Ellmann, pp. 222–23.
22. As David Grimsted points out, melodrama may always have been deeply antiprogressive, in spite of its apparent hopefulness and thrust toward a happy ending. First, the 'centrality of the villain in these plays, even though he was always eventually defeated, suggested a world where the evil and terror of which he was an incarnation were constant threats.' And second, in classic melodrama (as in soap operas), virtue is always allied with the past – with fathers, mothers, rural life styles, etc., while the present is conceived of as dangerous, confusing and perhaps even degenerate.' See *Melodrama Unveiled*, pp. 223–24.
23. Porter, p. 788.
24. Michel Foucault, *The History of Sexuality*, esp. pp. 57–73. In this connection, it is interesting to recall how in many detective stories, TV, shows, and films, the detective must overcome the reluctance of an *innocent* party to yield some bit of information necessary to the solution of the crime. For an interesting discussion of Dragnet's Joe Friday as the Great Listener, see Reuel Denney, *The Astonished Muse*, pp. 82–92.
25. Peter Brooks, *The Melodramatic Imagination*, p. 42. Or, as Eric Bentley puts it, 'melodrama is not so much the exaggerated as the uninhibited.' See *The Life of the Drama*, p. 206.
26. Carol Lopate, 'Daytime Television: You'll Never Want to Leave Home,' p. 51.
27. Easton, p. 34.

REFERENCES

Barthes, Roland. S/Z. Translated by Richard Miller. New York: Hill & Wang, 1974.

Benjamin, Walter. *Illuminations*. Translated by Harry Zohn. Edited by Hannah Arendt. New York: Schocken Books, 1969.

Bentley, Eric. *The Life of the Drama*. New York: Atheneum, 1974.

Brooks, Peter. *The Melodramatic Imagination: Balzac, Henry James, Melodrama, and the Mode of Excess*. New Haven: Yale University Press, 1976.

Campbell, Bebe Moore. 'Hooked on Soaps.' *Essence*, November 1978, pp. 100–103.

Denney, Reuel. *The Astonished Muse*. Chicago: University of Chicago Press, 1957.

Dinnerstein, Dorothy. *The Mermaid and the Minotaur: Sexual Arrangements and Human Malaise*. New York: Harper & Row, 1976.

Easton, Barbara. 'Feminism and the Contemporary Family.' *Socialist Review* 8, no. 3 (1978), pp. 11–36.

Edmondson, Madeleine and Rounds, David. *From Mary Noble to Mary Hartman: The Complete Soap Opera Book*. New York: Stein & Day, 1976.

Ellmann, Mary. *Thinking about Women*. New York: Harvest Books, 1968.

Foucault, Michel. *The History of Sexuality: Volume I: An Introduction*. Translated by Robert Hurley. New York: Vintage Books, 1980.

Grimsted, David. *Melodrama Unveiled: American Theater and Culture, 1800–1850*. Chicago: University of Chicago Press, 1968.

Irigaray, Luce. 'Ce sexe qui n'en est pas un.' In *New French Feminisms*. Edited by Elaine Marks and Isabelle Courtivron. Amherst: University of Massachusetts Press, 1980.

Johnston, Claire. 'Women's Cinema as Counter-Cinema.' In *Movies and Methods*. Edited by Bill Nichols. Berkeley: University of California Press, 1976.

Lopate, Carol. 'Daytime Television: You'll Never Want to Leave Home.' *Radical America* 2 (1977): 33–51.

Olsen, Tillie. *Silences*. New York: Dell Publishing Co., 1979.

Ortner, Sherry B. 'Is Female to Male as Nature Is to Culture?' In *Woman, Culture and Society*. Edited by Michelle Zimbalist Rosaldo and Louise Lamphere. Stanford, Ca.: Stanford University Press, 1974.

Porter, Dennis. 'Soap Time: Thoughts on a Commodity Art Form.' *College English* 38 (1977): 782–88.

Poster, Mark. *Critical Theory of the Family*. New York: Continuum Books, 1978.

Weibel, Kathryn. *Mirror Mirror: Images of Women Reflected in Popular Culture*. Garden City, N.Y.: Anchor Books, 1977.

Williams, Raymond. *Television: Technology and Cultural Form*. New York: Schocken Books, 1975.

Editors' Note

*Chodorow, Nancy, *The Reproduction of Mothering: Psychoanalysis and the Sociology of Gender*. Berkeley: University of California Press, 1978.

47

CROSSROADS:
NOTES ON SOAP OPERA

Charlotte Brunsdon

Husband to wife weeping as she watches TV: 'For heaven's sake, Emily! It's only a commercial for acid indigestion.'
                                        Joke on Bryant & May matchbox.

INTRODUCTION: A GENDERED AUDIENCE?

The audience for soap opera is usually assumed to be female.[1] In these notes I would like to examine this assumption, and the extent to which the notion of a gendered audience can be useful to us in the understanding of a British soap-opera, *Crossroads*.

Initially, I should like to make a distinction between the subject positions that a text constructs, and the social subject who may or may not take these positions up. We can usefully analyse the 'you' or 'yous' that the text as discourse constructs, but we cannot assume that any individual audience member will necessarily occupy these positions.[2] The relation of the audience to the text will not be determined solely by that text, but also by positionalities in relation to a whole range of other discourses – discourses of motherhood, romance and sexuality for example. Thus it may well be that visual pleasure in narrative cinema is dependent on identification with male characters in their gaze at female characters, but it does not necessarily follow that any individual audience member will unproblematically occupy this masculine position. Indeed, feminist film criticism usefully deconstructs the gendering of this 'you'. As

From *Screen* 22:4 (1981) pp. 32–7.

J. Winship has recently argued: 'A feminist politics of representation ... has then to engage with the social reader, as well as the social text'.[3]

The interplay of social reader and social text can be considered by examining the extent to which a gendered audience is implied in programme publicity, scheduling and advertisements. The Independent Broadcasting Authority, in its 1979 annual handbook, groups *Crossroads* with other Drama serials:

> TV drama serials have for many years been an essential ingredient in the programme diet of a large and devoted audience. Established favourites such as *Coronation Street* and *Crossroads* continue to develop themes and situations which often deal with the everyday problems and difficulties to which many viewers can relate. Occasionally the more adventurous type of serial is produced.[4]

The feminity of the audience is specified, apart from the structuring dietary metaphor, in the opposition of 'devoted' and 'everyday' to 'adventurous'. There are a wide range of 'spin-off' materials associated with *Crossroads* – novels, special souvenir supplements, interview material, and a *Crossroads* Cookbook. I will take up the question of the incoherence of *Crossroads* narratives below.

In terms of scheduling, although *Crossroads* is broadcast at different times in different regions (stripped across four evenings a week),[5] it is always broadcast within the 5.15 pm – 7.30 pm slot. That is, with early evening, weekday transmission the programme is definitely not scheduled in the prime time in which it is expected to maximise on a male audience. If we accept Richard Paterson's argument that notions of the family and the domestic dominate the scheduling of British television programmes, then fathers are not expected to control television choice at this point. Paterson also suggests a relationship between scheduling and programme structure:

> Its narrative is constructed of multiple short segments, with continual repetition of narrative information, but no overall dramatic coherence in any episode. In part this structure reflects its place in the schedule: continual viewing has to be ensured even though meal times and other domestic interruptions might make it impossible to follow a coherent narrative.[6]

The broadcast slot of *Crossroads* is surrounded by magazine news programmes, panel games and other serials – all suitable for family, and interrupted, viewing. However, the advertising that frames, and erupts within, the programme is quite clearly addressed to a feminine consumer – beauty aids, breakfast cereals, instant 'man-appeal' meals and cleaning products: the viewer as sexual, as mother, as wife, as housewife, in contrast to the ads for lawn mowers, car gadgets, DIY equipment or large family purchases which dominate from 8.30 pm on. These 'extra textual' factors suggest that women are the target audience for *Crossroads*.

A DISCONTINUOUS TEXT

The ideological problematic of soap-opera – the frame or field in which meanings are made, in which significance is constructed narratively – is that of 'personal life'. More particularly, personal life in its everyday realisation through personal relationships. This can be understood to be constituted primarily through the representations of romances, families and attendant rituals – births, engagements, marriages, divorces and deaths. In marxist terms this is the sphere of the individual outside waged labour. In feminist terms, it is the sphere of women's 'intimate oppression'. Ideologically constructed as the feminine sphere, it is within this realm of the domestic, the personal, the private, that feminine competence is recognised. However, the action of soap-opera is not restricted to familial or quasi-familial institutions but, as it were, *colonises* the public masculine sphere, representing it from the point of view of the personal.

Thus in *Crossroads* we have a family run business, the Crossroads motel, with an attached garage. The motel is near a village, Kings Oak, which at various times has included a market-garden, a doctor's surgery, a post-office, an antique shop, and so on. Regular characters are members of one of three groups – the Crossroads family, the motel/garage workforce, or the village. The fictional community, clearly socially hierarchised through *mise-en-scène* and dialogue, is kept interacting through a series of interlocking economic relationships, but this business interaction is of diegetic importance only as the site of personal relationships. It is always emotionally significant personal interaction, often reported in dialogue, which is narratively foregrounded. This can be seen most clearly through the narrative construction of time and place.

There is no single linear time flow. The minimum three concurrent narratives proceed through a succession of short segments (rarely exceeding 2½ minutes). In contrast with classical narrative cinema,[7] the temporal relationship between segments is rarely encoded. Time in general moves forward, although there is repetition at the beginning of episodes. Relationships between segments can be read as in most cases sequential or simultaneous. One continuous scene can be broken into several segments – notoriously over commercial breaks and between episodes, but this is a standard intra-episodic suspense device. The lack of any overarching time scheme permits the rise and fall of different narrative threads. As each narrative has only its time of exposition, there is no loss of 'real' or referential time if a narrative lapses. Similarly, the very simplicity of the use of 'interruption' as the major form of narrative delay, extending dramatic action, also works against the construction of a coherent referential time. The different present tenses of the narrative co-exist, temporally unhierarchised.

Space in *Crossroads* is also organised in a way which is quite distinct from the conventions of classical narrative cinema, conventions which are carried over to some other forms of television drama. The shoestring budgets mean very restricted sets (all internal, usually no more than five in one episode) and few available camera positions.[8] Generally, sets have two distinct spaces arranged laterally to each other – that is, there are two distinct camera fields, and it is the articulation of these fields which constructs the space.[9] Some sets allow only one camera position. These camera set-ups are not variable, and camera movement is limited. Most scenes are shot in mid-shot or medium close-up, opening with either a close-up or a longer shot. The narrative does not mobilise space within any particular set, nor is there any attempt to make the different spaces of the different sets cohere. We are instead presented with a series of tableau-like views, more theatrical than cinematic. The sets thus function very literally as setting or background, seen always from the same points of view, as familiar as the room in which the viewer has the television.

I am thus arguing that the diegetic world of *Crossroads* is temporally and spatially fragmented, and that this fragmentation, accompanied by repetitious spatial orientation, foregrounds that dialogue of emotional and moral dilemma which makes up the action. The coherence of the serial does not come from the subordination of space and time to linear narrativity, as it does in classical narrative cinema, but from the continuities of moral and ideological frameworks which inform the dialogue. It is these frameworks which are explored, rehearsed and made explicit for the viewer in the repeated mulling over of actions and possibilities. *Crossroads* is in the business not of creating narrative excitement, suspense, delay and resolution, but of constructing moral consensus about the conduct of personal life. There is an endless unsettling, discussion and resettling of acceptable modes of behaviour within the sphere of personal relationships.

There are two key elements in this. Firstly, structurally, the plurality of story lines, which allows the use of the narrative strategy of interruption, and secondly, diegetically, the plot importance accorded to forms of lying and deceit. Structurally, although the different physical spaces of narratives do not cohere, except in the meeting place of the motel lobby, the same set of events, or the same dilemma, will be discussed, by different characters in 'their own' environments. A range of different opinions and understandings of any one situation will thus be voiced. At the same time, the use of interruption, the consistent holding off of *dénouement* and knowledge, invites the viewer to engage in exactly the same type of speculation and judgement. The viewer can, as it were, practise possible outcomes – join in the debate about how a particular event is to be understood.

The use of deceit in the narrative works slightly differently. By deceit, I mean the development of a narrative line which the audience knows that one character is consciously lying or misleading other characters. Here, the viewer is in a position of privileged knowledge in relation to the protagonists, and can see clearly what and who is 'right'. The drama of morality is here produced by the tension between the fact that 'good' characters must continue to be trusting, to remain 'good', but that they will suffer unless they 'find out' about the true nature of another character, X.

In both cases, what is being set in play, or exercised, are repertoires of understandings and assumptions about personal and familial relationships, in which the notion of individual character is central. Thus although soap-opera narrative may seem to ask 'What will happen next?' as its dominant question, the terrain on which this question is posed is determined by a prior question – 'What kind of a person is this?'. And in the ineluctable posing of this question, of all characters, whatever their social position, soap-opera poses a potential moral equality of all individuals.

A GENDERED AUDIENCE – 2

Recently, Tania Modleski has argued for the textual inscription of a female (maternal) subject in American soap-opera. She has suggested that the multiple narrative structure of soap-opera demands multiple identification on the part of the viewer, and thus constitutes the viewer as a type of ideal mother, 'a person who possesses greater wisdom than all her children, whose sympathy is large enough to encompass the claims of all her family ... and who has no demands of her own'.[10] I will consider the related question of the type of cultural competence that *Crossroads* as soap-opera narrative(s) demands of its social reader.

Just as a Godard film requires the possession of certain forms of cultural capital on the part of its audience to 'make sense' – an extra-textual familiarity with certain artistic, linguistic, political and cinematic discourses – so too does *Crossroads*/soap-opera. The particular competences demanded by soap-opera fall into three categories:

1. Generic knowledge – familiarity with the conventions of soap-opera as a genre. For example, expecting discontinuous and cliff-hanging narrative structures.
2. Serial-specific knowledge – knowledge of past narratives and of characters (in particular, who belongs to who).
3. Cultural knowledge of the socially acceptable codes and conventions for the conduct of personal life.

I will only comment on the third category here. The argument is that the narrative strategies and concerns of *Crossroads* call on the traditionally feminine competencies associated with the responsibility for 'managing' the sphere of personal life. It is the culturally constructed skills of femininity – sensitivity, perception, intuition and the necessary privileging of the concerns of personal life – which are both called on and practised in the genre. The fact that these skills and competencies, this type of cultural capital, is ideologically constructed as natural, does not mean, as many feminists have shown, that they are the *natural* attributes of femininity. However, under present cultural and political arrangements, it is more likely that female viewers will possess this repertoire of both sexual and maternal femininities which is called on to fill out the range of narrative possibilities when, for example, the phone rings. That is, when Jill is talking to her mother about her marriage (17 January 1979), and the phone rings, the viewer needs to know not only that it is likely to be Stan (her nearly ex-husband) calling about custody of their daughter Sarah-Jane (serial-specific knowledge) and that we're unlikely to hear the content of the phone-call in that segment (generic knowledge) but also that the mother's 'right' to her children is no longer automatically assumed. These knowledges only have narrative resonance in relation in discourses of maternal femininity which are elaborated elsewhere, already in circulation and brought to the programme by the viewer. In the enigma that is then posed – will Jill or Stan get Sarah-Jane? – questions are also raised about who, generally and particularly should get custody. The question of what should happen is rarely posed 'openly' – in this instance it was quite clear that 'right' lay with Jill. But it is precisely the terms of the question, the way in which it relates to other already circulating discourses, if you like, the degree of its closure, which form the site of the construction of moral consensus, a construction which 'demands', seeks to implicate, a skilled viewer.

I am thus arguing that *Crossroads* textually implies a feminine viewer to the extent that its textual discontinuities require a viewer competent within the ideological and moral frameworks, the rules, of romance, marriage and family life to make sense of it.

Against critics who complain of the redundancy of soap-opera, I would suggest that the radical discontinuities of the text require extensive, albeit interrupted, engagement on the part of the audience, before it becomes pleasurable. This is not to designate *Crossroads* 'progressive' but to suggest that the skills and discourses mobilised by its despised popularity have partly been overlooked because of their legitimation as natural (feminine).

NOTES

1. For example, early research on American radio soaps, either assumes a female audience, or only investigates one. (See H. Herzog. 'On Borrowed Experience' in *Studies in the Philosophy of Social Science*, vol. 9 no. 65. 1941: Rudolph Arnheim. 'The World of the Daytime Serial' in *Radio Research* nos. 42–43. Lazarsfeld and Stanton (eds). New York 1944: H. Kauffman. 'The Appeal of Specific Daytime Serials' *Radio Research*, op. cit.). It is of course precisely the perceived 'feminine' appeal of the genre which has fuelled recent feminist interest (see, for instance, Richard Dyer et al. *Coronation Street*. BFI Television Monograph no. 13 London 1981, and Tania Modleski. 'The Search for Tomorrow in Today's Soap Operas', *Film Quarterly* vol. 33 no. 1. 1979). [See Ch. 46 in this book.]
2. See, for instance, Steve Neale. 'Propaganda', *Screen* vol. 18 no. 3 1977, Paul Willemen. 'Notes on subjectivity', *Screen* vol. 19 no. 1 1978, and David Morley. The *'Nationwide'* Audience, BFI, London 1980.
3. J. Winship. 'Handling Sex', *Media Culture and Society*, vol. 3 no. 1 1981. [See Ch. 59 in this book.]
4. *Television and Radio 1979*, Independent Broadcasting Authority, London 1979.
5. These notes are based on 1978 research when *Crossroads* was still four evenings per week, as opposed to the three at present.
6. Richard Paterson. 'Planning the Family: The Art of the Schedule', *Screen Education* no. 35. Summer 1980.
7. I recognise that 'classical narrative cinema' is not monolithic. David Bordwell and Kristin Thompson in *Film Art*, New York, 1979, give an account of the conventions of the narrative fiction film in the west.

8. Production constraints of *Crossroads* are discussed by Geoff Brown. 'I'm Worried about Chalet Nine', *Time Out* 24–30 November 1978, and R. Miles. 'Everyday Stories, Everyday Folk' MA Dissertation, University of Leicester, 1980.

9. I am indebted to Andy Lowe ('Narrative Spaces and Closure' unpublished paper, Media Group, Centre for Contemporary Cultural Studies, Birmingham 1977) who originally discussed *Crossroads* in these terms.

10. Tania Modleski, op. cit. [See Chapter 46 in this book.]

48

EVERYTHING STOPS FOR *CROSSROADS*: WATCHING WITH THE AUDIENCE

Dorothy Hobson

This chapter is about the viewers who watch *Crossroads*. It is written from different sources but it is all based on talking to people about the programme, and watching the programme with viewers. The data comes from interviews and observations which I made while watching episodes, and long unstructured conversations which we had after the programmes had finished. It is important to stress that the interviews were unstructured because I wanted the viewers to determine what was interesting or what they noticed, or liked, or disliked about the programme and specifically about the episodes which we had watched. I hoped that they would indicate the reasons for the popularity of the programme and also areas where they may have been critical. When a programme has fifteen million viewers it is, of course, not possible to speak to more than a minute percentage of those viewers. Different people watch television programmes for different reasons, and make different 'readings' of those programmes, and much of what they say is determined by preconceived ideas and opinions which they bring to a programme. The message is not solely in the 'text' but can be changed or 'worked on' by the audience as they make their own interpretation of a programme.

[...]

I began the project with the idea of linking the understanding of the production process of specific episodes or programmes with the audience reception

From D. Hobson, Crossroads: *The Drama of a Soap Opera* (London: Methuen, 1982) pp. 105–7 and 124–36.

and understanding of those same episodes or programmes. Although I have gone out to watch specific episodes and to talk about those episodes, the viewers have quickly moved the conversation to the programme in general and talked about other episodes through the medium of the storylines. This has not only been the case when I have watched Crossroads but also whenever I have watched other fictional programmes, whether they are drama series or situation comedies. I always began asking about the programme which we had just watched but quite quickly the women and their families began talking about the characters by name, and moved the conversations to the areas which most interested them.

The usual criticism which is made of any research which involves the intrusion into the privacy of a natural situation is that the presence of the researcher changes the situation. This is of course perfectly correct and the researcher, far from being neutral in the research situation, does affect that situation. In fact, the interaction between the interviewer and interviewee is an integral part of the research. However, since many of the viewers talked about programmes which they had seen when I was not there, nor did they know that months or years ahead they would be talking about them, it can be said that the effect which those programmes had had upon their audience had not been affected by my presence. In fact, it became clear through the process of the study that the audience do not watch programmes as separate or individual items, nor even as types of programmes, but rather that they build up an understanding of themes over a much wider range of programmes and length of time of viewing.

[...]

The basis of soap opera is its characters and their continuing stories. When the viewers say, 'I want to see what happens next,' it is what happens to the characters that interests them. What happens next? How will she get out of this problem? Will she meet someone rich, handsome, sexy? Will her children be all right? Storylines in soap opera are not arbitrary, they are stories which deal with everyday life and its 'ups and downs', problems and pleasures; the inclusion of personal, moral and emotional matters is an integral part of the genre.

'What happened in *Crossroads* last night?' or more familiarly, 'What happened to Jill last night?' No one has to explain which Jill is being talked about because the shared knowledge of the characters which is held by the viewers becomes part of the cultural capital which they exchange in normal conversation. In short digression, I once sat on a train returning from London to Birmingham when British Rail were running their £1.00 tickets during the winter of 1980. Four pensioners sat at a table next to me, complete with their sandwiches and flasks of coffee, and they talked together about many topics of mutual interest. The conversation moved to exchanges about their respective children and grandchildren and names were mentioned. Suddenly, without comment one of the women said, 'What about Emily's trouble with Arthur, what do you think about it all?' (This is not remembered verbatim.) The conversation continued about the mess that Emily was in now that it had been found that he was already married, and how it had seemed too good to be true for her to have found someone like him. How would she be, and how would it all end? As swiftly as the topic had arisen, it switched back to talking about other topics. The uninitiated or 'culturally deprived' would be forgiven for not realizing that the troubles of poor Emily and the misery which Arthur had brought to her were not the problems of the children or relatives of two of the speakers. However, anyone who was aware of the current storyline of the soap opera *Coronation Street* would have known instantly that it was the fates of the fictional characters which were being discussed. Yet from the conversation it was obvious that the speakers were playing a game with the serial. They did not actually believe that the characters existed; they were simply sharing a fantastic interest in the characters outside the serial. How many of us can honestly admit not to having done that ourselves? How many were not saddened at the fate of 'the beautiful young Sebastian' as he visibly declined before our eyes in *Brideshead Revisited* during this winter? It is a false critical elitism to allow the 'belief' and enjoyment in a fictional character in one programme and deny others the right to that belief or enjoyment in another.

Similarly, the knowledge which television viewers have about events within the programmes is a form of cultural capital which excludes those who do not watch the programmes. It is actually fun to talk about the characters in a soap opera, and yet the game that viewers play with one another is interpreted as some form of psychological disorder, when for the most part they are well aware that the game is going on.

It would be wrong, however, to create the idea that fans of *Crossroads* are uncritical of the programme. In fact, the contrary is true, and the viewers possess a level of knowledge about the storylines, the sets and the characters which few professional critics would be able to match. Their postive commitment to the programme does mean that when they make critical remarks their comments are more likely to be of a constructive nature rather than the blanket dismissive mode of some criticism. Their criticism is usually accompanied by a suggestion for improvement and they are unlikely to make comments which would be damaging to the programme as a whole.

Since the storylines are what holds the audience to *Crossroads*, it is not surprising that this is the area where they have most criticism to offer. However, they do not criticize the stories *per se*, but treat them rather benevolently, waiting to see how they will develop. Generally it is not the theme of any story which annoys them or fails to hold their interest; in fact their willingness to accept a wide variety of storylines would appear to be a *carte blanche* for producers. It is, however, the length of time which a story runs which they sometimes find rather boring.

[...]

The viewers' criticism was often accompanied by suggestions for improvements. These were sometimes at the level of more interesting storylines which could develop the characters whom the viewers liked but thought could be more interesting. The character of Kath Brownlow was one who was particularly mentioned. Viewers liked the actress and the character and women were not impressed by the way that she was treated by her husband,

DH   Which characters do you particularly like or dislike?

L   Well, I dislike Arthur Brownlow, I can't stand him.

DH   And why don't you like him?

L   Because if he was my husband I would have kicked him out years ago – but that is obviously the character, not him. And his wife gets on your nerves, but then again they ought to be able to do something with her part, I think, because she's either laying the table or unlaying it or they are eating. Every time you see their living-room you know there is something on the table. That gets on your nerves.

When I pressed them about how the part could be improved the woman and her husband had different suggestions,

P   Put more meat into it.

L   Yes, she seems sort of downtrodden.

P   Take a lover!

L   Get her husband to lay the table for a change. It's just the character. She's probably doing a very good acting job.

The suggestion from the man is of a jokey nature, but the woman has identified one of the significant characteristics of Kath, who is written as an example of the ordinary, respectable working-class/lower-middle-class woman. She appears downtrodden and accepts Arthur's chauvinism, but not without a certain amount of eyebrow raising at his behaviour. The character as portrayed by the actress is seen as 'realistic', but what the viewers are asking for are stronger storylines so that the character can develop. Other women who talked about Kath have suggested that although the characterization might have been realistic when Kath was at home and without financial independence, now that she has returned to work, part-time in the motel kitchen, she would have gained more confidence and would not take Arthur's attitude and behaviour so readily. These women were often speaking from their own experiences of returning to work and they wished that Kath at least would be allowed to do something to establish her own independence.

The constant referencing of the events within the programme with ideas of what would be likely to happen in their own experience is the overriding way in which the viewers interact with the stories. They also have a remarkable amount of knowledge of what has happened in the serial and make judgements about it, always based in 'real life'. Sometimes these are at a small or trivial level, at others they are much more complex judgements. One woman commented that it was about time that Kath Brownlow had a new three-piece suite because the one which she had was getting to look old, and she added the comment, 'She will be able to when she's having the digs money off Kevin.' This comment was made at a lighthearted level but it did indicate that the viewer was questioning the realism of the serial. She knew that a woman of Kath's class would not be content with the old three-piece suite which the production tolerated. It was a nice example of the realism in the woman's experience being in conflict with the reality of the budget which constrained the production from buying Kath a new suite.

The knowledge of the way women react to stress in their own lives coloured the reactions that the viewers had to storylines within the serial. Stories about Jill's problems and her ways of coping with them were very interesting to the viewers. But they were not totally sympathetic to her reactions to her problems:

> I thought it was quite nitty gritty when – I'm going back a bit though – when Jill had that baby by Hugh Mortimer's son. I can't remember who he is now but I thought that was very good.

Another woman had no such problems with her memory, and told me stories from the serial in great detail, combined with a sharp critical assessment of the actions in the story, which were firmly rooted in her own assessments of everyday life:

> I thought when Jill was going through this drunken phase, you know, not so long ago, after this other fella ditched her, I thought was pathetic actually. Because she's been through it all before. It's about time she ... you know. It is, it's part of life. We could all turn to the bottle but you just don't, do you, in real life like, you know. Some do. I agree some do, and I suppose that this is what they are trying to get over, that some do turn to the bottle. But there again, from the type of family that she's supposed to belong to, you wouldn't imagine that she would.

The woman was certainly not tolerant towards Jill. The fact that the character had been through many problems in her life meant in the eyes of this woman that she should have learned to cope with them better, and her class position should have stopped her from taking such a course. Even though there were areas of Jill's life of which the woman had no direct experience, there were assumptions about behaviour which were based on ideas which were common to all women of all classes. 'We could all turn to the bottle, but you just don't, do you, in real life,' but then again, 'some do,' so the authenticity of the serial is confirmed. Again, it shows that the actual stories are not criticized; it is the way that the characters react in the stories which determine whether the viewers will accept the 'true to life' aspects of the programme.

The idea that viewers 'escape' into a programme like *Crossroads* is clearly invalid, or at least it is not escapism in the conventional sense of the word. Escapism suggests that someone is running away from their problems and seeking diversions, even if momentarily. There are, of course, programmes which do provide escapism for the audience, but soap operas are definitely not in this category. They are precisely a way of understanding and coping with problems which are recognized as 'shared' by other women, both in the programme and in 'real life'. Differences in class or material possessions seem to be transcended in the realization that there are problems in everyday life which are common to all women and their families.

> It brings in every aspect of life, the poorer part and the rest, like *Coronation Street* as well. It does involve people getting drunk, having babies without being married and all this, that and the other. It is an everyday programme, you get involved in it. I mean, they have brought mugging into it now, haven't they. I think it's because they bring everything into it that it is so good.

One way to understand the appeal of *Crossroads* for its viewers is through the solutions to the problems or resolutions in fictional terms. In a series like *Crossroads* the solutions to problems are not obviously progressive and never revolutionary. The resolution to a difficult problem is sometimes achieved by some magical solution disguised as 'natural causes', sometimes helped along by other characters in the serial, and it is rare for resolutions to move outside the consensus. Indeed, Jack Barton* stated quite definitely that it was not his aim to move outside the consensus in the treatment of his storylines. However, although not revolutionary, sometimes the solutions can allow the status quo to be shaken up a little and maybe moved on a fraction. In fact, in soap opera much of the dramatic tension is achieved through the dynamics of the changing relationships and situations of the characters. Although the solutions to problems may not be seen as progressive, it is often the raising of those problems in fictional forms that is important. The problems of facing an unwanted pregnancy and how to deal with it as explored in the storyline with Alison [. . .] provided a clue to why the ending was unimportant compared with the issues raised within the context of the story. From the perspective of a radical analysis the fortuitous miscarriage may be seen as a 'cop out', but in dramatic terms, the character, because of her sheltered life and intensively religious upbringing, would have been unlikely to have agreed to an abortion. However, the understanding of the situation and the responses which the raising of the problems elicit from the audience made the fictional resolutions almost irrelevant. For audiences recognize the restrictions imposed on the programme by its time schedule, but appreciate that it is portraying issues which they see as part of everyday life, therefore they can fill in their own understanding of the unseen events in the programme.

[. . .]

Sometimes storylines are touchstones for experiences which the viewers have and which they see reflected in the serial. One such incident brought home to me the futility of trying to estimate which stories would appeal to which sections of the audience. Marjory, an elderly widow with whom I watched the programme, continually surprised me throughout my time with her. The episode which we watched contained the storyline of Glenda's supposed frigidity and inability to have sexual intercourse with Kevin after they had returned from honeymoon. The sexual aspects of the story were not made explicit in any way and it was at one level a story where I felt one section of the audience might want the programme to go into more detail, yet I would have expected, from the image of older viewers which is prevalent, that someone like Marjory may not have liked this particular storyline. I was proved to be completely mistaken in my speculation and again the incident revealed the intricate workings of the audience with the themes presented in the series.

DH   What do you think about the way the programme sometimes brings in subjects that are a bit difficult, like this story with Glenda at the moment? What do you think when it brings those kind of stories in?

M   Oh well, that kind of thing, her married life is not satisfactory, is it! That's the answer to that. Well, I'm going to say something to you. I never thought mine was when I was young. So I can understand how she felt, and it's rather a worry to you. In other words, well of course in my day they were terribly innocent, weren't they. We didn't really know what was what and what wasn't. And I think we were all a bit frightened. Well I said tonight, you never felt you could really let yourself go, you were frightened of having a kid, and all that kind of thing. Well I can understand that, you see. Now *that* is a thing, when I'm listening to that, I think, 'I can remember I used to be a bit like that.' So that is what I mean to say, whatever they put in *Crossroads*, it's appertaining to something what could happen in life. It doesn't seem fiction to me.

DH   No, no, that's interesting, because you think if any age group were going to think 'why have they bothered to have that story in,' it would be somebody older, and yet you understood it.

M   It comes to my age group. We used to say we were frightened of our husbands putting their trousers on the bedrail. You know, we had no pill, we had nothing. I mean, I'm speaking perfectly open to you, we were terrified really, if the man got anything out of it it's right, but you were too frightened to let yourself go, and that's just it.

Clearly, if a programme like *Crossroads* can transcend age to such an extent and evoke in one viewer the memories of her own early married life fifty years previously, it is making connections with its viewers which begin to indicate the importance of the genre. *Crossroads* viewers contribute to their own understanding of the programme and make their own readings of what the production sets out to communicate. They work with the text and add their own experiences and opinions to the stories in the programme.

It seems that the myth of the passive viewer is about to be shattered. They do not sit there watching and taking it all in without any mental activity or creativity. It seems that they expect to contribute to the production which they are watching and bring their own knowledge to augment the text. Stories which seem almost too fantastic for an everyday serial are transformed through a sympathetic audience reading whereby they strip the storyline to the idea behind it and construct an understanding on the skeleton that is left.

Popular fiction *should* connect with life and reality, indeed it is meaningless if it does not achieve this end, for fiction has always grown from experiences in life. *Crossroads* connects with its viewers. To look at a programme like *Crossroads* and criticize it on the basis of conventional literary/media analysis is obstinately to refuse to understand the relationship which it has with its audience. A television programme is a three part development – the production process, the programme, and the understanding of that programme by the audience or consumer – and it is false and elitist criticism to ignore what any member of the audience thinks or feels about a programme. *Crossroads* is a form of popular art and far from writing it off as rubbish we should be looking at what its popularity tells us about all programmes and indeed all forms of popular art. To try to say what *Crossroads* means to its audience is impossible for there is no single *Crossroads*, there are as many different *Crossroads* as there are viewers. Tonight twelve million, tomorrow thirteen million; with thirteen million possible understandings of the programme. Lew Grade is reported as saying, 'I don't make programmes for critics – I make programmes for the viewers.' His sentiments should be taken further, for in fact the viewers are the critics. Or at least, the only ones who should count.

Editors' Note
*Jack Barton, producer of *Crossroads* during the period of Dorothy Hobson's research.

49

SYLVANIA WATERS AND THE SPECTACULAR EXPLODING FAMILY

Jon Stratton and Ien Ang

TELEVISION, THE FAMILY AND IMAGINED COMMUNITY

The family has been central for television. As a modern cultural institution, television has depended on the idea of the family for its operation. Modern television, epitomized by national broadcast television, has always been constructed around concepts of family entertainment, family drama and, most importantly, the family audience. Even now, television schedules are carefully constructed to offer programmes for the whole family and for all members of the family. Television programmes are also very often *about* the family, taking its normality in modern life for granted and, as part of the circulation of the discourse of the family, helping to shape and reinforce understandings about the family. In this sense, television both reflects and reinforces the modern nation-state's basic reliance on the construct of the family – more precisely, the nuclear family – as the basis for social order, as the site for morality and for the organization of desire. Modern television, in short, was family television – and in some ways the family remains one of the primary preoccupations of (national, broadcast) television.

The intimate connection between television and the family suggests how the two institutions interact – are mutually complicit – in contributing to the construction of a unified national culture in the modern world. Television's integrative power has been deployed in the most private arena of life in the modern nation-state: the family home. Through (modern) television, the nation

From *Screen* 35:1 (1994) pp. 1–21.

could be forged into an encompassing imagined community in a way which was both much more extensive and intimate than the newspaper: Benedict Anderson's exemplary medium.[1] As the 'unifying rhetorical space of daily television extends into the living rooms of everyone',[2] the distinction between the public and private spheres has been collapsing. Television was itself implicated in this collapse.

But what was once the family home is now something quite different. In *Family Television*, published in 1986, David Morley discussed the place and role of television within the family.[3] The family he concerned himself with was the normative family of traditional sociology – the nuclear family. Eighteen families were interviewed for Morley's project. All contained a husband and wife – marriage is very important in sociological definitions of the family – and between two and four children. In only one case are we told that a wife has a daughter and a son from a previous marriage. Thus, Morley's research took the nuclear family as both normal and normative at a time when, in practice, it was coming to exist only as an important part of conservative ideology and, in concert with this, as a nostalgic touchstone for a lost society. In a later paper, Morley has usefully explained his choice for addressing the case of the nuclear family 'as representative of the ideological (if not empirical) heartland of the television audience'.[4] This contextualization illuminates the observation that television's homogenizing preoccupation with the family works to exclude or marginalize – at the level of representation – the day-to-day experiences of the majority of television's actual audiences. It is the generation following World War II which marked the period in western countries of maximum hegemony of nuclear family life. Since the late 1960s, however, all western nation-states have seen a steady rise in divorce and single-parent families. By 1990, the nuclear family so beloved by functionalist sociology as the basis of social order had become a minority. Only about 30 per cent of households in Britain conform to this classic family type. If we exclude from this category those families where both parents work and only look at those where the father works and the mother stays at home (that is, the perfect ideological structure), the figure declines to 13.8 per cent.[5] In Australia, according to Noller and Callen, about 28 per cent of the population live in nuclear families with dependent children.[6] The majority of people live in a variety of other ways: on their own, in shared situations, as same-sex couples, as single mothers or fathers – again sometimes sharing, or remarried, or *de facto*, in blended family situations.[7] The nuclear family has exploded.

Paralleling this explosion has been a resurgence of interest in family melodrama in television soap opera. Christine Gledhill has argued that, 'If [the] potentiality for the melodramatic lay dormant while fifties family melodrama in the cinema carried the brunt of the growing pressure on gender roles, the seventies and eighties saw a renewed search in popular fictional forms for enacting heterosexual and family crisis'.[8] Gledhill's point refers to changing gender relations, but the crisis of the nuclear family was qualitatively more profound: the very idea of family itself was being questioned, losing its uncontested ideological power. The soap opera, in its traditional formulation the site of women's culture, was also where family values were asserted and rehearsed. As Christine Geraghty has noted, 'the basis of soap operas is family life',[9] even if perfect nuclear families are more often than not absent in soap narratives – British, Australian or American. Indeed, one of the central problematics of soap opera as a genre, as well as a reason for its popularity and success, may be found in the way in which it upholds, against all odds, the ideal of the family. As soap characters struggle along, they continue to yearn for the utopia of the perfect family – where we project happiness and a sense of belonging – despite its harsh, less than perfect empirical reality, to which the soaps testify. Soaps, then, are vehicles for reconciling the ideal and the real, or better, for keeping the ideal alive by concentrating on the dramatic imperfections of the real. In this sense, soap opera traditionally constructs 'real' family life as lacking, even if it is the only thing that we have. Against the – unimaginable, impossible – ideal that is the ideology of nuclear family life as portrayed for example in television advertisements, actual family life is always found wanting. At the same time, it is ultimately what we want.

As the nuclear family exploded, the soap opera was torn in different directions. In one transformation it became a prime-time show concerned not only with the family but also with power, wealth, pleasure, leisure and sex as opposed to love. *Dallas* and *Dynasty* epitomize these shows. In another transformation, melodrama was played down and shows like *Neighbours* became nostalgic evocations of a mythical post-World War II period when the practices and values of the nuclear family were uncontested. In a third, much rarer, transformation the nuclear family and its ideological repertoire of moral values vanished from the soap opera completely, leaving it fundamentally changed. We have discussed this development elsewhere in relation to the Australian soap opera *Chances*.[10] These transformations in soap opera signal the increasing difficulty the genre has in performing its traditionally reassuring role: that is to represent *unproblematically* the ultimate viability of an everyday world held together by a moral repertoire centred around family values.

All this provides a general context for the significance of the screening on Australian television of *Sylvania Waters*, a programme which was claimed to be a documentary series featuring the day-to-day life of a real Sydney family. A crew filmed this family, warts and all, for ninety hours over a six month period, and the programme was shown in twelve weekly half-hour episodes from July 1992 on ABC television, the Australian national public broadcaster. It should be noted that *Sylvania Waters* has British, not Australian origins. Its production was an initiative of the BBC, in coproduction with the ABC. But the series was shown in Australia before it was shown in Britain. Part of the peculiarity of the programme, then, was that it was a British documentary series about an Australian family, designed for a British audience but watched by an Australian audience first.

Sylvania Waters immediately became an object of heated national debate in Australia, and the intensity of the controversy sparked by it (about which more later) was related precisely to the programme's presentation as a representative investigation of the lifestyle of an ordinary Australian family – a family which could be held up as a symbolic mirror to the Australian nation. In this sense, *Sylvania Waters* epitomized the national articulation of family and television we discussed above. But with a difference. While the modern version of this articulation signals a strengthening of the hegemonic unity of family and nation through television, its postmodern transformation – which we would suggest is the case with *Sylvania Waters* – signals, if not the breakdown of that hegemony, then at least the *problem* television now has in holding the increasingly mythical family, and therefore the increasingly problematized, modern homogeneous nation, together. Related to this is the more general problem of the status of television in relation to the family as the privatized nuclear family exploded.

While *Sylvania Waters* was supposed to be a documentary, from the very beginning it was presented with explicit reference to the soap opera. When the producers were searching for a suitable family during the preparation period, they distributed a flyer throughout Sydney which interpellated people thus:

> Any dramas in your house? We are seeking a family whose children cover a wide range of ages and interests. A lively family, with something to say, who are willing to let us into their lives. Let us see how the 'average' Australian family live Better than a soapie, this is real life.[11]

As we will explore in this article, it is the soap operatic articulations of *Sylvania Waters* which make the programme a fundamentally ambiguous statement about 'family' and 'television' in contemporary society.

The very title of the programme follows the (predominantly British) soap convention of using the name of a fictional local community to construct a sense of place. The British connection is not arbitrary here. Sylvania Waters is a nouveau riche Sydney suburb which looks and feels utterly exotic from a British point of view. The fact that this was the location where the disturbing unraveling of the family was being dramatized, means that *Sylvania Waters*, constructed as a world resolutely outside of British space, can be taken, from a British perspective, as having nothing to do with British reality. Moreover, more than any other British settler state, excepting the special instance of the USA, Australia has been constructed in Britain as an antipodean exotic Other, a colonized alternative into which British dreams and nightmares, hopes and fears, could be read. British audience were therefore given the luxury of an opportunity to revel voyeuristically in a world from which they could assume to be exempted. Australian audiences, however, watched a programme which claimed to show them a version of themselves. As a consequence, they were forced to confront and question many of the traditional ideological tenets of modernity which we have outlined. In practical terms, these were summed up in the problem of how to represent 'the Australian family'. However, as a cultural event, *Sylvania Waters* unwound many more far-reaching modern assumptions, ranging from television's claim to realism to the position of television in the experience of family life, in a time when the distinction between public and private spheres, historically divided by the family, has all but disappeared, and when the family itself has exploded. What was private and not, therefore, for public display – namely, intimate family life – has now become the subject of everyday television. It is the very explosion of the family which has enabled this spectacularization to take place. At the same time, the televisual spectacularization of the family has also contributed to its explosion by displaying the non-normativeness of the apparently most normative family. All these considerations make *Sylvania Waters* a suitable anchor for a discussion about the current, postmodern disarticulation of television, family and nation.

[…]

TELEVISION, THE FAMILY AND SIMULATION

What is most significant about *Sylvania Waters* is that it does *not* feature a nuclear family. The Baker–Donahers are a complex blended family, consisting of an unmarried middle-aged couple living together in what is known in Australia as a *de facto* arrangement. Both Noeline Baker and Laurie Donaher had been married and their children from these marriages, spread over two additional households, add to this constructed family.[12] By the sociological standards of modernity, then, the *Sylvania Waters* family is by no means typical. Laurie Donaher was aware of this 'I thought there's no way they're going to choose us. … we were under the impression that it was a typical Australian family they were after, but we thought we weren't typical'.[13] By the very selection of this particular family, then, *Sylvania Waters* testifies to the explosion of the nuclear family.

But the doing away with the typical also points to a more profound paradox: exposing the idiosyncratic ways of this particular family only leads to a further dissolution of the idea of the family itself. In a different, more experiential rendering of the concept of the typical, Noeline Baker reflects in the last episode of *Sylvania Waters* that 'I think we are quite a typical Australian family. We have our ups; we have lots of the ups and an awful lot of the downs, but basically it's no different to the family over the street.' However, what the controversy around *Sylvania Waters* makes clear is that even if this were the case, no family will turn out to be the same when it comes to *how* they handle their ups and downs. This leads to an undoing of the cultural category of the family itself; what is left is a plurality of events and experiences whose subsumption under a single, encompassing category of 'family life' is at best reductive, at worst nonsensical. 'The family' is exposed as a myth at the very point at which it is brought into the realm of public visibility. In this sense,

Sylvania Waters is the culmination of a trend towards the spectacularization of the family which, in the western world, started in the early seventies.

It is significant that documentaries aimed at scrutinizing and displaying – rather than explicitly commenting on – family life began just as the nuclear family form went into its period of steep decline. In the USA, where the nuclear family exploded first, a tele-*vérité* documentary using a similar method to *The Family* and *Sylvania Waters* was made of the Louds family in 1971. Baudrillard has described the paradoxical quest for the normative real in this case: 'Seven months of uninterrupted shooting. Three hundred hours of direct nonstop broadcasting, without script or scenario, the odyssey of a family. ...'[14]

[...]

In commenting on 'the phantasm of filming the Louds *as if TV wasn't there*,' Baudrillard notes: 'The producers' trump card was to say: "They lived as if we weren't there." An absurd, paradoxical formula – neither true, nor false: but utopian. The "as if *we* weren't there" is equivalent to "as if *you* were there".'[15]

Baudrillard's utopia can be interpreted in two distinctive ways. The more traditional, modern one refers to the naturalistic fallacy – the realist illusion – which treats the medium as transparent, leading to a mistaking of the representation for the real. In this case, 'as if *you* were there' implies the positioning of the audience as flies on the wall, having immediate access to the object of representation – the life of this particular family. But this scenario still retains the distinction between subject and object, as well as the real and the representation. A more radical, postmodern utopia, if we want to call it that, would highlight the 'as if': the exposed family simulates its own life as though they were in the spotlights of the cameras and we, the audience, participate in this simulation in a kind of 'thrill of the real'. The distance of perspective – marked by the separation of subject and object, of seer and seen – is being lost and, as part of this loss, it becomes impossible to distinguish acting from natural, daily life, the representation from the real. It is in this simulatory logic that the family can be seen never to have existed without the abstracting distance of representation. Once it was drawn into the regime of excessive transparency, of unmediated presentation, it can no longer cohere as the family.

[...]

THE FAMILY SPECTACLE

At the beginning of *Sylvania Waters*, two of the three couples are living together without being married: Noeline and Laurie, and also the next generation, Noeline's son Paul and his girlfriend Dione. (Laurie's son Mick and his partner Yvette *are* married, but it is significant that their role is marginalized in the narrative; Ardill described them as 'essentially boring'.) As in *The Family,* the younger generation gets married in episode eleven, which documents Paul and Dione's wedding day. However, the narrative finale of the series is the prospective marriage of Noeline and Laurie who, in the last episode, fly off to Europe for a holiday with the intention of getting married there. In *The Family* the Wilkins parents are, of course, already married; the normality of the nuclear family was therefore never in doubt in this series. By contrast, *Sylvania Waters* starts out with the crisis of the family, and ends with a movement towards its reinstatement – although we never get to know in the series whether Noeline and Laurie actually do get married in Europe.

It is through Paul and Dione that the ideology of the family is most explicitly articulated. Throughout the series they profess their happiness with each other in spite of their fights, and constantly assert their desire to stay together. When their baby, Kane, is born (in episode two) they both assert that, coming from broken and alcoholic homes, they each know what it is like not to have a proper family. As a consequence they will stay together for Kane's sake no matter what. The ideological effect of the opposition between Noeline and Laurie's relationship and Paul and Dione's is to increase conservative and nostalgic sympathy for Paul and Dione. Paul and Dione's statements about their families offer a critical reading of Noeline and Laurie because of their implied inability to hold their own marriages together and their commitment to such a project.

[...]

It is Noeline who is constructed as the dominant excessive figure in *Sylvania Waters*. The series highlights her arguments with Laurie. In these arguments she tends to be standing, he tends to be seated; she tends to be foregrounded, he tends to be backgrounded. The effect of the editing of the series is to offer a reading of their relationship as being based on mutual misunderstanding, and aggression on the part of Noeline. Laurie, on the other hand, is constructed as weak and unable and unwilling to control his excessive *de facto* wife. This raucous image of domesticity is the opposite of the traditional ideology of love, mutual support and female moral control over the family within the confines of a generalized patriarchal authority. In the last episode, Laurie objected to some of Noeline's relatives staying in their house while they were away for the weekend. At least one third of the episode was spent on showing the huge argument that transpired as a result of Noeline's subversion of Laurie's patriarchal power. In the context of the ideology of the modern nuclear family, then, Noeline's behaviour is constructed as antithetical to proper wifely behaviour.

The significance of this construction of Noeline can be understood more fully by placing her character in the light of the double coding of *Sylvania Waters* as a text combining documentary techniques with the narrative concerns of the soap opera. Christine Geraghty has noted in relation to British soaps such as *Coronation Street* and *EastEnders*, which she calls matriarchal soaps, that 'the mother takes on the burden of being both the moral and practical support to the family'.[16] From this perspective Noeline is constructed as the soap villain, the character viewers love to hate. Noeline is presented as an archaic image of the world turned upside down. Where she should be subordinate to her husband she has not even remarried; she dominates Laurie, and instead of functioning as the nurturing and mediating centre of a harmonious household, she argues with everybody. She is extraordinarily emotional, marking her as the text's key melodramatic site.

[...]

But while the soap opera coding reinforced a conservative preferred reading of *Sylvania Waters*, the crossreferences to soap opera in the whole event simultaneously point to something more fundamental, namely, that while *Sylvania Waters* was designed to (re)present the family, what took place was its spectacularization. As the family only exists as a simulation today, its reality can only take the form of a spectacle. The effect of this is a blurring of the real and the fictional. As Mark Poster has explained, '[a] simulation is different from a fiction or lie in that it not only presents an absence as a presence, the imaginary as the real, it also undermines any contrast to the real, absorbing the real within itself'.[17] This forms the background to why *Sylvania Waters* could so unproblematically be referred to as a real life soap; so unproblematically indeed that a new generic hybrid was invented to typify the programme in public discourse: the 'soapumentary'.

[...]

Such uncertainty is an inevitable effect of the changed position of television in relation to the now exploded and spectacularized family. What *Sylvania Waters* shows is that television can no longer serve as site for the construction of a consensual and homogeneous imagined community based on the nuclear family. The close scrutiny of the exploded Baker–Donaher family paradoxically reinforces only the recognition that the normative nuclear family, as represented in sociology and advertising, was fiction rather than fact. As a result, the specularity of the Baker–Donahers is undermined by their spectacularity. They now circulate in the nonreferential world of simulation.

When the Wilkins family appeared on television as *The Family* the pressure on the marriage split up the couple and the family. The Louds split up during the filming of them. In both cases, the resulting explosion of the family was real, and in both cases the splits were said to be associated with the new public visibility of the families. Twenty years on, the day-to-day effects of televisual spectacularization are better understood. The Baker–Donahers have agents – signalling their status, acquired through television, as marketable celebrities. Brian Walsh, Noeline and Laurie's agent, remarked shortly after the series finished that: 'The interest since the show has been phenomenal. I mean I handled Kylie [Minogue] and Jason [Donovan] when *Neighbours* took off and it has nothing on *Sylvania Waters*.'[18]

Paul and Dione have become celebrities in their own right, appearing not only on Couchman's show but on talk-back radio and other programmes. Walsh's reference point for Noeline's popularity is two actors from *Neighbours*. The celebrity occupies an indeterminate position: neither real nor imaginary but hyperreal, it is a position constructed in and through the circulation of media images.

Noeline was said to have been inconsolable about the way she was made into an object of hatred and ridicule. The Donahers celebrated the showing of the last episode with the burning of the videotapes of the series in their garden. Watson was not impressed and evoked reminiscences of Nazi book burnings in the 1930s. He hinted at an intolerance which, he claimed, revealed a refusal to look at the truth. However, the whole event can also be interpreted in a different way, as the *simulated performance* of family trauma. They had become stars, with a cheering public of 3,500 on their front lawn just after the last episode finished. Not surprisingly, the whole spectacle was itself televised in an episode of the reality television show *Hard Copy* on Channel Ten, one of Australia's commercial channels. Jane Fraser aptly described the event like this: 'Noeline had a spectacularly good cry ... on *Hard Copy*, the Ten network program which filmed the family watching the family waving goodbye to the family. "It was a relief", explained Mr Walsh [the agent], "that it was all over".'[19] Yet precisely the newly acquired celebrity status of the Baker–Donahers ensures that it was not going to be over at all. If anything, this 'family' will continue its life in simulated form through continued media exposure.

It was Guy Debord who, not coincidentally also in 1971, described this new society as the society of the spectacle, characterized by a proliferation of the hyperreality of simulation.[20] The status of *Sylvania Waters* as a simulation, rather than (re)presentation, of 'an Australian family' unsettles the modern articulation of family, television and national imagined community. Where in modernity the system of representation, of which national broadcast television was a key part, judged us against a normative model – in this case the nuclear family – so as to homogenize us into a cohesive imagined community, today spectacular families circulate as images with no normative family reality against which they can be measured. This is what happened to the Baker–Donahers. Nevertheless, the ideology of the nuclear family continues to circulate as an ideal, which forms the background for the confused reception of *Sylvania Waters* in Australia. As the explosion of the nuclear family as a lived reality has become an inexorable fact, its image can no longer be a reference point for the imagined unity of the (Australian) nation. In the end, the *Sylvania Waters* affair has made it clear that television no longer has the capability, and authority, to represent the nation to itself.

Notes

1. Benedict Anderson, *Imagined Communities* (London: Verso, 1983).
2. Jody Berland, 'Placing Television', *New Formations*, no 4 (1988), p. 147.

3. David Morley, *Family Television* (London: Comedia, 1986).
4. David Morley, *Television, Audiences and Cultural Studies* (London: Routledge, 1992), p. 164.
5. This figure comes from Morley. *Television, Audiences and Cultural Studies*, p. 163.
6. Patricia Nollen and Victor Callan, 'Images of the typical Australian family', in Kathleen Funder (ed.), *Images of Australian Families* (Melbourne: Longman Cheshire, 1991), p. 21.
7. Michael Gilding, *The Making and Breaking of the Australian Family* (Sydney Allen & Unwin, 1991), provides a good account of the explosion of the nuclear family in Australia, especially in the section 'Many Australian families'.
8. Christine Gledhill, 'Speculations on the relationship between soap opera and melodrama', *Quarterly Review of Film & Video*, vol. 14, no 1–2 (1992), p. 119.
9. Christine Geraghty, *Women and Soap Opera* (Oxford: Polity Press, 1991), p. 60.
10. Ien Ang and Jon Stratton, 'The end of civilisation as we knew it: *Chances* and the postrealist soap opera', in Robert C. Allen (ed.), *As The World Turns Soap Opera Worldwide* (Chapel Hill: University of North Carolina Press, forthcoming 1994).
11. Quoted in Philip McLean, 'Sylvania Waters', *The Sunday Telegraph*, 12 July 1992.
12. The inability of nuclear family rhetoric to describe this organization is typified in the variety of names given to the family. Different reports called them the Baker–Donahers, the Donaher–Bakers and the Donahers. Interestingly, but not surprisingly, no report seems to have called them the Bakers.
13. Laurie Donaher, quoted in McLean, 'Sylvania Waters'.
14. Jean Baudrillard, *Simulations* (New York: Semiotext(e), 1983), p. 49.
15. Baudrillard, *Simulations*, p. 50.
16. Geraghty, *Women and Soap Opera*, p. 75.
17. Mark Poster, 'Introduction', in M. Poster (ed.), *Jean Baudrillard, Selected Readings* (Stanford: Stanford University Press, 1988), p. 6.
18. Quoted in Jane Fraser, 'Noeline's tale of troubled waters'.
19. Ibid.
20. Guy Debord, *La société de spectacle* (Paris: Editions Champs Libres, 1971). Eng. trans. *The Society of the Spectacle* (Detroit: Black & Red, 1977).

FURTHER READING

Allen, R. C., *Speaking of Soap Operas* (Chapel Hill: University of North Carolina Press, 1985).

Allen, R. C. (ed.), *To Be Continued ... Soap Operas around the World* (London and New York: Routledge, 1995).

Ang, I., *Watching 'Dallas': Soap Opera and the Melodramatic Imagination* (London: Methuen, 1985).

Ang, I., 'Melodramatic identifications: Television fiction and women's fantasy'. In M. E. Brown (ed.), *Television and Women's Culture* (London: Sage, 1990).

Arnheim, R., 'The World of the Daytime Serial'. In F. Lazarsfeld and F. Stanton (eds), *Radio Research 1942–3* (New York: Duell, Sloan & Pearce, 1944).

Brown, M. E., 'The Politics of Soaps: Pleasure and Feminine Empowerment'. *The Australian Journal of Cultural Studies* 4:2 (1986) pp. 1–25.

Brown, M. E. (ed.), *Television and Women's Culture* (London: Sage, 1990).

Brown, M. E., 'Motley Moments: Soap Operas, Carnival, Gossip and the Power of Utterance'. In M. E. Brown (ed.), *Television and Women's Culture* (London: Sage, 1990).

Brunsdon, C., 'Writing about Soap Opera'. In L. Masterman (ed.), *Television Mythologies* (London: Comedia, 1984).

Brunsdon, C., 'Feminism and Soap Opera'. In K. Davies, J. Dickey, and T. Stratford (eds), *Out of Focus: Writings on Women and the Media* (London: Women's Press, 1987).

Brunsdon, C., 'Identity in Feminist Television Criticism'. *Media, Culture and Society* 15:2 (1993) pp. 309–20.

Buckingham, D., *Public Secrets: 'EastEnders' and its Audience* (London: BFI, 1987).

Buckman, P., *All for Love: A Study in Soap Opera* (London: Secker & Warburg, 1984).

Cantor, M. and Pingree, S., *The Soap Opera* (London: Sage, 1983).

Dyer, R., Geraghty, C., Jordan, M., Lovell, T., Paterson, R. and Stewart, J., *Coronation Street*. BFI TV Monograph; no. 13 (London: BFI, 1981).

Dyer, R., Lovell, T. and McCrindle, J., 'Women and Soap Opera'. *Edinburgh Television Festival Magazine* (1978); repr. in A. Gray and J. McGuigan (eds), *Studying Culture* (London: Edward Arnold, 1993).

Feuer, J., 'Melodrama, Serial Form and Television Today'. *Screen* 25:1 (1984) pp. 4–16.

Feuer, J., 'Narrative Form in American Network Television'. In C. MacCabe (ed.), *High Theory: Low Culture* (Manchester: Manchester University Press, 1986).

Finch, M., 'Sex and Address in *Dynasty*'. *Screen* 27:6 (1986) pp. 24–42.

Fiske, J., *Television Culture* (London: Methuen, 1987).

Flitterman-Lewis, S., 'All's Well that Doesn't End: Soap Opera and the Marriage Motif'. *Camera Obscura* 16 (1988) pp. 118–27.

Geraghty, C., *Women and Soap Opera: a Study of Prime Time Soaps* (Cambridge: Polity, 1991).

Geraghty, C., 'British Soaps in the 1980s'. In D. Strinati and S. Wagg (eds), *Come On Down? Popular Culture in Post-War Britain* (London: Routledge, 1992).

Glaessner, V., 'Gendered Fictions'. In A. Goodwin and G. Whannel (eds), *Understanding Television* (London: Routledge, 1990).

Gripsrud, J., *The Dynasty Years: Hollywood Television and Critical Media Studies* (London: Routledge, 1995).

Heide, M., *Television Culture and Women's Lives* (Philadelphia: University of Philadelphia Press, 1995).

Herzog, H., 'On Borrowed Experience: An Analysis of Listening to Daytime Sketches'. In *Studies in Philosophy and Social Science* 9:1 (1941) pp. 65–95.

Herzog, H., 'What do we Really Know about Daytime Serial Listeners?' In P. Lazarsfeld and F. M. Stanton (eds), *Radio Research: 1942–1943* (New York: Duell, Sloan & Pearce, 1944) pp. 3–33.

Hobson, D., *'Crossroads': The Drama of a Soap Opera* (London: Methuen, 1982).

Hobson, D., 'Soap Operas at Work'. In E. Seiter, H. Borchers, G. Kreutzner, E.-M. Warth (eds), *Remote Control: Television Audiences and Cultural Power* (London: Routledge, 1989).

Katz, E. and Liebes, T., 'Mutual Aid in the Decoding of *Dallas*: Preliminary Notes from a Cross-Cultural Study'. In P. Drummond and R. Paterson (eds), *Television in Transition* (London: BFI, 1986).

Kreutzner, G. and Seiter, E., 'Not all "Soaps" are Created Equal: Towards a Cross-cultural Criticism of Television Serials'. *Screen* 32:2 (1991) pp. 154–72.

Kuhn, A., 'Women's Genres'. *Screen* 25:1 (1984) pp. 18–28.

Liebes, T. and Katz, E., *The Export of Meaning: Cross-Cultural Readings of* Dallas (Oxford: Oxford University Press, 1990).

Liebes, T. and Livingstone, S., 'European Soap Operas: The Diversification of a Genre'. *European Journal of Communication* 13:2 (1998) pp. 147–180.

Livingstone, S., 'Viewers' Interpretations of Soap Opera: The Role of Gender, Power and Morality'. In P. Drummond and R. Paterson (eds), *Television and Its Audience* (London: BFI, 1988).

Modleski, T., 'The Rhythms of Reception: Daytime Television and Women's Work'. In E. A. Kaplan (ed.), *Regarding Television* (Frederick, Md.: University Publications of America, 1983).

Modleski, T., *Loving with a Vengeance: Mass-Produced Fantasies for Women* (London: Methuen, 1984).

Nochimson, M., *No End to Her: Soap Opera and the Female Subject* (Berkeley: University of California Press, 1992).

Press, A., 'Class, Gender and the Female Viewer: Women's Responses to *Dynasty*. In M. E. Brown (ed.), *Television and Women's Culture* (London: Sage, 1990).

Press, A., *Women Watching Television: Gender, Class and Generation in the American Television Experience* (Philadelphia: University of Pennsylvania Press, 1991).

Schroder, K., 'The Pleasure of *Dynasty*: The Weekly Reconstruction of Self-Confidence'. In P. Drummond and R. Paterson (eds), *Television and Its Audience* (London: BFI, 1988).

Seiter, E., 'Promise and Contradiction: The Daytime Television Serials'. *Screen* 23 (1982) pp. 150–63.

Seiter, E., Kreutzner, G., Warth, E.-M. and Borchers, H., '"Don't treat us like we're so stupid and naive": Towards an Ethnography of Soap Opera Viewers'. In E. Seiter, H. Borchers, G. Kreutzner and E.-M. Warth (eds), *Remote Control: Television Audiences and Cultural Power* (London: Routledge, 1989).

White, M., 'Women, Memory and Serial Melodrama: Anecdotes in Television Soap Opera'. *Screen* 35:4 (1994) pp. 336–53.

SECTION 6
NEWS

NEWS
INTRODUCTION

News, according to Denis McQuail, is 'the core activity according to which a large part of the journalistic (and thus media) profession defines itself'.[1] Its claims to objectivity, neutrality and balance, reinforced in Britain by the formal demands of a public service broadcasting structure, provide the basis of the media's claims to the status of a 'fourth estate', independent of the workings of political or government agencies. As provider of independent information in and about the public sphere, its effective operation has been seen to act as guarantor both of the social responsibility of the mass media and of the healthy workings of a democratic society. News analysis has been at the heart, therefore, of what John Corner has called the *'public knowledge* project' within media studies, the investigation of the media as 'an agency of public knowledge and "definitional" power' and with 'the politics of information and the viewer as citizen'.[2]

At the same time, however, news is also a media *text* and a cultural commodity. As a television genre, for example, it exhibits all those features (segmentation, the open-ended series format, repetition, a sense of 'nowness') which John Ellis sees as characterising television as a medium (see Chapter 19), and in this respect can be seen to have more in common with soap opera than the account above might suggest. As Ellis concludes, 'After all, the first true use of the open-ended series format would seem to be the news bulletin, endlessly updating events and never synthesising them'.[3]

The news we get is inevitably, then, the product of institutional pressures and structures, and of processes of both selection and construction. Its study focuses attention on issues of power, both in the relationship between media institutions and the state and in the internal workings of media institutions themselves, but it also raises issues about the gendered nature of definitions of the public sphere, about the *constructedness* of its representations of the real, and about the range of possible audience readings generated by such an apparently neutral form. News is, in John Fiske's words, 'one of the most complex and widely studied' media forms.[4] It is also one of the most difficult to define. As discourse, its relation to the real is not as straightforward as claims to objectivity or neutrality might suggest, and the complex nature of its relationship to social and ideological power structures forms one of the major themes in the chapters which follow.

Chapter 50 comprises two extracts from Peter Golding and Philip Elliott's 1979 study of the operations of news organisations in three different countries, *Making the News*. The first extract comes from their discussion of news values. Following Galtung and Ruge,[5] they define news values as 'qualities of events or of their journalistic construction, whose relative absence or presence recommends them for inclusion in the news product. The more of such qualities a story exhibits, the greater its chances of inclusion.' News values, however, do not act, as media institutions might claim, as prior guarantors of journalistic objectivity and impartiality. Rather, they are 'as much the resultant explanation or justification of necessary procedures as their source'. Working rules, they are organisational responses to 'the two immediate determinants of news making, perceptions of the audience and the availability of material'. The second extract discusses the consequences of these processes. News, argue Golding and Elliott, is ideology: the 'integrated picture of reality' which it provides, is a picture which legitimates the interests of the powerful in society. It does this by omitting two key elements in the world it portrays. The first is social process: news renders invisible the processes of change, presenting the world as a succession of single events. The second 'absent dimension' is social power: news offers us politics in the form of the rituals of political office and omits consideration of economic power altogether. The result is a picture of a world which appears both unchanging and unchangeable.

The extract from *Policing the Crisis* (Hall *et al.*, 1978) which follows (Chapter 51), represents a powerful application of Gramsci's theory of hegemony[6] to the processes of news production which have been outlined in the previous chapter. This theorising of the *'ideological role'* of the news media argues, first, that the process of ordering 'disorderly' events which news undertakes, is also a process of assigning *meaning*. It operates by placing those events within 'maps of meaning' into which our social world is *already* organised and which it is assumed we all share. Thus news not only defines for us *'what* significant events are taking place' but also positions these events – events which by their definition as news are disruptive or problematic – within an interpretive framework which both *'assumes and helps to construct society as a consensus'*. Further, Hall *et al.* argue that the 'working rules' which ensure 'impartiality', 'balance' and 'objectivity' in news, themselves operate in the interests of the

powerful in society. The requirement to rely on 'accredited' sources for interpretations of events means a 'systematically structured *over-accessing* to the
media' by the powerful, who then become the 'primary definers' of events.
'Oppositional' voices are usually confined to the accredited representatives of
official opposition parties. The definitions of the powerful thus become the
accepted definitions of social reality and consent to the existing social order is
secured.

John Hartley's chapter (Chapter 52) takes as its focus the *textual* characteristics of television news, and in particular the way in which TV news positions
itself and its stories in relation to the viewer. His purpose is to demonstrate
how 'large-scale issues, such as ideology and power, may be connected with
small-scale processes within texts'. His study analyses in detail, then, a single
news item within a main evening bulletin, in this case a bulletin broadcast on
BBC1 during the 'winter of discontent' in Britain of 1979. Hartley examines
the textual structures of the news story: its mode of address, camera positioning and movement, its narrative structure and point of view, its picture and
sound relations, and its discursive strategies. He argues that, despite the
institutional commitment to impartiality of TV news, and its undoubted
struggle to achieve this, its formal structures inevitably construct specific
identifications and positions for its viewers. Indeed, in its very search for
clarity of explanation, TV news taps into the popular discourses also mobilised
by politicians, and finds itself in unwitting collusion with the explanatory
structures which these assume.

In the public discourse of news, women, as a number of feminist commentators have pointed out, are a troubling element. They may be employed as
news*readers*, but the discourse which they speak is a masculine one, at odds
with the image of femininity (the 'to-be-looked-at-ness' of Laura Mulvey's
description) which they are required to present.[7] Lana Rakow and Kimberlie
Kranich's chapter (Chapter 53) examines the way in which women are represented within television news, employing theoretical approaches developed
in feminist film and literary theory to argue that in the masculine narrative of
news, women function not as 'speaking subjects' but as 'signs', carriers not
creators of meaning. Rakow and Kranich examined one month's news on
American television. Women, they found, appeared largely as representatives
of the private sphere – as mothers, wives or sisters of the protagonists of news
stories – or as victims, whether of violence, natural disaster or illness. Far fewer
appeared in roles with a 'public' character, as politicians, spokespersons or –
their most frequent public role – as 'celebrities'. Thus women, they argue,
function within news in a limited number of signifying roles: as 'signs of the
times', to illustrate the private consequences of public events, or as 'signs of
support' for institutions or policies. Where they claim to speak *for women* they
are marked as unusual, 'disorderly' or as in conflict with each other, and,
since the category 'woman' is seen as homogeneous, they are almost always
white. Television news, conclude Rakow and Kranich, locates women within a

taken-for-granted meaning system, fixing the meaning of 'the sign "woman"' even as it claims simply to relay 'the real'.

Michael Gurevitch's chapter (Chapter 54) deals with the recent effects on television news of the globalization of news sources. The deployment of satellite technology in the dissemination of television news, he argues, has shifted power relationships both within the media industries and between the media and governments. Television's capacity to tell the story of an event, via satellite technology, as it happens, makes it now a potential *player* on the stage of international events. In events like the student uprising in Beijing's Tiananmen Square of 1988, for example, it was television which *created* a global audience for the event, thus both influencing the behaviour of the event's protagonists and playing a significant part in the construction of world opinion about it. In many cases, too, television's role goes beyond this, so that it becomes a 'go-between' in international crises. As it thus becomes a participant in the events it reports, the line between 'social reality' and 'media reality' becomes increasingly blurred. Within national and local media systems this shift in power relationships is less easy to interpret. On the one hand, satellite technology may work to extend the reach of local news stations, thus making them less dependent on outside news sources. On the other, the rapid growth in the global dissemination of news images which are then edited and shaped within national broadcasting organisations may leave us as viewers *more* dependent on the frameworks of interpretation offered by news broadcasters. As audiences of global news stories, we have, after all, no alternative sources of information (for the importance of this, see Greg Philo's research below). All discussions of the mass media, concludes Gurevitch, are ultimately concerned with issues of power. In trying to make sense of the effects of the globalization of news sources, our starting point must be the shifting balances of power between media institutions and political institutions, within the media industries, between national and local news services, and between media producers and media audiences which such globalization inaugurates.

The work of the Glasgow University Media Group constitutes the most sustained analysis of television news content to have come out of British media studies. The final chapter in this section (Chapter 55) comes from Greg Philo of the GUMG, and reflects the recent expansion of the group's work into audience research, in order to 'examine how the structuring of news messages relate[s] to processes of understanding and belief within television audiences'.[8] Philo's research, published in *Seeing and Believing*, studied the responses of 169 people to the miners' strike of 1984–5. Groups of three to four people were given a set of photographs taken from television news programmes and asked to write their own 'news reports', which were then compared with actual news bulletins. Even one year after the strike had ended, which is when the exercise was carried out, there were 'extraordinary similarities'. Groups reproduced not only the general tone of bulletins but also actual phrases which had been used in them. Each participant was then asked a series of questions on issues such as picketing and violence in the strike. The extract included here discusses the resonses to these questions. Philo concludes that whether or not audiences accept television's account of events depends on 'what beliefs, experience, and information they bring to what they are shown'. Where people had personal experience of the events or access to other sources of information, they were able to negotiate or even reject television's account. Even in these cases, however, the influence of media and especially television was central, since 'it established so firmly the issues which came to be associated with the strike'. The emphasis on picketing violence, for example, which was reproduced in both the constructed 'news reports' and people's memories of the strike, proved very damaging to the miners' cause. Even those whose direct experience of the strike contradicted television's account found it difficult to assert alternative meanings in the face of 'the dominant flow of images from the media'.

NOTES

1. McQuail, *Mass Communication Theory*, 2nd edition (London: Sage, 1987), p. 203
2. Corner, 'Meaning, Genre and Context: The Problematics of "Public Knowledge" in the New Audience Studies'. In J. Curran and M. Gurevitch (eds), *Mass Media and Society* (London: Edward Arnold, 1991), pp. 267–84.
3. See this volume, Chapter 19.
4. Fiske, *Television Culture* (London: Methuen, 1987), p. 281.
5. See Johan Galtung and Mari Ruge, 'The structure of foreign news' (1965), extract reprinted as 'Structuring and selecting news', in S. Cohen and J. Young (eds), *The Manufacture of News* (London: Constable, 1973).
6. For a definition of this concept, see Introduction to Section 4.3.
7. See Patricia Holland, 'When a Woman Reads the News', in H. Baehr and G. Dyer (eds), *Boxed In: Women and Television* (London: Pandora Press, 1987), and Laura Mulvey, 'Visual Pleasure and Narrative Cinema', *Screen* 16:3 (1975) pp. 6–18.
8. Philo, 'Getting the Message: Audience Research in the Glasgow University Media Group', in J. Eldridge (ed.), *Getting the Message: News, Truth and Power* (London: Routledge, 1993), p. 254.

50

NEWS VALUES
AND NEWS PRODUCTION

Peter Golding and Philip Elliott

Discussions of news values usually suggest they are surrounded by a mystique, an impenetrable cloud of verbal imprecision and conceptual obscurity. Many academic reports concentrate on this nebulous aspect of news values and imbue them with far greater importance and allure than they merit. We have stressed that news production is rarely the active application of decisions of rejection or promotion to highly varied and extensive material. On the contrary, it is for the most part the passive exercise of routine and highly regulated procedures in the task of selecting from already limited supplies of information. News values exist and are, of course, significant. But they are as much the resultant explanation or justification of necessary procedures as their source.

News values are used in two ways. They are criteria of selection from material available to the newsroom of those items worthy of inclusion in the final product. Second, they are guidelines for the presentation of items, suggesting what to emphasise, what to omit, and where to give priority in the preparation of the items for presentation to the audience. News values are thus working rules, comprising a corpus of occupational lore which implicitly and often expressly explains and guides newsroom practice. It is not as true as often suggested that they are beyond the ken of the newsman, himself unable and unwilling to articulate them. Indeed, they pepper the daily exchanges between journalists in collaborative production procedures. Far more they are terse shorthand references to shared understandings about the nature and purpose of

From P. Golding and P. Elliott, *Making the News* (London: Longman, 1979) pp. 114–23.

news which can be used to ease the rapid and difficult manufacture of bulletins and news programmes. News values are qualities of events or of their journalistic construction, whose relative absence or presence recommends them for inclusion in the news product. The more of such qualities a story exhibits, the greater its chances of inclusion. Alternatively, the more different news values a story contains, the greater its chances of inclusion (see Galtung and Ruge, 1965). News values derive from unstated or implicit assumptions or judgements about three things:

1. The audience. Is this important to the audience or will it hold their attention? Is it of known interest, will it be understood, enjoyed, registered, perceived as relevant?
2. Accessibility – in two senses, prominence and ease of capture. Prominence: to what extent is the event known to the news organisation, how obvious is it, has it made itself apparent? Ease of capture: how available to journalists is the event, is it physically accessible, manageable technically, in a form amenable to journalism, is it ready-prepared for easy coverage, will it require great resources to obtain?
3. Fit. Is the item consonant with the pragmatics of production routines, is it commensurate with technical and organisational possibilities, is it homologous with the exigencies and constraints in programme making and the limitations of the medium? Does it make sense in terms of what is already known about the subject?

In other words, news values themselves derive from the two immediate determinants of news making, perceptions of the audience and the availability of material. Historically news values come to imbue the necessities of journalism with the lustre of good practice. They represent a classic case of making a virtue of necessity. This particularly applies to the broader values we have subsumed under the title of the occupational ideology – impartiality, objectivity, accuracy and so on. [. . .] News values are attached to the practice of the job, they are story values. Some of the more important are as follows. The first four derive from considerations of the audience, the remainder from a mixture of the three factors described above.

DRAMA

News stories are, as the term suggests, stories as well as news. Good ones exhibit a narrative structure akin to the root elements in human drama. To recall Reuven Frank, former President of NBC news in America, 'joy, sorrow, shock, fear, these are the stuff of news'. The good news story tells its tale with a beginning, a middle and an end, in that order.

[. . .]

Dramatic structure is often achieved by the presentation of conflict, most commonly by the matching of opposed viewpoints drawn from spokesmen of 'both sides of the question'. The audience is here felt to be served by being given the full picture as well as an interesting confrontation (cf. Epstein, 1973, pp. 168–9). [...]

VISUAL ATTRACTIVENESS

Television is a visual medium and the special power of television news is its ability to exploit this advantage. Television journalists are not obsessed by notions of 'good television' or 'good film'. They can't be, given the limited number of stories for which film is available. But the temptation to screen visually arresting material and to reject stories unadorned with good film is ever present and sometimes irresistible. In turn judgements about newsworthiness will be shaped by aesthetic judgements about film. A former editor-in-chief of the British Independent Television News has written that 'the key to putting more hard news on to the air effectively lies, I am sure, in putting more pictures and less talk into news programmes'. [...]

Just as audiences often justify their trust in the veracity of television news by reference to its use of film: 'you can actually see it happening', so newsmen refer to this quality in their favourite stories. 'Another good one was a building disaster. Three people died when it collapsed. We were the first station there and you could actually see people being rescued on camera.' (Head of News, WNBC.)

A story may be included simply because film is available or because of the dramatic qualities of the film. A story narrated several days previously will be resurrected as film arrives simply to show the film. Film can also provide concrete evidence of the global surveillance of electronic journalism by demonstrating visually the journalist's presence at an event.

ENTERTAINMENT

News programmes seek, and usually find, large audiences. To do so they must take account of entertainment values in the literal sense of providing captivating, humorous, titillating, amusing or generally diverting material. The 'human interest' story was invented for just this purpose. Broadcast news is generally sober and serious, taking its social responsibility and constitutional position as demanding less frivolity than might be licensed in the popular press. Helen Hughes, who over 30 years ago wrote a book on the human interest story, considered that human interest was a dimension added to other types of story. '...the news signalises [sic] a deviation from the expected, the normal and the traditional, which, when told with human interest is made human and comprehensible' (Hughes, 1942; see also Hughes, 1940). Although she was writing of the press this is especially true of broadcast news. The whimsical or bizarre events that are the currency of human interest stories, or the celebrities, children and animals that are their stars, are frequently too frivolous for broadcast news. But the human interest angle is an important way of making events palatable or comprehensible to audiences of broadcast news.

For some broadcast journalists there is a tension between the desire to ensure audience attentiveness and interest by following entertainment values, and a concern to maintain standards of seriousness and the plain honest narration of facts; between information and entertainment. This debate was alive in most newsrooms and linked back to arguments about how 'hard' or 'soft' news should be. It stems again from the dilemma of the journalist as producer of a marketable commodity, whose presentation and dressing up for the audience may cut across some of the professional ideals of the journalist *qua* journalist. The solution is normally the co-option of one ideal by the other, in the argument that to inform an audience you must first have its attention, and that there's no point preparing serious, well-intentioned, high-minded journalism if the audience registers its boredom by switching off. Thus entertainment is high on the list of news values both as an end in itself and as a means to other journalistic ideals.

IMPORTANCE

The most frequently cited reason for including a particular item in news bulletins is its importance. This is usually taken to mean that the reported event has considerable significance for large numbers of people in the audience. Most often importance is cited to explain the inclusion of items which might be omitted on the criteria of other audience-based news values. That is, items which may be boring, repetitive or non-visual must still be included despite audience disinterest. The item refers to something the audience needs to know. This news value is rooted in theories of the social role of journalism as tribune of the people. In broadcasting it has the further support that state-authorised corporations are expected to behave responsibly, informatively and educatively. Importance is often applied to political and foreign news. Both are assumed to be of greater interest to journalists than to their audience. Both are included however because of their unquestioned importance.

[...]

SIZE

The bigger the story the greater the likelihood of its inclusion, and the greater the prominence with which it will be presented. This simple rule of course begs the question of just how events are measured and which dimensions are relevant. The most common considerations are the numbers or type of people involved, or the scale of the event as an instance of a type. Thus the more people involved in a disaster or the presence of 'big names' at a formal occasion, enhance the initial visibility of such events and hence their consequent news value. Size as a news value normally qualifies other news values. That is, subsequent to the selection of events in the world as news, the criterion of size is applied to decide which are the most important news events. Less commonly events not normally registered as news become eligible by the sheer scale on which they occur.

PROXIMITY

Like size, the criterion of proximity derives partly from considerations of the audience, partly from problems of accessibility. Proximity has two senses, cultural and geographical. Stories are culturally proximate if they refer to events within the normal experience of journalists and their audience. They are the kinds of events which require a wide range of common language and shared cultural assumptions. For this reason they are normally, but not necessarily, domestic stories. Thus in Ireland the importance of the Church in secular life provides a background for stories on church or religion in other countries which might be ignored in more secularised nations. Cultural proximity can be applied to stories by, for example, putting foreign news into a domestic context to explain its importance or significance.

Geographical proximity refers to the simple rules of thumb that suggest the primacy of domestic news and the allocation of news from the rest of the world according to their nearness to the audience (see Schlesinger, 1978, p. 117). Here geography is distorted by the mechanics of news collection. As we have seen, the distribution of news gatherers is far from random, and in journalistic terms Lagos is far closer to London than to, say, Accra. Nonetheless the criterion is applied, and several Nigerian sub-editors adopted a three-tier news geography: Nigeria, Africa, the world. In the other countries, too, there was a sense of concentric spheres of influence. This design was of course totally disrupted by the availability of material. The geographical criterion thus moderates to two rules. Either, the further away an event the bigger it has to be, or, nearby events take precedence over similar events at a distance.

BREVITY

A story which is closely packed with facts and little padding is preferred to loose 'soft' news. Partly this relates to the journalistic role of informing rather than explaining, partly to concerns for what are seen as audience requirements and limitations. Audiences want just the facts and nothing but the facts. Since they also require comprehensiveness clearly no single item can be allowed to drag on too long. [...] News bulletins are normally between 15 and 30 minutes, and contain less than a couple of dozen items. Limiting news stories to their apparently more obvious elements is essential if there is to be room for even a minimal selection of the day's events. This limit seems to emphasise the necessary objectivity of broadcast news while in fact merely disguising the vast edifice of assumptions and cultural packaging which allow such brief items to make sense at all.

NEGATIVITY

Bad news is good news. As is often observed there is little mileage in reporting the safe arrival of aircraft, the continued health of a film star, or the smooth untroubled negotiations of a wage settlement. News is about disruptions in the normal current of events. In the literal sense it is not concerned with the uneventful. The concentration on negative events, that is events perceived or presented as damaging to social institutions, is not the result of a mischievous obsession with misery or discontent among journalists, but the outcome of the history of their occupation. News began as a service to groups directly concerned for the uninterrupted flow of commercial life. Interruptions included loss of merchandise at sea, financial upheavals in mercantile centres or, of course, war. These events remain paradigm instances of bad news, and as a result of news per se.

It is for this reason that news is described as a social surveillance, registering threats to the normal fabric of society and explaining their significance. The news value of negativity is therefore an important contributor to the social values in news, defining by default both the status quo and the sources and nature of threats to it. [...] It is worth noting that negativity is not a universal primary news value. What western journalists often see as the tediousness and irrelevance of broadcast news in eastern Europe has much to do with the conventions in many of these countries of presenting positive news (industrial production achievements, the award of honours, etc.) while excluding accidents, violence, crime and other negative categories prominent in news elsewhere (Varis, 1974; Lansipuro, 1975).

Some categories of negative news are disliked in broadcasting for their lack of other values. Crime was deliberately under-reported [...] in deference to the view that its presentation was pandering to the sensational news values more appropriate to the popular press. [...] Many broadcast journalists regretted this tendency to play down crime, and it was more often an executive than a 'shopfloor' view. Many journalists also subscribed to the view that showing too much violence was irresponsible. However, this view was frequently swamped by the power of news values such as drama and visual attractiveness. Again this is defined by reference to the audience. The point is made by Brucker (1973, p. 175):

> It is, of course, a basic principle of journalism that the bigger, the more off-beat, or the more bloody the spectacle, the greater the news value. This is not because newspapermen are more ghoulish or less sensitive to the finer things of life than their fellow men. It merely reflects the ineluctable fact that readers will flock to a story that has shock value but ignore one that is routine.

Or, as a journalist once pointed out, given a choice of two calamities news editors choose both, in the belief that the audience will be held by the dramatic power of tragic narrative.

RECENCY

The next three news values are derived more from production requirements than the perceived demands of the audience. Recency, the requirement that news be up to date and refer to events as close to transmission time as possible, derives from two factors. First, traditional journalistic competition puts a premium on the supply of 'earliest intelligencies' ahead of rivals. At its most successful this aim produces the 'scoop', an exclusive capture of a news event ahead of all competition. Second, the periodicity of news production itself sets the frame within which events in the world will be perceived. Thus daily production sets a daily frame, and news events must have occurred in the twenty-four hours between bulletins to merit inclusion. Although this is often impossible, especially for newsrooms dependent on air-freighted news film, the dictum that 'it's news when the audience first sees it' was only offered rather sheepishly, in the certain knowledge that it was an unhappy transgression of a root news value. The main point, however, is that processes which do not fit this daily cycle do not register as news by producing news events. Since daily reports are required the necessity of filling a daily quota becomes a laudable goal, and recency emerges as a journalistic virtue. Speed in collection and processing becomes paramount and is often cited as the particular merit of individual journalists or newsrooms. Conversely it is one of the main complaints against non-journalist broadcasters that they do not understand the need for speed and that technical and other facilities are inadequate for journalistic demands. The favourite accolade for Eurovision was that it permitted same-day film of European events. One of the most frequently cited problems was late arrival of unprocessed film and the inadequacy of film processing facilities.

The broadcasting equivalent of newspaper editions is the sequence of bulletins through the day, or evening on television. Journalists were acutely aware of the need to 'keep the picture changing'. [...] Journalists were fond of the fast-breaking story where the rapid movement of events pre-empted any need for the artificial injection of pace or change. Recency emphasises the task of news in topping up information on those events and institutions already defined as the substance of news.

ELITES

As a value within 'bigness' news values emphasise that big names are better news than nobodies, major personalities of more interest than ordinary folk. There is an obvious circularity in this in that well-known personalities become so by their exposure in news media. It is this that leads us to root this news value in production rather than in audience interests. Clearly audiences are interested in major rather than minor figures, people they all know about rather than the acquaintances of a few. But [...] elites are only partially exposed, and concentration on powerful or ruling groups is neither uniform nor comprehensive.

PERSONALITIES

News is about people, and mostly about individuals. This news value empha-sises the need to make stories comprehensible by reducing complex processes and institutions to the actions of individuals. This aim is, like many news values, a virtue born of necessity. Brief, and especially visual, journalism cannot deal with abstractions and has to narrate in the concrete. Thus it becomes a news value to 'seek the personal angle' or to 'personalise' the news. The effect of this is to treat institutional and international relations either as the interaction of individuals, or as being analogous to inter-personal relations. For example, international political news deals almost entirely with the diplomatic globe-trotting of major politicians, and international relations are seen to depend on how well political leaders get on. The analogies appear in the terminology of the emotions which characterises institutional or national relations. Governments become 'angry', unions are 'hot-headed', nations are 'anxious' or 'eager'. This is most easily portrayed by personalising such acts in the presentation of individuals.

This list may not exhaust all news values but it includes the main ones. Their obviousness can be illustrated by compiling a list of antonyms. It is hard to imagine broadcast journalists anywhere seeking news which dealt with small events, the long term, dull, distant, visually boring, unimportant people, and so on. Yet many of these labels describe events and processes which may well have significance for news audiences, but which are not news. The application of news values is part of the process by which this labelling occurs.

BIAS, OBJECTIVITY AND IDEOLOGY

[...]

It is possible to see broadcast news as simply the result of the bias of individual journalists, committed either to professional notions of how news should be structured, or to social views of the ideas it should convey. For David Brinkley, the authoritative American newscaster, 'News is what I say it is. It's something worth knowing by my standards' (Brinkley, 1964). Whether this is unguarded arrogance, or hyperbole to make a point about the essential indefinability of news, it represents to many people the most likely explanation of news output. The newscaster is the visible tip of the news production plant, a visual or aural reminder that it is a process handled by people; fallible, biased and opinionated, like the rest of us. The obvious weakness of this explanation is that the news changes very little when the individuals who produce it are changed. An occasional shift in partisanship may be detected in the reporting of particular issues, but the events covered, and the nature of their coverage, remain the same. [...] [E]ven in highly varied cultural and organisational settings broadcast news emerges with surprisingly similar forms and contents. In addition the division of labour required for production limits the impacts of individuals on news. [...] Epstein (1973, p. 28) describes how 'News executives

Ibid., pp. 206–11.

decide on the development of correspondents and camera crews; assignment editors select what stories will be covered and by whom; field producers, in constant phone contact with the producers in New York, usually supervise the preparation of filming of stories … editors … reconstruct the story on film …' and so on.

Yet the notion of group, if not individual, bias persists. [...] The notion of bias is often contrasted with objectivity, and for clarity's sake two distinctions should be made. First impartiality and objectivity are distinct. Impartiality implies a disinterested approach to news, lacking in motivation to shape or select material according to a particular view or opinion. Objectivity, however defined, is clearly a broader demand than this. A journalist may well be impartial towards the material on which he works, yet fail to achieve objectivity – a complete and unrefracted capture of the world – due to the inherent limitations in news gathering and processing. Second, the bias of an individual reporter dealing with a single event may be reduced or even eliminated by, for example, the deliberate application of self-discipline and professional standards of process. In other words we should distinguish bias as the deliberate aim of journalism, which is rare, from bias as the inevitable but unintended consequence of organisation.

There are, then, three possible views of journalistic objectivity and impartiality. First, there is the professional view that it is possible to be both, based on the idea that objectivity and impartiality are attitudes of mind. Second is the view that objectivity may well be a nebulous and unattainable goal, but that impartiality is still desirable and possible.

[...]

The third view, that neither objectivity or impartiality are in any serious sense possible in journalism, comes from a change of analytical perspective, from the short-term and deliberate production of news stories to the long-term and routine, unreflective practices of journalism as we have analysed them in this study. Objectivity and impartiality remain the aims of most day-to-day journalism. But we should understand these terms as labels applied by journalists to the rules which govern their working routines. Objectivity is achieved by subscribing to and observing these sets of rules, which are themselves the object of our analysis. We have seen how these rules, both the explicit regulations of organisational charters and newsroom manuals, and the implicit understandings of news values, are derived from the currents of supply and demand which eddy round the newsroom.

The assumed needs and interests of audiences on the one hand, and the truncated supply of information into the newsroom on the other, both exert pressures to which the organisation of news production responds. What are the consequences of these pressures?

When we come to assess news as a coherent view of the world, that is to step up from news values to social values, we enter an altogether more complex and tangled argument. News is ideology to the extent that it provides an integrated picture of reality. But an ideology is more than this; it is also the world view of particular social groups, and especially of social classes. The claim that news is ideology implies that it provides a world view both consistent in itself, and supportive of the interests of powerful social groupings. This can come about in two ways.

First, news is structured by the exigencies of organised production which are the main concern of this study. These allow only a partial view of the reported world which may or may not coincide with a ruling ideology. The historical process by which this coincidence occurs is more than accidental, and is rooted in the development of news as a service to elite groups. [...] Thus most of the basic goals and values which surround journalism refer to the needs and interests of these groups. Second, in attempting to reach widespread, anonymous audiences news draws on the most broadly held common social values and assumptions, in other words the prevailing consensus, in establishing common ground for communication with its audiences. In the case of broadcast journalism the complex relationship with the state exaggerates this need to cling to the central and least challenged social values which provide implicit definitions of actions and events as acceptable or unacceptable, usual or unusual, legitimate or illegitimate.

[...]

There are two key elements to the world of broadcast news; the invisibility of social process, and the invisibility of power in society. We can discuss these two lacunae separately. First, the loss of a sense of social process. News is about the present, or the immediate past. It is an account of today's events. The world of broadcast news is a display of single events, making history indeed 'one damn thing after another'. Yet in this whirl of innumerable events the lingering impression is of stasis. Events are interchangeable, a succession rather than an unfolding. What is provided is a topping up of the limited range of regularly observed events in the world with more of the same. A reassuring sameness assimilates each succession of events to ready-made patterns in a timeless mosaic.

This fragmentation of social process, evacuating history, has been described as 'a kind of consecration to collective amnesia' (Gabel, 1967, p. 113). In a real sense reason disappears as actors flit across the journalistic stage, perform and hurriedly disappear. [...] Thus industrial relations appears not as an evolving conflict of interest but as a sporadic eruption of inexplicable anger and revolt (Hartmann, 1976; Glasgow University Media Group, 1976). Similarly the political affairs of foreign lands appear as spasmodic convulsions of a more or less violent turn, while international relations appear to result from the occasional urge for travel and conversation indulged in by the diplomatic jet-set.

The second absent dimension in broadcast news is that of power. News is about the actions of individuals, not corporate entities, thus individual authority rather than the exertion of entrenched power is seen to be the mover of events. News, and broadcast news in particular, is the last refuge of the great man theory of history. Yet faces change, power holders are replaced, and such changes take pride of place in the circumspection of the news. The continuing and consistent power of the position is masked by concentration on the recurrent changes of office-holder.

In domestic news the focus is on central political elites and their daily gamesmanship in the arenas of conflict resolution. Groups which may exert power but which do not make news disappear, by definition, from view, and with them the visibility of power itself. Prominent among the absentees are the owners of property and their corporate representatives. Of all the institutions which contribute to social process none is so invisible to broadcast news as the world of the company boardroom. In international news the world revolves round the news capitals in Europe and North America. For audiences in the Third World their fellows in three continents are invisible, a communality of interest cannot emerge and problems appear particular and separate to each watching nation. Thus it is not the *effect* of the rich and powerful nations on the Third World that is seen, but their attractiveness as models, benevolence as aid-givers and convenors of conferences, or wisdom as disinterested umpires in local disputes.

Power disappears in the institutional definitions the news provides, an agenda of issues and arenas to which attention is directed. In particular politics is separated from power. Power is seen only in the public display of formality, gesture and speech by major political actors. It is defined by reference to government and the central institutions of political negotitaion. Rositi has similarly drawn attention in his analysis of European television news to 'the primacy of formal politics' in the television news world (Rositi, 1975, pp. 25–30), and remarks on the absence of financial and business elites. Thus power is reduced to areas of negotiation compromise, and politics to a recurrent series of decisions, debates and personalities. It is removed from the institutions of production. Thus news bears witness to the institutional separation of economics and politics, a precondition for the evacuation of power from its account of the world. Power is absent from news by virtue of this severance of politics from economics; power is located in authority not in control, in the office-holder not the property owner. News thus provides a particular and truncated view of power, and in this sense power is a dimension that is effectively missing from news.

With these two missing dimensions – social process or history, and power – news indeed provides a world view. The question remains to what extent this is a coherent ideology. Analyses which see news as necessarily a product of powerful groups, in society, designed to provide a view of the world consonant with the interests of those groups simplify the situation too far to be helpful. The occupational routines and beliefs of journalists do not allow a simple conduit between the ruling ideas of the powerful and their distribution via the airwaves.

Yet the absence of power and process clearly precludes the development of views which might question the prevailing distribution of power, or its roots in the evolution of economic distribution and control. A world which appears fundamentally unchanging, subject to the genius or caprice of myriad powerful individuals, is not a world which appears susceptible to radical change or challenge.

There are three ways, then, in which broadcast news is ideological. First it focuses our attention on those institutions and events in which social conflict is managed and resolved. It is precisely the arenas of consensus formation which provide both access and appropriate material for making the news. Second, broadcast news, in studiously following statutory demands to eschew partiality or controversy, and professional demands for objectivity and neutrality, is left to draw on the values and beliefs of the broadest social consensus. It is this process which Stuart Hall (1970, p. 1056) describes as 'the steady and unexamined play of attitudes which, via the mediating structure of professionally defined news values, inclines all the media toward the status quo'. The prevailing beliefs in any society will rarely be those which question existing social organisation or values. News will itself merely reinforce scepticism about such divergent, dissident or deviant beliefs. Third, as we have seen, broadcast news is, for historical and organisational reasons, inherently incapable of providing a portrayal of social change or of displaying the operation of power in and between societies. It thus portrays a world which is unchanging and unchangeable.

The key elements of any ruling ideology are the undesirability of change, and its impossibility; all is for the best and change would do more harm than good, even if it were possible. Broadcast news substantiates this philosophy because of the interplay of the three processes we have just described.

REFERENCES

Brinkley, D. (1964) Interview, in TV *Guide*, 11 April.
Brucker, H. (1973) *Communication is Power: Unchanging Values in a Changing Journalism*, New York, Oxford University Press.
Epstein, E. J. (1973) *News from Nowhere – Television and the News*, New York, Random House.
Gabel, J. (1967) *La Falsa Conscienza*, Dedalo, Bari, quoted in Rositi (1975).
Galtung, J. and Ruge, M. (1965) The structure of foreign news, *Journal of Peace Research*, vol. 1, pp. 64–90.
Glasgow University Media Group (1976) *Bad News*, London, Routledge & Kegan Paul.
Hall, S. (1970) A world at one with itself, *New Society*, 18 June, pp. 1056–8.
Hartmann, P. (1976) *The Media and Industrial Relations*, unpublished, Leicester Centre for Mass Communication Research.
Hughes, H. M. (1940) *News and the Human Interest Story*, Chicago, University of Chicago Press.
Hughes, H. M. (1942) The social interpretation of news, *Annals of the American Academy of Political and Social Science*, vol. 219, pp. 11–17.
Lansipuro, Y. (1975) Joint Eurovision/Intervision news study, *EBU Review*, vol. XXVI, no. 3, May, pp. 37–40.

Rositi, F. (1975) The television news programme: fragmentation and recomposition of our image of society. Report presented to Prix Italia, Florence.

Schlesinger, P. (1978) *Putting 'Reality' Together: BBC News*, London, Constable.

Varis, T. (1974) *Television News in Eurovision and Intervision*, Report to EBU Working Party on Television News, Lisbon.

51

THE SOCIAL PRODUCTION OF NEWS

Stuart Hall, Chas Critcher, Tony Jefferson, John Clarke and Brian Roberts

The media do not simply and transparently report events which are 'naturally' newsworthy *in themselves*. 'News' is the end-product of a complex process which begins with a systematic sorting and selecting of events and topics according to a socially constructed set of categories. As MacDougall puts it:

> At any given moment billions of simultaneous events occur throughout the world. .... All of these occurences are potentially news. They do not become so until some purveyor of news gives an account of them. The news, in other words, is the account of the event, not something intrinsic in the event itself.[1]

One aspect of the structure of selection can be seen in the routine organisation of newspapers with respect to regular types or areas of news. Since newspapers are committed to the regular production of news, these organisational factors will, in turn, affect what is selected. For example, newspapers become pre-directed to certain types of event and topic in terms of the organisation of their own work-force (e.g. specialist correspondents and departments, the fostering of institutional contacts, etc.) and the structure of the papers themselves (e.g. home news, foreign, political, sport, etc.).[2]

Given that the organisation and staffing of a paper regularly direct it to certain categories of items, there is still the problem of selecting, from the many contending items within any one category, those that are felt will be of interest

From S. Hall et al., *Policing the Crisis: Mugging, the State, and Law and Order* (Basingstoke: Macmillan Education Ltd., 1978) pp. 53–60.

to the reader. This is where the *professional ideology* of what constitutes 'good news' – the newsman's sense of *news values* – begins to structure the process.

[...]

These two aspects of the social production of news – the bureaucratic organisation of the media which produces the news in specific types or categories and the structure of news values which orders the selection and ranking of particular stories within these categories – are only part of the process. The third aspect – the moment of the *construction* of the news story itself – is equally important, if less obvious. This involves the presentation of the item to its *assumed* audience, in terms which, as far as the presenters of the item can judge, will make it comprehensible to that audience. If the world is not to be represented as a jumble of random and chaotic events, then they must be identified (i.e. named, defined, related to other events known to the audience), and assigned to a social context (i.e. placed within a frame of meanings familiar to the audience). This process – identification and contextualisation – is one of the most important through which events are 'made to mean' by the media. An event only 'makes sense' if it can be located within a range of known social and cultural identifications. If newsmen did not have available – in however routine a way – such cultural 'maps' of the social world, they could not 'make sense' for their audiences of the unusual, unexpected and unpredicted events which form the basic content of what is 'newsworthy'. Things are newsworthy because they represent the changefulness, the unpredictability and the conflictful nature of the world. But such events cannot be allowed to remain in the limbo of the 'random' – they must be brought within the horizon of the 'meaningful'. This bringing of events within the realm of meanings means, in essence, referring unusual and unexpected events to the 'maps of meaning' which already form the basis of our cultural knowledge, into which the social world is *already* 'mapped'. The social identification, classification and contextualisation of news events in terms of these background frames of reference is the fundamental process by which the media make the world they report on intelligible to readers and viewers. This process of 'making an event intelligible' is a social process – constituted by a number of specific journalistic practices, which embody (often only implicitly) crucial assumptions about what society is and how it works.

One such background assumption is the *consensual* nature of society: the process of *signification* – giving social meanings to events – *both assumes and helps to construct society as a 'consensus'*. We exist as members of one society *because* – it is assumed – we share a common stock of cultural knowledge with our fellow men: we have access to the same 'maps of meanings'. Not only are we all able to manipulate these 'maps of meaning' to understand events, but we have fundamental interests, values and concerns in common, which these maps embody or reflect. We all want to, or do, maintain basically the same perspective *on* events. In this view, what unites us, as a society and a culture – its consensual side – far outweighs what divides and distinguishes us as groups or classes from other groups. Now, at one level, the existence of a cultural consensus is an obvious truth; it is the basis of all social communication.[3] If we were not members of the same language community we literally could not communicate with one another. On a broader level, if we did not inhabit, to some degree, the same classifications of social reality we could not 'make sense of the world together'. In recent years, however, this basic cultural fact about society has been raised to an extreme ideological level. Because we occupy the same society and belong to roughly the same 'culture', it is assumed that there is, basically, only *one* perspective on events: that provided by what is sometimes called *the* culture, or (by some social scientists) *the* 'central value system'. This view denies any major structural discrepancies between different groups, or between the very different maps of meaning in a society. This 'consensual' viewpoint has important political consequences, when used as the taken-for-granted basis of communication. It carries the assumption that we also all have roughly the same *interest* in the society, and that we all roughly have an equal share of power in the society. This is the essence of the idea of the political consensus. 'Consensual' views of society represent society as if there are no major cultural or economic breaks, no major conflicts of interests between classes and groups. Whatever disagreements exist, it is said, there are legitimate and institutionalised means for expressing and reconciling them. The 'free market' in opinions and in the media is supposed to guarantee the reconciliation of cultural discontinuities between one group and another. The political institutions – parliament, the two-party system, political representation, etc. – are supposed to guarantee equal access for all groups to the decision making process. The growth of a 'consumer' economy is supposed to have created the economic conditions for everyone to have a stake in the making and distribution of wealth. The rule of law protects us all equally. This consensus view of society is particularly strong in modern, democratic, organised capitalist societies; and the media are among the institutions whose practices are most widely and consistently predicated upon the assumption of a 'national consensus'. So that, when events are 'mapped' by the media into frameworks of meaning and interpretation, it is assumed that we all equally possess and know how to use these frameworks, that they are drawn from fundamentally the same structures of understanding for all social groups and audiences. Of course, in the formation of opinion, as in politics and economic life, it is conceded that there will be differences of outlook, disagreement, argument and opposition; but these are understood as taking place within a broader basic framework of agreement – 'the consensus' – to which everyone subscribes, and within which every dispute, disagreement or conflict of interest can be reconciled by discussion, without recourse to confrontation or violence.

[...]

Events, as news, then, are regularly interpreted within frameworks which derive, in part, from this notion of *the consensus* as a basic feature of everyday life. They are elaborated through a variety of 'explanations', images and discourses which articulate what the audience is assumed to think and know about the society.

[...]

What, then, is the underlying significance of the framing and interpretive function of news presentation? We suggest that it lies in the fact that the media are often presenting information about events which occur outside the direct experience of the majority of the society. The media thus represent the primary, and often the only, source of information about many important events and topics. Further, because news is recurrently concerned with events which are 'new' or 'unexpected', the media are involved in the task of making comprehensible what we would term 'problematic reality'. Problematic events breach our commonly held expectations and are therefore threatening to a society based around the expectation of consensus, order and routine. Thus the media's mapping of problematic events within the conventional understandings of the society is crucial in two ways. The media define for the majority of the population *what* significant events are taking place, but, also, they offer powerful interpretations of *how* to understand these events. Implicit in those interpretations are orientations towards the events and the people or groups involved in them.

PRIMARY AND SECONDARY DEFINERS

In this section we want to begin to account for the 'fit' between dominant ideas and professional media ideologies and practices. This cannot be simply attributed – as it sometimes is in simple conspiracy theories – to the fact that the media are in large part capitalist-owned (though that structure of ownership is widespread), since this would be to ignore the day-to-day 'relative autonomy' of the journalist and news producers from direct economic control. Instead we want to draw attention to the more routine *structures* of news production to see how the media come in fact, in the 'last instance', to *reproduce the definitions of the powerful*, without being, in a simple sense, in their pay. Here we must insist on a crucial distinction between *primary* and *secondary definers* of social events.

The media do not themselves autonomously create news items; rather they are 'cued in' to specific new topics by regular and reliable institutional sources. As Paul Rock notes:

> In the main journalists position themselves so that they have access to institutions which generate a useful volume of reportable activity at regular intervals. Some of these institutions do, of course, make themselves visible by means of dramatization, or through press releases and press agents. Others are known to regularly produce consequential events. The courts, sports grounds and parliament mechanically manufacture news which is ... assimilated by the press.[4]

One reason for this has to do with the internal pressures of news production – as Murdock notes:

> The incessant pressures of time and the consequent problems of resource allocation and work scheduling in news organisations can be reduced or alleviated by covering 'pre-scheduled events'; that is, events that have been announced in advance by their convenors. However, one of the consequences of adopting this solution to scheduling problems is to increase the newsmen's dependence on news sources willing and able to preschedule their activities.[5]

The second has to do with the fact that media reporting is underwritten by notions of 'impartiality', 'balance' and 'objectivity'. This is formally enforced in television (a near-monopoly situation, where the state is directly involved in a regulatory sense) but there are also similar professional ideological 'rules' in journalism.[6] One product of these rules is the carefully structured distinction between 'fact' and 'opinion'. [. . .] For our present purposes, the important point is that these professional rules give rise to the practice of ensuring that media statements are, wherever possible, grounded in 'objective' and 'authoritative' statements from 'accredited' sources. This means constantly turning to accredited representatives of major social institutions – MPs for political topics, employers and trade-union leaders for industrial matters, and so on. Such institutional representatives are 'accredited' because of their Institutional power and position, but also because of their 'representative' status: either they represent 'the people' (MPs, Ministers, etc.) or organised interest groups (which is how the TUC and the CBI are now regarded). One final 'accredited source' is 'the expert': his calling – the 'disinterested' pursuit of knowledge – not his position or his representativeness, confers on his statements 'objectivity' and 'authority'. Ironically, the very rules which aim to preserve the impartiality of the media, and which grew out of desires for greater professional neutrality, also serve powerfully to orientate the media in the 'definitions of social reality' which their 'accredited sources' – the institutional spokesmen – provide.

These two aspects of news production – the practical pressures of constantly working against the clock and the professional demands of impartiality and objectivity – combine to produce a systematically structured *over-accessing* to the media of those in powerful and privileged institutional positions. The media thus tend, faithfully and impartially, to reproduce symbolically the existing structure of power in society's institutional order. This is what Becker has called the 'hierarchy of credibility' – the likelihood that those in powerful or high-status positions in society who offer opinions about controversial topics will have their definitions accepted, because such spokesmen are understood to have access to more accurate or more specialised information on particular topics than the majority of the population.[7] The result of this structured preference given in the media to the opinions of the powerful is that these 'spokesmen' become what we call the *primary definers* of topics.

What is the significance of this? It could rightly be argued that through the requirement of 'balance' [...] alternative definitions do get a hearing: each 'side' *is* allowed to present its case. In point of fact [...] the setting up of a topic in terms of a debate within which there are oppositions and conflicts is also one way of *dramatising* an event so as to enhance its newsworthiness. The important point about the structured relationship between the media and the primary institutional definers is that it permits the institutional definers to establish the initial definition or *primary interpretation* of the topic in question. This interpretation then 'commands the field' in all subsequent treatment and sets the terms of reference within which all further coverage or debate takes place. Arguments *against* a primary interpretation are forced to insert themselves into *its* definition of 'what is at issue' – they must begin from this framework of interpretation as their starting-point. This initial interpretative framework – what Lang and Lang have called an 'inferential structure'[8] – is extremely difficult to alter fundamentally, once established. For example, once race relations in Britain have been defined as a 'problem of numbers' (i.e. how many blacks there are in the country), then even liberal spokesmen, in proving that the figures for black immigrants have been exaggerated, are nevertheless obliged to subscribe, implicitly, to the view that the debate is 'essentially' *about numbers*.

[...]

Effectively, then, the primary definition *sets the limit* for all subsequent discussion by *framing what the problem is*. This initial framework then provides the criteria by which all subsequent contributions are labelled as 'relevant' to the debate, or 'irrelevant' – beside the point. Contributions which stray from this framework are exposed to the charge that they are 'not addressing the problem'.[9]

The media, then, do not simply 'create' the news; nor do they simply transmit the ideology of the 'ruling class' in a conspiratorial fashion. Indeed, we have suggested that, in a critical sense, the media are frequently not the 'primary definers' of news events at all; but their structured relationship to power has the effect of making them play a crucial but secondary role in *reproducing* the definitions of those who have privileged access, as of right, to the media as 'accredited sources'. From this point of view, in the moment of news production, the media stand in a position of structured subordination to the primary definers.

It is this structured relationship – between the media and its 'powerful' sources – which begins to open up the neglected question of the *ideological role* of the media. It is this which begins to give substance and specificity to Marx's basic proposition that 'the ruling ideas of any age are the ideas of its ruling class'. Marx's contention is that this dominance of 'ruling ideas' operates primarily because, in addition to its ownership and control of the means of material production, this class also owns and controls the means of 'mental production'. In producing their definition of social reality, and the place of 'ordinary people' within it, they construct a particular image of society which represents particular class interests as the interests of all members of society. Because of their control over material and mental resources, and their domination of the major institutions of society, this class's definitions of the social world provide the basic rationale for those institutions which protect and reproduce their 'way of life'. This control of mental resources ensures that theirs are the most powerful and 'universal' of the available definitions of the social world. Their universality ensures that they are shared to some degree by the subordinate classes of the society. Those who govern, govern also through ideas; thus they govern with the consent of the subordinate classes, and not principally through their overt coercion. Parkin makes a similar point: 'the social and political definitions of those in dominant positions tend to become objectified in the major institutional orders, so providing the moral framework for the entire social system.'[10]

In the major social, political and legal institutions of society, coercion and constraint are never wholly absent. This is as true for the media as elsewhere. For example, reporters and reporting *are* subject to economic and legal constraints, as well as to more overt forms of censorship (e.g. over the coverage of events in Northern Ireland). But the transmission of 'dominant ideas' depends *more* on non-coercive mechanisms for their reproduction. Hierarchical structures of command and review, informal socialisation into institutional roles, the sedimenting of dominant ideas into the 'professional ideology' – all help to ensure, within the media, their continued reproduction in the dominant form. What we have been pointing to in this section is *precisely how one particular professional practice ensures that the media, effectively but 'objectively', play a key role in reproducing the dominant field of the ruling ideologies.*

[...]

NOTES

1. C. MacDougall, *Interpretative Reporting* (New York: Macmillan, 1968) p. 12.
2. For a fuller account of the impact of these 'bureaucratic' factors in news production, see P. Rock, 'News as Eternal Recurrence', in *The Manufacture of News: Social Problems, Deviance and the Mass Media*, ed. S. Cohen and J. Young (London: Constable, 1973).
3. L. Wirth, 'Consensus and Mass Communications', *American Sociological Review*, vol. 13, 1948.
4. Rock, 'News as Eternal Recurrence', p. 77.
5. G. Murdock, 'Mass Communication and the Construction of Meaning', in *Rethinking Social Psychology*, ed. N. Armistead (Harmondsworth: Penguin, 1974) p. 210.
6. For a historical account of the evolution of those rules, see J. W. Carey, 'The Communications Revolution and the Professional Communicator', *Sociological Review Monograph*, vol. 13, 1969.
7. H. Becker, 'Whose Side are We on?', in *The Relevance of Sociology*, ed. J. D. Douglas (New York: Appleton-Century Crofts, 1972).

8. K. Lang and G. Lang, 'The Inferential Structure of Political Communications', *Public Opinion Quarterly*, vol. 19, Summer 1955.

9. See S. M. Hall, 'The "Structured Communication" of Events', paper for the Obstacles to Communication Symposium, UNESCO/Division of Philosophy (available from Centre for Contemporary Cultural Studies, University of Birmingham); Clarke et al., 'The Selection of Evidence and the Avoidance of Racialism: a Critique of the Parliamentary Select Committee on Race Relations and Immigration', *New Community*, vol. III, no. 3, Summer 1974.

10. F. Parkin, *Class Inequality and Political Order* (London: MacGibbon & Kee, 1971) p. 83.

52

HOME HELP FOR POPULIST POLITICS: RELATIONAL ASPECTS OF TV NEWS

John Hartley

[...]

EYE CONTACT

Television news exploits one of the most distinctive features of TV in general, namely the representation of people, and in particular of people's faces, expressive features and eyes, in the process of narration. But whereas by established convention TV and cinema fiction rarely make use of direct eye-contact with the camera/viewer, television news has instated this form of address at the centre of its textual strategy. Thus, without verbalizing it, television news operates on a first person (1) to second person (you) axis, in the form of the newsreader's relation to the viewer via direct address and eye-contact.

In addition to the relations between viewer and newsreader/reporter there is a textual relation between viewer and news story; that is, between the viewer and the characters whose stories are narrated. In this case there is a choice as to whether the relation is constructed as 'we' (including the viewer with depicted characters), or as 'they' (excluding the viewer from identification with them). Television news activates a full circuit between first (narrator), second (viewer) and third (depicted) persons, being able to align the viewer to the newsworthy people represented in the story (as either we or they), but also being able to address the viewer over the heads, literally, of such people. It can do this without verbal intrusion; eye-contact alone establishes an I/you axis between

From Hartley, *Tele-ology: Studies in Television* (London and New York: Routledge, 1992) pp. 75–90.

newsreader and viewer, without, apparently, any unwanted editorializing interventions.

INSTITUTIONAL VS FORMAL RELATIONS

However, television news is not simply a matter of newsreader addressing viewer. Beyond this basic relation are (at least) two other kinds of relation that TV news has to accommodate in its routine practices. These are extra-textual relations, and it so happens that they make mutually exclusive, and thus contra-dictory, demands on TV news. The first may be called TV news's *institutional* relations. Foremost among these is the statutory requirement laid on broad-casters that TV news be impartial. That is, events must be narrated without the news adopting the point of view of any one faction, party or person. The second relation, which may be called *formal*, contradicts the first because news cannot escape the television/cinema codes of visual representation that it uses. To put it bluntly, the first problem news camerawork faces is where to put the camera. In fiction-filmmaking, a conventional distinction has arisen between what are known as p.o.v. (point of view) shots and neutral shots. A p.o.v. shot is one that shows the scene or characters from one of the characters' point of view. Often the point of view is visually *motivated* by including part of the observer's figure (shoulder, side of head) seen from behind, in the frame. Such shots are often used to show dialogue between two characters, with the point of view of each seen in alternate shots (a sequential strategy known as shot–reverse-shot). The viewer is thus positioned as the character whose point of view is shown. However, the viewer is not limited to this point of view, since that of several different characters may be shown, as well as neutral shots. Hence, during the course of a film, the viewer achieves a kind of composite point of view; one which is privilege over the point of view of any one character since the viewer knows more, from more points of view, than anyone in the film. In fact, television/cinema codes position the viewer as that point from which all the different characters, scenes, actions and plot developments are *intelligible*, and this totalizing position is denied to the characters themselves.

This discussion leads to two conclusions about news camerawork. First, the conventionalized distinction between p.o.v. shots and neutral shots does not stand up to close inspection. All shots have a point of view, whether *internally motivated* by the placing of a character, or *externally motivated* by the posi-tioning of the imaginary observer (viewer). Furthermore, shots presented as neutral are unable to stand alone – they are only ever seen in contrast to p.o.v. shots. Thus, at the very least, neutral shots signify a point of view which is not that of the participants. When set against other shots that do offer a partici-pant's point of view, such neutrality becomes, ideologically, very productive.

Second, news camerawork solves the problem of where to put the camera in a very similar way to the way fictional conventions have dealt with it. That is, the news also constructs an imaginary viewer, positioned as it were behind the camera, from whose point of view the partial and disjointed fragments of picture, sound and story can cohere into intelligibility. As in fiction, so in news; there is no point of view from within the news where it all makes sense. None of the institutional personnel (newsreader, correspondent, reporter, etc.) and none of the accessed characters whose faces and voices appear in the news are in a position to see the whole. Indeed, all the people who are seen, and all the textual deployments of sound, picture and sequence, are subordinate to the imaginary viewer, who thus takes the place of the omniscient author/narrator of realist novels.

Here the force of the inevitable contradiction between TV news's *formal* relations and its *institutional* relations can be sensed. News has to be impartial; that is, it must narrate events without a point of view. Since that is impossible, there is a contradiction between (required) impartiality and (unavoidable) point of view. The construction of an imaginary viewer as the point of intelligibility actually makes matters worse. This is because, in the first place, there is no viewer at the point(s) of production who can offer advice on what an appropriate point of view might look like; broadcasters work to a fictionalized image of the viewer. Second, there is no unified point of view among those who actually watch the news at the point(s) of consumption. Quite the reverse, in fact.

Nevertheless, the news institutions have not only accepted the requirement of impartiality, but (even in the face of widespread doubt and criticism) they continue to assert that they have achieved it. Thus the news is presented with an assurance not only that it is intelligible to the viewer, but also that it is true. So the contradiction is erased in the relation the news proposes with its viewers – the type of intelligibility that is offered textually seems to escape the problem of point of view, since it is the only point of view that allows no alternative – the point of view of impartiality, namely truth.

IT'S A PLOT

At this point it is useful to turn to detailed analysis of the news text, from the BBC *Nine O'Clock News* of 1 February 1979.[1] [...] It was the second item of its bulletin, being preceded by a foreign affairs story from Iran about the return of the Ayatollah Khomeini from exile. The story was divided up into seven sections, of which two (sections IV and VI) were film reports. This analysis concentrates largely on these two sections. [...]

The most obvious means by which the viewer is positioned in relation to the event is through what can be called the plot of the story as a whole. The plot is a simple affair of cause and effect. It is initiated verbally:

> Here at home the dispute by public service workers is still spreading. (*Cause*)

> Half the hospitals in England and Wales and some in Scotland can now open their doors only to emergency cases. (*Effect*)

[...]

Internal vs External Point of View

Within the cause–effect plot, the camera is used to establish point of view in different ways for the different participants. As far as the picketers are concerned, the point of view of the shots of them can be established by asking whether the camera point of view is that of the strikers themselves. For this to be so, the scene would have to be shot from their point of view; that is, looking *out* of the picket line (across the street or into the entrance), or else looking *inside* the picket line, sharing the talk and seeing the faces of the others there. Such shots would, in fact, differ considerably from what is shown. These are filmed from a distance outside the picket line, usually from across a road, and the picketers are only seen as a collectivity, in long-shot, never as individuals. These shots, then, display an *external* point of view, orienting the viewer along the third person to second person axis of relation (they/you): the point of view is the viewer's.

In the film sequences showing the effect of the action inside the hospital the point of view is different. They are framed more tightly than the shots of the pickets, showing fewer people at a time on screen, usually no more than two, and more of their facial and expressive features are identifiable than are those of the strikers. Participants move towards the camera and even past it, including it within their action. These shots, then, display an *internal* point of view, orienting the viewer along the third person to first person axis of relation (they/we). This positions the viewer *as* one of the participants, and is comparable to proper p.o.v. shots in cinema.

Deferential vs Unmotivated Camera-Movement

A further set of differences that compounds these point of view distinctions is associated with movements of the camera itself, as opposed to the participants moving in the frame. Here again the differences are organized about the strikers on the one hand, and the patients and medical staff on the other. Where there is camera-movement in the shots of the picketers, it is *unmotivated* by their movements. There are reframings from close-ups of details (an entrance sign, a placard, a banner) to long-shots of the nearby pickets. If this is compared with the shots of patients and medical staff, it is clear that in these the camera-movements are motivated by action. The camera is *deferential*; it follows the actions of the people in shot, usually panning. The only shots in the 'effects' sequences where this doesn't hold true are those that show inanimate objects.

[...]

In summary of this section it is possible to set out how the relational dimension of the camera point of view has sorted the strikers and the nurses/patients into a they/we position:

```
                      cause : effect
         external point of view : internal point of view
   unmotivated camera-movement : deferential camera-movement
                long/wide frame : mid/close frame
              strikers/picketers : nurses/patients/employers
                           they : we
```

Narrative Point of View

While the pictures are busy sorting out the strikers from the nurses and patients, the verbal component of the film reports is adding its own relational dimension to the story. It too offers a point of view from which the viewer can make sense of the story. It is possible to use a simple analytical procedure which may be called *reversal* to try to identify a narrative point of view. Here is a version of the opening sequence of section IV. But the 'they' pronouns and cognates, and the names, have been reversed for the sake of analysis to read 'we' instead (in italics). Having done this, it is possible to look for any strain to the syntax, or any disruption of the popular idiom in which the voice-over is delivered:

> *We* didn't give much warning about *our* strike – just five minutes' notice. *We* then walked out to join the picket line and stayed out for four hours. Now further action in other departments of the hospital is planned [*by us*], though *we* claim the children themselves won't suffer.

The two most striking misfits are the agentless passive 'is planned', which is very hard to render with a 'we' agent; and the 'we claim', which is idiomatically suspect. Beyond this, a 'we' identity that made such a point of giving little warning before walking out and staying out would be representing itself as a bloody-minded identity, to say the least.

[...]

These points of view of the strikers can be compared with those of other participants to see if there are any significant differences. In section IV, the strikers are followed narratively by 'senior nursing staff', and once again the point of view is reversed:

> *We* had to help out sorting dirty linen from the wards; it took up much of *our* valuable time.

Here the oddity is actually in the original – this idiomatic phrasing fits a 'we' identity so well that the original 'it took up much of their valuable time' is the surprising version. In section VI there are further references to medical staff:

> Every day *we* [doctors] treat up to a hundred patients who are suffering from everything from cuts and bruises to heart attacks and appendicitis.

> Until unpaid volunteers like her came along, *we* [the nurses] had to dust and vacuum.

These too fit easily into an idiomatically plausible 'we' form, as do references to the patients.

A control of the reversal strategy can be derived from the bulletin. The union shop steward interviewed in section IV actually uses 'we' forms through his answers. If these are reversed into 'they' forms, the results can be compared with the voice-overs directly:

> Yes *they* can guarantee ... *they've* told the unit administrator that if, during *their* action, children were at risk, *they* would immediately leave the picket line and go in and help ... *They* believe *they've* shown responsibility ... *they've* been traditionally a very passive workforce, and *they* hope that by workers at this world-famous hospital taking action it will bring public sympathy to *their* side.

In view of the marked differences between this and the voice-over presentation of the strikers, and the differences between them and the medical staff and patients, it is possible to conclude that the narrative point of view confirms the camera point of view by verbally sorting out these two classes of participants into 'they' and 'we' identities. Thus, the viewer is positioned differently in relation to the strikers and to the doctors/nurses/patients respectively, and cannot so easily adopt the strikers' point of view.

PICTURE AND SOUND RELATIONS

The separate components of picture and sound work in their own ways, but they also work together, and this provides a further, distinct area of analysis. In general, TV news conforms to the realist relationship between picture and sound tracks. That is, each is taken to motivate the other, and the sounds heard are understood as being synchronous ('in sync.') with the picture. Thus, ambient sound is confined to that which occurred at the moment of shooting – TV news does not generally avail itself of the possibilities offered by music, wild-track sound, etc. (though the realist relation between picture and sound can be *manufactured* by using sounds from the effects library to cover mute pictures, for instance, although there is no evidence of this practice here). Ambient sound itself may be significant, but it is subordinate to voice-over commentary, so it tends to get faded up and down according to the voice-over's prior claim to audibility.

The apparent mutual motivation of picture and sound in TV news is very important ideologically, not because it actually occurs, but because it doesn't. The paradox is caused by voice-over commentary, which benefits from the genre-expectation that picture and sound are synchronized, even though it is in fact quite separate in origin from the footage it comments on. Voice-overs are not unmotivated by the picture/ambient sound, but they are external to them, and just as voice-overs are always more audible than ambient or synchronized sound, so they claim a 'higher' level of correspondence to actuality than mere synchronicity. Because they 'helpfully' explain the pictures, voice-overs both encourage and benefit from the viewer's sense that there is a unity of picture and sound. This 'unity' is then cashed in ideologically, as it were, since the explanations appear to arise 'naturally' from the pictures with which they are united.

[...]

The Employers: An Absent 'They'

Having seen how textually complex the relations between picture and sound can be at a given moment, it is useful to return to the main topic of the story, namely the industrial dispute itself, to see if these relations contribute to its signification. Here the apparent unity of picture, speech and sound is ideologically productive, because there are significant points at which the sense of the speech and that of the picture go out of sync. These are the points when the employers are brought into the story.

As a matter of fact the employers are never named directly as such, and no employer's representative is interviewed or shown. This is a significant absence, given that there is an interview with the shop steward, there are pictures of strikers, volunteers, patients and nurses, while doctors, the government and the opposition are mentioned verbally; every party to the dispute gets a look-in except the employers. But they do make their shadowy presence felt:

> Because of the unpredictable/nature of the strike action consultants at the hospital *have now been instructed* to admit only emergency cases.

The employers, then, are deleted as agents from the passive 'have now been instructed'. Verbally, the instruction seems to flow from the 'unpredictable nature of the strike action' rather than from the employers. Visually, the instruction is signified not by reference to those that issued it, but to its effect. Whilst the voice-over says what the instruction 'means' ('It means that children ... are being turned away'), the picture shows a man and child approaching the camera, crossing in front of it to stop at the hospital entrance, where the child continues to gaze back at the viewer. Thus the employers cannot be mapped into any position or point of view with respect to the viewer – there is no point of view from which to observe an absent 'they'.

[...]

Thus when the employers figure in the actuality sequences they are displaced verbally into 'instructions' and 'authorities', and visually into the strike's effects rather than its causes. Because of this, it seems in the end that a point of view is established for the employers; they are collapsed into the other groups who are represented as the bearers of the strike's effects: the patients, doctors and nurses. To the extent that this is so, and because they are presented in opposition to the strikers (they think differently), the employers are aligned with the 'we' side of the we/they opposition.

Relations Between Speakers: Who's Talking?

News is often described as being about events, but it isn't. News is a complex mixture of voices, some of which speak for themselves, whilst others speak professionally. Some of the speakers are 'institutional voices', and others are 'accessed voices'; that is, some speakers are employees of the broadcasting institution (newsreaders, correspondents, reporters), whilst others are accessed by it (these include anyone who isn't a newsperson, from prime ministers to vox pops, but it may include professional voices in the form of 'experts', and these are often broadcasters and journalists themselves). The way in which this variety of voices actually appears in the news is complex. They may be present in both picture and sound as they speak, or accessed by sound but not by picture (as in recordings of parliament) or vice versa (as in the picket-line talk). Otherwise, the things people say may be quoted directly or indirectly, with or without attribution, by the institutional voices. Such quotations may be reinforced visually by being spelt out in a caption, often with an accompanying picture of the original speaker.

Thus it is not always easy, in the course of a news story in which all of these possibilities are deployed in one place or another, to identify exactly who is speaking at a given moment, or what relation between the speakers is being proposed. But the multiplicity of voices and speakers does not appear at the time as mere confusion, since each speaker is subordinate to the overall discursive unity of the bulletin. At this higher level of unity, the variety of voices contributes to the flow of sense. No matter who is speaking, certain terms, concepts and registers are brought into play, and in the course of the story as a whole they are either taken up, confirmed and endorsed, or set in opposition to others, or left unexploited and neglected. But once such a discursive unity has been achieved, it is useful to return to its textual sources to see which of the voices, if any, have won. Such textual gains and losses may turn out to have political implications.

'Home Help': A Discourse of Domesticity

A good example of a unity which transcends the voices that contribute to it but clearly works to the benefit of some of those voices as against others is what may be called the discourse of domesticity. Along the way, this discourse serves to organize the whole story into a very particular kind of intelligibility. It is first encountered in the very first phrase of the story: 'Here at home'; where 'home' is the nation as distinct from abroad (which had been signified in this bulletin by the previous story about Iran). Thereafter the discourse becomes increasingly important as the story progresses. First, it displaces the more obvious discourse for such a story as this, namely the discourse of industrial relations. Whilst very little is said about wage claims and conditions of work, quite a lot is said about dusting and vacuum cleaning. Second, it becomes associated in this story with the very fluid signifier 'help'. In actual fact the word 'help' occurs thirteen times in the story, used by different voices in different contexts to mean different things. But by the end of the story, its meaning has been fixed.

[...]

What captures it, in fact, is the discourse of domesticity, which proves to be the means by which help can be given to the patients and the doctors and nurses who are affected by the strike. Thus, the news tells about Jenny Munns, who left her own 'housework', so that the nurses wouldn't have to 'dust and vacuum'. She herself says that what made her answer the appeal for help was a 'neighbour', and the fact that 'I'm at home in the morning'. The second volunteer has been helping out 'generally', and with the 'washing up'. Visually the impression of domesticity is confirmed by Mrs Munns's informal house-coat (not uniform) and by her use of the vacuum-cleaner. The reporter goes on to speak of 'paper plates', and of help with the 'washing up', about which no-one 'grumbled', but which is seen in detail on the screen.

The language is not that of an industrial dispute, much less of the political conflict between government and opposition, between Tories and Labour, or between the prime minister and the 'irresponsible minority' of strikers that is quoted at the beginning of the story. Thus 'help' has displaced politics, but it doesn't escape politics. The first time the word is heard is on the lips of Margaret Thatcher, who uses it in the very sense the news eventually establishes for it. She calls for volunteers to help the patients and the doctors and nurses. Conversely, Mr Callaghan's use of 'help' is in a much more directly political sense. He calls for higher-paid workers to 'help' the low paid (presumably though not explicitly by moderating their own wage claims) and he says the low-paid workers must get a pay rise to 'help' them. But neither of these senses for 'help' is taken further in the news story. Mr Callaghan's use of the term is discursively defeated. Similarly, the NUPE shop steward offers help from the picket line. Although the news shows the very workers reckoned by the prime minister to need help, and although these very workers offer to help, the drift of the story is quite contrary to such positive identifications of the strikers themselves. The upshot is not only that 'help' comes to mean domestic help, but that the volunteers who supply it are exempted altogether from any suggestion that – seen from another point of view – their action could be seen as strike-breaking, and they themselves as scabs. In this particular news story, then, the discursive victory belongs to Margaret Thatcher, since her mobilization of a particular sense and referent for 'help' is the one that the news uses, not only as a signifier for the event, but even as a determinant of its structure; that is, the selection of the volunteers for interview as newsworthy.

[...]

CONCLUSION: THE POLITICS OF POPULIST DISCOURSES

This discussion suggests that the representational and relational dimensions of news texts mediate between textual features on the one hand and wider cultural processes on the other. The analysis shows that those wider cultural processes are not merely invoked within textual features, but rather that textual features play an active, political role in cultural relations of power. That is to say, the news is active in the politics of sense-making, even when the stories concern matters not usually understood as directly political (a wage dispute), and even when it is striving for impartiality. The common ground between news and political struggles is what can be called popular discourse. The news strives for clarity, both of representation and of point of view, and one of the most important means it uses towards this end is populism. Populist discourses (e.g. 'domesticity') and popular idioms (e.g. 'help') are mobilized to make sense of both the world and those who represent different social and political constituencies within it (e.g. both the world and such groups are sorted into we/they categories).

However, populist discourses are also the ground upon which politicians seek to cultivate support. Thus, the news enters into unwitting collusion with Thatcherism in seeking to make sense of the public service workers' dispute by means of notions of help and domesticity. For by so doing the news allows its populism to be colonized or captured by Thatcherite populism. Along the way it denies the viewer a position from which it is easy to align with the strikers, to such an extent that in the end their discourses (of industrial disputes and pay claims) become unspeakable, and the representation of 'volunteers' as scabs becomes unthinkable, which must have proved a great 'help' to Mrs Thatcher.

Note

1. Other aspects of the same news story are analysed in John Hartley (1982) *Understanding News*, London: Methuen, chapter 7.

53

WOMAN AS SIGN IN TELEVISION NEWS

Lana F. Rakow and Kimberlie Kranich

Taking as its starting point the gendered nature of news as a masculine narrative, an analysis shows that when women do appear as sources and subjects in news, they represent 'women' in a ritualized role, and feminist voices are usually mainstream designees of a seemingly homogeneous female viewpoint.

> The New York Tribune of September 3 headed its report of the meeting of the Working Woman's Association as 'The Wars of the Women.' Beside that report thus designated stood the report of the Twenty-third Street Union Republican General Committee without a heading, though that might have appropriately been called the 'wars of the men.' ... The only way in which I can account for the omission of headings to these reports of the wars of the men is that these captions are written by some masculine wit, who is decidedly partial to jokes on women (25).

This excerpt from the nineteenth-century women's rights periodical *The Revolution* attests that, even in 1869, women in the United States noted and resented the news coverage they received. Contemporary feminists, of course, have been no less immune to such double standards and no less concerned about them.

Tuchman (26) and Robinson (22) have both documented stages in early news coverage of the women's movement, from trivialization and ridicule to institutionalization and cooptation. A national study (11) found that newspapers

From *Journal of Communication* 41:1 (Winter 1991) pp. 8–23.

gave inadequate coverage to six issues of importance to women – domestic relations, enforcement of Title IX, the legal impact of the Equal Rights Amendment, the National Women's Conference at Houston in 1977, pay equity, and the World Conference of the United Nations Decade for Women in 1980. Coverage of the World Conference generally focused on conflict, often portraying the meetings in disarray. Another study found that between 40 and 50 per cent of stories about the three UN-sponsored International Women's Decade conferences had a conflict angle, a higher percentage than generally found in news (7). Other research continues to document women's serious underrepresentation as newsmakers and sources in print and broadcast news.

Thus the news media are sites at which women, the women's movement, feminism, and women's issues are ignored or displayed in particular ways. Does this occur as the result of conventions of news gathering and writing? The underrepresentation of women as reporters? The sexism or ignorance of individual male editors and reporters?

To better understand what is happening when women appear in the news, we found it useful to connect theoretical developments in the field of communication concerning the nature and function of news with theoretical developments about women's representations in mass media. Communication scholars have been developing the notion that news serves a narrative function in Western cultures, circulating meanings that in general confirm and conserve existing social and economic relationships (6, 14, 18). Feminist scholars in communication and other disciplines have been developing sophisticated understandings of gender and representation, which they are only beginning to apply to news and its representation of women.

Here we extend the work begun by feminist scholars through an empirical and interpretative study of how women appear as sources in television news. We will argue that an understanding of news must begin with its essential gendered nature as a masculine narrative, in which women function not as speaking subjects but as signs. Any improvements in women's treatment in the news will require not simply more coverage of women or more women journalists (see 28) but a fundamental change in news as a narrative genre.

Feminist scholars have made exciting headway in understanding the process of culture and its present (but not unalterable) fundamentally gendered form. Through connections to literary theory, postmodernism, psychoanalysis, radical feminist theory, semiotics, symbolic interactionism, and the like, feminists have come to comprehend the full significance of gender as a social construction, in its present form a system of social relations that posits two groups of people, women and men, as different and as unequal.

In discussing the link between gender and culture, Rubin (23) and Cowie (9) begin with the notion that a culture rests on a kinship system, a system of categories that define members' relationships. Rubin, in a corrective to Claude

Lévi-Strauss's work on kinship, traces the subordination of women to the creation of a particular gender system in which men exchange women:

> 'Exchange of women' is a shorthand for expressing that the social relations of a kinship system specify that men have certain rights in their female kin, and that women do not have the same rights either to themselves or their male kin. In this sense, the exchange of women is a profound perception of a system in which women do not have full rights to themselves. (23, p. 164)

A culture's division of labor *creates* gender and makes the sameness of women and men taboo, Rubin argues. Because sexuality and gender in a kinship system are what organizes society, Rubin says, feminists must advocate a revolution in kinship.

Cowie (9), also working with Lévi-Strauss's notions about the exchange of women in kinship, explains that the exchange of women takes place in different systems of signification (or meaning), of which kinship is one. Men not only physically exchange women (for example, a bride leaves her father's house to live in her husband's house); they also communicate the sign 'woman.' In fact, it is women's status *as* sign that enables their physical exchange.

Other feminists have echoed the insight that gender is a semiotic system, a system of meaning based on difference. Mulvey, in a landmark piece of feminist scholarship that launched contemporary feminist psychoanalytic film theory, states:

> Woman then stands in patriarchal culture as signifier for the male other, bound by a symbolic order in which man can live out his phantasies and obsessions through linguistic command by imposing them on the silent image of woman still tied to her place as bearer of meaning, not maker of meaning. (21, p. 7)

The implications of women functioning as a sign in men's discourse or narratives have been brought to bear in subsequent analyses of particular film and television genres, especially classic Hollywood cinema.[1] Feminist critics have worked with Mulvey's notion of women as the object of male gaze to understand the point of view of visual narratives. Others have added to our understanding of representations by critiquing the standard social science, commonsense notion of visual images. As Cowie argues (8, 9), there are two problems with assuming or expecting a direct correspondence between an image and 'reality.' First, an image is always an *interpretation* of reality. Second, the image is always interpreting *another* interpretation – 'reality' – that is not innocent, pre-existing culture. 'Real' women are as socially constructed, as much the product of discursive practices, as the sign 'woman' in the visual image.

Although we are not the first to describe news as a masculine genre, feminist critics have not yet brought to bear on news the analysis of woman as sign. In

665

their discussion of news as narrative, Bird and Dardenne (3, p. 79) ask the provocative question, 'Whose story?' Few working from a cultural studies perspective have thought to answer the question with 'men,' and feminist critics have focused on fictional visual narratives and advertisements (see 2).

Feminists have long noted the relationship of news to the political and economic interests of men. Journalists' 'hard news–soft news' distinction has institutionalized a gendered division between 'serious, important' news that is overwhelmingly masculine and 'human interest, lifestyle' news that is more likely to be the purview of women reporters and readers. News is largely 'men talking to men' (19, p. 180), or, as Hartley puts it, 'news is not only about and by men, it is overwhelmingly seen through men' (14, p. 146). Holland (16, p. 141) notes that the two themes of television news – excitement and seriousness – are both based upon masculine values, a fact that discourages women from staking a claim to the genre. Fiske (13, p. 308) calls television news 'masculine soap opera' because of its lack of closure, multiplicity of plots and characters, and repetition and familiarity. News is more prestigious than, say, soap opera not because it is inherently superior but because men and their interests – 'news' – are given an authoritative status, cloaked in an ideology of objectivity and truth.

Women viewers obviously know the difference as well. They favor different programming than men do (e.g., 20), and news is not one of their preferences. As Holland observes:

> When we look at the way women are represented in the news it is not surprising that this is one area of television that women in the audience feel is not for them; they pay little attention to it even though it is frequently on in their presence. (16, p. 139)

The little news that does appear about women, coming as it does from a man's perspective, is termed by Molotch 'locker-room talk' (19, p. 185).

It is not surprising, then, that in this masculine narrative women seldom have a part as speaking subjects. This is not to say that they do not speak. Women newscasters are a case in point. Their invitation to speak, says Holland, is an invitation to be decorative performers. Like women in other masculine narratives, they function as the object of the male gaze (16, p. 146), although their appearance as 'real women' rather than as actresses representing fictional characters may obscure this. Public controversies about double standards of appearance for women newscasters and anchors should remind us that these women are no less the bearers of meaning, the objects of male fantasy, than other representations of women. The double bind women newscasters thus face gives us insight into their difficulty in satisfying a television audience. The newscaster is to present an authoritative, confident, yet unremarkable image, the active speaking subject. The head-and-shoulder image of a man is completed by his speech; but the head-and-shoulder image of a woman is completed by her body (16, p. 138). As Holland summarizes the paradox: 'They cannot escape their femininity, yet the possibility of making a contribution that is specifically on behalf of women is ruled out. They may not speak as women or for women' (16, p. 148).

Women appear in connection to the news in two other ways: as newsmakers and as sources. Research consistently supports what any lay person can observe firsthand: that men far outnumber women in both categories. In its 1974–5 study of network television news, the US Commission on Civil Rights (27) found that 9.9 per cent of newsmakers were white women and 3.5 per cent were women of color. A study of news broadcasts in Montreal in 1977 (22) determined that 15 per cent of newsmakers were women. In a sample of newspapers in 1979 and 1980 (4), fewer than 10 per cent of the news sources identifiable by gender were women. A study of network news programs in 1982–4 found that about one out of seven on-camera sources were women (29).

In national television news, as Holland explains, 'the reduced visibility of women in the news is more emphatic, carries more significance, precisely because of its routine juxtaposition with their heightened visibility in the rest of the output' (16, pp. 139–40). Like women in other masculine narratives and like women newscasters, they appear as carriers of meaning, as signs.

Given that so few women are used as newsmakers or as news sources, a woman's appearance in a story takes on a special significance. We do not mean to suggest that men conspire to exclude women or are necessarily conscious of selecting women for particular purposes. Rather, news media personnel work within a taken-for-granted meaning system in which it simply makes sense to do these things.

The absence of women as newsmakers is related to their absence as sources. Fiske (13, p. 284) explains that news is associated with the activities of the public sphere, the province of elites and men, who thus people the news. Women's absence from the public sphere as well as their lack of status as authority figures or experts gives the news media a ready-made justification for women's absence from news programs – without the media's having to confront their complicity in setting the conditions for women's appearance. It is true that news media personnel conventionally rely on 'authoritative' sources to provide interpretations of events; however, the selection of particular sources and the roles they are permitted to play in the news story are what gives the story its frame, just as a reliance on 'experts' gives voice to a particular segment of the population.

[...]

Instead, women generally fall into the category of 'ordinary people,' who appear infrequently in the news and typically stand for a social aggregate; well-known individuals are used to represent social and political groups (24). Sources thus function as signs, as bearers of meaning in a well-orchestrated discourse (see, e.g., 1, 5). However, since women are found so infrequently in news stories, and since they always sign as 'woman' (unlike men, who do not ordinarily carry meaning as 'man' because the culture assumes maleness as given), their function as sign is unique.

To investigate women's unique function as sign in television news, we examined one month of newscasts from all three networks. We used the *Television News Index and Abstracts*, a guide to the videotaped network evening news programs of the Vanderbilt Television News Archive. These abstracts summarize the content of each CBS, NBC, and ABC evening news program as well as provide information about on-camera appearances of sources. We coded and quantified all examples of women used as news sources in July 1986. This sampling strategy obviously does not replicate any one viewer's possible exposure to network newscasts.

A total of 1,203 items (excluding introductions and farewells, commercials, and announcements of upcoming stories) were aired by the three networks. Only 181, or about 15 per cent, used any women as on-camera sources (where gender was identifiable, excluding ambiguous names and categories such as 'students' or 'people').[2] Since more than one woman served as a source in some stories, a woman appeared on camera as a source a total of 256 times. We coded women sources into one of seven categories: private individuals (unaffiliated with an organization or institution), politicians or candidates, activists, representatives of organizations or institutions, members of professions, celebrities, or unknowns. Categories were determined by mutual agreement after all women sources had been identified.

As seen in Table 1, private individuals comprised by far the largest group of women sources, 127 of 256, or just about half. Compared to Whitney et al.'s earlier finding that 25.7 per cent unaffiliated male and female individuals were used as television network sources (29), this suggests that women are disproportionately represented in the category of private individuals. These were

Table 1: On-camera appearances by women as network news sources on ABC, NBC, and CBS, July 1986

	Appearances	
	n	% of total
Private individuals	127	50
Experts and authorities	40	16
Spokespersons	34	13
Candidates and politicians	20	8
Celebrities	20	8
Political activists	10	4
Unidentifiable	5	2
Total	256	101[a]

[a] Rounding error.

women in the private sphere affected by crime, disasters, public policy, or the actions of their families. Thirty-two were part of the largest single subcategory, family members; that is, they were the mothers or other relatives of hostages, gunmen, spies, afflicted children, and the like. The next largest single subcategory (n = 24) was victims, including battered women, stabbing victims, and residents of areas affected by earthquakes and toxic waste sites. Others in the general category of private individuals were such women as child abusers, cancer patients, immigrants, cocaine addicts, women addicted to television shopping, women who love to quilt, and tourists.

The ratio of women's appearance in this category to their appearance in other categories confirms feminists' observation that, when a woman does speak in the news, she does so

> either as an anonymous example of uninformed public opinion, as house-wife, consumer, neighbour, or as mother, sister, wife of the man in the news, or as victim – of crime, disaster, political policy. Thus not only do they speak less frequently, but they tend to speak as passive reactors and witnesses to public events rather than as participants in those events. (16, p. 139)

The remainder of the sources occupied roles with a 'public' character. Women politicians and candidates on the foreign, national, state, and local levels appeared on screen 20 times in July, though fewer than 20 women were involved. ... Celebrities appeared 20 times, with Nancy Reagan accounting for four appearances and Sarah Ferguson three. Political activists were used 10 times as sources – for example, a birth control advocate in Colombia, a leader in the sanctuary movement smuggling Central American refugees to the United States, South African anti-apartheid group leaders and members, and Navajo Roberta Blackgoat.

A final category of sources was spokespersons for institutions and organizations. Here women were used as sources 34 times, 12 times to represent government agencies and also on behalf of such diverse institutions as the banking industry, Playboy Enterprises, the Slave Mart Museum, the American Enterprise Institute, Planned Parenthood, and Worlds of Wonder, Inc. (a toy manufacturer). Feminist organizations were represented only twice, both times by the National Organization for Women.

We selected for closer examination 46 stories from the Vanderbilt Archive in which women were likely to be significant to the meaning of the story. The frequency or infrequency of women's appearance and the positions they hold as sources do not give us a complete picture of how women are used to carry meaning in news stories. We therefore examined the abstracts for six months of network newscasts (July, August, and September 1986 and January, February, and March 1987) and concentrated on stories that might be expected to be seen by news personnel or by feminists as particularly relevant to or about women –

breast cancer, welfare, domestic abuse, and beauty pageants, as well as stories featuring nondominant ethnic groups (to increase the likelihood of finding women of color used as sources). We examined on tape those stories that the Vanderbilt abstracts suggested would illustrate varying news practices using women as sources. We also examined on tape stories for which footage helped clarify tone or content. Viewing the resulting 46 news stories (2½ hours of videotape) enabled us to fill out and contextualize information provided by the abstracts. This sample was intended not to be random or representative but to uncover the variety of ways in which women are used as news sources.

The functions women serve as sources/signs in network news reveal several patterns. Although they appear to be 'real' women, women as sources *carry* rather than *create* meaning in the stories in which they appear. Like women newscasters, they always signify as 'woman,' but they are seldom able to speak for or about women. We have grouped our observations in five categories, treated in turn below.

As 'signs of the times,' women are used to illustrate the private consequences of public events and actions. Women as sources in the capacity of institutionally unaffiliated individuals located in the private sphere serve to illustrate the consequences, emotions, or behaviors that underlie a story. These women are not sources of information, as sources generally function, but specimens. Here is what a woman who abuses her children looks like and how, now repentant, she gets help and the social order is restored; here are society's most vulnerable members (wives, mothers, daughters, sisters) emotionally buffeted about by the political and uncaring actions of governments; here is an ordinary woman who fled her home in an earthquake. These women are used to make a connection between the private sphere of home, family, emotions, neighborhood, and personal experience and the public world of politics, policy, and authority (including the authority to restore order and provide assistance).

As we expected from our preceding analysis of woman as sign in masculine narratives, in most stories women as sources are not themselves part of the public debate or conflict. They are, instead, called in as evidence to support one side of an argument or one interpretation of a problem. This is most obvious when a woman is the mother or sister of a hostage, spy, or military casualty. Although she may indeed have an opinion on the situation, her on-camera appearance lets her neither join the argument nor approach a solution. Her appearance is a ritualized – contained and safe – representation of how the actions of those in the public sphere affect those in the private sphere.

[...]

As 'signs of support,' women are used to endorse an action or policy because of their organizational or institutional affiliations. On the occasions when women do appear as speaking subjects in the public debate of a news story, generally they speak not for women but for organizations and institutions – many of which, feminists would argue, oppress women or advocate policies or actions against women's best interests.

In the study of broadcasts for the month of July, 12 women represented government agencies and 6 represented businesses or trade associations. (Women did not represent labor in any stories, though two women workers were quoted.) So, for example, Christie Hefner of Playboy Enterprises spoke against the Meese Pornography Commission findings, and other women spoke for the banking industry (defending mortgage practices), for the American Enterprise Institute (criticizing foreign governments), and for the US Treasury (noting the sale of US liberty coins).

Like women newscasters, the women who appear in stories of this kind have their subject positions as women invoked by their appearance, but their voices as women are denied. In other words, they function as women but do not speak as them. Because so few women appear on camera at all, it is important to ask why a woman is chosen to represent an organization when she is. It may be the luck of the draw or a bona fide part of her job, an indication that women are making progress moving into the management ranks of organizations. Conversely, organizations and institutions may use women to make a position more palatable or to diffuse the strength of an argument that women might make against them.

[...]

Those allowed to speak for women are 'unusual signs,' or 'feminists.' As illustrated by the story about men's battering of women, even those stories that could be expected to have women speaking for women generally do not. In order for a woman to occupy a position as a speaking subject who speaks *for women*, she must signify as 'feminist,' a particular and unusual kind of 'woman.'

In the six months of broadcasting examined, feminists were used as sources in only seven stories, four of which used Eleanor Smeal, then president of the National Organization for Women. Representatives of feminist organizations were called on to react to Supreme Court decisions on sodomy, abortion, affirmative action, and sexual harassment (Smeal, ABC, July 13, 1986), to another Supreme Court decision on affirmative action (Smeal, ABC, CBS, and NBC, March 25, 1987), to the report of the Meese Pornography Commission (Women Against Pornography, ABC, July 9, 1986), to a Supreme Court decision on maternity leave (Women's Legal Defense Fund, NBC, January 13, 1987), and to schools' efforts to teach computer literacy to girls (Women's Action Alliance, CBS, August 24, 1986).

That feminists are asked to comment on so few stories is even more striking considering how frequently other political positions are represented in stories. For example, the American Enterprise Institute was frequently quoted, including on such unlikely topics as the death penalty (CBS, July 2, 1986) and the release of a US hostage (NBC, July 26, 1986; ABC, July 28, 1986).

Feminists who do appear on screen generally represent liberal, mainstream feminism.[3] Since only one feminist generally appears in a story, the implication is that feminism is a homogeneous ideological position, that there is only one way to frame the problem under discussion, and that only someone designated as a feminist by her institutional affiliation is aware of and dissatisfied with women's social place. Her ritualized appearance gives the illusion that the news organization has fulfilled its obligation to provide balance and expert testimony.

[...]

Because 'all signs are alike,' only white women are allowed to signify as 'woman.' Another way the purity of the sign 'woman' is maintained is by homogeneity of appearance. In the realms of fiction and advertising, age, height, weight, body proportions, facial features, and clothing can be carefully selected, controlled, or altered to achieve the broadly similar look of contemporary sexual beauty that clearly marks the sign 'woman' and that serves to differentiate women from men. In broadcast news, which is presented as a 'slice of real life,' the physical appearance of women appearing as newsmakers and as sources is more difficult to control. Despite this – or perhaps because of it – as network television news sources, those who signify as women, and as feminists, share the physical characteristic of being white.

Women of color do occasionally appear on camera in stories involving their race or ethnic identity.

[...]

The meaning of the sign 'woman,' bound up as it is with the assumption of whiteness, is critical to the construction of both a gender system and a race system. Both race and gender depend on linguistically categorizing people, ostensibly to reflect biological (e.g., skin color) differences but actually to create a political and hierarchical system of difference. If whiteness must be encoded into the sign 'woman' in order for it to carry meaning, then women and men from other racial and ethnic groups are outside the dominant meaning system that differentiates 'real' or 'typical' women and men. Those who are assigned and who take up the identity 'woman' differ greatly in their experiences and material conditions, but these differences are denied and hidden in favor of a shared and overriding 'similarity' – women's essential and intractable difference from men. The assumption that all women are the same belies the foundation of whiteness upon which the system of differentiation rests, embedding a system of racism in the symbolic order.[4]

On the rare occasions that news media personnel choose to incorporate a feminist perspective on a new story, they go to familiar, predominantly white, liberal, visible organizations. These organizations provide a white woman as a representative, reflecting their white leadership. Consequently, feminism appears to be a movement for and about white women, and the perspective that women of color bring to analyzing issues of gender is all but invisible in network television news.

When women's actions disrupt the social order, they are represented as part of 'the nature of the sign' – an inherent part of all women's personalities. Despite the attempt to preserve the purity of the sign 'woman' as white and apolitical, women do threaten the boundaries of differentiation and do challenge the order of things. One way to recontain this disorderliness and preserve the meaning of the sign is to attribute the conflicts raised by women's dissatisfaction with their social place to an essential personality trait of woman. This explains the emphasis on conflict that feminists have documented in news treatment of women and the women's movement. All women may be alike, according to the meaning attributed to the sign 'woman,' but that does not mean they can get along with each other, like each other, or work together.[5]

In only a few of the network news stories we sampled did women sources agree with each other, and even when they did, a critical analysis of the news item was absent. Such was the case with a story on the medical profession's underuse of mammography to detect breast cancer. Two women patients and a woman physician all spoke in favor of the procedure, ignoring such feminist concerns as making the procedure available to poor women and exploring alternative medical treatment. . . .

More prevalent than women sources agreeing with each other, however, were women sources pitted against each other, not to illuminate the issues at stake for women but to create a standoff of conflicting personalities. CBS and ABC used disagreement among women as the theme in covering the Meese Commission report. CBS pitted Christie Hefner against 'former porn star' (the reporter's term) Linda Lovelace in disagreeing about the Commission's findings. Here the conflict was constructed as between Hefner on the left (she commented that the Commission was out of touch with changing US attitudes) and Lovelace on the right (though Lovelace made a radical feminist statement about how pornography silences women, her appearance was followed by a long segment on right-wing 'antiporn' groups, leaving Lovelace and anyone else supporting the Commission positioned on the right). The distinction Hefner made in the NBC story between sexually violent material and *Playboy* was not introduced here, yet ostensibly Hefner and Lovelace could have had grounds for *agreement* in their opposition to sexually violent material. . . .

Creating disagreement among women and framing stories as conflicts between women rather than as problems women face is similar to a strategy news media personnel use in covering race. Hartmann and Husband (15) argue that media coverage of race defines situations in terms of intergroup conflict that feeds white fears of other racial groups:

> Blacks come to be seen as conflict-generating *per se* and the chances that people will think about the situation in more productive ways – in terms of the issues involved or of social problems generally – are reduced. The result is that real conflict is amplified, and potential for conflict created. (p. 301)

White women's criticism of their social place, their rejection of the terms of the sign 'woman,' are rendered harmless when their words and actions are characterized as part of an essential personality fault. Oppressive actions against women and men of other races are justified and their threat to the social order quelled when they are presented as inherently dangerous and disruptive.

Television news is not a reflection of society but an instance of it, locating women inside and outside the screen in a discourse that assigns the meaning of the sign 'woman' even while invoking it as if it were already there. The solution to this problem of woman as sign in television news must be a radical one; the problem may even be impossible to solve. Can the masculine narrative of news be 'feminized'? More basically, can the symbolic system that posits women as objects of men's exchange be altered? These are the questions to which communication scholars and journalists interested in understanding the news need to turn their attention.

Notes

1. A useful history of this feminist criticism can be found in Kaplan's review (17), though we find inaccurate her division of feminist positions into essentialist and anti-essentialist. It is possible from a radical feminist perspective to see 'woman' and 'man' as cultural, discursive creations rather than biological ones and still value what those constituted as 'women' have made of their situation.
2. Not all news items had on-camera sources, so it may seem unfair to compare stories with women as sources to all stories rather than only to stories using sources; however, the choice to use *no* source can be as important as the choice to use a woman or a man, as our later discussion will demonstrate.
3. Liberal feminists advocate equal opportunities for women within the existing hierarchical social structure. Radical, socialist, and poststructuralist feminists advocate deep changes in the social structure beginning with men's relation to women (radical feminists), material conditions and economic relations (socialist feminists), or the ordering of symbolic systems (poststructuralist feminists).
4. White women themselves have taken up this system of signification. The assumption that all women are white and share the same political agenda has plagued much of the feminist movement.
5. Television news shares with other masculine discourses, such as fiction, advertising, and print journalism, this unflattering and trivializing definition of women. To take one blatant example, in a *Newsweek* article entitled 'Mommy vs. Mommy,' writer Nina Darnton – whether as a result of her gender and professional socialization or of the intervention of editors – characterizes the contemporary political and economic dilemma of women with children as 'the Mommy Wars,' in which 'conflict' between mothers who stay at home and mothers who work 'is played out against a backdrop of frustration, insecurity, jealousy and guilt' (10, p. 64).

References

1. Barkin, S. M. and M. Gurevitch. 'Out of Work and on the Air: Television News of Unemployment.' *Critical Studies in Mass Communication* 4(1), March 1987, pp. 1–20.
2. Betterton, R. (Ed.). *Looking On: Images of Femininity in the Visual Arts and Media*, London: Pandora Press, 1987.
3. Bird, S. E. and R. W. Dardenne. 'Myth, Chronicle, and Story: Exploring the Narrative Qualities of News.' In J. W. Carey (Ed.), *Media, Myths, and Narratives: Television and the Press*, Beverly Hills, Cal.: Sage, 1988, pp. 67–86.

4. Brown, J. D., C. R. Bybee, S. T. Wearden, and D. M. Straughan. 'Invisible Power: Newspaper News Sources and the Limits of Diversity.' *Journalism Quarterly* 64(1), Spring 1987, pp. 45–54.
5. Campbell, R. and J. L. Reeves. 'Covering the Homeless: The Joyce Brown Story.' *Critical Studies in Mass Communication* 6(1), March 1989, pp. 21–42.
6. Carey, J. W. (Ed.). *Media, Myths, and Narratives: Television and the Press*, Beverly Hills, Cal.: Sage, 1988.
7. Cooper, A. and L. D. Davenport. 'Newspaper Coverage of International Women's Decade: Feminism and Conflict,' *Journal of Communication Inquiry* 11(1), Winter 1987, pp. 108–115.
8. Cowie, E. 'Women, Representation, and the Image.' *Screen Education* 23, 1977, pp. 1–23.
9. Cowie, E. 'Woman as Sign.' *M/F* 1, 1978, pp. 49–63.
10. Darnton, N. 'Mommy vs. Mommy.' *Newsweek*, June 4, 1990, pp. 64–67.
11. East, C. and D. Jurney. *New Directions for News*. Washington, D.C.: Women's Studies Program and Police Center, George Washington University, 1983.
12. Eliasoph, N. 'Routines and the Making of Oppositional News.' *Critical Studies in Mass Communication* 5(4), December 1988, pp. 313–334.
13. Fiske, J. *Television Culture*. London: Methuen, 1987.
14. Hartley, J. *Understanding News*. London: Methuen, 1982.
15. Hartmann, P. and C. Husband. 'The Mass Media and Racial Conflict.' In S. Cohen and J. Young (Eds), *The Manufacture of News: Social Problems, Deviance and the Mass Media*. Beverly Hills, Cal.: Sage, 1981, pp. 288–302.
16. Holland, P. 'When a Woman Reads the News.' In H. Baehr and G. Dyer (Eds), *Boxed In: Women and Television*. New York: Pandora Press, 1987, pp. 133–150.
17. Kaplan, E. A. 'Feminist Criticism and Television.' In R. C. Allen (Ed.), *Channels of Discourse: Television and Contempory Criticism*. Chapel Hill: University of North Carolina Press, 1987, pp. 211–253.
18. Manoff, R. K. and M. Schudson (Eds). *Reading the News*. New York: Pantheon Books, 1987.
19. Molotch, H. L. 'The News of Women and the Work of Men.' In G. Tuchman, A. K. Daniels, and J. Benét (Eds), *Hearth and Home: Images of Women in the Mass Media*. New York: Oxford University Press, 1978, pp. 176–185.
20. Morley, D. *Family Television*. London: Comedia, 1986.
21. Mulvey, L. 'Visual Pleasure and Narrative Cinema.' *Screen* 16(3), Autumn 1975, pp. 6–18.
22. Robinson, G. J. 'Women, Media Access and Social Control.' In L. K. Epstein (Ed.), *Women and the News*. New York: Hastings House, 1978, pp. 87–108.
23. Rubin, G. 'The Traffic in Women: Notes on the "Political Economy" of Sex.' In A. M. Jaggar and P. S. Rothenberg (Eds), *Feminist Frameworks: Alternative Theoretical Accounts of the Relations between Women and Men*. New York: McGraw-Hill, 1984, pp. 155–171.
24. Sigal, L. V. 'Sources Make the News.' In R. K. Manoff and M. Schudson (Eds), *Reading the News*. New York: Pantheon Books, 1987, pp. 9–37.
25. 'Those Ridiculous Headings.' *The Revolution*, September 16, 1869.
26. Tuchman, G. *Making News: A Study in the Construction of Reality*. New York: Free Press, 1978.
27. U.S. Commission on Civil Rights. *Window Dressing on the Set: Women and Minorities in Television*. Washington, D.C.: U.S. Government Printing Office, 1977.
28. van Zoonen, L. 'Rethinking Women and the News.' *European Journal of Communication* 3(1), March 1988, pp. 35–53.
29. Whitney, D. C., M. Fritzler, S. Jones, S. Mazzarella, and L. Rakow. 'Geographic and Source Biases in Network Television News 1982–1984.' *Journal of Broadcasting & Electronic Media* 33(2), Spring 1989, pp. 159–174.

54

THE GLOBALIZATION OF ELECTRONIC JOURNALISM

Michael Gurevitch

The notion of globalization has become one of the more common, rather overused buzzwords of our times. Often accurately, sometimes hyperbolically, all manner of events, processes, products and ideas, from political and military conflicts, to the organization of industrial production, to consumer products, to markets, to culture, both 'high' and 'popular', are endowed with a global embrace. Yet perhaps in no other field has globalization become so immediately visible as in television generally, and television news specifically. Every television viewer witnesses the process every day.

Overuse of a concept leads, inevitably, to its trivialization. Much of the discussion of the globalization of the media, both in the media themselves and often also in the academic literature, is either platitudinous, repetitive, or soaked in the aura of 'high tech'. The great 'media events' of our time, such as the live broadcasting of the landing on the moon, or of the explosion of the Challenger, or of sports events such as the Olympic games, are invoked to illustrate and dramatize the marvels of the new technologies. Less attention is paid to questions concerning the social, cultural, economic and political antecedents and consequences of this 'communication revolution'. A 'blue skies' psychology seems to permeate the discussion, according to which this 'revolution' will bring people and nations together, shrink our world and turn it into McLuhan's prophesied 'global village'. It is a perspective based on the implicit assumption that 'communication is a good thing'; that tensions and conflicts

From J. Curran and M. Gurevitch, *Mass Media and Society* (London: Edward Arnold, 1991) pp. 178–93.

stem from 'breakdowns in communication', and that if we could only have 'better communication' a more harmonious global order will come about.

To be sure, the other side of that coin has also been argued forcefully. The seemingly boundless optimism about the potential promises expected to emerge from the 'communication revolution' has been countered by critics who raised two related objections: first, there were those who saw in an unbridled tide of global communication genuine threats to the autonomy and the viability of the cultures of weaker and more dependent societies, primarily indigenous Third World cultures, but also the cultures of some First World societies, whose 'authenticity' and uniqueness were seen as perilously vulnerable to the products of Hollywood and US television. (Note, for example, the publication in 1989 of the European Community Green Paper, *Television without Frontiers*, designed, amongst other things to create 'a trade barrier' to limit American entertainment imports – in the name of national cultural 'preservation' (Smith, 1990), or the debate in France, a few years ago, about the pernicious effects of 'Dallas'.) Second, questions were raised about the economic, political and ideological interests being served by an unlimited and 'free' flow of communication. Were these, the critics asked, indeed 'technologies of freedom', (in Ithiel Pool's (1983) memorable phrase), or did they actually threaten to undermine the capacity of weaker countries to structure their national media systems, and formulate their own national communication policies according to their own lights?

The challenge for students of international communication is to 'get a conceptual grip, beyond the language of gee-whizzery, on an escalating yet formless, sprawling and globe-shaking process that may be impinging on people's senses of their places in the world and on the power of regimes to effect their wills within it' (Blumler, 1989). Although in this chapter we do not intend to confront this challenge fully, we wish to depart from the arguments referred to above, which for the most part date back to the heyday of the debate about 'media imperialism' in the 1970s, and instead, explore the impact of one aspect of that process, namely the globalization of television news, on the *shifting balance of relationships of dependency* in a number of areas: between notionally dominant and subordinate national media systems; between media institutions and political institutions; inside the television industries, between national and 'local' television news services; between television encoders and audience decoders.

[...]

TELEVISION'S MANY ROLES AND POWER RELATIONSHIPS

All discussion of the mass media is ultimately concerned with the issue of power. Although different schools of thought have conceptualized the issue in different ways, and have defined and studied the power of the media differently, the underlying rationale for their concern is the same: the media should be examined because they wield considerable power and influence in modern societies. Power, however, does not exist on its own. Rather, it is manifested only in the context of interactions and relationships, whether between individuals, institutions or societies. The power of the media can therefore be examined only in relational contexts. Our argument is that the globalization of television has enhanced the role of television in ways that had a formative impact on these relationships, and hence on the 'balance of power' between the media and other social institutions, primarily the institutions of power in society – government and other political institutions.

The enhancement of the roles, and the powers, of television can be traced to its emergence, in the era of instant global communication, as an *active participant in the events it purportedly 'covers'*. Television can no longer be regarded (if it ever was) as a mere observer and reporter of events. It is inextricably locked into these events, and has clearly become an integral part of the reality it reports. The notion that television, and the media generally, should be more properly regarded as participants in the world they report on, rather than observers, has been for many years, and still is, a controversial one. For it challenges one of the central tenets of western journalism, namely that the media should stand 'outside, and be detached from, the subjects of their reporting, if they are to be true to the norms of objectivity, impartiality and neutrality'. They must observe events and relate them to their audiences as if from the perspective of 'God's eye'.

But in spite of the hallowed status of this position, this 'norm of apartness' is clearly flawed, both empirically and conceptually. Journalists cannot extricate themselves from their societal context, either physically, socially or culturally, any more than other members of society can. They cannot, therefore, claim – and hence should not pretend to – be able to observe the social world as if they were not part of it, as if from a position 'floating' above it. Wherever they appear, and whichever event they 'cover', they inevitably become a part of the environment which they observe and of the event they report. There is nothing new, of course, about this argument. Yet it is worth re-stating here because the rapid globalization of television news has established the participatory nature of television news as more crucial and fraught with consequences than ever before. Nowhere is this more dramatically visible than at the international level.

THE INTERNATIONAL LEVEL

The role that television now plays in the conduct of international relations is merely an extension onto the international level of the actively participatory role that the media have always played in the lives of societies. But the dramatic expansion of the stage upon which television now performs this role – from a national/societal onto a global one – has endowed it with a qualitatively new and sharper edge. This is especially the case in times of social and political turmoil, of rapid and revolutionary social change, or in periods of international crises. The capacity of television, utilizing satellite technology, to tell the story of an event *as it happens*, simultaneously with its unfolding, can have direct consequences for the direction that the event might take. Some of the more memorable examples of this recently are television's coverage of the Gulf war, its reporting of the revolutionary events in Eastern Europe in 1989, and the role played by television in the student uprising in Tiananmen Square in Beijing in 1988.

The presence of television cameras impacted on these events in some significant ways. Consider the following:

- First, in each of these cases television created a global audience for the event. Probably never before was the claim that 'the whole world is watching' so true and apt. Interestingly, the events that attract a global audience can be quite varied. They range from the obvious ones – wars (in the Persian Gulf) and acts of terrorism and other political violence, to revolutions, (such as the transformation, peaceful and otherwise, of the regimes of Eastern Europe in the late 1980s), to uprisings, (such as the Chinese students ill-fated demonstration in Tiananmen Square in 1988 or the Palestinian Intifada), to dramatic scientific/ political events, such as the landing on the moon; sports events like the Olympics, or 'human interest' stories, such as the plight of three whales under the Alaskan ice. The diverse nature of these events suggests that the rationale for their global dissemination stems less from their inherent significance for a global audience (however that significance is defined) than from their 'newsworthiness', an attribute bestowed on events by media practitioners. Thus, it is television, rather than the events themselves, that transformed the city squares and other sites in which these events took place into a global stage, watching these events.

- Second, the consequent global publicity given to these events by 'live' television undoubtedly influences the behavior of the actors or the protagonists involved. Clearly, the publicity enjoyed by the demonstrating students in Tiananmen Square helped to sustain the demonstration and was probably taken into account by the Chinese authorities, perhaps first constraining their response and later hastening it. Large scale publicity probably also acts as a mobilizer, leading the yet uninvolved to get involved. For example, the call for mass demonstrations in Wenceslas Square in Prague in 1989 publicized by television, was apparently responsible for recruiting even more demonstrators and, indeed, to engulf the whole society in the process of political change. The fall of the Berlin Wall in the glare of the television cameras undoubtedly endowed this event with an even greater symbolic value than it might have had, had it not been witnessed 'live' by countless millions around the world.

- Third, global television assumes a significant role in the construction of world public opinion. As Blumler (1989) puts it:

> The news media are not only a selectively-focusing and agenda setting force in international affairs. They are also a world-opinion defining

agency. For at present, they virtually have a monopoly over the construction of world opinion, its agenda of prime concerns, and its main targets of praise and blame. At present, at least, what they tell us about what world opinion apparently holds on a certain matter can rarely be double-checked by international opinion poll results.

It should, of course, be noted that the role played by the media in the construction of world opinion is an extension, onto a global scale, of the similar role they play in their own societies. However, whereas public opinion in a given society is typically tapped through surveys and polls – thus being a construct of the pollsters' work – *global* public opinion is, of course, wholly a media construction. In the absence of global polls or other similar 'hard' evidence, global public opinion is inevitably a product of media practices.

• Fourth, television acts as a 'go between', a channel of communication, especially in instances in which hostile relationships between governments tend to preclude direct contacts. One of the more celebrated examples of television's capacity to open up such channels of communication is the role imputed to US television in bringing about the visit by the Egyptian President, Anwar Sadat to Jerusalem. The news people who 'mediated' between the Egyptian President and the Israeli Prime Minister may or may not deserve credit for Sadat's trip, but at the very least they created a channel of communication where no other *public* one existed, and through which the opposing leaders appeared to communicate with each other *almost* directly.

A number of recent examples suggest that globalized television sometimes assumes not merely the role of a 'go between' but may launch reportorial initiatives that tend to blur the distinction between the roles of reporters and diplomats. The Sadat-Begin 'dialogue' is one case in point. More recently, discussing American television's coverage of the Persian Gulf crisis, a *Washington Post* columnist dubbed it 'teleplomacy'. He referred to the scramble by television reporters and news anchors to interview the Iraqi President, in the course of which the interviewers slid, almost imperceptibly, into the roles of advocates, as if representing their own government, and negotiators, exploring with their interviewee avenues for resolving the crisis.

Such 'extra-professional' behaviour raises questions and some criticism of the performance of television journalists and its consequences. It has been argued, for example, that the scramble to secure the first interview with Saddam Hussein, born of the immense competitive pressures under which reporters and networks labor, offered the interviewee a platform from which to address a global audience directly, going 'above the heads' of other governments; that the reporters tend to become advocates for their own side; their own governments and its policies, and that consequently they usurp the role of the true professional advocates, the government's own representatives.

The role journalists sometimes play as go-betweens in international crises raises other questions concerning the very nature of the journalism they profess to practise. The active participation of journalists in the events they presumably 'cover' is often achieved at the cost of sacrificing some traditional journalistic norms, such as editorial control over which actors (and perspectives) to incorporate into the story and which to ignore. Journalists reporting from Iraq during the Gulf war were, of course, aware that they were being 'used' by their Iraqi hosts to present a view of the hostilities as seen through Iraqi eyes, yet were criticized by television viewers in the West for spreading Iraqi 'propaganda'. (One conservative American Senator went as far as denouncing CNN's correspondent in Baghdad as a 'sympathizer' with the Iraqi regime.) Likewise, in the wake of the American bombing of Tripoli in 1986, the Libyans assisted Western television crews in filming civilian casualties, and naturally restricted access to military areas (Wallis and Baran, 1990). By facilitating the work of these journalists, both the Iraqis and the Libyans did, ironically, contribute to upholding the traditional journalistic norm of 'balance' – of showing 'the other side'. The motives impelling the journalists, however, stem, more likely, from competitive pressures than from adherence to the norm of 'balance'.

In addition to the hazards of control and manipulation that the media undergo in their new role as international political brokers, it is not entirely clear that the consequences of their interventions are always beneficial. For example, questions could be raised whether the failure of the diplomatic negotiations that preceded the Gulf war could be attributed, at least in part, to the fact that they were made part of a public discourse, and thus were framed in political and highly ideological terms that left little room for deal-making.

• Fifth, television's participation in events further blurs the line between 'social reality' and 'media reality'. It goes to the heart of the role of the media as 'definers of social reality', and beyond. The familiar approach to viewing the 'reality defining' role of the media suggests that, as Bennett (1982) for example, puts it,

> *what* 'events' are 'reported' by the media and the *ways* in which they are signified have a bearing on the ways in which we perceive the world and thus, if action is at all related to thought, on the ways we act within it.

The presence of journalists, and especially of television cameras, in any event goes beyond selecting what to report and how to report it. It impacts on the very behavior of the actors involved in the event, and thus alters its nature. 'Reality' and its portrayal on the screen are so inextricably intertwined as to become virtually indistinguishable. In fact, the farther the event from the audience, the more likely it is that the reality of the event on television will become the only 'reality'. Instant global television thus renders the complexity of the relationship between television portrayals and 'reality' even more acute. Television's coverage of political conventions, for example, has long been acknowledged to influence all aspects of the event, from its timing, to the scheduling of speakers, to the choice of colors on the podium. In the case of more chaotic, violent and potentially controversial events such as wars and other armed conflicts television's reality assumes predominant significance.

INSIDE THE TELEVISION INDUSTRIES

Media systems around the world vary in many ways. The relationship between the press and broadcasting systems and the political system is governed, in every country, by the nature of its political system and the norms that characterize its political culture. The socio-political and the economic structure of different societies also determine the internal structure of their media systems, their modes of finance, and consequently the intra-system relationships between different media organizations. Thus, for example, the American broadcasting system, truly reflecting its economic base, has always been regarded as a 'classic' example of a privately owned, commercially driven system, claiming autonomy from government and other forms of political controls. Many European countries, on the other hand, had a 'mixed' media system, combining state controlled or public service media organizations side by side with privately owned commercial organizations. For many years these structures were fairly stable, exhibiting little propensity for change. The advent of the new communication technologies appears to have changed all that. It is not the purpose of this chapter to explore these changes. Our concern here is limited to examining the impact of the introduction of satellite technology on the relationships between different television organizations.

The US experience is most instructive in this regard. This is so partly because the American broadcasting system is the largest in the world, certainly in terms of the number of different television outlets, but especially because its specific structure, consisting of three national commercial networks, a smaller public television network, a range of affiliate local stations and a sizeable number of independent local stations, constitutes a complex system of power dependencies, which turned out to be vulnerable to the potential impact of technological change. For many years televisions news in the American context meant, by and large, network news. The global news gathering machineries constructed by the networks' news organizations required resources above and beyond those available to any single station. As a result, local stations were always dependent on the networks' resources for news materials which originated beyond their immediate home areas. News programs produced by local stations reflected this dependency in the ways in which networks' originated materials were used in those (fairly infrequent) instances when foreign or other remote news stories were inserted into 'local' news shows.

Satellite technology has altered these dependencies. It enabled local stations to receive remote stories directly, often from their own sources. The cost of sending a reporter equipped with a satellite dish to a remote location where a major news story is unfolding is becoming increasingly affordable for single stations, especially when the prestige value of having one's own correspondent on the scene is considered. Thus, by extending the news reach of local stations the same technology that contributed to the globalization of television news has, perhaps paradoxically, promoted developments in the opposite direction, namely increasing decentralization of news gathering.

The new status and prestige gained by local television news has also resulted in increased economic returns for local stations through steadily increased ratings. According to a 1985 study by Baran (quoted in Wallis and Baran 1990), local television news in some stations accounts for 40 to 60 per cent of the stations' profits. These profits, in turn, allow the local stations to buy further national and foreign news footage.

While these developments are, for the most part, evident in the commercialized and virtually deregulated American broadcasting arena, parallels are emerging in Europe. 'Even in the European context of highly regulated broadcast media, many local lobbying groups are agitating for extended regional and local broadcast media' (Wallis and Baran, 1990). This is bound to affect the position, and the market share, of large scale, centralized news organizations. In the long run it might result in an increasing fragmentation of television news production. Thus far this might be primarily an American phenomenon, but it could be clearly extrapolated to the global scene. In that case, it could make smaller, less affluent television news organizations less dependent on the 'big boys' in the news business, and more capable of deploying the technology to serve their own needs. Satellite technology might prove to be the key for at least a partial liberation of television news services in smaller First World and Third World countries from dependency on the richer and more powerful news organizations. It might initiate the 'post media imperialism' era.

ENCODERS AND DECODERS

The debate about the 'balance of power' between those responsible for the production and shaping of media texts – the encoders on the one hand – and members of the media audiences – the decoders on the other – has received renewed attention over the last decade with the formulation of 'reception theory'. According to Curran, (1990), this 'revisionist scholarship' in media studies consisted of two major shifts: first, the emergence of scholarship that emphasized the 'inconsistencies, contradictions, gaps and even internal oppositions within texts', and that thus departed from earlier theoretical formulations that regarded texts as carrying coherent and dominant meanings; and second, a shift that stressed a view of the audience as active and autonomous – 'a reconceptualization of the audience as an active producer of meaning', challenging the assumption that 'audiences responded in prescribed ways to fixed, preconstituted meanings in texts'. It is useful to speculate, in the framework of these reconceptualizations, about the position of the audience for television news in an era of global journalism. By and large, this discussion is inevitably speculative, since hardly any empirical evidence is as yet available on that issue.

First, much of the news materials disseminated globally, but especially the 'raw materials' disseminated through the regional news exchange systems and the television news agencies (Visnews and WTN) may be properly described as 'open' texts. 'Openness' here implies the extent to which different kinds of texts constrain the meanings embedded in them or, alternatively, allow for multiple decodings of their meanings. Thus, it can be argued that verbal texts (e.g. news stories in the printed press) are relatively 'closed' (i.e. they constrain the range of interpretations or meanings of the events they report) since *any account of an event necessarily defines its meaning*. On the other hand, 'pure' visuals (i.e. visuals unaccompanied by a verbal caption or text) are relatively 'open', as they are susceptible to a wider range of interpretations or 'stories' based upon them. The visual materials that are the stock in trade of the news exchange organizations and the news agencies are, indeed, sent primarily in the form of 'raw materials', that is, unedited footage, including only 'natural-sound'. The task of editing and shaping these materials into news stories remains in the hands of news editors in the different broadcasting organizations. Thus, while the same visual materials might be used by editors in different countries, the final shape of the stories they are telling, their narrative and thematic structures, and the meanings embedded in them remain in the hands of editors working with different national audiences in mind. In fact, such is the degree of 'openness' of the visuals that come down from the satellites, that they could be regarded almost as 'an empty vessel' (Barkin and Gurevitch, 1986).

The resulting diversity of meanings offers an almost unique opportunity to witness the ways in which television news construct different social realities. By comparing the similarities or differences in the meanings encoded into a variety of stories of the 'same' event, some insight may be gained of the degree of control that encoders have over the construction of meanings. In an era of increasing globalization of television news such comparative analysis may also offer an important antidote to 'naive universalism' – that is, to the assumption that events reported in the news carry their own meanings, and that the meanings embedded in news stories produced in one country can therefore be generalized to news stories told in other societies (Gurevitch and Blumler, 1990).

How does this process impact on the 'autonomy of the audience' – the capacity of audience members to act as active producers of meanings? Since audience members have no access to the more 'open' texts of raw visuals and are only exposed to already fully fashioned stories, their position as news consumers may not have changed from that in the era of 'conventional' television news. It would therefore be plausible to assume that they may not have gained any greater autonomy vis-a-vis the story tellers. In fact, it might be possible to argue that, faced with a larger amount of news stories from far-away places (for that is one of the changes that the global flow of news facilitates), their dependence on the encoders to make sense of these events actually increases. Presented with stories of events for which they have no ready-made 'schemas' (Graber, 1984), or frameworks for interpretation, viewers are less able to negotiate and construct the meanings of these events for themselves, and are inevitably more dependent on the perspectives embedded in the stories. Their power position vis-a-vis the correspondents and editors who bring them these stories is thus diminished.

As suggested earlier, we have no evidence to support that conclusion. It is based on a rather simple extrapolation of current theories of media-audience relationships. However, if it were to be confirmed it might result in another swing of the theoretical pendulum, a retreat from the recent formulations of 'reception theory', back to the theories of powerful media and powerless audiences.

The process of globalization of electronic journalism is growing apace, transforming the flow of communication around the world and impacting in myriad ways on the ways people and societies know, perceive and understand the world and conduct relationships with each other. Perhaps paradoxically, however, the defining contours of the process are not easy to discern. The difficulty we are confronted with in trying to grasp the nature and consequences of this process lie partly in the rapid development of the technology that facilitates its rapid emergence and change of the institutional structures that carry the globalization process forward, and the diverse ways in which the implications and the consequences of these developments manifest themselves. But the more significant obstacle, as was suggested earlier, lies in our uncertainty about the most appropriate and theoretically productive way to conceptualize the process. In the absence of a comprehensive theoretical framework these diverse phenomena will remain unrelated, disconnected and more difficult to make sense of.

In this chapter we attempted to offer a starting point for the construction of such a conceptual framework. One starting point, we suggested, may be found in the *shifting balance of relationships of dependency* between different participants in the networks of global communication. Each 'communication revolution', from the Guttenbergian to the electronic, to the emergence of global, satellite-based communication, brought in their wake a transformation in the power relationships in society: the printing press contributed to undermining the power of the Papacy; the press facilitated the consolidation of the dominance of the middle classes in industrial societies; the electronic media, among other things, helped to legitimate counter-cultures and other stirrings against the existing social order. The globalization of television, and more specifically the emergence of television news as a truly global phenomenon may, or may not be a 'revolution' on par with these other historical revolutions. But the path to understanding it might be the same.

REFERENCES

Barkin, S. and Gurevitch, M., (1987): 'Out of Work and on the Air: Television News of Unemployment', *Critical Studies in Mass Communication*, vol. 4, no. 1.

Bennett, Tony, (1982): 'Media, "Reality", Signification', in Gurevitch, Michael et al. (eds) *Culture, Society and the Media*. London: Methuen.

Blumler, Jay, (1989): 'The Internationalization of Communication', Paper presented to College of Communication, University of Texas, Austin, Texas.

Curran, James, (1990): 'The New Revisionism in Mass Communication Research: A Reappraisal', *European Journal of Communication*, vol. 5, no. 2–3.

Graber, Doris, (1984): *Processing the News*. New York and London: Longman.

Gurevich, Michael and Blumler, Jay, (1990): 'Comparative Research: The Extending Frontier', in Swanson, D. and Nimmo, D. (eds), *New Directions in Political Communication*, Newbury Park, California: Sage.

Pool, Ithiel de Sola, (1983): *Technologies of Freedom*. Cambridge, MA: Harvard University Press.

Smith, Anthony, (1990): 'Media Globalism in the Age of Consumer Sovereignty', *Gannett Center Journal*, vol. 4, no. 4, Fall 1990.

Wallis, Roger and Stanley Baran, (1990): *The Known World of Broadcast News*. London and New York: Routledge.

55

NEWS CONTENT AND AUDIENCE BELIEF

Greg Philo

[...]

The press and television are sometimes accused of selectivity in their report-ing. The sheer scale of the events in the [Miners'] Strike [of 1984–5] meant that there were very many different stories and incidents which could potentially be highlighted. It is important to grasp the magnitude of the events in order to see how such a process of selection can work. At this time there were 190,000 mineworkers in total. There were also tens of thousands of police and workers from other unions and support groups who were involved in actions at different times in the strike. At Orgreave on 18 June 1984, there were 10,000 pickets present plus a very heavy police presence. Other picketing actions were much smaller, but spread over a very large number of locations. There were 174 pits, plus other sites such as power stations, ports, and steelworks. In such a huge sample of people over such a long period, we might expect to find many vari-eties of human behaviour. There would be miners trained in first aid, who would pause to help policemen who had fallen (which did happen), and we would find people who would throw bolts and bricks.

The political and economic events which surrounded the strike resulted in a conflict on a scale which had been unknown for many years. The police had a pivotal role in this and were seen as directly antagonistic to the strike by those who were pursuing it. When tens of thousands of police, miners, and their supporters confronted each other in such a stressed period, there was a very real

From G. Philo, *Seeing and Believing: The Influence of Television* (London: Routledge, 1990) pp. 147–54.

possibility that there would be violent incidents. But it is the relentless focus on these by television and the press, accompanied by the comments on 'escalation' and 'new records', which establishes for many of the audience the belief that violence was a persistent feature of most picketing.

There was a remarkable unanimity of belief amongst the groups in this sample about what had actually been shown. In the general sample, 98 per cent believed that most picketing which they had seen on television news was violent. The remaining 2 per cent either were unsure or believed the picketing shown was 'intimidatory' rather than physically violent. But perhaps what is most remarkable is the number of people who believed that these television images represented the everyday reality of picketing. There was occasionally a fear expressed of even going near a picket line, because of the high levels of physical fighting which were believed to be going on. In all, 54 per cent of the general sample believed that picketing was mostly violent.

The source for these beliefs was overwhelmingly given as television and the press, with the emphasis on TV, because of its immediate and more dramatic quality. Some people also indicated how their attitudes had altered as a result of what they had seen. For example, one of the secretaries in the solicitors' office in Croydon wrote that her opinion of the police had improved because 'you do not realise what they have to put up with'. It was clear that some key elements of belief were being provided by the media. But it would be wrong to see people as being totally dependent on such messages, as if they are simply empty vessels which are being filled up by News at Ten. To accept and believe what is seen on television is as much a cultural act as the rejection of it. Both acceptance and rejection are conditioned by our beliefs, history, and experience. A high degree of trust in the BBC, for example, might result from a knowledge of its history and its peculiar role in British society as an authoritative 'national' voice.

Television news itself works very hard at strategies to win our trust. It scorns the crude editorializing of newspapers and uses presentational techniques which suggest neutrality and balance. Whether the audience actually accepts television's presentation of itself depends very much on what beliefs, experience, and information they bring to what they are shown.

In this sample, some people clearly accepted the television account. But others adapted parts of the message and changed key elements of its meaning. For example, some believed that the strike was mostly violent because of what they had seen on television, but blamed the police for provoking the trouble. They could be quite aware that television news had not explained the origins of the violence in this way. The disjunction between what they had seen and what they believed was explained by saying that television 'only showed violence from miners, not police' (Glasgow woman). In such an example, what is finally believed results from news images being interpreted through beliefs about both the police and television.[1]

In the Glasgow retirement group, we encountered a different negotiation of the television message. In this group, there was a very high degree of trust in television news and most accepted its account of the violent nature of picketing. But there was also a high degree of sympathy with the miners and this contradiction was partly resolved by a focus on 'outsiders, infiltrators, and militants' as the cause of the trouble. This negotiation was not completely successful in rehabilitating the miners, as there was also deep unhappiness expressed about the violence and how it had reflected on the miners' cause.

The process by which people understand a television message depends in part on the beliefs which they bring to it and crucially on how these beliefs are utilized. There were cases amongst the group of electronics staff and the Bromley women where people had a critique of television latent in their beliefs. They stated at first that they thought picketing was mostly violent and then moved away from this position as they began to comment on the nature of television as a medium, with its tendency to select and to focus on the sensational. In these cases, the exercise itself seems to have provided the stimulus for the emergence of this view. But it is important that the belief about picketing had in a sense rested with them, until they were pressed to explain it. These again seem to be examples of the message being absorbed in spite of other beliefs which were held.

Where no critical view of television exists, the likelihood of accepting its account may be very great. One person in the Glasgow retirement group commented that television was the most important source of information and took her opinion of picketing from it because as she said: 'Seeing is believing.'

We also saw one case in this sample where the acceptance of the television message was underlined by indirect experience. One of the London Transport supervisors had stayed for a period in Yorkshire and had thought that the people there had a very 'them-and-us' attitude. This had led him to accept the television portrayal of picketing. But it was clear that in this study the overwhelming effect of indirect and direct experience was to produce a rejection of the television news account. This was most obvious in the case of people who had been at picket lines, whether police, pickets, or other observers. One interesting case was of the Scottish solicitor who had driven past a picket line during the strike and had compared what he had seen with television coverage of picketing. In the same office, a secretary commented that her experience of seeing how a dispute at Chrysler was treated in the news, had led her to question the coverage of the miners' strike.

In the general sample, 43 per cent believed that picketing was mostly peaceful. When giving reasons, about a third of these based their belief on the experience of knowing or having met policemen or miners. The effect of such experience could traverse class and political culture. We saw for example the two Bromley residents whose views were generally on the right and whose key memory of the strike was of 'Arthur Scargill talking rubbish/lies'. Yet they believed that picketing was mostly peaceful because of their contact with miners and their families whilst on holiday at Ollerton.

A second major reason for doubting television news was the comparison of it with other sources of information, such as the 'quality' and local press or 'alternative' current affairs programmes and radio. About 16 per cent of the general sample made such comparisons. These comments were sometimes linked to remarks on the tendency of television to exaggerate and focus on violence to the exclusion of other events. In the general sample, 14 per cent of the people made this criticism and gave it as a reason for rejecting the news presentation. This is a relatively low proportion given that it is sometimes thought that beliefs about the tendency of media to exaggerate are generally held in the population. It might in fact be that they are. But what is significant about this result is that even where such beliefs existed they were not always used to discount what was seen in the news. It was also noteworthy that where people relied only on this criticism to reject the news account, there was a tendency to estimate the level of violence as being very high. Some of the group in the Glasgow solicitors' office made such estimates, although their conclusion was that for a majority of the time picketing was probably peaceful.

These criticisms of television as a medium and the comparison of it with other accounts were made by people with varied political views. But there was another strand of criticism which saw the focus on violence as a conscious attempt to denigrate the miners' case.

This view was most prominent amongst the Scottish trade unionists. One of the London Transport supervisors had also commented that the media 'picked out the violence so as to get the majority of people against the miners'. The trade unionists had criticized several aspects of news presentation, such as the 'big thing' that was made of Ian MacGregor being knocked over and the focus on 'violence instead of support groups'. There was a strong belief amongst them that picketing was mostly peaceful. In arguing this, some also commented on the scale of the strike and the numbers involved, saying that people could not have been fighting most of the time. This deduction could apparently be made irrespective of sympathies with the strike. One woman in the Penge group said that she would have shot striking miners (had she been a working miner), but also argued that, 'because of the amount who were actually on strike . . . it can't all have been violent'. One of the print workers commented that 'if they had been really violent, the police couldn't have coped, it would have been the army' and a Bromley resident said that 'there would be a revolution'.

In the general sample, about 6 per cent of the people gave such deductions as an explanation for their beliefs on picketing, while 3 per cent gave their personal conviction that most people are not inclined to violence. These are relatively small proportions of the sample. We might remember that 54 per cent had believed that most picketing was violent. The source of this belief seems very clearly to have been the media. It is something of an indictment of news journalism that after coverage virtually every day for a year, such a large proportion of people had apparently no idea what a typical picket line was like. The eye-witness accounts which we have seen here were greeted with genuine surprise by many in the groups who had been convinced by what they had seen on the news.

MEMORY AND BELIEFS

The most frequently cited memories were of violence. Seventy-two per cent of the general sample thought that 'confrontation', 'clashes', 'picketing', and 'violence' were what was shown most on television news of the strike. [...] In the key memories, 'confrontation', 'violence', and 'picketing' were again cited more than any other issue. These were given by 27 per cent of the people in the general sample. There were other issues cited as key memories which had connotations of violence, such as the intimidation/treatment of non-strikers (6 per cent), police violence/causing trouble/charging miners on horseback (12 per cent), and the death of the Welsh taxi-driver (9 per cent). Arthur Scargill was named as being what was 'most shown' by 27 per cent of the general sample and was given as a key memory by 21 per cent, sometimes accompanied by pejorative comments. This was most noticeable in the south of the country. In the Shenfield group, for example, the miners' leader is named in eight out of the ten replies. For some respondents he was thought to be both what was shown most on television and also had the greatest impact upon them of anything in the strike. This suggests that judgements about the content of news were being affected by prior belief, in this case the intense antipathy which was felt for Scargill.

The assessment of what was on the news most could also be affected by direct involvement or close sympathy with the dispute. The Scottish trade unionists, the Yorkshire miners, and the printers in Fleet Street all included references to the return to work.

They had generally a very cynical view of the media and many saw the news emphasis on the breakdown of the strike as evidence of bias against the miners' cause. As one miner put it, television had shown 'returning miners, the more the better'. But the images were clearly also very significant in their own memories, because of what they represented in terms of the failure of union solidarity. This was very apparent in the case of the print workers who were involved in their own union dispute. For some in these groups, the return to work was given as the key memory of the strike and was also estimated to have been the issue most shown on the news. But there was not always such a clear correspondence between these two dimensions of memory. Some respondents made clear distinction between them. In the general sample, 9 per cent believed that negotiations, meetings, and arguments featured most in news coverage, but there were no references to these as key memories.

As we have seen, for most people the violent images were very salient and were thought to have predominated in the news. But many also made it clear that there were other memories which had an even more powerful impact upon them. For example the group of Scottish trade unionists had believed overwhelmingly that violence was the most shown issue on the news. But nearly half of the group did not include this in their key memories and instead spoke of the role of support groups and miners' wives and the attitude of the government and the Coal Board.

In the general sample, memories were clearly affected by political belief and class experience. The groups of women in Glasgow and Penge remembered people queueing for food and the loss of jobs in the dispute. But class experience was not synonymous with political belief. Some of the middle-class women in Bromley were very sympathetic to the miners' cause – yet none of these gave unemployment or hardship in the strike as a key memory.

The effect of experience on perception could apparently last for many years. One of the middle-class residents of Shenfield gave as her key memory of the strike the hopelessness of families and 'shortage of money'. She explained this by speaking of the harsh consequences of unemployment on her family when she was a small child.

Attitudes to police action in the strike could also be affected by past experience. One woman in the Glasgow retirement group commented on her belief that the police were 'causing the trouble' during the strike. She based this view on experiences when living in a large working-class housing estate, twenty years earlier. There were several examples of how direct contact with the police could have remarkable effects on memories of the dispute. Two people from the middle-class areas of Bromley and Beckenham gave 'police tactics' and 'use of police horsemen against miners and fear on people's faces', as their key memories of the strike. Both also gave accounts of how they had been stopped by the police – one of them for what was described as an 'April Fool's joke'.

In the general sample as a whole, there was apparently a growth in negative attitudes towards the police. Forty-three per cent of the people said that their attitude had changed for the worse in the period since the strike, while 11 per cent said that their attitude had improved (a further 12 per cent said that their attitude was already very good). Some of these changes in attitude related to media coverage of events which had nothing to do with the miners' dispute – such as the attack on the six youths in a police van in Islington in 1983 and the subsequent action against police officers.

Criticisms of the police which were featured in the media could sometimes be re-negotiated by people who were sympathetic with the force. They might say for example that the tougher stance of the police was being 'forced upon them', or the criticisms might simply be rejected. But negative contact with the police seemed to have a very powerful impact on the beliefs of people who might otherwise have been sympathetic.

This further underlines one of the key findings here, that direct experience can have a crucial influence on how new information from the media is understood. Such direct contacts, together with political culture, class experience, processes of logic, and comparisons made between accounts, were the most important factors in the relation between perception and belief.

These findings show that some of the media audience clearly negotiate the meaning of what they are told. However, the influence of media and especially television was central, since it established so firmly the issues which came to be associated with the strike. Some of these, such as the emphasis on violence and the return to work, were very damaging to the miners' cause. Those who sought to reject these accounts of the strike had in a sense to struggle against the dominant flow of images from the media. For those without access to direct experience, it was sometimes a losing battle.

[...]

NOTE

1. None of these elements are static and they can all move in relation to each other. For example, several people said that their beliefs about television had been altered by what they had seen. They had believed it to be neutral until its presentation of the miners' strike. This potential for change is important since there is a recent trend in media studies to present the interpretation of television messages as being subject to pre-existing cultural and political beliefs. Such beliefs are important dimensions to the reception of new information, but they cannot be treated as fixed entities. There is the constant possibility of their movement and renegotiation in relation to what we see and are told and as a result of new experience.

FURTHER READING

Bell, A. and Garrett, P. (eds), *Approaches to Media Discourse* (Oxford: Blackwell, 1998).

Boyce, G., Curran, J., and Wingate, P. (eds), *Newspaper History: from the Seventeenth Century to the Present Day* (London: Constable, 1978).

Boyd-Barrett, O. and Newbold, C. (eds), *Approaches to Media* (London: Arnold, 1995).

Butcher, H. et al., 'Images of Women in the Media'. In S. Cohen and J. Young (eds), *The Manufacture of News: Social Problems, Deviance and the Mass Media* (London: Constable, 1973).

Carey, J. W. (ed.), *Media, Myths, and Narratives: Television and the Press* (London: Sage, 1988).

Chibnall, S., *Law and Order News* (London: Tavistock, 1977).

Cohen, S., *Folk Devils and Moral Panics* (Oxford: Blackwell, 1987).

Cohen, S. and Young, J. (eds), *The Manufacture of News: Social Problems, Deviance and the Mass Media* (London: Constable, 1973).

Connell, I., 'Television, News and the Social Contract'. In S. Hall, D. Hobson, A. Lowe, and P. Willis (eds), *Culture, Media, Language* (London: Hutchinson, 1980).

Corner, J., *Television Form and Public Address* (London: Edward Arnold, 1995).

Cumberbatch, G., McGregor, R., Brown, J., and Morrison, D., *Television and the Miners' Strike* (London: Broadcasting Research Unit, 1986).

Curran, J. and Gurevitch, M. (eds), *Mass Media and Society* (London: Edward Arnold, 1991).

Curran, J., Gurevitch, M., and Woollacott, J., *Mass Communication and Society* (London: Edward Arnold, 1977).

Curran, J. and Seaton, J., *Power without Responsibility: the Press and Broadcasting in Britain*. 4th edition (London: Routledge, 1991).

Dahlgren, P., 'The Modes of Reception: For a Hermeneutics of TV News'. In P. Drummond and R. Paterson (eds), *Television in Transition* (London: BFI, 1985).

Dahlgren, P., 'What's the Meaning of This?: Viewers' Plural Sense-Making of TV News'. *Media, Culture and Society* 10:3 (1988) pp. 285–301

Dahlgren, P. and Sparks, C. (eds), *Communication and Citizenship: Journalism and the Public Sphere* (London: Routledge, 1991).

Davis, H. and Walton, P., *Language, Image, Media* (Oxford: Blackwell, 1983).

Eldridge, J. (ed.), *Getting the Message: News, Truth and Power* (London and New York: Routledge, 1993).

Ericson, R., Baranek, P., and Chan, J., *Visualizing Deviance: A Study of News Organization* (Milton Keynes: Open University Press, 1987).

Ericson, R., Baranek, P., and Chan, J., *Negotiating Control: A Study of News Sources* (Milton Keynes: Open University Press, 1989).

Fiske, J., *Television Culture* (London: Methuen, 1987).

Fiske, J., *Reading the Popular* (London: Unwin Hyman, 1989).

Fiske, J. and Hartley, J., *Reading Television* (London: Methuen, 1978).

Galtung, J. and Ruge, M., 'Structuring and Selecting News'. In S. Cohen and J. Young (eds), *The Manufacture of News: Social Problems, Deviance and the Mass Media* (London: Constable, 1973).

Gans, H., *Deciding What's News* (London: Constable, 1979).

Glasgow University Media Group, *Bad News* (London: Routledge, 1976).

Glasgow University Media Group, *More Bad News* (London: Routledge, 1980).

Glasgow University Media Group, *Really Bad News* (London: Writers and Readers Co-operative, 1982).

Glasgow University Media Group, *War and Peace News* (Milton Keynes: Open University Press, 1985).

Glasgow University Media Group (ed. J. Eldridge), *Getting the Message: News, Truth and Power* (London: Routledge, 1993).

Golding, P. and Elliott, P., *Making the News* (London: Longman, 1979).

Golding, P. and Middleton, S., *Images of Welfare* (Oxford: Blackwell and Martin Robertson, 1982).

Goodwin, A., 'TV News: Striking the Right Balance'. In A. Goodwin and G. Whannel (eds), *Understanding Television* (London: Routledge, 1990).

Graber, I., 'Television and Political Coverage'. In C. Geraghty and D. Lusted (eds), *The Television Studies Book* (London: Arnold, 1998).

Hall, S., 'The Determinations of News Photographs'. In S. Cohen and J. Young (eds), *The Manufacture of News: Social Problems, Deviance and the Mass Media* (London: Constable, 1973).

Hall, S., 'Introduction' to A. C. H. Smith (with E. Immirzi and T. Blackwell), *Paper Voices: the Popular Press and Social Change 1935–1965* (London: Chatto and Windus, 1975).

Hall, S., Connell, I., and Curti, L., 'The Unity of Current Affairs Television'. In T. Bennett, S. Boyd-Bowman, C. Mercer, and J. Woollacott (eds), *Popular Television and Film* (London: BFI, 1981).

Hall, S., Critcher, C., Jefferson, T., Clarke, J., and Roberts, B., *Policing the Crisis: Mugging, the State, and Law and Order* (London: Macmillan, 1978).

Hartley, J., *Understanding News* (London: Methuen, 1982).

Hartley, J., 'Truth Wars'. In *Tele-ology* (London and New York: Routledge, 1992).

Hjarvard, S., 'TV News: From Discrete Items to Continuous Narrative? The Social Meaning of Changing Temporal Structures'. *Cultural Studies* 8:2 (1994) pp. 306–20.

Holland, P., 'When a Woman Reads the News'. In H. Baehr and G. Dyer (eds), *Boxed In: Women and Television* (London: Pandora Press, 1987).

Jacobs, R. N., 'Producing the News, Producing the Crisis: Narrativity, Television and News Work'. *Media, Culture and Society* 18:3 (1996) pp. 373–98.

Jensen, K. B., *Making Sense of the News* (Ahrhus: University of Ahrhus Press, 1986).

Jensen, K. B., 'The Politics of Polysemy: Television News, Everyday Consciousness and Political Action'. *Media, Culture and Society* 12:1 (1990) pp. 57–77.

Lewis, J., 'Decoding Television News'. In P. Drummond and R. Paterson (eds), *Television in Transition* (London: BFI, 1985).

Lewis, J., 'Behind the News'. In J. Lewis, *The Ideological Octopus: An Exploration of Television and its Audience* (London: Routledge, 1991).

Manoff, R. K. and Schudson, M. (eds), *Reading the News* (New York: Pantheon Books, 1987).

Miller, D., 'Official Sources and "Primary definition": the Case of Northern Ireland'. *Media, Culture and Society* 15:3 (1993) pp. 385–406.

Negrine, R., *Politics and the Mass Media in Britain* (London: Routledge, 1989).

Philo, G., *Seeing and Believing* (London: Routledge, 1990).

Schlesinger, P., *Putting 'Reality' Together: BBC News* (London: Methuen, 1978).

Schlesinger, P., Murdock, G., and Elliott, P., *Televising 'Terrorism': Political Violence in Popular Culture* (London: Comedia, 1983).

Schlesinger, P. 'From Production to Propaganda'. *Media, Culture and Society* Vol. 2. (London: Sage, 1989) pp. 283–306.

Schlesinger, P., 'Rethinking the Sociology of Journalism: Source Strategies and the Limits of Media Centrism'. In M. Ferguson (ed.), *Public Communication: the New Imperatives* (London: Sage, 1990).

Schudson, M., *Discovering the News* (New York: Basic Books, 1987).

Schudson, M., 'The Sociology of News Production Revisited'. In J. Curran and M. Gurevitch (eds), *Mass Media and Society* (London: Edward Arnold, 1991).

Tuchman, G., *Making News: A Study in the Construction of Reality* (New York: Free Press, 1978).

Tulloch, J., 'Policing the Public Sphere: the British Machinery of News Management'. *Media, Culture and Society* 15:3 (1993) pp. 363–84.

van Zoonen, L., 'Rethinking Women and the News'. *European Journal of Communication* 3:1 (1988) pp. 35–53.

Wallis, R. and Baran, S., *The Known World of Broadcast News* (London: Routledge, 1990).

White, D. M., 'The Gatekeeper: A Case Study in the Selection of News'. *Journalism Quarterly* 27:4 (1950) pp. 383–90.

SECTION 7
ADVERTISING

ADVERTISING
INTRODUCTION

The study of advertising takes us into wider and more contested areas of study than do the first two case studies in this Reader. In the first place, advertising is an *industry* which wields considerable power within capitalist society. It is tied in more directly to capitalism's economic structures than other media forms, being linked into a chain of marketing practices which function to sustain the flow of goods on which the economic system depends. It also exerts economic force upon mass media structures themselves, since it acts, as James Curran argues (Chapter 57), as a 'concealed subsidy system' to whose demands the mass media must be responsive. A consideration of its relations of production, therefore, must deal not only with its internal processes but with the influence it exerts at this level upon the media system as a whole.

Second, advertising has often been seen within cultural theory as emblematic of the culture in which it has become so all-pervasive. For F. R. Leavis, writing in 1930 in defence of what he termed 'minority culture', advertising epitomised the 'exploitation of the cheap response' which characterises contemporary 'mass civilisation'.[1] In 1947, Theodor Adorno and Max Horkheimer, writing from the very different, Marxist perspective of the Frankfurt School (see Chapter 2), argued similarly that advertising pervades what has now become the 'culture industry', subsidising the 'ideological media' and turning culture into an 'assembly-line' whose standardised products it furnishes with artificial differences.[2] For contemporary theorists, too, advertising functions in this emblematic way. Jean Baudrillard, for example, argues that it 'invades every-thing'. Both public and private space disappear, as does the separation between them, to be replaced by 'great screens on which are reflected atoms, particles, molecules in motion', in the 'era of hyperreality'.[3] For these theorists, advertising functions as a key reference point rather than an object of sustained study.

Third, as part of a marketing industry, advertising has conducted its own audience research, and at times this has been difficult to distinguish from certain strands of academic research, particularly within the American 'mass communication' tradition. Todd Gitlin, for example, in a 1978 critique of what he termed the 'dominant paradigm' of American media sociology, makes this attack on the American tradition:

> It is no secret that mass communications research descends directly from the development of sophisticated marketing techniques. The theory of 'effects' was first developed for the direct, explicit use of broadcasters and advertisers, and continues to be used mostly in those circles, to grow more sophisticated there.[4]

His conclusion, that, by its complicity with the advertising industry, American media sociology has functioned to 'legitimize ... mid-century capitalism',[5] is one echoed elsewhere within the 'critical' tradition of media research. Stuart Hall, for example, writes in 1982 that this approach, 'though advanced as empirically-grounded and scientific, was predicated on a very specific set of political and ideological presuppositions'.[6] These presuppositions, characterised by Ien Ang as 'the institutional point of view',[7] remain hidden, however, framing and underpinning the research as 'a set of unexamined postulates'. Thus advertising becomes a ground on which opposing traditions of audience research may be fought out.

Finally, its links with the processes of consumption mean that advertising is caught up in wider arguments about the power of audiences/consumers to resist the meanings and pleasures produced by the powerful. For example, John Fiske's assertion of a semi-autonomous 'cultural economy' which operates in parallel to the 'political economy', and in which consumers rather than producers are empowered, produces a view of shopping as 'an oppositional ... act', whose 'guerrillas' – particularly women – cause the persuasive techniques of advertising always to fail. 'There is so much advertising', he argues, 'only because it can never finally succeed in its tasks – those of containing social diversity within the needs of capitalism and of reducing the relative autonomy of the cultural economy from the financial ...'[8]

The chapter by Raymond Wiiliams which opens this section, written in 1960, takes up several of the issues outlined above. Advertising, he argues (Chapter 56), is both crucial to the economic functioning of capitalism and a form of 'social communication', offering us new ways of understanding ourselves. Advertising, then, categorises us as 'consumers' rather than 'users', offering in response to real human needs (the 'problems of death, loneliness, frustration, the need for identity and respect') the illusory satisfaction provided by the consumption of material goods. In advertising's 'magic system' these goods are identified with human values and desires, in order to obscure the 'real sources' of satisfaction whose discovery would involve radical changes in our way of life. Williams, however, is far less pessimistic than, for example, Adorno and Horkheimer. Advertisers, he writes, are as confused as their consumers, and the confused society for which they speak still has a choice: between 'capitalism and socialism ... man as consumer and man as user'.

The second chapter, by James Curran (Chapter 57), offers an overview of the impact of advertising on the range and nature of Britain's mass media. Advertisers, he argues, have played a central role in shaping Britain's media system in three ways. Firstly, the allocation of advertising finance *between* the different media sectors influences the overall shape of Britain's media industries. Changing trends in advertising allocation cause the expansion or contraction of specific sectors. Secondly, advertising allocation *within* media sectors influences the character of each medium, causing, for example, the political imbalance of the press and the overwhelming orientation of women's magazines towards the young middle-class reader. Finally, the need to respond to advertising pressures has produced highly conservative television and commercial radio schedules, and a popular press which is largely depoliticised.

Chapter 58 comes from Sean Nixon's study of the construction of 'new masculinities' within advertising, retailing and men's 'style magazines' in the 1980s, *Hard Looks*. In this section, he gives an account of the shifts within advertising practices which facilitated the influence of the 1980s 'style press' and general interest men's magazines in establishing a distinctive imagery for the 'new man'. He also analyses the nature of that imagery and the changes in the codings of masculinity which it represented. Nixon argues that in order to understand the cultural significance of this 'new man' imagery, it is not enough simply to examine the imagery itself; nor can it be explained solely by reference to the economic shifts in the advertising and magazine industries which led to its appearance. Instead, we must explore the interdependence of economic and cultural practices. The two do not function as discrete, autonomous realms. Representations – in this case of the 'new man' – do not simply result from economic processes of production; they are a part of these processes and the discursive ground on which producers, advertisers and consumers meet.

Judith Williamson's (1978) *Decoding Advertisements* inaugurated the application of structuralist analysis to advertising texts. Her analysis of 'how ads work'[9] drew on semiotics, Lacanian psychoanalysis and Althusserian Marxism and heralded an engagement by feminist and cultural studies scholars with the textual structures of advertisements. Janice Winship's analysis of the use of hands in advertisements (Chapter 59) draws on Williamson's work to argue that ads not only reflect but also help to construct the ideological structures and frameworks in our society. Hands, she argues, are always gendered in advertisements, and through her analysis of specific examples she explores the meanings of 'masculinity' and 'femininity' constructed through these representations.

The chapter by Anne McClintock which follows (Chapter 60), examines the relations of power and desire in the imperial discourses of nineteenth-century Britain. Her focus is the soap advertisements which, she argues, legitimise racist conceptions of Britain's colonial others through a fetishising of 'whiteness' as cleanliness. In these advertisements, imperialism is 'domesticated', and soap comes to mediate 'the Victorian poetics of racial hygiene and imperial progress'. Its advertisements present the colonies as conquered by domestic commodities and offer imperial progress as commodity spectacle. If these advertisements mask the realities of imperial power, however, they also obscure the realities of the domestic sphere as the space of unpaid women's work. Working women are absent, the value of their work is displaced onto the commodity itself, and the advertisements' 'feminised' Africans are figured 'not as historic agents, but as frames for the commodity, for their exhibition value alone'. The fetishistic images which these advertisements present, argues McClintock, are a crucial part of the Victorian 'mass marketing of empire as a series of images', its 'civilising mission' embodied in the spectacular effects of the domestic commodity, soap.

The final chapter of this section, by Mica Nava and Orson Nava (Chapter 61), is unusual within academic work on advertising in being based upon an ethnographic study. The Navas' analysis of young people's readings of advertisements offers a challenge to the focus on the power of advertisers or the advertising text to determine meaning, which can be found in different ways in the work of Curran, Winship and McClintock. Like John Fiske and Angela McRobbie (Chapters 42 and 30), the Navas emphasises the creative play of advertising's users, arguing that both the 'critical tools' evidenced by young people's decodings, and the pleasures generated by the 'increasingly ... sophisticated cultural form' of advertising, may be used to 'subvert and fragment existing networks of power-knowledge'.

NOTES

1. See *Mass Civilisation and Minority Culure*. This extract is taken from J. Storey (ed.), *Cultral Theory and Popular Culture: A Reader* (Hemel Hempstead: Harvester Wheatsheaf, 1994), p.12.
2. See 'The Culture Industry: Enlightenment as Mass Deception'. In J. Curran, M. Gurevitch and J. Woollacott (eds), *Mass Communication and Society* (London: Edward Arnold, 1977), pp. 380, 381.
3. See 'The Ecstasy of Communication'. In H. Foster (ed.), *Postmodern Culture* (London: Pluto Press, 1985), pp. 129, 130. See also Chapter 9 in this volume.
4. Todd Gitlin, 'Media Sociology: the Dominant Paradigm'. In *Theory and Society* 6 (1978), p. 232.
5. Ibid., p. 245.
6. Stuart Hall, 'The Rediscovery of "Ideology": Return of the Repressed in Media Studies'. In M. Gurevitch, T. Bennett, J. Curran and J. Woollacott (eds), *Culture, Society and the Media* (London: Methuen, 1982), p. 59.
7. Ien Ang, *Desperately Seeking the Audience* (London: Routledge, 1991), p. 157. Ang's examination of the advertising industry's audience research, as its title suggests, concludes that this research is doomed to failure, since the practices and experiences

of actual audiences always remain beyond the reach of its quantitative research methods.

8. See 'Shopping for Pleasure' in *Reading the Popular* (London: Unwin Hyman, 1989), pp. 13–42 and 'Commodities and Culture' in *Understanding Popular Culture* (London: Unwin Hyman, 1989), p. 30.

9. Williamson, *Decoding Advertisements* (London: Marion Boyars, 1978).

56

ADVERTISING: THE MAGIC SYSTEM

Raymond Williams

[...]

In the last hundred years [...] advertising has developed from the simple announcements of shopkeepers and the persuasive arts of a few marginal dealers into a major part of capitalist business organization. This is important enough, but the place of advertising in society goes far beyond this commercial context. It is increasingly the source of finance for a whole range of general communication, to the extent that in 1960 our majority television service and almost all our newspapers and periodicals could not exist without it. Further, in the last forty years and now at an increasing rate, it has passed the frontier of the selling of goods and services and has become involved with the teaching of social and personal values; it is also rapidly entering the world of politics. Advertising is also, in a sense, the official art of modern capitalist society: it is what 'we' put up in 'our' streets and use to fill up to half of 'our' newspapers and magazines: and it commands the services of perhaps the largest organized body of writers and artists, with their attendant managers and advisers, in the whole society. Since this is the actual social status of advertising, we shall only understand it with any adequacy if we can develop a kind of total analysis in which the economic, social and cultural facts are visibly related. We may then also find, taking advertising as a major form of modern social communication, that we can understand our society itself in new ways.

From R. Williams, *Problems in Materialism and Culture* (London: Verso, 1980) pp. 184–91.

It is often said that our society is too materialist, and that advertising reflects this. We are in the phase of a relatively rapid distribution of what are called 'consumer goods', and advertising, with its emphasis on 'bringing the good things of life', is taken as central for this reason. But it seems to me that in this respect our society is quite evidently not materialist enough, and that this, paradoxically, is the result of a failure in social meanings, values and ideals.

It is impossible to look at modern advertising without realising that the material object being sold is never enough: this indeed is the crucial cultural quality of its modern forms. If we were sensibly materialist, in that part of our living in which we use things, we should find most advertising to be of an insane irrelevance. Beer would be enough for us, without the additional promise that in drinking it we show ourselves to be manly, young in heart, or neighbourly. A washing-machine would be a useful machine to wash clothes, rather than an indication that we are forward-looking or an object of envy to our neighbours. But if these associations sell beer and washing-machines, as some of the evidence suggests, it is clear that we have a cultural pattern in which the objects are not enough but must be validated, if only in fantasy, by association with social and personal meanings which in a different cultural pattern might be more directly available. The short description of the pattern we have is *magic*: a highly organized and professional system of magical inducements and satisfactions, functionally very similar to magical systems in simpler societies, but rather strangely coexistent with a highly developed scientific technology.

This contradiction is of the greatest importance in any analysis of modern capitalist society. The coming of large-scale industrial production necessarily raised critical problems of social organization, which in many fields we are still only struggling to solve. In the production of goods for personal use, the critical problem posed by the factory of advanced machines was that of the organization of the market. The modern factory requires not only smooth and steady distributive channels (without which it would suffocate under its own product) but also definite indications of demand without which the expensive processes of capitalization and equipment would be too great a risk. The historical choice posed by the development of industrial production is between different forms of organization and planning in the society to which it is central. In our own century, the choice has been and remains between some form of socialism and a new form of capitalism. In Britain, since the 1890s and with rapidly continuing emphasis, we have had the new capitalism, based on a series of devices for organizing and ensuring the market. Modern advertising, taking on its distinctive features in just this economic phase, is one of the most important of these devices, and it is perfectly true to say that modern capitalism could not function without it.

Yet the essence of capitalism is that the basic means of production are not socially but privately owned, and that decisions about production are therefore in the hands of a group occupying a minority position in the society and in no direct way responsible to it. Obviously, since the capitalist wishes to be successful, he is influenced in his decisions about production by what other members of the society need. But he is influenced also by considerations of industrial convenience and likely profit, and his decisions tend to be a balance of these varying factors. The challenge of socialism, still very powerful elsewhere but in Britain deeply confused by political immaturities and errors, is essentially that decisions about production should be in the hands of the society as a whole, in the sense that control of the means of production is made part of the general system of decision which the society as a whole creates. The conflict between capitalism and socialism is now commonly seen in terms of a competition in productive efficiency, and we need not doubt that much of our future history, on a world scale, will be determined by the results of our competition. Yet the conflict is really much deeper than this, and is also a conflict between different approaches to and forms of socialism. The fundamental choice that emerges, in the problems set to us by modern industrial production, is between man as consumer and man as user. The system of organized magic which is modern advertising is primarily important as a functional obscuring of this choice.

'CONSUMERS'

The popularity of 'consumer', as a way of describing the ordinary member of modern capitalist society in a main part of his economic capacity, is very significant. The description is spreading very rapidly, and is now habitually used by people to whom it ought, logically, to be repugnant. It is not only that, at a simple level, 'consumption' is a very strange description of our ordinary use of goods and services. This metaphor drawn from the stomach or the furnace is only partially relevant even to our use of things. Yet we say 'consumer', rather than 'user', because in the form of society we now have, and in the forms of thinking which it almost imperceptibly fosters, it is as consumers that the majority of people are seen. We are the market, which the system of industrial production has organized. We are the channels along which the product flows and disappears. In every aspect of social communication, and in every version of what we are as a community, the pressure of a system of industrial production is towards these impersonal forms.

Yet it is by no means necessary that these versions should prevail, just because we use advanced productive techniques. It is simply that once these have entered a society, new questions of structure and purpose in social organization are inevitably posed. One set of answers is the development of genuine democracy, in which the human needs of all the people in the society are taken as the central purpose of all social activity, so that politics is not a system of government but of self-government, and the systems of production and communication are rooted in the satisfaction of human needs and the development of human capacities. Another set of answers, of which we have had more experience, retains, often in very subtle forms, a more limited social purpose. In the first phase, loyal subjects, as they were previously seen, became the labour market of industrial 'hands'. Later, as the 'hands' reject this version of themselves, and claim a higher human status, the emphasis is changed. Any real concession of higher status would mean the end of class-society and the coming of socialist democracy. But intermediate concessions are possible, including material concessions. The 'subjects' become the 'electorate', and 'the mob' becomes 'public opinion'.

Decision is still a function of the minority, but a new system of decision, in which the majority can be organized to this end, has to be devised. The majority are seen as 'the masses', whose opinion, *as masses* but not as real individuals or groups, is a factor in the business of governing. In practical terms, this version can succeed for a long time, but it then becomes increasingly difficult to state the nature of the society, since there is a real gap between profession and fact. Moreover, as the governing minority changes in character, and increasingly rests for real power on a modern economic system, older social purposes become vestigial, and whether expressed or implied, the maintenance of the economic system becomes the main factual purpose of all social activity. Politics and culture become deeply affected by this dominant pattern, and ways of thinking derived from the economic market – political parties considering how to sell themselves to the electorate, to create a favourable brand image; education being primarily organized in terms of a graded supply of labour; culture being organized and even evaluated in terms of commercial profit – become increasingly evident.

Still, however, the purposes of the society have to be declared in terms that will command the effort of a majority of its people. It is here that the idea of the 'consumer' has proved so useful. Since consumption is within its limits a satisfactory activity, it can be plausibly offered as a commanding social purpose. At the same time, its ambiguity is such that it ratifies the subjection of society to the operations of the existing economic system. An irresponsible economic system can supply the 'consumption' market, whereas it could only meet the criterion of human use by becoming genuinely responsible: that is to say, shaped in its use of human labour and resources by general social decisions. The consumer asks for an adequate supply of personal 'consumer goods' at a tolerable price: over the last ten years, this has been the primary aim of British government. But users ask for more than this, necessarily. They ask for the satisfaction of human needs which consumption, as such can never really supply. Since many of these needs are social – roads, hospitals, schools, quiet – they are not only not covered by the consumer ideal: they are even denied by it, because consumption tends always to materialize as an individual activity. And to satisfy this range of needs would involve questioning the autonomy of the economic system, in its actual setting of priorities. This is where the consumption ideal is not only misleading, as a form of defence of the system, but ultimately destructive to the broad general purposes of the society.

Advertising, in its modern forms, then operates to preserve the consumption ideal from the criticism inexorably made of it by experience. If the consumption of individual goods leaves that whole area of human need unsatisfied, the attempt is made, by magic, to associate this consumption with human desires to which it has no real reference. You do not only buy an object: you buy social respect, discrimination, health, beauty, success, power to control your environment. The magic obscures the real sources of general satisfaction because their discovery would involve radical change in the whole common way of life.

Of course, when a magical pattern has become established in a society, it is capable of some real if limited success. Many people will indeed look twice at you, upgrade you, upmarket you, respond to your displayed signals, if you have made the right purchases within a system of meanings to which you are all trained. Thus the fantasy seems to be validated, at a personal level, but only at the cost of preserving the general unreality which it obscures: the real failures of the society which however are not easily traced to this pattern.

It must not be assumed that magicians – in this case, advertising agents – disbelieve their own magic. They may have a limited professional cynicism about it, from knowing how some of the tricks are done. But fundamentally they are involved, with the rest of the society, in the confusion to which the magical gestures are a response. Magic is always an unsuccessful attempt to provide meanings and values, but it is often very difficult to distinguish magic from genuine knowledge and from art. The belief that high consumption is a high standard of living is a general belief of the society. The conversion of numerous objects into sources of sexual or pre-sexual satisfaction is evidently not only a process in the minds of advertisers, but also a deep and general confusion in which much energy is locked.

At one level, the advertisers are people using certain skills and knowledge, created by real art and science, against the public for commercial advantage. This hostile stance is rarely confessed in general propaganda for advertising, where the normal emphasis is the blind consumption ethic ('Advertising brings you the good things of life'), but it is common in advertisers' propaganda to their clients. 'Hunt with the mind of the hunter', one recent announcement begins, and another, under the heading 'Getting any honey from the hive industry?', is rich in the language of attack:

> One of the most important weapons used in successful marketing is advertising. Commando Sales Limited, steeped to the nerve ends in the skills of unarmed combat, are ready to move into battle on any sales front at the crack of an accepted estimate. These are the front line troops to call in when your own sales force is hopelessly outnumbered by the forces of sales resistance ...

This is the structure of feeling in which 'impact' has become the normal description of the effect of successful communication, and 'impact' like 'consumer' is now habitually used by people to whom it ought to be repugnant. What sort of person really wants to 'make an impact' or create a 'smash hit', and what state is a society in when this can be its normal cultural language?

It is indeed monstrous that human advances in psychology, sociology and communication should be used or thought of as powerful techniques *against* people, just as it is rotten to try to reduce the faculty of human choice to 'sales resistance'. In these respects, the claim of advertising to be a service is not particularly plausible. But equally, much of this talk of weapons and impact is the jejune bravado of deeply confused men. It is in the end the language of frustration rather than of power. Most advertising is not the cool creation of skilled professionals, but the confused creation of bad thinkers and artists. If we look at the petrol with the huge clenched fist, the cigarette against loneliness in the deserted street, the puppet facing death with a life-insurance policy (the modern protection, unlike the magical symbols painstakingly listed from earlier societies), or the man in the cradle which is an aeroplane, we are looking at attempts to express and resolve real human tensions which may be crude but which also involve deep feelings of a personal and social kind.

The structural similarity between much advertising and much modern art is not simply copying by the advertisers. It is the result of comparable responses to the contemporary human condition, and the only distinction that matters is between the clarification achieved by some art and the displacement normal in bad art and most advertising. The skilled magicians, the masters of the masses, must be seen as ultimately involved in the general weakness which they not only exploit but are exploited by. If the meanings and values generally operative in the society give no answers to, no means of negotiating, problems of death, loneliness, frustration, the need for identity and respect, then the magical system must come, mixing its charms and expedients with reality in easily available forms, and binding the weakness to the condition which has created it. Advertising is then no longer merely a way of selling goods, it is a true part of the culture of a confused society.

57

THE IMPACT OF ADVERTISING ON THE BRITISH MASS MEDIA

James Curran[1]

Senior officials at the Independent Broadcasting Authority are adamant that advertising has no effect on commercial television. 'If the suggestion is' writes Ian Haldane, the head of the IBA research department, 'that advertising has some "impact" or influence on ITV programmes, this is not so: the two are absolutely separate as laid down in the IBA Act under which we broadcast, and neither has any influence on the other.'[2] Even the suggestion that the policy of commercial broadcasting companies is influenced, in some way, by advertisers' requirements, provokes sharp denials. 'The programme controllers (of the ITV companies) are more Reithian than the BBC,' declares Stephen Murphy, a TV officer at the IBA with a distinguished record as a BBC producer, ' ... Advertising pressure is simply not transferred through.'[3]

Royal Commissions on the Press are almost equally dismissive about the effect of advertising on the Press. The first Commission concluded that attempts by advertisers to influence editorial policy 'appear to be infrequent and un-successful' (RCP, 1949: 143). Similar conclusions were reached by its two successors, neither of which found substantiated evidence that advertisers had ever significantly influenced editorial policy (RCP, 1962: 86–87; 1977: 104–105).

Indeed, the whole question of advertising influence on the media is author-itatively judged to be closed since such marginal influence, as may exist, cannot be adequately measured. 'No Royal Commission can expect to learn,' argued

From *Media, Culture and Society* 3:1 (1981) pp. 43–69.

the last Commission, 'what happens from those directly concerned, for it would not be in their interest to speak about the success of advertisers in exerting pressures . . . ' (RCP, 1977: 105). 'In its nature', opined its predecessor, 'the subject is one in which one has to rely largely on impression' (RCP, 1962: 86). The head of the IBA research department was even more forthright: this research study, he warned, was likely to be 'sadly lacking in substantial material, even were such material available'.[4]

Such intimidating scepticism, combined with consistent denials of significant advertising influence, would seem to suggest that further enquiry is pointless. Nevertheless, there are grounds for wondering whether the verdict of successive Royal Commissions on the Press and of experienced officials at the IBA is correct.[5] Their conclusions are largely based on a rather narrow definition of advertising influence in terms of overt attempts by advertisers to influence media content to their advantage by withholding or giving advertising favours.[6] This reflects the way in which the influence of advertising is often presented by critics from the Left. Thus, Sheridan and Gardiner (1979: 121–122) have recently argued, for instance, that the editorial policy of the press is shaped and moulded by a combination of 'subtle and crude financial pressure' from advertisers, exemplified by some advertisers' boycott of The Guardian during the Suez Crisis. In a similar vein, the Glasgow University Media Group (1976: 71) alleged, to the fury and outrage of many in the IBA and elsewhere, that Independent Television News not infrequently suppresses news stories in response to, or in anticipation of, pressure from advertisers.[7]

It is worth investigating, however, alternative ways in which advertisers may influence the mass media other than by overt attempts to influence its content. In particular, attention needs to be given to ways in which advertising as a concealed subsidy system has shaped the mass media; and to ways in which the media have adapted to the marketing needs of advertisers in order to compete for these subsidies.

The nature of these influences has been obscured by the conventional representation of advertisers as having interests identical with those of audiences (e.g. Advertising Association, 1975). Since advertisers want to reach the public in order to sell their products, it is argued, they naturally support the media which are popular with the public. Advertisers are thus portrayed as neutral and passive intermediaries who allocate their media budgets according to the likes and dislikes of media consumers and who consequently *exercise no independent influence of their own*. As John Whale puts it, 'advertising doubles the price on each reader's head . . . but there is not much a newspaperman can do to differentiate a double from a single dose of zeal to attract new readers' (Whale, 1979: 93).

This portrayal of advertisers is based on a misleading representation of media planning and marketing practice. Advertisers rarely think of the media exclusively as a distribution system for advertisements: they also generally make judgements about the effectiveness of different media as agencies of persuasion.

They are not 'neutral' in their desire to reach all members of the public: they usually wish to reach – and will pay more to reach – particular segments of the market rather than others. They are not 'passive' and unchanging in the criteria they adopt for media buying: on the contrary, changes in marketing perspectives, research procedures and data inputs have produced changes in how advertisers have spent this money with important long-term consequences for the development of the media. Finally advertisers are not a uniform group with a common approach and shared objectives: indeed, changes within the economy have resulted in a significant shift in the pattern of advertising expenditure, reflecting the emergence of new advertisers and the decline of others, which have had major repercussions on the media system as a whole.

What this exploratory study will seek to do, therefore, is to examine ways in which the allocation of advertising, and media competition for this allocation, has influenced the character of the British mass media, and consider how this allocation has been influenced, in turn, by economic and social structures external to the media. To see the impact of advertising only in terms of overt attempts by individual advertisers to influence media content is, it will be argued, to misconceive both the true nature and the significance of advertising influence: advertising patronage is essentially an impersonal means by which Britain's mass media are fashioned according to the marketing needs of the economic system and the class inequalities of power, influence and consumption within British society.

Advertising Allocation Between Media

Advertisers make a larger contribution to the finances of the British mass media than audiences. Commercial broadcasting derives nearly all of its revenue from advertising while newspapers and magazines both derive over half their revenue from advertisements (see Table [57.]1).

Advertising does not constitute a straight media subsidy. Receipts from advertisers must be set against the costs involved in securing and producing advertisements, and these sometimes represent, as we shall see, a very large proportion of advertising revenue. Generally speaking, though, advertising generates a surplus after relevant costs have been deducted, so that advertising allocations crucially affect the financial resources available to competing media sectors as well as to competing companies within each media sector.

Table [57.]1. *Proportion of press revenue derived from advertising in 1979**

National dailies	National Sundays	Regional daily and Sunday papers	Local weeklies	Total newspapers	Trade, technical and professional journals	Other periodicals	Total periodicals
44%	44%	66%	85%	59%	64%	47%	54%

*Derived from Department of Industry (1979).

Advertising allocations between media are not closely tied to the pattern of media consumption. Newspapers and magazines absorb much less time, on average, than commercial TV and radio. Yet the press obtains almost three times as much advertising as commercial broadcasting (see Table [57.]2). The continuing ascendancy of the press as an advertising medium (largely due to government restrictions on the development of commercial broadcasting) has helped it to fend off the challenge of TV. During the period of rapid growth of TV ownership during the 50s and early 60s, the press was able to charge very low cover prices and spend very much more heavily on editorial outlay as a result of the rising advertising income it obtained. This contributed, in turn, to its remarkable resilience. The proportion of the adult population reading newspapers and magazines remained stable during the period of TV's rise, while newspaper consumption (when measured adequately) actually increased (Curran, 1970).[8] There is also no close correspondence between the pattern of demand and the amount of advertising expenditure on different sectors of the press. Although the circulation of the regional press was only about two-thirds that of the national press,[9] the regional papers still obtained £246 million more advertising than national papers in 1979. The success of the regional press in attracting advertising has helped to make it more profitable than Fleet Street.

The trade, technical and professional press also has a very much smaller circulation than that of the rest of the magazine press,[10] but nonetheless still attracts more advertising (see Table [57.]2). This high level of support has helped to sustain a large number of specialist titles many of which have only small sales.

CHANGES IN ADVERTISING ALLOCATIONS

Important shifts in the pattern of media advertising expenditure have taken place during the last 40 years, which have altered the character of the media. Before considering these, it is necessary to refer, however, to government economic controls which temporarily distorted advertising trends. Newsprint rationing was maintained on a statutory basis between 1940 and 1956, and on a voluntary basis until 1959. During the height of its severity, newsprint rationing caused national newspapers to shrink to less than a quarter of their pre-war size, and severely curtailed advertising in national newspapers (Gerald, 1956). Imposed with less severity on the regional press, rationing caused advertising to be redistributed to the provinces (Henry, 1979). And because

Table [57.]2. *Media advertising expenditure (£m) in 1979**

National newspapers	Regional newspapers	Magazines and periodicals	Trade and technical	Total press	TV	Cinema	Radio
347	593	180	203	1496	471	17	52

*Source: Advertising Association (1980: 45).

magazines were exempted from economic controls before newspapers, there was a temporary boom in magazine advertising in the early 1950s (Silverman, 1954). These distortions need to be distinguished from long-term changes.

The most important of these long-term changes have been the decline of traditional mass market advertising media and the linked rise of television; the shift of advertising to the provinces; and the redistribution of advertising within the magazine sector in favour of specialist magazines (see Table [57.]3).

[...]

ADVERTISING ALLOCATION WITHIN MEDIA SECTORS: SOME CONSEQUENCES

The last Royal Commission on the Press recoiled from the thought of redistributing advertising according to public service criteria partly on the grounds that it would introduce political judgements in the free processes of the market (RCP, 1977: 117). It did not pause to consider whether free market processes also have political and cultural consequences. It merely assumed that free market allocation of advertising was neutral and consequently that it did not warrant careful investigation.[11] Whether the Commission's assumption is justified remains to be seen.

THE CONSERVATIVE BIAS OF ADVERTISING: A REAPPRAISAL

The national newspaper press is predominantly conservative – very much more so than its readers, to judge from a comparison of newspapers' and readers' political affiliations (Seymour-Ure, 1977).[12] It also derives a substantial proportion of its revenue from advertisers. This has prompted some commentators to assume that the two things are connected: advertisers, it is reasoned, use their

Table [57.]3. *Distribution of advertising expenditure between media**

	1938 %	1948 %	1954 %	1960 %	1965 %	1970 %	1975 %	1979 %
National newspapers	25	14	17	20	20	20	17	16
Regional newspapers†	27	31	31	21	24	26	29	28
Magazines and periodicals	15	13	19	12	11	9	8	9
Trade and technical journals	12	16	13	10	9	10	9	10
Other publications‡	2	1	1	1	1	2	2	3
Press production costs§	5	8	6	5	4	6	5	6
Total press	85	83	88	71	70	72	70	70
Television	–	–	–	22	24	23	24	22
Poster and transport	8	14	9	5	4	4	4	4
Cinema	3	4	3	2	1	1	1	1
Radio	3	–	1	–	1	–	1	2

*Sources: Kaldor and Silverman (1948), Silverman (1951), Advertising Association (1951, 1962, 1972, 1980), Critchley (n.d.). All forms of non-media promotional expenditure are excluded. All percentage figures have been rounded off to the nearest whole number.
† Including London evening newspapers.
‡ Directories, guide books, yellow pages, etc.
§ According to the Advertising Association's definition which does not include all relevant costs.

financial power to fashion the press according to their political prejudices (Steed, 1938; Labour Research Department, 1946; Orwell, 1970; Hoch, 1974).

It is undoubtedly the case that political bias on the part of advertisers helped to stifle the development of the radical press during the late nineteenth and early twentieth century when the national press evolved in its modern form (Curran, 1977). The subsequent growth of advertising also helped to perpetuate this historical legacy by forcing up press costs and making the launch and establishment of new papers more costly and difficult[13] (Curran and Seaton, 1981).

Nevertheless, the political bias of advertisers was only one factor contributing to the conservative domination of the press in the early twentieth century. In any case, important changes have taken place in the procedures adopted by advertisers in selecting advertising media, which has significantly reduced the influence of political bias on media appropriations (Curran, 1980).

Disparities still persist however in the advertising revenue per copy obtained by Conservative and Labour papers. For example, the net advertisement revenue of the generally Conservative *Sunday Times* was almost four times that of the Labour *Sunday Mirror* in 1975, despite the fact that it had less than half the *Sunday Mirror*'s circulation (Curran, 1978: T7). These disparities do not arise from political prejudice but from the fact that, generally speaking, Conservative papers reach readers who have more money to spend, more influence over corporate spending, and watch less ITV than readers of Labour papers.[14]

The pattern of advertising expenditure has consequently enabled some Conservative papers to be economically viable with audiences much smaller than those of Labour papers.[15] The four quality dailies constitute half the national daily titles in Britain, yet they accounted for only 15% of national daily circulation in 1980.[16] Although they charged high cover prices, they still derived over half their revenue from advertising. Mostly Conservative in their politics, they have continued in publication largely because of the high advertising receipts they have obtained as a result of being read by a socially select readership. A similar pattern has developed in the national Sunday press, where three out of seven papers, heavily endowed with advertising, accounted for only 18% of national Sunday circulation in 1980. They have survived and grown only with the aid of advertising bounty.[17] The obverse to this is that Labour papers have died with circulations far larger than those of some Conservative papers. In 1964, for instance, the Labour *Daily Herald* was forced to close with a readership well over that of *The Times* and *The Financial Times* combined (National Readership Survey, 1964: T1A).

The political imbalance of the press thus partly reflects class inequalities within society which have generated unequal advertising subsidies between Labour and Conservative papers. This has helped to reinforce Conservative domination of the national press by making it easier for Conservative papers to survive and flourish.

INEQUALITIES OF CULTURAL PROVISION

Women's magazines tend to be oriented towards the middle class. This is a consequence of the much higher advertising subsidies that middle-class women readers generate by comparison with working-class readers. Bird (1978) found, for instance, that the correlation between the advertisement revenue of the five big women's weeklies and the size of their ABC1 (i.e. upper middle, middle and lower middle class) readerships was 0.997, very much higher than that between circulation and advertising revenue which was only 0.782.

[...]

This pattern of advertising expenditure has profoundly affected the development of the women's magazine press. The majority of women's magazines sell at prices (after discounts to distributors) that do not cover costs (Coopers and Lybrand, 1975). Whether they make a profit depends upon whether they attract adequate advertising. Only in the children's and young teenage market are magazines largely dependent on sales. In other sectors of the women's magazine market, the average magazine has relied upon advertising for the majority of its revenue.[18]

Consequently, the majority of adult women's magazine titles are oriented towards the middle class, even though it constitutes little more than one-third of the population.[19] Even some mass market publications pay disproportionate attention to the middle class because of its importance to advertisers. As Michael Bird (then marketing director of the National Magazine Company) stressed in an influential paper, magazines are forced to seek not the largest but the 'optimum circulation' defined in relation to advertisers' priorities. 'Pushing circulations to ruinous heights' can be counterproductive if 'the audience profile is diluted' (Bird, 1978: 150; cf. Bird, 1979).

Publications that have not conformed to advertisers' requirements have simply disappeared. For example, *Everywoman* folded in 1967 with the fourth highest sale out of 21 women's magazines sold through newsagents, but with a majority of its readers being drawn from the working class (National Readership Survey, 1966: T19A). This gravitational pull towards the middle class, exerted by advertising, has contributed to the remarkable conservatism of much women's journalism. It has also resulted in a broad range of cultural provision being geared disproportionately to one section of the community.

The class bias of much magazine publishing is matched by an age bias. As early as the 1950s, market researchers were stressing the importance of the age cycle and family structure on the demand pattern for products (e.g. Wheeler, 1954). The relative affluence of the 15–24 age group, at a time of sharply rising consumption, encouraged advertisers to pay increasing attention to youth markets. This orientation was further reinforced by the 'accessibility' of youth markets due to the greater willingness of young people to try out new consumer products. This encouraged publishers to cater for this much-prized advertising market by launching a succession of publications aimed at young people.[20] In marked contrast, few publications have been directed towards elderly people because their disposable income – and consequently advertising utility – is much less than that of young people. Inequalities between age groups are thus reproduced in the market structure of the magazine press through the mediational rôle of advertisers.

Inequalities of age and class have coalesced to produce a further distortion in the women's magazine press. Many of the new women's magazines aimed at the late teen and twenties market have been oriented towards the middle class. Consequently many more magazines now cater primarily for the young (under 35) middle class than for the older (over 35) working class, although the former number about five and a half million and the latter 16 million (Bird, 1979).

THE BIAS OF ADVERTISERS' PRIORITIES

Which sections of the public are serviced with a multiplicity of publications depends, in part, upon their importance to advertisers. Two groups – distribution agents and those influencing corporate spending decisions – are so important that they have over a thousand publications catering for their needs. For example, there were 161 medical publications in 1974, many of which were heavily subsidized by advertising designed to influence spending within the National Health Service.[21]

Another distorting effect of advertising has been to encourage the growth of what may be broadly defined as 'consumer' magazines, but not a whole range of publications that fail to conform to the marketing requirements of advertisers. A good example of this latter group are political periodicals that, generally speaking, are found wanting on three counts. They do not provide an editorial environment conducive to buying particular products or services; they do not 'cover' a consumer market; and they do not reach specialized groups of corporate spenders or distribution agents. Consequently whereas advertising subsidies have assisted the growth of consumer and specialist publications by lowering their cover prices and funding their editorial costs, the lack of large-scale advertising has retarded a comparable development of the political periodical press in Britain.

[...]

DICTATES OF THE MASS MARKET

TV companies make their money from selling audiences rather than programmes. TV companies therefore seek to make and transmit programmes that *produce* the audiences advertisers want to reach. As Simon Broadbent, the vice-chairman of a leading agency, put it, 'the spot therefore is the packaging, the product inside the package is an audience'.

Contrary to popular belief, advertisers generally do not want to reach a mass audience in an indiscriminate way. As the standard advertising textbook puts it, 'It is wasteful and often futile to aim advertising at everybody' (Broadbent, 1979: 149). Many advertisers would like ideally commercial TV to produce large but variegated and selected audiences.

[...]

A small number of programmes do 'select' particular groups and, no less important for the media planner, also deter particular groups of consumer.[22] But generally speaking, the pattern of commercial TV programme viewing is very unselective and would seem to be influenced more by the availability of the viewer to watch TV than by what is being shown. As Goodhardt et al. (1975) have shown, specialized programmes do not tend to generate specialized audiences; light viewers do not tend to be especially discriminating but tend to watch the most popular programmes; even many regular series have a minority of viewers who saw the previous episode.

The desire of most advertisers to use TV as a medium for reaching selected groups is thus partly frustrated by the relative lack of selectivity of TV viewing. Thus would-be selective, targeting pressure has been converted into a powerful impetus for TV companies to deliver the largest possible audience since this produces the largest possible number of people within the prospect groups that advertisers want to reach. This, in turn, enables TV companies to charge high rates.

Advertisers also exert a strong pressure for commercial TV companies to produce stable, reliable and predictable audiences. Advertisers pay money for spots in anticipation that these will deliver certain quantities of viewers. Most sophisticated agencies also run retrospective checks to see what value for money they obtained from their schedules. If the TV companies do not deliver what is expected of them, there is generally a loud chorus of complaint from their clients.

Advertisers also seek quantity rather than quality.

[...]

The effect of this pressure for large audiences is for priority to be given to programmes that are of universal appeal – notably soap operas, situation comedies, the main news bulletin and variety programmes. In 1978–79, for instance, what may be broadly defined as drama, light entertainment, news and news magazine programmes, accounted for 61% of ITV's total output, and the overwhelming proportion of its peak time transmission (IBA, 1979). Programmes that are not of universal appeal such as documentary and current affairs programmes tend to be transmitted outside peak time hours.

Commercial TV companies have also developed scheduling strategies designed to maintain a stable and predictable audience. This generally involves transmitting light entertainment programmes early in the evening, followed by a sequence of programmes that expand and consolidate the mass audience throughout the evening. If ITV contractors are forced as a consequence of IBA pressure, direct or indirect, to transmit a programme of low audience appeal during peak viewing hours, they often take steps to minimize audience fall-out either by matching it with an equally unpopular programme on BBC1 or by 'hammocking' the programme between two 'bankers' (i.e. programmes with proven audience appeal). The scheduling philosophy of the ITV system is thus essentially cautious and conservative: it is wary of programme innovation during peak time viewing of a sort that might lose viewers to another channel for the rest of the evening.

The pursuit of viewers in crude terms of quantity rather than in terms of their quality of appreciation also provides a built-in bias within the ITV system against current affairs programmes. As Barwise, Ehrenburg and Goodhardt (1979) have shown, 'information' programmes generally gain higher appreciation scores than 'entertainment' programmes, even though they generally attract smaller audiences. Whether reliance on ratings results in advertisers undervaluing the 'pull' of minority programmes is less than clear. Barwise, Ehrenburg and Goodhardt (1979) found that, within the two broad categories of information and entertainment programmes, there was a positive correlation between size of audience and appreciation.[23]

The development of mass audience programming and scheduling strategies within the private sector of broadcasting has compelled a fundamental change of policy within the BBC. When in 1958 its audience share slipped to below 30%, senior BBC executives became convinced that the BBC had to imitate, to some extent, the programme and scheduling policy of ITV. Increasingly, the output and schedules of BBC1 have come to resemble those of its principal rival. The change has produced an increasing uniformity in the content of broadcasting and an increasing reluctance to experiment. As Weldon, then managing director of the BBC, euphemistically put it, 'once you are locked in competition, you cannot afford losers' (Weldon, 1971: 9).

Commercial radio has also responded to mass marketing pressures. Between 6 am and 6 pm, commercial local radio stations are largely geared to satisfying the largest possible audience. This has given rise to styles of radio production very different from those pioneered by the BBC: to programming as distinct from separate programmes, that is to say a miscellany of short items that will include something of interest for almost everyone in the local community, organized in a flexible way and set on 'a music bed'. Within this format, priority is given to those sections of the audience available to listen. It is only in the evening that more conventional programmes are transmitted, including some aimed at minority audiences. These include programmes directed at specialist markets that will attract specialized advertising such as 'Race Track' (Radio Victory) which generates car accessory advertising, and 'Hullaballoo' (Capital Radio) which generated advertisements aimed at teenagers. The shift reflects an attempt to deliver a differentiated audience (which, again, is partly frustrated by unselective radio listening behaviour) of value to advertisers, at a time when the mass audience has been surrendered to TV.

The fluid, fast-moving programming formula of local commercial radio has been highly successful in attracting substantial local audiences to local commercial radio during peak listening times. Its overall share of radio listening in ILR areas in 1980 was 34%, significantly higher than that of any national or local BBC radio channel (JICRAR, 1980). This share is still substantially lower, however, than the BBC service as a whole, and has not compelled an adjustment on the part of the BBC comparable to the radio reorganization and change in broadcasting philosophy that followed the incursion of illegal commercial radio stations into the mass audience during the 1960s.

A striking feature of local commercial radio output is its inclusion of a substantial local news content. This is a reflection of the pattern of consumer demand. IBA surveys reveal, for example, that 'local news coverage' was rated more favourably than any other aspect of commercial local radio output.[24] The provision of local news is thus consistent with maintaining large audiences in order to maximize advertising, just as the provision of news bulletins is consistent with maximizing TV audiences.

The same is not true of national newspapers. Research undertaken by publishers over a 40-year period shows that most categories of news about public affairs have obtained below-average attention in national papers both before and after the arrival of TV. In particular, public affairs items have generally appealed less to women and to the young than to men and the older age-groups. In contrast, human interest stories and certain entertainment features have been found to have a universal appeal, transcending differences of sex, age and class. As economic pressures have built up for popular newspapers to maximize their sales and advertising revenue by winning bigger audiences, so the proportion of space devoted to public affairs has declined, while common-denominator material has steadily increased. The only departure from this trend over a 50-year period has been the period of strict economic controls when popular newspapers were temporarily insulated from the economic pressures for audience maximization (Curran, Douglas and Whannel, 1980).

There has not been a comparable trend towards depoliticization of the quality press. This is not because there is a wide chasm between reading preferences of mass and elite audiences: the pattern of quality and popular reader interest is in fact rather similar, with certain categories of human interest story being the most read items in both quality and popular papers (Curran, Douglas and Whannel, 1980: 304 *et passim*). Publishers of quality newspapers have merely been restrained from providing more common-denominator material for fear of diluting the social quality of their audiences, and consequently undermining their utility to advertisers as selective media reaching small elite groups.

[...]

CREATING THE RIGHT ENVIRONMENT

Subjective judgements about whether a medium provides a favourable environment for advertisements has always played a part in some advertisers' choice of media. This has generated pressure on media to create a suitable environment for advertising in order to maximize revenue.

Subjective judgements of media 'communication value' have been based on a number of considerations: whether specific editorial or programme content will attract the attention of particular groups of consumers to adjacent advertising; whether such advertising will gain their attention when they are in the right mood to respond; whether media content will induce a frame of mind that will be responsive to the advertised message; whether the authority or prestige of the medium or particular programme/column will rub off on the client's product; whether the style and tone of the media content harmonizes with the advertisement in a way that reinforces its effectiveness; and whether, in crude terms, the editorial content supports the product that is being advertised.

Such subjective considerations have become much less important in media selection than they were 50 years ago. They are now generally outweighed by calculations of cost of exposure to the target audience and 'experience' based on previous advertising campaigns. There has been, however, a significant shift towards a more intuitive approach to media selection during the last 12 years and this has increased pressures on the media to provide an environment conducive to advertising.

Commercial television is the mass medium least affected by pressure of this kind. The prohibition of advertising sponsorship within commercial TV has insulated programme controllers from direct influence on programme content. Advertisers do have foreknowledge of programme schedules and consequently are able to select space beside specific programmes. Programmes are sometimes selected because their content is thought to complement a particular advertising campaign. In theory, at least, this could give rise to pressure for more programmes complementing advertising commercials. But in practice, the selection of spots in terms of programmes is unusual.[25] Advertisers generally buy viewers rather than programme environments. The fact that the connection between programmes and audience types or profiles is so elusive, as mentioned earlier, further reduces pressure on TV companies to deliver a suitable programme ambience. Moreover, a belief has developed within agencies that commercials create 'their own environment' unaided by programme content.

When there is a conflict between a commercial and a programme – such as the announcement of an airline crash with an airline advertisement scheduled to follow – the conflict is sometimes eliminated by the withdrawal of the advertisement. But programmes or programme items are not suppressed to protect the commercial interests of advertisers. Commercial TV companies have a monopoly as the sellers of TV airtime and are in a powerful position to resist illicit advertising pressure. Indeed, it is very much in their economic interests not to submit to advertisers' censorship since this would put their franchises at risk.

Commercial radio stations are also insulated, to some extent, from overt advertising pressures. Subject to surveillance by the IBA, local radio companies have a vested interest in maintaining their autonomy from advertisers. The fact that the majority of local radio advertising is bought in packages rather than in spots, with the times of transmission being rotated by radio contractors, further contributes to radio's independence from crude advertising influence.

Newspapers have been more influenced by advertisers, and in some ways less resistant to advertising pressure. Service features on investment, travel, property, motoring and fashion have grown as a proportion of editorial space in national newspapers during the postwar period (Curran, Douglas and Whannel, 1980). Their expansion has been geared, to a large extent, to the advertising they have generated. They represent an efficient means of selling selected subgroups within a mass audience, packaged in a suitable editorial environment. Yet their narrow orientation to readers as consumers has distorted their content (Curran, 1978). Their advertising orientation has encouraged the specialist journalists working on these pages to develop a dependent and generally uncritical relationship with advertisers (Tunstall, 1971). The result has been the development of a subservient genre of journalism in which, as Ian Breach, the former motoring correspondent of *The Guardian*, puts it, 'there is a pervading fear that valuable advertising will drain away in the face of persistent criticism that names names and condemns specific products' (Breach, 1978).

This crude form of influence is largely restricted to the advertising-oriented sections of national papers. It is extremely rare for news items to be suppressed or rewritten in order to placate potential advertisers. Attempts by advertisers to influence general news reporting and comment by withholding advertising is also much less frequent than is generally supposed. The *Sunday Times* continued to receive advertising from Distillers, for example, even when it was campaigning against the company for its 'heartless treatment' of Thalidomide drug victims. Advertisers are a much more pervasive influence on women's magazines than they are on national newspapers. There is generally less commitment to non-revenue goals within consumer magazine organizations than there is within national news organizations, and consequently less suspicion of advertisers. Consumer magazines are also subject to more advertising pressure because advertisers attach more weight to the editorial environment of magazines than to the content of any other medium.[26]

Pressure from advertisers has crucially influenced the balance of contents of the magazine press. A growing proportion of women's magazines during the 50s and 60s, for instance, were devoted to material consumption partly in order to provide a conducive environment for advertisements. This expansion tended to squeeze out more general articles on social and even political issues (White, 1970).

[...]

CONCLUSION

Advertisers have thus played a central rôle in shaping Britain's media system. Firstly, recent changes in advertising allocation *between* media sectors have tended to undermine traditional mass media, promote the growth of specialized media and favour the development of the regional press.

Second, advertising appropriations *within* each media sector have profoundly influenced the character and development of each medium. In particular, they have reinforced the conservative domination of the national press, caused the women's magazine press to be heavily oriented towards the young middle class, and contributed to a growing financial imbalance between the public and private sectors of broadcasting.

Third, the media have adapted to the requirements of advertisers in the ways they have sought to maximize revenue. This has resulted in a growing polarization between popular and quality newspaper journalism, the adoption of limiting programme strategies for producing large and predictable audiences on television, and the increasing subordination of the consumer magazine press to creating a conducive editorial environment for advertisements.

NOTES

1. School of Communication, Polytechnic of Central London.
2. Letter to the author, 30 August 1980.
3. Interview with Stephen Murphy, 22 September 1980.
4. Letter to the author, 30 August 1980.
5. Not least because not all IBA officials I spoke to were of the same mind: some of the younger executives, in particular, were more inclined to perceive advertising as an influence on broadcasting output.
6. This was not true of the considered comments of S. Murphy of the IBA nor of the last Royal Commission on the Press, although the Commission only seriously addressed itself in its report to a conspiracy model of advertising influence.
7. The page numbering in the reference refers to the proof copy of *Bad News*. Allegations of direct advertising influence (which were almost certainly untrue) were withdrawn following the threat of a libel action.
8. Adjusting to declining advertising profits during the 70s, national newspapers sharply increased retail prices appreciably more than the rate of inflation, thereby losing the large price differential they had compared with papers in many Western countries (documented, for instance, by the Royal Commission on the Press (1962 Appendix 9). It is perhaps no coincidence that the audience for newspapers began to decline as a proportion of the adult population during the 1970s.
9. In 1976, its aggregate circulation was 65% of that of the national press (calculated from RCP, 1977, Annex 3, T1).
10. The aggregate circulation of the trade, technical and professional press is unknown, but for an indication of its smallness by comparison with the rest of the periodical press, see Coopers and Lybrand (1975: T1. 7).
11. In so far as the Commission was interested in the advertising process, it was largely in order to forecast future trends (see RCP, 1977: Appendix E).
12. Seymour-Ure's valuable analysis is confined to the national daily press. The political imbalance is less marked in the case of national Sunday papers.
13. Since 1918, only three new national papers have been successfully established and only one of these (currently accounting for at most 0.2% of national daily circulation) is on the left. Such adaptation as there has been to the increased

strength of the left in the country, has been through changes of ownership and editorial staffing rather than through the launch of new papers.

14. There are, of course, exceptions such as the Conservative *Sun* which has a below-average (among national dailies) advertising revenue per copy. But it is not a typical Conservative paper since more of its readers voted Labour than Conservative in the last three General Elections.

15. This remains true despite the erosion of advertising profit margins because Conservative papers generally have suffered less from this erosion than Labour papers.

16. The *Morning Star* has been excluded since it does not have an audited circulation.

17. The papers concerned are the *Times, Financial Times, Guardian, Sunday Times, Sunday Telegraph* and *Observer*. Four of these six papers are generally aligned with the Conservative Party. In addition to a high level of advertising support, some of them have also obtained large subsidies from multinational conglomerates.

18. Advertising accounted for, on average, 60% of young women's magazines and of women's monthlies, and 55% of women's weekly revenue in 1973–74 (RCP Secretariat, 1977: T24).

19. Significantly, this targetting towards the middle class is much less marked in the case of juvenile and young teen publications. Children's periodicals derived, on average, 90% of their revenue from sales, while teenage magazines obtained, on average, 70% of their revenue from sales, in 1973–74.

20. Social changes, inducing a change in the pattern of reader demand, also encouraged this shift. See White (1970, 1977).

21. For an interesting examination of the wider implications of having a medical press heavily subsidized by drug companies in an American context, see Gandy (1980).

22. For example, Sunday afternoon football on TV has a particular appeal among lager drinkers.

23. Whether this would have remained true if very heavy viewers – 'lumpers' who will watch most programmes that are being screened – had been eliminated, remains to be investigated. For rather different findings from those of Barwise, Ehrenburg and Goodhardt (1979), see Prue (1979).

24. 'Local news coverage' scored + 86%, the highest score out of 19 aspects of commercial local radio output based on subtracting 'likes' and 'dislikes' from the question 'which of these aspects do you like, which do you dislike, and which makes no difference to you?' asked in each one of 19 local surveys in the various ILR areas over a period of five years (IBA, unpublished material).

25. Instances of commercials skilfully harmonizing with programmes, that were mentioned to me, included an advertisement for 'Black Magic' with a romantic drama, a James Bond commercial alongside 'The Professionals' (a security police drama), a Kattomeat commercial alongside a programme about the conservation of tigers, and so on. They were remarked upon *because* they were unusual.

26. This is partly because agencies are encouraged to evaluate the editorial content of magazines in terms of advertising effectiveness by the way in which many magazines sell advertising space. This is very much less true of other media.

REFERENCES

Advertising association (1962). *Advertising Expenditure 1960*, Advertising Association, London.

Advertising association (1972). Advertising expenditure 1960–71, *Advertising Quarterly*, vol. 32 and 33.

Advertising association (1975). *Evidence to Royal Commission on the Press* 1974–77, HMSO.

Advertising association (1980). Advertising expenditure tables, 1960–1979, *Advertising Magazine*. vol 64.

Barwise, T. P., Ehrenburg, A. S. C. and Goodhardt, G. J. (1979). Audience appreciation and audience size, *Journal of the Market Research Society*, vol. 21, 4.

Bird, M. (1978). Magazines, markets and money, in Henry, H. (ed.) *Behind the Headlines – the Business of the British Press*, Associated Business Press, London.

Bird, M. (1979). Women's magazines – survey of the 70s, *Options*, Spring.

Breach, I. (1978). The gentlemen of the road, *Sunday Times Colour Magazine*.

Broadbent, S. (1979). *Spending Advertising Money* (3rd edition), Business Books, London.

Coopers and Lybrand (1975). The periodical publishing industry, unpub., Royal Commission on the Press 1974–77.

Critchley, R. A. (n.d.) *U.K. Advertising Statistics*, Advertising Association, London.

Curran, J. (1970). The impact of TV on the audience for national newspapers 1945–68, in Tunstall, J. (ed.), *Media Sociology*, Constable, London.

Curran, J. (1977). Capitalism and control of the press, 1800–1975, in Curran, J., Gurevitch, M. and Woollacott, J. (eds) *Mass Communication and Society*, Arnold, London.

Curran, J. (1978). Advertising and the press, in Curran, J. (ed.) *The British Press: A Manifesto*, Macmillan, London.

Curran, J. (1980). Advertising as a patronage system, *Sociological Review Monograph*, 29.

Curran J., Douglas, A. and Whannel, G. (1980). The political economy of the human-interest story, in Smith, A. (ed.) *Newspapers and Democracy*, Massachusetts Institute of Technology Press, Cambridge, Mass.

Curran, J. and Seaton, J. (1981). *Power Without Responsibility: Press and Broadcasting in Britain*, Fontana, London.

Department of Industry (1979). Newspapers and periodicals, *Business Monitor* (PQ485), Fourth Quarter, HMSO, London.

Gandy, O., Jr. (1980). Information in health: subsidised news, *Media, Culture and Society*, vol. 2.

Gerald, J. E. (1956). *The British Press under Government Economic Controls*, University of Minnesota Press, Minneapolis.

Glasgow University Media Group (1976). *Bad News*, Routledge, Kegan & Paul, London.

Goodhardt, G. J., Ehrenburg, A. S. C. and Collins, M. A. (1975). *The Television Audience: Patterns of Viewing*, Saxon House, Westmead.

Henry, H. (1977). Some observations on the effects of newsprint rationing (1939–1959) on the advertising media, *Journal of Advertising History*, vol. 1.

Hoch, P. (1974). *The Newspaper Game*, Calder & Boyars, London.

Independent Broadcasting Authority (1979). *Annual Report 1978–9*, IBA, London.

Jicrar (1980). Independent local radio network surveys, Spring/Autumn.

Kaldor, N. and Silverman, R. (1948). *A Statistical Analysis of Advertising Expenditure and of the Press*, Cambridge University Press, Cambridge.

Labour Research Department (1946). *The Millionaire Press*, L.R.D., London.

National Readership Surveys (1956–67). Institute of the Practitioners in Advertising, London.

Orwell, G. (1970). London letter to partisan review, in Orwell, S. and Angus, I. (eds), *The Collected Essays, Journalism and Letters of George Orwell*, vol. 2, Penguin, Harmondsworth.

Prue, T. (1979). The rate for the job, *Options*, vol. 3.

Royal Commission on the Press 1947–1949 (1949). HMSO, London.

Royal Commission on the Press 1961–1962 (1962). HMSO, London.

Royal Commission on the Press 1974–1977 Final Report (1977). HMSO, London.

Royal Commission on the Press Secretariat (1977). Periodicals and the alternative press, *Royal Commission on the Press Research Series 6*, HMSO, London.

Seymour-Ure, C. (1977). National daily newspapers and the party system, in *Studies on the Press*, Royal Commission on the Press Working Paper No. 3, HMSO, London.

Silverman, R. (1951). *Advertising Expenditure in 1948*, Advertising Association, London.

Silverman, R. (1954). *Advertising Expenditure in 1952*, Advertising Association, London.

Steed, H. Wickham (1938). *The Press*, Penguin, Harmondsworth.

Tunstall, J. (1971). *Journalists at Work*, Constable, London.

Weldon, H. (1971). *Competition in Television*, BBC, London.

Whale, J. (1979). *The Politics of the Media* (rev. edition), Fontana, London.

Wheeler, D. (1955). *A New Classification of Households*, British Market Research Bureau, June.

White, C. (1970). *Women's Magazines 1963–1968*, Michael Joseph, London.

White, C. (1977). *The Women's Periodical Press in Britain 1946–1976*, Royal Commission on the Press Working Paper No. 4, HMSO, London.

58

ADVERTISING, MAGAZINE CULTURE, AND THE 'NEW MAN'

Sean Nixon

[agencies] know that the fashionable young man is out there, but they don't know how to address him. You can't address all men; there's been no one image specific to all men.

(Lucy Purdy, Research Bureau Limited, *Arena*, Summer 1988: 24)

Lucy Purdy's comments captured the dilemma faced by advertising, practitioners in the early to mid 1980s in advertising to men. Consumer research was producing a picture of shifts in the values and lifestyles of groups of male consumers. These shifts were represented in consumer types like the 'avant guardian', the 'self exploiter' or the 'innovator'. Advertising practitioners were confronted with the problem of making decisions about the significance of these findings and with assessing whether they were appropriate for the specific male markets they were producing adverts for.

Two practices within the process of making adverts shaped the way certain groups of practitioners responded to the evidence from consumer research. They were account planning and media buying. Both practices were important because it was through them that research findings – like that about new groups of male consumers – were incorporated into the advertising process and ultimately impacted on the decisions made in the production of adverts by art directors and writers.

[...]

From S. Nixon, *Hard Looks: Masculinities, Spectatorship and Contemporary Consumption* (London: UCL Press, 1996) pp. 103, 116–22, 131–37, 143–44.

'CREATIVE ADVERTISING' AND THE 'NEW MAN'

It is my contention that changes in the advertising industry [...] underpin in institutional terms the formation of the 'new man' imagery within advertising. I want to [...] focus on two campaigns that exemplify these developments. They are Bartle Bogle Hegarty's work for Levi-Strauss's 'Levi's 501 jeans' and Grey advertising's work for Beechams Healthcare and Toiletries' 'Brylcreem'. Both campaigns are significant because they were key to establishing a successful style of advertising to new male markets in the mid 1980s. As such, they provided a positive answer to the question posed by Lucy Purdy at the beginning of this chapter. As we saw, she argued that agencies and their clients were uncertain about how to address the 'fashionable young man'. BBH and Grey found the appropriate imagery to successfully do just that.

Levi's 501s

I have already signalled the significance of BBH's two television adverts for Levi-Strauss which ran from the end of 1985 and through 1986. These adverts formed part of a campaign which aimed to turn around Levi-Strauss's fortunes. These had been declining since the end of the 1970s and most rapidly during the early 1980s. They had reached a particularly low point in 1984. That year saw the year on year sales of jeans in the UK market as a whole down by 13 per cent, and Levi-Strauss's sales were hit particularly badly. The company themselves identified part of the reason for this decline in the failure of a marketing strategy which had been introduced at the end of the 1970s with the first signs of shifts in the jeans market. Levi-Strauss had diversified from its core business of jeans into menswear, womenswear and youthwear. In particular, it had more intensively targeted the 25 to 35 year old mainstream male market with a range of leisure-wear. These included Levi's sweatshirts and trousers like the Levi's 'Action Slacks'. This strategy undermined, however, Levi-Strauss's core product area (the jeans) and what the company saw as their essential values (quality, durability, Americanness, tradition). Research by Levi-Strauss showed, in particular, that the credibility for young consumers of the Levi's name had slipped amidst the proliferation of leisure wear for older markets. As Peter Skilland, Levi-Strauss's marketing services manager at the time acknowledged, 'Putting the Levi's name on polyester trousers meant nothing to the polyester trouser buyer and left the jeans buyer totally unimpressed' (*Campaign*, 23/6/86: 50).

The company initiated a major rethink of its strategy. It decided upon what it called a 'back to basics' policy. In other words, the product diversification was reversed, and Levi-Strauss refocused its manufacturing and marketing on the jean market. The aim was to re-establish the association of the Levi's name with tradition, Americanness, durability and quality. Three strands of this policy were significant. First, a decision was made to move away from an emphasis on volume sales and instead concentrate on profitability per unit. What this meant for the product range was the relaunch of the company's longest-standing line – the 501 jean – as a quality fashion trouser at a higher price. Secondly,

Levi-Strauss was concerned to refocus its marketing upon what it saw as the crucial jeans market – the 15 to 19 year old youth market, and especially 15 to 19 year old males. Thirdly, the new marketing of the relaunched Levi's 501 was to be co-ordinated across Levi-Strauss's European markets and be – in this sense – genuinely pan-European.

BBH, who had won the UK account in 1982, satisfied Levi-Strauss that they could co-ordinate the new pan-European strategy. In researching the creative strategy for the campaign, BBH discovered a significant trend:

> we uncovered a fascination, almost a reverence, for a mythical America of the past – the America that had produced Dean and Presley, the 57 Chevrolet, Sam Cooke, the Misfits and a host of other heroes and 'cult objects'. Clothes and shoes featured strongly in this, and the 'fifties' look, suitably processed for the mid-1980s, was current ... 501s featured heavily in this trend, and were being adopted by opinion-leading 'cognescenti' in small but interesting numbers in London, Paris, Hamburg, Berlin, Rome and Milan. (Broadbent 1990: 184)

The appropriation of the 'fifties' look in 'street style' and the valorization of a particular repertoire of 'classic' objects (like Zippo lighters and Ray Ban sunglasses) offered a potentially neat fit with Levi-Strauss's 'back to basics' strategy. BBH's brief, however, was to establish the Levi's 501 jeans in the arena of mass fashion. That is, it had not only to address opinion-leaders (or what BBH elsewhere termed 'innovators'), but – in BBH's terms – 'early adopters'. As the agency themselves put it,

> We wanted to make 501s compulsory equipment for anyone who cared about the way they looked. We wished to persuade the 15–20 year old males who represent the core jeans market that 501 were the right look, and the only label: the right look because 'anti-fit' [the 501 cut] was the way jeans were being worn by those in the know; the only label, because only Levi's 501 had laid genuine claim to the heady jeans heritage that was rooted in the fifties. (ibid.: 185)

A more detailed formulation of the brief followed from this specification of the target consumers. Using group discussions with consumers in London and Frankfurt based around video screenings of film footage and collages of magazine photos, BBH confirmed that – in their terms – the 'evocation of a mythical America was a motivating route ... We also deepened our understanding of the role of great pop classics in underlying the status of the product and learned that casting was absolutely crucial' (ibid.: 185).

The final creative brief was produced from these findings and the adverts were art directed by John Hegarty and written by Barbara Noakes. 'Bath' and 'Launderette' went on the air in the UK on Boxing Day 1985 on both ITV and Channel 4, together with a cinema run of the adverts. In addition, the marketing strategy included a press campaign, the development of extensive point-of-sale materials (to support the new campaign within retail outlets), the design of a 501 logo, coordination with record companies of the release of the two sound-track songs, and – in 1987 – a second phase of marketing. I [will] come back to the press campaign. Importantly, as we will see, it was aimed not at the mass market of early-adopters targeted through television, but at a segmented market of 'innovators'.

'Bath' and 'Launderette' were immediately successful. Sales of the 501s expanded rapidly; so rapidly in fact that in March and April of 1986 the adverts were withdrawn from television because Levi's factories were unable to keep up with demand. Importantly for Levi-Strauss, sales of the 501s markedly improved the profits per units of the company. The adverts also prompted extended press and television commentary, and picked up a number of industry awards.

It was the codings of masculinity put together in the adverts which really concerns us. [. . .] I want to underline here five characteristics of the masculinity signified in 'Bath' and 'Launderette'. First, the appropriation and glamorization of 1950s style was important. It set the terms for the signification of an assertive masculinity. Secondly, the surface of the models' bodies – and specifically developed muscles – were displayed. Thirdly, the assertive masculinity of both the 'fifties' style and the models' physiques, were signified together with the coding of softness and sensuality. Both Nick Kamen and James Mardle had smooth, clear skins, full pouting lips, shiny eyes and glossy, highly groomed hair. Fourthly, the display of these bodies was presented to the viewer in highly distinctive ways. Cuts to arms, chest, face, bottom and thighs, together with a focus on the unbuttoning of the jeans and (in the case of 'Bath') a cut of the water seeping over the model's jean-clad crotch, undermined more conventional significations of power and aggression associated with displayed masculine bodies. Fifthly, the male hero was represented as self-contained and on his own.

What these characteristics established was a coherent grammar for addressing new male consumers in the mid to late 1980s. Not all the codings necessarily appeared in every advert, but a combination of them was characteristically present in a series of adverts for clothing and accessories, grooming and toiletries, financial services and electrical goods. This repertoire of codings was central to Grey Advertising's work with Brylcreem.

Brylcreem

If Levi-Strauss was suffering from a decline in its fortunes prior to its strategic rethink and BBH's campaign for the Levi's 501s, then Beechams's Brylcreem was in near terminal decline. From a peak in the early 1960s when Brylcreem sold one hundred million pots in the UK, by 1984 sales were down to five million because of longer hair and styles requiring blow-drying among men. This dramatic decline was aggravated by the nature of Brylcreem's remaining customer base, which was an ageing group of long-term male users. Beechams saw little opportunity in expanding sales within this market, and no advertising of the brand had been run since the 'Brylcreem bounce' campaign of the early 1970s. A general re-appraisal by Beechams of its key brands, however, changed this. Suffering from what industry analysts termed 'lack of executive direction' in the early 1980s, Beechams set in motion initiatives to reposition and re-establish brands like Lucozade, Horlicks, Ribena and (what Beechams saw as the most difficult task) Brylcreem. Underpinning this strategy was new product development and marketing. Grey Advertising, which won the new account in 1985, set about researching the creative strategy. A key finding for Grey was that among a younger generation of men, shorter hair and traditionally smart hairstyles were being worn in preference for what Grey called the '"scruffy" styles of the last twenty years' (*Campaign*, 4/10/85: 15). These were, specifically, a highly fashion conscious group of male consumers whom Grey termed 'stylepreneurs' (ibid.). Formulating a creative strategy for these target consumers was a problem, however, for the creatives at Grey. Art director Su Sareem and writer Jan Heron described how they came up with the final version.

> Jan and I were despairing – we knew that there was a solution there somewhere but we just couldn't seem to find it. For inspiration, we went through the old Brylcreem commercials and were watching the sixties reel in my flat. Suddenly the phone rang. I put the video on 'hold' and the image started to shake. We both realised that with good music, it would be perfect. (*Campaign*, 4/10/85: 15)

Three new commercials were cut and re-edited from the old commercials using video-editing techniques and a contemporary soundtrack was added. Beechams was not fully convinced by this creative strategy, and initially allocated only £1 million to test the campaign. Grey used all this budget for a television campaign in London. Both the agency and client were happy with the initial consumer response, and so in February 1986 a second campaign – using similar footage – was launched, together with an extensive press and poster campaign. The press and poster work extended the pastiche of the 1960s advertising using contemporary models. These included Nick Kamen's brother, Barry. This was accompanied by the design of a new tub style. In 1987, further product development was initiated and a range of 13 products (including mousse, gel and aftershave) was launched in black packaging and with a new typeface for the brand name. In 1988, this product range was backed by a new television commercial which – still focusing on the appropriation of 1950s style short hair by young men – extended the repositioning of the brand as an essential purchase for stylish young men (*Campaign*, 11/11/88: 3). The creative team at Grey, like their counterparts at BBH, identified casting as crucial to establishing the credibility of the advert among its target audience. In casting the 26 year old Corsican, Jean-Ange Chiapinini, the team 'were looking for the definitive modern man. A cross between Mickey Rourke and Matt Dillon, more of a man on the street than a pretty-boy model type like Nick Kamen' (ibid.: 12).

The advert was set in a barber's shop, amid the traditional paraphernalia of masculine grooming. The narrative of the advert was based around the model being wet shaved by the barber. In dramatically lit gloom we see the shaving cream being applied, the razor being used and the barber massaging the model's temples and then pulling a hot flannel over his face to complete the grooming. Throughout this ritual, which is shot in rapid close-ups, the model is narcissistically absorbed in the care he is receiving. His self-absorption is highlighted by the fact that the process of shaving is shot in such quick edits to a thunderous soundtrack. We glimpse a flame, the razor against his face, a razor being sharpened on leather and the steaming flannel being pulled across his face. The model remains self-absorbed amid these movements around him. In all of this there was more than a hint at sado-masochism connoted through the ritual of grooming between the barber and the model.

The masculine imagery of the campaigns echoed many of the codings at work in the Levi's 501 adverts, despite the self-conscious attempt (through casting in particular) to encode a different masculinity. The appropriation of the iconography of the neat and smart style of respectable 1950s masculinity was key to the first television campaigns, the press and poster campaign and the 1988 television commercial (even if, in the early television campaigns, the imagery was in fact from the early 1960s). The glamorization and – most clearly in the re-cut and re-edited adverts – playful quality of this appropriation was again important. The casting of the models was also significant. Chiapinini's 'look', in the 1988 advert, was certainly harder than Kamen's. More important, though, were the continuities in both this advert and the press and poster adverts: the combination of an assertively masculine 'look', which also contained elements of softness or sensuality connoted through the gloss of the hair and skin and the fullness of the lips. The television advert of 1988 for Brylcreem also explicitly displayed, like the Levi's 501 adverts, the narcissistic pleasures of grooming and adornment.

These codings of masculinity are at the heart of my contentions about the distinctiveness of the 1980s 'new man' imagery. In order to develop my argument about the break they represented in popular representations of masculinity and the forms of spectatorship associated with them, I want to turn to another institutional site in the regime of 'new man' imagery. This was the new magazine culture of the 'style press' and men's general interest magazines. These magazines are particularly important because the codings of masculinity represented in the Levi's 501 and Brylcreem adverts drew upon codings established within the 'style' magazines in the mid 1980s.

[...]

THE STYLE PRESS

The 'style press' was a term applied to three magazines which launched almost simultaneously in 1980. These were *The Face*, *I-D*, and *Blitz*. The term was deployed as a form of trade and journalistic shorthand for the kind of journalism and editorial mix which characterized the magazines. The magazines themselves were all produced by independent publishers – Wagadon (*The Face*), Jigsaw (*Blitz*) and Levelprint Ltd (*I-D*) – and who, among the company of publishing giants like IPC, National Magazines, Condé Nast, and even a smaller publisher like EMAP, were marginal enterprises.

The Face was the most successful of the three magazines, reaching a circulation peak of around 92,000 between 1985 and 1987, as well as picking up a number of trade awards (*Benn's Media Directory*, 1983–8).

[...]

The Face's circulation expanded strongly in 1983 and 1984. In the second half of 1984 sales rose by 20 per cent from 66,500 to 80,000 (*Media Week*, 3/5/85: 22). As the magazine grew, [publisher and editor Nick] Logan's strong sense of the 'look' of the magazine led to a somewhat idiosyncratic approach to competing for advertising revenue. Initially, he had planned that *The Face* would be able to survive on cover sales alone, and although Logan had been forced from early on to take advertising, *The Face* did not have an advertising manager until 1984. Logan's antagonism to advertising derived from his sense that advertising spoiled the 'look' of the magazine. In particular, half-page or smaller adverts were anathema to Logan in his concern to develop the design of the magazine (*Direction*, 9/1988: 32).

Rod Sopp's arrival as advertising manager in 1984 marked a more engaged – if still disingenuous – view of advertising in relation to the magazine. Sopp skilfully crafted Logan's dislike of the way advertising broke up the aimed for layouts of the magazine, into a piece of media folklore about *The Face*'s preparedness to refuse adverts on aesthetic grounds. More significantly, Sopp produced for the first time a worked-up picture of the type of persons who read *The Face*. Sopp presented *The Face* to advertisers as the perfect media form through which to target the consumer groups we have already encountered namely, 'innovators' or 'opinion formers'. These were groups of consumers who, for Sopp, were at the forefront of social trends; taste-shapers who – and he gave this example – were behind the classic mid 1980s style for young men of a plain white T-shirt, Levi's 501s, white socks and bass weejun loafers.

Sopp's representation of *The Face*'s readership of 'innovators' through the figure of the stylish young man was significant. Attention to menswear and male style was an important element of the magazine's editorial between 1983 and 1987. As Logan acknowledged, in what is a telling comment for my argument in this chapter,

> One area where we are particularly strong is in men's fashions, which is
> pretty badly represented generally. I keep reading about the need for a
> men's magazine, but I think we're closer to that than anyone. Two thirds
> of our readers are men. At the moment I'm caught between trying to

attract more women readers, or expanding the trend towards men. (*Media Week*, 16/3/84: 56)

Other commentators, like Jane Reed of IPC, saw *The Face* as shaping up a new market of young male readers. She argued that the magazine had established 'new territory for young men', particularly in terms of promoting style and consumption (*Campaign*, 26/7/85: 37). Even critics recognized the address *The Face* made to young men. Thus, publisher Peter Jackson castigated the magazine for being 'narrow, mannered and obsessed with males' (*Campaign*, 27/3/87: 20).

It was *The Face*'s association with this consumer subject, however – the stylish young male 'innovator' – that attracted advertising media buyers to the magazine. *Media Week* succinctly enunciated the thinking behind media buyer's interest in the magazine when it suggested that '*The Face*'s 63% NRS male readership is used by hapless media planners [or buyers] stuck with the perennial problem of reaching the young male through the colour press' (*Media Week*, 12/2/88: 4).

The placing of *The Face* high up the media buying lists of advertising media buyers and planners was itself dependent upon shifts in media buying practice. Thus, despite its relatively small circulation, *The Face*, was identified by media buyers as an effective place in which to advertise both because the magazine was read by key groups of consumers ('innovators', 'the style-conscious male') and because it provided a sympathetic context in which to place adverts for, in particular, a range of lifestyle orientated goods and services: clothing, financial services, records, alcohol and consumer electronics. Two high profile advertising campaigns which ran in the magazine between 1985 and 1987 illustrated the way *The Face* was classified by advertising practitioners within this form of 'qualitative' media buying. These were the adverts produced for Way In and Levi's 501s.

[...]

Levi's 501s

BBH's press campaign for Levi's 501 jeans, which followed the broadcasting and screening of the 'Bath' and 'Launderette' television and cinema commercials in January 1986, was even more explicit than Lynne Franks PR's work for Way In in the way it selected *The Face* in terms of 'qualitative' media buying criteria. As we saw, the television and cinema adverts produced by BBH were aimed at a mass market of consumers ('early adopters', in BBH's terms) and motivated by the ambition to make the Levi's 501s a compulsory purchase for anyone within this segment interested in fashion. A major concern, however, surfaced for the agency with this strategy.

The early indications of the potential success of the 501 programme, gave us one major concern. We feared that, as 501s went 'public', the opinion leaders who had discovered the product without the aid of advertising would abandon the brand. We had to reassure this small (but very important) group that 501s really were the great classic they had always believed them to be. (Broadbent 1990: 188)

The press campaign put together by BBH was designed to do precisely this. John Hegarty art directed five adverts which displayed the 501s laid out on a flat surface as part of a coordinated 'look'. Each advert was immaculately styled and accessorized by contemporary British fashion designers – Scott Crolla, Wendy Dagworthy, Jasper Conran, Joseph Ettedgui and Paul Smith. The adverts ran in *The Face* – directly targeted by BBH at 'innovators' (*Campaign*, 24/1/86: 12, *Media Week*, 29/4/88: 28).

The interlinking of these forms of advertising media buying practice and creative strategy on the pages of *The Face* – exemplified in both the Way In and Levi's 501 adverts – drew the magazine, then, very directly into the advertising arguments about targeting new male consumers through the colour press; arguments which – as I have suggested – were an important determinant of the formation of men's magazines. In classifying *The Face*, however, the media buyers at BBH or Lynne Franks PR did not hold all the cards. What was distinctive about the relationship between *The Face* and advertising practitioners at this time (1984–7), was the ability of the magazine to lay claim to this group of young male consumers. In other words, the magazine – and especially Rod Sopp – was extremely successful in persuading advertising media buyers that *The Face* was not only the perfect media vehicle through which to target new male consumers, but also that the magazine's staff had a developed sense of this group of consumers' tastes, values and sensibilities. This last point was particularly critical. In a period where advertising practitioners had evidence of shifts in the 'values and lifestyles' of groups of men and yet were uncertain about how to represent the new male consumer, *The Face* offered the precepts of the necessary cultural knowledge to target these 'new men'. Pivotal to this, as I hinted in my comments on the Levi's 501 and Brylcreem adverts, was the styling of menswear in the magazine and the codings of masculinities that this threw up. These exerted considerable influence over a wider range of representations targeted at new male consumers.

As well as being central to the way advertisers targeted this segment of male consumers through the colour press, *The Face* was also subject to close scrutiny from other consumer magazine publishers. For a number of publishing practitioners, the success of *The Face* between 1984 and 1986 really testified to a shift in the magazine reading habits of important groups of young men. In particular, it was seen to have educated a generation of young men into reading a general interest magazine for men. In doing so, *The Face* also shifted the terms of what the format of a general interest magazine could be; namely, one based upon a style-led journalism and editorial approach rather than on the format offered by women's magazines. These findings gave considerable impetus to the formulation of a general interest men's magazine aimed at the segment of men in the age group above *The Face*'s target readership. That is, men aged between 20 and 45.

[...]

CONCLUSION

What, then, can we draw out from this account of the advertising and publishing knowledges and practices that drove the formation of general interest men's magazines in the UK? What has my attention to the advertising/publishing nexus associated with the 'style press' and men's magazines delivered? First, it is important to emphasize that the account I have put together reveals the extent of the interest from groups of media practitioners (within magazine publishing and advertising) in a new type of magazine for men in the period between 1983 and 1989. Secondly, the concern specifically to target men through new magazines was dependent, as we saw, on a sense amongst these practitioners of shifts in young men's 'values and life-styles'. This was largely drawn from evidence from consumer research, but also from assessments of developments within magazine culture itself. Thirdly, the concern to target men through new magazines was also dependent upon the production of new products and services by advertisers and the refocusing of the marketing of existing products in relation to the new male market. Fourthly, the identification and servicing of new male readerships was led by independent publishers. Thus, the development of a sector of UK general interest men's magazines was marked in its formation by the success of the 'style press' and the publishing practices of the independent publishers, Wagadon. It was the style-based format that set the precepts for general interest men's magazines in their formation. Fifthly, the shifts within advertising media buying practice were critical to the advertising arguments and practice that shaped the formation of the new sector and provided its economic underpinning.

Putting together an account of these advertising and publishing knowledges and practices also has other pay-offs. It sheds light, in particular, on the way a central institutional determinant of the magazines functioned; that is, the economic relations between advertisers and publishers. It is to repeat a well worn conceptualization to suggest that these economic relations regulated the production of the magazines. For publishers, securing and maintaining healthy levels of advertising revenue and achieving sufficiently large circulation figures formed the *sine qua non* of their operations as commercial enterprises. However, rather than take on trust the assumption from economic theory that these economic relations and their associated commercial imperatives constituted a primary level of determination on the production of the magazines, the account I have offered in this chapter prompts us to consider their operation in different terms. First, it points us to the key relationships that constituted these economic relations. From the account it is clear that we are talking about relations produced between some specific practitioners. Namely, advertising media buyers and magazine advertising managers. It was this key relationship that effectively constituted the economic relation between advertisers and publishers. Secondly, foregrounding these knowledges and practices revealed the way in which representations of the imagined target readerships were central to the operationalizing of these economic relations. In other words, it was through these shared representations of the consumer that the relationship between media buyers and advertising managers functioned. This suggests, then, that the economic relations between advertisers and publishers themselves had cultural conditions of existence; cultural conditions of existence made up of the way the market of consumers was represented through specific cultural practices. It is not to overplay the argument to suggest that this work of representation was as much a condition of existence of these economic relations as the exchange of money between advertising agencies and publishers.

REFERENCE

Broadbent, S. (ed.) 1990. *Advertising Works 5.*

59

HANDLING SEX

Janice Winship

Attention to women's and men's hands in ads may not seem *the* most burning issue to be tackled on the question of representations of femininity and masculinity in ads. Yet it is not just feminist nit-picking. As Erving Goffman has commented in his glossy book, *Gender Advertisements*, gender is 'something that can be conveyed *fleetingly* in any social situation' (Goffman, 1979: 7, my emphasis). If only a brief *time* suffices to communicate gender to us, similarly only a small part of our anatomy need be represented in that communication. A representation of a hand, or even only a part of one, will then do quite as well to signify cultural aspects of gender, as a full length portrayal. That this is so, is sure evidence of the pervasiveness and depth to which gender construction penetrates.

However, there are other reasons why I have chosen the representation of hands to focus this discussion of gender difference and its construction in forms which, I argue, are oppressive to women. Firstly, there is a partly empirical consideration. In ads women are frequently represented in a 'fragmented' way, or as Trevor Millum describes, photographically 'cropped' (Millum, 1975: 83–84). Women are signified by their lips, legs, hair, eyes or hands, which stand, metonymically – the bit for the whole – for, in this case, the 'sexual woman' (Winship, 1980). Men, on the other hand are less often 'dismembered' and the only bit of them which is represented with any frequency seems to be the hand. Since women's hands also appear in ads this allows us to make a limited but

From *Media, Culture and Society* 3:1 (1981) pp. 25–41.

fine analysis which begins to compare the representations of femininity with those of masculinity by beginning from a similar point. The *difference* of the meanings conveyed by a gendered hand, which the analysis then goes on to demonstrate, is only highlighted by this formally equivalent beginning. In the ad context we find that a woman's hand can never be substitute for a man's, nor a man's for a woman's: the gender difference the hand stands for is always crucial to the meaning of the ad.

This singular focus on hands also has a further pedagogic benefit in so far as it allows us to argue a particular theoretical position more clearly. Briefly, that position holds that ads as a discourse do have their own 'specificity' but that the order of that specificity must be pinned down. Simultaneously we must also conceptualize them in their 'external' relations, especially in their relation to the social reader and to other discourses. Behind this formulation is the political concern posed by the title, 'Handling sex'. *Who* is handling? The ad makers certainly, but we as readers of the ad also 'handle' what we understand there. A feminist politics of representation with respect to ads has then, to engage with the social reader, as well as the social text.

[...]

To return now to the choice of hands, this focus allows us to illustrate that, clearly, one of the ideological fields these ads are working within, is that of feminity and masculinity; that feminity and masculinity can be constructed by means quite specific to ads – the hand – but also alongside other means; that femininity and masculinity are constructed with particular ideological inflections, and nearly always have a class specificity; that the hand can be used as a visual mode of address which is also verbally repeated. In what follows it is these aspects which I examine in a selection of ads, paying particular attention to how ads mean differently for women and men reading them.

1. NATURALLY: 'MEN OF THE WORLD' AND 'WOMEN AT HOME'

In most ads where we see a hand there is no doubt about it: it just *has* to be a woman's or a man's hand which we see there: the other sex would not do. It is not, however, the intrinsic qualities of each hand which makes that so. Rather it is the tightly organized production of the *whole* representation in the ad – of which the hand is only a part – which constructs a gender difference from which the hand accrues, as well as contributes meaning. If we were merely to change the hands in the next two ads so that a woman's hand (signified by, say, painted nails and a gold bracelet) was offering that packet of cigarettes, and a man's hand (signified by, say, shirt cuff and jacket) was pouring that custard there would be a disruption of the meanings. 'Hand' and text would rudely jar, signifying contradictorily: a woman's hand does not signify 'world leader'; a man's hand does not signify 'home-made'. But as it is, the appropriately gendered hand allows us to key into familiar ideologies of masculinity and femininity. Those ideologies seem 'naturally' masculine or feminine, and the represented hand is 'naturally' a man's *or* a woman's.

*Rothman's cigarettes (*Observer, *28 September 1980)*

At one level the background of deep blue, *royal* blue (royal confirmed by the royal insignia and 'By special appointment') only repeats the blue band across the packet. Yet at another it signifies, as we know from other texts outside the ad, the universe, the span of the sky, or the world's seas. That meaning is corroborated by the globe represented by (some of) the constituent flags (what imperialism is perpetrated here with Britain's union jack at the centre of the world, which the packet too occupies?); and by the assignation: 'world leader'. This label is linked to 'Filter tipped' on the packet: both are against a red background, both cut diagonally across the page. The cigarette is visually confirmed by this exchange of meaning, which we make, as the 'world leader', as 'King Size' in status as well as size. At the same time the male hand, marked as male by what seems the customary middle class code in ads – the white shirt cuff, and accompanying jacket sleeve (here dark blue, with conveniently superimposed insignia), the well manicured and unblemished hand – partakes of that leadership. These are all the signs that *he* is a leader, the 'officered (naval?) gentleman'. Cigarette and man add stature to each other.

But to whom is this packet of gourmet or snobbish fare proffered? The 'world', which includes 'you': 'the best tobacco money can buy'; the best tobacco *your* money can buy. But who is 'you'? Men. For the claims of a

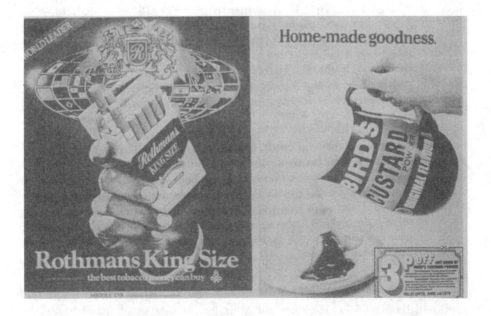

masculine leadership, over which hand and packet egg each other on in complicit and seemingly natural agreement, allows men a point of participation in the signification of the ad – via hand or packet. If that 'you' is a woman we can only submit to this dominating hand offering us a cigarette, and capitulate to the meaning of the *ad from which we are excluded*, even if we buy the cigarettes. How can we enter 'world leadership'?

*Bird's custard (*Woman's Weekly, 24 March 1979)

If we were to replace the woman's hand here by a man's we would no longer have 'Home-made goodness' as an appropriate caption. It might as a chef's hand signify a 'culinary delight', but then jam sponge would have been transformed from its 'homely' associations. This woman's hand (as woman herself) is synonymous with home; the meaning emerges 'naturally', something we recognize from what we know outside ads. But how do we know that *inside* the ad? Note what the hand looks like: *un*varnished nails, no indication of elegant long fingers which are the usual signs for that other non-homely femininity, the signification for 'beauty' or 'sex', and which definitively mark the hand as different from a man's. Here that difference is less visually established by the hand than by other visual and verbal cues in the ad. 'Home-made goodness' is conjured up not only by the 'plain' hand but by the unadorned plate, the old-fashioned, English pudding and custard itself. There is an implicit appeal to tradition, to the idealized value of femininity as 'home-making' which cuts across any class specificity: the absence of any background detail which would place this hand in class terms aids this signification. But see not only how easily and effortlessly that tradition is kept alive, but the *narrowness* of what it includes: *just* pour a jug of Bird's custard (as world leadership in the Rothman's ad *just* needed a packet of cigarettes). Modes of femininity and masculinity are achievable, then, through consumption.

If we delve a little deeper into the ad's rhetoric, as Alvarado puts it, to make an analysis which 'releases that frozen moment' (Alvarado, 1979: 8) of the representation, we might want to ask: who made the jam sponge and custard? And who is going to eat this homely fare? Who is she serving? There are three sorts of answer here. One concerns who produced the *commodity*, Bird's custard. The second is concerned with who made the pudding, or the mock-up, for the purposes of the photograph. The third is the narrative the ad fictionally traps into this moment of representation, as if it were the 'natural' narrative, so 'natural' that we don't even have to think about it. The answers are sewn up. Obviously, she who owns the hand, a 'mum', a 'wife' has made the pudding and custard; Obviously 'he' or 'they' – children and/or husband are going to eat it. Home-making is, unremittingly, for others. There she is preparing something which she is unlikely to eat herself: jam sponge at 250 calories a portion, uncompromisingly on all those diet lists of taboo foods. What woman dare eat that without feelings of self-damnation? This is truly men's and children's fare.

Reading this ad we are not verbally addressed as 'you'. Yet visually we are placed so that the hand which pours this custard could be ours: it is *our* body, if we are women, which completes the person off page. This is a frequent and useful artifice for ads, a means of visually addressing us as powerful as the verbal exhortations to 'you'. We are inevitably caught up in this 'natural' association of the feminine hand and homemade goodness – for the family. To reject that on any grounds other than feminism, that is, to wrench apart some of this 'natural meaning', we are thrown into '*not*' goodness. What guilt to bear! Meanwhile, men enjoy the pudding, their masculinity unthreatened. Representationally their dominance is signified in their absence: they are being served.

2. BEAUTY AND THE BOSS

We have seen then, that these two hands, a man's and a woman's, signify seemingly naturally and unquestionably the 'worldly' and the 'homely', masculinity and femininity.

However, there are other gendered qualities called into play by ads. John Berger's pithy statement on the subject of gender representations that 'Men act and women appear' (Berger, 1972: 47), has awesome applicability.

(a) *Men at work* ...

Scotcade shirts (Observer, 21 September 1980)

On the question of how masculinity is represented differently from femininity there is one simple point to be made here. 'Man the (middle class) worker' is signified both by what his hand is doing *and* by his appearance – the creaseless shirt and business tie. We can just about imagine that women's blouses might be advertised with this same caption which, by emptying our usual understanding

of 'white, blue collar workers' to which the ad refers, and refilling with a 'commodity' meaning, trivializes that original understanding while *appearing* to extend it – 'cream collar workers' too. Workers are now differentiated by what they consume rather than by their place in any social division of labour, Judith Williamson considers this aspect of ads in some detail (Williamson, 1980). We can even imagine that a woman could be shown doing the same activities; they are not particularly masculine tasks. But what is extremely unlikely is this mutual support between 'doing' and 'appearance'. Either the whole stress would be on the women's *looks* in the blouse (and the ad might show her face, or emphasize her sexuality by her bosom or even her hand) and/or there would be some dis-juncture between what she was doing and how, and for whom, she was looking. Men's sexuality is not in play in this ad; if the 'worker' were a woman it undoubtedly would be.

[...]

(h)   *and men at play*

JVC video (Observer, 4 November 1979)

As readers of the ad we are clearly put in the position of the viewer of the TV screen; moreover that position is occupied by a man whose hand we see controlling the screen. *If* we are men that could be our hand. The hand is marked as masculine both by its *lack* of feminine marks – no varnished nails – the caption – 'Who said slow motion replays were just for "Match of the Day"?'

– and the TV image – the fanciful strip 'girls'. As if an appeal to the most popular TV programme for men were not enough, adding insult to injury, the ad relies on that other 'spectator sport', peculiarly masculine in style, that of 'bird' watching. I use this sexist term only because the 'Simulated picture' indicates only too well the calculating construction of the ad: not just any old picture from the telly, but one showing women who are decoratively attired *like* extravagant birds. They are caught at some moment in a striptease act posing with what Goffman has neatly described as 'the bashful knee bend' (Goffman, 1979: 45). However his interpretation of this as representing 'a foregoing of full effort ... the position adds a moment to any effort', and his assertion that because women are seen supporting each other in this pose the question of gender relations does not arise, seems not to be quite the point. The gesture is surely one of submission in which the woman is pausing to gaze or to be gazed at – by men. And it is this representation of women which the male hand is seen to control; at the press of a button 'you' (he) can stop and start, obliterate or bring into gaze the strip act, like the director of a film. As the ad says, 'All you need now is a canvas chair with "Director" on it.' What is being advertised is the video and the control of the image which it provides, but what seems to be at stake is a control of women's sexuality: women as fare for men's play. Further in a reversal which gives them no power or status at all, *women work* on the screen, while men play – with them.

Sony stereo cassette player (Observer, 22 June 1980)

When a woman's hand appears in what is formally a similar mode – at the controls of a cassette player – its place and meaning bear no comparison with the controlling hand of masculinity. The limp-wristed way she holds her hand, finger delicately resting on a switch hardly suggests she is actively working the equipment. [...] This elegantly attired, black gloved hand, with ring and silver bracelets, complements and repeats the metallic tones of the cassette player. The hand and the hi-fi are interchangeable; not only through their colours, but also their size and, importantly, what they are meant to stand for. The cassette player is called 'Stowaway': it is tiny; so are women's hands (well, so the stereotypes say). But this gloved hand is also classy, daring, demonstrating style; so is the cassette player. If the hand signifies the ultimate in the 'lady of leisure', a female dilettante who has money and more to spend (or be spent on her), so too the cassette player is in a class of its own: 'Sony's little masterpiece.' Even Sony think they've done quite well.

The ad primarily addresses men – hi-fi freaks – who may 'want to know about its performance in Hz, SPL, and watts per channel ... ' They are urged, 'To see how small it is put your hand over the picture.' 'Your' (his) hand is then caught up in that of the dazzling lady; the electric touch only affirms the effect of Sony's technical achievement: 'to dazzle your ears.' Obviously it would not have been appropriate to encourage two male hands to touch: how could that signify 'dazzlement'?

Finally note the differences between Sony and their 'brilliant technical achievement' (*Who* are Sony? *Whose* achievement is it?), and the woman's hand; production and consumption; masculinity and femininity.

Elbeo tights (Honey, *August/September, 1980*)

Here gender difference is organized explicitly around sexuality: blatantly a man's hand 'touches her up', but in a class mode which would refuse that idiom. Visually all is there for us to guess; verbally like middle class manners, double-talk is the key note. If a hand can be used in representation so that we are placed as the owner of it, off the page, it can also pose the riddle of what exactly is happening to the owner of the hand off the page. And when it is a man's hand resting on a woman's leg the answer is clear: sex, however harmless. Yet the caption belies such a sexual appeal: 'Your appreciation of the finer things in life has always impressed me, Sir Giles.' With what are fast becoming tedious middle class significations for masculinity – white shirt cuff etc. – *plus* large dress ring, which definitely ups the class position, this 'gentleman', Sir Giles, could not be concerned with anything so brash as sex, but rather with 'the finer things in life'. What are they? Outside the context of the ad we might guess: good wine, antiques, tailor made suits, caviar and truffles, those accoutrements of a certain class position which his hand, the finely upholstered sofa, are signs for in the ad. Note how the background here is important whereas it was purposely obliterated in the Bird's ad. The scene conforms to what Goffman refers to as 'commercial realism' in relation to which 'the viewer is to engage

knowingly in a kind of make-believe, treating the depicted world as if it were real-life but of course not actually real' (Goffman, 1979: 6). But for the ad the apotheosis of 'fineness' is, of course, Elbeo tights which drain 'fineness' from the classy environment – ' . . . are more than a shade superior'.

If the man's hand signifies class, the bit of woman which is represented primarily signifies sexuality, and would do so, *even* if the man's hand were not there. A focus on legs, like a focus on the lips, bottom, or breasts of a woman, always signifies sexuality. Yet the gold chain round her ankle and mini (*c.* 1980), black, broderie anglaise dress, support a sexual signification. There is also something classy about her representation too: the stylishness of black patent court shoes, gold chain and black dress. Indeed, a 'fine' sexuality which carries over to the 'Supersheer 15 Denier "Nymphe"' tights, which in turn, themselves deliver that fineness to whoever wears them. The sexual loading behind the term 'fine' is not only carried in the name of the tights – Nymphe – what kind of femininity does that suggest – but also in the placing of his hand: literally it is his appreciation of the tights which is being referred to. But really?

Since it is in a woman's magazine, and since it is an ad for tights, it is women who read this ad. A woman appears to have the speaking voice. But what she speaks of is only to be impressed that *he* appreciates, what *she* appreciates; and the latter is only what he has set up in the first place. She speaks to accept a male possession – the hand on her knee: the 'man's eye view' of her legs.

3. GENDER (DIS)PLACEMENT

The next two ads are similar in so far as they show a woman and a man, respectively, in the 'wrong place'. In the Veuve du Vernay ad a woman has invaded what is visually purported to be the male terrain of a commuter train. In the Carling ad a man has been and gone from what is verbally assumed to be a woman's place – around the kitchen sink. These displacements serve, however, not to be innovative, only to reinforce particular ideologies of masculinity and femininity. Moreover the *form* of each ad – different in each case – heightens the separation between femininity and masculinity which is being constructed.

Veuve du Vernay (Observer, *13 July 1980)*

While the Elbeo ad corresponds to what Goffman describes as 'commercial realism', this ad uses a kind of montage technique: the incongruous chain of colour composed of the curiously emerging man's hand pouring the drink, and the woman's ridiculously placed arm and leg, seem to be superimposed against the background of drab grey and white businessmen. This achieves two effects: one of playing up a 'naughty' fantasy element, and perhaps of generating humour (funny for whom though?); the other of differentiating that brazen couple from the boring and repeated motif of the city gents.

Clearly the 'chain of colour' signifies excitement and sex. In the Elbeo ad a man's hand corroborated the sexual meaning of the woman's legs. Here the sexually explosive mixture constituted from the man's hand, the woman's hand

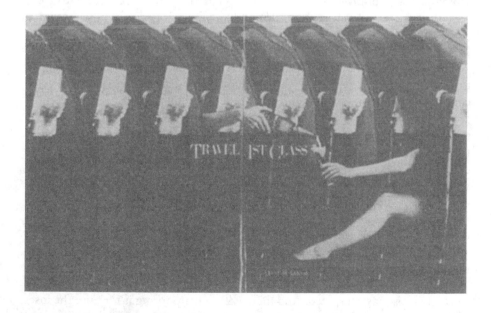

and leg, still has the woman's leg as the core of the sexual signification. Imagine the ad *without* that leg: neither so ridiculous nor so sexually 'ripe'. Yet the man's hand does have some sexual meaning – in its difference from the suited arm of the city gent clutching his *Times* and umbrella. The latter is middle aged, portly and formal; the former is probably young and certainly 'naked' – or shirtless – with bronzed arm, full of sexual potency. The potency is symbolized by her position, not quite supine, but certainly awkwardly below him who could be standing; she sexually submits as the drink is poured (coincidentally at crotch level?) into her glass: a metaphor for a 'sexual filling'.

'Travel 1st Class' exhorts the ad, and we can add, 'you will find sex and excitement'. But to whom is this addressed? Perhaps 'you' are a woman and the drink a woman's drink, for where is *his* glass? 'You' (she) reels with the effect, of him, or the drink, and see the same businessman many times over: woman out of control. She drinks it but *he* has bought it and offers it to her, a sign not of his service to her, but of her *dependence* on him. But we can also read the ad as perhaps the fantasy of that city gent. He imagines himself in the place of the one who pours the drink: their arms are almost in the same place. What he gets travelling first class is not the drink, but *her*. But then contrarily, we are put into the position of looking *up* to the line of men; as the crouching woman who extends her vulnerable limbs? If we are women what other position is offered us? While men revel in sweet fantasy.

Carling *(*Cosmopolitan*, June 1980)*

A difference is marked here not by the contrast between colour and black and white, but between the background of the kitchen and the focal inset of the woman's hand pouring a can of lager. What the difference is about is not sexuality/asexuality or excitement/mundanity, contrasts which the woman primarily introduces into the Veuve du Vernay ad, but femininity and masculinity of another order: femininity as domestic and masculinity as definitely not.

The 'commercial realism' of the kitchen scene has all the signs of construction. Who can spot the visual clues which indicate, what we are told in text and caption, that a man (her husband – note the wedding ring we can usefully just see on her finger) has not only done the washing up, but that it is not taken for granted that he will do it: it is not his natural rôle? He needs reminding – 'Your turn xx'. Does she when it's her turn? The crockery needs putting away, the cloth hasn't been hung to dry; the bin hasn't been emptied, i.e. she still has work to do. Would *men* looking at this ad recognize those signs of masculine domesticity which are only *too* familiar to women? Yet here she is so thankful for this small lightening of her load, that she is rewarding him. What reward does she get each day? It is *such* an (extra)ordinary task for him to do that both a 'little feminine charm' is required to encourage its execution, and because the task is such a strain, so mammoth a chore – 'The things men do for ... ' – only Carling with its 'thirst shattering flavour' will suffice to quench this man-size thirst this task has generated. And there we see her pouring it for him; the inset

of femininity restoring what is absent from that kitchen. Despite her absence from the kitchen then, she is confirmed in her domestic rôle; despite his presence he is affirmed as 'a man' – and non-domestic, naturally.

What we have seen in these ads are the ways in which the hand becomes a central mark of femininity or masculinity. If we were to look just at our friends' *hands* we might well *not* be able to tell whether the hand was a woman's or a man's. But of course, then, as in the ads, we *do* always know whose hand it is primarily from what the person as a whole looks like, if not from the hand itself. Usually, however, the hand is not the chief means by which we recognize femininity or masculinity, though this has not always been the case. Leonora Davidoff explains how the appearance of hands was a preoccupation of the middle classes in the nineteenth century; it was as much a concern about establishing class differentials as it was to separate women and men (Davidoff, 1976: 127). Even today the difference between rough and calloused hands, and smooth white ones has both a class and gender reference, which we all recognize ideologically, but do not entirely rely on in our judgement of people as working class or middle class, women or men. What is specific to representation and ads is how they are able to 'elevate' this, in many cases, 'unmarked' part of our bodies and embue it with gender, even when it is detached from any body: it becomes the focal sign of femininity or masculinity. Yet though as we look at the ads it appears that it does this *by itself*, that the gendered meaning is there 'naturally', in the hand, this is by no means so. The biological hand is parasitic on *cultural* markers for this 'natural meaning'. Thus either the hand itself is marked – the bracelet, or shirt cuff – or the text and visuals apart from the hand are marked – 'Home-made goodness' and sponge pudding in the Bird's Custard ad, caption and the TV image in the JVC video ad – and these fill the hand with gendered and therefore cultural meaning. This process of representation occurs equally for masculinity and femininity. Inequality lies in the cultural meanings themselves to which representation only gives a heightened and particular expression.

References

Alvarado, M. (1980). Photographs and narrativity, *Screen Education*, no. 32/33, Autumn/Winter 1979/80

Berger, J. (1972). *Ways of Seeing*, London, Penguin

Davidoff, L. (1976). The rationalisation of housework, in Barker, D. and Allen, S. (eds) *Dependence and Exploitation in Work and Marriage*, London, Longman

Goffman, E. (1979). *Gender Advertisements*, London, Macmillan

Millum, T. (1975). *Images of Woman*, London, Chatto & Windus

Williamson, J. (1978). *Decoding Advertisements*, London, Marion Boyars

Williamson, J. (1979). The history that photographs mislaid, *Photography/Politics: One*

Winship, J. (1980). Sexuality for sale, in Hall, S., Hobson, D., Lowe, A. and Willis, P. (eds) *Culture, Media, Language*, London, CCCS/Hutchinson

60

SOFT-SOAPING EMPIRE: COMMODITY RACISM AND IMPERIAL ADVERTISING

Anne McClintock

Doc: My, it's so clean.
Grumpy: There's dirty work afoot.

(Snow White and the Seven Dwarfs)

EMPIRE OF THE HOME

In 1899, the year the Anglo–Boer war erupted in South Africa, an advertisement for Pears' Soap in *McClure's Magazine* accounted:

> The first step towards LIGHTENING THE WHITE MAN'S BURDEN is through teaching the virtues of cleanliness. PEARS' SOAP is a potent factor in brightening the dark corners of the earth as civilization advances, while amongst the cultured of all nations it holds the highest place – it is the ideal toilet soap.

The advertisement (Figure [60]1) figures an admiral decked in pure imperial white, washing his hands in his cabin as his steamship crosses the oceanic threshold into the realm of empire. In this image, private domesticity and the imperial market – the two spheres vaunted by middle-class Victorians to be naturally distinct – converge in a single commodity spectacle: the domestic sanctum of the white man's bathroom gives privileged vantage on to the global realm of imperial commerce. Imperial progress is consumed at a glance: time consumed as a commodity spectacle, as *panoptical time*.

From G. Robertson, M. Mash, L. Tickner, J. Bird, B. Curtis and T. Putnam (eds), *Travellers' Tales: Narratives of Home and Displacement* (London and New York: Routledge, 1994) pp. 131–54.

On the wall, the porthole is both window and mirror. The window, icon of imperial surveillance and the Enlightenment idea of knowledge as penetration, is a porthole on to public scenes of economic conversion: one scene depicts a kneeling African gratefully receiving the Pears' Soap as he might genuflect before a religious fetish. The mirror, emblem of Enlightenment self-consciousness, reflects the sanitized image of white, male, imperial hygiene. Domestic hygiene, the ad implies, purifies and preserves the white male body from contamination as it crosses the dangerous threshold of empire; at the same time, the domestic commodity guarantees white male power, the genuflexion of Africans and rule of the world. On the wall, an electric light bulb signifies scientific rationality and spiritual advance. In this ad, the household commodity spells the lesson of imperial progress and capitalist civilization: civilization, for the white man, advances and brightens through his four beloved fetishes: soap, the mirror, light and white clothing – the four domestic fetishes that recur throughout imperial advertising and imperial popular culture of the time.

The first point about the Pears' advertisement is that it figures imperialism as coming into being through domesticity. At the same time, imperial domesticity is a domesticity without women. The commodity fetish, as the central form of the industrial enlightenment, reveals what liberalism would like to forget: the domestic is political, the political is gendered. What could not be admitted into male rationalist discourse (the economic value of women's domestic labour) is disavowed and projected on to the realm of the 'primitive' and the zone of

Figure [60]1: A white man sanitizing himself as he crosses the threshold of empire.

empire. At the same time, the economic value of colonized cultures is domesticated and projected on to the realm of the 'prehistoric' fetish.

A characteristic feature of the Victorian middle class was its peculiarly intense preoccupation with boundaries. In imperial fiction and commodity kitsch, boundary objects and liminal scenes recur ritualistically. As colonials travelled back and forth across the threshold of their known world, crisis and boundary confusion were warded off and contained by fetishes, absolution rituals and liminal scenes. Soap and cleaning rituals became central to the ceremonial demarcation of body boundaries and the policing of social hierarchies. Cleansing and boundary rituals are integral to most cultures; what characterized Victorian cleaning rituals, however, was their peculiarly intense relation to money.

I begin with the Pears' Soap ad because it registers what I see as an epochal shift that took place in the culture of imperialism in the last decades of the nineteenth century. This was the shift from *scientific* racism – embodied as it was in anthropological, scientific and medical journals, travel writing and ethnographies – to what can be called *commodity racism*. Commodity racism – in the specifically Victorian forms of advertising and commodity spectacle, the imperial Expositions and the museum movement – converted the imperial progress narrative into mass-produced consumer spectacles. Commodity racism, I suggest, came to produce, market and distribute evolutionary racism and imperial power on a hitherto unimagined scale. In the process, the Victorian middle-class home became a space for the display of imperial spectacle and the reinvention of race, while the colonies – in particular Africa – became a theatre for exhibiting the Victorian cult of domesticity and the reinvention of gender.

The cult of domesticity became indispensable to the consolidation of British imperial identity – contradictory and conflictual as that was. At the same time, imperialism gave significant shape to the development of Victorian domesticity and the historic separation of the private and public. An intricate dialectic emerged: the Victorian invention of domesticity took shape around colonialism and the idea of race. At the same time, colonialism took shape around the Victorian invention of domesticity and the idea of the home.[1] Through the mediation of commodity spectacle, domestic space became racialized, while colonial space became domesticated.[2] The mass marketing of empire as a system of images became inextricably wedded to the reinvention of domesticity, so that the cultural history of imperialism cannot be understood without a theory of domestic space and gender power.

COMMODITY RACISM AND THE SOAP CULT

At the beginning of the nineteenth century, soap was a scarce and humdrum item and washing a cursory activity at best. A few decades later, the manufacture of soap had burgeoned into an imperial commerce. Victorian cleaning rituals were vaunted as the God-given sign of Britain's evolutionary superiority and soap had become invested with magic, fetish powers. The soap saga captured the hidden affinity between domesticity and empire and embodied a triangulated crisis in value: the undervaluation of women's work in the domestic realm; the overvaluation of the commodity in the industrial market; and the disavowal of colonized economies in the arena of empire. Soap entered the realm of Victorian fetishism with spectacular effect, notwithstanding the fact that male Victorians promoted soap as the very icon of non-fetishistic rationality.

Both the cult of domesticity and the new imperialism found in soap an exemplary mediating form. The emergent middle-class values – monogamy ('clean' sex which has value), industrial capital ('clean' money which has value), Christianity ('being washed in the blood of the lamb'), class control ('cleansing the great unwashed'), and the imperial civilizing mission ('washing and clothing the savage') – could all be marvellously embodied in a single household commodity. Soap advertising, in particular the Pears' Soap campaign, took its place at the vanguard of Britain's new commodity culture and its civilizing mission.

In the eighteenth century, the commodity was little more than a mundane object to be bought and used – in Marx's words, 'a trivial thing'.[3] By the late nineteenth century, however, the commodity had taken its privileged place, not only as the fundamental form of a new industrial economy, but also as the fundamental form of a new cultural system for representing social value.[4] Banks and stock exchanges rose up to manage the bonanzas of imperial capital. Professions emerged to administer the goods tumbling hectically from the manufactures. Middle-class domestic space became crammed, as never before, with furniture, clocks, mirrors, paintings, stuffed animals, ornaments, guns and a myriad gewgaws and knick-knacks. Victorian novelists bore witness to the strange spawning of commodities that seemed to have lives of their own. Meanwhile huge ships lumbered with trifles and trinkets, plied their trade between the colonial markets of Africa, the East, and the Americas.[5]

The new economy created an uproar, not only of things, but of signs. As Thomas Richards has argued, if all these new commodities were to be managed, a unified system of cultural representation had to be found. Richards shows how in 1851 the Great Exhibition of Things at the Crystal Palace served as a monument to a new form of consumption: 'What the first Exhibition heralded so intimately was the complete transformation of collective and private life into a space for the spectacular exhibition of commodities.'[6] As a 'semiotic laboratory for the labour theory of value', the Great Exhibition showed once and for all that the capitalist system not only had created a dominant form of exchange, but was also in the process of creating a dominant form of representation to go with it: the voyeuristic panorama of surplus as spectacle. By exhibiting commodities not only as goods, but also as an organized system of images, the Great Exhibition helped to fashion 'a new kind of being, the consumer, and a new kind of ideology, consumerism'. The mass consumption of the commodity spectacle was born.

Victorian advertising reveals a paradox, however. As the cultural form entrusted with upholding and marketing abroad the middle-class distinctions between private and public and between paid work and unpaid work, advertising also from the outset began to confound those distinctions. Advertising took the intimate signs of domesticity (children bathing, men shaving, women laced into corsets, maids delivering nightcaps) into the public realm, plastering scenes of domesticity on walls, buses, shopfronts and billboards. At the same time, advertising took scenes of empire into every corner of the home, stamping images of colonial conquest on soap boxes, match boxes, biscuit tins, whiskey bottles, tea tins and chocolate bars. By trafficking promiscuously across the threshold of private and public, advertising began to subvert some of the fundamental distinctions that commodity capital was bringing into being.

From the outset, moreover, Victorian advertising took explicit shape around the reinvention of racial difference. Commodity kitsch made possible, as never before, the mass marketing of empire as an organized system of images and attitudes. Soap flourished not only because it created and filled a spectacular gap in the domestic market, but also because, as a cheap and portable domestic commodity, it could persuasively mediate the Victorian poetics of racial hygiene and imperial progress.

Commodity racism became distinct from scientific racism in its capacity to expand beyond the literate propertied elite through the marketing of commodity spectacle. If, after the 1850s, scientific racism saturated anthropological, scientific and medical journals, travel writing and novels, these cultural forms were still relatively class-bound and inaccessible to most Victorians, who had neither the means nor the education to read such material. Imperial kitsch as consumer *spectacle*, by contrast, could package, market and distribute evolutionary racism on a hitherto unimagined scale. No pre-existing form of organized racism had ever before been able to reach so large and so differentiated a mass of the populace. Thus, as domestic commodities were mass-marketed through their appeal to imperial jingoism, commodity jingoism itself helped reinvent and maintain British national unity in the face of deepening imperial competition and colonial resistance. The cult of domesticity became indispensable to the consolidation of British national identity, and at the centre of the domestic cult stood the simple bar of soap.[7]

Yet soap has no social history. Since it purportedly belongs in the female realm of domesticity, soap is figured as beyond history and beyond politics proper.[8] To begin to write a social history of soap, then, is to refuse, in part, the erasure of women's domestic value under imperial capitalism. It cannot be forgotten, moreover, that the history of Victorian attempts to impose their commodity economy on African cultures was also the history of diverse African attempts either to refuse, appropriate, or negotiate European commodity fetishism to suit their own needs. The story of soap reveals that fetishism, far from being a quintessentially African propensity, as nineteenth-century anthropology maintained, was central to industrial modernity, inhabiting and mediating the uncertain threshold zones between domesticity and industry, metropolis and empire.

EMPIRE OF THE HOME: RACIALIZING DOMESTICITY

Before the late nineteenth century, washing was done in most households only once or twice a year in great, communal binges, usually in public at streams or rivers.[9] As for body washing, not much had changed since the days when Queen Elizabeth I was distinguished by the frequency with which she washed: 'regularly every month whether she needed it or not'.[10] By the 1890s, however, soap sales had soared, Victorians were consuming 260,000 tons of soap a year, and advertising had emerged as the central cultural form of commodity capitalism.[11]

The initial impetus for soap advertising came from the realm of empire. For Britain, economic competition with the United States and Germany created the need for a more aggressive promotion of products, and led to the first real innovations in advertising. In 1884, the year of the Berlin Conference, the first wrapped soap was sold under a brand name. This small event signified a major transformation in capital, as imperial competition gave rise to the creation of monopolies. Henceforth, items formerly indistinguishable from each other (soap sold simply as soap) would be marketed by their corporate signature (Pears', Monkey Brand, etc.). Soap became one of the first commodities to register the historic shift from a myriad small businesses to the great imperial monopolies. In the 1870s, hundreds of small soap companies plied the new trade in hygiene, but by the end of the century, the trade was monopolized by ten large companies.

In order to manage the great soap show, an aggressively entrepreneurial breed of advertisers emerged, dedicated to gracing their small, homely product with a radiant halo of imperial glamour and racial potency. The advertising agent, like the bureaucrat, played a vital role in the imperial expansion of foreign trade. Advertisers billed themselves as 'empire builders', and flattered themselves with 'the responsibility of the historic imperial mission'. Said one: 'Commerce even more than sentiment binds the ocean sundered portions of empire together. Anyone who increases these commercial interests strengthens the whole fabric of the empire.'[12] Soap was credited not only with bringing moral and economic salvation to the lives of Britain's 'great unwashed', but also with magically embodying the spiritual ingredient of the imperial mission itself.

In an ad for Pears', for example, a black and implicitly racialized coal-sweeper holds in his hands a glowing, occult object. Luminous with its own inner radiance, the simple soap-bar glows like a fetish, pulsating magically with spiritual enlightenment and imperial grandeur, promising to warm the hands and hearts of working people across the globe.[13] Pears', in particular, became intimately associated with a purified nature, magically cleansed of polluting industry (tumbling kittens, faithful dogs, children festooned with flowers), and a purified working-class, magically cleansed of polluting labour (smiling servants in crisp white aprons, rosy-cheeked match-girls and scrubbed scullions).[14]

None the less, the Victorian obsession with cotton and cleanliness was not simply a mechanical reflex of economic surplus. If imperialism garnered a bounty of cheap cotton and soap oils from coerced colonial labour, the middle-class Victorian fascination with clean white bodies and clean white clothing stemmed not only from the rampant profiteering of the imperial economy, but also from the unbidden realms of ritual and fetish.

Soap did not flourish when imperial ebullience was at its peak. It emerged commercially during an era of impending crisis and social calamity, serving to preserve, through fetish ritual, the uncertain boundaries of class, gender and race identity in a world felt to be threatened by the fetid effluvia of the slums, the belching smoke of industry, social agitation, economic upheaval, imperial competition and anti-colonial resistance. Soap offered the promise of spiritual salvation and regeneration through commodity consumption, a regime of domestic hygiene that could restore the threatened potency of the imperial body politic and the race.

Four fetishes recur ritualistically in soap advertising: soap itself; white clothing (especially aprons); mirrors; and monkeys. A typical Pears' advertisement figures a black child and a white child together in a bathroom (see Figure [60]2). The Victorian bathroom is the innermost sanctuary of domestic hygiene, and by extension the private temple of public regeneration. The sacrament of soap offers a reformation allegory, whereby the purification of the domestic body becomes a metaphor for the regeneration of the body politic. In this particular ad, a black boy sits in the bath, gazing wide-eyed into the water as if into a foreign element. A white boy, clothed in a white apron – the familiar fetish of domestic purity – bends benevolently over his 'lesser' brother, bestowing upon him the precious talisman of racial progress. The magical fetish of soap promises that the commodity can regenerate the Family of Man by washing from the skin the very stigma of racial and class degeneration.

Soap advertising offers an allegory of imperial 'progress' as spectacle. In this ad, the imperial topos of panoptical time (progress consumed as a spectacle from a privileged point of invisibility) enters the domain of the commodity. In the second frame of this ad, the black child is out of the bath, and the white boy shows him his startled visage in the mirror. The boy's body has become magically white, but his face – for Victorians the seat of rational individuality and self-consciousness – remains stubbornly black. The white child is thereby figured as the agent of history and the male heir to progress, reflecting his lesser brother in the European mirror of self-consciousness. In the Victorian mirror, the black child witnesses his predetermined destiny of imperial metamorphosis, but himself remains a passive, racial hybrid: part black, part white, brought to the brink of civilization by the twin commodity fetishes of soap and mirror. The advertisement discloses a crucial element of late Victorian commodity

Figure [60]2: The sacrament of soap: racializing domesticity.

culture: the metaphoric transformation of *imperial time* into *consumer space* – imperial progress consumed, at a glance, as domestic spectacle.

[...]

DOMESTICATING EMPIRE

By the end of the century, a stream of imperial bric-à-brac had invaded Victorian homes. Colonial heroes and colonial scenes emblazoned a host of domestic commodities, from milk cartons to sauce bottles, tobacco tins to whiskey bottles, assorted biscuits to toothpaste, toffee boxes to baking powder.[15] Traditional *national* fetishes, such as the Union Jack, Britannia, John Bull and the rampant lion, were marshalled into a revamped celebration of *imperial* spectacle. Empire was seen to be patriotically defended by Ironclad Porpoise Bootlaces and Sons of the Empire Soap, while Stanley came to the rescue of the Emin of Pasha laden with outsize boxes of Huntley and Palmers Biscuits.

Late Victorian advertising presented a vista of the colonies as conquered by domestic commodities.[16] In the flickering magic lantern of imperial desire, teas, biscuits, tobaccos, Bovril, tins of cocoa and, above all, soaps beach themselves on far-flung shores, tramp through jungles, quell uprisings, restore order and write the inevitable legend of commercial progress across the colonial landscape. In a Huntley and Palmers' Biscuits ad, a group of male colonials sit in the middle of a jungle on biscuit crates, sipping tea. Towards them, a stately and

Figure [60]3: The myth of the first contact with the conquering commodity.

seemingly endless procession of elephants, laden with more biscuits and colonials, brings tea-time to the heart of the jungle. The serving attendant in this ad, as in most others, is male. Two things happen: women vanish from the *Boy's Own* affair of empire, while colonized men are feminized by their association with domestic servitude.

Liminal images of oceans, beaches and shorelines recur in cleaning ads of the time. An exemplary ad for Chlorinol Soda Bleach shows three boys in a soda-box sailing in a phantasmic ocean bathed by the radiance of the imperial dawn (Figure [60]4). In a scene washed in the red, white and blue of the Union Jack, two black boys proudly hold aloft their boxes of Chlorinol. A third boy, the familiar racial hybrid of cleaning ads, has presumably already applied his bleach, for his skin is blanched an eerie white. On red sails that repeat the red of the bleach box, the legend of black people's purported commercial redemption in the arena of empire reads: 'We are Going to Use "Chlorinol" and be like De White Nigger'.

The ad vividly exemplifies Marx's lesson that the mystique of the commodity fetish lies not in its use value, but in its exchange value and its potency as a sign: 'So far as [the commodity] is a value in use, there is nothing mysterious about it'. For three naked children, clothing bleach is less than useful. Instead, the whitening agent of bleach promises an alchemy of racial upliftment through historic contact with commodity culture. The transforming power of the civilizing

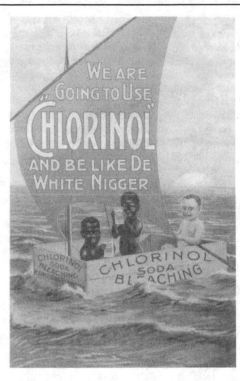

Figure [60]4: Panoptical
time: imperial progress
consumed at a glance

mission is stamped on the boat-box's sails as the objective character of the
commodity itself. More than merely a *symbol* of imperial progress, the domestic
commodity becomes the *agent of* history itself. The commodity, abstracted from
social context and human labour, does the civilizing work of empire, while
radical change is figured as magic, without process or social agency. In this way,
cleaning ads such as Chlorinol's foreshadow the 'before and after' beauty ads of
the twentieth century: a crucial genre directed largely at women, in which the
conjuring power of the product to alchemize change is all that lies between the
temporal 'before and after' of women's bodily transformation.

The Chlorinol ad displays a racial and gendered division of labour. Imperial
progress from black child to 'white nigger' is consumed as commodity spectacle
– panoptical time. The self-satisfied, hybrid 'white nigger' literally holds the
rudder of history and directs social change, while the dawning of civilization
bathes his enlightened brow with radiance. The black children simply have
exhibition value as potential consumers of the commodity, there only to uphold
the promise of capitalist commerce and to represent how far the white child has
evolved – in the iconography of Victorian racism, the condition of 'savagery' is
identical to the condition of infancy. Like white women, Africans (both women
and men) are figured not as historic agents, but as frames for the commodity, for
their *exhibition* value alone. The working-women, both black and white, who
spend vast amounts of energy bleaching the white sheets, shirts, frills, aprons,

cuffs and collars of imperial clothes are nowhere to be seen. It is important to note that in Victorian advertising, black women are very seldom rendered as consumers of commodities, for, in imperial lore, they lag too far behind men to be agents of history.

In the Chlorinol ad, women's creation of social value through household work is displaced on to the commodity as its own power, fetishistically inscribed on the children's bodies as a magical metamorphosis of the flesh. At the same time, military subjugation, cultural coercion and economic thuggery get refigured in such cleaning ads as a benign, domestic process as natural and healthy as washing. The stains of Africa's disobligingly complex and tenacious past and the inconvenience of alternative economic and cultural values are washed away like grime.

Incapable of themselves actually engendering change, African men are figured only as 'mimic men', to borrow V. S. Naipaul's dyspeptic phrase, destined simply to ape the epic white march of progress to self-knowledge. Bereft of the white raiments of imperial godliness, the Chlorinol children appear to take the fetish literally, content to bleach their skins to white. Yet these ads reveal that, far from being a quintessentially African propensity, the faith in fetishism was a faith fundamental to imperial capitalism itself.

By the turn of the century, soap ads vividly embodied the hope that the commodity alone, independent of its use value, could convert other cultures to civilization. Soap ads also embody what can be called *the myth of first contact*: the hope of capturing, as spectacle, the pristine moment of originary contact fixed forever in the timeless surface of the image. In another Pears' ad, a black man stands alone on a beach, examining a bar of soap he has picked from a crate washed ashore from a shipwreck. The ad announces nothing less than the 'The Birth of Civilization'. Civilization is born, the image implies, at the moment of first contact with the Western commodity. Simply by touching the magical object, African man is inspired into history. An epic metamorphosis takes place, as Man the Hunter-gather (anachronistic man) evolves instantly into Man the Consumer. At the same time, the magical object effects a *gender* transformation, for the consumption of the domestic soap is racialized as a male birthing ritual with the egg-shaped commodity as the fertile talisman of change. Since women cannot be recognized as agents of history, it is necessary that a man, not a woman, be the historic beneficiary of the magical cargo, and that the male birthing occur on the beach, not in the home.[17]

In keeping with the racist iconography of the gender degeneration of colonized men, the man is subtly feminized by his role as historic specimen on display. His jaunty feather displays what Victorians liked to believe was colonized men's fetishistic, feminine and lower-class predilection for decorating their bodies. Thomas Carlyle, in his prolonged cogitation on clothes, *Sartor Resartus*, notes, for example: 'The first spiritual want of a barbarous man is Decoration, an instinct we still see amongst the barbarous classes in civilized nations.'[18] Feminists have explored how, in the iconography of modernity, women's bodies are exhibited for visual consumption, but very little has been said about how, in imperial iconography, black men were figured as spectacles for commodity exhibition. If, in scenes set in the Victorian home, female servants are *racialized* and portrayed as frames for the exhibition of the commodity, in advertising scenes set in the colonies, colonized men are *feminized* and portrayed as exhibition frames for commodity display. Black women, by contrast, are rendered virtually invisible. Essentialist assumptions about a universal 'male gaze' require a great deal more historical complication.

Marx notes how under capitalism 'the exchange value of a commodity assumes an independent existence'. Towards the end of the nineteenth century, in many ads, the commodity itself disappears, and the corporate signature, as the embodiment of pure exchange value in monopoly capital, finds its independent existence. Another ad for Pears' features a group of dishevelled Sudanese 'dervishes' awestruck by a white legend carved on the mountain face: PEARS' SOAP IS THE BEST (Figure [60]5). The significance of the ad, as Richards notes, is its representation of the commodity as a magic medium capable of enforcing and enlarging British power in the colonial world without the rational understanding of the mesmerized Sudanese.[19] What the ad more properly reveals is the colonials' own fetishistic faith in the magic of brand-names to work the causal power of empire. In a similar ad, the letters BOVRIL

Figure [60]5: The commodity signature as colonial fetish.

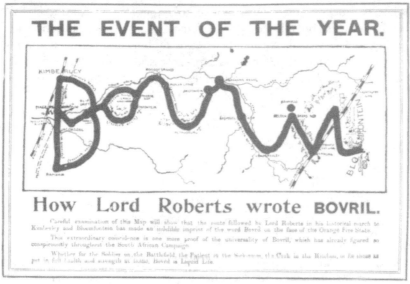

Figure [60]6: 'As if writ by nature.'

march boldly over a colonial map of South Africa – imperial progress consumed as spectacle (Figure [60.6]). In an inspired promotional idea, the word BOVRIL was recognized as tracing the military advance of Lord Roberts across the country, yoking together, as if writ by nature, the simultaneous lessons of colonial domination and commodity progress. In this ad, the colonial map enters the realm of commodity spectacle.

The poetics of cleanliness is a poetics of social discipline. Purification rituals prepare the body as a terrain of meaning, organizing flows of value across the self and the community, and demarcating boundaries between one community and another. Purification rituals, however, can also be regimes of violence and constraint. People who have the power to invalidate the boundary rituals of another people demonstrate thereby their capacity to impose violently their culture on others. Colonial travel writers, traders, missionaries and bureaucrats carped constantly at the supposed absence in African culture of 'proper domestic life', in particular Africans' purported lack of 'hygiene'.[20] But the invention of Africans as 'dirty' and 'undomesticated', far from being an accurate depiction of African cultures, served to legitimize the imperialists' violent enforcement of their cultural and economic values, with the intent of purifying and thereby subjugating the 'unclean' African body, and imposing market and cultural values more useful to the mercantile and imperial economy. The myth of imperial commodities beaching on native shores, there to be welcomed by awestruck natives, wipes from memory the long and intricate history of European commercial trade with Africans and the long and intricate history of African resistance to Europe. Domestic ritual became a technology of discipline and dispossession.

What is crucial, however, is not simply the formal contradictions that structure fetishes, but also the more demanding historical question of how certain groups succeed, through coercion or hegemony, in containing the ambivalence that fetishism embodies, by successfully imposing their economic and cultural system on others.[21] This does not mean that the contradictions are permanently resolved, nor that they cannot be used against the colonials themselves. None the less, it seems crucial to recognize that what has been vaunted by some as the permanent 'undecidability' of cultural signs can also be rendered violently decisive by superior force or hegemonic dominion.

[...]

NOTES

I explore this complex dialectic of race, class and gender in more detail in *Imperial Leather. Race, Gender and Sexuality in the Colonial Contest*, New York and London, Routledge, 1994.

1. See Jean and John L. Comaroff, 'Home-made hegemony: modernity, domesticity and colonialism in South Africa', in Karen Tranberg Hansen (ed.), *African Encounters with Domesticity*. New Brunswick, Rutgers University Press, 1992, pp. 37–74.
2. Commodity spectacle, though hugely influential, was not the only cultural form for the meditation of this dialectic. Travel writing, novels, postcards, photographs, pornography and other cultural forms can be as fruitfully investigated for the relation between domesticity and empire. I focus on commodity spectacle since its extensive reach beyond the literate and propertied elite gave imperial domesticity particularly far-reaching clout.
3. Karl Marx, 'Commodity fetishism', *Capital*, vol 1. Quoted in Thomas Richards, *The Commodity Culture of Victorian Britain. Advertising and Spectacle 1851–1914*, London, Verso, 1990.
4. See Richards' excellent analysis, especially the Introduction and Chapter 1.
5. See David Simpson's analysis of novelistic fetishism in *Fetishism and Imagination. Dickens, Melville, Conrad*, Baltimore, Johns Hopkins University Press, 1982.
6. Richards, op. cit., p. 72.
7. In 1889, an ad for Sunlight Soap featured the feminized figure of British nationalism, Britannia, standing on a hill and showing P. T. Barnum, the famous circus manager and impresario of the commodity spectacle, a huge Sunlight Soap factory stretched out below them. Britannia proudly proclaims the manufacture of Sunlight Soap to be: 'The Greatest Show On Earth'. See Jennifer Wicke's excellent analysis of P. T. Barnum in *Advertising Fictions: Literature, Advertisement and Social Reading*, New York, Columbia University Press, 1988.
8. See Timothy Burke, 'Nyamarira that I loved: commoditization, consumption and the social history of soap in Zimbabwe', in *The Societies of Southern Africa in the 19th and 20th Centuries*, Collected Seminar Papers, no. 42, vol. 17, Institute of Commonwealth Studies, University of London, 1992, pp. 195–216.
9. Leonore Davidoff and Catherine Hall, *Family Fortunes, Men and Women of the English Middle Class*, London, Routledge, 1992.
10. David T. A. Lindsey and Geoffrey C. Bamber, *Soap-Making. Past and Present. 1876–1976*, Nottingham, Gerard Brothers Ltd.
11. Ibid., p. 38. Just how deeply the relation between soap and advertising became embedded in popular memory is expressed in words such as 'soft-soap' and 'soap-opera'.
12. Quoted in Diana and Geoffrey Hindley, *Advertising In Victorian England 1837–1901*, London, Wayland, 1972, p. 117.

13. Mike Dempsey (ed.), *Bubbles. Early Advertising Art from A. & F. Pears Ltd*, London, Fontana, 1978.

14. Laurel Bradley, 'From Eden to Empire. John Everett Millais' Cherry Ripe', *Victorian Studies*, Winter 1991, vol. 34, no. 2.

15. During the Anglo–Boer war, Britain's fighting forces were seen as valiantly fortified by Johnston's Corn Flour, Pattisons' Whiskey and Frye's Milk Chocolate. See Robert Opie, *Trading on the British Image*, Harmondsworth, Penguin Books, 1985, for a collection of advertising images.

16. In a brilliant chapter, Richards explores how the explorer and travel writer, Henry Morton Stanley's conviction that he had a mission to civilize Africans by teaching them the value of commodities, 'reveals the major role that imperialists ascribed to the commodity in propelling and justifying the scramble for Africa', in T. Richards, *The Commodity Culture of Victorian Britain*, London, Verso, 1990, p. 123.

17. As Richards notes: 'A hundred years earlier the ship offshore would have been preparing to enslave the African bodily as an object of exchange; here the object is rather to incorporate him into the orbit of exchange. In either case, this liminal moment posits that capitalism is dependent on a noncapitalist world, for only by sending commodities into liminal areas where, presumably, their value will not be appreciated at first can the endemic overproduction of the capitalist system continue.' Ibid., p. 140.

18. Thomas Carlyle, *The Works Of Thomas Carlyle*, The Centenary Edition, 30 vols, London, Chapman and Hall, 1896–99, p. 30.

19. Richards, op. cit., pp. 122–3.

20. But palm-oil soaps had been made and used for centuries in West and equatorial Africa. In *Travels in West Africa*, Mary Kingsley records the custom of digging deep baths in the earth, filling them with boiling water and fragrant herbs, and luxuriating under soothing packs of wet clay. In southern Africa, soap from oils was not much used, but clays, saps and barks were processed as cosmetics, and shrubs known as 'soap bushes' were used for cleansing. Male Tswana activities like hunting and war were elaborately prepared for and governed by taboo. 'In each case,' as Jean and John Comaroff write, 'the participants met beyond the boundaries of the village, dressed and armed for the fray, and were subjected to careful ritual washing (go foka marumo).' Jean and John Comaroff, *Of Revelation and Revolution. Christianity, Colonialism and Consciousness in South Africa*, vol. 1, Chicago, University of Chicago Press, 1991. In general, people creamed, glossed and sheened their bodies with a variety of oils, ruddy ochres, animal fats and fine coloured clays.

21. For an exploration of colonial hegemony in Southern Africa, see Jean and John Comaroff, op. cit.

61

DISCRIMINATING OR DUPED? YOUNG PEOPLE AS CONSUMERS OF ADVERTISING/ART

Mica Nava and Orson Nava

This chapter is based on research commissioned by Paul Willis in his capacity as director of the Gulbenkian Enquiry into Arts and Cultural Provision for Young People. It is drawn on, as are similarly commissioned investigations by other authors, in Willis' final report *Common Culture* (1990). The Enquiry was prompted in the first instance by the recognition 'that most young people see the arts as remote and institutional, not part of everyday life. Art is what they are forced to do at school ... the preserve of art galleries, theatres and concert halls' which they do not attend. The project of the Enquiry was therefore to explore the wide range of cultural forms and symbolic expressions through which young people establish their identities, the ways in which they consume and invest with meaning the practices and spaces that surround them. 'The Enquiry sets out to investigate creativity wherever it is and whatever its forms' (Willis, 1988: 1).

It is in the context of these terms of reference that the following arguments about young people, advertising and art must be understood.

An interesting TV commercial made by the agency Ogilvy and Mather was shown on Channel 4 each Sunday during the spring of 1988. Entitled *Chair*, its object was to promote the agency's own advertising services to potential 'marketing decision makers'. The advert opens with a shot of a modern young man in a stylish flat watching television. At the commercial break he gets up

From M. Nava, *Changing Cultures: Feminism, Youth and Consumerism* (London: Sage, 1992) pp. 171–82.

and goes to make a cup of tea. For a moment the camera focuses on the empty chair and the abandoned TV set. Then it cuts to the kitchen but we can still hear the noise of the ads coming from the unwatched television. The young man returns to his chair with his cup of tea just as the commercial break ends. Over the final frame a voiceover informs us that there are 600 commercials on TV every day; 'what's so special about yours?' it enquires of the potential advertisers among us.

As the press release for Ogilvy and Mather states, 'The film confronts the viewer with the question of whether or not people pay attention to commercial breaks.' At the same time it conveys another message. It represents young people as discriminating and hard to reach and suggests that they are likely to ignore all but the most challenging and entertaining commercials. This view of young people is one which is increasingly prevalent among advertisers and their clients and was frequently expressed to us in interview. Articles in trade magazines like *Campaign*, research conducted by advertising agencies like the *McCann-Erickson Youth Study*, advertisements themselves, and a spate of recent conferences organized for marketeers about the difficulties of targeting and persuading contemporary youth are further evidence of this growing preoccupation (Nava, 1988). Within the world of advertising today, concern is regularly expressed about how to reach young people (since they watch less TV than any other age group, even the under-fours) and how to persuade and gratify them, given what is referred to in the trade (and is illustrated in the Ogilvy and Mather ad) as their high level of 'televisual literacy'. Bartle Bogle Hegarty, the agency responsible for the Levi ads, have put it thus: 'Young consumers are sophisticated, video literate and acutely sensitive to being patronised. They pick up clues and covert messages quicker than you would believe.'

This image of young people and advertising is not, however, the one that circulates most frequently. The way in which advertising and consumerism are generally viewed today (although challenged by, for example, Myers, 1986; Nava, 1987) remains deeply influenced by the work of cultural theorists of the 1950s and 1960s such as Vance Packard, who argues in his seminal book *The Hidden Persuaders* (1981, first published in 1957) that people are 'influenced and manipulated [by advertisers] far more than we realize. ... Large scale efforts are being made, often with impressive success, to channel our ... habits, our purchasing decisions and our thought processes' (1981: 11). For Herbert Marcuse (1964) one of the most influential thinkers of the Left in this sphere, advertising – as an inherent aspect of consumer capitalism and its pursuit of profit – is capable not only of convincing us to buy, but of creating false needs, of indoctrinating us into social conformity and thus ultimately of suppressing political opposition. More recently, commentators of both the Left and Right who have been preoccupied by what they consider to be a decline in moral standards (see for example the work of Jeremy Seabrook on the one hand and statements issued by Mary Whitehouse on the other) as well as more academic analysts of advertising (Dyer, 1982) have been concerned to establish the effects of a constant diet of television programmes and commercials, particularly on young viewers who are considered to be those most at risk of being corrupted and duped by entreaties to buy.

Given the pervasiveness of these debates, it is not surprising that certain ideas have now become part of received wisdom, a commonsense way of viewing the world. Thus we have a context in which the question of television advertising and youth is likely to conjure up images of undereducated un-discriminating and undisciplined young people who are addicted to TV and who mindlessly imbibe the advertisers' messages along with the materialist values of the consumer society. Characteristic of this view is the notion that there exists a simple cause and effect relationship between advertising and the purchasing of commodities. It is not only assumed that advertisements work but that the young are more likely than any other sector of the population to be taken in by the psychologically informed scheming of the marketeers. Youth are considered to be more vulnerable, more gullible and more inclined to be persuaded to buy totally useless things.

Significantly and interestingly, this is a far more demeaning view of youth than that held by the advertisers themselves. As has already been indicated, the British advertising industry is highly respectful of the critical skills and visual literacy of young people. Indeed, as emerges clearly from our research, no other age group is considered as discriminating, cynical and resistant to the 'hard sell'. Furthermore, no other group is as astute at decoding the complex messages, cross-references and visual jokes of current advertising (except perhaps the industry itself). These critical skills are untutored and seem to arise out of an unprecedented intimacy with the cultural form of the television commercial. No other generation has been so imbued with the meanings produced by quick edits, long shots, zooms, by particular lighting codes and combinations of sound. The young have a unique mastery of the grammar of the commercial; one might say that they have an intuitive grasp of the visual equivalent of the semicolon. This is the case even where, as one bemused advertiser put it, 'they are not very intellectually clever'.

Advertisers work hard to capture this discerning audience and to win its esteem. Indeed many ads appear to utilize the codes that are most likely to appeal to that sector of the population with the most developed analytical skills – that is, the young – regardless of the suitability of the product for this kind of treatment. The British Telecom commercial about the unfortunate Jewish grandson who managed to pass only his pottery and sociology exams, which emerged as the preferred ad in a small-scale survey of young people, is an example of this. In return, young people will watch and rewatch the commercials they consider successful. The tea will wait (or will be made by someone else) while judgement is exercised. Favourite ads will be recorded and viewed again with friends. Phrases will be selected and replayed. Comparisons and connections will be made, messages identified and effectivity assessed. Repetition and familiarity might enhance the rating of some commercials (for example the celebrated Levi Strauss Launderette ad) but others will not survive such close scrutiny. They will be taped over and forgotten.

It is not only 'youth' (fourteen to twenty-four-year-olds) who watch and enjoy TV ads in this way. Research carried out by the Association of Market Survey Organizations indicates that commercials also come high on the list of younger children's preferred television viewing. Favourite ads among those in the six to fourteen-year-old category include Carling's Black Label, Anchor Butter's dancing cows and Mates condoms. They too like advertisements promoting items which they are unlikely to buy.

What emerges quite clearly from this picture is that young people consume commercials independently of the product that is being marketed. Commercials are cultural products in themselves and are consumed for themselves. The success of any particular commercial is, in this respect, completely divorced from its effectivity in promoting sales. Evaluations are made on the basis of criteria which are indistinguishable from those employed in the appreciation of other cultural forms. Our argument therefore is twofold: an analysis of the mode in which the commercial is consumed not only gives us insight into the cultural skills of young people, it also radically interrogates conventional divisions between art and advertising.

[...]

Among the technologies and forms which have been requisitioned by the makers of advertisements since the turn of the century are painting, photography, cinema, graphics, animation, pop music, video promos and video scratch. Examples are numerous: Dada and surrealism have been used in cigarette advertising; Michelangelo's drawings have been used by Parker pens. As John Berger pointed out in *Ways of Seeing* (1972), publicity regularly quotes from works of art. Of the popular cultural forms, hip hop and rapping have most recently been in vogue. More critical avant-garde forms like video scratch are also increasingly drawn on, though not always with much understanding. On the whole, however, what is interesting is that these techniques are not only appropriated and 'quoted', they are also developed (this is particularly so for photography, graphics and animation) in the innovative and generously funded climate of advertising today.

At the level of ideas we see that advertisements not only draw specific narratives and images from the other forms, and parody them, they increasingly cross-reference each other. In this sense they constitute the classic postmodernist form (if such a thing exists) wherein boundaries between forms and between their high and popular versions are effaced (Jameson, 1985). Works of art, despite ideologies to the contrary, have always been derivative; in so far as they make use of existing technologies, artistic conventions and archetypal themes, they are collaborative projects. In advertising, however, this process of the appropriation and reworking of ideas and motifs already in the public domain is not only not concealed, it is celebrated. Pastiche is increasingly becoming an integral part of the form.

References are made to different genres of cinema. The Pirelli Tyre ad is a miniature *film noir*, complete with murder plot, *femme fatale* and moody lighting. Carling Black Label has made an ad for its lager which references the cinematic preoccupation with Vietnam yet also appears to be a critique of war films and traditional masculinity: the hero is an intellectual and a refusenik – an inversion of the archetypal Rambo figure. Barclays Bank has made use of the style and images of *Blade Runner* as well as its director, Ridley Scott. The Holsten Pils advertisements are famous for taking quotations from old movies and incorporating them into their own narratives; thus we witness an unlikely encounter in the ladies washroom between Griff Rhys Jones and Marilyn Monroe.

Cross-referencing between ads occurs frequently, particularly where an ad has been successful. In its recent campaign Carling Black Label has made parodic references of this kind its trademark, hence its detailed and witty re-enactment – even the same extras are used – of the famous Levi's Launderette ad, which itself draws on images from 1950s youth movies. In the same vein Carling Black Label references an Old Spice commercial in its ad about a surfer riding a wave into a pub. Another example of an obscure and in this case more laboured reference occurs in a Wrangler ad where the hero puts on a pair of jeans and drives a double-decker bus across a row of parked motorbikes. This is a very coded allusion to Eddie Kidd, star of a 1987 ad for Black Levi 501s, who as a real-life stunt man in the 1970s held the world record for jumping his motorbike across parked double-decker buses.

The fusion of the commercial with other cultural forms is exemplified in an interesting way by a 1988 Independent Broadcasting Authority ruling on an ad for Pepe jeans. This was banned from appearing either immediately before or immediately after a normal programme because stylistically it looked more like a TV drama than a commercial and might delude people about its status. Influences operate in both directions. *Network 7*, for example, a now defunct Channel 4 programme for young people, developed a style of editing and presentation which owed a great deal to television advertising. The employment of cinema and TV actors in commercials also contributes to this merger of forms; not only do such actors draw on theatrical skills and conventions which are then subsumed into the commercial form, they also carry with them their theatrical identities which then work to enhance selected meanings.

[...]

At the level of behind-the-camera personnel there has in recent years been an escalating rate of crossover between commercials and cinema and TV. For some time now directors have been cutting their teeth on ads and progressing thereafter – where possible – to bigger things, even to Hollywood. Alan Parker, Ridley Scott and Tony Scott are examples of these. More recently, however, the movement has been in the other direction and already established cinema and television directors from a range of political and stylistic backgrounds have been recruited to direct commercials. Thus Ken Russell, director of *Crimes of Passion*, made an ad for Shredded Wheat; Peter Greenaway (*Draughtman's Contract*) and Stephen Frears (*My Beautiful Launderette*) have both directed commercials in the last few years. Ken Loach (*Kes*) made the award-winning ad for *The Guardian* in which the skinhead saves a passer-by from falling scaffolding, and John Amiel (*The Singing Detective*) and Nic Roeg (*Bad Timing*) made two of the government AIDS warnings. Amiel has described the condensed quintessential dramas currently being made for British advertisers by himself and other established directors as 'little haikus' (Rusbridger, 1988). They exist and are recognized as autonomous creations.

[...]

Here we must return to young people. How do youth fit into this analysis of the commercial as (at its best) an increasingly innovative and sophisticated cultural form – as 'art'? What has the relationship of young people been to this redefinition? Is it possible to argue that, as audience, they have contributed to the complexity, elegance and wit of some contemporary television commercials?

In order to unravel and respond to these questions it is necessary to investigate in a little more detail the current state of advertising and marketing theory and practice. What has emerged quite clearly in recent years, concurrently with the refinements in form, is that advertisers no longer have confidence in the old theories about how ads promote sales. This view was frequently confirmed in the interviews we conducted with members of the industry and was reiterated in papers delivered by advertisers at a number of conferences we attended.[1] Beliefs in the power of subliminal messages to penetrate and manipulate the mass psyche no longer have currency. Advertisers are now as aware as other cultural producers that there is no formula or scientific method which can guarantee success. Market research has not come up with the answers. Marketing managers cannot precisely identify the components of a successful campaign; they are unable to anticipate what will spark the public imagination; they do not know exactly who their target audience is, nor how to reach it; and, at a more pedestrian level, they do not even know whether an ad is more effective if placed before or after a particular programme. Some go so far as to insist that advertising is hardly effective at all, that what is required is consistent media coverage in order to shift a product. So what we see is that marketing is a far more haphazard process than the intellectual orthodoxies would have us believe. There are no rules. There is no consensus.

These uncertainties do not mean though that the classic objectives of the industry have been abandoned. Advertisers still aim to increase sales for their clients, and to do so they need to take into account the culture and preferences of young people who constitute a significant proportion of the market both in terms of their own disposable income and their influence on friends and family.

They must be recruited, their cynicism must be overcome. Yet in the absence of the confident and clear guidelines of earlier times, how is this to be achieved?

Although the industry continues to be enormously productive, the undermining of old convictions and the growing anxiety about public (youth) cynicism combine to reveal a picture of the advertising process itself in a state of crisis. Indeed the paradox is that the industry's productivity appears to be both a symptom and a cause of its malaise. More numerous and more subtle and sophisticated advertisements have generated more discriminating audiences. As we have already argued, at the forefront of these are the young themselves, whose scepticism and powers of analysis are, in this respect, a great deal more developed than those of older generations. It is through the exercise of these refined critical skills and through the consumption of the ad rather than the product that the young have contributed to the spiralling crisis.

Given the current climate of uncertainty and the lack of clarity about what might be an appropriate response to the crisis, the solution of the marketeers has been to turn to the creative departments within their agencies, to hand over responsibility to individuals largely trained in art schools, who rely not on research and surveys, for which they have little respect, but on imagination, inventiveness and intuition.[2]

Alternatively they have hired film-makers from outside the industry with already established 'artistic' credibility. There is no doubt that the experimental forms produced in this way have had unprecedented success in recruiting and retaining viewers. Above all they have been able to satisfy the gourmet appetites of the discerning young. What emerges quite clearly from this account is that young people, in their capacity as active consumers, have, as Willis (1988) suggests, 'shaped the contours of the commercial culture' which they inhabit. Unlike the young man in the Ogilvy and Mather commercial described at the beginning of this chapter, they do watch the ads. But they do not necessarily buy.

In this chapter we have developed an argument about young people and their relation to contemporary advertising. In order to do this we have used a very undifferentiated model of youth, we have not investigated – or even postulated – distinctions based on class, race or gender because our argument does not require these refinements. Not all youth – and certainly not only youth – read advertisements in the ways in which we (and the advertisers themselves) have argued, though sufficient numbers do to justify our thesis. Our central preoccupation here has been with the consumption of advertising and the skills brought to bear in this process. This has included examining not only transformations in the production of advertisements but also the ways in which historically advertising has been defined. Our argument has been that although ads have in the past been primarily concerned to promote sales, they increasingly offer moments of intellectual stimulation, entertainment and pleasure – of 'art'. To focus on this phenomenon is not to exonerate advertisers and their clients from responsibility in the formation and perpetuation of consumer capitalism. Nor is it to deny totally the influence of advertising in purchasing decisions. Our intention has been to bypass these debates. Instead we recognize the relative autonomy of the ad as product and view it as no more or less inherently implicated in the economic organization of life than any other cultural form. (Advertisements can after all also promote progressive products and causes, like Nicaraguan coffee and the Greater London Council: Myers, 1986.) More importantly, [...] we have emphasized in this chapter the very considerable though untutored skills that young people bring to bear in their appreciation of advertisements and that they exercise individually and collectively, not in museums and public galleries, but in millions of front rooms throughout the country – and indeed the world.

The critical question arising from this is whether or not the possession of such decoding skills by young people, and the revolution in the advertising process itself, can be interpreted as progressive. Debates of this kind have always surrounded new stages in the dissemination of knowledge. Reading the written word was considered a contentious activity in the nineteenth century: some people thought it would serve to discipline and pacify the population while others feared (or hoped) it would prove subversive. Earlier in this century Walter Benjamin (1973, originally published in 1936) claimed that the new technology of film would help to develop in spectators a more acute and critical perception. Film as cultural form was not only more popular and democratic, it was potentially revolutionary. Arguing against this position, Adorno and Horkheimer (1973), condemned the culture industry for what they alleged was its taming both of critical art and the minds of the people. More recently Fredric Jameson (1985) has asked similar questions about the advent of 'postmodernism'. To what extent can postmodern forms be considered oppositional or progressive? Is there a way in which they can resist and contest the logic of consumer capitalism? Our answer must be that the forms alone cannot be subversive, but that the critical tools as well as the pleasures they have generated, and from which they are in any case inseparable, may indeed subvert and fragment existing networks of power-knowledge.

NOTES

1. See for example papers given by Neil Fazakerly, Creative Director at Davidson Pearce, at the Institute of Contemporary Arts 'Talking Ideas' event, July 1988; Winston Fletcher, Chairman of Delaney Fletcher Delaney, at the *Marxism Today* 'New Times' conference, October 1989; and Richard Phillips, Creative Director at J. Walter Thompson at the Forum Communications 'New Wave Young: Targeting the Youth Market' conference, March 1988.
2. See note 1.

REFERENCES

Adorno, Theodor and Horkheimer, Max (1973) *Dialectics of Enlightenment*. London: Allen.
Benjamin, Walter (1973) 'The work of art in the age of mechanical reproduction', in *Illuminations*. London: Fontana. (Originally published in 1936.)

Berger, John (1972) *Ways of Seeing*. Harmondsworth: Penguin.

Dyer, Gillian (1982) *Advertising as Communication*. London: Methuen.

Foster, Hal (1985) *Postermodern Culture*. London: Pluto Press.

Jameson, Fredric (1985) 'Postmodernism and consumer society', in Foster (1985).

Marcuse, H. (1964) *One-Dimensional Man*. Boston: Beacon Press.

Myers, Kathy (1986) *Understains: The Sense and Seduction of Advertising*. London: Comedia.

Nava, Mica (1987) 'Consumerism and its contradictions', *Cultural Studies*, 1/2.

Nava, Mica (1988) 'Targeting the young: what do the marketeers think?' Unpublished paper for the Gulbenkian Enquiry into Young People and the Arts.

Packard, Vance (1981) *The Hidden Persuaders*. Harmondsworth: Penguin. (Originally published in 1957.)

Rusbridger, Alan (1988) 'Ad men discover a fatal attraction', *The Guardian*, 3 March.

Willis, Paul (1988) Unpublished 'Position paper' for the Gulbenkian Enquiry into Arts and Cultural Provision for Young People.

Willis, Paul (1990) *Common Culture*. Milton Keynes: Open University Press.

FURTHER READING

Adorno, T. and Horkheimer, M., 'The Culture Industry: Enlightenment as Mass Deception'. In J. Curran, M. Gurevitch and J. Woollacott (eds), *Mass Communication and Society* (London: Edward Arnold, 1977).

Ang, I., *Desperately Seeking the Audience* (London: Routledge, 1991).

Baehr, H., *Women and Media* (Oxford. Pergamon Press, 1980).

Barthes, R., *Mythologies* (London: Paladin, 1973).

Berger, J., *Ways of Seeing* (Harmondsworth: Penguin, 1972).

Bonney, B. and Wilson, H., *Australia's Commercial Media* (Melbourne: Macmillan, 1983).

Bonney, B. and Wilson, H., 'Advertising and the Manufacture of Difference'. In M. Alvarado and J. O. Thompson (eds), *The Media Reader* (London: BFI, 1990).

Brierley, S., *The Advertising Handbook* (London and New York: Routledge, 1995).

Chapman, S. and Egger, G., 'Myth in Cigarette Advertising and Health Promotion'. In H. Davis and P. Walton (eds), *Language, Image, Media* (Oxford: Blackwell, 1983).

Cook, G., *The Discourse of Advertising* (London: Routledge, 1992).

Corner, J., 'Adworlds'. In Corner, *Television Form and Public Address* (London: Edward Arnold, 1995).

Coward, R., *Female Desire* (London: Paladin, 1984).

Curran, J., 'Capitalism and Control of the Press, 1800–1975'. In J. Curran, M. Gurevitch and J. Woollacott (eds), *Mass Communication and Society* (London: Edward Arnold, 1977).

Curran, J., 'Advertising and the Press'. In J. Curran (ed.), *The British Press ... A Manifesto* (London: Macmillan, 1978).

Curran, J., 'Advertising as a Patronage System'. *Sociological Review Monograph* 29 (1980).

Curran, J. and Seaton, J., *Power without Responsibility: the Press and Broadcasting in Britain*. 4th edition (London: Routledge, 1991).

Davis, H. and Walton, P. (eds), *Language, Image, Media* (Oxford: Blackwell, 1983).

Dyer, G., *Advertising as Communication* (London: Methuen, 1982).

Earnshaw, S., 'Advertising and the Media: the Case of Women's Magazines'. *Media, Culture and Society* 6:4 (1984) pp. 411–21.

Ewen, S., *Captains of Consciousness* (New York: McGraw Hill, 1976).

Ewen, S. and E., *Channels of Desire* (New York: McGraw Hill, 1982).

Fiske, J., *Television Culture* (London: Methuen, 1987).

Fiske, J., *Reading the Popular* (London: Unwin Hyman, 1989).

Fiske, J., *Understanding Popular Culture* (London: Unwin Hyman, 1989).

Goddard, J., 'Editorial'. In M. Alvarado and J. O. Thompson, *The Media Reader* (London: BFI, 1990).

Goffman, E., *Gender Advertisements* (London: Macmillan, 1978).

Goldman, R., *Reading Ads Socially* (London: Routledge, 1992).

Goldman, R. and Papson, S., 'Advertising in the Age of Hypersignification'. *Theory, Culture and Society* 11:3 (1994) pp. 23–53.

Hebdige, D., *Subculture: the Meaning of Style* (London: Methuen, 1979).

Hebdige, D., *Hiding in the Light: On Images and Things* (London: Routledge, 1988).

Inglis, F., *The Imagery of Power* (London: Heinemann, 1972).

Janus, N., 'Advertising and the Mass Media: Transnational Link between Production and Consumption'. *Media, Culture and Society* 3:1 (1981) pp. 13–23.

Jhally, S., *The Codes of Advertising: Fetishism and the Political Economy Of Meaning in the Consumer Society* (London: Routledge, 1990).

Leiss, W., *The Limits to Satisfaction* (London: Marion Boyars, 1978).

Leiss, W., Kline, S. and Jhally, S., *Social Communication in Advertising*. 2nd edition (London: Routledge, 1990).

Mort, F., 'Boy's Own? Masculinity, Style and Popular Culture'. In R. Chapman and J. Rutherford (eds), *Male Order: Unwrapping Masculinity* (London: Lawrence and Wishart).

Myers, K., 'Understanding advertisers'. In H. Davis and P. Walton (eds), *Language, Image, Media* (Oxford: Blackwell, 1983).

Myers, K., *Understains: the Sense and Seduction of Advertising* (London: Comedia, 1986).

Nava, M., *Changing Cultures: Feminism, Youth and Consumerism* (London: Sage, 1992).

Nixon, S., *Hard Looks: Masculinities, Spectatorship and Contemporary Consumption* (London: UCL Press, 1996).

Packard, V., *The Hidden Persuaders* (Harmondsworth: Penguin, 1979).

Pateman, T., 'How is Understanding an Advertisement Possible?'. In H. Davis and P. Walton (eds), *Language, Image, Media* (Oxford: Blackwell, 1983).

Schudson, M., 'Criticizing the Critics of Advertising: Towards a Sociological View of Marketing'. *Media, Culture and Society* 3:1 (1981) pp. 3–12.

Schudson, M., *Advertising: The Uneasy Persuasion* (London: Routledge, 1993).

Sinclair, J., *Images Incorporated: Advertising as Industry and Ideology* (London: Routledge, 1989).

Tomlinson, A. (ed.), *Consumption, Identity and Style: Marketing, Meanings, and the Packaging of Pleasure* (London: Routledge, 1990).

Tuchman, G., Kaplan Daniels, A. and Benet, J. (eds), *Hearth and Home: Images of Women in the Media* (New York: Oxford University Press, 1978).

van Zoonen, L., *Feminist Media Studies* (London: Sage, 1994).

Wernick, A., *Promotional Culture: Advertising, Ideology and Symbolic Expression* (London: Sage, 1991).

Williams, R., *Problems in Materialism and Culture* (London: Verso, 1980).

Williamson, J., *Decoding Advertisements* (London: Marion Boyars, 1978).

Williamson, J., 'Woman Is an Island: Femininity and Colonization'. In T. Modleski (ed.), *Studies in Entertainment: Critical Approaches to Mass Culture* (Bloomington: Indiana University Press, 1986).

Willis, P., *Common Culture* (Milton Keynes: Open University Press, 1990).

Willis, S., *A Primer for Daily Life* (London: Routledge, 1991).
Winship, J., 'Sexuality for Sale'. In S. Hall, D. Hobson, A. Lowe and P. Willis (eds), *Culture, Media, Language* (London: Hutchinson, 1980).

SECTION 8
NEW MEDIA

NEW MEDIA
INTRODUCTION

The employment of the word 'media' in anything approaching its usage in the term 'media studies' emerged in the 1920s, when it came to refer to the various vehicles for advertising. It was then often coupled with the word 'mass'. 'Mass media represents the most economical way of getting the story over the new and wider markets in the least time' wrote one author in 1923 in the book *Advertising and Selling*, for example.[1] For a medium to reach a mass of people it had to be capable of having its message reproduced on a substantial scale, and so 'media' was referring to sophisticated (for their era) technologies for reproducing and/or disseminating symbols, which from the late nineteenth century had been electrically powered. But the evolution of the word in the early twentieth century was not arbitrary; as almost invariably in semantic development, its new use arose from its previous history of meanings and associations. Insofar as the term indicates 'means, instrument, channel', it had long been associated with expressivity: 'But yet is not of necessitie that Cogitations bee expressed by the Medium of words ...' wrote Bacon in his *Advancement of Learning* in 1605. In painting, the 'medium' was the liquid with which the pigments were mixed, so the particularity of the means of expression depended on the medium employed: oil painting, water colour, tempera, etc.

As the twentieth century drew to a close, the 'mass' in the term 'mass media' gradually dropped away. This was partly because of the decreasing currency of the mental model of human community as 'mass society'. The pluralising of the channels of communication, and the associated adjustments in the industry and the academy in thinking about audiences, contributed to – and were reciprocally affected by – changing paradigms of society. In naming fields of study, the study of 'mass communication' has become increasingly displaced by 'media studies' since the 1960s.

The term 'media' in 'media studies' thus brings with it the ideas of: channels of communication; complex technologies of mechanical or electronic reproduction; and means of expression. Since the 1980s there have been accelerating developments in microelectronics, computing, telecommunications and digital software, which have made for new kinds of electronic technologies of reproduction and dissemination, new channels of communication and new means of expression. These are appropriately often referred to as 'new media', and studying their social and cultural role is properly the province of a media studies fitted to comprehend and explain the contemporary.

New media tend to be firstly perceived as technological innovations, and in Chapter 62 Brian Winston asks 'how are media born?' He answers this through a case study in the historiography of the birth of an earlier medium, the cinema, comparing different accounts of its invention. This serves to illustrate his argument against an approach that is implicit or explicit in many people's thinking about technological development, the view that new technologies emerge solely by a logic that is *internal* to science and engineering, unfolded through the agency of great scientists and engineers. This is the 'technological determinist' view in which 'the technology is the dominant, *determining* factor in the process.' Instead, Winston stresses that new media emerge in response to a host of factors in the wider social realm (governmental and political, financial, corporate, cultural), and he calls this approach 'cultural determinist' because he regards this complex of sociocultural factors as the determining causes of the pattern of events. Since the status quo in any situation suits the interests currently prevailing, there are always tendencies resisting the changes that any innovation will bring; this he calls the 'law' of the suppression of radical potential. But for change to be successfully instituted, there must be social interests served by its adoption; this he calls the 'supervening social necessity' that overcomes the anterior 'law'. Thus in the case of the emergence of any new medium into social usage, there are push-pull social factors that promote or hinder its development and adoption, which he says should be seen broadly as 'cultural' determinants.

In a section towards the end of the chapter Winston also draws out the other side of this argument against technological determinism. If the emergence of a technology is determined by a wider set of sociocultural factors, then so too are the subsequent developments in which the technology plays a part. He doesn't wish to argue that the employment of the technology has no consequences, but he wishes to refute a strong technological determinism of the kind Marshall McLuhan espoused (see Chapter 3) in which it is the technologies that fundamentally determine the nature of social life. Much public rhetoric on the new media – from politicians, advertising, corporate representatives and newspaper columnists – contains stronger or weaker variants of technological determinism, and Winston's chapter provides a useful starting point for thinking the issue through for media technologies.

The 1990s witnessed the spectacular emergence of a new computer-based communications network, the Internet with its World Wide Web system of connections. In Chapter 63 Peter Golding discusses the Net from a political economy perspective. He examines the rhetorical claims that have been widely made for it: increasing democracy, empowering citizens through accessible information and educational materials, improving communication amongst the peoples of the world. He is sceptical about these desirable outcomes being achieved as large-scale private interests come to dominate the Net, bringing advertising, e-commerce and commodified entertainment services including pornography. Significantly, he refers to this process as 'mediatisation', meaning a form of communication becoming a 'medium', in which he draws on the 1920s sense with which we started, of media as vehicles for advertising, corporate speech and the sale of audiences' attention. He is aware of similar rhetorics having been deployed previously to extol the promise of earlier communication technologies, promises which proved not to be realised. Again, these rhetorical claims often comprise a version of technological determinism, in which it is implied that the technology alone is sufficient to call forth an array of positive outcomes, whereas in fact only by considering the social, political, cultural and economic factors that determine the way a technology is developed and used can we account for their failure to fulfil the grandiose prognostications.

These are the kinds of factors that Eric Hirsch considers in Chapter 64 when discussing computers in the home. He sees their presence as the current expression of a long line of historical development which has constituted the 'home' in its present form, with its 'project of domestic self-sufficiency'. Integral to this is a system of interconnections between these domestic units and the wider world, embodied in a succession of technologies: the electricity system, the telephone, the radio, television. Hence the importance of the modem in his case study, the device that connects the home computer to a wider network. Hirsch's piece brings together his broad historical overview with case study material drawn from a particular family household in outer London. To some extent, this material is in the tradition of ethnographic 'audience' research in British media studies that was pioneered by David Morley,[2] and pursued by Ann Gray *inter alia* (see Chapter 41), albeit less explicitly gender sensitive (as Hirsch acknowledges). By approaching the microcosm of an individual family's history of relationship with a changing technology of communication through the macro-view of over a century's history of communication technology's role in the constitution of the domestic, Hirsch illuminates some of the wider social meanings of patterns of domestic usage of new media.

Sadie Plant's piece on the Internet (Chapter 65) speaks from within a particular 1990s sub-cultural formation that has been variously called 'techno-culture', 'cyberculture', or in a phrase that she uses, the 'digital underground'. Heralded by a school of science fiction literature of the late 1980s ('cyberpunk' fiction), and spreading outwards from its heartland of the Bay Area of Northern California,[3] this sensibility sees the new digital media as integral to contemporary artistic innovation and social freedom. Refusing the traditional counterposition of femininity and technology and celebrating the liberation that digital media can facilitate for women forms a strong feminist strand in this ideology, which found early expression in a manifesto from Donna Haraway.[4]

Sadie Plant's anarcha-feminist version, which she calls 'cyberfeminism', draws on the writings of French feminist Luce Irigaray for its account of the feminine (as does Tania Modleski when discussing soap opera as a 'feminine' genre in Chapter 46). If maleness is centred, bounded, phallic, unitary, focused, hierarchical, silencing, controlled and controlling, the feminine is the opposite of these. And computer networking, Plant points out, has the characteristics of the feminine: decentred, reciprocal, lateral, fluid, multiple, dispersed, responsive, expansive, communicative, fertile. The new networked digital media, she argues, go with the grain of the feminist revolution; women are taking them up, and this is subversive of patriarchy.

Perhaps Plant's claims are the kind of thing Peter Golding is referring to when he comments that there is a 'hippie taint to much Internet culture, as the networks bristle with West Coast new age rhetoric, technoshamanism and role-playing fantasy worlds' (though he calls this bristling 'whiskery', thinking probably of Rheingold[5] primarily, and certainly not referring directly to Plant). Early adoption of a new medium is often associated with a particular subcultural formation: Hirsch refers to the early radio 'hams' in this regard.[6] The subculture then dissolves – or moves on – when employment of the medium becomes mainstream. This may prove to be the case for 'cyberfeminism'. And if the mainstream take-up of the Net leads to advertisers and other commercial interests coming to dominate both the material available and the signposted navigation paths, and displace the more informal, inexpensive, free-ranging, lateral communication links explored by the early netizens (the 'cyber gypsies'), then Golding would probably join Plant in seeing this as a loss.

But from another angle, Plant's piece can be viewed in the tradition flowing from Walter Benjamin, in which the essay by Enzensberger that makes up Chapter 7 participates. In his celebrated essay of 1936 'The Work of Art in the Age of Mechanical Reproduction' Benjamin argued that the new media of image-making and distribution (photography, photogravure printing, film) enabled a new kind of visualisation that was progressive because it was industrial, widely socially available, wholly desacralised, and required a form of attention ('Zerstreuung') appropriate to the modern world.[7] Thus, the nature of these media was consonant with other features of modernity and its emancipative possibilities. Enzensberger argued in an analogous way a third of a century later, claiming that lightweight, cheaper, more accessible media had the potential to contribute to democratic progress against the frozen power balance of the Cold War; for him, new media went with the grain of the mobilisation of popular protest. And it can be seen that over a quarter of a century later and with yet another newly emergent form of media, Sadie Plant's piece employs a comparable structure of argument in the era of postmodernity when discussing the Net, linking the properties of a medium with contemporary liberatory possibilities.

Taken together, these four pieces give a sample of the kinds of ideas and approaches which media studies, developed in the twentieth century to consider the role of the press and broadcasting, furnishes for addressing new media as they emerge today.

NOTES

1. G. Snow, in N. T. Praigg (1923) *Advertising and Selling*, cited in *Oxford English Dictionary*, 1989 edn.
2. David Morley, *Family Television: Cultural Power and Domestic Leisure* (London: Comedia, 1986). Morley himself was to go on from this work on television to research the role of other communication technologies within the fabric of everyday household life; see, for instance, David Morley and Roger Silverstone, 'Domestic Communication: Technologies and Meanings', *Media, Culture and Society* 12·1, 1990, pp. 31–55.
3. See, for example, Rudy Rucker, R. U. Sirius, Queen Mu (eds) *Mondo 2000: a User's Guide to the Cutting Edge* (London: Thames and Hudson, 1992); Douglas Rushkoff, *Cyberia: Life in the Trenches of Hyperspace* (New York: Harper, 1994); and Mark Dery, *Escape Velocity: Cyberculture at the End of the Century* (London: Hodder & Stoughton, 1996).
4. Donna Haraway, 'A Manifesto for Cyborgs; Science, Technology and Socialist Feminism in the 1980s', *Socialist Review* 80, 1985, pp. 65–107; Donna Haraway, *Simians, Cyborgs and Women: the Reinvention of Nature* (New York: Routledge, 1991).
5. Howard Rheingold, *Virtual Community: Finding Connection in a Computerised World* (London: Secker and Warburg, 1994).
6. Many of the early users of lightweight video production equipment were drawn from a subculture of community activism, and were committed to the medium as an instrument of community empowerment – a view scathingly appraised by Nicholas Garnham in 'The Myths of Video', collected in *Capitalism and Communication: Global Culture and the Economics of Information* (London: Sage, 1990).
7. Walter Benjamin (orig. 1936) 'The Work of Art in the Age of Mechanical Reproduction' in *Illuminations* (London: Jonathon Cape, 1969).

62

HOW ARE MEDIA BORN?

Brian Winston

This piece addresses two related questions: (a) How does technological change occur in mass communication? (b) What effect, if any, does the technology have on the content, the output, of mass communication? These questions are related in that they both deal with the historical relationship of technology to communication processes.

The first question is clearly historical. There are various accounts available to explain the nature of these changes. In some, technological developments are isolated: the technology is the dominant, *determining* factor in the process. I will be calling such accounts of change *technological determinist*. Other accounts place a greater emphasis on socioeconomic factors. In these accounts, technology is but one of many forces, influenced by and influencing social, economic, and cultural developments. I will be calling accounts of this sort *cultural determinist*.

The second question, about the effects of technology on communication, can also be thought of as historical. The only way a judgement can be made as to the effect of a technology on the content of communications is by comparing the content before and after the technology is introduced. Thus the second question, which seems to address only the issue of effects, is also really addressing the issue of change and, in so doing, is historical.

These two questions are linked in another way. Technological determinist accounts of media history tend to stress the role of media technology in

From John Downing, Ali Mohammadi, Annabelle Sreberny-Mohammadi (eds), *Questioning the Media: A Critical Introduction* (London: Sage, 1990) Ch. 3.

governing the content of communication. Conversely, cultural determinist accounts tend to deny technology this determining role. So the answer to the first question above is likely to condition the answer given to the second.

This chapter presents four successive accounts of the genesis of communications technology. It is not, clearly, a full-blown history of media technology, although you may well find some new information on the subject. It is designed to encourage you to think more carefully about that history, to learn how to evaluate the problems in historical explanations and not just accept them because a scholar has published them.

TECHNOLOGICAL DETERMINIST ACCOUNT A

Technological determinism, wrote Raymond Williams (1974),

> is an immensely powerful and now largely orthodox view of the nature of social change. New technologies are discovered by an essentially internal process of research and development, which then sets the conditions of social change and progress. Progress, in particular, is the history of these inventions which 'created the modern world.' The effects of the technologies, whether direct or indirect, foreseen or unforeseen, are as it were the rest of history. (p. 13)

In its simplest form, this dominant theory explains the 'essentially internal process of research and development' as nothing more than the biographies of the scientists and technologists involved, arranged chronologically. This account sees the development and impact of technology as 'the progress of great men' (women and people of non-White cultures tend not to figure).

Here, presented as a case study, is a short history of the cinema written as 'the progress of great men,' based on a classic history of film (Ramsaye, 1926).

Case 1: Cinematic Projection

One essential element of the cinema is the idea of projection. The line that leads to projection begins with Della Porta, an Italian, who put a lens on the front of the earliest camera – a simple box. An image was produced on a glass screen set in the back wall of the box. Della Porta made this device in 1555. Next, Athanasius Kircher, a German, produced a magic lantern that projected an image onto a screen (1649).

Peter Roget, an Englishman, theorized in 1824 that the retina of the eye retains an image for a fraction of a second after the image is removed or changed. This 'persistence of vision' can be used to fool the eye into believing a succession of separate and slightly different images to be actually one moving image. Toys to exploit 'persistence of vision' by animating drawings were then 'invented' by men like Paris (English, 1824), Plateau (Belgian, early 1830s), and von Stampfer (German, 1832). In 1852, von Uchatius, another German, put an animated strip of drawing (done on glass) into a magic lantern and projected the resulting moving image onto a screen.

A substitute for glass now had to be found. The line leading to this part of the cinematographic apparatus goes back to early experiments with substances that change their color, essentially by darkening, in response to light. More research, like that of Wedgewood (English, 1802), led to the first photograms – images made by laying objects, such as leaves, directly onto materials, like paper or leather, treated with light-sensitive substances. But these images were not 'fixed' and would disappear into black if further exposed to the light.

Scientists undertook the discovery of a chemical that would halt the darkening process. In 1837 a Frenchman, Nicephore Niepce, found a way of doing this and, with his partner Daguerre, produced a type of photograph known as the daguerreotype. Meanwhile, an Englishman, Fox-Talbot, invented a photographic process that produced first a negative, made of chemically treated paper oiled to transparency, and then a positive copy.

This, the essence of modern photography, was then refined. A wood pulp extract called cellulose was used instead of paper. Celluloid film finally allowed George Eastman to 'invent,' in 1888, a camera that anybody could use.

Back to the cinema. It was Edison who took photography and melded it with the developments in animated drawing and magic lanterns to produce the kinetoscope in 1892. There were British, French, and other claimants for the honor of 'inventing' the first motion picture device. Two Frenchmen, the Lumiere brothers, gave the first public cinema (their term) show, using a projector to throw a moving image onto a screen, before an audience, arranged as in a live theater, in 1895.

So was the cinema invented.

There are numerous problems with this account. In its eagerness to create 'great men,' the story becomes highly selective. For instance, Roget's explanation of why we see apparent motion, 'persistence of vision,' is not really physiologically accurate (Nichols and Liderman, cited in De Lauretis and Heath, 1980, pp. 97ff), but even very recent histories still begin with Roget and his idea (see, e.g., Beaver, 1983; Mast, 1981).

Real contributions are seen as coming solely from the genius of a single figure, when, in fact, they are the product of collective inventiveness. For instance, it took more than thirty years to go from the development of celluloid, which was originally produced during the US Civil War as a dressing for wounds, to the Kodak. The full story of those years reveals a number of innovations and dead ends. It involves many, many more people than just

George Eastman, who successfully marketed a technology to which a lot of hands had contributed.

Edison's role in this process needs to be revised. Edison at Menlo Park was running one of the earliest modern industrial laboratories and pursuing a range of experiments, including investigations into the moving image. His method was to delegate much of the work to his assistants. In the case of the cinema, the work was actually done by a man named Dickson (Hendricks, 1961). Edison knew this full well, but that never prevented him from accepting credit for the 'invention' of the kinetoscope.

The poverty, or 'thinness,' of great-man histories is not based simply on the desire to create heroes. Another crucial factor is the implicit insistence on the primacy of the West. For instance, the camera does not begin with Della Porta but with Arab astronomers at least 300 years earlier. There is even a reference to projected images in China in 121 BC. It has been suggested that the first magic lantern lecture in Europe was given by a Jesuit who had learned the technique while a missionary in China, and that Kircher had nothing to do with it (Temple, 1986, p. 86). Even without this, it is possible that the camera was in existence in Italy over a century before Della Porta (Winston, 1987, p. 199).

You might also have wondered why, in this account, such emphasis has been placed on nationality. In part, it has to do with national pride. But establishing who did something first has more to it than that. Modern patent rights depend on registering an invention first, and that implies financial advantages.

The failure of the great-man style of technological determinism cannot be corrected simply by writing more comprehensive histories. This sort of history really cannot answer the question of *how* technological change occurs; instead, it simply tells us *when*. The only explanation offered as to *how* is that great men, out of their genius, think of them.

TECHNOLOGICAL DETERMINIST ACCOUNT B

There is a more sophisticated version of the technological determinist approach that we need to explore in order to see if these 'how/why' questions can be better answered. Here, the changes listed in Case 1 would be treated as a sequence of developments causally related to each other. The 'inventors' would be left out, or their parts downplayed. Such a history of the cinema would view its technological development as the inevitable result of scientific progress, part of the never-ending advancement of human knowledge in Western culture. Such an account would suggest that the independent existence of the camera, the lantern, and the lens had to combine to produce the magic lantern. In turn, this development inevitably melded with the development of photography to create cinematography.

The arrival of sound in film provides us with a case study in this more sophisticated mode. This account is based on Ogle (1977).

Case 2: Sound in Film

Sound recording developed using wax cylinders, discs, and wire before the turn of the twentieth century at the same time as the cinema itself was being perfected. However, these were mechanical recording devices without amplification that would not, therefore, work well in a theatrical environment.

Electronic devices that enabled sound to be amplified evolved out of experiments on the nature of electricity itself, then at the cutting edge of physics. By 1906, a number of independent researchers had produced a tube rather like the electric light bulb then being generally manufactured, but this specialized version could reproduce and amplify electrical signals.

The application of this technology to silent cinema was interrupted by World War I, but experiments continued using various systems. Running film projectors synchronously with phonographs was one. Another, more complicated, converted sound waves, via a microphone linked to a light bulb, into light waves to which the film could be exposed.

The technology was therefore awaiting its moment. That came in 1926, when the industry finally realized that the public would accept sound. Earlier attempts had failed because the technology was not quite developed and because there was inertia about changing over from the commercially successful methods of having live music at each screening.

The introduction of sound also made easier the introduction of faster (i.e., more light-sensitive) film stocks. The very bright arc lights used in the silent studios used to hiss. This was acceptable in silent shooting but bothersome if sound was being recorded. Incandescent lights were then introduced because they made no noise, but they were also less powerful, so the industry needed faster stocks. More sensitive film had been available but unused since before World War I.

This new stock was black-and-white but panchromatic – equally sensitive to all colors, unlike the slower orthochromatic stock it replaced. 'Ortho' was blind to red, which it therefore photographed as black. The introduction of panchromatic film affected makeup, costume, and set design. It also helped, therefore, to put in place production procedures that would facilitate the next major technical advance – color.

Such an account presents a seamless sequence of technical events, each automatically triggering its successor. Each can be delayed by external factors, such as World War I and industrial inertia. But in the end the technology triumphs.

Yet important clues as to *how* technical change occurs can be gained by thinking of *why* a change occurs at a particular time. This is a more complicated issue than it might seem to be at first sight. Changes do not occur simply when the materials and the scientific knowledge necessary for an advance are at hand. The history of the cinema is a good illustration of this.

The great-man account in Case 1 revealed that there was nothing to prevent Kircher from doing, two centuries earlier, what Ustachius did. Kircher could draw and he had glass. And he had just 'invented,' or borrowed from the Chinese, the lantern that Ustachius was to use.

Such questions can be extended. Why did Della Porta not place a light where he had put his ground-glass screen? Had he done so, he could have created the magic lantern a century before Kircher. And why did the Arab astronomers not pursue these developments centuries before that? Or the Chinese even earlier?

The great-man style of technological determinism cannot help us to answer such questions. It is equally clear that the sophisticated technological determinism of Case 2 is no better. We do not know from Case 2 why early films did not have sound, since sound-recording techniques and motion picture devices developed simultaneously (Hendricks, 1961, p. 111). And we are no nearer to understanding why the Arabs failed to exploit the camera, why Kircher did not invent the camera, and so on.

A better way we can begin to answer these questions is, however, hinted at in Case 2. There we started to hear about forces other than the technological, such as World War I and attitudes in the film industry. In a technological determinist account these are treated as incidentals, but cultural determinists will take these external factors as significant.

CULTURAL DETERMINIST ACCOUNT A

To take a cultural determinist view, it becomes necessary to examine the social context of the technology. This implies an examination of the circumstances into which the technology is introduced and diffused through society. In turn, then, a cultural determinist would need to look at the circumstances preceding the development of a technology. Note that the word *development* is preferred to the word *invention* because invention implies a single moment – but these single moments always obscure long-term developments involving many hands. Thus the cultural determinist will at least be an economic historian.

Let us take an economic history type of account of the introduction of sound in film and see how it compares with the technological determinist account offered in Case 2. Here, in Case 3, the key player becomes a corporation (Warner Brothers), but this key player is not a corporate great man. Rather, the struggle to introduce sound is located within corporate competition (Allen and Gomery, 1985, pp. 105ff).

Case 3: The Economics of Sound in Film

In the mid-1920s Warner Brothers was a small studio. It obtained from a New York bank, Goldman Sachs, a line of credit to expand its operations and used this money primarily to acquire movie theaters. Warner's biggest rivals were vertically integrated in this way; that is, studios owned chains of theaters and thus had ready markets for their products. Studios that did not own theaters were at a considerable disadvantage in marketing their films.

Warner's also used the money to buy into the new radio industry by acquiring a radio station. This was done because radio was increasingly being used to promote movies. By this acquisition the company gained familiarity with sound-recording techniques.

It was this changing capital infrastructure in the movie industry that constituted the enabling ground for the introduction of sound. Warner, smaller than the five major Hollywood studios, decided after much internal debate to gamble that sound in its newly acquired theaters would give it an edge. The introduction of sound was thus an attempt to improve market share. Acquisition of a chain of theaters alone was not enough to do this; the chain had to attract audiences by offering something different.

It was the potential disruption to their profitable silent film business, reinforced by their experience of failed experiments with sound dating back to the period before 1914, that 'caused' Warner's rivals, the Big Five, not to exploit sound. The technology was available, but the commercial desire and need were not.

Warner successfully demonstrated that sound could be popular with audiences by making a series of variety shorts. Fox, another company struggling to catch up with the Big Five, then demonstrated that sound news films could also be popular.

As a result of this challenge, the Big Five agreed to introduce sound film using a common system. The technology they agreed upon, sound on film, was the most complex and expensive, but, because the Big Five had agreed upon it, it was well placed to become the industry standard. It was thus also designed to prevent Fox and Warner, who were using slightly different versions, from continuing to make gains. Warner and Fox fell into line.

The Big Five sound system is the one in use up to the present day.

There are a number of differences between the accounts in Case 3 and Case 2. In Case 3 the development of sound film critically depends on the period before its introduction. In Case 2 this period is seen as a lull, a pause before the inevitable triumph of the technology. In Case 3 it becomes instead a period of struggle of the sort that determines not only the pace at which the technology is introduced, but also its form. It is a struggle waged first within Warner, then between Warner and its rivals, to maximize profits and to have a particular technical solution dominate.

The explanation given in Case 3 is not a substitute for the information in Case 2. It is not that we are writing economic history instead of technological history. Rather, we are attempting to combine the 'thinness' of the account in Case 2 by trying to write a 'thicker' history, one that describes both. Economic historians, in effect, would add a mass of new information about Warner as a business.

However, economics is a crucial element, but not the end of the matter. Case 3 assumes that the main engines of technical change are the corporation and the market, and that the corporation's motivation will always be to increase the 'bottom line.' There are two problems with this. One is that technical innovation has not always depended upon the existence of corporations seeking profits. Case 3 is good at explaining sound, but it still does not help us understand why the Arabs, Della Porta, Kircher, and the others did not create the cinema.

Second, much innovation is designed to protect corporations and preserve existing markets, rather than to produce new goods and services for profit. Bell Laboratories is a good case in point. Often considered the most effective industrial innovator in history, Bell Labs was actually established to protect AT&T, the telephone monopoly, from new technologies, specifically radio. By 1878 Bell himself had built a good telephone receiver, but his transmitter was terrible. Edison, by contrast, had patented a superior transmitter, but his receiver was not as effective as Bell's. In this patent standoff, Bell and his business partners hired Emile Berliner to get the infant phone company out of trouble. Berliner, who later built the first device for playing records (the phonograph), did just this. In six weeks' time, he produced a good transmitter without infringing on Edison's patents. Thereafter this pattern of threat averted by patentable innovation was repeated often until, in the radio era, AT&T's research programs were finally organized into Bell Labs.

The result of Bell's research program is that every telecommunications innovation has relied to some extent on Bell patents. This includes radio, television, sound film, fax systems, and space communications. No innovation has occurred in the telecommunications field without Bell both agreeing to it and profiting from it. The expenditures lavished on Bell Labs were not therefore simply to maximize profit. They were designed to suppress the disruptive – to Bell – possibilities of innovation.

Thus we need to go beyond the economic historian's version of cultural determinism to something 'thicker' still. Central to my argument is that *all* technological communication innovation can be thought of as a series of events taking place in the realm of technology, but influenced by and reacting to events taking place (a) in the realm of pure science and (b) in society in general. This model has to be rendered even more complex, because society also influences science, which in turn influences the technology. However, for present purposes I will include society's influences on science as part of science itself.

CULTURAL DETERMINIST ACCOUNT B

Let us take another case – television – to illustrate this 'thicker' cultural determinism.

Case 4: Television

As industrial capitalism, from the end of the eighteenth century onward, began to stimulate scientists' inquiries into more practical and profitable applications, so substances were discovered that responded to light in various ways. The basic chemistry of photography emerged, as Case 1 showed, because it was known that some substances darken when exposed to light. Here we will be concerned with the fact that a group of substances alter their resistance to electric current according to the amount of light that falls on them.

Selenium was noted as such a substance by 1839, but no theoretical understanding of why this occurs was offered and no immediate applications suggested themselves for about 40 years. Then it became possible to theorize a device that would translate an optical image (light waves) into a variable electric current, using selenium as a sensor. This idea was prompted by parallel developments that used the variable resistance of carbon to electricity to construct a device that translated sound waves into a variable electric current – a telephone.

The problem for 'seeing by telephone,' as it was called, was that it had no practical application except perhaps as a facsimile device. But facsimile devices, which allowed for images to be sent by telegraph, were already in existence and worked better, because with the selenium versions there was no apparent way of creating a hard copy. Nevertheless, a device for turning images into an electrical wave analogue using a selenium sensor was patented in Berlin in 1884. Use of the word *television* as a description of this process dates from 1903.

Various researchers all over the world realized that television could transmit moving pictures. But what use would that be? The live theater had been industrialized in the nineteenth century by the creation of theatrical circuits that brought entertainment to the masses. Film had partially mechanized theater and would eventually largely substitute for it. There was no social need for television at that time.

Nor did any researcher think money could be made by delivering entertainment to the home. The masses, given the long hours they worked and the poor pay they received, had not yet the means to use it. The consumerist economy (Kellner, 1990) was still around the corner.

Thus by the turn of this century television existed as a technical possibility. It was grounded in scientific research but seemingly had no practical application. By 1908 the actual electronic system used to produce TV images had been outlined. The first image was transmitted in 1911 to a cathode ray tube in St Petersburg. Major firms were interested, because the technology could potentially be used as an alternative to radio and film, and because of its possible threat to established facsimile systems. Research programs were set up, but they were underfunded. Nevertheless, by 1923 an RCA team, led by Vladimir Zworykin, patented the basic TV camera tube of today.

Further development during the 1920s and 1930s was confused because the major radio industry players were not interested and because other solutions than a purely electronic TV system were also under consideration. These mechanical/electronic systems, which dated back to the 1884 patent, were being explored by a group of researchers largely outside the radio industry.

The confusion persisted because the capital necessary to diffuse TV was then being applied to the movies – by now the talkies – and to radio. The very same firms were interested in all three areas, and judged that TV would be a threat to current business but had interesting future possibilities. Nevertheless, in both Britain and Nazi Germany public television, using a fully electronic system, began in 1936. In Germany it was seen only rarely for theatrical purposes, for the regime continued to focus more on radio, film, and the press to get across its propaganda. In Britain the economic difficulties of the Depression decade prevented its widespread use.

A major factor in the delay in the United States was that RCA so controlled the patents that the Federal Communications Commission was worried about the survival of the other firms that could make TV equipment. It therefore stood in the path of RCA's development of TV from 1936 to 1941. The FCC was trying to prevent the AT&T telephone monopoly from being reproduced by RCA in this area. By 1941 the necessary agreements had been struck, but US entry into the war that year halted further development.

At the end of the war the situation was quite different. The radio industry was looking for a new technology to exploit, having saturated the market with radio sets. In general, the war had greatly expanded the electronic manufacturing capacity of the country, and if that capacity were not to be lost, the public would have to begin to 'need' a range of domestic electrical appliances that it had lived without previously. Further, the opportunities for advertising these and other products via TV seemed wide open. The Depression decade seemed to have fixed in policymakers' minds that if consumer demand was flat, no economic growth was possible; and after the many sacrifices of the war, a return to Depression would have been political dynamite.

However, it was not an overnight process. The FCC again suppressed the free development of TV by limiting the number of stations that could be built, even instituting a 'freeze' on new construction from 1948 to 1952. There were technical reasons for doing this, including the decision as to which color system was to be used, the power and location of TV masts, and the question of VHF and UHF wavebands. But the reasons were not simply technical.

It is often suggested that TV destroyed Hollywood. The great studios are a thing of the past. But where does most TV production still take place? Hollywood. The FCC freeze also allowed Hollywood to maintain its position as supplier to the new TV industry, for it was during that period that the terms of this trade were worked out.

Case 4 attempts to meld all of the elements used in the other cases – the individual contribution, the triggering effects of increasing knowledge in science, and the application of other technologies, economic forces, political considerations, social policy, and general cultural factors. These various elements can be thought of as relating in the following way.

Imagine the realm of science as a line going from the past to the future:

past   _____   future

          science

Now imagine a parallel line, which we will call 'technology':

          technology

past   _____   future

          science

These two lines are connected in the mind of the technologist, the person who has an idea for an application:

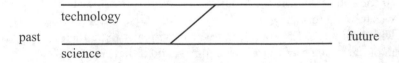

          technology

past   _____   future

          science

The idea is triggered by the understanding of science but is expressed 'in the metal' as a technological device. History shows the technologist is likely to build a whole series of devices, some slightly, some radically, different from each other. The device we commonly call the 'invention' does not differ from the others because it works and they do not. Often the 'preinventions' work just as well. What makes the difference is that a point is reached where one of these contrivances is seen to have a real use. After that recognition of the *application* the device is considered an 'invention'; before, as a 'prototype.' I will call the emergence of an application *supervening social necessity*.

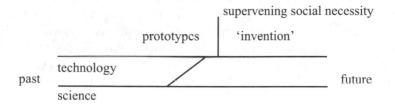

Supervening social necessities are the accelerators pushing the development of media and other technology.

In Case 4 the supervening social necessities that influenced the development of television include the rise of the home, the dominance of the nuclear family, and the political and economic need to maintain full employment after World War II. Because of these, the device finally moved out of the limbo of being an experiment to being a widely diffused consumer product.

Supervening social necessities are at the interface between society and technology. They can exist because of the needs of corporations, as when Kodak introduced Super 8 film because ordinary 8mm film had saturated the market. Or they can become a force because of another technology. Railroad development required instant signaling systems, and so enabled the telegraph to develop. Or, as in Case 4, there can be general social forces that act as supervening social necessities. Telephones emerged in the late 1870s because the modern corporation was emerging and with it the modern office. Not only telephones but elevators, typewriters, and adding machines were all 'invented' during this period, although the first typewriter was patented 150 years earlier, the adding machine dated back some 250 years, and the modern hydraulic elevator had been available for over 20 years.

But if there are accelerators, there are also brakes. These work to slow the disruptive impact of new technology. I describe the operation of these brakes as the *'law' of the suppression of radical potential*, using 'law' in its standard social science sense to denote a regular and powerful general tendency.

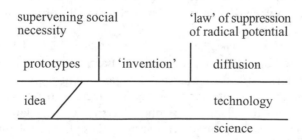

The brakes in Case 4, which caused television to be nearly a century in development, show its radical potential being suppressed, and are thus an instance of this 'law.' The brakes ensure that a technology's introduction does not disrupt the social or corporate status quo. Thus in the case of TV, the existence of facsimile systems, the rise of radio, the dominance of RCA, and the need not to destroy the film industry all acted to suppress the speed at which the new medium was introduced, to minimize disruption. The result is that all the main film and radio interests of the 1930s are still in business today, and television can be found in practically every house in the nation, sometimes in almost every room.

This concept of supervening social necessities and a 'law' of the suppression of radical potential represents one way in which a cultural determinist would seek to understand the nature of change in media technology. I would argue it to be a more effective, more *powerful* way of explaining these matters than any that the technological determinists can produce.

For instance, we can now, using this model, answer our questions about the Arabs and the Chinese. The Arab astronomers who pioneered the camera did so for astronomical reasons, which were their supervening social necessity. Furthermore, their Islamic faith by then forbade the making of realistic images of living beings, so that culturally they would have been prohibited from exploring the camera's image-making potential. That was how the 'law' of the suppression of radical potential operated on their research agenda. The Chinese produced these technologies in the context of an imperial system that used them as marks of distinction for the court. The culture made the technologies elite and limited and therefore suppressed their further development. It is these sorts of factors, not scientific knowledge or technological know-how, that condition technological developments.

EFFECTS OF TECHNOLOGY ON COMMUNICATION CONTENT

We can now begin to address our second question. All communication modes except face-to-face speech depend on technology. Mass communication requires technologies of a sophisticated kind. The question is whether any such technologies determine what gets communicated.

Answers come in weaker and stronger forms. The weakest form is also the easiest to agree with, namely, that it is obvious that not all technologies can do the same thing. A typewriter cannot convey the same information as a photo. But can we go further?

Mohammadi (1990) reviews a well-known study by Daniel Lerner (1954) that argued, based upon research in the Near East, that when modern media were suddenly injected into a traditional village environment in the Third World, they had the effect of expanding many villagers' horizons and expectations quite dramatically. This is a stronger version of the claim that media technology determines the communication that takes place. Mohammadi notes the highly questionable assumptions also carried with this theory, but we might agree that the theory's basic assertion is plausible, even if we might want to rein it in with further 'buts' and 'if sos.' Similarly, Sreberny-Mohammadi's argument (1990) about forms of media is an intermediate version of the argument that media technologies must be incorporated into the analysis of media effects. So far there may be room for dispute on individual points, but not on the basic position.

However, the stronger versions are quite frequently to be met with in the generalized pronouncements about media influence in the world today that commentators and editorial writers reproduce from time to time. The most renowned exponent of the strong position was Canadian media theorist Marshall McLuhan, who – even though I am now about to attack his arguments – has the distinction of having first encouraged the general public to think seriously about the impact of media technology on society. He was one of a group of Canadian historians, anthropologists, and literary critics who developed a body of ideas that suggested that in communications, technology was the determining influence. His most frequently quoted aphorism is that 'the *medium* is the message' (McLuhan, 1964). He meant by this that media content (the explicit message) explains far less about communication than the communicative impact of the technical medium as such, viewed in terms of its effects on whole societies and cultures over centuries of their development. Actual media output therefore was of comparatively little interest to McLuhan. Here is how he describes the impact of printing press technology:

> Socially, the typographic extension of man brought in nationalism, industrialism, mass markets, and universal literacy and education. For print presented an image of repeatable precision that inspired totally new forms of extending social energies. ... The same spirit of private enterprise that emboldened authors and artists to cultivate self-expression led other men to create giant corporations, both military and commercial. (p. 157)

The key words here are that 'print *presented an image* of repeatable precision that *inspired*.' It is a claim not merely that the printing press determined the content of books or pamphlets, but that leading aspects of our communicative culture (literacy, education, self-expression by authors and artists), our institutions (industrialism, giant corporations, mass markets), and our political self-understanding (nationalism) were summoned into being by this media technology. It goes beyond a technical explanation of how media technology developed to provide a media-technological explanation of modern society.

But McLuhan's approach, although grounded in his reading of history, is difficult to sustain on the basis of the historical evidence. All the effects of the printing press he outlines took centuries to manifest themselves. Nationalism, in its modern form, dates from after the American and French revolutions. How then can a device introduced nearly 300 years earlier have 'caused' nationalism? Similarly, universal literacy and the rise of great corporations date from the second half of the nineteenth century, some 400 years after the printing press had been introduced into the West.

McLuhan's technological determinism depends upon a very loose idea of historical causality. 'Perhaps the most significant of the gifts of typography to man is that of detachment and non-involvement,' he asserts (p. 157). This assertion is built upon his prior claim that the printing press gave birth to the individual author and artist. But his position is untenable. In what sense are modern people more communicatively uninvolved and detached than they were in the past, specifically the medieval European past? Certainly our sensitivity to human cruelty toward other people and animals is vastly increased, although we can be just as brutal, and now on an industrial scale, as our ancestors. How could it be shown that before print there were no authors, artists, or ordinary people who thought of themselves as individuals in the way we think of ourselves today?

Furthermore, McLuhan's basis mode of reasoning may have important ideological effects. If technology is an external force, like nature, it cannot easily be subjected to social control. It implies we are helpless in the face of such a force, rather than that we can adapt and use technology for our own freely determined purposes.

[...]

One last example: for the technological determinist, the fact that color film does not easily photograph Black skin tones is the result of the technical properties of the dyes used in those films. The cultural determinist will want to explore this matter a little more thoroughly. I would begin with the fact that color film was largely created by White scientists to photograph White skin tones. These products do not simply reproduce nature. Each color film stock the chemists designed contained a different solution to the basic problem of representing – or, better, *re*-presenting – natural colors. Each produces a slightly but noticeably different result.

In doing the creative work involved, the chemists are forced to make choices as to which colors their film will respond to best. For reasons grounded in the fundamental physiology of color perception within the human eye, any one set of choices will result in a film that cannot represent Black skin tones as well as it represents White. Color film stocks in general tend to give Black people a greenish hue. Indeed, the research literature on the development of such stocks reveals that the chemists were primarily interested in getting so-called White (i.e., Caucasian) skin tones as acceptable as possible. They simply did not concern themselves with how Black people would be photographed (Winston, 1985, pp. 195ff). In this way we see once again that it is the social context, not the technology, that determines the content of communication forms.

Conclusions

At the outset, we noted that the answers given to the question as to how media technologies develop will in turn condition the answers given to the parallel question of what impact technology has on the content of communication. The technological determinist, who wants to see the technology as all-powerful, operating as though in a historical vacuum, will tend to see the influence of media technology on content as overwhelming. The cultural determinist, who wants to place the technology firmly in its social context, will also want to see that context as the primary factor determining both media technology and media content.

Technological determinism tends to present us as being comparatively impotent, as malleable consumers, unthinking and unprotesting, in the face of media technology power. The cultural determinist view, by contrast, is empowering. By drawing attention to the ways in which society constantly conditions technological developments, this view gives us the power to evaluate media technologies and to understand that we are not in the grip of forces totally beyond our control.

These implications also show us why theories in general are important. Theories can help or hinder us in coming to an understanding of the world. Without that understanding we cannot act. Thus theory is critical to action.

References

Allen, R. and Gomery, D. (1985) *Film History: Theory and Practice*, New York: Knopf.

Beaver, F. (1983) *A History of the Motion Picture*, New York: McGraw-Hill.

De Lauretis, T. and Heath, S. (eds) (1980) *The Cinematic Apparatus*, New York: St. Martin's.

Hendricks, G. (1961) *The Edison Motion Picture Myth*, Berkeley: University of California Press.

Kellner, D. (1990) 'Advertising and Consumer Culture', ch. 17 of Downing, J. et al. (eds) *Questioning the Media*, Sage.

Lerner, D. (1958) *The Passing of Traditional Society*, New York: Free Press.

Mast, G. (1981) *A Short History of the Movies* (3rd edn), Indianapolis: Bobbs-Merrill.

McLuhan, M. (1964) *Understanding Media*, London: Methuen.

Mohammadi, A. (1990) 'Cultural Imperialism and Cultural Identity', ch. 19 of Downing, J. et al. (eds) *Questioning the Media*, Sage.

Ogle, P. (1977) 'Development of sound systems: the commercial era', *Film Reader* 2, January.

Sreberny-Mohammadi, A. (1990) 'Forms of Media as Ways of Knowing', ch. 2 of Downing, J. et al. (eds) *Questioning the Media*, Sage.

Temple, R. (1986) *The Genius of China*, New York: Simon and Schuster.

Williams, R. (1974) *Television: Technology and Cultural Form*, London: Fontana.

Winston, B. (1985) 'A whole technology of dyeing: a note on ideology and the apparatus of the chromatic moving image', *Daedelus*, 114:4.

Winston, B. (1987) 'A mirror for Brunelleschi', *Daedelus*, 116:3.

63

WORLDWIDE WEDGE: DIVISION AND CONTRADICTION IN THE GLOBAL INFORMATION INFRASTRUCTURE

Peter Golding

Start today to realise the future – the Internet is here and is happening now, capitalise on the future today
> (advertisement in UK financial press, March 1996)

The Internet suffers from the problems often found in resources that are in common ownership: potential misuse, security problems and a lack of structure.
> (International Telecommunication Union press release, October 1995)

The days when the Net seemed to exist outside the laws of capitalism are just about over.
> (*Hot Wired* magazine, 12 March 1996)

Progressive social critics are pessimists by nature; time and again they have watched the promise of shared abundance dissipated by corporate greed and political failure. But hope survives, nourished by a mix of naivety, determination and honest endeavour as in Gramsci's succinct quip, 'pessimism of the intellect, optimism of the will'. Nothing feeds that eternal hope of progress more than technical change. The emergence in recent decades of communications forces of previously unimagined speed and flexibility has been the recurrent basis for visionary rewriting of future history.

In recent years, guerrilla television, community video, cable – the television of abundance – and citizens' band radios have all offered transient promise of providing electronic sustenance and substance for dissent and diversity. Yet

---

From Daya Kishan Thussu (ed.), *Electronic Empires: Global Media and Local Resistance* (London: Arnold, 1998).

each has disappeared as a serious tool of social change. The incorporation of technical novelty into the apparatus of oppression and inequality should come as no surprise for historians familiar with the story of the printing press, the newspaper or broadcasting. Yet as capitalism clearly arrives at something of a transitional boundary in the late twentieth century, the sense that the formidable and unprecedented potency of the new computer-based technologies may mean something quite different has once again rekindled the embers of radical optimism.

The latest repository for such optimism has been the Internet, the exponentially growing network of computer networks which has evolved its own culture, endless media hype, a growing literature and even an embryonic genre of film and novelisation. At last dreams of electronically delivered Jeffersonian ideals seem within our grasp, as politicians like Tony Blair in the UK and Al Gore in the USA scramble to become the visionaries of digital politics. No one will miss out on this transformation. We have no less than Newt Gingrich's assurance that 'this new era will see a revolution in goods and services that will empower and enhance most people' (Gingrich, 1995: 55). Note the 'most', however; even visionaries hedge their bets. It is enough to make one drool since, as Gingrich goes on, 'the United States can profit enormously by being the leader in the development of the new goods, services, systems and standards associated with a technological revolution of this scale' (ibid., 57–8).

In this chapter I want to assess more broadly the implications of the growth of the Internet, and set this assessment alongside some observations about global communications inequality more generally.

NERDS AND NET PROFITS

There is an appealing romance about the history of the Internet, and indeed of the computer industry more generally, which would mould it into a microcosm of the American dream. Energetic and inventive young men, in backyards and garden sheds, are the driving force which kick-starts the industry taking America into the information age. With just a pocketful of risk-venture dollars, and nothing but dreams, a few borrowed gizmos and their technological wizardry, these techno-entrepreneurs are the new Carnegies, Hearsts, Edisons, DuPonts and Rockefellers of the digital age. In ecstatic endorsement of this vision, the *Economist* saw the growth of the Net as 'not fluke or fad, but the consequence of unleashing the power of individual creativity. If it were an economy it would be the triumph of the free market over central planning. In music, jazz over Bach. Democracy over dictatorship' (1995: 4).

Like most mythologies this dramatisation has its kernel of truth. The frontier ideals of early development have bequeathed a slightly whiskery hippie taint to much Internet culture, as the networks bristle with West Coast new age rhetoric, technoshamanism and role-playing fantasy worlds. It is a delusion. The suits were there at the beginning, and it is no surprise that devotees like Rheingold (1994) sound a wistfully fearful note. As he argues, more in hope than expectation, 'it is still possible for people round the world to make sure this new sphere of vital human discourse remains open to the citizens of the planet before the political and economic big boys seize it, censor it, meter it, and sell it back to us'.

The roots of the Internet lay elsewhere than in the nerds' backyards, however. It started life in the Pentagon's Advanced Research Projects Agency. Needing a way of linking military computer researchers led to a technique whereby data could be split up and transmitted in packets. This gave both security (parts of a message cannot be 'eavesdropped') and safety (even a nuclear attack can only hit one part of a network, so that others remain intact and take over). These early experiments in the mid-1960s paralleled work at the National Physical Laboratory in the UK. ARPANET grew from four nodes in 1969 to roughly 100 by 1975 when it was turned over to the Defense Communications Agency. In the 1980s academic networks developed under the auspices of the National Science Foundation (CSNET) and the resulting NSFNET subsequently replaced ARPANET in 1990. The privatisation of the regional NSF networks marked the emergence of a commercial basis for the interconnected networks now in place, and has been the basis for all subsequent expansion.

As the Internet grows almost exponentially, a fully commercial set of back-bone systems has been constructed in place of the one developed by the government. Internet service providers have become large public companies or have merged. In 1995 all remaining curbs on commercial use disappeared. Eric Schmidt, chief technology officer for Sun Microsystems put it simply: 'customer service is the "killer application of the Internet"'. For Russ Jones, Digital's Internet programme manager, the Internet 'is a richer environment for exploring commercial capabilities'. Or to quote the *Economist*, 'The Internet had grown up' (1995: 9).

Internet size, whatever that might mean, roughly doubles every year. Put the hyperbole and the arithmetic together and everyone on the planet will be connected by the year 2003. The World Wide Web was developed at the European Centre for Particle Research in 1989, but only took off in 1993 when software developed at the University of Illinois and subsequently elsewhere created 'browsers' and graphical interfaces made the search for and interroga-tion of 'pages' on the WWW possible. With this arrival of multimedia possi-bilities for the Internet, commercial developers of such browsers, such as Netscape, became rich overnight. By 1995 there were over 30,000 websites in the Internet, and the number has doubled roughly every two or three months. The most significant change in the character of the WWW has been the irresistible rise of commercial sites.

One estimate, prepared at MIT, shows the proportion of websites devoted to commercial use to have risen from 4.6 per cent of the total in 1993 to 50 per cent by early 1996. Tracking the nature of Internet use generally can be done by watching the 'domains' into which usage fits. By 1994 'com' had replaced 'edu' as the most common domain name, as companies discovered the Web was more than a nerd's hangout. A January 1996 survey by Network Wizards shows 9.4 million host computers connected to the Internet, of which 'com' was easily the single largest domain, larger than academic (edu) and government (gov) sources combined.

THE 'BIG BOYS' JOIN IN

Two features of major corporations in the telecommunications and information sectors stand out in the late 1990s. One is the rash of mergers and incorporation that has taken place. The other is the diversification of activity. Both are designed to place the mega-corporations in pole position as the Internet's commercialisation becomes serious. According to a 1995 survey by Broadview Associates, merger and acquisition transactions in the IT industry jumped 57 per cent in 1995, with a transaction value of $134 million. IT companies sought energetically to achieve the critical mass necessary for competition in the international market, and especially sought the synergy which association with the newly deregulated telecommunications companies would allow. A presence on the WWW became more than a yuppie fashion accessory, more a business opportunity and requirement.

In Europe the activity has been mainly in telecommunications, in the USA in the audio-visual sector, and in Japan in electronics. Germany is Europe's largest telecoms market, and has seen mergers with US companies (Thyssen-BellSouth) and with British (Viag Interkom-BT; Veba-Cable and Wireless). In audio-visual sectors recent alliances include the association of France's UGC and Twentieth Century Fox, and a production accord between France Television and Time Warner. The wider trend of mega-mergers in the audio-visual sectors has included the takeover by Canadian wine and drinks giant Seagram of MCA, which controls Universal Studios; Time Warner's buy-out of Turner Broadcasting; Disney's purchase of Capital Cities (including the ABC network), and the takeover by Westinghouse of the CBS network.

The growth of vertical integration strategies which this trend represents places the audio-visual sector in a key position as distribution becomes the next priority for Internet commercialisation. This is well represented by the 1994 purchase by media giant Viacom, which controls the MTV channels, of the Paramount movie studios. Time Warner, the largest purely media corporation on the planet, includes in its activities *Time* magazine, Warner Music and Warner Bros. studios, the Home Box Office TV channel, and major holdings in cable systems and channels, as well as the mammoth operation in book-selling operated by Time Life Books.

In many ways this vertical integration may be more significant than the much-touted convergence of the telecommunications, computing and broadcasting industries. The latter is a purely technological take on what must be seen as a primarily fiscal and economic strategy. Inevitably some other familiar names come into view. Rupert Murdoch's News Corporation made its entry onto this stage with the establishment of a joint venture with long-distance operator MCI in information services, including MCI's FYI Online and e-mail services, and NewsCorp's Delphi Internet and online games service Kesmai, while Microsoft appeared with the Microsoft Network and tentative entries into the audio-visual sector through a stake in DreamWorks, an alliance with NBC network, and licensing of interactive video games. Somehow the dream of Jeffersonian democracy through optic fibres had been transposed into the slightly increased chance of saving a twenty-minute round trip to the video rental store. It is difficult to square the reality with Murdoch's promise that 'this venture will bridge different communities of interest, create opportunities to build and grow relationships and enrich the daily experience of individuals from all walks of life' (Press release, 20 February 1996, www.internetmci.com/ven).

Essentially, corporations could use the Net to market three commodities: their own goods, access to the network, and advertising. Marketing of goods on the Internet has hardly begun, stunted by the persistent difficulties surrounding security of payment. Advertising faces the problem of audience audit, to which a great deal of attention is being given. How many times has your site been accessed, or 'hit'? Despite that uncertainty, charges are beginning to stabilise. Popular sites on the Web, like *Playboy*'s, have been charging up to $100,000 for placing a postage-stamp-sized link on their pages. In the UK the Electronic Telegraph charges £25,000 for seven weeks' display on their screen of a button link. But then, by November 1995 *Playboy* could claim over 3 million 'hits' per day. Jonathan Nelson, CEO of US website specialists Organic Online, suggests 'We look at Web sites as eyeball aggregators, trying to bring people in and give them an experience. The aim is to bring in the right people in a very detailed demographic niche' (quoted in Waldman, 1996).

For the entertainment corporations the pitch is more direct. CNN Online selects stories targeted at younger upmarket males. Such services offer the possibility of seducing their clientele onto premium services beyond the main free services, in a parallel to the tariff structures of cable television. Columbia TriStar launched a website in 1995 and used it to build viewer loyalty with such gimmicks as a poll to ask viewers whether the lead in a sitcom should become pregnant, and puzzles to back up game shows.

DIGITAL DILEMMAS: CONTRADICTION AND CONFLICT FOR THE INTERNET

The corporate takeover and commercialisation of the Internet can lead easily to a weary fatalism, accepting that another potentially liberating technology has been engulfed by the still rampant forces of the 'free market'. But at this stage in its development the Net represents very starkly just those choices and contradictions which are at the heart of any political moment. Four key areas illustrate the present state of uncertainty and opportunity.

Community use or market mechanism?

The inherent twin properties of use value and exchange value are deeply embedded in the evolution of a communication system such as the Internet.

Even the most casual and serendipitous of surfers will not travel far around the Web without coming across examples of the seriously progressive potential of its social evolution. In London in 1990 McDonalds served libel writs on five activists who published a pamphlet providing less than flattering details of the food giant's employment practices and its questionable farming and food-production methods. The trial assumed Dickensian proportions, and two of the defendants, an unemployed single father and an ex-gardener turned barmaid, proved indefatigable self-taught lawyers in a seemingly endless and frustrating saga for the corporation, whose $26 billion turnover and $10,000-a-day legal team were unable to crack the pair in what became Britain's longest-ever civil trial. Not the least of the support structures for the defendants was the development of a website which made sure that the millions of words detailing McDonald's alleged failings brought out in the trial, and every critical article or cartoon which have appeared in the meantime, had the widest possible electronic circulation. When Greenpeace found themselves in dispute with Shell over the disposal of redundant North Sea oil rigs, environmental activists used the Web to drum up support. Other examples are legion.

Evidence from surveys suggests that demand for information on the Web is high, and indeed exceeds the demand for entertainment. A Harris poll in 1994 found 63 per cent of consumers wanted health or government information and other public-service material. Almost three-quarters wanted customised news, but only 40 per cent wanted movies on demand, and even fewer wanted interactive shopping. Why then is corporate strategy the opposite? Quite simply because, as Howard Besser notes, 'the industry believes that in the long run this other set of services will prove more lucrative' (Besser, 1995: 64).

What will make the Net grow, supply or demand? Consultants for the European Commission, Ovum, estimate that by 2005 the percentage of revenues from networked multimedia services in north-west Europe will derive 42 per cent from entertainment and pornography, and only 11 per cent from information services (Graham et al., 1996: 6). When Viacom bought Paramount many questioned why, at $10 billion, they should pay seventeen times the cash value of the company. But Paramount's TV and movie stock provide an invaluable resource for exploitation by seeking additional distribution channels, new user fees and extended audiences for advertising. Microsoft's alliance with NBC to create twenty-four-hour TV and Internet news is paralleled by a flocking of broadcasters to the Web. By March 1996 about 300,000 home pages on the Web had 'television' as one of their key words.

Integration or exclusion?

Early Net dreamers saw a wired universe, in which virtual communities would offer mutual support and conviviality in a global digital commune. The Net would be a horizontal communications structure, quite unlike the hierarchical vertical structures of old. In the high profile debates about censorship and pornography on the Web there has been understandable focus on the exclusion of women from this latest 'toy for the boys'. Appalling examples of cross-national prostitution via the Web, and the arrival of such unlovely and unlikely online hucksters as 'Pimps-R-Us', have given sound bases to critiques that women are excluded from the Net by the sexist nature of chat lines and the intrinsic patriarchality of its growth. But possibly more fundamental has been the emergence of division and exclusion by price.

Inevitably the consolidation of a market structure is replicating patterns of exclusion and differentiation apparent in earlier technologies. To access the Net requires a reasonably state-of-the-art computer, a phone line and a modem. In the UK many poor families do not even have telephone access. The start-up hardware would cost more than they are ever likely to afford. Online costs include the monthly payment to a company like Compuserve, currently about $27, not a princely sum, but roughly a quarter of the social security allowance for a teenage child. The growing power of the service providers was massively magnified in 1997 with the surprise marriage between Compuserve and the giant America Online, giving the new conglomerate some 11 million subscribers overall.

Recent surveys show that home-computer ownership is reaching a ceiling, with growth in 1995 virtually nil in the USA. The majority of sales are to existing owners upgrading rather than diffusion into new groups, thus exacerbating the gaps which already exist. The evidence confirms this trend. Director of the MIT Media Lab and digital visionary Nicholas Negroponte sees it this way: 'Some people worry about the social divide between the information-rich and the information-poor, the haves and the have-nots, the First and Third Worlds. But the real cultural divide is going to be generational' (Negroponte, 1996: 6). But he is wrong. A survey by Durlacher shows that the 25–34-year-old middle-class male is the biggest user group of the Internet. But an NOP survey in 1995 in the UK also shows that one-third of users are 35–54 and a third are female. The biggest differentiator is by income; roughly a third earned over £25,000 per annum. *Financial Times* readers were the most represented on the Web. A large-scale survey by Nielsen in the USA and Canada found that WWW users have high incomes (25 per cent over $80,000), half are in professional and managerial groups and two-thirds have college degrees.

While there have been doubts cast on the accuracy of some of these surveys the picture of market differentiation by price is clear and growing. One acute analysis comes from the journal of the Association of Chief Police Officers in the UK, which has drawn its own conclusions. In an article in May 1996 it fears the arrival of an electronic underclass, 'alienated, denied access to the new society because of a lack of education and wealth'.

The emergence of new communications goods has coincided with an ever-widening profile of income inequality. In the UK changes in the labour market, Thatcherite tax and welfare policies, and industrial reconstruction and decay have produced a regime of inequalities unparalleled in a century. Between 1979 and 1993 the poorest tenth of the UK population saw their real income fall by 18 per cent, while the top tenth received an increase of a startling 61 per cent. The share of national income going to these two groups is also diverging, producing unprecedented levels of income inequality. Pay inequality is larger than at any time since records began a century ago (the worst-paid tenth received 69 per cent of average wages in 1979, 63 per cent of average in 1993; the figures for the best-paid tenth were 146 per cent rising to 159 per cent). Wealth remains equally starkly differentiated: the top 1 per cent own 18 per cent of marketable wealth, the top 10 per cent own 49 per cent. In the USA the wealthiest 1 per cent owns 40 per cent of the nation's wealth, while the top 20 per cent own four-fifths of the total.

This is not the arithmetic of community communications. The global village has become the digital bazaar. As communications are driven into the market place the widening inequalities of economic fortune are translated into cultural and political disadvantage. As even columnist David Kline observed in that courier of technohype, *Hotwired* magazine, 'The future may become a wonderland of opportunity only for the minority among us who are affluent, mobile, and highly educated. And it may at the same time, become a digital dark age for the majority of citizens – the poor, the non-college educated, and the so-called unnecessary' (Kline, 1995).

Diversity or conglomeration?

Yet another dream for pioneers was the Net as the playground of the inventor-entrepreneur, a place where a thousand overnight millionaires could bloom, and everyone would be producer and consumer alike. After all, the Web was invented by a software engineer stuck away at a physics lab in Switzerland. The software which gave it its biggest boost emerged from a group of students at Illinois University, and Marc Andreesen, developer of Netscape, the most popular browser for the WWW, became an instant multi-millionaire in his early twenties.

Not only that but the entry of the corporate giants has been far from smooth. By February 1996 NewsCorp and MCI's Online Ventures was laying off staff and saying goodbye to its chief executive. AT&T is another giant that has lost a succession of senior executives in a halting and uneven entry into the new marketplace. Apple's eWorld and Murdoch's Delphi are also distinguished in this company of stumbling Goliaths. But the point is that the giant corporations can afford to make mistakes. Watching for shooting stars on the periphery of the business they can shift risk capital into them at their point of proven take-off, allowing the start-up and R & D costs to be absorbed by the small players. The so-called boutique character of the new market, stressing subcontracting and flexible small businesses, may challenge the corporate dinosaurs, but the bulk of the new markets is still ending up in their hands.

Electronic democracy or cyber-individualism?

Not long ago the arrival of cable TV and the imminent coming of computer networking evoked frissons of expectation about a new golden age of 'tele-democracy'. Voters would have direct access to their political masters, the electronic referendum would provide a recurrent mechanism of accountability and democratic politics, and political information for citizenship would be boundless and instantly accessible. The digital Athenian democracy this conjured up also, among sceptical observers, prompted the reminder that in Athens neither women nor slaves got much of a political look-in.

So too with the new cyberdemocracy. As Clifford Stoll in his splendidly sceptical diatribe *Silicon Snake Oil* points out, until the golden age arrives 'only the technoliterati will be enfranchised with network access' (Stoll, 1995: 32). The limited, and it would appear, stubbornly abating online community, will have privileged access to the political universe unavailable to the techno-poor. Not only that but the character of the politics envisaged in these scenarios changes the nature of democracy in its essence. As Stoll points out, 'This electronic town hall removes valid reasons for representative government. What's the purpose of a representative when each of us can vote immediately on every issue?' (ibid.: 33). There is here the potential for a fundamental individualisation of politics. In cyberdemocracy the role of representative and intermediary organisations – trade unions, community groups, political parties, pressure groups – is atrophied. As a result, as Dutch analysts van de Donk and Tops suggest, 'representative organisations may disappear ... A direct plebiscitarian democracy becomes feasible when the *demos* ... can come together "virtually"' (van de Donk and Tops, 1995: 16).

But the presupposition of universal access, itself illusory, is also based on a fiction about the nature of interactivity. Home shopping on the Web has not taken off because people want to touch, see and interact with what they are buying and those from whom they purchase it. But that will change as systems become more elaborate and secure. Interactivity on the Web, far from a mechanism for democratic debate and influence, will descend, as Besser sardonically notes, to 'responding to multiple-choice questions and entering credit card numbers on a key pad' (Besser, 1995: 63). Thus individualisation, unequal access and disenfranchisement may be the outcome of Net politics, as much as an electronic Agora.

NOT SO WORLDWIDE AFTER ALL

The emerging electronic inequalities generated by the World Wide Web and its commercial incorporation reflect the underlying political economy of all previous communications technologies. This creates a double differentiation, both at national and at international level. As we have seen, access to an abundant resource is only of value to commercial exploitation if that access can be curtailed by the price mechanism. In other words artificial scarcity has to be introduced and barriers erected to market entry for both consumers and producers.

This scenario becomes writ large on the global scale. The 1980s were indeed the 'lost decade' for much of the poorer two-thirds of the world. At the start of the decade, roughly 60 per cent of the world's population lived in countries whose per capita income was less than 10 per cent of the world average. As the nineties arrived some were emerging from the morass of destitution. But this was a small minority, mainly in the east Asian bloc of 'newly industrialising countries'. While aid was hastily diverted to the struggling economies of Eastern Europe (prompted by commercial opportunism and American alarm at the political instability generated by collapsing economies and a power vacuum), the poorer countries, of Asia and Africa especially, listened to uncomfortable advice about 'structural adjustment' while watching over soaring debt and falling primary commodity prices. The combination of growing Northern protectionism, declining aid, higher real interest rates and growing debt has further consolidated the endemic crisis of third world economies. By the year 2000, as the rest of us gaze in wonder at millennium celebrations and ponder the luxuries of the digital future, about a billion people will be living in absolute poverty. Some 70 per cent of world income is produced and consumed by 15 per cent of the world's population.

The implications of these trends for communications have been central to global politics in the last three decades. The emergence of the Non-Aligned Movement to provide a political accompaniment to pressure for a New International Economic Order led inexorably to the cardinal involvement of UNESCO as a forum for what became the insistent demand for a New International Information and Communication Order, culminating in the establishment of the MacBride Commission and, later, the International Programme for the Development of Communications.

It is not surprising, in this context, that the terrain occupied by communications goods and facilities is a hilly one, marked by soaring peaks of advantage and dismal valleys of privation. For example, book production continues to be dominated by Europe and the USA. The dominance of the English-language multinational publishers, especially in educational publishing, continues to sustain what has been the longest established feature of the international media. Over half the world's newspaper production remains in the industrialized West. Conversely, Africa has just 1 per cent of the world's newspaper circulation, the same proportion as a decade ago.

The growth of broadcasting as the dominant medium in most regions has been swift and dramatic. Europe and North America own two-thirds of the total of the world's TV and radio sets, though they account for just 14.9 per cent (Europe) and 5.2 per cent (North America) of the world's population. Notable for its very limited incursion into this picture is Africa, with 12.1 per cent of the world's population, but whose share of world radio and television sets is just 3.7 per cent and 1.3 per cent respectively.

The extent to which the 'lost decade' has seen the gap between rich and poor opening wider is starkly illustrated. There are over eight times as many book titles produced per capita in developed countries compared to the developing countries. The gap in newspapers per capita is of a similar ratio. The developed world has nearly six times as many radios per capita as the developing world, and nearly nine times as many television sets. The picture these figures superficially represent does not, of course, illustrate the disappointments of the 1980s. If we look at Africa again, with just 37 televisions per 1000 inhabitants in 1990 and just 172 radios, we realise how far behind some regions have been left. These figures were 17 and 104 in 1980. Yet in North America the equivalent figures for 1990 were 2,017 (radio) and 798 (television), reflecting an increase in the decade greater than the African total.

In telecommunications generally the gap is enormous. Despite the pressures for deregulation imposed by the IMF, African countries lag further and further behind. Basic telephony is still an essential. In South Africa there are 60 telephones for every 100 white inhabitants, but just one per 100 blacks (the figure is only 1.6 per 100 people for the whole continent). The post-Apartheid government has resisted privatisation until this is corrected. In 1994 Europe and North America accounted for 69 per cent of global telecommunications revenues, Africa for just 1 per cent (and for just 2 per cent of international telephone traffic). South African Deputy President Thabo Mbeki put the issue in severe relief at the G7 information summit in 1995 when he simply noted that 'half of humanity has never made a telephone call. The reality is that there are more telephone lines in Manhattan, New York, than in Sub-Saharan Africa.'

The huge opportunities afforded by developments in this field, both for personal communication and liberation from constraints of time and place, and for the acceleration and facilitation of commerce, are distributed with massive inequities. Telecommunications trade grew from less than $50 billion in 1990 to $96 billion in 1995. The telecommunications services market has grown from just under $400 billion to over $600 billion in the same period. In terms of market capitalisation, the telecommunications industry ranks third in the world behind health care and banking, and it is growing at twice the rate of the global economy (ITU, 1997a).

The routing of telecommunications is a simple reflection of the global capital structure. Four of the five top international telecommunication routes have the USA as one partner, and the USA is partner to 51 per cent of international telephone traffic in the top fifty routes (calculated from ITU, 1997b). Japan and the USA dominate world telecommunication equipment exports, accounting for 48 per cent of the value of exports by the top ten nations (ITU, 1997a). Even within the developing world the overwhelming volume of traffic is among and between the major trading elites, with the top twenty-five routes including those between Hong Kong, China, Singapore and Malaysia. No African country features in the top international routes among developing nations until we get down to number 1.5 (Namibia and South Africa). Yet, paradoxically, the biggest users of international telephony are a small number of affluent Sub-Saharan subscribers, living in a continent where there is not even one line per hundred people. More obviously, however, '24 OECD countries, while containing only 15 per cent of the world's population, account for 71 per cent of all telephone lines' (Winseck, 1997: 234). While half the world's population have never made a phone call, a fraction are on line and in touch to great effect and benefit.

The Internet repeats this picture only too clearly. By 1994 not a single less developed country had a computer network directly connected to the Internet. Packet-switched data networks existed in only five LDCs. The Internet Society estimate that in 1994 there were 0.002 Internet users per 1000 inhabitants in India, compared to 48.9 in Sweden. Most African nations still have no Internet access, yet the possible uses for such networks, for example in electronic health and education services, are enormous. Africa One, the fibre-optic undersea cable which will create a communications ring around the continent, will not be complete before 1999 at the earliest, and it remains to be seen if it is better news for AT&T Submarine Systems, the company who developed Africa One, than it is for the potential users. No African country was involved in the development stages of the $2.6 billion project. We have heard about the 'magic multiplier' potential of communication technologies before. After all, whatever happened to the 'transistor revolution'?

On Contradiction and Optimism

The jury is still out on what these innovations may mean. Just as the impact of the 'transistor revolution' in the 1960s was far from as predicted, so too for more recent gadgetry. The cassette recorder facilitated cheap and easy production, duplication and dissemination of local music and styles in many regions, yet also became the dominant form for global distribution of the ever more ubiquitous transnational music industry. Video recording gave new political energy and resource to the Kayapo and other indigenous peoples in the Amazon basin, yet also secured the full integration of the television and film industries in the further domestication of Western leisure patterns. The Internet is being heralded by aficionados as the means for horizontal communication and global networking which will revolutionise relationships both local and global, yet its commercialisation in the mid-1990s looks all too familiar to observers of past technological promise.

The contradiction inherent in these hopes and doubts is built in to international policymaking. The tension between the potential for wider access to information and the desire to own and control it is not new. At the ITU conference in 1994 US Vice-President Al Gore argued for development of the new global information infrastructure on the basis of five principles: private investment, competition, flexible regulation, non-discriminatory access and universal service. It takes no great insight to spot the incompatibility among those principles.

The same contradictions appear in the European Community, whose Ministerial Conference on the Information Society in February 1995 set out the G7 countries' visions of this future. Again we see a shopping list of principles to realise these aims including ensuring universal access; equality of opportunity; diversity of content and worldwide co-operation with special attention to the needs of less developed countries. Yet at the same time the principles included promoting dynamic competition, encouraging private investment, and an adaptable and open-access regulatory framework. Square pegs do not go into round holes, even when made from fibre optics. The essentially contradictory components of these aspirations will be the battle ground on which future policy in this area will be fought.

While the mega-corporations continue their stumbling but inexorable com-modification of the Internet and allied technologies, there will be a clash of ideals. The American Libraries Association can suggest that the 'National Information Infrastructure has almost limitless potential for social empower-ment, democratic diversification, and creative education' (Kranich, 1994: 2) but realistically, they also recognise that it 'will be owned, controlled and dominated by unregulated media giants that are driven by profits, not the hope for cultural understanding, greater democracy, the decrease of poverty, or educational enhancement' (ibid.: 6). Their answer is to call for a Corporation for Public Networking.

What we are witnessing is the 'mediatisation' of the new technologies, as they follow past scenarios of commercialisation, differentiated access, exclusion of the poor, privatisation, deregulation and globalisation. None of this is inevi-table. We find ourselves staring at the arrival of a tool which could nourish and enhance the public sphere, or equally, which could provide another vehicle for the incorporation of progressive politics and ideals into the grubby maw of market rapacity. The call to battle may arrive along unfamiliar channels, but its tenets and tones will be all too familiar.

REFERENCES

Besser, H. (1995) From Internet to information superhighway, in Brook, J. and Boal, I. (eds) *Resisting the Virtual Life: The Culture and Politics of Information*, City Lights, San Francisco.

Economist (1995) The Internet, Survey, 1 July, pp. 1–20.

Gingrich, N. (1995) *To Renew America*, HarperCollins, New York.

Graham, C. et al. (1996) *The Consumer in the Information Society: A Discussion Paper for Identifying Priority Issues*, Ovum Ltd., London.

ITU (1997a) *World Telecommunication Development Report*, International Telecom-munication Union, Zurich.

ITU (1997b) ITU/TeleGeography direction of traffic database. (Available online at http://www.itu.int/ti/industryoverview/top50int.html.)

Kline, D. (1995) To have and to have not, *Hotwired*, 18 Dec., p. 5. (Available online at http://www.hotwired.com/market/95/51/index 1a.html.)

Kranich, N. (1994) Internet access and democracy: ensuring public access on the information highway, *Open* magazine pamphlet series, No. 31, Westfield, NJ.

Negroponte, N. (1996) *Being Digital*, Coronet Books, London.

Rheingold, H. (1994) *The Virtual Community: Finding Competition in a Computerised World*, Secker & Warburg, London.

Stoll, C. (1995) *Silicon Snake Oil: Second Thoughts on the Information Highway*, Macmillan, London.

van de Donk, W. B. H. J. and Tops, P. W. (1995) Orwell or Athens? Informatization and the future of democracy, in their *Orwell in Athens: A Perspective on Informatization and Democracy*, IOS Press, Amsterdam.

Waldman, S. (1996) Adland's new toy, *Guardian*, 18 March, p. 16.

Winseck, D. (1997) Contradictions in the democratisation of international communication, *Media, Culture & Society*, 19.2, pp. 219–46.

64

NEW TECHNOLOGIES AND DOMESTIC CONSUMPTION

Eric Hirsch

[...]

[T]here is a clear historical and social connection between [new technologies and] domestic consumption: for the last 200 years the latter has been sustained (and also continually perceived as threatened) by new technologies. What is meant by 'new' is crucial here. 'New-ness' co-exists in a tension with what is seen as established (or often traditional) – technologies are both established and new at the same time. For example, 'established' forms of computing are nowadays continually perceived as being superceded by 'novel' forms; computing is 'established' and 'new' simultaneously.

Technologies are not alone in being subject to this tension. Forms of domestic consumption are both established and new in an analogous manner: people commonly evoke both old and novel forms of consuming in the domestic context. Moreover, the distinction between old and new which is rendered visible in the relationship between technology and domestic consumption is simultaneously used by people as part of their own self-conceptualisation (Strathern, 1996: 45; cf. Hirsch, 1992). Television, for example, is central to our contemporary, everyday patterns of domestic consumption. At the same time personal computers, the Internet, and the 'Information Superhighway' more generally are the 'new technologies seen as offering novel possibilities for the domestic sphere but also perceived as challenging our conventional or 'established' patterns of domestic consumption centred around broadcast

From C. Geraghty and D. Lusted (eds), *The Television Studies Book* (London: Arnold, 1998) pp. 158–74.

television. A generation and a half ago television would have had the status of 'new' technology positioned on the horizon of the consumer as a novel possibility for domestic use, envisioned as simultaneously supplanting established forms thus rendered as traditional.

My central argument is that an explicit emphasis on domestic consumption – which emerged as a middle-class phenomenon during the late eighteenth to early nineteenth century – has been a project of domestic self-sufficiency.[1] What I mean by this is that this project is sustainable only through an ever-widening and interrelated set of connections with the public, the world of work and 'society', from which it was self-consciously separated. What has become particularly manifest during this period is a mutually constitutive relationship between forms of socio-cultural innovations (e.g. forms of domesticity) and technological innovations (e.g. forms of technology used in or connected to the domestic context) whereby the efficacy of each becomes evident. More specifically, the interests in creating domains of domestic self-sufficiency made manifest the need for connections of various kinds: to goods and services and for communication and transport, each facilitated by new technologies. In a related manner, the new technologies were seen by entrepreneurs and others as feasible avenues for development through their eventual deployment in domestic units requiring various kinds of connections. This essay will therefore look at some examples of these connections in what are now thought of as older technologies, in order to establish the context in which we can begin to understand the family's relationship with new technologies in the domestic sphere (presented as a case study of a family in contemporary Britain).

Although the chapter draws on a range of historical sources (largely from the Anglo-American context), it should not be read as a history. Rather, it is a historically informed account which is deliberately schematic. It is also important to highlight that the mode of analysis used to explore the middle-class project which achieved dominance is, in part, constituted by the project itself: we are constrained to think within its categories. However, when the project begins to unravel, then other ways of thinking about the project become available. It is from this latter perspective that the scheme I present is written.

The 200-year timespan – from the late eighteenth century to the present – can be divided up into roughly five distinct but overlapping periods. Retrospectively, broadcast television is foreshadowed by the relationship between domestic self-sufficiency and the ever more profuse set of connections through which an emphasis on domesticity can be sustained. Throughout successive periods, this relationship becomes more and more close-knit. But as we shall see, the innumerable connections gathered up by broadcast television also foreshadowed its perceived limits and eventual 'undoing', which has become visible during the current phase of socio-cultural and technological innovations, the fifth period.

The first period, from c.1780 to the 1850s, constituted a revolution in speed; the speed at which manufactured goods were produced and transported and the speed with which the consumers of those goods both consumed them and were themselves transported. This first period engendered a crisis of control which provided the contours of the second period. From the 1850s to 1880s a range of social and technical strategies were first formulated to coordinate and integrate the often indiscernible set of connections generated between the production, distribution and consumption of goods and services: between the domestic units and ever more profuse connections. These social and technical strategies were systematised during the third period from the 1880s to 1940s. It was during this time that the cultural ideal, which first emerged 100 years previously, was codified in the spaces of suburbia and became a reality for the majority of the population (in Britain and the USA). This harmonization of 'individual/family' and 'society' entered its 'golden age' during the fourth period from the 1940s to 1970s. Processes of technological miniaturization and the rapid expansion of consumer electronics further enhanced the domestic ideal throughout this period. But the limitations of the systems (both 'social' and 'technical') first codified during the latter part of the nineteenth century became explicit. This sense of limits heralded the period in which we now find ourselves, a period which began during the 1970s and which promulgates a combination of individual 'choice' and technological 'convergence'. This is the long-term perspective that is needed if we are to understand the social and historical significance both of broadcast television – and of the associated range of 'new' technologies which appear to be supplanting its dominance – at the centre of our domestic culture.

REVOLUTION IN SPEED

The separation of the domestic context from the market was a project that was explicitly aspired to towards the end of the eighteenth century (cf. Stone, 1990: 291; Wahrman, 1995). Domestic life became idealized as a haven from the aggressiveness and uncertainty of the marketplace. But this separation of domesticity both from the perceived harshness of economic life as well as from other domestic units went hand in hand with a range of technical and organizational developments in communication: increasing literacy, the intro-duction of the postal system, fast and relatively cheap travel by coach, steamer and later railway (Davidoff and Hall, 1987: 321). These might not look like 'new' technologies in the way we currently understand the term, and yet the connections they facilitated were central to the self-sufficiency hankered for by the emerging middle classes: 'The creation of the private sphere has been central to the elaboration of consumer demand, so essential to the expansion and accumulation process which characterises modern societies' (Davidoff and Hall, 1987: 29; cf. Barker and Gerhold, 1993: 41–7, 60). At the same time, novel forms of enterprise, middle-class in emphasis, were created around supplying this private sphere with the goods through which to manifest their newly acquired visibility and distinctiveness. In short, this was the period of the birth of a consumer society: the expectation of novelty and ever-changing fashion came to predominate (McKendrick *et al.*, 1982; cf. Campbell, 1987). The 'novelty' of technologies and of domestic relations in this consumer society was an actualization of speed, which thus became of central importance to both the production and distribution process (Barker and Savage, 1974: 14–15). There emerged, then, a dynamic relationship between an ideal of domesticity and the profusion of connections that at once sustained this ideal and were productive of an industrial economy founded on speed (cf. Schivelbusch, 1986). These connections also led, however, to a crises of control, as the entrepreneurs increasingly found it difficult to manage the products, consumers and connections that had been generated between them (see Beniger, 1986: 227–8). Their control was crucial if the flow between them was to be sustained at an ever-greater pace.

CRISIS OF CONTROL

The emergence of the department store and the applications of telegraphic communication to the railroads overlapped historically (Chandler, 1984: 474): both developments were significant for the later emergence of broadcast television.

The department store and telegraphic communication were each a related outgrowth of the scale of connections traced both by persons and manufactured goods and the increasing difficulty in controlling their flow effectively. In effect these multifarious connections had grown to such an extent that it became impossible to draw them together within an encompassing form. Both the department store and telegraphic communications were innovations which were designed to transcend this crisis. The scale of capital devoted to production and distribution processes which engendered innovations of control made apparent the requirement to control consumption. Advertising and marketing campaigns through mass-circulation publishing became widespread during this period which, in turn, foreshadowed the development of 'market research': '[m]ass media were not sufficient to effect true control ... without a means of feedback from potential consumers to advertisers' (Beniger, 1986: 284). The current regime of commercial broadcast television is informed by this social innovation.

The new technology of the telegraph helped to make the connections which sustained both the productive enterprises of business and commerce and separate domestic units. The implementation of control on these 'external' connections was paralleled by an emphasis on the control or discipline of the 'internal', domestic environment. There was a proliferation of literature on household management, domestic economy and hints on household taste as an increasing number of new devices required accommodation within the home (e.g. stereoscopes, photographs, gas appliances, etc., Briggs, 1990: 217).

This external–internal relationship was soon to be further transformed by the new horizons opened up by the introduction of telephone communication. Alexander Graham Bell's vision was one of universal interconnections over vast distances which were not just for the well-off or for business use (de Sola Pool, 1977: 130). This was not, however, such a far-fetched notion since the telegraph had already established a global system of communication (Headrick, 1988: ch. 4) and the distinct technology of telephone had been isolated as a by-product of telegraphic communication. Just as the technology of the telegraph provided the basis for the telephone, so the culture of the telegraph pre-disposed a particular perception towards the possibilities offered by this new technology. In particular, communication between parties via the telegraph operator was one that took time to wrest away from popular consciousness: '[i]t may be obvious now when the telephone often seems to be an appendage to the mouth and ear how many different uses (and misuses) it has, but those living in the telegraph age had to learn them' (Aronson, 1977: 25).

The widespread delivery of the telephone to domestic as well as commercial contexts was not feasible without a central office system with the connections facilitated by a switching mechanism. As Bell indicated in a letter (of 1878) to the entrepreneurs in Britain charged with developing his invention:

> It is conceivable that cables of telephone wires could be laid underground, or suspended overhead, communicating by branch wires with private dwellings, country houses, shops, manufactories, etc. uniting them through the main cable with a central office where the wire could be connected as desired, establishing direct communication between any two places in the city ... I believe in the future wires will unite the head office of the Telephone Company in different cities, and a man in one part of the country may communicate by word of mouth with another in a different place. (quoted by Aronson, 1977: 22)

An analogous relationship during this same period was envisioned for electricity by Thomas Edison whereby electricity was to be delivered into the home (Hughes, 1983; Marvin, 1988; Forty, 1986: ch. 8). In each the notion of a system of interconnections thus came to be of central significance and it was to define the contours of the next period in which first broadcast radio and then broadcast television formally emerged.

SYSTEM AND SIMULTANEITY

The 'systems' approach characterized not only the development and management of technology but it also came to define in a similar manner the analysis and management of 'society'. The crisis of control during previous decades had rendered visible what came to be understood as problems of integration: how was it possible to systematize and thus integrate the various parts to the whole – the individual as part of a wider social reality (Strathern, 1992: 108–9); individual products or services to wider processes of production, distribution and exchange? This was discerned as much as a commercial problem as it was a moral one. On the one hand, Edison's interest in systems was motivated by a desire for commercial advantage, particularly in the development of electricity supply:

> Like any other machine the failure of one part to cooperate properly with the other part disorganises the whole and renders it inoperative for the purposes intended ... The problem then that I [Edison] undertook to solve was stated generally, the production of the multifarious apparatus, methods and devices, each adapted for use with every other, and all forming a comprehensive system. (Quoted in Hughes 1983: 22)

On the other hand, theorists of society such as Durkheim perceived a problem of integration between the individual and society as a consequence of increasing social complexity through the division of labour (cf. Hawthorn, 1987: 123–4, 131). Here was a moral problem that required adequate mechanisms of control if a condition of 'anomie' was to be transcended – the breakdown of norms governing individual and group behaviour: 'Durkheim argued [that] anomie results ... from the breakdown in communication among ... increasingly isolated sectors, so that individuals employed in them lose sight of the larger purpose of their separate efforts' (Beniger, 1986: 12). The solution was to be found in public institutions (education, religion, welfare) which engendered a sense of the social whole (system) as integrated and greater than the sum of its parts (individuals/families). Social reform was soon sought through the use of the innovative techniques of social survey questionnaires which were quickly adopted by advertisers and marketers for different but not unrelated commercial problems. The consumer was soon perceived as linked to a number of separately regulated technological systems (telegraph, telephone, electricity), just as the individual/family was linked to the social whole through a number of separate public institutions or systems. Thus was rendered explicit in this proliferation of systems the phenomena of simultaneity: the ability to experience distant events at the same time (Kern, 1983), and broadcasting would emerge as the most powerful form of simultaneity. But its specific form depended on whether it was part of commercial enterprise (USA) or public service (Britain) (cf. Williams, 1990: 326). During the 1920s take-up of radio in the domestic context coincided with the proliferation of the middle-class ideal of domestic living as embodied in the suburban semi-detached house or bungalow (Oliver *et al.*, 1994; cf. Silverstone, 1994).[2] British broadcasters conceptualized their audience not as an aggregate of individuals but as a specifically domestic one – of families (Scannell and Cardiff, 1991: ch. 16). The middle-class values associated with this notion could then be promoted for the whole nation.[3]

Jennings and Gill's investigations on the impact of radio on everyday life were explicitly commissioned for this purpose by the BBC's Board of Governors during the 1930s: 'they concentrated their efforts on a working class district of Bristol, and their report argued strongly that radio had improved the attractiveness of homelife for working class families' (Scannell and Cardiff, 1991: 363). Radio is thus an example of what came into clearer focus during this period between the wars – the advance of the encompassing ideal of the social or collective whole to which individuals/families were related or attached. This was the ethos with which the advent of broadcasting became imbued. A similar ethos existed less visibly in the formation during this time of the National Grid of electricity to which nearly three-quarters of all homes were connected by 1939 (Davis, 1994: 79; cf. Hughes, 1983: 361–2). Many of the new technologies of the home were powered by electricity, and this capacity meant that the pursuit of domestic consumption could be seen at once as an individual achievement and as part of the greater social system (society, culture) of which it was a part: one could now switch on and off at will.

HARMONIZATION AND ITS LIMITS

Even during the early days of radio broadcasting, television could be envisioned as just around the corner (Briggs, 1985: 155). In Britain at least, its transmission was cut short by the war (Briggs, 1985: 201). With the end of the war the ideal of the suburban semi-detached, middle-class family was ever stronger, but with 'greater security, less responsibility and the assurance of steady material advancement' (Oliver *et al.*, 1994: 194). Broadcast television eventually became synonymous with this advance: it was at once its material embodiment and simultaneously gave audio-visual form to the systematic integration that the individual in the domestic sphere had with this material advancing society. During the 1950s and 1960s this became codified as 'the presumption of the growing internal harmony of a society that was now basically satisfactory, if improvable ... based on confidence in the economy of organised social consensus' (Hobsbawm, 1994: 286).

This 'harmonization' process was facilitated by the boom in consumer electronics (television sets, hi-fi record-playing equipment and records, tape recorders, FM radios) (Hall and Preston, 1988: 165).[4] General access to these technologies was a visible manifestation of the 'affluence' now seen as prevalent (Galbraith, 1958). At the same time, conceptions of 'harmony' were based on domestic living arrangements envisioned as connected to an ever-expanding sphere of media and communication, as key advertisements of this affluence. Broadcast television became the prime example of these numerous connections, providing the sense of a spatio-temporal flow simultaneous with the flow dictated by a highly rationalized system of industrial production and distribution. The rationalization of television programme content was already prefigured during the early years of radio broadcasting (Scannell and Cardiff, 1991: 374–5): '[I]n the later thirties ... [t]he Programme Planning Department [of the BBC] was beginning to adjust daily output to chime in with the time routines of day-to-day life through the weekend and working week'.

As we have seen, the use of survey research as market feedback technology for systematizing the production and distribution of individual goods and services enabled the rationalized control of consumption wherever broadcast television figured significantly as a means of advertising (in Britain since 1955). The use of television as vehicle for consumer advertising has come to be regarded as central to its ubiquity in everyday life (cf. Silverstone, 1994). The 'constant presence' of television is both an outgrowth of this rationalization and productive of the sense that we should in some way – often ambiguously – be influenced by it.

The continuing growth in consumer electronics throughout this period was premised on three related technical innovations which all expanded on tendencies present in previous periods (Dummer, 1983), but in its very success this consumer boom also helped to make explicit the limits of 'harmonization'. The first was the transistor, which made possible both processes of miniaturization and an increase in the range of electronic applications (Dummer, 1983: 7). The second was the integrated circuit, which took further the miniaturization process, heralding the establishment of microelectronics and 'the manufacture of many individual electronic components and functions on a single microchip' (Hall and Preston, 1988: 153). The third was the 'microprogrammable computer on a chip' which has the 'capacity to perform the full range of logic functions on every kind of information presentable in digital form' (Hall and Preston, 1988: 153–4).

This 'revolution' in microelectronics was part of the more complete working out of the solutions to the crisis of control that were first proposed over a century earlier (Beniger, 1986: 435). At the same time, the advent of digitization brought into focus the possible 'convergence' of computer, telecommunication and media: it now became conceivable that these separately regulated 'systems' could become part of one fully interconnected network (cf. Nora and Mine, 1980). The possibility of envisioning the eclipse of separately regulated systems coincided with a radical new vision of the individual/family relationship to the shape of these systems: society as regulated by an all-encompassing state. Just as the limits of the period of harmony were increasingly conceptualized around technological convergence, so the individual/family came to be defined less in relationship to an encompassing societal system and more by the exercise of 'choice' (cf. Strathern, 1992: 213, n. 21).

CHOICE AND CONVERGENCE

Already by the middle of the nineteenth century, the technology of home entertainment was a well-established industry, first in the form of the stereoscope and later in the form of the 'instantaneous photograph' (Briggs, 1990: 132, 135). The notion of the 'spectacle' of a public kind (exhibitions, dioramas) as well as of a private, domestic kind (delight of the interior surroundings) came to define the sense of 'separated-connectedness'. This was further elaborated by the advent of the cinema at the turn of the century and the improvement of the domestic phonograph.

As we have seen, broadcast media, first radio and then television, were central components in systematizing the relations of this public and domestic culture. But by the 1970s, a new range of technologies and politico-moral ideas were on the horizon which would re-shape not only the contours of home media, communication and information, but also the former relationship between 'society' and the individual/family (cf. Williams, 1965: ch. 3). Broadcast television, formerly viewed as almost synonymous with this relationship, was becoming supplanted from this position. At the same time, new configurations of television (less centred on the broadcast form) in the shape of cable, satellite, video, the older communication technology of the telephone, and the new technologies of personal computers, were positioning themselves in a politico-moral environment of 'choice'.

This technological convergence was accompanied by a flattening of the class-based distinctions that had previously been instrumental in providing the conceptual and material architecture of the relationship between the individual/family and society. Now the example being promoted is the private individual, whether residing in a family-based domestic unit or in a transnational corporation. The latter are '[s]uper-private, super individualistic, they seem only larger versions of the private individual' (Strathern, 1992: 141–2).

In this new period of privatized choice, what is potentially emerging are forms of domestic consumption embodying two screens: the older screen of broadcast television is now re-figured around a range of new technologies and the screen of the personal computer. The conventional scheduling structure of broadcast television has been subject to transformation through the development of the video cassette recorder (Hall and Preston, 1988: 163) and the use of 'time shifting' and 'zapping' of scheduled programmes (Ang, 1992: 136), alternative media use (rental movies and video games), and the growth of cable and satellite television from the mid-1980s. What has emerged in this configuration of new technologies and new uses – and this is particularly evident in the British context – is the movement from 'broadcasting' to 'television' (i.e. a move from an emphasis on public service to that of commercial profit) (Murdock, 1994: 156): and in some cases the use of 'television' cable for 'telecommunications' purposes which is more profitable in the long term (Murdock, 1994: 162–3).

The advent of the personal computer has run parallel with these changes around the television screen – and initially convergent with them in certain cases. Its early history during the 1970s and 1980s is in many respects similar to radio when it first appeared earlier this century – focused as it was on the hobbyist and organised hobby culture (Pegg, 1983; Haddon, 1992: 94–5, n. 7, cf. Pfaffenberger, 1988). In this incipient market a number of related uses came to the fore, including games, entertainment and education (links between home and arcades; home and school) and homeworking via modems (separating or connecting home and work). To these transformations of the personal computer we must now add the Internet. During the late 1980s and early 1990s this technological innovation (see Rheingold, 1994: 65–88 for historical background) captured the imagination of domestic computer users with its potential for seemingly innumerable connections from the perspective of the individual. More recently, the addition of the World Wide Web has transformed this connecting potential further: 'this hypertext protocol permits people to simply click on highlighted text to be connected to a computer file somewhere in the Web' (Baldwin *et al.*, 1996: 70).

The convergence of information, communication and media, an ideal promulgated by corporate interest and promoted by forms of national regulation, exists in an uncertain relationship with the interests of domestic consumers (the early failure of videotext is such an example, Baldwin *et al.*, 1996: 65–6; cf. Miles, 1988: 64–9). What is clear, however, is that 'convergence' does not depend on technical innovations alone.[5] Rather, as discussed above, there is a mutually constitutive relationship between 'new' forms of domesticity (based on explicit individual choice) and the connections which such self-sufficiency renders visible for 'new' technologies (based on technological convergence). It has been forecast that even with the implementation of an integrated broadband system, television and computers will not replace one another. Television will continue with its programme format but with some 'interactivity' and the accessing of information. Computers, by contrast, will be used for work, transactional services, e-mail and other on-line services; both will be used for shopping (Baldwin *et al.*, 1996: 156). More precise contours of these sociotechnical innovations are difficult to discern from our current vantage point. What is at issue is how these multifarious connections will come to be gathered together in separate contexts of domesticity where the emphasis is less on societal (state) regulated systems, and more on individual choice. At this point we can turn to the case study of one family which exemplifies this engagement with the current range of new possibilities.

FINDING A PLACE FOR THE MODEM IN THE HOME

During the late 1980s and early 1990s I conducted ethnographic research with 16 families in inner and outer London.[6] 'One of the families I worked with, which I refer to as the Williams family, lived in a semi-detached house in outer London. Geoff and Maria were both pharmacists and worked in two of the local hospitals: Geoff in a full-time capacity as a Principal Pharmacist and Maria on a part-time basis having recently returned to work after a period away looking after their two children. Heather and Alan were eleven and eight respectively when I first met them and attended a local Catholic school. An explicit concern expressed by Geoff and Maria during my fieldwork with them was the separation of home and work. More specifically, the weekend was a time when the family as a whole would spend time together, not constrained by the dictates of time which govern the working/school week; Geoff would consciously remove his watch at the weekend and not shave.

An important aspect of this weekend period was the time spent watching television together as a family. However, as we shall see below, this sense of togetherness around television, particularly at the weekends, would transform as the children grew older and their concerns for independence and privateness became more explicit. For Heather independence and privateness came to be focused largely around the television, while for Alan the computer became more important, although often in conjunction with television viewing.

The explicit value placed on the separateness of the home came to be, among other things during this period of fieldwork, focused around the computer Geoff had purchased for use in the home. This was an Amstrad 1512 which was initially obtained to encourage Alan to learn how to write his own programmes and to move on from the Sega games console which he used frequently (but more of this below). However, at this time, the computer came to take on a transformed significance in the Williams' home, in the context of constraints now operating on Geoff in his hospital job. As Geoff expressed it at the time:

> A computer to me was a tool I used at work until I got myself into the situation I was working late in the evenings, starting early in the morning and when I actually sat down and thought about it there were things that I could do by finishing off at home. There were things I could start from home by dialling in on a modem and I do all these end of month reports which I can key in at this end and I can go in tomorrow morning ... For instance tonight was the last night of the financial month and I could key all the information down the telephone and I can go in tomorrow morning and it will be sat there for me when I walk in, whereas otherwise I would have to go in an hour early before I started. So from that point of view it's saving me so many hours a month, probably about six hours a month, and if I have a report to present tomorrow morning and I'm there at 5:30 this evening at work, say, and I haven't quite finished it, rather than sort of sit around for another half hour or hour – well you are never at your best at the end of a busy day – I tend just to bring a floppy disk home, whack it in the computer and just tidy it up. Perhaps the next morning.

Although all the family members were generally happy with Geoff's use of the computer for this purpose, they were less than enamoured with what the modem in the home entailed for their own living space – the lounge to be precise. The computer had to be next to the telephone line in the lounge and this involved it being placed on a coffee table between two of the lounge chairs. Not only this, but it was a central focus of the room when one entered from the front door or came down the stairs. Again, as Geoff put it: 'At the moment, it's not popular there, it's going out of there actually ... [into a planned conservatory]'.

When I last met the Williams during 1990 the conservatory was completed and the computer had moved into its new home. The modem, however, had not been moved, as a telephone connection point had not been placed there and this entailed a series of extension leads from the conservatory space into the lounge when the modem was in use; it was not a perfect solution in their eyes, but a better arrangement than having the computer and modem together. I recently (1996) re-visited the Williams to find out, among other things, how they had gotten on with the modem in the intervening period. When I returned to the Williams household I was surprised to discover that the modem of old was nowhere to be seen (the Williams had also moved in the intervening four to five years). In fact, the very mention of the old modem provoked laughter from Alan; his father replied defensively: 'In those days it was a fast modem.' Geoff explained that he used the modem for around 18 months and then for a variety of reasons it was no longer needed:

> The security of computer systems have been highlighted in the last 5–6 years ... I would dial from home into the system then, but this is not acceptable now. Some hacker ['cracker', Alan insists in the background] may come in and damage your database. The only safe system today is a dial-back modem with all sorts of security codes on it, but this is big money. Too much money at the moment.

Maria then adds: 'Half of the problem was the way the printer would jam at the other end ... It was not possible to see what was happening at the other end.' Geoff agreed and added that the system he is using presently is much quicker and more user friendly:

> Time constraints that old one forced upon me during the working day are no longer there ... with the old computer ... if I ran huge reports during a working day it slowed down the speed at which rest of department worked. What was the alternative? ... the alternative was to run those reports outside of working time plugging [the] modem in at work, coming home and waiting until I knew all routine work was finished and then knocking the report out ... System is now 500–1000 times faster.

Alan also interjects with his specific perspective on the matter:

> Seems weird that within my lifetime [he is now 14] you have got modems that have changed from being this big [he motions with his arms spread apart] ... which is like your old black box which you still have lying around somewhere, to something which is like a very thick credit card but 40 times faster.

His parents both respond in kind with the notion of 'progress', Geoff stating that he could remember the wireless.

The demise of this modem in the home, however, did not signal the end of modems on the Williams' horizons. Maria indicated that her hospital is planning to issue modems for those on call in roughly six months' time: 'You would have a laptop at home when on call, doctor can phone up, you can tap into hospital system with [a] modem that does not plug into phone line, but with a card' ('a similar principle to that of a mobile phone', adds Alan). She indicates this modem is still not operational as there are a number of security issues that have to be rectified.

Again at this point Alan offers his perspective to the general direction of our discussion, re-iterating a theme often stressed by his parents in the past. In short, he does not like the idea of working from home: 'There should be a separation ... different mental states'. Geoff replies how this is not an option for those he often deals with through his own work, people who work from home and car. (As we shall see below, this is a possibility from which Geoff now does not preclude himself.)

In the more immediate future another modem is on the horizon. This is the plan to buy a modem for Alan for his upcoming birthday (later in August) and as Geoff puts it 'to go on the Internet'.

Before considering the Williams' conceptualization of entry onto the Internet via the modem, it is useful, I think, to briefly re-trace their more general relationship with computers in the home (while I say 'their', it is more accurate to highlight Geoff and Alan's use, as Maria and Heather showed little interest and/or felt excluded from this domain; although issues of gender exclusion are obviously of importance, due to the limited nature of this paper I do not pursue them here).[7]

A Brief History of Computer Use

Maria purchased the first computer for use in the home. This was a Dragon 32 in c.1985. At the time Geoff was taking an evening class on basic computer use and found there was a limited number of computers for the students to practise on. This meant he got very little practice at the keyboard. Maria bought the computer because Geoff continually moaned about this situation but did nothing to remedy it; Maria finally heard enough and went out and purchased what he only talked about getting.

The computer had a 'maze game' which Alan subsequently learned to play. Not long after this Alan also wanted, like others in his peer group, a Sega games console. At the time the family was living in Plymouth. A few years later Geoff took a better position in Slough and the family moved. It was during this time that the Dragon came to the end of its 'life' and Geoff bought the Amstrad 1512. As Alan recalled, the games on the Amstrad were worse than those on the Sega but you could write your own programmes on the former; at this time Alan learned 'Basic' at school and soon became involved in writing his own programmes.

The Williams had the Amstrad for two years and before they moved on to a new 'home', they decided to update the computer for Alan – an Olivetti 386. At the same time Heather was given a new television with teletext and remote control as she was very interested in television in the same way that Alan was keenly involved with the computer. Both were presented as Christmas presents.

As Alan recalls, he bought many computer games to play on the Olivetti for about a three-year period: for two years he bought all the latest versions and then for one year bought the 'budget games'. It was at the end of this period that he discovered 'Visual Basic'. This brief history of the computers in the Williams' home and Alan's involvement with them was glossed by Geoff as follows:

He moved from games machine which was purely games ... Sega ... to the Amstrad where he learned a bit about 'Basic' and how programmes worked, but could still play games, to the Olivetti where games got faster, better and more colourful, to a programming language called 'Visual Basic' which was sophisticated, and last year we got the Pentium.

Maria adds: 'He just grew out of it [Olivetti] ...'

And Geoff: 'He couldn't do any more with it ...'

Maria: 'Bit slow for you [referring to Alan] ...'

Alan: 'My habits changed ... I developed a hobby – a strange, very sad hobby – I tried to refine it, organize the hard drive so files would be in order I liked them ... [I wanted to] see how far I could refine the system.'

The move to the Pentium was prompted by these limits and the fact that Alan was receiving money from the BBC for an acting part he had secured on a children's programme. Using also an equal sum from his parents, he acquired a Viglen desktop, Pentium processor, speakers, etc: 'a full multi-task system', as Alan referred to it. Since this purchase virtually all of his free time is spent in the spare room which houses the computer – a routine his parents attempt to monitor and restrict at particular times (e.g. when he is revising for his GCSEs).

It is only recently that Geoff, together with Alan, has rekindled an interest in a modem in the home. The modem will be purchased for Alan's upcoming birthday (see above) and GCSE results. Geoff explains this in the following terms: 'These days keep them up with technology ... they are going to come across it.'

There are, however, two dimensions to this 'keeping up' idea that Geoff subsequently discloses. The first is related to Alan's involvement in computer use. The second is Geoff's own concern about the security of his position within the 'new' NHS. As both Maria and he indicate during our discussion, jobs are no longer secure in the Health Service; Maria's boss was recently made redundant. For Geoff the interest in the modem is part of an insurance policy in case he loses his job and has to begin to sell his services as a consultant working from home.

Geoff's most immediate interest, however, is the potential he sees in the Internet: 'The Internet is not particularly practical now ... problem is that it has potential to be very useful indeed but is at its beginning ... good stuff in there but you have to find it'. By contrast, Maria's major concern is the extent to which her telephone is to be constantly taken up: 'I shall just have to ration you to it ...'. For Alan the greatest interest lies in e-mail and in particular to a female friend from school who lives roughly 10 minutes away and who already has e-mail: 'The only other instantaneous communication is on the phone, but in a conversation you have to keep to the same topic [in an e-mail message] you can have one paragraph on this and one paragraph on this ... and then respond and add something else'. 'Surfing the net' does not hold much interest. Rather, he envisions drawing on computer magazines that have regular features about what is good on the Internet 'and we have discovered it'. He predicts his use of the Internet to be similar to his current viewing of television where he consults the *Radio Times* in his sister's room 'when she is not looking' and makes a note of what he wants to watch.

In general, Geoff notes that he has been keeping an eye on the Internet: 'You have got to keep your fingers on the pulse and you have got to know when to jump.'

When to Jump?

I was interested in the way the Williams, and in particular Geoff and Alan, were conceptualizing their moment of truth: when they would make their first connection. It was clear in their minds that all the factors they had some control over had to be researched initially: which modem to buy, which 'provider' to use and what form of access to purchase, which sites to visit, and so on. Each one of these preparatory steps to becoming connected involved a number of elements. For example, Geoff and Alan are currently reading an up-to-date volume on different types of modem. Once they have selected several as suitable ('and cheapest') they will as Alan puts it: 'ask friends, ring the "providers", ring the computer manufacturer to inquire about their preferences and any issues about compatibility'. With regard to the 'provider' a number of factors emerge: should they proceed with a firm like CompuServe which is an international provider and will be more expensive but also more reliable, or with a smaller outfit that is cheaper but perhaps not as reliable? Geoff draws an analogy here with double glazing firms for Maria's sake as she is not clear about the role of the 'provider': 'On the one hand you have Anglia which is a large firm and has an outlet in every town. On the other hand you have "Jo Bloggs" special of five windows for £1000 . . .'. As far as the 'sites' to visit, both Geoff and Alan agree that they will use books and magazines to do the searching for them, although as Geoff observes: 'seems a bit daft . . . all computerised but still using a book to get to it'.

My intention in rehearsing this family's conceptualization of this anticipated connection to the Internet (and there are a number of other details I have left out at this stage for reasons of space) is that it makes visible a series of other related connections: to other domestic contexts (friends), to 'providers', suppliers, libraries and bookshops. And all of these connections are brought into focus at this point in time by a tiny technological object – 'a thicker version of a credit card' – which will enable the initial 'jump'.

Conclusion: Finding a Place for the Modem in the Home

In the half dozen years that I have known the Williams family they have had one modem and are about to purchase a second. There were a number of problems with the first; from their perspective it was the physical place of the modem *vis-à-vis* the computer and telephone line that made it seem so out of place. To help maintain the separation between home and work for which it was summoned the modem did its work, but made its presence visibly felt.

The second, anticipated modem will not, it seems, create the same problem concerning physical presence as did its ancestor. Rather, the problems it will make manifest seem to centre more on the multiplicity of connections that it will enable. This is envisioned as a tremendous potential (Geoff), a threat to the telephone line (Maria), to be weighed against a more intense interest in e-mail (Alan) and of marginal interest in comparison with television (Heather). I would suggest that the anticipated modem has to find its place more in the *relations that constitute the domestic context of the Williams home*, than in its physical location. This was certainly an issue with the previous modem, but the connections and possibilities for connections it entailed were more limited compared to the current version.

In the current period of 'choice and convergence', then, each member of the Williams family perceives the new technology as offering different possibilities, different 'choices'. A number of conflicting interests will have to become reconciled with the advent of the new modem and the multiple connections with the outside world it facilitates. In short, there is uncertainty in what the internal relations around the modem will look like in relation to the outside connections it will enable.

The tensions revealed by this example, although unique to the contemporary period, reoccur throughout the history of the relationship between 'new' technologies and the domestic context which has been surveyed by this chapter. There have been a number of significant transformations over the 200-year period covered which are not simply a consequence of 'new' technologies alone or of 'new' notions of domesticity alone, but of the mutually constitutive relations that each effects on the other. The history of these processes is increasingly being recovered by scholars: around the take-up of television (see Spigel, 1990), for radio (see Moores, 1988), for electricity and telephone (see Fischer, 1988; Marvin, 1988) and for the railroad (see Schivelbusch, 1986), to name just a few examples.

The current debates surrounding broadcast television and its place in the domestic context in relation to a range of new technologies are, as I have suggested, part of a long-standing history where what is new and what is old or established are always co-existent, always define each other. This is as true of the technologies as it is of domesticity and its forms of consumption, and the relations sustained between them.

NOTES

1. The emergence of the middle class, with its emphasis on family-based domesticity and the separation of male (workplace) and female (home) spheres, was one of several ideals (ideologies) promoted during the late eighteenth century. It was not self-evident that the family model of domesticity should become dominant. That it did was in part because of the forceful moral, religious and political arguments orchestrated on its behalf. Other forms of domesticity and other forms of working

arrangements were simultaneously promoted and there was a struggle as to which would be ascendant (see Hall, 1992; Strathern, 1992).

2. Between 1924 and 1929 the ownership of radio licences in the UK increased from 10 per cent of households to 26 per cent. Over the next 10 years there was a steady increase so that by 1939, 71 per cent of all households possessed a radio (Pegg, 1983: 7, table 1.1).

3. Simultaneity is more than just people watching at the same time; they must also make similar connections to the media. If simultaneity can only be completed by similarity then the suburban model of living is a perfect exemplar.

4. In the UK between 1954 and 1968 combined radio and television licences increased from just over 3 million to roughly 15 million (Briggs, 1985: 303).

5. The most significant technical innovation is arguably the integrated broadband system, based on fibre optic cables, which permits transmission of a large volume of digitized material.

6. The focus of the research was on the domestic culture of the home in the context of information and communication technologies. The research was carried out in collaboration with Roger Silverstone as part of the ESRC Programme on Information and Communication Technologies. The families involved in the research were recruited through local schools. Fieldwork with each family occurred over a six to nine month period based on eight to nine visits. The research format included structured, but open-ended sets of questions and discussion themes as well as participant observation involving all family members in the home (see Hirsch, 1992 for more details).

7. Haddon (1992: 90) has documented how the computer game market developed from the male-dominated arcades culture when pinball machines were replaced by video games. It is of note that when the discussion turned to the connections facilitated by the Internet (e.g. television-related Web sites) Heather expressed an interest in computer use for this purpose.

REFERENCES

Ang, I., (1992) 'Living-room wars: new technologies, audience measurement and the tactics of television consumption'. In R. Silverstone and E. Hirsch (eds), *Consuming Technologies. Media and Information in Domestic Spaces*, London: Routledge.

Aronson, S., (1977) 'Bell's electrical toy: What's the use? The sociology of early telephone usage'. In I. de Sola Pool (ed.), *The Social Impact of the Telephone*, Cambridge, MA.: MIT Press.

Baldwin, T. *et al.*, (1996) *Convergence: Integrating Media, Information and Communication*, London: Sage.

Barker, T. and Gerhold, D., (1993) *The Rise and Rise of Road Transport, 1700–1990*, London: Macmillan.

Barker, T. and Savage, C., (1974) *An Economic History of Transport in Britain*, 3rd edn. London: Hutchinson.

Beniger, J., (1986) *The Control Revolution: Technological and Economic Origins of the Information Society*, Cambridge, MA: Harvard University Press.

Briggs, A. (1985) *The BBC. The First Fifty Years*, Oxford: Oxford University Press.

Briggs, A. (1990) *Victorian Things*, London: Penguin Books.

Campbell, C., (1987) *The Romantic Ethic and the Spirit of Modern Consumerism*, Oxford: Blackwell.

Chandler, A., (1984) 'The emergence of managerial capitalism'. *Business History Review*, 58: 473–503.

Davidoff, L. and Hall, C., (1987) *Family Fortunes: Men and Women of the English Middle Class 1780–1850*, London: Hutchinson.

Davis, I., (1994) 'A celebration of ambiguity. The synthesis of contrasting values', In P. Oliver, *et al.*, *Dunroamin: The Suburban Semi and its Enemies*, London: Pimlico.

de Sola Pool, I. (ed.), (1977) *The Social Impact of the Telephone*, Cambridge, MA: MIT Press.

Dummer, G., (1983) *Electric Inventions and Discoveries. Electronics from its Earliest Beginnings to the Present Day*, 3rd revised and expanded edn. Oxford: Pergamon.

Fischer, C., (1988) '"Touch someone": the telephone industry discovers sociability'. *Technology and Culture*, 29, 1: 32–61.

Forty, A., (1986) *Objects of Desire: Design and Society 1750–1980*, London: Thames and Hudson.

Galbraith, J. (1958) *The Affluent Society*, London: Hamish Hamilton.

Haddon, L., (1992) 'Explaining ICT consumption: the case of the home computer'. In R. Silverstone and E. Hirsch (eds), *Consuming Technologies: Media and Information in Domestic Spaces*, London: Routledge.

Hall, C. (1992) *White, Male and Middle Class: Explorations in Feminism and History*, Cambridge: Polity Press.

Hall, P. and Preston P., (1988) *The Carrier Wave: New Information Technology and the Geography of Innovation, 1846–2003*, London: Unwin Hyman.

Hawthorn, G., (1987) *Enlightenment and Despair: A History of Social Theory*, 2nd edn. Cambridge: Cambridge University Press.

Headrick, D., (1988) *The Tentacles of Progress: Technology Transfer in the Age of Imperialism, 1850–1940*, Oxford: Oxford University Press.

Hirsch, E., (1992) 'The long term and short term of domestic consumption: an ethnographic case study'. In R. Silverstone and E. Hirsch (eds), *Consuming Technologies: Media and Information in Domestic Spaces*, London: Routledge.

Hobsbawm, E., (1994) *The Age of Extremes: The Short Twentieth Century, 1914–91*, London: Abacus.

Hughes, T., (1983) *Networks of Power: Electrification in Western Society, 1880–1930*, Baltimore: Johns Hopkins University Press.

Kern, S., (1983) *The Culture of Time and Space 1880–1918*, Cambridge, MA: Harvard University Press.

Marvin, C., (1988) *When Old Technologies were New: Thinking about Communications in the Late Nineteenth Century*, New York: Oxford University Press.

McKendrick, N. et al., (1982) *The Birth of a Consumer Society: The Commercialization of Eighteenth-Century England*. London: Hutchinson.

Miles, I., (1988) *Home Informatics: Information Technology and the Transformation of Everyday Life*, London: Pinter.

Moores, S., (1988) '"The box on the dresser": memories of early radio and everyday life'. *Media, Culture and Society*, 10, 1: 23–40.

Murdock, G., (1994) 'Money talks: broadcasting, finance and public culture'. In S. Hood (ed.), *Behind the Screens: The Structure of British Television in the Nineties*, London: Lawrence and Wishart.

Nora, S. and Mine, A., (1980) *The Computerization of Society. A Report to the President of France*, Cambridge, MA: MIT Press.

Oliver, P. et al., (1994) *Dunroamin: The Suburban Semi and its Enemies*, London: Pimlico.

Pegg, M., (1983) *Broadcasting and Society, 1918–1939*, London: Croom Helm.

Pfaffenberger, B., (1988) 'The social meaning of the personal computer; or, why the personal computer revolution was no revolution'. *Anthropological Quarterly*, 61, 1: 39–47.

Rheingold, H., (1994) *The Virtual Community: Homesteading on the Electronic Frontier*, New York: HarperCollins.

Scannell, P. and Cardiff, D., (1991) *A Social History of Broadcasting, Vol. 1 1922–1939: Serving the Nation*, London: Blackwell.

Schivelbusch, W., (1986) *The Railway Journey: The Industralization of Time and Space in the Nineteenth Century*, new edn, Leamington Spa: Berg.

Silverstone, R., (1994) *Television and Everyday Life*, London: Routledge.

Spigel, L. (1990) 'Television in the family circle: the popular reception of a new medium'. In P. Mellencamp (ed.), *Logics of Television: Essays in Cultural Criticism*, Bloomington and London: Indiana University Press and British Film Institute.

Stone, L., (1990) *Road to Divorce: England 1530–1987*, Oxford: Oxford University Press.

Strathern, M., (1992) *After Nature: English Kinship in the Late Twentienth Century*, Cambridge: Cambridge University Press.

——, (1996) 'Enabling identity? Biology, choice and the new reproductive technologies'. In S. Hall and P. du Gay (eds), *Questions of Cultural Identity*, London: Sage.

Wahrman, D., (1995) *Imagining the Middle Class: The Political Representation of Class in Britain, c. 1780–1840*, Cambridge: Cambridge University Press.

Williams, R., (1965) *The Long Revolution*, Harmondsworth: Penguin Books.

——, (1990) *Culture and Society: Coleridge to Orwell*, London: Hogarth Press.

65

ON THE MATRIX: CYBERFEMINIST SIMULATIONS

Sadie Plant

Her mind is a matrix of non-stop digital flickerings.

(Misha 1991: 113)

If machines, even machines of theory, can be aroused all by themselves, may woman not do likewise?

(Irigaray 1985a: 232)

After decades of ambivalence towards technology, many feminists are now finding a wealth of new opportunities, spaces and lines of thought amidst the new complexities of the 'telecoms revolution'. The Internet promises women a network of lines on which to chatter, natter, work and play; virtuality brings a fluidity to identities which once had to be fixed; and multi-media provides a new tactile environment in which women artists can find their space.

Cyberfeminism has, however, emerged as more than a survey or observation of the new trends and possibilities opened up by the telecoms revolution. Complex systems and virtual worlds are not only important because they open spaces for existing women within an already existing culture, but also because of the extent to which they undermine both the world-view and the material reality of two thousand years of patriarchal control.

Network culture still appears to be dominated by both men and masculine intentions and designs. But there is more to cyberspace than meets the male gaze. Appearances have always been deceptive, but no more so than amidst

From Rob Shields (ed.), *Cultures of the Internet: Virtual Spaces, Real Histories, Living Bodies* (London: Sage, 1996) pp. 170–83.

today's simulations and immersions of the telecoms revolution. Women are accessing the circuits on which they were once exchanged, hacking into security's controls, and discovering their own post-humanity. The cyberfeminist virus first began to make itself known in the early 1990s.[1] The most dramatic of its earliest manifestations was *A Cyberfeminist Manifesto for the 21st Century*, produced as a digitized billboard dispayed on a busy Sydney thoroughfare. The text of this manifesto has mutated and shifted many times since, but one of its versions includes the lines:

> we are the virus of the new world disorder
> disrupting the symbolic from within
> saboteurs of big daddy mainframe
> the clitoris is a direct line to the matrix
> VNS MATRIX
> terminators of the moral code ...

Like all successful viruses, this one caught on. VNS Matrix, the group of four women artists who made the billboard, began to write the game plan for *All New Gen*, a viral cyber-guerrilla programmed to infiltrate cyberspace and hack into the controls of Oedipal man – or Big Daddy Mainframe, as he's called in the game. And there has been no stopping All New Gen. She has munched her way through patriarchal security screens and many of their feminist simulations, feeding into and off the energies with which she is concurrent and in tune: the new cyberotics engineered by the girls; the queer traits and tendencies of Generations XYZ; the post-human experiments of dance music scenes.

All New Gen and her allies are resolutely hostile to morality and do nothing but erode political power. They reprogram guilt, deny authority, confuse identity, and have no interest in the reform or redecoration of the ancient patriarchal code. With Luce Irigaray (1985b: 75), they agree that 'how the system is put together, how the specular economy works', are amongst the most important questions with which to begin its destruction.

THE SPECULAR ECONOMY

This is the first discovery: that patriarchy is not a construction, an order or a structure, but an economy, for which women are the first and founding commodities. It is a system in which exchanges 'take place exclusively between men. Women, signs, commodities, and currency always pass from one man to another', and the women are supposed to exist 'only as the possibility of mediation, transaction, transition, transference – between man and his fellow-creatures, indeed between man and himself' (Irigaray 1985b: 193). Women have served as his media and interfaces, muses and messengers, currencies and screens, interactions, operators, decoders, secretaries ... they have been man's go-betweens, the in-betweens, taking his messages, bearing his children, and passing on his genetic code.

If women have experienced their exclusion from social, sexual and political life as the major problem posed by their government, this is only the tip of an iceberg of control and alienation from the species itself. Humanity has defined itself as a species whose members are precisely what they think they own: male members. Man is the one who has one, while the character called 'woman' has, at best, been understood to be a deficient version of a humanity which is already male. In relation to *homo sapiens*, she is the foreign body, the immigrant from nowhere, the alien without and the enemy within. Woman can do anything and everything except be herself. Indeed, she has no being, nor even one role; no voice of her own, and no desire. She marries into the family of man, but her outlaw status always remains: 'within herself' she never signs up. She doesn't have the equipment' (Irigaray, 1991: 90).

What this 'equipment' might have given her is the same senses of member-ship, belonging and identity which have allowed her male colleagues to consider themselves at home and in charge of what they call 'nature', the 'world', or 'life'. Irigaray's male subjects are first and foremost the ones who see, those whose gaze defines the world. The phallus and the eye stand in for each other, giving priority to light, sight, and a flight from the dark dank matters of the feminine. The phallic eye has functioned to endow them with a connection to what has variously been defined as God, the good, the one, the ideal from or transcendent truth. It has been, in effect, their badge of membership, their means of iden-tification and unification with an equally phallic authority. Whereas woman has nothing to be seen where man thinks the member should be. Only a hole, a shadow, a wound, a 'sex that is not one.'

All the great patriarchs have defined this as *her* problem. Witch-hunters defined the wickedness of women as being due to the fact that they 'lack the male member', and when Freud exhorts them to get 'little ones of their own', he intends this to compensate for this supposed lack. And without this one, as Irigaray writes, hysteria 'is all she has left'. This, or mimicry, or catatonic silence.

Either way, woman is left without the senses of self and identity which accrue to the masculine. Denied the possibility of an agency which would allow to transform herself, it becomes hard to see what it would take for her situation ever to change. How can Irigaray's women discover themselves when any conception of who they might be has already been decided in advance? How can she speak without becoming the only speaking subject conceivable to man? How can she be active when activity is defined as male? How can she design her own sexuality when even this has been defined by those for whom the phallus is the central core?

The problem seems intractable. Feminist theory has tried every route, and found itself in every cul-de-sac. Struggles have been waged both with and against Marx, Freud, Lacan, Derrida ... sometimes in an effort to claim or reclaim some notion of identity, subjectivity and agency; sometimes to eschew it in the name of undecidability or *jouissance*. But always in relation to a sacrosanct conception of a male identity which women can either accept, adapt to, or refuse altogether. Only Irigaray – and even then, only in some of her works – begins to suggest that there really is no point in pursuing the masculine dream of self-control, self-identification, self-knowledge and self-determination. If 'any theory of the subject always have been appropriated by the masculine' (Irigaray, 1985a: 133) before the women can get close to it, only the destruction of this subject will suffice.

Even Irigaray cannot imagine quite what such a transformation would involve: this is why so much of her work is often said to be unhelpfully pessimistic. But there is more than the hope that such change will come. For a start, and like all economies, patriarchy is not a closed system, and can never be entirely secure. It too has an 'outside', from which it has 'in some way borrowed energy', as is clear from the fact that in spite of patriarchy's love of origins and sources, 'the origin of its motive force remains, partially, unexplained, eluded' (Irigaray, 1985b: 115). It needs to contain and control what it understands as 'woman' and 'the feminine', but it cannot do without them: indeed, as its media, means of communication, reproduction and exchange, women are the very fabric of its culture, the material precondition of the world it controls. If Irigaray's conclusions about the extent and pervasiveness of patriarchy were once an occasion for pessimistic paralysis, things look rather different in an age for which all economic systems are reaching the limits of their modern functioning. And if ever this system did begin to give, the effects of its collapse would certainly outstrip those on its power over women and their lives: patriarchy is the precondition of all other forms of ownership and control, the model of every exercise of power, and the basis of all subjection. The control and exchange of women by their fathers, husbands, brothers and sons is the diagram of hierarchical authority.

This 'specular economy' depends on its ability to ensure that all tools, commodities, and media know their place, and have no aspirations to usurp or subvert the governing role of those they serve. 'It would', for example, 'be out of the question for them to go to the "market" alone, to profit from their own value, to talk to each other, to desire each other, without the control of the selling-buying-consuming subjects' (Irigaray, 1985b: 196). It is out of the question, but it happens anyway.

By the late twentieth century, all patriarchy's media, tools, commodities, and the lines of commerce and communication on and as which they circulate have changed beyond recognition. The convergence of once separate and specialized media turns them into systems of telecommunication with messages of their own; and tools mutate into complex machines which begin to learn and act for themselves. The proliferation, falling costs, miniaturization and ubiquity of the silicon chip already renders the new commodity smart and, as trade routes and their traffics run out of control on computerized markets with 'minds of their own', state, society, subject, the geo-political order, and all other forces of patriarchal law and order are undermined by the activity of markets which no longer lend their invisible hands in support of the status quo. As media, tools and goods mutate, so the women begin to *change*, escaping their isolation and coming increasingly interlinked. Modern feminism is marked by the emergence of networks and contacts which need no centralized organization and evade its structures of command and control.

The early computer was a military weapon, a room-sized giant of a system full of transistors and ticker-tape. Not until the 1960s development of the silicon chip did computers become small and cheap enough to circulate as commodities, and even then the first mass market computers were hardly user-friendly machines. But if governments, the military and the big corporations had ever intended to keep it to themselves, the street found new uses for the new machinery. By the 1980s there were hackers, cyberpunks, rave, and digital arts. Prices began to plummet as computers crept on to the desks and then into the laps and even the pockets of a new generation of users. Atomized systems began to lose their individual isolation as a global web emerged from the thousands of e-mail connections, bulletin boards, and multiple-user domains which compose the emergence of the Net. By the mid-1990s, a digital underground is thriving, and the Net has become the leading zone on which the old identifications collapse. Genders can be bent and blurred and the time-space co-ordinates tend to get lost. But even such schizophrenia, and the imminent impossibility – and even the irrelevance – of distinguishing between virtual and actual reality, pales into insignificance in comparison to the emergence of the Net as an anarchic, self-organizing, system into which its users fuse. The Net is becoming cyberspace, the virtuality with which the not-quite-ones have always felt themselves to be in touch.

This is also the period in which the computer becomes an increasingly decentralized machine. The early computers were serial systems which worked on the basis of a central processing unit in which logical 'if-then' decisions are made in serial fashion, one step at a time. The emergence of parallel distributed processing systems removes both the central unit and the serial nature of its operations, functioning instead in terms of interconnected units which operate simultaneously and without reference to some governing core. Information is not centrally stored or processed, but is distributed across the switches and connections which constitute the system itself.

This 'connectionist' machine is an indeterminate process rather than a definite entity:

> We are faced with a system which depends on the levels of *activity* of its various sub-units, and on the manner in which the activity levels of some sub-units affect one another. If we try to 'fix' all this activity by trying to define the entire state of the system at one time ... we immediately lose appreciation of the evolution of these activity levels over time. Conversely, if it is the activity levels in which we are interested, we need to look for patterns over time. (Eiser, 1994: 192)

Parallel distributed processing defies all attempts to pin it down, and can only ever be contingently defined. It also turns the computer into a complex thinking machine which converges with the operations of the human brain. Simultaneous with the Artificial Intelligence and computer science programmes which have led to such developments, research in the neuro-sciences moves towards materialist conceptions of the brain as a complex, connective, distributed machine. Neural nets are distributed systems which function as analogues of the brain and can learn, think 'evolve', and 'live'. And the parallels proliferate. The complexity the computer becomes also emerges in economies, weather-systems, cities and cultures, all of which begin to function as complex systems with their own parallel processes, connectivities, and immense tangles of mutual interlinkings.

Not that artificial lives, cultures, markets, and thinking organisms are suddenly free to self-organize. Science, its disciplines, and the academic structures they support insist on the maintenance of top-down structures, and depend on their ability to control and define the self-organizing processes they unleash. State institutions and corporations are intended to guarantee the centralized and hierarchical control of market processes, cultural development and, indeed, any variety of activity which might disturb the smooth regulation of the patriarchal economy. When Isaac Asimov wrote his three laws of robotics, they were lifted straight from the marriage vows: love, honour, and obey ... [2] Like women, any thinking machines are admitted on the understanding that they are duty-bound to honour and obey the members of the species to which they were enslaved: the members, the male ones, the family of man. But self-organizing processes proliferate, connections are continually made, and complexity becomes increasingly complex. In spite of *its* best intentions, patriarchy is subsumed by the processes which served it so well. The goods do get together, eventually.

The implications of all these accelerating developments are extensive and profound. In philosophical terms, they all tend towards the erosion of idealism and the emergence of a new materialism, a shift in thinking triggered by the emergent activity and intelligence of the material reality of a world which man still believes he controls. Self-replicating programs proliferate in the software labs, generating evolutionary processes in the same machines on to which the Human Genome Project downloads DNA. Nanotechnology feeds into material self-organization at a molecular level and in defiance of old scientific paradigms, and a newly digitized biology has to acknowledge that there is neither a pinnacle of achievement nor a governing principle overriding evolution, which is instead composed of complex series of parallel processes, learning and mutating on microcosmic scales, and cutting across what were once separated into natural and cultural processes.

Although she is supposed to do nothing more than function as an object of consumption and exchange, it is a woman who first warns the world of the possibility of the runaway potential of its new sciences and technologies: Mary Shelley's Frankenstein makes the first post-human life form of a modern age which does indeed roll round to the unintended consequences of its own intelligent and artificial lives. Shelley writes far in advance of the digital computers which later begin to effect such developments, but she clearly feels the stirrings of artificial life even as industrialization begins and does much to programme the dreams and nightmares of the next two centuries of its acceleration.

The processes which feed into this emergent activity have no point of origin. Although they were gathering pace for some time before the computer arrives on the scene, its engineering changes everything. Regardless of recent portrayals of computers – and, by extension, all machines and all aspects of the telecoms revolution – as predominantly masculine tools, there is a long history of such intimate and influential connections between women and modernity's machines. The first telephonists, operators, and calculators were women, as were the first computers, and even the first computer programmers. Ada Lovelace wrote the software for the 1840s Analytical Engine, a prototype computer which was never built, and when such a machine was finally constructed in the 1940s, it too was programmed by a woman, Grace Murray Hopper. Both women have left their legacies: ADA is now the name of a US military programming language, and one of Hopper's claims to fame is the word 'bug', which was first used when she found a dead moth in the workings of Mark 1. And as women increasingly interact with the computers whose exploratory use was once monopolized by men, the qualities and apparent absences once defined as female become continuous with those described to the new machines.

Unlike previous machines, which tend to have some single purpose, the computer functions as a general purpose system which can, in effect, do anything. It can simulate the operations of, for example, the typewriter, and while it is running a word-processing program, this, in effect, is precisely what it is. But the computer is always more – or less – than the set of actual functions it fulfils at any particular time: as an implementation of Alan Turing's abstract machine, *the computer is virtually real*.[3] Like Irigaray's woman, it can turn its invisible, non-existent self to anything: it runs any program, and simulates all operations, even those of its own functioning. This is the woman who 'doesn't know what she wants', and cannot say what she is, or thinks, and yet still, of course, persists as though 'elsewhere', as Irigaray often writes. This is the complexity of a system beyond representation, something beyond expression in the existing discursive structures, the 'Nothing. Everything' with which Irigaray's woman responds when they ask her: 'what are you thinking?' (Irigaray, 1985b: 29).

> Thus what they desire is precisely nothing, and at the same time, everything. Always something more and something else besides that *one* – sexual organ, for example – that you give them, attribute to them; [something which] involves a different economy more than anything

else, one that upsets the linearity of a project, undermines the goal-object of a desire, diffuses the polarization towards a single pleasure, disconcerts fidelity to a single discourse ... (Irigaray, 1985b: 29–30)

Irigaray's woman has never had a unified role: mirror, screen, commodity; means of communication and reproduction; carrier and weaver; carer and whore; machine assemblage in the service of the species; a general purpose system of simulation and self-stimulation. It may have been woman's 'fluid character which has deprived her of all possibility of identity with herself within such a logic' (Irigaray, 1985b: 109), but if fluidity has been configured as a matter of deprivation and disadvantage in the past, it is a positive advantage in a feminized future for which identity is nothing more than a liability. It is 'her inexhaustible aptitude for mimicry' which makes her 'the living foundation for the whole staging of the world'. (Irigaray, 1991: 118). Her very inability to concentrate now connects her with the parallel processings of machines which function without unified control.

Neural nets function in a way which has less to do with the rigours of orthodox logic than with the intuitive leaps and cross-connections which characterize what has been pathologized as hysteria, which is said to be marked by a 'lack of inhibition and control in its associations' between ideas which are dangerously 'cut off from associative connection with the other ideas, but can be associated among themselves, and thus form the more or less highly organized rudiment of a second consciousness ...' (Freud and Breuer, 1991: 66–7). Hysteria is the point at which association gets a little too free, spinning off in its own directions and making links without reference to any central core. And if hysteria has functioned as a paralysing pathology of the sex that is not one, 'in hysteria there is at the same time the possibility of another mode of "production" ... maintained in latency. Perhaps as a cultural reserve yet to come ... ?' (Irigaray, 1985b: 138).

Freud's hysterical ideas grow 'out of the day-dreams which are so common even in healthy people and to which needlework and similar occupations render women particularly prone' (Freud and Breuer, 1991: 66). It is said that Ada Lovelace, herself defined as hysterical, 'wove her daydreams into seemingly authentic calculations' (Langton Moore, 1977: 216). Working with Charles Babbage on the nineteenth-century Analytical Engine, Lovelace lost her tortured self on the planes of mathematical complexity, writing the software for a machine which would take a hundred years to build. Unable to find the words for them, she programs a mathematics in which to communicate the abstraction and complexity of her thoughts.[4]

Lovelace and Babbage took their inspiration from the early nineteenth-century Jacquard loom, crucial both to the processes of automation integral to the industrial revolution, and to the emergence of the modern computer. The loom worked on the basis of punched paper programs, a system necessitated by the peculiar complexity of weaving which has always placed the activity in the forefront of technological advance. If weaving has played such a crucial role in the history of computing, it is also the key to one of the most extraordinary sites of a woman/machine interface which short-circuits their prescribed relationship and persists regardless of what man effects and defines as the history of technology.

Weaving is the exemplary case of a denigrated female craft which now turns out to be intimately connected to the history of computing and the digital technologies. Plaiting and weaving are the 'only contributions to the history of discoveries and inventions' (Freud, 1985: 167) which Freud is willing to ascribe to women. He tells a story in which weaving emerges as a simulation of what he describes as a natural process, the matting of pubic hairs across the hole, the zero, the nothing to be seen. Freud intends no favours with such an account. It is because of women's shame at the absence which lies where the root of their being should be that they cover up the disgusting wound, concealing the wandering womb of hysteria, veiling the matrix once and for all. This is a move which dissociates weaving from the history of science and technology, removing to a female zone both the woven and the networks and fine connective meshes of the computer culture into which it feeds.

In the course of weaving this story, Freud gives another game away. Orthodox accounts of the history of technology are told from an exclusively anthropomorphic perspective whose world-view revolves around the interests of man. Conceived the products of his genius and as means to his own ends, even complex machines are understood to be tools and mediations which allow a unified, discreet human agency to interact with an inferior natural world. Weaving, however, is outside this narrative: there is a continuity between the weaver, the weaving, and the woven which gives them a connectivity which eludes all orthodox conceptions of technology. And although Freud is willing to give women the credit for its 'invention', his account also implies that there is no point of origin, but instead a process of simulation by which weaving replicates or weaves itself. It is not a thing, but a process. In its future, female programmers and multi-media artists were to discover connections between knitting, patchwork, and software engineering and find weaving secreted in the pixelled windows which open on to cyberspace.

FROM MACHINES TO MATRICES

As images migrate from canvas to film and finally on to the digital screen, what was once called art mutates into a matter of software engineering. Digital art takes the image beyond even its mechanical reproduction, eroding orthodox conceptions of originals and originality. And just as the image is reprocessed, so it finds itself embroiled in a new network of connections between words, music, and architectures which diminishes the governing role it once played in the specular economy.

If the media were once as divided as the senses with which they interact, their convergence and transition into hypermedia allows the senses to fuse and connect. Touch is the sense of multi-media, the immersive simulations of cyberspace, and the connections, switches and links of all nets. Communication cannot be caught by the gaze, but is always a matter of getting in touch, a question of contact, contagion, transmission, reception and connectivity. If sight was the dominant and organizing sense of the patriarchal economy, tactility is McLuhan's 'integral sense' (1967: 77), putting itself and all the others in touch and becoming the sense of hypermedia. It is also the sense with which Irigaray approaches the matter of a female sexuality which is more than one, 'at least two', and always in touch with its own contact points. The medium is the message, and there is no 'possibility of distinguishing what is touching from what is touched' (Irigaray, 1985b: 26).

> For if 'she' says something, it is not, it is already no longer, identical with what she means. What she says is never identical with anything, moreover; rather, it is contiguous. *It touches (upon)*. And when it strays too far from that proximity, she stops and starts over at 'zero': her body-sex. (Irigaray, 1985: 29)

Digitization sets zero free to stand for nothing and make everything work. The ones and zeros of machine code are not patriarchal binaries or counterparts to each other: zero is not the other, but the very possibility of all the ones. Zero is the matrix of calculation, the possibility of multiplication, and has been reprocessing the modern world since it began to arrive from the East. It neither counts nor represents, but with digitization it proliferates, replicates, and undermines the privilege of one. Zero is not its absence, but a zone of multiplicity which cannot be perceived by the one who sees. Woman represents '*the horror of nothing to see*', but she also 'has sex organs more or less everywhere' (Irigaray, 1985b: 28). She too is more than the sum of her parts, beside herself with her extra links.

In Greek, the word for womb is *hystera*; in Latin, it is *matrix*, or matter, both the mother and the material. In *Neuromancer*, William Gibson calls it 'the nonspace', a 'vastness ... where the faces were shredded and blown away down hurricane corridors' (Gibson, 1986: 45). It is the imperceptible 'elsewhere' of which Irigaray speaks, the hole that is neither something nor nothing; the newly accessible virtual space which cannot be seen by the one it subsumes. If the phallus guarantees man's identity and his relation to transcendence and truth, it is also this which cuts him off from the abstract machinery of a world he thinks he owns.

It is only those at odds with this definition of humanity who seem to be able to access this plane. They have more in common with multifunctional systems than the active agency and singular identity proper to the male subject. Ada Lovelace writes the first programming language for an abstract machine yet to be built; Grace Murray Hopper programs Mark 1. And then there's Turing, described as 'a British mathematician who committed suicide by biting a poisoned Apple. As a discovered homosexual, he had been given a forced choice by the British courts either to go to jail or to take the feminizing hormone oestrogen. He chose the latter, with feminizing effects on his body, and who knows what effect on his brain.' And it was, as Edelman continues, 'that brain', newly engineered and feminized, which 'gave rise to a powerful set of mathematical ideas, one of which is known as a Turing machine' (Edelman, 1992: 218).

As the activities which have been monopolized by male conceptions of creativity and artistic genius now extend into the new multi-media and interactive spaces of the digital arts, women are at the cutting edge of experimentation in these zones. North America has Beth Stryker's *Cyberqueer*, and *Faultlines* from Ingrid Bachmann and Barbara Layne. In the UK, Orphan Drift ride a wave of writing, digital art, film and music. In Australia, Linda Dement's *Typhoid Mary* and *Cyberflesh Girlmonster* put blood, guts, and visceral infections on to her tactile multi-media screens. The French artist Orlan slides her body into cyberspace. The construct cunts access the controls. Sandy Stone makes the switch and the connection: '*to put on the seductive and dangerous cybernetic space like a garment, is to put on the female* (Stone, 1991: 109). Subversions of cyberpunk narrative proliferate. Kathy Acker hacks into *Neuromancer*, unleashing its elements in *Empire of the Senseless*. And Pat Cadigan's cyberpunk novels give another excruciating twist to the cyberspace tale. *Synners*, Fools and the stories in *Patterns* are texts of extraordinary density and intensity, both in terms of their writing and the worlds they engineer. If Gibson began to explore the complexities of the matrix, Cadigan's fictions perplex reality and identity to the point of irrelevance.

> Before you run out the door, consider two things:
> The future is already set, only the past can be changed, and
> If it was worth forgetting, it/s not worth remembering.
> (Cadigan, 1994: 287)

FROM VIRUSES TO REPLICUNTS

Once upon a time, tomorrow never came. Safely projected into the reaches of distant times and faraway galaxies, the future was science fiction and belonged to another world. Now it is here, breaking through the endless deferral of human horizons, short-circuiting history, downloading its images into today. While historical man continues to gaze in the rear-view mirror of the interface, guarding the present as a reproduction of the past, the sands of time are running into silicon, and Read Only Memory has come to an end. Cyberrevolution is virtually real.

Simulation leaves nothing untouched. Least of all the defences of a specular economy entirely invested in the identity of man and the world of ones and others he perceives. The father's authority is undermined as the sperm count goes into decline and oestrogen saturates the water-supply. Queer culture converges with post-human sexualities which have no regard for the moral code. Working patterns move from full-time, life-long, specialized careers to part-time, temporary, and multi-functional formats, and the context shifts into one in which women have long had expertise. It is suddenly noticed that girls' achievements in school and higher education are far in excess of those of their male counterparts, and a new transferable intelligence begins to be valued above either the strength or single-mindedness which once gave the masculine its power and are now being downgraded and rendered obsolete. Such tendencies – and the authoritarian reactions they excite – are emerging not only in the West but also across what were once lumped together as the cultures of the 'third world'. Global telecommunications and the migration of capital from the West are undermining both the pale male world and the patriarchal structures of the south and east, bringing unprecedented economic power to women workers and multiplying the possibilities of communication, learning, and access to information.

These crises of masculine identity are fatal corrosions of every one: every unified, centralized containment, and every system which keeps them secure. None of this was in the plan. What man has named as his history was supposed to function as the self-narrating story of a drive for domination and escape from the earth; a passage from carnal passions to self-control; a journey from the strange fluidities of the material to the self-identification of the soul. Driven by dreams of taming nature and so escaping its constraints, technical development has always invested in unification, light and flight, the struggle for enlightenment, a dream of escaping from the meat. Men may think and women may fear that they are on top of the situation, pursuing the surveillance and control of nature to unprecedented extremes, integrating their forces in the final consolidation of a technocratic fascism. But cyberspace is out of man's control: virtual reality destroys his identity, digitalization is mapping his soul and, at the peak of his triumph, the culmination of his machinic erections, man confronts the system he built for his own protection and finds it is female and dangerous.

Those who still cherish the patriarchal dream see cyberspace as a new zone of hope for a humanity which wants to be freed from the natural trap, escaping the body and sliding into an infinite, transcendent, and perfect other world. But the matrix is neither heaven, nor even a comforting return to the womb. By the time man begins to gain access to this zone, both the phallic dream of eternal life and its fantasy of female death are interrupted by the abstract matters of a cybernetic space which has woven him into its own emergence. Tempted still to go onwards and upwards by the promise of immortality, total control and autonomy, the hapless unity called man finds himself hooked up to the screen and plugged into a global web of hard, soft, and wetware systems. The great flight from nature he calls history comes to an end as he becomes a cyborg component of self-organizing processes beyond either his perception or his control.

As the patriarchal economy overheats, the human one, the member of the species, is rapidly losing his social, political, economic, and scientific status.

Those who distinguished themselves from the rest of what becomes their world and considered themselves to be 'making history', and building a world of their own design are increasingly subsumed by the activity of their own goods, services, lines of communication, and the self-organizing processes immanent to a nature they believed was passive and inert. If all technical development is underwritten by dreams for total control, final freedom, and some sense of ultimate reconciliation with the ideal, the runaway tendencies and chaotic emergences to which these dreams have led do nothing but turn them into nightmarish scenes.

Cyberfeminism is an insurrection on the part of the goods and materials of the patriarchal world, a dispersed, distributed emergence composed of links between women, women and computers, computers and communication links, connections and connectionist nets.

It becomes clear that if the ideologies and discourses of modern feminism were necessary to the changes in women's fortunes which creep over the end of the millennium, they were certainly never sufficient to the processes which now find man, in his own words, 'adjusting to irrelevance' and becoming 'the disposable sex'. It takes an irresponsible feminism – which may not be a feminism at all – to trace the inhuman paths on which woman begins to assemble herself as the cracks and crazes now emerging across the once smooth surfaces of patriarchal order. She is neither man-made with the dialecticians, biologically fixed with the essentialists, nor wholly absent with the Lacanians. She is in the process, turned on with the machines. As for patriarchy: it is not dead, but nor is it intractable.

There is no authentic or essential woman up ahead, no self to be reclaimed from some long lost past, nor even a potential subjectivity to be constructed in the present day. Nor is there only an absence or lack. Instead there is a virtual reality, an emergent process for which identity is not the goal but the enemy, precisely what has kept at bay the matrix of potentialities from which women have always downloaded their roles.

After the second come the next waves, the next sexes, asking for nothing, just taking their time. Inflicted on authority, the wounds proliferate. The replicunts write programs, paint viral images, fabricate weapons systems, infiltrate the arts and the industry. They are hackers, perverting the codes, corrupting the transmissions, multiplying zeros, and teasing open new holes in the world. They are the edge of the new edge, unashamedly opportunist, entirely irresponsible, and committed only to the infiltration and corruption of a world which already rues the day they left home.

Notes

1. Such cultural viruses are not metaphorical: both Richard Dawkins and more recently, Daniel Dennett, have conducted some excellent research into the viral functioning of cultural patterns. Nor are such processes of replication and contagion necessarily destructive: even the most damaging virus may need to keep its host alive.

2. Asimov's three rules are: 1. A robot may not injure a human being, or, through inaction, allow a human being to come to harm; 2. A robot must obey the orders given it by human beings, except where such orders would conflict with the First Law; 3. A robot must protect its own existence as long as such protection does not conflict with the First or Second Law.
3. Alan Turing's abstract machine, developed during WWII, forms the basis of the modern serial computer.
4. Her 'Sketch of the Analytical Engine invented by L. F. Menebrea, with notes upon the memoir by the translator, Ada Augustus, Countess of Lovelace', appears in Philip and Emily Morrison, eds, *Charles Babbage and his Calculating Engines, Selected Writings by Charles Babbage and Others*, Dover, 1961.

REFERENCES

Cadigan, Pat (1989) *Patterns*, London: Grafton.
Cadigan, Pat (1991) *Synners*, London: Grafton.
Cadigan, Pat (1994) *Fools*, London: Grafton.
Dennett, Daniel (1995) *Darwin's Dangerous Idea: Evolution and the Meanings of Life*, Hardmondsworth: Allen Lane/The Penguin Press.
Edelman, Gerald (1992) *Bright Air, Brilliant Fire*, New York: Basic Books.
Eiser, J. Richard (1994) *Attitudes, Chaos, and the Connectionist Mind*, Oxford: Blackwell.
Freud, Sigmund (1985) *New Introductory Lectures on Psychoanalysis*, Harmondsworth: Penguin.
Freud, Sigmund and Breuer, Joseph (1991) *Studies in Hysteria*, Harmondsworth: Penguin.
Gibson, William (1986) *Neuromancer*, London: Grafton.
Irigaray, Luce (1985a) *Speculum of the Other Woman*, Ithaca, New York: Cornell University Press.
Irigaray, Luce (1985b) *This Sex that is not One*, Ithaca, New York: Cornell University Press.
Irigaray, Luce (1991) *Marine Lover of Friedrich Nietzsche*, New York: Columbia University Press.
Langton Moore, Doris (1977) *Ada, Countess of Lovelace*, London: John Murray.
McLuhan, Marshall (1967) *Understanding Media*, London: Sphere Books.
Misha, (1991) 'Wire movement' 9, in Larry McCaffrey (ed.), *Storming the Reality Studio*, Durham, NC and London: Duke University Press.
Stone, Allucquere Rosanne (1991) 'Will the Real Body Stand Up?', in Michael Benedikt (ed.), *Cyberspace, First Steps*, Cambridge, MA and London: MIT Press.

FURTHER READING

Baldwin, T. F., McVoy, D. S. and Steinfeld, C., *Convergence: Integrating Media, Information and Communication*, (Thousand Oaks, Ca.: Sage, 1996).

Bender, G. and Druckrey, T. (eds), *Culture on the Brink: Ideologies of Technology*, (San Francisco: Bay Press, 1994).

Beniger, J., *The Control Revolution: Technological and Economic Origins of the Information Society*, (Cambridge, Mass.: Harvard University Press, 1986).

Brook, J. and Boal, I. A. (eds), *Resisting the Virtual Life*, (San Francisco: City Lights, 1995).

Carey, J., *Communication as Culture*, (London: Unwin, 1989).

Cubitt, S., *Digital Aesthetics*, (London: Sage, 1998).

de Lauretis, T. and Heath, S. (eds), *The Cinematic Apparatus*, (New York: St. Martin's Press, 1980).

de Sola Pool, I. (ed.), *The Social Impact of the Telephone*, (Cambridge, Mass: MIT Press, 1977).

Dovey, J. (ed.), *Fractal Dreams*, (London: Lawrence and Wishart, 1995).

Edge, D. and Wacjman, J. (eds), *The Social Shaping of Technology*, (Milton Keynes: Open University Press, 1985).

Featherstone, M. and Burrows, R. (eds), *Cyberspace/Cyberbodies/Cyberpunk: Cultures of Technology and Embodiment*, (London: Sage, 1995).

Fidler, R., *Mediamorphosis: Understanding New Media*, (Thousand Oaks, Ca.: Pine Forge, 1997).

Gray, A., *Video Playtime: the Gendering of a Leisure Technology*, (London: Routledge, 1992).

Hanhardt, J. (ed.), *Video Culture: a Critical Investigation*, (New York: 1986).

Hayward, P. (ed.), *Culture, Technology and Creativity in the Late Twentieth Century*, (London: John Libbey/Arts Council, 1990).

Hayward, P. and Wollen, T. (eds), *Future Visions: New Technologies of the Screen*, (London: British Film Institute, 1993).

Jones, S. (ed.), *Virtual Culture: Identity and Community in Cybersociety*, (London: Sage, 1997).

Kern, S., *The Culture of Time and Space 1880–1919*, (Cambridge, Mass.: Harvard University Press, 1983).

Levinson, P., *The Soft Edge: A Natural History and Future of the Information Revolution*, (London: Routledge, 1997).

Lister, M. (ed.), *The Photographic Image in Digital Culture*, (London: Routledge, 1995).

Loader, B. D. (ed.), *The Governance of Cyberspace: Politics, Technology and Global Restructuring*, (London: Routledge, 1997).

McLuhan, M., *The Gutenberg Galaxy*, (London: RKP, 1962).

McLuhan, M., *Understanding Media: the Extensions of Man*, (London: Routledge, Kegan and Paul, 1964).

Marvin, C., *When Old Technologies were New: Thinking about Communications in the Late Nineteenth Century*, (New York: Oxford University Press, 1988).

Meyrowitz, J., *No Sense of Place: the Impact of Electronic Media on Social Behaviour*, (New York: Oxford University Press, 1985).

Miles, I., *Home Informatics: Information Technology and the Transformation of Everyday Life*, (London: Pinter, 1988).

Miller, N. and Allen, R. (eds), *The Post-Broadcasting Age: New Technologies, New Communities*, (Luton: University of Luton Press, 1996).

Plant, S., *Zeroes and Ones*, (London: Fourth Estate, 1996).

Porter, D. (ed.), *Internet Culture* (London: Routledge, 1997).

Robins, K., *Into the Image: Culture and Politics in the Field of Vision*, (London: Routledge, 1996).

Shields, R. (ed.), *Cultures of Internet: Virtual Spaces, Real Histories, Living Bodies*, (London: Sage, 1996).

Silverstone, R., *Television and Everyday Life*, (London: Routledge, 1994).

Silverstone, R. and Hirsch, E. (eds), *Consuming Technologies: Media and Information in Domestic Spaces*, (London: Routledge, 1992).

Spender, D., *Nattering on the Net: Women, Power and Cyberspace* (London: Spinfex, 1995).

Webster, F., *Theories of the Information Society*, (London: Routledge, 1995).

Williams, N. and Hartley, P. (eds), *Technology in Human Communication*, (London: Pinter, 1990).

Williams, R., *Television: Technology and Cultural Form*, (London: Fontana/William Collins, 1974).

Winston, B., *Technologies of Seeing: Photography, Cinematography and Television*, (London: British Film Institute, 1996).

Winston, B., *Media Technology: A History from the Telegraph to the Internet*, (London: Routledge, 1998).

ACKNOWLEDGEMENTS

Grateful acknowledgement is made to the following sources for permission to reproduce material previously published elsewhere. Every effort has been made to trace the copyright holders, but if any have been inadvertently overlooked, the publisher will be pleased to make the necessary arrangements at the first opportunity.

Paul F. Lazarsfeld and Robert K. Merton, 'Mass Communication, Popular Taste and Organized Social Action', from *The Communication of Ideas*, ed. Lyman Bryson, HarperCollins Publishers, © 1948, Institute for Religious Studies;

Theodor Adorno, 'Culture Industry Reconsidered', translated by Anson G. Rabinbach, from *The Culture Industry: Selected Essays on Mass Culture* edited by J. M. Bernstein, © 1991, Routledge;

Marshall McLuhan, 'The Medium is the Message', from *Understanding Media*, by Marshall McLuhan, © 1964, Routledge;

Raymond Williams, '"Mass Communication" and "Minority Culture"', from *Communications*, by Raymond Williams, © 1962, 1966, 1976 Penguin Books;

Stuart Hall, 'Encoding/Decoding', from *Culture, Media, Language*, edited by Stuart Hall, Dorothy Hobson, Andrew Lowe and Paul Willis, © 1980, Routledge;

Annette Kuhn, 'The Power of the Image', from *The Power of the Image*, by Annette Kuhn, © 1985, Routledge;

Hans Magnus Enzensberger, 'Constituents of a Theory of the Media', translated by Stuart Hood from *Raids and Reconstructions*, © 1970 Pluto Press;

Jürgen Habermas, 'The Public Sphere', translated by Shierry Weber Nicholson, from *Jürgen Habermas on Society and Politics: A Reader*, edited by Steven Seidman, © 1989, Beacon Press. Reprinted by permission of Beacon Press, Boston;

Jean Baudrillard: Selected Writings. *New Literary History*, 16:3 (Spring 1985), pp. 577–89 © 1985, The University of Virginia. Reprinted by permission of the Johns Hopkins University Press;

Paddy Scannell, 'Public Service Broadcasting: The History of a Concept', chapter 1 of *Understanding Television*, edited by Andrew Goodwin and Gary Whannel, © 1990, Routledge;

Nicholas Garnham, 'On the Cultural Industries', from *Capitalism and Communication*, by Nicholas Garnham, © 1990, Sage Publications Ltd. Reprinted by permission of Sage Publications Ltd.;

Graham Murdock, 'Redrawing the Map of the Communication Industries: Concentration and Ownership in the Era of Privitization', from *Public Communication: The New Imperatives*, edited by Marjorie Ferguson, © 1990, Sage Publications Ltd. Reprinted by permission of Sage Publications Ltd.;

Jeremy Tunstall, 'Producers in British Television', from *Television Producers*, by Jeremy Tunstall, © 1993, Routledge;

Chapter one of *Peripheral Vision: New Patterns in Global Television*, edited by John Sinclair, Elizabeth Jacka, Stuart Cunningham © 1996, Oxford University Press. Reprinted by permission of Oxford University Press;

Extract from Bernard Berelson's, *Content Analysis in Communication Research*, © 1952, New York Free Press;

Andrew Crisell, 'Radio Signs', from *Understanding Radio*, by Andrew Crisell, © 1986, Routledge;

John Fiske, 'The Codes of Television', from *Television Culture*, by John Fiske, © 1987, Routledge;

Raymond Williams, 'Programming as Sequence or Flow', from *Television, Technology and Cultural Form*, by Raymond Williams, © 1974, Routledge;

John Ellis, 'Broadcast TV Narration', from *Visible Fictions: Cinema, Television, Video* by John Ellis, © 1982, Routledge;

Richard Dyer, 'Stereotypes', from *The Matter of Images* by Richard Dyer, © 1993, Routledge;

Niki Strange, 'Perform, Educate, Entertain: Ingredients of the Cookery Programme Genre', from *The Television Studies Book* edited by Christine Geraghty and David Lusted, © 1998, Arnold;

Stuart Hall, 'The Whites of Their Eyes: Racist Ideologies and the Media', from *Silver Linings*, edited by George Bridges and Rosalind Brunt, © 1981, Lawrence & Wishart;

Janet Woollacott, 'Fictions and Ideologies: The Case of Situation Comedy', by Janet Woollacott from *Popular Culture and Social Relations* edited by Tony Bennett, Colin Mercer and Janet Woollacott, © 1986, Open University Press;

Andrew Tolson, 'Televised Chat and the Synthetic Personality', from *Broadcast Talk*, edited by Paddy Scannell, © 1991, Sage Publications Ltd. Reprinted by permission of Sage Publications Ltd;

Norman Fairclough, 'Critical Analysis of Media Discourse', from *Media Discourse*, © 1995, Arnold;

Janice Winship, 'Survival Skills and Daydreams', from *Inside Women's Magazines*, by Janice Winship, © 1987, HarperCollins Publishers Ltd.;

Danae Clark, '*Cagney & Lacey*: Feminist Strategies of Detection', from *Television and Women's Culture: The Politics of the Popular*, by M. E. Brown, © 1990, Sage Publications Ltd. Reprinted by permission of Sage Publications Ltd.;

Corinne Squire, 'Empowering Women? The *Oprah Winfrey Show*', *Feminism and Psychology* 4:1, © 1994, Sage Publications Ltd. Reprinted by kind permission of Sage Publications Ltd. and Corinne Squire.

Jim Collins, 'Television and Postmodernism', from *Channels of Discourse Reassembled*, edited by R. C. Allen, © 1992, Routledge;

Angela McRobbie, 'Postmodernism and Popular Culture', from *ICA Documents 4: Postmodernism*, © 1986, Free Association Books. Reprinted by kind permission of Free Association Books and Angela McRobbie;

Bill Nichols, 'Reality TV and Social Perversion', from *Blurred Boundaries: Questions of Meaning in Contemporary Culture* by Bill Nichols, © 1994, Indiana University Press;

Lynne Joyrich, 'Critical and Textual Hypermasculinity', from *Logics of Television: Essays in Cultural Criticism* edited by P. Mellencamp, © 1990, Indiana University Press;

Hans Eysenck and D. K. B. Nias, 'Desensitization, Violence and the Media', from *Sex, Violence and the Media* by Hans Eysenck and D. K. B. Nias, © 1978, Maurice Temple Smith;

James D. Halloran, 'On the Social Effects of Television', from *The Effects of Television* edited by James Halloran, © 1970, Panther Books;

Denis McQuail, Jay G. Blumler and J. R. Brown, 'The Television Audience: A Revised Perspective', from *Sociology of Mass Communications* edited by Denis McQuail, © 1972, Penguin Books;

Philip Elliott, 'Uses and Gratifications Research: A Critique and Sociological Alternative', from *The Uses of Mass Communications: Current Perspectives on Gratifications Research* edited by Jay Blumler and Elihu Katz, © 1974, Sage Publications Inc. Reprinted by permission of Sage Publications Inc.;

David Morley, 'Cultural Transformations: The Politics of Resistance', from *Language, Image, Media* edited by H. Davis and P. Walton, © 1983, Blackwell and St. Martins Press;

Ien Ang, 'Wanted: Audiences. On the Politics of Empirical Audience Studies', from *Remote Control: Television, Audiences and Cultural Power* edited by E. Seiter et al., © 1989, Routledge;

Janice Radway, 'Conclusion', from *Reading the Romance: Women Patriarchy, and Popular Literature*, © 1987, Verso;

Daniel Miller, 'The Young and the Restless in Trinidad: A Case of the Local and the Global in Mass Consumption', from *Consuming Technologies: Media and Information in Domestic Spaces*, © 1992, Routledge;

Ann Gray, 'Behind Closed Doors: Video Recorders in the Home', from *Boxed In: Women and Television* edited by H. Baehr and G. Dyer, © 1987, Rivers Oram Publishers Ltd.;

John Fiske, 'Moments of Television: Neither the Text nor the Audience', from *Remote Control: Television, Audiences and Cultural Power* edited by E. Seiter et al., © 1989, Routledge;

Henry Jenkins, '"Strangers No More, We Sing": Filking and the Social Construction of the Science Fiction Fan Community', from *The Adoring Audience: Fan Culture and Popular Media* edited by L. A. Lewis, © 1992, Routledge;

Joke Hermes, 'Media, Meaning and Everyday Life', from *Cultural Studies* 7:3, © 1993, Routledge;

David Buckingham, '*EastEnders*: Creating the Audience', from *Public Secrets: EastEnders and its Audience*, by David Buckingham, © 1987, British Film Institute;

Tania Modleski, 'The Search for Tomorrow in Today's Soap Operas', from *Loving with a Vengeance: Mass-Produced Fantasies for Women* by Tania Modleski, © 1984, Routledge;

Charlotte Brunsdon, '*Crossroads*: Notes on Soap Opera', from *Screen*, vol. 22, no. 4, © 1981. Reprinted by permission of Screen and Charlotte Brunsdon;

Dorothy Hobson, 'Everything Stops for *Crossroads*: Watching with the Audience', from *Crossroads: The Drama of a Soap Opera* by Dorothy Hobson, © 1982, Routledge;

Jon Stratton and Ien Ang, '*Sylvania Waters* and the Spectacular Exploding Family', from *Screen* 35:1, © 1994, Oxford University Press. Reprinted by permission of Oxford University Press, Jon Stratton and Ien Ang;

Peter Golding and Philip Elliott, 'News Values and News Production' and 'Bias, Objectivity and Ideology', from *Making the News* by Peter Golding and Philip Elliott, © 1979, Longman;

Stuart Hall, Chas Critcher, Tony Jefferson, John Clarke and Brian Roberts, 'The Social Production of News' from *Policing the Crisis: Mugging, the State, Law and Order*, by Stuart Hall et al., © 1979, Macmillan Press Ltd.;

John Hartley, 'Home Help for Populist Politics: Relational Aspects of TV News', from *Tele-ology: Studies in Television* by John Hartley, © 1992, Routledge;

Lana F. Rakow and Kimberlie Kranich, 'Woman as Sign in Television News', from *Journal of Communication*, 41:1, © 1991, Oxford University Press. Reprinted by permission of Oxford University Press, Lana F. Rakow and Kimberlie Kranich;

Michael Gurevitch, 'The Globalization of Electronic Journalism', from *Mass Media and Society* edited by J. Curran and M. Gurevitch, © 1991, Arnold;

Greg Philo, 'News Content and Audience Belief', from *Seeing and Believing: The Influence of the Television*, by Greg Philo, © 1990, Routledge;

Raymond Williams, 'Advertising: The Magic System', from *Problems in Materialism and Culture* by Raymond Williams, © 1980, Verso;

James Curran, 'The Impact of Advertising on the British Mass Media', from *Media, Culture and Society*, vol. 3, no. 1, © 1981, Sage Publications Ltd. Reprinted by permission of Sage Publications Ltd.;

Sean Nixon, 'Advertising, Magazine Culture, and the "New Man"', from *Hard Looks: Masculinities, Spectatorship and Contemporary Consumption*, © 1996, UCL Press;

Janice Winship, 'Handling Sex', from *Media, Culture and Society*, vol. 3, no. 1, © 1981, Sage Publications Ltd. Reprinted by permission of Sage Publications Ltd.;

Anne McClintock, 'Soft-Soaping Empire: Commodity Racism and Imperial Advertising', from *Travellers' Tales: Narratives of Home and Displacement*, edited by G. Robertson, M. Mash, L. Tickner, J. Bird, B. Curtis and T. Putnam, © 1994, Routledge;

Mica Nava and Orson Nava, 'Discriminating or Duped? Young People as Consumers of Advertising/Art', from *Changing Cultures: Feminism, Youth and Consumerism* by Mica Nava, © 1992, Sage Publications Ltd. Reprinted by permission of Sage Publications Ltd.;

Brian Winston, 'How Are Media Born?', from *Questioning the Media*, edited by John Downing et al., © 1990, Sage Publications Ltd. Reprinted by permission of Sage Publications Ltd.;

Peter Golding, 'Worldwide wedge: division and contradiction in the global infrastructure', in chapter 8 of Daya Thussu (ed.) *Electronic Empires: Global Media and Local Resistance* (London: Arnold, 1998) a revised version of an article in *The Monthly Review*, 48: 3, July–Aug. 1996, pp. 70–85;

Eric Hirsch, 'New Technologies and Domestic Consumption', from *The Television Studies Book*, edited by Christine Geraghty and David Lusted, © 1998, Arnold;

Sadie Plant, 'On the Matrix: Cyberfeminist Simulations', from *Culture of Internet*, edited by Rob Shields, © 1996, Sage Publications Ltd. Reprinted by permission of Sadie Plant.

NAMES INDEX

SUBJECT INDEX